Problems and Solutions
in Mathematical Finance

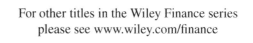

For other titles in the Wiley Finance series
please see www.wiley.com/finance

Problems and Solutions in Mathematical Finance

Volume 2: Equity Derivatives

Eric Chin, Dian Nel and Sverrir Ólafsson

WILEY

A catalogue record for this book is available from the British Library.

ISBN 978-1-119-96582-4 (hardback) ISBN 978-1-119-96610-4 (ebk)
ISBN 978-1-119-96611-1 (ebk)   ISBN 978-1-119-19219-0 (obk)

Cover design: Cylinder
Cover image: © Attitude/Shutterstock

Set in 10/12pt Times by Aptara Inc., New Delhi, India
Printed in Great Britain by TJ International Ltd, Padstow, Cornwall, UK

青取之於藍而青於藍
荀子勸學

"Blue dye is derived from the indigo plant and surpassed its parental colour"
Xunzi, *An Exhortation to Learning*

Contents

Preface

Mathematical finance is a highly challenging and technical discipline. Its fundamentals and applications are best understood by combining a theoretically solid approach with extensive exercises in solving practical problems. That is the philosophy behind all four volumes in this series on mathematical finance. This second of four volumes in the series *Problems and Solutions in Mathematical Finance* is devoted to the discussion of equity derivatives. In the first volume we developed the probabilistic and stochastic methods required for the successful study of advanced mathematical finance, in particular different types of pricing models. The techniques applied in this volume assume good knowledge of the topics covered in Volume 1. As we believe that good working knowledge of mathematical finance is best acquired through the solution of practical problems, all the volumes in this series are built up in a way that allows readers to continuously test their knowledge as they work through the texts.

This second volume starts with the analysis of basic derivatives, such as forwards and futures, swaps and options. The approach is bottom up, starting with the analysis of simple contracts and then moving on to more advanced instruments. All the major classes of options are introduced and extensively studied, starting with plain European and American options. The text then moves on to cover more complex contracts such as barrier, Asian and exotic options. In each option class, different types of options are considered, including time-independent and time-dependent options, or non-path-dependent and path-dependent options.

Stochastic financial models frequently require the fixing of different parameters. Some can be extracted directly from market data, others need to be fixed by means of numerical methods or optimisation techniques. Depending on the context, this is done in different ways. In the risk-neutral world, the drift parameter for the geometric Brownian motion (Black–Scholes model) is extracted from the bond market (i.e., the returns on risk-free debt). The volatility parameter, in contrast, is generally determined from market prices, as the so-called implied volatility. However, if a stochastic process is to be fitted to known price data, other methods need to be consulted, such as maximum-likelihood estimation. This method is applied to a number of stochastic processes in the chapter on volatility models.

In all option models, volatility presents one of the most important quantities that determine the price and the risk of derivatives contracts. For this reason, considerable effort is put into their discussion in terms of concepts, such as implied, local and stochastic volatilities, as well as the important volatility surfaces.

At the end of this volume, readers will be equipped with all the major tools required for the modelling and the pricing of a whole range of different derivatives contracts. They will therefore be ready to tackle new techniques and challenges discussed in the next two volumes, including interest-rate modelling in Volume 3 and foreign exchange/commodity derivatives in Volume 4.

As in the first volume, we have the following note to the student/reader: Please try hard to solve the problems on your own before you look at the solutions!

About the Authors

Eric Chin is a quantitative analyst at an investment bank in the City of London where he is involved in providing guidance on price testing methodologies and their implementation, formulating model calibration and model appropriateness on commodity and credit products. Prior to joining the banking industry he worked as a senior researcher at British Telecom investigating radio spectrum trading and risk management within the telecommunications sector. He holds an MSc in Applied Statistics and an MSc in Mathematical Finance both from University of Oxford. He also holds a PhD in Mathematics from University of Dundee.

Dian Nel has more than 10 years of experience in the commodities sector. He currently works in the City of London where he specialises in oil and gas markets. He holds a BEng in Electrical and Electronic Engineering from Stellenbosch University and an MSc in Mathematical Finance from Christ Church, Oxford University. He is a Chartered Engineer registered with the Engineering Council UK.

Sverrir Ólafsson is Professor of Financial Mathematics at Reykjavik University; a Visiting Professor at Queen Mary University, London and a director of Riskcon Ltd, a UK based risk management consultancy. Previously he was a Chief Researcher at BT Research and held academic positions at The Mathematical Departments of Kings College, London; UMIST Manchester and The University of Southampton. Dr Ólafsson is the author of over 95 refereed academic papers and has been a key note speaker at numerous international conferences and seminars. He is on the editorial board of three international journals. He has provided an extensive consultancy on financial risk management and given numerous specialist seminars to finance specialists. In the last five years his main teaching has been MSc courses on Risk Management, Fixed Income, and Mathematical Finance. He has an MSc and PhD in mathematical physics from the Universities of Tübingen and Karlsruhe respectively.

1
Basic Equity Derivatives Theory

In finance, an equity derivative belongs to a class of derivative instruments whose underlying asset is a stock or stock index. Hence, the value of an equity derivative is a function of the value of the stock or index. With a growing interest in the stock markets of the world, and the prevalence of employee stock options as a form of compensation, equity derivatives continue to expand with new product structures continuously being offered. In this chapter, we introduce the concept of equity derivatives with emphasis on forwards, futures, option contracts and also different types of hedging strategies.

1.1 INTRODUCTION

Among the many equity derivatives that are actively traded in the market, options and futures are by far the most commonly traded financial instruments. The following is the basic vocabulary of different types of derivatives contracts:

- **Option** A contract that gives the holder the right but not the obligation to buy or sell an asset for a fixed price (strike/exercise price) at or before a fixed expiry date.
- **Call Option** A contract that gives the holder the right to buy an asset for a fixed price (strike/exercise price) at or before a fixed expiry date.
- **Put Option** A contract that gives the holder the right to sell an asset for a fixed price (strike/exercise price) at or before a fixed expiry date.
- **Payoff** Difference between the market price and the strike price depending on derivative type.
- **Intrinsic Value** The payoff that would be received/paid if the option was exercised when the underlying asset is at its current level.
- **Time Value** Value that the option is above its intrinsic value. The relationship can be written as

$$\text{Option Price} = \text{Intrinsic Value} + \text{Time Value}.$$

- **Forward/Futures** A contract that obligates the buyer and seller to trade an underlying, usually a commodity or stock price index, at some specified time in the future. The difference between a forward and a futures contract is that forwards are over-the-counter (OTC) products which are customised agreements between two counterparties. In contrast, futures are standardised contracts traded on an official exchange and are marked to market on a daily basis. Hence, futures contracts do not carry any credit risk (the risk that a party will not meet its contractual obligations).
- **Swap** An OTC contract in which two counterparties exchange cash flows.
- **Stock Index Option** A contract that gives the holder the right but not the obligation to buy or sell a specific amount of a particular stock index for an agreed fixed price at or before

a fixed expiry date. As it is not feasible to deliver an actual stock index, this contract is usually settled in cash.

- **Stock Index Futures** A contract that obligates the buyer and seller to trade a quantity of a specific stock index on an official exchange at a price agreed between two parties with delivery on a specified future date. Like the stock index option, this contract is usually settled in cash.
- **Strike/Exercise Price** Fixed price at which the owner of an option can buy (for a call option) or sell (for a put option) the underlying asset.
- **Expiry Date/Exercise Date** The last date on which the option contract is still valid. After this date, the option contract becomes worthless.
- **Delivery Date** The last date by which the underlying commodity or stock price index (usually cash payment based on the underlying stock price index) for a forward/futures contract must be delivered to fulfil the requirements of the contract.
- **Discounting** Multiplying an amount by a discount factor to compute its present value (discounted value). It is the opposite of compounding, where interest is added to an amount so that the added interest also earns interest from then on. If we assume the risk-free interest rate r is a constant and continuously compounding, then the present value at time t of a certain payoff M at time T, for $t < T$, is $M e^{-r(T-t)}$.
- **Hedge** An investment position intended to reduce the risk from adverse price movements in an asset. A hedge can be constructed using a combination of stocks and derivative products such as options and forwards.
- **Contingent Claim** A claim that depends on a particular event such as an option payoff, which depends on a stock price at some future date.

Within the context of option contracts we subdivide them into *option style* or *option family*, which denotes the class into which the type of option contract falls, usually defined by the dates on which the option may be exercised. These include:

- **European Option** An option that can only be exercised on the expiry date.
- **American Option** An option that can be exercised any time before the expiry date.
- **Bermudan Option** An option that can only be exercised on predetermined dates. Hence, this option is intermediate between a European option and an American option.

Unless otherwise stated, all the options discussed in this chapter are considered to be European.

Option Trading

In option trading, the transaction involves two parties: a buyer and a seller.

- The buyer of an option is said to take a *long position* in the option, whilst the seller is said to take a *short position* in the option.
- The buyer or owner of a call (put) option has the right to buy (sell) an asset at a specified price by paying a premium to the seller or writer of the option, who will assume the obligation to sell (buy) the asset should the owner of the option choose to exercise (enforce) the contract.

- The payoff of a call option at expiry time T is defined as

$$\Psi(S_T) = \max\{S_T - K, 0\}$$

where S_T is the price of the underlying asset at expiry time T and K is the strike price. If $S_T > K$ at expiry, then the buyer of the call option should exercise the option by paying a lower amount K to obtain an asset worth S_T. However, if $S_T \leq K$ then the buyer of the call option should not exercise the option because it would not make any financial sense to pay a higher amount K to obtain an asset which is of a lower value S_T. Here, the option expires worthless.

In general, the profit earned by the buyer of the call option is

$$\Upsilon(S_T) = \max\{S_T - K, 0\} - C(S_t, t; K, T)$$

where $C(S_t, t; K, T)$ is the premium paid at time $t < T$ (written on the underlying asset S_t) in order to enter into a call option contract.

Neglecting the premium for buying an option, a call option is said to be *in-the-money* (ITM) if the buyer profits when the option is exercised ($S_T > K$). In contrast, a call option is said to be *out-of-the-money* (OTM) if the buyer loses when the option is exercised ($S_T < K$). Finally, a call option is said be to *at-the-money* (ATM) if the buyer neither loses nor profits when the option is exercised ($S_T = K$). Figure 1.1 illustrates the concepts we have discussed.

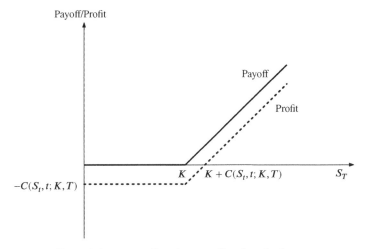

Figure 1.1   Long call option payoff and profit diagram.

- The payoff of a put option at expiry time T is defined as

$$\Psi(S_T) = \max\{K - S_T, 0\}$$

where S_T is the price of the underlying asset at expiry time T and K is the strike price. If $K > S_T$ at expiry, then the buyer of the put option should exercise the option by selling the asset worth S_T for a higher amount K. However, if $K \leq S_T$ then the buyer of the put option should not exercise the option because it would not make any financial sense to sell the asset worth S_T for a lower amount K. Here, the option expires worthless.

In general, the profit earned by the buyer of the put option is

$$\Upsilon(S_T) = \max\{K - S_T, 0\} - P(S_t, t; K, T)$$

where $P(S_t, t; K, T)$ is the premium paid at time $t < T$ (written on the underlying asset S_t) in order to enter into a put option contract.

Neglecting the premium for buying an option, a put option is said to be ITM if the buyer profits when the option is exercised ($K > S_T$). In contrast, a put option is said to be OTM if the buyer loses when the option is exercised ($K < S_T$). Finally, a put option is said to be ATM if the buyer neither loses nor profits when the option is exercised ($S_T = K$). Figure 1.2 illustrates the concepts we have discussed.

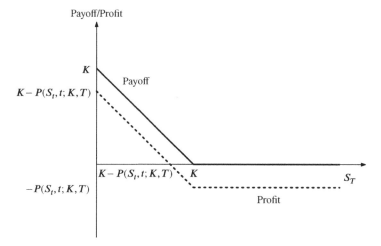

Figure 1.2   Long put option payoff and profit diagram.

Forward Contract

In a forward contract, the transaction is executed between two parties: a buyer and a seller.

- The buyer of the underlying commodity or stock index is referred to as the *long side* whilst the seller is known as the *short side*.
- The contractual obligation to buy the asset at the agreed price on a specified future date is known as the *long position*. A long position profits when the price of an asset rises.
- The contractual obligation to sell the asset at the agreed price on a specified future date is known as the *short position*. A short position profits when the price of an asset falls.
- For a long position, the payoff of a forward contract at the delivery time T is

$$\Pi_T = S_T - F(t, T)$$

where S_T is the spot price (or market price) at the delivery time T and $F(t, T)$ is the forward price initiated at time $t < T$ to be delivered at time T.

- For a short position, the payoff of a forward contract at the delivery time T is

$$\Pi_T = F(t,T) - S_T$$

where S_T is the spot price (or market price) at the delivery time T and $F(t,T)$ is the forward price initiated at time $t < T$ to be delivered at time T.
- Since there is no upfront payment to enter into a forward contract, the profit at delivery time T is the same as the payoff of a forward contract at time T. Figure 1.3 illustrates the concepts we have discussed.

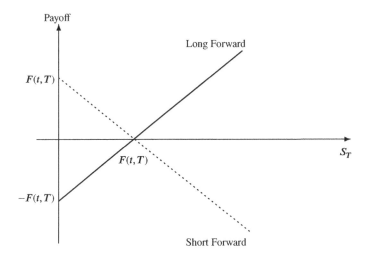

Figure 1.3   Long and short forward payoffs diagram.

Futures Contract

Similar to a forward contract, a futures contract is also an agreement between two parties in which the buyer agrees to buy an underlying asset from the seller. The delivery of the asset occurs at a specified future date, where the price is determined at the time of initiation of the contract. As in the case of a forward contract, it costs nothing to enter into a futures contract. However, the differences between futures and forwards are as follows:

- In a futures contract, the terms and conditions are standardised where trading takes place on a formal exchange with deep liquidity.
- There is no default risk when trading futures contracts, since the exchange acts as a counterparty guaranteeing delivery and payment by use of a clearing house.
- The clearing house protects itself from default by requiring its counterparties to settle profits and losses or mark to market their positions on a daily basis.
- An investor can hedge his/her future position by engaging in an opposite transaction before the delivery date of the contract.

In the futures market, margin is a performance guarantee. It is money deposited with the clearing house by both the buyer and the seller. There is no loan involved and hence, no interest is charged. To safeguard the clearing house, the exchange requires buyers/sellers to post margin (i.e., deposit funds) and settle their accounts on a daily basis. Prior to trading, the trader must post margin with their broker who in return will post margin with the clearing house.

- **Initial Margin** Money that must be deposited in order to initiate a futures position.
- **Maintenance Margin** Minimum margin amount that must be maintained; when the margin falls below this amount it must be brought back up to its initial level. Margin calculations are based on the daily settlement price, the average of the prices for trades during the closing period set by the exchange.
- **Variation Margin** Money that must be deposited to bring it back to the initial margin amount. If the account margin is more than the initial margin, the investor can withdraw the funds for new positions.
- **Settlement Price** Known also as the closing price for a stock. The settlement price is the price at which a derivatives contract settles once a given trading day has ended. The settlement price is used to calculate the margin at the end of each trading day.
- **Marking-to-Market** Process of adding gains to or subtracting losses from the margin account daily, based on the change in the settlement prices from one day to the next.

Termination of a futures position can be achieved by:

- An offsetting trade (known as a back-to-back trade), entering into an opposite position in the same contract.
- Payment of cash at expiration for a cash-settlement contract.
- Delivery of the asset at expiration.
- Exchange of physicals.

Stock Split (Divide) Effect

When a company issues a stock split (e.g., doubling the number of shares), the price is adjusted so as to keep the net value of all the stock the same as before the split.

Stock Dividend Effect

When dividends are paid during the life of an option contract they will inadvertently affect the price of the stock or asset. Here, the direction of the stock price will be determined based on the choice of the company whether it pays dividends to its shareholders or reinvests the money back in the business. Since we may regard dividends as a cash return to the shareholders, the reinvestment of the cash back into the business could create more profit and, depending on market sentiment, lead to an increase in stock price. Conversely, paying dividends to the shareholders will effectively reduce the stock price by the amount of the dividend payment, and as a result will affect the premium prices of options as well as futures and forwards.

Hedging Strategies

In the following we discuss how an investor can use options to design investment strategies with specific views on the stock price behaviour in the future.

- **Protective** This hedging strategy is designed to insure an investor's asset position (long buy or short sell).

An investor who owns an asset and wishes to be protected from falling asset values can insure his asset by buying a put option written on the same asset. This combination of owning an asset and purchasing a put option on that asset is called a protective put.

In contrast, an investor shorting an asset who will experience a loss if the asset price rises in value can insure his position by purchasing a call option written on the same asset. Such a combination of selling an asset and purchasing a call option on that asset is called a protective call.

- **Covered** This hedging strategy involves the investor writing an option whilst holding an opposite position on the asset. The motivation for doing so is to generate additional income by receiving premiums from option buyers, and this strategy is akin to selling insurance. When the writer of an option has no position in the underlying asset, this form of option writing is known as naked writing.

  In a covered call, the investor would hold a long position on an asset and sell a call option written on the same asset.

  In a covered put, the investor would short sell an asset and sell a put option written on the same asset.

- **Collar** This hedging strategy uses a combination of protective strategy and selling options to collar the value of an asset position within a specific range. By using a protective strategy, the investor can insure his asset position (long or short) whilst reducing the cost of insurance by selling an option.

  In a purchased collar, the strategy consists of a protective put and selling a call option whilst in a written collar, the strategy consists of a protective call and selling a put option.

- **Synthetic Forward** A synthetic forward consists of a long call, $C(S_t, t; K, T)$ and a short put, $P(S_t, t; K, T)$ written on the same asset S_t at time t with the same expiration date $T > t$ and strike price K.

  At expiry time T, the payoff is

$$C(S_T, T; K, T) - P(S_T, T; K, T) = S_T - K$$

and, assuming a constant risk-free interest rate r and by discounting the payoff back to time t, we have

$$C(S_t, t; K, T) - P(S_t, t; K, T) = S_t - Ke^{-r(T-t)}.$$

The above equation is known as the *put–call parity*, tying the relationship between options and forward markets together.

- **Bull Spread** An investor who enters a bull spread expects the stock price to rise and wishes to exploit this.

  For a bull call spread, it is composed of

$$\text{Bull Call Spread} = C(S_t, t; K_1, T) - C(S_t, t; K_2, T)$$

which consists of buying a call at time t with strike price K_1 and expiry T and selling a call at time t with strike price K_2, $K_2 > K_1$ and same expiry T.

  For a bull put spread, it is composed of

$$\text{Bull Put Spread} = P(S_t, t; K_1, T) - P(S_t, t; K_2, T)$$

which consists of buying a put at time t with strike price K_1 and expiry T and selling a put at time t with strike price K_2, $K_2 > K_1$ and same expiry T.

- **Bear Spread** The strategy behind the bear spread is the opposite of a bull spread. Here, the investor who enters a bear spread expects the stock price to fall.

  For a bear call spread, it is composed of

$$\text{Bear Call Spread} = C(S_t.t; K_2, T) - C(S_t, t; K_1, T)$$

  which consists of selling a call at time t with strike price K_1 and expiry T and buying a call at time t with strike price K_2, $K_2 > K_1$ and same expiry T.

  For a bear put spread, it is composed of

$$\text{Bear Put Spread} = P(S_t, t; K_2, T) - P(S_t, t; K_1, T)$$

  which consists of selling a put at time t with strike price K_1 and expiry T and buying a put at time t with strike price K_2, $K_2 > K_1$ and same expiry T.

- **Butterfly Spread** The investor who enters a butterfly spread expects that the stock price will not change significantly. It is a neutral strategy combining bull and bear spreads.

- **Straddle** This strategy is used if an investor believes that a stock price will move significantly, but is unsure in which direction. Here such a strategy depends on the volatility of the stock price rather than the direction of the stock price changes.

  For a long straddle, it is composed of

$$\text{Long Straddle} = C(S_t, t; K, T) + P(S_t, t; K, T)$$

  which consists of buying a call and a put option at time t with the same strike price K and expiry T.

  For a short straddle, it is composed of

$$\text{Short Straddle} = -C(S_t, t; K, T) - P(S_t, t; K, T)$$

  which consists of selling a call and a put option at time t with the same strike price K and expiry T.

- **Strangle** The strangle hedging strategy is a variation of the straddle with the key difference that the options have different strike prices but expire at the same time.

- **Strip/Strap** The strip and strap strategies are modifications of the straddle, principally used in volatile market conditions. However, unlike a straddle which has an unbiased outlook on the stock price movement, investors who use a strip (strap) strategy would exploit on downward (upward) movement of the stock price.

1.2 PROBLEMS AND SOLUTIONS

1.2.1 Forward and Futures Contracts

1. Consider an investor entering into a forward contract on a stock with spot price $10 and delivery date 6 months from now. The forward price is $12.50. Draw the payoff diagrams for both the long and short forward position of the contract.

   Solution: See Figure 1.4.

□

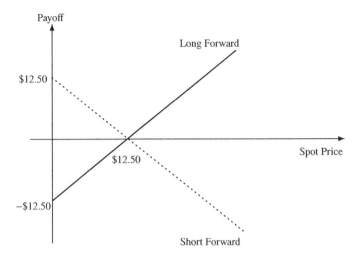

Figure 1.4   Long and short forward payoff diagram.

2. In terms of credit risk, is a forward contract riskier than a futures contract? Explain.

   Solution: Given that forward contracts are traded OTC between two parties and futures contracts are traded on exchanges which require margin accounts, forward contracts are riskier than futures contracts. ☐

3. Suppose ABC company shares are trading at $25 and pay no dividends and that the risk-free interest rate is 5% per annum. The forward price for delivery in 1 year's time is $28. Draw the payoff and profit diagrams for a long position for this contract.

   Solution: As there is no cost involved in entering into a forward contract, the payoff and profit diagrams coincide (see Figure 1.5).

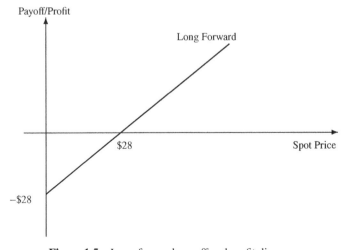

Figure 1.5   Long forward payoff and profit diagram.

☐

4. Consider a stock currently worth $100 per share with the risk-free interest rate 2% per annum. The futures price for a 1-year contract is worth $104. Show that there exists an arbitrage opportunity by entering into a short position in this futures contract.

Solution: At current time $t = 0$, a speculator can borrow $100 from the bank, buy the stock and short a futures contract.

At delivery time $T = 1$ year, the outstanding loan is now worth $100e^{0.02 \times 1} = \$102.02$. By delivering the stock to the long contract holder and receiving $104, the speculator can make a riskless profit of $104 - \$102.02 = \$1.98$.

$\square$

5. Let the current stock price be $75 with the risk-free interest rate 2.5% per annum. Assume the futures price for a 1-year contract is worth $74. Show that there exists an arbitrage opportunity by entering into a long position in this futures contract.

Solution: At current time $t = 0$, a speculator can short sell the stock, invest the proceeds in a bank account at the risk-free rate and then long a futures contract.

At time $T = 1$ year, the amount of money in the bank will grow to $75e^{0.025 \times 1} = \$76.89$. After paying for the futures contract which is priced at $74, the speculator can then return the stock to its owner. Thus, the speculator can make a riskless profit of $76.89 - \$74 = \$2.89$.

$\square$

6. An investor holds a long position in a stock index futures contract with a delivery date 3 months from now. The value of the contract is $250 times the level of the index at the start of the contract, and each index point movement represents a gain or a loss of $250 per contract. The futures contract at the start of the contract is valued at $250,000, and the initial margin deposit is $15,000 with a maintenance margin of $13,750 per contract.

Table 1.1 shows the stock index movement over a 4-day period.

Table 1.1   Daily closing stock index.

Day	Closing Stock Index
1	1002
2	994
3	998
4	997

Calculate the initial stock index at the start of the contract. By setting up a table, calculate the daily marking-to-market, margin balance and the variation margin over a 4-day period.

Solution: Since the futures contract is valued at $250,000 at the start of the contract, the initial stock index is $\frac{250,000}{250} = 1000$.

Table 1.2 displays the daily marking-to-market, margin balance and the variation margin in order to maintain the maintenance margin.

On Day 0, the initial balance is the initial margin requirement of $15,000 while on Day 1, as the change in the stock index is increased by 2 points, the margin balance is increased by $250 \times 2 = \$500$. On Day 2, the margin balance is $13,500 which is below the maintenance margin level of $13,750. Therefore, a deposit of $1,500 is needed to

Table 1.2   Daily movements of stock index.

Day	Required Deposit	Closing Stock Index	Daily Change	Marking-to-Market	Margin Balance	Variation Margin
0	$15,000	1000	0	0	$15,000	0
1	0	1002	+2	$500	$15,500	0
2	0	994	−8	−$2,000	$13,500	$1,500
3	$1,500	998	+4	$1,000	$16,000	0
4	0	997	−1	−$250	$15,750	0

bring the margin back to the margin requirement of $15,000. Hence, the variation margin is $1,500 occurring on Day 2.

□

7. An investor wishes to enter into 10 stock index futures contracts where the value of a contract is $250 times the level of the index at the start of the contract and each index point movement represents a gain or a loss of $250 per contract. The stock index at the start of the contract is 1,000 points and the initial margin deposit is 10% of the total futures contract value.

Let the continuously compounded interest rate be 5% which can be earned on the margin balance and the maintenance margin be 85% of the initial margin deposit. Suppose the investor position is marked on a weekly basis. What does the maximum stock index need to be in order for the investor to receive a margin call on week 1.

Solution: At the start of the contract the total futures contract value is $250 \times 1,000 \times 10 = $2,500,000$ and the initial margin deposit is $\$2,500,000 \times \frac{10}{100} = \$250,000$. The maintenance margin is therefore $\$250,000 \times \frac{85}{100} = \$187,500$.

To describe the movement of the stock index for week 1, see Table 1.3.

Table 1.3   Movement of stock index on week 1.

Week	Closing Stock Index	Weekly Change	Marking-to-Market	Margin Balance	Variation Margin
0	1000	0	0	$250,000	0
1	x	$x - 1000$	$2,500$ $\times(x - 1000)$	$250,000$ $+ \$2,500$ $\times(x - 1000)$	$187,500

Thus, in order to invoke a margin call we can set

$$2500(x - 1000) + 250,000 = 187,500$$

$$x = 975.$$

Therefore, if the stock index were to fall to values below 975 points then a margin call will be issued on week 1.

□

8. Let S_t denote the price of a stock with a dividend payment $\delta \geq 0$ at time t. What is the price of the stock immediately after the dividend payment?

Solution: Let S_t^+ denote the price of the stock immediately after the dividend payment. Therefore,

$$S_t^+ = S_t - \delta.$$

$\square$

9. Consider the price of a futures contract $F(t,T)$ with delivery time T on a stock with price S_t at time t ($t < T$). Suppose the stock does not pay any dividends. Show that under the no-arbitrage condition the futures contract price is

$$F(t,T) = S_t e^{r(T-t)}$$

where r is the risk-free interest rate.

Solution: We prove this result via contradiction.

If $F(t,T) > S_t e^{r(T-t)}$ then at time t an investor can short the futures contract worth $F(t,T)$ and then borrow an amount S_t from the bank to buy the asset. By time T the bank loan will amount to $S_t e^{r(T-t)}$. Since $F(t,T) > S_t e^{r(T-t)}$ then using the money received at delivery time T, the investor can pay off the loan, deliver the asset and make a risk-free profit $F(t,T) - S_t e^{r(T-t)} > 0$.

In contrast, if $F(t,T) < S_t e^{r(T-t)}$ then at time t an investor can long the futures contract, short sell the stock valued at S_t and then put the money in the bank. By time T the money in the bank will grow to $S_t e^{r(T-t)}$ and after returning the stock (from the futures contract) the investor will make a risk-free profit $S_t e^{r(T-t)} - F(t,T) > 0$.

Therefore, under the no-arbitrage condition we must have $F(t,T) = S_t e^{r(T-t)}$.

$\square$

10. Consider the price of a futures contract $F(t,T)$ with delivery time T on a stock with price S_t at time t ($t < T$). Throughout the life of the futures contract the stock pays discrete dividends $\delta_i, i = 1, 2, \ldots, n$ where $t < t_1 < t_2 < \cdots < t_n < T$. Show that under the no-arbitrage condition the futures contract price is

$$F(t,T) = S_t e^{r(T-t)} - \sum_{i=1}^{n} \delta_i e^{r(T-t_i)}$$

where r is the risk-free interest rate.

Solution: Suppose that over the life of the futures contract the stock pays dividends δ_i at time $t_i, i = 1, 2, \ldots, n$ where $t < t_1 < t_2 < \cdots < t_n < T$. When dividends are paid, the stock price S_t is reduced by the present values of all the dividends paid, that is

$$S_t - \sum_{i=1}^{n} \delta_i e^{-r(t_i-t)}.$$

Hence, using the same steps as discussed in Problem 1.2.1.9 (page 12), the futures price is

$$F(t,T) = \left(S_t - \sum_{i=1}^{n} \delta_i e^{-r(t_i-t)} \right) e^{r(T-t)}$$

$$= S_t e^{r(T-t)} - \sum_{i=1}^{n} \delta_i e^{r(T-t_i)}.$$

$\square$

11. Consider the number of stocks owned by an investor at time t as A_t where each of the stocks pays a continuous dividend yield D. Assume that all the dividend payments are reinvested in the stock. Show that the number of stocks owned by time T $(t < T)$ is

$$A_T = A_t e^{D(T-t)}.$$

Next consider the price of a futures contract $F(t,T)$ with delivery time T on a stock with price S_t at time t $(t < T)$. Suppose the stock pays a continuous dividend yield D. Using the above result, show that under the no-arbitrage condition the futures contract price is

$$F(t,T) = S_t e^{(r-D)(T-t)}$$

where r is the risk-free interest rate.

Solution: We first divide the time interval $[t,T]$ into n sub-intervals such that $t_i = t + \dfrac{i(T-t)}{n}$, $i = 1, 2, \ldots, n$ with $t_0 = t$ and $t_n = T$. By letting the dividend payment at time t_i be

$$\delta_i = \frac{D(T-t)}{n} S_t$$

for $i = 1, 2, \ldots, n$, and because all the dividends are reinvested in the stock, the number of stocks held becomes

$$A_{t_1} = A_{t_0} \left[1 + \frac{D(T-t)}{n} \right]$$

$$A_{t_2} = A_{t_1} \left[1 + \frac{D(T-t)}{n} \right] = A_{t_0} \left[1 + \frac{D(T-t)}{n} \right]^2$$

$$A_{t_3} = A_{t_2} \left[1 + \frac{D(T-t)}{n} \right] = A_{t_0} \left[1 + \frac{D(T-t)}{n} \right]^3$$

$$\vdots$$

$$A_{t_n} = A_{t_{n-1}} \left[1 + \frac{D(T-t)}{n} \right] = A_{t_0} \left[1 + \frac{D(T-t)}{n} \right]^n.$$

Because $A_{t_0} = A_t$ and $A_{t_n} = A_T$, therefore

$$A_T = A_t \left[1 + \frac{D(T-t)}{n}\right]^n$$

and taking limits $n \to \infty$ we have

$$\lim_{n\to\infty} A_T = A_t \lim_{n\to\infty} \left[1 + \frac{D(T-t)}{n}\right]^n = A_t e^{D(T-t)}.$$

From the above result we can deduce that investing one stock at time t will lead to a total growth of $e^{D(T-t)}$ by time T. Hence, if we start by buying $e^{-D(T-t)}$ number of stocks S_t at time t it will grow to one stock at time T. The total value of the stock at time t is therefore

$$S_t e^{-D(T-t)}$$

and following the arguments in Problem 1.2.1.9 (page 12) the futures price is

$$F(t,T) = S_t e^{-D(T-t)} e^{r(T-t)}$$
$$= S_t e^{(r-D)(T-t)}.$$

$\square$

12. Suppose an asset is currently worth \$20 and the 6-month futures price of this asset is \$22.50. By assuming the stock does not pay any dividends and the risk-free interest rate is the same for all maturities, calculate the 1-year futures price of this asset.

Solution: By definition the futures price is

$$F(t,T) = S_t e^{r(T-t)}$$

where t is the time of the start of the contract, T is the delivery time, S_t is the spot price at time t and r is the risk-free interest rate.
   By setting $t = 0$, $S_0 = \$20$ and $T_1 = 0.5$ years we have

$$F(0, T_1) = S_0 e^{rT_1} = \$22.50.$$

Hence,

$$r = 2\log\left(\frac{22.50}{20}\right) = 2\log 1.125.$$

Therefore, for a 1-year futures price, $T_2 = 1$ year

$$F(0, T_2) = S_0 e^{rT_2} = \$20 e^{2\log 1.125 \times 1} = \$25.31.$$

$\square$

13. Assume an investor buys 100,000 stocks of XYZ company and holds them for 3 years. Each of the stocks held pays a continuous dividend yield of 4% per annum and the investor

reinvests all the dividends when they are paid. Calculate the additional number of shares the investor would have at the end of 3 years.

Solution: Let $A_0 = 100{,}000$, $D = 0.04$ and $T = 3$ years. Therefore, by the end of 3 years, the number of shares owned by the investor is

$$A_T = A_0 e^{DT} = 100{,}000 e^{0.04 \times 3} = 112{,}749.69.$$

Therefore, the additional number of shares the investor has by the end of year 3 is

$$A_T - A_0 = 112{,}749.69 - 100{,}000 = 12{,}749.69 \simeq 12{,}749.$$

$\square$

14. Let the current stock price be \$30 with two dividend payments in 6 months and 9 months from today of \$1.50 and \$1.80, respectively. The continuously compounded risk-free interest rate is 5% per annum. Find the price of a 1-year futures contract.

Solution: Let $S_0 = \$30$, $t_1 = \frac{6}{12} = 0.5$ years, $t_2 = \frac{9}{12} = 0.75$ years, $\delta_1 = \$1.50$, $\delta_2 = \$1.80$, $r = 0.05$ and $T = 1$ year.
Therefore, the price of a 1-year futures contract is

$$\begin{aligned}
F(0,T) &= S_0 e^{rT} - \delta_1 e^{r(T-t_1)} - \delta_2 e^{r(T-t_2)} \\
&= 30 e^{0.05 \times 1} - 1.50 e^{0.05 \times (1 - 0.5)} - 1.80 e^{0.05 \times (1 - 0.75)} \\
&= \$28.18.
\end{aligned}$$

$\square$

15. Let the current price of a stock be \$12.75 that pays a continuous dividend yield D. Suppose the risk-free interest rate is 6% per annum and the price of a 6-month forward contract is \$13.25. Find D.

Solution: Let $S_0 = \$12.50$, $r = 0.06$, $T = 0.5$ years and $F(0,T) = \$13.25$. Since $F(0,T) = S_0 e^{(r-D)T}$,

$$12.75 e^{(0.06 - D) \times 0.5} = 13.25$$
$$D = 0.06 - \log\left(\frac{13.25}{12.75}\right) \times \frac{1}{0.5}$$
$$= 0.020395.$$

Hence, the dividend yield is $D = 2.0395\%$ per annum.

$\square$

1.2.2 Options Theory

1. Consider a long call option with strike price $K = \$100$. The current stock price is $S_t = \$105$ and the call premium is \$10. What is the intrinsic value of the call option at time t? Find the payoff and profit if the spot price at the option expiration date T is $S_T = \$120$. Draw the payoff and profit diagrams.

Solution: By defining $S_t = \$105$, $S_T = \$120$, $K = \$100$ and the call premium as $C(S_t, t; K, T) = \$10$, the intrinsic value of the call option at time t is

$$\Psi(S_t) = \max\{S_t - K, 0\} = \max\{105 - 100, 0\} = \$5.$$

At expiry time T, the payoff is

$$\Psi(S_T) = \max\{S_T - K, 0\} = \max\{120 - 100, 0\} = \$20$$

and the profit is

$$\Upsilon(S_T) = \Psi(S_T) - C(S_t, t; K, T) = \$20 - \$10 = \$10.$$

Figure 1.6 shows the payoff and profit diagrams for a long call option at the expiry time T. Here the profit diagram is a vertical shift of the call payoff based on the premium paid.

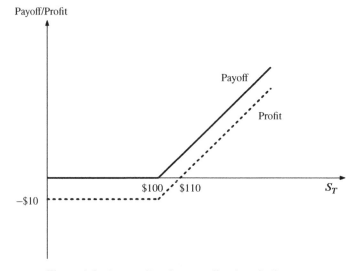

Figure 1.6   Long call option payoff and profit diagrams.

□

2. Consider a long put option with strike price $K = \$100$. The current stock price is $S_t = \$80$ and the put premium is \$5. What is the intrinsic value of the put option at time t? Find the payoff and profit if the spot price at the option expiration date T is $S_T = \$75$. Draw the payoff and profit diagrams.

Solution: By defining $S_t = \$80$, $S_T = \$75$, $K = \$100$ and the put premium as $P(S_t, t; K, T) = \$5$, the intrinsic value of the call option at time t is

$$\Psi(S_t) = \max\{K - S_t, 0\} = \max\{100 - 80, 0\} = \$20.$$

At expiry time T, the payoff is

$$\Psi(S_T) = \max\{K - S_T, 0\} = \max\{100 - 75, 0\} = \$25$$

and the profit is

$$\Upsilon(S_T) = \Psi(S_T) - P(S_t, t; K, T) = \$25 - \$5 = \$20.$$

Figure 1.7 shows the payoff and profit diagrams for a long put option at the expiry time T. Here the profit diagram is a vertical shift of the put payoff based on the premium paid.

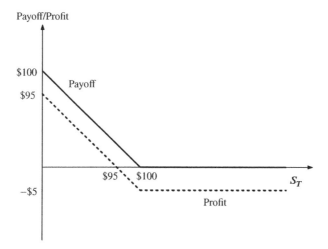

Figure 1.7   Long put option payoff and profit diagrams.

□

3. At time t we consider a long call option with a strike price K and a long forward contract with price K on the same underlying asset S_t. The premium for the call option is $C(S_t, t; K, T)$. Draw the profit diagram for these two financial instruments at the option expiry date T.

   Under what conditions is the call option more profitable than the forward contract, and vice versa?

   Solution: Figure 1.8 shows the profit diagram for a long call and a long forward contract at expiry date T.

   At time T the break even at the profit level is at $S_T = K - C(S_t, t; K, T)$. Therefore, if the stock $S_T \leq K - C(S_t, t; K, T)$ then the call option is more profitable as the loss is fixed with the amount of premium paid. However, if $S_T > K - C(S_t, t; K, T)$ then the forward contract is more profitable since there is no cost in entering a forward contract.

   □

4. At time t we consider a long put option with strike price K and a short forward contract with price K on the same underlying asset S_t. The premium for the put option is $P(S_t, t; K, T)$. Draw the profit diagram for these two financial instruments at the option expiry date T.

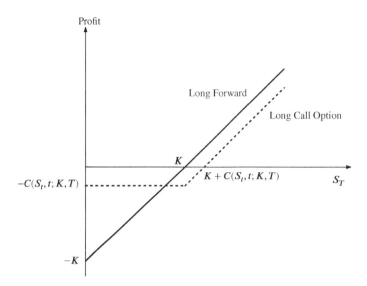

Figure 1.8 Long call option and long forward profit diagrams.

Under what conditions is the put option more profitable than the forward contract, and vice versa?

Solution: Figure 1.9 shows the profit diagram for a long put and a short forward contract at expiry date T.

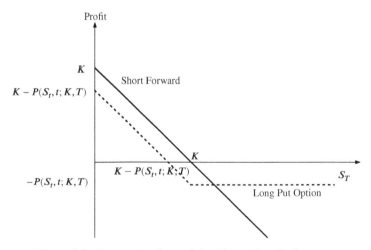

Figure 1.9 Long put option and short forward profit diagrams.

At time T the break-even point is at $S_T = K + P(S_t, t; K, T)$. Therefore, if the stock $S_T \geq K + P(S_t, t; K, T)$ then the put option is more profitable as the loss is fixed with the amount of premium paid. However, if $S_T < K + P(S_t, t; K, T)$ then the forward contract is more profitable since there is no cost in entering a forward contract.

$\square$

5. Consider a short call option with strike price $K = \$100$. The current stock price is $S_t = \$105$ and the call premium is $\$10$. What is the intrinsic value of the call option at time t? Find the payoff and profit if the spot price at the option expiration date T is $S_T = \$120$. Draw the payoff and profit diagrams.

Solution: By defining $S_t = \$105$, $S_T = \$120$, $K = \$100$ and the call premium as $C(S_t, t; K, T) = \$10$, the intrinsic value of the short call option at time t is

$$\Psi(S_t) = -\max\{S_t - K, 0\} = \min\{K - S_t, 0\} = \min\{100 - 105, 0\} = -\$5.$$

At expiry time T, the payoff is

$$\Psi(S_T) = -\max\{S_T - K, 0\} = \min\{K - S_T, 0\} = -\min\{100 - 120, 0\} = -\$20$$

and the profit is

$$\Upsilon(S_T) = \Psi(S_T) + C(S_t, t; K, T) = -\$20 + \$10 = -\$10.$$

Figure 1.10 shows the payoff and profit diagram for a short call option at the expiry time T. Here the profit diagram is a vertical shift of the short call payoff based on the premium received.

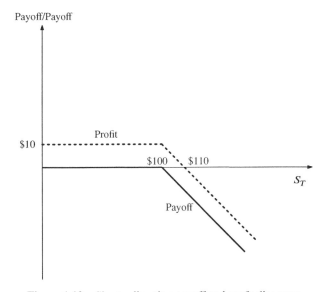

Figure 1.10   Short call option payoff and profit diagrams.

□

6. Consider a short put option with strike price $K = \$100$. The current stock price is $S_t = \$80$ and the put premium is $\$5$. What is the intrinsic value of the put option at time t? Find the payoff and profit if the spot price at the option expiration date T is $S_T = \$75$. Draw the payoff and profit diagrams.

Solution: By defining $S_t = \$80$, $S_T = \$75$, $K = \$100$ and the put premium as $P(S_t, t; K, T) = \$5$, the intrinsic value of the short put option at time t is

$$\Psi(S_t) = -\max\{K - S_t, 0\} = \min\{S_t - K, 0\} = \min\{80 - 100, 0\} = -\$20.$$

At expiry time T, the payoff is

$$\Psi(S_T) = -\max\{K - S_T, 0\} = \min\{S_T - K, 0\} = \min\{75 - 100, 0\} = -\$25$$

and the profit is

$$\Upsilon(S_T) = \Psi(S_T) + P(S_t, t; K, T) = -\$25 + \$5 = -\$20.$$

Figure 1.11 shows the payoff and profit diagrams for a short put option at the expiry time T. Here the profit diagram is a vertical shift of the short put payoff based on the premium received.

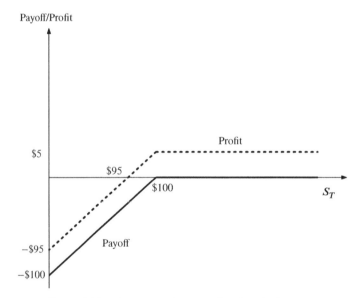

Figure 1.11   Short put option payoff and profit diagrams.

□

7. At time t we consider a short call option with strike price K and a short forward contract with price K on the same underlying asset S_t and expiry time $T > t$. The premium for the call option is $C(S_t, t; K, T)$ at time t. Draw the profit diagram for these two financial instruments at the option expiry time T.

   Under what conditions is the call option more profitable than the forward contract, and vice versa?

Solution: Figure 1.12 shows the profit diagram for a short call and a short forward contract at expiry time T.

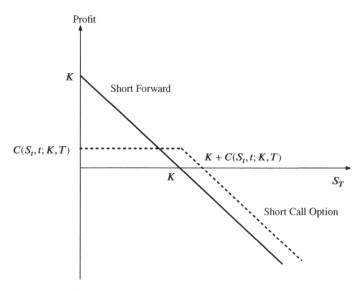

Figure 1.12   Short call option and short forward profit diagrams.

At time T the break-even point is at $S_T = K - C(S_t, t; K, T)$. Therefore, if the stock $S_T \leq K - C(S_t, t; K, T)$ then the forward contract is more profitable as the short call profit is fixed with the amount of premium received. However, if $S_T > K - C(S_t, t; K, T)$ then the forward contract is less profitable since the short call is augmented by the amount of premium paid to it.

$\qquad\qquad\qquad\qquad\qquad\qquad\qquad\qquad\qquad\qquad\qquad\qquad\qquad\qquad\qquad$ $\square$

8. At time t we consider a short put option with strike price K and a long forward contract with price K on the same underlying asset S_t and expiry time $T > t$. The premium for the put option is $P(S_t, t; K, T)$. Draw the profit diagram for these two financial instruments at the option expiry time T.

   Under what conditions is the put option more profitable than the forward contract, and vice versa?

   Solution: Figure 1.13 shows the profit diagram for a short put and a long forward contract at expiry time T.

   At time T the break-even point is at $S_T = K + P(S_t, t; K, T)$. Therefore, if the stock $S_T \geq K + P(S_t, t; K, T)$ then the forward contract is more profitable as the short put profit is fixed by the amount of premium received. However, if $S_T < K + P(S_t, t; K, T)$ then the forward contract is less profitable since the short put is augmented by the amount of premium paid to it.

$\qquad\qquad\qquad\qquad\qquad\qquad\qquad\qquad\qquad\qquad\qquad\qquad\qquad\qquad\qquad$ $\square$

9. *Put–Call Parity I.* At time t we consider a non-dividend-paying stock with spot price S_t and a risk-free interest rate r. Show that by taking a long European call option price at time t, $C(S_t, t; K, T)$ and a short European put option price at time t, $P(S_t, t; K, T)$ on the same

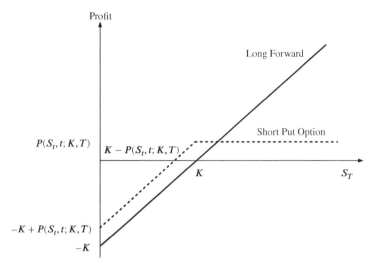

Figure 1.13   Short put option and long forward profit diagrams.

underlying stock S_t, strike price K and expiry time T ($t < T$) we have

$$C(S_t, t; K, T) - P(S_t, t; K, T) = S_t - Ke^{-r(T-t)}.$$

Solution: At time t we define the call option price as $C(S_t, t; K, T)$ and the put option price as $P(S_t, t; K, T)$, and we set the portfolio Π_t as

$$\Pi_t = C(S_t, t; K, T) - P(S_t, t; K, T).$$

At expiry time T

$$
\begin{aligned}
\Pi_T &= C(S_T, T; K, T) - P(S_T, T; K, T) \\
&= \max\{S_T - K, 0\} - \max\{K - S_T, 0\} \\
&= \begin{cases} S_T - K & \text{if } S_T \geq K \\ \\ S_T - K & \text{if } S_T < K \end{cases} \\
&= S_T - K.
\end{aligned}
$$

In order for the portfolio to generate a guaranteed K at expiry time T, at time t we can discount the final value of the portfolio to

$$C(S_t, t; K, T) - P(S_t, t; K, T) = S_t - Ke^{-r(T-t)}$$

since a share valued at S_t will be worth S_T at expiry time T.

$\square$

10. *Put–Call Parity II.* At time t we consider a discrete dividend-paying stock with spot price S_t where the stock pays dividend $\delta_i \geq 0$ at time t_i, $i = 1, 2, \ldots, n$ for $t < t_1 < t_2 < \cdots <$

$t_n < T$. Show that by taking a long European call option $C(S_t, t; K, T)$ and a short European put option $P(S_t, t; K, T)$ on the same underlying stock S_t, strike price K and expiry time T $(t < T)$ we have

$$C(S_t, t; K, T) - P(S_t, t; K, T) = S_t - \sum_{i=1}^{n} \delta_i e^{-r(t_i - t)} - K e^{-r(T-t)}$$

where r is the risk-free interest rate.

Solution: At time t we set up the portfolio Π_t as

$$\Pi_t = C(S_t, t; K, T) - P(S_t, t; K, T)$$

and at expiry time T

$$
\begin{aligned}
\Pi_T &= C(S_T, T; K, T) - P(S_T, T; K, T) \\
&= \max\{S_T - K, 0\} - \max\{K - S_T, 0\} \\
&= \begin{cases} S_T - K & \text{if } S_T \geq K \\ S_T - K & \text{if } S_T < K \end{cases} \\
&= S_T - K.
\end{aligned}
$$

In order for the portfolio to generate one stock S_T with guaranteed K at expiry time T, at time t we can discount the final value of the portfolio to

$$C(S_t, t; K, T) - P(S_t, t; K, T) = S_t - \sum_{i=1}^{n} \delta_i e^{-r(t_i - t)} - K e^{-r(T-t)}$$

since when dividends are paid the stock price S_t is reduced by the present value of all the dividends paid.

$\square$

11. *Put–Call Parity III.* At time t we consider a continuous dividend-paying stock with spot price S_t where D is the continuous dividend yield and r is the risk-free interest rate. Show that by taking a long European call option $C(S_t, t; K, T)$ and a short European put option $P(S_t, t; K, T)$ on the same underlying stock S_t, strike price K and expiry time T $(t < T)$ we have

$$C(S_t, t; K, T) - P(S_t, t; K, T) = S_t e^{-D(T-t)} - K e^{-r(T-t)}.$$

Solution: At time t we define the call option price as $C(S_t, t; K, T)$ and the put option price as $P(S_t, t; K, T)$, and we set the portfolio Π_t as

$$\Pi_t = C(S_t, t; K, T) - P(S_t, t; K, T).$$

At expiry time T

$$\Pi_T = C(S_T, T; K, T) - P(S_T, T; K, T)$$
$$= \max\{S_T - K, 0\} - \max\{K - S_T, 0\}$$
$$= \begin{cases} S_T - K & \text{if } S_T \geq K \\ S_T - K & \text{if } S_T < K \end{cases}$$
$$= S_T - K.$$

In order for the portfolio to generate one stock S_T with guaranteed K at expiry time T, at time t we can discount the final value of the portfolio to

$$C(S_t, t; K, T) - P(S_t, t; K, T) = S_t e^{-D(T-t)} - K e^{-r(T-t)}$$

since $e^{-D(T-t)}$ number of shares valued at $S_t e^{-D(T-t)}$ will become one share worth S_T at expiry time T.

□

12. At time t we consider a call option with strike price $K = \$100$. Calculate the intrinsic value of this option if the current spot price is $S_t = \$105$, $S_t = \$100$ or $S_t = \$95$ and state whether it is ITM, OTM or ATM.

Solution: At time t the intrinsic call option value is $\Psi(S_t) = \max\{S_t - K, 0\}$. Hence, if $S_t = \$105$

$$\Psi(S_t) = \max\{105 - 100, 0\} = \$5$$

and since $S_t > K$, the intrinsic value of the call option is ITM.
  As for $S_t = \$100$

$$\Psi(S_t) = \max\{100 - 100, 0\} = 0$$

and because $\Psi(S_t) = 0$ and $S_t = K$, the intrinsic value of the call option is ATM.
  Finally, for $S_t = \$95$

$$\Psi(S_t) = \max\{95 - 100, 0\} = 0$$

and since $S_t < K$, the intrinsic value of the call option is OTM.

□

13. At time t we consider a put option with strike price $K = \$100$. Compute the intrinsic value of this option if the current spot price is $S_t = \$105$, $S_t = \$100$ or $S_t = \$95$ and state whether it is ITM, OTM or ATM.

Solution: At time t the intrinsic put option value is $\Psi(S_t) = \max\{K - S_t, 0\}$. Hence, if $S_t = \$105$

$$\Psi(S_t) = \max\{100 - 105, 0\} = 0$$

and since $S_t > K$, the intrinsic value of the put option is OTM.
  As for $S_t = \$100$

$$\Psi(S_t) = \max\{100 - 100, 0\} = 0$$

and because $\Psi(S_t) = 0$ and $S_t = K$, the intrinsic value of the put option is ATM.

Finally, for $S_t = \$95$

$$\Psi(S_t) = \max\{100 - 95, 0\} = \$5$$

and since $S_t < K$, the intrinsic value of the put option is OTM.

□

14. Suppose we have a quote for a 3-month European put option, with a strike price $K = \$60$ of $\$1.25$. The current stock price $S_0 = \$62$ and the risk-free interest rate $r = 5\%$ per annum. Owing to small trading in call options, there is no listing for the 3-month \$60 call (a call option price with strike \$60 expiring in 3 months). Suppose the stock does not pay any dividends then find the price of the 3-month European call option.

Solution: We first denote $C(S_0, 0; K, T)$ and $P(S_0, 0; K, T)$ as the call and put option prices, respectively at time $t = 0$ with strike price K and option expiry time $T = 3$ months. Given $P(S_0, 0; K, T) = \$1.25$ and $T = \frac{3}{12} = 0.25$ years, by rearranging the put–call parity we can write

$$C(S_0, 0; K, T) = P(S_0, 0; K, T) + S_0 - Ke^{-rT}$$
$$= \$1.25 + \$62 - 60e^{-0.05 \times 0.25}$$
$$= \$4.00.$$

Hence, if the 3-month \$60 call is available, it should be priced at \$4.00.

□

15. At time t we consider a European call option $C(S_t, t; K, T)$ and a European put option $P(S_t, t; K, T)$ on the same underlying asset S_t, strike price K and expiry time T. Suppose the underlying asset pays a continuous dividend yield D and there is a risk-free interest rate r, then under what condition is a European call option more expensive than a European put option?

Solution: From the put–call parity

$$C(S_t, t; K, T) - P(S_t, t; K, T) = S_t e^{-D(T-t)} - Ke^{-r(T-t)}$$

then $C(S_t, t; K, T) > P(S_t, t; K, T)$ if

$$S_t e^{-D(T-t)} - Ke^{-r(T-t)} > 0$$

or

$$S_t > Ke^{-(r-D)(T-t)}.$$

□

16. Suppose that a 6-month European call option, with a strike price of $K = \$85$, has a premium of $\$2.75$. The futures price for a 6-month contract is worth \$75 and the risk-free rate $r = 5\%$ per annum. Find the price of a 6-month European put option with the same strike price.

Solution: At initial time $t = 0$ we denote $C(S_0, 0; K, T)$ and $P(S_0, 0; K, T)$ as the call and put option prices, respectively on the underlying asset S_0, strike K and expiry time $T = 6$

months. Let the expiry time $T = \frac{6}{12} = 0.5$ years, $C(S_0, 0; K, T) = \$2.75$ and set the futures price $F(0, T) = \$75$. From the put–call parity we have

$$C(S_0, 0; K, T) - P(S_0, 0; K, T) = S_0 e^{-DT} - K e^{-rT}$$

where D is the continuous dividend yield. Since

$$F(0, T) = S_0 e^{(r-D)T}$$

we can write

$$P(S_0, 0; K, T) = C(S_0, 0; K, T) - (F(0, T) - K)e^{-rT}$$

and by substituting $C(S_0, 0; K, T) = \$2.75$, $F(0, T) = \$75$, $K = \$85$, $r = 0.05$ and $T = 0.5$ years, the put option price is

$$P(S_0, 0; K, T) = \$2.75 - (\$75 - \$85)e^{-0.05 \times 0.5} = \$12.50.$$

□

17. Suppose a 12-month European call option, with a strike price of $K = \$35$, has a premium of 2.15. The stock pays a dividend valued at 1.50 four months from now and another dividend valued at 1.75 eight months from now. Given that the current stock price is $S_0 = \$32$ and the risk-free rate $r = 5\%$ per annum, find the price of a 12-month European put option with the same strike price.

    Solution: Using the put–call parity for a stock with discrete dividends at time $t = 0$ we have

$$C(S_0, 0; K, T) - P(S_0, 0; K, T) = S_0 - \delta_1 e^{-rt_1} - \delta_2 e^{-rt_2} - K e^{-rT}$$

where $S_0 = \$32$, $\delta_1 = \$1.50$, $t_1 = \frac{4}{12} = \frac{1}{3}$ years, $\delta_2 = \$1.75$, $t_2 = \frac{8}{12} = \frac{2}{3}$ years, $K = \$35$, $r = 0.05$ and $T = 1$ year with European call option price $C(S_0, 0; K, T) = \$2.15$ and unknown European put option price $P(S_0, 0; K, T)$.
    Thus,

$$P(S_0, 0; K, T) = C(S_0, 0; K, T) - S_0 + \delta_1 e^{-rt_1} + \delta_2 e^{-rt_2} + K e^{-rT}$$
$$= 2.15 - 32 + 1.50 e^{-0.05 \times \frac{1}{3}} + 1.75 e^{-0.05 \times \frac{2}{3}} + 35 e^{-0.05}$$
$$= \$6.61.$$

□

18. Consider a European put option priced at 2.50 with strike price 22 and a European call option priced at 4.75 with strike price 30. What are the maximum losses to the writer of the put and the buyer of the call?

Solution: At time t the maximum loss of a short put is $-K + P(S_t, t; K, T)$ where K is the strike price, $T > t$ is the expiry date and $P(S_t, t; K, T)$ is the put option price. Therefore, the maximum loss of a short put is $-\$22 + \$2.50 = -\$19.50$.

In contrast, the maximum loss to the buyer of the call option is the premium paid, that is $-\$4.75$.

□

19. Let the current stock price be \$35 and the European put option is ITM by \$3.50. Find the corresponding strike price.

Solution: At current time t, the intrinsic value of the put option is defined as

$$\Psi(S_t) = \max\{K - S_t, 0\}$$

where S_t and K are the current stock price and strike price, respectively.

Given $S_t = \$35$, $\Psi(S_t) = \$3.50$ and since $K > S_t$ (intrinsic value is ITM), then

$$K - \$35 = \$3.50 \quad \text{or} \quad K = \$38.50.$$

□

20. Given the current spot price $S_0 = \$55$ we consider a European call option and a European put option with premiums \$1.98 and \$0.79, respectively on a common strike price $K = \$58$ and having the same expiry time T. By setting the risk-free interest rate $r = 3\%$ per annum, find T.

Solution: From the put–call parity at time $t = 0$,

$$C(S_0, 0; K, T) + P(S_0, 0; K, T) = S_0 - Ke^{-rT}$$

where the call option $C(S_0, 0; K, T) = \$1.98$ and the put option $P(S_0, 0; K, T) = \$0.79$. Substituting $S_0 = \$55$, $K = \$58$ and $r = 0.03$, we have

$$1.98 - 0.79 = 55 - 58e^{-0.03 \times T}$$
$$1.19 = 55 - 58e^{-0.03 \times T}$$

and solving the equation, we have

$$e^{-0.03 \times T} = 0.9278$$

or

$$T \simeq 2.5 \text{ years.}$$

□

1.2.3 Hedging Strategies

1. *Covered Call.* A covered call is an investment strategy constructed by buying a stock and selling an OTM call option on the same stock.

Explain why a call writer would set up this portfolio trading strategy and show that this strategy is undertaken for $C(S_t, t; K, T) \geq S_t - K$ where $C(S_t, t; K, T)$ is the call option price written on stock S_t with strike price K at time t with option expiry time $T > t$.

Draw the profit diagram of this strategy at expiry time T $(T > t)$.

Solution: In writing a covered call where the writer owns the stock, the writer can cover the obligation of delivering the stock if the holder of the call exercises the option at expiry date. In addition, by writing a covered call, the writer assumes the stock price will not be higher than the strike price and thus enhance his income by receiving the call option's premium. In contrast, if the stock price declines in value then the writer will lose money.

At time T the payoff of this portfolio is

$$
\begin{aligned}
\Psi(S_T) &= S_T - C(S_T, T; K, T) \\
&= S_T - \max\{S_T - K, 0\} \\
&= \begin{cases} K & \text{if } S_T \geq K \\ S_T & \text{if } S_T < K \end{cases}
\end{aligned}
$$

whilst the profit is

$$
\Upsilon(S_T) = \begin{cases} K - S_t + C(S_t, t; K, T) & \text{if } S_T \geq K \\ S_T - S_t + C(S_t, t; K, T) & \text{if } S_T < K \end{cases}
$$

where we need to deduct the cost of acquiring S_t and also to add the call option premium at the start of the contract.

Since the break-even point occurs when $S_T = S_t - C(S_t, t; K, T)$ where $\Upsilon(S_T) = 0$, in order for the strategy to take place we require $S_t - C(S_t, t; K, T) \geq K$ or $C(S_t, t; K, T) \leq S_t - K$.

Figure 1.14 shows the profit diagram of a covered call.

Since $C(S_t, t; K, T) \leq S_t - K$, the maximum gain from this strategy is $K - S_t + C(S_t, t; K, T) \geq 0$ whilst the maximum loss is $-S_t + C(S_t, t; K, T) \leq 0$.

$\square$

2. *Covered Put.* A covered put is a hedging strategy constructed by selling a stock and selling an OTM put option on the same stock.

Explain why a put writer would set up this portfolio trading strategy and show that this strategy is undertaken for $P(S_t, t; K, T) \geq K - S_t$ where $P(S_t, t; K, T)$ is the put option price written on stock S_t with strike price K at time t and expiry time $T > t$.

Draw the profit diagram of this strategy at expiry time T $(T > t)$.

Solution: In writing a covered put the writer expects the stock price will decline in value relative to the strike and thus enhance his income by receiving the put option's premium. By selling the stock short, the writer does not need to worry if the stock price drops further. However, if the stock price is much greater than the strike price at expiry then the writer will lose money.

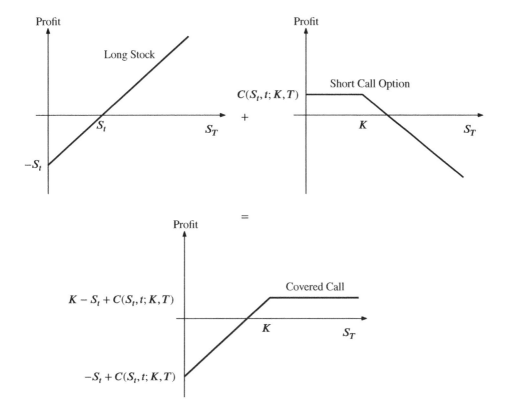

Figure 1.14   Construction of a covered call.

At time T the payoff of this portfolio is

$$\Psi(S_T) = -S_T - P(S_T, T; K, T)$$
$$= -S_T - \max\{K - S_T, 0\}$$
$$= \begin{cases} -S_T & \text{if } S_T \geq K \\ -K & \text{if } S_T < K \end{cases}$$

whilst the profit is

$$\Upsilon(S_T) = \Psi(S_T) + S_t + P(S_t, t; K, T)$$
$$= \begin{cases} S_t - S_T + P(S_t, t; K, T) & \text{if } S_T \geq K \\ S_t - K + P(S_t, t; K, T) & \text{if } S_T < K \end{cases}$$

where we need to add the sale of S_t and also the put option premium received at the start of the contract.

Since the break-even point occurs when $S_T = S_t + P(S_t, t; K, T)$ where $\Upsilon(S_T) = 0$, this strategy is undertaken when $S_t + P(S_t, t; K, T) \geq K$ or $P(S_t, t; K, T) \geq S_t - K$.

For a detailed construction of a covered put, see Figure 1.15.

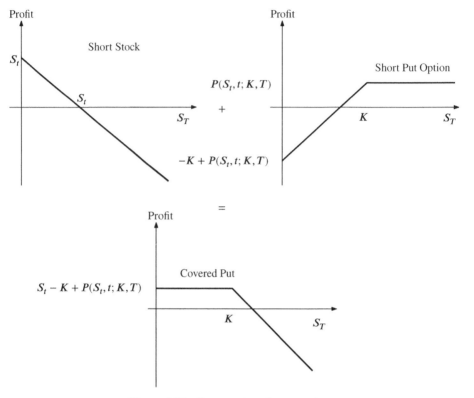

Figure 1.15   Construction of a covered put.

Since $P(S_t, t; K, T) \geq K - S_t$, the maximum gain from this strategy is capped at $S_t - K + P(S_t, t; K, T) \geq 0$ whilst the loss is unlimited.

$\square$

3. *Protective Call.* A protective call is an investment strategy constructed by selling a stock and buying an OTM call option on the same stock.

Explain why a call holder would set up this portfolio trading strategy and show that this strategy is undertaken for $C(S_t, t; K, T) \geq S_t - K$ where $C(S_t, t; K, T)$ is the call option price written on stock S_t with strike price K at time t and expiry time $T > t$.

Draw the profit diagram of this strategy at expiry time T $(T > t)$.

Solution: In buying a protective call the investor strategy is to protect profits from the rising stock price with respect to the strike price. By selling the stock the call holder assumes that the stock price will decline further. If the stock price is less than the strike at expiry time then the option will not be exercised and the call buyer will only lose the premium paid.

At time T the payoff of this portfolio is

$$\Psi(S_T) = -S_T + C(S_T, T; K, T)$$
$$= -S_T + \max\{S_T - K, 0\}$$
$$= \begin{cases} -K & \text{if } S_T \geq K \\ -S_T & \text{if } S_T < K \end{cases}$$

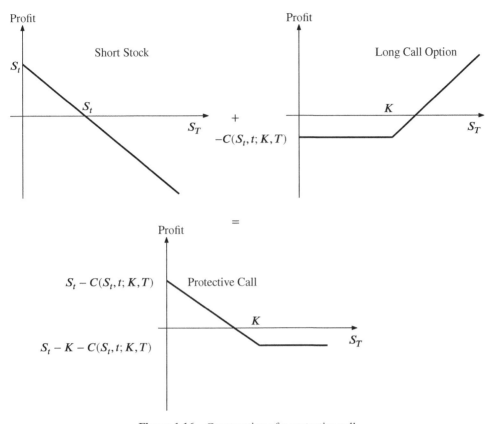

Figure 1.16   Construction of a protective call.

whilst the profit is

$$
\begin{aligned}
\Upsilon(S_T) &= \Psi(S_T) + S_t - C(S_t, t; K, T) \\
&= \begin{cases} S_t - K - C(S_t, t; K, T) & \text{if } S_T \geq K \\ S_t - S_T - C(S_t, t; K, T) & \text{if } S_T < K \end{cases}
\end{aligned}
$$

where we need to add the sale of the stock at time t and deduct the call option premium paid at the beginning of the contract.

Since the break-even point occurs when $S_T = S_t - C(S_t, t; K, T)$ so that $\Upsilon(S_T) = 0$, this strategy should be undertaken when $S_t - C(S_t, t; K, T) \leq K$ or $C(S_t, t; K, T) \geq S_t - K$.

Figure 1.16 shows the profit diagram of a protective call.

From the profit formula we can see that the protective call has a maximum upside gain of $S_t - C(S_t, t; K, T)$, which is the difference between the sale of the stock and the call option premium, and a limited loss of $S_t - K - C(S_t, t; K, T) \leq 0$.

$\square$

4. *Protective Put.* A protective put is a hedging strategy constructed by buying a stock and buying an OTM put option on the same stock.

   Explain why a put buyer would set up this portfolio trading strategy and show that this strategy is undertaken for $P(S_t, t) \geq K - S_t$ where $P(S_t, t; K, T)$ is the put option price written on stock S_t with strike price K at time t and expiry time $T > t$.

   Draw the profit diagram of this strategy at expiry time T ($T > t$).

Solution: In buying a protective put the investor strategy is to protect profits from the stock declining in value with respect to the strike price. By owning the stock the put holder can cover the obligation of delivering the stock to the put writer if the option is exercised at expiry time. If the stock price is above the strike at expiry time then the option will not be exercised and the put buyer will only lose the premium paid.

At time T the payoff of this portfolio is

$$\Psi(S_T) = S_T + P(S_T, T; K, T)$$
$$= S_T + \max\{K - S_T, 0\}$$
$$= \begin{cases} S_T & \text{if } S_T \geq K \\ K & \text{if } S_T < K \end{cases}$$

whilst the profit is

$$\Upsilon(S_T) = \begin{cases} S_T - S_t - P(S_t, t; K, T) & \text{if } S_T \geq K \\ K - S_t - P(S_t, t; K, T) & \text{if } S_T < K \end{cases}$$

where we need to deduct both the cost of acquiring S_t and the put option premium paid at the beginning of the contract.

Since the break-even point occurs when $S_T = S_t + P(S_t, t; K, T)$ so that $\Upsilon(S_T) = 0$, this strategy is undertaken if $S_t + P(S_t, t; K, T) \geq K$ or $P(S_t, t; K, T) \geq K - S_t$.

Figure 1.17 shows the profit diagram of a protective put.

From the profit formula we can see that the protective put has an unlimited upside gain and, because $P(S_t, t; K, T) \geq K - S_t$, it has a limited loss of $K - S_t - P(S_t, t; K, T) \leq 0$.

□

5. At time t consider a writer of a covered call on a \$35 stock with a strike price of \$40. The premium of the call option is \$1.75. Calculate the writer's maximum gain and loss at expiry time $T > t$.

Solution: At time t at the start of the contract let $S_t = \$35$, $K = \$40$ and the call option price $C(S_t, t; K, T) = \$1.75$.

From Problem 1.2.3.1 (page 28) the maximum gain of a covered call at expiry time T ($T > t$) is

$$\Upsilon_G(S_T) = K - S_t + C(S_t, t; K, T) = 40 - 35 + 1.75 = \$6.75$$

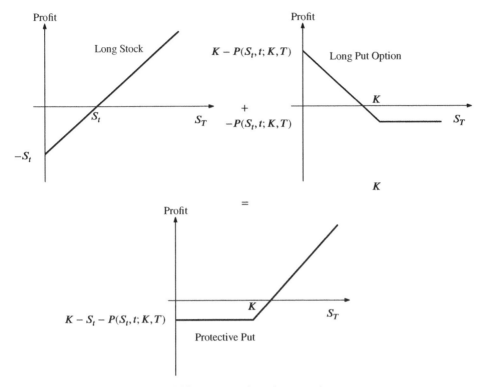

Figure 1.17   Construction of a protective put.

and the maximum loss is

$$\Upsilon_L(S_T) = -S_t + C(S_t, t; K, T) = -35 + 1.75 = -\$33.25.$$

□

6. At time t a writer short sells a stock for \$33 and sells a put option with strike price \$25 for \$1.75. What is the maximum gain and loss for the writer of this protective put at expiry time $T > t$?

   Solution: At current time t we let the spot price of the stock be $S_t = \$33$, strike $K = \$25$ and put option price $P(S_t, t; K, T) = \$1.75$. Therefore, from Problem 1.2.3.4 (page 33)

   $$\text{Maximum Gain of Protective Put} = +\infty$$

   and

   $$\begin{aligned}
   \text{Maximum Loss of Protective Put} &= K - S_t - P(S_t, t; K, T)\\
   &= \$25 - \$33 - \$1.75\\
   &= -\$9.75.
   \end{aligned}$$

   □

7. *Bull Call Spread.* A bull call spread is a hedging position designed to buy a call option $C(S_t, t; K_1, T)$ with strike K_1 and simultaneously sell a call option $C(S_t, t; K_2, T)$ with

strike K_2, $K_1 \leq K_2$ on the same underlying asset S_t and having the same expiry time T $(T > t)$.

Show that

$$C(S_t, t; K_1, T) \geq C(S_t, t; K_2, T), \quad K_1 \leq K_2$$

and draw the payoff and profit diagrams of a bull call spread.

Discuss under what conditions an investor should invest in such a hedging strategy.

Solution: We first assume $C(S_t, t; K_1, T) < C(S_t, t; K_2, T)$ and we set up a portfolio

$$\Pi_t = C(S_t, t; K_1, T) - C(S_t, t; K_2, T) < 0.$$

At expiry time T

$$
\begin{aligned}
\Pi_T &= C(S_T, T; K_1) - C(S_T, T; K_2) \\
&= \max\{S_T - K_1, 0\} - \max\{S_T - K_2, 0\} \\
&= \begin{cases} 0 & \text{if } S_T \leq K_1 \\ S_T - K_1 & \text{if } K_1 < S_T \leq K_2 \\ K_2 - K_1 & \text{if } S_T > K_2 \end{cases} \\
&\geq 0
\end{aligned}
$$

which constitutes an arbitrage opportunity. Therefore, $C(S_t, t; K_1, T) \geq C(S_t, t; K_2, T)$, $K_1 \leq K_2$.

At time T the payoff of this hedging strategy is

$$
\begin{aligned}
\Psi(S_T) &= C(S_T, T; K_1, T) - C(S_T, T; K_2, T) \\
&= \max\{S_T - K_1, 0\} - \max\{S_T - K_2, 0\} \\
&= \begin{cases} 0 & \text{if } S_T \leq K_1 \\ S_T - K_1 & \text{if } K_1 < S_T \leq K_2 \\ K_2 - K_1 & \text{if } S_T > K_2 \end{cases}
\end{aligned}
$$

and the corresponding profit is

$$
\begin{aligned}
\Upsilon(S_T) &= \Psi(S_T) - C(S_t, t; K_1, T) + C(S_t, t; K_2, T) \\
&= \begin{cases} C(S_t, t; K_2, T) - C(S_t, t; K_1, T) & \text{if } S_T \leq K_1 \\ S_T - K_1 + C(S_t, t; K_2, T) - C(S_t, t; K_1, T) & \text{if } K_1 < S_T \leq K_2 \\ K_2 - K_1 + C(S_t, t; K_2, T) - C(S_t, t; K_1, T) & \text{if } S_T > K_2 \end{cases}
\end{aligned}
$$

where the break-even point is $S_T = K_1 + C(S_t, t; K_1, T) - C(S_t, t; K_2, T)$ so that $\Upsilon(S_T) = 0$.

Figure 1.18 shows the payoff and profit diagrams of a bull call spread.

Based on the payoff and profit diagrams of a bull call spread, this hedging strategy would appeal to investors who have a bullish sentiment that the stock price

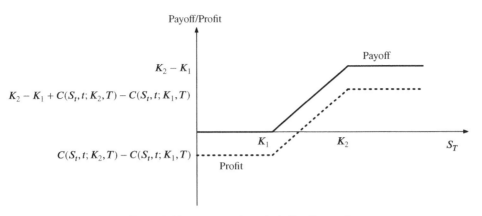

Figure 1.18   Construction of a bull call spread.

will increase in value relative to the strike prices K_1 and K_2. Hence, if $S_T > K_1 + C(S_t,t;K_1,T) - C(S_t,t;K_2,T)$ then the investor would make a profit but capped at a maximum gain of $K_2 - K_1 + C(S_t,t;K_2,T) - C(S_t,t;K_1,T) > 0$. However, if $S_T < K_1 + C(S_t,t;K_1,T) - C(S_t,t;K_2,T)$ then the investor would make a loss but limited to the difference between premiums received and paid.

$\qquad\qquad\qquad\qquad\qquad\qquad\qquad\qquad\qquad\qquad\qquad\qquad\qquad\qquad\quad\square$

8. *Bull Put Spread.* A bull put spread is an investment strategy constructed by buying a put option $P(S_t,t;K_1,T)$ with strike K_1 and simultaneously selling a put option $P(S_t,t;K_2,T)$ with strike K_2, $K_1 \leq K_2$ on the same underlying asset S_t and having the same expiry time T $(T > t)$.

 Show that

$$P(S_t,t;K_2,T) \geq P(S_t,t;K_1,T), \quad K_1 \leq K_2$$

and draw the payoff and profit diagrams of a bull put spread.

 Discuss under what conditions an investor should invest in such an investment strategy.

Solution: We first assume $P(S_t,t;K_2,T) < P(S_t,t;K_1,T)$ and we set up a portfolio

$$\Pi_t = P(S_t,t;K_2,T) - P(S_t,t;K_1,T) < 0.$$

At expiry time T

$$
\begin{aligned}
\Pi_T &= P(S_T,T;K_2,T) - P(S_T,T;K_1,T) \\
&= \max\{K_2 - S_T, 0\} - \max\{K_1 - S_T, 0\} \\
&= \begin{cases} K_2 - K_1 & \text{if } S_T \leq K_1 \\ K_2 - S_T & \text{if } K_1 < S_T \leq K_2 \\ 0 & \text{if } S_T > K_2 \end{cases} \\
&\geq 0
\end{aligned}
$$

which constitutes an arbitrage opportunity. Therefore, $P(S_t,t;K_2,T) \geq P(S_t,t;K_1,T)$, $K_1 \leq K_2$.

At time T the payoff of this hedging strategy is

$$\Psi(S_T) = P(S_T,T;K_1,T) - P(S_T,T;K_2,T)$$

$$= \max\{K_1 - S_T,0\} - \max\{K_2 - S_T,0\}$$

$$= \begin{cases} K_1 - K_2 & \text{if } S_T \leq K_1 \\ S_T - K_2 & \text{if } K_1 < S_T \leq K_2 \\ 0 & \text{if } S_T > K_2 \end{cases}$$

and the corresponding profit is

$$\Upsilon(S_T) = \Psi(S_T) - P(S_t,t;K_1,T) + P(S_t,t;K_2,T)$$

$$= \begin{cases} K_1 - K_2 + P(S_t,t;K_2,T) - P(S_t,t;K_1,T) & \text{if } S_T \leq K_1 \\ S_T - K_2 + P(S_t,t;K_2,T) - P(S_t,t;K_1,T) & \text{if } K_1 < S_T \leq K_2 \\ P(S_t,t;K_2,T) - P(S_t,t;K_1,T) & \text{if } S_T > K_2 \end{cases}$$

where the break-even point is $S_T = K_2 + P(S_t,t;K_1,T) - P(S_t,t;K_2,T)$ so that $\Upsilon(S_T) = 0$.

Figure 1.19 shows the payoff and profit diagrams of a bull put spread.

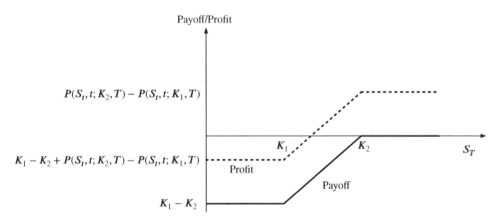

Figure 1.19   Construction of a bull put spread.

Based on the payoff and profit diagrams of a bull put spread, this hedging strategy would appeal to investors who have a bullish sentiment that the stock price will increase in value relative to the strike prices K_1 and K_2. Hence, if $S_T > K_2 + P(S_t,t;K_1,T) - P(S_t,t;K_2,T)$ then the investor would make a profit but capped at a maximum gain based on the difference between the put premiums received and paid. However, if $S_T < K_2 + P(S_t,t;K_1,T) - P(S_t,t;K_2,T)$ then the investor would make a loss but limited to a maximum loss of $K_1 - K_2 + P(S_t,t;K_2,T) - P(S_t,t;K_1,T) < 0$.

□

9. *Bear Call Spread.* A bear call spread is a hedging position designed to sell a call option $C(S_t, t; K_1, T)$ with strike K_1 and simultaneously buy a call option $C(S_t, t; K_2, T)$ with strike K_2, $K_1 \leq K_2$ on the same underlying asset S_t and having the same expiry time T $(T > t)$.

Show that

$$C(S_t, t; K_1, T) \geq C(S_t, t; K_2, T), \quad K_1 \leq K_2$$

and draw the payoff and profit diagrams of a bear call spread.

Discuss under what conditions an investor should invest in such a hedging strategy.

Solution: To show that $C(S_t, t; K_1, T) \geq C(S_t, t; K_2, T)$ for $K_1 \leq K_2$ see Problem 1.2.3.7 (page 34).

At time T the payoff of this hedging strategy is

$$
\begin{aligned}
\Psi(S_T) &= -C(S_T, T; K_1, T) + C(S_T, T; K_2, T) \\
&= -\max\{S_T - K_1, 0\} + \max\{S_T - K_2, 0\} \\
&= \begin{cases} 0 & \text{if } S_T \leq K_1 \\ K_1 - S_T & \text{if } K_1 < S_T \leq K_2 \\ K_1 - K_2 & \text{if } S_T > K_2 \end{cases}
\end{aligned}
$$

and the corresponding profit is

$$
\begin{aligned}
\Upsilon(S_T) &= \Psi(S_T) + C(S_t, t; K_1, T) - C(S_t, t; K_2, T) \\
&= \begin{cases} C(S_t, t; K_1, T) - C(S_t, t; K_2, T) & \text{if } S_T \leq K_1 \\ K_1 - S_T + C(S_t, t; K_1, T) - C(S_t, t; K_2, T) & \text{if } K_1 < S_T \leq K_2 \\ K_1 - K_2 + C(S_t, t; K_1, T) - C(S_t, t; K_2, T) & \text{if } S_T > K_2 \end{cases}
\end{aligned}
$$

where the break-even point is $S_T = K_1 + C(S_t, t; K_1, T) - C(S_t, t; K_2, T)$ so that $\Upsilon(S_T) = 0$.

Figure 1.20 is the payoff and profit diagrams of a bear call spread.

Based on the payoff and profit diagrams of a bear call spread, this hedging strategy would appeal to investors who have a bearish attitude that the stock price will decrease in value relative to the strike prices K_1 and K_2. Hence, if $S_T < K_1 + C(S_t, t; K_1, T) - C(S_t, t; K_2, T)$ then the investor would make a profit but capped at a maximum gain based on the difference between the call premiums received and paid. On the other hand, if $S_T > K_1 + C(S_t, t; K_1, T) - C(S_t, t; K_2, T)$ then the investor would make a loss but limited to a maximum loss of $K_1 - K_2 + C(S_t, t; K_1, T) - C(S_t, t; K_2, T) < 0$.

$\square$

10. *Bear Put Spread.* A bear put spread is an investment strategy constructed by selling a put option $P(S_t, t; K_1, T)$ with strike K_1 and simultaneously buying a put option $P(S_t, t; K_2, T)$ with strike K_2, $K_1 \leq K_2$ on the same underlying asset S_t and having the same expiry time T $(T > t)$.

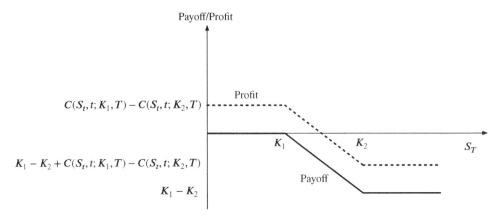

Figure 1.20   Construction of a bear call spread.

Show that

$$P(S_t, t; K_2, T) \geq P(S_t, t; K_1, T), \quad K_1 \leq K_2$$

and draw the payoff and profit diagrams of a bear put spread.

Discuss under what conditions an investor should invest in such an investment strategy.

Solution: To show that $P(S_t, t; K_2, T) \geq P(S_t, t; K_1, T)$ for $K_1 \leq K_2$ see Problem 1.2.3.8 (page 36).

At time T the payoff of this hedging strategy is

$$\Psi(S_T) = -P(S_T, T; K_1, T) + P(S_T, T; K_2, T)$$
$$= -\max\{K_1 - S_T, 0\} + \max\{K_2 - S_T, 0\}$$
$$= \begin{cases} K_2 - K_1 & \text{if } S_t \leq K_1 \\ K_2 - S_T & \text{if } K_1 < S_T \leq K_2 \\ 0 & \text{if } S_T > K_2 \end{cases}$$

and the corresponding profit is

$$\Upsilon(S_T) = \Psi(S_T) + P(S_t, t; K_1, T) - P(S_t, t; K_2, T)$$
$$= \begin{cases} K_2 - K_1 + P(S_t, t; K_1, T) - P(S_t, t; K_2, T) & \text{if } S_T \leq K_1 \\ K_2 - S_T + P(S_t, t; K_1, T) - P(S_t, t; K_2, T) & \text{if } K_1 < S_T \leq K_2 \\ P(S_t, t; K_1, T) - P(S_t, t; K_2, T) & \text{if } S_T > K_2 \end{cases}$$

where the break-even point is $S_T = K_2 + P(S_t, t; K_1, T) - P(S_t, t; K_2, T)$ so that $\Upsilon(S_T) = 0$.

Figure 1.21 shows the payoff and profit diagrams of a bear put spread.

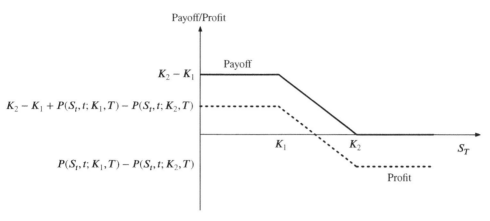

Figure 1.21   Construction of a bear put spread.

From the payoff and profit diagrams of a bear put spread we can see that this hedging strategy would appeal to investors who have a bearish attitude that the stock price will decrease in value relative to the strike prices K_1 and K_2. Hence, if $S_T < K_2 + P(S_t, t; K_1, T) - P(S_t, t; K_2, T)$ then the investor would make a profit but capped at a maximum gain of $K_2 - K_1 + P(S_t, t; K_1, T) - P(S_t, t; K_2, T)$. However, if $S_T > K_2 + P(S_t, t; K_1, T) - P(S_t, t; K_2, T)$ then the investor would make a loss but limited to a maximum loss of $P(S_t, t; K_1, T) - P(S_t, t; K_2, T) < 0$.

□

11. *Box Spread.* A long box spread is an investment strategy constructed by buying a bull call spread $C(S_t, t; K_1, T) - C(S_t, t; K_2, T)$ and buying a bear put spread $P(S_t, t; K_2, T) - P(S_t, t; K_1, T)$ with strikes K_1 and K_2, $K_1 \leq K_2$ on the same underlying asset S_t and having the same expiry time T $(T > t)$. Let the risk-free interest rate be r and the stock pays a continuous dividend D.

Show that the premium paid to enter into this portfolio strategy is the same as the present value of the payoff.

Show also that at time T the profit based on this strategy is independent of the terminal stock price S_T.

Give a financial interpretation of this investment strategy.

Solution: At initial time t the portfolio is worth

$$\Pi_t = C(S_t, t; K_1, T) - C(S_t, t; K_2, T) + P(S_t, t; K_2, T) - P(S_t, t; K_1, T)$$

and from the put–call parity

$$C(S_t, t; K_1, T) - P(S_t, t; K_1, T) = S_t e^{-D(T-t)} - K_1 e^{-r(T-t)}$$

and

$$C(S_t, t; K_2, T) - P(S_t, t; K_2, T) = S_t e^{-D(T-t)} - K_2 e^{-r(T-t)}.$$

Therefore,

$$\Pi_t = (K_2 - K_1)e^{-r(T-t)}.$$

At expiry time T the portfolio is

$$
\begin{aligned}
\Pi_T &= C(S_T, T; K_1, T) - C(S_T, T; K_2, T) \\
&\quad + P(S_T, T; K_2, T) - P(S_T, T; K_1, T) \\
&= \max\{S_T - K_1, 0\} - \max\{K_1 - S_T, 0\} \\
&\quad - \max\{S_T - K_2, 0\} + \max\{K_2 - S_T, 0\} \\
&= \begin{cases} K_2 - K_1 & \text{if } S_T \leq K_1 \\[2mm] K_2 - K_1 & \text{if } K_1 < S_T \leq K_2 \\[2mm] K_2 - K_1 & \text{if } S_T > K_2 \end{cases} \\
&= K_2 - K_1.
\end{aligned}
$$

Thus, at time t we can discount back the final value of the portfolio to become

$$\Pi_t = (K_2 - K_1)e^{-r(T-t)}$$

which is also the price of the premium paid.

The profit of entering such a hedging strategy is therefore

$$
\begin{aligned}
\Upsilon(S_T) &= \Pi_T - \Pi_t \\
&= (K_2 - K_1)(1 - e^{-r(T-t)}) \\
&> 0
\end{aligned}
$$

which guarantees a positive cash flow irrespective of the terminal stock price value S_T. Thus, the box spread is clearly an arbitrage opportunity provided the transaction cost is low.

□

12. At current time $t = 0$ a stock is trading at \$20 and for a risk-free interest rate of 4% per annum the prices of 6-month European options are given in Table 1.4.

Table 1.4   European option prices for different strikes.

Strike Price	European Call	European Put
\$20	\$1.98	\$1.58
\$27	\$1.21	\$7.68

Determine the payoff, premium paid and profit at the expiry time for a box spread constructed by buying a 20-strike European call, selling a 27-strike European call, selling a 20-strike European put and buying a 27-strike European put.

Solution: By setting $S_0 = \$20$, $K_1 = \$20$, $K_2 = \$27$, $r = 0.04$ and $T = \frac{6}{12} = 0.5$ years, from Problem 1.2.3.11 (page 40) the payoff of a box spread is

$$\Psi(S_T) = K_2 - K_1 = \$27 - \$20 = \$7.$$

The premium paid is therefore

$$\Psi(S_0) = (K_2 - K_1)e^{-rT} = \$7e^{-0.04 \times 0.5} = \$6.86$$

and the profit is

$$\Upsilon(S_T) = \Psi(S_T) - \Psi(S_0) = \$7 - \$6.86 = \$0.14.$$

$\square$

13. *Purchased Collar.* A purchased collar is a hedging strategy whereby at time t an investor buys an asset S_t, buys a put option $P(S_t, t; K_1, T)$ with strike price K_1 and sells a call option $C(S_t, t; K_2, T)$ with strike price K_2, $K_1 < K_2$ on the same underlying S_t and having the same expiry time $T(T > t)$.

Show that in order to prevent any arbitrage opportunity

$$S_t + P(S_t, t; K_1, T) - C(S_t, t; K_2, T) \geq 0.$$

Draw the profit diagram and give a financial interpretation of this hedging strategy.

Solution: We assume at time t that $S_t + P(S_t, t; K_1, T) - C(S_t, t; K_2, T) < 0$ and we set up a portfolio

$$\Psi(S_t) = S_t + P(S_t, t; K_1, T) - C(S_t, t; K_2, T) < 0.$$

At expiry time T

$$\begin{aligned}
\Psi(S_T) &= S_T + P(S_T, T; K_1, T) - C(S_T, T; K_2, T) \\
&= S_T + \max\{K_1 - S_T, 0\} - \max\{S_T - K_2, 0\} \\
&= \begin{cases} K_1 & \text{if } S_T \leq K_1 \\ S_T & \text{if } K_1 < S_T \leq K_2 \\ K_2 & \text{if } S_T > K_2 \end{cases} \\
&\geq 0
\end{aligned}$$

which is an arbitrage opportunity. Hence, $S_t + P(S_t, t; K_1, T) - C(S_t, t; K_2, T) \geq 0$.

Given that the investor has paid for both the stock S_t and the put premium $P(S_t, t; K_1, T)$ and simultaneously received $C(S_t, t; K_2, T)$, the profit at expiry time T is

$$\Upsilon(S_T) = \Psi(S_T) + C(S_t, t; K_2, T) - P(S_t, t; K_1, T) - S_t$$

where $\Psi(S_T) = S_T + P(S_T, T; K_1, T) - C(S_T, T; K_2, T)$ is the payoff of the purchased collar contract. Thus,

$$
\Upsilon(S_T) = \begin{cases}
K_1 + C(S_t, t; K_2, T) - P(S_t, t; K_1, T) - S_t & \text{if } S_T \leq K_1 \\
S_T + C(S_t, t; K_2, T) - P(S_t, t; K_1, T) - S_t & \text{if } K_1 < S_T \leq K_2 \\
K_2 + C(S_t, t; K_2, T) - P(S_t, t; K_1, T) - S_t & \text{if } S_T > K_2
\end{cases}
$$

with break even at $S_T = S_t + P(S_t, t; K_1, T) - C(S_t, t; K_2, T) \geq 0$.

Figure 1.22 shows the payoff and profit diagrams of a purchased collar.

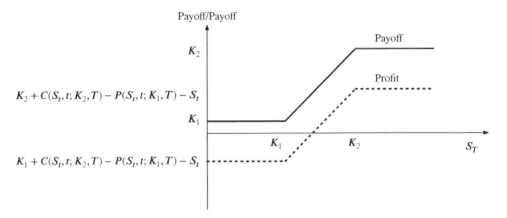

Figure 1.22   Construction of a purchased collar.

From the combination of options and asset we can see that the purchased collar is a hedging strategy consisting of buying a protective put and selling a call option. By buying a protective put the investor is able to insure the asset, whilst selling a call reduces the cost of insurance. Therefore, this position would be beneficial when the asset price $S_T > S_t + P(S_t, t; K_1, T) - C(S_t, t; K_2, T)$ (up to a maximum gain of $K_2 + C(S_t, t; K_2, T) - P(S_t, t; K_1, T) - S_t$) but if $S_T < S_t + P(S_t, t; K_1, T) - C(S_t, t; K_2, T)$ then the investor would lose money (up to a maximum loss of $K_1 + C(S_t, t; K_2, T) - P(S_t, t; K_1, T) - S_t$).

$\square$

14. *Written Collar.* A written collar is an investment strategy whereby at time t an investor would sell an asset S_t, sell a put option $P(S_t, t; K_1, T)$ with strike price K_1 and buy a call option $C(S_t, t; K_2, T)$ with strike price K_2, $K_1 < K_2$ on the same underlying S_t and having the same expiry time $T > t$.

Show that in order to prevent any arbitrage opportunity

$$
S_t + P(S_t, t; K_1, T) - C(S_t, t; K_2, T) \geq 0.
$$

Draw the payoff and profit diagrams and give a financial interpretation of this hedging strategy.

Solution: To show that at time t, $S_t + P(S_t, t; K_1, T) - C(S_t, t; K_2, T) \geq 0$ see Problem 1.2.3.13 (page 42).

At expiry time T the payoff is

$$\Psi(S_T) = -S_T - P(S_T, T; K_1, T) + C(S_T, T; K_2, T)$$
$$= -S_T - \max\{K_1 - S_T, 0\} + \max\{S_T - K_2, 0\}$$
$$= \begin{cases} -K_1 & \text{if } S_T \leq K_1 \\ -S_T & \text{if } K_1 < S_T \leq K_2 \\ -K_2 & \text{if } S_T > K_2 \end{cases}$$

while the profit at expiry time T is

$$\Upsilon(S_T) = \Psi(S_T) + S_t + P(S_t, t; K_1, T) - C(S_t, t; K_2, T)$$
$$= \begin{cases} -K_1 + S_t + P(S_t, t; K_1, T) - C(S_t, t; K_2, T) & \text{if } S_T \leq K_1 \\ -S_T + S_t + P(S_t, t; K_1, T) - C(S_t, t; K_2, T) & \text{if } K_1 < S_T \leq K_2 \\ -K_2 + S_t + P(S_t, t; K_1, T) - C(S_t, t; K_2, T) & \text{if } S_T > K_2 \end{cases}$$

with break even at $S_T = S_t + P(S_t, t; K_1, T) - C(S_t, t; K_2, T) \geq 0$.

Figure 1.23 shows the payoff and profit diagrams of a written collar.

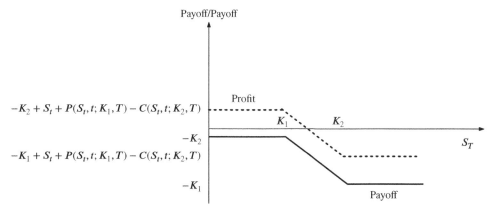

Figure 1.23   Construction of a written collar.

Given the combination of options and asset we can see that the written collar is a hedging strategy consisting of buying a protective call and selling a put option. By buying a protective call the investor is able to insure the short sale of the asset, whilst selling a put reduces the cost of insurance. Hence, this position would be beneficial when the asset price declines $S_T < S_t + P(S_t, t; K_1, T) - C(S_t, t; K_2, T)$ (up to a maximum gain of $-K_2 + S_t + P(S_t, t; K_1, T) - C(S_t, t; K_2))$ but if $S_T > S_t + P(S_t, t; K_1, T) - C(S_t, t; K_2, T)$ then the investor would lose money (up to a maximum loss of $-K_1 + S_t + P(S_t, t; K_1, T) - C(S_t, t; K_2, T))$.

□

15. *Long Straddle.* A long straddle is an investment strategy whereby at time t an investor would buy a call option $C(S_t, t; K, T)$ and buy a put option $P(S_t, t; K, T)$ on the same strike K using the same stock S_t and having the same expiry time T $(t < T)$.

   Draw the payoff and profit diagrams of this investment strategy and give a financial interpretation based on this combination of options portfolio.

Solution: We consider at time t that there is a stock worth S_t and for a strike price K the investor buys a call option $C(S_t, t; K, T)$ and a put option $P(S_t, t; K, T)$ on the same stock S_t with expiry time T.

   The payoff at time T is

$$\Psi(S_T) = C(S_T, T; K, T) + P(S_T, T; K, T)$$
$$= \max\{S_T - K, 0\} + \max\{K - S_T, 0\}$$
$$= \begin{cases} K - S_T & \text{if } S_T \leq K \\ S_T - K & \text{if } S_T > K \end{cases}$$

and the profit is

$$\Upsilon(S_T) = \Psi(S_T) - C(S_t, t; K, T) - P(S_t, t; K, T)$$
$$= \begin{cases} K - S_T - C(S_t, t; K, T) - P(S_t, t; K, T) & \text{if } S_T \leq K \\ S_T - K - C(S_t, t; K, T) - P(S_t, t; K, T) & \text{if } S_T > K \end{cases}$$

with break even at the profit level occurring at $S_T = K - C(S_t, t; K, T) - P(S_t, t; K, T)$ (provided $C(S_t, t; K, T) + P(S_t, t; K, T) \leq K$) and $S_T = K + C(S_t, t; K, T) + P(S_t, t; K, T)$.

   Figure 1.24 shows the payoff and profit diagrams of a long straddle.

   From the profit diagram we can see that the investor would make an unlimited profit if $S_T > K + C(S_t, t; K, T) + P(S_t, t; K, T)$ or a limited profit if $S_T < K - C(S_t, t; K, T) - P(S_t, t; K, T)$. In contrast, the maximum loss for the investor is the cost of purchasing the option. Hence, this strategy is dependent on how high the volatility of the stock is rather than the direction of the stock price. In short, the profit at expiry time relies on how much the stock price moves instead of whether it is increasing or decreasing in value.

□

16. *Short Straddle.* A short straddle is an investment strategy where at time t an investor would sell a call option $C(S_t, t; K, T)$ and sell a put option $P(S_t, t; K, T)$ on the same strike K using the same stock S_t and having the same expiry time T $(t < T)$.

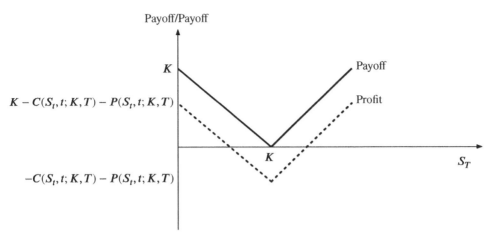

Figure 1.24 Construction of a long straddle.

Draw the payoff and profit diagrams of this investment strategy and give a financial interpretation based on this combination of options portfolio.

Solution: We consider at time t that there is a stock worth S_t and for a strike price K the writer sells a call option $C(S_t, t; K, T)$ and a put option $P(S_t, t; K, T)$ on the same stock S_t with expiry time T.

The payoff at time T is

$$\Psi(S_T) = -C(S_T, T; K, T) - P(S_T, T; K, T)$$
$$= -\max\{S_T - K, 0\} - \max\{K - S_T, 0\}$$
$$= \begin{cases} S_T - K & \text{if } S_T \leq K \\ K - S_T & \text{if } S_T > K \end{cases}$$

and the profit is

$$\Upsilon(S_T) = \Psi(S_T) + C(S_t, t; K, T) + P(S_t, t; K, T)$$
$$= \begin{cases} S_T - K + C(S_t, t; K, T) + P(S_t, t; K, T) & \text{if } S_T \leq K \\ K - S_T + C(S_t, t; K, T) + P(S_t, t; K, T) & \text{if } S_T > K \end{cases}$$

with break even at the profit level occurring either at $S_T = K - C(S_t, t; K, T) - P(S_t, t; K, T)$ (provided $C(S_t, t; K, T) + P(S_t, t; K, T) \leq K$) or $S_T = K + C(S_t, t; K, T) + P(S_t, t; K, T)$.

Figure 1.25 illustrates the payoff and profit diagrams of a short straddle.

From the profit diagram we can see that the writer would make an unlimited loss if $S_T > K + C(S_t, t; K, T) + P(S_t, t; K, T)$ or a limited loss if $S_T < K - C(S_t, t; K, T) - P(S_t, t; K, T)$. In contrast, the maximum gain for the writer is only the options premium received. Thus, unlike the long straddle, the short straddle depends very much on low

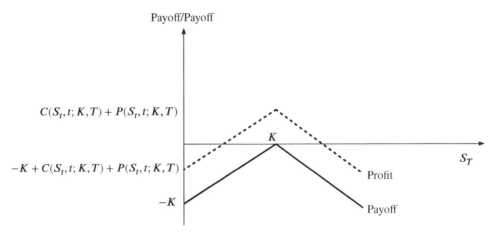

Payoff/Payoff

$C(S_t, t; K, T) + P(S_t, t; K, T)$

$-K + C(S_t, t; K, T) + P(S_t, t; K, T)$

K

S_T

Profit

$-K$

Payoff

Figure 1.25   Construction of a short straddle.

volatility and is most profitable if $S_T = K$. Hence, this strategy is dependent on the volatility of the stock rather than the direction of the stock price, and the writer who sells this portfolio of options would bet on the low volatility of the stock price.

□

17. Consider an investor buying a 35-strike call option and a 25-strike put option on a stock for prices of \$0.69 and \$0.52, respectively. Both of the options have the same expiry time of 6 months from now. Given that the current price of a stock is \$28 and the risk-free interest rate is $r = 3\%$ per annum, what is the position of this investment strategy? Find the profit and determine the break-even price of this hedging position at expiry time.

Solution: Let $S_0 = \$28$, $K_1 = \$25$, $K_2 = \$35$, $T = \frac{6}{12} = \frac{1}{2}$ years and we can write the portfolio at time $t = 0$ as

$$\Pi_0 = P(S_0, 0; K_1, T) + C(S_0, 0; K_2, T)$$

where $P(S_0, 0; K_1, T) = \$0.52$ is the put option price with strike $K_1 = \$25$ and $C(S_0, 0; K_2, T) = \$0.69$ is the call option price with strike price $K_2 = \$35$.

Since $K_1 < K_2$ and the options have the same expiry time on the same underlying asset price, the position is a long straddle.

At expiry time T the payoff is

$$\Psi(S_T) = P(S_T, T; K_1, T) + C(S_T, T; K_2, T)$$
$$= \max\{K_1 - S_T, 0\} + \max\{S_T - K_2, 0\}$$
$$= \begin{cases} K_1 - S_T & \text{if } S_T \le K_1 \\ K_1 - K_2 & \text{if } K_1 < S_T \le K_2 \\ S_T - K_2 & \text{if } S_T > K_2. \end{cases}$$

Given the total cost of the premium paid is $P(S_0,0;K_1,T) + C(S_0,0;K_2,T) = \$0.52 + \$0.69 = \$1.21$, the profit at expiry time T is

$$\Upsilon(S_T) = \Psi(S_T) - \$1.21$$

$$= \begin{cases} \$25 - S_T - \$1.21 & \text{if } S_T \leq K_1 \\ \$25 - \$35 - \$1.21 & \text{if } K_1 < S_T \leq K_2 \\ S_T - \$35 - \$1.21 & \text{if } S_T > K_2 \end{cases}$$

$$= \begin{cases} \$23.79 - S_T & \text{if } S_T \leq K_1 \\ -\$11.21 & \text{if } K_1 < S_T \leq K_2 \\ S_T - \$36.21 & \text{if } S_T > K_2 \end{cases}$$

with break-even points occurring at $S_T = \$23.79$ and $S_T = \$36.21$.

$\square$

18. *Long Strangle.* A long strangle is a hedging technique where at time t an investor would buy a put option $P(S_t,t;K_1,T)$ with strike K_1 and buy a call option $C(S_t,t;K_2,T)$ with strike K_2, $K_1 < K_2$ on the same stock S_t and having the same expiry time T ($t < T$).

   Draw the payoff and profit diagrams of this investment strategy and give a financial interpretation based on this combination of options portfolio.

Solution: At expiry time T the payoff of a long strangle portfolio is

$$\Psi(S_T) = P(S_T;T;K_1,T) + C(S_T;T;K_2,T)$$
$$= \max\{K_1 - S_T, 0\} + \max\{S_T - K_2, 0\}$$

$$= \begin{cases} K_1 - S_T & \text{if } S_T \leq K_1 \\ 0 & \text{if } K_1 < S_T \leq K_2 \\ S_T - K_2 & \text{if } S_T > K_2. \end{cases}$$

Given that the investor paid for the call and put premiums at time t, the profit at expiry time T is

$$\Upsilon(S_T) = \Psi(S_T) - P(S_t,t;K_1,T) - C(S_t,t;K_2,T)$$

$$= \begin{cases} K_1 - S_T - P(S_t,t;K_1,T) - C(S_t,t;K_2,T) & \text{if } S_T \leq K_1 \\ -P(S_t,t;K_1,T) - C(S_t,t;K_2,T) & \text{if } K_1 < S_T \leq K_2 \\ S_T - K_2 - P(S_t,t;K_1) - C(S_t,t;K_2) & \text{if } S_T > K_2 \end{cases}$$

with break even occurring at $S_T = K_1 - P(S_t, t; K_1, T) - C(S_t, t; K_2, T)$ (provided $P(S_t, t; K_1, T) + C(S_t, t; K_2, T) \le K_1$) and $S_T = K_2 + C(S_t, t; K_1, T) + P(S_t, t; K_1, T)$.

Figure 1.26 shows the payoff and profit diagrams of a long strangle.

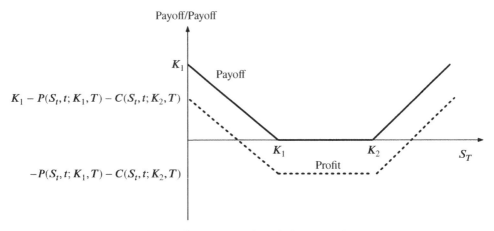

Figure 1.26   Construction of a long strangle.

Like the long straddle, the long strangle also exploits the volatility of the stock price where the profit is based on how much the price of the stock moves instead of its direction. Here the investor makes a positive gain at the expiry time T if $S_T > K_2 + P(S_t; t; K_1, T) + C(S_t, t; K_2, T)$ (unlimited gain) and if $S_T < K_1 - P(S_t, t; K_1, T) - C(S_t, t; K_2, T)$ (gain limited to $K_1 - P(S_t, t; K_1, T) - C(S_t, t; K_2, T)$). As for the downward risk, this strategy has a limited risk which is only the cost of the premiums paid and there is a range between the strikes in which the loss is unaffected by the change in stock price. Hence, this strategy is more suitable for high-volatility stocks.

$\square$

19. *Short Strangle.* A short strangle is a hedging technique where at time t a writer would sell a put option $P(S_t, t; K_1, T)$ with strike K_1 and sell a call option $C(S_t, t; K_2, T)$ with strike K_2, $K_1 < K_2$ on the same stock S_t and having the same expiry time T ($t < T$).

Draw the payoff and profit diagrams of this investment strategy and give a financial interpretation based on this combination of options portfolio.

Solution: At expiry time T the payoff of a short strangle portfolio is

$$\Psi(S_T) = -P(S_T; T; K_1, T) - C(S_T; T; K_2, T)$$
$$= -\max\{K_1 - S_T, 0\} - \max\{S_T - K_2, 0\}$$
$$= \begin{cases} S_T - K_1 & \text{if } S_T \le K_1 \\ 0 & \text{if } K_1 < S_T \le K_2 \\ K_2 - S_T & \text{if } S_T > K_2. \end{cases}$$

Given that the investor received the call and put premiums at time t, the profit at expiry time T is

$$\Upsilon(S_T) = \Psi(S_T) + P(S_t, t; K_1, T) + C(S_t, t; K_2, T)$$

$$= \begin{cases} S_T - K_1 + P(S_t, t; K_1, T) + C(S_t, t; K_2, T) & \text{if } S_T \leq K_1 \\ P(S_t, t; K_1, T) + C(S_t, t; K_2, T) & \text{if } K_1 < S_T \leq K_2 \\ K_2 - S_T + P(S_t, t; K_1, T) + C(S_t, t; K_2, T) & \text{if } S_T > K_2 \end{cases}$$

with break even occurring at $S_T = K_1 - P(S_t, t; K_1, T) - C(S_t, t; K_2, T)$ (provided $P(S_t, t; K_1, T) + C(S_t, t; K_2, T) \leq K_1$) and $S_T = K_2 + P(S_t, t; K_1, T) + C(S_t, t; K_2, T)$. Figure 1.27 shows the payoff and profit diagrams of a short strangle.

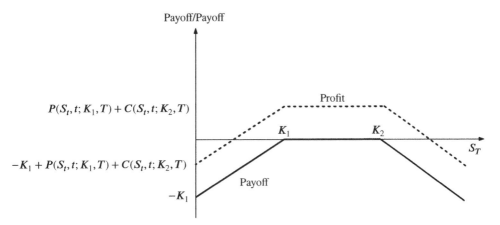

Figure 1.27   Construction of a short strangle.

Like the short straddle, the short strangle also exploits the low volatility of the stock price where the maximum profit is attained from the premiums received. But unlike the short straddle, this contract has a range between the strikes in which the gain is a constant value and unaffected by the change in strike price S_T. In contrast, by taking a short position of a strangle, the writer is exposed to a limited loss if $S_T < K_1 - P(S_t, t; K_1, T) - C(S_t, t; K_2, T)$ and an unlimited loss if $S_T > K_2 + P(S_t, t; K_1, T) + C(S_t, t; K_2, T)$. Hence, this strategy is more suitable for low-volatility stocks.

□

20. *Long Strip.* A long strip is an investment strategy where at time t an investor would buy a call option $C(S_t, t; K, T)$ and buy two put options $P(S_t, t; K, T)$ with strike K on the same stock S_t and having the same expiry time T $(t < T)$.
    Draw the payoff and profit diagrams of this investment strategy and give a financial interpretation based on this combination of options portfolio.

Solution: At expiry time T the payoff of this portfolio of options is

$$\Psi(S_T) = C(S_T, T; K, T) + 2P(S_T, T; K, T)$$
$$= \max\{S_T - K, 0\} + 2\max\{K - S_T, 0\}$$
$$= \begin{cases} 2(K - S_T) & \text{if } S_T \leq K \\ S_T - K & \text{if } S_T > K. \end{cases}$$

Given that the investor paid for the options premiums, the profit at expiry time T is

$$\Upsilon(S_T) = \Psi(S_T) - C(S_t, t; K, T) - 2P(S_t, t; K, T)$$
$$= \begin{cases} 2(K - S_T) - C(S_t, t; K, T) - 2P(S_t, t; K, T) & \text{if } S_T \leq K \\ S_T - K - C(S_t, t; K, T) - 2P(S_t, t; K, T) & \text{if } S_T > K \end{cases}$$

with break even at $S_T = K - \frac{1}{2}\left(C(S_t, t; K, T) + 2P(S_t, t; K, T)\right)$ (provided $C(S_t, t; K, T) + 2P(S_t, t; K, T) \leq 2K$) and $S_T = K + C(S_t, t; K, T) + 2P(S_t, t; K, T)$.

Figure 1.28 shows the payoff and profit diagrams of a long strip.

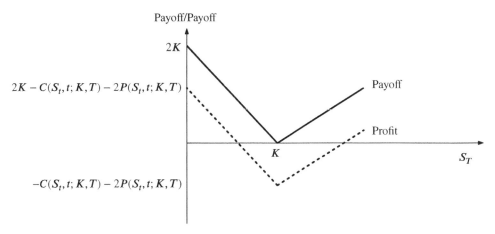

Figure 1.28   Construction of a long strip.

From the profit diagram we can see that the investor would make an unlimited profit if

$$S_T > K + C(S_t, t; K, T) + 2P(S_t, t; K, T)$$

or a limited profit if

$$S_T < K - \frac{1}{2}(C(S_t, t; K, T) + 2P(S_t, t; K, T)).$$

In contrast, the maximum loss for the investor is the cost of purchasing the options. Hence, like the long straddle, this strategy is also dependent on how high the volatility of the stock is rather than the direction of the stock price. However, the only difference between a long straddle and a long strip is that in the latter the strategy exploits more the fall in the stock price as the profit is much higher.

□

21. *Short Strip.* A short strip is an investment strategy where at time t an investor would sell a call option $C(S_t, t; K, T)$ and sell two put options $P(S_t, t; K, T)$ with strike K on the same stock S_t and having the same expiry time T $(t < T)$.

Draw the payoff and profit diagrams of this investment strategy and give a financial interpretation based on this combination of options portfolio.

Solution: At expiry time T the payoff of this portfolio of options is

$$\Psi(S_T) = -C(S_T, T; K, T) - 2P(S_T, T; K, T)$$
$$= -\max\{S_T - K, 0\} - 2\max\{K - S_T, 0\}$$
$$= \begin{cases} 2(S_T - K) & \text{if } S_T \leq K \\ \\ K - S_T & \text{if } S_T > K. \end{cases}$$

Given that the writer received the options premium, the profit at expiry time T is

$$\Upsilon(S_T) = \Psi(S_T) + C(S_t, t; K, T) + 2P(S_t, t; K, T)$$
$$= \begin{cases} 2(S_T - K) + C(S_t, t; K, T) + 2P(S_t, t; K, T) & \text{if } S_T \leq K \\ \\ K - S_T + C(S_t, t; K, T) + 2P(S_t, t; K, T) & \text{if } S_T > K \end{cases}$$

with break even at $S_T = K - \frac{1}{2}\left(C(S_t, t; K, T) + 2P(S_t, t; K, T)\right)$ (provided $C(S_t, t; K, T) + 2P(S_t, t; K, T) \leq 2K$) and $S_T = K + C(S_t, t; K, T) + 2P(S_t, t; K, T)$.

Figure 1.29 illustrates the payoff and profit diagrams of a short strip.

From the profit diagram we can see that the writer would make an unlimited loss if

$$S_T > K + C(S_t, t; K, T) + 2P(S_t, t; K, T)$$

or a limited loss if

$$S_T < K - \frac{1}{2}(C(S_t, t; K, T) + 2P(S_t, t; K, T)).$$

In contrast, the maximum gain is the premium received from the options. Hence, like the short straddle, this strategy is also dependent on how high the volatility of the stock is rather than the direction of the stock price. Here the writer bets that the stock price will remain stagnant but incurs a smaller loss if the stock price rises in value.

□

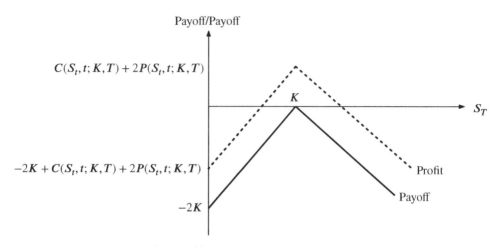

Figure 1.29   Construction of a short strip.

22. *Long Strap.* A long strap is a hedging technique where at time t an investor buys two call options $C(S_t, t; K, T)$ and one put option $P(S_t, t; K, T)$ with strike K on the same stock S_t and having the same expiry time T ($t < T$).

 Draw the payoff and profit diagrams of this investment strategy and give a financial interpretation based on this combination of options portfolio.

Solution: At expiry time T the payoff of this portfolio of options is

$$\Psi(S_T) = 2C(S_T, T; K, T) + P(S_T, T; K, T)$$
$$= 2\max\{S_T - K, 0\} + \max\{K - S_T, 0\}$$
$$= \begin{cases} K - S_T & \text{if } S_T \leq K \\ 2(S_T - K) & \text{if } S_T > K. \end{cases}$$

Given that the investor paid for an options premium, the profit at expiry time T is

$$\Upsilon(S_T) = \Psi(S_T) - 2C(S_t, t; K, T) - P(S_t, t; K, T)$$
$$= \begin{cases} K - S_T - 2C(S_t, t; K, T) - P(S_t, t; K, T) & \text{if } S_T \leq K \\ 2(S_T - K) - 2C(S_t, t; K, T) - P(S_t, t; K, T) & \text{if } S_T > K \end{cases}$$

with break even at $S_T = K - 2C(S_t, t; K, T) - P(S_t, t; K, T)$ (provided $2C(S_t, t; K, T) + P(S_t, t; K, T) \leq K$) and $S_T = K + \frac{1}{2}\left(2C(S_t, t; K, T) + P(S_t, t; K, T)\right)$.

 Figure 1.30 shows the payoff and profit diagrams of a long strap.

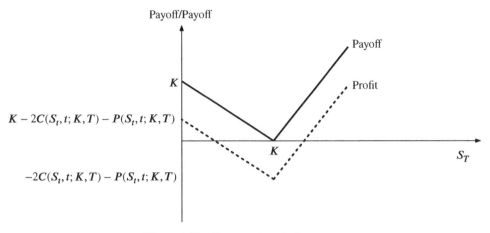

Figure 1.30   Construction of a long strap.

From the profit diagram we can see that the investor would make an unlimited profit if

$$S_T > K + \frac{1}{2}(2C(S_t, t; K, T) + P(S_t, t; K, T))$$

or a limited profit if

$$S_T < K - 2C(S_t, t; K, T) - P(S_t, t; K, T)$$

whilst the maximum loss for the investor is the cost of purchasing the options. Thus, like the long straddle, this strategy is also dependent on how high the volatility of the stock is rather than the direction of the stock price. However, the only difference between a long straddle and a long strap is that in the latter the strategy exploits more the rise in the stock price as the profit is much higher.

□

23. *Short Strap.* A short strap is a hedging technique where at time t a writer sells two call options $C(S_t, t; K, T)$ and one put option $P(S_t, t; K, T)$ with strike K on the same stock S_t and having the same expiry time T $(t < T)$.

Draw the payoff and profit diagrams of this investment strategy and give a financial interpretation based on this combination of options portfolio.

Solution: At expiry time T the payoff of this portfolio of options is

$$\Psi(S_T) = -2C(S_T, T; K, T) - P(S_T, T; K, T)$$
$$= -2\max\{S_T - K, 0\} - \max\{K - S_T, 0\}$$
$$= \begin{cases} S_T - K & \text{if } S_T \leq K \\ 2(K - S_T) & \text{if } S_T > K. \end{cases}$$

Given that the writer received the options premium, the profit at expiry time T is

$$\Upsilon(S_T) = \Psi(S_T) + 2C(S_t, t; K, T) + P(S_t, t; K, T)$$

$$= \begin{cases} S_T - K + 2C(S_t, t; K, T) + P(S_t, t; K, T) & \text{if } S_T \leq K \\ 2(K - S_T) + 2C(S_t, t; K, T) + P(S_t, t; K, T) & \text{if } S_T > K \end{cases}$$

with break even at $S_T = K - 2C(S_t, t; K, T) - P(S_t, t; K, T)$ (provided $2C(S_t, t; K, T) + P(S_t, t; K, T) \leq K$) and $S_T = K + C(S_t, t; K, T) + \frac{1}{2}P(S_t, t; K, T)$.

Figure 1.31 shows the payoff and profit diagrams of a short strap.

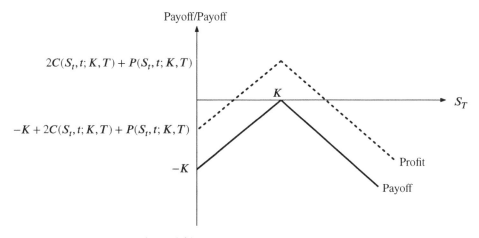

Figure 1.31   Construction of a short strap.

Based on the profit diagram we can see that the writer would make an unlimited loss if

$$S_T > K + C(S_t, t; K, T) + \frac{1}{2}P(S_t, t; K, T)$$

or a limited loss if

$$S_T < K - 2C(S_t, t; K, T) - P(S_t, t; K, T).$$

In contrast, the maximum gain is the premium received from the options. Hence, like the short straddle, this strategy is also dependent on how high the volatility of the stock is rather than the direction of the stock price. Here, the writer bets that the stock is price will remain stagnant but incurs a smaller loss if the stock price falls in value.

□

24. *Butterfly Spread (Using Call Options).* A butterfly spread is a hedging technique that, at time t and for strikes $K_1 < K_2 < K_3$, is constructed by buying one call option $C(S_t, t; K_1, T)$, buying one call option $C(S_t, t; K_3, T)$ and selling two call options $C(S_t, t; K_2, T)$ on the same stock S_t and having the same expiry time T ($t < T$).

Draw the payoff and profit diagrams of this hedging strategy with $K_2 = \frac{1}{2}(K_1 + K_3)$.

Solution: At expiry time T the payoff of a butterfly spread is

$$\Psi(S_T) = C(S_T,T;K_1,T) + C(S_T,T;K_3,T) - 2C(S_T,T;K_2,T)$$
$$= \max\{S_T - K_1, 0\} + \max\{S_T - K_3, 0\} - 2\max\{S_T - K_2, 0\}$$
$$= \begin{cases} 0 & \text{if } S_T \leq K_1 \\ S_T - K_1 & \text{if } K_1 < S_T \leq K_2 \\ 2K_2 - K_1 - S_T & \text{if } K_2 < S_T \leq K_3 \\ 2K_2 - K_1 - K_3 & \text{if } S_T > K_3 \end{cases}$$

and by setting $\Pi_t = C(S_t,t;K_1,T) + C(S_t,t;K_3,T) - 2C(S_t,t;K_2,T)$ the corresponding profit is

$$\Upsilon(S_T) = \Psi(S_T) - \Pi_t.$$

Hence, provided

$$-K_1 \leq C(S_t,t;K_1,T) + C(S_t,t;K_3,T) - 2C(S_t,t;K_2,T) \leq 2K_2 - 1$$

then break even occurs at

$$S_T = K_1 + C(S_t,t;K_1,T) + C(S_t,t;K_3,T) - 2C(S_t,t;K_2,T)$$

and

$$S_T = 2K_2 - K_1 - C(S_t,t;K_1,T) - C(S_t,t;K_3,T) + 2C(S_t,t;K_2,T).$$

Figure 1.32 shows the payoff and profit diagrams of a butterfly spread using call options with $K_2 = \frac{1}{2}(K_1 + K_3)$.

□

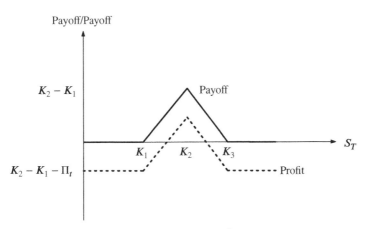

Figure 1.32   Construction of a butterfly spread with $K_2 = \frac{1}{2}(K_1 + K_3)$ and Π_t the net premium paid.

25. *Butterfly Spread (Using Put Options).* A butterfly spread is a hedging technique that, at time t and for strikes $K_1 < K_2 < K_3$, is constructed by buying one put option $P(S_t, t; K_1, T)$, buying one put option $P(S_t, t; K_3, T)$ and selling two put options $P(S_t, t; K_2, T)$ on the same stock S_t and having the same expiry time T $(t < T)$.

  Draw the payoff and profit diagrams of this hedging strategy with $K_2 = \frac{1}{2}(K_1 + K_3)$.

Solution: At expiry time T the payoff of a butterfly spread is

$$
\begin{aligned}
\Psi(S_T) &= P(S_T, T; K_1, T) + P(S_T, T; K_3, T) - 2P(S_T, T; K_2, T) \\
&= \max\{K_1 - S_T, 0\} + \max\{K_3 - S_T, 0\} - 2\max\{K_2 - S_T, 0\} \\
&= \begin{cases}
K_1 + K_3 - 2K_2 & \text{if } S_T \leq K_1 \\[2mm]
S_T + K_3 - 2K_2 & \text{if } K_1 < S_T \leq K_2 \\[2mm]
K_3 - S_T & \text{if } K_2 < S_T \leq K_3 \\[2mm]
0 & \text{if } S_T > K_3
\end{cases}
\end{aligned}
$$

and by setting $\Pi_t = P(S_t, t; K_1, T) + P(S_t, t; K_3, T) - 2P(S_t, t; K_2, T)$ the corresponding profit is

$$
\Upsilon(S_T) = \Psi(S_T) - \Pi_t.
$$

Hence, provided

$$
K_3 - 2K_2 \leq P(S_t, t; K_1, T) + P(S_t, t; K_3, T) - 2P(S_t, t; K_2, T) \leq K_3
$$

then break even occurs at

$$
S_T = 2K_2 - K_3 + P(S_t, t; K_1, T) + P(S_t, t; K_3, T) - 2P(S_t, t; K_2, T)
$$

and

$$
S_T = K_3 - P(S_t, t; K_1, T) - P(S_t, t; K_3, T) + 2P(S_t, t; K_2, T).
$$

Figure 1.33 shows the payoff and profit diagrams of a butterfly spread using put options with $K_2 = \frac{1}{2}(K_1 + K_3)$.

  □

26. *Butterfly Spread (Using Straddle and Strangle).* A butterfly spread is a hedging technique that, at time t and for strikes $K_1 < K_2 < K_3$, is constructed by selling a straddle:
  - sell a call option $C(S_t, t; K_2, T)$ with strike K_2
  - sell a put option $P(S_t, t; K_2, T)$ with strike K_2
  and buying a strangle:
  - buy a call option $C(S_t, t; K_1, T)$ with strike K_1
  - buy a put option $P(S_t, t; K_3, T)$ with strike K_3
  on the same stock S_t and having the same option expiry time T $(t < T)$.

  Draw the payoff and profit diagrams of this investment strategy with $K_2 = \frac{1}{2}(K_1 + K_3)$.

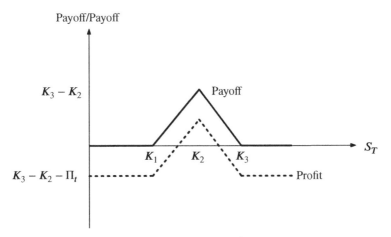

Figure 1.33 Construction of a butterfly spread with $K_2 = \frac{1}{2}(K_1 + K_3)$ and Π_t the net premium paid.

Solution: At expiry time T the payoff of a butterfly spread is

$$\Psi(S_T) = C(S_T, T; K_1, T) + P(S_T, T; K_3, T)$$
$$-C(S_T, T; K_2, T) - P(S_T, T; K_2, T)$$
$$= \max\{S_T - K_1, 0\} + \max\{K_3 - S_T, 0\}$$
$$- \max\{S_T - K_2, 0\} - \max\{K_2 - S_T, 0\}$$
$$= \begin{cases} K_3 - K_1 & \text{if } S_T \leq K_1 \\ \\ S_T + K_3 - K_1 - K_2 & \text{if } K_1 < S_T \leq K_2 \\ \\ -S_T + K_2 + K_3 - K_1 & \text{if } K_2 < S_T \leq K_3 \\ \\ K_2 - K_1 & \text{if } S_T > K_3 \end{cases}$$

and by setting $\Pi_t = C(S_t, t; K_1, T) + P(S_t, t; K_3, T) - C(S_t, t; K_2, T) - P(S_t, t; K_2, T)$ the corresponding profit is

$$\Upsilon(S_T) = \Psi(S_T) - \Pi_t.$$

Hence, provided

$$-K_1 - K_2 + K_3 \leq \frac{C(S_t, t; K_1, T) + P(S_t, t; K_3, T)}{-C(S_t, t; K_2, T) - P(S_t, t; K_2, T)} \leq -K_1 + K_2 + K_3$$

break even occurs at

$$S_T = K_2 + K_3 - K_1 - C(S_t, t; K_1, T) - P(S_t, t; K_3, T)$$
$$+ C(S_t, t; K_2, T) + P(S_t, t; K_2, T)$$

and

$$S_T = K_1 + K_2 - K_3 + C(S_t, t; K_1, T) + P(S_t, t; K_3, T)$$
$$- C(S_t, t; K_2, T) - P(S_t, t; K_2, T).$$

Figure 1.34 shows the payoff and profit diagrams of a butterfly spread with $K_2 = \frac{1}{2}(K_1 + K_3)$.

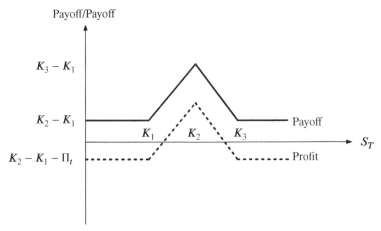

Figure 1.34   Construction of a butterfly spread with $K_2 = \frac{1}{2}(K_1 + K_3)$ and Π_t the net premium paid.

27. What is the financial motivation for an investor to enter into a butterfly spread contract?

Solution: Given three strike prices $K_1 < K_2 < K_3$, a butterfly spread can be constructed with a combination of call options, put options or by combining a straddle and a strangle.

At expiry time T for $0 < S_T^{min} < S_T^{max}$ such that the profit of a butterfly spread $\Upsilon(S_T^{min}) = 0$ and $\Upsilon(S_T^{max}) = 0$ then the investor would make a limited loss if the stock price $S_T > S_T^{max}$ or $S_T < S_T^{min}$. In contrast, the maximum gain for the investor occurs when $S_T = K_2$.

Thus, the investor buying a butterfly spread would speculate that the stock price at expiry time T will be between K_1 and K_3 in which the strategy will be most profitable. In essence, by exploiting simultaneously both the low and high volatilities of the stock price based on the combination of options, the investor purchasing a butterfly spread would bet that the stock price will stay close to K_2.

28. *Condor Spread (Using Call Options).* A condor spread is a hedging technique that, at time t and for strikes $K_1 < K_2 < K_3 < K_4$, is constructed by buying one call option $C(S_t, t; K_1, T)$, buying one call option $C(S_t, t; K_4, T)$, selling one call option $C(S_t, t; K_2, T)$ and selling one call option $C(S_t, t; K_3, T)$ on the same stock S_t and having the same option expiry time T $(t < T)$.

Draw the payoff and profit diagrams of this hedging strategy with $K_2 - K_1 = K_4 - K_3$.

Solution: Based on the construction of the options, the payoff at expiry time T is

$$\Psi(S_T) = C(S_T, T; K_1, T) - C(S_T, T; K_2, T)$$
$$-C(S_T, T; K_3, T) + C(S_T, T; K_4, T)$$
$$= \max\{S_T - K_1, 0\} - \max\{S_T - K_2, 0\}$$
$$- \max\{S_T - K_3, 0\} + \max\{S_T - K_4, 0\}$$

$$= \begin{cases} 0 & \text{if } S_T \leq K_1 \\ \\ S_T - K_1 & \text{if } K_1 < S_T \leq K_2 \\ \\ K_2 - K_1 & \text{if } K_2 < S_T \leq K_3 \\ \\ K_2 - K_1 + K_3 - S_T & \text{if } K_3 < S_T \leq K_4 \\ \\ K_2 - K_1 + K_3 - K_4 & \text{if } S_T > K_4 \end{cases}$$

and by setting $\Pi_t = C(S_t, t; K_1, T) - C(S_t, t; K_2, T) - C(S_t, t; K_3, T) + C(S_t, t; K_4, T)$ the corresponding profit is

$$\Upsilon(S_T) = \Psi(S_T) - \Pi_t.$$

Hence, provided

$$-K_1 \leq \frac{C(S_t, t; K_1, T) - C(S_t, t; K_2, T)}{-C(S_t, t; K_3, T) + C(S_t, t; K_4, T)} \leq -K_1 + K_2 + K_3$$

then break even occurs at

$$S_T = K_1 + C(S_t, t; K_1, T) - C(S_t, t; K_2, T) - C(S_t, t; K_3, T) + C(S_t, t; K_4, T)$$

and

$$S_T = K_2 - K_1 + K_3 - C(S_t, t; K_1, T) + C(S_t, t; K_2, T)$$
$$+ C(S_t, t; K_3, T) - C(S_t, t; K_4, T).$$

Figure 1.35 shows the payoff and profit diagrams of a condor spread using call options with $K_2 - K_1 = K_4 - K_3$.

$\square$

29. *Condor Spread (Using Put Options).* A condor spread is a hedging technique that, at time t and for strikes $K_1 < K_2 < K_3 < K_4$, is constructed by buying one put option $P(S_t, t; K_1, T)$, buying one put option $P(S_t, t; K_4, T)$, selling one put option $P(S_t, t; K_2, T)$ and selling one put option $P(S_t, t; K_3, T)$ on the same stock S_t and having the same expiry time T ($t < T$).

Draw the payoff and profit diagrams of this hedging strategy with $K_2 - K_1 = K_4 - K_3$.

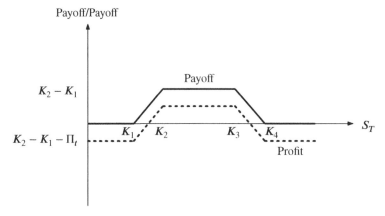

Figure 1.35   Construction of a condor spread with $K_2 - K_1 = K_4 - K_3$ and Π_t the net premium paid.

Solution: Based on the construction of the put options, the payoff at expiry time T is

$$
\begin{aligned}
\Psi(S_T) &= P(S_T, T; K_1, T) - P(S_T, T; K_2, T) \\
&\quad - P(S_T, T; K_3, T) + P(S_T, T; K_4, T) \\
&= \max\{K_1 - S_T, 0\} - \max\{K_2 - S_T, 0\} \\
&\quad - \max\{K_3 - S_T, 0\} + \max\{K_4 - S_T, 0\} \\
&= \begin{cases}
K_1 - K_2 - K_3 + K_4 & \text{if } S_T \leq K_1 \\
S_T - K_2 - K_3 + K_4 & \text{if } K_1 < S_T \leq K_2 \\
K_4 - K_3 & \text{if } K_2 < S_T \leq K_3 \\
K_4 - S_T & \text{if } K_3 < S_T \leq K_4 \\
0 & \text{if } S_T > K_4
\end{cases}
\end{aligned}
$$

and by setting $\Pi_t = P(S_t, t; K_1, T) - P(S_t, t; K_2, T) - P(S_t, t; K_3, T) + P(S_t, t; K_4, T)$ the corresponding profit is

$$
\Upsilon(S_T) = \Psi(S_T) - \Pi_t.
$$

Hence, provided

$$
-K_2 - K_3 + K_4 \leq \frac{P(S_t, t; K_1, T) - P(S_t, t; K_2, T)}{-P(S_t, t; K_3, T) + P(S_t, t; K_4, T)} \leq K_4
$$

then break even occurs at

$$S_T = K_2 + K_3 - K_4 + P(S_t, t; K_1, T) - P(S_t, t; K_2, T)$$
$$- P(S_t, t; K_3, T) + P(S_t, t; K_4, T)$$

and

$$S_T = K_4 - P(S_t, t; K_1, T) + P(S_t, t; K_2, T) + P(S_t, t; K_3, T) - P(S_t, t; K_4, T).$$

Figure 1.36 shows the payoff and profit diagrams of a condor spread using put options with $K_2 - K_1 = K_4 - K_3$.

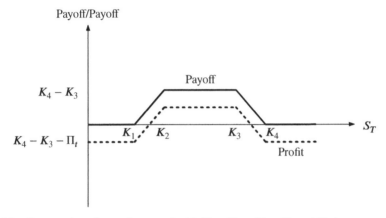

Figure 1.36   Construction of a condor spread with $K_2 - K_1 = K_4 - K_3$ and Π_t the net premium paid.

□

30. Explain the financial motivation for an investor to enter into a condor spread contract.

Solution: Using four different strike prices $K_1 < K_2 < K_3 < K_4$, a condor spread can be constructed with a combination of call options or put options.

At expiry time T for $0 < S_T^{\min} < S_T^{\max}$ such that the profit of a condor spread $\Upsilon(S_T^{\min}) = 0$ and $\Upsilon(S_T^{\max}) = 0$ then the investor would make a limited loss if the stock price $S_T > S_T^{\max}$ or $S_T < S_T^{\min}$.

Thus, the investor who invests in a condor spread speculates that the stock price at expiry time T will be between K_2 and K_3 in which the strategy will be most profitable. But unlike a butterfly spread, a condor spread has a much wider profit range at the expense of a higher premium paid. Thus, this contract is profitable for the investor who has a neutral outlook on the market.

□

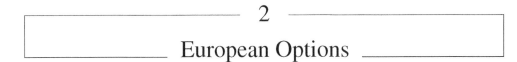

2

European Options

Options are one of the basic building blocks in finance and European options are the most common type of equity derivatives. They give the holder of the contract the right but not the obligation to enter into a future transaction only at the expiry date of the contract. In short, for buyers of European options, their right of exercise is only at expiration of the contract. As discussed in Chapter 1, a combination of such options with other products provides a multitude of trading strategies for hedgers, investors, traders and speculators.

2.1 INTRODUCTION

Central to the pricing of European options are the Black–Scholes (or Black–Scholes–Merton) formula and the martingale pricing theory. In the Black–Scholes–Merton formulation, there are two major approaches which arrive at the same partial differentiation equation formula:

- delta hedging strategy
- self-financing trading strategy

Delta Hedging Strategy
In 1973, Fischer Black and Myron Scholes published their paper "The pricing of options and corporate liabilities" in *The Journal of Political Economy* with the aim of deriving a theoretical valuation formula to price European options. The principal idea behind their theory is to hedge the option by buying/selling the underlying asset in such a way as to eliminate risk. This type of hedging is called delta hedging. Conceptually, at time t the hedging portfolio Π_t can be expressed by

$$\Pi_t = V - \Delta S_t$$

consisting of a long position in the option V and a Δ number of short positions in the asset S_t. Before the formula was derived, they made the following assumptions:

- The risk-free interest rate is known and is constant over time.
- The asset price follows a geometric Brownian motion.
- The asset pays no dividends during the life of the option.
- The option is European-style, which can only be exercised at expiry date.
- No transaction costs are associated with buying or selling the asset/option.
- Trading of the asset can take place continuously.
- Short selling is permitted.

Under these assumptions the option value depends only on the price of the asset and time, and on parameters which are taken to be known constants (i.e, $V = V(S_t, t)$). In addition, over "short" time intervals, the stochastic part of the change in the option price is perfectly correlated with changes in the stock price, i.e.,

$$d\Pi_t = dV - \Delta dS_t.$$

By writing the stochastic process of the asset price S_t as a geometric Brownian motion

$$\frac{dS_t}{S_t} = \mu dt + \sigma dW_t$$

where μ is the drift or expected rate of return, σ is a constant volatility and W_t is the standard Wiener process on the probability space $(\Omega, \mathcal{F}, \mathbb{P})$, and expanding $V(S_t, t)$ in a Taylor series about (S_t, t) and subsequently apply Itō's lemma we eventually have

$$dV = \frac{\partial V}{\partial t}dt + \frac{\partial V}{\partial S_t}dS_t + \frac{1}{2}\frac{\partial^2 V}{\partial S_t^2}(dS_t)^2 + \dots$$

$$= \left(\frac{\partial V}{\partial t} + \frac{1}{2}\sigma^2 S_t^2 \frac{\partial^2 V}{\partial S_t^2} + \mu S_t \frac{\partial V}{\partial S_t}\right)dt + \sigma S_t \frac{\partial V}{\partial S_t}dW_t.$$

As a result

$$d\Pi_t = \left(\frac{\partial V}{\partial t} + \frac{1}{2}\sigma^2 S_t^2 \frac{\partial^2 V}{\partial S_t^2} + \mu S_t \left(\frac{\partial V}{\partial S_t} - \Delta\right)\right)dt + \sigma S_t \left(\frac{\partial V}{\partial S_t} - \Delta\right)dW_t.$$

By choosing the portfolio weight $\Delta = \dfrac{\partial V}{\partial S_t}$ to eliminate all market risk, and from the assumption that the risk-free portfolio must have an expected return equal to the risk-free rate r, the governing partial-differential (or Black–Scholes) equation for an option price at time t, $V(S_t, t)$ is

$$\frac{\partial V}{\partial t} + \frac{1}{2}\sigma^2 S_t^2 \frac{\partial^2 V}{\partial S_t^2} + r S_t \frac{\partial V}{\partial S_t} - rV(S_t, t) = 0.$$

Note that in the Black–Scholes equation the drift parameter is not present, and this shows that the value of an option is independent of the rate of change of an underlying asset. The only parameters that affect the option price are the risk-free interest rate and the volatility of the asset underlying. As a result of this important argument, we may have a situation whereby two parties may differ in their estimate of the asset price growth, yet still agree on the price of an option.

Self-Financing Trading Strategy
In the same year, Robert C. Merton published "Theory of rational option pricing" in *The Bell Journal of Economics and Management Science* where an alternative derivation of the Black–Scholes model is presented via the construction of a self-financing trading strategy.

By definition, at time $t \in [0, T]$, the trading strategy (ϕ_t, ψ_t) of holding ϕ_t shares of risky asset S_t and ψ_t units of risk-free asset B_t having a portfolio value

$$\Pi_t = \phi_t S_t + \psi_t B_t$$

is called self-financing (or a self-financing portfolio) if and only if

$$d\Pi_t = \phi_t d S_t + \psi_t d B_t$$

implying that the change in portfolio value is due to changes in market conditions and not to either infusion or extraction of funds.

By definition, the contingent claim $V(S_T, T)$ is said to be attainable if there exists an admissible strategy worth $\Pi_T = V(S_T, T)$ at the option expiry time T. Here, the trading strategy (ϕ_t, ψ_t) is admissible if the portfolio $\Pi_t = \phi_t S_t + \psi_t B_t$ is self-financing and if $\Pi_t \geq -\alpha$ almost surely for some $\alpha > 0$ (i.e., a finite credit line).

In the absence of arbitrage, at every time $t \in [0, T]$, $V(S_t, t)$ must be equal to the portfolio value Π_t such that

$$\Pi_t = V(S_t, t).$$

Otherwise, an arbitrage opportunity occurs. At time $t \in [0, T]$, to replicate the option $V(S_t, t)$, we can now form the following self-financing portfolio

$$V(S_t, t) = \phi_t S_t + \psi_t B_t.$$

Let the risk-free asset price B_t and the risky asset price S_t have the following diffusion process

$$d B_t = r B_t dt \quad \text{and} \quad d S_t = \mu S_t dt + \sigma S_t d W_t$$

where r is the risk-free interest rate, μ is the asset drift rate, σ is the asset price volatility which are all constants and $\{W_t : 0 \leq t \leq T\}$ is a standard Wiener process on the probability space $(\Omega, \mathcal{F}, \mathbb{P})$.

Applying Taylor series on dV and using Itō's lemma, we eventually have

$$dV = \frac{\partial V}{\partial S_t} d S_t + \left(\frac{\partial V}{\partial t} + \frac{1}{2} \sigma^2 S_t^2 \frac{\partial^2 V}{\partial S_t^2} \right) dt.$$

Since the trading strategy (ϕ_t, ψ_t) is self-financing if and only if

$$d V = \phi_t d S_t + \psi_t d B_t = \phi_t d S_t + r B_t \psi_t dt$$

equating both of the equations we have

$$r B_t \psi_t = \frac{\partial V}{\partial t} + \frac{1}{2} \sigma^2 S_t^2 \frac{\partial^2 V}{\partial S_t^2} \quad \text{and} \quad \phi_t = \frac{\partial V}{\partial S_t}$$

and substituting the results into

$$V(S_t, t) = \phi_t S_t + \psi_t B_t$$

we have the Black–Scholes equation

$$\frac{\partial V}{\partial t} + \frac{1}{2}\sigma^2 S_t^2 \frac{\partial^2 V}{\partial S_t^2} + r S_t \frac{\partial V}{\partial S_t} - rV(S_t, t) = 0.$$

For a constant strike $K > 0$, if the terminal payoff at time $T > t$ is

$$V(S_T, T; K, T) = \begin{cases} \max\{S_T - K, 0\} & \text{for European call option} \\ \max\{K - S_T, 0\} & \text{for European put option} \end{cases}$$

with boundary conditions

$$V(0, t; K, T) = \begin{cases} 0 & \text{for European call option} \\ Ke^{-r(T-t)} & \text{for European put option} \end{cases}$$

and

$$\lim_{S_t \to \infty} V(S_t, t; K, T) = \begin{cases} S_t & \text{for European call option} \\ 0 & \text{for European put option} \end{cases}$$

then by solving the Black–Scholes equation via the the heat equation, the closed-form solution for the European call or put option price at time t is

$$V(S_t, t; K, T) = \begin{cases} S_t \Phi(d_+) - Ke^{-r(T-t)}\Phi(d_-) & \text{for European call option} \\ Ke^{-r(T-t)}\Phi(-d_-) - S_t \Phi(-d_+) & \text{for European put option} \end{cases}$$

where

$$d_\pm = \frac{\log(S_t/K) + (r - D \pm \frac{1}{2}\sigma^2)(T - t)}{\sigma \sqrt{T - t}}$$

and $\Phi(x) = \dfrac{1}{\sqrt{2\pi}} \displaystyle\int_{-\infty}^{x} e^{-\frac{1}{2}u^2} du$ is the cumulative distribution function (cdf) of a standard normal.

Given that the values of the European call and put options contain the function for the cdf of a standard normal distribution, we can see that the option prices have a relationship with the probability density function of the asset S_t which is log normally distributed. From the Feynman–Kac formula, we can infer that the option price can be interpreted as the discounted expected value of the payoff at expiry time T. This leads us to the subject of risk-neutral valuation of contingent claims via the martingale pricing theory.

Martingale Pricing Theory

As the name suggests, martingale pricing is based on the notion of equivalent martingale measure and risk-neutral valuation. Without loss of generality, assume we are in the Black–Scholes world with an economy consisting of a risky asset or stock S_t following a geometric Brownian motion and a risk-free asset B_t growing at a continuously compounded interest rate r of the form

$$\frac{dS_t}{S_t} = \mu dt + \sigma dW_t, \quad \frac{dB_t}{B_t} = r\,dt$$

where μ is the stock drift, σ is the stock volatility and W_t is a standard Wiener process on the probability space $(\Omega, \mathcal{F}, \mathbb{P})$.

Definition 2.1 (Equivalent Martingale Measure) *Let $(\Omega, \mathcal{F}, \mathbb{P})$ be the probability space satisfying the usual conditions and let $\mathbb{Q}$ be another probability measure on $(\Omega, \mathcal{F}, \mathbb{Q})$. The probability measure $\mathbb{Q}$ is said to be an equivalent measure or risk-neutral measure if it satisfies*

- *$\mathbb{Q} \sim \mathbb{P}$.*
- *The discounted price process $\{B_t^{-1} S_t^{(i)}\}$, $i = 1, 2, \ldots, m$ are martingales under $\mathbb{Q}$, that is*

$$\mathbb{E}^{\mathbb{Q}}\left(B_u^{-1} S_u^{(i)} \middle| \mathcal{F}_t \right) = B_t^{-1} S_t^{(i)}$$

for all $0 \leq t \leq u \leq T$.

From the definition of an equivalent martingale measure, we can now state Girsanov's theorem which tells us how to convert from the physical measure $\mathbb{P}$ to the risk-neutral measure $\mathbb{Q}$.

Theorem 2.2 (Girsanov's Theorem) *Let $\{W_t : 0 \leq t \leq T\}$ be a $\mathbb{P}$-standard Wiener process on the probability space $(\Omega, \mathcal{F}, \mathbb{P})$ and let $\mathcal{F}_t$, $0 \leq t \leq T$ be the associated Wiener process filtration. Suppose θ_t is an adapted process, $0 \leq t \leq T$ and consider*

$$Z_t = e^{-\int_0^t \theta_s dW_s - \frac{1}{2} \int_0^t \theta_s^2 ds}.$$

If

$$\mathbb{E}^{\mathbb{P}}\left(e^{\frac{1}{2} \int_0^T \theta_t^2 dt} \right) < \infty$$

*then Z_t is a positive $\mathbb{P}$-martingale for $0 \le t \le T$. By changing the measure $\mathbb{P}$ to a measure $\mathbb{Q}$
such that*

$$\mathbb{E}^{\mathbb{P}}\left(\left.\frac{d\mathbb{Q}}{d\mathbb{P}}\right|\mathscr{F}_t\right) = \left.\frac{d\mathbb{Q}}{d\mathbb{P}}\right|_{\mathscr{F}_t} = Z_t$$

then $\widetilde{W}_t = W_t + \int_0^t \theta_u\,du$ is a $\mathbb{Q}$-standard Wiener process.

Finally, as far as pricing of contingent claims $V(S_T,T)$ we can obtain the risk-neutral valuation approach given in the following theorem.

Theorem 2.3 *Assume that an equivalent martingale measure $\mathbb{Q}$ exists, and let $V(S_T,T)$ be an attainable contingent claim generated by an admissible self-financing trading strategy. Under the filtration $\mathscr{F}_t$, the European option price at time t is given by*

$$V(S_t,t) = B_t\mathbb{E}^{\mathbb{Q}}\left[\left.B_T^{-1}V(S_T,T)\right|\mathscr{F}_t\right] = e^{-r(T-t)}\mathbb{E}^{\mathbb{Q}}[V(S_T,T)|\mathscr{F}_t].$$

Remark 2.4 *Consider the stochastic differential equation (SDE)*

$$dX_t = \mu(X_t,t)dt + \sigma(X_t,t)dW_t$$

with $\mathbb{E}\left[\left(\int_0^t \sigma(X_s,s)^2 ds\right)^2\right] < \infty$, then X_t is a martingale if and only if X_t is driftless (i.e., $\mu(X_t,t) = 0$).

Since

$$\frac{d\left(\dfrac{S_t}{B_t}\right)}{\left(\dfrac{S_t}{B_t}\right)} = \frac{dS_t}{S_t} - \frac{dB_t}{B_t} - \frac{dS_t}{S_t}\frac{dB_t}{B_t} + \left(\frac{dB_t}{B_t}\right)^2$$

$$= (\mu - r)dt + \sigma dW_t$$

and by writing $d\widetilde{W}_t = dW_t + \theta dt$ where θ is a constant and $\widetilde{W}_t$ a $\mathbb{Q}$-standard Wiener process, and applying Girsanov's theorem to $d\left(\dfrac{S_t}{B_t}\right)\Big/\left(\dfrac{S_t}{B_t}\right)$, we obtain

$$\frac{d\left(\dfrac{S_t}{B_t}\right)}{\left(\dfrac{S_t}{B_t}\right)} = (\mu - r - \theta\sigma)dt + \sigma d\widetilde{W}_t.$$

To make S_t/B_t a $\mathbb{Q}$-martingale, we set

$$\theta = \frac{\mu - r}{\sigma}.$$

Thus, there is a unique θ which makes the discounted asset price process driftless, which is equivalent to saying that there is a unique change of measure which makes the discounted asset price a martingale under the risk-neutral measure.

Hence, under the risk-neutral measure $\mathbb{Q}$, the asset price follows the diffusion process

$$\frac{dS_t}{S_t} = r\,dt + \sigma d\,\widetilde{W}_t$$

and solving the SDE for $T > t$ and under the filtration $\mathcal{F}_t$ we have

$$\log\left(\frac{S_T}{S_t}\right)\bigg|\,\mathcal{F}_t \sim \mathcal{N}\left(\left(r - \frac{1}{2}\sigma^2\right)(T - t), \sigma^2(T - t)\right).$$

Thus, the European call option at time t with strike price K and expiry time $T > t$ is

$$\begin{aligned}
C(S_t, t; K, T) &= e^{-r(T-t)}\mathbb{E}^{\mathbb{Q}}\left[\max\{S_T - K, 0\}\big|\,\mathcal{F}_t\right]\\
&= e^{-r(T-t)}\mathbb{E}^{\mathbb{Q}}\left[(S_T - K)\mathbb{1}_{\{S_T \geq K\}}\big|\,\mathcal{F}_t\right]\\
&= e^{-r(T-t)}\left\{\mathbb{E}^{\mathbb{Q}}\left[S_T\mathbb{1}_{\{S_T \geq K\}}\big|\,\mathcal{F}_t\right] - K\mathbb{E}^{\mathbb{Q}}\left[\mathbb{1}_{\{S_T \geq K\}}\big|\,\mathcal{F}_t\right]\right\}\\
&= e^{-r(T-t)}\left\{\mathbb{E}^{\mathbb{Q}}\left[S_T\mathbb{1}_{\{S_T \geq K\}}\big|\,\mathcal{F}_t\right] - K\mathbb{Q}\left(S_T \geq K\big|\,\mathcal{F}_t\right)\right\}
\end{aligned}$$

whilst the European put option at time t with strike price K and expiry time $T > t$ is

$$\begin{aligned}
P(S_t, t; K, T) &= e^{-r(T-t)}\mathbb{E}^{\mathbb{Q}}\left[\max\{K - S_T, 0\}\big|\,\mathcal{F}_t\right]\\
&= e^{-r(T-t)}\mathbb{E}^{\mathbb{Q}}\left[(K - S_T)\mathbb{1}_{\{S_T \leq K\}}\big|\,\mathcal{F}_t\right]\\
&= e^{-r(T-t)}\left\{K\mathbb{E}^{\mathbb{Q}}\left[\mathbb{1}_{\{S_T \leq K\}}\big|\,\mathcal{F}_t\right]\right\} - \mathbb{E}^{\mathbb{Q}}\left[S_T\mathbb{1}_{\{S_T \leq K\}}\big|\,\mathcal{F}_t\right]\\
&= e^{-r(T-t)}\left\{K\mathbb{Q}\left(S_T \leq K\big|\,\mathcal{F}_t\right) - \mathbb{E}^{\mathbb{Q}}\left[S_T\mathbb{1}_{\{S_T \leq K\}}\big|\,\mathcal{F}_t\right]\right\}.
\end{aligned}$$

Continuous-Time Limit of Binomial Model

The binomial model or lattice approach is an alternative way to describe the evolution of the stochastic asset price process in discrete time. Following the seminal work of Cox, Ross and Rubinstein (1979), for each time step Δt, if the asset price begins at S_t at time t, then at time $t + \Delta t$ the asset can either move up to a value uS_t or move down to a value dS_t with risk-neutral probabilities π and $1 - \pi$, respectively where u and $d = 1/u$ are fixed constants such that $0 < d < e^{r\Delta t} < u$. The condition $d = 1/u$ is used to ensure that the lattice is symmetrical and is recombinant. Here, an up movement in the asset price for one node followed by a down movement in the asset price for the next node generates the same asset price as a down movement in the first node followed by an up movement in the next node.

Assuming that the asset price follows a geometric Brownian motion under the risk-neutral measure $\mathbb{Q}$

$$\log\left(\frac{S_{t+\Delta t}}{S_t}\right) \sim \mathcal{N}\left[\left(r - \frac{1}{2}\sigma^2\right)\Delta t, \sigma^2\Delta t\right]$$

and by matching the first and second moments up to $O(\Delta t)$

$$\mathbb{E}^Q\left(S_{t+\Delta t}\big| S_t\right) = \pi u S_t + (1-\pi) d S_t$$
$$\mathbb{E}^Q\left(S_{t+\Delta t}^2\big| S_t\right) = \pi u^2 S_t^2 + (1-\pi) d^2 S_t^2$$

we eventually have

$$u = e^{\sigma \Delta t}, \quad d = e^{-\sigma \Delta t} \quad \text{and} \quad \pi = \frac{e^{r \Delta t} - d}{u - d}.$$

Once we have built up a lattice of possible asset prices up to the option expiry time T, $T > t$ we can work backwards to price the option. Under the risk-neutral probability measure $\mathbb{Q}$, the European call option price at any node is given as the discounted expected value using the move up option and the move down option values multiplied by their respective risk-neutral probabilities. Thus, the option price corresponding to a node for time t is calculated as

$$V(S_t, t) = e^{-r \Delta t} \left[\pi V(u S_t, t + \Delta t) + (1-\pi) V(d S_t, t + \Delta t)\right].$$

To show that the Black–Scholes equation can be obtained as a limiting case in continuous time of the binomial model, we first take Taylor expansions of $V(u S_t, t + \Delta t)$ and $V(d S_t, t + \Delta t)$ so that

$$V(u S_t, t + \Delta t) = V(S_t + (u-1) S_t, t + \Delta t)$$
$$= V(S_t, t) + \frac{\partial V}{\partial t} \Delta t + \frac{\partial V}{\partial S_t}(u-1) S_t + \frac{1}{2} \frac{\partial^2 V}{\partial S_t^2}(u-1)^2 S_t^2$$
$$+ O\left((\Delta t)^2\right) + O\left((u-1)^3 S_t^3\right)$$

and

$$V(d S_t, t + \Delta t) = V(S_t + (d-1) S_t, t + \Delta t)$$
$$= V(S_t, t) + \frac{\partial V}{\partial t} \Delta t + \frac{\partial V}{\partial S_t}(d-1) S_t + \frac{1}{2} \frac{\partial^2 V}{\partial S_t^2}(d-1)^2 S_t^2$$
$$+ O\left((\Delta t)^2\right) + O\left((d-1)^3 S_t^3\right).$$

Hence,

$$\pi V(u S_t, t + \Delta t) + (1-\pi) V(d S_t, t + \Delta t) - e^{r \Delta t} V(S_t, t) = 0$$

becomes

$$\frac{\partial V}{\partial t} \Delta t + \frac{1}{2}\left[\pi(u-1)^2 + (1-\pi)(d-1)^2\right] S_t^2 \frac{\partial^2 V}{\partial S_t^2} + \left[\pi(u-1) + (1-\pi)(d-1)\right] S_t \frac{\partial V}{\partial S_t}$$

$$+ \left(1 - e^{r \Delta t}\right) V(S_t, t) + O\left((\Delta t)^2\right) + O\left((u-1)^3 S_t^3\right) + O\left((d-1)^3 S_t^3\right) = 0.$$

Taking first-order approximations

$$1 - e^{r\Delta t} = -r\Delta t + O((\Delta t)^2)$$
$$\pi(u - 1) + (1 - \pi)(d - 1) = r\Delta t + O((\Delta t)^2)$$
$$\pi(u - 1)^2 + (1 - \pi)(d - 1)^2 = \sigma^2 \Delta t + O((\Delta t)^2)$$

and because

$$O\left((u - 1)^3 S_t^3\right) = O((\Delta t)^3), O\left((d - 1)^3 S_t^3\right) = O((\Delta t)^3)$$

and by substituting the above information into the equation and dividing it by Δt, we have

$$\frac{\partial V}{\partial t} + \frac{1}{2}\sigma^2 S_t^2 \frac{\partial^2 V}{\partial S_t^2} + rS_t \frac{\partial V}{\partial S_t} - rV(S_t, t) + O(\Delta t) = 0.$$

Taking limits $\Delta t \to 0$, we finally obtain the Black–Scholes equation

$$\frac{\partial V}{\partial t} + \frac{1}{2}\sigma^2 S_t^2 \frac{\partial^2 V}{\partial S_t^2} + rS_t \frac{\partial V}{\partial S_t} - rV(S_t, t) = 0.$$

The Greeks

In this section we present the "Greeks", which are the sensitivities of the option prices with respect to the variables (i.e., asset price and time) and the parameters used as inputs to the Black–Scholes formula. The importance of Greeks lies mainly in the construction of portfolio and dynamic hedging, since the sign and magnitude of the Greeks provide an indication of how much the option price increases or decreases in value when the variables/parameters change. Note that the Greek for a written option is opposite in sign to its purchased option counterpart.

Tables 2.1 and 2.2 list the most common Greeks used for risk management.

Table 2.1 Delta and gamma for European options.

Name	Symbol	Definition	Description
Delta	Δ	$\dfrac{\partial V}{\partial S_t}$	• Calculates the rate of change of the theoretical Black–Scholes formula with respect to asset price. • Commonly used as a percentage of the total number of shares in an option contract. • Delta for a call option is always positive. Thus, an increase in stock price increases the call option value. • Delta for a put option is always negative. Thus, an increase in strike price decreases the put option value. • Maximum delta value occurs when it is near the strike price.
Gamma	Γ	$\dfrac{\partial^2 V}{\partial S_t^2}$	• Calculates the rate of change of the delta with respect to the asset price or second partial derivatives of the option with respect to the asset price. • Gamma is identical for call and put options, and is positive. Thus, both call and put options are convex functions. • Gamma is maximum when it is near the strike price and decreases its value when it is away from the strike price.

Table 2.2 Vega, rho and theta for European options.

Name	Symbol	Definition	Description
Vega	ν	$\dfrac{\partial V}{\partial \sigma}$	• Calculates the rate of change of the theoretical Black–Scholes formula with respect to the asset price volatility. • Vega is identical for call and put options and is positive. Thus, higher volatility increases both call and put option prices. • Usually measures how much an option price will change as volatility increases or decreases by 1%.
Rho	ρ	$\dfrac{\partial V}{\partial r}$	• Calculates the rate of change of the theoretical Black–Scholes formula with respect to the risk-free interest rate. • Higher interest rates increase (decrease) call (put) option price. • Lower interest rates increase (decrease) put (call) option price.
Theta	θ	$\dfrac{\partial V}{\partial t}$	• Calculates the rate of change of the theoretical Black–Scholes formula with respect to the passage of time. • Theta has its maximum absolute value when the call option is ATM.

Extension of Black–Scholes Model

The assumptions of the Black–Scholes model can be relaxed further to obtain closed-form formulas for European options on the following.

• Asset-paying dividends (fixed discrete dividends, discrete or continuous dividend yield). For asset S_t which pays a sequence of fixed discrete dividends D_i at time t_{D_i}, $i = 1, 2, \ldots, n$ such that $t < t_{D_1} < t_{D_2} < \cdots < t_{D_n}$, the Black–Scholes equation becomes

$$\frac{\partial V}{\partial t} + \frac{1}{2}\sigma^2 S_t^2 \frac{\partial^2 V}{\partial S_t^2} + \left(r S_t - \sum_{i=1}^{n} D_i \delta(t - t_{D_i}) \right) \frac{\partial V}{\partial S_t} - rV(S_t, t) = 0$$

where $\delta(t - t_{D_i})$ is the Dirac delta function centred at t_{D_i}.

For asset S_t paying continuous dividend yield D, the Black–Scholes equation becomes

$$\frac{\partial V}{\partial t} + \frac{1}{2}\sigma^2 S_t^2 \frac{\partial^2 V}{\partial S_t^2} + (r - D)S_t \frac{\partial V}{\partial S_t} - rV(S_t, t) = 0.$$

• Time-dependent continuous dividend yield, risk-free interest rate and volatility. For asset S_t paying time-dependent continuous dividend yield D_t with time-dependent volatility σ_t and risk-free interest rate r_t, the Black–Scholes equation becomes

$$\frac{\partial V}{\partial t} + \frac{1}{2}\sigma_t^2 S_t^2 \frac{\partial^2 V}{\partial S_t^2} + (r_t - D_t)S_t \frac{\partial V}{\partial S_t} - r_t V(S_t, t) = 0.$$

- Incorporating the effects of transaction costs in the hedging portfolio.
  By setting the following transaction costs in buying or selling an asset S_t which pays continuous dividend yield D:
  (i) a fixed cost at each transaction, κ_1
  (ii) a cost proportional to the number of assets traded, $\kappa_2|v|$
  (iii) a cost proportional to the value of the assets traded, $\kappa_3|v|S_t$
  where $\kappa_1, \kappa_2, \kappa_3 > 0$, $v > 0$ (for buying assets) and $v < 0$ (for selling assets), the Black–Scholes equation with transaction costs at time interval δt becomes

$$\frac{\partial V}{\partial t} + \frac{1}{2}\tilde{\sigma}^2 S_t^2 \frac{\partial^2 V}{\partial S_t^2} + (r - \tilde{D})S_t\frac{\partial V}{\partial S_t} - rV(S_t,t) - \frac{\kappa_1}{\delta t} = 0$$

where

$$\tilde{D} = D + \kappa_2\sigma\sqrt{\frac{2}{\pi\delta t}}\left|\frac{\partial^2 V}{\partial S_t^2}\right|\left(\frac{\partial V}{\partial S_t}\right)^{-1} \quad \text{and} \quad \tilde{\sigma}^2 = \sigma^2 - \kappa_3\sigma\sqrt{\frac{2}{\pi\delta t}}\text{sgn}\left(\frac{\partial^2 V}{\partial S_t^2}\right)$$

such that $\text{sgn}(x) = \dfrac{x}{|x|}$.
- Discontinuous jumps in asset price.
  For an asset S_t paying continuous dividend yield D and having a jump process such that J_t is the jump size variable, the Black–Scholes equation becomes

$$\frac{\partial V}{\partial t} + \frac{1}{2}\sigma^2 S_t^2 \frac{\partial^2 V}{\partial S_t^2} + \left[r - D - \mathbb{E}_J(J_t - 1)\right]S_t\frac{\partial V}{\partial S_t} - rV(S_t,t)$$

$$+ \lambda\mathbb{E}_J\left[V(J_t S_t, t) - V(S_t,t)\right] = 0$$

where the expectation $\mathbb{E}_J(\cdot)$ is taken over the jump component.

Criticisms of Black–Scholes Model

Given that the Black–Scholes model with European payoffs has closed-form solutions, one of the main advantages is to be able to calculate option prices analytically. In addition, the Black–Scholes formula is also easy to understand intuitively without the need to evaluate it using expensive numerical methods.

Unfortunately, some of the assumptions in the formula are questionable under the current economic and market conditions. One major criticism is the assumption of stock prices moving in a manner referred to as a random walk (stock price moves up and down with the same probability) and the stock returns following a normal distribution. Empirical tests have shown that there are significant fat tails (leptokurtic) and asymmetry (skewness) in the stock returns. Another major weakness of the Black–Scholes framework is that the volatility at the time of buying/selling the option remains unchanged until the option expiry date. This is simply not true. Nevertheless, even with the availability of option valuation models incorporating either stochastic volatility or fat tails which are more expensive to evaluate, the Black–Scholes model still continues to be used due to its robustness and tractability. After all, the model has only one unobservable parameter and that is the volatility.

2.2 PROBLEMS AND SOLUTIONS

2.2.1 Basic Properties

1. Consider a European call option with price $C(S_t, t; K, T)$ where S_t is the spot price at time $t < T$, T is the expiry date of the option and K is the strike price. Show that the call option is greater than or equal to its intrinsic value

$$C(S_t, t; K, T) \geq \max\{S_t - K, 0\}.$$

Solution: We assume $C(S_t, t; K, T) < \max\{S_t - K, 0\}$ and at time t we set up the following portfolio

$$\Pi_t = C(S_t, t; K, T) - \max\{S_t - K, 0\} < 0.$$

At expiry time T

$$
\begin{aligned}
\Pi_T &= C(S_T, T; K, T) - \max\{S_T - K, 0\} \\
&= \max\{S_T - K, 0\} - \max\{S_T - K, 0\} \\
&= 0
\end{aligned}
$$

which is an arbitrage opportunity. Therefore, $C(S_t, t; K, T) \geq \max\{S_t - K, 0\}$.

$\square$

2. Consider a European put option with price $P(S_t, t; K, T)$ where S_t is the spot price at time $t < T$, T is the expiry date of the option and K is the strike price. Show that the put option is greater than or equal to its intrinsic value

$$P(S_t, t; K, T) \geq \max\{K - S_t, 0\}.$$

Solution: We assume $P(S_t, t; K, T) < \max\{K - S_t, 0\}$ and at time t we set up the following portfolio

$$\Pi_t = P(S_t, t; K, T) - \max\{K - S_t, 0\} < 0.$$

At expiry time T

$$
\begin{aligned}
\Pi_T &= P(S_T, T; K, T) - \max\{K - S_T, 0\} \\
&= \max\{K - S_T, 0\} - \max\{K - S_T, 0\} \\
&= 0
\end{aligned}
$$

which is an arbitrage opportunity. Therefore, $P(S_t, t; K, T) \geq \max\{K - S_t, 0\}$.

$\square$

3. Let $C(S_t, t; K, T)$ be the price of a European call option where S_t is the spot price at time $t < T$, T is the expiry date of the option and K is the strike price. Show that

$$C(S_t, t; K, T) \leq S_t.$$

Solution: We assume at time t, $C(S_t, t; K, T) > S_t$ and we set up the portfolio

$$\Pi_t = S_t - C(S_t, t; K, T) < 0.$$

At time T

$$
\begin{aligned}
\Pi_T &= S_T - C(S_T, T; K, T) \\
&= S_T - \max\{S_T - K, 0\} \\
&= \begin{cases} S_T & \text{if } S_T \le K \\ K & \text{if } S_T > K \end{cases} \\
&> 0
\end{aligned}
$$

which is an arbitrage opportunity. Therefore, $C(S_t, t; K, T) \le S_t$.

$\square$

4. Let $P(S_t, t; K, T)$ be the price of a European put option where S_t is the spot price at time $t < T$, T is the expiry date of the option and K is the strike price. Show that

$$P(S_t, t; K, T) \le K.$$

Solution: We assume at time t, $P(S_t, t; K, T) > K$ and we set up the portfolio

$$\Pi_t = K - P(S_t, t; K, T) < 0.$$

At time T

$$
\begin{aligned}
\Pi_T &= K - P(S_T, T; K, T) \\
&= K - \max\{K - S_T, 0\} \\
&= \begin{cases} S_T & \text{if } S_T \le K \\ K & \text{if } S_T > K \end{cases} \\
&> 0
\end{aligned}
$$

which is an arbitrage opportunity. Therefore, $P(S_t, t; K, T) \le K$.

$\square$

5. Consider a European call option $C(S_t, t; K, T)$ with strike price K where S_t is the spot price of a risky asset at time $t < T$, with T the expiry time of the option. Assume that S_t pays a continuous dividend yield D, then show that

$$C(S_t, t; K, T) \ge \max\{S_t e^{-D(T-t)} - K e^{-r(T-t)}, 0\}$$

where r is the risk-free interest rate.

Solution: We assume $C(S_t, t; K, T) < \max\{S_t e^{-D(T-t)} - Ke^{-r(T-t)}, 0\}$ and we set up a portfolio

$$\Pi_t = C(S_t, t; K, T) - \max\{S_t e^{-D(T-t)} - Ke^{-r(T-t)}, 0\} < 0.$$

At time T

$$\begin{aligned}\Pi_T &= C(S_T, t; K, T) - \max\{S_T - K, 0\} \\ &= \max\{S_T - K, 0\} - \max\{S_T - K, 0\} \\ &= 0\end{aligned}$$

which is an arbitrage opportunity and hence a contradiction. Therefore, $C(S_t, t; K, T) \geq \max\{S_t e^{-D(T-t)} - Ke^{-r(T-t)}, 0\}$.

N.B. We can also show this result using the put–call parity $C(S_t, t; K, T) - P(S_t, t; K, T) = S_t e^{-D(T-t)} - Ke^{-r(T-t)}$, where $P(S_t, t; K, T)$ is the European put option on the same strike price K and expiry time T. Thus,

$$\begin{aligned}C(S_t, t; K, T) &= P(S_t, t; K, T) + S_t e^{-D(T-t)} - Ke^{-r(T-t)} \\ &\geq S_t e^{-D(T-t)} - Ke^{-r(T-t)} \\ &\geq \max\{S_t e^{-D(T-t)} - Ke^{-r(T-t)}, 0\}\end{aligned}$$

since $C(S_t, t; K, T) \geq 0$ and $P(S_t, t; K, T) \geq 0$.

$\square$

6. Consider a European put option $P(S_t, t; K, T)$ with strike price K where S_t is the spot price of a risky asset at time $t < T$, with T the expiry time of the option. Assume that S_t pays a continuous dividend yield D, then show that

$$P(S_t, t; K, T) \geq \max\{Ke^{-r(T-t)} - S_t e^{-D(T-t)}, 0\}$$

where r is the risk-free interest rate.

Solution: We assume $P(S_t, t; K, T) < \max\{Ke^{-r(T-t)} - S_t e^{-D(T-t)}, 0\}$ and we set up a portfolio

$$\Pi_t = P(S_t, t; K, T) - \max\{Ke^{-r(T-t)} - S_t e^{-D(T-t)}, 0\} < 0.$$

At time T

$$\begin{aligned}\Pi_T &= P(S_T, T; K, T) - \max\{K - S_T, 0\} \\ &= \max\{K - S_T, 0\} - \max\{K - S_T, 0\} \\ &= 0\end{aligned}$$

which is an arbitrage opportunity and hence a contradiction. Therefore, $P(S_t, t; K, T) \geq \max\{Ke^{-r(T-t)} - S_t e^{-D(T-t)}, 0\}$.

N.B. Like its European call option counterpart, we can also show this result using the put–call parity $C(S_t, t; K, T) - P(S_t, t; K, T) = S_t e^{-D(T-t)} - K e^{-r(T-t)}$ where $C(S_t, t; K, T)$ is the European call option on the same strike price K and expiry time T. Thus,

$$
\begin{aligned}
P(S_t, t; K, T) &= C(S_t, t; K, T) + K e^{-r(T-t)} - S_t e^{-D(T-t)} \\
&\geq K e^{-r(T-t)} - S_t e^{-D(T-t)} \\
&\geq \max\{ K e^{-r(T-t)} - S_t e^{-D(T-t)}, 0 \}
\end{aligned}
$$

since $C(S_t, t; K, T) \geq 0$ and $P(S_t, t; K, T) \geq 0$.

$\square$

7. Consider a European call option $C(S_t, t; K, T)$ with strike price K where S_t is the spot price of a risky asset at time $t < T$, with T the expiry time of the option. If the stock pays a sequence of discrete dividends D_i at time t_i, $i = 1, 2, \ldots, n$, $t < t_1 < t_2 < \cdots < t_n < T$ and by denoting r as the risk-free interest rate show that

$$
C(S_t, t; K, T) \geq \max \left\{ S_t - \sum_{i=1}^{n} D_i e^{-r(t_i - t)} - K e^{-r(T-t)}, 0 \right\}.
$$

Solution: Using the put–call parity $C(S_t, t; K, T) - P(S_t, t; K, T) = S_t - \sum_{i=1}^{n} D_i e^{-r(t_i - t)} - K e^{-r(T-t)}$ where $P(S_t, t; K, T)$ is the European put option on the same strike price K and expiry time T. Therefore,

$$
\begin{aligned}
C(S_t, t; K, T) &= P(S_t, t; K, T) + S_t - \sum_{i=1}^{n} D_i e^{-r(t_i - t)} - K e^{-r(T-t)} \\
&\geq S_t - \sum_{i=1}^{n} D_i e^{-r(t_i - t)} - K e^{-r(T-t)} \\
&\geq \max \left\{ S_t - \sum_{i=1}^{n} D_i e^{-r(t_i - t)} - K e^{-r(T-t)}, 0 \right\}
\end{aligned}
$$

since $C(S_t, t; K, T) \geq 0$ and $P(S_t, t; K, T) \geq 0$.

$\square$

8. Consider a European put option $P(S_t, t; K, T)$ with strike price K where S_t is the spot price of a risky asset at time $t < T$, with T the expiry time of the option. If the stock pays a sequence of discrete dividends D_i at time t_i, $i = 1, 2, \ldots, n$, $t < t_1 < t_2 < \cdots < t_n < T$ and by denoting r as the risk-free interest rate show that

$$
P(S_t, t; K, T) \geq \max \left\{ K e^{-r(T-t)} - S_t + \sum_{i=1}^{n} D_i e^{-r(t_i - t)}, 0 \right\}.
$$

Solution: Using the put–call parity $C(S_t, t; K, T) - P(S_t, t; K, T) = S_t - \sum_{i=1}^{n} D_i e^{-r(t_i - t)} - K e^{-r(T-t)}$ where $C(S_t, t; K, T)$ is the European call option on the same strike price K and expiry time T. Thus,

$$P(S_t, t; K, T) = C(S_t, t; K, T) + Ke^{-r(T-t)} - S_t + \sum_{i=1}^{n} D_i e^{-r(t_i-t)}$$

$$\geq Ke^{-r(T-t)} - S_t + \sum_{i=1}^{n} D_i e^{-r(t_i-t)}$$

$$\geq \max \left\{ Ke^{-r(T-t)} - S_t + \sum_{i=1}^{n} D_i e^{-r(t_i-t)}, 0 \right\}$$

since $C(S_t, t; K, T) \geq 0$ and $P(S_t, t; K, T) \geq 0$.

□

9. A stock price is currently worth \$25 and it pays a continuous dividend yield of 2.29%. Given that the risk-free interest rate is 4% find the lower bound for an 8-month European put option on the stock with strike price \$30.

   Solution: At initial time $t = 0$ we set the current stock price $S_0 = \$25$, strike $K = \$30$, dividend yield $D = 2.29\%$, risk-free interest rate $r = 4\%$ and expiry time $T = \frac{8}{12} = \frac{2}{3}$ years. By setting $P(S_0, 0; K, T)$ as the European put option at time $t = 0$ its lower bound is

$$P(S_0, 0; K, T) \geq \max\{K e^{-rT} - S_0 e^{-DT}, 0\}$$

$$= \max\{30e^{-0.04 \times \frac{2}{3}} - 25e^{-0.029 \times \frac{2}{3}}, 0\}$$

$$= \max\{4.69, 0\}$$

$$= \$4.69.$$

□

10. Consider a 6-month European call option on a discrete dividend-paying stock having a strike price of \$33. The current stock price is worth \$35 and dividends of \$1.00 and \$1.25 are expected to be paid in two months and four months, respectively. Given that the risk-free interest rate is 2.5% find the lower bound for the European call option price.

    Solution: At initial time $t = 0$ we let the current stock price $S_0 = \$35$, strike $K = \$33$, discrete dividends $D_1 = \$1.00$ at time $t_1 = \frac{2}{12} = \frac{1}{6}$ years, $D_2 = \$1.25$ at time $t_2 = \frac{4}{12} = \frac{1}{3}$ years, risk-free interest rate $r = 2.5\%$ and expiry time $T = \frac{6}{12} = \frac{1}{2}$ years. By denoting $C(S_0, 0; K, T)$ as the European call option at time $t = 0$, its lower bound is

$$C(S_0, 0; K, T) \geq \max\{S_0 - D_1 e^{-rt_1} - D_2 e^{-rt_2} - Ke^{-rT}, 0\}$$

$$= \max\{35 - e^{-0.025 \times \frac{1}{6}} - 1.25e^{-0.025 \times \frac{1}{3}} - 33e^{-0.025 \times \frac{1}{2}}, 0\}$$

$$= \max\{0.1745, 0\}$$

$$= \$0.17.$$

□

11. Consider two European call options $C(S_t, t; K, T_1)$ and $C(S_t, t; K, T_2)$ having expiry times T_1 and T_2 with $T_1 < T_2$, S_t is the spot price at time t and K is the common strike price. Show that for a non-dividend-paying stock

$$C(S_t, t; K, T_1) \leq C(S_t, t; K, T_2)$$

for $T_1 < T_2$.

Solution: We assume $C(S_t, t; K, T_1) > C(S_t, t; K, T_2)$ where at time t we can set up a portfolio

$$\Pi_t = C(S_t, t; K, T_2) - C(S_t, t; K, T_1) < 0.$$

At time T_1, the portfolio is now worth

$$\Pi_{T_1} = C(S_{T_1}, T_1; K, T_2) - \max\{S_{T_1} - K, 0\}$$

$$= \begin{cases} C(S_{T_1}, T_1; K, T_2) & \text{if } S_{T_1} \leq K \\ C(S_{T_1}, T_1; K, T_2) - S_{T_1} + K & \text{if } S_{T_1} > K. \end{cases}$$

Since $C(S_{T_1}, T_1; K, T_2) \geq S_{T_1} - K$ we have $\Pi_{T_1} \geq 0$, which is a contradiction. Therefore, $C(S_t, t; K, T_1) \leq C(S_t, t; K, T_2)$ for $T_1 < T_2$.

□

12. Consider two European put options $P(S_t, t; K, T_1)$ and $P(S_t, t; K, T_2)$ having expiry times T_1 and T_2 with $T_1 < T_2$, S_t is the spot price at time t and K is the common strike price. Show that for a non-dividend-paying stock

$$P(S_t, t; K, T_1) \leq P(S_t, t; K, T_2)$$

for $T_1 < T_2$.

Solution: We assume $P(S_t, t; K, T_1) > P(S_t, t; K, T_2)$ where at time t we can set up a portfolio

$$\Pi_t = P(S_t, t; K, T_2) - P(S_t, t; K, T_1) < 0.$$

At time T_1, the portfolio is now worth

$$\Pi_{T_1} = P(S_{T_1}, T_1; K, T_2) - \max\{K - S_{T_1}, 0\}$$

$$= \begin{cases} P(S_{T_1}, T_1; K, T_2) & \text{if } S_{T_1} \geq K \\ P(S_{T_1}, T_1; K, T_2) - K + S_{T_1} & \text{if } S_{T_1} < K. \end{cases}$$

Since $P(S_{T_1}, T_1; K, T_2) \geq K - S_{T_1}$ we have $\Pi_{T_1} \geq 0$, which is a contradiction. Therefore, $P(S_t, t; K, T_1) \leq P(S_t, t; T_2)$ for $T_1 < T_2$.

□

13. For a non-dividend-paying stock we consider a 3-month European call option with strike
$51 and a 6-month European call with strike $52 with premiums $4.50 and $4.17, respectively. Let the risk-free interest rate be 10% and show that we can construct an arbitrage
opportunity portfolio.

Solution: At time $t = 0$ we denote S_0 as the current stock price, strikes $K_1 = \$4.50$,
$K_2 = \$4.17$, expiry times $T_1 = \frac{3}{12} = \frac{1}{4}$ years, $T_2 = \frac{6}{12} = \frac{1}{2}$ years and risk-free interest rate
$r = 10\%$.

We denote the 3-month European call option with strike $K_1 = \$51$ and the 6-month
European call option with strike $K_2 = \$52$ as $C(S_0, 0; K_1, T_1) = \$4.50$ and
$C(S_0, 0; K_2, T_2) = \$4.17$, respectively.

At time $t = 0$ we set up the following portfolio

$$\Pi_0 = C(S_0, 0; K_2, T_2) - C(S_0, 0; K_1, T_1)$$
$$= \$4.17 - \$4.50$$
$$= -\$0.33.$$

At time T_1

$$\Pi_{T_1} = C(S_{T_1}, T_1; K_2, T_2) - C(S_{T_1}, T_1; K_1, T_1)$$
$$= C(S_{T_1}, T_1; K_2, T_2) - \max\{S_{T_1} - K_1, 0\}$$
$$= \begin{cases} C(S_{T_1}, T_1; K_2, T_2) & \text{if } S_{T_1} \leq K_1 \\ C(S_{T_1}, T_1; K_2, T_2) - S_{T_1} + K_1 & \text{if } S_{T_1} > K_1 \end{cases}$$
$$\geq \begin{cases} C(S_{T_1}, T_1; K_2, T_2) & \text{if } S_{T_1} \leq K_1 \\ S_{T_1} - K_2 e^{-r(T_2-T_1)} - S_{T_1} + K_1 & \text{if } S_{T_1} > K_1 \end{cases}$$
$$= \begin{cases} C(S_{T_1}, T_1; K_2, T_2) & \text{if } S_{T_1} \leq K_1 \\ K_1 - K_2 e^{-r(T_2-T_1)} & \text{if } S_{T_1} > K_1. \end{cases}$$

Given $C(S_{T_1}, T_1; K_2, T_2) \geq 0$ and $K_1 - K_2 e^{-r(T_2-T_1)} = 51 - 52 e^{-0.1 \times \frac{1}{4}} = \$0.28 > 0$, the
portfolio $\Pi_{T_1} \geq 0$ which is an arbitrage opportunity.

In contrast, at time T_2

$$\Pi_{T_2} = C(S_{T_2}, T_2; K_2, T_2) = \max\{S_{T_2} - K_2, 0\} \geq 0$$

which is also an arbitrage opportunity.

Thus, by setting up the portfolio at time $t = 0$

$$\Pi_0 = C(S_0, 0; K_2, T_2) - C(S_0, 0; K_1, T_1)$$

we can guarantee an arbitrage opportunity.

□

14. Consider two European call options $C(S_t, t; K_1, T)$ and $C(S_t, t; K_2, T)$ having strike prices K_1 and K_2, respectively with $K_1 < K_2$, S_t is the spot price at time t and $T > t$ is the expiry time. Show that

$$0 \le C(S_t, t; K_1, T) - C(S_t, t; K_2, T) \le K_2 - K_1$$

for $K_1 < K_2$.

Solution: We first assume $C(S_t, t; K_1, T) < C(S_t, t; K_2, T)$ where at time t we can set up a portfolio

$$\Pi_t = C(S_t, t; K_1, T) - C(S_t, t; K_2, T) < 0.$$

At expiry time T

$$
\begin{aligned}
\Pi_T &= C(S_T, T; K_1, T) - C(S_T, T; K_2, T) \\
&= \max\{S_T - K_1, 0\} - \max\{S_T - K_2, 0\} \\
&= \begin{cases}
0 & \text{if } S_T \le K_1 \\
S_T - K_1 & \text{if } K_1 < S_T \le K_2 \\
K_2 - K_1 & \text{if } S_T > K_2.
\end{cases}
\end{aligned}
$$

Hence, $\Pi_T \ge 0$ which is a contradiction.

We next assume $C(S_t, t; K_1, T) - C(S_t, t; K_2, T) > K_2 - K_1$ where at time t we set up the following portfolio

$$\Pi_t = K_2 - K_1 - C(S_t, t; K_1, T) + C(S_t, t; K_2, T) < 0.$$

At expiry time T

$$
\begin{aligned}
\Pi_T &= K_2 - K_1 - C(S_T, T; K_1, T) + C(S_T, T; K_2, T) \\
&= K_2 - K_1 - \max\{S_T - K_1, 0\} + \max\{S_T - K_2, 0\} \\
&= \begin{cases}
K_2 - K_1 & \text{if } S_T \le K_1 \\
K_2 - S_T & \text{if } K_1 < S_T \le K_2 \\
0 & \text{if } S_T > K_2.
\end{cases}
\end{aligned}
$$

Hence, $\Pi_T \ge 0$ which is also a contradiction.

Therefore,

$$0 \le C(S_t, t; K_1, T) - C(S_t, t; K_2, T) \le K_2 - K_1$$

for $K_1 < K_2$.

$\square$

15. Consider two European put options $P(S_t, t; K_1, T)$ and $P(S_t, t; K_2, T)$ having strike prices K_1 and K_2, respectively with $K_1 < K_2$, S_t is the spot price at time t and $T > t$ is the expiry time. Show that

$$0 \leq P(S_t, t; K_2, T) - P(S_t, t; K_1, T) \leq K_2 - K_1$$

for $K_1 < K_2$.

Solution: We first assume $P(S_t, t; K_2, T) < P(S_t, t; K_1, T)$ where at time t we can set up a portfolio

$$\Pi_t = P(S_t, t; K_2, T) - P(S_t, t; K_1, T) < 0.$$

At expiry time T

$$\begin{aligned} \Pi_T &= P(S_T, T; K_2, T) - P(S_T, T; K_1, T) \\ &= \max\{K_2 - S_T, 0\} - \max\{K_1 - S_T, 0\} \\ &= \begin{cases} K_2 - K_1 & \text{if } S_T < K_1 \\ K_2 - S_T & \text{if } K_1 \leq S_T < K_2 \\ 0 & \text{if } S_T \geq K_2. \end{cases} \end{aligned}$$

Hence, $\Pi_T \geq 0$ which is a contradiction.

We next assume $P(S_t, t; K_2, T) - P(S_t, t; K_1, T) > K_2 - K_1$ where at time t we set up the following portfolio

$$\Pi_t = K_2 - K_1 - P(S_t, t; K_2, T) + P(S_t, t; K_1, T) < 0.$$

At expiry time T

$$\begin{aligned} \Pi_T &= K_2 - K_1 - P(S_T, T; K_2, T) + P(S_T, T; K_1, T) \\ &= K_2 - K_1 - \max\{K_2 - S_T, 0\} + \max\{K_1 - S_T, 0\} \\ &= \begin{cases} 0 & \text{if } S_T < K_1 \\ S_T - K_1 & \text{if } K_1 \leq S_T < K_2 \\ K_2 - K_1 & \text{if } S_T \geq K_2. \end{cases} \end{aligned}$$

Hence, $\Pi_T \geq 0$ which is also a contradiction.

Therefore,

$$0 \leq P(S_t, t; K_2, T) - P(S_t, t; K_1, T) \leq K_2 - K_1$$

for $K_1 < K_2$.

$\square$

16. Consider two European call options $C(S_t, t; K_1, T)$ and $C(S_t, t; K_2, T)$ having strike prices K_1 and K_2, respectively with $K_1 < K_2$, S_t is the spot price at time t and $T > t$ is the expiry time. Given the risk-free interest rate r show that

$$0 \leq C(S_t, t; K_1, T) - C(S_t, t; K_2, T) \leq (K_2 - K_1)e^{-r(T-t)}$$

for $K_1 < K_2$.

Solution: From Problem 2.2.1.14 (page 81) we have shown that

$$C(S_t, t; K_1, T) - C(S_t, t; K_2, T) \geq 0.$$

In order to show that

$$C(S_t, t; K_1, T) - C(S_t, t; K_2, T) \leq (K_2 - K_1)e^{-r(T-t)}$$

we note that from the put–call parity

$$C(S_t, t; K_1, T) = P(S_t, t; K_1, T) + S_t - K_1 e^{-r(T-t)}$$
$$C(S_t, t; K_2, T) = P(S_t, t; K_2, T) + S_t - K_2 e^{-r(T-t)}.$$

Taking differences, we have

$$C(S_t, t; K_1, T) - C(S_t, t; K_2, T) = (K_2 - K_1)e^{-r(T-t)} + P(S_t, t; K_1, T)$$
$$- P(S_t, t; K_2, T)$$

and since $P(S_t, t; K_1, T) - P(S_t, t; K_2, T) \leq 0$ (see Problem 2.2.1.15, page 82)

$$C(S_t, t; K_1, T) - C(S_t, t; K_2, T) \leq (K_2 - K_1)e^{-r(T-t)}$$

for $K_1 < K_2$.

□

17. Consider two European put options $P(S_t, t; K_1, T)$ and $P(S_t, t; K_2, T)$ having strike prices K_1 and K_2, respectively with $K_1 < K_2$, S_t is the spot price at time t and $T > t$ is the expiry time. Given the risk-free interest rate r show that

$$0 \leq P(S_t, t; K_2, T) - P(S_t, t; K_1, T) \leq (K_2 - K_1)e^{-r(T-t)}$$

for $K_1 < K_2$.

Solution: From Problem 2.2.1.15 (page 82) we have

$$P(S_t, t; K_2, T) - P(S_t, t; K_1, T) \geq 0.$$

In order to show that

$$P(S_t, t; K_2, T) - P(S_t, t; K_1, T) \leq (K_2 - K_1)e^{-r(T-t)}$$

we note that from the put–call parity

$$P(S_t, t; K_2, T) = C(S_t, t; K_2, T) - S_t + K_2 e^{-r(T-t)}$$
$$P(S_t, t; K_1, T) = C(S_t, t; K_1, T) - S_t + K_1 e^{-r(T-t)}.$$

Taking differences, we have

$$P(S_t, t; K_2, T) - P(S_t, t; K_1, T) = (K_2 - K_1) e^{-r(T-t)} + C(S_t, t; K_2, T)$$
$$-C(S_t, t; K_1, T)$$

and since $C(S_t, t; K_2, T) - C(S_t, t; K_1, T) \leq 0$ (see Problem 2.2.1.14, page 81)

$$P(S_t, t; K_2, T) - P(S_t, t; K_1, T) \leq (K_2 - K_1) e^{-r(T-t)}$$

for $K_1 < K_2$.

□

18. Let the prices of two European put options with strikes \$50 and \$53 be \$1.50 and \$5.00, respectively where both options have the same time to expiry.
    (a) Is the no-arbitrage condition violated?
    (b) Suggest a spread position so that the portfolio will ensure an arbitrage opportunity.

    Solution: We assume the options are priced at time t with spot price S_t and we let $K_1 = \$50$ and $K_2 = \$53$ so that $P(S_t, t; K_1, T) = \$1.50$ and $P(S_t, t; K_2, T) = \$5.00$ where $T > t$ are the options' expiry time.
    (a) Since $P(S_t, t; K_2, T) - P(S_t, t; K_1, T) = \$5.00 - \$1.50 > K_2 - K_1 = \$53 - \$50$ for $K_1 < K_2$, this violates the condition $P(S_t, t; K_2, T) - P(S_t, t; K_1, T) \leq K_2 - K_1$.
    (b) We let the portfolio at time t be

$$\Pi_t = P(S_t, t; K_1, T) - P(S_t, t; K_2, T) = \$1.50 - \$5.00 = -\$3.50$$

    where at time T, the portfolio will be worth

$$\Pi_T = \max\{50 - S_T, 0\} - \max\{53 - S_T, 0\}$$

$$= \begin{cases} -3 & \text{if } S_T \leq 50 \\ S_T - 53 & \text{if } 50 < S_T \leq 53 \\ 0 & \text{if } S_T > 53. \end{cases}$$

Hence, the profit at time T is

$$\Upsilon_T = \Pi_T - \Pi_t$$

$$= \begin{cases} 0.50 & \text{if } S_T \leq 50 \\ S_T - 49.50 & \text{if } 50 < S_T \leq 53 \\ 3.50 & \text{if } S_T > 53 \end{cases}$$

$$> 0.$$

Thus, $\Upsilon_T > 0$, which shows that the portfolio $\Pi_t = P(S_t, t; K_1, T) - P(S_t, t; K_2, T)$ provides an arbitrage opportunity.

□

19. The Black–Scholes formulae for the value of a European call option $C(S_t, t; K, T)$ and a European put option $P(S_t, t; K, T)$ are

$$C(S_t, t; K, T) = S_t e^{-D(T-t)} \Phi(d_+) - K e^{-r(T-t)} \Phi(d_-)$$

$$P(S_t, t; K, T) = K e^{-r(T-t)} \Phi(-d_-) - S_t e^{-D(T-t)} \Phi(-d_+)$$

with $d_\pm$ given by

$$d_\pm = \frac{\log(S_t/K) + (r - D \pm \frac{1}{2}\sigma^2)(T - t)}{\sigma\sqrt{T - t}}.$$

$\Phi(\cdot)$ is the cdf of a standard normal, S_t is the spot price at time $t < T$, T is the expiry date of the option, K is the strike price, r is the risk-free interest rate, D is the continuous dividend yield and σ is the spot price volatility. In the following limits show that the values of the call and put prices satisfy

(a) $\displaystyle\lim_{t \to T} C(S_t, t; K, T) = \max\{S_T - K, 0\}$, $\displaystyle\lim_{t \to T} P(S_t, t; K, T) = \max\{K - S_T, 0\}$

(b) $\displaystyle\lim_{\sigma \to 0} C(S_t, t; K, T) = \begin{cases} S_t e^{-D(T-t)} - K e^{-r(T-t)} & \text{if } S_t > K e^{-(r-D)(T-t)} \\ 0 & \text{if } S_t \leq K e^{-(r-D)(T-t)} \end{cases}$

$\displaystyle\lim_{\sigma \to 0} P(S_t, t; K, T) = \begin{cases} 0 & \text{if } S_t \geq K e^{-(r-D)(T-t)} \\ K^{-r(T-t)} - S_t e^{-D(T-t)} & \text{if } S_t < K e^{-(r-D)(T-t)} \end{cases}$

(c) $\lim\limits_{\sigma\to\infty} C(S_t,t;K,T) = S_t e^{-D(T-t)}$, $\lim\limits_{\sigma\to\infty} P(S_t,t;K,T) = Ke^{-r(T-t)}$

(d) $\lim\limits_{D\to\infty,\sigma>0} C(S_t,t;K,T) = 0$, $\lim\limits_{D\to\infty,\sigma>0} P(S_t,t;K,T) = Ke^{-r(T-t)}$

(e) $\lim\limits_{T\to\infty,\sigma>0} C(S_t,t;K,T) = \begin{cases} S_t & \text{if } D = 0 \\ 0 & \text{if } D > 0 \end{cases}$

$\lim\limits_{T\to\infty,\sigma>0} P(S_t,t;K,T) = \begin{cases} K & \text{if } r = 0 \\ 0 & \text{if } r > 0. \end{cases}$

Solution:

(a) For the case $t \to T$

$$\lim_{t\to T} d_\pm = \lim_{t\to T}\left\{ \frac{\log(S_t/K)}{\sigma\sqrt{T-t}} + \left(\frac{r-D}{\sigma} \pm \frac{1}{2}\sigma\right)\sqrt{T-t} \right\}$$

$$= \begin{cases} +\infty & \text{if } S_T > K \\ 0 & \text{if } S_T = K \\ -\infty & \text{if } S_T < K. \end{cases}$$

Hence,

$$\lim_{t\to T} C(S_t,t;K,T) = \begin{cases} S_T - K & \text{if } S_T > K \\ 0 & \text{if } S_T \le K \end{cases}$$

$$\lim_{t\to T} P(S_t,t;K,T) = \begin{cases} K - S_T & \text{if } S_T < K \\ 0 & \text{if } S_T \ge K \end{cases}$$

or

$$\lim_{t\to T} C(S_t,t;K,T) = \max\{S_T - K, 0\}$$

$$\lim_{t\to T} P(S_t,t;K,T) = \max\{K - S_T, 0\}.$$

(b) For the case $\sigma \to 0$

$$\lim_{\sigma \to 0} d_{\pm} = \lim_{\sigma \to 0} \left\{ \frac{\log(S_t/K) + (r - D)(T - t)}{\sigma \sqrt{T - t}} \pm \frac{1}{2}\sigma\sqrt{T - t} \right\}$$

$$= \begin{cases} +\infty & \text{if } S_t > Ke^{-(r-D)(T-t)} \\ 0 & \text{if } S_t = Ke^{-(r-D)(T-t)} \\ -\infty & \text{if } S_t < Ke^{-(r-D)(T-t)}. \end{cases}$$

Therefore,

$$\lim_{\sigma \to 0} C(S_t, t; K, T) = \begin{cases} S_t e^{-D(T-t)} - Ke^{-r(T-t)} & \text{if } S_t > Ke^{-(r-D)(T-t)} \\ 0 & \text{if } S_t \leq Ke^{-(r-D)(T-t)} \end{cases}$$

and

$$\lim_{\sigma \to 0} P(S_t, t; K, T) = \begin{cases} 0 & \text{if } S_t \geq Ke^{-(r-D)(T-t)} \\ K^{-r(T-t)} - S_t e^{-D(T-t)} & \text{if } S_t < Ke^{-(r-D)(T-t)}. \end{cases}$$

(c) For the case $\sigma \to \infty$

$$\lim_{\sigma \to \infty} d_{\pm} = \lim_{\sigma \to \infty} \left\{ \frac{\log(S_t/K) + (r - D)(T - t)}{\sigma \sqrt{T - t}} \pm \frac{1}{2}\sigma\sqrt{T - t} \right\} = \pm\infty.$$

Therefore,

$$\lim_{\sigma \to \infty} C(S_t, t; K, T) = S_t e^{-D(T-t)}$$

and

$$\lim_{\sigma \to \infty} P(S_t, t; K, T) = Ke^{-r(T-t)}.$$

(d) For the case $D \to \infty$ and $\sigma > 0$

$$\lim_{D \to \infty, \sigma > 0} d_{\pm} = \lim_{D \to \infty, \sigma > 0} \left\{ \frac{\log(S_t/K) + (r \pm \frac{1}{2}\sigma^2)(T - t)}{\sigma \sqrt{T - t}} - \frac{D}{\sigma}\sqrt{T - t} \right\}$$

$$= -\infty.$$

Hence,

$$\lim_{D\to\infty,\sigma>0} C(S_t,t;K,T) = 0$$

and

$$\lim_{D\to\infty,\sigma>0} P(S_t,t;K,T) = Ke^{-r(T-t)}.$$

(e) For the case $T \to \infty$, $\sigma > 0$ and if $D > 0$, $r > 0$ and because $0 \leq \Phi(d_\pm) \leq 1$, $0 \leq \Phi(-d_\pm) \leq 1$

$$\lim_{T\to\infty,\sigma>0} C(S_t,t;K,T) = 0, \lim_{T\to\infty} P(S_t,t;K,T) = 0.$$

For the case $T \to \infty$, $\sigma > 0$ and if $D = 0$, $r > 0$ we have

$$\lim_{T\to\infty,\sigma>0} d_+ = \lim_{T\to\infty,\sigma>0} \left\{ \frac{\log(S_t/K)}{\sigma\sqrt{T-t}} + \left(\frac{r}{\sigma} + \frac{1}{2}\sigma\right)\sqrt{T-t} \right\}$$
$$= +\infty.$$

Hence,

$$\lim_{T\to\infty,\sigma>0} C(S_t,t;K,T) = S_t$$

and

$$\lim_{T\to\infty,\sigma>0} P(S_t,t;K,T) = 0.$$

Finally, for the case $T \to \infty$, $\sigma > 0$ and if $D > 0$, $r = 0$ we have

$$\lim_{T\to\infty,\sigma>0} d_- = \lim_{T\to\infty,\sigma>0} \left\{ \frac{\log(S_t/K)}{\sigma\sqrt{T-t}} - \left(\frac{D}{\sigma} + \frac{1}{2}\sigma\right)\sqrt{T-t} \right\}$$
$$= -\infty.$$

Therefore,

$$\lim_{T\to\infty,\sigma>0} C(S_t,t;K,T) = 0, \quad \lim_{T\to\infty,\sigma>0} P(S_t,t;K,T) = K.$$

Collectively, we can deduce

$$\lim_{T\to\infty,\sigma>0} C(S_t,t;K,T) = \begin{cases} S_t & \text{if } D = 0 \\ 0 & \text{if } D > 0 \end{cases}$$

and

$$\lim_{T\to\infty,\sigma>0} P(S_t,t;K,T) = \begin{cases} K & \text{if } r = 0 \\ 0 & \text{if } r > 0. \end{cases}$$

$\square$

2.2.2 Black–Scholes Model

1. *Black–Scholes Equation with Stock Paying Continuous Dividend Yield I.* Let $\{W_t : t \geq 0\}$ be a $\mathbb{P}$-standard Wiener process on the probability space $(\Omega, \mathcal{F}, \mathbb{P})$ and let the stock price S_t follow a geometric Brownian motion (GBM) with the following SDE

$$\frac{dS_t}{S_t} = \mu dt + \sigma dW_t$$

where μ is the drift parameter and σ is the volatility parameter. In addition, let B_t be the risk-free asset having the following differential equation

$$dB_t = r B_t dt$$

where r denotes the risk-free interest rate.

Assume that the stock S_t pays a continuous dividend yield D. Intuitively, explain why the above SDE can be written as

$$dS_t = (\mu - D)S_t dt + \sigma S_t dW_t.$$

By considering a delta-hedging portfolio involving both an option $V(S_t, t)$ which can only be exercised at expiry time T and a stock S_t, derive the Black–Scholes equation for a stock that pays continuous dividend yield.

Solution: Given that dividend yield is defined as the proportion of asset price paid out per unit time, when a dividend is paid out, the stock price S_t is reduced by $DS_t dt$. Therefore, we can write

$$dS_t = (\mu - D)S_t dt + \sigma S_t dW_t.$$

At time t we let the value of a portfolio Π_t be

$$\Pi_t = V(S_t, t) - \Delta S_t$$

where it involves buying one unit of option $V(S_t, t)$ and selling Δ units of S_t. Since the investor receives $DS_t dt$ for every unit of asset held, and because the investor holds $-\Delta S_t$, the portfolio changes by an amount $-\Delta D\, S_t dt$ and therefore the change in portfolio Π_t is

$$d\Pi_t = dV - \Delta(dS_t + D\, S_t dt)$$
$$= dV - \Delta dS_t - \Delta D\, S_t dt.$$

Expanding $V(S_t, t)$ using Taylor's theorem

$$dV = \frac{\partial V}{\partial t} dt + \frac{\partial V}{\partial S_t} dS_t + \frac{1}{2} \frac{\partial^2 V}{\partial S_t^2} \left(dS_t\right)^2 + \dots$$

and by substituting $dS_t = (\mu - D)\, S_t dt + \sigma S_t dW_t$ and subsequently applying Itō's lemma we have

$$dV = \left[\frac{\partial V}{\partial t} + \frac{1}{2}\sigma^2 S_t^2 \frac{\partial^2 V}{\partial S_t^2} + (\mu - D)\, S_t \frac{\partial V}{\partial S_t} \right] dt + \sigma S_t \frac{\partial V}{\partial S_t} dW_t.$$

Substituting back into $d\Pi_t$ and rearranging the terms we have

$$d\Pi_t = \left(\frac{\partial V}{\partial t} + \frac{1}{2}\sigma^2 S_t^2 \frac{\partial^2 V}{\partial S_t^2} + (\mu - D)\, S_t \frac{\partial V}{\partial S_t} \right) dt + \sigma S_t \frac{\partial V}{\partial S_t} dW_t$$
$$- \Delta \left[(\mu - D)\, S_t dt + \sigma S_t dW_t \right] - \Delta D\, S_t dt$$
$$= \left(\frac{\partial V}{\partial t} + \frac{1}{2}\sigma^2 S_t^2 \frac{\partial^2 V}{\partial S_t^2} + (\mu - D)\, S_t \frac{\partial V}{\partial S_t} - \mu \Delta S_t \right) dt$$
$$+ \sigma S_t \left(\frac{\partial V}{\partial S_t} - \Delta \right) dW_t.$$

To eliminate the random component we choose

$$\Delta = \frac{\partial V}{\partial S_t}$$

which leads to

$$d\Pi_t = \left(\frac{\partial V}{\partial t} + \frac{1}{2}\sigma^2 S_t^2 \frac{\partial^2 V}{\partial S_t^2} - D S_t \frac{\partial V}{\partial S_t} \right) dt.$$

Under the no-arbitrage condition the return on the amount Π_t invested at a risk-free interest rate would see a growth of

$$d\Pi_t = r\Pi_t dt$$

where r is the risk-free rate and hence we have

$$r\Pi_t dt = \left(\frac{\partial V}{\partial t} + \frac{1}{2}\sigma^2 S_t^2 \frac{\partial^2 V}{\partial S_t^2} - DS_t \frac{\partial V}{\partial S_t} \right) dt$$

$$r\left(V(S_t,t) - \Delta S_t\right) dt = \left(\frac{\partial V}{\partial t} + \frac{1}{2}\sigma^2 S_t^2 \frac{\partial^2 V}{\partial S_t^2} - DS_t \frac{\partial V}{\partial S_t} \right) dt$$

$$r\left(V(S_t,t) - S_t \frac{\partial V}{\partial S_t}\right) = \frac{\partial V}{\partial t} + \frac{1}{2}\sigma^2 S_t^2 \frac{\partial^2 V}{\partial S_t^2} - DS_t \frac{\partial V}{\partial S_t}$$

and finally

$$\frac{\partial V}{\partial t} + \frac{1}{2}\sigma^2 S_t^2 \frac{\partial^2 V}{\partial S_t^2} + (r - D) S_t \frac{\partial V}{\partial S_t} - rV(S_t,t) = 0$$

which is the Black–Scholes equation for a stock which pays continuous dividend yield.

$\square$

2. *Black–Scholes Equation with Stock Paying Continuous Dividend Yield II.* Let $\{W_t : t \geq 0\}$ be a $\mathbb{P}$-standard Wiener process on the probability space $(\Omega, \mathcal{F}, \mathbb{P})$ and let the stock price S_t follow a GBM with the following SDE

$$\frac{dS_t}{S_t} = (\mu - D)dt + \sigma dW_t$$

where μ is the drift parameter, D is the continuous dividend yield and σ is the volatility parameter. In addition, let B_t be the risk-free asset having the following differential equation

$$dB_t = r B_t dt$$

where r denotes the risk-free interest rate.

At time t we consider a trader who has a portfolio valued at Π_t, given as

$$\Pi_t = \phi_t S_t + \psi_t B_t$$

holding ϕ_t shares of stock and ψ_t units being invested in a risk-free asset B_t. Let the option price at time t be $V(S_t,t)$; the contingent claim $V(S_T,T)$ is said to be attainable if there exists an admissible strategy worth $\Pi_T = V(S_T,T)$ at the option expiry time T, $T > t$.

In the absence of arbitrage, show that $\Pi_t = V(S_t,t)$, $t \in [0,T]$.

Finally, show that the portfolio (ϕ_t, ψ_t) is self-financing if and only if $V(S_t,t)$ satisfies the Black–Scholes equation for a stock that pays continuous dividend yield.

Solution: Assume there is a risk-free interest rate r where an investor can invest in a money market account. At time t, if $\Pi_t > V(S_t,t)$ then the investor can sell the portfolio Π_t and use the proceeds to buy the option $V(S_t,t)$, making a profit $\Pi_t - V(S_t,t) > 0$ and saving it in a risk-free money-market account. At time T both of the asset values are identical,

$\Pi_T = V(S_T, T)$, with the value of the bought option covering the sold portfolio and making a risk-free profit $(\Pi_t - V(S_t, t))e^{r(T-t)}$.

Alternatively, at time t if $\Pi_t < V(S_t, t)$ then an investor can sell the option $V(S_t, t)$ and buy the portfolio Π_t, also making an instant profit $V(S_t, t) - \Pi_t > 0$, and the proceeds can go into the money-market account. At time T the asset values are equal, $\Pi_T = V(S_T, T)$, with the value of the bought portfolio covering the sold option and making a risk-free profit $(V(S_t, t) - \Pi_t)e^{r(T-t)}$.

Therefore, under the no-arbitrage condition we must have $\Pi_t = V(S_t, t)$.

At time $t \in [0, T]$, to replicate the option $V(S_t, t)$, let the self-financing portfolio be

$$V(S_t, t) = \phi S_t + \psi_t B_t.$$

By applying Taylor's theorem on dV

$$dV = \frac{\partial V}{\partial t} dt + \frac{\partial V}{\partial S_t} dS_t + \frac{1}{2} \frac{\partial^2 V}{\partial S_t^2} (dS_t)^2 + \dots$$

and since $(dS_t)^2 = ((\mu - D)S_t dt + \sigma S_t dW_t)^2 = \sigma^2 S_t^2 dt$ such that $(dt)^\nu = 0$, $\nu \geq 2$ we have

$$dV = \frac{\partial V}{\partial t} dt + \frac{\partial V}{\partial S_t} dS_t + \frac{1}{2} \sigma^2 S_t^2 \frac{\partial^2 V}{\partial S_t^2} dt$$

$$= \frac{\partial V}{\partial S_t} dS_t + \left(\frac{\partial V}{\partial t} + \frac{1}{2} \sigma^2 S_t^2 \frac{\partial^2 V}{\partial S_t^2} \right) dt.$$

Since the trader will receive $DS_t dt$ for every stock held, the portfolio (ϕ_t, ψ_t) is self-financing if and only if

$$dV = \phi_t dS_t + \psi_t dB_t + \phi_t DS_t dt = \phi_t dS_t + (rB_t \psi_t + \phi_t DS_t) dt.$$

By equating both of the equations we have

$$rB_t \psi_t + \phi_t DS_t = \frac{\partial V}{\partial t} + \frac{1}{2} \sigma^2 S_t^2 \frac{\partial^2 V}{\partial S_t^2} \quad \text{and} \quad \phi_t = \frac{\partial V}{\partial S_t}$$

and substituting the above two equations into

$$V = \phi_t S_t + \psi_t B_t$$

we have

$$\frac{\partial V}{\partial t} + \frac{1}{2} \sigma^2 S_t^2 \frac{\partial^2 V}{\partial S_t^2} + (r - D)S_t \frac{\partial V}{\partial S_t} - rV(S_t, t) = 0.$$

$\square$

3. *Black–Scholes Equation with Stock Paying Discrete Dividends.* Let $\{W_t : t \geq 0\}$ be a $\mathbb{P}$-standard Wiener process on the probability space $(\Omega, \mathcal{F}, \mathbb{P})$ and let the stock price S_t follow the SDE

$$\frac{dS_t}{S_t} = \mu dt + \sigma dW_t$$

where μ is the drift parameter and σ is the volatility parameter. In addition, let B_t be the risk-free asset having the following differential equation

$$dB_t = rB_t dt$$

where r denotes the risk-free interest rate.

Assume the asset S_t pays a sequence of fixed dividends D_i at time t_{D_i}, $i = 1, 2, \ldots, n$ such that $t < t_{D_1} < t_{D_2} < \cdots < t_{D_n}$. Explain intuitively why the SDE for S_t can be written as

$$dS_t = \left(\mu S_t - \sum_{i=1}^{n} D_i \delta(t - t_{D_i}) \right) dt + \sigma S_t dW_t$$

where $\delta(t - t_{D_i})$ is the Dirac delta function centred at t_{D_i}.

By considering a hedging portfolio involving both an option $V(S_t, t)$ which can only be exercised at expiry time $T > t_{D_n}$ and a stock S_t, show that $V(S_t, t)$ satisfies the following differential equation

$$\frac{\partial V}{\partial t} + \frac{1}{2}\sigma^2 S_t^2 \frac{\partial^2 V}{\partial S_t^2} + \left(rS_t - \sum_{i=1}^{n} D_i \delta(t - t_{D_i}) \right) \frac{\partial V}{\partial S_t} - rV(S_t, t) = 0.$$

Solution: When a discrete dividend D_i is paid at time t_{D_i}, the asset price S_t is reduced by the same amount. However, for the time between dividend payment dates, S_t still follows a GBM process. Hence, we can write

$$dS_t = \left(\mu S_t - \sum_{i=1}^{n} D_i \delta(t - t_{D_i}) \right) dt + \sigma S_t dW_t.$$

At time t we let the value of a portfolio Π_t be

$$\Pi_t = V(S_t, t) - \Delta S_t$$

where it involves buying one unit of option $V(S_t, t)$ and selling Δ units of S_t. At times $t_{D_1}, t_{D_2}, \ldots, t_{D_n}$, the owner of the portfolio receives $D_1, D_2, \ldots, D_n$ dividend payments for every asset held. Therefore, the change in portfolio Π_t becomes

$$d\Pi_t = dV - \Delta\left(dS_t + \sum_{i=1}^{n} D_i\delta(t - t_{D_i})dt\right)$$
$$= dV - \Delta(\mu S_t dt + \sigma S_t dW_t).$$

Expanding $V(S_t, t)$ using Taylor's theorem

$$dV = \frac{\partial V}{\partial t}dt + \frac{\partial V}{\partial S_t}dS_t + \frac{1}{2}\frac{\partial^2 V}{\partial S_t^2}\left(dS_t\right)^2 + \dots$$

and by substituting $dS_t = \left(\mu S_t - \sum_{i=1}^{n} D_i\delta(t - t_{D_i})\right)dt + \sigma S_t dW_t$ and applying Itō's lemma we have

$$dV = \left[\frac{\partial V}{\partial t} + \frac{1}{2}\sigma^2 S_t^2\frac{\partial^2 V}{\partial S_t^2} + \left(\mu S_t - \sum_{i=1}^{n} D_i\delta(t - t_{D_i})\right)\frac{\partial V}{\partial S_t}\right]dt + \sigma S_t\frac{\partial V}{\partial S_t}dW_t.$$

Hence,

$$d\Pi_t = \left(\frac{\partial V}{\partial t} + \frac{1}{2}\sigma^2 S_t^2\frac{\partial^2 V}{\partial S_t^2} + \left(\mu S_t - \sum_{i=1}^{n} D_i\delta(t - t_{D_i})\right)\frac{\partial V}{\partial S_t} - \mu\Delta S_t\right)dt$$
$$+ \sigma S_t\left(\frac{\partial V}{\partial S_t} - \Delta\right)dW_t.$$

Setting $\Delta = \dfrac{\partial V}{\partial S_t}$ to eliminate the random component leads to

$$d\Pi_t = \left(\frac{\partial V}{\partial t} + \frac{1}{2}\sigma^2 S_t^2\frac{\partial^2 V}{\partial S_t^2} - \sum_{i=1}^{n} D_i\delta(t - t_{D_i})\frac{\partial V}{\partial S_t}\right)dt.$$

Under the no-arbitrage condition the return on the portfolio Π_t invested in a risk-free interest rate would see a growth of

$$d\Pi_t = r\Pi_t dt$$

where r is the risk-free interest rate and hence we have

$$r\Pi_t dt = \left(\frac{\partial V}{\partial t} + \frac{1}{2}\sigma^2 S_t^2 \frac{\partial^2 V}{\partial S_t^2} - \sum_{i=1}^{n} D_i \delta(t - t_{D_i}) \frac{\partial V}{\partial S_t} \right) dt$$

$$r\left(V(S_t, t) - \Delta S_t \right) dt = \left(\frac{\partial V}{\partial t} + \frac{1}{2}\sigma^2 S_t^2 \frac{\partial^2 V}{\partial S_t^2} - \sum_{i=1}^{n} D_i \delta(t - t_{D_i}) \frac{\partial V}{\partial S_t} \right) dt$$

$$r\left(V(S_t, t) - S_t \frac{\partial V}{\partial S_t} \right) = \frac{\partial V}{\partial t} + \frac{1}{2}\sigma^2 S_t^2 \frac{\partial^2 V}{\partial S_t^2} - \sum_{i=1}^{n} D_i \delta(t - t_{D_i}) \frac{\partial V}{\partial S_t}$$

which eventually leads to

$$\frac{\partial V}{\partial t} + \frac{1}{2}\sigma^2 S_t^2 \frac{\partial^2 V}{\partial S_t^2} + \left(rS_t - \sum_{i=1}^{n} D_i \delta(t - t_{D_i}) \right) \frac{\partial V}{\partial S_t} - rV(S_t, t) = 0$$

which is a Black–Scholes equation with stock paying discrete dividend payments.

□

4. *European Option Valuation (PDE Approach).* Let $\{W_t : t \geq 0\}$ be a $\mathbb{P}$-standard Wiener process on the probability space $(\Omega, \mathscr{F}, \mathbb{P})$ and let the stock price S_t follow a GBM with the following SDE

$$\frac{dS_t}{S_t} = (\mu - D)\, dt + \sigma dW_t$$

where μ is the drift parameter, D is the dividend yield, σ is the volatility parameter and let r denote the risk-free interest rate.

Let $C(S_t, t; K, T)$ be the price of a European call option with strike K and expiry time $T > t$, satisfying the Black–Scholes equation

$$\frac{\partial C}{\partial t} + \frac{1}{2}\sigma^2 S_t^2 \frac{\partial^2 C}{\partial S_t^2} + (r - D)S_t \frac{\partial C}{\partial S_t} - rC(S_t, t; K, T) = 0$$

with boundary conditions

$$C(S_T, T; K, T) = \max\{S_T - K, 0\}, C(0, t; K, T) = 0$$

$$C(S_t, t; K, T) \sim S_t e^{-D(T-t)} \text{ as } S_t \to \infty.$$

With the introduction of variables x, τ and $\upsilon(x, \tau)$ defined by

$$S_t = Ke^x, t = T - \frac{\tau}{\frac{1}{2}\sigma^2}, C(S_t, t; K, T) = K\upsilon(x, \tau)$$

show that the Black–Scholes equation is reduced to

$$\frac{\partial v}{\partial \tau} = \frac{\partial^2 v}{\partial x^2} + k_1 \frac{\partial v}{\partial x} - k_0 v$$

with boundary condition

$$v(x,0) = \max\{e^x - 1\}$$

where $k_1 = \dfrac{(r - D - \frac{1}{2}\sigma^2)}{\frac{1}{2}\sigma^2}$ and $k_0 = \dfrac{r}{\frac{1}{2}\sigma^2}$.

Using a change of variables $v(x,\tau) = e^{\alpha x + \beta \tau} u(x,\tau)$ show that by setting

$$\alpha = -\frac{1}{2}k_1 \quad \text{and} \quad \beta = -\frac{1}{4}k_1^2 - k_0$$

the problem is reduced to a diffusion equation of the form

$$\frac{\partial u}{\partial \tau} = \frac{\partial^2 u}{\partial x^2}, u(x,0) = f(x)$$

where $f(x) = \max\{e^{\frac{1}{2}(k_1+1)x} - e^{\frac{1}{2}k_1 x}, 0\}$ for $-\infty < x < \infty$ and $\tau > 0$.
Given the solution

$$u(x,\tau) = \frac{1}{2\sqrt{\pi\tau}} \int_{-\infty}^{\infty} f(z) e^{-\frac{(x-z)^2}{4\tau}} \, dz$$

deduce that

$$C(S_t,t;K,T) = S_t e^{-D(T-t)} \Phi(d_+) - K e^{-r(T-t)} \Phi(d_-)$$

where

$$d_\pm = \frac{\log(S_t/K) + (r - D \pm \frac{1}{2}\sigma^2)(T - t)}{\sigma\sqrt{T - t}}$$

and $\Phi(x)$ is the standard normal cdf

$$\Phi(x) = \int_{-\infty}^{x} \frac{1}{\sqrt{2\pi}} e^{-\frac{1}{2}u^2} \, du.$$

Solution: A European call option with value $C(S_t,t;K,T)$ satisfies the Black–Scholes equation

$$\frac{\partial C}{\partial t} + \frac{1}{2}\sigma^2 S_t^2 \frac{\partial^2 C}{\partial S_t^2} + (r - D)S_t \frac{\partial C}{\partial S_t} - rC(S_t,t;K,T) = 0$$

with conditions

$$C(S_T, T; K, T) = \max\{S_T - K, 0\}, C(0, t; K, T) = 0$$

$$C(S_t, t; K, T) \sim S_t e^{-D(T-t)} \text{ as } S_t \to \infty.$$

First we transform the Black–Scholes equation by making it dimensionless, setting

$$S_t = Ke^x, t = T - \frac{\tau}{\frac{1}{2}\sigma^2}, C(S_t, t; K, T) = Kv(x, \tau)$$

and write

$$\frac{\partial C}{\partial t} = \frac{\partial C}{\partial \tau}\frac{\partial \tau}{\partial t} = -\frac{1}{2}K\sigma^2\frac{\partial v}{\partial \tau}, \frac{\partial C}{\partial S_t} = \frac{\partial C_t}{\partial x}\frac{\partial x}{\partial S_t} = \frac{K}{S_t}\frac{\partial v}{\partial x}$$

and

$$\frac{\partial^2 C}{\partial S_t^2} = \frac{\partial}{\partial S_t}\left(\frac{\partial C}{\partial S_t}\right)$$

$$= \frac{\partial}{\partial S_t}\left(\frac{\partial C}{\partial x}\frac{\partial x}{\partial S_t}\right)$$

$$= \frac{\partial}{\partial S_t}\left(\frac{\partial C}{\partial x}\right)\frac{\partial x}{\partial S_t} + \frac{\partial}{\partial S_t}\left(\frac{\partial x}{\partial S_t}\right)\frac{\partial C}{\partial x}$$

$$= \frac{\partial}{\partial x}\frac{\partial x}{\partial S_t}\left(\frac{\partial C}{\partial x}\right)\frac{\partial x}{\partial S_t} - \left(\frac{1}{S_t^2}\right)\frac{\partial C}{\partial x}$$

$$= \frac{\partial^2 C}{\partial x^2}\left(\frac{\partial x}{\partial S_t}\right)^2 - \left(\frac{1}{S_t^2}\right)\frac{\partial C}{\partial x}$$

$$= \frac{K}{S_t^2}\left(\frac{\partial^2 v}{\partial x^2} - \frac{\partial v}{\partial x}\right).$$

By substituting the above expressions back into the Black–Scholes equation we have

$$\frac{\partial v}{\partial \tau} = \frac{\partial^2 v}{\partial x^2} - \frac{\partial v}{\partial x} + \frac{r - D}{\frac{1}{2}\sigma^2}\frac{\partial v}{\partial x} - \frac{r}{\frac{1}{2}\sigma^2}v(x, \tau)$$

or

$$\frac{\partial v}{\partial \tau} = \frac{\partial^2 v}{\partial x^2} + k_1\frac{\partial v}{\partial x} - k_0 v(x, \tau)$$

where $k_1 = \dfrac{(r - D - \frac{1}{2}\sigma^2)}{\frac{1}{2}\sigma^2}$ and $k_0 = \dfrac{r}{\frac{1}{2}\sigma^2}$.

As for the boundary condition

$$C(S_T, T; K, T) = \max \{ S_T - K, 0 \}$$

it becomes

$$Kv(x, 0) = \max \{ K e^x - K, 0 \}$$

or

$$v(x, 0) = \max \{ e^x - 1, 0 \} .$$

In order to simplify the partial differential equation (PDE) we let

$$v(x, \tau) = e^{\alpha x + \beta \tau} u(x, \tau)$$

with

$$\frac{\partial v}{\partial \tau} = \beta e^{\alpha x + \beta \tau} u(x, \tau) + e^{\alpha x + \beta \tau} \frac{\partial u}{\partial \tau}$$

$$\frac{\partial v}{\partial x} = \alpha e^{\alpha x + \beta \tau} u(x, \tau) + e^{\alpha x + \beta \tau} \frac{\partial u}{\partial x}$$

$$\frac{\partial^2 v}{\partial x^2} = \alpha^2 e^{\alpha x + \beta \tau} u(x, \tau) + \alpha e^{\alpha x + \beta \tau} \frac{\partial u}{\partial x} + \alpha e^{\alpha x + \beta \tau} \frac{\partial u}{\partial x} + e^{\alpha x + \beta \tau} \frac{\partial^2 u}{\partial x^2}$$

$$= e^{\alpha x + \beta \tau} \left(\alpha^2 u(x, \tau) + 2\alpha \frac{\partial u}{\partial x} + \frac{\partial^2 u}{\partial x^2} \right) .$$

Substituting the above expressions back into the PDE yields

$$\beta u(x, \tau) + \frac{\partial u}{\partial \tau} = \alpha^2 u + 2\alpha \frac{\partial u}{\partial x} + \frac{\partial^2 u}{\partial x^2} + k_1 \left(\alpha u + \frac{\partial u}{\partial x} \right) - k_0 u(x, \tau)$$

or

$$\frac{\partial^2 u}{\partial x^2} + \left(2\alpha + k_1 \right) \frac{\partial u}{\partial x} + \left(\alpha^2 + k_1 \alpha - k_0 - \beta \right) u(x, \tau) = \frac{\partial u}{\partial \tau} .$$

In order to reduce the above problem to the form

$$\frac{\partial^2 u}{\partial x^2} = \frac{\partial u}{\partial \tau}$$

we let

$$\beta = \alpha^2 + k_1 \alpha - k_0 \quad \text{and} \quad 2\alpha + k_1 = 0$$

which gives

$$\alpha = -\frac{1}{2} k_1 \quad \text{and} \quad \beta = -\frac{1}{4} k_1^2 - k_0 .$$

Therefore,

$$v(x, \tau) = e^{\alpha x + \beta \tau} u(x, \tau)$$
$$= e^{-\frac{1}{2}k_1 x - (\frac{1}{4}k_1^2 + k_0)\tau} u(x, \tau)$$

where

$$\frac{\partial^2 u}{\partial x^2} = \frac{\partial u}{\partial \tau}, x \in (-\infty, \infty), \tau > 0$$

with

$$u(x, 0) = e^{\alpha x} v(x, 0)$$
$$= e^{\frac{1}{2}k_1 x} \max \left\{ e^x - 1, 0 \right\}$$
$$= \max \{ e^{(\frac{1}{2}k_1 + 1)x} - e^{\frac{1}{2}k_1 x}, 0 \}$$

or

$$f(x) = \max \{ e^{(\frac{1}{2}k_1 + 1)x} - e^{\frac{1}{2}k_1 x}, 0 \}.$$

The solution to the diffusion equation

$$\frac{\partial^2 u}{\partial x^2} = \frac{\partial u}{\partial \tau}, x \in (-\infty, \infty), \tau > 0$$

is given by

$$u(x, \tau) = \frac{1}{2\sqrt{\pi \tau}} \int_{-\infty}^{\infty} f(z) e^{-\frac{(x-z)^2}{4\tau}} dz.$$

Using the changing of variables we let $y = \dfrac{z - x}{\sqrt{2\tau}}$

$$u(x, \tau) = \frac{1}{2\sqrt{\pi \tau}} \int_{-\infty}^{\infty} f(x + \sqrt{2\tau} y) e^{-\frac{1}{2}y^2} \sqrt{2\tau} dy.$$

Since $f(x + \sqrt{2\tau} y) = \min \{ e^{\frac{1}{2}k_1 (x + \sqrt{2\tau} y)} (e^{x + \sqrt{2\tau} y} - 1), 0 \} > 0$ if $y > -\dfrac{x}{\sqrt{2\tau}}$

$$u(x, \tau) = \frac{1}{\sqrt{2\pi}} \int_{-\frac{x}{\sqrt{2\tau}}}^{\infty} \left[e^{(\frac{1}{2}k_1 + 1)(x + \sqrt{2\tau} y)} - e^{\frac{1}{2}k_1 (x + \sqrt{2\tau} y)} \right] e^{-\frac{1}{2}y^2} dy$$
$$= I_1 - I_2$$

where

$$I_1 = \frac{1}{\sqrt{2\pi}} \int_{-\frac{x}{\sqrt{2\tau}}}^{\infty} e^{(\frac{1}{2}k_1 + 1)(x + \sqrt{2\tau} y) - \frac{1}{2}y^2} dy$$

and

$$I_2 = \frac{1}{\sqrt{2\pi}} \int_{-\frac{x}{\sqrt{2\tau}}}^{\infty} e^{\frac{1}{2}k_1(x+\sqrt{2\tau}y)-\frac{1}{2}y^2} \, dy.$$

To calculate I_1 we have

$$\begin{aligned}
I_1 &= \frac{1}{\sqrt{2\pi}} \int_{-\frac{x}{\sqrt{2\tau}}}^{\infty} e^{(\frac{1}{2}k_1+1)(x+\sqrt{2\tau}y)-\frac{1}{2}y^2} \, dy \\
&= \frac{e^{(\frac{1}{2}k_1+1)x+(\frac{1}{2}k_1+1)^2\tau}}{\sqrt{2\pi}} \int_{-\frac{x}{\sqrt{2\tau}}}^{\infty} e^{-\frac{1}{2}(y-(\frac{1}{2}k_1+1)\sqrt{2\tau})^2} \, dy.
\end{aligned}$$

Let $s = y - (\frac{1}{2}k_1 + 1)\sqrt{2\tau}$ then

$$\begin{aligned}
I_1 &= \frac{e^{(\frac{1}{2}k_1+1)x+(\frac{1}{2}k_1+1)^2\tau}}{\sqrt{2\pi}} \int_{-\frac{x}{\sqrt{2\tau}}-(\frac{1}{2}k_1+1)\sqrt{2\tau}}^{\infty} e^{-\frac{1}{2}s^2} \, ds \\
&= e^{(\frac{1}{2}k_1+1)x+(\frac{1}{2}k_1+1)^2\tau} \Phi\left(d_+\right)
\end{aligned}$$

where $\Phi\left(d_+\right) = \frac{1}{\sqrt{2\pi}} \int_{-\infty}^{d_+} e^{-\frac{1}{2}s^2} \, ds$ and $d_+ = \frac{x}{\sqrt{2\tau}} + \left(\frac{1}{2}k_1 + 1\right)\sqrt{2\tau}$.

Using the same techniques we can write I_2 as

$$I_2 = e^{\frac{1}{2}k_1 x + \frac{1}{4}k_1^2 \tau} \Phi\left(d_-\right)$$

where $d_- = \frac{x}{\sqrt{2\tau}} + \frac{1}{2}k_1\sqrt{2\tau}$.

Thus,

$$u(x, \tau) = e^{(\frac{1}{2}k_1+1)x+(\frac{1}{2}k_1+1)^2\tau}\Phi(d_+) + e^{\frac{1}{2}k_1 x + \frac{1}{4}k_1^2\tau}\Phi(d_-)$$

and from $C(S_t, t; K, T) = Kv(x, \tau) = Ke^{\alpha x + \beta \tau}u(x, \tau)$ we eventually have

$$C(S_t, t; K, T) = Ke^{x+(k_1-k_0+1)\tau}\Phi(d_+) - Ke^{-k_0\tau}\Phi(d_-)$$

where $\alpha = -\frac{1}{2}k_1$ and $\beta = -\frac{1}{4}k_1^2 - k_0$.

Finally, by substituting $k_1 = \dfrac{(r - D - \frac{1}{2}\sigma^2)}{\frac{1}{2}\sigma^2}$ and $k_0 = \dfrac{r}{\frac{1}{2}\sigma^2}$ we have

$$C(S_t, t; K, T) = S_t e^{-D(T-t)}\Phi(d_+) - Ke^{-r(T-t)}\Phi(d_-)$$

where

$$d_{\pm} = \frac{\log(S_t/K) + (r - D \pm \frac{1}{2}\sigma^2)(T - t)}{\sigma\sqrt{T - t}}.$$

N.B. Using the put–call parity we can show that the price of a European put option is

$$P(S_t, t; K, T) = Ke^{-r(T-t)}\Phi(-d_-) - S_t e^{-D(T-t)}\Phi(-d_+).$$

$\square$

5. *European Option Valuation (Probabilistic Approach).* Let $\{W_t : t \geq 0\}$ be a $\mathbb{P}$-standard Wiener process on the probability space $(\Omega, \mathcal{F}, \mathbb{P})$ and let the asset price S_t follow a GBM with the following SDE

$$\frac{dS_t}{S_t} = (\mu - D)\,dt + \sigma dW_t$$

where μ is the drift parameter, D is the continuous dividend yield and σ is the volatility parameter. Using Itō's lemma show that under the risk-neutral measure $\mathbb{Q}$ the conditional distribution of S_T given S_t is

$$S_T | S_t \sim \log\text{-}\mathcal{N}\left[\log S_t + (r - D - \frac{1}{2}\sigma^2)(T - t), \sigma^2(T - t)\right]$$

where r is the risk-free interest rate and $T > t$.

From the Feynman–Kac formula the European call option with strike K and expiry time T is given by

$$C(S_t, t; K, T) = e^{-r(T-t)}\mathbb{E}^{\mathbb{Q}}\left[\max\{S_T - K, 0\} \big| \mathcal{F}_t\right]$$

where $\mathbb{E}^{\mathbb{Q}}(\cdot)$ is the expectation under the risk-neutral measure $\mathbb{Q}$.

Using the risk-neutral valuation approach show that the European call option price is

$$C(S_t, t; K, T) = S_t e^{-D(T-t)}\Phi(d_+) - Ke^{-r(T-t)}\Phi(d_-)$$

where

$$d_{\pm} = \frac{\log\left(S_t/K\right) + (r - D \pm \frac{1}{2}\sigma^2)(T - t)}{\sigma\sqrt{T - t}}$$

and $\Phi(x)$ is the standard normal cdf

$$\Phi(x) = \int_{-\infty}^{x} \frac{1}{\sqrt{2\pi}} e^{-\frac{1}{2}u^2}\,du.$$

Finally, deduce that the European put option price with strike K and expiry time T is

$$P(S_t, t; K, T) = Ke^{-r(T-t)}\Phi(-d_-) - S_t e^{-D(T-t)}\Phi(-d_+).$$

Solution: From Girsanov's theorem, under the risk-neutral measure $\mathbb{Q}$ we can write

$$\frac{dS_t}{S_t} = (r - D)\,dt + \sigma dW_t^{\mathbb{Q}}$$

such that $W_t^{\mathbb{Q}} = W_t + \left(\dfrac{\mu - r}{\sigma}\right)t$ is a $\mathbb{Q}$-standard Wiener process. Using Itō's lemma we can show that for $t < T$

$$d(\log S_t) = \frac{dS_t}{S_t} - \frac{1}{2}\left(\frac{dS_t}{S_t}\right)^2 + \dots$$

$$= (r - D)\,dt + \sigma dW_t^{\mathbb{Q}} - \frac{1}{2}\sigma^2 dt$$

$$= \left(r - D - \frac{1}{2}\sigma^2\right)dt + \sigma dW_t^{\mathbb{Q}}.$$

Integrating over time we have

$$\int_t^T d(\log S_u) = \int_t^T \left(r - D - \frac{1}{2}\sigma^2\right)du + \int_t^T \sigma\,dW_u^{\mathbb{Q}}$$

$$\log\left(\frac{S_T}{S_t}\right) = \left(r - D - \frac{1}{2}\sigma^2\right)(T - t) + \sigma W_{T-t}^{\mathbb{Q}}$$

where $W_{T-t}^{\mathbb{Q}} \sim \mathcal{N}(0, T - t)$. Hence, conditional on S_t we can write

$$S_T | S_t \sim \log\text{-}\mathcal{N}\left[\log S_t + \left(r - D - \frac{1}{2}\sigma^2\right)(T - t), \sigma^2(T - t)\right].$$

Under the risk-neutral measure $\mathbb{Q}$ we can write the European call option price as

$$C\left(S_t, t; K, T\right) = e^{-r(T-t)}\mathbb{E}^{\mathbb{Q}}\left[\max\{S_T - K, 0\}|\mathcal{F}_t\right]$$

$$= e^{-r(T-t)}\int_0^\infty \max\{S_T - K, 0\}f(S_T | S_t)dS_T.$$

Here, for a log normally distributed random variable $\log X \sim \mathcal{N}\left(\mu, \sigma^2\right)$ the probability density function (pdf) is

$$f_X\left(x; \mu, \sigma\right) = \frac{1}{x\sigma\sqrt{2\pi}}e^{-\frac{1}{2}\left(\frac{\log x - \mu}{\sigma}\right)^2}, \; x > 0$$

and we can thus write

$$f\left(S_T|S_t\right) = \frac{1}{S_T\sigma\sqrt{2\pi(T-t)}}e^{-\frac{1}{2}\left(\frac{\log S_T-\log S_t-(r-D-\frac{1}{2}\sigma^2)(T-t)}{\sigma\sqrt{T-t}}\right)^2}, \quad S_T > 0$$

or

$$f\left(S_T|S_t\right) = \frac{1}{S_T\sigma\sqrt{2\pi(T-t)}}e^{-\frac{1}{2}\left(\frac{\log S_T-m}{\sigma\sqrt{T-t}}\right)^2}, \quad S_T > 0$$

where $m = \log S_t + \left(r - D - \frac{1}{2}\sigma^2\right)(T-t)$. Therefore,

$$C\left(S_t,t;K,T\right) = e^{-r(T-t)}\int_0^K \max\{S_T - K,0\}f(S_T|S_t)\,dS_T$$
$$+e^{-r(T-t)}\int_K^\infty \max\{S_T - K,0\}f(S_T|S_t)\,dS_T$$
$$= e^{-r(T-t)}\int_K^\infty (S_T - K)f(S_T|S_t)\,dS_T$$
$$= I_1 - I_2$$

where

$$I_1 = e^{-r(T-t)}\int_K^\infty S_T f(S_T|S_t)\,dS_T \quad \text{and} \quad I_2 = e^{-r(T-t)}\int_K^\infty K f(S_T|S_t)\,dS_T.$$

Solving I_1 we have

$$I_1 = e^{-r(T-t)}\int_K^\infty S_T f(S_T|S_t)\,dS_T$$
$$= e^{-r(T-t)}\int_K^\infty \frac{1}{\sigma\sqrt{2\pi(T-t)}}e^{-\frac{1}{2}\left(\frac{\log S_T-m}{\sigma\sqrt{T-t}}\right)^2}\,dS_T$$

and by letting $u = \dfrac{\log S_T - m}{\sigma\sqrt{T-t}}$ we then have

$$I_1 = \frac{e^{m-r(T-t)}}{\sqrt{2\pi}}\int_{\frac{\log K-m}{\sigma\sqrt{T-t}}}^\infty e^{-\frac{1}{2}u^2+\sigma u\sqrt{T-t}}\,du.$$

Using the sum of squares

$$-\frac{1}{2}u^2 + \sigma u\sqrt{T-t} = -\frac{1}{2}\left[\left(u - \sigma\sqrt{T-t}\right)^2 - \sigma^2(T-t)\right]$$

we can simplify I_1 to become

$$
I_1 = \frac{e^{m-r(T-t)}}{\sqrt{2\pi}} \int_{\frac{\log K - m}{\sigma\sqrt{T-t}}}^{\infty} e^{-\frac{1}{2}\left[\left(u-\sigma\sqrt{T-t}\right)^2 - \sigma^2(T-t)\right]} d\,u
$$

$$
= e^{m-r(T-t)+\frac{1}{2}\sigma^2(T-t)} \int_{\frac{\log K - m}{\sigma\sqrt{T-t}}}^{\infty} \frac{1}{\sqrt{2\pi}} e^{-\frac{1}{2}\left(u-\sigma\sqrt{T-t}\right)^2} d\,u.
$$

By setting $v = u - \sigma\sqrt{T-t}$ and substituting $m = \log S_t + \left(r - D - \frac{1}{2}\sigma^2\right)(T-t)$ we eventually have

$$
I_1 = S_t e^{-D(T-t)} \Phi\left(\frac{\log(S_t/K) + (r - D + \frac{1}{2}\sigma^2)(T-t)}{\sigma\sqrt{T-t}}\right).
$$

Similarly for I_2 we have

$$
I_2 = e^{-r(T-t)} \int_K^{\infty} K f(S_T)\, dS_T
$$

$$
= e^{-r(T-t)} \int_K^{\infty} \frac{1}{S_T \sigma \sqrt{2\pi(T-t)}} e^{-\frac{1}{2}\left(\frac{\log S_T - m}{\sigma\sqrt{T-t}}\right)^2} dS_T
$$

and by setting $u = \dfrac{\log S_T - m}{\sigma\sqrt{T-t}}$ and substituting $m = \log S_t + \left(r - D - \frac{1}{2}\sigma^2\right)(T-t)$

$$
I_2 = e^{-r(T-t)} K \int_{\frac{\log K - m}{\sigma\sqrt{T-t}}}^{\infty} \frac{1}{\sqrt{2\pi}} e^{-\frac{1}{2}u^2} d\,u
$$

$$
= K e^{-r(T-t)} \left[1 - \Phi\left(\frac{\log K - m}{\sigma\sqrt{T-t}}\right)\right]
$$

$$
= K e^{-r(T-t)} \Phi\left(\frac{\log(S_t/K) + (r - D - \frac{1}{2}\sigma^2)(T-t)}{\sigma\sqrt{T-t}}\right).
$$

Therefore,

$$
C(S_t, t; K, T) = S_t e^{-D(T-t)} \Phi\left(d_+\right) - K e^{-r(T-t)} \Phi\left(d_-\right)
$$

where

$$d_\pm = \frac{\log(S_t/K) + (r - D \pm \frac{1}{2}\sigma^2)(T - t)}{\sigma\sqrt{T - t}}.$$

Using the put–call parity

$$C(S_t, t; K, T) - P(S_t, t; K, T) = S_t e^{-D(T-t)} - Ke^{-r(T-t)}$$

the European put option is

$$\begin{aligned}
P(S_t, t; K, T) &= C(S_t, t; K, T) - S_t e^{-D(T-t)} S_t + Ke^{-r(T-t)} \\
&= S_t e^{-D(T-t)}\Phi(d_+) - Ke^{-r(T-t)}\Phi(d_-) - S_t e^{-D(T-t)} + Ke^{-r(T-t)} \\
&= -S_t e^{-D(T-t)}\left[1 - \Phi(d_+)\right] + Ke^{-r(T-t)}\left[1 - \Phi(d_-)\right] \\
&= Ke^{-r(T-t)}\Phi(-d_-) - S_t e^{-D(T-t)}\Phi(-d_+).
\end{aligned}$$

$\square$

6. *Martingale Property.* Let $\{W_t : t \geq 0\}$ be a $\mathbb{P}$-standard Wiener process on the probability space $(\Omega, \mathcal{F}, \mathbb{P})$ and let the asset price S_t follow the following SDE

$$\frac{dS_t}{S_t} = (\mu - D)dt + \sigma dW_t$$

where μ is the drift parameter, D is the continuous dividend yield and σ is the volatility parameter. In addition, let r be the risk-free interest rate.

We define the price of a European call option priced at time t with strike price K and expiry time T, $t < T$ as

$$C(S_t, t; K, T) = S_t e^{-D(T-t)}\Phi(d_+) - Ke^{-r(T-t)}\Phi(d_-)$$

where

$$d_\pm = \frac{\log(S_t/K) + (r - D \pm \frac{1}{2}\sigma^2)(T - t)}{\sigma\sqrt{T - t}}$$

and $\Phi(\cdot)$ is the cdf of a standard normal.

Show that $e^{-rt}C(S_t, t; K, T)$ is a martingale under the risk-neutral measure $\mathbb{Q}$.

Solution: Under the risk-neutral measure $\mathbb{Q}$, S_t follows

$$\frac{dS_t}{S_t} = (r - D)dt + \sigma dW_t^{\mathbb{Q}}$$

where $W_t^{\mathbb{Q}} = W_t + \left(\frac{\mu - r}{\sigma}\right)t$ is a $\mathbb{Q}$-standard Wiener process.

Using Itō's lemma we can easily show for $T > t$

$$\log\left(\frac{S_T}{S_t}\right) \sim \mathcal{N}\left[\left(r - D - \frac{1}{2}\sigma^2\right)(T - t), \sigma^2(T - t)\right]$$

with density function for S_T

$$f(S_T|S_t) = \frac{1}{S_T \sigma \sqrt{2\pi(T - t)}} e^{-\frac{1}{2}\left(\frac{\log(S_T/S_t) - (r - D - \frac{1}{2}\sigma^2)(T-t)}{\sigma\sqrt{T-t}}\right)^2}.$$

To show that $e^{-rt}C(S_t, t; K, T)$ is a $\mathbb{Q}$-martingale we note the following.

(a) For $t < \tau < T$ and by setting $d_{\pm}^{\tau} = \dfrac{\log(S_{\tau}/K) + (r - D \pm \frac{1}{2}\sigma^2)(T - \tau)}{\sigma\sqrt{T - \tau}}$

$$\mathbb{E}^{\mathbb{Q}}\left[e^{-r\tau}C(S_{\tau}, \tau; K, T)\middle|\mathcal{F}_t\right] = \mathbb{E}^{\mathbb{Q}}\left[e^{-r\tau}\left\{S_{\tau}e^{-D(T-\tau)}\Phi(d_{+}^{\tau})\right.\right.$$
$$\left.\left. - Ke^{-r(T-\tau)}\Phi(d_{-}^{\tau})\right\}\middle|\mathcal{F}_t\right]$$
$$= e^{-r\tau - D(T-\tau)}\mathbb{E}^{\mathbb{Q}}\left[S_{\tau}\Phi(d_{+}^{\tau})\middle|\mathcal{F}_t\right]$$
$$- Ke^{-rT}\mathbb{E}^{\mathbb{Q}}\left[\Phi(d_{-}^{\tau})\middle|\mathcal{F}_t\right]$$
$$= I_1 - I_2$$

where $I_1 = e^{-r\tau - D(T-\tau)}\mathbb{E}^{\mathbb{Q}}\left[S_{\tau}\Phi(d_{+}^{\tau})\middle|\mathcal{F}_t\right]$ and $I_2 = Ke^{-rT}\mathbb{E}^{\mathbb{Q}}\left[\Phi(d_{-}^{\tau})\middle|\mathcal{F}_t\right]$.
   For the case

$$I_1 = e^{-r\tau - D(T-\tau)}\mathbb{E}^{\mathbb{Q}}\left[S_{\tau}\Phi(d_{+}^{\tau})\middle|\mathcal{F}_t\right]$$
$$= e^{-r\tau - D(T-\tau)}$$
$$\times \int_0^{\infty} S_{\tau}\Phi\left(\frac{\log(S_{\tau}/K) + (r - D + \frac{1}{2}\sigma^2)(T - \tau)}{\sigma\sqrt{T - \tau}}\right)f(S_{\tau}|S_t)\,dS_{\tau}$$

and by setting $x = \dfrac{\log(S_{\tau}/S_t) - (r - D - \frac{1}{2}\sigma^2)(\tau - t)}{\sigma\sqrt{\tau - t}}$ we have

$$I_1 = S_t e^{-r\tau - D(T-\tau) + (r - D - \frac{1}{2}\sigma^2)(\tau - t)}$$
$$\times \int_{-\infty}^{\infty} \Phi\left(\frac{m + x\sigma\sqrt{\tau - t}}{\sigma\sqrt{T - \tau}}\right)\frac{1}{\sqrt{2\pi}}e^{-\frac{1}{2}(x^2 - 2x\sigma\sqrt{\tau - t})}\,dx$$

or

$$I_1 = S_t e^{-r\tau - D(T-\tau) + (r-D)(\tau - t)}$$

$$\times \int_{-\infty}^{\infty} \Phi\left(\frac{m + x\sigma\sqrt{\tau - t}}{\sigma\sqrt{T - \tau}}\right) \frac{1}{\sqrt{2\pi}} e^{-\frac{1}{2}(x - \sigma\sqrt{\tau - t})^2} dx$$

where $m = \log(S_t/K) + (r - D + \frac{1}{2}\sigma^2)(T - \tau) + (r - D - \frac{1}{2}\sigma^2)(\tau - t)$.
By setting $y = x - \sigma\sqrt{\tau - t}$ we have

$$I_1 = S_t e^{-r\tau - D(T-\tau) + (r-D)(\tau - t)}$$

$$\times \int_{-\infty}^{\infty} \Phi\left(\frac{m + \sigma^2(\tau - t) + y\sigma\sqrt{\tau - t}}{\sigma\sqrt{T - \tau}}\right) \frac{1}{\sqrt{2\pi}} e^{-\frac{1}{2}y^2} dy$$

or

$$I_1 = S_t e^{-r\tau - D(T-t)} \int_{-\infty}^{\infty} \Phi\left(\frac{d_+ + \rho y}{\sqrt{1 - \rho^2}}\right) \frac{1}{\sqrt{2\pi}} e^{-\frac{1}{2}y^2} dy$$

where $\rho = \sqrt{\dfrac{\tau - t}{T - t}}$. From Problem 1.2.2.14 of *Problems and Solutions in Mathematical Finance, Volume 1: Stochastic Calculus* we can deduce

$$I_1 = S_t e^{-rt - D(T-t)} \Phi(\infty, d_+, -\rho)$$
$$= S_t e^{-rt - D(T-t)} \Phi(d_+)$$

where $d_+ = \dfrac{\log(S_t/K) + (r - D + \frac{1}{2}\sigma^2)(T - t)}{\sigma\sqrt{T - t}}$.

In contrast, for

$$I_2 = Ke^{-rT} \mathbb{E}^{\mathbb{Q}}\left[\Phi(d_-^\tau)\big|\, \mathscr{F}_t\right]$$

$$= Ke^{-rT} \int_0^{\infty} \Phi\left(\frac{\log(S_\tau/K) + (r - D - \frac{1}{2}\sigma^2)(T - \tau)}{\sigma\sqrt{T - \tau}}\right) f(S_\tau|S_t)\, dS_\tau$$

and by setting $x = \dfrac{\log(S_\tau/S_t) - (r - D - \frac{1}{2}\sigma^2)(\tau - t)}{\sigma\sqrt{\tau - t}}$ we have

$$I_2 = Ke^{-rT}$$

$$\times \int_{-\infty}^{\infty} \Phi\left(\frac{\log(S_t/K) + (r - D - \frac{1}{2}\sigma^2)(T - t) + x\sigma\sqrt{\tau - t}}{\sigma\sqrt{T - \tau}}\right) \frac{1}{\sqrt{2\pi}} e^{-\frac{1}{2}x^2} dx$$

$$= Ke^{-rT} \int_{-\infty}^{\infty} \Phi\left(\frac{d_- + \rho x}{\sqrt{1 - \rho^2}}\right) \frac{1}{\sqrt{2\pi}} e^{-\frac{1}{2}x^2} dx$$

$$= Ke^{-rT} \Phi(\infty, d_-, -\rho)$$

$$= Ke^{-rT} \Phi(d_-)$$

where $\rho = \sqrt{\dfrac{\tau - t}{T - t}}$ and $d_- = \dfrac{\log(S_t/K) + (r - D - \frac{1}{2}\sigma^2)(T - t)}{\sigma\sqrt{T - t}}$.

Therefore,

$$\mathbb{E}^{\mathbb{Q}}\left[e^{-r\tau}C(S_\tau, \tau; K, T)\big| \mathcal{F}_t\right] = e^{-rt}\left[S_t e^{-D(T-t)}\Phi(d_+) - Ke^{-r(T-t)}\Phi(d_-)\right]$$

$$= e^{-rt}C(S_t, t; K, T).$$

(b) Since $\left|e^{-rt}C(S_t, t; K, T)\right| = e^{-rt}C(S_t, t; K, T)$ and because $C(S_t, t; K, T) < S_t < \infty$ therefore

$$\mathbb{E}^{\mathbb{Q}}\left[\left|e^{-rt}C(S_t, t; K, T)\right|\right] = \mathbb{E}^{\mathbb{Q}}\left[e^{-rt}C(S_t, t; K, T)\right] < e^{-rt}S_t < \infty.$$

(c) Given that $e^{-rt}C(S_t, t; K, T)$ is a function of S_t, hence it is $\mathcal{F}_t$-adapted.
   From the results of (a) – (c) we have shown that $e^{-rt}C(S_t, t; K, T)$ is a Q-martingale.

N.B. Using the same steps we can also show that $e^{-rt}P(S_t, t; K, T)$ is a Q-martingale where $P(S_t, t; K, T)$ is the European put option price with strike K and expiry time T where the stock pays a continuous dividend yield.

□

7. *Invariance Property I.* Let the price of a European option $V(S_t, t)$ satisfy the Black–Scholes equation

$$\frac{\partial V}{\partial t} + \frac{1}{2}\sigma^2 S_t^2 \frac{\partial^2 V}{\partial S_t^2} + (r - D)S_t \frac{\partial V}{\partial S_t} - rV(S_t, t) = 0$$

where S_t is the spot price of a stock at time t, σ is the stock volatility, r is the constant risk-free interest rate, D is the continuous dividend yield and T is the option expiry time.
   Show that $V(\lambda S_t, t)$ is also a solution of the Black–Scholes equation for $\lambda > 0$.
   Give a financial interpretation of this property.

Solution: Let $W(S_t, t) = V(\lambda S_t, t)$ and by setting $\hat{S}_t = \lambda S_t$ we have

$$\frac{\partial W}{\partial t} = \frac{\partial V}{\partial t}, \quad \frac{\partial W}{\partial S_t} = \frac{\partial V}{\partial \hat{S}_t} \frac{\partial \hat{S}_t}{\partial S_t} = \lambda \frac{\partial V}{\partial \hat{S}_t}$$

$$\frac{\partial^2 W}{\partial S_t^2} = \frac{\partial}{\partial S_t} \left(\frac{\partial W}{\partial S_t} \right) = \frac{\partial}{\partial S_t} \left(\lambda \frac{\partial V}{\partial \hat{S}_t} \right) = \lambda \frac{\partial^2 V}{\partial \hat{S}_t^2} \frac{\partial \hat{S}_t}{\partial S_t} = \lambda^2 \frac{\partial^2 V}{\partial \hat{S}_t^2}.$$

By substituting the above expressions into

$$\frac{\partial W}{\partial t} + \frac{1}{2}\sigma^2 S_t^2 \frac{\partial^2 W}{\partial S_t^2} + (r - D)S_t \frac{\partial W}{\partial S_t} - rW(S_t, t)$$

we have

$$\frac{\partial W}{\partial t} + \frac{1}{2}\sigma^2 S_t^2 \frac{\partial^2 W}{\partial S_t^2} + (r - D)S_t \frac{\partial W}{\partial S_t} - rW(S_t, t)$$

$$= \frac{\partial V}{\partial t} + \frac{1}{2}\sigma^2 \lambda^2 S_t^2 \frac{\partial^2 V}{\partial \hat{S}_t^2} + (r - D)\lambda S_t \frac{\partial V}{\partial \hat{S}_t} - rV(\hat{S}_t, t)$$

$$= \frac{\partial V}{\partial t} + \frac{1}{2}\sigma^2 \hat{S}_t^2 \frac{\partial^2 V}{\partial \hat{S}_t^2} + (r - D)\hat{S}_t \frac{\partial V}{\partial \hat{S}_t} - rV(\hat{S}_t, t)$$

$$= 0.$$

Thus, the Black–Scholes equation is invariant under the change of variable $\hat{S}_t = \lambda S_t$ for $\lambda > 0$.

Given that both $V(S_t, t)$ and $V(\lambda S_t, t)$, $\lambda > 0$ satisfy the Black–Scholes equation, the price of a European option scales with the underlying stock price.

$\square$

8. *Invariance Property II.* Let $V_{bs}(S_t, t; K, T)$ denote the Black–Scholes formula at time t for a European option with expiry T, $T > t$, strike K, given S_t is the spot price of a stock at time t, σ is the stock volatility, D is the continuous dividend yield, and let r be the constant risk-free interest rate.

Prove that for any constant $\alpha > 0$,

$$V_{bs}(\alpha S_t, t; K, T) = \alpha V_{bs}(S_t, t; K/\alpha, T).$$

Solution: By definition

$$V_{bs}(S_t, t; K, T) = \delta S_t e^{-D(T-t)} \Phi(\delta d_+) - \delta K e^{-r(T-t)} \Phi(\delta d_-)$$

$$d_\pm = \frac{\log(S_t/K) + (r - D \pm \frac{1}{2}\sigma^2)(T - t)}{\sigma\sqrt{T - t}}$$

$$\delta = \begin{cases} +1 & \text{for European call option} \\ -1 & \text{for European put option.} \end{cases}$$

For any constant $\alpha > 0$,

$$V_{bs}(\alpha S_t, t; K, T) = \alpha \delta S_t e^{-D(T-t)} \Phi(\delta d_+) - \delta K e^{-r(T-t)} \Phi(\delta d_-)$$

$$d_\pm = \frac{\log(\alpha S_t / K) + (r - D \pm \frac{1}{2}\sigma^2)(T-t)}{\sigma\sqrt{T-t}}$$

$$= \frac{\log(S_t/(K/\alpha)) + (r - D \pm \frac{1}{2}\sigma^2)(T-t)}{\sigma\sqrt{T-t}}.$$

Thus,

$$V_{bs}(\alpha S_t, t; K, T) = \alpha \left[\delta S_t e^{-D(T-t)} \Phi(\delta d_+) - \delta(K/\alpha) e^{-r(T-t)} \Phi(\delta d_-) \right]$$
$$= \alpha V_{bs}(S_t, t; K/\alpha, T).$$

N.B. For example in a one-for-two stock split (holder of one share before the split will hold two shares after the split), with the introduction of new shares the value of the stock price and the strike price will be scaled by half. Thus, the value of the option prices will also be halved.

□

9. *Higher Derivatives Property.* We consider the value of a European option $V(S_t, t)$ satisfying the following Black–Scholes equation

$$\frac{\partial V}{\partial t} + \frac{1}{2}\sigma^2 S_t^2 \frac{\partial^2 V}{\partial S_t^2} + (r - D)S_t \frac{\partial V}{\partial S_t} - rV(S_t, t) = 0$$

where S_t is the spot price of a stock at time t, σ is the stock volatility, r is the constant risk-free interest rate, D is the continuous dividend yield and $T > t$ is the option expiry time.

Using mathematical induction show that

$$W^{(n)}(S_t, t) = S_t^n \frac{\partial^n V}{\partial S_t^n}$$

also satisfy the Black–Scholes equation for any $n = 1, 2, \ldots$

Solution: Let $W^{(n)}(S_t, t) = S_t^n \dfrac{\partial^n V}{\partial S_t^n}$, $n = 1, 2, \ldots$

For $n = 1$ we have $W^{(1)}(S_t, t) = S_t \dfrac{\partial V}{\partial S_t}$ and by differentiation

$$\frac{\partial W^{(1)}}{\partial t} = S_t \frac{\partial}{\partial t}\left(\frac{\partial V}{\partial S_t}\right), \quad S_t \frac{\partial W^{(1)}}{\partial S_t} = S_t \frac{\partial}{\partial S_t}\left(S_t \frac{\partial V}{\partial S_t}\right) = S_t \left(\frac{\partial V}{\partial S_t} + S_t \frac{\partial^2 V}{\partial S_t^2}\right)$$

and

$$S_t^2 \frac{\partial^2 W^{(1)}}{\partial S_t^2} = S_t^2 \left[\frac{\partial}{\partial S_t} \left(\frac{\partial V}{\partial S_t} + S_t \frac{\partial^2 V}{\partial S_t^2} \right) \right]$$

$$= 2S_t^2 \frac{\partial^2 V}{\partial S_t^2} + S_t^3 \frac{\partial^3 V}{\partial S_t^3}$$

$$= S_t \frac{\partial}{\partial S_t} \left(S_t^2 \frac{\partial^2 V}{\partial S_t^2} \right).$$

Substituting $\dfrac{\partial W^{(1)}}{\partial t}$, $S_t \dfrac{\partial W^{(1)}}{\partial S_t}$ and $S_t^2 \dfrac{\partial^2 W^{(1)}}{\partial S_t^2}$ into

$$\frac{\partial W^{(1)}}{\partial t} + \frac{1}{2}\sigma^2 S_t^2 \frac{\partial^2 W^{(1)}}{\partial S_t^2} + (r - D)S_t \frac{\partial W^{(1)}}{\partial S_t} - rW^{(1)}(S_t,t)$$

we have

$$\frac{\partial W^{(1)}}{\partial t} + \frac{1}{2}\sigma^2 S_t^2 \frac{\partial^2 W^{(1)}}{\partial S_t^2} + (r - D)S_t \frac{\partial W^{(1)}}{\partial S_t} - rW^{(1)}(S_t,t)$$

$$= S_t \frac{\partial}{\partial t}\left(\frac{\partial V}{\partial S_t}\right) + \frac{1}{2}\sigma^2 S_t \frac{\partial}{\partial S_t}\left(S_t^2 \frac{\partial^2 V}{\partial S_t^2}\right) + (r - D)S_t \frac{\partial}{\partial S_t}\left(S_t \frac{\partial V}{\partial S_t}\right) - rS_t \frac{\partial V}{\partial S_t}$$

$$= S_t \frac{\partial}{\partial S_t}\left(\frac{\partial V}{\partial t} + \frac{1}{2}\sigma^2 S_t^2 \frac{\partial^2 V}{\partial S_t^2} + (r - D)S_t \frac{\partial V}{\partial S_t} - rV(S_t,t)\right)$$

$$= 0.$$

Hence, $W^{(1)}(S_t,t) = S_t \dfrac{\partial V}{\partial S_t}$ is a solution of the Black–Scholes equation.

Assume that $W^{(n)}(S_t,t) = S_t^n \dfrac{\partial^n V}{\partial S_t^n}$ is also a solution of the Black–Scholes equation such that

$$S_t^n \frac{\partial}{\partial S_t^n}\left(\frac{\partial V}{\partial t} + \frac{1}{2}\sigma^2 S_t^2 \frac{\partial^2 V}{\partial S_t^2} + (r - D)S_t \frac{\partial V}{\partial S_t} - rV(S_t,t)\right) = 0.$$

For the case of $W^{(n+1)}(S_t,t) = S_t^{n+1} \dfrac{\partial^{n+1} V}{\partial S_t^{n+1}}$ we first differentiate

$$\frac{\partial}{\partial S_t}\left[S_t^n \frac{\partial}{\partial S_t^n}\left(\frac{\partial V}{\partial t} + \frac{1}{2}\sigma^2 S_t^2 \frac{\partial^2 V}{\partial S_t^2} + (r - D)S_t \frac{\partial V}{\partial S_t} - rV(S_t,t)\right)\right] = 0$$

and we then have

$$nS_t^{n-1}\frac{\partial^n}{\partial S_t^n}\left(\frac{\partial V}{\partial t}+\frac{1}{2}\sigma^2 S_t^2\frac{\partial^2 V}{\partial S_t^2}+(r-D)S_t\frac{\partial V}{\partial S_t}-rV(S_t,t)\right)$$

$$+S_t^n\frac{\partial^{n+1}}{\partial S_t^{n+1}}\left(\frac{\partial V}{\partial t}+\frac{1}{2}\sigma^2 S_t^2\frac{\partial^2 V}{\partial S_t^2}+(r-D)S_t\frac{\partial V}{\partial S_t}-rV(S_t,t)\right)$$

$$=0.$$

By multiplying the above equation with S_t we obtain

$$nS_t^n\frac{\partial^n}{\partial S_t^n}\left(\frac{\partial V}{\partial t}+\frac{1}{2}\sigma^2 S_t^2\frac{\partial^2 V}{\partial S_t^2}+(r-D)S_t\frac{\partial V}{\partial S_t}-rV(S_t,t)\right)$$

$$+S_t^{n+1}\frac{\partial^{n+1}}{\partial S_t^{n+1}}\left(\frac{\partial V}{\partial t}+\frac{1}{2}\sigma^2 S_t^2\frac{\partial^2 V}{\partial S_t^2}+(r-D)S_t\frac{\partial V}{\partial S_t}-rV(S_t,t)\right)$$

$$=0$$

and since

$$S_t^n\frac{\partial}{\partial S_t^n}\left(\frac{\partial V}{\partial t}+\frac{1}{2}\sigma^2 S_t^2\frac{\partial^2 V}{\partial S_t^2}+(r-D)S_t\frac{\partial V}{\partial S_t}-rV(S_t,t)\right)=0$$

we therefore have

$$S^{n+1}\frac{\partial^{n+1}}{\partial S_t^{n+1}}\left(\frac{\partial V}{\partial t}+\frac{1}{2}\sigma^2 S_t^2\frac{\partial^2 V}{\partial S_t^2}+(r-D)S_t\frac{\partial V}{\partial S_t}-rV(S_t,t)\right)=0.$$

Hence, $W^{(n+1)}(S_t,t)=S_t^{n+1}\dfrac{\partial^{n+1}V}{\partial S_t^{n+1}}$ is also a solution of the Black–Scholes equation. Thus, from mathematical induction we have shown that $S_t^n\dfrac{\partial^n V}{\partial S_t^n}$ satisfies the Black–Scholes equation for $n=1,2,\ldots$

□

10. Let the Black–Scholes equation for the price of a European option $V(S_t,t)$ on an underlying asset priced S_t at time t be

$$\frac{\partial V}{\partial t}+\frac{1}{2}\sigma^2 S_t^2\frac{\partial^2 V}{\partial S_t^2}+(r-D)S_t\frac{\partial V}{\partial S_t}-rV(S_t,t)=0$$

where σ is the constant volatility, r is the constant risk-free interest rate and D is the constant dividend yield.

Show that if

$$V(S_t, t) = f(S_t)g(t)$$

then

$$\frac{g'(t)}{g(t)} = -\left[\frac{\frac{1}{2}\sigma^2 S_t^2 f''(S_t) + (r - D)S_t \, f'(S_t) - rf(S_t)}{f(S_t)} \right].$$

Explain why g and f satisfy the following ordinary differential equations (ODEs)

$$g'(t) - \lambda g(t) = 0$$

and

$$\frac{1}{2}\sigma^2 S_t^2 f''(S_t) + (r - D)S_t \, f'(S_t) - (r - \lambda)f(S_t) = 0$$

for a constant λ.

Hence, conditional on λ find all solutions of the Black–Scholes equation.

Solution: If $V(S_t, t)$ can be separated as a product $V(S_t, t) = f(S_t)g(t)$ then

$$\frac{\partial V}{\partial t} = f(S_t)g'(t), \quad \frac{\partial V}{\partial S_t} = f'(S_t)g(t) \quad \text{and} \quad \frac{\partial^2 V}{\partial S_t^2} = f''(S_t)g(t)$$

and by substituting them into the Black–Scholes equation we have

$$\frac{\partial V}{\partial t} + \frac{1}{2}\sigma^2 S_t^2 \frac{\partial^2 V}{\partial S_t^2} + (r - D)S_t \frac{\partial V}{\partial S_t} - rV(S_t, t)$$

$$= f(S_t)g'(t) + \frac{1}{2}\sigma^2 S_t^2 f''(S_t)g(t) + (r - D)S_t \, f'(S_t)g(t) - rf(S_t)g(t)$$

$$= f(S_t)g'(t) + g(t)\left[\frac{1}{2}\sigma^2 S_t^2 f''(S_t) + (r - D)S_t \, f'(S_t) - rf(S_t)\right]$$

$$= 0.$$

Hence,

$$\frac{g'(t)}{g(t)} = -\left[\frac{\frac{1}{2}\sigma^2 S_t^2 f''(S_t) + (r - D)S_t \, f'(S_t) - rf(S_t)}{f(S_t)} \right].$$

Given that the left-hand side of the equation is a function of t whilst the right-hand side is a function of S_t, both equations must be equal to a constant λ. Thus,

$$g'(t) - \lambda g(t) = 0$$

and

$$\frac{1}{2}\sigma^2 S_t^2 f''(S_t) + (r - D)S_t \, f'(S_t) - (r - \lambda) \, f(S_t) = 0.$$

For the first-order ODE $g'(t) - \lambda g(t) = 0$, by setting the integrating factor

$$I = e^{-\int \lambda dt} = e^{-\lambda t}$$

we have

$$\frac{d}{dt}\left(e^{-\lambda t} g(t)\right) = 0$$

or

$$g(t) = C_g e^{\lambda t}$$

where C_g is a constant value.

As for solving $\frac{1}{2}\sigma^2 S_t^2 \, f''(S_t) + (r - D)S_t f'(S_t) - (r - \lambda)f(S_t) = 0$, which is a second-order ODE, we let $f(S_t) = C S_t^m$ where C is a constant. By substituting

$$f(S_t) = C S_t^m, f'(S_t) = mC S_t^{m-1} \quad \text{and} \quad f''(S_t) = m(m-1)C S_t^{m-2}$$

we eventually have

$$\frac{1}{2}\sigma^2 m^2 + (r - D - \frac{1}{2}\sigma^2)m - (r - \lambda) = 0.$$

Hence, by solving the above quadratic equation

$$m = \frac{-(r - D - \frac{1}{2}\sigma^2) \pm \sqrt{(r - D - \frac{1}{2}\sigma^2)^2 + 2\sigma^2(r - \lambda)}}{\sigma^2}$$

where we need to consider three cases of roots of m.

First, if $\lambda < r + \frac{1}{2\sigma^2}(r - D - \frac{1}{2}\sigma^2)^2$ then the solution of the ODE is of the form

$$f(S_t) = A_f S_t^{m_+} + B_f S_t^{m_-}$$

where

$$m_+ = \frac{-(r - D - \frac{1}{2}\sigma^2) + \sqrt{(r - D - \frac{1}{2}\sigma^2)^2 + 2\sigma^2(r - \lambda)}}{\sigma^2} > 0$$

$$m_- = \frac{-(r - D - \frac{1}{2}\sigma^2) - \sqrt{(r - D - \frac{1}{2}\sigma^2)^2 + 2\sigma^2(r - \lambda)}}{\sigma^2} < 0$$

and A_f, B_f are unknown constants. Thus,

$$V(S_t, t) = f(S_t)g(t) = C_1 e^{\lambda t} S_t^{m_+} + C_2 e^{\lambda t} S_t^{m_-}$$

where $C_1 = A_f C_g$ and $C_2 = B_f C_g$.

Second, if $\lambda = r + \dfrac{1}{2\sigma^2}\left(r - D - \dfrac{1}{2}\sigma^2\right)^2$ then

$$f(S_t) = C_f S_t^m$$

where $m = -\dfrac{1}{\sigma^2}(r - D - \dfrac{1}{2}\sigma^2)$ and C_f is a constant. Therefore,

$$V(S_t, t) = f(S_t)g(t) = C e^{\lambda t} S_t^m$$

where $C = C_f C_g$.

Third, if $\lambda > r + \dfrac{1}{2\sigma^2}(r - D - \dfrac{1}{2}\sigma^2)^2$ then we have complex roots for m so that

$$f(S_t) = K_1 S_t^{\alpha + i\beta} + K_2 S_t^{\alpha - i\beta}$$

where $\alpha = -\dfrac{1}{\sigma^2}(r - D - \dfrac{1}{2}\sigma^2)$, $\beta = \dfrac{1}{\sigma^2}\sqrt{-(r - D - \dfrac{1}{2}\sigma^2)^2 - 2\sigma^2(r - \lambda)}$ and K_1, K_2 are constants.

From the identity $e^{i\theta} = \cos\theta + i\sin\theta$ we can write the solution of the second-order ODE as

$$f(S_t) = C_f^{(1)} S_t^\alpha \cos\left(\beta \log S_t\right) + C_f^{(2)} S_t^\alpha \sin\left(\beta \log S_t\right)$$

where $C_f^{(1)}$ and $C_f^{(2)}$ are constants. Therefore,

$$V(S_t, t) = f(S_t)g(t) = C_1 e^{\lambda t} S_t^\alpha \cos\left(\beta \log S_t\right) + C_2 e^{\lambda t} S_t^\alpha \sin\left(\beta \log S_t\right)$$

where $C_1 = C_f^{(1)} C_g$ and $C_2 = C_f^{(2)} C_g$.

$\square$

11. *Discrete Dividends I – Escrowed Dividend Model.* We consider at time t a European option $V(S_t, t; K, T)$ with strike K written on a stock priced at S_t paying a dividend δ at time t_δ, $t_\delta < T$ where $T > t$ is the option expiry time.

Using no-arbitrage arguments explain why

$$S_{t_\delta^+} = S_{t_\delta^-} - \delta, \quad 0 \le \delta \le S_{t_\delta^-}$$

$$V(S_{t_\delta^-}, t_\delta^-; K, T) = V(S_{t_\delta^-} - \delta, t_\delta^+; K, T)$$

where t_δ^- and t_δ^+ are the time immediately before and after the dividend is paid, respectively.

Hence, deduce that

$$
V(S_t, t; K, T) = \begin{cases} V_{bs}(S_t - \delta e^{-r(t_\delta - t)}, t; K, T) & \text{if } 0 < t < t_\delta \\[2mm] V_{bs}(S_t, t; K, T) & \text{if } t_\delta < t \le T \end{cases}
$$

where $V_{bs}(S_t, t; K, T)$ is a European option with strike K and expiry time T written on a non-dividend-paying stock S_t satisfying the Black–Scholes equation

$$
\frac{\partial V_{bs}}{\partial t} + \frac{1}{2}\sigma^2 S_t^2 \frac{\partial^2 V_{bs}}{\partial S_t^2} + rS_t \frac{\partial V_{bs}}{\partial S_t} - rV_{bs}(S_t, t; K, T) = 0
$$

$$
V_{bs}(S_T, T; K, T) = \begin{cases} \max\{S_T - K, 0\} & \text{if option is a call} \\[2mm] \max\{K - S_T, 0\} & \text{if option is a put} \end{cases}
$$

where σ is the stock volatility and r is the risk-free interest rate.

Finally, deduce that if there are $n > 1$ dividends $\delta_1, \delta_2, \ldots, \delta_n$ to be paid by the stock at time $t_{\delta_1} < t_{\delta_2} < \cdots < t_{\delta_n}$, respectively where $t < t_{\delta_1}$ and $t_{\delta_n} < T$ then

$$
V(S_t, t; K, T) = \begin{cases} V_{bs}\left(S_t - \displaystyle\sum_{i=1}^{n} \delta_i e^{-r(t_{\delta_i} - t)}, t; K, T\right) & \text{if } 0 \le t < t_{\delta_1} < t_{\delta_2} < \cdots < t_{\delta_n} \\[4mm] V_{bs}(S_t, t; K, T) & \text{if } t_{\delta_n} < t \le T. \end{cases}
$$

Solution: At time t_δ the stock pays out a discrete dividend δ and to ensure there is no arbitrage opportunity we need to show

$$
S_{t_\delta^+} = S_{t_\delta^-} - \delta.
$$

Assume that $S_{t_\delta^+} < S_{t_\delta^-} - \delta$ then we can sell the stock at $t = t_\delta^-$, forfeiting the dividend at time $t = t_\delta$, and buy back the stock at time t_δ^+. Hence, the profit is

$$
\text{Profit} = S_{t_\delta^-} - \delta - S_{t_\delta^+} > 0
$$

which is an arbitrage opportunity.

In contrast, if $S_{t_\delta^+} > S_{t_\delta^-} - \delta$ then the strategy is to buy the stock at $t = t_\delta^-$, collecting the dividend at time $t = t_\delta$ and selling it afterwards. Thus, the profit is

$$
\text{Profit} = -S_{t_\delta^-} + \delta + S_{t_\delta^+} > 0
$$

which is also an arbitrage opportunity. Hence, $S_{t_\delta^+} = S_{t_\delta^-} - \delta$ and since $S_{t_\delta^+} \ge 0$ therefore $0 \le \delta \le S_{t_\delta^-}$.

Given that the option holder does not receive the dividend, the option value cannot jump across time t_δ. Therefore,

$$V(S_{t_\delta^-}, t_\delta^-; K, T) = V(S_{t_\delta^+}, t_\delta^+; K, T).$$

That is, the value of the option is the same immediately before the dividend date as well as immediately after the dividend date. Thus, the option price remains continuous in S_{t_δ} even though S_{t_δ} is not continuous.

Since $S_{t_\delta^+} = S_{t_\delta^-} - \delta$ therefore

$$V(S_{t_\delta^-}, t_\delta^-; K, T) = V(S_{t_\delta^-} - \delta, t_\delta^+; K, T).$$

If the option is priced at time $0 \leq t < t_\delta$ then at expiry T

$$V(S_T, T; K, T) = V_{bs}(S_T - \delta e^{r(T-t_\delta)}, T; K, T)$$

since δ being paid at time t_δ will grow at a risk-free interest rate r.

In contrast, if the option is priced at $t > t_\delta$ and because no dividends are paid thereafter, the option payoff at time T is $V(S_T, T; K, T) = V_{bs}(S_T, T; K, T)$. Therefore, by discounting the option payoff back to time t we can write

$$V(S_t, t; K, T) = \begin{cases} V_{bs}(S_t - \delta e^{-r(t_\delta - t)}, t; K, T) & \text{if } 0 \leq t < t_\delta \\ V_{bs}(S_t, t; K, T) & \text{if } t_\delta < t \leq T. \end{cases}$$

Finally, for the case when we have $n > 1$ dividends, we use an iterative method to prove the desired results.

For the case when $t_{\delta_n} < t < T$ and because there are no more dividends being paid, we have

$$V(S_t, t; K, T) = V_{bs}(S_t, t; K, T).$$

For $t < t_{\delta_n} < T$ and given that a dividend δ_n is paid at time t_{δ_n}, then

$$V(S_t, t; K, T) = V_{bs}(S_t - \delta_n e^{-r(t_{\delta_n} - t)}, t; K, T)$$

with spot price reset to $\tilde{S}_t = S_t - \delta_n e^{-r(t_{\delta_n} - t)}$.

When $t < t_{\delta_{n-1}} < t_{\delta_n} < T$ then, following the same arguments as before

$$V(S_t, t; K, T) = V_{bs}(\tilde{S}_t - \delta_{n-1} e^{-r(t_{\delta_{n-1}} - t)}, t; K, T)$$
$$= V_{bs}(S_t - \delta_{n-1} e^{-r(t_{\delta_{n-1}} - t)} - \delta_n e^{-r(t_{\delta_n} - t)}, t; K, T)$$

with spot price now reset to $\tilde{S}_t = S_t - \delta_{n-1} e^{-r(t_{\delta_{n-1}} - t)} - \delta_n e^{-r(t_{\delta_n} - t)}$.

Hence, for the case when $t < t_{\delta_1} < t_{\delta_2} < \cdots < t_{\delta_n} < T$ we can deduce that

$$V(S_t, t; K, T) = V_{bs}(\tilde{S}_t - \delta_1 e^{-r(t_{\delta_{n-1}} - t)}, t; K, T)$$

where $\tilde{S}_t = S_t - \sum_{i=2}^{n} \delta_i e^{-r(t_{\delta_i} - t)}$. Thus,

$$V(S_t, t; K, T) = \begin{cases} V_{bs}\left(S_t - \sum_{i=1}^{n} \delta_i e^{-r(t_{\delta_i} - t)}, t; K, T \right) & \text{if } 0 \le t < t_{\delta_1} < t_{\delta_2} < \cdots < t_{\delta_n} \\[4mm] V_{bs}(S_t, t; K, T) & \text{if } t_{\delta_n} < t \le T. \end{cases}$$

$\square$

12. *Discrete Dividends II – Forward Dividend Model.* We consider at time t a European option $V(S_t, t; K, T)$ with strike K written on a stock S_t paying a dividend δ at time t_δ, $t_\delta < T$ where $T > t$ is the option expiry time.

Using no-arbitrage arguments explain why

$$S_{t_\delta^+} = S_{t_\delta^-} - \delta, \quad 0 \le \delta \le S_{t_\delta^-}$$

$$V(S_{t_\delta^-}, t_\delta^-; K, T) = V(S_{t_\delta^-} - \delta, t_\delta^+; K, T)$$

where t_δ^- and t_δ^+ are the time immediately before and after the dividend is paid, respectively. Hence, deduce that

$$V(S_t, t; K, T) = \begin{cases} V_{bs}(S_t, t; K + \delta e^{r(T - t_\delta)}, T) & \text{if } 0 < t < t_\delta \\[4mm] V_{bs}(S_t, t; K, T) & \text{if } t_\delta < t \le T \end{cases}$$

where $V_{bs}(S_t, t; K, T)$ is a European option with strike K and expiry time T written on a non-dividend-paying stock S_t satisfying the Black–Scholes equation

$$\frac{\partial V_{bs}}{\partial t} + \frac{1}{2}\sigma^2 S_t^2 \frac{\partial^2 V_{bs}}{\partial S_t^2} + rS_t \frac{\partial V_{bs}}{\partial S_t} - rV_{bs}(S_t, t; K, T) = 0$$

$$V_{bs}(S_T, T; K, T) = \begin{cases} \max\{S_T - K, 0\} & \text{if option is a call} \\[4mm] \max\{K - S_T, 0\} & \text{if option is a put} \end{cases}$$

where σ is the stock volatility and r is the risk-free interest rate.

Finally, deduce that if there are $n > 1$ dividends $\delta_1, \delta_2, \ldots, \delta_n$ to be paid by the stock at time $t_{\delta_1} < t_{\delta_2} < \cdots < t_{\delta_n}$, respectively where $t < t_{\delta_1}$ and $t_{\delta_n} < T$ then

$$V(S_t, t; K, T) = \begin{cases} V_{bs}\left(S_t, t; K + \sum_{i=1}^{n} \delta_i e^{r(T-t_{\delta_i})}, T\right) & \text{if } 0 \leq t < t_{\delta_1} < t_{\delta_2} < \cdots < t_{\delta_n} \\[4mm] V_{bs}(S_t, t; K, T) & \text{if } t_{\delta_n} < t \leq T. \end{cases}$$

Solution: See Problem 2.2.2.11 (page 115) for the first part of the solutions.

Using the same arguments as in Problem 2.2.2.11 (page 115) we note that if the option is priced at time $0 \leq t < t_\delta$ then at expiry time T

$$V(S_T, T; K, T) = V_{bs}(S_T - \delta e^{r(T-t_\delta)}, T; K, T)$$
$$= \begin{cases} \max\left\{ S_T - \delta e^{r(T-t_\delta)} - K, 0 \right\} & \text{for a European call option} \\[3mm] \max\left\{ K - S_T + \delta e^{r(T-t_\delta)}, 0 \right\} & \text{for a European put option} \end{cases}$$
$$= \begin{cases} \max\left\{ S_T - \left(K + \delta e^{r(T-t_\delta)} \right), 0 \right\} & \text{for a European call option} \\[3mm] \max\left\{ \left(K + \delta e^{r(T-t_\delta)} \right) - S_T, 0 \right\} & \text{for a European put option} \end{cases}$$
$$= V_{bs}(S_T, T; K + \delta e^{r(T-t_\delta)}, T).$$

By discounting the option payoff back to time t, we eventually have

$$V(S_t, t; K, T) = \begin{cases} V_{bs}(S_t, t; K + \delta e^{r(T-t_\delta)}, T) & \text{if } 0 < t < t_\delta \\[3mm] V_{bs}(S_t, t; K, T) & \text{if } t_\delta < t \leq T. \end{cases}$$

Following the same iterative analysis as presented in Problem 2.2.2.11 (page 115) we can easily deduce that for $n > 1$ number of dividends the option price is

$$V(S_t, t; K, T) = \begin{cases} V_{bs}\left(S_t, t; K + \sum_{i=1}^{n} \delta_i e^{r(T-t_{\delta_i})}, T\right) & \text{if } 0 \leq t < t_{\delta_1} < t_{\delta_2} < \cdots < t_{\delta_n} \\[4mm] V_{bs}(S_t, t; K, T) & \text{if } t_{\delta_n} < t \leq T. \end{cases}$$

$\square$

13. *Discrete Dividends III – Bos–Vandermark Model.* We consider at time t a European option $V(S_t, t; K, T)$ with strike K written on a stock S_t paying a dividend δ at time t_δ, $t_\delta < T$ where $T > t$ is the option expiry time.

Using no-arbitrage arguments explain why

$$S_{t_\delta^+} = S_{t_\delta^-} - \delta, \quad 0 \le \delta \le S_{t_\delta^-}$$

$$V(S_{t_\delta^-}, t_\delta^-; K, T) = V(S_{t_\delta^-} - \delta, t_\delta^+; K, T)$$

where t_δ^- and t_δ^+ are the time immediately before and after the dividend is paid, respectively. By setting $\lambda_t \in [0, 1]$, deduce that

$$V(S_t, t; K, T) = \begin{cases} V_{bs}(S_t - \lambda_t \delta e^{-r(t_\delta - t)}, t; K + (1 - \lambda_t)\delta e^{r(T-t_\delta)}, T) & \text{if } 0 < t < t_\delta \\ V_{bs}(S_t, t; K, T) & \text{if } t_\delta < t \le T \end{cases}$$

where $V_{bs}(S_t, t; K, T)$ is a European option with strike K and expiry time T written on a non-dividend-paying stock S_t satisfying the Black–Scholes equation

$$\frac{\partial V_{bs}}{\partial t} + \frac{1}{2}\sigma^2 S_t^2 \frac{\partial^2 V_{bs}}{\partial S_t^2} + rS_t \frac{\partial V_{bs}}{\partial S_t} - rV_{bs}(S_t, t; K, T) = 0$$

$$V_{bs}(S_T, T; K, T) = \begin{cases} \max\{S_T - K, 0\} & \text{if option is a call} \\ \max\{K - S_T, 0\} & \text{if option is a put} \end{cases}$$

where σ is the stock volatility and r is the risk-free interest rate.

Finally, find the option price if there are $n > 1$ dividends $\delta_1, \delta_2, \ldots, \delta_n$ to be paid by the stock at time $t_{\delta_1} < t_{\delta_2} < \cdots < t_{\delta_n}$, respectively where $t < t_{\delta_1}$ and $t_{\delta_n} < T$, and $\lambda_t^{(i)} \in [0, 1]$, $i = 1, 2, \ldots, n$.

Solution: See Problem 2.2.2.11 (page 115) for the first part of the solutions.

Using the same arguments as in Problems 2.2.2.11 (page 115) and 2.2.2.12 (page 118) we note that if the option is priced at time $0 \le t < t_\delta$ then at expiry time T

$$V(S_T, T; K, T)$$
$$= V_{bs}(S_T - \delta e^{r(T-t_\delta)}, T; K, T)$$
$$= \begin{cases} \max\{S_T - \delta e^{r(T-t_\delta)} - K, 0\} & \text{for a call option} \\ \max\{K - S_T + \delta e^{r(T-t_\delta)}, 0\} & \text{for a put option} \end{cases}$$

$$= \begin{cases} \max\left\{S_T - \lambda_t \delta e^{r(T-t_\delta)} - (1-\lambda_t)\delta e^{r(T-t_\delta)} - K, 0\right\} & \text{for a call option} \\ \max\left\{K - S_T + \lambda_t \delta e^{r(T-t_\delta)} + (1-\lambda_t)\delta e^{r(T-t_\delta)}, 0\right\} & \text{for a put option} \end{cases}$$

$$= \begin{cases} \max\left\{S_T - \lambda_t \delta e^{r(T-t_\delta)} - \left(K + (1-\lambda_t)\delta e^{r(T-t_\delta)}\right), 0\right\} & \text{for a call option} \\ \max\left\{\left(K + (1-\lambda_t)\delta e^{r(T-t_\delta)}\right) - \left(S_T - \lambda_t \delta e^{r(T-t_\delta)}\right), 0\right\} & \text{for a put option} \end{cases}$$

$$= V_{bs}(S_T - \lambda_t \delta e^{r(T-t_\delta)}, T; K + (1-\lambda_t)\delta e^{r(T-t_\delta)}, T).$$

By discounting the option payoff back to time t, we eventually have

$$V(S_t, t; K, T) = \begin{cases} V_{bs}(S_t - \lambda_t \delta e^{-r(t_\delta - t)}, t; K + (1-\lambda_t)\delta e^{r(T-t_\delta)}, T) & \text{if } 0 < t < t_\delta \\ V_{bs}(S_t, t; K, T) & \text{if } t_\delta < t \leq T. \end{cases}$$

Following the same iterative analysis as presented in Problem 2.2.2.11 (page 115) we can easily deduce that for $n > 1$ number of dividends and $\lambda_t^{(i)} \in [0,1]$, $i = 1, 2, \ldots, n$, the option price is

$$V(S_t, t; K, T) = V_{bs}\left(S_t - \sum_{i=1}^{n} \lambda_t^{(i)} \delta_i e^{-r(t_{\delta_i} - t)}, t; K + \sum_{i=1}^{n} (1 - \lambda_t^{(i)})\delta_i e^{r(T-t_{\delta_i})}, T\right)$$

if $0 \leq t < t_{\delta_1} < \cdots < t_{\delta_n}$ and

$$V(S_t, t; K, T) = V_{bs}(S_t, t; K, T)$$

if $t_{\delta_n} < t \leq T$.

$\square$

14. *Discrete Dividend Yields.* We consider at time t a European option $V(S_t, t; K, T)$ with strike K written on a stock S_t paying a discrete dividend yield D at time t_D, $t_D < T$ where T is the option expiry time.

Using no-arbitrage arguments explain why

$$S_{t_D^+} = (1 - D)S_{t_D^-}, \quad 0 \leq D \leq 1$$

$$V(S_{t_D^-}, t_D^-; K, T) = V((1-D)S_{t_D^-}, t_D^+; K, T)$$

where t_D^- and t_D^+ are the times immediately before and after the dividend yield is paid, respectively.

Hence, deduce that

$$V(S_t, t; K, T) = \begin{cases} V_{bs}\big((1-D)S_t, t; K, T\big) & \text{if } 0 \leq t < t_D \\ \\ V_{bs}(S_t, t; K, T) & \text{if } t_D < t \leq T \end{cases}$$

where $V_{bs}(S_t, t; K, T)$ is a European option with strike K and expiry time T written on a non-dividend-paying stock S_t satisfying the Black–Scholes equation

$$\frac{\partial V_{bs}}{\partial t} + \frac{1}{2}\sigma^2 S_t^2 \frac{\partial^2 V_{bs}}{\partial S_t^2} + rS_t \frac{\partial V_{bs}}{\partial S_t} - rV_{bs}(S_t, t; K, T) = 0$$

$$V_{bs}(S_T, T; K, T) = \begin{cases} \max\{S_T - K, 0\} & \text{if option is a call} \\ \\ \max\{K - S_T, 0\} & \text{if option is a put} \end{cases}$$

where σ is the stock volatility and r is the risk-free interest rate.

Finally, deduce if there are $n > 1$ dividend yields $D_1, D_2, \ldots, D_n$ to be paid by the stock at time $t_{D_1} < t_{D_2} < \cdots < t_{D_n}$, respectively where $t < t_{D_1}$ and $t_{D_n} < T$ then

$$V(S_t, t; K, T) = V_{bs}\big(\beta_n S_t, t; K, T\big)$$

where $\beta_n = \prod_{i=1}^{n}(1 - D_i)$.

Solution: At time t_D the stock pays out a discrete dividend DS_{t_D} and to ensure there is no arbitrage opportunity we need to show

$$S_{t_D^+} = (1 - D)S_{t_D^-}.$$

Assume that $S_{t_D^+} < (1-D)S_{t_D^-}$ then an investor can sell the stock at $t = t_D^-$, forfeiting the dividend at time $t = t_D$, and buy back the stock at time t_δ^+. Hence, the profit is

$$\text{Profit} = S_{t_D^-} - DS_{t_D^-} - S_{t_D^+} > 0$$

which is an arbitrage opportunity.

In contrast, if $S_{t_D^+} > (1-D)S_{t_D^-}$ then the investor can buy the stock at $t = t_D^-$, collecting the dividend at time $t = t_D$ and selling it afterwards. Thus, the profit is

$$\text{Profit} = -S_{t_D^-} + DS_{t_D^-} + S_{t_D^+} > 0$$

which is also an arbitrage opportunity. Hence, $S_{t_D^+} = (1-D)S_{t_D^-}$ and since $S_{t_D^+} \geq 0$ therefore $0 \leq DS_{t_D^-} \leq S_{t_D^-}$ or $0 \leq D \leq 1$.

Given that the option holder does not receive the dividend, the option value cannot jump across time t_D. Therefore,

$$V(S_{t_D^-}, t_D^-; K, T) = V(S_{t_D^+}, t_D^+; K, T).$$

That is, the value of the option is the same immediately before the dividend date as well as immediately after the dividend date. Hence, the option price remains continuous in S_{t_D} even though S_{t_D} is not continuous.

Since $S_{t_D^+} = (1 - D)S_{t_D^-}$ therefore

$$V(S_{t_D^-}, t_D^-; K, T) = V((1 - D)S_{t_D^-}, t_D^+; K, T).$$

If the option is priced at time $0 < t < t_D$ then at expiry T we can set

$$V(S_T, T; K, T) = V_{bs}((1 - D)S_T, T; K, T).$$

In contrast, if the option is priced at $t > t_D$ and because no dividends are paid thereafter, the payoff at time T is $V(S_T, T; K, T) = V_{bs}(S_T, T; K, T)$.

Therefore, by discounting the option payoff back to time t we can write

$$V(S_t, t; K, T) = \begin{cases} V_{bs}((1 - D)S_t, t; K, T) & \text{if } 0 \le t < t_\delta \\ \\ V_{bs}(S_t, t; K, T) & \text{if } t_\delta < t \le T. \end{cases}$$

Finally, for the case when we have $n > 1$ dividends, we use an iterative method to prove the desired results.

For the case when $t_{D_n} < t < T$ and because there are no more dividends being paid, we have

$$V(S_t, t; K, T) = V_{bs}(S_t, t; K, T).$$

For $t < t_{D_n} < T$ and given that a dividend D_n is paid at time t_{D_n}, then

$$V(S_t, t; K, T) = V_{bs}((1 - D_n)S_t, t; K, T)$$

with spot price reset to $\tilde{S}_t = (1 - D_n)S_t$.

When $t < t_{D_{n-1}} < t_{D_n} < T$ then, following the same arguments as before

$$V(S_t, t; K, T) = V_{bs}((1 - D_{n-1})\tilde{S}_t, t; K, T)$$
$$= V_{bs}((1 - D_{n-1})(1 - D_n)S_t, t; K, T)$$

with spot price now reset to $\tilde{S}_t = (1 - D_{n-1})(1 - D_n)S_t$.

Hence, for the case when $t < t_{D_1} < t_{D_2} < \cdots < t_{D_n} < T$ we can deduce that

$$V(S_t, t; K, T) = V_{bs}((1 - D_1)\tilde{S}_t, t; K, T)$$

where $\tilde{S}_t = S_t \prod_{i=2}^{n} (1 - D_i)$. Thus,

$$V(S_t, t; K, T) = V_{bs}\left(S_t \prod_{i=1}^{n}(1 - D_i), t; K, T\right)$$

for $t < t_{D_1} < t_{D_2} < \cdots < t_{D_n} < T$.

$\square$

15. *Market Price of Risk.* Let $\{W_t : t \geq 0\}$ be a $\mathbb{P}$-standard Wiener process on the probability space $(\Omega, \mathscr{F}, \mathbb{P})$. Suppose the stock price S_t follows the following SDE

$$dS_t = (\mu - D)S_t dt + \sigma S_t dW_t$$

where μ is the drift parameter, D is the continuous dividend yield, σ is the volatility parameter, and let r denote the risk-free interest rate.

By considering a portfolio Π_t holding only one option $V(S_t, t)$ which is only exercised at expiry $T > t$ and using the Black–Scholes equation show that

$$d\Pi_t - r\Pi_t dt = \sigma S_t \frac{\partial V}{\partial S_t}\left(dW_t + \lambda dt\right)$$

where $\lambda = \dfrac{\mu - r}{\sigma}$ is known as the market price of risk.

Is the portfolio riskless? Interpret the function λ.

Solution: At time t we let the value of a portfolio Π_t be

$$\Pi_t = V(S_t, t)$$

and the change in portfolio Π_t becomes

$$d\Pi_t = dV.$$

Expanding $V(S_t, t)$ using Taylor's theorem

$$dV = \frac{\partial V}{\partial t}dt + \frac{\partial V}{\partial S_t}dS_t + \frac{1}{2}\frac{\partial^2 V}{\partial S_t^2}\left(dS_t\right)^2 + \ldots$$

and by substituting $dS_t = (\mu - D)S_t dt + \sigma S_t dW_t$ and applying Itô's lemma we have

$$d\Pi_t = \left[\frac{\partial V}{\partial t} + \frac{1}{2}\sigma^2 S_t^2 \frac{\partial^2 V}{\partial S_t^2} + (\mu - D)S_t \frac{\partial V}{\partial S_t}\right]dt + \sigma S_t \frac{\partial V}{\partial S_t}dW_t.$$

Hence,

$$
d\Pi_t - r\Pi_t dt = \left[\frac{\partial V}{\partial t} + \frac{1}{2}\sigma^2 S_t^2 \frac{\partial^2 V}{\partial S_t^2} + (\mu - D) S_t \frac{\partial V}{\partial S_t} - rV(S_t, t)\right] dt
$$
$$
+ \sigma S_t \frac{\partial V}{\partial S_t} dW_t
$$

and from the Black–Scholes equation

$$
\frac{\partial V}{\partial t} + \frac{1}{2}\sigma^2 S_t^2 \frac{\partial^2 V}{\partial S_t^2} + (r - D) S_t \frac{\partial V}{\partial S_t} - rV(S_t, t) = 0
$$

we have

$$
d\Pi_t - r\Pi_t dt = (\mu - r) S_t \frac{\partial V}{\partial S_t} dt + \sigma S_t \frac{\partial V}{\partial S_t} dW_t
$$
$$
= \sigma S_t \frac{\partial V}{\partial S_t}\left(dW_t + \frac{\mu - r}{\sigma} dt\right)
$$
$$
= \sigma S_t \frac{\partial V}{\partial S_t}\left(dW_t + \lambda dt\right)
$$

where $\lambda = \dfrac{\mu - r}{\sigma}$.

Given the presence of dW_t, the portfolio is not riskless.

By accepting a certain level of risk, $\lambda = \dfrac{\mu - r}{\sigma}$ can be interpreted as the excess return above the risk-free interest rate.

$\square$

16. *Black–Scholes Model with Transaction Costs.* Let $\{W_t : t \geq 0\}$ be a $\mathbb{P}$-standard Wiener process on the probability space $(\Omega, \mathcal{F}, \mathbb{P})$ and let the asset price S_t follow a GBM with the following SDE

$$
\frac{dS_t}{S_t} = (\mu - D) dt + \sigma dW_t
$$

where μ is the drift parameter, D is the continuous dividend yield, σ is the volatility parameter, and let r be the risk-free interest rate from a money-market account.

We consider incorporating a transaction cost in buying or selling the asset which has three components:

(i) a fixed cost at each transaction, κ_1

(ii) a cost proportional to the number of assets traded, $\kappa_2|v|$

(iii) a cost proportional to the value of the assets traded, $\kappa_3|v|S_t$

where $\kappa_1, \kappa_2, \kappa_3 > 0$, $v > 0$ (for buying assets) and $v < 0$ (for selling assets).

Show that $\mathbb{E}\left(|W_t|\right) = \sqrt{\dfrac{2t}{\pi}}$.

By considering a hedging portfolio involving buying an option $V(S_t, t)$ which can only be exercised at expiry time $T > t$, selling Δ numbers of asset S_t plus transaction costs, using Itō's lemma show that after a time interval $\delta t > 0$, $V(S_t, t)$ satisfies

$$\frac{\partial V}{\partial t} + \frac{1}{2}\tilde{\sigma}^2 S_t^2 \frac{\partial^2 V}{\partial S_t^2} + (r - \tilde{D})S_t \frac{\partial V}{\partial S_t} - rV(S_t, t) - \frac{\kappa_1}{\delta t} = 0$$

where

$$\tilde{D} = D + \kappa_2 \sigma \sqrt{\frac{2}{\pi \delta t}} \left| \frac{\partial^2 V}{\partial S_t^2} \right| \left(\frac{\partial V}{\partial S_t} \right)^{-1} \quad \text{and} \quad \tilde{\sigma}^2 = \sigma^2 - \kappa_3 \sigma \sqrt{\frac{2}{\pi \delta t}} \, \text{sgn}\left(\frac{\partial^2 V}{\partial S_t^2} \right)$$

such that $\text{sgn}(x) = \dfrac{x}{|x|}$.

Can the option price following a transaction cost model be negative?

Solution: For the first part of the problem, given $W_t \sim \mathcal{N}(0, t)$ then from Problem 1.2.2.11 of *Problems and Solutions in Mathematical Finance, Volume 1: Stochastic Calculus*, $|W_t|$ follows a folded normal distribution, $|W_t| \sim \mathcal{N}_f(0, t)$. Therefore, $\mathbb{E}(|W_t|) = \sqrt{\dfrac{2t}{\pi}}$.

At time t we let the value of a portfolio Π_t be

$$\Pi_t = V(S_t, t) - \Delta S_t$$

where it involves buying one unit of option $V(S_t, t)$ and selling Δ units of S_t. The continuous dividend yield is defined as the proportion of the asset price paid out per unit time. At time interval $\delta t > 0$, since we receive $DS_t \delta t$ for every asset held and the change in transaction costs is $\kappa_1 + \kappa_2|\delta\Delta| + \kappa_3|\delta\Delta|S_t$, the change in portfolio Π_t is

$$\delta\Pi_t = \delta V - \Delta(\delta S_t + DS_t\delta t) - (\kappa_1 + \kappa_2|\delta\Delta| + \kappa_3|\delta\Delta|S_t).$$

Expanding $V(S_t, t)$ using Taylor's theorem

$$\delta V = \frac{\partial V}{\partial t}\delta t + \frac{\partial V}{\partial S_t}\delta S_t + \frac{1}{2}\frac{\partial^2 V}{\partial S_t^2}(\delta S_t)^2 + \ldots$$

and by substituting $\delta S_t = (\mu - D)S_t\delta t + \sigma S_t\delta W_t$ and subsequently applying Itō's lemma we have

$$\delta V = \left[\frac{\partial V}{\partial t} + \frac{1}{2}\sigma^2 S_t^2 \frac{\partial^2 V}{\partial S_t^2} + (\mu - D)S_t\frac{\partial V}{\partial S_t} \right]\delta t + \sigma S_t\frac{\partial V}{\partial S_t}\delta W_t.$$

Substituting back into $\delta\Pi_t$ and rearranging the terms we have

$$
\delta\Pi_t = \left(\frac{\partial V}{\partial t} + \frac{1}{2}\sigma^2 S_t^2 \frac{\partial^2 V}{\partial S_t^2} + (\mu - D)\,S_t\frac{\partial V}{\partial S_t} \right)\delta t + \sigma S_t \frac{\partial V}{\partial S_t}\delta W_t
$$
$$
- \Delta\left[(\mu - D)\,S_t\delta t + \sigma S_t\delta W_t\right] - \Delta D S_t\delta t
$$
$$
- (\kappa_1 + \kappa_2|\delta\Delta| + \kappa_3|\delta\Delta|S_t)
$$
$$
= \left(\frac{\partial V}{\partial t} + \frac{1}{2}\sigma^2 S_t^2 \frac{\partial^2 V}{\partial S_t^2} + (\mu - D)\,S_t\frac{\partial V}{\partial S_t} - \mu\Delta S_t \right)\delta t
$$
$$
+ \sigma S_t \left(\frac{\partial V}{\partial S_t} - \Delta \right)\delta W_t - (\kappa_1 + \kappa_2|\delta\Delta| + \kappa_3|\delta\Delta|S_t).
$$

To eliminate the random component we choose

$$
\Delta = \frac{\partial V}{\partial S_t}
$$

which leads to

$$
\delta\Pi_t = \left(\frac{\partial V}{\partial t} + \frac{1}{2}\sigma^2 S_t^2 \frac{\partial^2 V}{\partial S_t^2} - D S_t\frac{\partial V}{\partial S_t} \right)\delta t - (\kappa_1 + \kappa_2|\delta\Delta| + \kappa_3|\delta\Delta|S_t).
$$

To find $|\delta\Delta|$ we note that

$$
\delta\Delta = \frac{\partial V}{\partial S_t}(S_t + \delta S_t, t + \delta t) - \frac{\partial V}{\partial S_t}(S_t, t)
$$
$$
= \frac{\partial V}{\partial S_t}(S_t, t) + \delta S_t \frac{\partial^2 V}{\partial S_t^2}(S_t, t) + \delta t \frac{\partial^2 V}{\partial t \partial S_t}(S_t, t) + \ldots - \frac{\partial V}{\partial S_t}(S_t, t)
$$
$$
= \delta S_t \frac{\partial^2 V}{\partial S_t^2}(S_t, t) + \delta t \frac{\partial^2 V}{\partial t \partial S_t}(S_t, t) + \ldots
$$

and because $\delta S_t = \sigma S_t \phi\sqrt{\delta t} + \mathcal{O}(\delta t)$ such that $\phi \sim \mathcal{N}(0, 1)$ we have

$$
\delta\Delta = \sigma S_t \frac{\partial^2 V}{\partial S_t^2}\phi\sqrt{\delta t} + \mathcal{O}(\delta t) \approx \sigma S_t \frac{\partial^2 V}{\partial S_t^2}\phi\sqrt{\delta t}.
$$

Thus, the expected number of assets bought or sold becomes

$$
\mathbb{E}(|\delta\Delta|) = \sigma S_t \sqrt{\frac{2\delta t}{\pi}}\left|\frac{\partial^2 V}{\partial S_t^2}\right|.
$$

Under the no-arbitrage condition the expected return on the amount Π_t invested in a risk-free interest rate would see a growth of

$$\mathbb{E}(\delta\Pi_t) = r\mathbb{E}(\Pi_t)\delta t$$

and hence we have

$$r\mathbb{E}(\Pi_t)\delta t = \left(\frac{\partial V}{\partial t} + \frac{1}{2}\sigma^2 S_t^2 \frac{\partial^2 V}{\partial S_t^2} - DS_t\frac{\partial V}{\partial S_t}\right)\delta t$$
$$-(\kappa_1 + \kappa_2\mathbb{E}(|\delta\Delta|) + \kappa_3\mathbb{E}(|\delta\Delta|)S_t)$$

$$r\left(V(S_t,t) - \Delta S_t\right)\delta t = \left(\frac{\partial V}{\partial t} + \frac{1}{2}\sigma^2 S_t^2 \frac{\partial^2 V}{\partial S_t^2} - DS_t\frac{\partial V}{\partial S_t}\right)\delta t$$
$$-\left(\kappa_1 + \kappa_2\sigma S_t\sqrt{\frac{2\delta t}{\pi}}\left|\frac{\partial^2 V}{\partial S_t^2}\right| + \kappa_3\sigma S_t^2\sqrt{\frac{2\delta t}{\pi}}\left|\frac{\partial^2 V}{\partial S_t^2}\right|\right)$$

$$r\left(V(S_t,t) - S_t\frac{\partial V}{\partial S_t}\right) = \frac{\partial V}{\partial t} + \frac{1}{2}\sigma^2 S_t^2 \frac{\partial^2 V}{\partial S_t^2} - DS_t\frac{\partial V}{\partial S_t}$$
$$-\frac{\kappa_1}{\delta t} - \kappa_2\sigma S_t\sqrt{\frac{2}{\pi\delta t}}\left|\frac{\partial^2 V}{\partial S_t^2}\right| - \kappa_3\sigma S_t^2\sqrt{\frac{2}{\pi\delta t}}\left|\frac{\partial^2 V}{\partial S_t^2}\right|$$

and after rearranging terms we finally have the Black–Scholes equation with transaction costs

$$\frac{\partial V}{\partial t} + \frac{1}{2}\widetilde{\sigma}^2 S_t^2\frac{\partial^2 V}{\partial S_t^2} + (r - \widetilde{D})S_t\frac{\partial V}{\partial S_t} - rV(S_t,t) - \frac{\kappa_1}{\delta t} = 0$$

where

$$\widetilde{D} = D + \kappa_2\sigma\sqrt{\frac{2}{\pi\delta t}}\left|\frac{\partial^2 V}{\partial S_t^2}\right|\left(\frac{\partial V}{\partial S_t}\right)^{-1} \quad \text{and} \quad \widetilde{\sigma}^2 = \sigma^2 - \kappa_3\sigma\sqrt{\frac{2}{\pi\delta t}}\,\mathrm{sgn}\left(\frac{\partial^2 V}{\partial S_t^2}\right).$$

By considering the case when $\kappa_2 = \kappa_3 = 0$, the Black–Scholes equation with transaction costs becomes

$$\frac{\partial V}{\partial t} + \frac{1}{2}\sigma^2 S_t^2\frac{\partial^2 V}{\partial S_t^2} + (r - D)S_t\frac{\partial V}{\partial S_t} - rV(S_t,t) - \frac{\kappa_1}{\delta t} = 0.$$

The solution to the above equation can be negative by setting $V(S_t,t) = -\dfrac{\kappa_1}{r\delta t} < 0$.

$\square$

17. *Merton Model.* Let $(\Omega, \mathscr{F}, \mathbb{P})$ be a probability space and let $\{W_t : t \geq 0\}$ be a $\mathbb{P}$-standard Wiener process and $\{N_t : t \geq 0\}$ be a Poisson process with intensity $\lambda > 0$ relative to the same filtration $\mathscr{F}_t, t \geq 0$. Suppose the stock price S_t follows a jump diffusion process with

the following SDE

$$\frac{dS_t}{S_{t^-}} = (\mu - D)\,dt + \sigma dW_t + (J_t - 1)dN_t$$

where

$$dN_t = \begin{cases} 1 & \text{with probability } \lambda dt \\ 0 & \text{with probability } 1 - \lambda dt \end{cases}$$

with μ being the drift parameter, D the continuous dividend yield, σ the volatility parameter and J_t the jump size variable. Let r denote the risk-free interest rate and assume that J_t, W_t and N_t are mutually independent.

By considering a hedging portfolio involving both an option $V(S_t, t)$ which can only be exercised at expiry time $T \geq t$ and a stock S_t, and assuming that the jump component is uncorrelated with the market, show that $V(S_t, t)$ satisfies

$$\frac{\partial V}{\partial t} + \frac{1}{2}\sigma^2 S_t^2 \frac{\partial^2 V}{\partial S_t^2} + \left[r - D - \mathbb{E}_J(J_t - 1) \right] S_t \frac{\partial V}{\partial S_t} - rV(S_t, t)$$
$$+ \lambda \mathbb{E}_J \left[V(J_t S_t, t) - V(S_t, t) \right] = 0$$

where the expectation $\mathbb{E}_J(\cdot)$ is taken over the jump component.

Solution: At time t we let the value of a portfolio Π_t be

$$\Pi_t = V(S_t, t) - \Delta S_t$$

where it involves buying one unit of option $V(S_t, t)$ and selling Δ units of S_t. Since we receive $DS_t dt$ for every asset held and because we hold $-\Delta S_t$, our portfolio changes by an amount $\Delta DS_t dt$ and therefore the change in portfolio Π_t is

$$d\Pi_t = dV - \Delta(dS_t + DS_t dt) = dV - \Delta dS_t - \Delta DS_t dt.$$

Expanding $V(S_t, t)$ using Taylor's theorem

$$dV = \frac{\partial V}{\partial t}dt + \frac{\partial V}{\partial S_t}dS_t + \frac{1}{2!}\frac{\partial^2 V}{\partial S_t^2}\left(dS_t\right)^2 + \frac{1}{3!}\frac{\partial^3 V}{\partial S_t^3}\left(dS_t\right)^3 + \dots$$

and substituting $\dfrac{dS_t}{S_t} = (\mu - D)\,dt + \sigma dW_t + (J_t - 1)dN_t$ where $S_{t^-} = S_t$ and subsequently applying Itô's lemma we have

$$dV = \frac{\partial V}{\partial t} dt + \frac{\partial V}{\partial S_t} \left[(\mu - D) S_t dt + \sigma S_t dW_t + (J_t - 1) S_t dN_t \right]$$

$$+ \frac{1}{2!} \frac{\partial^2 V}{\partial S_t^2} \left[\sigma^2 S_t^2 dt + (J_t - 1)^2 S_t^2 dN_t \right] + \frac{1}{3!} \frac{\partial^3 V}{\partial S_t^3} \left[(J_t - 1)^3 S_t^3 dN_t \right] + \dots$$

$$= \left[\frac{\partial V}{\partial t} + \frac{1}{2} \sigma^2 S_t^2 \frac{\partial^2 V}{\partial S_t^2} + (\mu - D) S_t \frac{\partial V}{\partial S_t} \right] dt + \sigma S_t \frac{\partial V}{\partial S_t} dW_t$$

$$+ \left[(J_t - 1) S_t \frac{\partial V}{\partial S_t} + \frac{1}{2!} (J_t - 1)^2 S_t^2 \frac{\partial^2 V}{\partial S_t^2} + \frac{1}{3!} (J_t - 1)^3 S_t^3 \frac{\partial^3 V}{\partial S_t^3} + \dots \right] dN_t$$

$$= \left[\frac{\partial V}{\partial t} + \frac{1}{2} \sigma^2 S_t^2 \frac{\partial^2 V}{\partial S_t^2} + (\mu - D) S_t \frac{\partial V}{\partial S_t} \right] dt + \sigma S_t \frac{\partial V}{\partial S_t} dW_t$$

$$+ \left[V(J_t S_t, t) - V(S_t, t) \right] dN_t.$$

Substituting back into $d\Pi_t$ and rearranging terms we have

$$d\Pi_t = \left[\frac{\partial V}{\partial t} + \frac{1}{2} \sigma^2 S_t^2 \frac{\partial^2 V}{\partial S_t^2} + (\mu - D) S_t \frac{\partial V}{\partial S_t} \right] dt + \sigma S_t \frac{\partial V}{\partial S_t} dW_t$$

$$+ \left[V(J_t S_t, t) - V(S_t, t) \right] dN_t - \Delta \left[(\mu - D) S_t dt + \sigma S_t dW_t + (J_t - 1) S_t dN_t \right]$$

$$- \Delta D S_t dt$$

$$= \left[\frac{\partial V}{\partial t} + \frac{1}{2} \sigma^2 S_t^2 \frac{\partial^2 V}{\partial S_t^2} + (\mu - D) S_t \frac{\partial V}{\partial S_t} - \mu \Delta S_t \right] dt + \sigma S_t \left[\frac{\partial V}{\partial S_t} - \Delta \right] dW_t$$

$$+ \left[V(J_t S_t, t) - V(S_t, t) - \Delta (J_t - 1) S_t \right] dN_t.$$

To eliminate the random component so as to ensure the profit or loss is riskless, we choose

$$\Delta = \frac{\partial V}{\partial S_t}$$

and hence

$$d\Pi_t = \left[\frac{\partial V}{\partial t} + \frac{1}{2} \sigma^2 S_t^2 \frac{\partial^2 V}{\partial S_t^2} - D S_t \frac{\partial V}{\partial S_t} \right] dt$$

$$+ \left[V(J_t S_t, t) - V(S_t, t) - (J_t - 1) S_t \frac{\partial V}{\partial S_t} \right] dN_t.$$

Given that the jump component is uncorrelated with the market and under the no-arbitrage condition, the return on the amount Π_t invested in a risk-free interest rate would see a growth of

$$\mathbb{E}_J(d\Pi_t) = r\Pi_t dt$$

and because $J_t \perp\!\!\!\perp N_t$ we have

$$r\Pi_t dt = \left[\frac{\partial V}{\partial t} + \frac{1}{2}\sigma^2 S_t^2 \frac{\partial^2 V}{\partial S_t^2} - DS_t \frac{\partial V}{\partial S_t}\right] dt$$

$$+ \mathbb{E}_J \left[V(J_t S_t, t) - V(S_t, t) - (J_t - 1)S_t \frac{\partial V}{\partial S_t}\right] \mathbb{E}_J(dN_t)$$

$$r\left[V(S_t, t) - \Delta S_t\right] dt = \left\{\frac{\partial V}{\partial t} + \frac{1}{2}\sigma^2 S_t^2 \frac{\partial^2 V}{\partial S_t^2} - DS_t \frac{\partial V}{\partial S_t}\right.$$

$$\left. - \lambda \mathbb{E}_J(J_t - 1)S_t \frac{\partial V}{\partial S_t} + \lambda \mathbb{E}_J \left[V(J_t S_t, t) - V(S_t, t)\right]\right\} dt$$

$$r\left[V(S_t, t) - S_t \frac{\partial V}{\partial S_t}\right] = \frac{\partial V}{\partial t} + \frac{1}{2}\sigma^2 S_t^2 \frac{\partial^2 V}{\partial S_t^2} - DS_t \frac{\partial V}{\partial S_t}$$

$$- \lambda \mathbb{E}_J(J_t - 1) S_t \frac{\partial V}{\partial S_t} + \lambda \mathbb{E}_J \left[V(J_t S_t, t) - V(S_t, t)\right]$$

and finally

$$\frac{\partial V}{\partial t} + \frac{1}{2}\sigma^2 S_t^2 \frac{\partial^2 V}{\partial S_t^2} + \left[r - D - \mathbb{E}_J(J_t - 1)\right] S_t \frac{\partial V}{\partial S_t} - rV(S_t, t)$$

$$+ \lambda \mathbb{E}_J \left[V(J_t S_t, t) - V(S_t, t)\right] = 0$$

which is the partial differentiation equation of $V(S_t, t)$ under the jump diffusion price process.

□

18. *European Option Valuation on Merton Model.* Let $(\Omega, \mathscr{F}, \mathbb{P})$ be a probability space and let $\{W_t : t \geq 0\}$ be a $\mathbb{P}$-standard Wiener process and $\{N_t : t \geq 0\}$ be a Poisson process with intensity $\lambda > 0$ relative to the same filtration $\mathscr{F}_t, t \geq 0$. Suppose the asset price S_t follows a jump diffusion process with the following SDE

$$\frac{dS_t}{S_{t^-}} = (\mu - D) dt + \sigma dW_t + (J_t - 1)dN_t$$

where

$$dN_t = \begin{cases} 1 & \text{with probability } \lambda dt \\ 0 & \text{with probability } 1 - \lambda dt \end{cases}$$

with μ being the drift parameter, D the continuous dividend yield, σ the volatility parameter and J_t the jump size variable which follows a log-normal distribution $\log J_t \sim \mathcal{N}(\mu_J, \sigma_J^2)$. Let r denote the risk-free interest rate and assume that J_t, W_t and N_t are mutually independent.

By assuming that the jump component is uncorrelated with the market, using Itō's formula show that under the equivalent martingale measure $\mathbb{Q}_M$ the conditional distribution of S_T given S_t and $N_{T-t} = n$, $n = 0, 1, 2, \ldots$ and $t < T$ can be expressed as

$$\log S_T | \{S_t, N_{T-t} = n\} \sim \mathcal{N}\left[\log S_t + \left(r - \widetilde{D} - \frac{1}{2}\widetilde{\sigma}^2\right)(T-t), \widetilde{\sigma}^2(T-t)\right]$$

where $\widetilde{D} = D + \lambda\left(e^{\mu_J + \frac{1}{2}\sigma_J^2} - 1\right) - \dfrac{n}{T-t}\left(\mu_J + \frac{1}{2}\sigma_J^2\right)$ and $\widetilde{\sigma}^2 = \sigma^2 + \dfrac{n\sigma_J^2}{T-t}$.

Hence, show that the European call option price at time $t \leq T$ with strike $K > 0$ and expiry time T is

$$C_m(S_t, t; K, T) = e^{-r(T-t)}\sum_{n=0}^{\infty}\frac{e^{-\lambda(T-t)}[\lambda(T-t)]^n}{n!}C_{bs}(S_t, t; K, T)$$

where

$$C_{bs}(S_t, t; K, T) = S_t e^{-\widetilde{D}(T-t)}\Phi(\widetilde{d}_+) - Ke^{-r(T-t)}\Phi(\widetilde{d}_-)$$

such that $\widetilde{d}_\pm = \dfrac{\log(S_t/K) + (r - \widetilde{D} \pm \frac{1}{2}\widetilde{\sigma}^2)(T-t)}{\widetilde{\sigma}\sqrt{T-t}}$ and $\Phi(x) = \displaystyle\int_{-\infty}^{x}\frac{1}{\sqrt{2\pi}}e^{-\frac{1}{2}u^2}\,du$.

Solution: From Problem 5.2.4.4 of *Problems and Solutions in Mathematical Finance, Volume 1: Stochastic Calculus*, under the equivalent martingale measure $\mathbb{Q}_M$ we can express the jump diffusion process as

$$\frac{dS_t}{S_{t^-}} = \left(r - D - \lambda(\bar{J} - 1)\right)dt + \sigma d\widetilde{W}_t + (J_t - 1)dN_t$$

where $\bar{J} = \mathbb{E}^{\mathbb{P}}(J_t) = e^{\mu_J + \frac{1}{2}\sigma_J^2}$, $\widetilde{W}_t = W_t - \left(\dfrac{\mu - r + \lambda(\bar{J}-1)}{\sigma}\right)t$ is a $\mathbb{Q}_M$-standard Wiener process and $N_t \sim$ Poisson(λt).

Using the results of Problem 5.2.2.3 of *Problems and Solutions in Mathematical Finance, Volume 1: Stochastic Calculus* we can write

$$S_T = S_t e^{(r-D-\lambda(\bar{J}-1)-\frac{1}{2}\sigma^2)(T-t)+\sigma\widetilde{W}_{T-t}}\prod_{i=1}^{N_{T-t}}J_i$$

where $J_i \sim$ log-$\mathcal{N}(\mu_J, \sigma_J^2)$, $i = 1, 2, \ldots, N_{T-t}$ is a sequence of independent and identically distributed random variables and $\widetilde{W}_{T-t} \sim \mathcal{N}(0, T-t)$. By independence of J_i, $i = 1, 2, \ldots, N_{T-t}$, $\widetilde{W}_{T-t}$ and N_{T-t} we have

$$\log S_T | \{S_t, N_{T-t} = n\} \sim \mathcal{N}\left[\log S_t + \left(r - D - \lambda\left(e^{\mu_J + \frac{1}{2}\sigma_J^2} - 1\right) - \frac{1}{2}\sigma^2\right)(T-t)\right.$$
$$\left. + n\mu_J, \sigma^2(T-t) + n\sigma_J^2\right].$$

By setting

$$\log S_T \,\big|\, \{S_t, N_{T-t} = n\} \sim \mathcal{N}\left[\log S_t + \left(r - \tilde{D} - \frac{1}{2}\tilde{\sigma}^2\right)(T-t), \tilde{\sigma}^2(T-t)\right]$$

where $\tilde{D}$ and $\tilde{\sigma}$ are the "continuous dividend" and "volatility" of the asset price S_t following a GBM process we can therefore set

$$\left(r - \tilde{D} - \frac{1}{2}\tilde{\sigma}^2\right)(T-t) = \left(r - D - \lambda\left(e^{\mu_J + \frac{1}{2}\sigma_J^2} - 1\right) - \frac{1}{2}\sigma^2\right)(T-t) + n\mu_J$$

$$\tilde{\sigma}^2(T-t) = \sigma^2(T-t) + n\sigma_J^2.$$

Solving the equations simultaneously we have

$$\tilde{D} = D + \lambda\left(e^{\mu_J + \frac{1}{2}\sigma_J^2} - 1\right) - \frac{n}{T-t}\left(\mu_J + \frac{1}{2}\sigma_J^2\right) \quad \text{and} \quad \tilde{\sigma}^2 = \sigma^2 + \frac{n\sigma_J^2}{T-t}.$$

From the definition of a European call option price with strike $K > 0$ and expiry time $T \geq t$

$$C_m(S_t, t; K, T) = e^{-r(T-t)}\mathbb{E}^{\mathbb{Q}_M}\left[\max\{S_T - K, 0\}\,\big|\,\mathscr{F}_t\right]$$

$$= e^{-r(T-t)}\sum_{n=0}^{\infty}\mathbb{Q}_M(N_{T-t} = n)\mathbb{E}^{\mathbb{Q}_M}\left[\max\{S_T - K, 0\}\,\big|\,\mathscr{F}_t, N_{T-t} = n\right]$$

$$= e^{-r(T-t)}\sum_{n=0}^{\infty}\left\{\frac{e^{-\lambda(T-t)}[\lambda(T-t)]^n}{n!}\right.$$

$$\times \mathbb{E}^{\mathbb{Q}_M}\left[\max\{S_T - K, 0\}\,\big|\,\mathscr{F}_t, N_{T-t} = n\right]\Big\}$$

where the term $\dfrac{e^{-\lambda(T-t)}[\lambda(T-t)]^n}{n!}$ is the probability of n jumps in time period $(t, T]$. Since the conditional distribution of S_T given S_t and $N_{T-t} = n$ can be written as

$$\log S_T \,\big|\, \{S_t, N_{T-t} = n\} \sim \mathcal{N}\left[\log S_t + \left(r - \tilde{D} - \frac{1}{2}\tilde{\sigma}^2\right)(T-t), \tilde{\sigma}^2(T-t)\right]$$

therefore from Problem 2.2.2.5 (page 101) the conditional call option

$$\mathbb{E}^{\mathbb{Q}_M}\left[\max\{S_T - K, 0\}\,\big|\,\mathscr{F}_t, N_{T-t} = n\right]$$

is simply the Black–Scholes call option price with dividend $\tilde{D}$ and volatility $\tilde{\sigma}$

$$\mathbb{E}^{\mathbb{Q}_M}\left[\max\{S_T - K, 0\}\,\big|\,\mathscr{F}_t, N_{T-t} = n\right] = C_{bs}(S_t, t; K, T)$$

where

$$C_{bs}(S_t, t; K, T) = S_t e^{-\widetilde{D}(T-t)} \Phi(\widetilde{d}_+) - K e^{-r(T-t)} \Phi(\widetilde{d}_-)$$

with $\widetilde{d}_\pm = \dfrac{\log(S_t/K) + (r - \widetilde{D} \pm \frac{1}{2}\widetilde{\sigma}^2)(T-t)}{\widetilde{\sigma}\sqrt{T-t}}$.

Hence, the explicit solution is

$$C_m(S_t, t; K, T) = e^{-r(T-t)} \sum_{n=0}^{\infty} \frac{e^{-\lambda(T-t)}[\lambda(T-t)]^n}{n!} C_{bs}(S_t, t; K, T).$$

$\square$

19. *Digital Option (PDE Approach).* Let $\{W_t : t \geq 0\}$ be a $\mathbb{P}$-standard Wiener process on the probability space $(\Omega, \mathscr{F}, \mathbb{P})$ and let the stock price S_t follow a GBM with the following SDE

$$\frac{dS_t}{S_t} = (\mu - D)\,dt + \sigma dW_t$$

where μ is the drift parameter, D is the continuous dividend yield, σ is the volatility, parameter, and let r denote the risk-free interest rate.

A digital (or cash-or-nothing) call option is a contract that pays \$1 at expiry time T if the spot price $S_T > K$ and nothing if $S_T \leq K$.

By denoting $C_d(S_t, t; K, T)$ as the price of a European digital call option satisfying the following PDE with boundary conditions

$$\frac{\partial C_d}{\partial t} + \frac{1}{2}\sigma^2 S_t^2 \frac{\partial^2 C_d}{\partial S_t^2} + (r - D)S_t \frac{\partial C_d}{\partial S_t} - rC_d(S_t, t; K, T) = 0$$

$$C_d(0, t; K, T) = 0, \quad C_d(S_T, T; K, T) = \mathbb{1}_{\{S_T > K\}}$$

and letting the solution of the SDE be in the form $C_d(S_t, t; K, T) = e^{\alpha x + \beta \tau} u(x, \tau)$ where $x = \log\left(S_t/K\right)$ and $\tau = \frac{1}{2}\sigma^2(T-t)$, show that by setting

$$\alpha = -\frac{1}{2}k_1 \quad \text{and} \quad \beta = -\frac{1}{4}k_1^2 - k_0$$

where $k_1 = \dfrac{r - D}{\frac{1}{2}\sigma^2} - 1$ and $k_0 = \dfrac{r}{\frac{1}{2}\sigma^2}$, the Black–Scholes equation for $C_d(S_t, t; K, T)$ is

$$\frac{\partial u}{\partial \tau} = \frac{\partial^2 u}{\partial x^2}, \quad u(x, 0) = f(x), \quad x \in (-\infty, \infty), \quad \tau > 0$$

where $f(x) = e^{\frac{1}{2}k_1 x} \mathbb{1}_{\{x > 0\}}$.

Given that the solution of $u(x, \tau)$ is

$$u(x, \tau) = \frac{1}{\sqrt{2\pi\tau}} \int_{-\infty}^{\infty} f(z)e^{-\frac{(x-\tau)^2}{4\tau}}\,dz$$

deduce that

$$C_d(S_t, t; K, T) = e^{-r(T-t)}\Phi\left(\frac{\log(S_t/K) + (r - D - \frac{1}{2}\sigma^2)(T - t)}{\sigma\sqrt{T - t}}\right).$$

Solution: Let $C_d(S_t, t; K, T) = e^{\alpha x + \beta \tau}u(x, \tau)$ where $x = \log\left(S_t/K\right)$ and $\tau = \frac{1}{2}\sigma^2(T - t)$. We have

$$\frac{\partial C_d}{\partial t} = \frac{\partial C_d}{\partial \tau}\cdot\frac{\partial \tau}{\partial t} = -\frac{1}{2}\sigma^2 e^{\alpha x + \beta \tau}\left[\frac{\partial u}{\partial \tau} + \beta u(x, \tau)\right]$$

$$\frac{\partial C_d}{\partial S_t} = \frac{\partial C_d}{\partial x}\cdot\frac{\partial x}{\partial S_t} = \frac{e^{\alpha x + \beta \tau}}{S_t}\left[\frac{\partial u}{\partial x} + \alpha u(x, \tau)\right]$$

and

$$\frac{\partial^2 C_d}{\partial S_t^2} = \frac{\partial}{\partial S_t}\left\{\frac{e^{\alpha x + \beta \tau}}{S_t}\left[\alpha u(x, \tau) + \frac{\partial u}{\partial x}\right]\right\}$$

$$= \frac{e^{\alpha x + \beta \tau}}{S_t^2}\left[\frac{\partial^2 u}{\partial x^2} + (2\alpha - 1)\frac{\partial u}{\partial x} + \alpha(\alpha - 1)u(x, \tau)\right].$$

By substituting the above expressions into the Black–Scholes equation for $C_d(S_t, t; K, T)$, we eventually have

$$\frac{1}{2}\sigma^2\left(\frac{\partial u}{\partial x^2} - \frac{\partial u}{\partial \tau}\right) + \frac{\partial u}{\partial x}\left[\frac{1}{2}\sigma^2(2\alpha - 1) + r - D\right]$$

$$+ u\left[\frac{1}{2}\sigma^2[\alpha(\alpha - 1) - \beta] + \alpha(r - D) - r\right] = 0.$$

To eliminate the terms $\dfrac{\partial u}{\partial x}$ and u we set

$$\frac{1}{2}\sigma^2(2\alpha - 1) + r - D = 0$$

$$\frac{1}{2}\sigma^2[\alpha(\alpha - 1) - \beta] + \alpha(r - D) - r = 0.$$

By solving the equations simultaneously we have

$$\alpha = -\frac{1}{2}k_1 \quad \text{and} \quad \beta = -\frac{1}{4}k_1^2 - k_0$$

where $k_1 = \dfrac{r - D}{\frac{1}{2}\sigma^2} - 1$ and $k_0 = \dfrac{r}{\frac{1}{2}\sigma^2}$.

Thus,

$$C_d(S_t, t; K, T) = e^{-\frac{1}{2}k_1 x - (\frac{1}{4}k_1^2 + k_0)\tau} u(x, \tau)$$

such that

$$u(x, 0) = e^{\frac{1}{2}k_1 x} C_d(S_T, T; K, T) = e^{\frac{1}{2}k_1 x} \mathbb{1}_{\{x>0\}}.$$

Writing the solution

$$u(x, \tau) = \frac{1}{2\sqrt{\pi \tau}} \int_{-\infty}^{\infty} f(z) e^{-\frac{(x-z)^2}{4\tau}} dz$$

$$= \frac{1}{2\sqrt{\pi \tau}} \int_{0}^{\tau} e^{\frac{1}{2}k_1 z - \frac{1}{4\tau}(x-z)^2} dz$$

$$= e^{\frac{(x+k_1\tau)^2 - x^2}{4\tau}} \int_{0}^{\infty} \frac{1}{2\sqrt{\pi \tau}} e^{-\frac{1}{2}\left(\frac{z-(x+k_1\tau)}{\sqrt{2\tau}}\right)^2} dz$$

$$= e^{\frac{(x+k_1\tau)^2 - x^2}{4\tau}} \int_{-\frac{(x+k_1\tau)}{\sqrt{2\tau}}}^{\infty} \frac{1}{\sqrt{2\pi}} e^{-\frac{1}{2}y^2} dy$$

$$= e^{\frac{(x+k_1\tau)^2 - x^2}{4\tau}} \Phi\left(\frac{x + k_1\tau}{\sqrt{2\tau}}\right)$$

hence

$$C_d(S_t, t; K, T) = e^{\alpha x + \beta \tau} u(x, \tau)$$

$$= e^{\alpha x + \beta \tau} e^{\frac{(x+k_1\tau)^2 - x^2}{4\tau}} \Phi\left(\frac{x + k_1\tau}{\sqrt{2\tau}}\right)$$

$$= e^{-k_0 \tau} \Phi\left(\frac{x + k_1\tau}{\sqrt{2\tau}}\right)$$

where $\alpha = -\frac{1}{2}k_1$ and $\beta = -\frac{1}{4}k_1^2 - k_0$.

Finally, by setting $x = \log\left(S_t/K\right)$ and $\tau = \frac{1}{2}\sigma^2(T-t)$ we have

$$C_d(S_t,t;K,T) = e^{-r(T-t)}\Phi\left(\frac{\log(S_t/K) + (r - D - \frac{1}{2}\sigma^2)(T-t)}{\sigma\sqrt{T-t}}\right).$$

N.B. Using the same techniques, for a digital (or cash-or-nothing) put which pays \$1 at expiry time T if the spot price $S_T < K$ and nothing if $S_T \geq K$ we can also show that the cash-or-nothing put price at time $t < T$ is

$$P_d(S_t,t;K,T) = e^{-r(T-t)}\Phi\left(\frac{-\log(S_t/K) - (r - D - \frac{1}{2}\sigma^2)(T-t)}{\sigma\sqrt{T-t}}\right).$$

□

20. *Digital Option (Probabilistic Approach).* Let $\{W_t : t \geq 0\}$ be a $\mathbb{P}$-standard Wiener process on the probability space $(\Omega, \mathcal{F}, \mathbb{P})$ and let the stock price S_t follow a GBM with the following SDE

$$\frac{dS_t}{S_t} = (\mu - D)\,dt + \sigma dW_t$$

where μ is the drift parameter, D is the continuous dividend yield, σ is the volatility parameter, and let r denote the risk-free interest rate.

A digital (or cash-or-nothing) call option is a contract that pays \$1 at expiry time T if the spot price $S_T > K$ and nothing if $S_T \leq K$. In contrast, a digital (or cash-or-nothing) put pays \$1 at expiry time T if the spot price $S_T < K$ and nothing if $S_T \geq K$.

By denoting $C_d(S_t,t;K,T)$ and $P_d(S_t,t;K,T)$ as the digital call and put option prices, respectively at time t, $t < T$ show using the risk-neutral valuation approach that

$$C_d(S_t,t;K,T) = e^{-r(T-t)}\Phi(d_-) \quad \text{and} \quad P_d(S_t,t;K,T) = e^{-r(T-t)}\Phi(-d_-)$$

where

$$d_- = \frac{\log(S_t/K) + (r - D - \frac{1}{2}\sigma^2)(T-t)}{\sigma\sqrt{T-t}} \quad \text{and} \quad \Phi(x) = \frac{1}{\sqrt{2\pi}}\int_{-\infty}^{x} e^{-\frac{1}{2}u^2}\,du.$$

Verify that the put–call parity for a digital option is

$$C_d(S_t,t;K,T) + P_d(S_t,t;K,T) = e^{-r(T-t)}.$$

Solution: From Girsanov's theorem, the spot price SDE under the risk-neutral measure $\mathbb{Q}$ is

$$\frac{dS_t}{S_t} = (r - D)dt + \sigma dW_t^{\mathbb{Q}}$$

where $W_t^{\mathbb{Q}} = W_t + \left(\dfrac{\mu - r}{\sigma}\right) t$ is a $\mathbb{Q}$-standard Wiener process.

By definition

$$\begin{aligned} C_d(S_t, t; K, T) &= e^{-r(T-t)} \mathbb{E}^{\mathbb{Q}}\left(\mathbb{1}_{\{S_T > K\}} \middle| \mathscr{F}_t \right) \\ &= e^{-r(T-t)} \left[1 \cdot \mathbb{Q}\left(S_T > K \middle| \mathscr{F}_t \right) + 0 \cdot \mathbb{Q}\left(S_T \leq K \middle| \mathscr{F}_t \right) \right] \\ &= e^{-r(T-t)} \mathbb{Q}\left(S_T > K \middle| \mathscr{F}_t \right). \end{aligned}$$

From Itō's lemma we can write

$$S_T = S_t e^{(r - D - \frac{1}{2}\sigma^2)(T-t) + \sigma W_{T-t}^{\mathbb{Q}}}, t < T.$$

Hence,

$$\begin{aligned} \mathbb{Q}\left(S_T > K \middle| \mathscr{F}_t \right) &= \mathbb{Q}\left(S_t e^{(r - D - \frac{1}{2}\sigma^2)(T-t) + \sigma W_{T-t}^{\mathbb{Q}}} > K \middle| \mathscr{F}_t \right) \\ &= \mathbb{Q}\left(W_{T-t}^{\mathbb{Q}} > \frac{\log(K/S_t) - (r - D - \frac{1}{2}\sigma^2)(T-t)}{\sigma} \middle| \mathscr{F}_t \right). \end{aligned}$$

Given that $W_{T-t}^{\mathbb{Q}} \sim \mathcal{N}(0, T-t)$, $Z = \dfrac{W_{T-t}^{\mathbb{Q}}}{\sqrt{T-t}} \sim \mathcal{N}(0, 1)$ and hence

$$\begin{aligned} \mathbb{Q}\left(S_T > K \middle| \mathscr{F}_t \right) &= \mathbb{Q}\left(\frac{W_{T-t}^{\mathbb{Q}}}{\sqrt{T-t}} > \frac{\log(K/S_t) - (r - D - \frac{1}{2}\sigma^2)(T-t)}{\sigma\sqrt{T-t}} \middle| \mathscr{F}_t \right) \\ &= \mathbb{Q}\left(Z > \frac{\log(K/S_t) - (r - D - \frac{1}{2}\sigma^2)(T-t)}{\sigma\sqrt{T-t}} \middle| \mathscr{F}_t \right) \\ &= \Phi(d_-) \end{aligned}$$

where $d_- = \dfrac{\log(S_t/K) + (r - D - \frac{1}{2}\sigma^2)(T-t)}{\sigma\sqrt{T-t}}$. Therefore,

$$C_d(S_t, t; K, T) = e^{-r(T-t)} \Phi(d_-).$$

In contrast, for a digital put option price, by definition

$$P_d(S_t, t; K, T) = e^{-r(T-t)} \mathbb{E}^{\mathbb{Q}} \left(\mathbb{I}_{\{S_T < K\}} \middle| \mathscr{F}_t \right)$$

$$= e^{-r(T-t)} \left[1 \cdot \mathbb{Q} \left(S_T < K \middle| \mathscr{F}_t \right) + 0 \cdot \mathbb{Q} \left(S_T \geq K \middle| \mathscr{F}_t \right) \right]$$

$$= e^{-r(T-t)} \mathbb{Q} \left(S_T < K \middle| \mathscr{F}_t \right)$$

and using the same techniques we can easily show that

$$\mathbb{Q} \left(S_T < K \middle| \mathscr{F}_t \right) = \Phi(-d_-)$$

and thus $P_d(S_t, t; K, T) = e^{-r(T-t)} \Phi(-d_-)$.
Finally, given that $\Phi(d_-) + \Phi(-d_-) = 1$

$$C_d(S_t, t; K, T) + P_d(S_t, t; K, T) = e^{-r(T-t)}.$$

$\square$

21. *Asset-or-Nothing Option (PDE Approach).* Let $\{W_t : t \geq 0\}$ be a $\mathbb{P}$-standard Wiener process on the probability space $(\Omega, \mathscr{F}, \mathbb{P})$ and let the stock price S_t follow a GBM with the following SDE

$$\frac{dS_t}{S_t} = (\mu - D) dt + \sigma dW_t$$

where μ is the drift parameter, D is the continuous dividend yield, σ is the volatility parameter, and let r denote the risk-free interest rate.

An asset-or-nothing call option is a contract that pays $S_T > 0$ at expiry time T if the spot price $S_T > K$ and nothing if $S_T \leq K$. In contrast, an asset-or-nothing put pays $S_T > 0$ at expiry time T if the spot price $S_T < K$ and nothing if $S_T \geq K$.

By denoting $C_a(S_t, t; K, T)$ as the price of an asset-or-nothing call option at time $t < T$ satisfying the following PDE with boundary conditions

$$\frac{\partial C_a}{\partial t} + \frac{1}{2}\sigma^2 S_t^2 \frac{\partial^2 C_a}{\partial S_t^2} + (r - D)S_t \frac{\partial C_a}{\partial S_t} - rC_a(S_t, t; K, T) = 0$$

$$C_a(0, t; K, T) = 0, \quad C_a(S_T, T; K, T) = S_T \mathbb{I}_{\{S_T > K\}}$$

and letting the solution of the PDE be in the form $C_a(S_t, t; K, T) = K e^{\alpha x + \beta \tau} u(x, \tau)$ where $x = \log(S_t / K)$ and $\tau = \frac{1}{2}\sigma^2(T - t)$, show that by setting

$$\alpha = -\frac{1}{2}k_1 \quad \text{and} \quad \beta = -\frac{1}{4}k_1^2 - k_0$$

where $k_1 = \dfrac{r - D}{\frac{1}{2}\sigma^2} - 1$ and $k_0 = \dfrac{r}{\frac{1}{2}\sigma^2}$, the Black–Scholes equation for $C_d(S_t, t; K, T)$ is

$$\frac{\partial u}{\partial \tau} = \frac{\partial^2 u}{\partial x^2}, \quad u(x, 0) = f(x), \quad x \in (-\infty, \infty), \tau > 0$$

where $f(x) = e^{(\frac{1}{2}k_1 + 1)x} \mathbb{I}_{\{x > 0\}}$.

Given that the solution

$$u(x, \tau) = \frac{1}{\sqrt{2\pi\tau}} \int_{-\infty}^{\infty} f(z) e^{-\frac{(x-\tau)^2}{4\tau}} \, dz$$

deduce that

$$C_a(S_t, t; K, T) = S_t e^{-D(T-t)} \Phi \left(\frac{\log(S_t/K) + (r - D + \frac{1}{2}\sigma^2)(T - t)}{\sigma \sqrt{T - t}} \right).$$

Solution: By setting $C(S_t, t; K, T) = K e^{\alpha x + \beta \tau} u(x, \tau)$ such that $x = \log\left(S_t/K\right)$, $\tau = \frac{1}{2}\sigma^2(T - t)$ and using the same steps as described in Problem 2.2.2.19 (page 134), we can show that

$$\frac{\partial u}{\partial \tau} = \frac{\partial^2 u}{\partial x^2}, \quad u(x, 0) = e^{(\frac{1}{2}k_1 + 1)x} \mathbb{I}_{\{x > 0\}}, \quad x \in (-\infty, \infty), \tau > 0$$

where $\alpha = -\dfrac{1}{2}k_1$, $\beta = -\dfrac{1}{4}k_1^2 - k_0$, $k_1 = \dfrac{r - D}{\frac{1}{2}\sigma^2} - 1$ and $k_0 = \dfrac{r}{\frac{1}{2}\sigma^2}$.

By solving the heat equation we have

$$u(x, \tau) = \frac{1}{2\sqrt{\pi\tau}} \int_0^{\infty} f(z) e^{-\frac{(x-z)^2}{4\tau}} \, dz$$

$$= \frac{1}{2\sqrt{\pi\tau}} \int_0^{\infty} e^{(\frac{1}{2}k_1 + 1)z - \frac{(x-z)^2}{4\tau}} \, dz$$

$$= e^{\frac{(x + (\frac{1}{2}k_1 + 1)\tau)^2 - x^2}{4\tau}} \int_0^{\infty} \frac{1}{2\sqrt{\pi\tau}} e^{-\frac{1}{2}\left(\frac{z - (x + (\frac{1}{2}k_1 + 1)\tau)}{\sqrt{2\tau}} \right)^2} \, dz$$

$$= e^{\frac{(x + (\frac{1}{2}k_1 + 1)\tau)^2 - x^2}{4\tau}} \int_{-\frac{x + (\frac{1}{2}k_1 + 1)\tau}{\sqrt{2\tau}}}^{\infty} \frac{1}{\sqrt{2\pi}} e^{-\frac{1}{2}y^2} \, dy$$

$$= e^{\frac{(x + (\frac{1}{2}k_1 + 1)\tau)^2 - x^2}{4\tau}} \Phi \left(\frac{x + (\frac{1}{2}k_1 + 1)\tau}{\sqrt{2\tau}} \right).$$

Therefore,

$$C(S_t, t; K, T) = K e^{\alpha x + \beta \tau} u(x, \tau)$$

$$= K e^{x + (k_1 - k_0 + 1)\tau} \Phi \left(\frac{x + (\frac{1}{2}k_1 + 1)\tau}{\sqrt{2\tau}} \right)$$

where $\alpha = -\frac{1}{2}k_1$ and $\beta = -\frac{1}{4}k_1^2 - k_0$.

By substituting $k_1 = \dfrac{r - D}{\frac{1}{2}\sigma^2} - 1$ and $k_0 = \dfrac{r}{\frac{1}{2}\sigma^2}$, the asset-or-nothing call option price is

$$C_a(S_t, t; K, T) = S_t e^{-D(T-t)} \Phi \left(\frac{\log(S_t/K) + (r - D + \frac{1}{2}\sigma^2)(T - t)}{\sigma\sqrt{T - t}} \right).$$

N.B. Using the same techniques we can also show that the asset-or-nothing put option price is

$$P_a(S_t, t; K, T) = S_t e^{-D(T-t)} \Phi \left(\frac{-\log\left(S_t/K\right) - \left(r - D + \frac{1}{2}\sigma^2\right)(T - t)}{\sigma\sqrt{T - t}} \right).$$

$\square$

22. *Asset-or-Nothing Option (Probabilistic Approach).* Let $\{W_t : t \geq 0\}$ be a $\mathbb{P}$-standard Wiener process on the probability space $(\Omega, \mathcal{F}, \mathbb{P})$ and let the stock price S_t follow a GBM with the following SDE

$$\frac{dS_t}{S_t} = (\mu - D)\, dt + \sigma\, dW_t$$

where μ is the drift parameter, D is the continuous dividend yield, σ is the volatility parameter, and let r denote the risk-free interest rate.

An asset-or-nothing call option is a contract that pays S_T at expiry time T if the spot price $S_T > K$ and nothing if $S_T \leq K$. In contrast, an asset-or-nothing put pays $S_T > 0$ at expiry time T if the spot price $S_T < K$ and nothing if $S_T \geq K$.

By denoting $C_a(S_t, t; K, T)$ and $P_a(S_t, t; K, T)$ as the asset-or-nothing call and put option prices, respectively at time t, $t < T$ show using the risk-neutral valuation approach that

$$C_a(S_t, t; K, T) = S_t e^{-D(T-t)} \Phi(d_+) \quad \text{and} \quad P_a(S_t, t; K, T) = S_t e^{-D(T-t)} \Phi(-d_+)$$

where

$$d_+ = \frac{\log(S_t/K) + (r - D + \frac{1}{2}\sigma^2)(T - t)}{\sigma\sqrt{T - t}} \quad \text{and} \quad \Phi(x) = \frac{1}{\sqrt{2\pi}} \int_{-\infty}^{x} e^{-\frac{1}{2}u^2} \, du.$$

Verify that the put–call parity for an asset-or-nothing option is

$$C_a(S_t, t; K, T) + P_a(S_t, t; K, T) = S_t e^{-D(T-t)}.$$

Solution: Using Girsanov's theorem, the spot price SDE under the risk-neutral measure $\mathbb{Q}$ is

$$\frac{dS_t}{S_t} = (r - D)dt + \sigma dW_t^{\mathbb{Q}}$$

where $W_t^{\mathbb{Q}} = W_t + \left(\frac{\mu - r}{\sigma}\right)t$ is a $\mathbb{Q}$-standard Wiener process. From Itō's lemma we can write

$$S_T = S_t e^{(r - D - \frac{1}{2}\sigma^2)(T-t) + \sigma W_{T-t}^{\mathbb{Q}}}, \quad t < T$$

such that

$$S_T | S_t \sim \log\text{-}\mathcal{N}\left[\log S_t + \left(r - D - \frac{1}{2}\sigma^2\right)(T - t), \sigma^2(T - t)\right].$$

By definition

$$C_a(S_t, t; K, T) = e^{-r(T-t)} \mathbb{E}^{\mathbb{Q}}\left(S_T \mathbb{1}_{\{S_T > K\}} \,\middle|\, \mathscr{F}_t\right)$$

$$= e^{-r(T-t)} \int_K^{\infty} S_T f(S_T | S_t) \, dS_T$$

such that

$$f\left(S_T | S_t\right) = \frac{1}{S_T \sigma \sqrt{2\pi(T - t)}} e^{-\frac{1}{2}\left(\frac{\log S_T - m}{\sigma\sqrt{T-t}}\right)^2}, \quad S_T > 0$$

where $m = \log S_t + \left(r - D - \frac{1}{2}\sigma^2\right)(T - t)$.

Hence, we can write

$$C_a(S_t, t; K, T) = e^{-r(T-t)} \int_K^{\infty} \frac{1}{\sigma\sqrt{2\pi(T - t)}} e^{-\frac{1}{2}\left(\frac{\log S_T - m}{\sigma\sqrt{T-t}}\right)^2} \, dS_T$$

and by letting $u = \dfrac{\log S_T - m}{\sigma\sqrt{T-t}}$ we have

$$C_a(S_t, t; K, T) = \frac{e^{m-r(T-t)}}{\sqrt{2\pi}} \int_{\frac{\log K-m}{\sigma\sqrt{T-t}}}^{\infty} e^{-\frac{1}{2}u^2 + \sigma u\sqrt{T-t}}\, du.$$

Using the sum of squares

$$-\frac{1}{2}u^2 + \sigma u\sqrt{T-t} = -\frac{1}{2}\left[\left(u - \sigma\sqrt{T-t}\right)^2 - \sigma^2(T-t)\right]$$

we can simplify the integral to become

$$C_a(S_t, t; K, T) = \frac{e^{m-r(T-t)}}{\sqrt{2\pi}} \int_{\frac{\log K-m}{\sigma\sqrt{T-t}}}^{\infty} e^{-\frac{1}{2}\left[\left(u - \sigma\sqrt{T-t}\right)^2 - \sigma^2(T-t)\right]}\, du$$

$$= e^{m-r(T-t)+\frac{1}{2}\sigma^2(T-t)} \int_{\frac{\log K-m}{\sigma\sqrt{T-t}}}^{\infty} \frac{1}{\sqrt{2\pi}} e^{-\frac{1}{2}\left(u - \sigma\sqrt{T-t}\right)^2}\, du.$$

Finally, by changing the variable once again with $v = u - \sigma\sqrt{T-t}$ and substituting $m = \log S_t + (r - D - \frac{1}{2}\sigma^2)(T-t)$ we eventually have

$$C_a(S_t, t; K, T) = S_t e^{-D(T-t)} \Phi\left(\frac{\log(S_t/K) + (r - D + \frac{1}{2}\sigma^2)(T-t)}{\sigma\sqrt{T-t}}\right).$$

As for the asset-or-nothing put option price, using similar arguments we can easily show that

$$P_d(S_t, t; K, T) = e^{-r(T-t)}\mathbb{E}^{\mathbb{Q}}\left(S_T \mathbb{1}_{\{S_T < K\}}\,\middle|\,\mathcal{F}_t\right)$$

$$= e^{-r(T-t)} \int_{-\infty}^{K} S_T f(S_T|S_t)\, dS_T$$

$$= S_t e^{-D(T-t)} \Phi\left(\frac{-\log(S_t/K) - (r - D + \frac{1}{2}\sigma^2)(T-t)}{\sigma\sqrt{T-t}}\right).$$

Thus,

$$C_a(S_t, t; K, T) = S_t e^{-D(T-t)}\Phi(d_+) \quad \text{and} \quad P_d(S_t, t; K, T) = S_t e^{-D(T-t)}\Phi(-d_+)$$

where

$$d_+ = \frac{\log(S_t/K) + (r - D + \frac{1}{2}\sigma^2)(T - t)}{\sigma\sqrt{T - t}}.$$

Because of the identity $\Phi(d_+) + \Phi(-d_+) = 1$, the put–call parity for an asset-or-nothing option is

$$C_a(S_t, t; K, T) + P_a(S_t, t; K, T) = S_t e^{-D(T-t)}.$$

$\square$

23. *Black Model.* From the Black–Scholes assumptions the price of a futures contract maturing at time $T > t$ on an asset with price S_t at time t is

$$F(t, T) = S_t e^{(r-D)(T-t)}$$

where D is the continuous dividend yield and r is the constant risk-free interest rate. Here, under the risk-neutral measure $\mathbb{Q}$ the asset price is assumed to follow a GBM process

$$\frac{dS_t}{S_t} = (r - D)\,dt + \sigma dW_t^{\mathbb{Q}}$$

where $\{W_t^{\mathbb{Q}} : t \geq 0\}$ is a $\mathbb{Q}$-standard Wiener process on the probability space $(\Omega, \mathcal{F}, \mathbb{Q})$ and σ is the asset volatility parameter.

By considering a hedging portfolio involving both a European option on futures $V(F(t, T), t)$ and a futures contract $F(t, T)$, show that the Black equation is

$$\frac{\partial V}{\partial t} + \frac{1}{2}\sigma^2 F(t, T)^2 \frac{\partial^2 V}{\partial F^2} - rV(F(t, T), t) = 0.$$

Solution: Let the value of the portfolio at time t be

$$\Pi_t = V(F(t, T), t) - \Delta F(t, T)$$

where it involves buying one unit of an option on futures $V(F(t, T), t)$ and selling Δ units of $F(t, T)$. The jump in the value of the portfolio in a single time step is

$$d\Pi_t = dV - \Delta dF$$

where, by expanding $V(F(t, T), t)$ using Taylor's theorem

$$dV = \frac{\partial V}{\partial t} + \frac{\partial V}{\partial F} dF + \frac{1}{2}\frac{\partial^2 V}{\partial F^2}(dF)^2 + \dots$$

Given $F(t,T) = S_t e^{(r-D)(T-t)}$ and $\dfrac{dS_t}{S_t} = (r-D)\,dt + \sigma\,dW_t^Q$ we can write

$$
\begin{aligned}
dF &= d\left(S_t e^{(r-D)(T-t)}\right) \\
&= e^{(r-D)(T-t)}\,dS_t - (r-D)S_t e^{(r-D)(T-t)}\,dt \\
&= e^{(r-D)(T-t)}\left[(r-D)S_t\,dt + \sigma S_t\,dW_t^Q\right] - (r-D)S_t e^{(r-D)(T-t)}\,dt \\
&= \sigma S_t e^{(r-D)(T-t)}\,dW_t^Q \\
&= \sigma F(t,T)\,dW_t^Q.
\end{aligned}
$$

From Itō's lemma

$$
(dW_t^Q)^2 = dt, \quad (dt)^2 = dW_t^Q dt = dt\,dW_t^Q = 0
$$

we have

$$
(dF)^2 = \sigma^2 F(t,T)^2 dt \quad \text{and} \quad (dF)^\nu = 0, \quad \nu > 2.
$$

Therefore,

$$
\begin{aligned}
dV &= \frac{\partial V}{\partial t}\,dt + \frac{\partial V}{\partial F}\,dF + \frac{1}{2}\frac{\partial^2 V}{\partial F^2}(dF)^2 + \dots \\
&= \left(\frac{\partial V}{\partial t} + \frac{1}{2}\sigma^2 F(t,T)^2 \frac{\partial^2 V}{\partial F^2}\right)dt + \sigma F(t,T)\frac{\partial V}{\partial F}\,dW_t^Q.
\end{aligned}
$$

By substituting dV into $d\Pi_t$ and rearranging terms, we have

$$
d\Pi_t = \left(\frac{\partial V}{\partial t} + \frac{1}{2}\sigma^2 F(t,T)^2 \frac{\partial^2 V}{\partial F^2}\right)dt + \sigma F(t,T)\left(\frac{\partial V}{\partial F} - \Delta\right)dW_t^Q.
$$

To ensure a risk-free portfolio we set

$$
\Delta = \frac{\partial V}{\partial F}
$$

which leads to

$$
d\Pi_t = \left(\frac{\partial V}{\partial t} + \frac{1}{2}\sigma^2 F(t,T)^2 \frac{\partial^2 V}{\partial F^2}\right)dt.
$$

Since it costs nothing to enter into a futures contract the cost of setting up the portfolio at time t is only $V(F(t,T),t)$, and therefore

$$
d\Pi_t = rV(F(t,T),t)dt.
$$

Thus,

$$rV(F(t,T),t)dt = \left(\frac{\partial V}{\partial t} + \frac{1}{2}\sigma^2 F(t,T)^2 \frac{\partial^2 V}{\partial F^2} \right) dt$$

or

$$\frac{\partial V}{\partial t} + \frac{1}{2}\sigma^2 F(t,T)^2 \frac{\partial^2 V}{\partial F^2} - rV(F(t,T),t) = 0.$$

□

24. Consider the value of a European option $V(S_t,t)$ satisfying the following Black–Scholes equation

$$\frac{\partial V}{\partial t} + \frac{1}{2}\sigma^2 S_t^2 \frac{\partial^2 V}{\partial S_t^2} + (r-D)S_t \frac{\partial V}{\partial S_t} - rV(S_t,t) = 0$$

where S_t is the spot price of a stock at time t, σ is the stock volatility, r is the constant risk-free interest rate, D is the continuous dividend yield and $T > t$ is the option expiry time.

Given that the price of a futures contract maturing at time T on an asset with price S_t at time t is

$$F(t,T) = S_t e^{(r-D)(T-t)}$$

derive the Black equation for a European option written on a futures contract $V(F(t,T),t)$.

Solution: Let $\hat{V}(S_t,t) = V(F(t,T),t)$ so that

$$\frac{\partial \hat{V}}{\partial t} = \frac{\partial V}{\partial t} + \frac{\partial V}{\partial F}\frac{\partial F}{\partial t}$$

$$= \frac{\partial V}{\partial t} - (r-D)S_t e^{(r-D)(T-t)} \frac{\partial V}{\partial F}$$

$$= \frac{\partial V}{\partial t} - (r-D)F(t,T)\frac{\partial V}{\partial F}$$

$$\frac{\partial \hat{V}}{\partial S_t} = \frac{\partial V}{\partial F}\frac{\partial F}{\partial S_t}$$

$$= e^{(r-D)(T-t)} \frac{\partial V}{\partial F}$$

$$= \left(\frac{F(t,T)}{S_t} \right) \frac{\partial V}{\partial F}$$

and

$$\frac{\partial^2 \hat{V}}{\partial S_t^2} = \frac{\partial}{\partial S_t}\left(e^{(r-D)(T-t)}\frac{\partial V}{\partial F}\right)$$

$$= e^{(r-D)(T-t)}\frac{\partial^2 V}{\partial F^2}\frac{\partial F}{\partial S_t}$$

$$= e^{2(r-D)(T-t)}\frac{\partial^2 V}{\partial F^2}$$

$$= \left(\frac{F(t,T)}{S_t}\right)^2\frac{\partial^2 V}{\partial F^2}.$$

By substituting $\hat{V}(S_t,t)$, $\dfrac{\partial \hat{V}}{\partial t}$, $\dfrac{\partial \hat{V}}{\partial S_t}$ and $\dfrac{\partial^2 \hat{V}}{\partial S_t^2}$ into

$$\frac{\partial \hat{V}}{\partial t} + \frac{1}{2}\sigma^2 S_t^2\frac{\partial^2 \hat{V}}{\partial S_t^2} + (r-D)S_t\frac{\partial \hat{V}}{\partial S_t} - r\hat{V}(S_t,t) = 0$$

we have

$$\frac{\partial V}{\partial t} - (r-D)F(t,T)\frac{\partial V}{\partial F} + \frac{1}{2}\sigma^2 S_t^2\left(\frac{F(t,T)}{S_t}\right)^2\frac{\partial^2 V}{\partial F^2}$$

$$+(r-D)S_t\left(\frac{F(t,T)}{S_t}\right)\frac{\partial V}{\partial F} - rV(F(t,T),t) = 0$$

or

$$\frac{\partial V}{\partial t} + \frac{1}{2}\sigma^2 F(t,T)^2\frac{\partial^2 V}{\partial F^2} - rV(F(t,T),t) = 0.$$

$\square$

25. Let the price of a futures contract maturing at time $T > t$ on an asset with price S_t at time t be

$$F(t,T) = S_t e^{(r-D)(T-t)}$$

where r is the constant risk-free interest rate and D is the continuous dividend yield. For a European option written on a futures contract $V(F(t,T),t)$ it satisfies the Black–Scholes equation

$$\frac{\partial V}{\partial t} + \frac{1}{2}\sigma^2 F(t,T)^2\frac{\partial^2 V}{\partial F^2} - rV(F(t,T),t) = 0.$$

Show that $\dfrac{F(t,T)}{B}V\left(\dfrac{B^2}{F(t,T)},t\right)$ is also a solution of the Black–Scholes equation for any constant B.

Show also that the prices of a European call option $C(F(t,T),t;K,\tau)$ and put option $P(F(t,T),t;K,\tau)$ on a futures contract with the same strike K and expiry time $\tau < T$ (i.e., the options expire before the futures contract maturity) have the following property

$$C(F(t,T),t;K,\tau) = \frac{F(t,T)}{K} P\left(\frac{K^2}{F(t,T)},t;K,\tau\right).$$

Solution: Let $W(F(t,T),t) = \dfrac{F(t,T)}{B} V\left(\hat{F}(t,T),t\right)$ where $\hat{F}(t,T) = \dfrac{B^2}{F(t,T)}$. By differentiation we have

$$\frac{\partial W}{\partial t} = \frac{F(t,T)}{B} \frac{\partial V}{\partial t}$$

$$\begin{aligned}
\frac{\partial W}{\partial F} &= \frac{1}{B} V(\hat{F}(t,T),t) + \frac{F(t,T)}{B} \frac{\partial V}{\partial \hat{F}} \frac{\partial \hat{F}}{\partial F} \\
&= \frac{1}{B} V(\hat{F}(t,T),t) + \frac{F(t,T)}{B} \frac{\partial V}{\partial \hat{F}} \left(-\frac{B^2}{F(t,T)}\right) \\
&= \frac{1}{B} V(\hat{F}(t,T),t) - \frac{B}{F(t,T)} \frac{\partial V}{\partial \hat{F}}
\end{aligned}$$

and

$$\begin{aligned}
\frac{\partial^2 W}{\partial F^2} &= \frac{1}{B} \frac{\partial V}{\partial \hat{F}} \frac{\partial \hat{F}}{\partial F} + \frac{B}{F(t,T)^2} \frac{\partial V}{\partial \hat{F}} - \frac{B}{F(t,T)} \frac{\partial^2 V}{\partial \hat{F}^2} \frac{\partial \hat{F}}{\partial F} \\
&= \frac{1}{B} \left(-\frac{B^2}{F(t,T)^2}\right) \frac{\partial V}{\partial \hat{F}} + \frac{B^2}{F(t,T)^2} \frac{\partial V}{\partial \hat{F}} + \left(\frac{B}{F(t,T)}\right)^3 \frac{\partial^2 V}{\partial \hat{F}^2} \\
&= \left(\frac{B}{F(t,T)}\right)^3 \frac{\partial^2 V}{\partial \hat{F}^2}.
\end{aligned}$$

Since

$$\frac{\partial W}{\partial t} + \frac{1}{2}\sigma^2 F(t,T)^2 \frac{\partial^2 W}{\partial F^2} - rW(F(t,T),t) = 0$$

therefore

$$\begin{aligned}
&\frac{F(t,T)}{B} \frac{\partial V}{\partial t} + \frac{1}{2}\sigma^2 F(t,T)^2 \left(\frac{B}{F(t,T)}\right)^3 \frac{\partial^2 V}{\partial \hat{F}^2} - r\left(\frac{F(t,T)}{B}\right) V\left(\hat{F}(t,T),t\right) \\
&= \frac{F(t,T)}{B} \left\{ \frac{\partial V}{\partial t} + \frac{1}{2}\sigma^2 \hat{F}(t,T)^2 \frac{\partial^2 V}{\partial \hat{F}^2} - rV(\hat{F}(t,T),t) \right\} \\
&= 0.
\end{aligned}$$

Hence,

$$\frac{\partial V}{\partial t} + \frac{1}{2}\sigma^2 \hat{F}(t,T)^2 \frac{\partial^2 V}{\partial \hat{F}^2} - rV(\hat{F}(t,T),t) = 0$$

which shows that $\dfrac{F(t,T)}{B}V\left(\dfrac{B^2}{F(t,T)},t\right)$ is also a solution of the Black–Scholes equation for any constant B.

Finally, to show that $C(F(t,T),t;K,\tau) = \dfrac{F(t,T)}{K}P\left(\dfrac{K^2}{F(t,T)},t;K,\tau\right)$ at the option expiry τ

$$\frac{F(\tau,T)}{K}P\left(\frac{K^2}{F(\tau,T)},\tau;K,\tau\right) = \frac{F(\tau,T)}{K}\max\left\{K - \frac{K^2}{F(\tau,T)},0\right\}$$

$$= \max\{F(\tau,T) - K\}$$

$$= C(F(\tau,T),\tau;K,\tau).$$

By discounting the payoffs back to time t we have

$$C(F(t,T),t;K,\tau) = \frac{F(t,T)}{K}P\left(\frac{K^2}{F(t,T)},t;K,\tau\right).$$

$\square$

26. Consider the price of a futures contract $F(t,T)$ with delivery time T on a stock with price S_t at time t ($t < T$). Throughout the life of the futures contract the stock pays discrete dividends $\delta_i, i = 1,2,\ldots,n$ where $t < t_1 < t_2 < \cdots < t_n < T$. Under the no-arbitrage condition the futures contract price is

$$F(t,T) = S_t e^{r(T-t)} - \sum_{i=1}^{n}\delta_i e^{r(T-t_i)}$$

where r is the risk-free interest rate.

By considering a European option on the futures $V(F(t,T),t)$, show that the Black–Scholes equation is

$$\frac{\partial V}{\partial t} + \frac{1}{2}\sigma^2\left(F(t,T) + \sum_{i=1}^{n}\delta_i e^{r(T-t_i)}\right)^2\frac{\partial^2 V}{\partial F^2} - rV(F(t,T),t) = 0$$

where σ is the stock volatility.

Solution: Let $\hat{V}(S_t,t) = V(F(t,T),t)$; differentiating with respect to t and S_t we have

$$\frac{\partial \hat{V}}{\partial t} = \frac{\partial V}{\partial t} + \frac{\partial V}{\partial F}\frac{\partial F}{\partial S_t} = \frac{\partial V}{\partial t} - rS_t e^{r(T-t)}\frac{\partial V}{\partial F}$$

$$\frac{\partial \hat{V}}{\partial S_t} = \frac{\partial V}{\partial F}\frac{\partial F}{\partial S_t} = e^{r(T-t)}\frac{\partial V}{\partial F}$$

and

$$\frac{\partial^2 \hat{V}}{\partial S_t^2} = \frac{\partial}{\partial S_t}\left(e^{r(T-t)}\frac{\partial V}{\partial F}\right) = e^{r(T-t)}\frac{\partial^2 V}{\partial F^2}\frac{\partial F}{\partial S_t} = e^{2r(T-t)}\frac{\partial^2 V}{\partial F^2}.$$

Given that

$$\frac{\partial \hat{V}}{\partial t} + \frac{1}{2}\sigma^2 S_t^2 \frac{\partial^2 \hat{V}}{\partial S_t^2} + r S_t \frac{\partial \hat{V}}{\partial S_t} - r\hat{V}(S_t, t) = 0$$

we have

$$\frac{\partial V}{\partial t} - r S_t e^{r(T-t)}\frac{\partial V}{\partial F} + \frac{1}{2}\sigma^2 S_t^2 e^{2r(T-t)}\frac{\partial^2 V}{\partial F^2} + r S_t e^{r(T-t)}\frac{\partial V}{\partial F} - rV(F(t,T),t) = 0$$

or

$$\frac{\partial V}{\partial t} + \frac{1}{2}\sigma^2\left(F(t,T) + \sum_{i=1}^{n}\delta_i e^{r(T-t_i)}\right)^2 \frac{\partial^2 V}{\partial F^2} - rV(F(t,T),t) = 0.$$

$\square$

27. Let the price of a futures contract maturing at time T on an asset with price S_t at time t, $t < T$ be

$$F(t,T) = S_t e^{(r-D)(T-t)}$$

where r is the constant risk-free interest rate, D is the continuous dividend yield and σ is the asset volatility. For European call $C(F(t,T),t;K,T)$ and put $P(F(t,T),t;K,T)$ options written on a futures contract with expiry time T and strike price K, show that

$$C(F(t,T),t;K,T) = e^{-r(T-t)}\left[F(t,T)\Phi(d_1) - K\Phi(d_2)\right]$$

and

$$P(F(t,T),t;K,T) = e^{-r(T-t)}\left[K\Phi(-d_2) - F(t,T)\Phi(-d_1)\right]$$

where

$$d_{1,2} = \frac{\log\left(F(t,T)/K\right) \pm \frac{1}{2}\sigma^2(T-t)}{\sigma\sqrt{T-t}} \quad \text{and} \quad \Phi(x) = \int_{-\infty}^{x}\frac{1}{\sqrt{2\pi}}e^{-\frac{1}{2}u^2}\,du.$$

Show that the put–call parity relationship for options on futures is

$$C(F(t,T),t;K,T) - P(F(t,T),t;K,T) = e^{-r(T-t)}\left[F(t,T) - K\right].$$

Solution: For European call $C(S_t, t; K, T)$ and put $P(S_t, t; K, T)$ options written on S_t with strike price K and expiry time T, we have

$$C(S_t, t; K, T) = S_t e^{-D(T-t)} \Phi(d_+) - K e^{-r(T-t)} \Phi(d_-)$$

and

$$P(S_t, t; K, T) = K e^{-r(T-t)} \Phi(-d_-) - S_t e^{-D(T-t)} \Phi(-d_+)$$

where

$$d_\pm = \frac{\log(S_t/K) + (r - D \pm \frac{1}{2}\sigma^2)(T - t)}{\sigma\sqrt{T - t}}.$$

Since $F(t, T) = S_t e^{(r-D)(T-t)}$, by substituting $S_t = F(t, T) e^{-(r-D)(T-t)}$ we have

$$C(F(t,T), t; K, T) = e^{-r(T-t)} \left[F(t,T) \Phi(d_1) - K \Phi(d_2) \right]$$

and

$$P(F(t,T), t; K, T) = e^{-r(T-t)} \left[K \Phi(-d_2) - F(t,T) \Phi(-d_1) \right]$$

where

$$d_{1,2} = \frac{\log\left(F(t,T)/K\right) \pm \frac{1}{2}\sigma^2(T - t)}{\sigma\sqrt{T - t}}.$$

Given the identity $\Phi(d_1) + \Phi(-d_1) = 1$ and $\Phi(d_2) + \Phi(-d_2) = 1$ therefore

$$C(F(t,T), t; K, T) - P(F(t,T), t; K, T) = e^{-r(T-t)} [F(t,T) - K].$$

N.B. From the expressions of $C(F(t,T), t; K, T)$ and $P(F(t,T), t; K, T)$ we can deduce that options on futures contracts are independent on an asset that pays a continuous dividend yield.

□

28. *Arithmetic Brownian Motion.* Let $\{W_t : t \geq 0\}$ be a $\mathbb{P}$-standard Wiener process on the probability space $(\Omega, \mathscr{F}, \mathbb{P})$ and let the asset price S_t follow an arithmetic Brownian motion (ABM) with the following SDE

$$dS_t = (\mu - D)dt + \sigma dW_t$$

where μ is the drift parameter, D is the continuous dividend yield and σ is the volatility parameter. Using Itō's lemma show that under the risk-neutral measure $\mathbb{Q}$ the conditional distribution of S_T given S_t is

$$S_T | S_t \sim \mathcal{N}\left(S_t e^{(r-D)(T-t)}, \frac{\sigma^2}{2(r-D)}\left[e^{2(r-D)(T-t)} - 1\right]\right)$$

where r is the risk-free interest rate and $T > t$.

Using the risk-neutral valuation approach show that the European call option price at time t with strike K and expiry time T is

$$C(S_t, t; K, T) = \left(S_t e^{-D(T-t)} - K e^{-r(T-t)}\right)\Phi(d) + \hat{\sigma}\Phi'(d)$$

and from the put–call parity deduce that the European put option price at time t with strike K and expiry time T is

$$P(S_t, t; K, T) = \hat{\sigma}\Phi'(-d) - \left(S_t e^{-D(T-t)} - K e^{-r(T-t)}\right)\Phi(-d)$$

where

$$d = \frac{S_t e^{-D(T-t)} - K e^{-r(T-t)}}{\hat{\sigma}}, \quad \hat{\sigma} = \sigma\sqrt{\frac{e^{-2D(T-t)} - e^{-2r(T-t)}}{2(r-D)}}$$

and $\Phi(x)$ is the standard normal cdf

$$\Phi(x) = \int_{-\infty}^{x} \frac{1}{\sqrt{2\pi}} e^{-\frac{1}{2}u^2}\, du.$$

Solution: From Girsanov's theorem, under the risk-neutral measure $\mathbb{Q}$ the asset price follows the process

$$dS_t = (r - D)S_t dt + \sigma dW_t^{\mathbb{Q}}$$

where $W_t^{\mathbb{Q}} = W_t + \left(\dfrac{\mu - rS_t}{\sigma}\right) t$ is a $\mathbb{Q}$-standard. Further details on this change of measure can be found in Problem 4.2.3.7 of *Problems and Solutions in Mathematical Finance, Volume 1: Stochastic Calculus*.

From Taylor's theorem and from the application of Itō's lemma

$$d(e^{-(r-D)t}S_t) = -(r-D)e^{-(r-D)t}S_t dt + e^{-(r-D)t}dS_t$$

$$+ \frac{1}{2}(r-D)^2 e^{-(r-D)t}S_t(dt)^2 + \ldots$$

$$= -(r-D)e^{-(r-D)t}S_t dt + e^{-(r-D)t}((r-D)S_t dt + \sigma dW_t^{\mathbb{Q}})$$

$$= \sigma e^{-(r-D)t}dW_t^{\mathbb{Q}}.$$

Taking integrals

$$\int_t^T d(e^{-(r-D)u} S_u) = \int_t^T \sigma e^{-(r-D)u} dW_u^{\mathbb{Q}}$$

$$e^{-(r-D)T} S_T - e^{-(r-D)t} S_t = \sigma \int_t^T e^{-(r-D)u} dW_u^{\mathbb{Q}}$$

or

$$S_T = S_t e^{(r-D)(T-t)} + \sigma \int_t^T e^{(r-D)(T-u)} dW_u^{\mathbb{Q}}.$$

Since $\displaystyle\int_t^T e^{(r-D)(T-u)} dW_u^{\mathbb{Q}} \sim \mathcal{N}\left(0, \int_t^T e^{2(r-D)(T-u)} du\right)$ therefore

$$S_T | S_t \sim \mathcal{N}\left(S_t e^{(r-D)(T-t)}, \frac{\sigma^2}{2(r-D)}\left[e^{2(r-D)(T-t)} - 1\right]\right).$$

By writing $m = S_t e^{(r-D)(T-t)}$ and $s = \sigma\sqrt{\dfrac{e^{2(r-D)(T-t)} - 1}{2(r-D)}}$ so that the conditional pdf of S_T given S_t is

$$f(S_T | S_t) = \frac{1}{s\sqrt{2\pi}} e^{-\frac{1}{2}\left(\frac{S_T - m}{s}\right)^2}$$

then from the definition of a European call option

$$C(S_t, t; K, T) = e^{-r(T-t)} \mathbb{E}^{\mathbb{Q}}\left[\max\{S_T - K, 0\} \,\middle|\, \mathscr{F}_t\right]$$

$$= e^{-r(T-t)} \int_K^\infty (S_T - K) f(S_T | S_t) \, dS_T$$

$$= I_1 - I_2$$

where $I_1 = e^{-r(T-t)} \displaystyle\int_K^\infty S_T f(S_T | S_t) \, dS_T$ and $I_2 = K e^{-r(T-t)} \displaystyle\int_K^\infty f(S_T | S_t) \, dS_T$.

For case I_1 and by setting $z = \dfrac{S_T - m}{s}$ we can write

$$I_1 = e^{-r(T-t)} \int_K^\infty \frac{S_T}{s\sqrt{2\pi}} e^{-\frac{1}{2}\left(\frac{S_T-m}{s}\right)^2} dS_T$$

$$= e^{-r(T-t)} \int_{\frac{K-m}{s}}^\infty \frac{sz+m}{\sqrt{2\pi}} e^{-\frac{1}{2}z^2} dz$$

$$= s e^{-r(T-t)} \int_{\frac{K-m}{s}}^\infty \frac{z}{\sqrt{2\pi}} e^{-\frac{1}{2}z^2} dz + m e^{-r(T-t)} \int_{\frac{K-m}{s}}^\infty \frac{1}{\sqrt{2\pi}} e^{-\frac{1}{2}z^2} dz$$

$$= e^{-r(T-t)} \left[m\Phi\left(\frac{m-K}{s}\right) + s\Phi'\left(\frac{m-K}{s}\right) \right].$$

Using similar techniques for case I_2 we have

$$I_2 = Ke^{-r(T-t)} \int_K^\infty \frac{1}{s\sqrt{2\pi}} e^{-\frac{1}{2}\left(\frac{S_T-m}{s}\right)^2} dS_T$$

$$= Ke^{-r(T-t)} \int_{\frac{K-m}{s}}^\infty \frac{1}{\sqrt{2\pi}} e^{-\frac{1}{2}z^2} dz$$

$$= Ke^{-r(T-t)} \Phi\left(\frac{m-K}{s}\right).$$

By substituting $m = S_t e^{(r-D)(T-t)}$ and $s = \sigma\sqrt{\dfrac{e^{2(r-D)(T-t)}-1}{2(r-D)}}$ we have

$$\frac{m-K}{s} = \frac{S_t e^{(r-D)(T-t)} - K}{\sigma\sqrt{\dfrac{e^{2(r-D)(T-t)}-1}{2(r-D)}}}$$

$$= \frac{e^{r(T-t)}\left(S_t e^{-D(T-t)} - Ke^{-r(T-t)}\right)}{\sigma\sqrt{\dfrac{e^{2(r-D)(T-t)}-1}{2(r-D)}}}$$

$$= \frac{S_t e^{-D(T-t)} - Ke^{-r(T-t)}}{\hat{\sigma}}$$

where $\hat{\sigma} = \sigma\sqrt{\dfrac{e^{-2D(T-t)}-e^{-2r(T-t)}}{2(r-D)}}$ and hence the European call option price at time t is

$$C(S_t,t;K,T) = I_1 - I_2$$

$$= e^{-r(T-t)}\left[(m-K)\Phi\left(\frac{m-K}{s}\right) + s\Phi'\left(\frac{m-K}{s}\right)\right]$$

$$= \left(S_t e^{-D(T-t)} - Ke^{-r(T-t)}\right)\Phi(d) + \hat{\sigma}\Phi'(d)$$

where $d = \dfrac{S_t e^{-D(T-t)} - Ke^{-r(T-t)}}{\hat{\sigma}}$.

Finally, from the put–call parity relationship of European options

$$C(S_t, t; K, T) - P(S_t, t; K, T) = S_t e^{-D(T-t)} - K e^{-r(T-t)}$$

the equivalent European put option price at time t is

$$
\begin{aligned}
P(S_t, t; K, T) &= C(S_t, t; K, T) - S_t e^{-D(T-t)} + K e^{-r(T-t)} \\
&= \left(S_t e^{-D(T-t)} - K e^{-r(T-t)} \right) (\Phi(d) - 1) + \hat{\sigma} \Phi'(d) \\
&= \hat{\sigma} \Phi'(-d) - \left(S_t e^{-D(T-t)} - K e^{-r(T-t)} \right) \Phi(-d)
\end{aligned}
$$

since $\Phi'(x) = \dfrac{1}{\sqrt{2\pi}} e^{-\frac{1}{2}x^2}$ is an even function.

$\square$

29. Let $\{W_t : t \geq 0\}$ be a $\mathbb{P}$-standard Wiener process on the probability space $(\Omega, \mathcal{F}, \mathbb{P})$ and let the stock price S_t satisfy the following GBM process

$$\frac{dS_t}{S_t} = (\mu - D)dt + \sigma dW_t$$

where μ is the drift parameter, D is the continuous dividend yield, σ is the volatility parameter and let r denote the risk-free interest rate.

We consider a European-style option contract with strike K written on the stock S_t that pays amount

$$\Psi(S_T) = \log\left(\frac{S_T}{S_0}\right) - K$$

at the expiry time $T > t$ where S_0 is the initial stock price.

Using Itō's lemma find the SDE for $\log S_t$ under the risk-neutral measure $\mathbb{Q}$.

Hence, show that the price of the option struck at time t is

$$V(S_t, t; K, T) = e^{-r(T-t)} \left[\log\left(\frac{S_t}{S_0}\right) + \left(r - D - \frac{1}{2}\sigma^2\right)(T - t) - K \right].$$

Find the hedging ratio, the number of stocks to hold and the amount of cash needed to invest in a risk-free money market in order to hedge this option contract at time t.

Finally, by considering a European contract that pays

$$\Psi(S_T) = \left[\log\left(\frac{S_T}{S_0}\right) - K \right]^2$$

at expiry time T what is the option price of this contract at time t?

Solution: From Girsanov's theorem the SDE of S_t under the risk-neutral measure $\mathbb{Q}$ is

$$\frac{dS_t}{S_t} = (r - D)dt + \sigma dW_t^{\mathbb{Q}}$$

where $W_t^{\mathbb{Q}} = W_t + \left(\dfrac{\mu - r}{\sigma}\right)t$ is a $\mathbb{Q}$-standard Wiener process.

From Taylor's expansion

$$d(\log S_t) = \frac{dS_t}{S_t} - \frac{1}{2}\left(\frac{dS_t}{S_t}\right)^2 + \ldots$$

and using Itō's lemma we eventually have

$$d(\log S_t) = \left(r - D - \frac{1}{2}\sigma^2\right)dt + \sigma dW_t^{\mathbb{Q}}.$$

Taking integrals

$$\int_t^T d\log S_u = \int_t^T \left(r - D - \frac{1}{2}\sigma^2\right)du + \int_t^T \sigma\, dW_u^{\mathbb{Q}}$$

$$\log\left(\frac{S_T}{S_t}\right) = \left(r - D - \frac{1}{2}\sigma^2\right)(T - t) + \sigma W_{T-t}^{\mathbb{Q}}$$

such that

$$\log\left(\frac{S_T}{S_t}\right) \sim \mathcal{N}\left[\left(r - D - \frac{1}{2}\sigma^2\right)(T - t), \sigma^2(T - t)\right].$$

Hence, the option price at time t is

$$V(S_t, t; K, T) = e^{-r(T-t)}\mathbb{E}^{\mathbb{Q}}\left[\Psi(S_T)\big|\,\mathcal{F}_t\right]$$

$$= e^{-r(T-t)}\mathbb{E}^{\mathbb{Q}}\left[\log\left(\frac{S_T}{S_0}\right) - K\,\bigg|\,\mathcal{F}_t\right]$$

$$= e^{-r(T-t)}\mathbb{E}^{\mathbb{Q}}\left[\log\left(\frac{S_T}{S_t}\right) + \log\left(\frac{S_t}{S_0}\right) - K\,\bigg|\,\mathcal{F}_t\right]$$

$$= e^{-r(T-t)}\left[\log\left(\frac{S_t}{S_0}\right) + \left(r - D - \frac{1}{2}\sigma^2\right)(T - t) - K\right].$$

At time t,

$$V(S_t, t; K, T) = \phi_t S_t + \psi_t$$

where ϕ_t is the number of units of S_t and ψ_t is the amount of cash invested in the risk-free money market. By partial differentiation with respect to S_t we therefore have

$$\phi_t = \frac{\partial V}{\partial S_t} = \frac{e^{-r(T-t)}}{S_t}$$

and hence

$$
\begin{aligned}
\psi_t &= V(S_t, t; K, T) - \phi_t S_t \\
&= e^{-r(T-t)} \left[\log\left(\frac{S_t}{S_0}\right) + \left(r - D - \frac{1}{2}\sigma^2\right)(T - t) - K - 1 \right].
\end{aligned}
$$

For the case when the payoff is $\Psi(S_T) = \left[\log\left(\frac{S_T}{S_0}\right) - K \right]^2$, the option price at time t is

$$
\begin{aligned}
V(S_t, t; K, T) &= e^{-r(T-t)} \mathbb{E}^{\mathbb{Q}} \left[\left(\log\left(\frac{S_T}{S_0}\right) - K \right)^2 \middle| \mathcal{F}_t \right] \\
&= e^{-r(T-t)} \mathbb{E}^{\mathbb{Q}} \left[\left(\log\left(\frac{S_T}{S_t}\right) + \log\left(\frac{S_t}{S_0}\right) - K \right)^2 \middle| \mathcal{F}_t \right] \\
&= e^{-r(T-t)} \mathbb{E}^{\mathbb{Q}} \left[\left(\log\left(\frac{S_T}{S_t}\right) - \left(r - D - \frac{1}{2}\sigma^2\right)(T - t) \right. \right. \\
&\qquad \left. \left. + \left(r - D - \frac{1}{2}\sigma^2\right)(T - t) + \log\left(\frac{S_t}{S_0}\right) - K \right)^2 \middle| \mathcal{F}_t \right] \\
&= e^{-r(T-t)} \mathbb{E}^{\mathbb{Q}} \left[\left(\log\left(\frac{S_T}{S_t}\right) - \left(r - D - \frac{1}{2}\sigma^2\right)(T - t) \right)^2 \middle| \mathcal{F}_t \right] \\
&\quad + 2 e^{-r(T-t)} \mathbb{E}^{\mathbb{Q}} \left[\log\left(\frac{S_T}{S_t}\right) - \left(r - D - \frac{1}{2}\sigma^2\right)(T - t) \middle| \mathcal{F}_t \right] \\
&\qquad \times \mathbb{E}^{\mathbb{Q}} \left[\log\left(\frac{S_t}{S_0}\right) + \left(r - D - \frac{1}{2}\sigma^2\right)(T - t) - K \middle| \mathcal{F}_t \right] \\
&\quad + e^{-r(T-t)} \mathbb{E}^{\mathbb{Q}} \left[\left(\log\left(\frac{S_t}{S_0}\right) + \left(r - D - \frac{1}{2}\sigma^2\right)(T - t) - K \right)^2 \middle| \mathcal{F}_t \right].
\end{aligned}
$$

Since

$$
\frac{\log\left(\frac{S_T}{S_t}\right) - \left(r - D - \frac{1}{2}\sigma^2\right)(T - t)}{\sigma\sqrt{T - t}} \sim \mathcal{N}(0, 1)
$$

therefore

$$\left[\frac{\log\left(\frac{S_T}{S_t}\right) - \left(r - D - \frac{1}{2}\sigma^2\right)(T-t)}{\sigma\sqrt{T-t}}\right]^2 \sim \chi^2(1)$$

with

$$\mathbb{E}^{\mathbb{Q}}\left[\left(\frac{\log\left(\frac{S_T}{S_t}\right) - \left(r - D - \frac{1}{2}\sigma^2\right)(T-t)}{\sigma\sqrt{T-t}}\right)^2 \middle| \mathcal{F}_t\right] = 1$$

or

$$\mathbb{E}^{\mathbb{Q}}\left[\left(\log\left(\frac{S_T}{S_t}\right) - \left(r - D - \frac{1}{2}\sigma^2\right)(T-t)\right)^2 \middle| \mathcal{F}_t\right] = \sigma^2(T-t).$$

Hence,

$$V(S_t, t; K, T) = e^{-r(T-t)}\left\{\sigma^2(T-t)\right.$$

$$\left. + \left[\log\left(\frac{S_t}{S_0}\right) + \left(r - D - \frac{1}{2}\sigma^2\right)(T-t) - K\right]^2\right\}.$$

□

30. *Merton Model for Default of a Company I.* At time t, we assume the asset A_t of a company satisfies the SDE

$$\frac{dA_t}{A_t} = \mu dt + \sigma dW_t$$

where μ is the drift parameter, σ is the volatility and $\{W_t : t \geq 0\}$ is a standard Wiener process on the probability space $(\Omega, \mathcal{F}, \mathbb{P})$. Let r be the risk-free interest rate.

In financial accounting the asset A_t is a combination of equity E_t and debt D_t so that

$$A_t = E_t + D_t$$

where at time T, $t < T$ the debt holders will receive an amount $F > 0$ which is the face value of the debt if $A_T > F$ and the equity holders will receive the rest of the value of the company. Otherwise, the company will be in default and the debt holders will receive A_T and the equity holders will receive nothing.

By constructing the payoff diagrams for E_T and D_T, find the values of E_t and D_t for all $t < T$ under the Black–Scholes framework.

Solution: At time T, for the debt holders

$$D_T = \begin{cases} F & \text{if } A_T > F \\ A_T & \text{if } A_T \leq F \end{cases}$$

and hence, for the equity holders

$$E_T = A_T - D_T$$
$$= A_T - \begin{cases} F & \text{if } A_T > F \\ A_T & \text{if } A_T \leq F \end{cases}$$
$$= \begin{cases} A_T - F & \text{if } A_T > F \\ 0 & \text{if } A_T \leq F \end{cases}$$
$$= \max\{A_T - F, 0\}.$$

At terminal time T, the payoff diagram for equity shareholders is given in Figure 2.1. Mathematically

$$E_T = \max\{A_T - F, 0\}$$

is the payoff of a European call option on the assets with strike equal to the face value.

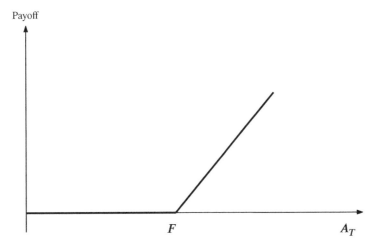

Figure 2.1 Payment to equity holders at time T.

Given that A_t follows a GBM process, the amount of equity E_t at time t is

$$E_t = C(A_t, t; F, T)$$

where

$$C(A_t, t; F, T) = A_t \Phi(d_+) - F e^{-r(T-t)} \Phi(d_-)$$

such that

$$d_\pm = \frac{\log(A_t/F) + (r \pm \frac{1}{2}\sigma^2)(T-t)}{\sigma\sqrt{T-t}} \quad \text{and} \quad \Phi(x) = \int_{-\infty}^{x} \frac{1}{\sqrt{2\pi}} e^{-\frac{1}{2}u^2} du.$$

In contrast, the payment to debt holders at time T is

$$D_T = \begin{cases} F & \text{if } A_T > F \\ A_T & \text{if } A_T \leq F \end{cases}$$
$$= \min\{F, A_T\}$$

or

$$D_T = \begin{cases} F & \text{if } A_T > F \\ A_T & \text{if } A_T \leq F \end{cases}$$
$$= \begin{cases} F & \text{if } A_T > F \\ F & \text{if } A_T \leq F \end{cases} - \begin{cases} 0 & \text{if } A_T > F \\ F - A_T & \text{if } A_T \leq F \end{cases}$$
$$= F - \max\{F - V_T, 0\}.$$

Therefore, the payoff diagram for the debt holders is given in Figure 2.2.
Thus,

$$D_T = \min\{F, A_T\} = F - \max\{F - A_T, 0\}$$

which is the difference between the face value and the payoff of a European put option with strike price equal to F. Thus, at time t the debt is equal to

$$D_t = F e^{-r(T-t)} - P(A_t, t; F, T)$$
$$= A_t - C(A_t, t; F, T)$$

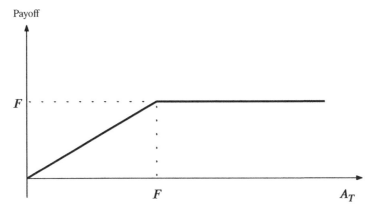

Figure 2.2   Payment to debt holders at time T.

where, from the put–call parity

$$P(A_t, t; F, T) = C(A_t, t; F, T) - A_t + Fe^{-r(T-t)}.$$

$\square$

31. *Generalised Black–Scholes Formula.* Let $\{W_t : t \geq 0\}$ be a $\mathbb{P}$-standard Wiener process on the probability space $(\Omega, \mathscr{F}, \mathbb{P})$ and let the asset price S_t have the following diffusion process

$$\frac{dS_t}{S_t} = (\mu_t - D_t)dt + \sigma_t dW_t$$

where μ_t, D_t and σ_t are time-dependent drift, continuous dividend yield and volatility functions, and let r_t be the time-dependent risk-free interest rate from a money-market account.

Under the risk-neutral measure $\mathbb{Q}$, deduce that the European option price at time t, written on S_t with strike price K expiring at T, $T > t$ is

$$V(S_t, t; K, T) = \delta S_t e^{-\int_t^T D_u du} \Phi(\delta d_+) - \delta K e^{-\int_t^T r_u du} \Phi(\delta d_-)$$

where

$$d_\pm = \frac{\log(S_t/K) + \int_t^T (r_u - D_u \pm \frac{1}{2}\sigma_u^2)\, du}{\sqrt{\int_t^T \sigma_u^2 du}}$$

$$\delta = \begin{cases} +1 & \text{for call option} \\ -1 & \text{for put option.} \end{cases}$$

Solution: Under the risk-neutral measure $\mathbb{Q}$, S_t follows

$$\frac{dS_t}{S_t} = (r_t - D_t)dt + \sigma_t dW_t^{\mathbb{Q}}$$

where $W_t^{\mathbb{Q}} = W_t + \int_0^t \frac{\mu_u - r_u}{\sigma_u} du$ is a $\mathbb{Q}$-standard Wiener process.

Hence, from Itō's lemma

$$d \log S_t = \frac{dS_t}{S_t} - \frac{1}{2}\left(\frac{dS_t}{S_t}\right)^2 + \ldots$$

$$= (r_t - D_t)dt + \sigma_t dW_t^{\mathbb{Q}} - \frac{1}{2}\sigma_t^2 dt$$

$$= \left(r_t - D_t - \frac{1}{2}\sigma_t^2\right)dt + \sigma_t dW_t^{\mathbb{Q}}.$$

Taking integrals

$$\int_t^T d \log S_u = \int_t^T \left(r_u - D_u - \frac{1}{2}\sigma_u^2\right)du + \int_t^T \sigma_u dW_u^{\mathbb{Q}}$$

or

$$\log\left(\frac{S_T}{S_t}\right) = \int_t^T \left(r_u - D_u - \frac{1}{2}\sigma_u^2\right)du + \int_t^T \sigma_u dW_u^{\mathbb{Q}}.$$

Since we can also write the Itō integral as

$$\int_t^T \sigma_u dW_u^{\mathbb{Q}} = \lim_{n\to\infty} \sum_{i=0}^{n-1} \sigma_{t_i}(W_{t_{i+1}}^{\mathbb{Q}} - W_{t_i}^{\mathbb{Q}})$$

where $t_i = t + i(T-t)/n$, $t = t_0 < t_1 < t_2 < \cdots < t_{n-1} < t_n = T$, $n \in \mathbb{N}$ and due to the stationary increment of a standard Wiener process, each term of $W_{t_{i+1}}^{\mathbb{Q}} - W_{t_i}^{\mathbb{Q}} \sim \mathcal{N}\left(0, \frac{T-t}{n}\right)$ is normally distributed multiplied by a deterministic term, therefore we can deduce that

$$\int_t^T \sigma_u dW_u^{\mathbb{Q}} \sim \mathcal{N}\left(0, \int_t^T \sigma_u^2 du\right)$$

and hence

$$\log\left(\frac{S_T}{S_t}\right) \sim \mathcal{N}\left[\int_t^T \left(r_u - D_u - \frac{1}{2}\sigma_u^2\right)du, \int_t^T \sigma_u^2 du\right]$$

or

$$\log\left(\frac{S_T}{S_t}\right) \sim \mathcal{N}\left[\left(\bar{r} - \bar{D} - \frac{1}{2}\bar{\sigma}^2\right)(T-t), \bar{\sigma}^2(T-t)\right]$$

where

$$\bar{r} = \frac{1}{T-t}\int_t^T r_u\, du, \quad \overline{D} = \frac{1}{T-t}\int_t^T D_u\, du, \quad \bar{\sigma}^2 = \frac{1}{T-t}\int_t^T \sigma_u^2\, du.$$

By analogy with the risk-neutral pricing methodology (see Problem 2.2.2.5, page 101), we can substitute the constants r, D and σ of the Black–Scholes formula with $\bar{r}$, $\overline{D}$ and $\bar{\sigma}$, respectively so that the price of European call $C(S_t, t; K, T)$ and put $P(S_t, t; K, T)$ options with strike K are

$$C(S_t, t; K, T) = S_t e^{-\overline{D}(T-t)}\Phi(d_+) - K e^{-\bar{r}(T-t)}\Phi(d_-)$$

$$P(S_t, t; K, T) = K e^{-\bar{r}(T-t)}\Phi(-d_-) - S_t e^{-\overline{D}(T-t)}\Phi(-d_+)$$

such that

$$d_\pm = \frac{\log(S_t/K) + (\bar{r} - \overline{D} \pm \frac{1}{2}\bar{\sigma}^2)(T-t)}{\bar{\sigma}\sqrt{T-t}}.$$

Substituting the values of $\bar{r}$, $\overline{D}$ and $\bar{\sigma}^2$ we finally have

$$C(S_t, t; K, T) = S_t e^{-\int_t^T D_u du}\Phi(d_+) - K e^{-\int_t^T r_u du}\Phi(d_-)$$

$$P(S_t, t; K, T) = S_t e^{-\int_t^T D_u du}\Phi(-d_+) - K e^{-\int_t^T r_u du}\Phi(-d_-)$$

where

$$d_\pm = \frac{\log(S_t/K) + \int_t^T (r_u - D_u \pm \frac{1}{2}\sigma_u^2)\, du}{\sqrt{\int_t^T \sigma_u^2 du}}.$$

$\square$

32. *Non-Dividend-Paying Asset Price as Numéraire.* Let $\{W_t : t \geq 0\}$ be a $\mathbb{P}$-standard Wiener process on the probability space $(\Omega, \mathcal{F}, \mathbb{P})$ and let the asset price S_t have the following diffusion process

$$\frac{dS_t}{S_t} = (\mu_t - D_t)dt + \sigma_t dW_t$$

where μ_t, D_t and σ_t are time-dependent drift, continuous dividend yield and volatility, functions, and let r_t be the time-dependent risk-free interest rate from a money-market account.

Show that under the risk-neutral measure $\mathbb{Q}$, $S_t e^{\int_0^t D_u du}$ follows a non-dividend diffusion process of the form

$$d\left(S_t e^{\int_0^t D_u du}\right) = r S_t e^{\int_0^t D_u du}dt + \sigma_t S_t e^{\int_0^t D_u du}dW_t^{\mathbb{Q}}$$

where $W_t^{\mathbb{Q}} = W_t + \int_0^t \frac{\mu_u - r_u}{\sigma_u}du$ is a $\mathbb{Q}$-standard Wiener process.

By definition the price of a European-style option with payoff $\Psi(S_T)$ at time $t < T$ is

$$V(S_t, t) = \mathbb{E}^{\mathbb{Q}}\left[e^{-\int_t^T r_u \, du} \Psi(S_T) \,\middle|\, \mathcal{F}_t \right]$$

where under the risk-neutral measure $\mathbb{Q}$, the risk-free money-market account acts as the numéraire.

By denoting $\mathbb{Q}_S$ as the equivalent martingale measure where the asset price $S_t e^{\int_0^t D_u \, du}$ is used as the numéraire and using

$$X_t = \left(S_t e^{\int_0^t D_u \, du} \right)^{-1} e^{\int_0^t r_u \, du}$$

as the discounted money-market account, show that under $\mathbb{Q}_S$ the asset price S_t now evolves according to the diffusion process

$$\frac{dS_t}{S_t} = (r_t - D_t + \sigma_t^2) dt + \sigma_t \, dW_t^{\mathbb{Q}_S}$$

where $W_t^{\mathbb{Q}_S} = W_t^{\mathbb{Q}} - \displaystyle\int_0^t \sigma_u \, du$ is a $\mathbb{Q}_S$-standard Wiener process.

Hence, show that for a strike price K the price $C_a(S_t, t; K, T)$ of a European asset-or-nothing call with terminal payoff

$$\Psi(S_T) = \begin{cases} S_T & \text{if } S_T > K \\ 0 & \text{if } S_T \le K \end{cases}$$

is given by

$$C_a(S_t, t; K, T) = S_t e^{-\int_t^T D_u \, du} \Phi(d_+)$$

where

$$d_+ = \frac{\log(S_t / K) + \int_t^T (r_u - D_u + \frac{1}{2}\sigma_u^2) \, du}{\sqrt{\int_t^T \sigma_u^2 \, du}} \quad \text{and} \quad \Phi(x) = \int_{-\infty}^x \frac{1}{\sqrt{2\pi}} e^{-\frac{1}{2}u^2} \, du.$$

Solution: From Girsanov's theorem, under the risk-neutral measure $\mathbb{Q}$, S_t follows

$$\frac{dS_t}{S_t} = (r_t - D_t) dt + \sigma_t \, dW_t^{\mathbb{Q}}$$

where $W_t^{\mathbb{Q}} = W_t + \int_0^t \dfrac{\mu_t - r_t}{\sigma_t}\,du$ is a $\mathbb{Q}$-standard Wiener process. From Itō's lemma

$$d\left(S_t e^{\int_0^t D_u du}\right) = D_t S_t e^{\int_0^t D_u du}dt + e^{\int_0^t D_u du}dS_t$$

$$= D_t S_t e^{\int_0^t D_u du}dt + e^{\int_0^t D_u du}\left[(r_t - D_t)S_t dt + \sigma_t dW_t^{\mathbb{Q}}\right]$$

$$= r_t S_t e^{\int_0^t D_u du}dt + \sigma_t S_t e^{\int_0^t D_u du}dW_t^{\mathbb{Q}}.$$

Given that $S_t e^{\int_0^t D_u du}$ is a non-dividend-paying asset and strictly positive, thus it can be used as a numéraire.

Under the change of numéraire for a payoff $\Psi(S_T)$

$$N_t^{(1)}\mathbb{E}^{\mathbb{Q}^{(1)}}\left[\left.\dfrac{\Psi(S_T)}{N_T^{(1)}}\right| \mathscr{F}_t\right] = N_t^{(2)}\mathbb{E}^{\mathbb{Q}^{(2)}}\left[\left.\dfrac{\Psi(S_T)}{N_T^{(2)}}\right| \mathscr{F}_t\right]$$

where for $i = 1, 2$, $N^{(i)}$ is a numéraire and $\mathbb{Q}^{(i)}$ is the measure under which the asset prices discounted by $N^{(i)}$ are $\mathbb{Q}^{(i)}$-martingales.

Under the risk-neutral measure $\mathbb{Q}$ we have

$$N_t^{(1)} = e^{\int_0^t r_u du} \text{ and } N_T^{(1)} = e^{\int_0^T r_u du}$$

and under the $\mathbb{Q}_S$ measure

$$N_t^{(2)} = S_t e^{\int_0^t D_u du} \text{ and } N_T^{(2)} = S_T e^{\int_0^T D_u du}.$$

Hence,

$$V(S_t, t) = \mathbb{E}^{\mathbb{Q}}\left[\left. e^{-\int_t^T r_u du}\Psi(S_T)\right| \mathscr{F}_t\right]$$

$$= e^{\int_0^t r_u du}\mathbb{E}^{\mathbb{Q}}\left[\left. \dfrac{\Psi(S_T)}{e^{\int_0^T r_u du}}\right| \mathscr{F}_t\right]$$

$$= S_t e^{\int_0^t D_u du}\mathbb{E}^{\mathbb{Q}_S}\left[\left. \dfrac{\Psi(S_T)}{S_T e^{\int_0^T D_u du}}\right| \mathscr{F}_t\right].$$

Given

$$\Psi(S_T) = \begin{cases} S_T & \text{if } S_T > K \\ 0 & \text{if } S_T \leq K \end{cases} = S_T \, \mathbb{I}_{\{S_T > K\}}$$

the asset-or-nothing call price under $\mathbb{Q}_S$ is

$$C_a(S_t, t; K, T) = S_t e^{\int_0^t D_u du} \mathbb{E}^{\mathbb{Q}_S} \left[\left. \frac{S_T \, \mathbb{I}_{\{S_T > K\}}}{S_T e^{\int_0^T D_u du}} \right| \mathcal{F}_t \right]$$

$$= S_t e^{-\int_t^T D_u du} \mathbb{E}^{\mathbb{Q}_S} \left[\left. \mathbb{I}_{\{S_T > K\}} \right| \mathcal{F}_t \right]$$

$$= S_t e^{-\int_t^T D_u du} \mathbb{Q}_S \left(S_T > K | \mathcal{F}_t \right).$$

Under $\mathbb{Q}_S$ the discounted money-market account is defined as

$$X_t = \left(S_t e^{\int_0^t D_u du} \right)^{-1} e^{\int_0^t r_u du}$$

where X_t is a $\mathbb{Q}_S$-martingale. Using Itō's lemma

$$dX_t = d \left(S_t^{-1} e^{\int_0^t (r_u - D_u) du} \right)$$

$$= (r_t - D_t) S_t^{-1} e^{\int_0^t (r_u - D_u) du} dt + e^{\int_0^t (r_u - D_u) du} d(S_t^{-1})$$

$$= (r_t - D_t) S_t^{-1} e^{\int_0^t (r_u - D_u) du} dt + S_t^{-1} e^{\int_0^t (r_u - D_u) du} \left(-\frac{dS_t}{S_t} + \left(\frac{dS_t}{S_t} \right)^2 + \dots \right)$$

$$= (r_t - D_t) X_t \, dt - X_t \left[(r_t - D_t) dt + \sigma_t dW_t^{\mathbb{Q}} \right] + \sigma^2 X_t dt$$

$$= -\sigma_t X_t dW_t^{\mathbb{Q}} + \sigma_t^2 X_t dt$$

$$= -\sigma_t X_t dW_t^{\mathbb{Q}_S}$$

where $W_t^{\mathbb{Q}_S} = W_t^{\mathbb{Q}} - \int_0^t \sigma_u \, du$ is a $\mathbb{Q}_S$-standard Wiener process.

By substituting $dW_t^{\mathbb{Q}} = dW_t^{\mathbb{Q}_S} + \sigma_t dt$ into $dS_t = (r_t - D_t) S_t dt + \sigma_t S_t dW_t^{\mathbb{Q}}$ the asset price diffusion process under $\mathbb{Q}_S$ becomes

$$\frac{dS_t}{S_t} = (r_t - D_t + \sigma_t^2) dt + \sigma_t dW_t^{\mathbb{Q}_S}.$$

To find the distribution of S_t we note that

$$d(\log S_t) = \frac{dS_t}{S_t} - \frac{1}{2} \left(\frac{dS_t}{S_t} \right)^2 + \dots$$

$$= (r_t - D_t + \sigma_t^2) dt + \sigma_t dW_t^{\mathbb{Q}_S} - \frac{1}{2} \sigma_t^2 dt$$

$$= \left(r_t - D_t + \frac{1}{2} \sigma_t^2 \right) dt + \sigma_t dW_t^{\mathbb{Q}_S}$$

and taking integrals

$$\log S_T = \log S_t + \int_t^T \left(r_u - D_u + \frac{1}{2} \sigma_u^2 \right) du + \int_t^T \sigma_u \, dW_u^{\mathbb{Q}_S}.$$

Since $W_t^{Q_S}$ is a $\mathbb{Q}_S$-martingale we have

$$\int_t^T \sigma_u \, dW_u^{Q_S} \sim \mathcal{N}\left(0, \int_t^T \sigma_u^2 \, du\right)$$

and hence

$$\log S_T \sim \mathcal{N}\left(\log S_t + \int_t^T \left(r_u - D_u + \frac{1}{2}\sigma_u^2\right) du, \int_t^T \sigma_u^2 \, du\right).$$

Therefore,

$$
\begin{aligned}
C_a(S_t, t; K, T) &= S_t e^{-\int_t^T D_u du} \mathbb{Q}_S \left(S_T > K \,\middle|\, \mathscr{F}_t\right) \\
&= S_t e^{-\int_t^T D_u du} \mathbb{Q}_S \left(\log S_T > \log K \,\middle|\, \mathscr{F}_t\right) \\
&= S_t e^{-\int_t^T D_u du} \\
&\quad \times \mathbb{Q}_S \left(Z > \frac{\log K - \log S_t - \int_t^T \left(r_u - D_u + \frac{1}{2}\sigma_u^2\right) du}{\sqrt{\int_t^T \sigma_u^2 du}} \,\middle|\, \mathscr{F}_t\right)
\end{aligned}
$$

where $Z \sim \mathcal{N}(0, 1)$.

Thus,

$$C_a(S_t, t; K, T) = S_t e^{-\int_t^T D_u du} \Phi(d_+)$$

where

$$d_+ = \frac{\log(S_t/K) + \int_t^T (r_u - D_u + \frac{1}{2}\sigma_u^2) \, du}{\sqrt{\int_t^T \sigma_u^2 du}} \quad \text{and} \quad \Phi(x) = \int_{-\infty}^x \frac{1}{\sqrt{2\pi}} e^{-\frac{1}{2}u^2} \, du.$$

$\square$

33. *European Option Price Under Stochastic Interest Rate I.* Let $\{W_t^S : t \geq 0\}$ and $\{W_t^r : t \geq 0\}$ be $\mathbb{P}$-standard Wiener processes on the probability space $(\Omega, \mathscr{F}, \mathbb{P})$ and let the asset price S_t have the following diffusion process

$$\frac{dS_t}{S_t} = (\mu_t - D_t)dt + \sigma_t dW_t^S$$

where μ_t, D_t and σ_t are time-dependent drift, continuous dividend yield and volatility functions and the risk-free interest rate r_t is assumed to follow an Ornstein-Uhlenbeck process (or Vasicek process in the interest-rate modelling world)

$$dr_t = \kappa(\theta - r_t)dt + \alpha dW_t^r$$

where κ, θ and α are constant parameters. In addition, we assume W_t^S and W_t^r are correlated with coefficient $\rho \in (-1,1)$,

$$dW_t^S \cdot dW_t^r = \rho dt.$$

Assume in the market there is a family of tradeable, risk-free zero-coupon bonds whose price at time t is $P(t,T)$ where they deliver a unit of currency at maturity T, $P(T,T) = 1$. The zero-coupon bond has the process

$$\frac{dP(t,T)}{P(t,T)} = \mu_p(t,T)dt + \sigma_p(t,T)dW_t^r$$

where $\mu_p(t,T)$ is the drift and $\sigma_p(t,T)$ is the volatility.

(a) By defining $\{Y_t : t \geq 0\}$ as a $\mathbb{P}$-standard Wiener process where $Y_t \perp\!\!\!\perp W_t^r$, show that we can write

$$W_t^S = \rho W_t^r + \sqrt{1-\rho^2} Y_t.$$

(b) At time t, we consider a trader who has a portfolio valued at Π_t holding ϕ_t units of risky asset S_t and ψ_t units invested in zero-coupon bonds. Using the two-dimensional Girsanov's theorem, show that under the risk-neutral measure $\mathbb{Q}$,

$$\frac{dS_t}{S_t} = (r_t - D_t)dt + \sigma_t d\widetilde{W}_t^S$$

$$\frac{dP(t,T)}{P(t,T)} = r_t dt + \sigma_p(t,T)d\widetilde{W}_t^r$$

$$dr_t = \left(\kappa(\theta - r_t) - \alpha\gamma_t\right)dt + \alpha d\widetilde{W}_t^r$$

where $\widetilde{W}^S = \rho\widetilde{W}_t^r + \sqrt{1-\rho^2}\widetilde{Y}_t$, $\widetilde{W}_t^r = W_t^r + \int_0^t \gamma_u\,du$, $\widetilde{Y}_t = Y_t + \int_0^t \lambda_u\,du$ are $\mathbb{Q}$-standard Wiener processes, $\gamma_t = \dfrac{\mu_p(t,T) - r_t}{\sigma_p(t,T)}$ is the market price of interest risk and $\rho\gamma_t + \sqrt{1-\rho^2}\lambda_t = \dfrac{\mu_t - r_t}{\sigma_t}$.

(c) Using Itō's formula, show that the zero-coupon bond price $P(t,T)$ satisfies the following PDE

$$\frac{\partial P}{\partial t} + \frac{1}{2}\alpha^2 \frac{\partial^2 P}{\partial r_t^2} + \left(\kappa(\theta - r_t) - \alpha\gamma_t\right)\frac{\partial P}{\partial r_t} - r_t P(t,T) = 0$$

$$P(T,T) = 1.$$

(d) Using the Feynman-Kac formula, state the price of the zero-coupon bond $P(t,T)$ at time t as an expectation.

Assuming the market price of risk γ_t is a constant value γ and by setting $\tilde{\theta} = \theta - \dfrac{\alpha\gamma}{\kappa}$, show that the solution of $P(t,T)$ can be written in the form

$$P(t,T) = e^{A(t,T)-r_t B(t,T)}$$

where

$$A(t,T) = \left(\tilde{\theta} - \frac{1}{2}\left(\frac{\alpha}{\kappa}\right)^2\right)(B(t,T) - T + t) - \frac{\alpha^2}{4\kappa}B(t,T)^2,$$

$$B(t,T) = \frac{1}{\kappa}\left(1 - e^{-\kappa(T-t)}\right) \quad \text{and} \quad \sigma_p(t,T) = -\frac{\alpha}{\kappa}\left(1 - e^{-\kappa(T-t)}\right).$$

(e) By denoting $\mathbb{Q}_T$ as the T-forward measure where the zero-coupon bond price is used as the numéraire, show that under the $\mathbb{Q}_T$ measure, the risky asset S_t, zero-coupon bond $P(t,T)$ and the interest rate r_t follow the diffusions

$$\frac{dS_t}{S_t} = \left(r_t - D_t + \rho\sigma_t\sigma_p(t,T)\right)dt + \sigma_t d\widehat{W}_t^S$$

$$\frac{dP(t,T)}{P(t,T)} = \left(r_t + \sigma_p(t,T)^2\right)dt + \sigma_p(t,T)d\widehat{W}_t^r$$

$$dr_t = \left(\kappa(\theta - r_t) + \alpha(\sigma(t,T) - \gamma_t)\right)dt + \alpha d\widehat{W}_t^r$$

where $\widehat{W}_t^S = \widetilde{W}_t^S - \displaystyle\int_0^t \rho\sigma_p(u,T)\,du$ and $\widehat{W}_t^r = \widetilde{W}_t^r - \displaystyle\int_0^t \sigma_p(u,T)\,du$ are $\mathbb{Q}_T$-standard Wiener processes.

(f) Finally, under $\mathbb{Q}_T$ show that for a payoff

$$\Psi(S_T) = \max\left\{S_T - K, 0\right\}$$

the European call option price with strike price K under stochastic interest rate is

$$C_{\text{stochIR}}(S_t, r_t, t; K, T) = S_t e^{-\int_t^T D_u du}\Phi(d_+) - KP(t,T)\Phi(d_-)$$

where

$$d_{\pm} = \frac{\log\left(S_t/(P(t,T)K)\right) - \int_t^T \left(D_u \mp \frac{1}{2}\sigma(u,T)^2\right) du}{\sqrt{\int_t^T \sigma(u,T)^2\, du}}$$

$$\sigma(t,T) = \sqrt{\sigma_t^2 + \sigma_p(t,T)^2 - 2\rho\sigma_t\sigma_p(t,T)}$$

$$\sigma_p(t,T) = -\frac{\alpha}{\kappa}\left(1 - e^{-\kappa(T-t)}\right)$$

$$\Phi(x) = \int_{-\infty}^{x} \frac{1}{\sqrt{2\pi}} e^{-\frac{1}{2}u^2}\, du.$$

Solution:

(a) By writing $W_t^S = \rho W_t^r + \sqrt{1-\rho^2}\, Y_t$ we have the following properties

$$\mathbb{E}(W_t^S) = \mathbb{E}\left(\rho W_t^r + \sqrt{1-\rho^2}\, Y_t\right) = \rho\mathbb{E}(W_t^r) + \sqrt{1-\rho^2}\,\mathbb{E}(Y_t) = 0$$

and

$$\mathrm{Var}(W_t^S) = \mathrm{Var}(\rho W_t^r + \sqrt{1-\rho^2}\, Y_t) = \rho^2\mathrm{Var}(W_t^r) + (1-\rho^2)\mathrm{Var}(Y_t) = t$$

since $W_t^r \perp\!\!\!\perp Y_t$

Given both $W_t^r \sim \mathcal{N}(0,t)$, $Y_t \sim \mathcal{N}(0,t)$ and $W_t^r \perp\!\!\!\perp Y_t$ therefore

$$\rho W_t^r + \sqrt{1-\rho^2}\, Y_t \sim \mathcal{N}(0,t).$$

From Itō's formula and taking note that $W_t^r \perp\!\!\!\perp W_t$

$$\begin{aligned}
dW_t^S \cdot dW_t^r &= d(\rho W_t^r + \sqrt{1-\rho^2}\, Y_t) \cdot dW_t^r \\
&= (\rho dW_t^r + \sqrt{1-\rho^2}\, dY_t) \cdot dW_t^r \\
&= \rho (dW_t^r)^2 + \sqrt{1-\rho^2}\, dY_t \cdot dW_t^r \\
&= \rho dt.
\end{aligned}$$

Thus, we can write $W_t^S = \rho W_t^r + \sqrt{1-\rho^2}\, Y_t$.

(b) We first define,

$$\widetilde{Y}_t = Y_t + \int_0^t \lambda_u\, du$$

$$\widetilde{W}_t^r = W_t^r + \int_0^t \gamma_u\, du$$

where λ_t is the market price of asset risk and γ_t is the market price of interest rate risk. Since $Y_t \perp\!\!\!\perp W_t^r$ therefore we can easily deduce $\widetilde{Y}_t \perp\!\!\!\perp \widetilde{W}_t^r$.

From the two-dimensional Girsanov's theorem, there exist a risk-neutral measure $\mathbb{Q}$ on the filtration $\mathscr{F}_s$, $0 \le s \le t$ defined by the Radon-Nikodým process,

$$\frac{d\mathbb{Q}}{d\mathbb{P}} = Z_t = e^{-\frac{1}{2}\int_0^t \lambda_u^2 du - \int_0^t \lambda_u dY_u} \cdot e^{-\frac{1}{2}\int_0^t \gamma_u^2 du - \int_0^t \gamma_u dW_u^r}$$

so that $\widetilde{Y}_t$ and $\widetilde{W}_t^r$ are $\mathbb{Q}$-standard Wiener processes and $\widetilde{Y}_t \perp\!\!\!\perp \widetilde{W}_t^r$.

Let the portfolio Π_t be defined as

$$\Pi_t = \phi_t S_t + \psi_t P(t, T)$$

where ϕ_t units are invested in risky asset S_t and ψ_t units are invested in zero-coupon bond $P(t, T)$. Given the holder of the portfolio will receive $D_t S_t dt$ for every risky asset held, thus

$$
\begin{aligned}
d\Pi_t &= \phi_t \left(dS_t + D_t S_t dt \right) + \psi_t dP(t, T) \\
&= \phi_t \left(\mu_t S_t dt + \sigma_t S_t dW_t^S \right) \\
&\quad + \psi_t \left(\mu_p(t, T) P(t, T) dt + \sigma_p(t, T) P(t, T) dW_t^r \right) \\
&= r_t \Pi_t dt + \phi_t S_t \left[(\mu_t - r_t) dt + \sigma_t \left(\rho dW_t^r + \sqrt{1 - \rho^2} dY_t \right) \right] \\
&\quad + \psi_t P(t, T) \left[\left(\mu_p(t, T) - r_t \right) dt + \sigma_p(t, T) dW_t^r \right]
\end{aligned}
$$

By substituting

$$
\begin{aligned}
dW_t^r &= d\widetilde{W}_t^r - \gamma_t dt \\
dY_t &= d\widetilde{Y}_t - \lambda_t dt
\end{aligned}
$$

into $d\Pi_t$ we have

$$
\begin{aligned}
d\Pi_t &= r_t \Pi_t dt \\
&\quad + \phi_t S_t \Big[(\mu_t - r_t) dt \\
&\qquad + \sigma_t \left(\rho d\widetilde{W}_t^r - \rho \gamma_t dt + \sqrt{1 - \rho^2} d\widetilde{Y}_t - \sqrt{1 - \rho^2} \lambda_t dt \right) \Big] \\
&\quad + \psi_t P(t, T) \left[\left(\mu_p(t, T) - r_t \right) dt + \sigma_p(t, T) \left(d\widetilde{W}_t^r - \gamma_t dt \right) \right] \\
&= r_t \Pi_t dt \\
&\quad + \phi_t S_t \left[\left(\mu_t - r_t - \left(\rho \gamma_t + \sqrt{1 - \rho^2} \lambda_t \right) \sigma_t \right) dt \right. \\
&\qquad \left. + \sigma_t \left(\rho d\widetilde{W}_t^r + \sqrt{1 - \rho^2} d\widetilde{Y}_t \right) \right] \\
&\quad + \psi_t P(t, T) \left[\left(\mu_p(t, T) - r_t - \gamma_t \sigma_p(t, T) \right) dt + \sigma_p(t, T) d\widetilde{W}_t^r \right].
\end{aligned}
$$

By writing $B_t = e^{\int_0^t r_u du}$ so that $dB_t = r_t B_t dt$, and under the risk-neutral measure $\mathbb{Q}$, both $\widetilde{W}_t^r$ and $\widetilde{W}_t$ are $\mathbb{Q}$-martingales. In order for the discounted $B_t^{-1} \Pi_t$ to be a $\mathbb{Q}$-martingale,

$$
\begin{aligned}
d(B_t^{-1}\Pi_t) &= -r_t B_t^{-1}\Pi_t dt + B_t^{-1} d\Pi_t \\
&= B_t^{-1}\phi_t S_t \left[\left(\mu_t - r_t - \left(\rho\gamma_t + \sqrt{1-\rho^2}\lambda_t\right)\sigma_t\right) dt \right. \\
&\quad \left. + \sigma_t \left(\rho d\widetilde{W}_t^r + \sqrt{1-\rho^2}d\widetilde{Y}_t\right)\right] \\
&\quad + B_t^{-1}\psi_t P(t,T)\left[\left(\mu_p(t,T) - r_t - \gamma_t \sigma_p(t,T)\right) dt + \sigma_p(t,T)d\widetilde{W}_t^r\right]
\end{aligned}
$$

we require

$$
\rho\gamma_t + \sqrt{1-\rho^2}\lambda_t = \frac{\mu_t - r_t}{\sigma_t} \quad \text{and} \quad \gamma_t = \frac{\mu_p(t,T) - r_t}{\sigma_p(t,T)}.
$$

Hence, by substituting

$$
\begin{aligned}
dW_t^r &= d\widetilde{W}_t^r - \gamma_t dt, \\
dY_t &= d\widetilde{Y}_t - \lambda_t dt, \\
\rho\gamma_t + \sqrt{1-\rho^2}\lambda_t &= \frac{\mu_t - r_t}{\sigma_t}
\end{aligned}
$$

into

$$
dS_t = (\mu_t - D_t)S_t dt + \sigma_t S_t \left(\rho dW_t^r + \sqrt{1-\rho^2}dY_t\right)
$$

we have

$$
\begin{aligned}
dS_t &= (\mu_t - D_t)S_t dt \\
&\quad + \sigma_t S_t \left(\rho d\widetilde{W}_t^r - \rho\gamma_t dt + \sqrt{1-\rho^2}d\widetilde{Y}_t - \sqrt{1-\rho^2}\lambda_t dt\right) \\
&= (\mu_t - D_t)S_t dt + \sigma_t S_t \left(\rho d\widetilde{W}_t^r + \sqrt{1-\rho^2}d\widetilde{Y}_t\right) \\
&\quad - \sigma_t S_t \left(\rho\gamma_t + \sqrt{1-\rho^2}\lambda_t\right) dt \\
&= (\mu_t - D_t)S_t dt + \sigma_t S_t \left(\rho d\widetilde{W}_t^r + \sqrt{1-\rho^2}d\widetilde{Y}_t\right) \\
&\quad - \sigma_t S_t \left(\frac{\mu_t - r_t}{\sigma_t}\right) dt \\
&= (r_t - D_t)S_t dt + \sigma_t S_t \left(\rho d\widetilde{W}_t^r + \sqrt{1-\rho^2}d\widetilde{Y}_t\right) \\
&= (r_t - D_t)S_t dt + \sigma_t S_t d\widetilde{W}_t^S
\end{aligned}
$$

where $\widetilde{W}_t^S = \rho\widetilde{W}_t^r + \sqrt{1-\rho^2}\widetilde{Y}_t$.

On the other hand, by substituting

$$dW_t^r = d\widetilde{W}_t^r - \gamma_t dt,$$
$$\gamma_t = \frac{\mu_p(t,T) - r_t}{\sigma_p(t,T)}$$

into

$$dP(t,T) = \mu_p(t,T)P(t,T)dt + \sigma_p(t,T)P(t,T)dW_t^r,$$
$$dr_t = \kappa(\theta - r_t)dt + \alpha dW_t^r$$

the zero-coupon bond price and the instantaneous interest rate under the $\mathbb{Q}$-measure become

$$\begin{aligned}
dP(t,T) &= \mu_p(t,T)P(t,T)dt + \sigma_p(t,T)P(t,T)\left(d\widetilde{W}_t^r - \gamma_t dt\right) \\
&= \mu_p(t,T)P(t,T)dt + \sigma_p(t,T)P(t,T)d\widetilde{W}_t^r \\
&\quad -\sigma_p(t,T)\left(\frac{\mu_p(t,T) - r_t}{\sigma_p(t,T)}\right)dt \\
&= r_t P(t,T)dt + \sigma_p(t,T)P(t,T)d\widetilde{W}_t^r
\end{aligned}$$

and

$$\begin{aligned}
dr_t &= \kappa(\theta - r_t)dt + \alpha\left(d\widetilde{W}_t^r - \gamma_t dt\right) \\
&= \left(\kappa(\theta - r_t) - \alpha\gamma_t\right)dt + \alpha d\widetilde{W}_t^r.
\end{aligned}$$

(c) From Itō's formula,

$$\begin{aligned}
dP(t,T) &= \frac{\partial P}{\partial t}dt + \frac{\partial P}{\partial r_t}dr_t + \frac{1}{2}\frac{\partial^2 P}{\partial r_t^2}(dr_t)^2 + \cdots \\
&= \frac{\partial P}{\partial t}dt + \frac{\partial P}{\partial r_t}\left[\left(\kappa(\theta - r_t) - \alpha\gamma_t\right)dt + \alpha d\widetilde{W}_t^r\right] + \frac{1}{2}\alpha^2\frac{\partial^2 P}{\partial r_t^2}dt \\
&= \left[\frac{\partial P}{\partial t} + \frac{1}{2}\alpha^2\frac{\partial^2 P}{\partial r_t^2} + \left(\kappa(\theta - r_t) - \alpha\gamma_t\right)\frac{\partial P}{\partial r_t}\right]dt + \alpha\frac{\partial P}{\partial r_t}d\widetilde{W}_t^r.
\end{aligned}$$

By equating coefficients with

$$dP(t,T) = r_t P(t,T)dt + \sigma_p(t,T)P(t,T)d\widetilde{W}_t^r$$

we will have

$$\frac{\partial P}{\partial t} + \frac{1}{2}\alpha^2\frac{\partial^2 P}{\partial r_t^2} + \left(\kappa(\theta - r_t) - \alpha\gamma_t\right)\frac{\partial P}{\partial r_t} - r_t P(t,T) = 0$$

and

$$\sigma_p(t,T) = \alpha \frac{\partial P}{\partial r_t} P(t,T)^{-1}$$

with boundary condition

$$P(T,T) = 1.$$

(d) From the Feynman-Kac formula, under the risk-neutral measure $\mathbb{Q}$, the solution of the PDE at time t is given by

$$P(t,T) = \mathbb{E}^{\mathbb{Q}}\left[e^{-\int_t^T r_u du} P(T,T) \middle| \mathscr{F}_t \right] = \mathbb{E}^{\mathbb{Q}}\left[e^{-\int_t^T r_u du} \middle| \mathscr{F}_t \right].$$

By setting $\gamma_t = \gamma$ where γ is a constant value and writing $\widetilde{\theta} = \theta - \dfrac{\alpha\gamma}{\kappa}$, we therefore have

$$dr_t = \kappa(\widetilde{\theta} - r_t)dt + \alpha d\widetilde{W}_t^r.$$

Solving the SDE directly,

$$\int_t^T dr_u = \int_t^T \left(\kappa(\widetilde{\theta} - r_u) \right) du + \alpha \int_t^T d\widetilde{W}_u^r$$

$$r_T = r_t = \kappa\widetilde{\theta}(T-t) - \kappa \int_t^T r_u \, du + \alpha \int_t^T d\widetilde{W}_u^r$$

which we finally have

$$-\int_t^T r_u \, du = \frac{1}{\kappa}(r_T - r_t) - \widetilde{\theta}(T-t) - \frac{\alpha}{\kappa} \int_t^T d\widetilde{W}_u^r.$$

From Problem 3.2.2.10 of *Problems and Solutions of Mathematical Finance 1: Stochastic Calculus*, we can write

$$r_T = r_t e^{-\kappa(T-t)} + \widetilde{\theta}\left(1 - e^{-\kappa(T-t)}\right) + \int_t^T \alpha e^{-\kappa(T-u)} d\widetilde{W}_u^r$$

and substituting it to the above equation

$$-\int_t^T r_u \, du = r_t \left(\frac{1 - e^{-\kappa(T-t)}}{\kappa} \right) + \widetilde{\theta}\left(\frac{1 - e^{-\kappa(T-t)}}{\kappa} - T + t \right)$$

$$+ \frac{\alpha}{k} \int_t^T \left(e^{-\kappa(T-u)} - 1 \right) d\widetilde{W}_u^r$$

or

$$-\int_t^T r_u\, du = -r_t B(t,T) + \widetilde{\theta}\left(B(t,T) - T + t\right)$$

$$+\frac{\alpha}{k}\int_t^T \left(e^{-\kappa(T-u)} - 1\right) d\widetilde{W}_u^r$$

where $B(t,T) = \dfrac{1}{\kappa}\left(1 - e^{-\kappa(T-t)}\right)$.

Taking mean, we have

$$\mathbb{E}^{\mathbb{Q}}\left[-\int_t^T r_u\, du\,\middle|\, \mathcal{F}_t\right] = -r_t B(t,T) + \widetilde{\theta}\left(B(t,T) - T + t\right)$$

since

$$\mathbb{E}^{\mathbb{Q}}\left[\frac{\alpha}{k}\int_t^T \left(e^{-\kappa(T-u)} - 1\right) d\widetilde{W}_u^r\,\middle|\, \mathcal{F}_t\right] = 0$$

and variance,

$$\text{Var}^{\mathbb{Q}}\left[-\int_t^T r_u\, du\,\middle|\, \mathcal{F}_t\right] = \left(\frac{\alpha}{k}\right)^2 \mathbb{E}^{\mathbb{Q}}\left[\left[\int_t^T \left(e^{-\kappa(T-s)} - 1\right) d\widetilde{W}_s^r\right]^2\,\middle|\, \mathcal{F}_t\right]$$

$$= \left(\frac{\alpha}{k}\right)^2 \mathbb{E}^{\mathbb{Q}}\left[\int_t^T \left(e^{-\kappa(T-u)} - 1\right)^2 du\,\middle|\, \mathcal{F}_t\right]$$

$$= -\left(\frac{\alpha}{k}\right)^2 \left(\frac{1 - e^{-\kappa(T-t)}}{\kappa} - T + t\right)$$

$$-\frac{\alpha^2}{2\kappa}\left(\frac{1}{\kappa^2} + \frac{e^{-2\kappa(T-t)}}{\kappa^2} - \frac{2e^{-\kappa(T-t)}}{\kappa^2}\right)$$

$$= -\left(\frac{\alpha}{k}\right)^2 \left(B(t,T) - T + t\right) - \frac{\alpha^2}{2\kappa}B(t,T)^2.$$

Since $r_T \sim \mathcal{N}\left(r_t e^{-\kappa(T-t)} + \widetilde{\theta}\left(1 - e^{-\kappa(T-t)}\right), \dfrac{\alpha^2}{\kappa}\left[1 - e^{-2\kappa(T-t)}\right]\right)$, we can deduce that

$$-\int_t^T r_u\, du \sim \mathcal{N}\left(-r_t B(t,T) + \widetilde{\theta}\left(B(t,T) - T + t\right),\right.$$

$$\left.-\left(\frac{\alpha}{k}\right)^2 \left(B(t,T) - T + t\right) - \frac{\alpha^2}{2\kappa}B(t,T)^2\right).$$

Thus,

$$P(t,T) = \mathbb{E}^{\mathbb{Q}} \left[e^{-\int_t^T r_u du} \middle| \mathscr{F}_T \right]$$

$$= e^{-r_t B(t,T) + \widetilde{\theta}(B(t,T) - T + t) - \frac{1}{2}\left(\frac{\alpha}{k}\right)^2 (B(t,T) - T + t) - \frac{\alpha^2}{4\kappa} B(t,T)^2}$$

$$= e^{A(t,T) - r_t B(t,T)}$$

where

$$A(t,T) = \left(\widetilde{\theta} - \frac{1}{2}\left(\frac{\alpha}{\kappa}\right)^2 \right) (B(t,T) - T + t) - \frac{\alpha^2}{4\kappa} B(t,T)^2$$

and

$$B(t,T) = \frac{1}{\kappa}\left(1 - e^{-\kappa(T-t)} \right).$$

Thus, the volatility of the zero-coupon bond is given as

$$\sigma_p(t,T) = \alpha \frac{\partial P}{\partial r_t} P(t,T)^{-1}$$

$$= -\alpha B(t,T)$$

$$= -\frac{\alpha}{\kappa}\left(1 - e^{-\kappa(T-t)} \right).$$

(e) Under the risk-neutral measure $\mathbb{Q}$, the discounted zero-coupon bond $B_t^{-1} P(t,T)$ is a $\mathbb{Q}$-martingale. Hence, we can deduce

$$\frac{d\left(B_t^{-1} P(t,T)\right)}{B_t^{-1} P(t,T)} = \frac{dP(t,T)}{P(t,T)} - \frac{dB_t}{B_t} - \frac{dP(t,T)}{P(t,T)}\frac{dB_t}{B_t} + \left(\frac{dB_t}{B_t}\right)^2$$

$$= r_t dt + \sigma_p(t,T) d\widetilde{W}_t^r - r_t dt$$

$$= \sigma_p(t,T) d\widetilde{W}_t^r$$

is a $\mathbb{Q}$-martingale.

From Itō's formula,

$$d\left(\log\left(B_t^{-1} P(t,T)\right)\right) = \frac{d\left(B_t^{-1} P(t,T)\right)}{B_t^{-1} P(t,T)} - \frac{1}{2}\left(\frac{d\left(B_t^{-1} P(t,T)\right)}{B_t^{-1} P(t,T)}\right)^2 + \dots$$

$$= \sigma_p(t,T) d\widetilde{W}_t^r - \frac{1}{2}\sigma_p(t,T)^2 dt$$

and solving the differential equation we have

$$\log\left(\frac{B_t^{-1} P(t,T)}{B_0^{-1} P(0,T)}\right) = \int_0^t \sigma_p(u,T)\, d\widetilde{W}_u^r - \frac{1}{2}\int_0^t \sigma_p(u,T)^2\, du$$

or

$$\frac{B_t^{-1} P(t,T)}{B_0^{-1} P(0,T)} = e^{\int_0^t \sigma_p(u,T) d\widetilde{W}_t^r - \frac{1}{2} \int_0^t \sigma_p(u,T)^2 du}$$

where $B_0 = 1$.

From Girsanov's theorem, we can define a T-forward measure $\mathbb{Q}_T$, given by the Radon-Nikodým derivative

$$
\begin{aligned}
\frac{d\mathbb{Q}_T}{d\mathbb{Q}}\bigg|_{\mathcal{F}_t} &= \frac{P(t,T)}{P(0,T)} \bigg/ \frac{B_t}{B_0} \\
&= \frac{B_t^{-1} P(t,T)}{B_0^{-1} P(0,T)} \\
&= e^{-\int_0^t (-\sigma_p(u,T)) d\widetilde{W}_u^r - \frac{1}{2} \int_0^t \sigma_p(u,T)^2 du}
\end{aligned}
$$

so that $\widehat{W}_t^r = \widetilde{W}_t^r - \int_0^t \sigma_p(u,T)\, du$ is a $\mathbb{Q}_T$-standard Wiener process.

In a similar vein, we can also set

$$\widetilde{W}_t^r = \rho \widetilde{W}_t^S + \sqrt{1-\rho^2}\, \widetilde{Z}_t$$

where $\widetilde{W}_t^S$ and $\widetilde{Z}_t$ are $\mathbb{Q}$-standard Wiener processes and $\widetilde{W}_t^S \perp \widetilde{Z}_t$.

Thus, we can write

$$
\begin{aligned}
dP(t,T) &= r_t P(t,T) dt + \sigma_p(t,T) P(t,T) d\widetilde{W}_t^r \\
&= r_t P(t,T) dt + \sigma_p(t,T) P(t,T) \left(\rho d\widetilde{W}_t^S + \sqrt{1-\rho^2} d\widetilde{Z}_t \right)
\end{aligned}
$$

and we can deduce

$$
\begin{aligned}
d\left(\log\left(B_t^{-1} P(t,T)\right)\right) &= \frac{d\left(B_t^{-1} P(t,T)\right)}{B_t^{-1} P(t,T)} - \frac{1}{2}\left(\frac{d\left(B_t^{-1} P(t,T)\right)}{B_t^{-1} P(t,T)}\right)^2 + \dots \\
&= \rho \sigma_p(t,T) d\widetilde{W}_t^S - \frac{1}{2}\rho^2 \sigma_p(t,T)^2 dt \\
&\quad + \sqrt{1-\rho^2}\, \sigma_p(t,T) d\widetilde{Z}_t - \frac{1}{2}(1-\rho^2)\sigma_p(t,T)^2 dt
\end{aligned}
$$

and hence

$$
\begin{aligned}
\frac{B_t^{-1} P(t,T)}{B_0^{-1} P(0,T)} = {}& e^{\int_0^t \rho\sigma_p(u,T) d\widetilde{W}_t^S - \frac{1}{2}\int_0^t \rho^2 \sigma_p(u,T)^2 du} \\
& \times e^{\int_0^t \sqrt{1-\rho^2}\sigma_p(u,T) d\widetilde{Z}_t - \frac{1}{2}\int_0^t (1-\rho^2)\sigma_p(u,T)^2 du}.
\end{aligned}
$$

From the two-dimensional Girsanov's theorem, there exist a T-forward measure $\mathbb{Q}_T$ on the filtration $\mathscr{F}_s$, $0 \leq s \leq t$ defined by the Radon-Nikodým process,

$$\frac{d\mathbb{Q}_T}{d\mathbb{Q}} = e^{-\int_0^t (-\rho\sigma_p(u,T))d\widetilde{W}_u^S - \frac{1}{2}\int_0^t \rho^2 \sigma_p(u,T)^2 du}$$

$$\times e^{-\int_0^t (-\sqrt{1-\rho^2}\sigma_p(u,T))d\widetilde{Z}_u - \frac{1}{2}\int_0^t (1-\rho^2)\sigma_p(u,T)^2 du}$$

so that $\widehat{W}_t^S = \widetilde{W}_t^S - \int_0^t \rho\sigma_p(u,T)\,du$ and $\widehat{Z}_t = \widetilde{Z}_t - \int_0^t \sqrt{1-\rho^2}\sigma_p(u,T)\,du$ are $\mathbb{Q}_T$-standard Wiener processes and $\widehat{W}_t^S \perp\!\!\!\perp \widehat{Z}_t$.

Hence, under the $\mathbb{Q}_T$ measure,

$$\frac{dS_t}{S_t} = (r_t - D_t)dt + \sigma_t\left(d\widehat{W}_t^S + \rho\sigma_p(t,T)dt\right)$$

$$= \left(r_t - D_t + \rho\sigma_t\sigma_p(t,T)\right)dt + \sigma_t d\widehat{W}_t^S,$$

$$\frac{dP(t,T)}{P(t,T)} = r_t dt + \sigma_p(t,T)\left(d\widehat{W}_t^r + \sigma_p(t,T)dt\right)$$

$$= \left(r_t + \sigma_p(t,T)^2\right)dt + \sigma_p(t,T)d\widehat{W}_t^r$$

and

$$dr_t = \left(\kappa(\theta - r_t) - \alpha\gamma_t\right)dt + \alpha\left(d\widehat{W}_t^r + \sigma_p(t,T)dt\right)$$

$$= \left(\kappa(\theta - r_t) + \alpha(\sigma_p(t,T) - \gamma_t)\right)dt + \alpha d\widehat{W}_t^r.$$

(f) Under the change of numéraire for a payoff $\Psi(S_T)$

$$N_t^{(1)}\mathbb{E}^{\mathbb{Q}^{(1)}}\left[\left.\frac{\Psi(S_T)}{N_T^{(1)}}\right|\mathscr{F}_t\right] = N_t^{(2)}\mathbb{E}^{\mathbb{Q}^{(2)}}\left[\left.\frac{\Psi(S_T)}{N_T^{(2)}}\right|\mathscr{F}_t\right]$$

where for $i = 1, 2$, $N^{(i)}$ is a numéraire and $\mathbb{Q}^{(i)}$ is the measure under which the asset prices discounted by $N^{(i)}$ are $\mathbb{Q}^{(i)}$-martingales.

Under the risk-neutral measure $\mathbb{Q}$ we have

$$N_t^{(1)} = e^{\int_0^t r_u du} \quad \text{and} \quad N_T^{(1)} = e^{\int_0^T r_u du}$$

and under the T-forward measure $\mathbb{Q}_T$

$$N_t^{(2)} = P(t,T) \quad \text{and} \quad N_T^{(2)} = P(T,T) = 1.$$

Hence, with the change of numéraire from the risk-neutral measure $\mathbb{Q}$ to the T-forward measure $\mathbb{Q}_T$, the European call option price at time t under stochastic interest rate is

$$
\begin{aligned}
C_{\mathrm{stochIR}}(S_t, r_t, t; K, T) &= \mathbb{E}^{\mathbb{Q}}\left[e^{-\int_t^T r_u du} \max\{S_T - K, 0\} \middle| \mathscr{F}_t \right] \\
&= e^{\int_0^t r_u du} \mathbb{E}^{\mathbb{Q}}\left[\frac{\max\{S_T - K, 0\}}{e^{\int_0^T r_u du}} \middle| \mathscr{F}_t \right] \\
&= P(t,T) \mathbb{E}^{\mathbb{Q}_T}\left[\frac{\max\{S_T - K, 0\}}{P(T,T)} \middle| \mathscr{F}_t \right] \\
&= P(t,T) \mathbb{E}^{\mathbb{Q}_T}\left[\max\left\{ \frac{S_T}{P(T,T)} - K, 0 \right\} \middle| \mathscr{F}_t \right].
\end{aligned}
$$

From Itô's formula,

$$
\begin{aligned}
\frac{d\left(P(t,T)^{-1}S_t\right)}{P(t,T)^{-1}S_t} &= \frac{dS_t}{S_t} - \frac{dP(t,T)}{P(t,T)} - \left(\frac{dS_t}{S_t}\right)\left(\frac{dP(t,T)}{P(t,T)}\right) + \left(\frac{dP(t,T)}{P(t,T)}\right)^2 \\
&= \left(r_t - D_t + \rho\sigma_t\sigma_p(t,T)\right)dt + \sigma_t d\widehat{W}_t^S \\
&\quad - \left(r_t + \sigma_p(t,T)^2\right)dt - \sigma_p(t,T)d\widehat{W}_t^r - \rho\sigma_t\sigma_p(t,T)dt \\
&\quad + \sigma_p(t,T)^2 dt \\
&= -D_t dt + \sigma_t d\widehat{W}_t^S - \sigma_p(t,T)d\widehat{W}_t^r \\
&= -D_t dt + \sigma(t,T)d\widehat{V}_t
\end{aligned}
$$

where

$$
\sigma(t,T) = \sqrt{\sigma_t^2 + \sigma_p(t,T)^2 - 2\rho\sigma_t\sigma_p(t,T)}
$$

and

$$
d\widehat{V}_t = \frac{\sigma_t d\widehat{W}_t^S - \sigma_p(t,T)d\widehat{W}_t^r}{\sqrt{\sigma_t^2 + \sigma_p(t,T)^2 - 2\rho\sigma_t\sigma_p(t,T)}}
$$

is a $\mathbb{Q}_T$-standard Wiener process.

Hence, by solving the geometric Brownian motion process,

$$
\log\left(\frac{P(T,T)^{-1}S_T}{P(t,T)^{-1}S_t} \right) \sim \mathcal{N}\left(-\int_t^T \left(D_u + \frac{1}{2}\sigma(u,T)^2\right) du, \int_t^T \sigma(u,T)^2\, du \right).
$$

Following Problem 1.2.2.7 of *Problems and Solutions in Mathematical Finance, Stochastic Calculus, Volume 1*, the European call option price at time t under stochastic interest rate is

$$C_{\text{stochIR}}(S_t, r_t, t; K, T) = S_t e^{-\int_t^T D_u du} \Phi(d_+) - K P(t,T) \Phi(d_-)$$

where

$$d_\pm = \frac{\log\left(S_t/(P(t,T)K)\right) - \int_t^T \left(D_u \mp \frac{1}{2}\sigma(u,T)^2\right) du}{\sqrt{\int_t^T \sigma(u,T)^2\, du}},$$

$$\sigma(t,T) = \sqrt{\sigma_t^2 + \sigma_p(t,T) - 2\rho\sigma_t\sigma_p(t,T)}$$

and

$$\sigma_p(t,T) = -\frac{\alpha}{\kappa}\left(1 - e^{-\kappa(T-t)}\right).$$

$\square$

34. *European Option Price Under Stochastic Interest Rate II.* Let $\{W_t^S : t \geq 0\}$ and $\{W_t^r : t \geq 0\}$ be $\mathbb{P}$-standard Wiener processes on the probability space $(\Omega, F, \mathbb{P})$ and let the asset price S_t have the following diffusion process

$$\frac{dS_t}{S_t} = (\mu_t - D_t)dt + \sigma_t dW_t^S$$

where μ_t, D_t and σ_t are time-dependent drift, continuous dividend yield and volatility functions and the risk-free interest rate r_t is assumed to follow an Ornstein-Uhlenbeck process (or Vasicek process in the interest-rate modelling world)

$$dr_t = \kappa(\theta - r_t)dt + \alpha dW_t^r$$

where κ, θ and α are constant parameters. In addition, we assume W_t^S and W_t^r are correlated with coefficient $\rho \in (-1, 1)$,

$$dW_t^S \cdot dW_t^r = \rho dt.$$

Assume that in the market there is a family of tradeable, risk-free zero-coupon bonds whose price at time t is $P(t,T)$ where they deliver a unit of currency at maturity T, $P(T,T) = 1$. The zero-coupon bond has the process

$$\frac{dP(t,T)}{P(t,T)} = \mu_p(t,T)dt + \sigma_p(t,T)dW_t^r$$

where $\mu_p(t,T)$ is the drift and $\sigma_p(t,T)$ is the volatility

(a) By considering a hedging portfolio involving an option $V(S_t, r_t, t)$ under stochastic interest rate which can only be exercised on the option expiry time $T > t$, a risky asset S_t and a zero-coupon bond $P(t, T)$ show that $V(S_t, r_t, t)$ satisfies the following PDE

$$\frac{\partial V}{\partial t} + \frac{1}{2}\sigma_t^2 S_t^2 \frac{\partial^2 V}{\partial S_t^2} + \frac{1}{2}\alpha^2 \frac{\partial^2 V}{\partial r_t^2} + \rho\alpha\sigma_t S_t \frac{\partial^2 V}{\partial S_t \partial r_t} + (r_t - D_t)S_t \frac{\partial V}{\partial S_t}$$

$$+ \left(\kappa(\theta - r_t) - \alpha\gamma_t\right)\frac{\partial V}{\partial r_t} - r_t V(S_t, r_t, t) = 0$$

with boundary condition

$$V(S_T, r_T, T) = \Psi(S_T)$$

where $\gamma_t = \dfrac{\mu_p(t, T) - r_t}{\sigma_p(t, T)}$ is the market price of risk of the interest rate and $\Psi(S_T)$ is the option payoff.

(b) Using Itō's formula, show that the zero-coupon bond price $P(t, T)$ satisfies the following PDE

$$\frac{\partial P}{\partial t} + \frac{1}{2}\alpha^2 \frac{\partial^2 P}{\partial r_t^2} + \left(\kappa(\theta - r_t) - \alpha\gamma_t\right)\frac{\partial P}{\partial r_t} - r_t P(t, T) = 0$$

with boundary condition

$$P(T, T) = 1.$$

(c) Assuming $\gamma_t = \gamma$ where γ is a constant value, $\tilde{\theta} = \theta - \dfrac{\alpha\gamma}{\kappa}$ and writing the price of a zero-coupon bond maturing at time T in the affine function form

$$P(t, T) = e^{A(t,T) - r_t B(t,T)}$$

with boundary conditions

$$A(T, T) = 0, \quad B(T, T) = 0$$

find the functions of $A(t, T)$ and $B(t, T)$ by solving the PDE satisfied by $P(t, T)$. Hence, show the volatility of the zero-coupon bond to be

$$\sigma_p(t, T) = -\frac{\alpha}{\kappa}\left(1 - e^{-\kappa(T-t)}\right).$$

(d) To reduce the dimensionality of the PDE satisfied by $V(S_t, r_t, t)$, let

$$\hat{S}_t = \frac{S_t}{P(t, T)} \quad \text{and} \quad \hat{V}(\hat{S}_t, t) = \frac{V(S_t, r_t, t)}{P(t, T)}$$

and using the zero-coupon bond price PDE, show that $\widehat{V}(\widehat{S}_t, t)$ satisfies

$$\frac{\partial \widehat{V}}{\partial t} + \frac{1}{2}\sigma(t,T)^2 \widehat{S}_t \frac{\partial^2 \widehat{V}}{\partial \widehat{S}_t^2} - D_t \widehat{S}_t \frac{\partial \widehat{V}_t}{\partial \widehat{S}_t} = 0$$

with boundary condition

$$\widehat{V}(\widehat{S}_t, T) = \Psi(\widehat{S}_T)$$

where $\sigma(t,T) = \sqrt{\sigma_t^2 + \sigma_p(t,T)^2 - 2\rho\sigma_t\sigma_p(t,T)}$ and $\Psi(\widehat{S}_T) = \dfrac{\Psi(S_T)}{P(T,T)}$.

(e) Finally, for a payoff

$$\Psi(S_T) = \max\left\{ K - S_T, 0 \right\}$$

deduce that the European put option price with strike price K under stochastic interest rate is

$$P_{\text{stochIR}}(S_t, r_t, t; K, T) = KP(t,T)\Phi(-d_-) - S_t e^{-\int_t^T D_u du}\Phi(-d_+)$$

where

$$d_\pm = \frac{\log\left(S_t/(P(t,T)K)\right) - \displaystyle\int_t^T \left(D_u \mp \frac{1}{2}\sigma(u,T)^2\right) du}{\sqrt{\int_t^T \sigma(u,T)^2\, du}},$$

$$\sigma(t,T) = \sqrt{\sigma_t^2 + \sigma_p(t,T)^2 - 2\rho\sigma_t\sigma_p(t,T)},$$

$$\sigma_p(t,T) = -\frac{\alpha}{\kappa}\left(1 - e^{-\kappa(T-t)}\right)$$

and

$$\Phi(x) = \int_{-\infty}^x \frac{1}{\sqrt{2\pi}} e^{-\frac{1}{2}u^2}\, du.$$

Solution:

(a) We let the portfolio at time t be

$$\Pi_t = V(S_t, r_t, t) - \Delta_1 S_t - \Delta_2 P(t,T)$$

where it consists of purchasing one unit of option, and selling Δ_1 and Δ_2 units of risky asset S_t and zero-coupon bond $P(t,T)$ respectively. Since the holder of the portfolio receives $D_t S_t dt$ for every asset held and because the investor holds $-\Delta_1 S_t$, the portfolio changes by an amount $-\Delta_1 D_t S_t dt$ and therefore the change in portfolio Π_t is

$$
\begin{aligned}
d\Pi_t &= dV - \Delta_1(dS_t + D_t S_t dt) - \Delta_2 dP(t, T) \\
&= dV - \Delta_1 dS_t - \Delta_1 D_t S_t dt - \Delta_2 dP(t, T) \\
&= dV - \Delta_1 \left(\mu_t S_t dt + \sigma_t S_t dW_t^S \right) \\
&\quad -\Delta_2 \left(\mu_p(t, T) P(t, T) dt + \sigma_p(t, T) P(t, T) dW_t^r \right) \\
&= dV - \left(\Delta_1 \mu_t S_t + \Delta_2 \mu_p(t, T) P(t, T) \right) dt - \Delta_1 \sigma_t S_t dW_t^S \\
&\quad -\Delta_2 \sigma_p(t, T) P(t, T) dW_t^r.
\end{aligned}
$$

Expanding $V(S_t, r_t, t)$ using Taylor's theorem

$$
\begin{aligned}
dV &= \frac{\partial V}{\partial t} dt + \frac{\partial V}{\partial S_t} dS_t + \frac{\partial V}{\partial r_t} dr_t + \frac{1}{2} \frac{\partial^2 V}{\partial t^2} (dt)^2 + \frac{1}{2} \frac{\partial^2 V}{\partial S_t^2} (dS_t)^2 \\
&\quad + \frac{1}{2} \frac{\partial^2 V}{\partial r_t^2} (dr_t)^2 + \frac{\partial^2 V}{\partial t \partial S_t} (dt)(dS_t) + \frac{\partial^2 V}{\partial t \partial r_t} (dt)(dr_t) \\
&\quad + \frac{\partial^2 V}{\partial S_t \partial r_t} (dS_t)(dr_t) + \dots
\end{aligned}
$$

and substituting $dS_t = (\mu_t - D_t) S_t dt + \sigma_t S_t dW_t^S$ and $dr_t = \kappa(\theta - r_t) + \alpha dW_t^r$, and applying Itō's lemma,

$$
\begin{aligned}
dV &= \left(\frac{\partial V}{\partial t} + \frac{1}{2} \sigma_t^2 S_t^2 \frac{\partial^2 V}{\partial S_t^2} + \frac{1}{2} \alpha^2 \frac{\partial^2 V}{\partial r_t^2} + \rho \alpha \sigma_t S_t \frac{\partial^2 V}{\partial S_t \partial r_t} \right. \\
&\quad \left. + (\mu_t - D_t) S_t \frac{\partial V}{\partial S_t} + \kappa(\theta - r_t) \frac{\partial V}{\partial r_t} \right) dt + \sigma_t S_t \frac{\partial V}{\partial S_t} dW_t^S + \alpha \frac{\partial V}{\partial r_t} dW_t^r.
\end{aligned}
$$

Substituting back into $d\Pi_t$ and rearranging the terms, we have

$$
\begin{aligned}
d\Pi_t &= \left(\frac{\partial V}{\partial t} + \frac{1}{2} \sigma_t^2 S_t^2 \frac{\partial^2 V}{\partial S_t^2} + \frac{1}{2} \alpha^2 \frac{\partial^2 V}{\partial r_t^2} + \rho \alpha \sigma_t S_t \frac{\partial^2 V}{\partial S_t \partial r_t} \right. \\
&\quad \left. + (\mu_t - D_t) S_t \frac{\partial V}{\partial S_t} + \kappa(\theta - r_t) \frac{\partial V}{\partial r_t} - \Delta_1 \mu_t S_t - \Delta_2 \mu_p(t, T) P(t, T) \right) dt \\
&\quad + \sigma_t S_t \left(\frac{\partial V}{\partial S_t} - \Delta_1 \right) dW_t^S + \left(\alpha \frac{\partial V}{\partial r_t} - \Delta_2 \sigma_p(t, T) P(t, T) \right) dW_t^r.
\end{aligned}
$$

To eliminate the random components, we set

$$
\Delta_1 = \frac{\partial V}{\partial S_t} \quad \text{and} \quad \Delta_2 = \alpha \sigma_p(t, T)^{-1} P(t, T)^{-1} \frac{\partial V}{\partial r_t}
$$

leading to

$$
d\Pi_t = \left[\frac{\partial V}{\partial t} + \frac{1}{2}\sigma_t^2 S_t^2 \frac{\partial^2 V}{\partial S_t^2} + \frac{1}{2}\alpha^2 \frac{\partial^2 V}{\partial r_t^2} + \rho\alpha\sigma_t S_t \frac{\partial^2 V}{\partial S_t \partial r_t} - D_t S_t \frac{\partial V}{\partial S_t} \right.
$$
$$
\left. + \left(\kappa(\theta - r_t) - \alpha \frac{\mu_p(t,T)}{\sigma_p(t,T)} \right) \frac{\partial V}{\partial r_t} \right] dt.
$$

Under no arbitrage condition, the return on the amount Π_t invested in a interest rate would see a growth of

$$
d\Pi_t = r_t \Pi_t dt
$$

and hence we have

$$
r_t \left(V(S_t, r_t, t) - S_t \frac{\partial V}{\partial S_t} - \frac{\alpha}{\sigma_p(t,T)} \frac{\partial V}{\partial r_t} \right) dt
$$
$$
= \left[\frac{\partial V}{\partial t} + \frac{1}{2}\sigma_t^2 S_t^2 \frac{\partial^2 V}{\partial S_t^2} + \frac{1}{2}\alpha^2 \frac{\partial^2 V}{\partial r_t^2} + \rho\alpha\sigma_t S_t \frac{\partial^2 V}{\partial S_t \partial r_t} - D_t S_t \frac{\partial V}{\partial S_t} \right.
$$
$$
\left. + \left(\kappa(\theta - r_t) - \alpha \frac{\mu_p(t,T)}{\sigma_p(t,T)} \right) \frac{\partial V}{\partial r_t} \right] dt.
$$

Removing dt and rearranging the terms we finally have the Black-Scholes equation under stochastic interest rate

$$
\frac{\partial V}{\partial t} + \frac{1}{2}\sigma_t^2 S_t^2 \frac{\partial^2 V}{\partial S_t^2} + \frac{1}{2}\alpha^2 \frac{\partial^2 V}{\partial r_t^2} + \rho\alpha\sigma_t S_t \frac{\partial^2 V}{\partial S_t \partial r_t} + (r_t - D_t)S_t \frac{\partial V}{\partial S_t}
$$
$$
+ \left(\kappa(\theta - r_t) - \alpha\gamma_t \right) \frac{\partial V}{\partial r_t} - r_t V(S_t, r_t, t) = 0
$$

with boundary condition

$$
V(S_T, r_T, T) = \Psi(S_T)
$$

where $\gamma_t = \dfrac{\mu_p(t,T) - r_t}{\sigma_p(t,T)}$ is the market price of risk of the interest rate.

(b) To find the PDE satisfied by the zero-coupon bond $P(t,T)$, from Taylor's theorem

$$
dP(t,T) = \frac{\partial P}{\partial t}dt + \frac{\partial P}{\partial r_t}dr_t + \frac{1}{2}\frac{\partial^2 P}{\partial r_t^2}(dr_t)^2 + \dots
$$

and substituting $dr_t = \kappa(\theta - r_t)dt + \alpha dW_t^r$ and using Itō's formula

$$
dP(t,T) = \left(\frac{\partial P}{\partial t} + \frac{1}{2}\alpha^2 \frac{\partial^2 P}{\partial r_t^2} + \kappa(\theta - r_t)\frac{\partial P}{\partial r_t} \right) dt + \alpha \frac{\partial P}{\partial r_t}dW_t^r.
$$

By equating coefficients with $dP(t,T) = \mu_p(t,T)P(t,T)dt + \sigma_p(t,T)P(t,T)dW_t^r$ we have

$$\mu_p(t,T) = \left(\frac{\partial P}{\partial t} + \frac{1}{2}\alpha^2 \frac{\partial^2 P}{\partial r_t^2} + \kappa(\theta - r_t)\frac{\partial P}{\partial r_t} \right) P(t,T)^{-1}$$

and

$$\sigma_p(t,T) = \alpha P(t,T)^{-1}\frac{\partial P}{\partial r_t}.$$

Substituting the expressions of $\mu_p(t,T)$ and $\sigma_p(t,T)$ into the market price of risk formula

$$\gamma_t = \frac{\mu_p(t,T) - r_t}{\sigma_p(t,T)}$$

we will have

$$\frac{\partial P}{\partial t} + \frac{1}{2}\alpha^2\frac{\partial^2 P}{\partial r_t^2} + \left(\kappa(\theta - r_t) - \alpha\gamma_t \right)\frac{\partial P}{\partial r_t} - r_t P(t,T) = 0$$

with boundary condition

$$P(T,T) = 1.$$

(c) By setting $\gamma_t = \gamma$ where γ is a constant value and writing $\widetilde{\theta} = \theta - \dfrac{\alpha\gamma}{\kappa}$, we therefore have

$$\frac{\partial P}{\partial t} + \frac{1}{2}\alpha^2\frac{\partial^2 P}{\partial r_t^2} + \left(\kappa(\widetilde{\theta} - r_t) \right)\frac{\partial P}{\partial r_t} - r_t P(t,T) = 0$$

with boundary condition

$$P(T,T) = 1.$$

By substituting

$$\frac{\partial P}{\partial t} = \left(\frac{\partial A}{\partial t} - r_t\frac{\partial B}{\partial t} \right)P(t,T), \quad \frac{\partial P}{\partial r_t} = -B(t,T)P(t,T), \quad \frac{\partial^2 P}{\partial r_t^2} = B(t,T)^2 P(t,T)$$

into the PDE and equating coefficients we eventually have

$$\frac{\partial B}{\partial t} = \kappa B(t,T) - 1$$

$$\frac{\partial A}{\partial t} = \kappa\widetilde{\theta}B(t,T) - \frac{1}{2}\alpha^2 B(t,T)^2.$$

Solving $\dfrac{\partial B}{\partial t} - \kappa B(t,T) = -1$ we let the integrating factor be $I = e^{-\kappa t}$, and thus

$$\frac{d}{dt}\left(e^{-\kappa t}B(t,T)\right) = -e^{-\kappa t}$$

$$e^{-\kappa t}B(t,T) = \frac{e^{-\kappa t}}{\kappa} + C$$

where C is a constant.

At time $t = T$, $B(T,T) = 0$ and hence $C = -\dfrac{e^{-\kappa T}}{\kappa}$. Thus,

$$B(t,T) = \frac{1}{\kappa}\left(1 - e^{-\kappa(T-t)}\right).$$

Solving $\dfrac{\partial A}{\partial t} = \kappa\widetilde{\theta}B(t,T) - \dfrac{1}{2}\alpha^2 B(t,T)^2$ and because $A(T,T) = 0$, we have

$$A(t,T) = \frac{1}{2}\alpha^2\int_t^T B(u,T)\,du - \kappa\widetilde{\theta}\int_t^T B(u,T)\,du.$$

Since

$$\int_t^T B(u,T)\,du = \frac{1}{\kappa}\int_t^T \left(1 - e^{-\kappa(T-u)}\right)du$$

$$= \frac{1}{\kappa}\left(T - t - \frac{1}{\kappa}\left(1 - e^{-\kappa(T-t)}\right)\right)$$

$$= \frac{1}{\kappa}\left(T - t - B(t,T)\right)$$

and

$$\int_t^T B(u,T)^2\,du = \frac{1}{\kappa^2}\int_t^T \left(1 - 2e^{-\kappa(T-u)} + e^{2\kappa(T-u)}\right)du$$

$$= \frac{1}{\kappa^2}\left(T - t - 2B(t,T)\right) + \frac{1}{2\kappa}\left(\frac{1 - e^{-2\kappa(T-t)}}{\kappa^2}\right)$$

$$= \frac{1}{\kappa^2}\left(T - t - B(t,T) - \frac{\kappa}{2}B(t,T)^2\right)$$

we have

$$A(t,T) = \frac{1}{2}\left(\frac{\alpha}{\kappa}\right)^2\left(T - t - B(t,T) - \frac{\kappa}{2}B(t,T)^2\right) - \widetilde{\theta}\left(T - t - B(t,T)\right)$$

$$= \left(\widetilde{\theta} - \frac{1}{2}\left(\frac{\alpha}{\kappa}\right)^2\right)\left(B(t,T) - T + t\right) - \frac{\alpha^2}{4\kappa}B(t,T)^2.$$

Therefore, the bond price is

$$P(t, T) = e^{A(t,T) - r_t B(t,T)}$$

where

$$A(t, T) = \left(\tilde{\theta} - \frac{1}{2} \left(\frac{\alpha}{\kappa} \right)^2 \right) (B(t, T) - T + t) - \frac{\alpha^2}{4\kappa} B(t, T)^2$$

and

$$B(t, T) = \frac{1}{\kappa} \left(1 - e^{-\kappa(T-t)} \right).$$

Furthermore, the volatility of the zero-coupon bond is given as

$$\sigma_p(t, T) = \alpha \frac{\partial P}{\partial r_t} P(t, T)^{-1}$$

$$= -\alpha B(t, T)$$

$$= -\frac{\alpha}{\kappa} \left(1 - e^{-\kappa(T-t)} \right).$$

(d) By setting

$$\widehat{S}_t = \frac{S_t}{P(t, T)} \quad \text{and} \quad \widehat{V}(\widehat{S}_t, t) = \frac{V(S_t, r_t, t)}{P(t, T)}$$

we have the following

$$\frac{\partial V}{\partial t} = \widehat{V}(\widehat{S}_t, t) \frac{\partial P}{\partial t} + P(t, T) \frac{\partial \widehat{V}}{\partial t} + \frac{\partial \widehat{V}}{\partial \widehat{S}_t} \frac{\partial \widehat{S}_t}{\partial t} P(t, T)$$

$$= \widehat{V}(\widehat{S}_t, t) \frac{\partial P}{\partial t} + P(t, T) \frac{\partial \widehat{V}}{\partial t} - \frac{S_t}{P(t, T)^2} \frac{\partial \widehat{V}}{\partial \widehat{S}_t} \frac{\partial P}{\partial t} P(t, T)$$

$$= \widehat{V}(\widehat{S}_t, t) \frac{\partial P}{\partial t} + P(t, T) \frac{\partial \widehat{V}}{\partial t} - \widehat{S}_t \frac{\partial \widehat{V}}{\partial \widehat{S}_t} \frac{\partial P}{\partial t},$$

$$\frac{\partial V}{\partial S_t} = \frac{\partial \widehat{V}}{\partial \widehat{S}_t} \frac{\partial \widehat{S}_t}{\partial S_t} P(t, T) = \frac{\partial \widehat{V}}{\partial \widehat{S}_t},$$

$$\frac{\partial^2 V}{\partial S_t^2} = \frac{\partial}{\partial S_t} \left(\frac{\partial \widehat{V}}{\partial \widehat{S}_t} \right) = \frac{\partial^2 \widehat{V}}{\partial \widehat{S}_t^2} \frac{\partial \widehat{S}_t}{\partial S_t} = \frac{1}{P(t, T)} \frac{\partial^2 \widehat{V}}{\partial \widehat{S}_t^2},$$

$$\frac{\partial V}{\partial r_t} = P(t,T)\frac{\partial \widehat{V}}{\partial \widehat{S}_t}\frac{\partial \widehat{S}_t}{\partial r_t} + \widehat{V}(\widehat{S}_t,t)\frac{\partial P}{\partial r_t}$$

$$= -P(t,T)\frac{\partial \widehat{V}}{\partial \widehat{S}_t}\frac{S_t}{P(t,T)^2}\frac{\partial P}{\partial r_t} + \widehat{V}(\widehat{S}_t,t)\frac{\partial P}{\partial r_t}$$

$$= -\widehat{S}_t\frac{\partial \widehat{V}}{\partial \widehat{S}_t}\frac{\partial P}{\partial r_t} + \widehat{V}(\widehat{S}_t,t)\frac{\partial P}{\partial r_t},$$

$$\frac{\partial^2 V}{\partial S_t \partial r_t} = \frac{\partial^2 V}{\partial r_t \partial S_t} = \frac{\partial}{\partial r_t}\left(\frac{\partial \widehat{V}}{\partial \widehat{S}_t}\right) = \frac{\partial^2 \widehat{V}}{\partial \widehat{S}_t^2}\frac{\partial \widehat{S}_t}{\partial r_t} = -\frac{\widehat{S}_t}{P(t,T)}\frac{\partial^2 \widehat{V}}{\partial \widehat{S}_t^2}\frac{\partial P}{\partial r_t},$$

$$\frac{\partial^2 V}{\partial r_t^2} = -\frac{\partial \widehat{S}_t}{\partial r_t}\frac{\partial \widehat{V}}{\partial \widehat{S}_t}\frac{\partial P}{\partial r_t} - \widehat{S}_t\frac{\partial^2 V}{\partial r_t \partial \widehat{S}_t}\frac{\partial P}{\partial r_t} - \widehat{S}_t\frac{\partial \widehat{V}}{\partial \widehat{S}_t}\frac{\partial^2 P}{\partial r_t^2} + \frac{\partial \widehat{V}}{\partial \widehat{S}_t}\frac{\partial \widehat{S}_t}{\partial r_t}\frac{\partial P}{\partial r_t}$$

$$+ \widehat{V}(\widehat{S}_t,t)\frac{\partial^2 P}{\partial r_t^2}$$

$$= -\left(\frac{\partial \widehat{S}_t}{\partial P}\frac{\partial P}{\partial r_t}\right)\frac{\partial \widehat{V}}{\partial \widehat{S}_t}\frac{\partial P}{\partial r_t} + \frac{\widehat{S}_t^2}{P(t,T)}\frac{\partial^2 \widehat{V}}{\partial \widehat{S}_t^2}\left(\frac{\partial P}{\partial r_t}\right)^2 - \widehat{S}_t\frac{\partial \widehat{V}}{\partial \widehat{S}_t}\frac{\partial^2 P}{\partial r_t^2}$$

$$+ \frac{\partial \widehat{V}}{\partial \widehat{S}_t}\left(\frac{\partial \widehat{S}_t}{\partial P}\frac{\partial P}{\partial r_t}\right)\frac{\partial P}{\partial r_t} + \widehat{V}(\widehat{S}_t,t)\frac{\partial^2 P}{\partial r_t^2}$$

$$= \frac{\widehat{S}_t^2}{P(t,T)}\frac{\partial^2 \widehat{V}}{\partial \widehat{S}_t^2}\left(\frac{\partial P}{\partial r_t}\right)^2 - \widehat{S}_t\frac{\partial \widehat{V}}{\partial \widehat{S}_t}\frac{\partial^2 P}{\partial r_t^2} + \widehat{V}(\widehat{S}_t,t)\frac{\partial^2 P}{\partial r_t^2}.$$

Substituting the above expressions into the Black-Scholes model under stochastic interest rate, dividing it by $P(t,T)$ and taking note that $\sigma_p(t,T) = \alpha P(t,T)^{-1}\frac{\partial P}{\partial r_t}$, we will eventually have

$$\frac{\partial \widehat{V}}{\partial t} + \frac{1}{2}\left(\sigma_t^2 + \sigma_p(t,T)^2 - 2\rho\sigma_t\sigma_p(t,T)\right)\widehat{S}_t^2\frac{\partial^2 \widehat{V}}{\partial \widehat{S}_t^2} - D_t\widehat{S}_t\frac{\partial \widehat{V}}{\partial \widehat{S}_t}$$

$$+ \left(\frac{\partial P}{\partial t} + \frac{1}{2}\alpha^2\frac{\partial^2 P}{\partial r_t^2} + \left(\kappa(\theta - r_t) - \alpha\gamma_t\right)\frac{\partial P}{\partial r_t} - r_t P(t,T)\right)\frac{\widehat{V}(\widehat{S}_t,t)}{P(t,T)}$$

$$- \left(\frac{\partial P}{\partial t} + \frac{1}{2}\alpha^2\frac{\partial^2 P}{\partial r_t^2} + \left(\kappa(\theta - r_t) - \alpha\gamma_t\right)\frac{\partial P}{\partial r_t} - r_t P(t,T)\right)\frac{\widehat{S}_t}{P(t,T)}\frac{\partial \widehat{V}}{\partial \widehat{S}_t} = 0.$$

Since

$$\frac{\partial P}{\partial t} + \frac{1}{2}\alpha^2\frac{\partial^2 P}{\partial r_t^2} + \left(\kappa(\theta - r_t) - \alpha\gamma_t\right)\frac{\partial P}{\partial r_t} - r_t P(t,T) = 0$$

therefore we have the reduced Black-Scholes equation of the form

$$\frac{\partial \widehat{V}}{\partial t} + \frac{1}{2}\sigma(t,T)^2 \widehat{S}_t^2 \frac{\partial^2 \widehat{V}}{\partial \widehat{S}_t^2} - D_t \widehat{S}_t \frac{\partial \widehat{V}}{\partial \widehat{S}_t} = 0$$

with boundary condition

$$\widehat{V}(\widehat{S}_T, T) = \Psi(\widehat{S}_T)$$

where

$$\sigma(t,T)^2 = \sigma_t^2 + \sigma_p(t,T)^2 - 2\rho\sigma_t\sigma_p(t,T) \quad \text{and} \quad \Psi(\widehat{S}_T) = \frac{\Psi(S_T)}{P(T,T)}.$$

(e) By writing $\widehat{P}_{bs}(\widehat{S}_t, t; K, T)$ as the European put option price at time t satisfying the reduced Black-Scholes equation with payoff

$$\widehat{P}_{bs}(\widehat{S}_T, T; K, T) = \frac{1}{P(T,T)} \max\{K - S_T, 0\} = \max\{K - \widehat{S}_T\}$$

where $\widehat{S}_T = \dfrac{S_T}{P(T,T)}$, $P(T,T) = 1$, K is the strike price and $T > t$, then the solution can be deduced as

$$\widehat{P}_{bs}(\widehat{S}_t, t; K, T) = K\Phi(-d_-) - \widehat{S}_t e^{-\int_t^T D_u du} \Phi(-d_+)$$

$$d_\pm = \frac{\log(\widehat{S}_t/K) - \int_t^T \left(D_u \mp \frac{1}{2}\sigma(u,T)^2\right) du}{\sqrt{\int_t^T \sigma(u,T)^2 \, du}}.$$

Hence, by setting back $\widehat{S}_t = P(t,T)^{-1} S_t$, the European put option price at time t under stochastic interest rate, $P_{\text{stochIR}}(S_t, r_t, t; K, T)$ is

$$P_{\text{stochIR}}(S_t, r_t, t; K, T) = P(t,T)\widehat{P}_{bs}(\widehat{S}_t, t; K, T)$$

$$= KP(t,T)\Phi(-d_-) - \widehat{S}_t P(t,T) e^{-\int_t^T D_u du} \Phi(-d_+)$$

$$= KP(t,T)\Phi(-d_-) - S_t e^{-\int_t^T D_u du} \Phi(-d_+)$$

where

$$d_\pm = \frac{\log\left(S_t/(P(t,T)K)\right) - \int_t^T \left(D_u \mp \frac{1}{2}\sigma(u,T)^2\right) du}{\sqrt{\int_t^T \sigma(u,T)^2 \, du}},$$

$$\sigma(t,T) = \sqrt{\sigma_t^2 + \sigma_p(t,T) - 2\rho\sigma_t\sigma_p(t,T)},$$

and

$$\sigma_p(t,T) = -\frac{\alpha}{\kappa}\left(1 - e^{-\kappa(T-t)}\right).$$

$\square$

2.2.3 Tree-Based Methods

1. *Risk-Neutral Approach.* At time t, the value of the stock is S_t and at time $T > t$, the price has moved to either uS_t or dS_t, $0 < d < u$. We assume under continuous compounding that there is a risk-free interest rate r and the stock pays a continuous dividend yield D where it follows a GBM process

$$\frac{dS_t}{S_t} = (\mu - D)dt + \sigma dW_t$$

such that μ is the drift, σ is the volatility and $\{W_t : t \geq 0\}$ is the $\mathbb{P}$-standard Wiener process on the probability space $(\Omega, \mathcal{F}, \mathbb{P})$.

Suppose $0 < d < e^{(r-D)(T-t)} < u$, show that the risk-neutral probabilities for upward and downward movement of the stock price are

$$\pi = \frac{e^{(r-D)(T-t)} - d}{u - d} \quad \text{and} \quad 1 - \pi = \frac{u - e^{(r-D)(T-t)}}{u - d}$$

respectively.

Prove that $0 < \pi < 1$.

Hence, find the market price of a European call option $V(S_t, t; K, T)$ which expires at time T with strike price K.

Solution: We first need to find the risk-neutral probabilities π, $1 - \pi$ for upward/downward movement of the stock price where, under the risk-neutral probability measure $\mathbb{Q}$

$$\mathbb{E}^{\mathbb{Q}}\left(S_T \mid S_t\right) = S_t e^{(r-D)(T-t)}.$$

Since the stock price would grow to either uS_t with probability π or dS_t with probability $1 - \pi$, we therefore have

$$\pi u S_t + (1 - \pi)dS_t = S_t e^{(r-D)(T-t)}$$

such that

$$\pi = \frac{e^{(r-D)(T-t)} - d}{u - d} \quad \text{and} \quad 1 - \pi = \frac{u - e^{(r-D)(T-t)}}{u - d}.$$

Since $0 < d < e^{(r-D)(T-t)} < u$ we have

$$e^{(r-D)(T-t)} - d > 0 \quad \text{and} \quad u - d > 0$$

and hence, $\pi > 0$. In addition, because $0 < e^{(r-D)(T-t)} - d < u - d$, therefore $\pi < 1$. Hence, the European call option price at time t is

$$V(S_t, t; K, T) = e^{-r(T-t)} \mathbb{E}^{\mathbb{Q}} \left[\max \left\{ S_T - K, 0 \right\} \middle| S_t \right]$$
$$= e^{-r(T-t)} \left[\pi \max \left\{ S_T - K, 0 \right\} + (1 - \pi) \max \left\{ S_T - K, 0 \right\} \right]$$
$$= e^{-r(T-t)} \left[\left(\frac{e^{(r-D)(T-t)} - d}{u - d} \right) \max \left\{ u S_t - K, 0 \right\} \right.$$
$$\left. + \left(\frac{u - e^{(r-D)(T-t)}}{u - d} \right) \max \left\{ d S_t - K, 0 \right\} \right].$$

$\square$

2. *Self-Financing Trading Strategy Approach.* At time t, the value of the stock is S_t and at time $T > t$, the price has moved to either uS_t or dS_t, $0 < d < u$. We assume under continuous compounding that there is a risk-free interest rate r and the stock pays a continuous dividend yield D.

Suppose $0 < d < e^{(r-D)(T-t)} < u$. Denoting $V(S_t, t; K, T)$ as the market price of a European put option which expires at time T with strike price K, show by setting up a portfolio

$$V(S_t, t; K, T) = \phi_t S_t + \psi_t$$

where ϕ_t is the number of units of S_t and ψ_t is the amount of cash invested in the money market that

$$\phi_t = e^{-D(T-t)} \left[\frac{V(uS_t, T) - V(dS_t, T)}{(u - d)S_t} \right]$$

and

$$\psi_t = e^{-r(T-t)} \left[\frac{uV(dS_t, T) - dV(uS_t, T)}{u - d} \right].$$

Hence, find the price of a European put option $V(S_t, t; K, T)$ which expires at time T with strike price K.

Solution: At time t, the portfolio is worth

$$V(S_t, t; K, T) = \phi_t S_t + \psi_t$$

where ϕ_t is the number of units of S_t and ψ_t is the amount of cash invested in the money market.

Given that S_t pays a continuous dividend yield D, then at time T the number of stocks and the amount of cash will grow to $\phi_t e^{D(T-t)}$ and $\psi_t e^{r(T-t)}$, respectively. Because S_T can either be $S_T = uS_t$ or $S_T = dS_t$, we can write

$$V(uS_t, T; K, T) = \phi_t e^{D(T-t)} uS_t + \psi_t e^{r(T-t)}$$

and

$$V(dS_t, T; K, T) = \phi_t e^{D(T-t)} dS_t + \psi_t e^{r(T-t)}.$$

Hence, by solving the two equations we have

$$\phi_t = e^{-D(T-t)} \left[\frac{V(uS_t, T; K, T) - V(dS_t, T; K, T)}{(u-d)S_t} \right]$$

and

$$\begin{aligned} \psi_t &= e^{-r(T-t)}(V(uS_t, T; K, T) - \phi_t e^{D(T-t)} uS_t) \\ &= e^{-r(T-t)} \left[\frac{uV(dS_t, T; K, T) - dV(uS_t, T; K, T)}{u-d} \right]. \end{aligned}$$

Finally, because

$$V(uS_t, T; K, T) = \max\{K - uS_t, 0\} \text{ and } V(dS_t, T; K, T) = \max\{K - dS_t, 0\}$$

therefore

$$\begin{aligned} V(S_t, t; K, T) &= \phi_t S_t + \psi_t \\ &= e^{-r(T-t)} \left[\left(\frac{e^{(r-D)(T-t)} - d}{u-d} \right) \max\{K - uS_t, 0\} \right. \\ &\qquad + \left. \left(\frac{u - e^{(r-D)(T-t)}}{u-d} \right) \max\{K - dS_t, 0\} \right]. \end{aligned}$$

$\square$

3. By referring to Problems 2.2.3.1 and 2.2.3.2 explain why, when we drop the assumption $0 < d < e^{(r-D)(T-t)} < u$, there is an arbitrage opportunity.

Solution: To show that there is an arbitrage opportunity if we drop the assumption $0 < d < e^{(r-D)(T-t)} < u$ we first assume $d \geq e^{(r-D)(T-t)}$ then, at time t, a speculator can borrow from the money market in order to buy stock worth S_t. At time T, the stock price is worth either uS_t or dS_t which is enough to pay off the money-market debt since $u > d \geq e^{(r-D)(T-t)}$. Hence, this provides an arbitrage.

In contrast, if $u \leq e^{(r-D)(T-t)}$, a speculator can short sell the stock worth S_t at time t and invest the proceeds in the money market whilst paying dividends to the owner of the stock. By time T, the money invested is worth $S_t e^{(r-D)(T-t)}$ and by replacing the cost of

the stock, and since $d < u \le e^{(r-D)(T-t)}$, the profit would either be $S_t(e^{(r-D)(T-t)} - u) \ge 0$
or $S_t(e^{(r-D)(T-t)} - d) \ge 0$ which is also an arbitrage.

$\square$

4. *Cox–Ross–Rubinstein Method.* At time t, the value of the asset is S_t and at time $t + \Delta t$,
$\Delta t > 0$ the asset price is either increased to uS_t or decreased to dS_t, $0 < d < u$. In addition,
under continuous compounding there is a risk-free interest rate r and the asset pays a
continuous dividend yield D. By assuming the asset price follows the geometric Brownian
motion such that under the risk-neutral measure $\mathbb{Q}$

$$\log\left(\frac{S_{t+\Delta t}}{S_t}\right) \sim \mathcal{N}\left[\left(r - D - \frac{1}{2}\sigma^2\right)\Delta t, \sigma^2 \Delta t\right]$$

where σ is the asset price volatility, show by using the first two moments of $S_{t+\Delta t}$ given
S_t that

$$\pi u + (1 - \pi)d = e^{(r-D)\Delta t}$$
$$\pi u^2 + (1 - \pi)d^2 = e^{(2(r-D)+\sigma^2)\Delta t}$$

where π and $1 - \pi$ are the risk-neutral probabilities of upward and downward movement
of the asset price, respectively.

By setting $u = \frac{1}{d}$ show that

$$u = A + \sqrt{A^2 - 1}, \quad d = A - \sqrt{A^2 - 1} \quad \text{and} \quad \pi = \frac{e^{(r-D)\Delta t} - d}{u - d}$$

where $A = \frac{1}{2}\left[e^{-(r-D)\Delta t} + e^{(r-D+\sigma^2)\Delta t}\right]$.

By expanding u and d up to $\mathcal{O}(\Delta t)$ show that

$$u = e^{\sigma\sqrt{\Delta t}} \quad \text{and} \quad d = e^{-\sigma\sqrt{\Delta t}}$$

and to ensure $\pi, 1 - \pi \in (0, 1)$ deduce that

$$0 < \Delta t < \left(\frac{\sigma}{r - D}\right)^2.$$

Solution: Since $\log\left(\frac{S_{t+\Delta t}}{S_t}\right) \sim \mathcal{N}\left[\left(r - D - \frac{1}{2}\sigma^2\right)\Delta t, \sigma^2 \Delta t\right]$, therefore the expectation
and variance of $S_{t+\Delta t}$ given S_t are

$$\mathbb{E}^{\mathbb{Q}}\left(S_{t+\Delta t}\mid S_t\right) = S_t e^{(r-D)\Delta t}$$

and

$$\text{Var}^{\mathbb{Q}}\left(S_{t+\Delta t}\mid S_t\right) = S_t^2 e^{2(r-D)\Delta t}\left(e^{\sigma^2\Delta t} - 1\right).$$

Thus,

$$
\begin{aligned}
\mathbb{E}^{Q}\left(S_{t+\Delta t}^{2}\,\big|\,S_{t}\right) &= \mathrm{Var}^{Q}\left(S_{t+\Delta t}\,\big|\,S_{t}\right) + \left[\mathbb{E}^{Q}\left(S_{t+\Delta t}\,\big|\,S_{t}\right)\right]^{2} \\
&= S_{t}^{2}e^{2(r-D)\Delta t}\left(e^{\sigma^{2}\Delta t}-1\right) + S_{t}^{2}e^{2(r-D)\Delta t} \\
&= S_{t}^{2}e^{(2(r-D)+\sigma^{2})\Delta t}.
\end{aligned}
$$

As the asset price at time $t + \Delta t$ could grow to either uS_{t} or dS_{t} with risk-neutral proba-bilities π and $1 - \pi$, respectively, therefore

$$
\begin{aligned}
\mathbb{E}^{Q}\left(S_{t+\Delta t}\,\big|\,S_{t}\right) &= \pi uS_{t} + (1-\pi)dS_{t} \\
\mathbb{E}^{Q}\left(S_{t+\Delta t}^{2}\,\big|\,S_{t}\right) &= \pi u^{2}S_{t}^{2} + (1-\pi)d^{2}S_{t}^{2}.
\end{aligned}
$$

Hence, by equating the continuous risk-neutral random walk and the discrete binomial model we have

$$
\begin{aligned}
\pi u + (1-\pi)d &= e^{(r-D)\Delta t} \\
\pi u^{2} + (1-\pi)d^{2} &= e^{(2(r-D)+\sigma^{2})\Delta t}.
\end{aligned}
$$

From

$$
\pi u + (1-\pi)d = e^{(r-D)\Delta t}
$$

we have

$$
\pi = \frac{e^{(r-D)\Delta t} - d}{u - d}.
$$

In addition, because

$$
\pi u^{2} + (1-\pi)d^{2} = e^{(2(r-D)+\sigma^{2})\Delta t}
$$

we can also write

$$
\pi = \frac{e^{(2(r-D)+\sigma^{2})\Delta t} - d^{2}}{u^{2} - d^{2}}.
$$

Thus,

$$
\frac{e^{(r-D)\Delta t} - d}{u - d} = \frac{e^{(2(r-D)+\sigma^{2})\Delta t} - d^{2}}{u^{2} - d^{2}}
$$

or

$$
u + d = \frac{e^{(2(r-D)+\sigma^{2})\Delta t} - d^{2}}{e^{(r-D)\Delta t} - d}.
$$

By setting $u = \dfrac{1}{d}$,

$$\frac{1}{d} + d = \frac{e^{(2(r-D)+\sigma^2)\Delta t} - d^2}{e^{(r-D)\Delta t} - d}$$

or

$$d^2 - 2Ad + 1 = 0$$

where $A = \dfrac{1}{2}\left[e^{-(r-D)\Delta t} + e^{(r-D+\sigma^2)\Delta t}\right]$. Hence,

$$d = A \pm \sqrt{A^2 - 1}$$

and because $d < u$ we can therefore set

$$d = A - \sqrt{A^2 - 1} \quad \text{and} \quad u = A + \sqrt{A^2 - 1}.$$

From Taylor's theorem we can expand A and A^2 as

$$\begin{aligned}
A &= \frac{1}{2}\left[e^{-(r-D)\Delta t} + e^{(r-D+\sigma^2)\Delta t}\right] \\
&= \frac{1}{2}\left[1 - (r - D)\Delta t + 1 + (r - D + \sigma^2)\Delta t + \mathcal{O}(\Delta t^2)\right] \\
&= 1 + \frac{1}{2}\sigma^2 \Delta t + \mathcal{O}(\Delta t^2)
\end{aligned}$$

and

$$\begin{aligned}
A^2 &= \frac{1}{4}\left[e^{-(r-D)\Delta t} + e^{(r-D+\sigma^2)\Delta t}\right]^2 \\
&= \frac{1}{4}\left[e^{-2(r-D)\Delta t} + 2e^{\sigma^2 \Delta t} + e^{2(r-D+\sigma^2)\Delta t}\right] \\
&= \frac{1}{4}\left[1 - 2(r - D)\Delta t + 2(1 + \sigma^2 \Delta t) + 1 + 2(r - D + \sigma^2)\Delta t\right] + \mathcal{O}(\Delta t^2) \\
&= 1 + \sigma^2 \Delta t + \mathcal{O}(\Delta t^2).
\end{aligned}$$

Therefore,

$$d = 1 - \sigma\sqrt{\Delta t} + \mathcal{O}(\Delta t) \quad \text{and} \quad u = 1 + \sigma\sqrt{\Delta t} + \mathcal{O}(\Delta t)$$

or

$$d = e^{-\sigma\sqrt{\Delta t}} \quad \text{and} \quad u = e^{\sigma\sqrt{\Delta t}}$$

since the terms $1 - \sigma\sqrt{\Delta t} + \mathcal{O}(\Delta t)$ and $1 + \sigma\sqrt{\Delta t} + \mathcal{O}(\Delta t)$ agree with $e^{-\sigma\sqrt{\Delta t}}$ and $e^{\sigma\sqrt{\Delta t}}$ up to $\mathcal{O}(\Delta t)$, respectively.

Finally, to ensure

$$0 < \frac{e^{(r-D)\Delta t} - d}{u - d} < 1$$

or

$$0 < \frac{e^{(r-D)\Delta t} - e^{-\sigma\sqrt{\Delta t}}}{e^{\sigma\sqrt{\Delta t}} - e^{-\sigma\sqrt{\Delta t}}} < 1$$

and by solving the inequality we have

$$0 < \Delta t < \left(\frac{\sigma}{r - D}\right)^2.$$

□

5. *Jarrow–Rudd Method.* At time t, the value of the asset is S_t and at time $t + \Delta t$, $\Delta t > 0$ the asset price is either increased to uS_t or decreased to dS_t, $0 < d < u$. In addition, under continuous compounding there is a risk-free interest rate r and the asset pays a continuous dividend yield D. By assuming the asset price follows the geometric Brownian motion such that under the risk-neutral measure $\mathbb{Q}$

$$\log\left(\frac{S_{t+\Delta t}}{S_t}\right) \sim \mathcal{N}\left[\left(r - D - \frac{1}{2}\sigma^2\right)\Delta t, \sigma^2 \Delta t\right]$$

where σ is the asset price volatility, show by using the first two moments of $S_{t+\Delta t}$ given S_t that

$$\pi u + (1 - \pi)d = e^{(r-D)\Delta t}$$
$$\pi u^2 + (1 - \pi)d^2 = e^{(2(r-D)+\sigma^2)\Delta t}$$

where π and $1 - \pi$ are the risk-neutral probabilities of upward and downward movement of the asset price, respectively.

By setting $\pi = \frac{1}{2}$ show that

$$d = e^{(r-D)\Delta t}\left(1 - \sqrt{e^{\sigma^2\Delta t} - 1}\right) \quad \text{and} \quad u = e^{(r-D)\Delta t}\left(1 + \sqrt{e^{\sigma^2\Delta t} - 1}\right)$$

and to ensure $0 < d < e^{(r-D)\Delta t} < u$, deduce that

$$0 < \Delta t < \frac{\log 2}{\sigma^2}.$$

Solution: To show

$$\pi u + (1 - \pi)d = e^{(r-D)\Delta t}$$
$$\pi u^2 + (1 - \pi)d^2 = e^{(2(r-D)+\sigma^2)\Delta t}$$

see Problem 2.2.3.4 (page 193).

By setting $\pi = \dfrac{1}{2}$ we have

$$u + d = 2e^{(r-D)\Delta t}$$
$$u^2 + d^2 = 2e^{(2(r-D)+\sigma^2)\Delta t}$$

and letting $u = 2e^{(r-D)\Delta t} - 1$ we have

$$d^2 - 2e^{(r-D)\Delta t}d + 2e^{(r-D)\Delta t} - e^{(2(r-D)+\sigma^2)\Delta t}$$

or

$$d = e^{(r-D)\Delta t}\left(1 \pm \sqrt{e^{\sigma^2 \Delta t} - 1}\right).$$

Since $d < u$ we therefore have

$$d = e^{(r-D)\Delta t}\left(1 - \sqrt{e^{\sigma^2 \Delta t} - 1}\right) \quad \text{and} \quad u = e^{(r-D)\Delta t}\left(1 + \sqrt{e^{\sigma^2 \Delta t} - 1}\right).$$

Finally, to ensure that $0 < d < e^{(r-D)\Delta t} < u$,

$$0 < e^{(r-D)\Delta t}\left(1 - \sqrt{e^{\sigma^2 \Delta t} - 1}\right) < e^{(r-D)\Delta t}$$

and solving the inequality we eventually obtain

$$0 < \Delta t < \frac{\log 2}{\sigma^2}.$$

$\square$

6. *Boyle Method.* We consider a trinomial model where at time t, the value of the asset is S_t and at time $t + \Delta t$, $\Delta t > 0$ the asset price is increased to uS_t, unchanged S_t or decreased to dS_t, $0 < d < u$. In addition, under continuous compounding there is a risk-free interest rate r and the asset pays a continuous dividend yield D. By assuming the asset price follows the geometric Brownian motion such that under the risk-neutral measure $\mathbb{Q}$

$$\log\left(\frac{S_{t+\Delta t}}{S_t}\right) \sim \mathcal{N}\left[\left(r - D - \frac{1}{2}\sigma^2\right)\Delta t, \sigma^2 \Delta t\right]$$

where σ is the asset price volatility, show by using the first two moments of $S_{t+\Delta t}$ given S_t that

$$\pi_1 u + \pi_2 + \pi_3 d = e^{(r-D)\Delta t}$$
$$\pi_1 u^2 + \pi_2 + \pi_3 d^2 = e^{(2(r-D)+\sigma^2)\Delta t}$$
$$\pi_1 + \pi_2 + \pi_3 = 1$$

where π_1, π_2 and π_3 are the risk-neutral probabilities of upward, unchanged and downward movement of the asset price, respectively.

By setting $u = \dfrac{1}{d}$ and $u = e^{\lambda \sigma \sqrt{\Delta t}}$, $\lambda > 0$ show that

$$\pi_1 = \frac{\left(e^{(2(r-D)+\sigma^2)\Delta t} - e^{(r-D)\Delta t}\right) e^{\lambda \sigma \sqrt{\Delta t}} - \left(e^{(r-D)\Delta t} - 1\right)}{(e^{\lambda \sigma \sqrt{\Delta t}} - 1)(e^{2\lambda \sigma \sqrt{\Delta t}} - 1)}$$

$$\pi_3 = \frac{\left(e^{(2(r-D)+\sigma^2)\Delta t} - e^{(r-D)\Delta t}\right) e^{2\lambda \sigma \sqrt{\Delta t}} - \left(e^{(r-D)\Delta t} - 1\right) e^{3\lambda \sigma \sqrt{\Delta t}}}{(e^{\lambda \sigma \sqrt{\Delta t}} - 1)(e^{2\lambda \sigma \sqrt{\Delta t}} - 1)}$$

$$\pi_2 = 1 - \pi_1 - \pi_3.$$

Solution: Since $\log\left(\dfrac{S_{t+\Delta t}}{S_t}\right) \sim \mathcal{N}\left[\left(r - D - \dfrac{1}{2}\sigma^2\right)\Delta t, \sigma^2 \Delta t\right]$, the expectation and variance of $S_{t+\Delta t}$ given S_t are

$$\mathbb{E}^{\mathbb{Q}}\left(S_{t+\Delta t}\mid S_t\right) = S_t e^{(r-D)\Delta t}$$

and

$$\mathrm{Var}^{\mathbb{Q}}\left(S_{t+\Delta t}\mid S_t\right) = S_t^2 e^{2(r-D)\Delta t}\left(e^{\sigma^2 \Delta t} - 1\right).$$

Thus,

$$\begin{aligned}
\mathbb{E}^{\mathbb{Q}}\left(S_{t+\Delta t}^2\mid S_t\right) &= \mathrm{Var}^{\mathbb{Q}}\left(S_{t+\Delta t}\mid S_t\right) + \left[\mathbb{E}^{\mathbb{Q}}\left(S_{t+\Delta t}\mid S_t\right)\right]^2 \\
&= S_t^2 e^{2(r-D)\Delta t}\left(e^{\sigma^2 \Delta t} - 1\right) + S_t^2 e^{2(r-D)\Delta t} \\
&= S_t^2 e^{(2(r-D)+\sigma^2)\Delta t}.
\end{aligned}$$

As the asset price at time $t + \Delta t$ could grow to uS_t, S_t or dS_t with risk-neutral probabilities π_1, π_2 and π_3, respectively, therefore

$$\mathbb{E}^{\mathbb{Q}}\left(S_{t+\Delta t}\mid S_t\right) = \pi_1 u S_t + \pi_2 S_t + \pi_3 d S_t$$

$$\mathbb{E}^{\mathbb{Q}}\left(S_{t+\Delta t}^2\mid S_t\right) = \pi_1 u^2 S_t^2 + \pi_2 S_t^2 + \pi_3 d^2 S_t^2.$$

Hence, by equating the continuous risk-neutral random walk and the discrete binomial model, and with the sum of probabilities of all mutually exclusive events equal to one, we have

$$\pi_1 u + \pi_2 + \pi_3 d = e^{(r-D)\Delta t}$$

$$\pi_1 u^2 + \pi_2 + \pi_3 d^2 = e^{(2(r-D)+\sigma^2)\Delta t}$$

$$\pi_1 + \pi_2 + \pi_3 = 1.$$

By setting $d = \dfrac{1}{u}$ and $\pi_2 = 1 - \pi_1 - \pi_3$ we can write the equations as

$$\pi_1(u - 1) + \pi_3 \left(\frac{1}{u} - 1 \right) = e^{(r-D)\Delta t} - 1$$

$$\pi_1(u^2 - 1) + \pi_3 \left(\frac{1}{u^2} - 1 \right) = e^{(2(r-D)+\sigma^2)\Delta t} - 1$$

or

$$\pi_1 u(u - 1) - \pi_3(u - 1) = u \left(e^{(r-D)\Delta t} - 1 \right)$$

$$\pi_1 u^2 (u^2 - 1) - \pi_3(u^2 - 1) = u^2 \left(e^{(2(r-D)+\sigma^2)\Delta t} - 1 \right).$$

By solving the equations simultaneously we have

$$\pi_1 = \frac{\left(e^{(2(r-D)+\sigma^2)\Delta t} - e^{(r-D)\Delta t} \right) u - \left(e^{(r-D)\Delta t} - 1 \right)}{(u - 1)(u^2 - 1)}$$

$$\pi_3 = \frac{\left(e^{(2(r-D)+\sigma^2)\Delta t} - e^{(r-D)\Delta t} \right) u^2 - \left(e^{(r-D)\Delta t} - 1 \right) u^3}{(u - 1)(u^2 - 1)}.$$

Hence, by setting $u = e^{\lambda \sigma \sqrt{\Delta t}}$ we have

$$\pi_1 = \frac{\left(e^{(2(r-D)+\sigma^2)\Delta t} - e^{(r-D)\Delta t} \right) e^{\lambda \sigma \sqrt{\Delta t}} - \left(e^{(r-D)\Delta t} - 1 \right)}{(e^{\lambda \sigma \sqrt{\Delta t}} - 1)(e^{2\lambda \sigma \sqrt{\Delta t}} - 1)}$$

$$\pi_3 = \frac{\left(e^{(2(r-D)+\sigma^2)\Delta t} - e^{(r-D)\Delta t} \right) e^{2\lambda \sigma \sqrt{\Delta t}} - \left(e^{(r-D)\Delta t} - 1 \right) e^{3\lambda \sigma \sqrt{\Delta t}}}{(e^{\lambda \sigma \sqrt{\Delta t}} - 1)(e^{2\lambda \sigma \sqrt{\Delta t}} - 1)}$$

with $\pi_2 = 1 - \pi_1 - \pi_3$.

$\square$

7. *Kamrad–Ritchken Method.* We consider a trinomial model where at time t, the value of the asset is S_t and at time $t + \Delta t$, $\Delta t > 0$ the asset price is increased to uS_t, unchanged S_t or decreased to dS_t, $0 < d < u$. In addition, under continuous compounding there is a risk-free interest rate r and the asset pays a continuous dividend yield D. By assuming the asset price follows the geometric Brownian motion such that under the risk-neutral measure $\mathbb{Q}$

$$\log \left(\frac{S_{t+\Delta t}}{S_t} \right) \sim \mathcal{N} \left[\left(r - D - \frac{1}{2} \sigma^2 \right) \Delta t, \sigma^2 \Delta t \right]$$

where σ is the asset price volatility, show by using the first two moments of $\log\left(\dfrac{S_{t+\Delta t}}{S_t}\right)$ given S_t that

$$\pi_1 \log u + \pi_3 \log d = \left(r - D - \frac{1}{2}\sigma^2\right)\Delta t$$

$$\pi_1(\log u)^2 + \pi_3(\log d)^2 = \sigma^2\Delta t + \left(r - D - \frac{1}{2}\sigma^2\right)^2 (\Delta t)^2$$

$$\pi_1 + \pi_2 + \pi_3 = 1$$

where π_1, π_2 and π_3 are the risk-neutral probabilities of upward, unchanged and downward movement of the asset price, respectively.

By setting $u = \dfrac{1}{d}$ and $u = e^{\lambda\sigma\sqrt{\Delta t}}$, $\lambda > 0$ show by taking an approximation up to $\mathcal{O}(\Delta t)$ that

$$\pi_1 = \frac{1}{2\lambda^2} + \frac{1}{2\lambda\sigma}\left(r - D - \frac{1}{2}\sigma^2\right)\sqrt{\Delta t}$$

$$\pi_2 = 1 - \frac{1}{\lambda^2}$$

$$\pi_3 = \frac{1}{2\lambda^2} - \frac{1}{2\lambda\sigma}\left(r - D - \frac{1}{2}\sigma^2\right)\sqrt{\Delta t}.$$

Finally, to ensure $\pi_1, \pi_2, \pi_3 \in (0,1)$ deduce that

$$\lambda > 1 \quad \text{and} \quad 0 < \sqrt{\Delta t} < \frac{\sigma}{\lambda}\left(r - D - \frac{1}{2}\sigma^2\right)^{-1}.$$

Solution: Under the risk-neutral measure $\mathbb{Q}$

$$\log\left(\frac{S_{t+\Delta t}}{S_t}\right) \sim \mathcal{N}\left[\left(r - D - \frac{1}{2}\sigma^2\right)\Delta t, \sigma^2\Delta t\right]$$

and we therefore have

$$\mathbb{E}^{\mathbb{Q}}\left[\log\left(\frac{S_{t+\Delta t}}{S_t}\right)\bigg| S_t\right] = \left(r - D - \frac{1}{2}\sigma^2\right)\Delta t$$

$$\mathbb{E}^{\mathbb{Q}}\left[\left\{\log\left(\frac{S_{t+\Delta t}}{S_t}\right)\right\}^2\bigg| S_t\right] = \mathrm{Var}^{\mathbb{Q}}\left[\log\left(\frac{S_{t+\Delta t}}{S_t}\right)\bigg| S_t\right]$$

$$+ \mathbb{E}^{\mathbb{Q}}\left[\log\left(\frac{S_{t+\Delta t}}{S_t}\right)\bigg| S_t\right]^2$$

$$= \sigma^2\Delta t + \left(r - D - \frac{1}{2}\sigma^2\right)(\Delta t)^2.$$

By matching the expectations within the trinomial model we have

$$\pi_1 \log\left(\frac{uS_t}{S_t}\right) + \pi_2 \log\left(\frac{S_t}{S_t}\right) + \pi_3 \log\left(\frac{dS_t}{S_t}\right) = \left(r - D - \frac{1}{2}\sigma^2\right)\Delta t$$

$$\pi\left[\log\left(\frac{uS_t}{S_t}\right)\right]^2 + \pi_2\left[\log\left(\frac{S_t}{S_t}\right)\right]^2 + \pi_3\left[\log\left(\frac{dS_t}{S_t}\right)\right]^2$$

$$= \sigma^2\Delta t + \left(r - D - \frac{1}{2}\sigma^2\right)(\Delta t)^2$$

or

$$\pi_1 \log u + \pi_3 \log d = \left(r - D - \frac{1}{2}\sigma^2\right)\Delta t$$

$$\pi_1 (\log u)^2 + \pi_3 (\log d)^2 = \sigma^2\Delta t + \left(r - D - \frac{1}{2}\sigma^2\right)(\Delta t)^2$$

$$\pi_1 + \pi_2 + \pi_3 = 1.$$

By setting $d = \dfrac{1}{u}$ we can write

$$(\pi_1 - \pi_3) \log u = \left(r - D - \frac{1}{2}\sigma^2\right)\Delta t$$

$$(\pi_1 + \pi_3)(\log u)^2 = \sigma^2\Delta t + \left(r - D - \frac{1}{2}\sigma^2\right)(\Delta t)^2$$

and by substituting $u = e^{\lambda\sigma\sqrt{\Delta t}}$

$$\pi_1 - \pi_3 = \frac{1}{\lambda\sigma}\left(r - D - \frac{1}{2}\sigma^2\right)\sqrt{\Delta t}$$

$$\pi_1 + \pi_3 = \frac{1}{\lambda^2} + \frac{1}{\lambda^2\sigma^2}\left(r - D - \frac{1}{2}\sigma^2\right)\Delta t.$$

By solving the two equations simultaneously we have

$$\pi_1 = \frac{1}{2\lambda^2} + \frac{1}{2\lambda\sigma}\left(r - D - \frac{1}{2}\sigma^2\right)\sqrt{\Delta t} + \frac{1}{2\lambda^2\sigma^2}\left(r - D - \frac{1}{2}\sigma^2\right)^2\Delta t$$

$$\pi_2 = 1 - \frac{1}{\lambda^2}$$

$$\pi_3 = \frac{1}{2\lambda^2} - \frac{1}{2\lambda\sigma}\left(r - D - \frac{1}{2}\sigma^2\right)\sqrt{\Delta t} - \frac{1}{2\lambda^2\sigma^2}\left(r - D - \frac{1}{2}\sigma^2\right)^2\Delta t$$

since $\pi_2 = 1 - \pi_1 - \pi_3$.

Hence, by taking an approximation up to $\mathcal{O}(\Delta t)$

$$\pi_1 = \frac{1}{2\lambda^2} + \frac{1}{2\lambda\sigma}\left(r - D - \frac{1}{2}\sigma^2\right)\sqrt{\Delta t}$$

$$\pi_2 = 1 - \frac{1}{\lambda^2}$$

$$\pi_3 = \frac{1}{2\lambda^2} - \frac{1}{2\lambda\sigma}\left(r - D - \frac{1}{2}\sigma^2\right)\sqrt{\Delta t}.$$

To ensure $\pi_1, \pi_2, \pi_3 \in (0,1)$ we require

$$0 < 1 - \frac{1}{\lambda^2} < 1 \quad \text{and} \quad 0 < \frac{1}{2\lambda^2} \pm \frac{1}{2\lambda\sigma}\left(r - D - \frac{1}{2}\sigma^2\right)\sqrt{\Delta t} < 1$$

or

$$\lambda > 1 \quad \text{and} \quad 0 < \sqrt{\Delta t} < \frac{\sigma}{\lambda}\left(r - D - \frac{1}{2}\sigma^2\right)^{-1}.$$

$\square$

8. *Continuous-Time Limit of Binomial Model.* In a discrete Black–Scholes world we consider the binomial method to calculate the price of a European option. At time t where the current spot price is S_t, we build a binomial tree of possible scenarios of future stock prices

$$S_i^{(j)} = u^i d^{i-j} S_t, \quad i = 0, 1, 2, \ldots, N, \quad j = 0, 1, 2, \ldots, i$$

such that $S_0^{(0)} = S_t$, N is the total number of time intervals, $u = e^{\sigma\sqrt{\Delta t}}$, $d = e^{-\sigma\sqrt{\Delta t}}$, $\Delta t = (T - t)/N$ is the size of the binomial time step, T is the option expiry time and σ is the stock price volatility.

The intermediate option price calculated at the m-th possible tree value and at the time step $t + n\Delta t$ where $m \le n \le N$ is given as

$$V\left(S_n^{(m)}, t + n\Delta t\right) = e^{-r\Delta t}\left[\pi V\left(uS_n^{(m)}, t + (n+1)\Delta t\right) + (1 - \pi)V\left(dS_n^{(m)}, t + (n+1)\Delta t\right)\right]$$

where $\pi = \dfrac{e^{(r-D)\Delta t} - d}{u - d}$ is the risk-neutral probability, r is the risk-free interest rate and D is the continuous dividend yield.

By expanding the Taylor series up to $\mathcal{O}(\Delta t^2)$, show that in the limit $\Delta t \to 0$ the intermediate option price satisfies the Black–Scholes equation

$$\frac{\partial V}{\partial t'} + \frac{1}{2}\sigma^2 S^2 \frac{\partial^2 V}{\partial S^2} + (r - D)S\frac{\partial V}{\partial S} - rV(S, t') = 0$$

where $S = S_n^{(m)}$ and $t' = t + n\Delta t$.

Solution: By setting $S = S_n^{(m)}$ and $t' = t + n\Delta t$ then from Taylor's expansion we have

$$V(uS, t' + \Delta t) = V(S + (u - 1)S, t' + \Delta t)$$
$$= V(S, t') + \frac{\partial V}{\partial S}(u - 1)S + \frac{\partial V}{\partial t'}\Delta t + \frac{1}{2}\frac{\partial^2 V}{\partial S^2}(u - 1)^2 S^2$$
$$+ O\left((\Delta t)^2\right) + O\left((u - 1)^3 S^3\right)$$

and

$$V(dS, t' + \Delta t) = V(S + (d - 1)S, t' + \Delta t)$$
$$= V(S, t') + \frac{\partial V}{\partial S}(d - 1)S + \frac{\partial V}{\partial t'}\Delta t + \frac{1}{2}\frac{\partial^2 V}{\partial S^2}(d - 1)^2 S^2$$
$$+ O\left((\Delta t)^2\right) + O\left((d - 1)^3 S^3\right).$$

By substituting Taylor's expansion into the intermediate European option price

$$V\left(S, t'\right) = e^{-r\Delta t}\left[\pi V\left(uS, t' + \Delta t\right) + (1 - \pi)V\left(dS, t' + \Delta t\right)\right]$$

we can write

$$\pi V\left(uS, t' + \Delta t\right) + (1 - \pi)V\left(dS, t' + \Delta t\right) - e^{r\Delta t}V(S, t')$$
$$= \frac{\partial V}{\partial t'}\Delta t + \frac{1}{2}\left[\pi(u - 1)^2 + (1 - \pi)(d - 1)^2\right]S^2\frac{\partial^2 V}{\partial S^2}$$
$$+ \left[\pi(u - 1) + (1 - \pi)(d - 1)\right]S\frac{\partial V}{\partial S} + \left(1 - e^{r\Delta t}\right)V(S, t')$$
$$+ O\left((\Delta t)^2\right) + O\left((u - 1)^3 S^3\right) + O\left((d - 1)^3 S^3\right).$$

Since

$$1 - e^{r\Delta t} = -r\Delta t + O\left((\Delta t)^2\right)$$

$$\pi(u - 1) + (1 - \pi)(d - 1) = \pi(u - d) + d - 1$$
$$= e^{(r-D)\Delta t} - 1$$
$$= (r - D)\Delta t + O\left((\Delta t)^2\right)$$

$$\pi(u - 1)^2 + (1 - \pi)(d - 1)^2 = \pi\left[(u - 1)^2 - (d - 1)^2\right] + (d - 1)^2$$
$$= \pi(u - d)(u + d - 2) + (d - 1)^2$$
$$= \left(e^{(r-D)\Delta t} - 1\right)\left(e^{\sigma\sqrt{\Delta t}} + e^{-\sigma\sqrt{\Delta t}} - 2\right)$$
$$+ \left(e^{-\sigma\sqrt{\Delta t}} - 1\right)^2$$
$$= \sigma^2\Delta t + O\left((\Delta t)^2\right)$$

and because

$$O\left((u-1)^3 S^3\right) = O\left((\Delta t)^3\right), O\left((d-1)^3 S^3\right) = O\left((\Delta t)^3\right)$$

therefore

$$\pi V\left(uS, t' + \Delta t\right) + (1 - \pi)V\left(dS, t' + \Delta t\right) - e^{r\Delta t}V(S, t')$$

$$= \frac{\partial V}{\partial t'}\Delta t + \frac{1}{2}\sigma^2 S^2 \frac{\partial^2 V}{\partial S^2}\Delta t + (r - D)S\frac{\partial V}{\partial S}\Delta t - rV(S, t')\Delta t + O\left((\Delta t)^2\right)$$

$$= \left[\frac{\partial V}{\partial t'} + \frac{1}{2}\sigma^2 S^2 \frac{\partial^2 V}{\partial S^2} + (r - D)S\frac{\partial V}{\partial S} - rV(S, t') + O(\Delta t)\right]\Delta t.$$

Since

$$\pi V\left(uS, t' + \Delta t\right) + (1 - \pi)V\left(dS, t' + \Delta t\right) - e^{r\Delta t}V(S, t') = 0$$

hence we can set

$$\frac{\partial V}{\partial t'} + \frac{1}{2}\sigma^2 S^2 \frac{\partial^2 V}{\partial S^2} + (r - D)S\frac{\partial V}{\partial S} - rV(S, t') + O(\Delta t) = 0.$$

By taking limits $\Delta t \to 0$ we have

$$\frac{\partial V}{\partial t'} + \frac{1}{2}\sigma^2 S^2 \frac{\partial^2 V}{\partial S^2} + (r - D)S\frac{\partial V}{\partial S} - rV(S, t') = 0.$$

$\square$

9. In a discrete-time Black–Scholes world, we consider the binomial tree model to calculate the price of a European call option. At time t where the current spot price is S_t, we build a tree of possible scenarios of future stock prices

$$S_i^{(j)} = u^j d^{i-j} S_t, i = 0, 1, \ldots, n, \quad j = 0, 1, 2, \ldots, i$$

such that $S_0^{(0)} = S_t$, n is the total number of time periods, $u = e^{\sigma\sqrt{\Delta t}}$, $d = e^{-\sigma\sqrt{\Delta t}}$, $\Delta t = (T - t)/n$ is the time step, T is the option expiry date and σ is the stock price volatility. Here $S_i^{(j)}$ denotes the j-th possible value of the stock price at time period i (or time step $t + i\Delta t$).

Show that the European call option price with strike K at time t is

$$V(S_t, t; K, T) = e^{-nr\Delta t} \sum_{j=0}^{n} \binom{n}{j} \pi^j (1 - \pi)^{n-j} \max\{u^j d^{n-j} S_t - K, 0\}$$

where $\pi = \dfrac{e^{(r-D)\Delta t} - d}{u - d}$ is the risk-neutral probability, r is the risk-free interest rate and D is the continuous dividend yield.

Solution: We prove this result via mathematical induction.

Let $n = 1$ where at time $T = t + \Delta t$, S_T can either be uS_t or dS_t with risk-neutral probabilities π and $1 - \pi$, respectively. Following Problem 2.2.3.1 (page 190), the price of a European call option at time t under the risk-neutral measure $\mathbb{Q}$ is

$$V(S_t, t; K, T) = e^{-r\Delta t}\mathbb{E}^{\mathbb{Q}}\left(\max\{S_T - K, 0\}\big| S_t\right)$$
$$= e^{-r(T-t)}\left[\pi \max\{uS_t - K, 0\} + (1 - \pi)\max\{dS_t - K, 0\}\right].$$

Hence, the result is true for $n = 1$.

We assume the result is true for $n = k$ such that

$$V(S_t, t; K, T) = e^{-rk\Delta t}\sum_{j=0}^{k}\binom{k}{j}\pi^j(1 - \pi)^{k-j}\max\{u^j d^{k-j}S_t - K, 0\}$$

$$= e^{-rk\Delta t}\left[(1 - \pi)^k \max\{d^k S_t - K, 0\}\right.$$
$$+ k\pi(1 - \pi)^{k-1}\max\{ud^{k-1}S_t - K, 0\}$$
$$+ \frac{k(k-1)}{2}\pi^2(1 - \pi)^{k-2}\max\{u^2 d^{k-2}S_t - K, 0\}$$
$$\left. + \cdots + \pi^k \max\{u^k S_t - K, 0\}\right]$$

$$= e^{-rk\Delta t}\left[(1 - \pi)^k V(d^k S_t, t + k\Delta t; K, T)\right.$$
$$+ k\pi(1 - \pi)^{k-1}V(ud^{k-1}S_t, t + k\Delta t; K, T)$$
$$+ \frac{k(k-1)}{2}\pi^2(1 - \pi)^{k-2}V(u^2 d^{k-2}S_t, t + k\Delta t; K, T)$$
$$\left. + \cdots + \pi^k V(u^k S_t, t + k\Delta t; K, T)\right]$$

where $V(u^j d^{k-j}S_t, t + k\Delta t; K, T) = \max\{u^j d^{k-j} - K, 0\}$ is the option's intrinsic value at time step $t + k\Delta t$, $j = 0, 1, 2, \ldots, k$.

For $n = k + 1$ we then have $k + 1$ possible stock prices at time step $t + (k + 1)\Delta t$ where $S_{k+1}^{(0)} = d^{k+1}S_t$, $S_{k+1}^{(1)} = ud^k S_t$, $S_{(k+1)}^{(2)} = u^2 d^{k-1}S_t$, $\ldots$, $S_{k+1}^{(k+1)} = u^{k+1}S_t$. Therefore,

$$V(d^k S_t, t + k\Delta t; K, T) = e^{-r\Delta t}\left[\pi \max\{ud^k S_t - K, 0\}\right.$$
$$\left. + (1 - \pi)\max\{d^{k+1}S_t - K, 0\}\right]$$
$$V(ud^{k-1}S_t, t + k\Delta t; K, T) = e^{-r\Delta t}\left[\pi \max\{u^2 d^{k-1}S_t - K, 0\}\right.$$
$$\left. + (1 - \pi)\max\{ud^k S_t - K, 0\}\right]$$
$$V(u^2 d^{k-2}S_t, t + k\Delta t; K, T) = e^{-r\Delta t}\left[\pi \max\{u^3 d^{k-2}S_t - K, 0\}\right.$$
$$\left. + (1 - \pi)\max\{u^2 d^{k-1}S_t - K, 0\}\right]$$
$$\vdots \qquad \vdots$$
$$V(u^k S_t, t + k\Delta t; K, T) = e^{-r\Delta t}\left[\pi \max\{u^{k+1}S_t - K, 0\}\right.$$
$$\left. + (1 - \pi)\max\{u^k dS_t - K, 0\}\right]$$

and by substituting the values into

$$
\begin{aligned}
V(S_t,t;K,T) = e^{-rk\Delta t} \big[& (1-\pi)^k V(d^k S_t, t+k\Delta t; k,T) \\
& + k\pi(1-\pi)^{k-1} V(ud^{k-1} S_t, t+k\Delta t; K,T) \\
& + \frac{k(k-1)}{2}\pi^2(1-\pi)^{k-2} V(u^2 d^{k-2} S_t, t+k\Delta t; K,T) \\
& + \cdots + \pi^k V(u^k S_t, t+k\Delta t; K,T) \big]
\end{aligned}
$$

we have

$$
\begin{aligned}
V(S_t,t;K,T) = e^{-r(k+1)\Delta t} \big[& (1-\pi)^{k+1}(1-\pi)\max\{d^{k+1} S_t - K, 0\} \\
& + (k+1)\pi(1-\pi)^k \max\{ud^k S_t - K, 0\} \\
& + \frac{(k+1)k}{2}\pi^2(1-\pi)^{k-1}\max\{u^2 d^{k-1} S_t - K, 0\} \\
& + \cdots + \pi^{k+1}\max\{u^{k+1} S_t - K, 0\} \big] \\
= e^{-r(k+1)\Delta t} \sum_{j=0}^{k+1} & \binom{k+1}{j}\pi^j(1-\pi)^{k+1-j}\max\{u^j d^{k+1-j} S_t - K, 0\}.
\end{aligned}
$$

Hence, the result is also true for $n = k + 1$. Thus, from mathematical induction we can deduce that the European call option price with strike K at time t is

$$
V(S_t,t;K,T) = e^{-rn\Delta t} \sum_{j=0}^{n} \binom{n}{j}\pi^j(1-\pi)^{n-j}\max\{u^j d^{n-j} S_t - K, 0\}
$$

where $n\Delta t = T - t$.

$\square$

10. In a discrete-time Black–Scholes world, we consider the binomial tree model to calculate the price of a European call option. At time t where the current spot price is S_t, we build a tree of possible scenarios of future stock prices

$$
S_i^{(j)} = u^j d^{i-j} S_t, \quad i = 0, 1, \ldots, n, \quad j = 0, 1, 2, \ldots, i
$$

such that $S_0^{(0)} = S_t$, n is the total number of time periods, $u = e^{\sigma\sqrt{\Delta t}}$, $d = e^{-\sigma\sqrt{\Delta t}}$, $\Delta t = (T-t)/n$ is the time step, T is the option expiry date and σ is the stock price volatility. Here $S_i^{(j)}$ denotes the j-th possible value of the stock price at time period i (or time step $t + i\Delta t$).

Let the European call option price with strike K at time t be

$$
C(S_t,t;K,T) = e^{-nr\Delta t} \sum_{j=0}^{n} \binom{n}{j}\pi^j(1-\pi)^{n-j}\max\{u^j d^{n-j} S_t - K, 0\}
$$

where $\pi = \dfrac{e^{(r-D)\Delta t} - d}{u - d}$ is the risk-neutral probability, r is the risk-free interest rate and D is the continuous dividend yield. By setting

$$m = \frac{\log\left(\dfrac{K}{S_t d^n}\right)}{\log\left(\dfrac{u}{d}\right)}$$

show that $C(S_t, t; K, T)$ can be written as

$$C(S_t, t; K, T) = S_t e^{-D(T-t)} \sum_{j\geq m}^{n} \binom{n}{j} \widetilde{\pi}^j (1 - \widetilde{\pi})^{n-j}$$

$$-K e^{-r(T-t)} \sum_{j\geq m}^{n} \binom{n}{j} \pi^j (1 - \pi)^{n-j}$$

where $\widetilde{\pi} = \pi u e^{-(r-D)\Delta t}$.

Finally, from the asymptotic property of a binomial distribution $Z \sim \text{Binomial}(n, p)$, $0 \leq p \leq 1$

$$\lim_{n\to\infty} Z \doteq \mathcal{N}(np, np(1 - p))$$

show that

$$\lim_{n\to\infty} C(S_t, t; K, T) = S_t e^{-D(T-t)} \Phi(d_+) - K e^{-r(T-t)} \Phi(d_-)$$

where

$$d_\pm = \frac{\log(S_t/K) + (r - D \pm \frac{1}{2}\sigma^2)(T - t)}{\sigma\sqrt{T - t}}$$

and $\Phi(x)$ is the standard normal cdf

$$\Phi(x) = \int_{-\infty}^{x} \frac{1}{\sqrt{2\pi}} e^{-\frac{1}{2}u^2} du.$$

Solution: By writing $m = \dfrac{\log\left(\dfrac{K}{S_t d^n}\right)}{\log\left(\dfrac{u}{d}\right)}$ so that

$$\max\{u^j d^{n-j} S_t - K, 0\} = \begin{cases} 0 & j < m \\ u^j d^{n-j} S_t - K & j \geq m \end{cases}$$

and setting $n\Delta t = T - t$ we can write

$$
\begin{aligned}
C(S_t, t; K, T) &= e^{-r(T-t)} \sum_{j=0}^{n} \binom{n}{j} \pi^j (1 - \pi)^{n-j} \max\{u^j d^{n-j} S_t - K, 0\} \\
&= e^{-r(T-t)} \sum_{j \geq m}^{n} \binom{n}{j} \pi^j (1 - \pi)^{n-j} \left(u^j d^{n-j} S_t - K \right) \\
&= S_t e^{-r(T-t)} \sum_{j \geq m}^{n} \binom{n}{j} (\pi u)^j ((1 - \pi)d)^{n-j} \\
&\quad - K e^{-r(T-t)} \sum_{j \geq m}^{n} \binom{n}{j} \pi^j (1 - \pi)^{n-j} \\
&= S_t e^{-D(T-t)} \sum_{j \geq m}^{n} \binom{n}{j} \left(\pi u e^{-(r-D)\Delta t} \right)^j \left((1 - \pi)d e^{-(r-D)\Delta t} \right)^{n-j} \\
&\quad - K e^{-r(T-t)} \sum_{j \geq m}^{n} \binom{n}{j} \pi^j (1 - \pi)^{n-j}.
\end{aligned}
$$

By setting $\widetilde{\pi} = \pi u e^{-(r-D)\Delta t}$ therefore

$$
\begin{aligned}
1 - \widetilde{\pi} &= 1 - \pi u e^{-(r-D)\Delta t} \\
&= e^{-(r-D)\Delta t} \left(e^{(r-D)\Delta t} - \pi u \right) \\
&= e^{-(r-D)\Delta t} \left(\pi(u - d) + d - \pi u \right) \\
&= (1 - \pi)d e^{-(r-D)\Delta t}.
\end{aligned}
$$

Hence,

$$
\begin{aligned}
C(S_t, t; K, T) &= S_t e^{-D(T-t)} \sum_{j \geq m}^{n} \binom{n}{j} \widetilde{\pi}^j (1 - \widetilde{\pi})^{n-j} \\
&\quad - K e^{-r(T-t)} \sum_{j \geq m}^{n} \binom{n}{j} \pi^j (1 - \pi)^{n-j} \\
&= S_t e^{-D(T-t)} \mathbb{P}(X \geq m) - K e^{-r(T-t)} \mathbb{P}(Y \geq m)
\end{aligned}
$$

where $X \sim \text{Binomial}(n, \widetilde{\pi})$ and $Y \sim \text{Binomial}(n, \pi)$.

Since

$$
\lim_{n \to \infty} X \doteqdot \mathcal{N}(n\widetilde{\pi}, \widetilde{\pi}(1 - \widetilde{\pi})) \quad \text{and} \quad \lim_{n \to \infty} Y \doteqdot \mathcal{N}(n\pi, n\pi(1 - \pi))
$$

therefore

$$\lim_{n\to\infty} C(S_t, t; K, T) = S_t e^{-D(T-t)} \Phi\left(\frac{n\tilde{\pi} - m}{\sqrt{n\tilde{\pi}(1 - \tilde{\pi})}}\right) - K e^{-r(T-t)} \Phi\left(\frac{n\pi - m}{\sqrt{n\pi(1 - \pi)}}\right)$$

$$= S_t e^{-D(T-t)} \Phi\left(\frac{\log(S_t/K) + n\tilde{\pi} \log(u/d) + n \log d}{\log(u/d)\sqrt{n\tilde{\pi}(1 - \tilde{\pi})}}\right)$$

$$- K e^{-r(T-t)} \Phi\left(\frac{\log(S_t/K) + n\pi \log(u/d) + n \log d}{\log(u/d)\sqrt{n\pi(1 - \pi)}}\right).$$

From Taylor's expansion

$$e^{(r-D)\Delta t} = 1 + (r - D)\Delta t + \mathcal{O}\left((\Delta t)^2\right)$$

$$e^{-(r-D)\Delta t} = 1 - (r - D)\Delta t + \mathcal{O}\left((\Delta t)^2\right)$$

$$e^{\sigma\sqrt{\Delta t}} = 1 + \sigma\sqrt{\Delta t} + \frac{1}{2}\sigma^2\Delta t + \mathcal{O}\left((\Delta t)^{\frac{3}{2}}\right)$$

$$e^{-\sigma\sqrt{\Delta t}} = 1 - \sigma\sqrt{\Delta t} + \frac{1}{2}\sigma^2\Delta t + \mathcal{O}\left((\Delta t)^{\frac{3}{2}}\right)$$

and taking limits

$$\lim_{n\to\infty} n\left[\pi \log\left(\frac{u}{d}\right) + \log d\right] = \lim_{n\to\infty}\left[n\left(\frac{e^{(r-D)\Delta t} - d}{u - d}\right)\log\left(\frac{u}{d}\right) + n\log d\right]$$

$$= \lim_{n\to\infty} n\left(e^{(r-D)\Delta t} - e^{-\sigma\sqrt{\Delta t}}\right)\lim_{n\to\infty}\frac{2\sigma\sqrt{\Delta t}}{e^{\sigma\sqrt{\Delta t}} - e^{-\sigma\sqrt{\Delta t}}}$$

$$- \lim_{n\to\infty} n\sigma\sqrt{\Delta t}$$

$$= \lim_{n\to\infty}\left[n\left(r - D - \frac{1}{2}\sigma^2\right)\Delta t + n\sigma\sqrt{\Delta t} + n\mathcal{O}\left((\Delta t)^{\frac{3}{2}}\right)\right]$$

$$\times \lim_{n\to\infty}\frac{2\sigma\sqrt{\Delta t}}{2\sigma\sqrt{\Delta t} + \mathcal{O}(\Delta t)} - \lim_{n\to\infty} n\sigma\sqrt{\Delta t}$$

$$= \left(r - D - \frac{1}{2}\sigma^2\right)(T - t)$$

$$\lim_{n\to\infty} n\left[\tilde{\pi}\log\left(\frac{u}{d}\right) + \log d\right] = \lim_{n\to\infty}\left[n\pi u e^{-(r-D)\Delta t}\log\left(\frac{u}{d}\right) + n\log d\right]$$

$$= \lim_{n\to\infty}\left[n\left(\frac{e^{(r-D)\Delta t} - d}{u - d}\right)u e^{-(r-D)\Delta t}\log\left(\frac{u}{d}\right) + n\log d\right]$$

$$= \lim_{n\to\infty}\left[n\left(\frac{u - e^{-(r-D)\Delta t}}{u - d}\right)\log\left(\frac{u}{d}\right) + n\log d\right]$$

$$= \lim_{n\to\infty} n\left(e^{\sigma\sqrt{\Delta t}} - e^{-(r-D)\Delta t}\right)\lim_{n\to\infty}\frac{2\sigma\sqrt{\Delta t}}{e^{\sigma\sqrt{\Delta t}} - e^{-\sigma\sqrt{\Delta t}}}$$

$$- \lim_{n\to\infty} n\sigma\sqrt{\Delta t}$$

$$= \lim_{n\to\infty}\left[n\left(r - D + \frac{1}{2}\sigma^2\right)\Delta t + n\sigma\sqrt{\Delta t} + n\mathcal{O}\left((\Delta t)^{\frac{3}{2}}\right)\right]$$

$$\times \lim_{n\to\infty}\frac{2\sigma\sqrt{\Delta t}}{2\sigma\sqrt{\Delta t} + \mathcal{O}(\Delta t)} - \lim_{n\to\infty} n\sigma\sqrt{\Delta t}$$

$$= \left(r - D + \frac{1}{2}\sigma^2\right)(T - t)$$

$$\lim_{n\to\infty} n\pi(1 - \pi)\left[\log\left(\frac{u}{d}\right)\right]^2 = \lim_{n\to\infty} n\left(\frac{e^{(r-D)\Delta t} - d}{u - d}\right)\left(\frac{u - e^{(r-D)\Delta t}}{u - d}\right)\left[\log\left(\frac{u}{d}\right)\right]^2$$

$$= \lim_{n\to\infty} n\left(e^{(r-D)\Delta t} - d\right)\left(u - e^{(r-D)\Delta t}\right)\left[\frac{\log(u/d)}{(u - d)}\right]^2$$

$$= \lim_{n\to\infty} n\left(e^{(r-D)\Delta t} - e^{-\sigma\sqrt{\Delta t}}\right)\left(e^{\sigma\sqrt{\Delta t}} - e^{(r-D)\Delta t}\right)$$

$$\times \left[\frac{\log(u/d)}{(u - d)}\right]^2$$

$$= \lim_{n\to\infty} n\left(\sigma^2\Delta t + \mathcal{O}(\Delta t^{\frac{3}{2}})\right)\lim_{n\to\infty}\left[\frac{2\sigma\sqrt{\Delta t}}{2\sigma\sqrt{\Delta t} + \mathcal{O}(\Delta t)}\right]^2$$

$$= \sigma^2(T - t)$$

and

$$\lim_{n\to\infty} n\tilde{\pi}(1 - \tilde{\pi})\left[\log\left(\frac{u}{d}\right)\right]^2 = \lim_{n\to\infty} n\pi(1 - \pi)e^{-2(r-D)\Delta t}\left[\log\left(\frac{u}{d}\right)\right]^2$$

$$= \lim_{n\to\infty} n\pi(1 - \pi)\left[\log\left(\frac{u}{d}\right)\right]^2\lim_{n\to\infty} e^{-2(r-D)\Delta t}$$

$$= \sigma^2(T - t)$$

such that using L'Hôpital's rule

$$\lim_{n\to\infty} \frac{2\sigma\sqrt{\Delta t}}{2\sigma\sqrt{\Delta t} + \mathcal{O}(\Delta t)} = \lim_{n\to\infty} \frac{2\sigma}{2\sigma + \mathcal{O}(\sqrt{\Delta t})} = 1.$$

Hence, we can write

$$\lim_{n\to\infty} C(S_t, t; K, T) = S_t e^{-D(T-t)}\Phi(d_+) - Ke^{-r(T-t)}\Phi(d_-)$$

where

$$d_\pm = \frac{\log(S_t/K) + (r - D \pm \frac{1}{2}\sigma^2)(T-t)}{\sigma\sqrt{T-t}}.$$

$\square$

11. Consider a binomial tree model for an underlying asset process $\{S_n : 0 \le n \le 3\}$ where $S_0 = 100$. Let

$$S_{n+1} = \begin{cases} uS_n & \text{with probability } \pi \\ \\ dS_n & \text{with probability } 1 - \pi \end{cases}$$

where $u = e^{\sigma\sqrt{\Delta t}}$ and $d = 1/u$, with σ the volatility and Δt the binomial time step. By assuming the risk-neutral interest rate $r = 5\%$, continuous dividend yield $D = 1\%$ and volatility $\sigma = 10\%$ we wish to price a European call option with strike $K = 95$ and expiry time $T = 1$ year in a 3-period binomial tree model.
(a) Find the risk-neutral probabilities π and $1 - \pi$.
(b) Find the price of the European call option.

Solution:
(a) Given $S_0 = 100$, $K = 95$, $r = 0.05$, $D = 0.01$, $\sigma = 0.1$ and time step $\Delta t = \frac{1}{3}$, then

$$u = e^{\sigma\sqrt{\Delta t}} = e^{\frac{0.1}{\sqrt{3}}} = 1.0594$$

and

$$d = e^{-\sigma\sqrt{\Delta t}} = e^{-\frac{0.1}{\sqrt{3}}} = 0.9439.$$

The risk-neutral probabilities are

$$\pi = \frac{e^{(r-D)\Delta t} - d}{u - d} = 0.6019$$

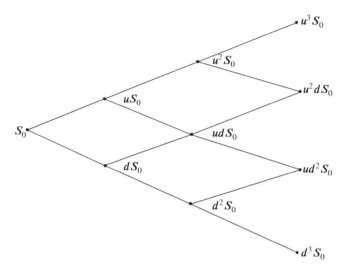

Figure 2.3 A 3-period binomial tree model.

and

$$1 - \pi = 1 - 0.6019 = 0.3981.$$

(b) The binomial tree in Figure 2.3 shows the price movement of S_0 in a 3-period binomial model.

By setting

$$S_i^{(j)} = u^j d^{i-j} S_0, \quad i = 0, 1, \ldots, n, \quad j = 0, 1, \ldots, i$$

the European call option price at each of the lattice points is

$$V_i^{(j)} = e^{-r\Delta t} \left[\pi V_{i+1}^{(j+1)} + (1 - \pi) V_{i+1}^{(j)} \right]$$

such that

$$V_n^{(j)} = \Psi(S_n^{(j)}) = \max \left\{ S_n^{(j)} - K, 0 \right\}$$

where $i = 0, 1, \ldots, n$ and $j = 0, 1, \ldots, i$.

Hence, at time period $n = 3$

$$
\begin{aligned}
V_3^{(0)} &= \Psi(S_3^{(0)}) \\
&= \max\{d^3 S_0 - K, 0\} \\
&= \max\{0.9439^3 \times 100 - 95, 0\} \\
&= 0
\end{aligned}
$$

$$V_3^{(1)} = \Psi(S_3^{(1)})$$
$$= \max\{ud^2 S_0 - K, 0\}$$
$$= \max\{1.0594 \times 0.9439^2 \times 100 - 95, 0\}$$
$$= 0$$

$$V_3^{(2)} = \Psi(S_3^{(2)})$$
$$= \max\{u^2 d S_0 - K, 0\}$$
$$= \max\{1.0594^2 \times 0.9439 \times 100 - 95, 0\}$$
$$= 10.9366$$

$$V_3^{(3)} = \Psi(S_3^{(3)})$$
$$= \max\{u^3 S_0 - K, 0\}$$
$$= \max\{1.0594^3 \times 100 - 95, 0\}$$
$$= 23.8995.$$

At time period $n = 2$

$$V_2^{(0)} = e^{-r\Delta t}\left[\pi V_3^{(1)} + (1 - \pi)V_3^{(0)}\right]$$
$$= e^{-\frac{0.05}{3}}[0.6019 \times 0 + 0.3981 \times 0]$$
$$= 0$$

$$V_2^{(1)} = e^{-r\Delta t}\left[\pi V_3^{(2)} + (1 - \pi)V_3^{(1)}\right]$$
$$= e^{-\frac{0.05}{3}}[0.6019 \times 10.9366 + 0.3981 \times 0]$$
$$= 6.4739$$

$$V_2^{(2)} = e^{-r\Delta t}\left[\pi V_3^{(3)} + (1 - \pi)V_3^{(2)}\right]$$
$$= e^{-\frac{0.05}{3}}[0.6019 \times 23.8995 + 0.3981 \times 10.9366]$$
$$= 18.4292.$$

At time period $n = 1$

$$V_1^{(0)} = e^{-r\Delta t}\left[\pi V_2^{(1)} + (1 - \pi)V_2^{(0)}\right]$$
$$= e^{-\frac{0.05}{3}}[0.6019 \times 6.4739 + 0.3981 \times 0]$$
$$= 3.8322$$

$$V_1^{(1)} = e^{-r\Delta t}\left[\pi V_2^{(2)} + (1 - \pi)V_2^{(1)}\right]$$
$$= e^{-\frac{0.05}{3}}[0.6019 \times 18.4292 + 0.3981 \times 6.4739]$$
$$= 13.4438$$

and finally at time period $n = 0$

$$V_0^{(0)} = e^{-r\Delta t} \left[\pi V_1^{(1)} + (1 - \pi) V_1^{(0)} \right]$$

$$= e^{-\frac{0.05}{3}} [0.6019 \times 13.4438 + 0.3981 \times 3.8322]$$

$$= 9.4585.$$

Therefore, the price of the European call based on a 3-period binomial model is $V_0^{(0)} = 9.4585$.

N.B. Take note that we can also obtain the same result by utilising the formula given in Problem 2.2.3.9 (page 204)

$$V_0^{(0)} = e^{-nr\Delta t} \sum_{j=0}^{n} \binom{n}{j} \pi^j (1 - \pi)^{n-j} \max\{u^j d^{n-j} S_0 - K, 0\}$$

$$= e^{-3 \times 0.05 \times \frac{1}{3}} \sum_{j=0}^{3} \binom{3}{j} 0.6019^j \times 0.3981^{n-j} \times V_3^{(j)}$$

$$= e^{-0.05} \left[0.3981^3 \times 0 + 3 \times 0.6019 \times 0.3981^2 \times 0 \right.$$

$$\left. + 3 \times 0.6019^2 \times 0.3981 \times 10.9366 + 0.6019^3 \times 23.8995 \right]$$

$$= 9.4585.$$

$\square$

12. Consider a binomial tree model for an underlying asset process $\{S_n : 0 \leq n \leq 3\}$ where $S_0 = 100$. Let

$$S_{n+1} = \begin{cases} u S_n & \text{with probability } \pi \\ d S_n & \text{with probability } 1 - \pi \end{cases}$$

where $u = e^{\sigma \sqrt{\Delta t}}$ and $d = 1/u$, with σ is the volatility and Δt the binomial time step. By assuming the risk-neutral interest rate $r = 5\%$ and the volatility $\sigma = 10\%$ we wish to price a European call option with strike $K = 95$ and expiry time $T = 1$ year in a 3-period binomial tree model where the stock price pays a discrete dividend $\delta = 1.00$ at time period 2.
(a) Find the risk-neutral probabilities π and $1 - \pi$.
(b) Find the price of the European call option.

Solution:
(a) Given $S_0 = 100$, $K = 95$, $r = 0.05$, $\delta = 1.00$, $\sigma = 0.1$ and time step $\Delta t = \frac{1}{3}$, then

$$u = e^{\sigma \sqrt{\Delta t}} = e^{\frac{0.1}{\sqrt{3}}} = 1.0594$$

and

$$d = e^{-\sigma\sqrt{\Delta t}} = e^{-\frac{0.1}{\sqrt{3}}} = 0.9439.$$

The risk-neutral probabilities are

$$\pi = \frac{e^{r\Delta t} - d}{u - d} = 0.6312$$

and

$$1 - \pi = 1 - 0.6312 = 0.3688.$$

(b) The 3-period binomial tree in Figure 2.4 shows the price movement of S_0 with discrete dividend payment at $n = 2$.

   By setting

$$S_i^{(j)} = \begin{cases} u^j d^{i-j} S_0 & i = 0, 1 \ j = 0, \dots, i \\ u^j d^{2-j} S_0 - \delta & i = 2, \ j = 0, \dots, i \end{cases}$$

and

$$S_3^{(0)} = d(d^2 S_0 - \delta), \ S_3^{(1)} = u(d^2 S_0 - \delta), \ S_3^{(2)} = d(ud S_0 - \delta)$$
$$S_3^{(3)} = u(ud S_0 - \delta), \ S_3^{(4)} = d(u^2 S_0 - \delta), \ S_3^{(5)} = u(u^2 S_0 - \delta)$$

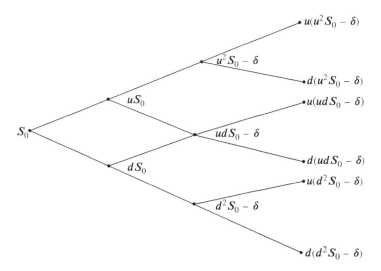

Figure 2.4   A 3-period binomial tree model with discrete dividend payment at time period $n = 2$.

the European call option price at each of the lattice points is

$$V_i^{(j)} = e^{-r\Delta t} \left[\pi V_{i+1}^{(j+1)} + (1 - \pi) V_{i+1}^{(j)} \right]$$

where $i = 0, 1$ and $j = 0, \dots, i$

$$V_2^{(0)} = e^{-r\Delta t} \left[\pi V_3^{(1)} + (1 - \pi) V_3^{(0)} \right]$$

$$V_2^{(1)} = e^{-r\Delta t} \left[\pi V_3^{(3)} + (1 - \pi) V_3^{(2)} \right]$$

$$V_2^{(2)} = e^{-r\Delta t} \left[\pi V_3^{(5)} + (1 - \pi) V_3^{(4)} \right]$$

such that

$$V_3^{(j)} = \Psi(S_3^{(j)}) = \max \left\{ S_3^{(j)} - K, 0 \right\}$$

for $j = 0, 1, \dots, 5$.

For time period $n = 3$, the payoffs are

$$V_3^{(0)} = \max\{d(d^2 S_0 - \delta) - K, 0\}$$
$$= \max\{0.9439(0.9439^2 \times 100 - 1) - 95, 0\}$$
$$= 0$$

$$V_3^{(1)} = \max\{u(d^2 S_0 - \delta) - K, 0\}$$
$$= \max\{1.0594(0.9439^2 \times 100 - 1) - 95, 0\}$$
$$= 0$$

$$V_3^{(2)} = \max\{d(ud S_0 - \delta) - K, 0\}$$
$$= \max\{0.9439(0.9439 \times 1.0594 \times 100 - 1) - 95, 0\}$$
$$= 0$$

$$V_3^{(3)} = \max\{u(ud S_0 - \delta) - K, 0\}$$
$$= \max\{1.0594(1.0594 \times 0.9439 \times 100 - 1) - 95, 0\}$$
$$= 9.8772$$

$$V_3^{(4)} = \max\{d(u^2 S_0 - \delta) - K, 0\}$$
$$= \max\{0.9439(1.0594^2 \times 100 - 1) - 95, 0\}$$
$$= 9.9927$$

$$V_3^{(5)} = \max\{u(u^2 S_0 - \delta) - K, 0\}$$
$$= \max\{1.0594(1.0594^2 \times 100 - 1) - 95, 0\}$$
$$= 22.8401.$$

At time period $n = 2$

$$V_2^{(0)} = e^{-r\Delta t} \left[\pi V_3^{(1)} + (1-\pi)V_3^{(0)} \right]$$

$$= e^{-\frac{0.05}{3}} [0.6312 \times 0 + 0.3688 \times 0]$$

$$= 0$$

$$V_2^{(1)} = e^{-r\Delta t} \left[\pi V_3^{(3)} + (1-\pi)V_3^{(2)} \right]$$

$$= e^{-\frac{0.05}{3}} [0.6312 \times 9.8772 + 0.3688 \times 0]$$

$$= 6.1314$$

$$V_2^{(2)} = e^{-r\Delta t} \left[\pi V_3^{(5)} + (1-\pi)V_3^{(4)} \right]$$

$$= e^{-\frac{0.05}{3}} [0.6312 \times 22.8401 + 0.3688 \times 9.9927]$$

$$= 17.8028.$$

At time period $n = 1$

$$V_1^{(0)} = e^{-r\Delta t} \left[\pi V_2^{(1)} + (1-\pi)V_2^{(0)} \right]$$

$$= e^{-\frac{0.05}{3}} [0.6312 \times 6.1314 + 0.3688 \times 0]$$

$$= 3.8062$$

$$V_1^{(1)} = e^{-r\Delta t} \left[\pi V_2^{(2)} + (1-\pi)V_2^{(1)} \right]$$

$$= e^{-\frac{0.05}{3}} [0.6312 \times 17.8028 + 0.3688 \times 6.1314]$$

$$= 13.2753$$

and finally at time period $n = 0$

$$V_0^{(0)} = e^{-r\Delta t} \left[\pi V_1^{(1)} + (1-\pi)V_1^{(0)} \right]$$

$$= e^{-\frac{0.05}{3}} [0.6312 \times 13.2753 + 0.3688 \times 3.8062]$$

$$= 9.6214.$$

Therefore, the price of the European call with discrete dividend based on a 3-period binomial model is $V_0^{(0)} = 9.6214$.

□

2.2.4   The Greeks

1. Let

$$d_{\pm} = \frac{\log(S_t/K) + (r - D \pm \frac{1}{2}\sigma^2)(T - t)}{\sigma\sqrt{T - t}}$$

where S_t is the spot price at time $t < T$, T is the expiry date of the option, K is the strike price, r is the risk-free interest rate, D is the continuous dividend yield and σ is the spot price volatility.

Show that

$$d_- = d_+ - \sigma\sqrt{T - t}$$

and

$$S_t e^{-D(T-t)} e^{-\frac{1}{2}d_+^2} = K e^{-r(T-t)} e^{-\frac{1}{2}d_-^2}.$$

Hence, deduce that

$$\frac{\partial d_+}{\partial S_t} = \frac{\partial d_-}{\partial S_t}$$

$$\frac{\partial d_+}{\partial K} = \frac{\partial d_-}{\partial K}$$

$$S_t e^{-D(T-t)}\frac{\partial \Phi(d_+)}{\partial S_t} = K e^{-r(T-t)}\frac{\partial \Phi(d_-)}{\partial S_t}$$

and

$$S_t e^{-D(T-t)}\frac{\partial \Phi(d_+)}{\partial K} = K e^{-r(T-t)}\frac{\partial \Phi(d_-)}{\partial K}$$

where $\Phi(\cdot)$ is the cdf of a standard normal.

Solution: From the definition

$$d_+ = \frac{\log(S_t/K) + (r - D + \frac{1}{2}\sigma^2)(T - t)}{\sigma\sqrt{T - t}}$$

$$d_- = \frac{\log(S_t/K) + (r - D - \frac{1}{2}\sigma^2)(T - t)}{\sigma\sqrt{T - t}}$$

we can write

$$d_+ - \sigma\sqrt{T-t} = \frac{\log(S_t/K) + (r - D + \frac{1}{2}\sigma^2)(T-t)}{\sigma\sqrt{T-t}} - \sigma\sqrt{T-t}$$

$$= \frac{\log(S_t/K) + (r - D + \frac{1}{2}\sigma^2)(T-t) - \sigma^2(T-t)}{\sigma\sqrt{T-t}}$$

$$= \frac{\log(S_t/K) + (r - D - \frac{1}{2}\sigma^2)(T-t)}{\sigma\sqrt{T-t}}.$$

Hence,

$$d_- = d_+ - \sigma\sqrt{T-t}.$$

As for the second result we note that

$$\frac{1}{2}\left(d_+^2 - d_-^2\right) = \frac{1}{2}\left(d_+^2 - d_+^2 + 2d_+\sigma\sqrt{T-t} - \sigma^2(T-t)\right)$$

$$= \log(S_t/K) + (r - D)(T-t)$$

from which follows that

$$S_t e^{-D(T-t)} e^{-\frac{1}{2}d_+^2} = K e^{-r(T-t)} e^{-\frac{1}{2}d_-^2}.$$

From $d_- = d_+ - \sigma\sqrt{T-t}$ and by differentiating with respect to S_t and K we have

$$\frac{\partial d_+}{\partial S_t} = \frac{\partial d_-}{\partial S_t}$$

and

$$\frac{\partial d_+}{\partial K} = \frac{\partial d_-}{\partial K}.$$

Since

$$\frac{\partial \Phi(d_+)}{\partial S_t} = \frac{\partial}{\partial S_t} \int_{-\infty}^{d_+} \frac{1}{\sqrt{2\pi}} e^{-\frac{1}{2}x^2} dx = \frac{1}{\sqrt{2\pi}} e^{-\frac{1}{2}d_+^2} \frac{\partial d_+}{\partial S_t}$$

$$\frac{\partial \Phi(d_-)}{\partial S_t} = \frac{\partial}{\partial S_t} \int_{-\infty}^{d_-} \frac{1}{\sqrt{2\pi}} e^{-\frac{1}{2}x^2} dx = \frac{1}{\sqrt{2\pi}} e^{-\frac{1}{2}d_-^2} \frac{\partial d_-}{\partial S_t}$$

$$\frac{\partial \Phi(d_+)}{\partial K} = \frac{\partial}{\partial K} \int_{-\infty}^{d_+} \frac{1}{\sqrt{2\pi}} e^{-\frac{1}{2}x^2} dx = \frac{1}{\sqrt{2\pi}} e^{-\frac{1}{2}d_+^2} \frac{\partial d_+}{\partial K}$$

$$\frac{\partial \Phi(d_-)}{\partial K} = \frac{\partial}{\partial K} \int_{-\infty}^{d_-} \frac{1}{\sqrt{2\pi}} e^{-\frac{1}{2}x^2} dx = \frac{1}{\sqrt{2\pi}} e^{-\frac{1}{2}d_-^2} \frac{\partial d_-}{\partial K}$$

and by substituting the terms $e^{-\frac{1}{2}d_+^2}$ and $e^{-\frac{1}{2}d_-^2}$ into $S_t e^{-D(T-t)} e^{-\frac{1}{2}d_+^2} = K e^{-r(T-t)} e^{-\frac{1}{2}d_-^2}$
and taking note that $\frac{\partial d_+}{\partial S_t} = \frac{\partial d_-}{\partial S_t}, \frac{\partial d_+}{\partial K} = \frac{\partial d_-}{\partial K}$, we have the relations

$$S_t e^{-D(T-t)} \frac{\partial \Phi(d_+)}{\partial S_t} = K e^{-r(T-t)} \frac{\partial \Phi(d_-)}{\partial S_t}$$

and

$$S_t e^{-D(T-t)} \frac{\partial \Phi(d_+)}{\partial K} = K e^{-r(T-t)} \frac{\partial \Phi(d_-)}{\partial K}.$$

$\square$

2. *Delta.* Let the Black–Scholes formulae for a European call option $C(S_t, t; K, T)$ and a European put option $P(S_t, t; K, T)$ be

$$C(S_t, t; K, T) = S_t e^{-D(T-t)} \Phi(d_+) - K e^{-r(T-t)} \Phi(d_-)$$
$$P(S_t, t; K, T) = K e^{-r(T-t)} \Phi(-d_-) - S_t e^{-D(T-t)} \Phi(-d_+)$$

with $d_\pm$ given by

$$d_\pm = \frac{\log(S_t/K) + (r - D \pm \frac{1}{2}\sigma^2)(T - t)}{\sigma\sqrt{T - t}}$$

such that $\Phi(\cdot)$ is the cdf of a standard normal, S_t is the spot price at time $t < T$, T is the expiry date of the option, K is the strike price, r is the risk-free interest rate, D is the continuous dividend yield and σ is the spot price volatility.

Without explicitly computing the partial derivatives of $d_\pm$ show that the delta of a European call, $\Delta_C = \frac{\partial C}{\partial S_t}$ and a European put, $\Delta_P = \frac{\partial P}{\partial S_t}$ are

$$\Delta_C = e^{-D(T-t)} \Phi(d_+) \quad \text{and} \quad \Delta_P = e^{-D(T-t)}(\Phi(d_+) - 1)$$

respectively.

Solution: Using the properties of Problem 2.2.4.1 (page 218) we note that

$$\Delta_C = \frac{\partial C}{\partial S_t}$$
$$= e^{-D(T-t)} \Phi(d_+) + S_t e^{-D(T-t)} \frac{\partial \Phi(d_+)}{\partial S_t} - K e^{-r(T-t)} \frac{\partial \Phi(d_-)}{\partial S_t}$$
$$= e^{-D(T-t)} \Phi(d_+).$$

Taking note that

$$\Phi(-d_\pm) = 1 - \Phi(d_\pm)$$

hence

$$\Delta_P = \frac{\partial P}{\partial S_t}$$

$$= Ke^{-r(T-t)}\frac{\partial}{\partial S_t}(1 - \Phi(d_-)) - e^{-D(T-t)}\Phi(-d_+) - S_t e^{-D(T-t)}\frac{\partial}{\partial S_t}(1 - \Phi(d_+))$$

$$= -Ke^{-r(T-t)}\frac{\partial\Phi(d_-)}{\partial S_t} - e^{-D(T-t)}\Phi(-d_+) + S_t e^{-D(T-t)}\frac{\partial\Phi(d_-)}{\partial S_t}$$

$$= -e^{-D(T-t)}\Phi(-d_+)$$

$$= e^{-D(t-t)}(\Phi(d_+) - 1).$$

$\square$

3. *Gamma.* Let the Black–Scholes formulae for a European call option $C(S_t, t; K, T)$ and a European put option $P(S_t, t; K, T)$ be

$$C(S_t, t; K, T) = S_t e^{-D(T-t)}\Phi(d_+) - Ke^{-r(T-t)}\Phi(d_-)$$
$$P(S_t, t; K, T) = Ke^{-r(T-t)}\Phi(-d_-) - S_t e^{-D(T-t)}\Phi(-d_+)$$

with $d_\pm$ given by

$$d_\pm = \frac{\log(S_t/K) + (r - D \pm \frac{1}{2}\sigma^2)(T - t)}{\sigma\sqrt{T - t}}$$

such that $\Phi(\cdot)$ is the cdf of a standard normal, S_t is the spot price at time $t < T$, T is the expiry date of the option, K is the strike price, r is the risk-free interest rate, D is the continuous dividend yield and σ is the spot price volatility.

Show that the gamma of a European call, $\Gamma_C = \dfrac{\partial^2 C}{\partial S_t^2}$ and a European put, $\Gamma_P = \dfrac{\partial^2 P}{\partial S_t^2}$

are equal such that

$$\Gamma = \frac{e^{-D(T-t)}e^{-\frac{1}{2}d_+^2}}{\sigma S_t\sqrt{2\pi(T - t)}} = \frac{Ke^{-r(T-t)}e^{-\frac{1}{2}d_-^2}}{\sigma S_t^2\sqrt{2\pi(T - t)}}$$

where $\Gamma = \Gamma_C = \Gamma_P$.

Solution: Using the results of Problem 2.2.4.2 (page 220) for a European call, the gamma is defined as

$$\Gamma_C = \frac{\partial^2 C}{\partial S_t^2} = \frac{\partial\Delta_C}{\partial S_t} = \frac{\partial}{\partial S_t}\left(e^{-D(T-t)}\Phi(d_+)\right) = e^{-D(T-t)}\Phi'(d_+)\frac{\partial d_+}{\partial S_t}.$$

Using similar steps, the gamma of a European put is

$$\Gamma_P = \frac{\partial^2 P}{\partial S_t^2} = \frac{\partial \Delta_P}{\partial S_t} = \frac{\partial}{\partial S_t}\left(e^{-D(t-t)}(\Phi(d_+) - 1)\right) = e^{-D(T-t)}\Phi'(d_+)\frac{\partial d_+}{\partial S_t}.$$

Hence,

$$\Gamma_C = \Gamma_P = e^{-D(T-t)}\Phi'(d_+)\frac{\partial d_+}{\partial S_t}$$

and by manipulating $\dfrac{\partial d_+}{\partial S_t}$,

$$\frac{\partial d_+}{\partial S_t} = \frac{\partial}{\partial S_t}\left\{\frac{\log(S_t/K) + (r - D + \frac{1}{2}\sigma^2)(T - t)}{\sigma\sqrt{T - t}}\right\} = \frac{1}{\sigma S_t\sqrt{T - t}}.$$

Therefore,

$$\Gamma_C = \Gamma_P = \frac{e^{-D(T-t)}\Phi'(d_+)}{\sigma S_t\sqrt{T - t}} = \frac{e^{-D(T-t)}e^{-\frac{1}{2}d_+^2}}{\sigma S_t\sqrt{2\pi(T - t)}}$$

where $\Phi'(x) = \dfrac{1}{\sqrt{2\pi}}e^{-\frac{1}{2}x^2}$.

In addition, from Problem 2.2.4.1 (page 218) we have the identity

$$S_t e^{-D(T-t)}e^{-\frac{1}{2}d_+^2} = K e^{-r(T-t)}e^{-\frac{1}{2}d_-^2}$$

and thus we can also write the gamma as

$$\Gamma_C = \Gamma_P = \frac{K e^{-r(T-t)}e^{-\frac{1}{2}d_-^2}}{\sigma S_t^2\sqrt{2\pi(T - t)}}.$$

□

4. *Dual Delta.* Let the Black–Scholes formulae of a European call option $C(S_t, t; K, T)$ and a European put option $P(S_t, t; K, T)$ be

$$C(S_t, t; K, T) = S_t e^{-D(T-t)}\Phi(d_+) - K e^{-r(T-t)}\Phi(d_-)$$
$$P(S_t, t; K, T) = K e^{-r(T-t)}\Phi(-d_-) - S_t e^{-D(T-t)}\Phi(-d_+)$$

with $d_\pm$ given by

$$d_\pm = \frac{\log(S_t/K) + (r - D \pm \frac{1}{2}\sigma^2)(T - t)}{\sigma\sqrt{T - t}}$$

such that $\Phi(\cdot)$ is the cdf of a standard normal, S_t is the spot price at time $t < T$, T is the expiry date of the option, K is the strike price, r is the risk-free interest rate, D is the continuous dividend yield and σ is the spot price volatility.

Show that the dual delta of a European call, $\dfrac{\partial C}{\partial K}$ and a European put, $\dfrac{\partial P}{\partial K}$ are

$$\frac{\partial C}{\partial K} = -e^{-r(T-t)}\Phi(d_-) \quad \text{and} \quad \frac{\partial P}{\partial K} = e^{-r(T-t)}\Phi(-d_-)$$

respectively.

Solution: Taking partial derivatives with respect to the strike price K

$$\frac{\partial C}{\partial K} = S_t e^{-D(T-t)}\frac{\partial}{\partial K}\Phi(d_+) - e^{-r(T-t)}\Phi(d_-) - Ke^{-r(T-t)}\frac{\partial}{\partial K}\Phi(d_-)$$

and

$$\frac{\partial P}{\partial K} = e^{-r(T-t)}\Phi(-d_-) + Ke^{-r(T-t)}\frac{\partial}{\partial K}\Phi(-d_-) - S_t e^{-D(T-t)}\frac{\partial}{\partial K}\Phi(-d_+).$$

For $\epsilon \in \{-1, 1\}$,

$$\frac{\partial}{\partial K}\Phi(\epsilon d_+) = \frac{-\epsilon}{\sigma K\sqrt{2\pi(T-t)}}e^{-\frac{1}{2}d_+^2} \quad \text{and} \quad \frac{\partial}{\partial K}\Phi(\epsilon d_-) = \frac{-\epsilon}{\sigma K\sqrt{2\pi(T-t)}}e^{-\frac{1}{2}d_-^2}$$

and using the properties of Problem 2.2.4.1 (page 218)

$$S_t e^{-D(T-t)}e^{-\frac{1}{2}d_+^2} = Ke^{-r(T-t)}e^{-\frac{1}{2}d_-^2}$$

we eventually have

$$\frac{\partial C}{\partial K} = -e^{-r(T-t)}\Phi(d_-) \quad \text{and} \quad \frac{\partial P}{\partial K} = e^{-r(T-t)}\Phi(-d_-).$$

$\square$

5. *Dual Gamma.* Let the Black–Scholes formulae for a European call option $C(S_t, t; K, T)$ and a European put option $P(S_t, t; K, T)$ be

$$C(S_t, t; K, T) = S_t e^{-D(T-t)}\Phi(d_+) - Ke^{-r(T-t)}\Phi(d_-)$$
$$P(S_t, t; K, T) = Ke^{-r(T-t)}\Phi(-d_-) - S_t e^{-D(T-t)}\Phi(-d_+)$$

with $d_\pm$ given by

$$d_\pm = \frac{\log(S_t/K) + (r - D \pm \frac{1}{2}\sigma^2)(T-t)}{\sigma\sqrt{T-t}}$$

such that $\Phi(\cdot)$ is the cdf of a standard normal, S_t is the spot price at time $t < T$, T is the expiry date of the option, K is the strike price, r is the risk-free interest rate, D is the continuous dividend yield and σ is the spot price volatility.

Show that the dual gamma of a European call, $\dfrac{\partial^2 C}{\partial K^2}$ and a European put, $\dfrac{\partial^2 P}{\partial K^2}$ are equal such that

$$\frac{\partial^2 C}{\partial K^2} = \frac{\partial^2 P}{\partial K^2} = \frac{e^{-r(T-t)}}{\sigma K \sqrt{2\pi(T-t)}} e^{-\frac{1}{2}d_-^2}.$$

Solution: From Problem 2.2.4.4 (page 222), taking partial derivatives with respect to K

$$\frac{\partial^2 C}{\partial K^2} = -e^{-r(T-t)}\frac{\partial}{\partial K}\Phi(d_-) \text{ and } \frac{\partial^2 P}{\partial K^2} = e^{-r(T-t)}\frac{\partial}{\partial K}\Phi(-d_-)$$

and since $\dfrac{\partial}{\partial K}\Phi(\epsilon d_-) = \dfrac{-\epsilon}{\sigma K \sqrt{2\pi(T-t)}} e^{-\frac{1}{2}d_-^2}$ for $\epsilon \in \{-1,1\}$, we have

$$\frac{\partial^2 C}{\partial K^2} = \frac{\partial^2 P}{\partial K^2} = \frac{e^{-r(T-t)}}{\sigma K \sqrt{2\pi(T-t)}e^{-\frac{1}{2}d_-^2}}.$$

$\square$

6. *Vega.* Let the Black–Scholes formulae for a European call option $C(S_t, t; K, T)$ and a European put option $P(S_t, t; K, T)$ be

$$C(S_t, t; K, T) = S_t e^{-D(T-t)}\Phi(d_+) - Ke^{-r(T-t)}\Phi(d_-)$$
$$P(S_t, t; K, T) = Ke^{-r(T-t)}\Phi(-d_-) - S_t e^{-D(T-t)}\Phi(-d_+)$$

with $d_\pm$ given by

$$d_\pm = \frac{\log(S_t/K) + (r - D \pm \frac{1}{2}\sigma^2)(T-t)}{\sigma\sqrt{T-t}}$$

such that $\Phi(\cdot)$ is the cdf of a standard normal, S_t is the spot price at time $t < T$, T is the expiry date of the option, K is the strike price, r is the risk-free interest rate, D is the continuous dividend yield and σ is the spot price volatility.

Without explicitly computing the partial derivatives of $d_\pm$ show that the vega of a European call, $\mathcal{V}_C = \dfrac{\partial C}{\partial \sigma}$ and a European put, $\mathcal{V}_P = \dfrac{\partial P}{\partial \sigma}$ are equal such that

$$\mathcal{V} = \sqrt{\frac{T-t}{2\pi}}S_t e^{-D(T-t)}e^{-\frac{1}{2}d_+^2} = \sqrt{\frac{T-t}{2\pi}}Ke^{-r(T-t)}e^{-\frac{1}{2}d_-^2}$$

where $\mathcal{V} = \mathcal{V}_C = \mathcal{V}_P$.

Hence, deduce that

$$\mathcal{V} = \sigma(T - t)S_t^2 \Gamma$$

where $\Gamma = \dfrac{\partial^2 C}{\partial S_t^2} = \dfrac{\partial^2 P}{\partial S_t^2}$.

Solution: For a European call the vega is defined as

$$\mathcal{V}_C = \frac{\partial C}{\partial \sigma}$$

$$= S_t e^{-D(T-t)} \frac{\partial \Phi(d_+)}{\partial d_+} \frac{\partial d_+}{\partial \sigma} - K e^{-r(T-t)} \frac{\partial \Phi(d_-)}{\partial d_-} \frac{\partial d_-}{\partial \sigma}$$

and using the identity $d_- = d_+ - \sigma\sqrt{T - t}$ we have

$$\frac{\partial d_-}{\partial \sigma} = \frac{\partial d_+}{\partial \sigma} - \sqrt{T - t}.$$

Hence,

$$\mathcal{V}_C = S_t e^{-D(T-t)} \frac{\partial \Phi(d_+)}{\partial d_+} \left(\frac{\partial d_-}{\partial \sigma} + \sqrt{T - t} \right) - K e^{-r(T-t)} \frac{\partial \Phi(d_-)}{\partial d_-} \frac{\partial d_-}{\partial \sigma}$$

$$= \left(S_t e^{-D(T-t)} \frac{\partial \Phi(d_+)}{\partial d_+} - K e^{-r(T-t)} \frac{\partial \Phi(d_-)}{\partial d_-} \right) \frac{\partial d_-}{\partial \sigma}$$

$$+ \sqrt{T - t} S_t e^{-D(T-t)} \frac{\partial \Phi(d_+)}{\partial d_+}$$

$$= \frac{1}{\sqrt{2\pi}} \left(S_t e^{-D(T-t)} e^{-\frac{1}{2}d_+^2} - K e^{-r(T-t)} e^{-\frac{1}{2}d_-^2} \right) \frac{\partial d_-}{\partial \sigma}$$

$$+ \sqrt{\frac{T - t}{2\pi}} S_t e^{-D(T-t)} e^{-\frac{1}{2}d_+^2}$$

$$= \sqrt{\frac{T - t}{2\pi}} S_t e^{-D(T-t)} e^{-\frac{1}{2}d_+^2}$$

since $S_t e^{-D(T-t)} e^{-\frac{1}{2}d_+^2} = K e^{-r(T-t)} e^{-\frac{1}{2}d_-^2}$.
Therefore,

$$\mathcal{V}_C = \sqrt{\frac{T - t}{2\pi}} S_t e^{-D(T-t)} e^{-\frac{1}{2}d_+^2} = \sqrt{\frac{T - t}{2\pi}} K e^{-r(T-t)} e^{-\frac{1}{2}d_-^2}.$$

As for the European put, we note that

$$\Phi(-d_\pm) = 1 - \Phi(d_\pm)$$

and hence we can write

$$P(S_t, t; K, T) = Ke^{-r(T-t)}(1 - \Phi(d_-)) - S_t e^{-D(T-t)}(1 - \Phi(d_+))$$
$$= Ke^{-r(T-t)} - S_t e^{-D(T-t)} + C(S_t, t; K, T).$$

Therefore,

$$\mathcal{V}_P = \frac{\partial P}{\partial \sigma} = \frac{\partial C}{\partial \sigma}$$

which implies

$$\mathcal{V}_P = \sqrt{\frac{T-t}{2\pi}} S_t e^{-D(T-t)} e^{-\frac{1}{2}d_+^2} = \sqrt{\frac{T-t}{2\pi}} Ke^{-r(T-t)} e^{-\frac{1}{2}d_-^2}.$$

Finally, by letting $\mathcal{V} = \mathcal{V}_C = \mathcal{V}_P$ and $\Gamma = \Gamma_C = \Gamma_P$ such that

$$\Gamma = \frac{e^{-D(T-t)} e^{-\frac{1}{2}d_+^2}}{\sigma S_t \sqrt{2\pi(T-t)}} = \frac{Ke^{-r(T-t)} e^{-\frac{1}{2}d_-^2}}{\sigma S_t^2 \sqrt{2\pi(T-t)}}$$

and by setting $e^{-D(T-t)} e^{-\frac{1}{2}d_+^2}$ or $e^{-r(T-t)} e^{-\frac{1}{2}d_-^2}$ in terms of Γ and substituting it into $\mathcal{V}$ we have

$$\mathcal{V} = \sigma(T-t) S_t^2 \Gamma.$$

$\square$

7. *Vomma.* Let the Black–Scholes formulae for a European call option $C(S_t, t; K, T)$ and a European put option $P(S_t, t; K, T)$ be

$$C(S_t, t; K, T) = S_t e^{-D(T-t)} \Phi(d_+) - Ke^{-r(T-t)} \Phi(d_-)$$
$$P(S_t, t; K, T) = Ke^{-r(T-t)} \Phi(-d_-) - S_t e^{-D(T-t)} \Phi(-d_+)$$

with $d_\pm$ given by

$$d_\pm = \frac{\log(S_t/K) + (r - D \pm \frac{1}{2}\sigma^2)(T-t)}{\sigma \sqrt{T-t}}$$

such that $\Phi(\cdot)$ is the cdf of a standard normal, S_t is the spot price at time $t < T$, T is the expiry date of the option, K is the strike price, r is the risk-free interest rate, D is the continuous dividend yield and σ is the spot price volatility.

Show that the vomma of a European call, $\dfrac{\partial \mathcal{V}_C}{\partial \sigma} = \dfrac{\partial^2 C}{\partial \sigma^2}$ and a European put, $\dfrac{\partial \mathcal{V}_P}{\partial \sigma} = \dfrac{\partial^2 P}{\partial \sigma^2}$ are equal such that

$$\frac{\partial \mathcal{V}}{\partial \sigma} = \sqrt{\frac{T-t}{2\pi}}\, S_t e^{-D(T-t)} e^{-\frac{1}{2}d_+^2} \frac{d_+ d_-}{\sigma} = \sqrt{\frac{T-t}{2\pi}}\, K e^{-r(T-t)} e^{-\frac{1}{2}d_-^2} \frac{d_+ d_-}{\sigma}$$

where $\dfrac{\partial \mathcal{V}}{\partial \sigma} = \dfrac{\partial \mathcal{V}_C}{\partial \sigma} = \dfrac{\partial \mathcal{V}_P}{\partial \sigma}$.

Hence, deduce that

$$\frac{\partial \mathcal{V}}{\partial \sigma} = \mathcal{V} \frac{d_+ d_-}{\sigma}$$

where $\mathcal{V} = \dfrac{\partial C}{\partial \sigma} = \dfrac{\partial P}{\partial \sigma}$.

Solution: From Problem 2.2.4.6 (page 224), both the European call and put options have the same vega

$$\mathcal{V} = \frac{\partial C}{\partial \sigma} = \frac{\partial P}{\partial \sigma}$$

where

$$\mathcal{V} = \sqrt{\frac{T-t}{2\pi}}\, S_t e^{-D(T-t)} e^{-\frac{1}{2}d_+^2} = \sqrt{\frac{T-t}{2\pi}}\, K e^{-r(T-t)} e^{-\frac{1}{2}d_-^2}.$$

By considering $\mathcal{V} = \sqrt{\dfrac{T-t}{2\pi}}\, S_t e^{-D(T-t)} e^{-\frac{1}{2}d_+^2}$ and taking partial differences with respect to σ,

$$\frac{\partial \mathcal{V}}{\partial \sigma} = -\sqrt{\frac{T-t}{2\pi}}\, S_t e^{-D(T-t)} e^{-\frac{1}{2}d_+^2} d_+ \frac{\partial d_+}{\partial \sigma}$$

and because

$$\frac{\partial d_+}{\partial \sigma} = \frac{\sigma^2 (T-t)^{\frac{3}{2}} - \left[\log(S_t/K) + (r - D + \frac{1}{2}\sigma^2)(T-t)\right]\sqrt{T-t}}{\sigma^2 (T-t)}$$

$$= -\frac{d_-}{\sigma}$$

therefore

$$\frac{\partial \mathcal{V}}{\partial \sigma} = \sqrt{\frac{T-t}{2\pi}}\, S_t e^{-D(T-t)} e^{-\frac{1}{2}d_+^2} \frac{d_+ d_-}{\sigma}.$$

In contrast, by setting $\mathcal{V} = \sqrt{\dfrac{T-t}{2\pi}} K e^{-r(T-t)} e^{-\frac{1}{2}d_-^2}$ and taking partial differences with respect to σ,

$$\frac{\partial \mathcal{V}}{\partial \sigma} = -\sqrt{\frac{T-t}{2\pi}} K e^{-r(T-t)} e^{-\frac{1}{2}d_-^2} d_- \frac{\partial d_-}{\partial \sigma}$$

and since

$$\frac{\partial d_-}{\partial \sigma} = \frac{-\sigma^2(T-t)^{\frac{3}{2}} - \left[\log(S_t/K) + (r - D - \frac{1}{2}\sigma^2)(T-t)\right]\sqrt{T-t}}{\sigma^2(T-t)}$$

$$= -\frac{d_+}{\sigma}$$

therefore

$$\frac{\partial \mathcal{V}}{\partial \sigma} = \sqrt{\frac{T-t}{2\pi}} K e^{-r(T-t)} e^{-\frac{1}{2}d_-^2} \frac{d_+ d_-}{\sigma}.$$

Because

$$\mathcal{V} = \sqrt{\frac{T-t}{2\pi}} S_t e^{-D(T-t)} e^{-\frac{1}{2}d_+^2} = \sqrt{\frac{T-t}{2\pi}} K e^{-r(T-t)} e^{-\frac{1}{2}d_-^2}$$

we can easily deduce

$$\frac{\partial \mathcal{V}}{\partial \sigma} = \mathcal{V} \frac{d_+ d_-}{\sigma}.$$

$\square$

8. *Theta.* Let the Black–Scholes formulae for a European call option $C(S_t, t; K, T)$ and a European put option $P(S_t, t; K, T)$ be

$$C(S_t, t; K, T) = S_t e^{-D(T-t)} \Phi(d_+) - K e^{-r(T-t)} \Phi(d_-)$$
$$P(S_t, t; K, T) = K e^{-r(T-t)} \Phi(-d_-) - S_t e^{-D(T-t)} \Phi(-d_+)$$

with $d_\pm$ given by

$$d_\pm = \frac{\log(S_t/K) + (r - D \pm \frac{1}{2}\sigma^2)(T-t)}{\sigma\sqrt{T-t}}$$

such that $\Phi(\cdot)$ is the cdf of a standard normal, S_t is the spot price at time $t < T$, T is the expiry date of the option, K is the strike price, r is the risk-free interest rate, D is the continuous dividend yield and σ is the spot price volatility.

Without explicitly computing the partial derivatives of $d_\pm$ show that the theta of a European call, $\Theta_C = \dfrac{\partial C}{\partial t}$ and a European put, $\Theta_P = \dfrac{\partial P}{\partial t}$ are

$$\Theta_C = \left(D\Phi(d_+) - \frac{\sigma e^{-\frac{1}{2}d_+^2}}{\sqrt{8\pi(T-t)}} \right) S_t e^{-D(T-t)} - \sigma K e^{-r(T-t)}\Phi(d_-)$$

and

$$\Theta_P = rKe^{-r(T-t)}\Phi(-d_-) - \left(D\Phi(-d_+) - \frac{\sigma e^{-\frac{1}{2}d_+^2}}{\sqrt{8\pi(T-t)}} \right) S_t e^{-D(T-t)}.$$

Solution: By definition

$$\frac{\partial C}{\partial t} = DS_t e^{-D(T-t)}\Phi(d_+) + S_t e^{-D(T-t)}\frac{\partial\Phi(d_+)}{\partial d_+}\frac{\partial d_+}{\partial t}$$
$$-rKe^{-r(T-t)}\Phi(d_-) - Ke^{-r(T-t)}\frac{\partial\Phi(d_-)}{\partial d_-}\frac{\partial d_-}{\partial t}.$$

Using the identity $d_- = d_+ - \sigma\sqrt{T-t}$ we have

$$\frac{\partial d_-}{\partial t} = \frac{\partial d_+}{\partial t} + \frac{\sigma}{2\sqrt{T-t}}$$

and since

$$\frac{\partial\Phi(d_\pm)}{\partial d_\pm} = \frac{1}{\sqrt{2\pi}}e^{-\frac{1}{2}d_\pm^2}$$

and

$$S_t e^{-D(T-t)}e^{-\frac{1}{2}d_+^2} = Ke^{-r(T-t)}e^{-\frac{1}{2}d_-^2}$$

we have

$$\frac{\partial C}{\partial t} = DS_t e^{-D(T-t)}\Phi(d_+) - rKe^{-r(T-t)}\Phi(d_-)$$
$$+ \frac{1}{\sqrt{2\pi}}S_t e^{-D(T-t)}e^{-\frac{1}{2}d_+^2}\frac{\partial d_+}{\partial t} - \frac{1}{\sqrt{2\pi}}Ke^{-r(T-t)}e^{-\frac{1}{2}d_-^2}\left(\frac{\partial d_+}{\partial t} + \frac{\sigma}{2\sqrt{T-t}} \right)$$
$$= DS_t e^{-D(T-t)}\Phi(d_+) - \left(r\Phi(d_-) + \frac{\sigma e^{-\frac{1}{2}d_-^2}}{\sqrt{8\pi(T-t)}} \right)Ke^{-r(T-t)}$$

or

$$\frac{\partial C}{\partial t} = \left(D\Phi(d_+) - \frac{\sigma e^{-\frac{1}{2}d_+^2}}{\sqrt{8\pi(T-t)}} \right) S_t e^{-D(T-t)} - \sigma K e^{-r(T-t)}\Phi(d_-).$$

From the put–call parity equation

$$P(S_t, t; K, T) = Ke^{-r(T-t)} - S_t e^{-D(T-t)} + C(S_t, t; K, T)$$

we have

$$\frac{\partial P}{\partial t} = rKe^{-r(T-t)} - DS_t e^{-D(T-t)} + \frac{\partial C}{\partial t}$$

$$= \left(r\Phi(-d_-) - \frac{\sigma e^{-\frac{1}{2}d_-^2}}{\sqrt{8\pi(T-t)}} \right) Ke^{-r(T-t)} - DS_t e^{-D(T-t)}\Phi(-d_+)$$

or

$$\frac{\partial P}{\partial t} = rKe^{-r(T-t)}\Phi(-d_-) - \left(D\Phi(-d_+) - \frac{\sigma e^{-\frac{1}{2}d_+^2}}{\sqrt{8\pi(T-t)}} \right) S_t e^{-D(T-t)}.$$

$\square$

9. *Rho.* Let the Black–Scholes formulae for a European call option $C(S_t, t; K, T)$ and a European put option $P(S_t, t; K, T)$ be

$$C(S_t, t; K, T) = S_t e^{-D(T-t)}\Phi(d_+) - Ke^{-r(T-t)}\Phi(d_-)$$
$$P(S_t, t; K, T) = Ke^{-r(T-t)}\Phi(-d_-) - S_t e^{-D(T-t)}\Phi(-d_+)$$

with $d_\pm$ given by

$$d_\pm = \frac{\log(S_t/K) + (r - D \pm \frac{1}{2}\sigma^2)(T-t)}{\sigma\sqrt{T-t}}$$

such that $\Phi(\cdot)$ is the cdf of a standard normal, S_t is the spot price at time $t < T$, T is the expiry date of the option, K is the strike price, r is the risk-free interest rate, D is the continuous dividend yield and σ is the spot price volatility.

Without explicitly computing the partial derivatives of $d_\pm$ show that the rho of a European call, $\rho_C = \frac{\partial C}{\partial r}$ and a European put, $\rho_P = \frac{\partial P}{\partial r}$ are

$$\rho_C = (T-t)Ke^{-r(T-t)}\Phi(d_-)$$

and

$$\rho_P = -(T-t)Ke^{-r(T-t)}\Phi(-d_-)$$

respectively.

Solution: Differentiating $C(S_t, t; K, T)$ with respect to r,

$$\frac{\partial C}{\partial r} = S_t e^{-D(T-t)} \frac{\partial \Phi(d_+)}{\partial d_+} \frac{\partial d_+}{\partial r} - K e^{-r(T-t)} \frac{\partial \Phi(d_-)}{\partial d_-} \frac{\partial d_-}{\partial r} + (T-t) K e^{-r(T-t)} \Phi(d_-).$$

Using the identity $d_- = d_+ - \sigma \sqrt{T-t}$ we have

$$\frac{\partial d_-}{\partial r} = \frac{\partial d_+}{\partial r}$$

and since

$$\frac{\partial \Phi(d_\pm)}{\partial d_\pm} = \frac{1}{\sqrt{2\pi}} e^{-\frac{1}{2} d_\pm^2}$$

and

$$S_t e^{-D(T-t)} e^{-\frac{1}{2} d_+^2} = K e^{-r(T-t)} e^{-\frac{1}{2} d_-^2}$$

we have

$$\frac{\partial C}{\partial r} = \frac{1}{\sqrt{2\pi}} \left(S_t e^{-D(T-t)} e^{-\frac{1}{2} d_+^2} - K e^{-r(T-t)} e^{-\frac{1}{2} d_-^2} \right) \frac{\partial d_+}{\partial r}$$
$$+ (T-t) K e^{-r(T-t)} \Phi(d_-)$$
$$= (T-t) K e^{-r(T-t)} \Phi(d_-).$$

Using the put–call parity

$$P(S_t, t; K, T) = K e^{-r(T-t)} - S_t e^{-D(T-t)} + C(S_t, t; K, T)$$

we have

$$\frac{\partial P}{\partial r} = -(T-t) K e^{-r(T-t)} \left(1 - \Phi(d_-) \right)$$
$$= -(T-t) K e^{-r(T-t)} \Phi(-d_-).$$

$\square$

10. *Psi.* Let the Black–Scholes formulae for a European call option $C(S_t, t; K, T)$ and a European put option $P(S_t, t; K, T)$ be

$$C(S_t, t; K, T) = S_t e^{-D(T-t)} \Phi(d_+) - K e^{-r(T-t)} \Phi(d_-)$$
$$P(S_t, t; K, T) = K e^{-r(T-t)} \Phi(-d_-) - S_t e^{-D(T-t)} \Phi(-d_+)$$

with $d_{\pm}$ given by

$$d_{\pm} = \frac{\log(S_t/K) + (r - D \pm \frac{1}{2}\sigma^2)(T - t)}{\sigma\sqrt{T - t}}$$

such that $\Phi(\cdot)$ is the cdf of a standard normal, S_t is the spot price at time $t < T$, T is the expiry date of the option, K is the strike price, r is the risk-free interest rate, D is the continuous dividend yield and σ is the spot price volatility.

Without explicitly computing the partial derivatives of $d_{\pm}$ show that the psi of a European call, $\psi_C = \dfrac{\partial C}{\partial D}$ and a European put, $\psi_P = \dfrac{\partial P}{\partial D}$ are

$$\psi_C = -(T - t)S_t e^{-D(T-t)}\Phi(d_+)$$

and

$$\psi_P = (T - t)S_t e^{-D(T-t)}\Phi(-d_+)$$

respectively.

Solution: Differentiating $C(S_t, t; K, T)$ with respect to D,

$$\frac{\partial C}{\partial D} = -(T - t)S_t e^{-D(T-t)}\Phi(d_+) + S_t e^{-D(T-t)}\frac{\partial \Phi(d_+)}{\partial d_+}\frac{\partial d_+}{\partial D}$$

$$- Ke^{-r(T-t)}\frac{\partial \Phi(d_-)}{\partial d_-}\frac{\partial d_-}{\partial D}.$$

Using the identity $d_- = d_+ - \sigma\sqrt{T - t}$ we have

$$\frac{\partial d_-}{\partial D} = \frac{\partial d_+}{\partial D}$$

and since

$$\frac{\partial \Phi(d_{\pm})}{\partial d_{\pm}} = \frac{1}{\sqrt{2\pi}}e^{-\frac{1}{2}d_{\pm}^2}$$

and

$$S_t e^{-D(T-t)}e^{-\frac{1}{2}d_+^2} = Ke^{-r(T-t)}e^{-\frac{1}{2}d_-^2}$$

we can deduce

$$S_t e^{-D(T-t)}e^{-\frac{1}{2}d_+^2}\frac{\partial d_+}{\partial D} = Ke^{-r(T-t)}e^{-\frac{1}{2}d_-^2}\frac{\partial d_-}{\partial D}.$$

Thus,

$$\frac{\partial C}{\partial D} = -(T-t)S_t e^{-D(T-t)}\Phi(d_+).$$

Finally, using the put–call parity

$$P(S_t, t; K, T) = C(S_t, t; K, T) + K e^{-r(T-t)} - S_t e^{-D(T-t)}$$

we have

$$\begin{aligned}
\frac{\partial P}{\partial D} &= \frac{\partial C}{\partial D} + (T-t)S_t e^{-D(T-t)} \\
&= -(T-t)S_t e^{-D(T-t)}\Phi(d_+) + (T-t)S_t e^{-D(T-t)} \\
&= (T-t)S_t e^{-D(T-t)}\left(1 - \Phi(d_+)\right) \\
&= (T-t)S_t e^{-D(T-t)}\Phi(-d_+).
\end{aligned}$$

$\square$

11. *Bos–Vandermark Model.* Let $\{W_t : t \geq 0\}$ be a $\mathbb{P}$-standard Wiener process on the probability space $(\Omega, \mathscr{F}, \mathbb{P})$ and let the stock price S_t follow a GBM with the following SDE

$$\frac{dS_t}{S_t} = \mu\, dt + \sigma\, dW_t$$

where μ is the drift parameter, σ is the volatility, and let r denote the risk-free interest rate. Assume the stock S_t pays a fixed discrete dividend Δ_D at time $t_{\Delta_D} > t$. For a strike price K, find the differential equation satisfied by the option $V(S_t, t; K, T)$ which can only be exercised at expiry time $T > t_{\Delta_D}$.

By setting $\lambda_t \in [0, 1]$ such that

$$\begin{aligned}
S_t^* &= S_t - \lambda_t \Delta_D e^{-r(t_{\Delta_D}-t)} \\
K^* &= K + (1 - \lambda_t)\Delta_D e^{r(T-t_{\Delta_D})}
\end{aligned}$$

show that for $t < t_{\Delta_D}$, the option premium price is

$$V(S_t, t; K, T) = V_{bs}(S_t^*, t; K^*, T)$$

satisfying

$$\Delta_D \left(\frac{\partial V_{bs}}{\partial S_t^*} + e^{r(T-t)}\frac{\partial V_{bs}}{\partial K^*}\right)\lambda_t' + \sigma^2 \left(\frac{1}{2}\Delta_D^2 e^{-r(t_{\Delta_D}-t)}\lambda_t^2 - \Delta_D S_t^* \lambda_t\right)\frac{\partial^2 V_{bs}}{\partial(S_t^*)^2} = 0$$

where $V_{bs}(\cdot)$ is the European option solution for zero discrete dividend.

By neglecting higher orders of $T - t$ and assuming $S_t^* \to K^*$, show that

$$\frac{\partial V_{bs}}{\partial S_t^*} + e^{r(T-t)}\frac{\partial V_{bs}}{\partial K^*} \approx \sigma^2(T - t)S_t^2 \frac{\partial^2 V_{bs}}{\partial(S_t^*)^2}$$

and finally by neglecting the contribution of Δ_D^2 deduce that

$$\lambda_t \approx \frac{T - t_{\Delta_D}}{T - t}.$$

You may assume that the cdf of the standard normal $\Phi(x)$ *can be approximated by the Marsaglia formula*

$$\Phi(x) = \frac{1}{2} + \phi(x)\left(x + \frac{x^3}{3} + \frac{x^5}{3 \cdot 5} + \cdots + \frac{x^{2n+1}}{3 \cdot 5 \cdot 7 \cdots (2n + 1)} + \ldots\right), n \in \mathbb{N}$$

where $\phi(x) = \dfrac{1}{\sqrt{2\pi}}e^{-\frac{1}{2}x^2}$.

Solution: For the first two results, refer to Problems 2.2.2.3 (page 93) and 2.2.2.13 (page 120).

Since

$$S_t^* = S_t - \lambda_t \Delta_D e^{-r(t_{\delta_D} - t)}$$
$$K^* = K + (1 - \lambda_t)\Delta_D e^{r(T - t_{\Delta_D})}$$

and from the identity $V(S_t, t; K, T) = V_{bs}(S_t^*, t; K^*, T)$ we have

$$
\begin{aligned}
\frac{\partial V}{\partial t} &= \frac{\partial V_{bs}}{\partial t} + \frac{\partial V_{bs}}{\partial S_t^*}\frac{\partial S_t^*}{\partial t} + \frac{\partial V_{bs}}{\partial K^*}\frac{\partial K^*}{\partial t} \\
&= \frac{\partial V_{bs}}{\partial t} + \frac{\partial V_{bs}}{\partial S_t^*}\left(-r\lambda_t \Delta_D e^{-r(t_{\Delta_D} - t)} - \Delta_D e^{-r(t_{\Delta_D} - t)}\lambda_t'\right) \\
&\quad + \frac{\partial V_{bs}}{\partial K^*}\left(-\Delta_D e^{r(T - t_{\Delta_D})}\lambda_t'\right) \\
&= \frac{\partial V_{bs}}{\partial t} - r\lambda_t \Delta_D e^{-r(t_{\Delta_D} - t)}\frac{\partial V_{bs}}{\partial S_t^*} - \Delta_D \lambda_t'\left(e^{-r(t_{\Delta_D} - t)}\frac{\partial V_{bs}}{\partial S_t^*} + e^{r(T - t_{\Delta_D})}\frac{\partial V_{bs}}{\partial K^*}\right)
\end{aligned}
$$

$$\frac{\partial V}{\partial S_t} = \frac{\partial V_{bs}}{\partial S_t^*}\frac{\partial S_t^*}{\partial S_t} = \frac{\partial V_{bs}}{\partial S_t^*}$$

and

$$\frac{\partial^2 V}{\partial S_t^2} = \frac{\partial}{\partial S_t}\left(\frac{\partial V_{bs}}{\partial S_t^*}\right) = \frac{\partial^2 V_{bs}}{\partial(S_t^*)^2}\frac{\partial S_t^*}{\partial S_t} = \frac{\partial^2 V_{bs}}{\partial(S_t^*)^2}.$$

By substituting the above results into the differential equation

$$\frac{\partial V}{\partial t} + \frac{1}{2}\sigma^2 S_t^2 \frac{\partial^2 V}{\partial S_t^2} + \left(rS_t - \Delta_D \cdot \delta(t - t_{\Delta_D})\right)\frac{\partial V}{\partial S_t} - rV(S_t, t; K, T) = 0$$

where $\delta(t - t_{\Delta_D})$ is the Dirac delta function centred at time $t = t_{\Delta_D}$, and after some algebraic manipulation we eventually arrive at

$$\delta\left(\frac{\partial V_{bs}}{\partial S_t^*} + e^{r(T-t)}\frac{\partial V_{bs}}{\partial K^*}\right)\lambda_t' + \sigma^2\left(\frac{1}{2}\Delta_D^2 e^{-r(t_{\Delta_D}-t)}\lambda_t^2 - \Delta_D S_t^*\lambda_t\right)\frac{\partial^2 V_{bs}}{\partial (S_t^*)^2} = 0.$$

Using the property $\Phi(x) = 1 - \Phi(-x)$ and from Problems 2.2.4.2 (page 220) and 2.2.4.4 (page 222), we have

$$\frac{\partial V_{bs}}{\partial S_t^*} + e^{r(T-t)}\frac{\partial V_{bs}}{\partial K^*} = \Phi(d_+) - \Phi(d_-).$$

From the definition

$$d_+^* = \frac{\log(S_t^*/K^*) + (r + \frac{1}{2}\sigma^2)(T - t)}{\sigma\sqrt{T - t}}$$

we can express

$$d_+^* = \left(\frac{r + \frac{1}{2}\sigma^2}{\sigma}\right)\sqrt{T - t} + O(\log(S_t^*/K^*))$$

$$(d_+^*)^2 = \left(\frac{r + \frac{1}{2}\sigma^2}{\sigma}\right)^2 (T - t) + O(\log(S_t^*/K^*))$$

$$(d_+^*)^3 = O((T - t)^{3/2}) + O(\log(S_t^*/K^*)).$$

Using Marsaglia's formula

$$\Phi(d_+^*) = \frac{1}{2} + \phi(d_+^*)\left(d_+^* + \frac{(d_+^*)^3}{3} + \ldots\right)$$

$$= \frac{1}{2} + \phi(d_+^*)\left(\frac{r + \frac{1}{2}\sigma^2}{\sigma}\right)\sqrt{T - t} + O((T - t)^{3/2})$$

$$+ O(\log(S_t^*/K^*))$$

and since $d_-^* = d_+^* - \sigma\sqrt{T-t}$, from Taylor's expansion

$$\phi(d_-^*) = \frac{1}{2} + \phi(d_-^*)\left(d_-^* + \frac{(d_-^*)^3}{3} + \cdots\right)$$

$$= \frac{1}{2} + \phi(d_+^* - \sigma\sqrt{T-t})\left(d_+^* - \sigma\sqrt{T-t} + \frac{(d_+^* - \sigma\sqrt{T-t})^3}{3} + \cdots\right)$$

$$= \frac{1}{2} + \left(\phi(d_+^*) - \sigma\phi'(d_+^*)\sqrt{T-t} + \frac{1}{2}\sigma^2\phi''(d_+^*)(T-t) + O((T-t)^{3/2})\right)$$

$$\times \left(\left(\frac{r - \frac{1}{2}\sigma^2}{\sigma}\right)\sqrt{T-t} + O((T-t)^{3/2}) + O(\log(S_t^*/K^*))\right)$$

$$= \frac{1}{2} + \phi(d_+^*)\left(\frac{r - \frac{1}{2}\sigma^2}{\sigma}\right)\sqrt{T-t} + O((T-t)^{3/2}) + O(\log(S_t^*/K^*)).$$

Thus,

$$\Phi(d_+^*) - \Phi(d_-^*) = \sigma\phi(d_+^*)\sqrt{T-t} + O((T-t)^{3/2}) + O(\log(S_t^*/K^*))$$

$$= \sigma\sqrt{\frac{T-t}{2\pi}}e^{-\frac{1}{2}(d_+^*)^2} + O((T-t)^{3/2}) + O(\log(S_t^*/K^*))$$

$$= \sigma^2(T-t)S_t^*\frac{\partial^2 V_{bs}}{\partial(S_t^*)^2} + O((T-t)^{3/2}) + O(\log(S_t^*/K^*))$$

since $\dfrac{\partial^2 V_{bs}}{\partial(S_t^*)^2} = \dfrac{e^{-\frac{1}{2}(d_+^*)^2}}{\sigma S_t^*\sqrt{2\pi(T-t)}}$ (see Problem 2.2.4.3, page 221).
Hence,

$$\frac{\partial V_{bs}}{\partial S_t^*} + e^{r(T-t)}\frac{\partial V_{bs}}{\partial K^*} = \sigma^2(T-t)S_t^*\frac{\partial^2 V_{bs}}{\partial(S_t^*)^2} + O((T-t)^{3/2}) + O(\log(S_t^*/K^*))$$

and ignoring higher orders of $T-t$ and assuming $S_t^* \to K^*$,

$$\frac{\partial V_{bs}}{\partial S_t^*} + e^{r(T-t)}\frac{\partial V_{bs}}{\partial K^*} \approx \sigma^2(T-t)S_t^*\frac{\partial^2 V_{bs}}{\partial(S_t^*)^2}.$$

By substituting the above result into

$$\Delta_D \left(\frac{\partial V_{bs}}{\partial S_t^*} + e^{r(T-t)} \frac{\partial V_{bs}}{\partial K^*} \right) \lambda_t' + \sigma^2 \left(\frac{1}{2} \Delta_D^2 e^{-r(t_{\Delta_D} - t)} \lambda_t^2 - \Delta_D S_t^* \lambda_t \right) \frac{\partial^2 V_{bs}}{\partial (S_t^*)^2} = 0$$

and neglecting the contribution of δ_D^2, we arrive at

$$\lambda_t' \approx \frac{\lambda_t}{T - t}.$$

Solving the first-order differentiation function,

$$\log \lambda_t \approx -\log(T - t) + C$$

where C is a constant. Since the discrete dividend Δ_D is paid at $t = t_{\Delta_D}$, therefore $\lambda_{t_{\Delta_D}} = 1$. Hence, we have $C = \log(T - t_{\Delta_D})$ and so

$$\lambda_t \approx \frac{T - t_{\Delta_D}}{T - t}.$$

$\square$

12. *Delta Hedging.* Assume we are in a Black–Scholes world where on day $t = 0$ a stock is trading at $S_0 = \$35$ per share. The stock price volatility is $\sigma = 25\%$ and it pays a continuous dividend yield $D = 2\%$. Suppose the writer of a European option sells a call option with strike $K = \$33$ on 1000 shares with time to expiration $T = 180$ days.

Given the risk-free interest rate $r = 5\%$ per annum, calculate the following.

(a) The call price and the corresponding delta at day 0. What is the writer's risk by selling a call option?

(b) The writer's trading strategy to maintain a delta-hedged portfolio on day 0. How much money does the writer need to borrow/put in a risk-free money market on day 0 in order to maintain a delta-hedged portfolio?

(c) The writer's profit if the stock price increases to \$35.50 on day 1. Calculate also the cost to keep the portfolio delta neutral.

(d) The writer's profit if the stock price falls to \$34.80 on day 2. Calculate also the cost to keep the portfolio delta neutral.

Note if $Z \sim \mathcal{N}(0, 1)$ *then the cumulative standard normal distribution function in the range* $[0, x]$, $x > 0$ *can be approximated by*

$$\mathbb{P}(0 < Z < x) = \frac{1}{\sqrt{2\pi}} \left(x - \frac{x^3}{6} + \frac{x^5}{40} - \frac{x^7}{336} + \frac{x^9}{3456} \right), 0 < x \ll 1.$$

Solution:

(a) On day 0 we have $S_0 = 35$, $K = 33$, $r = 0.05$, $D = 0.02$, $\sigma = 0.25$, $T = \frac{180}{365}$. From the Black–Scholes formula we can write the call option price as

$$C(S_0, 0; K, T) = S_0 e^{-DT} \Phi(d_1) - K e^{-rT} \Phi(d_2)$$

where

$$d_1 = \frac{\log\left(S_0/K\right) + (r - D + \frac{1}{2}\sigma^2)T}{\sigma\sqrt{T}}$$

$$= \frac{\log\left(35/33\right) + \left(0.05 - 0.02 + 0.5 \times 0.25^2\right)\frac{180}{365}}{0.25 \times \sqrt{\frac{180}{365}}}$$

$$= 0.5072$$

and

$$d_2 = d_1 - \sigma\sqrt{T} = 0.5072 - 0.25 \times \sqrt{\frac{180}{365}} = 0.3316.$$

Hence, from the polynomial approximation

$$\Phi(d_1) = \frac{1}{2} + \mathbb{P}(0 < Z < d_1)$$

$$= \frac{1}{2} + \frac{1}{\sqrt{2\pi}}\left(0.5072 - \frac{0.5072^3}{6} + \frac{0.5072^5}{40} - \frac{0.5072^7}{336} + \frac{0.5072^9}{3456}\right)$$

$$= 0.6940$$

and

$$\Phi(d_2) = \frac{1}{2} + \mathbb{P}(0 < Z < d_2)$$

$$= \frac{1}{2} + \frac{1}{\sqrt{2\pi}}\left(0.3316 - \frac{0.3316^3}{6} + \frac{0.3316^5}{40} - \frac{0.3316^7}{336} + \frac{0.3316^9}{3456}\right)$$

$$= 0.6299.$$

Therefore, on day 0 the call option price is

$$C(S_0, 0; K, T) = 35 \times e^{-0.02 \times \frac{180}{365}} \times 0.6940 - 33 \times e^{-0.05 \times \frac{180}{365}} \times 0.6299$$

$$= \$3.7712$$

and the corresponding delta is

$$\Delta_0 = e^{-DT}\Phi(d_1) = e^{-0.02 \times \frac{180}{365}} \times 0.6940 = 0.6872.$$

The risk of the call option writer is rising stock prices with respect to the option written on S_0.

(b) On day $t = 0$, let the hedging portfolio be

$$\Pi_0 = -C(S_0, 0; K, T) + \Delta S_0$$

where the call writer sells an option and buys Δ number of S_0. To maintain a delta-hedged portfolio we need

$$\frac{\partial \Pi_0}{\partial S_0} = 0$$

so that

$$\Delta = \frac{\partial C}{\partial S_0} = 0.6872.$$

That is, for each call option sold, the writer needs to buy 0.6872 units of $S_0 = \$35$.

To calculate how much money needs to be borrowed/put in a risk-free money market we replicate the derivative as

$$C(S_0, 0; K, T) = \Delta_0 S_0 + \psi_0$$

where ψ_0 is the amount of cash injected into the money market earning a risk-free interest rate $r = 5\%$.

Given $C(S_0, 0; K, T) = 3.7712$, $S_0 = 35$ and $\Delta_0 = 0.6872$ we have

$$\psi_0 = C(S_0, 0; K, T) - \Delta_0 S_0 = 3.7712 - 0.6872 \times 35 = -\$20.2808.$$

Thus, on day 0 the writer's trading strategy is to borrow $1000 \times \$20.2808 = \$20,280.80$ from the money market at $r = 5\%$ interest rate and purchase $1000 \times 0.6872 = 687.20$ units of $S_0 = \$35$.

(c) On day 1, $S_{\delta t} = 35.50$ where $\delta t = \frac{1}{365}$. The call option price is then

$$C(S_{\delta t}, \delta t; K, T) = S_{\delta t} e^{-D(T-\delta t)} \Phi(d_1) - K e^{-r(T-\delta t)} \Phi(d_2)$$

where

$$
\begin{aligned}
d_1 &= \frac{\log\left(S_{\delta t}/K\right) + (r - D + \frac{1}{2}\sigma^2)(T - \delta t)}{\sigma\sqrt{T - \delta t}} \\[2mm]
&= \frac{\log\left(35.50/33\right) + \left(0.05 - 0.02 + 0.5 \times 0.25^2\right)\frac{179}{365}}{0.25 \times \sqrt{\frac{179}{365}}} \\[2mm]
&= 0.5887
\end{aligned}
$$

and

$$d_2 = d_1 - \sigma\sqrt{T - \delta t} = 0.5887 - 0.25 \times \sqrt{\frac{179}{365}} = 0.4136.$$

Hence, from the polynomial approximation

$$\Phi(d_1) = \frac{1}{2} + \mathbb{P}(0 < Z < d_1)$$

$$= \frac{1}{2} + \frac{1}{\sqrt{2\pi}} \left(0.5887 - \frac{0.5887^3}{6} + \frac{0.5887^5}{40} - \frac{0.5887^7}{336} + \frac{0.5887^9}{3456} \right)$$

$$= 0.7720$$

and

$$\Phi(d_2) = \frac{1}{2} + \mathbb{P}(0 < Z < d_2)$$

$$= \frac{1}{2} + \frac{1}{\sqrt{2\pi}} \left(0.4136 - \frac{0.4136^3}{6} + \frac{0.4136^5}{40} - \frac{0.4136^7}{336} + \frac{0.4136^9}{3456} \right)$$

$$= 0.6604.$$

Therefore, on day 1 the call option price is

$$C(S_{\delta t}, \delta t; K, T) = 35.50 \times e^{-0.02 \times \frac{179}{365}} \times 0.7720 - 33 \times e^{-0.05 \times \frac{179}{365}} \times 0.6604$$

$$= \$4.1155$$

where

$$\text{Gains on option price sold} = 1000 \times (3.7712 - 4.1155) = -\$344.40$$

$$\text{Gains on share price purchased} = 1000 \times 0.6872 \times (35.50 - 35) = \$343.60$$

$$\text{1-Day interest} = 20{,}280.80 \times (1 - e^{0.05 \times \frac{1}{365}}) = -\$2.7783$$

so that

$$\text{Total profit on day 1} = -344.40 + 343.60 - 2.7783 = -\$3.4783.$$

The delta of the call option on day 1 is

$$\Delta_{\delta t} = e^{-D(T - \delta t)} \Phi(d_1) = e^{-0.02 \times \frac{179}{365}} \times 0.7220 = 0.7150$$

and to replicate the option

$$C(S_{\delta t}, \delta t; K, T) = \Delta_{\delta t} S_{\delta t} + \psi_{\delta t}$$

we have

$$\psi_{\delta t} = C(S_{\delta t}, \delta t; K, T) - \Delta_{\delta t} S_{\delta t} = 4.1155 - 0.7150 \times 35.50 = -\$21.2670.$$

Thus, on day 1, the writer needs to buy an additional $1000 \times (0.7150 - 0.6872) = 27.8$ units of $S_{\delta t} = \$35.50$ and borrow an additional $1000 \times (21.2670 - 20.2808) = \$986.20$ from the money market at $r = 5\%$ interest rate.

(d) On day 2, $S_{2\delta t} = 34.80$ where $\delta t = \frac{1}{365}$. The call option price is defined as

$$C(S_{2\delta t}, 2\delta t; K, T) = S_{2\delta t}e^{-D(T-2\delta t)}\Phi(d_1) - Ke^{-r(T-2\delta t)}\Phi(d_2)$$

where

$$
\begin{aligned}
d_1 &= \frac{\log\left(S_{2\delta t}/K\right) + (r - D + \frac{1}{2}\sigma^2)(T - 2\delta t)}{\sigma\sqrt{T - 2\delta t}} \\[2mm]
&= \frac{\log\left(34.80/33\right) + \left(0.05 - 0.02 + 0.5 \times 0.25^2\right)\frac{178}{365}}{0.25 \times \sqrt{\frac{178}{365}}} \\[2mm]
&= 0.4753
\end{aligned}
$$

and

$$d_2 = d_1 - \sigma\sqrt{T - 2\delta t} = 0.4753 - 0.25 \times \sqrt{\frac{178}{365}} = 0.3007.$$

Hence, from the polynomial approximation

$$
\begin{aligned}
\Phi(d_1) &= \frac{1}{2} + \mathbb{P}(0 < Z < d_1) \\[2mm]
&= \frac{1}{2} + \frac{1}{\sqrt{2\pi}}\left(0.4753 - \frac{0.4753^3}{6} + \frac{0.4753^5}{40} - \frac{0.4753^7}{336} + \frac{0.4753^9}{3456}\right) \\[2mm]
&= 0.6870
\end{aligned}
$$

and

$$
\begin{aligned}
\Phi(d_2) &= \frac{1}{2} + \mathbb{P}(0 < Z < d_2) \\[2mm]
&= \frac{1}{2} + \frac{1}{\sqrt{2\pi}}\left(0.3007 - \frac{0.3007^3}{6} + \frac{0.3007^5}{40} - \frac{0.3007^7}{336} + \frac{0.3007^9}{3456}\right) \\[2mm]
&= 0.6182.
\end{aligned}
$$

Therefore, on day 2 the call option price is

$$
\begin{aligned}
C(S_{2\delta t}, 2\delta t; K, T) &= 34.80 \times e^{-0.02 \times \frac{178}{365}} \times 0.6870 \\[2mm]
&\quad - 33 \times e^{-0.05 \times \frac{178}{365}} \times 0.6182 \\[2mm]
&= \$3.6182
\end{aligned}
$$

where

$$\text{Gains on option price sold} = 1000 \times (4.1155 - 3.6182) = \$497.30$$
$$\text{Gains on share price purchased} = 1000 \times 0.7150 \times (34.80 - 35.50)$$
$$= -\$500.50$$
$$\text{1-Day interest} = 21,267 \times (1 - e^{0.05 \times \frac{1}{365}}) = -\$2.9135$$

so that

$$\text{Total profit on day } 2 = 497.30 - 500.50 - 2.9135 = -\$6.1135.$$

The delta of the call option on day 2 is

$$\Delta_{2\delta t} = e^{-D(T-2\delta t)}\Phi(d_1) = e^{-0.02 \times \frac{178}{365}} \times 0.6870 = 0.6761$$

and to replicate the option

$$C(S_{2\delta t}, 2\delta t; K, T) = \Delta_{2\delta t}S_{2\delta t} + \psi_{2\delta t}$$

we have

$$\psi_{2\delta t} = C(S_{2\delta t}, 2\delta t; K, T) - \Delta_{2\delta t}S_{2\delta t}$$
$$= 3.6182 - 0.6761 \times 34.80$$
$$= -\$19.91008.$$

Thus, on day 2, the writer needs to sell $1000 \times (0.7150 - 0.6761) = 38.9$ units of $S_{2\delta t} = \$34.80$ and invest $1000 \times (21.2670 - 19.91008) = \$1356.92$ into the money market earning $r = 5\%$ interest rate.

$\square$

13. By referring to Problem 2.2.3.11 (page 211) find the trading strategy to hedge the option at the initial time period.

If the asset price moves down and up at time period $n = 1$ and $n = 2$, respectively, calculate the trading strategy to hedge this option.

Solution: At time period $n = 0$, let ϕ_0 and ψ_0 be the unit of the underlying asset S_0 and the amount of cash invested in the money market, respectively. At time period $n = 1$, the asset price can either be $S_1^{(0)} = dS_0$ or $S_1^1 = uS_0$ and ψ_0 will grow to $\psi_0 e^{r\Delta t}$. Thus, we can write

$$V_1^{(0)} = \phi_0 S_1^{(0)} + \psi_0 e^{r\Delta t}$$
$$V_1^{(1)} = \phi_0 S_1^{(1)} + \psi_0 e^{r\Delta t}.$$

Hence,

$$\phi_0 = \frac{V_1^{(1)} - V_1^{(0)}}{S_1^{(1)} - S_1^{(0)}} = \frac{V_1^{(1)} - V_1^{(0)}}{uS_0 - dS_0}$$

and

$$\psi_0 = e^{-r\Delta t}(V_1^{(0)} - \phi_0 S_1^{(0)}).$$

By substituting $V_1^{(0)} = 3.8322$, $V_1^{(1)} = 13.4438$, $S_1^{(0)} = d S_0 = 94.39$, $S_1^{(1)} = u S_0 = 105.94$, $r = 0.05$ and $\Delta t = \frac{1}{3}$ we have

$$\phi_0 = 0.8322 \quad \text{and} \quad \psi_0 = -73.4817$$

which implies we need to buy 0.8322 units of the underlying asset S_0 and borrow \$73.4817 from the money market at 5% interest rate.

At time period $n = 1$ we have $S_1 = S_1^{(0)} = d S_0$ and by setting ϕ_1 as the number of units of the underlying S_1 and ψ_1 as the amount of money invested in the money market, we can write the replication portfolio as

$$V_2^{(0)} = \phi_1 S_2^{(0)} + \psi_1 e^{r\Delta t}$$
$$V_2^{(1)} = \phi_1 S_2^{(1)} + \psi_1 e^{r\Delta t}.$$

Hence,

$$\phi_1 = \frac{V_2^{(1)} - V_2^{(0)}}{S_2^{(1)} - S_2^{(0)}} = \frac{V_2^{(1)} - V_2^{(0)}}{ud S_0 - d^2 S_0}$$

and

$$\psi_1 = e^{-r\Delta t}(V_2^{(0)} - \phi_1 S_2^{(0)}).$$

By substituting $V_2^{(0)} = 0$, $V_2^{(1)} = 6.4739$, $S_2^{(0)} = d^2 S_0 = 89.09$, $S_2^{(1)} = ud S_0 = 100$, $r = 0.05$ and $\Delta t = \frac{1}{3}$ we have

$$\phi_1 = 0.5936 \quad \text{and} \quad \psi_1 = -52.0360$$

where at time period $n = 1$ we now need to sell $0.8322 - 0.5936 = 0.2386$ units of the underlying asset $S_1 = \$94.39$ and invest $73.4817 - 52.0360 = \$21.4457$ into the money market earning 5% interest rate.

For time period 2, we set $S_2 = S_2^{(1)} = ud^2 S_0$ and we let ϕ_2 be the number of units of the underlying S_2 and ψ_2 be the amount of money invested in the money market. To replicate the payoff we have

$$V_3^{(1)} = \phi_2 S_3^{(1)} + \psi_2 e^{r\Delta t}$$
$$V_3^{(2)} = \phi_2 S_3^{(2)} + \psi_2 e^{r\Delta t}$$

and hence by solving the linear equations we have

$$\phi_2 = \frac{V_3^{(2)} - V_3^{(1)}}{S_3^{(2)} - S_3^{(1)}} = \frac{V_3^{(2)} - V_3^{(1)}}{u^2 d S_0 - u d^2 S_0}$$

and

$$\psi_2 = e^{-r\Delta t}(V_3^{(1)} - \phi_2 S_3^{(1)}).$$

Substituting $V_3^{(1)} = 0$, $V_3^{(2)} = 10.9366$, $S_3^{(1)} = u d^2 S_0 = 94.39$, $S_3^{(2)} = u^2 d S_0 = 105.94$, $r = 0.05$ and $\Delta t = \frac{1}{3}$ we have

$$\phi_2 = 0.9469 \quad \text{and} \quad \psi_2 = -89.8998$$

where we need to buy an additional $0.9469 - 0.5934 = 0.3535$ units of the underlying asset $S_2 = \$100$ and borrow an additional $89.8998 - 52.0360 = \$31.8638$ from the money market at 5% interest rate.

$\square$

14. At time t the stock price is trading at $S_t = \$40$ with delta $\Delta_t = 0.4127$ and gamma $\Gamma_t = 0.1134$. Estimate the new value of delta if $S_{t+\delta t} = \$42.75$ at time $t + \delta t$, $\delta t > 0$.

Solution: By definition, $\Gamma_t = \dfrac{\partial \Delta_t}{\partial S_t}$ which can be approximated by

$$\Gamma_t \approx \frac{\Delta_{t+\delta t} - \Delta_t}{S_{t+\delta t} - S_t}.$$

Hence,

$$\begin{aligned}
\Delta_{t+\delta t} &\approx \Delta_t + \Gamma_t(S_{t+\delta t} - S_t) \\
&= 0.4127 + 0.1134 \times (42.75 - 40) \\
&= 0.7246.
\end{aligned}$$

$\square$

15. Consider a stock trading at $S_t = \$49$ with volatility $\sigma_t = 35\%$ at time t. A European put option $P(S_t, t)$ on the stock is priced at $\$2.3217$ with vega $\mathcal{V}_t = 0.3796$. If the volatility increases by 0.5% at time $t + \delta t$, $\delta t > 0$, find the new put option price.

Solution: By definition, $\mathcal{V}_t = \dfrac{\partial P}{\partial \sigma_t}$ which can be approximated by

$$\mathcal{V}_t \approx \frac{P(S_{t+\delta t}, t + \delta t) - P(S_t, t)}{\sigma_{t+\delta t} - \sigma_t}.$$

Hence,

$$P(S_{t+\delta t}, t + \delta t) \approx P(S_t, t) + \mathcal{V}_t(\sigma_{t+\delta t} - \sigma_t)$$
$$= 2.3217 - 0.3796 \times 0.05$$
$$= 2.3407.$$

□

16. At time t, we have an asset price $S_t = \$37$ which pays a continuous dividend yield $D = 1.2\%$ with volatility $\sigma = 30\%$. By setting the risk-free interest rate $r = 8.5\%$ we let $C(S_t, t; K, T)$ be the European call option price having a strike price $K = \$35$ with time to expiry $T - t = 90$ days, where T is the option expiry time.

From the information given in Table 2.3 find the price of the European put option at time t.

Table 2.3   European call option Greek values.

European Call Option Greeks	Value
Δ_t	0.7110
Γ_t	0.0620
$\mathcal{V}_t$	0.0624
Θ_t (per calendar day)	−0.0146

Solution: From the Black–Scholes equation

$$\frac{\partial C}{\partial t} + \frac{1}{2}\sigma^2 S_t^2 \frac{\partial^2 C}{\partial S_t^2} + (r - D)S_t \frac{\partial C}{\partial S_t} - rC(S_t, t; K, T) = 0$$

or

$$\Theta_t + \frac{1}{2}\sigma^2 S_t^2 \Gamma_t + (r - D)S_t \Delta_t - rC(S_t, t; K, T) = 0.$$

Given that $\Theta_t = 0.0146$ is quoted per calendar day, then per year

$$\Theta_t = -0.0146 \times 365 = -5.3290.$$

Therefore, the call option price is

$$C(S_t, t; K, T) = \frac{1}{r}\left(\Theta_t + \frac{1}{2}\sigma^2 S_t^2 \Gamma_t + (r - D)S_t \Delta_t\right)$$

$$= \frac{1}{0.085}\left(-5.3290 + 0.5 \times 0.3^2 \times 37^2 \times 0.0620\right.$$

$$+ (0.085 - 0.012) \times 37 \times 0.7110)$$

$$= \$4.8344.$$

From put–call parity, the put option price is

$$P(S_t,t;K,T) = C(S_t,t;K,T) - S_t e^{-D(T-t)} + Ke^{-r(T-t)}$$
$$= 4.8344 - 37e^{-0.012\times\frac{90}{365}} + 35e^{-0.085\times\frac{90}{365}}$$
$$= \$2.2178.$$

□

17. Let $\{W_t : t \geq 0\}$ be a $\mathbb{P}$-standard Wiener process on the probability space $(\Omega, \mathcal{F}, \mathbb{P})$ and let the evolution of the asset price S_t have the following SDE

$$\frac{dS_t}{S_t} = (\mu - D)dt + \sigma dW_t$$

where μ is the drift parameter, D is the continuous dividend yield and σ is the asset price volatility. By setting r as the risk-free interest rate, a derivative security written on this asset has price $V(S_t,t)$ with payoff $\Psi(S_T)$ at expiry time T.

Show that the interest-rate sensitivity $\rho(S_t,t) = \dfrac{\partial V}{\partial r}$ satisfies the differential equation

$$\mathcal{L}_{BS}[\rho(S_t,t)] = V(S_t,t) - S_t \frac{\partial V}{\partial S_t}$$

with boundary condition $\rho(S_T,T) = 0$ where $\mathcal{L}_{BS}$ denotes the differential operator

$$\mathcal{L}_{BS} = \frac{\partial}{\partial t} + \frac{1}{2}\sigma^2 S_t^2 \frac{\partial^2}{\partial S_t^2} + (r-D)S_t\frac{\partial}{\partial S_t} - r.$$

Interpret this result financially.

By writing the solution of $\rho(S_t,t)$ in the form

$$\rho(S_t,t) = g(t)U(S_t,t)$$

with $U(S_T,T) = 0$, show that

$$\rho(S_t,t) = -(T-t)\left[V(S_t,t) - S_t\frac{\partial V}{\partial S_t}\right].$$

Solution: Since $V(S_t,t)$ satisfies

$$\frac{\partial V}{\partial t} + \frac{1}{2}\sigma^2 S_t^2 \frac{\partial^2 V}{\partial S_t^2} + (r-D)S_t\frac{\partial V}{\partial S_t} - rV(S_t,t) = 0$$

then by differentiating the Black–Scholes equation with respect to r we have

$$\frac{\partial}{\partial r}\left(\frac{\partial V}{\partial t} + \frac{1}{2}\sigma^2 S_t^2 \frac{\partial^2 V}{\partial S_t^2} + (r - D)S_t \frac{\partial V}{\partial S_t} - rV(S_t,t)\right) = 0$$

or

$$\frac{\partial}{\partial t}\left(\frac{\partial V}{\partial r}\right) + \frac{1}{2}\sigma^2 S_t^2 \frac{\partial^2}{\partial S_t^2}\left(\frac{\partial V}{\partial r}\right) + S_t \frac{\partial V}{\partial S_t} + (r - D)S_t \frac{\partial}{\partial S_t}\left(\frac{\partial V}{\partial r}\right) - V(S_t,t) - r\frac{\partial V}{\partial r} = 0.$$

By setting $\rho(S_t,t) = \dfrac{\partial V}{\partial r}$ we have

$$\frac{\partial \rho}{\partial t} + \frac{1}{2}\sigma^2 S_t^2 \frac{\partial^2 \rho}{\partial S_t^2} + (r - D)S_t \frac{\partial \rho}{\partial S_t} - r\rho(S_t,t) = V(S_t,t) - S_t \frac{\partial V}{\partial S_t}.$$

Because $V(S_T,T) = \Psi(S_T)$, thus $\dfrac{\partial V}{\partial r}(S_T,T) = \rho(S_T,T) = 0$.

Hence,

$$\mathcal{L}_{BS}[\rho(S_t,t)] = V(S_t,t) - S_t \frac{\partial V}{\partial S_t}$$

with boundary condition $\rho(S_T,T) = 0$.

If we set the delta of the option $\dfrac{\partial V}{\partial S_t} = \Delta$ then

$$\mathcal{L}_{BS}[\rho(S_t,t)] = V(S_t,t) - \Delta S_t$$

which is equivalent to a hedging portfolio used to construct the Black–Scholes equation.

By letting the solution of $\rho(S_t,t)$ be written as

$$\rho(S_t,t) = g(t)U(S_t,t)$$

where $g(t)$ is a function depending on time t, then by substituting it into the Black–Scholes differential operator

$$\begin{aligned}
\mathcal{L}_{BS}[\rho(S_t,t)] &= \mathcal{L}_{BS}[g(t)U(S_t,t)] \\
&= \frac{\partial}{\partial t}[g(t)U(S_t,t)] + \frac{1}{2}\sigma^2 S_t^2 \frac{\partial^2}{\partial S_t^2}[g(t)U(S_t,t)] \\
&\quad + (r - D)S_t \frac{\partial}{\partial S_t}[g(t)U(S_t,t)] - r[g(t)U(S_t,t)] \\
&= \frac{dg}{dt}U(S_t,t) + g(t)\mathcal{L}_{BS}[U(S_t,t)].
\end{aligned}$$

By setting $U(S_t,t) = V(S_t,t) - S_t \dfrac{\partial V}{\partial S_t}$ and since both $V(S_t,t)$ and $\dfrac{\partial V}{\partial S_t}$ satisfy the Black–Scholes equation (see Problem 2.2.2.9, page 110), therefore

$$\mathcal{L}_{BS}[U(S_t,t)] = \mathcal{L}_{BS}[V(S_t,t)] - \mathcal{L}_{BS}\left[S_t \frac{\partial V}{\partial S_t}\right] = 0.$$

Thus, we can set

$$\mathcal{L}_{BS}[\rho(S_t,t)] = \frac{dg}{dt}\left[V(S_t,t) - S_t \frac{\partial V}{\partial S_t}\right]$$

where $\dfrac{dg}{dt} = 1$ with boundary condition $g(T) = 0$.

Solving the first-order differential equation and taking note that $g(T) = 0$, we have

$$g(t) = -(T - t)$$

and hence

$$\rho(S_t,t) = -(T - t)\left[V(S_t,t) - S_t \frac{\partial V}{\partial S_t}\right].$$

$\square$

18. Let $\{W_t : t \geq 0\}$ be a $\mathbb{P}$-standard Wiener process on the probability space $(\Omega, \mathcal{F}, \mathbb{P})$ and let the asset price S_t follow a GBM process

$$\frac{dS_t}{S_t} = (\mu - D)dt + \sigma dW_t$$

where μ is the drift parameter, D is the continuous dividend yield and σ is the asset price volatility. By setting r as the risk-free interest rate, a derivative security written on this asset has price $V(S_t,t)$ with payoff $\Psi(S_T)$ at expiry time T.

Show that the volatility sensitivity $\mathcal{V}(S_t,t) = \dfrac{\partial V}{\partial \sigma}$ satisfies

$$\mathcal{L}_{BS}[\mathcal{V}(S_t,t)] + \sigma S_t^2 \Gamma(S_t,t) = 0$$

with boundary condition $\mathcal{V}(S_T,T) = 0$ where

$$\Gamma(S_t,t) = \frac{\partial^2 V}{\partial S_t^2}$$

is the gamma of the option price and $\mathcal{L}_{BS}$ denotes the differential operator

$$\mathcal{L}_{BS} = \frac{\partial}{\partial t} + \frac{1}{2}\sigma^2 S_t^2 \frac{\partial^2}{\partial S_t^2} + (r - D)S_t \frac{\partial}{\partial S_t} - r.$$

Let $U(S_t,t)$ be the price of another option that receives or pays $K(S_t,t)$ per unit time ($K(S_t,t) > 0$ denotes receiving an income whilst $K(S_t,t) < 0$ corresponds to a payment). By setting up a hedging portfolio show that $U(S_t,t)$ satisfies

$$\mathcal{L}_{BS}[U(S_t,t)] + K(S_t,t) = 0.$$

Further, show that if $U(S_T,T) = 0$ and $K(S_t,t) > 0$ for $0 \le t < T$ then $U(S_t,t) > 0$ for $0 \le t < T$.

Hence, deduce that if $\Gamma(S_t,t) > 0$ then $\mathcal{V}(S_t,t) > 0$ and finally show that

$$\mathcal{V}(S_t,t) = (T-t)\sigma S_t^2 \Gamma(S_t,t).$$

Solution: Since $V(S_t,t)$ satisfies

$$\frac{\partial V}{\partial t} + \frac{1}{2}\sigma^2 S_t^2 \frac{\partial^2 V}{\partial S_t^2} + (r-D)S_t \frac{\partial V}{\partial S_t} - rV(S_t,t) = 0$$

and by differentiating the Black–Scholes equation with respect to σ we have

$$\frac{\partial}{\partial \sigma}\left(\frac{\partial V}{\partial t} + \frac{1}{2}\sigma^2 S_t^2 \frac{\partial^2 V}{\partial S_t^2} + (r-D)S_t \frac{\partial V}{\partial S_t} - rV(S_t,t) \right) = 0$$

or

$$\frac{\partial}{\partial t}\left(\frac{\partial V}{\partial \sigma} \right) + \sigma S_t^2 \frac{\partial^2 V}{\partial S_t^2} + \frac{1}{2}\sigma^2 S_t^2 \frac{\partial^2}{\partial S_t^2}\left(\frac{\partial V}{\partial \sigma} \right) + (r-D)S_t \frac{\partial}{\partial S_t}\left(\frac{\partial V}{\partial \sigma} \right) - r\frac{\partial V}{\partial \sigma} = 0.$$

By setting $\mathcal{V}(S_t,t) = \dfrac{\partial V}{\partial \sigma}$ and $\Gamma(S_t,t) = \dfrac{\partial^2 V}{\partial S_t^2}$ we can write

$$\frac{\partial \mathcal{V}}{\partial t} + \frac{1}{2}\sigma^2 S_t^2 \frac{\partial^2 \mathcal{V}}{\partial S_t^2} + (r-D)S_t \frac{\partial \mathcal{V}}{\partial S_t} - r\mathcal{V}(S_t,t) + \sigma S_t^2 \Gamma(S_t,t) = 0$$

and using the differential operator $\mathcal{L}_{BS}$ we eventually have

$$\mathcal{L}_{BS}[\mathcal{V}(S_t,t)] + \sigma S_t^2 \Gamma(S_t,t) = 0$$

with boundary condition

$$\mathcal{V}(S_T,T) = \frac{\partial V}{\partial \sigma}(S_T,T) = \frac{\partial \Psi}{\partial \sigma}(S_T) = 0.$$

At time t we let the hedging portfolio Π_t be constructed by taking a long position on option $U(S_t,t)$ and short Δ units of S_t such that

$$\Pi_t = U(S_t,t) - \Delta S_t.$$

Since the asset pays a continuous dividend yield D and the option $U(S_t,t)$ receives/pays $K(S_t,t)$ per unit time, the instantaneous change in the portfolio is

$$d\Pi_t = dU + K(S_t,t)dt - \Delta(dS_t + DS_tdt)$$
$$= dU - \Delta dS_t + (K(S_t,t) - \Delta D S_t)dt.$$

Expanding $U(S_t,t)$ using Taylor's theorem we have

$$dU = \frac{\partial U}{\partial t}dt + \frac{\partial U}{\partial S_t}dS_t + \frac{1}{2}\frac{\partial^2 U}{\partial S_t^2}dS_t^2 + \ldots$$

Substituting $dS_t = (\mu - D)S_tdt + \sigma S_tdW_t$ and applying Itō's lemma

$$dU = \left(\frac{\partial U}{\partial t} + \frac{1}{2}\sigma^2 S_t^2\frac{\partial^2 U}{\partial S_t^2} + (\mu - D)S_t\frac{\partial U}{\partial S_t}\right)dt + \sigma S_t\frac{\partial U}{\partial S_t}dW_t.$$

Hence,

$$d\Pi_t = \left(\frac{\partial U}{\partial t} + \frac{1}{2}\sigma^2 S_t^2\frac{\partial^2 U}{\partial S_t^2} + (\mu - D)S_t\frac{\partial U}{\partial S_t} + K(S_t,t) - \mu\Delta S_t\right)dt$$
$$+\sigma S_t\left(\frac{\partial U}{\partial S_t} - \Delta\right)dW_t$$

and to eliminate the risk we set

$$\Delta = \frac{\partial U}{\partial S_t}$$

so that

$$d\Pi_t = \left(\frac{\partial U}{\partial t} + \frac{1}{2}\sigma^2 S_t^2\frac{\partial^2 U}{\partial S_t^2} + (\mu - D)S_t\frac{\partial U}{\partial S_t} + K(S_t,t) - \mu\Delta S_t\right)dt.$$

Under the no-arbitrage condition the return on the amount Π_t invested in a risk-free interest rate r would be

$$d\Pi_t = r\Pi_tdt$$

and taking into account that $\Delta = \dfrac{\partial V}{\partial S_t}$ we have

$$r\Pi_t dt = \left(\frac{\partial U}{\partial t} + \frac{1}{2}\sigma^2 S_t^2 \frac{\partial^2 U}{\partial S_t^2} + (\mu - D)S_t \frac{\partial U}{\partial S_t} \right.$$
$$\left. +K(S_t, t) - \mu \Delta S_t \right) dt$$

$$r(U(S_t, t) - \Delta S_t)dt = \left(\frac{\partial U}{\partial t} + \frac{1}{2}\sigma^2 S_t^2 \frac{\partial^2 U}{\partial S_t^2} + (\mu - D)S_t \frac{\partial U}{\partial S_t} \right.$$
$$\left. +K(S_t, t) - \mu \Delta S_t \right) dt$$

$$r\left(U(S_t, t) - S_t \frac{\partial U}{\partial S_t} \right) = \frac{\partial U}{\partial t} + \frac{1}{2}\sigma^2 S_t^2 \frac{\partial^2 U}{\partial S_t^2} + (\mu - D)S_t \frac{\partial U}{\partial S_t}$$
$$+K(S_t, t) - \mu S_t \frac{\partial U}{\partial S_t}$$

and finally we have

$$\frac{\partial U}{\partial t} + \frac{1}{2}\sigma^2 S_t^2 \frac{\partial^2 U}{\partial S_t^2} + (r - D)S_t \frac{\partial U}{\partial S_t} - rU(S_t, t) + K(S_t, t) = 0$$

or

$$\mathcal{L}_{BS}[U(S_t, t)] + K(S_t, t) = 0.$$

Assume that if $U(S_T, T) = 0$ and $K(S_t, t) > 0$ for $0 \leq t < T$ then $U(S_t, t) \leq 0$ for $0 \leq t < T$. Let the portfolio be

$$\widetilde{\Pi}_t = U(S_t, t) \leq 0$$

where the instantaneous change in the portfolio becomes

$$d\widetilde{\Pi}_t = dU(S_t, t) + K(S_t, t)dt.$$

Taking integrals and because $U(S_T, T) = 0$ and $K(S_t, t) > 0$ for $0 \leq t < T$

$$\widetilde{\Pi}_T - \widetilde{\Pi}_t = U(S_T, T) - U(S_t, t) + \int_t^T K(S_t, t)dt$$

$$\widetilde{\Pi}_T = U(S_T, T) + \int_t^T K(S_t, t)dt$$

$$= \int_t^T K(S_t, t)dt$$

$$> 0$$

which is a contradiction under the no-arbitrage condition. Therefore, $U(S_t, t) > 0$ for $0 \leq t < T$.

By comparing

$$\mathcal{L}_{BS}[V(S_t, t)] + \sigma S_t^2 \Gamma(S_t, t) = 0, \quad V(S_T, T) = 0$$

and

$$\mathcal{L}_{BS}[U(S_t, t)] + K(S_t, t) = 0, \quad U(S_T, T) = 0$$

we can deduce that if $K(S_t, t) = \sigma S_t^2 \Gamma(S_t, t) > 0$ then $U(S_t, t) = V(S_t, t) > 0$ for $0 \leq t < T$. Hence, for any option price, if the gamma is always positive then it has a positive vega.

Let $V(S_t, t) = g(t)\widetilde{K}(S_t, t)$ where $\widetilde{K}(S_t, t) = -\sigma S_t^2 \Gamma(S_t, t)$ and since $S_t^2 \dfrac{\partial^2 V}{\partial S_t^2}$ satisfies the Black–Scholes equation we have

$$
\begin{aligned}
\mathcal{L}_{BS}[V(S_t, t)] &= \mathcal{L}_{BS}[g(t)\widetilde{K}(S_t, t)] \\
&= \frac{\partial}{\partial t}[g(t)\widetilde{K}(S_t, t)] + \frac{1}{2}\sigma^2 S_t^2 \frac{\partial^2}{\partial S_t^2}[g(t)\widetilde{K}(S_t, t)] \\
&\quad +(r - D)S_t \frac{\partial}{\partial S_t}[g(t)\widetilde{K}(S_t, t)] - r[g(t)\widetilde{K}(S_t, t)] \\
&= \frac{dg}{dt}\widetilde{K}(S_t, t) + g(t)\mathcal{L}_{BS}[\widetilde{K}(S_t, t)] \\
&= \frac{dg}{dt}\widetilde{K}(S_t, t).
\end{aligned}
$$

Since $\mathcal{L}_{BS}[V(S_t, t)] = \widetilde{K}(S_t, t)$ then

$$\frac{dg}{dt} = 1$$

with boundary condition

$$g(T) = 1.$$

Solving the first-order differential equation we have

$$g(t) = -(T - t)$$

and hence

$$V(S_t, t) = -(T - t)\widetilde{K}(S_t, t) = (T - t)\sigma S_t^2 \Gamma(S_t, t).$$

$\square$

19. Let $\{W_t : t \geq 0\}$ be a $\mathbb{P}$-standard Wiener process on the probability space $(\Omega, \mathcal{F}, \mathbb{P})$ and at time t let the asset price S_t follow a GBM process

$$\frac{dS_t}{S_t} = (\mu - D)dt + \sigma dW_t$$

where μ is the drift parameter, D is the continuous dividend yield and σ is the asset price volatility.

Let the European call option $C(S_t, t; K, T)$ satisfy the following PDE

$$\frac{\partial C}{\partial t} + \frac{1}{2}\sigma^2 S_t^2 \frac{\partial^2 C}{\partial S_t^2} + (r - D)S_t \frac{\partial C}{\partial S_t} - rC(S_t, t; K, T) = 0$$

$$C(S_T, T; K, T) = \max\{S_T - K, 0\}$$

and the European digital call option price $C_d(S_t, t; K, T)$ satisfy

$$\frac{\partial C_d}{\partial t} + \frac{1}{2}\sigma^2 S_t^2 \frac{\partial^2 C_d}{\partial S_t^2} + (r - D)S_t \frac{\partial C_d}{\partial S_t} - rC_d(S_t, t; K, T) = 0$$

$$C_d(S_T, T; K, T) = \begin{cases} 1 & \text{if } S_T > K \\ 0 & \text{if } S_T \leq K \end{cases}$$

where r is the risk-free interest rate, K is the strike price and T is the option expiry time. Explain why, given

$$\frac{\partial}{\partial S_T} \max\{S_T - K, 0\} = \begin{cases} 1 & \text{if } S_T > K \\ 0 & \text{if } S_T \leq K \end{cases}$$

we have $C_d(S_t, t; K, T) \neq \Delta_C(S_t, t; K, T)$ where $\Delta_C(S_t, t; K, T) = \dfrac{\partial C}{\partial S_t}$.

Suppose $\hat{C}(S_t, t; K, T)$ is the price of another European call option with strike K and expiry time T where in this case the risk-free interest rate is $\hat{r}$, the continuous dividend yield $\hat{D}$ and volatility σ. By choosing appropriate $\hat{r}$ and $\hat{D}$ in terms of r, D and σ show that $C_d(S_t, t; K, T)$ and $\hat{\Delta}_C(S_t, t; K, T) = \dfrac{\partial \hat{C}}{\partial S_t}$ satisfy exactly the same Black–Scholes equation and payoff. Hence, deduce that

$$C_d(S_t, t; K, T) = e^{-r(T-t)}\Phi(d_-)$$

where

$$d_- = \frac{\log(S_t/K) + (r - D - \frac{1}{2}\sigma^2)(T - t)}{\sigma\sqrt{T - t}} \quad \text{and} \quad \Phi(x) = \int_{-\infty}^{x} \frac{1}{\sqrt{2\pi}}e^{-\frac{1}{2}u^2}\,du.$$

Solution: From the Black–Scholes equation

$$\frac{\partial C}{\partial t} + \frac{1}{2}\sigma^2 S_t^2 \frac{\partial^2 C}{\partial S_t^2} + (r-D)S_t \frac{\partial C}{\partial S_t} - rC(S_t,t;K,T) = 0$$

$$C(S_T,T;K,T) = \max\{S_T - K, 0\}$$

and by differentiating with respect to S_t

$$\frac{\partial}{\partial S_t}\left(\frac{\partial C}{\partial t} + \frac{1}{2}\sigma^2 S_t^2 \frac{\partial^2 C}{\partial S_t^2} + (r-D)S_t \frac{\partial C}{\partial S_t} - rC(S_t,t;K,T)\right) = 0$$

or

$$\frac{\partial}{\partial t}\left(\frac{\partial C}{\partial S_t}\right) + \sigma^2 S_t \frac{\partial^2 C}{\partial S_t^2} + \frac{1}{2}\sigma^2 S_t^2 \frac{\partial^2}{\partial S_t^2}\left(\frac{\partial C}{\partial S_t}\right)$$

$$+ (r-D)\frac{\partial C}{\partial S_t} + (r-D)S_t \frac{\partial}{\partial S_t}\left(\frac{\partial C}{\partial S_t}\right) - r\frac{\partial C}{\partial S_t} = 0.$$

By setting $\Delta_C(S_t,t;K,T) = \dfrac{\partial C}{\partial S_t}$ we have

$$\frac{\partial \Delta_C}{\partial t} + \frac{1}{2}\sigma^2 S_t^2 \frac{\partial^2 \Delta_C}{\partial S_t^2} + (r-D+\sigma^2)S_t \frac{\partial \Delta_C}{\partial S_t} - D\Delta_C(S_t,t;K,T) = 0$$

$$\Delta_C(S_T,T;K,T) = \begin{cases} 1 & \text{if } S_T > K \\ 0 & \text{if } S_T \leq K \end{cases}$$

which is not the same problem that $C_d(S_t,t;K,T)$ satisfies. Hence, $C_d(S_t,t;K,T) \neq \Delta_C(S_t,t;K,T)$.

For the case $\hat{C}(S_t,t;K,T)$, it satisfies

$$\frac{\partial \hat{C}}{\partial t} + \frac{1}{2}\sigma^2 S_t^2 \frac{\partial^2 \hat{C}}{\partial S_t^2} + (\hat{r}-\hat{D})S_t \frac{\partial \hat{C}}{\partial S_t} - \hat{r}\hat{C}(S_t,t;K,T) = 0$$

$$\hat{C}(S_T,T;K,T) = \max\{S_T - K, 0\}$$

and its delta $\hat{\Delta}_C(S_t,t;K,T) = \dfrac{\partial \hat{C}}{\partial S_t}$ satisfies

$$\frac{\partial \hat{\Delta}_C}{\partial t} + \frac{1}{2}\sigma^2 S_t^2 \frac{\partial^2 \hat{\Delta}_C}{\partial S_t^2} + (\hat{r}-\hat{D}+\sigma^2)S_t \frac{\partial \hat{\Delta}_C}{\partial S_t} - \hat{D}\hat{\Delta}_C(S_t,t;K,T) = 0$$

$$\hat{\Delta}_C(S_T,T;K,T) = \begin{cases} 1 & \text{if } S_T > K \\ 0 & \text{if } S_T \leq K. \end{cases}$$

By comparing the PDEs and payoffs satisfied by $C_d(S_t, t; K, T)$ and $\hat{\Delta}_C(S_t, t; K, T)$ and in order for

$$C_d(S_t, t; K, T) = \hat{\Delta}_C(S_t, t; K, T)$$

we can set $\hat{D} = r$ and $\hat{r} - \hat{D} + \sigma^2 = r - D$. Hence,

$$\hat{r} = 2r - D - \sigma^2 \quad \text{and} \quad \hat{D} = r.$$

Following Problem 2.2.4.2 (page 220) we have

$$C_d(S_t, t; K, T) = \hat{\Delta}_C(S_t, t; K, T)$$
$$= \frac{\partial}{\partial S_t} \hat{C}(S_t, t; K, T)$$
$$= e^{-\hat{D}(T-t)} \Phi(\hat{d}_+)$$

where $\hat{d}_+ = \dfrac{\log(S_t/K) + (\hat{r} - \hat{D} + \frac{1}{2}\sigma^2)(T - t)}{\sigma\sqrt{T - t}}$.

By substituting $\hat{r} = 2r - D - \sigma^2$ and $\hat{D} = r$ we have

$$e^{-\hat{D}(T-t)} = e^{-r(T-t)}$$

and

$$\hat{d}_+ = \frac{\log(S_t/K) + (r - D - \frac{1}{2}\sigma^2)(T - t)}{\sigma\sqrt{T - t}} = d_-.$$

Hence, $C_d(S_t, t; K, T) = e^{-r(T-t)} \Phi(d_-)$.

□

20. Let $\{W_t : t \geq 0\}$ be the standard Wiener process on the probability space $(\Omega, \mathcal{F}, \mathbb{P})$ where at time t the stock price S_t follows the following diffusion process

$$\frac{dS_t}{S_t} = (\mu - D)dt + \sigma dW_t$$

for constant drift μ, continuous dividend yield D and volatility σ. The risk-free interest rate is a constant r and a derivative security written on this asset has price $V(S_t, t)$ with payoff $\Psi(S_T)$ at expiry time T.

By defining the sensitivity of the option price with respect to the continuous dividend yield

$$\varphi(S_t, t) = \frac{\partial V}{\partial D}$$

show that

$$\mathcal{L}_{BS}[\varphi(S_t,t)] - S_t\frac{\partial V}{\partial S_t} = 0$$

with boundary condition $\varphi(S_T,T) = 0$ where $\mathcal{L}_{BS}$ denotes the Black–Scholes differential operator

$$\mathcal{L}_{BS} = \frac{\partial}{\partial t} + \frac{1}{2}\sigma^2 S_t^2 \frac{\partial^2}{\partial S_t^2} + (r-D)S_t\frac{\partial}{\partial S_t} - r.$$

Deduce that

$$\varphi(S_t,t) = -(T-t)S_t\frac{\partial V}{\partial S_t}$$

and give a financial interpretation of this result.

Solution: Given that $V(S_t,t)$ satisfies

$$\frac{\partial V}{\partial t} + \frac{1}{2}\sigma^2 S_t^2 \frac{\partial^2 V}{\partial S_t^2} + (r-D)S_t\frac{\partial V}{\partial S_t} - rV(S_t,t) = 0$$

and by differentiating the Black–Scholes equation with respect to D we have

$$\frac{\partial}{\partial D}\left(\frac{\partial V}{\partial t} + \frac{1}{2}\sigma^2 S_t^2 \frac{\partial^2 V}{\partial S_t^2} + (r-D)S_t\frac{\partial V}{\partial S_t} - rV(S_t,t)\right) = 0$$

or

$$\frac{\partial}{\partial t}\left(\frac{\partial V}{\partial D}\right) + \frac{1}{2}\sigma^2 S_t^2 \frac{\partial^2}{\partial S_t^2}\left(\frac{\partial V}{\partial D}\right) - S_t\frac{\partial V}{\partial S_t} + (r-D)S_t\frac{\partial}{\partial S_t}\left(\frac{\partial V}{\partial D}\right) - r\frac{\partial V}{\partial D} = 0.$$

By substituting $\varphi(S_t,t) = \dfrac{\partial V}{\partial D}$ we have

$$\frac{\partial\varphi}{\partial t} + \frac{1}{2}\sigma^2 S_t^2 \frac{\partial^2\varphi}{\partial S_t^2} + (r-D)S_t\frac{\partial\varphi}{\partial S_t} - r\varphi(S_t,t) - S_t\frac{\partial V}{\partial S_t} = 0$$

or in terms of the differential operator

$$\mathcal{L}_{BS}[\varphi(S_t,t)] - S_t\frac{\partial V}{\partial S_t} = 0$$

with boundary condition

$$\varphi(S_T,T) = \frac{\partial}{\partial D}V(S_T,T) = \frac{\partial}{\partial D}\Psi(S_T) = 0.$$

Let $\varphi(S_t, t) = g(t)U(S_t, t)$, where $U(S_t, t) = S_t \dfrac{\partial V}{\partial S_t}$. At expiry

$$\varphi(S_T, T) = g(T)U(S_T, T) = g(T)S_T \frac{\partial V}{\partial S_T} = 0.$$

Hence, $g(T) = 0$.

In addition,

$$\mathcal{L}_{BS}[\varphi(S_t, t)] = \mathcal{L}_{BS}[g(t)U(S_t, t)]$$

$$= \frac{\partial}{\partial t}[g(t)U(S_t, t)] + \frac{1}{2}\sigma^2 S_t^2 \frac{\partial^2}{\partial S_t^2}[g(t)U(S_t, t)]$$

$$+ (r - D)S_t \frac{\partial}{\partial S_t}[g(t)U(S_t, t)] - rg(t)U(S_t, t)$$

$$= \frac{dg}{dt}U(S_t, t) + g(t)\mathcal{L}_{BS}[U(S_t, t)]$$

$$= \frac{dg}{dt}S_t \frac{\partial V}{\partial S_t} + g(t)\mathcal{L}_{BS}\left[S_t \frac{\partial V}{\partial S_t}\right]$$

$$= S_t \frac{\partial V}{\partial S_t}.$$

Since $\mathcal{L}_{BS}\left[S_t \dfrac{\partial V}{\partial S_t}\right] = 0$ (see Problem 2.2.2.9, page 110) we have

$$\frac{dg}{dt} = 1.$$

Because $g(T) = 0$ we have

$$g(t) = -(T - t)$$

and therefore

$$\varphi(S_t, t) = -(T - t)S_t \frac{\partial V}{\partial S_t}.$$

By setting the option delta $\dfrac{\partial V}{\partial S_t} = \Delta_t$ we have

$$\mathcal{L}_{BS}[\varphi(S_t, t)] = \Delta_t S_t$$

which is equivalent to the number of shares needed to be bought or sold in a delta-hedging portfolio. Furthermore, because

$$\varphi(S_t,t) = -(T-t)\Delta_t S_t$$

then as the number of shares increases (decreases), the sensitivity of the option with respect to the continuous dividend yield also decreases (increases). In addition, because of the presence of the time to expiration $\tau = T - t$, we can see that any change in the dividend will have a bigger effect on longer-term options than shorter-term options.

$\square$

21. Let S_t be the price of an asset following a GBM process

$$\frac{dS_t}{S_t} = (\mu - D)dt + \sigma dW_t$$

where μ is the drift parameter, D is the continuous dividend yield, σ is the volatility and W_t is the standard Wiener process on the probability space $(\Omega, \mathcal{F}, \mathbb{P})$. Consider a digital (or cash-or-nothing) put option written on S_t with strike K having a terminal payoff $\Psi(S_T) = \mathbb{I}_{\{S_T < K\}}$ at expiry time $T > t$.

By considering a hedging portfolio consisting of long $1/\varepsilon$ European put option with strike $K + \varepsilon$ and short $1/\varepsilon$ European put option with strike K, show that as $\varepsilon \to 0$ the digital put option $P_d(S_t, t; K, T)$ is

$$P_d(S_t, t; K, T) = \frac{\partial P(S_t, t; K, T)}{\partial K}$$

where $P(S_t, t; K, T) = Ke^{-r(T-t)}\Phi(-d_-) - S_t e^{-D(T-t)}\Phi(-d_+)$ such that

$$d_\pm = \frac{\log(S_t/K) + (r - D \pm \frac{1}{2}\sigma^2)(T-t)}{\sigma\sqrt{T-t}} \quad \text{and} \quad \Phi(x) = \int_{-\infty}^{x} \frac{1}{\sqrt{2\pi}} e^{-\frac{1}{2}u^2} du.$$

Hence, deduce that the asset-or-nothing put option $P_a(S_t, t; K, T)$ with terminal payoff $\Psi(S_T) = S_T \mathbb{I}_{\{S_T < K\}}$ is

$$P_a(S_t, t; K, T) = K\frac{\partial P(S_t, t; K, T)}{\partial K} - P(S_t, t; K, T).$$

Solution: At time t the portfolio Π_t is worth

$$\Pi_t = \frac{P(S_t, t; K + \varepsilon, T) - P(S_t, t; K, T)}{\varepsilon}.$$

At expiry time T we have

$$\Pi_T = \frac{P(S_T,T;K+\varepsilon,T) - P(S_T,T;K,T)}{\varepsilon}$$

$$= \begin{cases} \frac{1}{\varepsilon}(K+\varepsilon - S_T) & \text{if } S_T < K+\varepsilon \\ 0 & \text{if } S_T \geq K+\varepsilon \end{cases} - \begin{cases} \frac{1}{\varepsilon}(K - S_T) & \text{if } S_T < K \\ 0 & \text{if } S_T \geq K \end{cases}$$

$$= \begin{cases} 1 & \text{if } S_T < K \\ \frac{1}{\varepsilon}(K - S_T + \varepsilon) & \text{if } K \leq S_T < K+\varepsilon \\ 0 & \text{if } S_T \geq K+\varepsilon. \end{cases}$$

Taking limits and from L'Hôpital's rule

$$\lim_{\varepsilon \to 0, S_T \to K} \frac{K - S_T + \varepsilon}{\varepsilon} = \lim_{\varepsilon \to 0, S_T \to K} \frac{-1+1}{1} = 0$$

therefore

$$\lim_{\varepsilon \to 0} \Pi_T = \begin{cases} 1 & \text{if } S_T < K \\ 0 & \text{if } S_T \geq K \end{cases}$$

$$= \mathbb{I}_{\{S_T < K\}}$$

which is equal to the payoff of a digital put option.

Hence, by discounting the payoff up to time t and using Taylor's theorem we have

$$P_d(S_t,t;K,T) = \lim_{\varepsilon \to 0} \frac{P(S_t,t;K+\varepsilon,T) - P(S_t,t;K,T)}{\varepsilon}$$

$$= \lim_{\varepsilon \to 0} \frac{P(S_t,t;K,T) + \frac{\partial P(S_t,t;K,T)}{\partial K}\varepsilon - P(S_t,t;K,T) + \mathcal{O}(\varepsilon^2)}{\varepsilon}$$

$$= \frac{\partial P(S_t,t;K,T)}{\partial K} + \lim_{\varepsilon \to 0} \mathcal{O}(\varepsilon)$$

$$= \frac{\partial P(S_t,t;K,T)}{\partial K}.$$

From Problem 2.2.2.21 (page 139) the closed-form solution for an asset-or-nothing put option price is

$$
\begin{aligned}
P_a(S_t, t; K, T) &= S_t e^{-D(T-t)}\Phi(-d_1)\\
&= Ke^{-r(T-t)}\Phi(-d_2) - P(S_t, t; K, T)\\
&= KP_d(S_t, t; K, T) - P(S_t, t; K, T)\\
&= K\frac{\partial P(S_t, t; K, T)}{\partial K} - P(S_t, t; K, T).
\end{aligned}
$$

N.B. By setting up a portfolio

$$
\Pi_t = \frac{C(S_t, t; K.T) - C(S_t, t; K + \varepsilon, T)}{\varepsilon}
$$

we can also show that the digital call option price is

$$
C_d(S_t, t; K, T) = -\frac{\partial C(S_t, t; K, T)}{\partial K}
$$

and the asset-or-nothing call option price is

$$
C_a(S_t, t; K, T) = -K\frac{\partial C(S_t, t; K, T)}{\partial K} + C(S_t, t; K, T)
$$

where $C(S_t, t; K, T) = S_t e^{-D(T-t)}\Phi(d_+) - Ke^{-r(T-t)}\Phi(d_-)$.

$\square$

22. *Boyle–Emanuel Method.* Let $V(S_t, t)$ denote the derivative security at time t on an asset S_t where S_t follows a GBM

$$
\frac{dS_t}{S_t} = (\mu - D)dt + \sigma dW_t
$$

where μ is the drift parameter, D is the continuous dividend yield, σ is the asset volatility and W_t is the standard Wiener process on the probability space $(\Omega, \mathscr{F}, \mathbb{P})$. Assume that $V(S_t, t)$ satisfies the Black–Scholes equation

$$
\frac{\partial V}{\partial t} + \frac{1}{2}\sigma^2 S_t^2 \frac{\partial^2 V}{\partial S_t^2} + (r - D)S_t\frac{\partial V}{\partial S_t} - rV(S_t, t) = 0
$$

with payoff $V(S_T, T) = \Psi(S_T)$ at expiry time T, $t < T$ and r is the risk-free interest rate.
Consider a trader setting up a hedging portfolio at time t

$$
\Pi_t = V(S_t, t) - \Delta(S_t, t)S_t
$$

where $\Delta(S_t, t) = \dfrac{\partial V}{\partial S_t}$ is the delta of $V(S_t, t)$. The portfolio is left unhedged for a small time $\delta t > 0$. By ignoring higher terms of $\mathcal{O}((\delta t)^{\frac{3}{2}})$ show that the hedging error (or return on the hedge) is

$$\varepsilon_t = (\Pi_{t+\delta t} - \Pi_t) - r\Pi_t \delta t$$

$$\approx \frac{1}{2}\sigma^2 S_t^2 \Gamma(S_t, t)(Z^2 - 1)\delta t$$

where $\Gamma(S_t, t) = \dfrac{\partial^2 V}{\partial S_t^2}$ and $Z^2 \sim \chi^2(1)$.

Find the expectation and variance of ε_t given S_t. Interpret the results financially if $V(S_t, t)$ is a European option and the market behaviour over the time between rehedges is volatile.

Solution: At time t the portfolio is worth

$$\Pi_t = V(S_t, t) - \Delta(S_t, t)S_t$$

and given that the portfolio is unhedged at time $t + \delta t$, and because the asset pays a continuous dividend yield D, we therefore have

$$\Pi_{t+\delta t} = V(S_{t+\delta t}, t + \delta t) - \Delta(S_t, t)(S_{t+\delta t} + DS_t \delta t).$$

In addition, since

$$\delta \Pi_t = \Pi_{t+\delta t} - \Pi_t$$

and under the no-arbitrage condition

$$\delta \Pi_t = r\Pi_t \delta t$$

the hedging error ε_t is

$$\begin{aligned}
\varepsilon_t &= (\Pi_{t+\delta t} - \Pi_t) - r\Pi_t \delta t \\
&= V(S_{t+\delta t}, t + \delta t) - \Delta(S_t, t)(S_{t+\delta t} + DS_t \delta t) - V(S_t, t) + \Delta(S_t, t)S_t \\
&\quad - rV(S_t, t)\delta t + r\Delta(S_t, t)S_t \delta t \\
&= V(S_{t+\delta t}, t + \delta t) - V(S_t, t) - rV(S_t, t)\delta t + (r - D)\Delta(S_t, t)S_t \delta t \\
&\quad - \Delta(S_t, t)\delta S_t
\end{aligned}$$

where $\delta S_t = S_{t+\delta t} - S_t$.

From Taylor's theorem

$$V(S_{t+\delta t}, t + \delta t) = V(S_t, t) + \frac{\partial V}{\partial S_t}\delta S_t + \frac{\partial V}{\partial t}\delta t + \frac{1}{2}\frac{\partial^2 V}{\partial S_t^2}(\delta S_t)^2 + \frac{1}{2}\frac{\partial^2 V}{\partial t^2}(\delta t)^2$$

$$+ \frac{\partial^2 V}{\partial S_t \partial t}(\delta S_t \delta t) + \dots$$

and by substituting $\delta S_t = (\mu - D)S_t \delta t + \sigma S_t \sqrt{\delta t} Z$ where $Z \sim \mathcal{N}(0,1)$ and $\Delta(S_t, t) = \dfrac{\partial V}{\partial S_t}$ we have

$$V(S_{t+\delta t}, t + \delta t) = V(S_t, t) + \Delta(S_t, t)\delta S_t + \frac{\partial V}{\partial t}\delta t + \frac{1}{2}\sigma^2 S_t^2 \frac{\partial^2 V}{\partial S_t^2} Z^2 \delta t + \mathcal{O}((\delta t)^{\frac{3}{2}})$$

where $Z^2 \sim \chi(1)$.

Substituting the result of $V(S_{t+\delta t}, t + \delta t)$ and by neglecting higher orders of $\mathcal{O}(\delta t^{\frac{3}{2}})$ we have

$$\varepsilon_t \approx \left[\frac{\partial V}{\partial t} + (r - D)\Delta(S_t, t)S_t - rV(S_t, t) \right] \delta t + \frac{1}{2}\sigma^2 S_t^2 Z^2 \delta t$$

$$= \frac{1}{2}\sigma^2 S_t^2 \frac{\partial^2 V}{\partial S_t^2}(Z^2 - 1)\delta t$$

$$= \frac{1}{2}\sigma^2 S_t^2 \Gamma(S_t, t)(Z^2 - 1)\delta t$$

since $\dfrac{\partial V}{\partial t} + \dfrac{1}{2}\sigma^2 S_t^2 \dfrac{\partial^2 V}{\partial S_t^2} + (r - D)S_t \dfrac{\partial V}{\partial S_t} - rV(S_t, t) = 0$.

Given S_t, the expectation and variance of ε_t are

$$\mathbb{E}(\varepsilon_t | S_t) \approx 0 \quad \text{and} \quad \text{Var}(\varepsilon_t | S_t) \approx \frac{1}{2}\left\{ \sigma^2 S_t^2 \Gamma(S_t, t)\delta t \right\}^2$$

since $\mathbb{E}(Z^2) = 1$ and $\text{Var}(Z^2) = 2$.

Finally, if $V(S_t, t)$ is a European option then $\Gamma(S_t, t) > 0$ (see Problem 2.2.4.3, page 221). Given that the market behaviour is volatile, $\text{Var}(\varepsilon_t | S_t)$ would increase since σ increases in value. Hence, $V(S_t, t)$ would also increase in value as the option price increases with volatility. Then the hedge portfolio would also rise because of the increase in the variance estimate of the hedging error.

$\square$

23. At time t a contract was written to sell 100 units of "strip" consisting of one European call option $C(S_t, t; K, T)$ and two European put options $P(S_t, t; K, T)$ written on a non-dividend-paying stock S_t with the same strike K and time to expiry $T - t = 270$ days, where T is the expiry time. The writer delta-hedged the contract at time t and since then has not rebalanced the portfolio. At time τ ($t < \tau$) the writer decided to close out the position with the information given in Table 2.4.

Table 2.4   European option prices and deltas.

Time	t	τ
Stock Price	$60	$65
Call Price	$6.4884	$7.3351
Put Price	$13.9466	$10.4433
Call Option Delta	0.4565	
Put Option Delta	−0.5435	

By assuming the risk-free interest rate r as a constant value, calculate the profit of the writer at time τ.

Solution: At time t we denote one unit of short strip as

$$V(S_t, t; K, T) = C(S_t, t; K, T) + 2P(S_t, t; K, T)$$

where $C(S_t, t; K, T)$ and $P(S_t, t; K, T)$ are the European call and put option prices written on S_t with the same strike K and expiry time T ($t < T$). Let the portfolio consist of short one unit of $V(S_t, t; K, T)$ and long Δ_t units of stock S_t so that

$$\Pi_t = -V(S_t, t; K, T) + \Delta_t S_t.$$

By differentiating the portfolio Π_t with respect to S_t

$$\frac{\partial \Pi_t}{\partial S_t} = -\frac{\partial V}{\partial S_t} + \Delta_t$$

and for the portfolio to be delta neutral we set $\dfrac{\partial \Pi_t}{\partial S_t} = 0$ and hence

$$\begin{aligned}
\Delta_t &= \frac{\partial V}{\partial S_t} \\
&= \frac{\partial C}{\partial S_t} + 2\frac{\partial P}{\partial S_t} \\
&= 0.4565 - 2 \times 0.5435 \\
&= -0.6305.
\end{aligned}$$

In order to replicate the option payoff $V(S_t, t; K, T)$ we let

$$V(S_t, t; K, T) = \Delta_t S_t + \Psi_t$$

where Ψ_t is the amount of cash invested in a risk-free money market. Hence,

$$\begin{aligned}
\Psi_t &= V(S_t, t; K, T) - \Delta_t S_t \\
&= C(S_t, t; K, T) + 2P(S_t, t; K, T) - \Delta_t S_t \\
&= 6.4884 + 2 \times 13.9466 + 0.6305 \times 60 \\
&= 72.2116.
\end{aligned}$$

Thus, to maintain a delta-hedged portfolio the writer needs to invest $100 \times 72.2116 = \$7{,}221.16$ into the money market and sell $100 \times 0.6304 = 63.04$ units of $S_t = \$60$.

In order to calculate the interest earned between time t and τ, from the put–call parity

$$C(S_t, t; K, T) - P(S_t, t; K, T) = S_t - Ke^{-r(T-t)}$$
$$C(S_\tau, \tau; K, T) - P(S_\tau, \tau; K, T) = S_\tau - Ke^{-r(T-\tau)}$$

and by substituting $C(S_t, t; K, T) = \$6.4884$, $C(S_\tau, \tau; K, T) = \$7.3351$, $P(S_t, t; K, T) = \$13.9466$, $P(S_\tau, \tau; K, T) = \$10.4433$, $S_t = \$60$ and $S_\tau = \$65$ we have

$$Ke^{-r(T-t)} = \$67.4582 \quad \text{and} \quad Ke^{-r(T-\tau)} = \$68.1082$$

such that

$$e^{r(\tau-t)} = \frac{68.1082}{67.4582}.$$

Hence,

$$\text{Gains on "strip" sold} = 100 \times [6.4884 + 2 \times 13.9466 - 7.3351$$
$$- 2 \times 10.4432]$$
$$= \$615.99$$
$$\text{Gains on share price purchased} = -100 \times 0.6305 \times (65 - 60)$$
$$= -\$315.25$$
$$\text{Interest earned} = 7{,}221.16 \times (e^{r(\tau-t)} - 1)$$
$$= 7{,}221.16 \left(\frac{68.1082}{67.4582} - 1\right)$$
$$= \$69.58$$

so that

$$\text{Total profit at time } \tau = 615.99 - 315.25 + 69.58 = \$370.32.$$

$\square$

24. At time t an investor has sold 1000 units of 33-strike call option on a non-dividend-paying stock S_t. From the information given in Table 2.5, calculate how many units of 35-strike call and stock the investor should buy/sell in order to maintain a delta and gamma-neutral portfolio.

Table 2.5 European call option Greek values for different strikes.

	33-Strike Call	35-Strike Call
Delta	0.6986	0.5217
Gamma	0.07584	0.06245

Solution: Let $K_1 = 33$ and $K_2 = 35$ denote the strike prices for 33-strike call $C(S_t, t; K_1, T)$ and 35-strike call $C(S_t, t; K_2, T)$ option prices, respectively, where T is the option expiry time.

Let the portfolios be constructed as follows:

$$\Pi_t^{(1)} = -C(S_t, t; K_1, T) + \Delta_t^{(1)} S_t$$
$$\Pi_t^{(2)} = C(S_t, t; K_2, T) - \Delta_t^{(2)} S_t$$

where $\Delta_t^{(1)}$ and $\Delta_t^{(2)}$ are the number of shares needed to be bought/sold for each of the portfolios $\Pi_t^{(1)}$ and $\Pi_t^{(2)}$, respectively.

In order to maintain gamma neutrality using 35-strike calls, we let the combined port-folios be

$$\Pi_t = n_1 \Pi_t^{(1)} + n_2 \Pi_t^{(2)}$$

where n_1 and n_2 are the numbers of $C(S_t, t; K_1, T)$ and $C(S_t, t; K_2, T)$ options needed to set the gamma of the portfolio Π_t to zero. By differentiating Π_t twice with respect to S_t we have

$$\frac{\partial^2 \Pi_t}{\partial S_t^2} = -n_1 \frac{\partial^2 C}{\partial S_t^2}(S_t, t; K_1, T) + n_2 \frac{\partial^2 C}{\partial S_t^2}(S_t, t; K_2, T)$$

and by setting $\dfrac{\partial^2 \Pi_t}{\partial S_t^2} = 0$

$$-n_1 \frac{\partial^2 C}{\partial S_t^2}(S_t, t; K_1, T) + n_2 \frac{\partial^2 C}{\partial S_t^2}(S_t, t; K_2, T) = 0.$$

Given $n_1 = 1000$, $\dfrac{\partial^2 C}{\partial S_t^2}(S_t, t; K_1) = 0.07584$ and $\dfrac{\partial^2 C}{\partial S_t^2}(S_t, t; K_2, T) = 0.06245$, we have $n_2 = 1214.4115$. Thus, to ensure that portfolio Π_t is gamma neutral the investor needs to buy 1214.4115 units of $C(S_t, t; K_2, T)$.

Finally, to delta-neutralise portfolio Π_t we note that

$$\frac{\partial \Pi_t}{\partial S_t} = n_1 \frac{\partial \Pi_t^{(1)}}{\partial S_t} + n_2 \frac{\partial \Pi_t^{(2)}}{\partial S_t}$$

$$= n_1 \left[-\frac{\partial C}{\partial S_t}(S_t, t; K_1, T) + \Delta_t^{(1)} \right] + n_2 \left[\frac{\partial C}{\partial S_t}(S_t, t; K_2, T) - \Delta_t^{(2)} \right]$$

$$= 0$$

or

$$n_1 \Delta_t^{(1)} - n_2 \Delta_t^{(2)} = n_1 \frac{\partial C}{\partial S_t}(S_t, t; K_1, T) - n_2 \frac{\partial C}{\partial S_t}(S_t, t; K_2, T)$$

$$= 1000 \times 0.6986 - 1214.4115 \times 0.5217$$

$$= 65.04152.$$

Hence, in order to delta-hedge the portfolio the investor needs to buy 65.04152 shares of S_t.

$\square$

3
American Options

In the previous chapter we concentrated solely on European options, but in most exchange-traded options nearly all stock and equity options are American options whilst stock indices are mainly European options. For a European option, the option price is only dependent on the underlying asset price at expiry and is independent of the path that the underlying asset price follows over the life of the option. Hence, the payoff is path independent and it follows that the discounted expected value of the payoff is also path independent. In contrast, an American option gives the holder of the contract the right but not the obligation to enter into a future transaction at any time until the expiry date of the contract. Therefore, American options belong to path-dependent options since they depend on the path of the underlying asset price prior to the option's expiry time. Given that investors have the freedom to exercise their American options any time during the life of the contract, naturally they are more expensive than European options which can only be exercised at expiry.

3.1 INTRODUCTION

As an American option value is greater than its equivalent European counterpart, it does not satisfy the same problem specification as the European option. Hence, the American option cannot satisfy the Black–Scholes equation. However, both have the same value at the option expiry time.

By setting $C_{am}(S_t, t; K, T)$ and $P_{am}(S_t, t; K, T)$ to be the American call and put option prices, respectively whilst $C_{bs}(S_t, t; K, T)$ and $P_{bs}(S_t, t; K, T)$ are the European call and put option prices, respectively with S_t being the common dividend-paying stock price at time t, $T > t$ being the option's expiry time, D being the continuous dividend yield, K being the common strike and r being the risk-free interest rate, we have the following properties for the call options

$$S_t e^{-D(T-t)} - K e^{-r(T-t)} \leq C_{bs}(S_t, t; K, T) \leq C_{am}(S_t, t; K, T) \leq S_t$$

and for the put options

$$K e^{-r(T-t)} - S_t e^{-D(T-t)} \leq P_{bs}(S_t, t; K, T) \leq P_{am}(S_t, t; K, T) \leq K.$$

For European options, the put–call parity is

$$C_{bs}(S_t, t; K, T) - P_{bs}(S_t, t; K, T) = S_t e^{-D(T-t)} - K e^{-r(T-t)}$$

whilst for American options, the put–call parity is

$$S_t e^{-D(T-t)} - K \leq C_{am}(S_t, t; K, T) - P_{am}(S_t, t; K, T) \leq S_t - K e^{-r(T-t)}.$$

Conceptually, the pricing formulations for the American option can be framed as follows:

- optimal stopping time formulation
- free boundary formulation
- linear complementarity formulation.

Optimal Stopping Time Formulation

Consider an American option with terminal payoff $\Psi(S_T)$ where T is the option expiry time and suppose the option is exercised at time $u \leq T$. Under the risk-neutral measure $\mathbb{Q}$, conditional on the filtration $\mathscr{F}_t$, the discounted price of the option at time $t \leq u$ with payoff at time u is given by

$$\mathbb{E}^{\mathbb{Q}} \left[e^{-r(u-t)} \Psi(S_u) \middle| \mathscr{F}_t \right]$$

where $\mathbb{E}^{\mathbb{Q}}$ denotes the expectation under the risk-neutral measure $\mathbb{Q}$, and under which the stock S_t follows the diffusion process

$$dS_t = (r - D)S_t dt + \sigma S_t dW_t^{\mathbb{Q}}$$

where r is the risk-free interest rate, D is the continuous dividend yield, σ is the stock volatility and $W_t^{\mathbb{Q}}$ is a $\mathbb{Q}$-standard Wiener process.

As the holder of the American option can exercise at any time during the life of the option contract, the American option price at time $t \leq u \leq T$ is

$$V(S_t, t) = \sup_{t \leq u \leq T} \mathbb{E}^{\mathbb{Q}} \left[e^{-r(u-t)} \Psi(S_u) \middle| \mathscr{F}_t \right]$$

where the supremum is taken over all possible stopping times u. The supremum is reached at the optimal stopping time τ such that

$$\tau = \inf_u \left\{ t \leq u \leq T : V(S_u, u) = \Psi(S_u) \right\}.$$

Note that the optimal stopping time problem is useful for theoretical arguments when formulating the problem via a probabilistic approach. However, it is impractical when it comes to numerical computation, except for special types of American options like immediate-touch options.

Free Boundary Formulation

The Black–Scholes equation which is satisfied by European options is no longer valid where early exercise is permitted. As the American option gives its holder much more flexibility over when to exercise it, it therefore has a higher value. When early exercise is permitted, the American option satisfies the Black–Scholes inequality

$$\frac{\partial V}{\partial t} + \frac{1}{2}\sigma^2 S_t^2 \frac{\partial^2 V}{\partial S_t^2} + (r - D)S_t \frac{\partial V}{\partial S_t} - rV(S_t, t) \leq 0$$

with constraints

$$V(S_t, t) \geq \Psi(S_t), \quad V(S_T, T) = \Psi(S_T)$$

where $\Psi(S_t)$ is the intrinsic value of the American option payoff at time t.

Thus, the problem of finding the option price value is known as a free boundary problem since the optimal exercise price is not known *a priori*. To decide when to exercise rather than holding the option, there are two criteria to adhere to:

- The option price can never be worth less than its intrinsic value; otherwise there will be an arbitrage opportunity.
- The holder of the option must exercise so as to give the option its maximum value.

At the optimal exercise boundary S_t^∞ the following hold:

- The option price and the intrinsic function must be continuous as functions of the stock price, S_t.
- The sensitivity of the option price with respect to the stock price, $\left. \dfrac{\partial V}{\partial S_t} \right|_{S_t = S_t^\infty}$ is contin-

  uous as a function of the stock price, S_t. This condition is known as the smooth pasting condition.

When trying to understand the local behaviour of American options, the free boundary formulation is an extremely useful tool. However, it is not a very practical method, since with the presence of free boundaries they have to be determined via expensive numerical strategies which are non-trivial.

Linear Complementarity Formulation

From the free boundary problem, the American option price $V(S_t, t)$ can be formulated further as a linear complementarity problem. In general, by writing $\mathcal{L}_{BS}$ to denote the Black–Scholes operator

$$\mathcal{L}_{BS} = \frac{\partial}{\partial t} + \frac{1}{2}\sigma^2 S_t^2 \frac{\partial^2}{\partial S_t^2} + (r - D)S_t \frac{\partial}{\partial S_t} - r$$

the linear complementarity formulation to determine the American option $V(S_t, t)$ is given as

$$\mathcal{L}_{BS}[V(S_t, t)] \leq 0, \quad V(S_t, t) \geq \Psi(S_t), \quad [V(S_t, t) - \Psi(S_t)] \cdot \mathcal{L}_{BS}[V(S_t, t)] = 0$$

such that

$$V(S_T, T) = \Psi(S_T) \quad \text{and} \quad \frac{\partial V}{\partial S_t} \text{ is continuous in } S_t.$$

There are several advantages to this formulation:

- The formulation does not explicitly contain a free boundary.
- The formulation is independent of the number of free boundaries.
- The free boundary is recovered from the solution.
- The problem can be solved numerically, such as using finite-difference approximations or numerical optimisation. However, for high-dimensional (multi-asset) American options, the numerical scheme is impractical. An alternative is to use the least-squares Monte Carlo method.

Binomial Option Pricing

The binomial formula can also be modified to evaluate American options. Like its European counterparts, the binomial formula for American options also consists of a lattice representing the movements of the stock price where the option is priced by working backwards through the lattice. For the case of American options, since there is a possibility of early exercise, at each node we take the maximum of the value of the option if it is held to expiration and the gain that could be realised with immediate exercise.

Thus, for an American call the value of the option at a node is given by

$$
C_{am}(S_t, t; K, T) = \max \left\{ S_t - K, \\
\quad e^{-r\Delta t} \left[\pi C_{am}(uS_t, t + \Delta t; K, T) + (1 - \pi)C_{am}(dS_t, t + \Delta t; K, T) \right] \right\}
$$

and for an American put it is given by

$$
P_{am}(S_t, t; K, T) = \max \left\{ K - S_t, \\
\quad e^{-r\Delta t} \left[\pi P_{am}(uS_t, t + \Delta t; K, T) + (1 - \pi)P_{am}(dS_t, t + \Delta t; K, T) \right] \right\}
$$

where S_t is the stock price at time t (equivalent to a node in a tree), r is the risk-free interest rate, K is the strike price, $T > t$ is the option expiry time, Δt is the binomial time step, π and $1 - \pi$ are the risk-neutral probabilities for the increase and decrease in the stock price, respectively.

In contrast, for the case of Bermudan options, since early exercise is only allowed on predetermined dates, the value of a Bermudan call option, $C_{berm}(S_t, t; K, T)$ at a node becomes

$$
C_{berm}(S_t, t; K, T)
$$

$$
= \begin{cases}
\max \left\{ S_t - K, \\
e^{-r\Delta t} \left[\pi C_{berm}(uS_t, t + \Delta t; K, T) + (1 - \pi)C_{berm}(dS_t, t + \Delta t; K, T) \right] \right\} & \text{early exercise is allowed} \\[2ex]
e^{-r\Delta t} \left[\pi C_{berm}(uS_t, t + \Delta t; K, T) + (1 - \pi)C_{berm}(dS_t, t + \Delta t; K, T) \right] & \text{early exercise is not allowed}
\end{cases}
$$

and the corresponding value of a Bermudan put option, $P_{berm}(S_t, t; K, T)$ is

$P_{berm}(S_t, t; K, T)$

$$= \begin{cases} \max \{ K - S_t, \\ e^{-r\Delta t} \left[\pi P_{berm}(uS_t, t + \Delta t; K, T) + (1 - \pi)P_{berm}(dS_t, t + \Delta t; K, T) \right] \} & \text{early exercise is allowed} \\ \\ e^{-r\Delta t} \left[\pi P_{berm}(uS_t, t + \Delta t; K, T) + (1 - \pi)P_{berm}(dS_t, t + \Delta t; K, T) \right] & \text{early exercise is not allowed.} \end{cases}$$

3.2 PROBLEMS AND SOLUTIONS

3.2.1 Basic Properties

1. Consider the American and European call options with prices $C_{am}(S_t, t; K, T)$ and $C_{bs}(S_t, t; K, T)$, respectively where S_t is the dividend-paying asset price at time $t < T$, T is the expiry time of the options and K is the common strike price. Show that

$$C_{bs}(S_t, t; K, T) \leq C_{am}(S_t, t; K, T) \leq C_{bs}(S_t, t; K, T) + S_t(1 - e^{-D(T-t)})$$

where D is the continuous dividend yield.

Solution: Assume $C_{am}(S_t, t; K, T) < C_{bs}(S_t, t; K, T)$ for all t. Therefore, at time t we can set up a portfolio with long one American call and short one European call options

$$\Pi_t = C_{am}(S_t, t; K, T) - C_{bs}(S_t, t; K, T) < 0.$$

Assume at time τ, $t \leq \tau \leq T$, that the American call option is exercised, giving a payoff

$$S_\tau - K > 0$$

and by exercising the American call option it gives us

$$\text{Net profit at time } \tau = S_\tau - K - C_{am}(S_\tau, \tau; K, T) + C_{bs}(S_\tau, \tau; K, T) > 0.$$

At expiry time T, and because we are holding the asset now worth S_T (bought at strike price K at time τ), then irrespective of whether the holder of the European call option exercises the option or not

$$\text{Net profit at time } T = \begin{cases} S_T - K & \text{if } S_T > K \\ \\ 0 & \text{if } S_T \leq K \end{cases}$$
$$\geq 0.$$

Hence, we always have a guaranteed positive return for the case when $S_t > K$, which implies the existence of an arbitrage opportunity.

In contrast, if the American call option is not exercised then at terminal time T

$$\Pi_T = C_{am}(S_T, T; K, T) - C_{bs}(S_T, T; K, T)$$
$$= \max\{S_T - K, 0\} - \max\{S_T - K, 0\}$$
$$= 0.$$

Hence, we also have an arbitrage opportunity. Therefore, we conclude that $C_{am}(S_t, t; K, T) \geq C_{bs}(S_t, t; K, T)$.

For the case $C_{am}(S_t, t; K, T) \leq C_{bs}(S_t, t; K, T) + S_t(1 - e^{-D(T-t)})$ we assume

$$C_{am}(S_t, t; K, T) > C_{bs}(S_t, t; K, T) + S_t(1 - e^{-D(T-t)})$$

and set up the following portfolio at time t

$$\Pi_t = C_{bs}(S_t, t; K, T) + S_t(1 - e^{-D(T-t)}) - C_{am}(S_t, t; K, T) < 0.$$

Assume at time $\tau, t \leq \tau \leq T$, that the American call option is exercised with payoff

$$S_\tau - K > 0.$$

Thus, the value of the portfolio at time τ is

$$\Pi_\tau = C_{bs}(S_\tau, \tau; K, T) + S_\tau(1 - e^{-D(T-\tau)}) - (S_\tau - K)$$
$$= C_{bs}(S_\tau, \tau; K, T) - S_\tau e^{-D(T-\tau)} + K$$
$$\geq S_\tau - K - S_\tau e^{-D(T-\tau)} + K$$
$$= S_\tau(1 - e^{-D(T-\tau)})$$
$$> 0$$

which is an arbitrage opportunity.

In addition, if the American call option is not exercised then at terminal time T, the portfolio is now worth

$$\Pi_T = C_{bs}(S_T, T; K, T) - C_{am}(S_T, T; K, T)$$
$$= \max\{S_T - K, 0\} - \max\{S_T - K, 0\}$$
$$= 0$$

which is also an arbitrage opportunity. Hence, $C_{am}(S_t, t; K, T) \leq C_{bs}(S_t, t; K, T) + S_t(1 - e^{-D(T-t)})$.

$\square$

2. Consider the American and European call options with prices $C_{am}(S_t, t; K, T)$ and $C_{bs}(S_t, t; K, T)$, respectively where S_t is the dividend-paying asset price at time $t < T$, T is the expiry time of the options and K is the common strike price. Show that

$$C_{bs}(S_t, t; K, T) \leq C_{am}(S_t, t; K, T) \leq C_{bs}(S_t, t; K, T) + \sum_{i=1}^{n} \delta_i e^{-r(t_i - t)}$$

where $\delta_1, \delta_2, \ldots, \delta_n$ is a sequence of discrete dividends paid at time $t_1, t_2, \ldots, t_n$, respectively where $t < t_1 < t_2 < \cdots < t_n < T$.

Solution: For the proof of the inequality $C_{am}(S_t, t; K, T) \geq C_{bs}(S_t, t; K, T)$ see Problem 3.2.1.1 (page 271).

For the case $C_{am}(S_t, t; K, T) \leq C_{bs}(S_t, t; K, T) + \sum_{i=1}^{n} \delta_i e^{-r(t_i - t)}$ we assume

$$C_{am}(S_t, t; K, T) > C_{bs}(S_t, t; K, T) + \sum_{i=1}^{n} \delta_i e^{-r(t_i - t)}$$

and set up the following portfolio at time t,

$$\Pi_t = C_{bs}(S_t, t; K, T) + \sum_{i=1}^{n} \delta_i e^{-r(t_i - t)} - C_{am}(S_t, t; K, T) < 0.$$

Assume at time τ, $t < t_1 < t_2 < \cdots < t_{k-1} < \tau < t_k < t_{k+1} < \cdots < t_n < T$, that the American call option is exercised by the owner with payoff

$$S_\tau - K > 0.$$

Thus the value of the portfolio at time τ is

$$\Pi_\tau = C_{bs}(S_\tau, \tau; K, T) + \sum_{i=k}^{n} \delta_i e^{-r(t_i - \tau)} - (S_\tau - K)$$

$$= C_{bs}(S_\tau, \tau; K, T) + \sum_{i=k}^{n} \delta_i e^{-r(t_i - \tau)} - S_\tau + K$$

$$\geq S_\tau - K + \sum_{i=k}^{n} \delta_i e^{-r(t_i - \tau)} - S_\tau + K$$

$$= \sum_{i=k}^{n} \delta_i e^{-r(t_i - \tau)}$$

$$> 0$$

which is an arbitrage opportunity.

In addition, if the American call option is not exercised then at terminal time T, the portfolio is now worth

$$\Pi_T = C_{bs}(S_T, T; K, T) - C_{am}(S_T, T; K, T)$$
$$= \max\{S_T - K, 0\} - \max\{S_T - K, 0\}$$
$$= 0$$

which is also an arbitrage opportunity. Hence, $C_{am}(S_t, t; K, T) \leq C_{bs}(S_t, t; K, T) + \sum_{i=1}^{n} \delta_i e^{-r(t_i - t)}$.

$\square$

3. Consider the American and European call options with prices $C_{am}(S_t, t; K, T)$ and $C_{bs}(S_t, t; K, T)$, respectively where S_t is the spot price at time $t < T$, T is the expiry time of the options and K is the common strike price. Let r be the risk-free interest rate. Show that if the stock does not pay dividends, then it is never optimal to exercise an American call option before expiry, i.e.

$$C_{am}(S_t, t; K, T) = C_{bs}(S_t, t; K, T)$$

but this is not true for an American put option.

Solution: Given that $C_{bs}(S_t, t; K, T) \geq \max\{S_t - K, 0\}$, the price of a European call option is always greater than the intrinsic value of an American call option. Therefore, it is inadvisable to exercise the American call option early since there is no incentive to hold onto the stock which pays no dividends, and hence $C_{am}(S_t, t; K, T) = C_{bs}(S_t, t; K, T)$.

By delaying the exercise of an American call option until expiry time, the holder will gain interest on the strike. However, by delaying the exercise of an American put option the holder would lose the interest gained on the strike.

N.B. Note that by setting the continuous dividend yield or discrete dividends to zero, from Problems 3.2.1.1 and 3.2.1.2 (see pages 271–273) we have

$$C_{bs}(S_t, t; K, T) \leq C_{am}(S_t, t; K, T) \leq C_{bs}(S_t, t; K, T)$$

or

$$C_{am}(S_t, t; K, T) = C_{bs}(S_t, t; K, T).$$

□

4. Consider the American and European put options with prices $P_{am}(S_t, t; K, T)$ and $P_{bs}(S_t, t; K, T)$, respectively where S_t is the spot price at time $t < T$, T is the expiry time of the options, K is the common strike price and r is the constant risk-free interest rate. Show that

$$P_{bs}(S_t, t; K, T) \leq P_{am}(S_t, t; K, T) \leq P_{bs}(S_t, t; K, T) + K(1 - e^{-r(T-t)}).$$

Solution: Assume that $P_{am}(S_t, t; K, T) < P_{bs}(S_t, t; K, T)$ for all t. Therefore, at time t we can set up a portfolio with long one American put and short one European put options,

$$\Pi_t = P_{am}(S_t, t; K, T) - P_{bs}(S_t, t; K, T) < 0.$$

Assume at time τ, $t \leq \tau \leq T$, that the American put option is exercised giving a payoff

$$K - S_\tau > 0.$$

Thus, by exercising the American put option it gives us

$$\text{Net profit at time } \tau = K - S_\tau - P_{am}(S_\tau, \tau; K, T) + P_{bs}(S_\tau, t; K, T) > 0$$

and we can invest K in the bank that will give us $Ke^{r(T-\tau)}$ at time T.

At expiry time T, and because we are holding $Ke^{r(T-\tau)}$ worth of cash, then irrespective of whether the holder of the European put option exercises the option or not, we are always guaranteed to have a positive return $Ke^{r(T-\tau)} - K \geq 0$ which implies an arbitrage opportunity. Therefore, $P_{am}(S_t, t; K, T) \geq P_{bs}(S_t, t; K, T)$.

In contrast, if the American put option is not exercised then at terminal time T

$$
\begin{aligned}
\Pi_T &= P_{am}(S_T, T; K, T) - P_{bs}(S_T, T; K, T) \\
&= \max\{K - S_T, 0\} - \max\{K - S_T, 0\} \\
&= 0.
\end{aligned}
$$

Hence, we also have an arbitrage opportunity. Therefore, we can conclude that $P_{am}(S_t, t; K, T) \geq P_{bs}(S_t, t; K, T)$.

For the case $P_{am}(S_t, t; K, T) \leq P_{bs}(S_t, t; K, T) + K(1 - e^{-r(T-t)})$ we assume

$$
P_{am}(S_t, t; K, T) > P_{bs}(S_t, t; K, T) + K(1 - e^{-r(T-t)})
$$

and set up the following portfolio at time t

$$
\Pi_t = P_{bs}(S_t, t; K, T) + K(1 - e^{-r(T-t)}) - P_{am}(S_t, t; K, T) < 0.
$$

Assume at time τ, $t \leq \tau \leq T$, that the American put option is exercised with the payoff

$$
K - S_\tau
$$

where $K > S_\tau$. Thus, the value of the portfolio at time τ is

$$
\begin{aligned}
\Pi_\tau &= P_{bs}(S_\tau, \tau; K, T) + K(1 - e^{-r(T-\tau)}) - (K - S_\tau) \\
&= P_{bs}(S_\tau, \tau; K, T) - Ke^{-r(T-\tau)} + S_\tau \\
&\geq K - S_\tau - Ke^{-r(T-\tau)} + S_\tau \\
&= K(1 - e^{-r(T-\tau)}) \\
&> 0
\end{aligned}
$$

which is an arbitrage opportunity.

In addition, if the American put option is not exercised then at terminal time T, the portfolio is now worth

$$
\begin{aligned}
\Pi_T &= P_{bs}(S_T, T; K, T) - P_{am}(S_T, T; K, T) \\
&= \max\{K - S_T, 0\} - \max\{K - S_T, 0\} \\
&= 0
\end{aligned}
$$

which is also an arbitrage opportunity. Hence, $P_{am}(S_t, t; K, T) \leq P_{bs}(S_t, t; K, T) + K(1 - e^{-r(T-t)})$.

$\square$

5. Consider the American and European put options with prices $P_{am}(S_t, t; K, T)$ and $P_{bs}(S_t, t; K, T)$, respectively where S_t is a dividend-paying asset price at time $t < T$, T is the expiry time of the options and K is the common strike price. Show that in the absence of a risk-free interest rate, $r = 0$ it is never optimal to exercise an American put option before expiry time, i.e.

$$P_{am}(S_t, t; K, T) = P_{bs}(S_t, t; K, T)$$

but this is not the case for an American call option.

Solution: Since $P_{bs}(S_t, t; K, T) \geq \max\{K - S_t, 0\}$, which is the intrinsic value of an American put option, and if $r = 0$ then by exercising the option early there is no financial gain in holding K in the money market. Therefore, it is never optimal to exercise an American put option before expiry time.

By delaying the exercise of an American put option until expiry time, the holder will gain dividend on the stock. However, by delaying the exercise of an American call option the holder would lose dividend gained on the stock.

N.B. Note that by setting the interest rate to zero, from Problem 3.2.1.4 (see page 274) we have

$$P_{bs}(S_t, t; K, T) \leq P_{am}(S_t, t; K, T) \leq P_{bs}(S_t, t; K, T)$$

or

$$P_{am}(S_t, t; K, T) = P_{bs}(S_t, t; K, T).$$

$\square$

6. Consider an American call option with price $C(S_t, t; K, T)$ where S_t is the spot price at time $t < T$, T is the expiry date of the option and K is the strike price. Show that

$$C(S_t, t; K, T) \geq \max\{S_t - K, 0\}.$$

Solution: We assume $C(S_t, t; K, T) < \max\{S_t - K, 0\}$ and at time t we set up the following portfolio

$$\Pi_t = C(S_t, t; K, T) - \max\{S_t - K, 0\} < 0$$

At expiry time T

$$\begin{aligned} \Pi_T &= C(S_T, T; K, T) - \max\{S_T - K, 0\} \\ &= \max\{S_T - K, 0\} - \max\{S_T - K, 0\} \\ &= 0 \end{aligned}$$

which is an arbitrage opportunity. Therefore, $C(S_t, t; K, T) \geq \max\{S_t - K, 0\}$.

N.B. We can also prove the following. Assume $S_t > K$ and let $C(S_t, t; K, T) < S_t - K$. Because $C(S_t, t; K, T) \geq 0$ an investor can then buy the option at time t and exercise it immediately, leading to a profit $S_t - K > 0$. The net profit is therefore $S_t - K -$

$C(S_t,t;K,T) > 0$, which in turn provides an arbitrage opportunity to the investor. Thus, $C(S_t,t;K,T) \geq \max\{S_t - K, 0\}$.

□

7. Let $C(S_t,t;K,T)$ be the price of an American call option where S_t is the spot price at time $t < T$, T is the expiry time of the option and K is the strike price. Show that

$$C(S_t,t;K,T) \leq S_t.$$

Solution: Assume that $C(S_t,t;K,T) > S_t$ and hence at time t we can sell an American call option $C(S_t,t;K,T)$ and buy a stock S_t, giving us a profit of $C(S_t,t;K,T) - S_t > 0$. Given that we own the stock, we can always cover the delivery of the stock should the option be exercised by the holder at any time until time T. Therefore, we are always guaranteed to have a positive return $\max\{S_t - K, 0\} \geq 0$ which implies an arbitrage opportunity. Therefore, $C(S_t,t;K,T) \leq S_t$.

□

8. For a non-dividend-paying asset, let $C(S_t,t;K,T)$ be the price of an American call option where S_t is the asset price at time $t < T$, T is the expiry time of the option, K is the strike price and r is a constant interest rate. Show that

$$C(S_t,t;K,T) \geq \max\{S_t - Ke^{-r(T-t)}, 0\}.$$

Solution: From the put–call parity for European options

$$C_{bs}(S_t,t;K,T) - P_{bs}(S_t,t;K,T) = S_t - Ke^{-r(T-t)}$$

where $C_{bs}(S_t,t;K,T)$ and $P_{bs}(S_t,t;K,T)$ are the European call and put option prices at time t written on S_t with common strike K and expiry time $T > t$.
We then have

$$\begin{aligned} C_{bs}(S_t,t;K,T) &= P_{bs}(S_t,t;K,T) + S_t - Ke^{-r(T-t)} \\ &\geq S_t - Ke^{-r(T-t)} \end{aligned}$$

since $P_{bs}(S_t,t;K,T) \geq 0$.
Because $C(S_t,t;K,T) \geq C_{bs}(S_t,t;K,T)$ we therefore have

$$C(S_t,t;K,T) \geq S_t - Ke^{-r(T-t)}.$$

Since $C(S_t,t;K,T) \geq 0$, then $C(S_t,t;K,T) \geq \max\{S_t - Ke^{-r(T-t)}, 0\}$.

□

9. Let $C(S_t,t;K,T)$ be the price of an American call option where S_t is the asset price at time $t < T$, T is the expiry time of the option, K is the strike price and r is a constant interest rate. Assume that the asset pays a continuous dividend yield D. Show that

$$C(S_t,t;K,T) \geq \max\{S_t e^{-D(T-t)} - Ke^{-r(T-t)}, 0\}.$$

Solution: From the put–call parity for European options

$$C_{bs}(S_t, t; K, T) - P_{bs}(S_t, t; K, T) = S_t e^{-D(T-t)} - K e^{-r(T-t)}$$

where $C_{bs}(S_t, t; K, T)$ and $P_{bs}(S_t, t; K, T)$ are the European call and put option prices at time t written on S_t with common strike K and expiry time $T > t$.

We then have

$$C_{bs}(S_t, t; K, T) = P_{bs}(S_t, t; K, T) + S_t e^{-D(T-t)} - K e^{-r(T-t)}$$
$$\geq S_t e^{-D(T-t)} - K e^{-r(T-t)}$$

since $P_{bs}(S_t, t; K, T) \geq 0$.

Because $C(S_t, t; K, T) \geq C_{bs}(S_t, t; K, T)$ we therefore have

$$C(S_t, t; K, T) \geq S_t e^{-D(T-t)} - K e^{-r(T-t)}.$$

Since $C(S_t, t; K, T) \geq 0$, then $C(S_t, t; K, T) \geq \max\{S_t e^{-D(T-t)} - K e^{-r(T-t)}, 0\}$.

$\square$

10. Let $C(S_t, t; K, T)$ be the price of an American call option where S_t is the asset price at time $t < T$, T is the expiry time of the option, K is the strike price and r is a constant interest rate. Assume that the asset pays a sequence of discrete dividends δ_i at time t_i, $i = 1, 2, \ldots, n$ where $t < t_1 < t_2 < \cdots < t_n < T$. Show that

$$C(S_t, t; K, T) \geq \max\left\{ S_t - \sum_{i=1}^{n} \delta_i e^{-r(t_i-t)} - K e^{-r(T-t)}, 0 \right\}.$$

Solution: From the put–call parity for European options

$$C_{bs}(S_t, t; K, T) - P_{bs}(S_t, t; K, T) = S_t - \sum_{i=1}^{n} \delta_i e^{-r(t_i-t)} - K e^{-r(T-t)}$$

where $C_{bs}(S_t, t; K, T)$ and $P_{bs}(S_t, t; K, T)$ are the European call and put option prices at time t written on S_t with common strike K and expiry time $T > t$.

We then have

$$C_{bs}(S_t, t; K, T) = P_{bs}(S_t, t; K, T) + S_t - \sum_{i=1}^{n} \delta_i e^{-r(t_i-t)} - K e^{-r(T-t)}$$

$$\geq S_t - \sum_{i=1}^{n} \delta_i e^{-r(t_i-t)} - K e^{-r(T-t)}$$

since $P_{bs}(S_t, t; K, T) \geq 0$.

Because $C(S_t, t; K, T) \geq C_{bs}(S_t, t; K, T)$ we therefore have

$$C(S_t, t; K, T) \geq S_t - \sum_{i=1}^{n} \delta_i e^{-r(t_i - t)} - Ke^{-r(T-t)}.$$

Since $C(S_t, t; K, T) \geq 0$, then

$$C(S_t, t; K, T) \geq \max \left\{ S_t - \sum_{i=1}^{n} \delta_i e^{-r(t_i - t)} - Ke^{-r(T-t)}, 0 \right\}.$$

□

11. Consider an American call option with price $C(S_t, t; K, T)$ where S_t is the spot price at time $t < T$, T is the expiry time of the option and K is the strike price. By assuming the stock does not pay dividends, should the holder of an American call option exercise the option if $S_t > K$ whilst believing that the future stock price will go below K?

Solution: If the option is sold at time t then

$$\begin{aligned} \text{Net profit} &= \text{Profit of option sold} - \text{Cost of option bought} \\ &= C(S_t, t; K, T) - C(S_t, t; K, T) \\ &= 0. \end{aligned}$$

On the contrary, if the holder does nothing at time t then

$$\text{Net profit} = -\text{Cost of option bought} = -C(S_t, t; K, T) < 0.$$

Since

$$C(S_t, t; K, T) \geq \max\{S_t - K, 0\} = S_t - K$$

and if the option is exercised at time t then

$$\begin{aligned} \text{Net profit} &= \text{Payoff at time } t - \text{Cost of option bought} \\ &= S_t - K - C(S_t, t; K, T) \\ &\leq 0. \end{aligned}$$

Therefore, the holder should sell the option rather than exercise it.

□

12. Consider an American put option with price $P(S_t, t; K, T)$ where S_t is the spot price at time $t < T$, T is the expiry time of the option and K is the strike price. Show that

$$P(S_t, t; K, T) \geq \max\{K - S_t, 0\}.$$

Solution: We assume $K > S_t$ and let

$$P(S_t, t; K, T) < K - S_t.$$

Because $P(S_t, t; K, T) \geq 0$ an investor can buy a put option at time t and exercise it immediately, leading to a profit $K - S_t > 0$. The net profit is therefore $K - S_t - P(S_t, t; K, T) > 0$, which in turn provides an arbitrage opportunity to the investor. Hence, $P(S_t, t; K, T) \geq \max\{K - S_t, 0\}$.

$\square$

13. Let $P(S_t, t; K, T)$ be the price of an American put option where S_t is the spot price at time $t < T$, T is the expiry time of the option and K is the strike price. Show that

$$P(S_t, t; K, T) \leq K.$$

Solution: Assume $P(S_t, t; K, T) > K$ and hence at time t we can sell an American put option $P(S_t, t; K, T)$ and deposit the money in the bank, earning a risk-free interest rate r which will give us at least $Ke^{r(\tau - t)}$ for $t \leq \tau \leq T$. Given that we own the cash, we can always cover the purchase of the stock for the price of K, should the option be exercised by the holder at any time until time T. Therefore, we are always guaranteed to have a positive return $\max\{K - S_t, 0\} \geq 0$, which implies an arbitrage opportunity. Therefore, $P(S_t, t; K, T) \leq K$.

$\square$

14. For a non-dividend-paying asset, let $P(S_t, t; K, T)$ be the price of an American put option where S_t is the asset price at time $t < T$, T is the expiry time of the option, K is the strike price and r is a constant interest rate. Show that

$$P(S_t, t; K, T) \geq \max\{Ke^{-r(T-t)} - S_t, 0\}.$$

Solution: From the put–call parity for European options

$$C_{bs}(S_t, t; K, T) - P_{bs}(S_t, t; K, T) = S_t - Ke^{-r(T-t)}$$

where $C_{bs}(S_t, t; K, T)$ and $P_{bs}(S_t, t; K, T)$ are the European call and put option prices at time t written on S_t with common strike K and expiry time $T > t$.

We then have

$$\begin{aligned} P_{bs}(S_t, t; K, T) &= C_{bs}(S_t, t; K, T) + Ke^{-r(T-t)} - S_t \\ &\geq Ke^{-r(T-t)} - S_t \end{aligned}$$

since $C_{bs}(S_t, t; K, T) \geq 0$.

Because $P(S_t, t; K, T) \geq P_{bs}(S_t, t; K, T)$ we have

$$P(S_t, t; K, T) \geq Ke^{-r(T-t)} - S_t.$$

Since $P(S_t, t; K, T) \geq 0$ therefore $P(S_t, t; K, T) \geq \max\{Ke^{-r(T-t)} - S_t, 0\}$.

$\square$

15. Let $P(S_t, t; K, T)$ be the price of an American put option where S_t is the asset price at time $t < T$, T is the expiry time of the option, K is the strike price and r is a constant interest rate. Assume that S_t pays a continuous dividend yield D. Show that

$$P(S_t, t; K, T) \geq \max\{Ke^{-r(T-t)} - S_t e^{-D(T-t)}, 0\}.$$

Solution: From the put–call parity for European options we have

$$C_{bs}(S_t, t; K, T) - P_{bs}(S_t, t; K, T) = S_t e^{-D(T-t)} - Ke^{-r(T-t)}$$

where $C_{bs}(S_t, t; K, T)$ and $P_{bs}(S_t, t; K, T)$ are the European call and put option prices at time t written on S_t with common strike K and expiry time $T > t$.
We then express

$$
\begin{aligned}
P_{bs}(S_t, t; K, T) &= C_{bs}(S_t, t; K, T) + Ke^{-r(T-t)} - S_t e^{-D(T-t)} \\
&\geq Ke^{-r(T-t)} - S_t e^{-D(T-t)}
\end{aligned}
$$

since $C_{bs}(S_t, t; K, T) \geq 0$.
Because $P(S_t, t; K, T) \geq P_{bs}(S_t, t; K, T)$ we have

$$P(S_t, t; K, T) \geq Ke^{-r(T-t)} - S_t e^{-D(T-t)}.$$

Since $P(S_t, t; K, T) \geq 0$ therefore $P(S_t, t; K, T) \geq \max\{Ke^{-r(T-t)} - S_t e^{-D(T-t)}, 0\}$.

$\square$

16. Let $P(S_t, t; K, T)$ be the price of an American put option where S_t is the asset price at time $t < T$, T is the expiry time of the option, K is the strike price and r is a constant interest rate. Assume that the asset pays a sequence of discrete dividends δ_i at time $t_i, i = 1, 2, \ldots, n$ where $t < t_1 < t_2 < \cdots < t_n < T$. Show that

$$P(S_t, t; K, T) \geq \max\left\{Ke^{-r(T-t)} - S_t + \sum_{i=1}^{n} \delta_i e^{-r(t_i-t)}, 0\right\}.$$

Solution: From the put–call parity for European options we have

$$C_{bs}(S_t, t; K, T) - P_{bs}(S_t, t; K, T) = S_t - \sum_{i=1}^{n} \delta_i e^{-r(t_i-t)} - Ke^{-r(T-t)}$$

where $C_{bs}(S_t, t; K, T)$ and $P_{bs}(S_t, t; K, T)$ are the European call and put option prices at time t written on S_t with common strike K and expiry time $T > t$.
We then have

$$
\begin{aligned}
P_{bs}(S_t, t; K, T) &= C_{bs}(S_t, t; K, T) + Ke^{-r(T-t)} - S_t + \sum_{i=1}^{n} \delta_i e^{-r(t_i-t)} \\
&\geq Ke^{-r(T-t)} - S_t + \sum_{i=1}^{n} \delta_i e^{-r(t_i-t)}
\end{aligned}
$$

since $C_{bs}(S_t, t; K, T) \geq 0$.

Because $P(S_t, t; K, T) \geq P_{bs}(S_t, t; K, T)$ we have

$$P(S_t, t; K, T) \geq Ke^{-r(T-t)} - S_t + \sum_{i=1}^{n} \delta_i e^{-r(t_i-t)}.$$

Since $P(S_t, t; K, T) \geq 0$ therefore

$$P(S_t, t; K, T) \geq \max \left\{ Ke^{-r(T-t)} - S_t + \sum_{i=1}^{n} \delta_i e^{-r(t_i-t)}, 0 \right\}.$$

□

17. *Put–Call Parity I.* Consider the American call and put options with prices $C(S_t, t; K, T)$ and $P(S_t, t; K, T)$, respectively where S_t is the spot price at time $t < T$, T is the expiry time of the options, K is the common strike price and r is a constant risk-free interest rate. Show that

$$S_t - K \leq C(S_t, t; K, T) - P(S_t, t; K, T) \leq S_t - Ke^{-r(T-t)}.$$

Solution: Since S_t does not pay any dividends, then

$$C(S_t, t; K, T) = C_{bs}(S_t, t; K, T)$$

where $C_{bs}(S_t, t; K, T)$ is the European call option price written on S_t at time t with strike price K and option expiry T.

In addition, from Problem 3.2.1.4 (page 274) we have

$$P_{bs}(S_t, t; K, T) \leq P(S_t, t; K, T) \leq P_{bs}(S_t, t; K, T) + K(1 - e^{-r(T-t)})$$

where $P_{bs}(S_t, t; K, T)$ is the European put option price written on S_t at time t with strike price K and option expiry T.

Thus,

$$\begin{aligned}
C(S_t, t; K, T) - P(S_t, t; K, T) &\geq C(S_t, t; K, T) - P_{bs}(S_t, t; K, T) \\
&\quad - K(1 - e^{-r(T-t)}) \\
&= C_{bs}(S_t, t; K, T) - P_{bs}(S_t, t; K, T) \\
&\quad - K(1 - e^{-r(T-t)}) \\
&= S_t - Ke^{-r(T-t)} - K(1 - e^{-r(T-t)}) \\
&= S_t - K
\end{aligned}$$

since $C_{bs}(S_t, t; K, T) - P_{bs}(S_t, t; K, T) = S_t - K^{-r(T-t)}$.

In contrast, using the put–call parity for European options again

$$C(S_t, t; K, T) - P(S_t, t; K, T) \le C(S_t, t; K, T) - P_{bs}(S_t, t; K, T)$$
$$= C_{bs}(S_t, t; K, T) - P_{bs}(S_t, t; K, T)$$
$$= S_t - Ke^{-r(T-t)}.$$

$\square$

18. *Put–Call Parity II.* Consider the American call and put options with prices $C(S_t, t; K, T)$ and $P(S_t, t; K, T)$, respectively where S_t is the spot price at time $t < T$ which pays a continuous dividend yield D, T is the expiry time of the options, K is the common strike price and r is a constant risk-free interest rate. Show that

$$S_t e^{-D(T-t)} - K \le C(S_t, t; K, T) - P(S_t, t; K, T) \le S_t - Ke^{-r(T-t)}.$$

Solution: From Problems 3.2.1.1 and 3.2.1.4 (pages 271–274) we have

$$C_{bs}(S_t, t; K, T) \le C(S_t, t; K, T) \le C_{bs}(S_t, t; K, T) + S_t(1 - e^{-D(T-t)})$$
$$P_{bs}(S_t, t; K, T) \le P(S_t, t; K, T) \le P_{bs}(S_t, t; K, T) + K(1 - e^{-r(T-t)})$$

where $C_{bs}(S_t, t; K, T)$ and $P_{bs}(S_t, t; K, T)$ are the European call and put option prices, respectively written on S_t at time t with strike price K and option expiry T.
   Thus,

$$C(S_t, t; K, T) - P(S_t, t; K, T) \ge C_{bs}(S_t, t; K, T) - P_{bs}(S_t, t; K, T)$$
$$-K(1 - e^{-r(T-t)})$$
$$= S_t e^{-D(T-t)} - Ke^{-r(T-t)} - K(1 - e^{-r(T-t)})$$
$$= S_t e^{-D(T-t)} - K$$

since $C_{bs}(S_t, t; K, T) - P_{bs}(S_t, t; K, T) = S_t e^{-D(T-t)} - K^{-r(T-t)}$.
   In contrast, using the put–call parity for European options again

$$C(S_t, t; K, T) - P(S_t, t; K, T) \le C_{bs}(S_t, t; K, T) + S_t(1 - e^{-D(T-t)})$$
$$-P_{bs}(S_t, t; K, T)$$
$$= C_{bs}(S_t, t; K, T) - P_{bs}(S_t, t; K, T)$$
$$+S_t(1 - e^{-D(T-t)})$$
$$= S_t e^{-D(T-t)} - Ke^{-r(T-t)} + S_t(1 - e^{-D(T-t)})$$
$$= S_t - Ke^{-r(T-t)}.$$

$\square$

19. *Put–Call Parity III.* Consider the American call and put options with prices $C(S_t, t; K, T)$ and $P(S_t, t; K, T)$, respectively where S_t is the spot price at time $t < T$ which pays a sequence of discrete dividends $\delta_1, \delta_2, \ldots, \delta_n$ at times $t_1, t_2, \ldots, t_n$, respectively, $t < t_1 <$

$t_2 < \cdots < t_n < T$, T is the expiry time of the options, K is the common strike price and r is a constant risk-free interest rate. Show that

$$S_t - \sum_{i=1}^{n} \delta_i e^{-r(t_i - t)} - K \le C(S_t, t; K, T) - P(S_t, t; K, T) \le S_t - K e^{-r(T-t)}.$$

Solution: From Problems 3.2.1.2 and 3.2.1.4 (pages 272–274) we have

$$C_{bs}(S_t, t; K, T) \le C(S_t, t; K, T) \le C_{bs}(S_t, t; K, T) + \sum_{i=1}^{n} \delta_i e^{-r(t_i - t)}$$

$$P_{bs}(S_t, t; K, T) \le P(S_t, t; K, T) \le P_{bs}(S_t, t; K, T) + K(1 - e^{-r(T-t)})$$

where $C_{bs}(S_t, t; K, T)$ and $P_{bs}(S_t, t; K, T)$ are the European call and put option prices, respectively written on S_t at time t with strike price K and option expiry T.

Thus,

$$\begin{aligned}
C(S_t, t; K, T) - P(S_t, t; K, T) &\ge C_{bs}(S_t, t; K, T) - P_{bs}(S_t, t; K, T) \\
&\quad - K(1 - e^{-r(T-t)}) \\
&= S_t - \sum_{i=1}^{n} \delta_i e^{-r(t_i - t)} - K^{-r(T-t)} \\
&\quad - K(1 - e^{-r(T-t)}) \\
&= S_t - \sum_{i=1}^{n} \delta_i e^{-r(t_i - t)} - K
\end{aligned}$$

since $C_{bs}(S_t, t; K, T) - P_{bs}(S_t, t; K, T) = S_t - \sum_{i=1}^{n} \delta_i e^{-r(t_i - t)} - K^{-r(T-t)}$.

In contrast, using the put–call parity for European options again

$$\begin{aligned}
C(S_t, t; K, T) - P(S_t, t; K, T) &\le C_{bs}(S_t, t; K, T) + \sum_{i=1}^{n} \delta_i e^{-r(t_i - t)} \\
&\quad - P_{bs}(S_t, t; K, T) \\
&= C_{bs}(S_t, t; K, T) - P_{bs}(S_t, t; K, T) \\
&\quad + \sum_{i=1}^{n} \delta_i e^{-r(t_i - t)} \\
&= S_t - \sum_{i=1}^{n} \delta_i e^{-r(t_i - t)} - K^{-r(T-t)} + \sum_{i=1}^{n} \delta_i e^{-r(t_i - t)} \\
&= S_t - K e^{-r(T-t)}.
\end{aligned}$$

□

20. Given that the continuously compounded risk-free interest rate is 2% per annum, what is the greatest lower bound of a 3-month American put option on a non-dividend-paying stock currently worth \$10 with strike price \$15?

Solution: Let $S_0 = 10$, $K = 15$, $T = \frac{3}{12} = 0.25$ years, $r = 0.02$, and let $P(S_0, 0; K, T)$ denote the American put option at time $t = 0$. As

$$P(S_0, 0; K, T) \geq \max\{K - S_0, 0\}$$

the greatest lower bound is then given by

$$P(S_0, 0; K, T) \geq \max\{15 - 10, 0\} = \$5.$$

$\square$

21. Given that the continuously compounded risk-free interest rate is 5% per annum, what is the greatest lower bound of a 6-month American call option on a non-dividend-paying stock currently worth $20 with strike price $15?

Solution: Let $S_0 = 20$, $K = 15$, $T = \frac{6}{12} = 0.5$ years, $r = 0.05$, and let $C(S_0, 0; K, T)$ denote the American call option at time $t = 0$. As

$$C(S_0, 0; K, T) \geq \max\{S_0 - Ke^{-rT}, 0\}$$

the greatest lower bound is given by

$$C(S_0, 0; K, T) \geq \max\{20 - 15 \times e^{-0.05 \times 0.5}, 0\} = \$5.37.$$

$\square$

22. Suppose that a trader holds an American call option on a non-dividend-paying stock with strike price $100 with expiry time 6 months from now. The continuously compounded interest rate is 5% and the current stock price is $110.
    (a) What happens if the trader exercises the call option now?
    (b) Does the trader have an advantage if he exercises the option at expiry time?
    (c) What would be the trader's strategy if he knew the stock price was going to fall?

Solution: Let the current time $t = 0$ so that $S_0 = 110$, $T = \frac{6}{12} = 0.5$, $r = 0.05$ and $K = 100$.
    (a) By exercising at time $t = 0$, the trader would pay $100 to own a stock which is worth $110. If the trader sells the stock, he would make an instant profit of $110 - \$100 = \$10$.
    (b) By delaying exercising the option, the trader can deposit $100 in a bank earning a risk-free interest rate $r = 5\%$ which, in 6 months' time, will be worth $100 \times e^{0.05 \times 0.5} = \$102.53$.
    At time T, if $S_T > 100$ the trader can exercise the call and pay $100 to own the stock. Therefore, he makes an extra profit of $2.53 compared with exercising the option now.
    In contrast, if $S_T \leq 100$ the trader would not exercise the option and would have $102.53 in the bank. Had the trader exercised the option at time $t = 0$, he would own stock worth 110 and, by selling the stock and putting the proceeds in the bank, it will grow to $110 \times e^{0.05 \times 0.5} = \$112.78$ in 6 months' time. Thus, if the trader only exercises the option at the expiry time and if $S_T \leq 100$ then he will be making a loss of $112.78 - \$102.53 = \$10.25$.

(c) If the trader exercises the call option now, he will pay \$100 for the stock and can sell it for \$110 and deposit the profit of \$10 in the bank. At time $T = 0.5$ the trader will earn $\$10 \times e^{0.05 \times 0.5} = \$10.25$.

Conversely, if he waits until expiry time, he can short sell the stock now and deposit \$110 in the bank, thus earning $\$110 \times e^{0.05 \times 0.5} = \$112.78$ in 6 months' time. To cover his short-selling activity he can exercise the call option at expiry time by paying \$100 for S_T. Thus, he makes a profit of \$12.78, which is more than the \$10.25 if he exercised immediately.

□

23. Consider an American put option on a non-dividend-paying stock with strike price \$12 with expiry time 8 months from now. The current stock price is \$10 and the continuously compounded interest rate is 5% per annum. Given that the price of the American put option is \$2.50, calculate the range of values for the corresponding American call option with the same strike price and expiry time.

Solution: Let the current time be $t = 0$, so that $S_0 = 10$, $T = \frac{8}{12} = \frac{2}{3}$ years, $r = 0.05$ and $K = 12$. By denoting $P(S_0, 0; K, T) = 2.50$ as the price of an American put option then, from the put–call parity, the corresponding American call option $C(S_0, 0; K, T)$ satisfies

$$P(S_0, 0; K, T) + S_0 - K \le C(S_0, 0; K, T) \le P(S_0, 0; K, T) + S_0 - Ke^{-rT}.$$

Thus,

$$2.5 + 10 - 12 \le C(S_0, 0; K, T) \le 2.5 + 10 - 12 \times e^{-0.05 \times \frac{2}{3}}$$

or

$$\$0.50 \le C(S_0, 0; K, T) \le \$0.89.$$

□

24. Consider two identical American call options $C(S_t, t; K, T_1)$ and $C(S_t, t; K, T_2)$ having expiry times T_1 and T_2 with $T_1 < T_2$, S_t is the spot price at time t and K is the common strike price. Show that

$$C(S_t, t; K, T_1) \le C(S_t, t; K, T_2)$$

for $T_1 < T_2$.

Solution: We assume $C(S_t, t; K, T_1) > C(S_t, t; K, T_2)$ where at time t we can set up a portfolio

$$\Pi_t = C(S_t, t; K, T_2) - C(S_t, t; K, T_1) < 0.$$

At time T_1, the portfolio is now worth

$$\Pi_{T_1} = C(S_{T_1}, T_1; K, T_2) - \max\{S_{T_1} - K, 0\}$$

$$= \begin{cases} C(S_{T_1}, T_1; K, T_2) & \text{if } S_{T_1} \leq K \\ C(S_{T_1}, T_1; K, T_2) - S_{T_1} + K & \text{if } S_{T_1} > K. \end{cases}$$

Since $C(S_{T_1}, T_1; K, T_2) \geq S_{T_1} - K$ then $\Pi_{T_1} \geq 0$, which is a contradiction. Therefore,

$$C(S_t, t; K, T_1) \leq C(S_t, t; K, T_2)$$

for $T_1 < T_2$.

$\square$

25. Consider two identical American put options $P(S_t, t; K, T_1)$ and $P(S_t, t; K, T_2)$ having expiry times T_1 and T_2 with $T_1 < T_2$, S_t is the spot price at time t and K is the common strike price. Show that

$$P(S_t, t; K, T_1) \leq P(S_t, t; K, T_2)$$

for $T_1 < T_2$.

Solution: We assume $P(S_t, t; K, T_1) > P(S_t, t; K, T_2)$ where at time t we can set up a portfolio

$$\Pi_t = P(S_t, t; K, T_2) - P(S_t, t; K, T_1) < 0.$$

At time T_1, the portfolio is now worth

$$\Pi_{T_1} = P(S_{T_1}, T_1; K, T_2) - \max\{K - S_{T_1}, 0\}$$

$$= \begin{cases} P(S_{T_1}, T_1; K, T_2) & \text{if } S_{T_1} \geq K \\ P(S_{T_1}, T_1; K, T_2) - K + S_{T_1} & \text{if } S_{T_1} < K. \end{cases}$$

Since $P(S_{T_1}, T_1; K, T_2) \geq K - S_{T_1}$ then $\Pi_{T_1} \geq 0$, which is a contradiction. Therefore,

$$P(S_t, t; K, T_1) \leq P(S_t, t; K, T_2)$$

for $T_1 < T_2$.

$\square$

26. Consider two identical American call options $C(S_t, t; K_1, T)$ and $C(S_t, t; K_2, T)$ having strike prices K_1 and K_2 with $K_1 < K_2$, S_t is the spot price at time t and $T > t$ is the expiry time. Show that

$$0 \le C(S_t, t; K_1, T) - C(S_t, t; K_2, T) \le K_2 - K_1$$

for $K_1 < K_2$.

Solution: We first assume $C(S_t, t; K_1, T) < C(S_t, t; K_2, T)$ where at time t we can set up a portfolio

$$\Pi_t = C(S_t, t; K_1, T) - C(S_t, t; K_2, T) < 0.$$

At expiry time T

$$
\begin{aligned}
\Pi_T &= C(S_T, T; K_1, T) - C(S_T, T; K_2, T) \\
&= \max\{S_T - K_1, 0\} - \max\{S_T - K_2, 0\} \\
&= \begin{cases} 0 & \text{if } S_T \le K_1 \\ S_T - K_1 & \text{if } K_1 < S_T \le K_2 \\ K_2 - K_1 & \text{if } S_T > K_2. \end{cases}
\end{aligned}
$$

Hence, $\Pi_T \ge 0$ which is a contradiction.

We next assume $C(S_t, t; K_1, T) - C(S_t, t; K_2, T) > K_2 - K_1$ where at time t we set up the following portfolio

$$\Pi_t = K_2 - K_1 - C(S_t, t; K_1, T) + C(S_t, t; K_2, T) < 0.$$

At expiry time T

$$
\begin{aligned}
\Pi_T &= K_2 - K_1 - C(S_T, T; K_1, T) + C(S_T, T; K_2, T) \\
&= K_2 - K_1 - \max\{S_T - K_1, 0\} + \max\{S_T - K_2, 0\} \\
&= \begin{cases} K_2 - K_1 & \text{if } S_T \le K_1 \\ K_2 - S_T & \text{if } K_1 < S_T \le K_2 \\ 0 & \text{if } S_T > K_2. \end{cases}
\end{aligned}
$$

Hence, $\Pi_T \ge 0$ which is also a contradiction.

Therefore,

$$0 \le C(S_t, t; K_1, T) - C(S_t, t; K_2, T) \le K_2 - K_1$$

for $K_1 < K_2$.

$\square$

27. Consider two identical American put options $P(S_t, t; K_1, T)$ and $P(S_t, t; K_2, T)$ having strike prices K_1 and K_2 with $K_1 < K_2$, S_t is the spot price at time t and $T > t$ is the expiry time. Show that

$$0 \leq P(S_t, t; K_2, T) - P(S_t, t; K_1, T) \leq K_2 - K_1$$

for $K_1 < K_2$.

Solution: We first assume $P(S_t, t; K_2, T) < P(S_t, t; K_1, T)$ where at time t we can set up a portfolio

$$\Pi_t = P(S_t, t; K_2, T) - P(S_t, t; K_1, T) < 0.$$

At expiry time T

$$
\begin{aligned}
\Pi_T &= P(S_T, T; K_2, T) - P(S_T, T; K_1, T) \\
&= \max\{K_2 - S_T, 0\} - \max\{K_1 - S_T, 0\} \\
&= \begin{cases} K_2 - K_1 & \text{if } S_T < K_1 \\ K_2 - S_T & \text{if } K_1 \leq S_T < K_2 \\ 0 & \text{if } S_T \geq K_2. \end{cases}
\end{aligned}
$$

Hence, $\Pi_T \geq 0$ which is a contradiction.

We next assume $P(S_t, t; K_2, T) - P(S_t, t; K_1, T) > K_2 - K_1$ where at time t we set up the following portfolio

$$\Pi_t = K_2 - K_1 - P(S_t, t; K_2, T) + P(S_t, t; K_1, T) < 0.$$

At expiry time T

$$
\begin{aligned}
\Pi_T &= K_2 - K_1 - P(S_T, T; K_2, T) + P(S_T, T; K_1, T) \\
&= K_2 - K_1 - \max\{K_2 - S_T, 0\} + \max\{K_1 - S_T, 0\} \\
&= \begin{cases} 0 & \text{if } S_T < K_1 \\ S_T - K_1 & \text{if } K_1 \leq S_T < K_2 \\ K_2 - K_1 & \text{if } S_T \geq K_2. \end{cases}
\end{aligned}
$$

Hence, $\Pi_T \geq 0$ which is also a contradiction.

Therefore,

$$0 \leq P(S_t, t; K_2, T) - P(S_t, t; K_1, T) \leq K_2 - K_1$$

for $K_1 < K_2$.

$\square$

28. Let the prices of two American call options with strikes \$50 and \$60 be \$2.50 and \$3.00, respectively where both options have the same time to expiry.
    (a) Is the no-arbitrage condition violated?
    (b) Suggest a spread position so that the portfolio will ensure an arbitrage opportunity.

Solution: We assume the options are priced at time t with spot price S_t and we let $K_1 = \$50$, $K_2 = \$60$ and $T > t$ is the expiry time so that $C(S_t, t; K_1, T) = \$2.50$ and $C(S_t, t; K_2, T) = \$3.00$.
(a) Since $C(S_t, t; K_1, T) < C(S_t, t; K_2, T)$ for $K_1 < K_2$, this violates the condition $C(S_t, t; K_1, T) \geq C(S_t, t; K_2, T)$.
(b) We let the portfolio at time t be

$$\Pi_t = C(S_t, t; K_1, T) - C(S_t, t; K_2, T) < 0$$

where at time T the portfolio will be worth

$$\Pi_T = \max\{S_T - 50, 0\} - \max\{S_T - 60, 0\}$$

$$= \begin{cases} 0 & \text{if } S_T \leq 50 \\ S_T - 50 & \text{if } 50 < S_T \leq 60 \\ 10 & \text{if } S_T > 60. \end{cases}$$

Thus, $\Pi_T \geq 0$ which shows that the portfolio $\Pi_t = C(S_t, t; K_1, T) - C(S_t, t; K_2, T)$ provides an arbitrage opportunity.

$\square$

29. At time t we consider an American put option on a non-dividend-paying stock S_t with strike price $K > S_t$ and r is the risk-free interest rate. The stock price is forecast to fall in value where at the expiry time T, $S_T < S_t$. Is it advisable to exercise the option early? If the stock pays a dividend $\delta > 0$ at intermediate time τ, $t < \tau < T$, should we exercise the option early?

Solution: If the option is exercised early at time t, the payoff is

$$\Psi(S_t) = \max\{K - S_t, 0\} = K - S_t.$$

If the option is exercised at expiry time T, the payoff is

$$\Psi(S_T) = \max\{K - S_T, 0\} = K - S_T.$$

Hence, the present value of the payoff at time t is

$$V(S_t, t; K, T) = Ke^{-r(T-t)} - S_t < K - S_t.$$

Therefore, it is advisable to exercise early if the stock price is forecast to fall in value.

If the stock pays a dividend at time τ then the present value of the payoff at time t is

$$V(S_t, t; K, T) = Ke^{-r(T-t)} - (S_t - \delta e^{-r(\tau - t)}) = Ke^{-r(T-t)} - S_t + \delta e^{-r(\tau - t)}.$$

Thus, early exercise is advisable if

$$Ke^{-r(T-t)} - S_t + \delta e^{-r(\tau - t)} < K - S_t$$

or

$$\delta e^{-r(\tau - t)} < K(1 - e^{-r(T-t)}).$$

$\square$

30. Consider an investor holding one American call option and one European call option on the same non-dividend-paying stock with strike price $K = \$50$. The price of the American call option is \$5 with time to expiry 8 months, whilst the European call option is priced at \$7 with time to expiry 6 months. The continuously compounded risk-free interest rate is $r = 5\%$. Show that the investor can construct an arbitrage portfolio.

Solution: At time $t = 0$ with spot price S_0 we denote the price of an American call option by

$$C_{am}(S_0, 0; K, T_1) = \$5 \quad \text{for } T_1 = \frac{8}{12} = \frac{2}{3} \text{ years}$$

and the European call option price by

$$C_{bs}(S_0, 0; K, T_2) = \$7 \quad \text{for } T_2 = \frac{6}{12} = \frac{1}{2} \text{ years.}$$

We first set up a portfolio at time $t = 0$

$$\Pi_0 = C_{am}(S_0, 0; K, T_1) - C_{bs}(S_0, 0; K, T_2) < 0.$$

At time $t = T_2$ we have

$$\begin{aligned}
\Pi_{T_2} &= C_{am}(S_{T_2}, T_2; K, T_1) - C_{bs}(S_{T_2}, T_2; K, T_2) \\
&= C_{am}(S_{T_2}, T_2; K, T_1) - \max\{S_{T_2} - K, 0\} \\
&= \begin{cases} C_{am}(S_{T_2}, T_2; K, T_1) & \text{if } S_{T_2} \leq K \\[2mm] C_{am}(S_{T_2}, T_2; K, T_1) - S_{T_2} + K & \text{if } S_{T_2} > K \end{cases} \\
&\geq \begin{cases} C_{am}(S_{T_2}, T_2; K, T_1) & \text{if } S_{T_2} \leq K \\[2mm] K(1 - e^{-r(T_1 - T_2)}) & \text{if } S_{T_2} > K \end{cases}
\end{aligned}$$

since $C_{am}(S_{T_2}, T_2; K, T_1) \geq S_{T_2} - Ke^{-r(T_1-T_2)}$. Further, because $C_{am}(S_{T_2}, T_2; K, T_1) \geq 0$, then $\Pi_{T_2} > 0$ which constitutes an arbitrage opportunity.

□

3.2.2 Time-Independent Options

1. *Generalised Perpetual American Option.* Consider an economy which consists of a risk-free asset and a stock, whose values at time t are B_t and S_t, respectively. Assume that these values evolve according to the following diffusion processes

$$dB_t = rB_t dt, \quad dS_t = (\mu - D)S_t dt + \sigma S_t dW_t$$

where D is the continuous dividend yield, r is the risk-free rate, μ is the stock price growth rate and $\sigma_t > 0$ is the stock price volatility. In addition, $\{W_t : 0 \leq t \leq T\}$ is the $\mathbb{P}$-standard Wiener process on the probability space $(\Omega, \mathscr{F}, \mathbb{P})$ and $\mathscr{F}_t, 0 \leq t \leq T$ is the filtration generated by the standard Wiener process.

Show that a perpetual American option $V(S_t)$ (which has not yet been exercised) satisfies the following second-order ODE

$$\frac{1}{2}\sigma^2 S_t^2 \frac{d^2V}{dS_t^2} + (r - D)S_t \frac{dV}{dS_t} - rV(S_t) = 0.$$

Show also that the general solution of the above equation is

$$V(S_t) = AS_t^{\alpha_+} + BS_t^{\alpha_-}$$

where A and B are unknown constants, $\alpha_+ > 0$ and $\alpha_- < 0$.

Solution: We consider a perpetual American option with an arbitrary payoff and because it is time independent we can denote the option price at time t as $V(S_t)$.

By setting a Δ-hedged portfolio

$$\Pi_t = V(S_t) - \Delta S_t$$

and because during time dt the stock pays out a continuous dividend $DS_t dt$ we have

$$d\Pi_t = dV - \Delta(dS_t + DS_t dt).$$

By Taylor's expansion and subsequently using Itō's lemma we can write

$$dV = \frac{dV}{dS_t}dS_t + \frac{1}{2}\frac{d^2V}{dS_t^2}(dS_t)^2 + \frac{1}{3!}\frac{d^3V}{dS_t^3}(dS_t)^3 + \cdots$$

$$= \frac{dV}{dS_t}\left[(\mu - D)S_t dt + \sigma dW_t\right] + \frac{1}{2}\sigma^2 S_t^2 \frac{d^2V}{dS_t^2}dt$$

$$= \left[\frac{1}{2}\sigma^2 S_t^2 \frac{d^2V}{dS_t^2} + (\mu - D)S_t \frac{dV}{dS_t}\right]dt + \sigma \frac{dV}{dS_t}dW_t$$

and

$$dS_t + DS_t dt = \mu S_t dt + \sigma S_t dW_t.$$

By substituting the above expressions into $d\Pi_t$ we have

$$d\Pi_t = \left[\frac{1}{2}\sigma^2 S_t^2 \frac{d^2 V}{dS_t^2} + (\mu - D)S_t \frac{dV}{dS_t} - \Delta \mu S_t \right] dt + \sigma \left[\frac{dV}{dS_t} - \Delta \right] dW_t.$$

To eliminate risk we set

$$\Delta = \frac{dV}{dS_t}$$

and hence

$$d\Pi_t = \left[\frac{1}{2}\sigma^2 S_t^2 \frac{d^2 V}{dS_t^2} - DS_t \frac{dV}{dS_t} \right] dt.$$

Given that there is no time limit to exercise the option, to avoid arbitrage we set

$$d\Pi_t = r\Pi dt$$

or

$$\left[\frac{1}{2}\sigma^2 S_t^2 \frac{d^2 V}{dS_t^2} - DS_t \frac{dV}{dS_t} \right] dt = r \left[V(S_t) - \frac{dV}{dS_t} S_t \right] dt.$$

Hence,

$$\frac{1}{2}\sigma^2 S_t^2 \frac{d^2 V}{dS_t^2} + (r - D)S_t \frac{dV}{dS_t} - rV(S_t) = 0.$$

To solve the second-order ODE we look for solutions of the form

$$V(S_t) = CS_t^m$$

where C is a constant. By substituting

$$V(S_t) = CS_t^m, \quad \frac{dV}{dS_t} = mCS_t^{m-1}, \quad \frac{d^2 V}{dS_t^2} = m(m-1)CS_t^{m-2}$$

into the ODE we have

$$\frac{1}{2}\sigma^2 m(m-1) + (r - D)m - r = 0$$

or

$$\frac{1}{2}\sigma^2 m^2 + \left(r - D - \frac{1}{2}\sigma^2\right) m - r = 0.$$

Hence,

$$m = \frac{-(r - D - \frac{1}{2}\sigma^2) \pm \sqrt{(r - D - \frac{1}{2}\sigma^2)^2 + 2\sigma^2 r}}{\sigma^2}.$$

Since

$$\sqrt{(r - D - \frac{1}{2}\sigma^2)^2 + 2\sigma^2 r} > (r - D - \frac{1}{2}\sigma^2)$$

the solution of the ODE must be of the form

$$V(S_t) = AS_t^{\alpha_+} + BS_t^{\alpha_-}$$

where A and B are unknown constants,

$$\alpha_+ = \frac{-(r - D - \frac{1}{2}\sigma^2) + \sqrt{(r - D - \frac{1}{2}\sigma^2)^2 + 2\sigma^2 r}}{\sigma^2} > 0$$

and

$$\alpha_- = \frac{-(r - D - \frac{1}{2}\sigma^2) - \sqrt{(r - D - \frac{1}{2}\sigma^2)^2 + 2\sigma^2 r}}{\sigma^2} < 0.$$

□

2. *Perpetual American Call Option.* By definition a perpetual American call option gives the holder the right but not the obligation to buy an underlying asset (where the current price at time t is S_t) for a specified strike price K at any time in the future with no expiry time. Assume that the price of the perpetual American call option $C(S_t)$ satisfies

$$\frac{1}{2}\sigma^2 S_t^2 \frac{d^2 C}{d S_t^2} + (r - D)S_t \frac{dC}{d S_t} - rC(S_t) = 0, \quad 0 < S_t < S^\infty$$

with boundary conditions

$$C(0) = 0, \quad C(S^\infty) = S^\infty - K$$

where r is the risk-free interest rate, D is the continuous dividend yield, σ is the constant volatility and $S^\infty > K$ denotes the unknown optimal exercise boundary such that for $S_t \geq S^\infty$ the option should be exercised whilst for $S_t < S^\infty$ the option should be held.

Show that

$$C(S_t) = \begin{cases} (S^\infty - K)\left(\dfrac{S_t}{S^\infty}\right)^{\alpha_+} & \text{if } S_t < S^\infty \\[4mm] S_t - K & \text{if } S_t \geq S^\infty \end{cases}$$

where

$$\alpha_+ = \frac{-(r - D - \frac{1}{2}\sigma^2) + \sqrt{(r - D - \frac{1}{2}\sigma^2)^2 + 2\sigma^2 r}}{\sigma^2} > 0.$$

Hence, show that the optimal exercise boundary is

$$S^\infty = \frac{\alpha_+ K}{\alpha_+ - 1}$$

and that for this optimal value the "smooth-pasting" condition

$$\Delta = \frac{dC}{dS_t}\bigg|_{S_t = S^\infty} = 1$$

is satisfied.

Deduce that if $D = 0$, it is not optimal to exercise the perpetual American call option.

Solution: Given that $S^\infty > K$ is the optimal exercise boundary then, for $S_t \geq S^\infty$, we can deduce that the perpetual American call option is equal to its intrinsic value, that is

$$C(S_t) = S_t - K, \quad S_t \geq S^\infty.$$

For $S_t < S^\infty$, $C(S_t)$ satisfies the second-order ODE and from Problem 3.2.2.1 (page 292) the general solution is

$$C(S_t) = AS_t^{\alpha_+} + BS_t^{\alpha_-}$$

where A and B are unknown constants,

$$\alpha_+ = \frac{-(r - D - \frac{1}{2}\sigma^2) + \sqrt{(r - D - \frac{1}{2}\sigma^2)^2 + 2\sigma^2 r}}{\sigma^2} > 0$$

and

$$\alpha_- = \frac{-(r - D - \frac{1}{2}\sigma^2) - \sqrt{(r - D - \frac{1}{2}\sigma^2)^2 + 2\sigma^2 r}}{\sigma^2} < 0.$$

From the initial conditions, for $S_t \to 0$, $C(S_t) \to 0$ and because $\alpha_- < 0$ we can set $B = 0$. Thus,

$$C(S_t) = A S_t^{\alpha_+}.$$

Because $S^\infty > K$ therefore $C(S^\infty) = S^\infty - K$. By continuity

$$A(S^\infty)^{\alpha_+} = S^\infty - K$$

or

$$A = (S^\infty - K)\left(\frac{1}{S^\infty}\right)^{\alpha_+}.$$

Therefore, for $S_t < S^\infty$

$$C(S_t) = (S^\infty - K)\left(\frac{S_t}{S^\infty}\right)^{\alpha_+}.$$

In order to find the optimal exercise boundary we differentiate $C(S_t)$ with respect to S^∞

$$
\begin{aligned}
\frac{dC}{dS^\infty} &= \left(\frac{S_t}{S^\infty}\right)^{\alpha_+} - \left(\frac{S_t}{S^\infty}\right)^{\alpha_+}\left[\frac{\alpha_+(S^\infty - K)}{S^\infty}\right] \\
&= \left(\frac{S_t}{S^\infty}\right)^{\alpha_+}\left[1 - \frac{\alpha_+(S^\infty - K)}{S^\infty}\right]
\end{aligned}
$$

and by setting $\dfrac{dC}{dS^\infty} = 0$ we have

$$S^\infty = \frac{\alpha_+ K}{\alpha_+ - 1}.$$

By differentiating $\dfrac{dC}{dS^\infty}$ once again with respect to S^∞

$$\frac{d^2C}{d(S^\infty)^2} = -\frac{\alpha_+}{S^\infty}\left(\frac{S_t}{S^\infty}\right)^{\alpha_+}\left[1 - \frac{\alpha_+(S^\infty - K)}{S^\infty}\right] - \left(\frac{S_t}{S^\infty}\right)^{\alpha_+}\frac{\alpha_+ K}{(S^\infty)^2}$$

and by substituting $S^\infty = \dfrac{\alpha_+ K}{\alpha_+ - 1}$ we have

$$\left.\frac{d^2C}{d(S^\infty)^2}\right|_{S^\infty = \frac{\alpha_+ K}{\alpha_+ - 1}} < 0.$$

Hence, $S^\infty = \dfrac{\alpha_+ K}{\alpha_+ - 1}$ is a local maximum point.

For $S_t < S^\infty$, $C(S_t) = (S^\infty - K)\left(\dfrac{S_t}{S^\infty}\right)^{\alpha_+}$ and by differentiating $C(S_t)$ with respect to S_t

$$\frac{dC}{dS_t} = \frac{\alpha_+(S^\infty - K)}{S^\infty}\left(\frac{S_t}{S^\infty}\right)^{\alpha_+ - 1}.$$

By taking limits

$$\lim_{S_t \to (S^\infty)^-}\frac{dC}{dS_t} = \frac{\alpha_+(S^\infty - K)}{S^\infty}$$

$$= \frac{\alpha_+\left(\dfrac{\alpha_+ K}{\alpha_+ - 1} - K\right)}{\dfrac{\alpha_+ K}{\alpha_+ - 1}}$$

$$= 1.$$

For $S_t \geq S^\infty$, $C(S_t) = S_t - K$ and by differentiating $C(S_t)$ with respect to S_t we have

$$\frac{dC}{dS_t} = 1$$

or

$$\lim_{S_t \to (S^\infty)^+}\frac{dC}{dS_t} = 1.$$

Since

$$\lim_{S_t \to (S^\infty)^-}\frac{dC}{dS_t} = \lim_{S_t \to (S^\infty)^+}\frac{dC}{dS_t} = 1$$

therefore the "smooth-pasting" condition $\Delta = \left.\dfrac{dC}{dS_t}\right|_{S_t = S^\infty} = 1$ is satisfied.

If $D = 0$ then

$$\alpha_+ = \frac{1}{\sigma^2}\left[-\left(r - \frac{1}{2}\sigma^2\right) + \sqrt{\left(r - \frac{1}{2}\sigma^2\right) + 2r\sigma^2}\right]$$

$$= \frac{1}{\sigma^2}\left[-\left(r - \frac{1}{2}\sigma^2\right) + \sqrt{\left(r - \frac{1}{2}\sigma^2\right)^2}\right]$$

$$= 1.$$

Hence,

$$\lim_{D \to 0} S^\infty = \lim_{\alpha \to 1} \frac{\alpha_+ K}{\alpha_+ - 1} = \infty$$

which implies it is never optimal to exercise the perpetual American call when $D = 0$.

$\square$

3. *Perpetual American Put Option.* By definition a perpetual American put option gives the holder the right but not the obligation to sell an underlying asset (where the current price at time t is S_t) for a specified strike price K at any time in the future with no expiry time. Assume that the price of the perpetual American put option $P(S_t)$ satisfies

$$\frac{1}{2}\sigma^2 S_t^2 \frac{d^2 P}{dS_t^2} + (r - D)S_t \frac{dP}{dS_t} - rP(S_t) = 0, \quad S_t > S^*$$

with boundary conditions

$$P(\infty) = 0, \quad P(S^*) = K - S^*$$

where r is the risk-free interest rate, D is the continuous dividend yield, σ is the constant volatility and $S^* < K$ denotes the unknown optimal exercise boundary such that for $S_t \leq S^*$ the option should be exercised whilst for $S_t > S^*$ the option should be held.

Show that

$$P(S_t) = \begin{cases} K - S_t & \text{if } S_t \leq S^* \\ (K - S^*)\left(\dfrac{S_t}{S^*}\right)^{\alpha_-} & \text{if } S_t > S^* \end{cases}$$

where

$$\alpha_- = \frac{-\left(r - D - \frac{1}{2}\sigma^2\right) - \sqrt{\left(r - D - \frac{1}{2}\sigma^2\right)^2 + 2\sigma^2 r}}{\sigma^2} < 0.$$

Hence, show that the optimal exercise boundary is

$$S^* = \frac{\alpha_- K}{\alpha_- - 1}$$

and for this optimal value the "smooth-pasting" condition

$$\Delta = \frac{dP}{dS_t}\bigg|_{S_t = S^*} = -1$$

is satisfied.

Deduce that if $r = 0$ then it is not optimal to exercise the perpetual put option.

Solution: Given that $S^* < K$ is the optimal exercise boundary then, for $S_t \leq S^*$, the perpetual American put option can be deduced to be equal to its intrinsic value, that is

$$P(S_t) = K - S_t, \quad S_t < S^*.$$

For $S_t > S^*$, $P(S_t)$ satisfies the second-order ODE and from Problem 3.2.2.1 (page 292) the general solution is

$$P(S_t) = AS_t^{\alpha_+} + BS_t^{\alpha_-}$$

where A and B are unknown constants,

$$\alpha_+ = \frac{-\left(r - D - \frac{1}{2}\sigma^2\right) + \sqrt{\left(r - D - \frac{1}{2}\sigma^2\right)^2 + 2\sigma^2 r}}{\sigma^2} > 0$$

and

$$\alpha_- = \frac{-\left(r - D - \frac{1}{2}\sigma^2\right) - \sqrt{\left(r - D - \frac{1}{2}\sigma^2\right)^2 + 2\sigma^2 r}}{\sigma^2} < 0.$$

From the initial conditions, for $S_t \to \infty$, $P(S_t) \to 0$ and because $\alpha_+ > 0$ we can set $A = 0$. Thus,

$$P(S_t) = BS_t^{\alpha_-}.$$

Because $P(S^*) = K - S^*$ by continuity

$$B(S^*)^{\alpha_-} = K - S^*$$

or

$$B = (K - S^*)\left(\frac{1}{S^*}\right)^{\alpha_-}.$$

Therefore, for $S_t > S^*$

$$P(S_t) = (K - S^*)\left(\frac{S_t}{S^*}\right)^{\alpha_-}.$$

To find the optimal exercise boundary we differentiate $P(S_t)$ with respect to S^*

$$\frac{dP}{dS^*} = -\left(\frac{S_t}{S^*}\right)^{\alpha_-} - \frac{\alpha_-(K - S^*)}{S^*}\left(\frac{S_t}{S^*}\right)^{\alpha_-}$$

$$= -\left(\frac{S_t}{S^*}\right)^{\alpha_-}\left[1 + \frac{\alpha_-(K - S^*)}{S^*}\right]$$

and by setting $\dfrac{dP}{dS^*} = 0$ we have

$$S^* = \frac{\alpha_- K}{\alpha_- - 1}.$$

By differentiating $\dfrac{dP}{dS^*}$ once again with respect to S^*

$$\frac{d^2 P}{d(S^*)^2} = \frac{\alpha_-}{S^*}\left(\frac{S_t}{S^*}\right)^{\alpha_-}\left[1 + \frac{\alpha_-(K - S^*)}{S^*}\right] + \left(\frac{S_t}{S^*}\right)^{\alpha_-}\frac{\alpha_- K}{(S^*)^2}$$

and by substituting $S^* = \dfrac{\alpha_- K}{\alpha_- - 1}$ we have

$$\left.\frac{d^2 P}{d(S^*)^2}\right|_{S^* = \frac{\alpha_- K}{\alpha_- - 1}} < 0.$$

Hence, $S^* = \dfrac{\alpha_- K}{\alpha_- - 1}$ is a local maximum point.

For $S_t > S^*$, $P(S_t) = (K - S^*)\left(\dfrac{S_t}{S^*}\right)^{\alpha_-}$ and by differentiating $P(S_t)$ with respect to S_t

$$\frac{dP}{dS_t} = \frac{\alpha_-(K - S^*)}{S^*}\left(\frac{S_t}{S^*}\right)^{\alpha_- - 1}.$$

By taking limits $S_t \to (S^*)^+$

$$\lim_{S_t \to (S^*)^+}\frac{dP}{dS_t} = \frac{\alpha_-\left(K - \dfrac{\alpha_- K}{\alpha_- - 1}\right)}{\dfrac{\alpha_- K}{\alpha_- - 1}}$$

$$= -1.$$

For $S_t \leq S^*$, $P(S_t) = K - S_t$ and by differentiating $P(S_t)$ with respect to S_t we have

$$\frac{dP}{dS_t} = -1$$

and by taking limits

$$\lim_{S_t \to (S^*)^-}\frac{dP}{dS_t} = -1.$$

Since $\lim\limits_{S_t \to (S^*)^-} \dfrac{dP}{dS_t} = \lim\limits_{S_t \to (S^*)^+} \dfrac{dP}{dS_t} = -1$ therefore the "smooth-pasting" condition $\Delta =$

$\dfrac{dP}{dS_t}\Big|_{S_t = S^*} = -1$ is satisfied.

If $r = 0$ then

$$\alpha_- = \frac{D + \frac{1}{2}\sigma^2 - \sqrt{\left(D + \frac{1}{2}\sigma^2\right)^2}}{\sigma^2}$$

$$= 0.$$

Therefore, the optimal exercise boundary S^* becomes

$$\lim_{r \to 0} S^* = \lim_{r \to 0} \frac{\alpha_- K}{\alpha_- - 1}$$

$$= 0.$$

Hence, if the risk-free interest rate is zero then it is not optimal to exercise the perpetual put option.

$\square$

4. Let $(\Omega, \mathcal{F}, \mathbb{P})$ be a probability space and let $\{W_t : t \geq 0\}$ be a $\mathbb{P}$-standard Wiener process on the probability space $(\Omega, \mathcal{F}, \mathbb{P})$. Suppose at time t that the stock price S_t follows the GBM process with the following SDE

$$dS_t = (\mu - D)S_t dt + \sigma S_t dW_t$$

and a risk-free asset B_t follows

$$dB_t = rB_t dt$$

where μ is the drift rate, D is the continuous dividend yield, σ is the asset price volatility and r is the risk-free interest rate.

For a constant λ show that $X_t = e^{\lambda W_t - \frac{1}{2}\lambda^2 t}$ is a martingale.

By setting $T = \min\{t \geq 0 : W_t = a + bt\}$ as the first-passage time of hitting the slope line $a + bt$ where a and b are constants, using the optimal stopping theorem show that the Laplace transform of its distribution is given by

$$\mathbb{E}\left(e^{-\theta T}\right) = e^{-a(b + \sqrt{b^2 + 2\theta})}, \quad \theta > 0.$$

We consider the perpetual American call and put options denoted by $C(S_t)$ and $P(S_t)$, respectively for a specified strike price K. Let $S^\infty > K$ and $S^* < K$ denote the unknown optimal exercise boundaries for the perpetual American call and put options, respectively. Here, for $S_t \geq S^\infty$ ($S_t > S^*$) the perpetual American call (put) option should be exercised (held) and for $S_t < S^\infty$ ($S_t \leq S^*$) the perpetual American call (put) option should be held (exercised).

Under the risk-neutral measure $\mathbb{Q}$ and using the Laplace transform for the distribution of the time to hit the optimal exercise boundaries show that

$$
C(S_t) = \begin{cases} (S^\infty - K)\left(\dfrac{S_t}{S^\infty}\right)^{\alpha_+} & \text{if } S_t < S^\infty \\[2ex] S_t - K & \text{if } S_t \geq S^\infty \end{cases}
$$

and

$$
P(S_t) = \begin{cases} K - S_t & \text{if } S_t \leq S^* \\[2ex] (K - S^*)\left(\dfrac{S_t}{S^*}\right)^{\alpha_-} & \text{if } S_t > S^* \end{cases}
$$

where

$$
\alpha_+ = \frac{-\left(r - D - \frac{1}{2}\sigma^2\right) + \sqrt{\left(r - D - \frac{1}{2}\sigma^2\right)^2 + 2\sigma^2 r}}{\sigma^2} > 0
$$

and

$$
\alpha_- = \frac{-\left(r - D - \frac{1}{2}\sigma^2\right) - \sqrt{\left(r - D - \frac{1}{2}\sigma^2\right)^2 + 2\sigma^2 r}}{\sigma^2} < 0.
$$

Solution: To show that $X_t = e^{\lambda W_t - \frac{1}{2}\lambda^2 t}$ is a martingale and the Laplace transform of the first-passage time distribution see Problems 2.2.3.3 and 2.2.4.7, respectively of *Problems and Solutions in Mathematical Finance, Volume 1: Stochastic Calculus*.

We first consider the perpetual American call option case where we let τ^∞ be the time to hit the unknown optimal exercise boundary S^∞ defined as

$$
\tau^\infty = \min\{u - t \geq 0 : S_u = S^\infty\}.
$$

From Girsanov's theorem, under the risk-neutral measure $\mathbb{Q}$ we have

$$
\frac{dS_t}{S_t} = (r - D)dt + \sigma dW_t^{\mathbb{Q}}
$$

where $W_t^{\mathbb{Q}} = W_t + \left(\dfrac{\mu - r}{\sigma}\right)t$ is a $\mathbb{Q}$-standard Wiener process.

Hence, the perpetual American call option price at time t is defined as

$$C(S_t) = \mathbb{E}^Q\left[e^{-r\tau^\infty}\max\{S_{\tau^\infty} - K, 0\}\Big| \mathscr{F}_t\right]$$

$$= \begin{cases} (S^\infty - K)\mathbb{E}^Q\left[e^{-r\tau^\infty}\Big|\mathscr{F}_t\right] & \text{if } S_t < S^\infty \\ S_t - K & \text{if } S_t \geq S^\infty. \end{cases}$$

By solving the SDE, for $u > t$ we have

$$S_u = S_t\exp\left[\left(r - D - \frac{1}{2}\sigma^2\right)(u - t) + \sigma W_{u-t}^Q\right]$$

and hence the hitting time τ^∞ becomes

$$\tau^\infty = \min\left\{u - t \geq 0 : S_t\exp\left[\left(r - D - \frac{1}{2}\sigma^2\right)(u - t) + \sigma W_{u-t}^Q\right] = S^\infty\right\}$$

$$= \min\left\{u - t \geq 0 : W_{u-t}^Q = \frac{1}{\sigma}\log\left(\frac{S^\infty}{S_t}\right) - \frac{1}{\sigma}\left(r - D - \frac{1}{2}\sigma^2\right)(u - t)\right\}$$

$$= \min\left\{v \geq 0 : W_v^Q = \frac{1}{\sigma}\log\left(\frac{S^\infty}{S_t}\right) - \frac{1}{\sigma}\left(r - D - \frac{1}{2}\sigma^2\right)v\right\}$$

where $v = u - t$.

Therefore, by setting $a = \frac{1}{\sigma}\log\left(\frac{S^\infty}{S_t}\right)$ and $b = -\frac{1}{\sigma}\left(r - D - \frac{1}{2}\sigma^2\right)$, the Laplace transform of the hitting-time distribution becomes

$$\mathbb{E}^Q\left[e^{-r\tau^\infty}\Big|\mathscr{F}_t\right] = e^{-a(b+\sqrt{b^2+2r})}$$

$$= \exp\left\{-\frac{1}{\sigma}\log\left(\frac{S^\infty}{S_t}\right)\left[-\frac{1}{\sigma}\left(r - D - \frac{1}{2}\sigma^2\right)\right.\right.$$

$$\left.\left.+\sqrt{\frac{1}{\sigma^2}\left(r - D - \frac{1}{2}\sigma^2\right)^2 + 2r}\right]\right\}$$

$$= \left(\frac{S_t}{S^\infty}\right)^{\alpha_+}$$

where

$$\alpha_+ = \frac{-\left(r - D - \frac{1}{2}\sigma^2\right) + \sqrt{\left(r - D - \frac{1}{2}\sigma^2\right)^2 + 2\sigma^2 r}}{\sigma^2} > 0.$$

Thus,

$$C(S_t) = \begin{cases} (S^\infty - K)\left(\dfrac{S_t}{S^\infty}\right)^{\alpha_+} & \text{if } S_t < S^\infty \\[2em] S_t - K & \text{if } S_t \geq S^\infty \end{cases}$$

such that $\lim_{S_t \to 0} C(S_t) = (S^\infty - K) \lim_{S_t \to 0} \left(\dfrac{S_t}{S^\infty}\right)^{\alpha_+} = 0$.

For the case of a perpetual American put option, let τ^* be the time to hit the unknown optimal exercise boundary S^* defined as

$$\tau^* = \min\{u - t \geq 0 : S_u = S^*\}$$

and the option price is defined as

$$P(S_t) = \mathbb{E}^{\mathbb{Q}}\left[e^{-r\tau^*}\max\{K - S_{\tau^*}, 0\}\,\Big|\,\mathscr{F}_t\right]$$

$$= \begin{cases} K - S_t & \text{if } S_t \leq S^* \\[1em] (K - S^*)\mathbb{E}^{\mathbb{Q}}\left[e^{-r\tau^*}\,\Big|\,\mathscr{F}_t\right] & \text{if } S_t > S^*. \end{cases}$$

Since $S_u = S_t \exp\left[\left(r - \frac{1}{2}\sigma^2\right)(u - t) + \sigma W_{u-t}^{\mathbb{Q}}\right]$ for $u > t$, and using the reflection principle of the Wiener process, the hitting time τ^* can be written as

$$\tau^* = \min\left\{u - t \geq 0 : W_{u-t}^{\mathbb{Q}} = \frac{1}{\sigma}\log\left(\frac{S^\infty}{S_t}\right) - \frac{1}{\sigma}\left(r - D - \frac{1}{2}\sigma^2\right)(u - t)\right\}$$

$$= \min\left\{u - t \geq 0 : -W_{u-t}^{\mathbb{Q}} = -\frac{1}{\sigma}\log\left(\frac{S^\infty}{S_t}\right) + \frac{1}{\sigma}\left(r - D - \frac{1}{2}\sigma^2\right)(u - t)\right\}$$

$$= \min\left\{u - t \geq 0 : \widetilde{W}_{u-t}^{\mathbb{Q}} = -\frac{1}{\sigma}\log\left(\frac{S^\infty}{S_t}\right) + \frac{1}{\sigma}\left(r - D - \frac{1}{2}\sigma^2\right)(u - t)\right\}$$

$$= \min\left\{v \geq 0 : \widetilde{W}_v^{\mathbb{Q}} = -\frac{1}{\sigma}\log\left(\frac{S^\infty}{S_t}\right) + \frac{1}{\sigma}\left(r - D - \frac{1}{2}\sigma^2\right)v\right\}$$

where $v = u - t$ and $\widetilde{W}_v^{\mathbb{Q}}$ is a $\mathbb{Q}$-standard Wiener process.

By setting $a = -\dfrac{1}{\sigma}\log\left(\dfrac{S^\infty}{S_t}\right)$ and $b = \dfrac{1}{\sigma}\left(r - D - \dfrac{1}{2}\sigma^2\right)$, the Laplace transform of the hitting-time distribution becomes

$$\mathbb{E}^{\mathbb{Q}}\left[e^{-r\tau^*}\,\Big|\,\mathscr{F}_t\right] = e^{-a(b + \sqrt{b^2 + 2r})}$$

$$= \exp\left\{\frac{1}{\sigma}\log\left(\frac{S^\infty}{S_t}\right)\left[\frac{1}{\sigma}\left(r - D - \frac{1}{2}\sigma^2\right)\right.\right.$$

$$+\sqrt{\frac{1}{\sigma^2}\left(r - D - \frac{1}{2}\sigma^2\right)^2 + 2r}\Bigg]\Bigg\}$$

$$= \left(\frac{S_t}{S^*}\right)^{\alpha_-}$$

where

$$\alpha_- = \frac{-\left(r - D - \frac{1}{2}\sigma^2\right) - \sqrt{\left(r - D - \frac{1}{2}\sigma^2\right)^2 + 2\sigma^2 r}}{\sigma^2} < 0.$$

Hence,

$$P(S_t) = \begin{cases} K - S_t & \text{if } S_t \leq S^* \\ (K - S^*)\left(\dfrac{S_t}{S^*}\right)^{\alpha_-} & \text{if } S_t > S^* \end{cases}$$

where $\displaystyle\lim_{S_t \to \infty} P(S_t) = (K - S^*)\lim_{S_t \to \infty}\left(\frac{S_t}{S^*}\right)^{\alpha_-} = 0.$

$\square$

3.2.3   Time-Dependent Options

1. Consider an economy which consists of a risk-free asset and a stock, whose values at time t are B_t and S_t, respectively. Assume that these values evolve according to the following diffusion processes

$$dB_t = rB_t dt, \quad dS_t = (\mu - D)S_t dt + \sigma S_t dW_t$$

such that D is the continuous dividend yield, r is the risk-free rate, μ is the stock price growth rate and σ_t is the stock price volatility. In addition, $\{W_t : t \geq 0\}$ is the $\mathbb{P}$-standard Wiener process on the probability space $(\Omega, \mathcal{F}, \mathbb{P})$.

Show that the American option $V(S_t, t)$ satisfies the following inequality

$$\frac{\partial V}{\partial t} + \frac{1}{2}\sigma^2 S_t^2 \frac{\partial^2 V}{\partial S_t^2} + (r - D)S_t \frac{\partial V}{\partial S_t} - rV(S_t, t) \leq 0$$

with constraint

$$V(S_t, t) \geq \Psi(S_t)$$

where $\Psi(S_t)$ is the intrinsic value of the American option at time t.

Solution: We first set up a Δ-hedged portfolio

$$\Pi_t = V(S_t, t) - \Delta S_t$$

and because during time dt the stock pays out a continuous dividend $DS_t dt$ we have

$$d\Pi_t = dV - \Delta(dS_t + DS_t dt).$$

By Taylor's expansion and subsequently using Itō's lemma we can write

$$dV = \frac{\partial V}{\partial t}dt + \frac{\partial V}{\partial S_t}dS_t + \frac{1}{2}\frac{\partial^2 V}{\partial S_t^2}(dS_t)^2 + \frac{1}{3!}\frac{\partial^3 V}{\partial S_t^3}(dS_t)^3 + \cdots$$

$$= \frac{\partial V}{\partial t}dt + \frac{\partial V}{\partial S_t}\left[(\mu - D)S_t dt + \sigma dW_t\right] + \frac{1}{2}\sigma^2 S_t^2 \frac{\partial^2 V}{\partial S_t^2}dt$$

$$= \left[\frac{\partial V}{\partial t} + \frac{1}{2}\sigma^2 S_t^2 \frac{\partial^2 V}{\partial S_t^2} + (\mu - D)S_t \frac{\partial V}{\partial S_t}\right]dt + \sigma \frac{\partial V}{\partial S_t}dW_t$$

and

$$dS_t + DS_t dt = \mu S_t dt + \sigma S_t dW_t.$$

By substituting the above expressions into $d\Pi_t$ we have

$$d\Pi_t = \left[\frac{\partial V}{\partial t} + \frac{1}{2}\sigma^2 S_t^2 \frac{\partial^2 V}{\partial S_t^2} + (\mu - D)S_t \frac{\partial V}{\partial S_t} - \Delta\mu S_t\right]dt$$

$$+ \sigma\left[\frac{\partial V}{\partial S_t} - \Delta\right]dW_t.$$

To eliminate the random component we set

$$\Delta = \frac{\partial V}{\partial S_t}$$

and hence

$$d\Pi_t = \left[\frac{\partial V}{\partial t} + \frac{1}{2}\sigma^2 S_t^2 \frac{\partial^2 V}{\partial S_t^2} - DS_t \frac{\partial V}{\partial S_t}\right]dt.$$

If we assume

$$d\Pi_t > r\Pi_t dt$$

then we would experience an arbitrage since a trader can borrow money at the risk-free rate and then set up a Δ-hedged portfolio such that the return from the portfolio is greater than the return from a bank.

Because there are times to exercise the option, the simple arbitrage argument used in the European options is not valid here. Hence, we can conclude that for an American option

$$d\Pi_t \le r\Pi_t dt$$

or

$$\left[\frac{\partial V}{\partial t} + \frac{1}{2}\sigma^2 S_t^2 \frac{\partial^2 V}{\partial S_t^2} - DS_t \frac{\partial V}{\partial S_t}\right]dt \le r\left[V(S_t,t) - \frac{\partial V}{\partial S_t}S_t\right]dt.$$

Therefore,

$$\frac{\partial V}{\partial t} + \frac{1}{2}\sigma^2 S_t^2 \frac{\partial^2 V}{\partial S_t^2} + (r-D)S_t\frac{\partial V}{\partial S_t} - rV(S_t,t) \le 0.$$

Here, for a European option, the inequality would become an equality.

Finally, from Problems 3.2.1.6 (page 276) and 3.2.1.12 (page 279) we can deduce that $V(S_t,t) \ge \Psi(S_t)$.

□

2. *Linear Complementarity Problem.* We consider the price of an American option $V(S_t,t)$ written on an underlying asset S_t at time t which satisfies the following inequality

$$\frac{\partial V}{\partial t} + \frac{1}{2}\sigma^2 S_t^2 \frac{\partial^2 V}{\partial S_t^2} + (r-D)S_t\frac{\partial V}{\partial S_t} - rV(S_t,t) \le 0$$

with constraint

$$V(S_t,t) \ge \Psi(S_t)$$

where $\Psi(S_t)$ is the option's intrinsic value, r is the risk-free interest rate, D is the continuous dividend yield and σ is the constant volatility.

Show that $V(S_t,t)$ with its corresponding intrinsic value $\Psi(S_t)$ satisfies the linear complementarity problem

$$\mathcal{L}_{BS}[V(S_t,t)] \le 0, \quad V(S_t,t) \ge \Psi(S_t), \quad [V(S_t,t) - \Psi(S_t)] \cdot \mathcal{L}_{BS}[V(S_t,t)] = 0$$

where $\mathcal{L}_{BS}$ denotes the differential operator

$$\mathcal{L}_{BS} = \frac{\partial}{\partial t} + \frac{1}{2}\sigma^2 S_t^2 \frac{\partial^2}{\partial S_t^2} + (r-D)S_t\frac{\partial}{\partial S_t} - r.$$

Solution: Suppose that $V(S_t,t) = \Psi(S_t)$. Then early exercise is optimal and by substituting $V(S_t,t) = \Psi(S_t)$ into the inequality we have

$$\frac{\partial \Psi}{\partial t} + \frac{1}{2}\sigma^2 S_t^2 \frac{\partial^2 \Psi}{\partial S_t^2} + (r-D)S_t\frac{\partial \Psi}{\partial S_t} - r\Psi(S_t) < 0$$

since the option's intrinsic value does not satisfy the Black–Scholes equation.

Hence,

$$V(S_t,t) = \Psi(S_t), \quad \mathcal{L}_{BS}[V(S_t,t)] < 0.$$

In contrast, if $V(S_t,t) > \Psi(S_t)$ then early exercise is not optimal and therefore

$$V(S_t,t) > \Psi(S_t), \quad \mathcal{L}_{BS}[V(S_t,t)] = 0.$$

Collectively we can write

$$\mathcal{L}_{BS}[V(S_t,t)] \leq 0, \quad V(S_t,t) \geq \Psi(S_t), \quad \left[V(S_t,t) - \Psi(S_t)\right] \cdot \mathcal{L}_{BS}[V(S_t,t)] = 0.$$

$\square$

3. *Continuous Limit of Binomial Model for American Options.* In a discrete-time Black–Scholes world, we consider the binomial tree model to calculate the price of an American option. At time t, where the current spot price is S_t, we build a tree of possible scenarios of future stock prices

$$S_i^{(j)} = u^j d^{i-j} S_t, \quad i = 0,1,\ldots,N, \quad j = 0,1,2,\ldots,i$$

such that $S_0^{(0)} = S_t$, N is the total number of time periods, $u = e^{\sigma\sqrt{\Delta t}}$, $d = e^{-\sigma\sqrt{\Delta t}}$, $\Delta t = (T-t)/N$ is the binomial time step, T is the expiry time and σ is the stock price volatility.

The intermediate American option price $V(S_n^{(m)}, t + n\Delta t)$ calculated at the m-th possible tree value and at time step $t + n\Delta t$, where $m \leq n$, $n \leq N$ is defined as

$$V(S_n^{(m)}, t + n\Delta t)$$
$$= \max\left\{\Psi(S_n^{(m)}), e^{-r\Delta t}\left[\pi V(uS_n^{(m)}, t+(n+1)\Delta t) + (1-\pi)V(dS_n^{(m)}, t+(n+1)\Delta t)\right]\right\}$$

where $\Psi(S_n^{(m)})$ is the option's intrinsic value, $\pi = \dfrac{e^{(r-D)\Delta t} - d}{u - d}$ is the risk-neutral probability, r is the risk-free interest rate and D is the continuous dividend yield.

Using Taylor's expansion up to $O(\Delta t)$ show that in the limit $\Delta t \to 0$ the binomial method approximates the continuous-time linear complementarity problem of the form

$$\mathcal{L}_{BS}[V(S,t')] \leq 0, \quad V(S,t') \geq \Psi(S), \quad \left[V(S,t') - \Psi(S)\right] \cdot \mathcal{L}_{BS}[V(S,t')] = 0$$

where $S = S_n^{(m)}$, $t' = t + n\Delta t$ and $\mathcal{L}_{BS}$ denotes the differential operator

$$\mathcal{L}_{BS} = \frac{\partial}{\partial t'} + \frac{1}{2}\sigma^2 S^2 \frac{\partial^2}{\partial S^2} + (r-D)S\frac{\partial}{\partial S} - r.$$

Solution: By setting $S = S_n^{(m)}$ and $t' = t + n\Delta t$, the intermediate American option price can be written as

$$V(S,t') = \max\left\{\Psi(S), e^{-r\Delta t}\left[\pi V(uS, t' + \Delta t) + (1-\pi)V(dS, t' + \Delta t)\right]\right\}$$

where we either have

$$V(S,t') = \Psi(S) \text{ and } V(S,t') > e^{-r\Delta t}\left[\pi V(uS,t'+\Delta t) + (1-\pi)V(dS,t'+\Delta t)\right]$$

or

$$V(S,t') > \Psi(S) \text{ and } V(S,t') = e^{-r\Delta t}\left[\pi V(uS,t'+\Delta t) + (1-\pi)V(dS,t'+\Delta t)\right].$$

By expanding $V(uS,t'+\Delta t)$ and $V(dS,t'+\Delta t)$ using Taylor's theorem and using the same steps as discussed in Problem 2.2.3.8 (page 202), we can write

$$\pi V(uS,t'+\Delta t) + (1-\pi)V(dS,t'+\Delta t) - e^{r\Delta t}V(S,t')$$
$$= \left[\frac{\partial V}{\partial t'} + \frac{1}{2}\sigma^2 S^2 \frac{\partial^2 V}{\partial S^2} + (r-D)S\frac{\partial V}{\partial S} - rV(S,t') + O(\Delta t)\right]\Delta t.$$

Since

$$\pi V(uS,t'+\Delta t) + (1-\pi)V(dS,t'+\Delta t) - e^{r\Delta t}V(S,t') = 0 \text{ and } V(S,t') > \Psi(S)$$

or

$$\pi V(uS,t'+\Delta t) + (1-\pi)V(dS,t'+\Delta t) - e^{r\Delta t}V(S,t') < 0 \text{ and } V(S,t') = \Psi(S)$$

we have

$$\frac{\partial V}{\partial t'} + \frac{1}{2}\sigma^2 S^2 \frac{\partial^2 V}{\partial S^2} + (r-D)S\frac{\partial V}{\partial S} - rV(S,t') + O(\Delta t) = 0 \text{ and } V(S,t') > \Psi(S)$$

or

$$\frac{\partial V}{\partial t'} + \frac{1}{2}\sigma^2 S^2 \frac{\partial^2 V}{\partial S^2} + (r-D)S\frac{\partial V}{\partial S} - rV(S,t') + O(\Delta t) < 0 \text{ and } V(S,t') = \Psi(S).$$

Hence, by taking limits $\Delta t \to 0$

$$\mathcal{L}_{BS}[V(S,t')] = 0 \text{ and } V(S,t') > \Psi(S)$$

or

$$\mathcal{L}_{BS}[V(S,t')] < 0 \text{ and } V(S,t') = \Psi(S).$$

Then we have

$$\mathcal{L}_{BS}[V(S,t')] \leq 0, \quad V(S,t') \geq \Psi(S), \quad \left[V(S,t') - \Psi(S)\right] \cdot \mathcal{L}_{BS}[V(S,t')] = 0.$$

$\square$

4. Consider a binomial tree model for an underlying asset process $\{S_n : 0 \le n \le 3\}$ where $S_0 = 100$. Let

$$
S_{n+1} = \begin{cases} u S_n & \text{with probability } \pi \\ d S_n & \text{with probability } 1 - \pi \end{cases}
$$

where $u = e^{\sigma \sqrt{\Delta t}}$ and $d = 1/u$ where σ is the volatility and Δt is the binomial time step. By assuming the risk-neutral interest rate $r = 5\%$, continuous dividend yield $D = 1\%$ and volatility $\sigma = 10\%$, we wish to price an American put option with strike $K = 105$ and expiry time $T = 1$ year in a 3-period binomial tree model.
(a) Find the risk-neutral probabilities π and $1 - \pi$.
(b) Find the price of the American put option.
(c) What is the trading strategy to hedge this option at the initial time period?

Solution:
(a) Given $S_0 = 100$, $K = 105$, $r = 0.05$, $D = 0.01$, $\sigma = 0.1$ and time step $\Delta t = \frac{1}{3}$, therefore

$$
u = e^{\sigma \sqrt{\Delta t}} = e^{\frac{0.1}{\sqrt{3}}} = 1.0594
$$

and

$$
d = e^{-\sigma \sqrt{\Delta t}} = e^{-\frac{0.1}{\sqrt{3}}} = 0.9439.
$$

The risk-neutral probabilities are

$$
\pi = \frac{e^{(r-D)\Delta t} - d}{u - d} = 0.6019
$$

and

$$
1 - \pi = 1 - 0.6019 = 0.3981.
$$

(b) The binomial tree in Figure 3.1 shows the price movement of S_0 in a 3-period binomial model.
By setting

$$
S_i^{(j)} = u^j d^{i-j} S_0, \quad i = 0, 1, \ldots, n, \quad j = 0, 1, \ldots, i
$$

the American put option price at each of the lattice points is

$$
V_i^{(j)} = \max \left\{ \Psi(S_i^{(j)}), e^{-r\Delta t} \left[\pi V_{i+1}^{(j+1)} + (1 - \pi) V_{i+1}^{(j)} \right] \right\}
$$

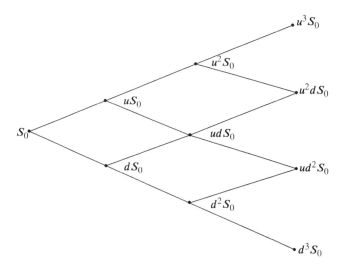

Figure 3.1 A 3-period binomial tree model.

such that

$$\Psi(S_i^{(j)}) = \max\left\{K - S_i^{(j)}, 0\right\}$$

where $i = 0, 1, \ldots, n$ and $j = 0, 1, \ldots, i$.

Hence, at time period $n = 3$

$$
\begin{aligned}
V_3^{(0)} &= \Psi(S_3^{(0)}) \\
&= \max\{K - d^3 S_0, 0\} \\
&= \max\{105 - 0.9439^3 \times 100, 0\} \\
&= 20.9035
\end{aligned}
$$

$$
\begin{aligned}
V_3^{(1)} &= \Psi(S_3^{(1)}) \\
&= \max\{K - ud^2 S_0, 0\} \\
&= \max\{105 - 1.0594 \times 0.9439^2 \times 100, 0\} \\
&= 10.6131
\end{aligned}
$$

$$
\begin{aligned}
V_3^{(2)} &= \Psi(S_3^{(2)}) \\
&= \max\{K - u^2 d S_0, 0\} \\
&= \max\{105 - 1.0594^2 \times 0.9439 \times 100, 0\} \\
&= 0
\end{aligned}
$$

$$
\begin{aligned}
V_3^{(3)} &= \Psi(S_3^{(3)}) \\
&= \max\{K - u^3 S_0, 0\} \\
&= \max\{105 - 1.0594^3 \times 100, 0\} \\
&= 0.
\end{aligned}
$$

At time period $n = 2$

$$V_2^{(0)} = \max\left\{\Psi(S_2^{(0)}, e^{-r\Delta t}\left[\pi V_3^{(1)} + (1-\pi)V_3^{(0)}\right]\right\}$$

$$= \max\left\{\max\left\{K - d^2 S_0, 0\right\}, e^{-r\Delta t}\left[\pi V_3^{(1)} + (1-\pi)V_3^{(0)}\right]\right\}$$

$$= \max\left\{\max\left\{105 - 0.9439^2 \times 100, 0\right\},\right.$$

$$\left. e^{-\frac{0.05}{3}}[0.6019 \times 10.6131 + 0.3981 \times 20.9035]\right\}$$

$$= \max\{15.9053, 14.4666\}$$

$$= 15.9053$$

$$V_2^{(1)} = \max\left\{\Psi(S_2^{(1)}, e^{-r\Delta t}\left[\pi V_3^{(2)} + (1-\pi)V_3^{(1)}\right]\right\}$$

$$= \max\left\{\max\left\{K - ud S_0, 0\right\}, e^{-r\Delta t}\left[\pi V_3^{(2)} + (1-\pi)V_3^{(1)}\right]\right\}$$

$$= \max\left\{\max\left\{105 - 1.0594 \times 0.9439 \times 100, 0\right\},\right.$$

$$\left. e^{-\frac{0.05}{3}}[0.6019 \times 0 + 0.3981 \times 10.6131]\right\}$$

$$= \max\{5.0032, 4.1552\}$$

$$= 5.0032$$

$$V_2^{(2)} = \max\left\{\Psi(S_2^{(2)}, e^{-r\Delta t}\left[\pi V_3^{(3)} + (1-\pi)V_3^{(2)}\right]\right\}$$

$$= \max\left\{\max\left\{K - u^2 S_0, 0\right\}, e^{-r\Delta t}\left[\pi V_3^{(3)} + (1-\pi)V_3^{(2)}\right]\right\}$$

$$= \max\left\{\max\left\{105 - 1.0594^2 \times 100, 0\right\},\right.$$

$$\left. e^{-\frac{0.05}{3}}[0.6019 \times 0 + 0.3981 \times 0]\right\}$$

$$= \max\{0, 0\}$$

$$= 0.$$

At time period $n = 1$

$$V_1^{(0)} = \max\left\{\Psi(S_1^{(0)}, e^{-r\Delta t}\left[\pi V_2^{(1)} + (1-\pi)V_2^{(0)}\right]\right\}$$

$$= \max\left\{\max\left\{K - d S_0, 0\right\}, e^{-r\Delta t}\left[\pi V_2^{(1)} + (1-\pi)V_2^{(0)}\right]\right\}$$

$$= \max\left\{\max\left\{105 - 0.9439 \times 100, 0\right\},\right.$$

$$\left. e^{-\frac{0.05}{3}}[0.6019 \times 5.0032 + 0.3981 \times 15.9053]\right\}$$

$$= \max\{10.61, 9.1889\}$$

$$= 10.61$$

$$V_1^{(1)} = \max\left\{\Psi(S_1^{(1)}, e^{-r\Delta t}\left[\pi V_2^{(2)} + (1-\pi)V_2^{(1)}\right]\right\}$$

$$= \max\left\{\max\{K - uS_0, 0\}, e^{-r\Delta t}\left[\pi V_2^{(2)} + (1-\pi)V_2^{(1)}\right]\right\}$$

$$= \max\{\max\{105 - 1.0594 \times 100, 0\},$$

$$e^{-\frac{0.05}{3}}[0.6019 \times 0 + 0.3981 \times 5.0032]\}$$

$$= \max\{0, 1.9589\}$$

$$= 1.9589$$

and finally at time period $n = 0$

$$V_0^{(0)} = \max\left\{\Psi(S_0^{(0)}, e^{-r\Delta t}\left[\pi V_1^{(1)} + (1-\pi)V_1^{(0)}\right]\right\}$$

$$= \max\left\{\max\{K - S_0, 0\}, e^{-r\Delta t}\left[\pi V_1^{(1)} + (1-\pi)V_1^{(0)}\right]\right\}$$

$$= \max\{\max\{105 - 100, 0\},$$

$$e^{-\frac{0.05}{3}}[0.6019 \times 1.9589 + 0.3981 \times 10.61]\}$$

$$= \max\{5, 5.3136\}$$

$$= 5.3136.$$

Therefore, the price of the American put based on a 3-period binomial model is $V_0^{(0)} = 5.3136$.

(c) At time period $n = 0$, let ϕ_0 and ψ_0 be the unit of the underlying asset S_0 and the amount of cash invested in the money market, respectively. At time period $n = 1$, the asset price can either be $S_1^{(0)} = dS_0$ or $S_1^1 = uS_0$ and ψ_0 will grow to $\psi_0 e^{r\Delta t}$. Thus, we can write

$$V_1^{(0)} = \phi_0 S_1^{(0)} + \psi_0 e^{r\Delta t}$$

$$V_1^{(1)} = \phi_0 S_1^{(1)} + \psi_0 e^{r\Delta t}.$$

Hence,

$$\phi_0 = \frac{V_1^{(1)} - V_1^{(0)}}{S_1^{(1)} - S_1^{(0)}} = \frac{V_1^{(1)} - V_1^{(0)}}{uS_0 - dS_0}$$

and

$$\psi_0 = e^{-r\Delta t}(V_1^{(0)} - \phi_0 S_1^{(0)}).$$

By substituting $V_1^{(0)} = 10.61$, $V_1^{(1)} = 1.9589$, $S_1^{(0)} = dS_0 = 94.39$, $S_1^{(1)} = uS_0 = 105.94$, $r = 0.05$ and $\Delta t = \frac{1}{3}$ we have

$$\phi_0 = -0.7490 \quad \text{and} \quad \psi_0 = 79.9642$$

which implies we need to sell -0.7778 units of the underlying asset S_0 and put $\$79.9642$ into the money market at 5% interest rate.

□

5. *Smooth-Pasting Condition for an American Call Option.* We consider an American call option, $C(S_t, t; K, T)$ with strike K written on an underlying asset priced at S_t at time t and $T > t$ is the option expiry time. Here the option has an unknown optimal exercise boundary S_t^∞ such that the option should be exercised if $S_t \geq S_t^\infty$ and held if $S_t < S_t^\infty$. By assuming $S_t^\infty > K$ show that the American call option satisfies the "smooth-pasting" condition

$$\left.\frac{\partial C}{\partial S_t}\right|_{S_t = S_t^\infty} = 1$$

at the optimal exercise boundary S_t^∞.

Solution: We prove this result via contradiction.

From definition, the value of an American call option can be written as

$$C(S_t, t; K, T) = \begin{cases} f(S_t, t; K, T) & \text{if } S_t < S_t^\infty \\ \\ S_t - K & \text{if } S_t \geq S_t^\infty \end{cases}$$

where $f(S_t, t; K, T)$ solves the Black–Scholes equation and $\dfrac{\partial C}{\partial S_t} = 1$ for $S_t \geq S_t^\infty$. For a graphical interpretation of the American call option see Figure 3.2.

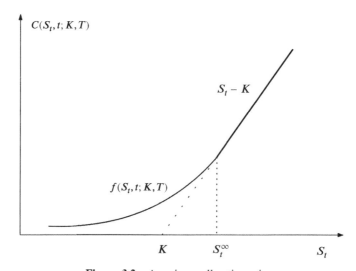

Figure 3.2   American call option price.

For $S_t < S^\infty$, suppose $\left.\dfrac{\partial C}{\partial S_t}\right|_{S_t=S_t^\infty} < 1$ then

$$C(S_t, t; K, T) < \max\{S_t - K, 0\}$$

which contradicts the fact that $C(S_t, t; K, T) \geq \max\{S_t - K, 0\}$.

Conversely if $\left.\dfrac{\partial C}{\partial S_t}\right|_{S_t=S_t^\infty} > 1$ then as the underlying asset price gets closer to S_t^∞ the value of the American call option can be increased by choosing a larger S^∞, which is a contradiction to the fact that S_t^∞ is the optimal exercise boundary.

Hence, in order to satisfy the optimal exercise strategy of an American call option we have

$$\left.\frac{\partial C}{\partial S_t}\right|_{S_t=S_t^\infty} = 1$$

where the two parts of $C(S_t, t; K, T)$ are joined smoothly without any discontinuity at $S_t = S_t^\infty$.

$\square$

6. *Smooth-Pasting Condition for an American Put Option.* We consider an American put option $P(S_t, t; K, T)$ with strike K written on an underlying asset priced at S_t at time t where $T > t$ is the option expiry time. Here the option has an unknown optimal exercise boundary S_t^* such that the option should be exercised if $S_t \leq S^*$ and held if $S_t > S_t^*$. By assuming $S_t^* < K$ show that the American put option satisfies the "smooth-pasting" condition

$$\left.\frac{\partial P}{\partial S_t}\right|_{S_t=S_t^*} = -1$$

at the optimal exercise boundary S_t^*.

Solution: We prove this result via contradiction.

From definition, the value of an American put option can be written as

$$P(S_t, t; K, T) = \begin{cases} K - S_t & \text{if } S_t \leq S_t^* \\ g(S_t, t; K, T) & \text{if } S_t > S_t^* \end{cases}$$

where $g(S_t, t; K, T)$ solves the Black–Scholes equation and $\dfrac{\partial P}{\partial S_t} = -1$ for $S_t \leq S_t^*$. For a graphical interpretation see Figure 3.3.

Suppose $\left.\dfrac{\partial P}{\partial S_t}\right|_{S_t=S_t^*} < -1$ then for $S_t > S_t^*$

$$P(S_t, t) < \max\{K - S_t, 0\}$$

which contradicts the fact that $P(S_t, t) \geq \max\{K - S_t, 0\}$.

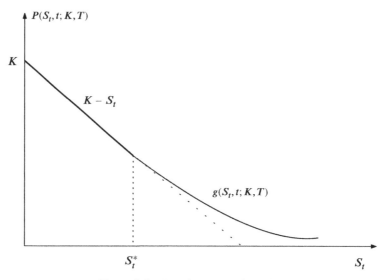

Figure 3.3 American put option price.

Conversely, if $\left.\dfrac{\partial P}{\partial S_t}\right|_{S_t=S_t^*} > -1$ then as the underlying asset price gets closer to S_t^* the value of the American put option can be increased by choosing a smaller S_t^*, which is a contradiction to the fact that S_t^* is the optimal exercise boundary.

Hence, in order to satisfy the optimal exercise strategy of an American put option we have

$$\left.\frac{\partial P}{\partial S_t}\right|_{S_t=S_t^*} = -1$$

where the two parts of $P(S_t,t;K,T)$ are joined smoothly without any discontinuity at $S_t = S_t^*$.

□

7. *American Call Option Asymptotic Optimal Exercise Boundary.* We consider an American call option price $C(S_t,t;K,T)$ written on an underlying asset priced at S_t at time t satisfying the following inequality

$$\frac{\partial C}{\partial t} + \frac{1}{2}\sigma^2 S_t^2 \frac{\partial^2 C}{\partial S_t^2} + (r-D)S_t\frac{\partial C}{\partial S_t} - rC(S_t,t;K,T) \le 0$$

with constraints

$$C(S_t,t;K,T) \ge \max\{S_t-K,0\}, \quad C(S_T,T;K,T) = \max\{S_T-K,0\}$$

where r is the risk-free interest rate, D is the continuous dividend yield, σ is the constant volatility, K is the strike price and $T > t$ is the option expiry time. The option has an unknown optimal exercise boundary $S_t^\infty \geq K$ where the option should be exercised if $S_t \geq S_t^\infty$ and held if $S_t < S_t^\infty$.

Show that for $D < r$

$$\lim_{t \to T} \frac{\partial C}{\partial t} \leq 0, \quad \text{for } K < \lim_{t \to T} S_t \leq \frac{rK}{D}$$

and

$$\lim_{t \to T} \frac{\partial C}{\partial t} > 0, \quad \text{for } \lim_{t \to T} S_t > \frac{rK}{D}$$

and hence deduce that $\lim_{t \to T} S_t^\infty = \frac{rK}{D}$.

For $D \geq r$ show that

$$\lim_{t \to T} S_t^\infty = K.$$

Finally, deduce that $\lim_{t \to T} S_t^\infty = K \max \left\{ \frac{r}{D}, 1 \right\}$.

Explain the financial implications if we set $D = 0$ or $r = 0$.

Solution: By considering the case when the American call option is not optimal to exercise, then the option price satisfies the Black–Scholes equation

$$\frac{\partial C}{\partial t} + \frac{1}{2}\sigma^2 S_t^2 \frac{\partial^2 C}{\partial S_t^2} + (r - D)S_t \frac{\partial C}{\partial S_t} - rC(S_t, t; K, T) = 0$$

with constraint

$$C(S_t, t; K, T) > \max\{S_t - K, 0\}.$$

For case $D < r$ we only consider $\lim_{t \to T} S_t > K$ such that

$$\lim_{t \to T} C(S_t, t; K, T) = \lim_{t \to T} S_t - K.$$

We then have

$$\lim_{t \to T} \frac{\partial C}{\partial t} = -\lim_{t \to T} \frac{1}{2}\sigma^2 S_t^2 \frac{\partial^2 C}{\partial S_t^2} - \lim_{t \to T}(r - D)S_t \frac{\partial C}{\partial S_t} + \lim_{t \to T} rC(S_t, t; K, T)$$

$$= -(r - D)\lim_{t \to T} S_t + r(\lim_{t \to T} S_t - K)$$

$$= D \lim_{t \to T} S_t - rK.$$

Suppose $\lim\limits_{t\to T}\dfrac{\partial C}{\partial t} > 0$, then expanding $C(S_t,t;K,T)$ using Taylor's theorem for $t\to T$ gives

$$\lim_{t\to T} C(S_t,t;K,T) = C(S_T,T;K,T) + \lim_{t\to T}\frac{\partial C}{\partial t}(t-T) + O((t-T)^2)$$
$$< C(S_T,T;K,T)$$
$$= S_T - K$$

which is a contradiction.

Therefore, in order to hold the option we have

$$\lim_{t\to T}\frac{\partial C}{\partial t} \le 0, \quad \text{for } K < \lim_{t\to T} S_t \le \frac{rK}{D}$$

and conversely

$$\lim_{t\to T}\frac{\partial C}{\partial t} > 0, \quad \text{for } \lim_{t\to T} S_t > \frac{rK}{D}$$

where the option should be exercised. Hence, the optimal exercise boundary is obtained by setting

$$\lim_{t\to T} S_t^\infty = \frac{rK}{D}.$$

For the case $D \ge r$ we assume $\lim\limits_{t\to T} S_t^\infty > K$ where early exercise is not optimal for $K < \lim\limits_{t\to T} S_t < \lim\limits_{t\to T} S_t^\infty$. Given $D \ge r$ and $\lim\limits_{t\to T} S_t > K$ therefore, by not exercising the option the interest earned on the strike is greater than the dividend lost from holding the asset, which is a contradiction. Hence,

$$\lim_{t\to T} S_t^\infty \le K.$$

Because $S_t^\infty \ge K, t < T$ we can deduce that

$$\lim_{t\to T} S_t^\infty = K.$$

In general we can write

$$\lim_{t\to T} S_t^\infty = \begin{cases} \dfrac{rK}{D} & \text{if } D < r \\[2mm] K & \text{if } D \ge r \end{cases}$$
$$= K \max\left\{\frac{r}{D}, 1\right\}.$$

If $D = 0$ then

$$\lim_{t \to T} S_t^\infty = \infty$$

which shows that it is never optimal to exercise an American call option before the expiry time.

In contrast, if $r = 0$ then

$$\lim_{t \to T} S_t^\infty = K$$

which implies that it is always optimal to exercise an American call option whenever the option is deep in the money.

$\square$

8. *American Put Option Asymptotic Optimal Exercise Boundary.* We consider an American put option price $P(S_t, t; K, T)$ written on an underlying asset priced at S_t at time t satisfying the following inequality

$$\frac{\partial P}{\partial t} + \frac{1}{2}\sigma^2 S_t^2 \frac{\partial^2 P}{\partial S_t^2} + (r - D)S_t \frac{\partial P}{\partial S_t} - rP(S_t, t; K, T) \le 0$$

with constraints

$$P(S_t, t; K, T) \ge \max\{K - S_t, 0\}, \quad P(S_T, T; K, T) = \max\{K - S_T, 0\}$$

where r is the risk-free interest rate, D is the continuous dividend yield, σ is the constant volatility, K is the strike price and $T > t$ is the option expiry time. The option has an unknown optimal exercise boundary $S_t^* \le K$ where the option should be exercised if $S_t \le S_t^*$ and held if $S_t > S_t^\infty$.

Show that for $D > r$

$$\lim_{t \to T} \frac{\partial P}{\partial t} \le 0, \quad \text{for } \frac{rK}{D} \le \lim_{t \to T} S_t < K$$

and

$$\lim_{t \to T} \frac{\partial P}{\partial t} > 0, \quad \text{for } \lim_{t \to T} S_t < \frac{rK}{D}$$

and hence deduce that $\lim_{t \to T} S_t^* = \dfrac{rK}{D}$.

For $D \le r$ show that

$$\lim_{t \to T} S_t^* = K.$$

Finally, deduce that $\lim_{t \to T} S_t^* = K \min\left\{\dfrac{r}{D}, 1\right\}$.

Explain the financial implications if we set $D = 0$ or $r = 0$.

Solution: We only consider the case when the American put option is not optimal to exercise where the option price satisfies the Black–Scholes equation

$$\frac{\partial P}{\partial t} + \frac{1}{2}\sigma^2 S_t^2 \frac{\partial^2 P}{\partial S_t^2} + (r - D)S_t \frac{\partial P}{\partial S_t} - rP(S_t, t; K, T) = 0$$

with constraint

$$P(S_t, t; K, T) > \max\{K - S_t, 0\}.$$

For case $D \le r$ we consider $\lim_{t \to T} S_t < K$ so that

$$\lim_{t \to T} P(S_t, t; K, T) = K - \lim_{t \to T} S_t.$$

We then have

$$\lim_{t \to T} \frac{\partial P}{\partial t} = -\lim_{t \to T} \frac{1}{2}\sigma^2 S_t^2 \frac{\partial^2 P}{\partial S_t^2} - \lim_{t \to T}(r - D)S_t \frac{\partial P}{\partial S_t} + \lim_{t \to T} rP(S_t, t; K, T)$$

$$= (r - D)\lim_{t \to T} S_t - r(\lim_{t \to T} S_t - K)$$

$$= rK - D\lim_{t \to T} S_t.$$

Suppose $\lim_{t \to T} \dfrac{\partial P}{\partial t} > 0$, then expanding $P(S_t, t; K, T)$ using Taylor's theorem for $t \to T$ gives

$$\lim_{t \to T} P(S_t, t; K, T) = P(S_T, T; K, T) + \lim_{t \to T} \frac{\partial P}{\partial t}(t - T) + O((t - T)^2)$$

$$< P(S_T, T; K, T)$$

$$= K - S_T$$

which is a contradiction.

Therefore, in order to hold the option we have

$$\lim_{t \to T} \frac{\partial P}{\partial t} \le 0, \quad \text{for } \frac{rK}{D} \le \lim_{t \to T} S_t < K$$

and conversely the option should be exercised when

$$\lim_{t \to T} \frac{\partial P}{\partial t} > 0, \quad \text{for } \lim_{t \to T} S_t < \frac{rK}{D}.$$

Hence, the optimal exercise boundary is obtained by setting

$$\lim_{t \to T} S^*_t = \frac{rK}{D}.$$

For the case $D \leq r$ we assume $\lim_{t \to T} S_t^* < K$ where early exercise is not optimal for $\lim_{t \to T} S_t^* < \lim_{t \to T} S_t < K$. Given $D \leq r$ and $\lim_{t \to T} S_t < K$ therefore, by not exercising the option the holder assumes the interest lost on the strike is lower than the dividend gained from holding the asset, which is a contradiction. Hence,

$$\lim_{t \to T} S_t^* \geq K.$$

Because $S_t^\infty \leq K, t < T$ we can deduce that

$$\lim_{t \to T} S_t^* = K.$$

In general, we can write

$$\lim_{t \to T} S_t^* = \begin{cases} \dfrac{rK}{D} & \text{if } D > r \\[2ex] K & \text{if } D \leq r \end{cases}$$

$$= K \min\left\{\frac{r}{D}, 1\right\}.$$

If $D = 0$ then

$$\lim_{t \to T} S_t^* = K$$

which implies it is always optimal to exercise an American put option whenever the option is deep in the money.

If $r = 0$ then

$$\lim_{t \to T} S_t^* = 0$$

which shows that when there is zero interest rate there is no financial gain in holding K from early exercise and therefore it is never optimal to exercise an American put option until expiry time. Thus, it is better to hold on to the option whilst earning dividend D from S_t till the expiry time.

□

9. *Upper Bound of American Option Price.* Let $V(S_t, t)$ be the price of an American option on an underlying asset S_t at time t with terminal payoff $\Psi(S_T)$ where T is the option expiry time. In addition, let r be the risk-free interest rate.

Under the risk-neutral measure $\mathbb{Q}$ and conditional on the filtration $\mathscr{F}_t$, we can express the option price as a *primal* problem

$$V(S_t, t) = \sup_{t \leq \tau \leq T} \mathbb{E}^{\mathbb{Q}}\left[e^{-r(T-\tau)}\Psi(S_\tau)\middle| \mathscr{F}_t\right]$$

where the supremum is taken over all possible stopping times τ, $\tau \in [t, T]$.

For arbitrary martingales M_t, show that

$$V(S_t,t) \leq \inf_M \mathbb{E}^Q \left[\max_{t \leq \tau \leq T} \left\{ e^{-r(T-\tau)} \Psi(S_\tau) - M_\tau \right\} \middle| \mathcal{F}_t \right] + M_t$$

where the right-hand side of the inequality is the *dual* problem.
    Hence, show that

$$V(S_t,t) \leq \mathbb{E}^Q \left[\max_{t \leq \tau \leq T} e^{-r(T-\tau)} \Psi(S_\tau) \middle| \mathcal{F}_t \right].$$

Solution: For an arbitrary martingale M_t

$$V(S_t,t) = \sup_{t \leq \tau \leq T} \mathbb{E}^Q \left[e^{-r(T-\tau)} \Psi(S_\tau) \middle| \mathcal{F}_t \right]$$

$$= \sup_{t \leq \tau \leq T} \mathbb{E}^Q \left[e^{-r(T-\tau)} \Psi(S_\tau) + M_\tau - M_\tau \middle| \mathcal{F}_t \right]$$

$$= \sup_{t \leq \tau \leq T} \left\{ \mathbb{E}^Q \left[e^{-r(T-\tau)} \Psi(S_\tau) - M_\tau \middle| \mathcal{F}_t \right] + \mathbb{E}^Q \left[M_\tau \middle| \mathcal{F}_t \right] \right\}$$

$$= \sup_{t \leq \tau \leq T} \mathbb{E}^Q \left[e^{-r(T-\tau)} \Psi(S_\tau) - M_\tau \middle| \mathcal{F}_t \right] + M_t$$

$$\leq \mathbb{E}^Q \left[\max_{t \leq \tau \leq T} \left\{ e^{-r(T-\tau)} \Psi(S_\tau) - M_\tau \right\} \middle| \mathcal{F}_t \right] + M_t.$$

Thus, taking the infimum

$$V(S_t,t) \leq \inf_M \mathbb{E}^Q \left[\max_{t \leq \tau \leq T} \left\{ e^{-r(T-\tau)} \Psi(S_\tau) - M_\tau \right\} \middle| \mathcal{F}_t \right] + M_t.$$

Setting $M_t = 0$, we have

$$V(S_t,t) \leq \mathbb{E}^Q \left[\max_{t \leq \tau \leq T} e^{-r(T-\tau)} \Psi(S_\tau) \middle| \mathcal{F}_t \right].$$

$\square$

10. *Black Approximation.* Consider an American call option written on an underlying asset S_t at time t with strike price K and option expiry time $T > t$. The asset pays one discrete dividend δ at time τ, $t < \tau < T$. In addition, let σ be the asset volatility and r be the risk-free interest rate.
    The Black approximation to price an American call option with a single dividend is given as

$$C_{am}(S_t,t;K,T) \approx \max \left\{ C_{bs}(S_t - \delta e^{-r(\tau-t)},t;K,T), C_{bs}(S_t,t;K,\tau) \right\}$$

where it is set as the maximum of two European options that expire at times T and τ such that

$$C_{bs}(X, t; Y, T) = X\Phi(d_+) - Ye^{-r(T-t)}\Phi(d_-)$$

$$d_{\pm} = \frac{\log(X/Y) + (r \pm \frac{1}{2}\sigma^2)(T-t)}{\sigma\sqrt{T-t}}$$

$$\Phi(x) = \int_{-\infty}^{x} \frac{1}{\sqrt{2\pi}} e^{-\frac{1}{2}u^2} du.$$

What do the first and second terms of the approximation symbolise?

Is the approximation value an upper or lower bound of the American call option price?

Finally, show that it is never optimal to exercise the American call option with a single discrete dividend when

$$\delta \leq K\left[1 - e^{-r(T-\tau)}\right].$$

Solution: The first term provides the European call option price value when the probability of early exercise is zero, whilst the second term assumes that the probability of early exercise before the ex-dividend date τ is one.

Since the two terms are sub-optimal values, therefore

$$C_{am}(S_t, t; K, T) \geq \max\left\{C_{bs}(S_t - \delta e^{-r(\tau-t)}, t; K, T), C_{bs}(S_t, t; K, \tau)\right\}.$$

To show that it is never optimal to exercise the American call option with one discrete dividend when

$$\delta \leq K\left[1 - e^{-r(T-\tau)}\right]$$

we first consider the possibility of early exercise prior to the dividend date τ.

If the option is exercised at time τ, the buyer of the call option receives

$$S_\tau - K.$$

If the option is not exercised before τ, the asset price will drop to

$$S_\tau - \delta.$$

Because the value of the call option

$$C_{am}(S_\tau, \tau; K, T) \geq S_\tau - \delta - K^{-r(T-\tau)}$$

therefore it is not optimal to exercise at time τ if

$$S_\tau - \delta - Ke^{-r(T-\tau)} \geq S_\tau - K$$

or

$$\delta \leq K \left[1 - e^{-r(T-\tau)}\right].$$

□

11. *Barone-Adesi and Whaley Formula.* Let $P_{am}(S_t, t; K, T)$ be the price of an American put option on an underlying asset S_t at time t such that it satisfies the Black–Scholes equation for $S_t > S_t^*$

$$\frac{\partial P_{am}}{\partial t} + \frac{1}{2}\sigma^2 S_t^2 \frac{\partial^2 P_{am}}{\partial S_t^2} + (r - D)S_t \frac{\partial P_{am}}{\partial S_t} - rP_{am}(S_t, t; K, T) = 0$$

$$P_{am}(S_t, t; K, T) > \max\{K - S_t, 0\}$$

where $S_t^* \leq K$ is the unknown optimal exercise boundary, K is the strike price, r is the risk-free interest rate, D is the continuous dividend yield, σ is the constant volatility and $T > t$ is the expiry time.

By writing the American put option price as

$$P_{am}(S_t, t; K, T) = P_{bs}(S_t, t; K, T) + \varepsilon(S_t, t; K, T)$$

where $P_{bs}(S_t, t; K, T)$ is the price of a European put option and $\varepsilon(S_t, t; K, T)$ is the early-exercise premium, show that for $S_t > S^*$, $\varepsilon(S_t, t; K, T)$ satisfies

$$\frac{\partial \varepsilon}{\partial t} + \frac{1}{2}\sigma^2 S_t^2 \frac{\partial^2 \varepsilon}{\partial S_t^2} + (r - D)S_t \frac{\partial \varepsilon}{\partial S_t} - r\varepsilon(S_t, t; K, T) = 0$$

$$\lim_{S_t \to 0} \varepsilon(S_t, t; K, T) = K(1 - e^{-r(T-t)}), \quad \lim_{S_t \to \infty} \varepsilon(S_t, t; K, T) = 0, \quad \lim_{t \to T} \varepsilon(S_t, t; K, T) = 0.$$

By setting $\varepsilon(S_t, t; K, T) = (1 - e^{-r(T-t)})v(S_t, t; K, T)$ show that for $S_t > S_t^*$, $v(S_t, t; K, T)$ satisfies

$$\frac{\partial v}{\partial t} + \frac{1}{2}\sigma^2 S_t^2 \frac{\partial^2 v}{\partial S_t^2} + (r - D)S_t \frac{\partial v}{\partial S_t} - \frac{r}{1 - e^{-r(T-t)}}v(S_t, t; K, T) = 0$$

$$\lim_{S_t \to 0} v(S_t, t; K, T) = K, \quad \lim_{S_t \to \infty} v(S_t, t; K, T) = 0, \quad \lim_{t \to T} v(S_t, t; K, T) = 0.$$

By assuming $\dfrac{\partial v}{\partial t} = 0$ show that the American put option can be approximated by

$$P_{am}(S_t, t; K, T) = P_{bs}(S_t, t; K, T) + AS_t^\alpha$$

where A is a constant,

$$\alpha = \frac{-(r - D - \frac{1}{2}\sigma^2) - \sqrt{\left(r - D - \frac{1}{2}\right)^2 + 2\sigma\tilde{r}}}{\sigma^2}$$

and

$$\tilde{r} = \frac{r}{1 - e^{-r(T-t)}}.$$

Finally, using the "smooth-pasting" condition and the solution of $P_{am}(S_t, t; K, T)$ at $S_t = S_t^*$, show that the constant A is

$$A = -\left[\frac{\Delta_E^* + 1}{\alpha(S_t^*)^{\alpha-1}}\right]$$

where $\Delta_E^* = \left.\dfrac{\partial P_{bs}}{\partial S_t}\right|_{S_t=S_t^*}$ with S_t^* satisfying the following equation

$$\left(\frac{\Delta_E^* + 1 - \alpha}{\alpha}\right) S_t^* + P_{bs}(S_t^*, t; K, T) - K = 0.$$

Solution: For $S_t > S_t^*$, both $P_{am}(S_t, t; K, T)$ and $P_{bs}(S_t, t; K, T)$ satisfy the Black–Scholes equation. Therefore, $\varepsilon(S_t, t; K, T)$ also satisfies

$$\frac{\partial\varepsilon}{\partial t} + \frac{1}{2}\sigma^2 S_t^2 \frac{\partial^2\varepsilon}{\partial S_t^2} + (r - D)S_t \frac{\partial\varepsilon}{\partial S_t} - r\varepsilon(S_t, t; K, T) = 0.$$

Given that

$$\varepsilon(S_t, t; K, T) = P_{am}(S_t, t; K, T) - P_{bs}(S_t, t; K, T)$$

as $S_t \to 0$, we have $P_{am}(S_t, t; K, T) \to K$ and $P_{bs}(S_t, t; K, T) \to Ke^{-r(T-t)}$.
Thus,

$$\lim_{S_t \to 0} \varepsilon(S_t, t; K, T) = K(1 - e^{-r(T-t)}).$$

In contrast, for the case when $S_t \to \infty$, we have $P_{am}(S_t, t; K, T) \to 0$ and $P_{bs}(S_t, t; K, T) \to 0$. Therefore,

$$\lim_{S_t \to \infty} \varepsilon(S_t, t; K, T) = 0.$$

Finally, for $t \to T$, both $P_{am}(S_t, t; K, T) \to \max\{K - S_T, 0\}$ and $P_{bs}(S_t, t; K, T) \to \max\{K - S_T, 0\}$, and so

$$\lim_{t \to T} \varepsilon(S_t, t; K, T) = 0.$$

By setting $\varepsilon(S_t, t; K, T) = (1 - e^{-r(T-t)})v(S_t, t)$ we have

$$\frac{\partial \varepsilon}{\partial t} = -re^{-r(T-t)}v(S_t, t; K, T) + (1 - e^{-r(T-t)})\frac{\partial v}{\partial t}$$

$$\frac{\partial \varepsilon}{\partial S_t} = (1 - e^{-r(T-t)})\frac{\partial v}{\partial S_t}, \frac{\partial^2 \varepsilon}{\partial S_t^2} = (1 - e^{-r(T-t)})\frac{\partial^2 v}{\partial S_t^2}$$

and substituting them into the Black–Scholes equation we eventually have

$$\frac{\partial v}{\partial t} + \frac{1}{2}\sigma^2 S_t^2 \frac{\partial^2 v}{\partial S_t^2} + (r - D)S_t \frac{\partial v}{\partial S_t} - \frac{r}{1 - e^{-r(T-t)}}v(S_t, t; K, T) = 0$$

such that

$$\lim_{S_t \to 0} v(S_t, t; K, T) = \lim_{S_t \to 0} \varepsilon(S_t, t; K, T)(1 - e^{-r(T-t)})^{-1} = K$$

$$\lim_{S_t \to \infty} v(S_t, t; K, T) = \lim_{S_t \to 0} \varepsilon(S_t, t; K, T)(1 - e^{-r(T-t)})^{-1} = 0$$

and

$$\lim_{t \to T} v(S_t, t; K, T) = \lim_{t \to T} \varepsilon(S_t, t; K, T)(1 - e^{-r(T-t)})^{-1} = 0.$$

By setting $\frac{\partial v}{\partial t} = 0$, the equation becomes

$$\frac{1}{2}\sigma^2 S_t^2 \frac{\partial^2 v}{\partial S_t^2} + (r - D)S_t \frac{\partial v}{\partial S_t} - \frac{r}{1 - e^{-r(T-t)}}v(S_t, t; K, T) = 0$$

and following the workings of the perpetual American options (see Problem 3.2.2.1, page 292) we can write the general solution as

$$v(S_t, t; K, T) = AS_t^\alpha + BS_t^\beta$$

where A and B are constants,

$$\alpha = \frac{-(r - D - \frac{1}{2}\sigma^2) - \sqrt{(r - D - \frac{1}{2})^2 + 2\sigma\tilde{r}}}{\sigma^2} < 0$$

and

$$\beta = \frac{-(r - D - \frac{1}{2}\sigma^2) + \sqrt{\left(r - D - \frac{1}{2}\right)^2 + 2\sigma\tilde{r}}}{\sigma^2} > 0$$

such that $\tilde{r} = \frac{r}{1 - e^{-r(T-t)}}$. From the initial condition, for $S_t \to \infty$, $v(S_t, t; K, T) \to 0$ and because $\beta > 0$ therefore $B = 0$. Hence,

$$v(S_t, t; K, T) = A S_t^\alpha.$$

Finally, at $S_t = S_t^*$ (see Problem 3.2.3.6, page 315) we have

$$P_{am}(S_t^*, t; K, T) = K - S_t^* \text{ and } \left.\frac{\partial P_{am}}{\partial S_t}\right|_{S_t=S_t^*} = -1$$

and by writing $\Delta_{bs}^* = \left.\frac{\partial P_{bs}}{\partial S_t}\right|_{S_t=S_t^*}$ we therefore have two equations

$$P_{bs}(S_t^*, t; K, T) + A(S_t^*)^\alpha = K - S_t^*$$
$$\Delta_{bs}^* + \alpha A(S_t^*)^{\alpha-1} = -1$$

and by solving them simultaneously

$$A = -\left[\frac{\Delta_{bs}^* + 1}{\alpha(S_t^*)^{\alpha-1}}\right]$$

and S_t^* satisfies

$$\left(\frac{\Delta_{bs}^* + 1 - \alpha}{\alpha}\right) S_t^* + P_{bs}(S_t^*, t; K, T) - K = 0.$$

$\square$

12. Consider a binomial tree model for an underlying asset process $\{S_n : 0 \le n \le 3\}$ following the Cox–Ross–Rubinstein model. With the initial asset price $S_0 = 100$, let

$$S_{n+1} = \begin{cases} uS_n & \text{with probability } \pi \\ dS_n & \text{with probability } 1 - \pi \end{cases}$$

where $u = e^{\sigma\sqrt{\Delta t}}$ and $d = 1/u$, with σ the volatility and Δt the binomial time step. Assuming the risk-free interest rate $r = 1\%$, continuous dividend yield $D = 0.5\%$ and volatility $\sigma = 8\%$, we wish to price a Bermudan call option with strike $K = 95$ and expiry time $T = 1$

year in a 3-period binomial tree model. For the Bermudan call option, early exercise is only
allowed in the fourth month of the contract.
(a) Find the risk-neutral probabilities π and $1 - \pi$.
(b) Find the price of the Bermudan call option.

Solution:
(a) Given $S_0 = 100$, $K = 95$, $r = 0.01$, $D = 0.005$, $\sigma = 0.08$ and time step $\Delta t = \frac{1}{3}$, then

$$u = e^{\sigma \sqrt{\Delta t}} = e^{\frac{0.08}{\sqrt{3}}} = 1.0472$$

and

$$d = e^{-\sigma \sqrt{\Delta t}} = \frac{1}{u} = \frac{1}{1.0472} = 0.9549.$$

Therefore, the risk-neutral probabilities are

$$\pi = \frac{e^{(r-D)\Delta t} - d}{u - d} = 0.5065$$

and

$$1 - \pi = 1 - 0.5065 = 0.4935.$$

(b) The binomial tree in Figure 3.4 shows the price movement of S_0 in a 3-period binomial
model.

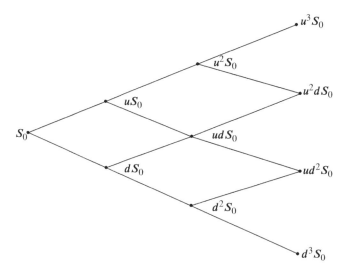

Figure 3.4   A 3-period binomial tree model.

By setting

$$S_i^{(j)} = u^j d^{i-j} S_0, \quad i = 0, 1, \ldots, n, \quad j = 0, 1, \ldots, i$$

the Bermudan call option price at each of the lattice points is

$$V_i^{(j)} = \begin{cases} \max\left\{ \Psi(S_i^{(j)}), \right. \\ \left. e^{-r\Delta t}\left[\pi V_{i+1}^{(j+1)} + (1-\pi)V_{i+1}^{(j)}\right]\right\} & \text{early exercise is allowed} \\ \\ e^{-r\Delta t}\left[\pi V_{i+1}^{(j+1)} + (1-\pi)V_{i+1}^{(j)}\right] & \text{early exercise is not allowed} \end{cases}$$

such that

$$\Psi(S_i^{(j)}) = \max\left\{ S_i^{(j)} - K, 0 \right\}$$

where $i = 0, 1, \ldots, n$ and $j = 0, 1, \ldots, i$.

Hence, at time period $n = 3$ (i.e., option expiry time $T = 1$ year)

$$\begin{aligned} V_3^{(0)} &= \Psi(S_3^{(0)}) \\ &= \max\{d^3 S_0 - K, 0\} \\ &= \max\{0.9549^3 \times 100 - 95, 0\} \\ &= 0 \end{aligned}$$

$$\begin{aligned} V_3^{(1)} &= \Psi(S_3^{(1)}) \\ &= \max\{ud^2 S_0 - K, 0\} \\ &= \max\{1.0472 \times 0.9549^2 \times 100 - 95, 0\} \\ &= 0.4873 \end{aligned}$$

$$\begin{aligned} V_3^{(2)} &= \Psi(S_3^{(2)}) \\ &= \max\{u^2 d S_0 - K, 0\} \\ &= \max\{1.0472^2 \times 0.9549 \times 100 - 95, 0\} \\ &= 9.7170 \end{aligned}$$

$$\begin{aligned} V_3^{(3)} &= \Psi(S_3^{(3)}) \\ &= \max\{u^3 S_0 - K, 0\} \\ &= \max\{1.0472^3 \times 100 - 95, 0\} \\ &= 19.8389. \end{aligned}$$

At time period $n = 2$ (i.e., $t = 8$ months) where early exercise is not allowed

$$V_2^{(0)} = e^{-r\Delta t} \left[\pi V_3^{(1)} + (1 - \pi)V_3^{(0)} \right]$$

$$= e^{-\frac{0.01}{3}} [0.5065 \times 0.4873 + 0.4935 \times 0]$$

$$= 0.2460$$

$$V_2^{(1)} = e^{-r\Delta t} \left[\pi V_3^{(2)} + (1 - \pi)V_3^{(1)} \right]$$

$$= e^{-\frac{0.01}{3}} [0.5065 \times 9.7170 + 0.4935 \times 0.4873]$$

$$= 5.1450$$

$$V_2^{(2)} = e^{-r\Delta t} \left[\pi V_3^{(3)} + (1 - \pi)V_3^{(2)} \right]$$

$$= e^{-\frac{0.01}{3}} [0.5065 \times 19.8389 + 0.4935 \times 9.7170]$$

$$= 14.7944.$$

At time period $n = 1$ (i.e., $t = 4$ months) where early exercise is allowed

$$V_1^{(0)} = \max \left\{ \Psi(S_1^{(0)}), e^{-r\Delta t} \left[\pi V_2^{(1)} + (1 - \pi)V_2^{(0)} \right] \right\}$$

$$= \max \left\{ \max \{ dS_0 - K, 0 \}, e^{-r\Delta t} \left[\pi V_2^{(1)} + (1 - \pi)V_2^{(0)} \right] \right\}$$

$$= \max \{ \max \{ 0.9549 \times 100 - 95, 0 \},$$

$$e^{-\frac{0.01}{3}} [0.5065 \times 5.1450 + 0.4935 \times 0.2460] \}$$

$$= \max \{ 0.4900, 2.7183 \}$$

$$= 2.7183$$

$$V_1^{(1)} = \max \left\{ \Psi(S_1^{(1)}), e^{-r\Delta t} \left[\pi V_2^{(2)} + (1 - \pi)V_2^{(1)} \right] \right\}$$

$$= \max \left\{ \max \{ uS_0 - K, 0 \}, e^{-r\Delta t} \left[\pi V_2^{(2)} + (1 - \pi)V_2^{(1)} \right] \right\}$$

$$= \max \{ \max \{ 1.0472 \times 100 - 95, 0 \},$$

$$e^{-\frac{0.01}{3}} [0.5065 \times 14.7944 + 0.4935 \times 5.1450] \}$$

$$= \max \{ 9.7200, 9.9990 \}$$

$$= 9.9990$$

and finally at time period $n = 0$ (i.e., $t = 0$) where early exercise is not allowed

$$V_0^{(0)} = e^{-r\Delta t} \left[\pi V_1^{(1)} + (1 - \pi)V_1^{(0)} \right]$$

$$= e^{-\frac{0.01}{3}} [0.5065 \times 9.9990 + 0.4935 \times 2.7183]$$

$$= 6.3847.$$

Therefore, the price of the Bermudan call option based on a 3-period binomial model is $V_0^{(0)} = 6.3847$.

$\hfill\square$

13. *One-Touch Option (PDE Approach).* Let $\{W_t : t \geq 0\}$ be a $\mathbb{P}$-standard Wiener process on the probability space $(\Omega, \mathcal{F}, \mathbb{P})$ and at time t, let the asset price S_t follow a GBM with the following SDE

$$\frac{dS_t}{S_t} = (\mu - D)\,dt + \sigma dW_t$$

where μ is the drift parameter, D is the continuous dividend yield and σ is the volatility parameter.

A one-touch call option is an American digital call option $C_{am}^d(S_t, t; K, T)$ that pays \$1 at the expiry time T if the underlying asset price S_u, $t \leq u \leq T$ is above the strike value K. If the underlying asset value has not reached the strike price by T then the option expires worthless.

As long as the option is not exercised then for $0 < S_t < K$, $C_{am}^d(S_t, t; K, T)$ satisfies the Black–Scholes equation

$$\frac{\partial C_{am}^d}{\partial t} + \frac{1}{2}\sigma^2 S_t^2 \frac{\partial^2 C_{am}^d}{\partial S_t^2} + (r - D)S_t \frac{\partial C_{am}^d}{\partial S_t} - rC_{am}^d(S_t, t; K, T) = 0$$

with boundary conditions

$$C_{am}^d(0, t; K, T) = 0, \quad C_{am}^d(K, t; K, T) = e^{-r(T-t)}, \quad C_{am}^d(S_T, T; K, T) = \mathbb{I}_{\{S_T \geq K\}}.$$

By writing the solution of $C_{am}^d(S_t, t; K, T)$ in the form

$$C_{am}^d(S_t, t; K, T) = C_{bs}^d(S_t, t; K, T) + P_{bs}^d(S_t, t; K, T) + V(S_t, t; K, T)$$

where $C_{bs}^d(S_t, t; K, T)$ and $P_{bs}^d(S_t, t; K, T)$ are the European digital call and put options satisfying

$$C_{bs}^d(S_t, t; K, T) + P_{bs}^d(S_t, t; K, T) = e^{-r(T-t)}$$

find the Black–Scholes equation for $V(S_t, t; K, T)$ together with its corresponding boundary conditions for $0 < S_t < K$.

Writing $V(S_t, t; K, T) = e^{\alpha x + \beta \tau} B(x, \tau)$ where $x = \log\left(\dfrac{S_t}{K}\right)$ and $\tau = \frac{1}{2}\sigma^2(T - t)$, show that by setting

$$\alpha = -\frac{1}{2}k_1 \quad \text{and} \quad \beta = -\frac{1}{4}k_1^2 - k_0$$

where $k_1 = \dfrac{r - D}{\frac{1}{2}\sigma^2} - 1$ and $k_0 = \dfrac{r}{\frac{1}{2}\sigma^2}$, the Black–Scholes equation for $V(S_t, t; K, T)$ is reduced to a heat equation of the form

$$\frac{\partial B}{\partial \tau} = \frac{\partial^2 B}{\partial x^2}$$

$$B(x, 0) = f(x), \quad B(0, \tau) = 0, x < 0.$$

Given that the solution of the heat equation is

$$B(x, \tau) = \frac{1}{2\sqrt{\pi\tau}} \int_{-\infty}^{0} f(z)e^{-(x-z)^2/4\tau}\,dz - \frac{1}{2\sqrt{\pi\tau}} \int_{0}^{\infty} f(-z)e^{-(x-z)^2/4\tau}\,dz$$

deduce that for $0 < S_t < K$

$$C_{am}^d(S_t, t; K, T) = C_{bs}^d(S_t, t; K, T) + \left(\frac{S_t}{K}\right)^{2\alpha} P_{bs}^d\left(\frac{K^2}{S_t}, t; K, T\right)$$

where

$$C_{bs}^d\left(X_t, t; K, T\right) = e^{-r(T-t)}\Phi\left(\frac{\log\left(X_t/K\right) + (r - D - \frac{1}{2}\sigma^2)(T - t)}{\sigma\sqrt{T - t}}\right)$$

and

$$P_{bs}^d\left(Y_t, t; K, T\right) = e^{-r(T-t)}\Phi\left(\frac{-\log\left(Y_t/K\right) - (r - D - \frac{1}{2}\sigma^2)(T - t)}{\sigma\sqrt{T - t}}\right)$$

respectively and

$$\Phi(x) = \frac{1}{\sqrt{2\pi}} \int_{-\infty}^{x} e^{-\frac{1}{2}u^2}\,du$$

is the standard normal cumulative density.

Solution: Given   that $C_{am}^d(S_t, t; K, T) = C_{bs}^d(S_t, t; K, T) + P_{bs}^d(S_t, t; K, T) + V(S_t, t; K, T)$ we can therefore express

$$\frac{\partial C_{am}^d}{\partial t} = \frac{\partial C_{bs}^d}{\partial t} + \frac{\partial P_{bs}^d}{\partial t} + \frac{\partial V}{\partial t}$$

$$\frac{\partial C_{am}^d}{\partial S_t} = \frac{\partial C_{bs}^d}{\partial S_t} + \frac{\partial P_{bs}^d}{\partial S_t} + \frac{\partial V}{\partial S_t}$$

and

$$\frac{\partial^2 C_{am}^d}{\partial S_t^2} = \frac{\partial^2 C_{bs}^d}{\partial S_t^2} + \frac{\partial^2 P_{bs}^d}{\partial S_t^2} + \frac{\partial^2 V}{\partial S_t^2}.$$

By substituting the above expressions into the Black–Scholes equation for $C_{am}^d(S_t, t; K, T)$ and taking note that

$$\frac{\partial C_{bs}^d}{\partial t} + \frac{1}{2}\sigma^2 S_t^2 \frac{\partial^2 C_{bs}^d}{\partial S_t^2} + (r - D)S_t \frac{\partial C_{bs}^d}{\partial S_t} - rC_{bs}^d(S_t, t; K, T) = 0, \quad 0 < S_t < K$$

and

$$\frac{\partial P_{bs}^d}{\partial t} + \frac{1}{2}\sigma^2 S_t^2 \frac{\partial^2 P_{bs}^d}{\partial S_t^2} + (r - D)S_t \frac{\partial P_{bs}^d}{\partial S_t} - rP_{bs}^d(S_t, t; K, T) = 0, \quad 0 < S_t < K$$

we have

$$\frac{\partial V}{\partial t} + \frac{1}{2}\sigma^2 S_t^2 \frac{\partial^2 V}{\partial S_t^2} + (r - D)S_t \frac{\partial V}{\partial S_t} - rV(S_t, t; K, T) = 0, \quad 0 < S_t < K$$

with boundary conditions

$$V(0, t; K, T) = 0, \quad V(K, t; K, T) = 0, \quad V(S_T, T; K, T) = -\mathbb{1}_{\{S_T < K\}}$$

since

$$C_{bs}^d(S_t, t; K, T) + P_{bs}^d(S_t, t; K, T) = e^{-r(T-t)}$$

and

$$V(S_T, T; K, T) = C_{am}(S_T, T; K, T) - C_{bs}^d(S_T, T; K, T) - P_{bs}^d(S_T, T; K, T)$$
$$= \mathbb{1}_{\{S_T \geq K\}} - 1.$$

Given that $V(S_t, t; K, T) = e^{\alpha x + \beta \tau} B(x, \tau)$ where $x = \log\left(\frac{S_t}{K}\right)$ and $\tau = \frac{1}{2}\sigma^2(T - t)$, we have

$$\frac{\partial V}{\partial t} = \frac{\partial V}{\partial \tau} \cdot \frac{\partial \tau}{\partial t} = -\frac{1}{2}\sigma^2 e^{\alpha x + \beta \tau}\left[\frac{\partial B}{\partial \tau} + \beta B(x, \tau)\right]$$

$$\frac{\partial V}{\partial S_t} = \frac{\partial V}{\partial x} \cdot \frac{\partial x}{\partial S_t} = \frac{e^{\alpha x + \beta \tau}}{S_t}\left[\frac{\partial B}{\partial x} + \alpha B(x, \tau)\right]$$

and

$$
\begin{aligned}
\frac{\partial^2 V}{\partial S_t^2} &= \frac{\partial}{\partial S_t}\left\{ \frac{e^{\alpha x + \beta \tau}}{S_t}\left[\alpha B(x,\tau) + \frac{\partial B}{\partial x}\right]\right\} \\
&= \frac{e^{\alpha x + \beta \tau}}{S_t^2}\left[\frac{\partial^2 B}{\partial x^2} + (2\alpha - 1)\frac{\partial B}{\partial x} + \alpha(\alpha - 1)B(x,\tau)\right].
\end{aligned}
$$

Substituting the above expressions into the Black–Scholes equation for $V(S_t, t; K, T)$ we eventually have

$$
\frac{1}{2}\sigma^2\left(\frac{\partial B}{\partial x^2} - \frac{\partial B}{\partial \tau}\right) + \frac{\partial B}{\partial x}\left[\frac{1}{2}\sigma^2(2\alpha - 1) + r - D\right]
$$
$$
+ B\left[\frac{1}{2}\sigma^2[\alpha(\alpha - 1) - \beta] + \alpha(r - D) - r\right] = 0
$$

and to eliminate the terms $\dfrac{\partial B}{\partial x}$ and B we set

$$
\frac{1}{2}\sigma^2(2\alpha - 1) + r - D = 0
$$
$$
\frac{1}{2}\sigma^2[\alpha(\alpha - 1) - \beta] + \alpha(r - D) - r = 0.
$$

By solving the equations simultaneously we have

$$
\alpha = -\frac{1}{2}k_1 \quad \text{and} \quad \beta = -\frac{1}{4}k_1^2 - k_0
$$

where $k_1 = \dfrac{r - D}{\frac{1}{2}\sigma^2} - 1$ and $k_0 = \dfrac{r}{\frac{1}{2}\sigma^2}$.

Hence,

$$
V(S_t, t; K, T) = e^{-\frac{1}{2}k_1 x - (\frac{1}{4}k_1^2 + k_0)\tau} B(x, \tau)
$$

with boundary conditions

$$
B(x, 0) = e^{\frac{1}{2}k_1 x} V(Ke^x, T; K, T) = -e^{\frac{1}{2}k_1 x}, \quad x < 0
$$

and

$$
B(0, \tau) = 0.
$$

By setting $f(x) = -e^{\frac{1}{2}k_1 x}$ and since

$$
B(x, \tau) = \frac{1}{2\sqrt{\pi\tau}}\int_{-\infty}^{0} f(z)e^{-(x-z)^2/4\tau}dz - \frac{1}{2\sqrt{\pi\tau}}\int_{0}^{\infty} f(-z)e^{-(x-z)^2/4\tau}dz
$$

we first let

$$B_1(x, \tau) = \frac{1}{2\sqrt{\pi\tau}} \int_{-\infty}^{0} f(z) e^{-(x-z)^2/4\tau} \, dz$$

$$= -e^{\frac{(x+k_1\tau)^2 - x^2}{4\tau}} \int_{-\infty}^{0} \frac{1}{2\sqrt{\pi\tau}} e^{-\frac{1}{2}\left(\frac{z-(x+k_1\tau)}{\sqrt{2\tau}}\right)^2} \, dz$$

$$= -e^{\frac{(x+k_1\tau)^2 - x^2}{4\tau}} \int_{-\infty}^{\frac{-x-k_1\tau}{\sqrt{2\tau}}} \frac{1}{\sqrt{2\pi}} e^{-\frac{1}{2}y^2} \, dy$$

$$= -e^{\frac{(x+k_1\tau)^2 - x^2}{4\tau}} \Phi\left(\frac{-x - k_1\tau}{\sqrt{2\tau}}\right).$$

In contrast,

$$B_2(x, \tau) = -\frac{1}{2\sqrt{\pi\tau}} \int_{0}^{\infty} f(-z) e^{-(x-z)^2/4\tau} \, dz$$

$$= e^{\frac{(x-k_1\tau)^2 - x^2}{4\tau}} \int_{0}^{\infty} \frac{1}{2\sqrt{\pi\tau}} e^{-\frac{1}{2}\left(\frac{z-(x-k_1\tau)}{\sqrt{2\tau}}\right)^2} \, dz$$

$$= e^{\frac{(x-k_1\tau)^2 - x^2}{4\tau}} \int_{-\frac{x-k_1\tau}{\sqrt{2\tau}}}^{\infty} \frac{1}{\sqrt{2\pi}} e^{-\frac{1}{2}y^2} \, dy$$

$$= e^{\frac{(x-k_1\tau)^2 - x^2}{4\tau}} \Phi\left(\frac{x - k_1\tau}{\sqrt{2\tau}}\right).$$

Thus,

$$B(x, \tau) = B_1(x, \tau) + B_2(x, \tau)$$

$$= -e^{\frac{(x+k_1\tau)^2 - x^2}{4\tau}} \Phi\left(\frac{-x - k_1\tau}{\sqrt{2\tau}}\right) + e^{\frac{(x-k_1\tau)^2 - x^2}{4\tau}} \Phi\left(\frac{x - k_1\tau}{\sqrt{2\tau}}\right)$$

such that

$$B(0, \tau) = -e^{k_1^2\tau^2} \Phi\left(-\frac{k_1\tau}{\sqrt{2\tau}}\right) + e^{k_1^2\tau^2} \Phi\left(-\frac{k_1\tau}{\sqrt{2\tau}}\right) = 0.$$

Hence,

$$V(S_t, t; K, T) = e^{\alpha x + \beta\tau} B(x, \tau)$$

$$= -e^{k_0\tau} \Phi\left(\frac{-x - k_1\tau}{\sqrt{2\tau}}\right) + e^{-k_1 x - k_0\tau} \Phi\left(\frac{x - k_1\tau}{\sqrt{2\tau}}\right)$$

$$= -e^{-r(T-t)}\Phi\left(\frac{-\log\left(S_t/K\right)-(r-D-\frac{1}{2}\sigma^2)(T-t)}{\sigma\sqrt{T-t}}\right)$$

$$+\left(\frac{S_t}{K}\right)^{2\alpha}e^{-r(T-t)}\Phi\left(\frac{-\log\left(K/S_t\right)-(r-D-\frac{1}{2}\sigma^2)(T-t)}{\sigma\sqrt{T-t}}\right)$$

$$= -P_{bs}^d(S_t,t;K,T)+\left(\frac{S_t}{K}\right)^{2\alpha}P_{bs}^d\left(\frac{K^2}{S_t},t;K,T\right).$$

Therefore, for $0 < S_t < K$ the one-touch call option is

$$C_{am}^d(S_t,t;K,T)=C_{bs}^d(S_t,t;K,T)+P_{bs}^d(S_t,t;K,T)+V(S_t,t;K,T)$$

$$= C_{bs}^d(S_t,t;K,T)+\left(\frac{S_t}{K}\right)^{2\alpha}P_{bs}^d\left(\frac{K^2}{S_t},t;K,T\right).$$

N.B. Using the same principles we can also show that for $K < S_t < \infty$, the one-touch put option price is

$$P_{am}^d(S_t,t;K,T)=P_{bs}^d(S_t,t;K,T)+\left(\frac{S_t}{K}\right)^{2\alpha}C_{bs}^d\left(\frac{K^2}{S_t},t;K,T\right).$$

$\square$

14. *One-Touch Option (Probabilistic Approach).* Let $\{W_t : t \geq 0\}$ be a $\mathbb{P}$-standard Wiener process on the probability space $(\Omega, \mathcal{F}, \mathbb{P})$ and at time t, let the asset price S_t follow a GBM with the following SDE

$$\frac{dS_t}{S_t} = (\mu - D)\,dt + \sigma dW_t$$

where μ is the drift parameter, D is the continuous dividend yield and σ is the volatility parameter.

A one-touch call option is an American digital call option $C_{am}^d(S_t,t;K,T)$ that pays \$1 at the expiry time T if the underlying asset price $S_u, t \leq u \leq T$ is above the strike value K. If the underlying asset value has not reached the strike price by T then the option expires worthless.

Show that under the risk-neutral measure $\mathbb{Q}$, for $0 < S_t < K$ the option price at time t can be written as

$$C_{am}^d(S_t,t;K,T)=e^{-r(T-t)}\mathbb{Q}\left(\max_{t\leq u\leq T}S_u > K\,\middle|\,\mathcal{F}_t\right)$$

where r is the risk-free interest rate.

By finding the running maximum of S_u, $t \leq u \leq T$ show that the one-touch call option price has a closed-form solution given as

$$C_{am}^d(S_t, t; K, T) = C_{bs}^d(S_t, t; K, T) + \left(\frac{S_t}{K}\right)^{2\alpha} P_{bs}^d\left(\frac{K^2}{S_t}, t; K, T\right)$$

where $0 < S_t < K$, $\alpha = \dfrac{1}{2}\left(1 - \dfrac{r - D}{\frac{1}{2}\sigma^2}\right)$, $C_{bs}^d(X_t, t; K, T)$ and $P_{bs}^d(Y_t, t; K, T)$ are the European digital call and put options defined as

$$C_{bs}^d\left(X_t, t; K, T\right) = e^{-r(T-t)}\Phi\left(\frac{\log(X_t/K) + (r - D - \frac{1}{2}\sigma^2)(T - t)}{\sigma\sqrt{T - t}}\right)$$

and

$$P_{bs}^d\left(Y_t, t; K, T\right) = e^{-r(T-t)}\Phi\left(\frac{-\log(Y_t/K) - (r - D - \frac{1}{2}\sigma^2)(T - t)}{\sigma\sqrt{T - t}}\right)$$

respectively and

$$\Phi(x) = \frac{1}{\sqrt{2\pi}}\int_{-\infty}^{x} e^{-\frac{1}{2}u^2}\,du$$

is the standard normal cumulative density.

Solution: Since the option is an American digital call with payout at time T then for non-early exercise time we would require $0 < S_t < K$. Hence, under the risk-neutral measure $\mathbb{Q}$ the one-touch call option price at time t becomes

$$C_{am}^d(S_t, t; K, T) = e^{-r(T-t)}\mathbb{E}^{\mathbb{Q}}\left[\mathbb{I}_{\{\max_{t \leq u \leq T} S_u > K\}}\middle| \mathcal{F}_t\right]$$

$$= e^{-r(T-t)}\mathbb{Q}\left(\max_{t \leq u \leq T} S_u \geq K\middle| \mathcal{F}_t\right)$$

such that

$$C_{am}^d(K, t; K, T) = e^{-r(T-t)}.$$

From Girsanov's theorem, under the risk-neutral measure $\mathbb{Q}$ we can easily show that S_t follows

$$\frac{dS_t}{S_t} = (r - D)\,dt + \sigma dW_t^{\mathbb{Q}}$$

where $W_t^{\mathbb{Q}} = W_t + \left(\dfrac{\mu - r}{\sigma}\right) t$ is a $\mathbb{Q}$-standard Wiener process. Using Itō's lemma we can show that for $t < T$

$$S_T = S_t e^{(r - D - \frac{1}{2}\sigma^2)(T-t) + \sigma W_{T-t}^{\mathbb{Q}}} = S_t e^{\sigma \widehat{W}_{T-t}}$$

where $\widehat{W}_{T-t} = v(T-t) + W_{T-t}^{\mathbb{Q}}$ and $v = \dfrac{1}{\sigma}(r - D - \dfrac{1}{2}\sigma^2)$.

By writing

$$M_{T-t} = \max_{t \leq u \leq T} \widehat{W}_{u-t}$$

therefore

$$\max_{t \leq u \leq T} S_u = S_t e^{\sigma M_{T-t}}.$$

By substituting the above expression into the option price we have

$$
\begin{aligned}
C_{am}^d(S_t, t; K, T) &= e^{-r(T-t)} \mathbb{Q}\left(S_t e^{\sigma M_{T-t}} \geq K \,\middle|\, \mathcal{F}_t \right) \\
&= e^{-r(T-t)} \left[1 - \mathbb{Q}\left(S_t e^{\sigma M_{T-t}} \leq K \,\middle|\, \mathcal{F}_t \right) \right] \\
&= e^{-r(T-t)} \left[1 - \mathbb{Q}\left(M_{T-t} \leq \frac{1}{\sigma} \log\left(\frac{K}{S_t}\right) \,\middle|\, \mathcal{F}_t \right) \right].
\end{aligned}
$$

From Problem 4.2.2.15 of *Problems and Solutions in Mathematical Finance, Volume 1: Stochastic Calculus* we can show that

$$
\begin{aligned}
\mathbb{Q}\left(M_{T-t} \leq \frac{1}{\sigma} \log(\frac{K}{S_t}) \,\middle|\, \mathcal{F}_t \right) &= \Phi\left(\frac{\frac{1}{\sigma}\log(K/S_t) - v(T-t)}{\sqrt{T-t}} \right) \\
&\quad - \left(\frac{S_t}{K}\right)^{-\frac{2v}{\sigma}} \Phi\left(\frac{-\frac{1}{\sigma}\log(K/S_t) - v(T-t)}{\sqrt{T-t}} \right).
\end{aligned}
$$

Hence,

$$
\begin{aligned}
C_{am}^d(S_t, t; K, T) &= e^{-r(T-t)} \left[1 - \Phi\left(\frac{\log(K/S_t) - (r - D - \frac{1}{2}\sigma^2)(T-t)}{\sigma\sqrt{T-t}} \right) \right] \\
&\quad + \left(\frac{S_t}{K}\right)^{2\alpha} e^{-r(T-t)} \Phi\left(\frac{-\log(K/S_t) - (r - D - \frac{1}{2}\sigma^2)(T-t)}{\sigma\sqrt{T-t}} \right)
\end{aligned}
$$

$$= e^{-r(T-t)} \Phi \left(\frac{\log(S_t/K) + (r - D - \frac{1}{2}\sigma^2)(T - t)}{\sigma \sqrt{T - t}} \right)$$

$$+ \left(\frac{S_t}{K} \right)^{2\alpha} e^{-r(T-t)} \Phi \left(\frac{-\log(K/S_t) - (r - D - \frac{1}{2}\sigma^2)(T - t)}{\sigma \sqrt{T - t}} \right)$$

$$= C_{bs}^d(S_t, t; K, T) + \left(\frac{S_t}{K} \right)^{2\alpha} P_{bs}^d \left(\frac{K^2}{S_t}, t; K, T \right)$$

where $\alpha = \dfrac{1}{2} \left(1 - \dfrac{r - D}{\frac{1}{2}\sigma^2} \right)$.

$\square$

15. *Immediate-Touch Option (PDE Approach).* Let $\{W_t : t \geq 0\}$ be a $\mathbb{P}$-standard Wiener process on the probability space $(\Omega, \mathcal{F}, \mathbb{P})$ and at time t, let the asset price S_t follow a GBM with the following SDE

$$\frac{dS_t}{S_t} = (\mu - D)\, dt + \sigma dW_t$$

where μ is the drift parameter, D is the continuous dividend yield and σ is the volatility parameter.

An immediate-touch call option is an American digital call option $C_d(S_t, t; K, T)$ that immediately pays \$1 if the underlying asset price S_u, $t \leq u \leq T$ is above the strike value K where T is the expiry time. If the underlying asset value has not reached the strike price by T then the option expires worthless, that is $C_d(S_T, T; K, T) = 0$, $0 < S_T < K$.

As long as the option is not exercised then for $0 < S_t < K$, $C_d(S_t, t; K, T)$ satisfies the Black–Scholes equation

$$\frac{\partial C_d}{\partial t} + \frac{1}{2}\sigma^2 S_t^2 \frac{\partial^2 C_d}{\partial S_t^2} + (r - D)S_t \frac{\partial C_d}{\partial S_t} - rC_d(S_t, t; K, T) = 0$$

with boundary conditions

$$C_d(0, t; K, T) = 0, \quad C_d(K, t; K, T) = 1.$$

By writing the solution of $C_d(S_t, t; K, T)$ in the form

$$C_d(S_t, t; K, T) = C^\infty(S_t) + C(S_t, t; K, T)$$

where $C^\infty(S_t)$ satisfies the perpetual call problem

$$\frac{1}{2}\sigma^2 S_t^2 \frac{d^2 C^\infty}{dS_t^2} + (r - D)S_t \frac{dC^\infty}{dS_t} - rC^\infty(S_t) = 0$$

with boundary conditions

$$C^\infty(0) = 0, \quad C^\infty(K) = 1$$

find $C^\infty(S_t)$ by solving the second-order ODE.

For $0 < S_t < K$ find the Black–Scholes equation for $C(S_t, t; K, T)$ together with its corresponding boundary conditions.

Writing $C(S_t, t; K, T) = e^{\alpha x + \beta \tau} B(x, \tau)$ where $x = \log\left(\dfrac{S_t}{K}\right)$ and $\tau = \frac{1}{2}\sigma^2(T - t)$ show that by setting

$$\alpha = -\frac{1}{2}(k - 1) \quad \text{and} \quad \beta = -\frac{1}{4}(k + 1)^2 - k'$$

where $k = \dfrac{r - D}{\frac{1}{2}\sigma^2}$ and $k' = \dfrac{D}{\frac{1}{2}\sigma^2}$, the Black–Scholes equation for $C(S_t, t; K, T)$ is reduced to a heat equation of the form

$$\frac{\partial B}{\partial \tau} = \frac{\partial^2 B}{\partial x^2}$$

$$B(x, 0) = f(x), \quad B(0, \tau) = 0, \quad x < 0.$$

Given that the solution of the heat equation with the above boundary conditions is

$$B(x, \tau) = \frac{1}{2\sqrt{\pi\tau}} \int_{-\infty}^{0} f(y)e^{-(x-y)^2/4\tau}dy - \frac{1}{2\sqrt{\pi\tau}} \int_{0}^{\infty} f(-y)e^{-(x-y)^2/4\tau}dy$$

deduce that for $0 < S_t < K$

$$C_d(S_t, t; K, T) = \left(\frac{S_t}{K}\right)^{\lambda_+} \Phi(d_+) + \left(\frac{S_t}{K}\right)^{\lambda_-} \Phi(d_-)$$

where

$$\lambda_\pm = \frac{-(r - D - \frac{1}{2}\sigma^2) \pm \sqrt{(r - D - \frac{1}{2}\sigma^2)^2 + 2\sigma^2 r}}{\sigma^2}$$

$$d_\pm = \frac{\log(S_t/K) \pm (T - t)\sqrt{(r - D - \frac{1}{2}\sigma^2)^2 + 2\sigma^2 r}}{\sigma\sqrt{T - t}}$$

and

$$\Phi(x) = \frac{1}{\sqrt{2\pi}} \int_{-\infty}^{x} e^{-\frac{1}{2}u^2} du$$

is the standard normal cdf.

Solution: Given that $C^\infty(S_t)$ satisfies the perpetual call problem then from Problem 3.2.2.2 (page 294), the solution of the ODE is

$$C(S_t) = AS_t^{\lambda_+}$$

where $\lambda_+ = \dfrac{-(r - D - \frac{1}{2}\sigma^2) + \sqrt{(r - D - \frac{1}{2}\sigma^2)^2 + 2\sigma^2 r}}{\sigma^2} > 0.$

Since $C^\infty(K) = 1$

$$A = K^{-\lambda_+}$$

and hence

$$C^\infty(S_t) = \left(\frac{S_t}{K}\right)^{\lambda_+}.$$

Since $C_d(S_t, t; K, T) = C^\infty(S_t) + C(S_t, t; K, T)$ we can write

$$\frac{\partial C_d}{\partial t} = \frac{\partial C}{\partial S_t}, \quad \frac{\partial C_d}{\partial S_t} = \frac{dC^\infty}{dS_t} + \frac{\partial C}{\partial S_t}, \quad \frac{\partial^2 C_d}{\partial S_t^2} = \frac{d^2 C^\infty}{dS_t^2} + \frac{\partial^2 C}{\partial S_t^2}$$

and by substituting them into the Black–Scholes equation for $C_d(S_t, t; K, T)$ and taking note that

$$\frac{1}{2}\sigma^2 S_t^2 \frac{d^2 C^\infty}{dS_t^2} + (r - D)S_t \frac{dC^\infty}{dS_t} - rC^\infty(S_t) = 0$$

we have

$$\frac{\partial C}{\partial t} + \frac{1}{2}\sigma^2 S_t^2 \frac{\partial^2 C}{\partial S_t^2} + (r - D)S_t \frac{\partial C}{\partial S_t} - rC(S_t, t; K, T) = 0, \quad 0 < S_t < K$$

with boundary conditions

$$C(0, t; K, T) = 0, \quad C(K, t; K, T) = 0, \quad C(S_T, T; K, T) = -\left(\frac{S_T}{K}\right)^{\lambda_+}, \quad 0 < S_T < K.$$

Given that $C(S_t, t; K, T) = e^{\alpha x + \beta \tau} B(x, \tau)$ where $x = \log\left(\dfrac{S_t}{K}\right)$ and $\tau = \frac{1}{2}\sigma^2(T - t)$ we have

$$\frac{\partial C}{\partial t} = \frac{\partial C}{\partial \tau} \cdot \frac{\partial \tau}{\partial t} = -\frac{1}{2}\sigma^2 e^{\alpha x + \beta \tau}\left[\frac{\partial B}{\partial \tau} + \beta B(x, \tau)\right]$$

$$\frac{\partial C}{\partial S_t} = \frac{\partial C}{\partial x} \cdot \frac{\partial x}{\partial S_t} = \frac{e^{\alpha x + \beta \tau}}{S_t}\left[\frac{\partial B}{\partial x} + \alpha B(x, \tau)\right]$$

and

$$\frac{\partial^2 C}{\partial S_t^2} = \frac{\partial}{\partial S_t}\left\{\frac{e^{\alpha x+\beta\tau}}{S_t}\left[\alpha B(x,\tau) + \frac{\partial B}{\partial x}\right]\right\}$$

$$= \frac{e^{\alpha x+\beta\tau}}{S_t^2}\left[\frac{\partial^2 B}{\partial x^2} + (2\alpha - 1)\frac{\partial B}{\partial x} + \alpha(\alpha - 1)B(x,\tau)\right].$$

By substituting the above expressions into the Black–Scholes equation for $C(S_t, t; K, T)$ we eventually have

$$\frac{1}{2}\sigma^2\left(\frac{\partial B}{\partial x^2} - \frac{\partial B}{\partial \tau}\right) + \frac{\partial B}{\partial x}\left[\frac{1}{2}\sigma^2(2\alpha - 1) + r - D\right]$$

$$+ B\left[\frac{1}{2}\sigma^2[\alpha(\alpha - 1) - \beta] + \alpha(r - D) - r\right] = 0.$$

To eliminate the terms $\dfrac{\partial B}{\partial x}$ and B we set

$$\frac{1}{2}\sigma^2(2\alpha - 1) + r - D = 0$$

$$\frac{1}{2}\sigma^2[\alpha(\alpha - 1) - \beta] + \alpha(r - D) - r = 0.$$

By solving the equations simultaneously we have

$$\alpha = -\frac{1}{2}(k - 1) \quad \text{and} \quad \beta = -\frac{1}{4}(k + 1)^2 - k'$$

where $k = \dfrac{r - D}{\frac{1}{2}\sigma^2}$ and $k' = \dfrac{D}{\frac{1}{2}\sigma^2}$.

Hence,

$$C(S_t, t; K, T) = e^{-\frac{1}{2}(k-1)x - \frac{1}{4}(k+1)^2\tau - k'\tau}B(x,\tau)$$

with boundary conditions

$$B(x, 0) = e^{\frac{1}{2}(k-1)x}C(S_T, T; K, T) = -e^{\frac{1}{2}(k-1)x}\left(\frac{Ke^x}{K}\right)^{\lambda_+} = -e^{\frac{1}{2}(k-1+2\lambda_+)x}, \quad x < 0$$

and

$$B(0, \tau) = 0.$$

By setting $f(x) = -e^{\frac{1}{2}(k-1+2\lambda_+)}$ then

$$B(x, \tau) = \frac{1}{2\sqrt{\pi\tau}}\int_{-\infty}^{0} f(y)e^{-(x-y)^2/4\tau}dy - \frac{1}{2\sqrt{\pi\tau}}\int_{0}^{\infty} f(-y)e^{-(x-y)^2/4\tau}dy$$

$$= B_1(x, \tau) + B_2(x, \tau)$$

where

$$B_1(x, \tau) = -\frac{1}{2\sqrt{\pi\tau}} \int_{-\infty}^{0} e^{-\frac{1}{2}\left(\frac{x-y}{\sqrt{2\tau}}\right)^2 + \frac{1}{2}(k-1+2\lambda_+)y} \, dy$$

and

$$B_2(x, \tau) = \frac{1}{2\sqrt{\pi\tau}} \int_{0}^{\infty} e^{-\frac{1}{2}\left(\frac{x-y}{\sqrt{2\tau}}\right)^2 - \frac{1}{2}(k-1+2\lambda_+)y} \, dy.$$

For the case $B_1(x, \tau)$ we have

$$B_1(x, \tau) = -\frac{1}{2\sqrt{\pi\tau}} \int_{-\infty}^{0} e^{-\frac{1}{2}\left(\frac{x-y}{\sqrt{2\tau}}\right)^2 + \frac{1}{2}(k-1+2\lambda_+)y} \, dy$$

$$= -e^{\frac{(x+(k-1+2\lambda_+)\tau)^2 - x^2}{4\tau}} \int_{-\infty}^{0} \frac{1}{2\sqrt{\pi\tau}} e^{-\frac{1}{2}\left(\frac{y-(x+(k-1+2\lambda_+)\tau)}{\sqrt{2\tau}}\right)^2} $$

$$= -e^{\frac{1}{2}x(k-1+2\lambda_+)+\frac{1}{4}\tau(k-1+2\lambda_+)^2} \int_{-\infty}^{-\left(\frac{x+(k-1+2\lambda_+)\tau}{\sqrt{2\tau}}\right)} \frac{1}{\sqrt{2\pi}} e^{-\frac{1}{2}z^2} \, dz$$

$$= -e^{\frac{1}{2}x(k-1+2\lambda_+)+\frac{1}{4}\tau(k-1+2\lambda_+)^2} \left(\Phi(d_+) - 1\right)$$

where $d_+ = \dfrac{x + \tau(k - 1 + 2\lambda_+)}{\sqrt{2\tau}}.$

For the case $B_2(x, \tau)$, using similar techniques we have

$$B_2(x, \tau) = \frac{1}{2\sqrt{\pi\tau}} \int_{0}^{\infty} e^{-\frac{1}{2}\left(\frac{x-y}{\sqrt{2\tau}}\right)^2 - \frac{1}{2}(k-1+2\lambda_+)y} \, dy$$

$$= e^{\frac{x^2 - (x+(k-1+2\lambda_+)\tau)^2}{4\tau}} \int_{0}^{\infty} \frac{1}{2\sqrt{\pi\tau}} e^{-\frac{1}{2}\left(\frac{y-(x-(k-1+2\lambda_+)\tau)}{\sqrt{2\tau}}\right)^2} \, dy$$

$$= e^{-\frac{1}{2}x(k-1+2\lambda_+)+\frac{1}{4}\tau(k-1+2\lambda_+)^2} \int_{\frac{(k-1+2\lambda_+)\tau-x}{\sqrt{2\tau}}}^{\infty} \frac{1}{\sqrt{2\pi}} e^{-\frac{1}{2}z^2} \, dz$$

$$= e^{-\frac{1}{2}x(k-1+2\lambda_+)+\frac{1}{4}\tau(k-1+2\lambda_+)^2} \Phi(d_-)$$

where $d_- = \dfrac{x - \tau(k - 1 + 2\lambda_+)}{2\sqrt{\tau}}.$

Thus,

$$
\begin{aligned}
B(x,\tau) &= B_1(x,\tau) + B_2(x,\tau) \\
&= -e^{\frac{1}{2}x(k-1+2\lambda_+)+\frac{1}{4}\tau(k-1+2\lambda_+)^2}\left(\Phi(d_+)-1\right) \\
&\quad + e^{-\frac{1}{2}x(k-1+2\lambda_+)+\frac{1}{4}\tau(k-1+2\lambda_+)^2}\Phi(d_-)
\end{aligned}
$$

where

$$
\begin{aligned}
B(0,\tau) &= -e^{\frac{1}{4}\tau(k-1+2\lambda_+)^2}\left[\Phi\left(\frac{(k-1+2\lambda_+)\tau}{\sqrt{2\tau}}\right)-1\right] \\
&\quad + e^{\frac{1}{4}\tau(k-1+2\lambda_+)^2}\Phi\left(-\frac{(k-1+2\lambda_+)\tau}{\sqrt{2\tau}}\right) \\
&= 0.
\end{aligned}
$$

Therefore, we can write

$$
\begin{aligned}
C(S_t,t;K,T) &= e^{-\frac{1}{2}(k-1)x-\frac{1}{4}(k+1)^2\tau-k'\tau}B(x,\tau) \\
&= e^{-\frac{1}{2}(k-1)x-\frac{1}{4}(k+1)^2\tau-k'\tau}\left[e^{-\frac{1}{2}x(k-1+2\lambda_+)+\frac{1}{4}\tau(k-1+2\lambda_+)^2}\Phi(d_-)\right] \\
&\quad -e^{-\frac{1}{2}(k-1)x-\frac{1}{4}(k+1)^2\tau-k'\tau}\left[e^{\frac{1}{2}x(k-1+2\lambda_+)+\frac{1}{4}\tau(k-1+2\lambda_+)^2}\left(\Phi(d_+)-1\right)\right] \\
&= e^{-x(k-1+\lambda_+)}\Phi(d_-) + e^{x\lambda_+}\left(\Phi(d_+)-1\right).
\end{aligned}
$$

By substituting $\lambda_+ = \dfrac{-(r-D-\frac{1}{2}\sigma^2)+\sqrt{(r-D-\frac{1}{2}\sigma^2)^2+2\sigma^2 r}}{\sigma^2}$, $x = \log\left(\dfrac{S_t}{K}\right)$, $\tau = \frac{1}{2}\sigma^2(T-t)$ and $k = \dfrac{r-D}{\frac{1}{2}\sigma^2}$ we have

$$
d_\pm = \frac{\log(S_t/K)\pm(T-t)\sqrt{(r-D-\frac{1}{2}\sigma^2)^2+2\sigma^2 r}}{\sigma\sqrt{T-t}}, \quad e^{-x(k-1+\lambda_+)} = \left(\frac{S_t}{K}\right)^{\lambda_-}
$$

and

$$
e^{x\lambda_+} = \left(\frac{S_t}{K}\right)^{\lambda_+}
$$

where $\lambda_- = \dfrac{-(r-D-\frac{1}{2}\sigma^2)-\sqrt{(r-D-\frac{1}{2}\sigma^2)^2+2\sigma^2 r}}{\sigma^2}$.

Therefore, for $0 < S_t < K$

$$C(S_t, t; K, T) = \left(\frac{S_t}{K}\right)^{\lambda_+} \left(\Phi(d_+) - 1\right) + \left(\frac{S_t}{K}\right)^{\lambda_-} \Phi(d_-)$$

and because $C_d(S_t, t; K, T) = C^\infty(S_t) + C(S_t, t; K, T)$ thus

$$C_d(S_t, t; K, T) = \left(\frac{S_t}{K}\right)^{\lambda_+} \Phi(d_+) + \left(\frac{S_t}{K}\right)^{\lambda_-} \Phi(d_-), \quad 0 < S_t < K.$$

N.B. Using similar steps we can also show the immediate-touch put option to be

$$P_d(S_t, t; K, T) = \left(\frac{S_t}{K}\right)^{\lambda_+} \Phi(-d_+) + \left(\frac{S_t}{K}\right)^{\lambda_-} \Phi(-d_-)$$

for $S_t > K$.

$\square$

16. *Immediate-Touch Option (Probabilistic Approach).* Let $\{W_t : t \geq 0\}$ be a $\mathbb{P}$-standard Wiener process on the probability space $(\Omega, \mathcal{F}, \mathbb{P})$ and at time t, let the asset price S_t follow a GBM with the following SDE

$$\frac{dS_t}{S_t} = (\mu - D)\, dt + \sigma dW_t$$

where μ is the drift parameter, D is the continuous dividend yield and σ is the volatility parameter.

By setting $\tau = \inf\{t \geq 0 : W_t = a + bt\}$ as the first-passage time of hitting the slope $a + bt$ where $a, b \in \mathbb{R}$, show that the pdf is

$$f_\tau(t) = \frac{|a|}{t\sqrt{2\pi t}} e^{-\frac{1}{2t}(a+bt)^2}.$$

An immediate-touch call option is an American digital call option $C_d(S_t, t; K, T)$ that immediately pays \$1 if the underlying asset price $S_u, t \leq u \leq T$ is above the strike value K where T is the expiry time. If the underlying asset value has not reached the strike price by T then the option expires, worthless, that is $C_d(S_T, T; K, T) = 0, 0 < S_T < K$.

Under the risk-neutral measure $\mathbb{Q}$ show that

$$C_d(S_t, t; K, T) = \int_0^{T-t} e^{-rv} f_\tau^{\mathbb{Q}}(v)\, dv$$

where $\tau = \inf\left\{t \geq 0 : W_t^{\mathbb{Q}} = w - \theta t\right\}$, $W_t^{\mathbb{Q}} = W_t + \left(\frac{\mu - r}{\sigma}\right) t$ is a $\mathbb{Q}$-standard Wiener process, $w = \frac{1}{\sigma} \log\left(\frac{K}{S_t}\right)$, $\theta = \frac{1}{\sigma}\left(r - D - \frac{1}{2}\sigma^2\right)$ and $f_\tau^{\mathbb{Q}}(t)$ is the pdf of τ under the $\mathbb{Q}$ measure.

By setting $\alpha = \sigma\theta$ and $\beta^2 = \alpha^2 + 2\sigma^2 r$ show that we can write

$$C_d(S_t, t; K, T) = \left(\frac{K}{S_t}\right)^{\frac{\alpha\pm\beta}{\sigma^2}} \int_0^{T-t} \frac{\log(K/S_t)}{\sigma v\sqrt{2\pi v}} e^{-\frac{1}{2\sigma^2 v}\left[\log\left(\frac{K}{S_t}\pm\beta v\right)\right]} dv.$$

Taking partial fractions of the form

$$\frac{\log\left(K/S_t\right)}{\sigma\sqrt{t}} = \frac{\log\left(K/S_t\right) - \beta t}{2\sigma\sqrt{t}} + \frac{\log\left(K/S_t\right) + \beta t}{2\sigma\sqrt{t}}$$

and by choosing appropriate integrands, show that for $0 < S_t < K$

$$C_d(S_t, t; K, T) = \left(\frac{S_t}{K}\right)^{\lambda_+} \Phi(d_+) + \left(\frac{S_t}{K}\right)^{\lambda_-} \Phi(d_-)$$

where

$$\lambda_\pm = \frac{-(r - D - \frac{1}{2}\sigma^2) \pm \sqrt{(r - D - \frac{1}{2}\sigma^2)^2 + 2\sigma^2 r}}{\sigma^2}$$

$$d_\pm = \frac{\log(S_t/K) \pm (T - t)\sqrt{(r - D - \frac{1}{2}\sigma^2)^2 + 2\sigma^2 r}}{\sigma\sqrt{T - t}}$$

and

$$\Phi(x) = \frac{1}{\sqrt{2\pi}} \int_{-\infty}^x e^{-\frac{1}{2}u^2} du$$

is the standard normal cumulative density.

Solution: In order to show that

$$f_\tau(t) = \frac{|a|}{t\sqrt{2\pi t}} e^{-\frac{1}{2t}(a+bt)^2}$$

which is the first-passage time density of a standard Wiener process hitting a slope, see Problem 4.2.2.16 of *Problems and Solutions in Mathematical Finance, Volume 1: Stochastic Calculus.*

From Girsanov's theorem, under the risk-neutral measure $\mathbb{Q}$ the SDE for the asset price is

$$\frac{dS_t}{S_t} = (r - D)dt + \sigma dW_t^{\mathbb{Q}}$$

where $W_t^{\mathbb{Q}} = W_t + \left(\dfrac{\mu - r}{\sigma}\right) t$ is a $\mathbb{Q}$-standard Wiener process. Hence, using Itō's lemma for $u > t$ we can write

$$S_u = S_t e^{\sigma \widehat{W}_{u-t}}$$

where $\widehat{W}_{u-t} = W_{u-t}^{\mathbb{Q}} + \theta(u - t)$, $\theta = \dfrac{1}{\sigma}\left(r - D - \dfrac{1}{2}\sigma^2\right)$.

By definition the immediate-touch call option price is

$$C_d(S_t, t; K, T) = \mathbb{E}^{\mathbb{Q}}\left(\max_{t \leq u \leq T} e^{-r(u-t)} \mathbb{I}_{\{S_u \geq K\}} \Big| \mathscr{F}_t\right)$$

$$= \mathbb{E}^{\mathbb{Q}}\left(\max_{t \leq u \leq T} e^{-r(u-t)} \mathbb{I}_{\{S_t e^{\sigma \widehat{W}_{u-t}} \geq K\}} \Big| \mathscr{F}_t\right)$$

$$= \mathbb{E}^{\mathbb{Q}}\left(\max_{t \leq u \leq T} e^{-r(u-t)} \mathbb{I}_{\{\widehat{W}_{u-t} \geq \frac{1}{\sigma}\log\left(\frac{K}{S_t}\right)\}} \Big| \mathscr{F}_t\right).$$

Since

$$\left\{\max_{t \leq u \leq T} S_u \geq K\right\} \Leftrightarrow \left\{\max_{t \leq u \leq T} \widehat{W}_{u-t} \geq \frac{1}{\sigma}\log\left(\frac{K}{S_t}\right)\right\} \Leftrightarrow \{\tau \leq T\}$$

where

$$\tau = \inf\left\{u \geq t : \widehat{W}_{u-t} = \frac{1}{\sigma}\log\left(\frac{K}{S_t}\right)\right\}$$

therefore

$$C_d(S_t, t; K, T) = \mathbb{E}^{\mathbb{Q}}\left(e^{-r(\tau-t)} \mathbb{I}_{\{\tau \leq T\}} \Big| \mathscr{F}_t\right)$$

$$= \int_t^T e^{-r(u-t)} f_\tau^{\mathbb{Q}}(u)\, du$$

where

$$f_\tau^{\mathbb{Q}}(u) = \frac{w}{(u-t)\sqrt{2\pi(u-t)}} e^{-\frac{1}{2(u-t)}(w - \theta(u-t))^2}, \qquad w = \frac{1}{\sigma}\log\left(\frac{K}{S_t}\right)$$

and

$$\theta = \frac{1}{\sigma}\left(r - D - \frac{1}{2}\sigma^2\right).$$

By letting $v = u - t$ we can write

$$C_d(S_t, t; K, T) = \int_0^{T-t} e^{-rv} \frac{w}{v\sqrt{2\pi v}} e^{-\frac{1}{2v}(w - \theta v)^2}\, dv.$$

Thus, by substituting $\alpha = \sigma\theta = r - D - \dfrac{1}{2}\sigma^2$, $\sigma w = \log\left(\dfrac{K}{S_t}\right)$, $\beta^2 = \alpha^2 + 2r\sigma^2$

$$
\begin{aligned}
C_d(S_t, t; K, T) &= \int_0^{T-t} e^{-rv} \frac{\log(K/S_t)}{\sigma v \sqrt{2\pi v}} e^{-\frac{1}{2\sigma^2 v}\left[\log\left(\frac{K}{S_t}\right) - \alpha v\right]^2} dv \\
&= \left(\frac{K}{S_t}\right)^{\frac{\alpha}{\sigma^2}} \int_0^{T-t} \frac{\log(K/S_t)}{\sigma v \sqrt{2\pi v}} e^{-\frac{1}{2\sigma^2 v}\left[\left\{\log\left(\frac{K}{S_t}\right)\right\}^2 + (\alpha^2 + 2r\sigma^2)v^2\right]} dv \\
&= \left(\frac{K}{S_t}\right)^{\frac{\alpha}{\sigma^2}} \int_0^{T-t} \frac{\log(K/S_t)}{\sigma v \sqrt{2\pi v}} e^{-\frac{1}{2\sigma^2 v}\left[\left\{\log\left(\frac{K}{S_t}\right)\right\}^2 + \beta^2 v^2\right]} dv \\
&= \left(\frac{K}{S_t}\right)^{\frac{\alpha}{\sigma^2}} \int_0^{T-t} \frac{\log(K/S_t)}{\sigma v \sqrt{2\pi v}} e^{-\frac{1}{2\sigma^2 v}\left\{\left[\log\left(\frac{K}{S_t}\right) \pm \beta v\right]^2 \mp 2\beta v \log\left(\frac{K}{S_t}\right)\right\}} dv \\
&= \left(\frac{K}{S_t}\right)^{\frac{\alpha \pm \beta}{\sigma^2}} \int_0^{T-t} \frac{\log(K/S_t)}{\sigma v \sqrt{2\pi v}} e^{-\frac{1}{2\sigma^2 v}\left[\log\left(\frac{K}{S_t}\right) \pm \beta v\right]^2} dv.
\end{aligned}
$$

By setting

$$
\frac{\log(K/S_t)}{\sigma\sqrt{v}} = \frac{\log(K/S_t) - \beta v}{2\sigma\sqrt{v}} + \frac{\log(K/S_t) + \beta v}{2\sigma\sqrt{v}}
$$

we have

$$
\begin{aligned}
C_d(S_t, t; K, T) &= \left(\frac{K}{S_t}\right)^{\frac{\alpha \pm \beta}{\sigma^2}} \int_0^{T-t} \frac{\log(K/S_t) - \beta v}{2\sigma\sqrt{2\pi v}} e^{-\frac{1}{2\sigma^2 v}\left[\log\left(\frac{K}{S_t}\right) \pm \beta v\right]^2} dv \\
&+ \left(\frac{K}{S_t}\right)^{\frac{\alpha \pm \beta}{\sigma^2}} \int_0^{T-t} \frac{\log(K/S_t) + \beta v}{2\sigma\sqrt{2\pi v}} e^{-\frac{1}{2\sigma^2 v}\left[\log\left(\frac{K}{S_t}\right) \pm \beta v\right]^2} dv.
\end{aligned}
$$

Hence, by selecting

$$
\begin{aligned}
C_d(S_t, t; K, T) &= \left(\frac{K}{S_t}\right)^{\frac{\alpha + \beta}{\sigma^2}} \int_0^{T-t} \frac{\log(K/S_t) - \beta v}{2\sigma\sqrt{2\pi v}} e^{-\frac{1}{2\sigma^2 v}\left[\log\left(\frac{K}{S_t}\right) + \beta v\right]^2} dv \\
&+ \left(\frac{K}{S_t}\right)^{\frac{\alpha - \beta}{\sigma^2}} \int_0^{T-t} \frac{\log(K/S_t) + \beta v}{2\sigma\sqrt{2\pi v}} e^{-\frac{1}{2\sigma^2 v}\left[\log\left(\frac{K}{S_t}\right) - \beta v\right]^2} dv
\end{aligned}
$$

and by setting

$$
x = \frac{\log(K/S_t) + \beta v}{2\sigma\sqrt{2\pi v}} \quad \text{and} \quad y = \frac{\log(K/S_t) - \beta v}{2\sigma\sqrt{2\pi v}}
$$

we eventually have

$$C_d(S_t, t; K, T) = \left(\frac{K}{S_t}\right)^{\frac{\alpha+\beta}{\sigma^2}} \int_{-\infty}^{\frac{-\log(K/S_t)-\beta(T-t)}{\sigma\sqrt{T-t}}} \frac{1}{\sqrt{2\pi}} e^{-\frac{1}{2}x^2} dx$$

$$+ \left(\frac{K}{S_t}\right)^{\frac{\alpha-\beta}{\sigma^2}} \int_{-\infty}^{\frac{-\log(K/S_t)+\beta(T-t)}{\sigma\sqrt{T-t}}} \frac{1}{\sqrt{2\pi}} e^{-\frac{1}{2}y^2} dy$$

$$= \left(\frac{K}{S_t}\right)^{\frac{\alpha+\beta}{\sigma^2}} \Phi\left(\frac{\log(S_t/K) - \beta(T-t)}{\sigma\sqrt{T-t}}\right)$$

$$+ \left(\frac{K}{S_t}\right)^{\frac{\alpha-\beta}{\sigma^2}} \Phi\left(\frac{\log(S_t/K) + \beta(T-t)}{\sigma\sqrt{T-t}}\right)$$

$$= \left(\frac{S_t}{K}\right)^{-\left(\frac{\alpha-\beta}{\sigma^2}\right)} \Phi\left(\frac{\log(S_t/K) + \beta(T-t)}{\sigma\sqrt{T-t}}\right)$$

$$+ \left(\frac{S_t}{K}\right)^{-\left(\frac{\alpha+\beta}{\sigma^2}\right)} \Phi\left(\frac{\log(S_t/K) - \beta(T-t)}{\sigma\sqrt{T-t}}\right).$$

By substituting $\alpha = r - D - \frac{1}{2}\sigma^2$ and $\beta = \sqrt{(r - D - \frac{1}{2}\sigma^2)^2 + 2r\sigma^2}$ we have, for $0 < S_t < K$

$$C_d(S_t, t; K, T) = \left(\frac{S_t}{K}\right)^{\lambda_+} \Phi(d_+) + \left(\frac{S_t}{K}\right)^{\lambda_-} \Phi(d_-)$$

where

$$\lambda_\pm = \frac{-(r - D - \frac{1}{2}\sigma^2) \pm \sqrt{(r - D - \frac{1}{2}\sigma^2)^2 + 2\sigma^2 r}}{\sigma^2}$$

and

$$d_\pm = \frac{\log(S_t/K) \pm (T-t)\sqrt{(r - D - \frac{1}{2}\sigma^2)^2 + 2\sigma^2 r}}{\sigma\sqrt{T-t}}.$$

$\square$

4

Barrier Options

In the last two chapters we have concentrated solely on European and American options which have a fixed strike and expiry date but different styles of exercise rights. In financial circles, these two types of derivatives are known as vanilla options, with the former also known as Black–Scholes options. In this chapter we will discuss barrier options, which are one of the most popular traded options that belong to a family of derivatives known as exotic options. Basically, an exotic option is a type of option which is neither a European nor an American option. Although they may have either European or American-style payoffs, exotic options have additional features that trigger the payoffs. The simplest exotic options are the digital and asset-or-nothing options which we have come across in Chapter 2. Another important difference between exotic options and vanilla options is that unlike vanilla options which are traded on major exchanges such as the Chicago Board Options Exchange, exotic options are usually traded OTC (i.e., without any supervision of an exchange). Hence these options are generally negotiated by brokers or dealers of the options' sellers and buyers, as to how the trades are to be settled in the future.

In finance, barrier options belong to a class of exotic options that can be terminated or activated when the threshold or barrier is crossed. These options are usually written on volatile stocks and given such a feature, barrier options are significantly cheaper than vanilla options. Hence, by trading such an option, it provides investors with an alternative hedging strategy without having to pay for the full vanilla price, which they believe is unlikely to occur in the lifetime of the option contract. By making the barrier be a function of time or paying a rebate when the barrier is triggered, there is a lot of flexibility for investors to express their view in the stock price movements within the contract. In addition, the option can also be easily extended to incorporate early-exercise features, but the solutions to such a problem usually depend on numerical methods. In this chapter, unless otherwise stated, we only consider European-style barrier options.

4.1 INTRODUCTION

Conceptually, barrier options are conditional options which are dependent on some barriers being breached (or triggered) in their contractual lives. As these options are either activated or deactivated when the asset price crosses a barrier, these options are path-dependent. However, these options are also known as weakly path-dependent, since we only need to know whether or not the barrier is triggered and we are not concerned about the asset price path.

Basically, there are two types of barrier options: knock-ins and knock-outs.

For a knock-in:

- If the option is an **up-and-in barrier option**, then the option is only active if the barrier is hit from below the barrier. Note that the option remains worthless if the asset price does not rise above the barrier. If at some point during the life of the option the barrier is hit, then the option will turn into a European option.

- If the option is a **down-and-in barrier option**, then the option is only active if the barrier is hit from above the barrier. Note that the option remains worthless if the asset price does not fall below the barrier. If at some point during the life of the option the barrier is hit, then the option will turn into a European option.

For a knock-out:

- If the option is an **up-and-out barrier option**, then the option is only active if the asset price is below the barrier. Here, the option becomes worthless if the asset price rises above the barrier (or the barrier is hit from below).
- If the option is a **down-and-out barrier option**, then the option is only active if the asset price is above the barrier. Here, the option becomes worthless if the asset price falls below the barrier (or the barrier is hit from above).

In–Out Parity

Just like the European and American options have their put–call parities, the barrier options have the in–out parity

$$V_{k/i}(S_t, t; K, B, T) + V_{k/o}(S_t, t; K, B, T) = V_{bs}(S_t, t; K, T)$$

where the sum of the knock-in option $V_{k/i}(S_t, t; K, B, T)$ and the knock-out option $V_{k/o}(S_t, t; K, B, T)$ with the same asset price S_t, strike K, barrier B and expiry time T is the same as the price of a European (Black–Scholes) option. From the above relationship, given that knock-ins and knock-outs have positive payoffs and hence positive option price values, we can immediately deduce that their option price values are less than the value of a European option. This is not unexpected, since barrier options have fewer rights than European options and thus they have a lower value.

By incorporating a rebate R payable at expiry T, we have the following property

$$V_{k/i}^R(S_t, t; K, B, T) + V_{k/o}^R(S_t, t; K, B, T) = V_{bs}(S_t, t; K, T) + Re^{-r(T-t)}$$

where $V_{k/i}^R(S_t, t; K, B, T)$ and $V_{k/o}^R(S_t, t; K, B, T)$ are knock-in and knock-out options with rebate R, respectively having the same asset price S_t, strike K, barrier B, expiry time T, and r is the constant risk-free interest rate.

In contrast, if the rebate R is payable at knock-out or knock-in time, the corresponding in–out parity is

$$V_{k/i}^R(S_t, t; K, B, T) + V_{k/o}^R(S_t, t; K, B, T) = V_{bs}(S_t, t; K, T) + R\left[\left(\frac{S_t}{B}\right)^{\lambda_+} + \left(\frac{S_t}{B}\right)^{\lambda_-}\right]$$

where

$$\lambda_\pm = \frac{-(r - D - \frac{1}{2}\sigma^2) \pm \sqrt{(r - D - \frac{1}{2}\sigma^2)^2 + 2\sigma^2 r}}{\sigma^2}.$$

Barrier Options Pricing

Under the Black–Scholes methodology we can solve the pricing issues of barrier options using both the probabilistic (martingale pricing) approach and partial differentiation equation (via the reflection principle) approach.

Probabilistic Approach

In the same vein as the martingale pricing framework of European options, we can also price barrier options via the risk-neutral expectation strategy. For instance, a knock-in barrier option payoff can be written as

$$
\Psi_{k/i}(S_T) = \begin{cases} \Psi(S_T)\,\mathbb{I}_{\{\max_{t \le u \le T} S_u \ge B\}} & \text{up-and-in option} \\[2mm] \Psi(S_T)\,\mathbb{I}_{\{\min_{t \le u \le T} S_u \le B\}} & \text{down-and-in option} \end{cases}
$$

whilst for a knock-out barrier option payoff

$$
\Psi_{k/o}(S_T) = \begin{cases} \Psi(S_T)\,\mathbb{I}_{\{\max_{t \le u \le T} S_u < B\}} & \text{up-and-out option} \\[2mm] \Psi(S_T)\,\mathbb{I}_{\{\min_{t \le u \le T} S_u > B\}} & \text{down-and-out option} \end{cases}
$$

where $\Psi(S_T)$ is the European option payoff at expiry time T.

In order to price this option we need to know the probability that the barrier will be triggered and also the probability that the option is exercised at expiry time. Hence, this requires the joint distribution of the Wiener process with drift (for the European option payoff) and its running maximum (for up-and-in and up-and-out options) or running minimum (for down-and-in and down-and-out options).

Without loss of generality, let $\{W_t : t \ge 0\}$ be a $\mathbb{P}$-standard Wiener process and if X_t is a Wiener process with drift $\mu \in \mathbb{R}$ in the form

$$
X_t = \mu t + W_t
$$

and by defining

$$
M_t^X = \max_{0 \le s \le t} X_s
$$

to be the running maximum of the process X_t up to time t, the cdf of the running maximum is

$$
\mathbb{P}(M_t^X \le x) = \Phi\left(\frac{x - \mu t}{\sqrt{t}}\right) - e^{2\mu x}\Phi\left(\frac{-x - \mu t}{\sqrt{t}}\right), \quad x \ge 0
$$

where $\Phi(\cdot)$ is the standard normal cdf. The joint density of (M_t^X, X_t) of the running maximum and the Wiener process is

$$f_{M_t^X, X_t}^{\mathbb{P}}(x, y) = \frac{2(2x - y)}{t\sqrt{2\pi t}} e^{\mu y - \frac{1}{2}\mu^2 t - \frac{1}{2t}(2x-y)^2}, \quad x \geq 0, x \geq y.$$

As for the running minimum of the process X_t up to time t,

$$m_t^X = \min_{0 \leq s \leq t} X_s$$

the cdf of the running minimum is

$$\mathbb{P}(m_t^X \leq x) = \Phi\left(\frac{x - \mu t}{\sqrt{t}}\right) + e^{2\mu x}\Phi\left(\frac{x + \mu t}{\sqrt{t}}\right), \quad x \leq 0$$

with the joint density of (m_t^X, X_t) of the running minimum and the Wiener process

$$f_{m_t^X, X_t}^{\mathbb{P}}(x, y) = \frac{-2(2x - y)}{t\sqrt{2\pi t}} e^{\mu y - \frac{1}{2}\mu^2 t - \frac{1}{2t}(2x-y)^2}, \quad x \leq 0, x \leq y.$$

For the derivation of the above formulae, see Problem 4.2.2.14 of *Problems and Solutions in Mathematical Finance, Volume 1: Stochastic Calculus*.

Partial Differentiation Equation Approach

In order to find the closed-form solutions of barrier options via the PDE method, we first consider the reflected solution of the Black–Scholes equation.

Theorem 4.1 *Suppose $V(S_t, t)$ satisfies the Black–Scholes equation (see below) with the asset S_t paying a continuous dividend yield D,*

$$\frac{\partial V}{\partial S_t} + \frac{1}{2}\sigma^2 S_t^2 \frac{\partial^2 V}{\partial S_t^2} + (r - D)S_t \frac{\partial V}{\partial S_t} - rV(S_t, t) = 0$$

then for any constant B (representing a barrier)

$$U(S_t, t) = \left(\frac{S_t}{B}\right)^{2\alpha} V\left(\frac{B^2}{S_t}, t\right)$$

also satisfies the Black–Scholes equation provided that $\alpha = \dfrac{1}{2}\left(1 - \dfrac{r - D}{\frac{1}{2}\sigma^2}\right)$. Note that S_t and B^2/S_t are on opposite sides of the barrier B for $S_t \neq B$ and coincide when $S_t = B$.

Let us begin by focussing on the up-and-out barrier option and note that we can consider only the knock-out options as the knock-in options' prices can be obtained easily from the in–out parity identity. If we consider the Black–Scholes equation for an asset S_t paying a continuous dividend yield D, the up-and-out barrier option $V_{u/o}(S_t, t; K, B, T)$ with strike price K and barrier B satisfies the PDE

$$\frac{\partial V_{u/o}}{\partial S_t} + \frac{1}{2}\sigma^2 S_t^2 \frac{\partial^2 V_{u/o}}{\partial S_t^2} + (r - D)S_t \frac{\partial V_{u/o}}{\partial S_t} - rV_{u/o}(S_t, t; K, B, T) = 0$$

provided the following boundary conditions are satisfied

$$0 < S_t < B, \quad t \leq T$$

$$V_{u/o}(B, t; K, B, T) = 0$$

$$V_{u/o}(S_T, T; K, B, T) = \Psi(S_T)$$

where $\Psi(S_T)$ is the European (Black–Scholes) payoff at expiry time T.

Given that the up-and-out barrier option has a European payoff at expiry T but becomes worthless on the barrier B, we can deduce that

$$V_{u/o}(S_t, t; K, B, T) = \widetilde{V}_{u/o}(S_t, t; K, B, T) - \widehat{V}_{u/o}(S_t, t; K, B, T)$$

so that $\widetilde{V}_{u/o}(S_t, t; K, B, T)$ satisfies the Black–Scholes equation

$$\frac{\partial \widetilde{V}_{u/o}}{\partial S_t} + \frac{1}{2}\sigma^2 S_t^2 \frac{\partial^2 \widetilde{V}_{u/o}}{\partial S_t^2} + (r - D)S_t \frac{\partial \widetilde{V}_{u/o}}{\partial S_t} - r\widetilde{V}_{u/o}(S_t, t; K, B, T) = 0$$

with truncated payoff

$$0 < S_t < B, \quad t \leq T$$

$$\widetilde{V}_{u/o}(S_T, T; K, B, T) = \Psi(S_T).$$

To account for the barrier, we therefore require $\widehat{V}(S_t, t; K, B, T)$ to satisfy

$$\widehat{V}_{u/o}(S_T, T; K, B, T) = 0$$

at expiry time T and

$$\widehat{V}_{u/o}(B, t; K, B, T) = \widetilde{V}_{u/o}(B, t; K, B, T)$$

on the barrier B.

To find the solution for $\hat{V}_{u/o}(S_t, t; K, B, T)$ we note that since $\left(\dfrac{S_t}{B}\right)^{2\alpha} \tilde{V}_{u/o}\left(\dfrac{B^2}{S_t}, t; K, B, T\right)$ with $\alpha = \dfrac{1}{2}\left(1 - \dfrac{r-D}{\frac{1}{2}\sigma^2}\right)$ also satisfies the Black–Scholes equation, we can thus set the solution of an up-and-out barrier option as

$$V_{u/o}(S_t, t; K, B, T) = \tilde{V}_{u/o}(S_t, t; K, B, T) - \left(\frac{S_t}{B}\right)^{2\alpha} \tilde{V}_{u/o}\left(\frac{B^2}{S_t}, t; K, B, T\right).$$

Since S_t and B^2/S_t are on opposite sides of the barrier B for $S_t \neq B$, therefore

$$\left(\frac{S_T}{B}\right)^{2\alpha} \tilde{V}\left(\frac{B^2}{S_T}, t; K, B, T\right) = 0$$

for all $0 < S_T < B$. Hence, one can easily check that the boundary conditions

$$V_{u/o}(S_T, T; K, B, T) = \Psi(S_T) \quad \text{and} \quad V_{u/o}(B, t; K, B, T) = 0$$

are satisfied. Using the in–out parity property, the up-and-in barrier option price $V_{u/i}(S_t, t; K, B, T)$ at time t, $t \leq T$ is

$$V_{u/i}(S_t, t; K, B, T) = V_{bs}(S_t, t; K, T) - V_{u/o}(S_t, t; K, B, T).$$

Following the same arguments, the down-and-out barrier option at time t is

$$V_{d/o}(S_t, t; K, B, T) = \tilde{V}_{d/o}(S_t, t; K, B, T) - \left(\frac{S_t}{B}\right)^{2\alpha} \tilde{V}_{d/o}\left(\frac{B^2}{S_t}, t; K, B, T\right)$$

where $\tilde{V}_{d/o}(S_t, t; K, B, T)$ satisfies the following Black–Scholes equation

$$\frac{\partial \tilde{V}_{d/o}}{\partial S_t} + \frac{1}{2}\sigma^2 S_t^2 \frac{\partial^2 \tilde{V}_{d/o}}{\partial S_t^2} + (r - D)S_t \frac{\partial \tilde{V}_{d/o}}{\partial S_t} - r\tilde{V}_{d/o}(S_t, t; K, B, T) = 0$$

with truncated payoff

$$S_t > B, \quad t \leq T$$

$$\tilde{V}_{d/o}(S_t, t; K, B, T) = \Psi(S_T).$$

Finally, with the application of the in–out parity property, the down-and-in barrier option price $V_{d/i}(S_t, t; K, B, T)$ at time t, $t \leq T$ is

$$V_{d/i}(S_t, t; K, B, T) = V_{bs}(S_t, t; K, T) - V_{d/o}(S_t, t; K, B, T).$$

4.2 PROBLEMS AND SOLUTIONS

4.2.1 Probabilistic Approach

1. *Up-and-Out/Up-and-In Call Options.* Let $\{W_t : t \geq 0\}$ be a $\mathbb{P}$-standard Wiener process on the probability space $(\Omega, \mathcal{F}, \mathbb{P})$ and let the asset price S_t follow a GBM with the following SDE

$$\frac{dS_t}{S_t} = (\mu - D)\,dt + \sigma dW_t$$

where μ is the drift parameter, D is the continuous dividend yield and σ is the volatility parameter. In addition, let r be the risk-free interest rate.

We consider a European up-and-out call option at time t, with expiry at time $T > t$, strike K and constant barrier $B > K$.

Explain why, for an up-and-out call option, we require $S_t < B$ and $B > K$, and show that the terminal payoff can be written as

$$\Psi(S_T) = \max\{S_T - K, 0\}\,\mathbb{1}_{\{\max\limits_{t \leq u \leq T} S_u < B\}}.$$

Using the identity

$$\frac{1}{\sqrt{2\pi T}} \int_L^U e^{aw - \frac{1}{2}(\frac{w}{\sqrt{T}})^2}\,dw = e^{\frac{1}{2}a^2 T}\left[\Phi\left(\frac{U - aT}{\sqrt{T}}\right) - \Phi\left(\frac{L - aT}{\sqrt{T}}\right)\right]$$

where $\Phi(x) = \displaystyle\int_{-\infty}^x \frac{1}{\sqrt{2\pi}}e^{-\frac{1}{2}u^2}\,du$ is the cdf of a standard normal, show that under the risk-neutral measure $\mathbb{Q}$, the up-and-out call option price at time t is

$$\begin{aligned}
C_{u/o}\left(S_t, t; K, B, T\right) = {} &C_{bs}\left(S_t, t; K, T\right) \\
&- \left[C_{bs}\left(S_t, t; B, T\right) + (B - K)C_d\left(S_t, t; B, T\right)\right] \\
&- \left(\frac{S_t}{B}\right)^{2\alpha}\left\{C_{bs}\left(\frac{B^2}{S_t}, t; K, T\right)\right. \\
&\left. - \left[C_{bs}\left(\frac{B^2}{S_t}, t; B, T\right) + (B - K)C_d\left(\frac{B^2}{S_t}, t; B, T\right)\right]\right\}
\end{aligned}$$

where $\alpha = \dfrac{1}{2}\left(1 - \dfrac{r - D}{\frac{1}{2}\sigma^2}\right)$, $C_{bs}\left(X, t; Y, T\right)$ and $C_d\left(X, t; Y, T\right)$ are the vanilla and digital call option prices defined as

$$
C_{bs}(X,t;Y,T) = Xe^{-D(T-t)}\Phi\left(\frac{\log(X/Y)+(r-D+\frac{1}{2}\sigma^2)(T-t)}{\sigma\sqrt{T-t}}\right)
$$
$$
-Ye^{-r(T-t)}\Phi\left(\frac{\log(X/Y)+(r-D-\frac{1}{2}\sigma^2)(T-t)}{\sigma\sqrt{T-t}}\right)
$$

and

$$
C_d(X,t;Y,T) = e^{-r(T-t)}\Phi\left(\frac{\log(X/Y)+(r-D-\frac{1}{2}\sigma^2)(T-t)}{\sigma\sqrt{T-t}}\right)
$$

respectively. Hence, deduce that the European up-and-in call option price at time t is

$$
C_{u/i}(S_t,t;K,B,T) = C_{bs}(S_t,t;B,T)
$$
$$
+(B-K)C_d(S_t,t;B,T)+\left(\frac{S_t}{B}\right)^{2\alpha}C_{bs}\left(\frac{B^2}{S_t},t;K,T\right)
$$
$$
-\left(\frac{S_t}{B}\right)^{2\alpha}\left[C_{bs}\left(\frac{B^2}{S_t},t;B,T\right)+(B-K)C_d\left(\frac{B^2}{S_t},t;B,T\right)\right].
$$

Solution: Since the option is an up-and-out call we require S_t for all t to be below the barrier B, otherwise it knocks out. Furthermore, we require $B > K$ for all time t, since if $B \leq K$ the option is worthless as no asset path would give a non-zero payoff. Therefore, the payoff of an up-and-out call option is

$$
\Psi(S_T) = \max\{S_T-K,0\}\,\mathbb{I}_{\{\max_{t\leq u\leq T}S_u<B\}}.
$$

Under the risk-neutral measure $\mathbb{Q}$, S_t follows

$$
\frac{dS_t}{S_t} = (r-D)\,dt+\sigma dW_t^{\mathbb{Q}}
$$

where $W_t^{\mathbb{Q}} = W_t+\left(\frac{\mu-r}{\sigma}\right)t$ is a $\mathbb{Q}$-standard Wiener process. Using Itō's lemma we can easily show that for $t<T$

$$
S_T = S_t e^{(r-D-\frac{1}{2}\sigma^2)(T-t)+\sigma W_{T-t}^{\mathbb{Q}}}
$$
$$
= S_t e^{\sigma\widehat{W}_{T-t}}
$$

where $\widehat{W}_{T-t} = v(T-t)+W_{T-t}^{\mathbb{Q}}$ and $v = \frac{1}{\sigma}(r-D-\frac{1}{2}\sigma^2)$. By writing

$$
M_{T-t} = \max_{t\leq u\leq T}\widehat{W}_{u-t}
$$

therefore

$$\max_{t \le u \le T} S_u = S_t e^{\sigma M_{T-t}}$$

and we can rewrite the payoff as

$$\Psi(S_T) = \max \left\{ S_T - K, 0 \right\} \, \mathbb{1}_{\left\{ \max_{t \le u \le T} S_u < B \right\}}$$

$$= \max \left\{ S_t e^{\sigma \widehat{W}_{T-t}} - K, 0 \right\} \, \mathbb{1}_{\left\{ S_t e^{\sigma M_{T-t}} < B \right\}}$$

$$= \left(S_t e^{\sigma \widehat{W}_{T-t}} - K \right) \mathbb{1}_{\left\{ S_t e^{\sigma M_{T-t}} < B, \, S_t e^{\sigma \widehat{W}_{T-t}} > K \right\}}$$

$$= \left(S_t e^{\sigma \widehat{W}_{T-t}} - K \right) \mathbb{1}_{\left\{ M_{T-t} < \frac{1}{\sigma} \log \left(\frac{B}{S_t} \right), \, \widehat{W}_{T-t} > \frac{1}{\sigma} \log \left(\frac{K}{S_t} \right) \right\}}.$$

Hence, the up-and-out call option price at time t is

$$C_{u/o}\left(S_t, t; K, B, T \right)$$

$$= e^{-r(T-t)} \mathbb{E}^{\mathbb{Q}} \left[\Psi(S_T) \big| \mathscr{F}_t \right]$$

$$= e^{-r(T-t)} \mathbb{E}^{\mathbb{Q}} \left[\left(S_t e^{\sigma \widehat{W}_{T-t}} - K \right) \mathbb{1}_{\left\{ M_{T-t} < \frac{1}{\sigma} \log \left(\frac{B}{S_t} \right), \, \widehat{W}_{T-t} > \frac{1}{\sigma} \log \left(\frac{K}{S_t} \right) \right\}} \bigg| \mathscr{F}_t \right]$$

$$= e^{-r(T-t)} \int_{w=\frac{1}{\sigma} \log \left(\frac{K}{S_t} \right)}^{w=\frac{1}{\sigma} \log \left(\frac{B}{S_t} \right)} \int_{m=w}^{m=\frac{1}{\sigma} \log \left(\frac{B}{S_t} \right)} \left(S_t e^{\sigma w} - K \right) f_{M, \widehat{W}}^{\mathbb{Q}}(m, w) \, dm \, dw$$

where

$$f_{M, \widehat{W}}^{\mathbb{Q}}(m, w) = \begin{cases} \dfrac{2(2m-w)}{(T-t)\sqrt{2\pi(T-t)}} e^{vw - \frac{1}{2}v^2(T-t) - \frac{1}{2}\left(\frac{2m-w}{\sqrt{T-t}} \right)^2} & m \ge 0, m \ge w \\ \\ 0 & \text{otherwise.} \end{cases}$$

Refer to Problem 4.2.2.14 of *Problems and Solutions in Mathematical Finance, Volume 1: Stochastic Calculus* for a derivation of the above density function.

Hence,

$$C_{u/o}\left(S_t, t; K, B, T\right)$$

$$= -e^{-r(T-t)} \int_{w=\frac{1}{\sigma}\log\left(\frac{K}{S_t}\right)}^{w=\frac{1}{\sigma}\log\left(\frac{B}{S_t}\right)} \left(S_t e^{\sigma w} - K\right)$$

$$\times \frac{1}{\sqrt{2\pi(T-t)}} e^{vw - \frac{1}{2}v^2(T-t) - \frac{1}{2}\left(\frac{2m-w}{\sqrt{T-t}}\right)^2} \Bigg|_{m=w}^{m=\frac{1}{\sigma}\log\left(\frac{B}{S_t}\right)} dw$$

$$= \frac{1}{\sqrt{2\pi(T-t)}} \int_{\frac{1}{\sigma}\log\left(\frac{K}{S_t}\right)}^{\frac{1}{\sigma}\log\left(\frac{B}{S_t}\right)} \left(S_t e^{\sigma w} - K\right) e^{-r(T-t) + vw - \frac{1}{2}v^2(T-t) - \frac{1}{2}\left(\frac{w}{\sqrt{T-t}}\right)^2} dw$$

$$- \frac{1}{\sqrt{2\pi(T-t)}} \int_{\frac{1}{\sigma}\log\left(\frac{K}{S_t}\right)}^{\frac{1}{\sigma}\log\left(\frac{B}{S_t}\right)} \left(S_t e^{\sigma w} - K\right) e^{-r(T-t) + vw - \frac{1}{2}v^2(T-t) - \frac{1}{2}\left(\frac{\frac{2}{\sigma}\log\left(\frac{B}{S_t}\right) - w}{\sqrt{T-t}}\right)^2} dw$$

$$= S_t I_1 - K I_2 - (S_t I_3 - K I_4)$$

where

$$I_1 = \frac{1}{\sqrt{2\pi(T-t)}} \int_{\frac{1}{\sigma}\log\left(\frac{K}{S_t}\right)}^{\frac{1}{\sigma}\log\left(\frac{B}{S_t}\right)} e^{-r(T-t) + \sigma w + vw - \frac{1}{2}v^2(T-t) - \frac{1}{2}\left(\frac{w}{\sqrt{T-t}}\right)^2} dw$$

$$I_2 = \frac{1}{\sqrt{2\pi(T-t)}} \int_{\frac{1}{\sigma}\log\left(\frac{K}{S_t}\right)}^{\frac{1}{\sigma}\log\left(\frac{B}{S_t}\right)} e^{-r(T-t) + vw - \frac{1}{2}v^2(T-t) - \frac{1}{2}\left(\frac{w}{\sqrt{T-t}}\right)^2} dw$$

$$I_3 = \frac{1}{\sqrt{2\pi(T-t)}} \int_{\frac{1}{\sigma}\log\left(\frac{K}{S_t}\right)}^{\frac{1}{\sigma}\log\left(\frac{B}{S_t}\right)} e^{-r(T-t) + \sigma w + vw - \frac{1}{2}v^2(T-t) - \frac{1}{2}\left(\frac{\frac{2}{\sigma}\log\left(\frac{B}{S_t}\right) - w}{\sqrt{T-t}}\right)^2} dw$$

$$I_4 = \frac{1}{\sqrt{2\pi(T-t)}} \int_{\frac{1}{\sigma}\log\left(\frac{K}{S_t}\right)}^{\frac{1}{\sigma}\log\left(\frac{B}{S_t}\right)} e^{-r(T-t) + vw - \frac{1}{2}v^2(T-t) - \frac{1}{2}\left(\frac{\frac{2}{\sigma}\log\left(\frac{B}{S_t}\right) - w}{\sqrt{T-t}}\right)^2} dw.$$

Using the identity

$$\frac{1}{\sqrt{2\pi T}} \int_L^U e^{aw - \frac{1}{2}\left(\frac{w}{\sqrt{T}}\right)^2} dw = e^{\frac{1}{2}a^2 T} \left[\Phi\left(\frac{U - aT}{\sqrt{T}}\right) - \Phi\left(\frac{L - aT}{\sqrt{T}}\right)\right]$$

we have

$$
I_1 = \frac{1}{\sqrt{2\pi(T-t)}} e^{-r(T-t)-\frac{1}{2}v^2(T-t)} \int_{\frac{1}{\sigma}\log\left(\frac{K}{S_t}\right)}^{\frac{1}{\sigma}\log\left(\frac{B}{S_t}\right)} e^{(v+\sigma)w-\frac{1}{2}\left(\frac{w}{\sqrt{T-t}}\right)^2} dw
$$

$$
= e^{-r(T-t)-\frac{1}{2}v^2(T-t)+\frac{1}{2}(v+\sigma)^2(T-t)} \left[\Phi\left(\frac{\frac{1}{\sigma}\log(B/S_t)-(v+\sigma)(T-t)}{\sqrt{T-t}} \right) \right.
$$

$$
\left. -\Phi\left(\frac{\frac{1}{\sigma}\log(K/S_t)-(v+\sigma)(T-t)}{\sqrt{T-t}} \right) \right]
$$

and knowing that $v = \frac{1}{\sigma}(r - D - \frac{1}{2}\sigma^2)$, we have

$$
I_1 = e^{-D(T-t)} \left[1 - \Phi\left(\frac{\log(S_t/B)+(r-D+\frac{1}{2}\sigma^2)(T-t)}{\sigma\sqrt{T-t}} \right) \right.
$$

$$
\left. -1 + \Phi\left(\frac{\log(S_t/K)+(r-D+\frac{1}{2}\sigma^2)(T-t)}{\sigma\sqrt{T-t}} \right) \right]
$$

$$
= e^{-D(T-t)} \left[\Phi\left(\frac{\log(S_t/K)+(r-D+\frac{1}{2}\sigma^2)(T-t)}{\sigma\sqrt{T-t}} \right) \right.
$$

$$
\left. -\Phi\left(\frac{\log(S_t/B)+(r-D+\frac{1}{2}\sigma^2)(T-t)}{\sigma\sqrt{T-t}} \right) \right].
$$

Similarly we can deduce

$$
I_2 = \frac{1}{\sqrt{2\pi(T-t)}} e^{-r(T-t)-\frac{1}{2}v^2(T-t)} \int_{\frac{1}{\sigma}\log\left(\frac{K}{S_t}\right)}^{\frac{1}{\sigma}\log\left(\frac{B}{S_t}\right)} e^{vw-\frac{1}{2}\left(\frac{w}{\sqrt{T-t}}\right)^2} dw
$$

$$
= e^{-r(T-t)-\frac{1}{2}v^2(T-t)+\frac{1}{2}v^2(T-t)}
$$

$$
\left[\Phi\left(\frac{\frac{1}{\sigma}\log(B/S_t)-v(T-t)}{\sqrt{T-t}} \right) - \Phi\left(\frac{\frac{1}{\sigma}\log(K/S_t)-v(T-t)}{\sqrt{T-t}} \right) \right]
$$

$$
= e^{-r(T-t)} \left[\Phi\left(\frac{\log(B/S_t)-(r-D-\frac{1}{2}\sigma^2)(T-t)}{\sigma\sqrt{T-t}} \right) \right.
$$

$$
\left. -\Phi\left(\frac{\log(K/S_t)-(r-D-\frac{1}{2}\sigma^2)(T-t)}{\sigma\sqrt{T-t}} \right) \right]
$$

$$
= e^{-r(T-t)} \left[\Phi\left(\frac{\log(S_t/K)+(r-D-\frac{1}{2}\sigma^2)(T-t)}{\sigma\sqrt{T-t}} \right) \right.
$$

$$
\left. -\Phi\left(\frac{\log(S_t/B)+(r-D-\frac{1}{2}\sigma^2)(T-t)}{\sigma\sqrt{T-t}} \right) \right].
$$

$$I_3 = \frac{1}{\sqrt{2\pi(T-t)}} e^{-r(T-t)-\frac{1}{2}v^2(T-t)-\frac{2}{\sigma^2(T-t)}\left(\log\left(\frac{B}{S_t}\right)\right)^2}$$

$$\times \int_{\frac{1}{\sigma}\log\left(\frac{K}{S_t}\right)}^{\frac{1}{\sigma}\log\left(\frac{B}{S_t}\right)} e^{\left[v+\sigma+\frac{2}{\sigma(T-t)}\log\left(\frac{B}{S_t}\right)\right]w-\frac{1}{2}\left(\frac{w}{\sqrt{T-t}}\right)^2} dw$$

$$= e^{-r(T-t)-\frac{1}{2}v^2(T-t)-\frac{2}{\sigma^2(T-t)}\left(\log\left(\frac{B}{S_t}\right)\right)^2+\frac{1}{2}\left[v+\sigma+\frac{2}{\sigma(T-t)}\log\left(\frac{B}{S_t}\right)\right]^2(T-t)}$$

$$\times \left[\Phi\left(\frac{\frac{1}{\sigma}\log(B/S_t) - \left[v+\sigma+\frac{2}{\sigma(T-t)}\log(B/S_t)\right](T-t)}{\sqrt{T-t}} \right) \right.$$

$$\left. -\Phi\left(\frac{\frac{1}{\sigma}\log(K/S_t) - \left[v+\sigma+\frac{2}{\sigma(T-t)}\log(B/S_t)\right](T-t)}{\sqrt{T-t}} \right) \right]$$

$$= e^{-D(T-t)} \left(\frac{S_t}{B}\right)^{-1-\frac{2(r-D)}{\sigma^2}} \left[\Phi\left(\frac{\log(B^2/(S_tK)) + (r-D+\frac{1}{2}\sigma^2)(T-t)}{\sigma\sqrt{T-t}} \right) \right.$$

$$\left. -\Phi\left(\frac{\log(B/S_t) + (r-D+\frac{1}{2}\sigma^2)(T-t)}{\sigma\sqrt{T-t}} \right) \right].$$

$$I_4 = \frac{1}{\sqrt{2\pi(T-t)}} e^{-r(T-t)-\frac{1}{2}v^2(T-t)-\frac{2}{\sigma^2(T-t)}\left(\log\left(\frac{B}{S_t}\right)\right)^2}$$

$$\times \int_{\frac{1}{\sigma}\log\left(\frac{K}{S_t}\right)}^{\frac{1}{\sigma}\log\left(\frac{B}{S_t}\right)} e^{\left[v+\frac{2}{\sigma(T-t)}\log\left(\frac{B}{S_t}\right)\right]w-\frac{1}{2}\left(\frac{w}{\sqrt{T-t}}\right)^2} dw$$

$$= e^{-r(T-t)-\frac{1}{2}v^2(T-t)-\frac{2}{\sigma^2(T-t)}\left(\log\left(\frac{B}{S_t}\right)\right)^2+\frac{1}{2}\left[v+\frac{2}{\sigma(T-t)}\log\left(\frac{B}{S_t}\right)\right]^2(T-t)}$$

$$\times \left[\Phi\left(\frac{\frac{1}{\sigma}\log(B/S_t) - \left[v+\frac{2}{\sigma(T-t)}\log(B/S_t)\right](T-t)}{\sqrt{T-t}} \right) \right.$$

$$\left. -\Phi\left(\frac{\frac{1}{\sigma}\log(K/S_t) - \left[v+\frac{2}{\sigma(T-t)}\log(B/S_t)\right](T-t)}{\sqrt{T-t}} \right) \right]$$

$$= e^{-r(T-t)} \left(\frac{S_t}{B}\right)^{1-\frac{2(r-D)}{\sigma^2}} \left[\Phi\left(\frac{\log(B^2/(S_tK)) + (r-D-\frac{1}{2}\sigma^2)(T-t)}{\sigma\sqrt{T-t}} \right) \right.$$

$$\left. -\Phi\left(\frac{\log(B/S_t) + (r-D-\frac{1}{2}\sigma^2)(T-t)}{\sigma\sqrt{T-t}} \right) \right].$$

Therefore,

$$
C_{u/o}\left(S_t, t; K, B, T\right)
$$

$$
= S_t I_1 - K I_2 - (S_t I_3 - K I_4)
$$

$$
= S_t e^{-D(T-t)} \Phi\left(\frac{\log(S_t/K) + (r - D + \frac{1}{2}\sigma^2)(T - t)}{\sigma\sqrt{T - t}}\right)
$$

$$
- S_t e^{-D(T-t)} \Phi\left(\frac{\log(S_t/B) + (r - D + \frac{1}{2}\sigma^2)(T - t)}{\sigma\sqrt{T - t}}\right)
$$

$$
- K e^{-r(T-t)} \Phi\left(\frac{\log(S_t/K) + (r - D - \frac{1}{2}\sigma^2)(T - t)}{\sigma\sqrt{T - t}}\right)
$$

$$
+ K e^{-r(T-t)} \Phi\left(\frac{\log(S_t/B) + (r - D - \frac{1}{2}\sigma^2)(T - t)}{\sigma\sqrt{T - t}}\right)
$$

$$
- S_t \left(\frac{S_t}{B}\right)^{-1-\frac{2(r-D)}{\sigma^2}} e^{-D(T-t)} \Phi\left(\frac{\log(B^2/(S_t K)) + (r - D + \frac{1}{2}\sigma^2)(T - t)}{\sigma\sqrt{T - t}}\right)
$$

$$
+ S_t \left(\frac{S_t}{B}\right)^{-1-\frac{2(r-D)}{\sigma^2}} e^{-D(T-t)} \Phi\left(\frac{\log(B/S_t) + (r - D + \frac{1}{2}\sigma^2)(T - t)}{\sigma\sqrt{T - t}}\right)
$$

$$
+ K \left(\frac{S_t}{B}\right)^{1-\frac{2(r-D)}{\sigma^2}} e^{-r(T-t)} \Phi\left(\frac{\log(B^2/(S_t K)) + (r - D - \frac{1}{2}\sigma^2)(T - t)}{\sigma\sqrt{T - t}}\right)
$$

$$
- K \left(\frac{S_t}{B}\right)^{1-\frac{2(r-D)}{\sigma^2}} e^{-r(T-t)} \Phi\left(\frac{\log(B/S_t) + (r - D - \frac{1}{2}\sigma^2)(T - t)}{\sigma\sqrt{T - t}}\right)
$$

$$
= C_{bs}\left(S_t, t; K, T\right) - C_{bs}\left(S_t, t; B, T\right) + (K - B)C_d\left(S_t, t; B, T\right)
$$

$$
- \left(\frac{S_t}{B}\right)^{1-\frac{2(r-D)}{\sigma^2}} C_{bs}\left(\frac{B^2}{S_t}, t; K, T\right) - \left(\frac{S_t}{B}\right)^{1-\frac{2(r-D)}{\sigma^2}} C_{bs}\left(\frac{B^2}{S_t}, t; B, T\right)
$$

$$
+ \left(\frac{S_t}{B}\right)^{1-\frac{2(r-D)}{\sigma^2}} (K - B)C_d\left(\frac{B^2}{S_t}, t; B, T\right)
$$

$$
= C_{bs}\left(S_t, t; K, T\right) - \left[C_{bs}\left(S_t, t; B, T\right) + (B - K)C_d\left(S_t, t; B, T\right)\right]
$$

$$
- \left(\frac{S_t}{B}\right)^{2\alpha} \left\{ C_{bs}\left(\frac{B^2}{S_t}, t; K, T\right) \right.
$$

$$
\left. - \left[C_{bs}\left(\frac{B^2}{S_t}, t; B, T\right) + (B - K)C_d\left(\frac{B^2}{S_t}, t; B, T\right)\right] \right\}
$$

where $\alpha = \dfrac{1}{2}\left(1 - \dfrac{r - D}{\frac{1}{2}\sigma^2}\right)$.

In contrast, for an up-and-in call option price its payoff at expiry T can be written as

$$\Psi(S_T) = \max\{S_T - K, 0\}\, \mathbb{I}_{\{\max_{t \leq u \leq T} S_u \geq B\}}$$

$$= \max\{S_T - K, 0\}\left(1 - \mathbb{I}_{\{\max_{t \leq u \leq T} S_u < B\}}\right)$$

$$= \max\{S_T - K, 0\} - \max\{S_T - K, 0\}\,\mathbb{I}_{\{\max_{t \leq u \leq T} S_u < B\}}.$$

Hence, under the risk-neutral measure $\mathbb{Q}$, the up-and-in call option price at time t is

$$C_{u/i}\left(S_t, t; K, B, T\right) = e^{-r(T-t)}\mathbb{E}\left[\max\{S_T - K, 0\}\middle|\mathscr{F}_t\right]$$

$$-e^{-r(T-t)}\mathbb{E}\left[\max\{S_T - K, 0\}\,\mathbb{I}_{\{\max_{t \leq u \leq T} S_u < B\}}\middle|\mathscr{F}_t\right]$$

$$= C_{bs}\left(S_t, t; K, T\right) - C_{u/o}\left(S_t, t; K, B, T\right)$$

$$= C_{bs}\left(S_t, t; B, T\right) + (B-K)C_d\left(S_t, t; B, T\right)$$

$$+ \left(\frac{S_t}{B}\right)^{2\alpha}\left\{C_{bs}\left(\frac{B^2}{S_t}, t; K, T\right)\right.$$

$$\left. - \left[C_{bs}\left(\frac{B^2}{S_t}, t; B, T\right) + (B-K)C_d\left(\frac{B^2}{S_t}, t; B, T\right)\right]\right\}.$$

$\square$

2. *Down-and-Out/Down-and-In Call Options.* Let $\{W_t : t \geq 0\}$ be a $\mathbb{P}$-standard Wiener process on the probability space $(\Omega, \mathscr{F}, \mathbb{P})$ and let the asset price S_t follow a GBM with the following SDE

$$\frac{dS_t}{S_t} = (\mu - D)\, dt + \sigma dW_t$$

where μ is the drift parameter, D is the continuous dividend yield and σ is the volatility parameter. We consider a European down-and-out call option at time t, with expiry at time $T > t$, strike K and constant barrier B.

Explain why, for a down-and-out European call, $S_t > B$, and show that the terminal payoff for $B \leq K$ or $B > K$ can be written as

$$\Psi(S_T) = \max\{S_T - K, 0\}\,\mathbb{I}_{\{\min_{t \leq u \leq T} S_u > B\}}.$$

Using the identity

$$\frac{1}{\sqrt{2\pi T}}\int_L^U e^{aw - \frac{1}{2}\left(\frac{w}{\sqrt{T}}\right)^2}\, dw = e^{\frac{1}{2}a^2 T}\left[\Phi\left(\frac{U - aT}{\sqrt{T}}\right) - \Phi\left(\frac{L - aT}{\sqrt{T}}\right)\right]$$

where $\Phi(x) = \int_{-\infty}^{x} \frac{1}{\sqrt{2\pi}} e^{-\frac{1}{2}u^2} du$ is the cdf of a standard normal, show that under the risk-neutral measure $\mathbb{Q}$, the down-and-out call option price at time t is

$$C_{d/o}\left(S_t, t; K, B, T\right) = C_{bs}\left(S_t, t; Z, T\right) + (Z - K) C_d\left(S_t, t; Z, T\right) - \left(\frac{S_t}{B}\right)^{2\alpha}$$

$$\times \left[C_{bs}\left(\frac{B^2}{S_t}, t; Z, T\right) + (Z - K) C_d\left(\frac{B^2}{S_t}, t; Z, T\right)\right]$$

where $Z = \max\{B, K\}$, $\alpha = \frac{1}{2}\left(1 - \frac{r - D}{\frac{1}{2}\sigma^2}\right)$, r is the risk-free interest rate, $C_{bs}(X, t; Y, T)$ and $C_d(X, t; Y, T)$ are the vanilla and digital call option prices defined as

$$C_{bs}\left(X, t; Y, T\right) = X e^{-D(T-t)} \Phi\left(\frac{\log(X/Y) + (r - D + \frac{1}{2}\sigma^2)(T - t)}{\sigma\sqrt{T - t}}\right)$$

$$- Y e^{-r(T-t)} \Phi\left(\frac{\log(X/Y) + (r - D - \frac{1}{2}\sigma^2)(T - t)}{\sigma\sqrt{T - t}}\right)$$

and

$$C_d\left(X, t; Y, T\right) = e^{-r(T-t)} \Phi\left(\frac{\log(X/Y) + (r - D - \frac{1}{2}\sigma^2)(T - t)}{\sigma\sqrt{T - t}}\right)$$

respectively. Hence, deduce that the European down-and-in call option price at time t is

$$C_{d/i}\left(S_t, t; K, B, T\right) = C_{bs}\left(S_t, t; K, T\right)$$

$$- C_{bs}\left(S_t, t; Z, T\right) - (Z - K) C_d\left(S_t, t; Z, T\right) + \left(\frac{S_t}{B}\right)^{2\alpha}$$

$$\times \left[C_{bs}\left(\frac{B^2}{S_t}, t; Z, T\right) + (Z - K) C_d\left(\frac{B^2}{S_t}, t; Z, T\right)\right].$$

Solution: We consider two cases for the down-and-out call option price when $B \leq K$ and $B > K$.

We require $S_t > B$ for all t so as to ensure the option would not knock out at the starting time t. Hence, for either $B \leq K$ or $B > K$, the payoff of a down-and-out call option is

$$\Psi(S_T) = \max\left\{S_T - K, 0\right\} \mathbb{I}_{\{\min_{t \leq u \leq T} S_u > B\}}.$$

Under the risk-neutral measure $\mathbb{Q}$, S_t follows

$$\frac{dS_t}{S_t} = (r - D)\, dt + \sigma\, dW_t^{\mathbb{Q}}$$

where $W_t^{\mathbb{Q}} = W_t + \left(\dfrac{\mu - r}{\sigma}\right)t$ is a $\mathbb{Q}$-standard Wiener process. From Itō's lemma, for $t < T$

$$S_T = S_t e^{(r-D-\frac{1}{2}\sigma^2)(T-t)+\sigma W_{T-t}^{\mathbb{Q}}}$$

$$= S_t e^{\sigma \widehat{W}_{T-t}}$$

where $\widehat{W}_{T-t} = v(T-t) + W_{T-t}^{\mathbb{Q}}$ and $v = \dfrac{1}{\sigma}(r - D - \dfrac{1}{2}\sigma^2)$. By writing

$$m_{T-t} = \min_{t \leq u \leq T} \widehat{W}_{u-t}$$

therefore

$$\min_{t \leq u \leq T} S_u = S_t e^{\sigma m_{T-t}}$$

and we can rewrite the payoff as

$$\Psi(S_T) = \max\left\{S_T - K, 0\right\} \mathbb{1}_{\{\min_{t \leq u \leq T} S_u > B\}}$$

$$= \max\left\{S_t e^{\sigma \widehat{W}_{T-t}} - K, 0\right\} \mathbb{1}_{\{S_t e^{\sigma m_{T-t}} > B\}}$$

$$= \begin{cases} \left(S_t e^{\sigma \widehat{W}_{T-t}} - K\right) \mathbb{1}_{\left\{S_t e^{\sigma m_{T-t}} > B, S_t e^{\sigma \widehat{W}_{T-t}} > K\right\}} & \text{if } B \leq K \\[12pt] \left(S_t e^{\sigma \widehat{W}_{T-t}} - K\right) \mathbb{1}_{\left\{S_t e^{\sigma m_{T-t}} > B, S_t e^{\sigma \widehat{W}_{T-t}} > B\right\}} & \text{if } B > K \end{cases}$$

$$= \begin{cases} \left(S_t e^{\sigma \widehat{W}_{T-t}} - K\right) \mathbb{1}_{\left\{m_{T-t} > \frac{1}{\sigma}\log\left(\frac{B}{S_t}\right), \widehat{W}_{T-t} > \frac{1}{\sigma}\log\left(\frac{K}{S_t}\right)\right\}} & \text{if } B \leq K \\[12pt] \left(S_t e^{\sigma \widehat{W}_{T-t}} - K\right) \mathbb{1}_{\left\{m_{T-t} > \frac{1}{\sigma}\log\left(\frac{B}{S_t}\right), \widehat{W}_{T-t} > \frac{1}{\sigma}\log\left(\frac{B}{S_t}\right)\right\}} & \text{if } B > K. \end{cases}$$

Case 1: $B \leq K$

The down-and-out call option price at time t is

$$C_{d/o}\left(S_t, t; K, B, T\right)$$

$$= e^{-r(T-t)}\mathbb{E}^{\mathbb{Q}}\left[\Psi(S_T)\big|\,\mathcal{F}_t\right]$$

$$= e^{-r(T-t)}\mathbb{E}^{\mathbb{Q}}\left[\left(S_t e^{\sigma \widehat{W}_{T-t}} - K\right) \mathbb{1}_{\left\{m_{T-t} > \frac{1}{\sigma}\log\left(\frac{B}{S_t}\right), \widehat{W}_{T-t} > \frac{1}{\sigma}\log\left(\frac{K}{S_t}\right)\right\}}\,\bigg|\,\mathcal{F}_t\right]$$

$$= e^{-r(T-t)}\int_{w=\frac{1}{\sigma}\log\left(\frac{K}{S_t}\right)}^{w=\infty}\int_{m=\frac{1}{\sigma}\log\left(\frac{B}{S_t}\right)}^{m=w}\left(S_t e^{\sigma w} - K\right)f_{m,\widehat{W}}^{\mathbb{Q}}(m, w)\,dm\,dw$$

where

$$f_{m,\widehat{W}}^{Q}(m,w) = \begin{cases} \dfrac{-2(2m-w)}{(T-t)\sqrt{2\pi(T-t)}} e^{vw-\frac{1}{2}v^2(T-t)-\frac{1}{2}\left(\frac{2m-w}{\sqrt{T-t}}\right)^2} & m \leq 0, m \leq w \\ \\ 0 & \text{otherwise.} \end{cases}$$

(See Problem 4.2.2.14 of *Problems and Solutions in Mathematical Finance, Volume 1: Stochastic Calculus* for the derivation of $f_{m,\widehat{W}}^{Q}(m,w)$.)

Thus,

$$C_{d/o}\left(S_t, t; K, B, T\right)$$

$$= -e^{-r(T-t)} \int_{w=\frac{1}{\sigma}\log\left(\frac{K}{S_t}\right)}^{w=\infty} \left(S_t e^{\sigma w} - K\right)$$

$$\times \frac{1}{\sqrt{2\pi(T-t)}} e^{vw-\frac{1}{2}v^2(T-t)-\frac{1}{2}\left(\frac{2m-w}{\sqrt{T-t}}\right)^2} \Bigg|_{m=\frac{1}{\sigma}\log\left(\frac{B}{S_t}\right)}^{m=w} dw$$

$$= e^{-r(T-t)} \int_{\frac{1}{\sigma}\log\left(\frac{K}{S_t}\right)}^{w=\infty} \left(S_t e^{\sigma w} - K\right) \frac{1}{\sqrt{2\pi(T-t)}} e^{vw-\frac{1}{2}v^2(T-t)-\frac{1}{2}\left(\frac{w}{\sqrt{T-t}}\right)^2} dw$$

$$- e^{-r(T-t)} \int_{\frac{1}{\sigma}\log\left(\frac{K}{S_t}\right)}^{w=\infty} \left(S_t e^{\sigma w} - K\right) \frac{1}{\sqrt{2\pi(T-t)}} e^{vw-\frac{1}{2}v^2(T-t)-\frac{1}{2}\left(\frac{\frac{2}{\sigma}\log\left(\frac{B}{S_t}\right)-w}{\sqrt{T-t}}\right)^2} dw$$

$$= S_t I_1 - K I_2 - (S_t I_3 - K I_4)$$

where

$$I_1 = \frac{1}{\sqrt{2\pi(T-t)}} \int_{\frac{1}{\sigma}\log\left(\frac{K}{S_t}\right)}^{w=\infty} e^{-r(T-t)+\sigma w+vw-\frac{1}{2}v^2(T-t)-\frac{1}{2}\left(\frac{w}{\sqrt{T-t}}\right)^2} dw$$

$$I_2 = \frac{1}{\sqrt{2\pi(T-t)}} \int_{\frac{1}{\sigma}\log\left(\frac{K}{S_t}\right)}^{w=\infty} e^{-r(T-t)+vw-\frac{1}{2}v^2(T-t)-\frac{1}{2}\left(\frac{w}{\sqrt{T-t}}\right)^2} dw$$

$$I_3 = \frac{1}{\sqrt{2\pi(T-t)}} \int_{\frac{1}{\sigma}\log\left(\frac{K}{S_t}\right)}^{w=\infty} e^{-r(T-t)+\sigma w+vw-\frac{1}{2}v^2(T-t)-\frac{1}{2}\left(\frac{\frac{2}{\sigma}\log\left(\frac{B}{S_t}\right)-w}{\sqrt{T-t}}\right)^2} dw$$

$$I_4 = \frac{1}{\sqrt{2\pi(T-t)}} \int_{\frac{1}{\sigma}\log\left(\frac{K}{S_t}\right)}^{w=\infty} e^{-r(T-t)+vw-\frac{1}{2}v^2(T-t)-\frac{1}{2}\left(\frac{\frac{2}{\sigma}\log\left(\frac{B}{S_t}\right)-w}{\sqrt{T-t}}\right)^2} dw.$$

Using the identity

$$\frac{1}{\sqrt{2\pi T}} \int_L^U e^{aw - \frac{1}{2}(\frac{w}{\sqrt{T}})^2}\, dw = e^{\frac{1}{2}a^2 T} \left[\Phi\left(\frac{U - aT}{\sqrt{T}}\right) - \Phi\left(\frac{L - aT}{\sqrt{T}}\right) \right]$$

and following the same steps as described in Problem 4.2.1.1 (page 357), we have

$$I_1 = e^{-D(T-t)}\left[1 - \Phi\left(\frac{\frac{1}{\sigma}\log(K/S_t) + (v + \sigma)(T - t)}{\sqrt{T - t}} \right) \right]$$

$$= e^{-D(T-t)}\Phi\left(\frac{\log(S_t/K) + (r - D + \frac{1}{2}\sigma^2)(T - t)}{\sigma\sqrt{T - t}} \right)$$

$$I_2 = e^{-r(T-t)}\left[1 - \Phi\left(\frac{\frac{1}{\sigma}\log(K/S_t) - v(T - t)}{\sqrt{T - t}} \right) \right]$$

$$= e^{-r(T-t)}\Phi\left(\frac{\log(S_t/K) + (r - D - \frac{1}{2}\sigma^2)(T - t)}{\sigma\sqrt{T - t}} \right)$$

$$I_3 = e^{-D(T-t)}\left(\frac{S_t}{B}\right)^{-1 - \frac{2(r-D)}{\sigma^2}}$$

$$\times \left[1 - \Phi\left(\frac{\frac{1}{\sigma}\log(K/S_t) - \left(v + \sigma + \frac{2}{\sigma(T - t)}\log(B/S_t)\right)(T - t)}{\sqrt{T - t}} \right) \right]$$

$$= e^{-D(T-t)}\left(\frac{S_t}{B}\right)^{-1 - \frac{2(r-D)}{\sigma^2}}\Phi\left(\frac{\log(B^2/(S_t K)) + (r - D + \frac{1}{2}\sigma^2)(T - t)}{\sigma\sqrt{T - t}} \right)$$

$$I_4 = e^{-r(T-t)}\left(\frac{S_t}{B}\right)^{1 - \frac{2(r-D)}{\sigma^2}}$$

$$\times \left[1 - \Phi\left(\frac{\frac{1}{\sigma}\log(K/S_t) - \left(v + \frac{2}{\sigma(T - t)}\log(B/S_t)\right)(T - t)}{\sqrt{T - t}} \right) \right]$$

$$= e^{-r(T-t)}\left(\frac{S_t}{B}\right)^{1 - \frac{2(r-D)}{\sigma^2}}\Phi\left(\frac{\log(B^2/(S_t K)) + (r - D - \frac{1}{2}\sigma^2)(T - t)}{\sigma\sqrt{T - t}} \right).$$

Therefore,

$$C_{d/o}\left(S_t, t; K, B, T\right)$$

$$= S_t I_1 - K I_2 - (S_t I_3 - K I_4)$$

$$= S_t e^{-D(T-t)} \Phi\left(\frac{\log(S_t/K) + (r - D + \frac{1}{2}\sigma^2)(T - t)}{\sigma\sqrt{T - t}}\right)$$

$$- K e^{-r(T-t)} \Phi\left(\frac{\log(S_t/K) + (r - D - \frac{1}{2}\sigma^2)(T - t)}{\sigma\sqrt{T - t}}\right)$$

$$- S_t e^{-D(T-t)} \left(\frac{S_t}{B}\right)^{-1-\frac{2(r-D)}{\sigma^2}} \Phi\left(\frac{\log(B^2/(S_t K)) + (r - D + \frac{1}{2}\sigma^2)(T - t)}{\sigma\sqrt{T - t}}\right)$$

$$- K e^{-r(T-t)} \left(\frac{S_t}{B}\right)^{1-\frac{2(r-D)}{\sigma^2}} \Phi\left(\frac{\log(B^2/(S_t K)) + (r - D - \frac{1}{2}\sigma^2)(T - t)}{\sigma\sqrt{T - t}}\right)$$

$$= C_{bs}\left(S_t, t; K, T\right) - \left(\frac{S_t}{B}\right)^{2\alpha} C_{bs}\left(\frac{B^2}{S_t}, t; K, T\right)$$

where $\alpha = \dfrac{1}{2}\left(1 - \dfrac{r - D}{\frac{1}{2}\sigma^2}\right)$.

Case 2: $B > K$

The down-and-out call option price at time t is

$$C_{d/o}\left(S_t, t; K, B, T\right)$$

$$= e^{-r(T-t)} \mathbb{E}^{\mathbb{Q}}\left[\Psi(S_T)\middle|\, \mathcal{F}_t\right]$$

$$= e^{-r(T-t)} \mathbb{E}^{\mathbb{Q}}\left[\left(S_t e^{\sigma \widehat{W}_{T-t}} - K\right) \mathbb{1}_{\left\{m_{T-t} > \frac{1}{\sigma}\log\left(\frac{B}{S_t}\right), \widehat{W}_{T-t} > \frac{1}{\sigma}\log\left(\frac{B}{S_t}\right)\right\}}\middle|\, \mathcal{F}_t\right]$$

$$= e^{-r(T-t)} \int_{w=\frac{1}{\sigma}\log\left(\frac{B}{S_t}\right)}^{w=\infty} \int_{m=\frac{1}{\sigma}\log\left(\frac{B}{S_t}\right)}^{m=w} \left(S_t e^{\sigma w} - K\right) f_{m,\widehat{W}}^{\mathbb{Q}}(m, w)\, dm\, dw$$

where

$$
f^{Q}_{m,\widehat{W}}(m, w) = \begin{cases} \dfrac{-2(2m-w)}{(T-t)\sqrt{2\pi(T-t)}} e^{vw-\frac{1}{2}v^2(T-t)-\frac{1}{2}\left(\frac{2m-w}{\sqrt{T-t}}\right)^2} & m \le 0, m \le w \\ \\ 0 & \text{otherwise.} \end{cases}
$$

Using the same steps as described in Case 1, we have

$$
C_{d/o}\left(S_t, t; K, B, T\right) = S_t I_1 - K I_2 - (S_t I_3 - K I_4)
$$

where

$$
I_1 = e^{-D(T-t)}\left[1 - \Phi\left(\frac{\frac{1}{\sigma}\log(B/S_t) + (v+\sigma)(T-t)}{\sqrt{T-t}}\right)\right]
$$

$$
= e^{-D(T-t)}\Phi\left(\frac{\log(S_t/B) + (r - D + \frac{1}{2}\sigma^2)(T-t)}{\sigma\sqrt{T-t}}\right)
$$

$$
I_2 = e^{-r(T-t)}\left[1 - \Phi\left(\frac{\frac{1}{\sigma}\log(B/S_t) - v(T-t)}{\sqrt{T-t}}\right)\right]
$$

$$
= e^{-r(T-t)}\Phi\left(\frac{\log(S_t/B) + (r - D - \frac{1}{2}\sigma^2)(T-t)}{\sigma\sqrt{T-t}}\right)
$$

$$
I_3 = e^{-D(T-t)}\left(\frac{S_t}{B}\right)^{-1-\frac{2(r-D)}{\sigma^2}}
$$

$$
\times \left[1 - \Phi\left(\frac{\frac{1}{\sigma}\log(B/S_t) - \left(v + \sigma + \frac{2}{\sigma(T-t)}\log(B/S_t)\right)(T-t)}{\sqrt{T-t}}\right)\right]
$$

$$
= e^{-D(T-t)}\left(\frac{S_t}{B}\right)^{-1-\frac{2(r-D)}{\sigma^2}}\Phi\left(\frac{\log(B/S_t) + (r - D + \frac{1}{2}\sigma^2)(T-t)}{\sigma\sqrt{T-t}}\right)
$$

$$I_4 = e^{-r(T-t)} \left(\frac{S_t}{B} \right)^{1 - \frac{2(r-D)}{\sigma^2}}$$

$$\times \left[1 - \Phi \left(\frac{\frac{1}{\sigma} \log(B/S_t) - \left(v + \frac{2}{\sigma(T-t)} \log(B/S_t) \right)(T-t)}{\sqrt{T-t}} \right) \right]$$

$$= e^{-r(T-t)} \left(\frac{S_t}{B} \right)^{1 - \frac{2(r-D)}{\sigma^2}} \Phi \left(\frac{\log(B/S_t) + (r - D - \frac{1}{2}\sigma^2)(T-t)}{\sigma\sqrt{T-t}} \right).$$

Therefore,

$$C_{d/o} \left(S_t, t; K, B, T \right) = C_{bs} \left(S_t, t; B, T \right) + (B - K) C_d \left(S_t, t; B, T \right) - \left(\frac{S_t}{B} \right)^{2\alpha}$$

$$\times \left[C_{bs} \left(\frac{B^2}{S_t}, t; B, T \right) + (B - K) C_d \left(\frac{B^2}{S_t}, t; B, T \right) \right]$$

where $\alpha = \frac{1}{2} \left(1 - \frac{r-D}{\frac{1}{2}\sigma^2} \right)$.

Hence, by setting $Z = \max\{B, K\}$ we can write

$$C_{d/o} \left(S_t, t; K, B, T \right) = C_{bs} \left(S_t, t; Z, T \right) + (Z - K) C_d \left(S_t, t; Z, T \right) - \left(\frac{S_t}{B} \right)^{2\alpha}$$

$$\times \left[C_{bs} \left(\frac{B^2}{S_t}, t; Z, T \right) + (Z - K) C_d \left(\frac{B^2}{S_t}, t; Z, T \right) \right].$$

For the case of the down-and-in call option price, by definition its payoff at expiry time T can be written as

$$\Psi(S_T) = \max \left\{ S_T - K, 0 \right\} \mathbb{1}_{\{ \min_{t \le u \le T} S_u \le B \}}$$

$$= \max \left\{ S_T - K, 0 \right\} \left(1 - \mathbb{1}_{\{ \min_{t \le u \le T} S_u > B \}} \right)$$

$$= \max \left\{ S_T - K, 0 \right\} - \max \left\{ S_T - K, 0 \right\} \mathbb{1}_{\{ \min_{t \le u \le T} S_u > B \}}.$$

Under the risk-neutral measure $\mathbb{Q}$, the down-and-in call option price at time t is

$$C_{d/i}\left(S_t, t; K, B, T\right)$$

$$= e^{-r(T-t)}\mathbb{E}\left[\max\left\{S_T - K, 0\right\}\middle|\mathcal{F}_t\right]$$

$$-e^{-r(T-t)}\mathbb{E}\left[\max\left\{S_T - K, 0\right\}\mathbb{I}_{\left\{\min_{t \leq u \leq T} S_u > B\right\}}\middle|\mathcal{F}_t\right]$$

$$= C_{bs}\left(S_t, t; K, T\right) - C_{d/o}\left(S_t, t; K, B, T\right)$$

$$= \begin{cases} \left(\dfrac{S_t}{B}\right)^{2\alpha} C_{bs}\left(\dfrac{B^2}{S_t}, t; K, T\right) & \text{if } B \leq K \\[4mm] C_{bs}\left(S_t, t; K, T\right) - C_{bs}\left(S_t, t; B, T\right) - (B - K)\,C_d\left(S_t, t; B, T\right) \\ + \left(\dfrac{S_t}{B}\right)^{2\alpha}\left[C_{bs}\left(\dfrac{B^2}{S_t}, t; B, T\right) + (B - K)\,C_d\left(\dfrac{B^2}{S_t}, t; B, T\right)\right] & \text{if } B > K \end{cases}$$

$$= C_{bs}\left(S_t, t; K, T\right) - C_{bs}\left(S_t, t; Z, T\right) - (Z - K)\,C_d\left(S_t, t; Z, T\right)$$

$$+ \left(\dfrac{S_t}{B}\right)^{2\alpha}\left[C_{bs}\left(\dfrac{B^2}{S_t}, t; Z, T\right) + (Z - K)\,C_d\left(\dfrac{B^2}{S_t}, t; Z, T\right)\right]$$

where $Z = \max\{B, K\}$.

$\square$

3. *Up-and-Out/Up-and-In Put Options.* Let $\{W_t : t \geq 0\}$ be a $\mathbb{P}$-standard Wiener process on the probability space $(\Omega, \mathcal{F}, \mathbb{P})$ and let the asset price S_t follow a GBM with the following SDE

$$\frac{dS_t}{S_t} = (\mu - D)\,dt + \sigma dW_t$$

where μ is the drift parameter, D is the continuous dividend yield and σ is the volatility parameter. We consider a European up-and-out put option at time t, with expiry at time $T > t$, strike K and constant barrier B.

Explain why, for an up-and-out European put, $S_t < B$, and show that the terminal payoff for $B \geq K$ or $B < K$ can be written as

$$\Psi(S_T) = \max\left\{K - S_T, 0\right\}\mathbb{I}_{\left\{\max_{t \leq u \leq T} S_u < B\right\}}.$$

Using the identity

$$\frac{1}{\sqrt{2\pi T}} \int_L^U e^{aw - \frac{1}{2}(\frac{w}{\sqrt{T}})^2} dw = e^{\frac{1}{2}a^2 T} \left[\Phi\left(\frac{U - aT}{\sqrt{T}}\right) - \Phi\left(\frac{L - aT}{\sqrt{T}}\right) \right]$$

where $\Phi(x) = \int_{-\infty}^x \frac{1}{\sqrt{2\pi}} e^{-\frac{1}{2}u^2} du$ is the cdf of a standard normal, show that under the risk-neutral measure $\mathbb{Q}$, the up-and-out put option price at time t is

$$P_{u/o}\left(S_t, t; K, B, T\right) = P_{bs}\left(S_t, t; Z, T\right) + (K - Z) P_d\left(S_t, t; Z, T\right) - \left(\frac{S_t}{B}\right)^{2\alpha}$$

$$\times \left[P_{bs}\left(\frac{B^2}{S_t}, t; Z, T\right) + (K - Z) P_d\left(\frac{B^2}{S_t}, t; Z, T\right) \right]$$

where $Z = \min\{B, K\}$, $\alpha = \frac{1}{2}\left(1 - \frac{r - D}{\frac{1}{2}\sigma^2}\right)$, r is the risk-free interest rate, $P_{bs}(X, t; Y, T)$ and $P_d(X, t; Y, T)$ are the vanilla and digital put option prices defined as

$$P_{bs}(X, t; Y, T) = Y e^{-r(T-t)} \Phi\left(\frac{-\log(X/Y) - (r - D - \frac{1}{2}\sigma^2)(T - t)}{\sigma\sqrt{T - t}}\right)$$

$$-X e^{-D(T-t)} \Phi\left(\frac{-\log(X/Y) - (r - D + \frac{1}{2}\sigma^2)(T - t)}{\sigma\sqrt{T - t}}\right)$$

and

$$P_d(X, t; Y, T) = e^{-r(T-t)} \Phi\left(\frac{-\log(X/Y) - (r - D - \frac{1}{2}\sigma^2)(T - t)}{\sigma\sqrt{T - t}}\right)$$

respectively. Hence, deduce that the European up-and-in put option price at time t is

$$P_{u/i}\left(S_t, t; K, B, T\right) = P_{bs}\left(S_t, t; K, T\right)$$

$$-P_{bs}\left(S_t, t; Z, T\right) - (K - Z) P_d\left(S_t, t; Z, T\right) + \left(\frac{S_t}{B}\right)^{2\alpha}$$

$$\times \left[P_{bs}\left(\frac{B^2}{S_t}, t; Z, T\right) + (K - Z) P_d\left(\frac{B^2}{S_t}, t; Z, T\right) \right].$$

Solution: We require $S_t < B$ so as to ensure the up-and-out put option would not knock out, especially at initiation of the contract.

For $B \geq K$ or $B < K$, the payoff of an up-and-out put option is therefore

$$\Psi(S_T) = \max\left\{K - S_T, 0\right\} \, \mathbb{1}_{\left\{\max_{t \leq u \leq T} S_u < B\right\}}.$$

Under the risk-neutral measure $\mathbb{Q}$, S_t follows

$$\frac{dS_t}{S_t} = (r - D)\,dt + \sigma dW_t^{\mathbb{Q}}$$

where $W_t^{\mathbb{Q}} = W_t + \left(\dfrac{\mu - r}{\sigma}\right) t$ is a $\mathbb{Q}$-standard Wiener process. From Itō's lemma, for $t < T$

$$S_T = S_t e^{(r - D - \frac{1}{2}\sigma^2)(T - t) + \sigma W_{T-t}^{\mathbb{Q}}}$$
$$= S_t e^{\sigma \widehat{W}_{T-t}}$$

where $\widehat{W}_{T-t} = v(T - t) + W_{T-t}^{\mathbb{Q}}$ and $v = \dfrac{1}{\sigma}(r - D - \dfrac{1}{2}\sigma^2)$. By writing

$$M_{T-t} = \max_{t \leq u \leq T} \widehat{W}_{u-t}$$

therefore

$$\max_{t \leq u \leq T} S_u = S_t e^{\sigma M_{T-t}}$$

and we can rewrite the payoff as

$$\Psi(S_T) = \max\left\{K - S_T, 0\right\} \, \mathbb{1}_{\left\{\max_{t \leq u \leq T} S_u < B\right\}}$$

$$= \max\left\{K - S_t e^{\sigma \widehat{W}_{T-t}}, 0\right\} \, \mathbb{1}_{\left\{S_t e^{\sigma M_{T-t}} < B\right\}}$$

$$=
\begin{cases}
\left(K - S_t e^{\sigma \widehat{W}_{T-t}}\right) \mathbb{1}_{\left\{S_t e^{\sigma M_{T-t}} < B, \, S_t e^{\sigma \widehat{W}_{T-t}} < K\right\}} & \text{if } B \geq K \\[2mm]
\left(K - S_t e^{\sigma \widehat{W}_{T-t}}\right) \mathbb{1}_{\left\{S_t e^{\sigma M_{T-t}} < B, \, S_t e^{\sigma \widehat{W}_{T-t}} < B\right\}} & \text{if } B < K
\end{cases}$$

$$=
\begin{cases}
\left(K - S_t e^{\sigma \widehat{W}_{T-t}}\right) \mathbb{1}_{\left\{M_{T-t} < \frac{1}{\sigma}\log\left(\frac{B}{S_t}\right), \, \widehat{W}_{T-t} < \frac{1}{\sigma}\log\left(\frac{K}{S_t}\right)\right\}} & \text{if } B \geq K \\[2mm]
\left(K - S_t e^{\sigma \widehat{W}_{T-t}}\right) \mathbb{1}_{\left\{M_{T-t} < \frac{1}{\sigma}\log\left(\frac{B}{S_t}\right), \, \widehat{W}_{T-t} < \frac{1}{\sigma}\log\left(\frac{B}{S_t}\right)\right\}} & \text{if } B < K.
\end{cases}$$

Case 1: $B \geq K$

The up-and-out put option price at time t is

$$P_{u/o}\left(S_t, t; K, B, T\right)$$

$$= e^{-r(T-t)}\mathbb{E}^{\mathbb{Q}}\left[\Psi(S_T)\big|\mathcal{F}_t\right]$$

$$= e^{-r(T-t)}\mathbb{E}^{\mathbb{Q}}\left[\left(K - S_t e^{\sigma\widehat{W}_{T-t}}\right)\mathbb{I}_{\left\{M_{T-t}<\frac{1}{\sigma}\log\left(\frac{B}{S_t}\right),\widehat{W}_{T-t}<\frac{1}{\sigma}\log\left(\frac{K}{S_t}\right)\right\}}\bigg|\mathcal{F}_t\right]$$

$$= e^{-r(T-t)}\int_{w=-\infty}^{w=\frac{1}{\sigma}\log\left(\frac{K}{S_t}\right)}\int_{m=w}^{m=\frac{1}{\sigma}\log\left(\frac{B}{S_t}\right)}\left(K - S_t e^{\sigma w}\right)f^{\mathbb{Q}}_{M,\widehat{W}}(m,w)\,dm\,dw$$

where

$$f^{\mathbb{Q}}_{M,\widehat{W}}(m,w) = \begin{cases} \dfrac{2(2m-w)}{(T-t)\sqrt{2\pi(T-t)}}e^{vw-\frac{1}{2}v^2(T-t)-\frac{1}{2}\left(\frac{2m-w}{\sqrt{T-t}}\right)^2} & m \geq 0, m \geq w \\[4mm] 0 & \text{otherwise.} \end{cases}$$

To derive the expression $f^{\mathbb{Q}}_{M,\widehat{W}}(m,w)$, see Problem 4.2.2.14 of *Problems and Solutions in Mathematical Finance, Volume 1: Stochastic Calculus*.

By switching the limits of the inner integral

$$P_{u/o}\left(S_t, t; K, B, T\right)$$

$$= e^{-r(T-t)}\int_{w=-\infty}^{w=\frac{1}{\sigma}\log\left(\frac{K}{S_t}\right)}\int_{m=\frac{1}{\sigma}\log\left(\frac{B}{S_t}\right)}^{m=w} -\left(K - S_t e^{\sigma w}\right)f^{\mathbb{Q}}_{M,\widehat{W}}(m,w)\,dm\,dw$$

$$= e^{-r(T-t)}\int_{w=-\infty}^{w=\frac{1}{\sigma}\log\left(\frac{K}{S_t}\right)}\int_{m=\frac{1}{\sigma}\log\left(\frac{B}{S_t}\right)}^{m=w} \left(S_t e^{\sigma w} - K\right)f^{\mathbb{Q}}_{M,\widehat{W}}(m,w)\,dm\,dw$$

$$= -e^{-r(T-t)}\int_{w=-\infty}^{w=\frac{1}{\sigma}\log\left(\frac{K}{S_t}\right)}\left(S_t e^{\sigma w} - K\right)\frac{1}{\sqrt{2\pi(T-t)}}e^{vw-\frac{1}{2}v^2(T-t)-\frac{1}{2}\left(\frac{w}{\sqrt{T-t}}\right)^2}\,dw$$

$$+e^{-r(T-t)}\int_{-\infty}^{w=\frac{1}{\sigma}\log\left(\frac{K}{S_t}\right)}\left(S_t e^{\sigma w} - K\right)\frac{1}{\sqrt{2\pi(T-t)}}e^{vw-\frac{1}{2}v^2(T-t)-\frac{1}{2}\left(\frac{\frac{2}{\sigma}\log\left(\frac{B}{S_t}\right)-w}{\sqrt{T-t}}\right)^2}\,dw$$

$$= -S_t I_1 + K I_2 + S_t I_3 - K I_4$$

where

$$I_1 = \frac{1}{\sqrt{2\pi(T-t)}} \int_{w=-\infty}^{w=\frac{1}{\sigma}\log\left(\frac{K}{S_t}\right)} e^{-r(T-t)+\sigma w+vw-\frac{1}{2}v^2(T-t)-\frac{1}{2}\left(\frac{w}{\sqrt{T-t}}\right)^2} dw$$

$$I_2 = \frac{1}{\sqrt{2\pi(T-t)}} \int_{w=-\infty}^{w=\frac{1}{\sigma}\log\left(\frac{K}{S_t}\right)} e^{-r(T-t)+vw-\frac{1}{2}v^2(T-t)-\frac{1}{2}\left(\frac{w}{\sqrt{T-t}}\right)^2} dw$$

$$I_3 = \frac{1}{\sqrt{2\pi(T-t)}} \int_{w=-\infty}^{w=\frac{1}{\sigma}\log\left(\frac{K}{S_t}\right)} e^{-r(T-t)+\sigma w+vw-\frac{1}{2}v^2(T-t)-\frac{1}{2}\left(\frac{\frac{2}{\sigma}\log\left(\frac{B}{S_t}\right)-w}{\sqrt{T-t}}\right)^2} dw$$

$$I_4 = \frac{1}{\sqrt{2\pi(T-t)}} \int_{w=-\infty}^{w=\frac{1}{\sigma}\log\left(\frac{K}{S_t}\right)} e^{-r(T-t)+vw-\frac{1}{2}v^2(T-t)-\frac{1}{2}\left(\frac{\frac{2}{\sigma}\log\left(\frac{B}{S_t}\right)-w}{\sqrt{T-t}}\right)^2} dw.$$

Using the identity

$$\frac{1}{\sqrt{2\pi T}} \int_L^U e^{aw-\frac{1}{2}\left(\frac{w}{\sqrt{T}}\right)^2} dw = e^{\frac{1}{2}a^2 T}\left[\Phi\left(\frac{U-aT}{\sqrt{T}}\right) - \Phi\left(\frac{L-aT}{\sqrt{T}}\right)\right]$$

and following the same steps as described in Problem 4.2.1.1 (page 357), we have

$$I_1 = e^{-D(T-t)}\Phi\left(\frac{\frac{1}{\sigma}\log(K/S_t) - (v+\sigma)(T-t)}{\sqrt{T-t}}\right)$$

$$= e^{-D(T-t)}\Phi\left(\frac{-\log(S_t/K) - (r-D+\frac{1}{2}\sigma^2)(T-t)}{\sigma\sqrt{T-t}}\right)$$

$$I_2 = e^{-r(T-t)}\Phi\left(\frac{\frac{1}{\sigma}\log(K/S_t) - v(T-t)}{\sqrt{T-t}}\right)$$

$$= e^{-r(T-t)}\Phi\left(\frac{-\log(S_t/K) - (r-D-\frac{1}{2}\sigma^2)(T-t)}{\sigma\sqrt{T-t}}\right)$$

$$I_3 = e^{-D(T-t)} \left(\frac{S_t}{B} \right)^{-1-\frac{2(r-D)}{\sigma^2}}$$

$$\times \Phi \left(\frac{\frac{1}{\sigma} \log(K/S_t) - \left(v + \sigma + \frac{2}{\sigma(T-t)} \log(B/S_t) \right)(T-t)}{\sqrt{T-t}} \right)$$

$$= e^{-D(T-t)} \left(\frac{S_t}{B} \right)^{-1-\frac{2(r-D)}{\sigma^2}}$$

$$\times \Phi \left(\frac{-\log(B^2/(S_t K)) - (r - D + \frac{1}{2}\sigma^2)(T-t)}{\sigma\sqrt{T-t}} \right)$$

$$I_4 = e^{-r(T-t)} \left(\frac{S_t}{B} \right)^{1-\frac{2(r-D)}{\sigma^2}}$$

$$\times \Phi \left(\frac{-\frac{1}{\sigma} \log(K/S_t) - \left(v + \frac{2}{\sigma(T-t)} \log(B/S_t) \right)(T-t)}{\sqrt{T-t}} \right)$$

$$= e^{-r(T-t)} \left(\frac{S_t}{B} \right)^{1-\frac{2(r-D)}{\sigma^2}}$$

$$\times \Phi \left(\frac{-\log(B^2/(S_t K)) - (r - D - \frac{1}{2}\sigma^2)(T-t)}{\sigma\sqrt{T-t}} \right).$$

Therefore,

$$P_{u/o} \left(S_t, t; K, B, T \right)$$

$$= -S_t I_1 + K I_2 + S_t I_3 - K I_4$$

$$= K e^{-r(T-t)} \Phi \left(\frac{-\log(S_t/K) - (r - D - \frac{1}{2}\sigma^2)(T-t)}{\sigma\sqrt{T-t}} \right)$$

$$-S_t e^{-D(T-t)} \Phi \left(\frac{-\log(S_t/K) - (r - D + \frac{1}{2}\sigma^2)(T-t)}{\sigma\sqrt{T-t}} \right)$$

$$+S_t e^{-D(T-t)} \left(\frac{S_t}{B} \right)^{-1-\frac{2(r-D)}{\sigma^2}} \Phi \left(\frac{-\log(B^2/(S_t K)) - (r - D + \frac{1}{2}\sigma^2)(T-t)}{\sigma\sqrt{T-t}} \right)$$

$$-K e^{-r(T-t)} \left(\frac{S_t}{B} \right)^{1-\frac{2(r-D)}{\sigma^2}} \Phi \left(\frac{-\log(B^2/(S_t K)) - (r - D - \frac{1}{2}\sigma^2)(T-t)}{\sigma\sqrt{T-t}} \right)$$

$$= P_{bs} \left(S_t, t; K, T \right) - \left(\frac{S_t}{B} \right)^{2\alpha} P_{bs} \left(\frac{B^2}{S_t}, t; K, T \right)$$

where $\alpha = \dfrac{1}{2}\left(1 - \dfrac{r - D}{\frac{1}{2}\sigma^2}\right)$.

Case 2: $B < K$

The up-and-out put option price at time t is

$$P_{u/o}\left(S_t, t; K, B, T\right)$$

$$= e^{-r(T-t)}\mathbb{E}^{\mathbb{Q}}\left[\Psi(S_T)|\mathcal{F}_t\right]$$

$$= e^{-r(T-t)}\mathbb{E}^{\mathbb{Q}}\left[\left(K - S_t e^{\sigma\widehat{W}_{T-t}}\right) \mathbb{1}_{\left\{M_{T-t}<\frac{1}{\sigma}\log\left(\frac{B}{S_t}\right),\widehat{W}_{T-t}<\frac{1}{\sigma}\log\left(\frac{B}{S_t}\right)\right\}}\Bigg|\mathcal{F}_t\right]$$

$$= e^{-r(T-t)}\int_{w=-\infty}^{w=\frac{1}{\sigma}\log\left(\frac{B}{S_t}\right)}\int_{m=w}^{m=\frac{1}{\sigma}\log\left(\frac{B}{S_t}\right)}\left(K - S_t e^{\sigma w}\right) f_{M,\widehat{W}}^{\mathbb{Q}}(m, w)\, dm dw$$

where

$$f_{M,\widehat{W}}^{\mathbb{Q}}(m, w) = \begin{cases} \dfrac{2(2m-w)}{(T-t)\sqrt{2\pi(T-t)}}e^{vw-\frac{1}{2}v^2(T-t)-\frac{1}{2}\left(\frac{2m-w}{\sqrt{T-t}}\right)^2} & m \geq 0, m \geq w \\ \\ 0 & \text{otherwise.} \end{cases}$$

By switching the limits of the inner integral

$$P_{u/o}\left(S_t, t; K, B, T\right)$$

$$= e^{-r(T-t)}\int_{w=-\infty}^{w=\frac{1}{\sigma}\log\left(\frac{B}{S_t}\right)}\int_{m=\frac{1}{\sigma}\log\left(\frac{B}{S_t}\right)}^{m=w}\left(S_t e^{\sigma w} - K\right) f_{M,\widehat{W}}^{\mathbb{Q}}(m, w)\, dm dw.$$

Hence, using the same steps as described in Case 1, we have

$$P_{u/o}\left(S_t, t; K, B, T\right) = -S_t I_1 + K I_2 + (S_t I_3 - K I_4)$$

where

$$I_1 = e^{-D(T-t)}\Phi\left(\frac{-\log(S_t/B) - (r - D + \frac{1}{2}\sigma^2)(T - t)}{\sigma\sqrt{T - t}}\right)$$

$$I_2 = e^{-r(T-t)} \Phi \left(\frac{-\log(S_t/B) - (r - D - \frac{1}{2}\sigma^2)(T-t)}{\sigma\sqrt{T-t}} \right)$$

$$I_3 = e^{-D(T-t)} \left(\frac{S_t}{B} \right)^{-1 - \frac{2(r-D)}{\sigma^2}} \Phi \left(\frac{-\log(B/S_t) - (r - D + \frac{1}{2}\sigma^2)(T-t)}{\sigma\sqrt{T-t}} \right)$$

$$I_4 = e^{-r(T-t)} \left(\frac{S_t}{B} \right)^{1 - \frac{2(r-D)}{\sigma^2}} \Phi \left(\frac{-\log(B/S_t) - (r - D + \frac{1}{2}\sigma^2)(T-t)}{\sigma\sqrt{T-t}} \right).$$

Therefore,

$$P_{u/o} \left(S_t, t; K, B, T \right) = P_{bs} \left(S_t, t; B, T \right) + (K - B) P_d \left(S_t, t; B, T \right) - \left(\frac{S_t}{B} \right)^{2\alpha}$$
$$\times \left[P_{bs} \left(\frac{B^2}{S_t}, t; B, T \right) + (K - B) P_d \left(\frac{B^2}{S_t}, t; B, T \right) \right]$$

where $\alpha = \frac{1}{2} \left(1 - \frac{r - D}{\frac{1}{2}\sigma^2} \right)$.

Hence, in general we have

$$P_{u/o} \left(S_t, t; K, B, T \right) = P_{bs} \left(S_t, t; Z, T \right) + (K - Z) P_d \left(S_t, t; Z, T \right) - \left(\frac{S_t}{B} \right)^{2\alpha}$$
$$\times \left[P_{bs} \left(\frac{B^2}{S_t}, t; Z, T \right) + (K - Z) P_d \left(\frac{B^2}{S_t}, t; Z, T \right) \right]$$

where $Z = \min\{B, K\}$.

For the case of up-and-in put option price, by definition its payoff at expiry time T can be written as

$$\Psi(S_T) = \max \left\{ K - S_T, 0 \right\} \mathbb{I}_{\{ \max_{t \le u \le T} S_u \ge B \}}$$

$$= \max \left\{ K - S_T, 0 \right\} \left(1 - \mathbb{I}_{\{ \max_{t \le u \le T} S_u < B \}} \right)$$

$$= \max \left\{ K - S_T, 0 \right\} - \max \left\{ K - S_T, 0 \right\} \mathbb{I}_{\{ \max_{t \le u \le T} S_u < B \}}.$$

Under the risk-neutral measure $\mathbb{Q}$, the up-and-in put option price at time t is

$$P_{u/i}\left(S_t, t; K, B, T\right)$$

$$= e^{-r(T-t)}\mathbb{E}\left[\max\left\{K - S_T, 0\right\}\middle|\mathcal{F}_t\right]$$

$$-e^{-r(T-t)}\mathbb{E}\left[\max\left\{K - S_T, 0\right\}\,\mathbb{1}_{\{\max\limits_{t\leq u\leq T} S_u < B\}}\middle|\mathcal{F}_t\right]$$

$$= P_{bs}\left(S_t, t; K, T\right) - P_{u/o}\left(S_t, t; K, T\right)$$

$$= \begin{cases} \left(\dfrac{S_t}{B}\right)^{2\alpha} P_{bs}\left(\dfrac{B^2}{S_t}, t; K, T\right) & \text{if } B \geq K \\[4mm] \left(\dfrac{S_t}{B}\right)^{2\alpha}\left[P_{bs}\left(\dfrac{B^2}{S_t}, t; B, T\right) + (K - B) P_d\left(\dfrac{B^2}{S_t}, t; B, T\right)\right] \\[4mm] \quad - (K - B) P_d\left(S_t, t; B, T\right) & \text{if } B < K \end{cases}$$

$$= P_{bs}\left(S_t, t; Z, T\right) + (K - Z) P_d\left(S_t, t; Z, T\right)$$

$$- \left(\dfrac{S_t}{B}\right)^{2\alpha}\left[P_{bs}\left(\dfrac{B^2}{S_t}, t; Z, T\right) + (K - Z) P_d\left(\dfrac{B^2}{S_t}, t; Z, T\right)\right]$$

where $Z = \min\{B, K\}$.

$\square$

4. *Down-and-Out/Down-and-In Put Options.* Let $\left\{W_t : t \geq 0\right\}$ be a $\mathbb{P}$-standard Wiener process on the probability space $(\Omega, \mathcal{F}, \mathbb{P})$ and let the asset price S_t follow a GBM with the following SDE

$$\frac{dS_t}{S_t} = (\mu - D)\,dt + \sigma dW_t$$

where μ is the drift parameter, D is the continuous dividend yield and σ is the volatility parameter. We consider a European down-and-out put option at time t, with expiry at time T ($T > t$), strike K and constant barrier $B < K$.

Explain why, for a down-and-out put option, $S_t > B$ and $B < K$, and show that the terminal payoff can be written as

$$\Psi(S_T) = \max\left\{K - S_T, 0\right\}\,\mathbb{1}_{\{\min\limits_{t\leq u\leq T} S_u > B\}}.$$

Using the identity

$$
\frac{1}{\sqrt{2\pi T}} \int_L^U e^{aw-\frac{1}{2}(\frac{w}{\sqrt{T}})^2} \, dw = e^{\frac{1}{2}a^2 T} \left[\Phi\left(\frac{U-aT}{\sqrt{T}}\right) - \Phi\left(\frac{L-aT}{\sqrt{T}}\right) \right]
$$

where $\Phi(x) = \displaystyle\int_{-\infty}^x \frac{1}{\sqrt{2\pi}} e^{-\frac{1}{2}u^2} \, du$ is the cdf of a standard normal, show that under the risk-neutral measure $\mathbb{Q}$, the down-and-out put option price at time t is

$$
\begin{aligned}
P_{d/o}\left(S_t, t; K, B, T\right) = {}& P_{bs}\left(S_t, t; K, T\right) \\
& - \left[P_{bs}\left(S_t, t; B, T\right) + (K-B) P_d\left(S_t, t; B, T\right) \right] \\
& - \left(\frac{S_t}{B}\right)^{2\alpha} \left\{ P_{bs}\left(\frac{B^2}{S_t}, t; K, T\right) \right. \\
& \left. - \left[P_{bs}\left(\frac{B^2}{S_t}, t; B, T\right) + (K-B) P_d\left(\frac{B^2}{S_t}, t; B, T\right) \right] \right\}
\end{aligned}
$$

where $\alpha = \dfrac{1}{2}\left(1 - \dfrac{r-D}{\frac{1}{2}\sigma^2}\right)$, r is the risk-free interest rate, $P_{bs}\left(X, t; Y, T\right)$ and $P_d\left(X, t; Y, T\right)$ are the vanilla and digital call option prices defined as

$$
\begin{aligned}
P_{bs}\left(X, t; Y, T\right) = {}& Y e^{-r(T-t)} \Phi\left(\frac{-\log(X/Y) - (r - D - \frac{1}{2}\sigma^2)(T-t)}{\sigma\sqrt{T-t}}\right) \\
& - X e^{-D(T-t)} \Phi\left(\frac{-\log(X/Y) - (r - D + \frac{1}{2}\sigma^2)(T-t)}{\sigma\sqrt{T-t}}\right)
\end{aligned}
$$

and

$$
P_d\left(X, t; Y\right) = e^{-r(T-t)} \Phi\left(\frac{-\log(X/Y) - (r - D - \frac{1}{2}\sigma^2)(T-t)}{\sigma\sqrt{T-t}}\right)
$$

respectively. Hence, deduce that the European up-and-in put option price at time t is

$$
\begin{aligned}
P_{d/i}\left(S_t, t; K, B, T\right) = {}& P_{bs}\left(S_t, t; B, T\right) + (K-B) P_d\left(S_t, t; B, T\right) \\
& + \left(\frac{S_t}{B}\right)^{2\alpha} \left\{ P_{bs}\left(\frac{B^2}{S_t}, t; K, T\right) \right. \\
& \left. - \left[P_{bs}\left(\frac{B^2}{S_t}, t; B, T\right) + (K-B) P_d\left(\frac{B^2}{S_t}, t; B, T\right) \right] \right\}.
\end{aligned}
$$

Solution: Since the option is a down-and-out put, we require $S_t > B$ to ensure that the option would not knock out at the starting time t. In addition, we require $B < K$ for all time t, since if $B \geq K$ the option will not pay out either at expiry or at the barrier. Therefore, the payoff of a down-and-out put option is

$$\Psi(S_T) = \max\left\{K - S_T, 0\right\} \, \mathbb{I}_{\{\min\limits_{t \leq u \leq T} S_u > B\}}.$$

Under the risk-neutral measure $\mathbb{Q}$, S_t follows

$$\frac{dS_t}{S_t} = (r - D)\,dt + \sigma dW_t^{\mathbb{Q}}$$

where $W_t^{\mathbb{Q}} = W_t + \left(\dfrac{\mu - r}{\sigma}\right)t$ is a $\mathbb{Q}$-standard Wiener process. Using Itō's lemma we can easily show that for $t < T$

$$S_T = S_t e^{(r - D - \frac{1}{2}\sigma^2)(T-t) + \sigma W_{T-t}^{\mathbb{Q}}}$$
$$= S_t e^{\sigma \widehat{W}_{T-t}}$$

where $\widehat{W}_{T-t} = v(T - t) + W_{T-t}^{\mathbb{Q}}$ and $v = \dfrac{1}{\sigma}(r - D - \dfrac{1}{2}\sigma^2)$. By writing

$$m_{T-t} = \min_{t \leq u \leq T} \widehat{W}_{u-t}$$

therefore

$$\min_{t \leq u \leq T} S_u = S_t e^{\sigma m_{T-t}}$$

and we can rewrite the payoff as

$$\Psi(S_T) = \max\left\{K - S_T, 0\right\} \, \mathbb{I}_{\{\min\limits_{t \leq u \leq T} S_u > B\}}$$
$$= \max\left\{K - S_t e^{\sigma \widehat{W}_{T-t}}, 0\right\} \, \mathbb{I}_{\{S_t e^{\sigma m_{T-t}} > B\}}$$
$$= \left(K - S_t e^{\sigma \widehat{W}_{T-t}}\right) \, \mathbb{I}_{\{S_t e^{\sigma m_{T-t}} > B, S_t e^{\sigma \widehat{W}_{T-t}} < K\}}$$
$$= \left(K - S_t e^{\sigma \widehat{W}_{T-t}}\right) \, \mathbb{I}_{\{m_{T-t} > \frac{1}{\sigma}\log\left(\frac{B}{S_t}\right), \widehat{W}_{T-t} < \frac{1}{\sigma}\log\left(\frac{K}{S_t}\right)\}}.$$

Hence, the down-and-out put option price at time t is

$$P_{d/o}\left(S_t, t; K, B, T\right)$$

$$= e^{-r(T-t)}\mathbb{E}^{\mathbb{Q}}\left[\Psi(S_T)\middle|\mathscr{F}_t\right]$$

$$= e^{-r(T-t)}\mathbb{E}^{\mathbb{Q}}\left[\left(K - S_t e^{\sigma\widehat{W}_{T-t}}\right)\mathbb{I}_{\left\{m_{T-t}>\frac{1}{\sigma}\log\left(\frac{B}{S_t}\right),\widehat{W}_{T-t}<\frac{1}{\sigma}\log\left(\frac{K}{S_t}\right)\right\}}\middle|\mathscr{F}_t\right]$$

$$= e^{-r(T-t)}\int_{w=\frac{1}{\sigma}\log\left(\frac{B}{S_t}\right)}^{w=\frac{1}{\sigma}\log\left(\frac{K}{S_t}\right)}\int_{m=\frac{1}{\sigma}\log\left(\frac{B}{S_t}\right)}^{m=w}\left(K - S_t e^{\sigma w}\right)f^{\mathbb{Q}}_{m,\widehat{W}}(m, w)\,dm\,dw$$

where

$$f^{\mathbb{Q}}_{m,\widehat{W}}(m, w) = \begin{cases} \dfrac{-2(2m-w)}{(T-t)\sqrt{2\pi(T-t)}}e^{vw-\frac{1}{2}v^2(T-t)-\frac{1}{2}\left(\frac{2m-w}{\sqrt{T-t}}\right)^2} & m \le 0, m \le w \\ \\ 0 & \text{otherwise.} \end{cases}$$

See Problem 4.2.2.14 of *Problems and Solutions in Mathematical Finance, Volume 1: Stochastic Calculus* to derive the expression $f^{\mathbb{Q}}_{M,\widehat{W}}(m, w)$.

By switching the limits of the inner integral

$$P_{u/o}\left(S_t, t; K, B, T\right)$$

$$= e^{-r(T-t)}\int_{w=\frac{1}{\sigma}\log\left(\frac{B}{S_t}\right)}^{w=\frac{1}{\sigma}\log\left(\frac{K}{S_t}\right)}\int_{m=w}^{w=\frac{1}{\sigma}\log\left(\frac{B}{S_t}\right)}\left(S_t e^{\sigma w} - K\right)f^{\mathbb{Q}}_{m,\widehat{W}}(m, w)\,dm\,dw$$

$$= -e^{-r(T-t)}\int_{w=\frac{1}{\sigma}\log\left(\frac{B}{S_t}\right)}^{w=\frac{1}{\sigma}\log\left(\frac{K}{S_t}\right)}\left(S_t e^{\sigma w} - K\right)\frac{1}{\sqrt{2\pi(T-t)}}e^{vw-\frac{1}{2}v^2(T-t)-\frac{1}{2}\left(\frac{w}{\sqrt{T-t}}\right)^2}\,dw$$

$$+e^{-r(T-t)}\int_{w=\frac{1}{\sigma}\log\left(\frac{B}{S_t}\right)}^{w=\frac{1}{\sigma}\log\left(\frac{K}{S_t}\right)}\left(S_t e^{\sigma w} - K\right)\frac{1}{\sqrt{2\pi(T-t)}}e^{vw-\frac{1}{2}v^2(T-t)-\frac{1}{2}\left(\frac{\frac{2}{\sigma}\log\left(\frac{B}{S_t}\right)-w}{\sqrt{T-t}}\right)^2}\,dw$$

$$= -S_t I_1 + K I_2 + (S_t I_3 - K I_4)$$

where

$$I_1 = \frac{1}{\sqrt{2\pi(T-t)}}\int_{\frac{1}{\sigma}\log\left(\frac{B}{S_t}\right)}^{\frac{1}{\sigma}\log\left(\frac{K}{S_t}\right)}e^{-r(T-t)+\sigma w+vw-\frac{1}{2}v^2(T-t)-\frac{1}{2}\left(\frac{w}{\sqrt{T-t}}\right)^2}\,dw$$

$$I_2 = \frac{1}{\sqrt{2\pi(T-t)}} \int_{\frac{1}{\sigma}\log\left(\frac{B}{S_t}\right)}^{\frac{1}{\sigma}\log\left(\frac{K}{S_t}\right)} e^{-r(T-t)+vw-\frac{1}{2}v^2(T-t)-\frac{1}{2}\left(\frac{w}{\sqrt{T-t}}\right)^2} \, dw$$

$$I_3 = \frac{1}{\sqrt{2\pi(T-t)}} \int_{\frac{1}{\sigma}\log\left(\frac{B}{S_t}\right)}^{\frac{1}{\sigma}\log\left(\frac{K}{S_t}\right)} e^{-r(T-t)+\sigma w+vw-\frac{1}{2}v^2(T-t)-\frac{1}{2}\left(\frac{\frac{2}{\sigma}\log\left(\frac{B}{S_t}\right)-w}{\sqrt{T-t}}\right)^2} \, dw$$

$$I_4 = \frac{1}{\sqrt{2\pi(T-t)}} \int_{\frac{1}{\sigma}\log\left(\frac{B}{S_t}\right)}^{\frac{1}{\sigma}\log\left(\frac{K}{S_t}\right)} e^{-r(T-t)+vw-\frac{1}{2}v^2(T-t)-\frac{1}{2}\left(\frac{\frac{2}{\sigma}\log\left(\frac{B}{S_t}\right)-w}{\sqrt{T-t}}\right)^2} \, dw.$$

Using the identity

$$\frac{1}{\sqrt{2\pi T}} \int_L^U e^{aw-\frac{1}{2}\left(\frac{w}{\sqrt{T}}\right)^2} \, dw = e^{\frac{1}{2}a^2 T} \left[\Phi\left(\frac{U-aT}{\sqrt{T}}\right) - \Phi\left(\frac{L-aT}{\sqrt{T}}\right) \right]$$

and knowing that $v = \frac{1}{\sigma}(r - D - \frac{1}{2}\sigma^2)$, we have

$$I_1 = e^{-D(T-t)} \left[\Phi\left(\frac{-\log(S_t/K)-(r-D+\frac{1}{2}\sigma^2)(T-t)}{\sigma\sqrt{T-t}}\right) \right.$$
$$\left. -\Phi\left(\frac{-\log(S_t/B)-(r-D+\frac{1}{2}\sigma^2)(T-t)}{\sigma\sqrt{T-t}}\right) \right]$$

$$I_2 = e^{-r(T-t)} \left[\Phi\left(\frac{-\log(S_t/K)-(r-D-\frac{1}{2}\sigma^2)(T-t)}{\sigma\sqrt{T-t}}\right) \right.$$
$$\left. -\Phi\left(\frac{-\log(S_t/B)-(r-D-\frac{1}{2}\sigma^2)(T-t)}{\sigma\sqrt{T-t}}\right) \right]$$

$$I_3 = e^{-D(T-t)} \left(\frac{S_t}{B}\right)^{-1-\frac{2(r-D)}{\sigma^2}} \left[\Phi\left(\frac{-\log(B^2/(S_t K))-(r-D+\frac{1}{2}\sigma^2)(T-t)}{\sigma\sqrt{T-t}}\right) \right.$$
$$\left. -\Phi\left(\frac{-\log(B/S_t)-(r-D+\frac{1}{2}\sigma^2)(T-t)}{\sigma\sqrt{T-t}}\right) \right]$$

$$I_4 = e^{-r(T-t)} \left(\frac{S_t}{B}\right)^{1-\frac{2(r-D)}{\sigma^2}} \left[\Phi\left(\frac{-\log(B^2/(S_t K))-(r-D-\frac{1}{2}\sigma^2)(T-t)}{\sigma\sqrt{T-t}}\right) \right.$$
$$\left. -\Phi\left(\frac{-\log(B/S_t)-(r-D-\frac{1}{2}\sigma^2)(T-t)}{\sigma\sqrt{T-t}}\right) \right].$$

Therefore,

$$P_{d/o}\left(S_t, t; K, B, T\right)$$

$$= -S_t I_1 + K I_2 + (S_t I_3 - K I_4)$$

$$= -S_t e^{-D(T-t)} \Phi\left(\frac{-\log(S_t/K) - (r - D + \frac{1}{2}\sigma^2)(T-t)}{\sigma\sqrt{T-t}}\right)$$

$$+ S_t e^{-D(T-t)} \Phi\left(\frac{-\log(S_t/B) - (r - D + \frac{1}{2}\sigma^2)(T-t)}{\sigma\sqrt{T-t}}\right)$$

$$+ K e^{-r(T-t)} \Phi\left(\frac{-\log(S_t/K) - (r - D - \frac{1}{2}\sigma^2)(T-t)}{\sigma\sqrt{T-t}}\right)$$

$$- K e^{-r(T-t)} \Phi\left(\frac{-\log(S_t/B) - (r - D - \frac{1}{2}\sigma^2)(T-t)}{\sigma\sqrt{T-t}}\right)$$

$$+ S_t \left(\frac{S_t}{B}\right)^{-1 - \frac{2(r-D)}{\sigma^2}} e^{-D(T-t)} \Phi\left(\frac{-\log(B^2/(S_t K)) - (r - D + \frac{1}{2}\sigma^2)(T-t)}{\sigma\sqrt{T-t}}\right)$$

$$- S_t \left(\frac{S_t}{B}\right)^{-1 - \frac{2(r-D)}{\sigma^2}} e^{-D(T-t)} \Phi\left(\frac{-\log(B/S_t) - (r - D + \frac{1}{2}\sigma^2)(T-t)}{\sigma\sqrt{T-t}}\right)$$

$$- K \left(\frac{S_t}{B}\right)^{1 - \frac{2(r-D)}{\sigma^2}} e^{-r(T-t)} \Phi\left(\frac{-\log(B^2/(S_t K)) - (r - D - \frac{1}{2}\sigma^2)(T-t)}{\sigma\sqrt{T-t}}\right)$$

$$+ K \left(\frac{S_t}{B}\right)^{1 - \frac{2(r-D)}{\sigma^2}} e^{-r(T-t)} \Phi\left(\frac{-\log(B/S_t) - (r - D - \frac{1}{2}\sigma^2)(T-t)}{\sigma\sqrt{T-t}}\right)$$

$$= P_{bs}\left(S_t, t; K, T\right) - \left[P_{bs}\left(S_t, t; B, T\right) + (K - B)P_d\left(S_t, t; B, T\right)\right] - \left(\frac{S_t}{B}\right)^{2\alpha}$$

$$\times \left\{P_{bs}\left(\frac{B^2}{S_t}, t; K, T\right) - \left[P_{bs}\left(\frac{B^2}{S_t}, t; B, T\right) + (K - B)P_d\left(\frac{B^2}{S_t}, t; B, T\right)\right]\right\}$$

where $\alpha = \frac{1}{2}\left(1 - \frac{r - D}{\frac{1}{2}\sigma^2}\right)$.

For the case of the down-and-in put option price, by definition its payoff at expiry time T can be written as

$$\Psi(S_T) = \max\left\{K - S_T, 0\right\} \, \mathbb{I}_{\left\{\min_{t \le u \le T} S_u \le B\right\}}$$

$$= \max\left\{K - S_T, 0\right\}\left(1 - \mathbb{I}_{\left\{\min_{t \le u \le T} S_u > B\right\}}\right)$$

$$= \max\left\{K - S_T, 0\right\} - \max\left\{K - S_T, 0\right\}\, \mathbb{I}_{\left\{\min_{t \le u \le T} S_u > B\right\}}.$$

Under the risk-neutral measure $\mathbb{Q}$, the down-and-in put option price at time t is

$$P_{d/i}\left(S_t, t; K, B, T\right) = e^{-r(T-t)}\mathbb{E}\left[\max\left\{K - S_T, 0\right\}\middle|\mathscr{F}_t\right]$$

$$-e^{-r(T-t)}\mathbb{E}\left[\max\left\{K - S_T, 0\right\}\mathbb{I}_{\left\{\min_{t \le u \le T} S_u > B\right\}}\middle|\mathscr{F}_t\right]$$

$$= P_{bs}\left(S_t, t; K, T\right) - P_{d/o}\left(S_t, t; K, T\right)$$

$$= P_{bs}\left(S_t, t; B, T\right) + (K - B)P_d\left(S_t, t; B, T\right)$$

$$+ \left(\frac{S_t}{B}\right)^{2\alpha}\left\{P_{bs}\left(\frac{B^2}{S_t}, t; K, T\right)\right.$$

$$\left. - \left[P_{bs}\left(\frac{B^2}{S_t}, t; B, T\right) + (K - B)P_d\left(\frac{B^2}{S_t}, t; B, T\right)\right]\right\}.$$

$\square$

4.2.2 Reflection Principle Approach

1. *Reflection Principle for Black–Scholes Equation.* Assume we are in the Black–Scholes world where at time t, the asset price S_t follows the SDE

$$dS_t = (\mu - D)S_t dt + \sigma S_t dW_t$$

where μ, D and σ are the drift, continuous dividend yield and volatility, respectively, W_t is the standard Wiener process and there is a risk-free asset which earns interest at a constant rate r. Let $V_{bs}(S_t, t; K, T)$ be the price of a European option satisfying the Black–Scholes equation

$$\frac{\partial V_{bs}}{\partial t} + \frac{1}{2}\sigma^2 S_t^2\frac{\partial^2 V_{bs}}{\partial S_t^2} + (r - D)S_t\frac{\partial V_{bs}}{\partial S_t} - rV_{bs}(S_t, t; K, T) = 0$$

with

$$V_{bs}(S_T, T; K, T) = \Psi(S_T)$$

where $\Psi(S_T)$ is the option payoff for a strike price K at expiry time $T > t$. Show that for a constant B, the function

$$U(S_t, t; K, T) = (S_t/B)^{2\alpha} V_{bs}(B^2/S_t, t; K, T)$$

satisfies

$$\frac{\partial U}{\partial t} + \frac{1}{2}\sigma^2 S_t^2 \frac{\partial^2 U}{\partial S_t^2} + \left[\sigma^2(1 - 2\alpha) - (r - D)\right] S_t \frac{\partial U}{\partial S_t}$$
$$- \left[r + \alpha\sigma^2 - 2\alpha(r - D + \alpha\sigma^2)\right] U(S_t, t; K, T) = 0.$$

Explain the significance of the above PDE if we set $\alpha = \dfrac{1}{2}\left(1 - \dfrac{r - D}{\frac{1}{2}\sigma^2}\right)$.

Solution: By setting $\xi = B^2/S_t$ we can write

$$U(S_t, t; K, T) = (S_t/B)^{2\alpha} V_{bs}(\xi, t; K, T).$$

Differentiating $U(S_t, t; K, T)$ with respect to t and S_t we have

$$\frac{\partial U}{\partial t} = \left(\frac{S_t}{B}\right)^{2\alpha} \frac{\partial V_{bs}}{\partial t}$$

$$\begin{aligned}
\frac{\partial U}{\partial S_t} &= 2\alpha S_t^{2\alpha-1} B^{-2\alpha} V_{bs}(\xi, t; K, T) + \left(\frac{S_t}{B}\right)^{2\alpha} \frac{\partial V_{bs}}{\partial \xi} \frac{\partial \xi}{\partial S_t} \\
&= 2\alpha S_t^{2\alpha-1} B^{-2\alpha} V_{bs}(\xi, t; K, T) - \left(\frac{S_t}{B}\right)^{2\alpha} \frac{\partial V_{bs}}{\partial \xi} \left(\frac{S_t}{B}\right)^2 \\
&= 2\alpha S_t^{2\alpha-1} B^{-2\alpha} V_{bs}(\xi, t; K, T) - S_t^{2\alpha-1} B^{-2\alpha} \xi \frac{\partial V_{bs}}{\partial \xi} \\
&= \frac{1}{S_t}\left(\frac{S_t}{B}\right)^{2\alpha} \left[2\alpha V_{bs}(\xi, t; K, T) - \xi \frac{\partial V_{bs}}{\partial \xi}\right]
\end{aligned}$$

and finally by differentiating $\dfrac{\partial U}{\partial S_t}$ with respect to S_t

$$
\begin{aligned}
\frac{\partial^2 U}{\partial S_t^2} &= -\frac{1}{S_t^2}\left(\frac{S_t}{B}\right)^{2\alpha}\left[2\alpha V_{bs}(\xi,t;K,T) - \xi\frac{\partial V_{bs}}{\partial \xi}\right] \\
&\quad + \frac{2\alpha}{S_t^2}\left(\frac{S_t}{B}\right)^{2\alpha}\left[2\alpha V_{bs}(\xi,t;K,T) - \xi\frac{\partial V_{bs}}{\partial \xi}\right] \\
&\quad + \frac{1}{S_t}\left(\frac{S_t}{B}\right)^{2\alpha}\left[2\alpha\frac{\partial V_{bs}}{\partial \xi}\frac{\partial \xi}{\partial S_t} - \frac{\partial \xi}{\partial S_t}\frac{\partial V_{bs}}{\partial \xi} - \xi\frac{\partial^2 V_{bs}}{\partial \xi^2}\frac{\partial \xi}{\partial S_t}\right] \\
&= \left(\frac{2\alpha-1}{S_t^2}\right)\left(\frac{S_t}{B}\right)^{2\alpha}\left[2\alpha V_{bs}(\xi,t;K,T) - \xi\frac{\partial V_{bs}}{\partial \xi}\right] \\
&\quad - \frac{1}{S_t^2}\left(\frac{S_t}{B}\right)^{2\alpha}\left[(2\alpha-1)\xi\frac{\partial V_{bs}}{\partial \xi} - \xi^2\frac{\partial^2 V_{bs}}{\partial \xi^2}\right] \\
&= \frac{1}{S_t^2}\left(\frac{S_t}{B}\right)^{2\alpha}\left[2\alpha(2\alpha-1)V_{bs}(\xi,t;K,T) - 2(2\alpha-1)\xi\frac{\partial V_{bs}}{\partial \xi} + \xi^2\frac{\partial^2 V_{bs}}{\partial \xi^2}\right].
\end{aligned}
$$

By substituting $\dfrac{\partial U}{\partial t}$, $\dfrac{\partial U}{\partial S_t}$ and $\dfrac{\partial^2 U}{\partial S_t^2}$ into

$$
\begin{aligned}
&\frac{\partial U}{\partial t} + \frac{1}{2}\sigma^2 S_t^2\frac{\partial^2 U}{\partial S_t^2} + \left[\sigma^2(1-2\alpha) - (r-D)\right]S_t\frac{\partial U}{\partial S_t} \\
&\quad - \left[r + \alpha\sigma^2 - 2\alpha(r - D + \alpha\sigma^2)\right]U(S_t,t;K,T)
\end{aligned}
$$

we have

$$
\begin{aligned}
&\frac{\partial U}{\partial t} + \frac{1}{2}\sigma^2 S_t^2\frac{\partial^2 U}{\partial S_t^2} + \left[\sigma^2(1-2\alpha) - (r-D)\right]S_t\frac{\partial U}{\partial S_t} \\
&\quad - \left[r + \alpha\sigma^2 - 2\alpha(r - D + \alpha\sigma^2)\right]U(S_t,t;K,T) \\
&= \left(\frac{S_t}{B}\right)^{2\alpha}\left\{\frac{\partial V_{bs}}{\partial t} + \frac{1}{2}\sigma^2\xi^2\frac{\partial^2 V_{bs}}{\partial \xi^2} + (r-D)\xi\frac{\partial V_{bs}}{\partial \xi} - rV_{bs}(\xi,t;K,T)\right\} \\
&= 0
\end{aligned}
$$

since $\dfrac{\partial V_{bs}}{\partial t} + \dfrac{1}{2}\sigma^2\xi^2\dfrac{\partial^2 V_{bs}}{\partial \xi^2} + (r-D)\xi\dfrac{\partial V_{bs}}{\partial \xi} - rV_{bs}(\xi,t;K,T) = 0$.

By setting $\alpha = \dfrac{1}{2}\left(1 - \dfrac{r-D}{\frac{1}{2}\sigma^2}\right)$ then $U(S_t,t;K,T) = \left(S_t/B\right)^{2\alpha}V_{bs}\left(B^2/S_t,t;K,T\right)$

satisfies

$$
\frac{\partial U}{\partial t} + \frac{1}{2}\sigma^2 S_t^2\frac{\partial^2 U}{\partial S_t^2} + (r-D)S_t\frac{\partial U}{\partial S_t} - rU(S_t,t;K,T) = 0.
$$

$\square$

2. *In–Out Parity.* Assume we are in the Black–Scholes world where at time t the asset price S_t follows the SDE

$$dS_t = (\mu - D)S_t dt + \sigma S_t dW_t$$

where μ, D and σ are the drift, continuous dividend yield and volatility, respectively, W_t is the standard Wiener process and there is a risk-free asset which earns interest at a constant rate r. Let $V_{bs}(S_t, t; K, T)$ be the price of a European option satisfying the Black–Scholes equation

$$\frac{\partial V_{bs}}{\partial t} + \frac{1}{2}\sigma^2 S_t^2 \frac{\partial^2 V_{bs}}{\partial S_t^2} + (r - D)S_t \frac{\partial V_{bs}}{\partial S_t} - rV_{bs}(S_t, t; K, T) = 0$$

with

$$V_{bs}(S_T, T; K, T) = \Psi(S_T)$$

where $\Psi(S_T)$ is the option payoff for a strike price K at expiry time $T > t$. Let $V_{u/o}(S_t, t; K, B, T), V_{u/i}(S_t, t; K, B, T), V_{d/o}(S_t, t; K, B, T)$ and $V_{d/i}(S_t, t; K, B, T)$ be the European up-and-out/in and European down-and-out/in options with common barrier B, strike price K and expiry time T. By setting up independent portfolios, show that

$$V_{u/o}(S_t, t; K, B, T) + V_{u/i}(S_t, t; K, B, T) = V_{bs}(S_t, t; K, T)$$

and

$$V_{d/o}(S_t, t; K, B, T) + V_{d/i}(S_t, t; K, B, T) = V_{bs}(S_t, t; K, T).$$

Solution: At time t, we first set up the portfolios $\Pi_u(S_t, t)$ and $\Pi_d(S_t, t)$ with each having the following options

$$\Pi_u(S_t, t) = V_{u/o}(S_t, t; K, B, T) + V_{u/i}(S_t, t; K, B, T)$$
$$\Pi_d(S_t, t) = V_{d/o}(S_t, t; K, B, T) + V_{d/i}(S_t, t; K, B, T).$$

For the case of $\Pi_u(S_t, t)$, at expiry time T only one of the two barrier options can be active. If barrier B is triggered ($S_T \geq B$), then

$$V_{u/o}(S_T, T; K, B, T) = 0 \text{ and } V_{u/i}(S_T, T; K, B, T) = \Psi(S_T).$$

However, if the barrier B is not triggered ($S_T < B$), then

$$V_{u/o}(S_T, T; K, B, T) = \Psi(S_T) \text{ and } V_{u/i}(S_T, T; K, B, T) = 0.$$

In the same vein for $\Pi_d(S_t, t)$, at expiry time T if the barrier B is triggered ($S_T \leq B$) then

$$V_{d/o}(S_T, T; K, B, T) = 0 \text{ and } V_{u/i}(S_T, T; K, B, T) = \Psi(S_T)$$

while if B is never triggered $(S_T > B)$ then

$$V_{d/o}(S_T, T; K, B, T) = \Psi(S_T) \text{ and } V_{d/i}(S_T, T; K, B, T) = 0.$$

Hence, at time T, the portfolios have the values

$$V_{u/o}(S_T, T; K, B, T) + V_{u/i}(S_T, T; K, B, T) = \Psi(S_T) = V_{bs}(S_T, T; K, T)$$
$$V_{d/o}(S_T, T; K, B, T) + V_{d/i}(S_T, T; K, B, T) = \Psi(S_T) = V_{bs}(S_T, T; K, T)$$

and by discounting them back to time t under the risk-neutral measure $\mathbb{Q}$, we have

$$V_{u/o}(S_t, t; K, B, T) + V_{u/i}(S_t, t; K, B, T) = V_{bs}(S_t, t; K, T)$$
$$V_{d/o}(S_t, t; K, B, T) + V_{d/i}(S_t, t; K, B, T) = V_{bs}(S_t, t; K, T).$$

$\square$

3. *Up-and-Out/In Barrier Options*. Assume we are in the Black–Scholes world where at time t the asset price S_t follows the SDE

$$dS_t = (\mu - D)S_t dt + \sigma S_t dW_t$$

where μ, D and σ are the drift, continuous dividend yield and volatility, respectively, W_t is the standard Wiener process and there is a risk-free asset which earns interest at a constant rate r.

Let $V_{bs}(S_t, t; K, T)$ be the price of a European option satisfying the Black–Scholes equation

$$\frac{\partial V_{bs}}{\partial t} + \frac{1}{2}\sigma^2 S_t^2 \frac{\partial^2 V_{bs}}{\partial S_t^2} + (r - D)S_t \frac{\partial V_{bs}}{\partial S_t} - rV_{bs}(S_t, t; K, T) = 0$$

with boundary condition

$$V_{bs}(S_T, T; K, T) = \Psi(S_T)$$

where $\Psi(S_T)$ is the option payoff for a strike price K at expiry time $T > t$. Let $V_{u/o}(S_t, t; K, B, T)$ and $V_{u/i}(S_t, t; K, B, T)$ be the European up-and-out/in options, respectively with common barrier B, strike price K and expiry time T.

Using the reflection principle, show that the formula for an up-and-out barrier option is

$$V_{u/o}(S_t, t; K, B, T) = \widehat{V}_{u/o}(S_t, t; K, B, T) - \left(\frac{S_t}{B}\right)^{2\alpha} \widehat{V}_{u/o}\left(\frac{B^2}{S_t}, t; K, B, T\right)$$

where $\alpha = \dfrac{1}{2}\left(1 - \dfrac{r-D}{\frac{1}{2}\sigma^2}\right)$ and $\widehat{V}_{u/o}(S_t, t; K, B, T)$ satisfies the following Black–Scholes equation

$$\frac{\partial \widehat{V}_{u/o}}{\partial t} + \frac{1}{2}\sigma^2 S_t^2 \frac{\partial^2 \widehat{V}_{u/o}}{\partial S_t^2} + (r-D)S_t \frac{\partial \widehat{V}_{u/o}}{\partial S_t} - r\widehat{V}_{u/o}(S_t, t; K, B, T) = 0$$

with discontinuous payoff

$$0 < S_t < B, \quad t \le T$$

$$\widehat{V}_{u/o}(S_T, T; K, B, T) = \Psi(S_T).$$

Deduce the general solution for the up-and-in barrier option price.

Solution: The up-and-out barrier option $V_{u/o}(S_t, t; K, B, T)$ with strike price K and barrier B satisfies the PDE

$$\frac{\partial V_{u/o}}{\partial t} + \frac{1}{2}\sigma^2 S_t^2 \frac{\partial^2 V_{u/o}}{\partial S_t^2} + (r-D)S_t \frac{\partial V_{u/o}}{\partial S_t} - rV_{u/o}(S_t, t; K, B, T) = 0$$

with the following boundary conditions

$$0 < S_t < B, \quad t \le T$$

$$V_{u/o}(B, t; K, B, T) = 0$$

$$V_{u/o}(S_T, T; K, B, T) = \Psi(S_T)$$

where $\Psi(S_T)$ is the European option (Black–Scholes) payoff at expiry T. As the up-and-out barrier option has a European payoff at expiry time T but becomes worthless on the barrier B, we can therefore write its solution as

$$V_{u/o}(S_t, t; K, B, T) = \widehat{V}_{u/o}(S_t, t; K, B, T) - \widetilde{V}_{u/o}(S_t, t; K, B, T)$$

so that $\widehat{V}_{u/o}(S_t, t; K, B, T)$ satisfies the Black–Scholes equation

$$\frac{\partial \widehat{V}_{u/o}}{\partial t} + \frac{1}{2}\sigma^2 S_t^2 \frac{\partial^2 \widehat{V}_{u/o}}{\partial S_t^2} + (r-D)S_t \frac{\partial \widehat{V}_{u/o}}{\partial S_t} - r\widehat{V}_{u/o}(S_t, t; K, B, T) = 0$$

with discontinuous payoff

$$0 < S_t < B, \quad t \le T$$

$$\widehat{V}_{u/o}(S_T, T; K, B, T) = \Psi(S_T)$$

whilst for $\widetilde{V}_{u/o}(S_t, t; K, B, T)$ we require on the barrier B

$$\widetilde{V}_{u/o}(B, t; K, B, T) = \widehat{V}_{u/o}(B, t; K, B, T)$$

and at expiry T

$$\widetilde{V}_{u/o}(S_T, T; K, B, T) = 0.$$

From the reflection principle (see Problem 4.2.2.1, page 386), by writing $\xi_t = \dfrac{B^2}{S_t}$

$$\widetilde{V}_{u/o}(S, t; K, B, T) = \left(\frac{S_t}{B}\right)^{2\alpha} \widehat{V}_{u/o}\left(\frac{B^2}{S_t}, t; K, B, T\right)$$

$$= \left(\frac{B}{\xi_t}\right)^{2\alpha} \widehat{V}_{u/o}(\xi_t, t; K, B, T)$$

with $\alpha = \dfrac{1}{2}\left(1 - \dfrac{r - D}{\frac{1}{2}\sigma^2}\right)$ also satisfies the Black–Scholes equation

$$\left(\frac{B}{\xi_t}\right)^{2\alpha}\left[\frac{\partial \widehat{V}_{u/o}}{\partial t} + \frac{1}{2}\sigma^2\xi_t^2\frac{\partial^2 \widehat{V}_{u/o}}{\partial \xi_t^2} + (r - D)\xi_t\frac{\partial \widehat{V}_{u/o}}{\partial \xi_t} - r\widehat{V}_{u/o}(\xi_t, t; K, B, T)\right] = 0$$

with the following boundary conditions

$$0 < \xi_t < B, \quad t \leq T$$

$$\left(\frac{B}{\xi_t}\right)^{2\alpha} \widehat{V}_{u/o}(\xi_T, T; K, B, T) = \left(\frac{B}{\xi_t}\right)^{2\alpha} \Psi(\xi_T)$$

or

$$\frac{\partial \widehat{V}_{u/o}}{\partial t} + \frac{1}{2}\sigma^2\xi_t^2\frac{\partial^2 \widehat{V}_{u/o}}{\partial \xi_t^2} + (r - D)\xi_t\frac{\partial \widehat{V}_{u/o}}{\partial \xi_t} - r\widehat{V}_{u/o}(\xi_t, t; K, B, T) = 0$$

with boundary conditions

$$0 < \xi_t < B, \quad t \leq T$$

$$\widehat{V}_{u/o}(\xi_T, T; K, B, T) = \Psi(\xi_T).$$

Thus, we can set

$$\tilde{V}_{u/o}(S_t, t; K, B, T) = \left(\frac{S_t}{B}\right)^{2\alpha} \hat{V}_{u/o}\left(\frac{B^2}{S_t}, t; K, B, T\right).$$

To test the boundary conditions, we note that at the barrier $S_t = B$ we have

$$\tilde{V}_{u/o}(B, t; K, B, T) = \left(\frac{B}{B}\right)^{2\alpha} \hat{V}_{u/o}\left(\frac{B^2}{B}, t; K, B, T\right) = \hat{V}_{u/o}(B, t; K, B, T)$$

whilst at expiry time T, we have

$$\tilde{V}_{u/o}(S_T, T; K, B, T) = \left(\frac{S_T}{B}\right)^{2\alpha} \hat{V}_{u/o}\left(\frac{B^2}{S_T}, T; K, B, T\right)$$

$$= \left(\frac{S_T}{B}\right)^{2\alpha} \Psi\left(\frac{B^2}{S_T}\right) \, \mathbb{1}_{\frac{B^2}{S_T} < B}$$

where for the reflection part, the payoff is only valid for $\dfrac{B^2}{S_T} < B$ or $S_T > B$.

Therefore, in the range $0 < S_T < B$ for an up-and-out option

$$\tilde{V}_{u/o}(S_T, T; K, B, T) = \left(\frac{S_T}{B}\right)^{2\alpha} \hat{V}_{u/o}\left(\frac{B^2}{S_T}, T; K, B, T\right) = 0.$$

Hence, the general solution of an up-and-out barrier option is

$$V_{u/o}(S_t, t; K, B, T) = \hat{V}_{u/o}(S_t, t; K, B, T) - \left(\frac{S_t}{B}\right)^{2\alpha} \hat{V}_{u/o}\left(\frac{B^2}{S_t}, t; K, B, T\right).$$

By writing the up-and-in barrier option as $V_{u/i}(S_t, t; K, B, T)$, from the in–out parity

$$V_{u/o}(S_t, t; K, B, T) + V_{u/i}(S_t, t; K, B, T) = V_{bs}(S_t, t; K, T)$$

where $V_{bs}(S_t, t; K, T)$ is the Black–Scholes formula for a European option written on asset price S_t with strike K and expiry time T. Thus, the up-and-in barrier option formula is

$$V_{u/i}(S_t, t; K, B, T) = V_{bs}(S_t, t; K, T) - V_{u/o}(S_t, t; K, B, T)$$

$$= V_{bs}(S_t, t; K, T) - \hat{V}_{u/o}(S_t, t; K, B, T)$$

$$+ \left(\frac{S_t}{B}\right)^{2\alpha} \hat{V}_{u/o}\left(\frac{B^2}{S_t}, t; K, B, T\right).$$

$\square$

4. *Down-and-Out/In Barrier Options.* Assume that at time t, the asset price S_t follows the SDE

$$dS_t = (\mu - D)S_t dt + \sigma S_t dW_t$$

where μ, D and σ are the drift, continuous dividend yield and volatility, respectively, W_t is the standard Wiener process and there is a risk-free asset which earns interest at a constant rate r.

Let $V_{bs}(S_t, t; K, T)$ be the price of a European option satisfying the Black–Scholes equation

$$\frac{\partial V_{bs}}{\partial t} + \frac{1}{2}\sigma^2 S_t^2 \frac{\partial^2 V_{bs}}{\partial S_t^2} + (r - D)S_t \frac{\partial V_{bs}}{\partial S_t} - rV_{bs}(S_t, t; K, T) = 0$$

with boundary condition

$$V_{bs}(S_T, T; K, T) = \Psi(S_T)$$

where $\Psi(S_T)$ is the option payoff for a strike price K at expiry time $T > t$. Let $V_{d/o}(S_t, t; K, B, T)$ and $V_{d/i}(S_t, t; K, B, T)$ be the European down-and-out/in options, respectively with common barrier B, strike price K and expiry time T.

Using the reflection principle, show that the formula for a down-and-out barrier option is

$$V_{d/o}(S_t, t; K, B, T) = \widehat{V}_{d/o}(S_t, t; K, B, T) - \left(\frac{S_t}{B}\right)^{2\alpha} \widehat{V}_{d/o}\left(\frac{B^2}{S_t}, t; K, B, T\right)$$

where $\alpha = \dfrac{1}{2}\left(1 - \dfrac{r - D}{\frac{1}{2}\sigma^2}\right)$ and $\widehat{V}_{d/o}(S_t, t; K, B, T)$ satisfies the following Black–Scholes equation

$$\frac{\partial \widehat{V}_{d/o}}{\partial t} + \frac{1}{2}\sigma^2 S_t^2 \frac{\partial^2 \widehat{V}_{d/o}}{\partial S_t^2} + (r - D)S_t \frac{\partial \widehat{V}_{d/o}}{\partial S_t} - r\widehat{V}_{d/o}(S_t, t; K, B, T) = 0$$

with truncated payoff

$$S_t > B, \quad t \le T$$

$$\widehat{V}_{d/o}(S_T, T; K, B, T) = \Psi(S_T).$$

Deduce the general solution for the down-and-in barrier option price.

Solution: By definition, the down-and-out barrier option $V_{d/o}(S_t, t; K, B, T)$ with strike price K and barrier B satisfies the PDE

$$\frac{\partial V_{d/o}}{\partial t} + \frac{1}{2}\sigma^2 S_t^2 \frac{\partial^2 V_{d/o}}{\partial S_t^2} + (r-D)S_t \frac{\partial V_{d/o}}{\partial S_t} - rV_{d/o}(S_t, t; K, B, T) = 0$$

with the following boundary conditions

$$S_t > B, \quad t \leq T$$

$$V_{d/o}(B, t; K, B, T) = 0$$

$$V_{d/o}(S_T, T; K, B, T) = \Psi(S_T)$$

where $\Psi(S_T)$ is the European option (Black–Scholes) payoff at expiry T. As the down-and-out barrier option has a European payoff at expiry time T but becomes worthless on the barrier B, we can therefore write its solution as

$$V_{d/o}(S_t, t; K, B, T) = \widehat{V}_{d/o}(S_t, t; K, B, T) - \widetilde{V}_{d/o}(S_t, t; K, B, T)$$

so that $\widehat{V}_{d/o}(S_t, t; K, B, T)$ satisfies the Black–Scholes equation

$$\frac{\partial \widehat{V}_{d/o}}{\partial t} + \frac{1}{2}\sigma^2 S_t^2 \frac{\partial^2 \widehat{V}_{d/o}}{\partial S_t^2} + (r-D)S_t \frac{\partial \widehat{V}_{d/o}}{\partial S_t} - r\widehat{V}_{d/o}(S_t, t; K, B, T) = 0$$

with discontinuous payoff

$$S_t > B, \quad t \leq T$$

$$\widehat{V}_{d/o}(S_T, T; K, B, T) = \Psi(S_T)$$

whilst for $\widetilde{V}_{d/o}(S_t, t; K, B, T)$, we require on the barrier B

$$\widetilde{V}_{d/o}(B, t; K, B, T) = \widehat{V}_{d/o}(B, t; K, B, T)$$

and at expiry T

$$\widetilde{V}_{d/o}(S_T, T; K, B, T) = 0.$$

From the reflection principle (see Problem 4.2.2.1, page 386), by writing $\xi_t = \dfrac{B^2}{S_t}$

$$\tilde{V}_{d/o}(S,t;K,B,T) = \left(\frac{S_t}{B}\right)^{2\alpha} \hat{V}_{d/o}\left(\frac{B^2}{S_t},t;K,B,T\right)$$

$$= \left(\frac{B}{\xi_t}\right)^{2\alpha} \hat{V}_{d/o}(\xi_t,t;K,B,T)$$

with $\alpha = \dfrac{1}{2}\left(1 - \dfrac{r-D}{\frac{1}{2}\sigma^2}\right)$ also satisfies the Black–Scholes equation

$$\left(\frac{B}{\xi_t}\right)^{2\alpha}\left[\frac{\partial \hat{V}_{d/o}}{\partial t} + \frac{1}{2}\sigma^2\xi_t^2\frac{\partial^2 \hat{V}_{d/o}}{\partial \xi_t^2} + (r-D)\xi_t\frac{\partial \hat{V}_{d/o}}{\partial \xi_t} - r\hat{V}_{d/o}(\xi_t,t;K,B,T)\right] = 0$$

with the following boundary conditions

$$\xi_t > B, \quad t \le T$$

$$\left(\frac{B}{\xi_t}\right)^{2\alpha} \hat{V}_{d/o}(\xi_T,T;K,B,T) = \left(\frac{B}{\xi_t}\right)^{2\alpha}\Psi(\xi_T)$$

or

$$\frac{\partial \hat{V}_{d/o}}{\partial t} + \frac{1}{2}\sigma^2\xi_t^2\frac{\partial^2 \hat{V}_{d/o}}{\partial \xi_t^2} + (r-D)\xi_t\frac{\partial \hat{V}_{d/o}}{\partial \xi_t} - r\hat{V}_{d/o}(\xi_t,t;K,B,T) = 0$$

with boundary conditions

$$\xi_t > B, \quad t \le T$$

$$\hat{V}_{d/o}(\xi_T,T;K,B,T) = \Psi(\xi_T).$$

Thus, we can set

$$\tilde{V}_{d/o}(S_t,t;K,B,T) = \left(\frac{S_t}{B}\right)^{2\alpha} \hat{V}_{d/o}\left(\frac{B^2}{S_t},t;K,B,T\right).$$

To test the boundary conditions, we note that at the barrier $S_t = B$ we have

$$\tilde{V}_{d/o}(B,t;K,B,T) = \left(\frac{B}{B}\right)^{2\alpha} \hat{V}_{d/o}\left(\frac{B^2}{B},t;K,B,T\right) = \hat{V}_{d/o}(B,t;K,B,T)$$

whilst at expiry time T, we have

$$
\tilde{V}_{d/o}(S_T, T; K, B, T) = \left(\frac{S_T}{B}\right)^{2\alpha} \hat{V}_{d/o}\left(\frac{B^2}{S_T}, T; K, B, T\right)
$$

$$
= \left(\frac{S_T}{B}\right)^{2\alpha} \Psi\left(\frac{B^2}{S_T}\right) \mathbb{1}_{\frac{B^2}{S_T} > B}
$$

where for the reflection part, the payoff is only valid for $\dfrac{B^2}{S_T} > B$ or $S_T < B$.

Therefore, in the range $S_T > B$ for a down-and-out option

$$
\tilde{V}_{d/o}(S_T, T; K, B, T) = \left(\frac{S_T}{B}\right)^{2\alpha} \hat{V}_{d/o}\left(\frac{B^2}{S_T}, T; K, B, T\right) = 0.
$$

Hence, the general solution of a down-and-out barrier option is

$$
V_{d/o}(S_t, t; K, B, T) = \hat{V}_{d/o}(S_t, t; K, B, T) - \left(\frac{S_t}{B}\right)^{2\alpha} \hat{V}_{d/o}\left(\frac{B^2}{S_t}, t; K, B, T\right).
$$

By writing the down-and-in barrier option as $V_{d/i}(S_t, t; K, B, T)$, from the in–out parity

$$
V_{d/o}(S_t, t; K, B, T) + V_{d/i}(S_t, t; K, B, T) = V_{bs}(S_t, t; K, T)
$$

where $V_{bs}(S_t, t; K, T)$ is the Black–Scholes formula for a European option written on asset price S_t with strike K and expiry time T. Thus, the down-and-in barrier option formula is

$$
V_{d/i}(S_t, t; K, B, T) = V_{bs}(S_t, t; K, T) - V_{d/o}(S_t, t; K, B, T)
$$

$$
= V_{bs}(S_t, t; K, T) - \hat{V}_{d/o}(S_t, t; K, B, T)
$$

$$
+ \left(\frac{S_t}{B}\right)^{2\alpha} \hat{V}_{d/o}\left(\frac{B^2}{S_t}, t; K, B, T\right).
$$

$\square$

5. *Up-and-Out/Up-and-In Call Options.* Let $\{W_t : t \geq 0\}$ be a $\mathbb{P}$-standard Wiener process on the probability space $(\Omega, \mathcal{F}, \mathbb{P})$ and let the asset price S_t follow a GBM with the following SDE

$$
\frac{dS_t}{S_t} = (\mu - D)\,dt + \sigma dW_t
$$

where μ is the drift parameter, D is the continuous dividend yield and σ is the volatility parameter. We consider a European up-and-out call option at time t, with expiry at time $T > t$, strike K and constant barrier $B > K$.

By constructing a payoff diagram and using the reflection principle, find the up-and-out call option price.

Furthermore, deduce the up-and-in call option price using the knock-in and knock-out parity relationship.

Solution: For the up-and-out barrier call option we know that the option expires worthless if the barrier B is reached, and since we are dealing with an up-and-out call option, the barrier B must be set above the strike K, i.e. $B > K$, otherwise the payoff will be knock-out (see Figure 4.1).

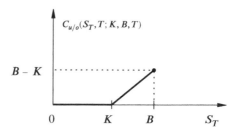

Figure 4.1 Up-and-out call payoff diagram.

The payoff diagram for the up-and-out call option $C_{u/o}(S_T, T; K, B, T)$ can be constructed with the following portfolio

$$\text{Portfolio} = \begin{pmatrix} \text{Long one call} \\ \text{with strike } K \end{pmatrix}$$
$$- \left[\begin{pmatrix} \text{Long one call} \\ \text{with strike } B \end{pmatrix} + \begin{pmatrix} \text{Long one digital call with} \\ \text{strike } B \text{ and payoff } (B - K) \end{pmatrix} \right]$$

which is illustrated in Figure 4.2.

At expiry time T we can therefore write the up-and-out call option price as

$$C_{u/o}\left(S_T, T; K, B, T\right) = C_{bs}\left(S_T, T; K, T\right)$$
$$- \left[C_{bs}\left(S_T, T; B, T\right) + (B - K) C_d\left(S_T, T; B, T\right)\right].$$

By discounting the entire payoff under the risk-neutral measure $\mathbb{Q}$ and using the reflection principle, we can write the solution for the up-and-out call option at time t as

$$C_{u/o}\left(S_t, t; K, B, T\right) = C_{bs}\left(S_t, t; K, T\right)$$
$$- \left[C_{bs}\left(S_t, t; B, T\right) + (B - K) C_d\left(S_t, t; B, T\right)\right]$$
$$- \left(\frac{S_t}{B}\right)^{2\alpha} \left\{ C_{bs}\left(\frac{B^2}{S_t}, t; K, T\right) \right.$$
$$\left. - \left[C_{bs}\left(\frac{B^2}{S_t}, t; B, T\right) + (B - K) C_d\left(\frac{B^2}{S_t}, t; B, T\right)\right] \right\}$$

where $\alpha = \dfrac{1}{2}\left(1 - \dfrac{r - D}{\frac{1}{2}\sigma^2}\right)$.

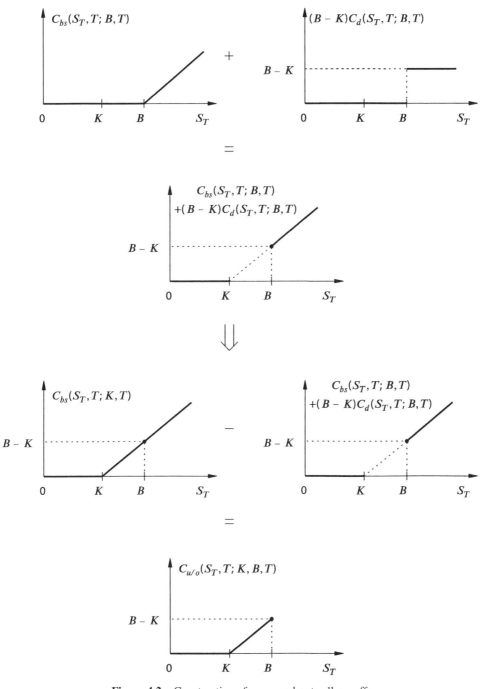

Figure 4.2   Construction of an up-and-out call payoff.

From the knock-in and knock-out parity relationship

$$C_{u/i}\left(S_t, t; K, B, T\right) + C_{u/o}\left(S_t, t; K, B, T\right) = C_{bs}\left(S_t, t; K, T\right)$$

therefore the up-and-in call option price at time t is

$$
\begin{aligned}
C_{u/i}\left(S_t, t; K, B, T\right) &= C_{bs}\left(S_t, t; K, T\right) - C_{u/o}\left(S_t, t; K, B, T\right) \\
&= C_{bs}\left(S_t, t; B, T\right) + (B-K)C_d\left(S_t, t; B, T\right) \\
&\quad + \left(\frac{S_t}{B}\right)^{2\alpha}\left\{ C_{bs}\left(\frac{B^2}{S_t}, t; K, T\right)\right. \\
&\quad \left. - \left[C_{bs}\left(\frac{B^2}{S_t}, t; B, T\right) + (B-K)C_d\left(\frac{B^2}{S_t}, t; B, T\right)\right]\right\}.
\end{aligned}
$$

□

6. *Down-and-Out/Down-and-In Call Options.* Let $\left\{W_t : t \geq 0\right\}$ be a $\mathbb{P}$-standard Wiener process on the probability space $(\Omega, \mathcal{F}, \mathbb{P})$ and let the asset price S_t follow a GBM with the following SDE

$$\frac{dS_t}{S_t} = (\mu - D)\,dt + \sigma dW_t$$

where μ is the drift parameter, D is the continuous dividend yield and σ is the volatility parameter. We consider a European down-and-out call option at time t, with expiry at time $T > t$, strike K and constant barrier B.

By constructing payoff diagrams for $B \leq K$ and $B > K$, and using the reflection principle, find the down-and-out call option prices.

Furthermore, using the knock-in and knock-out parity relationship, deduce the down-and-in call options.

Solution: From the definition of a down-and-out call option price, the payoff diagrams $B < K$ and $B > K$ are given in Figure 4.3.

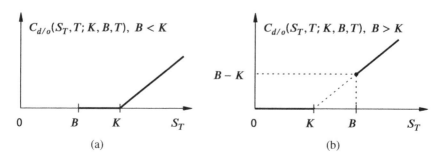

Figure 4.3 Down-and-out call payoff diagram for (a) $B \leq K$ and (b) $B > K$.

For the case when $B \leq K$, at expiry time T the down-and-out call option price is the same as a European call option price

$$C_{d/o}(S_T, T; K, B, T) = C_{bs}\left(S_T, T; K, T\right).$$

By discounting the entire payoff under the risk-neutral measure $\mathbb{Q}$ and using the reflection principle, we can write the solution for the down-and-out call option at time t as

$$C_{d/o}(S_t, t; K, B, T) = C_{bs}\left(S_t, t; K, T\right) - \left(\frac{S_t}{B}\right)^{2\alpha} C_{bs}\left(\frac{B^2}{S_t}, t; K, T\right)$$

where $\alpha = \dfrac{1}{2}\left(1 - \dfrac{r - D}{\frac{1}{2}\sigma^2}\right)$.

For the case when $B > K$, the payoff diagram for the down-and-out call option price $C_{d/o}(S_T, T; K, B, T)$ can be constructed with the following portfolio

$$\text{Portfolio} = \left(\begin{array}{c} \text{Long one call} \\ \text{with strike } B \end{array}\right) + \left(\begin{array}{c} \text{Long one digital call with} \\ \text{strike } B \text{ and payoff } (B - K) \end{array}\right)$$

where Figure 4.4 graphically illustrates the construction of the payoff.

Hence, at expiry time T we can write

$$C_{d/o}\left(S_T, T; K, B, T\right) = C_{bs}\left(S_T, T; B, T\right) + (B - K)C_d\left(S_T, T; B, T\right).$$

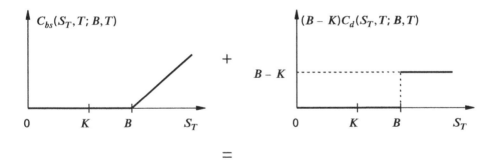

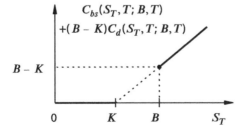

Figure 4.4 Down-and-out call payoff diagram for $B > K$.

By discounting the entire payoff under the risk-neutral measure $\mathbb{Q}$ and using the reflection principle, we can write the solution for the down-and-out call option for $B > K$ as

$$C_{d/o}\left(S_t, t; K, B, T\right) = C_{bs}\left(S_t, t; B, T\right) + (B - K)\,C_d\left(S_t, t; B, T\right) - \left(\frac{S_t}{B}\right)^{2\alpha}$$

$$\times \left[C_{bs}\left(\frac{B^2}{S_t}, t; B, T\right) + (B - K)\,C_d\left(\frac{B^2}{S_t}, t; B, T\right)\right].$$

Hence,

$$C_{d/o}\left(S_t, t; K, B, T\right) = \begin{cases} C_{bs}\left(S_t, t; K, T\right) \\ \quad - \left(\dfrac{S_t}{B}\right)^{2\alpha} C_{bs}\left(\dfrac{B^2}{S_t}, t; K, T\right) & \text{if } B \leq K \\[2em] C_{bs}\left(S_t, t; B, T\right) + (B - K)\,C_d\left(S_t, t; B, T\right) \\ \quad - \left(\dfrac{S_t}{B}\right)^{2\alpha}\left[C_{bs}\left(\dfrac{B^2}{S_t}, t; B, T\right)\right. & \text{if } B > K. \\ \quad \left. + (B - K)\,C_d\left(\dfrac{B^2}{S_t}, t; B, T\right)\right] \end{cases}$$

Since

$$C_{d/i}\left(S_t, t; K, B, T\right) + C_{d/o}\left(S_t, t; K, B, T\right) = C_{bs}\left(S_t, t; K, T\right)$$

therefore

$$C_{d/i}\left(S_t, t; K, B, T\right) = \begin{cases} \left(\dfrac{S_t}{B}\right)^{2\alpha} C_{bs}\left(\dfrac{B^2}{S_t}, t; K, T\right) & \text{if } B \leq K \\[2em] C_{bs}\left(S_t, t; K, T\right) - C_{bs}\left(S_t, t; B, T\right) \\ \quad - (B - K)\,C_d\left(S_t, t; B, T\right) + \left(\dfrac{S_t}{B}\right)^{2\alpha} & \text{if } B > K. \\ \quad \times \left[C_{bs}\left(\dfrac{B^2}{S_t}, t; B, T\right)\right. \\ \quad \left. + (B - K)\,C_d\left(\dfrac{B^2}{S_t}, t; B, T\right)\right] \end{cases}$$

□

7. *Up-and-Out/Up-and-In Put Options.* Let $\left\{W_t : t \geq 0\right\}$ be a $\mathbb{P}$-standard Wiener process on the probability space $(\Omega, \mathcal{F}, \mathbb{P})$ and let the asset price S_t follow a GBM with the following SDE

$$\frac{dS_t}{S_t} = (\mu - D)\,dt + \sigma\,dW_t$$

where μ is the drift parameter, D is the continuous dividend yield and σ is the volatility parameter. We consider a European up-and-out put option at time t, with expiry at time $T > t$, strike K and constant barrier B.

By constructing payoff diagrams for $B < K$ and $B \geq K$, and using the reflection principle, find the up-and-out put option prices.

Furthermore, using the knock-in and knock-out parity relationship, deduce the up-and-in put option price.

Solution: From the definition of an up-and-out put option price, the payoff diagrams for $B \geq K$ and $B < K$ are given in Figure 4.5.

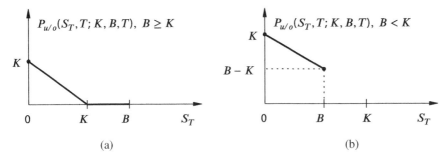

(a)   (b)

Figure 4.5   Up-and-out put payoff diagrams for (a) $B \geq K$ and (b) $B < K$.

For the case when $B \geq K$, at expiry time T the up-and-out put price is the same as a European put option price with strike K and therefore we can simply write

$$P_{u/o}(S_T, T; K, B, T) = P_{bs}\left(S_T, T; K, T\right).$$

By discounting the entire payoff under the risk-neutral measure $\mathbb{Q}$ and using the reflection principle, we can write the solution for the up-and-out put price as

$$P_{u/o}(S_t, t; K, B, T) = P_{bs}\left(S_t, t; K, T\right) - \left(\frac{S}{B}\right)^{2\alpha} P_{bs}\left(\frac{B^2}{S_t}, t; K, T\right)$$

where $\alpha = \dfrac{1}{2}\left(1 - \dfrac{r - D}{\frac{1}{2}\sigma^2}\right)$.

For the case when $B < K$, the payoff diagram for the up-and-out put option price $P_{u/o}(S_T, T; K, B, T)$ can be constructed with the following portfolio

$$\text{Portfolio} = \left(\begin{array}{c}\text{Long one put}\\\text{with strike } B\end{array}\right) + \left(\begin{array}{c}\text{Long one digital put with}\\\text{strike } B \text{ and payoff } (K - B)\end{array}\right)$$

where Figure 4.6 graphically illustrates the construction of the payoff.

Hence, at expiry time T we can write

$$P_{u/o}\left(S_T, T; K, B, T\right) = P_{bs}\left(S_T, T; B, T\right) + (K - B) P_d\left(S_T, T; B, T\right).$$

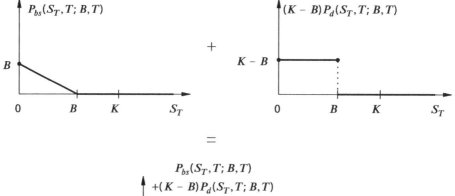

Figure 4.6   Up-and-out put payoff diagram for $B < K$.

By discounting the entire payoff under the risk-neutral measure $\mathbb{Q}$ and using the reflection principle, we can write the solution for the up-and-out put option for $B < K$ as

$$
P_{u/o}\left(S_t, t; K, B, T\right) = P_{bs}\left(S_t, t; B, T\right) + (K - B)\,P_d\left(S_t, t; B, T\right) - \left(\frac{S_t}{B}\right)^{2\alpha}
$$
$$
\times \left[P_{bs}\left(\frac{B^2}{S_t}, t; B, T\right) + (K - B)\,P_d\left(\frac{B^2}{S_t}, t; B, T\right)\right].
$$

Therefore,

$$
P_{u/o}\left(S_t, t; K, B, T\right) =
\begin{cases}
P_{bs}\left(S_t, t; K, T\right) - \left(\dfrac{S}{B}\right)^{2\alpha} P_{bs}\left(\dfrac{B^2}{S_t}, t; K, T\right) & \text{if } B \geq K \\[2em]
\begin{aligned}
&P_{bs}\left(S_t, t; B, T\right) + (K - B)\,P_d\left(S_t, t; B, T\right) \\
&- \left(\dfrac{S_t}{B}\right)^{2\alpha}\left[P_{bs}\left(\dfrac{B^2}{S_t}, t; B, T\right)\right. \\
&\left.+ (K - B)\,P_d\left(\dfrac{B^2}{S_t}, t; B, T\right)\right]
\end{aligned} & \text{if } B < K.
\end{cases}
$$

From the knock-in and knock-out parity relationship

$$
P_{u/i}\left(S_t, t; K, B, T\right) + P_{u/o}\left(S_t, t; K, B, T\right) = P_{bs}\left(S_t, t; K, T\right)
$$

the corresponding up-and-in put option price at time t becomes

$$
P_{u/i}\left(S_t, t; K, B, T\right) =
\begin{cases}
\left(\dfrac{S_t}{B}\right)^{2\alpha} P_{bs}\left(\dfrac{B^2}{S_t}, t; K, T\right) & \text{if } B \geq K \\[4ex]
P_{bs}\left(S_t, t; K, T\right) - P_{bs}\left(S_t, t; B, T\right) \\
- (K - B)\, P_d\left(S_t, t; B, T\right) \\
+ \left(\dfrac{S_t}{B}\right)^{2\alpha}\left[P_{bs}\left(\dfrac{B^2}{S_t}, t; B, T\right)\right. & \text{if } B < K. \\[2ex]
\left. + (K - B)\, P_d\left(\dfrac{B^2}{S_t}, t; B, T\right)\right]
\end{cases}
$$

$\square$

8. *Down-and-Out/Down-and-In Put Options.* Let $\left\{W_t : t \geq 0\right\}$ be a $\mathbb{P}$-standard Wiener process on the probability space $(\Omega, \mathcal{F}, \mathbb{P})$ and let the asset price S_t follow a GBM with the following SDE

$$
\frac{dS_t}{S_t} = (\mu - D)\, dt + \sigma dW_t
$$

where μ is the drift parameter, D is the continuous dividend yield and σ is the volatility parameter. We consider a European down-and-out put option at time t, with expiry at time $T > t$, strike K and constant barrier $B < K$.

By constructing a payoff diagram and using the reflection principle, find the down-and-out put option price.

Furthermore, deduce the down-and-in put option price using the knock-in and knock-out parity relationship.

Solution: For the down-and-out barrier put option we know that the option expires worthless if the barrier B is triggered, and since we are dealing with a down-and-out put option, the barrier B must be set below the strike K, i.e. $B < K$; otherwise the payoff will be knock-out (see Figure 4.7).

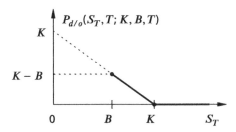

Figure 4.7   Down-and-out put payoff diagram for $B < K$.

The payoff for the down-and-out put option $P_{d/o}(S_T, T; K, B, T)$ can be constructed with the following portfolio

$$
\text{Portfolio} = \begin{pmatrix} \text{Long one put} \\ \text{with strike } K \end{pmatrix}
$$
$$
- \left[\begin{pmatrix} \text{Long one put} \\ \text{with strike } B \end{pmatrix} + \begin{pmatrix} \text{Long one digital put with} \\ \text{strike } B \text{ and payoff } (K - B) \end{pmatrix} \right]
$$

where Figure 4.8 graphically illustrates the construction of the payoff.

At expiry time T we can therefore write

$$
P_{d/o}\left(S_T, T; K, B, T \right) = P_{bs}\left(S_T, T; K, T \right)
$$
$$
- \left[P_{bs}\left(S_T, T; B, T \right) + (K - B)\, P_d\left(S_T, T; B, T \right) \right].
$$

By discounting the entire payoff under the risk-neutral measure $\mathbb{Q}$ and using the reflection principle, we can write the solution for the down-and-out put option as

$$
P_{d/o}\left(S_t, t; K, B, T \right) = P_{bs}\left(S_t, t; K, T \right)
$$
$$
- \left[P_{bs}\left(S_t, t; B, T \right) + (K - B)\, P_d\left(S_t, t; B, T \right) \right]
$$
$$
- \left(\frac{S_t}{B} \right)^{2\alpha} \left\{ P_{bs}\left(\frac{B^2}{S_t}, t; K, T \right) \right.
$$
$$
\left. - \left[P_{bs}\left(\frac{B^2}{S_t}, t; B, T \right) + (K - B)\, P_d\left(\frac{B^2}{S_t}, t; B, T \right) \right] \right\}
$$

where $\alpha = \dfrac{1}{2}\left(1 - \dfrac{r - D}{\frac{1}{2}\sigma^2} \right)$.

From the knock-in and knock-out parity relationship

$$
P_{d/i}\left(S_t, t; K, B, T \right) + P_{d/o}\left(S_t, t; K, B, T \right) = P_{bs}\left(S_t, t; K, T \right)
$$

the corresponding down-and-in put option price at time t is

$$
P_{d/i}\left(S_t, t; K, B, T \right) = P_{bs}\left(S_t, t; K, T \right) - P_{d/o}\left(S_t, t; K, B, T \right)
$$
$$
= P_{bs}\left(S_t, t; B, T \right) + (K - B)P_d\left(S_t, t; B, T \right)
$$
$$
+ \left(\frac{S_t}{B} \right)^{2\alpha} \left\{ P_{bs}\left(\frac{B^2}{S_t}, t; K, T \right) \right.
$$
$$
\left. - \left[P_{bs}\left(\frac{B^2}{S_t}, t; B, T \right) + (K - B)P_d\left(\frac{B^2}{S_t}, t; B, T \right) \right] \right\}.
$$

$\square$

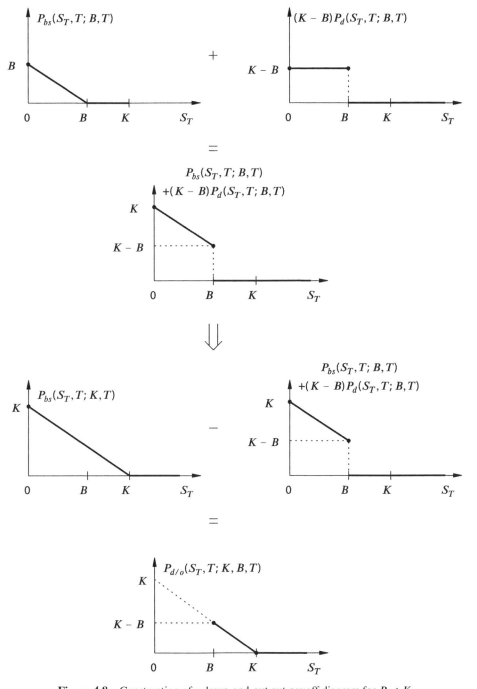

Figure 4.8   Construction of a down-and-out put payoff diagram for $B < K$.

4.2.3   Further Barrier-Style Options

1. *In–Out Parity with Rebate at Expiry.* Assume we are in the Black–Scholes world where at time $t < T$, the asset price S_t follows the SDE

$$dS_t = (\mu - D)S_t dt + \sigma S_t dW_t$$

where μ, D and $\sigma > 0$ are the drift, continuous dividend yield and volatility, respectively, W_t is the standard Wiener process and there is a risk-free asset which earns interest at a constant rate r. Let $V_{bs}(S_t, t; K, T)$ be the price of a European option satisfying the Black–Scholes equation

$$\frac{\partial V_{bs}}{\partial t} + \frac{1}{2}\sigma^2 S_t^2 \frac{\partial^2 V_{bs}}{\partial S_t^2} + (r - D)S_t \frac{\partial V_{bs}}{\partial S_t} - r V_{bs}(S_t, t; K, T) = 0$$

with boundary condition

$$V_{bs}(S_T, T; K, T) = \Psi(S_T)$$

where $\Psi(S_T)$ is the option payoff for a strike price K at expiry time T.

By incorporating a rebate R payable at expiry time T, we define $V_{u/o}^R(S_t, t; K, B, T)$, $V_{d/o}^R(S_t, t; K, B, T)$, $V_{u/i}^R(S_t, t; K, B, T)$ and $V_{d/i}^R(S_t, t; K, B, T)$ as the European up-and-out, down-and-out, up-and-in and down-and-in options, respectively with common barrier B, strike price K, rebate R and expiry time T.

Show by setting up independent portfolios that

$$V_{u/o}^R(S_t, t; K, B, T) + V_{u/i}^R(S_t, t; K, B, T) = V_{bs}(S_t, t; K, T) + R e^{-r(T-t)}$$

and

$$V_{d/o}^R(S_t, t; K, B, T) + V_{d/i}^R(S_t, t; K, B, T) = V_{bs}(S_t, t; K, T) + R e^{-r(T-t)}.$$

Solution: At time $t < T$, we first set up the portfolios $\Pi_u^R(S_t, t)$ and $\Pi_d^R(S_t, t)$ with each having the following options

$$\Pi_u^R(S_t, t) = V_{u/o}^R(S_t, t; K, B, T) + V_{u/i}^R(S_t, t; K, B, T)$$
$$\Pi_d^R(S_t, t) = V_{d/o}^R(S_t, t; K, B, T) + V_{d/i}^R(S_t, t; K, B, T).$$

First consider $\Pi_u^R(S_t, t)$ where at expiry time T, only one of the two barrier options can be active. If barrier B is triggered ($S_T \geq B$), then

$$V_{u/o}^R(S_T, T; K, B, T) = R \text{ and } V_{u/i}^R(S_T, T; K, B, T) = V_{u/i}(S_T, T; K, B, T)$$

where $V_{u/i}(S_T, T; K, B, T)$ is the European up-and-in barrier option payoff without rebate.

However, if the barrier B is not triggered ($S_T < B$), then

$$V_{u/o}^R(S_T, T; K, B, T) = V_{u/o}(S_T, T; K, B, T) \text{ and } V_{u/i}^R(S_T, T; K, B, T) = R$$

where $V_{u/o}(S_T, T; K, B, T)$ is the European up-and-out barrier option payoff without rebate.

In the same vein for $\Pi_d^R(S_t, t; K, B, T)$, at expiry time T if the barrier is triggered ($S_T \leq B$) then

$$V_{d/o}^R(S_T, T; K, B, T) = R \text{ and } V_{d/i}^R(S_T, T; K, B, T) = V_{d/i}(S_T, T; K, B, T)$$

where $V_{d/i}(S_T, T; K, B, T)$ is the European down-and-in barrier option payoff without rebate.

Finally, if B is never triggered ($S_T > B$) then

$$V_{d/o}^R(S_T, T; K, B, T) = V_{d/o}(S_T, T; K, B, T) \text{ and } V_{d/i}^R(S_T, T; K, B, T) = R$$

where $V_{d/o}(S_T, T; K, B, T)$ is the European down-and-out barrier option payoff without rebate.

Hence, at expiry time T we have

$$\begin{aligned}
V_{u/o}^R(S_T, T; K, B, T) + V_{u/i}^R(S_T, T; K, B, T) &= V_{u/o}(S_T, T; K, B, T) \\
&\quad + V_{u/i}(S_T, T; K, B, T) \\
&\quad + R\left[\mathbb{1}_{S_T \geq B} + \mathbb{1}_{S_T < B}\right] \\
&= V_{bs}(S_T, T; K, T) + R
\end{aligned}$$

and

$$\begin{aligned}
V_{d/o}^R(S_T, T; K, B, T) + V_{d/i}^R(S_T, T; K, B, T) &= V_{d/o}(S_T, T; K, B, T) \\
&\quad + V_{d/i}(S_T, T; K, B, T) \\
&\quad + R\left[\mathbb{1}_{S_T \leq B} + \mathbb{1}_{S_T > B}\right] \\
&= V_{bs}(S_T, T; K, T) + R.
\end{aligned}$$

By discounting the terminal payoffs back to time t, we can conclude that

$$V_{u/o}^R(S_t, t; K, B, T) + V_{u/i}^R(S_t, t; K, B, T) = V_{bs}(S_t, t; K, T) + R\, e^{-r(T-t)}$$

and

$$V_{d/o}^R(S_t, t; K, B, T) + V_{d/i}^R(S_t, t; K, B, T) = V_{bs}(S_t, t; K, B, T) + R\, e^{-r(T-t)}.$$

$\square$

2. *Up-and-Out/In with Rebates at Expiry.* Assume we are in the Black–Scholes world where at time $t < T$, the asset price S_t follows the SDE

$$dS_t = (\mu - D)S_t dt + \sigma S_t dW_t$$

where μ, D and $\sigma > 0$ are the drift, continuous dividend yield and volatility, respectively, W_t is the standard Wiener process and there is a risk-free asset which earns interest at a constant rate r.

Let $V_{bs}(S_t, t; K, T)$ be the price of a European option satisfying the Black–Scholes equation

$$\frac{\partial V_{bs}}{\partial t} + \frac{1}{2}\sigma^2 S_t^2 \frac{\partial^2 V_{bs}}{\partial S_t^2} + (r - D)S_t \frac{\partial V_{bs}}{\partial S_t} - rV_{bs}(S_t, t; K, T) = 0$$

with boundary condition

$$V_{bs}(S_T, T; K, T) = \Psi(S_T)$$

where $\Psi(S_T)$ is the option payoff for a strike price K at expiry time T.

By incorporating a rebate R payable at expiry T, we define $V_{u/o}^R(S_t, t; K, B, T)$ and $V_{u/i}^R(S_t, t; K, B, T)$ as the European up-and-out and European out-and-in options, respectively with common barrier B, strike price K, rebate R and expiry time T.

Using the put–call parity for European digital options and the reflection principle, show that the formula for an up-and-out barrier option incorporating a rebate R payable at expiry T is

$$V_{u/o}^R(S_t, t; K, B, T) = V_{u/o}(S_t, t; K, B, T)$$
$$+ R\left[C_d(S_t, t; B, T) + \left(\frac{S_t}{B}\right)^{2\alpha} P_d\left(\frac{B^2}{S_t}, t; B, T\right) \right]$$

where $V_{u/o}(S_t, t; K, B, T)$ is the European up-and-out barrier option without rebate, $\alpha = \frac{1}{2}\left(1 - \frac{r - D}{\frac{1}{2}\sigma^2}\right)$, $C_d(X, t; Y, T)$ and $P_d(X, t; Y, T)$ are the European digital call and put options defined as

$$C_d(X, t; Y, T) = e^{-r(T-t)}\Phi\left(\frac{\log(X/Y) + (r - D - \frac{1}{2}\sigma^2)(T - t)}{\sigma\sqrt{T - t}}\right)$$

and

$$P_d(X, t; Y, T) = e^{-r(T-t)}\Phi\left(\frac{-\log(X/Y) - (r - D - \frac{1}{2}\sigma^2)(T - t)}{\sigma\sqrt{T - t}}\right)$$

respectively.

Finally, deduce the general solution for the up-and-in barrier option price with a rebate R payable at expiry T.

Solution: For the up-and-out case, we can split the option price into two parts

$$V_{u/o}^R(S_t,t;K,B,T) = V_{u/o}(S_t,t;K,B,T) + \overline{V}_{u/o}^R(S_t,t;B,T)$$

where $V_{u/o}(S_t,t;K,B,T)$ is the usual European up-and-out barrier option price which only exists for $S_t < B$, whilst when the asset reaches the barrier (i.e. $S_t = B$) the option $\overline{V}_{u/o}^R(S_t,t;B,T)$ takes the form

$$\overline{V}_{u/o}^R(S_t,t;B,T) = R e^{-r(T-t)}.$$

From the put–call parity for European digital options we have

$$C_d(S_t,t;B,T) + P_d(S_t,t;B,T) = e^{-r(T-t)}$$

such that at expiry T

$$C_d(S_T,T;B,T) = \begin{cases} 0 & \text{if } S_T < B \\ 1 & \text{if } S_T \geq B \end{cases}$$

and

$$P_d(S_T,T;B,T) = \begin{cases} 1 & \text{if } S_T \leq B \\ 0 & \text{if } S_T > B. \end{cases}$$

Note that $P_d(S_t,t;B,T) \neq 0$ for $S_t \leq B$, $t \leq T$ but its reflection does vanish such that at expiry time T

$$\left(\frac{S_T}{B}\right)^{2\alpha} P_d\left(\frac{B^2}{S_T},T;B,T\right) = \left(\frac{S_T}{B}\right)^{2\alpha} \mathbb{1}_{\left\{\frac{B^2}{S_T} \leq B\right\}}$$

$$= \left(\frac{S_T}{B}\right)^{2\alpha} \mathbb{1}_{\{S_T \geq B\}}$$

where for the reflection part the payoff is only valid for $S_T \geq B$.

Since we only consider the range $0 < S_T < B$ for an up-and-out barrier option, we can set

$$\overline{V}_{u/o}^R(S_T,T;B,T) = R\left[C_d(S_T,T;B,T) + \left(\frac{S_T}{B}\right)^{2\alpha} P_d\left(\frac{B^2}{S_T},T;B,T\right)\right].$$

By discounting the entire payoff back to time t using the risk-free interest rate r, we have

$$\overline{V}_{u/o}^R(S_t, t; B, T) = R\left[C_d(S_t, t; B, T) + \left(\frac{S_t}{B}\right)^{2\alpha} P_d\left(\frac{B^2}{S_t}, t; B, T\right)\right]$$

where for $S_t = B$

$$\overline{V}_{u/o}^R(B, t; B, T) = R\left[C_d(B, t; B, T) + P_d(B, t; B, T)\right]$$

$$= R e^{-r(T-t)}.$$

Hence, by adding back the up-and-out barrier option without rebate, the general solution of an up-and-out barrier option with rebate payable at expiry T becomes

$$V_{u/o}^R(S_t, t; K, B, T) = V_{u/o}(S_t, t; K, B, T)$$

$$+ R\left[C_d(S_t, t; B, T) + \left(\frac{S_t}{B}\right)^{2\alpha} P_d\left(\frac{B^2}{S_t}, t; B, T\right)\right].$$

From the in–out parity for barriers with rebates at expiry

$$V_{u/o}^R(S_t, t; K, B, T) + V_{u/i}^R(S_t, t; K, B, T) = V_{bs}(S_t, t; K, T) + R e^{-r(T-t)}$$

where $V_{bs}(S_t, t; K, T)$ is the Black–Scholes formula for a European option written on asset S_t with strike K and expiry time T. Therefore, the up-and-in barrier option price with a rebate R payable at expiry T is

$$V_{u/i}^R(S_t, t; K, B, T) = V_{bs}(S_t, t; K, T) - V_{u/o}(S_t, t; K, B, T)$$

$$+ R\left[e^{-r(T-t)} - C_d(S_t, t; B, T)\right.$$

$$\left. - \left(\frac{S_t}{B}\right)^{2\alpha} P_d\left(\frac{B^2}{S_t}, t; B, T\right)\right].$$

$$\square$$

3. *Down-and-Out/In with Rebates at Expiry.* Assume we are in the Black–Scholes world where at time $t < T$, the asset price S_t follows the SDE

$$dS_t = (\mu - D)S_t dt + \sigma S_t dW_t$$

where μ, D and $\sigma > 0$ are the drift, continuous dividend yield and volatility, respectively, W_t is the standard Wiener process and there is a risk-free asset which earns interest at a constant rate r.

Let $V_{bs}(S_t, t; K, T)$ be the price of a European option satisfying the Black–Scholes equation

$$\frac{\partial V_{bs}}{\partial t} + \frac{1}{2}\sigma^2 S_t^2 \frac{\partial^2 V_{bs}}{\partial S_t^2} + (r - D)S_t \frac{\partial V_{bs}}{\partial S_t} - rV_{bs}(S_t, t; K, T) = 0$$

with

$$V_{bs}(S_T, T; K, T) = \Psi(S_T)$$

where $\Psi(S_T)$ is the option payoff for a strike price K at expiry time T. By incorporating a rebate R payable at expiry T, let $V_{d/o}^R(S_t, t; K, B, T)$ and $V_{d/i}^R(S_t, t; K, B, T)$ be the European up-and-out/in options, respectively with common barrier B, strike price K, rebate R and expiry time T.

Using the put–call parity for European digital options and the reflection principle, show that the formula for an up-and-out barrier option incorporating a rebate R payable at expiry T is

$$V_{d/o}^R(S_t, t; K, B, T) = V_{d/o}(S_t, t; K, B, T)$$

$$+ R\left[\left(\frac{S_t}{B}\right)^{2\alpha} C_d\left(\frac{B^2}{S_t}, t; B, T\right) + P_d(S_t, t; B, T)\right]$$

where $V_{d/o}(S_t, t; K, B, T)$ is the European down-and-out barrier option without rebate, $\alpha = \frac{1}{2}\left(1 - \dfrac{r - D}{\frac{1}{2}\sigma^2}\right)$, $C_d(X, t; Y, T)$ and $P_d(X, t; Y, T)$ are the European digital call and put options defined as

$$C_d(X, t; Y, T) = e^{-r(T-t)}\Phi\left(\frac{\log(X/Y) + (r - D - \frac{1}{2}\sigma^2)(T - t)}{\sigma\sqrt{T - t}}\right)$$

and

$$P_d(X, t; Y, T) = e^{-r(T-t)}\Phi\left(\frac{-\log(X/Y) - (r - D - \frac{1}{2}\sigma^2)(T - t)}{\sigma\sqrt{T - t}}\right)$$

respectively.

Finally, deduce the general solution for the down-and-in barrier option price with a rebate R payable at expiry T.

Solution: For the down-and-out case, we can split the option price into two parts

$$V_{d/o}^R(S_t, t; K, B, T) = V_{d/o}(S_t, t; K, B, T) + \overline{V}_{d/o}^R(S_t, t; B, T)$$

where $V_{d/o}(S_t, t; K, B, T)$ is the usual European up-and-out barrier option price which only exists for $S_t > B$, whilst when $S_t = B$ the option $\overline{V}_{d/o}^R(S_t, t; B, T)$ takes the form

$$\overline{V}_{d/o}^R(S_t, t; B, T) = R\, e^{-r(T-t)}.$$

From the put–call parity for European digital options we have

$$C_d(S_t, t; B, T) + P_d(S_t, t; B, T) = e^{-r(T-t)}$$

such that at expiry T

$$C_d(S_T, T; B, T) = \begin{cases} 0 & \text{if } S_T < B \\ 1 & \text{if } S_T \geq B \end{cases}$$

and

$$P_d(S_T, T; B, T) = \begin{cases} 1 & \text{if } S_T \leq B \\ 0 & \text{if } S_T > B. \end{cases}$$

Note that $C_d(S_t, t; B, T) \neq 0$ for $S_t \geq B$, $t \leq T$ but its reflection is where at expiry time T

$$\left(\frac{S_T}{B}\right)^{2\alpha} C_d\left(\frac{B^2}{S_T}, T; B, T\right) = \left(\frac{S_T}{B}\right)^{2\alpha} \mathbb{1}_{\left\{\frac{B^2}{S_T} \geq B\right\}}$$

$$= \left(\frac{S_T}{B}\right)^{2\alpha} \mathbb{1}_{\{S_T \leq B\}}$$

where for the reflection part the payoff is only valid for $S_T \leq B$.

Since we only consider the range $S_T > B$, for a down-and-out barrier option we can set

$$\overline{V}_{d/o}^R(S_T, T; B, T) = R\left[\left(\frac{S_T}{B}\right)^{2\alpha} C_d\left(\frac{B^2}{S_T}, T; B, T\right) + P_d(S_T, T; B, T)\right].$$

By discounting the entire payoff back to time t using the risk-free interest rate r, we have

$$\overline{V}_{d/o}^R(S_t, t; B, T) = R\left[\left(\frac{S_t}{B}\right)^{2\alpha} C_d\left(\frac{B^2}{S_t}, t; B, T\right) + P_d(S_t, t; B, T)\right]$$

where for $S_t = B$

$$\overline{V}_{d/o}^R(B, t; B, T) = R\left[C_d(B, t; B, T) + P_d(S_t, t; B, T)\right]$$
$$= R\, e^{-r(T-t)}.$$

Hence, by adding back the down-and-out barrier option without rebate, the general solution of a down-and-out barrier option with rebate payable at expiry T becomes

$$V_{d/o}^R(S_t, t; K, B, T) = V_{d/o}(S_t, t; K, B, T)$$

$$+ R\left[\left(\frac{S_t}{B}\right)^{2\alpha} C_d\left(\frac{B^2}{S_t}, t; B, T\right) + P_d(S_t, t; B, T)\right].$$

From the in–out parity for barriers with rebates at expiry

$$V_{d/o}^R(S_t, t; K, B, T) + V_{d/i}^R(S_t, t; K, B, T) = V_{bs}(S_t, t; K, T) + R e^{-r(T-t)}$$

where $V_{bs}(S_t, t; K, T)$ is the Black–Scholes formula for a European option written on asset S_t with strike K and expiry time T. Therefore, the down-and-in barrier option price with a rebate R payable at expiry T is

$$V_{d/i}^R(S_t, t; K, B, T) = V_{bs}(S_t, t; K, T) - V_{d/o}(S_t, t; K, B, T)$$

$$+ R\left[e^{-r(T-t)} - \left(\frac{S_t}{B}\right)^{2\alpha} C_d\left(\frac{B^2}{S_t}, t; B, T\right)\right.$$

$$\left. - P_d(S_t, t; B, T)\right].$$

$\square$

4. *Up-and-Out/In Barrier Options with Immediate Rebates.* Let $\{W_t : t \geq 0\}$ be a $\mathbb{P}$-standard Wiener process on the probability space $(\Omega, \mathscr{F}, \mathbb{P})$ and assume that we are in the Black–Scholes world where at time $t < T$, the asset price S_t follows the SDE

$$dS_t = (\mu - D)S_t dt + \sigma S_t dW_t$$

where μ, D and $\sigma > 0$ are the drift, dividend yield and volatility, respectively, and there is a risk-free asset which earns interest at a constant rate r. Let $V_{bs}(S_t, t; K, T)$ be the price of a European option satisfying the Black–Scholes equation

$$\frac{\partial V}{\partial t} + \frac{1}{2}\sigma^2 S_t^2 \frac{\partial^2 V}{\partial S_t^2} + (r - D)S_t \frac{\partial V}{\partial S_t} - rV(S_t, t; K, T) = 0$$

with

$$V_{bs}(S_T, T; K, T) = \Psi(S_T)$$

where $\Psi(S_T)$ is the option payoff for a strike price K at expiry time T.

By incorporating a rebate R payable at knock-out/knock-in time τ, $t \leq \tau \leq T$, let $V_{u/o}^R(S_t, t; K, B, T)$ and $V_{u/i}^R(S_t, t; K, B, T)$ be the European up-and-out and up-and-in barrier options, respectively with common barrier B, strike price K, rebate R and expiry time T.

By writing

$$V_{u/o}^R(S_t, t; K, B, T) = V_{u/o}(S_t, t; K, B, T) + \tilde{V}_{u/o}^R(S_t, t; B, T)$$

$$V_{u/i}^R(S_t, t; K, B, T) = V_{u/i}(S_t, t; K, B, T) + \tilde{V}_{u/i}^R(S_t, t; B, T)$$

where $V_{u/o}(S_t, t; K, B, T)$ and $V_{u/i}(S_t, t; K, B, T)$ are the European up-and-out and up-and-in barrier option prices without rebates, respectively, whilst $\tilde{V}_{u/o}^R(S_t, t; B, T)$ and $\tilde{V}_{u/i}^R(S_t, t; B, T)$ are the corresponding option prices associated with immediate rebate at knock-out/knock-in time, show that

$$\tilde{V}_{u/o}^R(S_t, t; K, B, T) = R\, C_d^{Am}(S_t, t; B, T)$$

$$\tilde{V}_{u/i}^R(S_t, t; K, B, T) = R\, P_d^{Am}(S_t, t; B, T)$$

where $C_d^{Am}(S_t, t; B, T)$ and $P_d^{Am}(S_t, t; B, T)$ are the immediate-touch call and put options, respectively defined as

$$C_d^{Am}(S_t, t; B, T) = \left(\frac{S_t}{B}\right)^{\lambda_+}\Phi(d_+) + \left(\frac{S_t}{B}\right)^{\lambda_-}\Phi(d_-)$$

and

$$P_d^{Am}(S_t, t; B, T) = \left(\frac{S_t}{B}\right)^{\lambda_+}\Phi(-d_+) + \left(\frac{S_t}{B}\right)^{\lambda_-}\Phi(-d_-)$$

such that

$$\lambda_\pm = \frac{-(r - D - \frac{1}{2}\sigma^2) - \sqrt{(r - D - \frac{1}{2}\sigma^2)^2 + 2\sigma^2 r}}{\sigma^2}$$

$$d_\pm = \frac{\log(S_t/B) \pm (T - t)\sqrt{(r - D - \frac{1}{2}\sigma^2) + 2\sigma^2 r}}{\sigma\sqrt{T - t}}$$

and

$$\Phi(x) = \int_{-\infty}^{x} \frac{1}{\sqrt{2\pi}} e^{-\frac{1}{2}u^2}\, du$$

is the cdf of a standard normal.

Finally, verify that

$$V_{u/o}^R(S_t, t; K, B, T) + V_{u/i}^R(S_t, t; K, B, T) = V_{bs}(S_t, t; K, T)$$

$$+ R\left[\left(\frac{S_t}{B}\right)^{\lambda_+} + \left(\frac{S_t}{B}\right)^{\lambda_-}\right].$$

Solution: At time t we first set up the portfolio $\Pi_u^R(S_t, t)$ having the following options:

$$\Pi_u^R(S_t, t) = V_{u/o}^R(S_t, t; K, B, T) + V_{u/i}^R(S_t, t; K, B, T)$$

where

$$V_{u/o}^R(S_t, t; K, B, T) = V_{u/o}(S_t, t; K, B, T) + \widetilde{V}_{u/o}^R(S_t, t; B, T)$$

$$V_{u/i}^R(S_t, t; K, B, T) = V_{u/i}(S_t, t; K, B, T) + \widetilde{V}_{u/i}^R(S_t, t; B, T).$$

At any time τ, $t \le \tau \le T$, only one of the two barrier options can be active. If barrier B is triggered, that is $\max_{t \le \tau \le T} S_\tau \ge B$ such that $V_{u/o}(S_t, t; K, B, T)$ vanishes, then under the risk-neutral measure $\mathbb{Q}$ the rebate price is

$$
\begin{aligned}
V_{u/o}^R(S_t, t; K, B, T) &= \widetilde{V}_{u/o}^R(S_t, t; B, T) \\
&= R\,\mathbb{E}^{\mathbb{Q}}\left[\left. \max_{t \le \tau \le T} e^{-r(T-\tau)}\, \mathbb{1}_{S_\tau \ge B} \right| \mathcal{F}_t \right] \\
&= R\, C_d^{Am}(S_t, t; B, T).
\end{aligned}
$$

Correspondingly, if $\max_{t \le \tau \le T} S_\tau \ge B$ then the rebate price $\widetilde{V}_{u/i}^R(S_t, t; B, T)$ vanishes so that

$$V_{u/i}^R(S_t, t; K, B, T) = V_{u/i}(S_t, t; K, T).$$

In contrast, if the barrier is not triggered, $\max_{t \le \tau \le T} S_\tau < B$, then under the risk-neutral measure $\mathbb{Q}$

$$V_{u/o}^R(S_t, t; K, B, T) = V_{u/o}(S_t, t; K, B, T)$$

and

$$
\begin{aligned}
V_{u/i}^R(S_t, t; K, B, T) &= \widetilde{V}_{u/i}^R(S_t, t; B, T) \\
&= R\,\mathbb{E}^{\mathbb{Q}}\left[\left. \max_{t \le \tau \le T} e^{-r(T-\tau)}\, \mathbb{1}_{S_\tau < B} \right| \mathcal{F}_t \right] \\
&= R\, P_d^{Am}(S_t, t; B, T).
\end{aligned}
$$

Thus, we can conclude that the European up-and-out/in barrier option prices with immediate rebates are

$$V_{u/o}^R(S_t, t; K, B, T) = V_{u/o}(S_t, t; K, B, T) + R\, C_d^{Am}(S_t, t; B, T)$$

$$V_{u/i}^R(S_t, t; K, B, T) = V_{u/i}(S_t, t; K, B, T) + R\, P_d^{Am}(S_t, t; B, T).$$

Finally, by substituting the values of $C_d^{Am}(S_t, t; B, T)$ and $P_d^{Am}(S_t, t; B, T)$ (see Problems 3.2.3.15 and 3.2.3.16, pages 339–345) and using the identity of standard normal density, we can express

$$V_{u/o}^R(S_t, t; K, B, T) + V_{u/i}^R(S_t, t; K, B, T) = V_{u/o}(S_t, t; K, B, T) + V_{u/i}(S_t, t; K, B, T)$$
$$+ R\left[C_d^{Am}(S_t, t; B, T) + P_d^{Am}(S_t, t; B, T)\right]$$
$$= V_{bs}(S_t, t; K, T)$$
$$+ R\left[\left(\frac{S_t}{B}\right)^{\lambda_+} + \left(\frac{S_t}{B}\right)^{\lambda_-}\right].$$

$\square$

5. *Down-and-Out/In Barrier Options with Immediate Rebates.* Let $\{W_t : t \geq 0\}$ be a $\mathbb{P}$-standard Wiener process on the probability space $(\Omega, \mathscr{F}, \mathbb{P})$ and assume that we are in the Black–Scholes world where at time $t < T$, the asset price S_t follows the SDE

$$dS_t = (\mu - D)S_t dt + \sigma S_t dW_t$$

where μ, D and $\sigma > 0$ are the drift, dividend yield and volatility, respectively, and there is a risk-free asset which earns interest at a constant rate r. Let $V_{bs}(S_t, t; K, T)$ be the price of a European option satisfying the Black–Scholes equation

$$\frac{\partial V}{\partial t} + \frac{1}{2}\sigma^2 S_t^2 \frac{\partial^2 V}{\partial S_t^2} + (r - D)S_t \frac{\partial V}{\partial S_t} - rV(S_t, t; K, T) = 0$$

with

$$V(S_T, T; K, T) = \Psi(S_T)$$

where $\Psi(S_T)$ is the option payoff for a strike price K at expiry time T. When incorporating a rebate R payable at knock-out/knock-in time τ, $t \leq \tau \leq T$, let $V_{d/o}^R(S_t, t; K, B, T)$ and $V_{d/i}^R(S_t, t; K, B, T)$ be the European down-and-out and down-and-in options, respectively with common barrier B, strike price K, rebate R and expiry time T.

By writing

$$V_{d/o}^R(S_t, t; K, B, T) = V_{d/o}(S_t, t; K, B, T) + \widetilde{V}_{d/o}^R(S_t, t; B, T)$$
$$V_{d/i}^R(S_t, t; K, B, T) = V_{d/i}(S_t, t; K, B, T) + \widetilde{V}_{d/i}^R(S_t, t; B, T)$$

where $V_{d/o}(S_t, t; K, B, T)$ and $V_{d/i}(S_t, t; K, B, T)$ are the European down-and-out and down-and-in barrier option prices without rebates, respectively, whilst $\widetilde{V}_{d/o}^R(S_t, t; B, T)$ and $\widetilde{V}_{d/i}^R(S_t, t; B, T)$ are the corresponding option prices associated with immediate rebate at knock-out/knock-in time, show that

$$\widetilde{V}_{d/o}^R(S_t, t; K, B, T) = R\,C_d^{Am}(S_t, t; B, T)$$
$$\widetilde{V}_{d/i}^R(S_t, t; K, B, T) = R\,P_d^{Am}(S_t, t; B, T)$$

where $C_d^{Am}(S_t, t; B, T)$ and $P_d^{Am}(S_t, t; B, T)$ are the immediate-touch call and put options, respectively defined as

$$C_d^{Am}(S_t, t; B, T) = \left(\frac{S_t}{B}\right)^{\lambda_+} \Phi(d_+) + \left(\frac{S_t}{B}\right)^{\lambda_-} \Phi(d_-)$$

and

$$P_d^{Am}(S_t, t; B, T) = \left(\frac{S_t}{B}\right)^{\lambda_+} \Phi(-d_+) + \left(\frac{S_t}{B}\right)^{\lambda_-} \Phi(-d_-)$$

such that

$$\lambda_{\pm} = \frac{-(r - D - \frac{1}{2}\sigma^2) - \sqrt{(r - D - \frac{1}{2}\sigma^2)^2 + 2\sigma^2 r}}{\sigma^2}$$

$$d_{\pm} = \frac{\log(S_t/B) \pm (T - t)\sqrt{(r - D - \frac{1}{2}\sigma^2) + 2\sigma^2 r}}{\sigma\sqrt{T - t}}$$

and

$$\Phi(x) = \int_{-\infty}^{x} \frac{1}{\sqrt{2\pi}} e^{-\frac{1}{2}u^2} du$$

is the cdf of a standard normal.

Finally, verify that

$$V_{d/o}^R(S_t, t; K, B, T) + V_{d/i}^R(S_t, t; K, B, T) = V_{bs}(S_t, t; K, T)$$

$$+ R\left[\left(\frac{S_t}{B}\right)^{\lambda_+} + \left(\frac{S_t}{B}\right)^{\lambda_-}\right].$$

Solution: At time t we first set up the portfolio $\Pi_d^R(S_t, t)$ having the following options

$$\Pi_d^R(S_t, t) = V_{d/o}^R(S_t, t; K, B, T) + V_{d/i}^R(S_t, t; K, B, T)$$

where

$$V_{d/o}^R(S_t, t; K, B, T) = V_{d/o}(S_t, t; K, B, T) + \tilde{V}_{d/o}^R(S_t, t; B, T),$$

$$V_{d/i}^R(S_t, t; K, B, T) = V_{d/i}(S_t, t; K, B, T) + \tilde{V}_{d/i}^R(S_t, t; B, T).$$

At any time τ, $t \leq \tau \leq T$, only one of the two barrier options can be active. If barrier B is triggered that is $\max_{t \leq \tau \leq T} S_\tau \leq B$ such that $V_{d/o}(S_t, t; K, B, T)$ vanishes then under the risk-neutral measure $\mathbb{Q}$ the rebate price is

$$V_{d/o}^R(S_t, t; K, B, T) = \widetilde{V}_{d/o}^R(S_t, t; B, T)$$

$$= R\,\mathbb{E}^\mathbb{Q}\left[\max_{t \leq \tau \leq T} e^{-r(T-\tau)}\, \mathbb{I}_{S_\tau \leq B}\,\middle|\, \mathcal{F}_t\right]$$

$$= R\,P_d^{Am}(S_t, t; B, T).$$

Correspondingly, if $\max_{t \leq \tau \leq T} S_\tau \leq B$ then the rebate price $\widetilde{V}_{d/i}^R(S_t, t; B, T)$ vanishes so that

$$V_{d/i}^R(S_t, t; K, B, T) = V_{d/i}(S_t, t; K, B, T).$$

Conversely if B is never triggered, $\max_{t \leq \tau \leq T} S_\tau > B$ then under the risk-neutral measure $\mathbb{Q}$

$$V_{d/o}^R(S_t, t; K, B, T) = V_{d/o}(S_t, t; K, B, T)$$

and

$$V_{d/i}^R(S_t, t; K, B, T) = \widetilde{V}_{d/i}^R(S_t, t; B, T)$$

$$= R\,\mathbb{E}^\mathbb{Q}\left[\max_{t \leq \tau \leq T} e^{-r(T-\tau)}\, \mathbb{I}_{S_\tau > B}\,\middle|\, \mathcal{F}_t\right]$$

$$= R\,C_d^{Am}(S_t, t; B, T).$$

Thus, we can conclude that the European down-and-out/in barrier option prices with immediate rebates are

$$V_{d/o}^R(S_t, t; K, B, T) = V_{d/o}(S_t, t; K, B, T) + R\,P_d^{Am}(S_t, t; B, T)$$
$$V_{d/i}^R(S_t, t; K, B, T) = V_{d/i}(S_t, t; K, B, T) + R\,C_d^{Am}(S_t, t; B, T).$$

Finally, by subsituting the values of $C_d^{Am}(S_t, t; B, T)$ and $P_d^{Am}(S_t, t; B, T)$ (see Problems 3.2.3.15 and 3.2.3.16, pages 339–345) and using the identity of standard normal density, we can write

$$V_{d/o}^R(S_t, t; K, B, T) + V_{d/i}^R(S_t, t; K, B, T) = V_{d/o}(S_t, t; K, B, T) + V_{d/i}(S_t, t; K, B, T)$$

$$+ R\left[P_d^{Am}(S_t, t; B, T) + C_d^{Am}(S_t, t; B, T)\right]$$

$$= V_{bs}(S_t, t; K, B, T)$$

$$+ R\left[\left(\frac{S_t}{B}\right)^{\lambda_+} + \left(\frac{S_t}{B}\right)^{\lambda_-}\right].$$

$\square$

6. *Reflection Principle Properties for Black–Scholes Equation.* Assume we are in the Black–Scholes world where at time t, the asset price S_t follows the SDE

$$dS_t = (\mu - D)S_t dt + \sigma S_t dW_t$$

where μ, D and $\sigma > 0$ are the drift, dividend yield and volatility, respectively, W_t is the standard Wiener process and there is a risk-free asset which earns interest at a constant rate r. Let $V(S_t, t; K, T)$ be the price of a European option satisfying the Black–Scholes equation

$$\frac{\partial V}{\partial t} + \frac{1}{2}\sigma^2 S_t^2 \frac{\partial^2 V}{\partial S_t^2} + (r - D)S_t \frac{\partial V}{\partial S_t} - rV(S_t, t; K, T) = 0$$

with

$$V(S_T, T; K, T) = \Psi(S_T)$$

where $\Psi(S_T)$ is the option payoff for a strike price K at expiry time T. Show that $S_t e^{-D(T-t)}$ and $Ke^{-r(T-t)}$ satisfy the Black–Scholes equation. Hence, deduce from the reflection principle that for a constant B

$$S_t \left(\frac{S_t}{B}\right)^{-1 - \frac{r-D}{\frac{1}{2}\sigma^2}} e^{-D(T-t)} \text{ and } K\left(\frac{S_t}{B}\right)^{1 - \frac{r-D}{\frac{1}{2}\sigma^2}} e^{-r(T-t)}$$

also satisfy the Black–Scholes equation.

Solution: By setting $V(S_t, t; K, T) = S_t e^{-D(T-t)}$ we have

$$\frac{\partial V}{\partial t} = DS_t e^{-D(T-t)}, \frac{\partial V}{\partial S_t} = e^{-D(T-t)} \text{ and } \frac{\partial^2 V}{\partial S_t^2} = 0$$

and substituting the partial derivatives into the Black–Scholes equation we have

$$\frac{\partial V}{\partial t} + \frac{1}{2}\sigma^2 S_t^2 \frac{\partial^2 V}{\partial S_t^2} + (r - D)S_t \frac{\partial V}{\partial S_t} - rV(S_t, t; K, T)$$

$$= DS_t e^{-D(T-t)} + (r - D)S_t e^{-D(T-t)} - rS_t e^{-D(T-t)}$$

$$= 0.$$

In contrast, by setting $V(S_t, t; K, T) = Ke^{-r(T-t)}$ and taking partial derivatives

$$\frac{\partial V}{\partial t} = rKe^{-r(T-t)}, \frac{\partial V}{\partial S_t} = 0 \text{ and } \frac{\partial^2 V}{\partial S_t^2} = 0$$

and substituting them into the Black–Scholes equation we have

$$\frac{\partial V}{\partial t} + \frac{1}{2}\sigma^2 S_t^2 \frac{\partial^2 V}{\partial S_t^2} + (r - D)S_t \frac{\partial V}{\partial S_t} - rV(S_t, t; K, T) = 0.$$

Therefore, we can conclude that both $S_t e^{-D(T-t)}$ and $Ke^{-r(T-t)}$ satisfy the Black–Scholes equation.

If $V(S_t, t; K, T)$ satisfies the Black–Scholes equation then from the reflection principle for a constant B, $(S_t/B)^{2\alpha} V\left(B^2/S_t, t; K, T\right)$ also satisfies the Black–Scholes equation provided $\alpha = \dfrac{1}{2}\left(1 - \dfrac{r - D}{\frac{1}{2}\sigma^2}\right)$.

Hence, using the reflection principle

$$\left(\frac{S_t}{B}\right)^{2\alpha}\left(\frac{B^2}{S_t}\right)e^{-D(T-t)} = S_t\left(\frac{S_t}{B}\right)^{2(\alpha-1)}e^{-D(T-t)} = S_t\left(\frac{S_t}{B}\right)^{-1-\frac{r-D}{\frac{1}{2}\sigma^2}}e^{-D(T-t)}$$

and

$$\left(\frac{S_t}{B}\right)^{2\alpha}Ke^{-r(T-t)} = K\left(\frac{S_t}{B}\right)^{1-\frac{r-D}{\frac{1}{2}\sigma^2}}e^{-r(T-t)}$$

would yield an additional two solutions to the Black–Scholes equation.

□

7. *Reflection Principle for Black Equation.* Assume we are in the Black–Scholes world where at time t, the asset price S_t follows the SDE

$$dS_t = (\mu - D)S_t dt + \sigma S_t dW_t$$

where μ, D and $\sigma > 0$ are the drift, dividend yield and volatility, respectively, W_t is the standard Wiener process and there is a risk-free asset which earns interest at a constant rate r. Recall that the price of a futures contract at delivery time T on an asset S_t at time t is $F(t, T) = S_t e^{(r-D)(T-t)}$ and for an option with value $V(F(t, T), t; K, \tau)$ on a futures $F(t, T)$ with strike price K, expiry time $\tau < T$ the corresponding Black formula is

$$\frac{\partial V}{\partial t} + \frac{1}{2}\sigma^2 F(t, T)^2 \frac{\partial^2 V}{\partial F^2} - rV(F(t, T), t; K, \tau) = 0.$$

Show that if $V(F(t, T), t; K, \tau)$ is a solution to the above equation, then so is

$$(F(t, T)/B)V\left(B^2/F(t, T), t; K, \tau\right)$$

for any constant B.

Hence, for a constant B, show that the prices of European call $C_{bs}(F(t, T), t; K, \tau)$ and put $P_{bs}(F(t, T), t; K, \tau)$ options on $F(t, T)$ with the same strike K and expiry $\tau < T$ have the following relationships

$$\frac{K}{B}C_{bs}\left(F(t, T), t; \frac{B^2}{K}, \tau\right) = \frac{F(t, T)}{B}P_{bs}\left(\frac{B^2}{F(t, T)}, t; K, \tau\right)$$

and

$$\frac{K}{B}P_{bs}\left(F(t, T), t; \frac{B^2}{K}, \tau\right) = \frac{F(t, T)}{B}C_{bs}\left(\frac{B^2}{F(t, T)}, t; K, \tau\right).$$

Solution: Let $\widehat{F}(t, T) = \dfrac{B^2}{F(t, T)}$ and define

$$\widehat{V}(F(t,T), t; K, \tau) = \frac{F(t,T)}{B} V\left(\widehat{F}(t,T), t; K, \tau\right).$$

By differentiating $\widehat{V}(F(t, T), t; K, \tau)$ with respect to t and $F(t, T)$ we have

$$\frac{\partial \widehat{V}}{\partial t} = \frac{F(t,T)}{B} \frac{\partial V}{\partial t}$$

$$\frac{\partial \widehat{V}}{\partial F} = \frac{V(\widehat{F}(t,T), t)}{B} + \frac{F(t,T)}{B} \frac{\partial V}{\partial \widehat{F}} \frac{\partial \widehat{F}}{\partial F}$$

$$= \frac{V(\widehat{F}(t,T), t)}{B} + \frac{F(t,T)}{B} \frac{\partial V}{\partial \widehat{F}} \left(-\frac{B^2}{F(t,T)^2}\right)$$

$$= \frac{V(\widehat{F}(t,T), t)}{B} - \frac{B}{F(t,T)} \frac{\partial V}{\partial \widehat{F}}$$

and

$$\frac{\partial^2 \widehat{V}}{\partial F^2} = \frac{1}{B} \frac{\partial V}{\partial \widehat{F}} \frac{\partial \widehat{F}}{\partial F} + \frac{B}{F(t,T)^2} \frac{\partial V}{\partial \widehat{F}} - \frac{B}{F(t,T)} \frac{\partial^2 V}{\partial \widehat{F}^2} \frac{\partial \widehat{F}}{\partial F}$$

$$= -\frac{B}{F(t,T)^2} \frac{\partial V}{\partial \widehat{F}} + \frac{B}{F(t,T)^2} \frac{\partial V}{\partial \widehat{F}} + \left(\frac{B}{F(t,T)}\right)^3 \frac{\partial^2 V}{\partial \widehat{F}^2}$$

$$= \left(\frac{B}{F(t,T)}\right)^3 \frac{\partial^2 V}{\partial \widehat{F}^2}.$$

By substituting the above expressions into the Black formula we have

$$\frac{\partial \widehat{V}}{\partial t} + \frac{1}{2}\sigma^2 F(t,T)^2 \frac{\partial^2 \widehat{V}}{\partial F^2} - r\widehat{V}(F(t,T), t; K, \tau)$$

$$= \frac{F(t,T)}{B} \frac{\partial V}{\partial t} + \frac{1}{2}\sigma^2 F(t,T)^2 \left(\frac{B}{F(t,T)}\right)^3 \frac{\partial^2 V}{\partial \widehat{F}^2} - r\frac{F(t,T)}{B} V(\widehat{F}(t,T), t; K, \tau)$$

$$= \frac{F(t,T)}{B} \left[\frac{\partial V}{\partial t} + \frac{1}{2}\sigma^2 F(t,T)^2 \left(\frac{B}{F(t,T)}\right)^2 \frac{\partial^2 V}{\partial \widehat{F}^2} - rV(\widehat{F}(t,T), t; K, \tau)\right]$$

$$= \frac{F(t,T)}{B} \left[\frac{\partial V}{\partial t} + \frac{1}{2}\sigma^2 \widehat{F}(t,T)^2 \frac{\partial^2 V}{\partial \widehat{F}^2} - rV(\widehat{F}(t,T), t; K, \tau)\right]$$

$$= 0$$

since

$$\frac{\partial V}{\partial t} + \frac{1}{2}\sigma^2 \widehat{F}(t,T)^2 \frac{\partial^2 V}{\partial \widehat{F}^2} - rV(\widehat{F}(t,T), t; K, \tau) = 0.$$

Hence, for a constant B, $(F(t,T)/B)V\left(B^2/F(t,T), t; K, \tau\right)$ also satisfies the Black formula.

Finally, to show the relationship between the call and put options on $F(t,T)$ we note that at expiry $\tau < T$

$$C_{bs}(F(\tau,T),\tau;K,\tau) = \max\{F(\tau,T) - K, 0\}$$
$$P_{bs}(F(\tau,T),\tau;K,\tau) = \max\{K - F(\tau,T), 0\}.$$

Thus,

$$
\begin{aligned}
\frac{F(\tau,T)}{B} P_{bs}\left(\frac{B^2}{F(\tau,T)}, \tau; K, \tau\right) &= \frac{F(\tau,T)}{B} \max\left\{K - \frac{B^2}{F(\tau,T)}, 0\right\} \\
&= \frac{F(\tau,T)}{B} \frac{K}{F(\tau,T)} \max\left\{F(\tau,T) - \frac{B^2}{K}, 0\right\} \\
&= \frac{K}{B} \max\left\{F(\tau,T) - \frac{B^2}{K}, 0\right\} \\
&= \frac{K}{B} C_{bs}\left(F(\tau,T), \tau; \frac{B^2}{K}, \tau\right)
\end{aligned}
$$

and similarly

$$
\begin{aligned}
\frac{F(\tau,T)}{B} C_{bs}\left(\frac{B^2}{F(\tau,T)}, \tau; K, \tau\right) &= \frac{F(\tau,T)}{B} \max\left\{\frac{B^2}{F(\tau,T)} - K, 0\right\} \\
&= \frac{F(\tau,T)}{B} \frac{K}{F(\tau,T)} \max\left\{\frac{B^2}{K} - F(\tau,T), 0\right\} \\
&= \frac{K}{B} \max\left\{\frac{B^2}{K} - F(\tau,T), 0\right\} \\
&= \frac{K}{B} P_{bs}\left(F(\tau,T), \tau; \frac{B^2}{K}, \tau\right).
\end{aligned}
$$

Hence, for all $t < \tau$ we can deduce that

$$\frac{K}{B} C_{bs}\left(F(t,T), t; \frac{B^2}{K}, \tau\right) = \frac{F(t,T)}{B} P_{bs}\left(\frac{B^2}{F(t,T)}, t; K, \tau\right)$$

and

$$\frac{K}{B} P_{bs}\left(F(t,T), t; \frac{B^2}{K}, \tau\right) = \frac{F(t,T)}{B} C_{bs}\left(\frac{B^2}{F(t,T)}, t; K, \tau\right).$$

$\square$

8. *Knock-Out and Knock-In Options on Futures.* Let $\{W_t : t \geq 0\}$ be a $\mathbb{P}$-standard Wiener process on the probability space $(\Omega, \mathcal{F}, \mathbb{P})$ and assume we are in the Black–Scholes world where at time t, the asset price S_t follows the SDE

$$dS_t = (\mu - D)S_t dt + \sigma S_t dW_t$$

where μ, D and $\sigma > 0$ are the drift, dividend yield and volatility, respectively, and there is a risk-free asset which earns interest at a constant rate r.

Given that the price of a futures contract at delivery time T on an asset S_t at time t is $F(t,T) = S_t e^{(r-D)(T-t)}$ and under the risk-neutral measure $\mathbb{Q}$, find the European up-and-out/in and down-and-out/in call and put options on futures at time t, expiring at time $\tau \leq T$ with strike price K and barrier B.

Solution: From Girsanov's theorem, under the risk-neutral measure $\mathbb{Q}$, S_t follows

$$\frac{dS_t}{S_t} = (r - D)dt + \sigma dW_t^{\mathbb{Q}}$$

where $W_t^{\mathbb{Q}} = \left(\frac{\mu - r}{\sigma}\right)t + W_t$ is a $\mathbb{Q}$-standard Wiener process. For $T > t$ and given $F(t,T) = S_t e^{(r-D)(T-t)}$, from Taylor's theorem

$$dF(t,T) = \frac{\partial F(t,T)}{\partial t}dt + \frac{\partial F(t,T)}{\partial S_t}dS_t + \frac{1}{2}\frac{\partial^2 F(t,T)}{\partial t^2}(dt)^2 + \cdots$$

and by applying Itō's lemma we have

$$\frac{dF(t,T)}{F(t,T)} = \sigma dW_t^{\mathbb{Q}}.$$

Hence, for $\tau \leq T$ the solution to the above SDE is

$$F(\tau,T) = F(t,T)e^{\sigma \widehat{W}_{\tau-t}}$$

where $\widehat{W}_{\tau-t} = -\frac{1}{2}\sigma(T-t) + W_{\tau-t}^{\mathbb{Q}}$.

By comparing both the SDEs for an asset price S_t and the futures price $F(t,T)$, the equivalent up-and-out/in and down-and-out/in call and put option prices for futures expiring at $\tau \leq T$ can by setting $r - D = 0$ and replacing S_t with $F(t,T)$ so that

$$C_{u/o}(F(t,T),t;K,\tau) = C_{bs}(F(t,T),t;K,\tau)$$
$$- \left[C_{bs}(F(t,T),t;B,\tau) + (B-K)C_d(F(t,T),t;B,\tau)\right]$$
$$- \frac{F(t,T)}{B}\left\{C_{bs}\left(\frac{B^2}{F(t,T)},t;K,\tau\right)\right.$$
$$- \left[C_{bs}\left(\frac{B^2}{F(t,T)},t;B,\tau\right)\right.$$
$$\left.\left. + (B-K)C_d\left(\frac{B^2}{F(t,T)},t;B,\tau,B\right)\right]\right\}$$

$$C_{u/i}(F(t,T),t;K,\tau) = C_{bs}(F(t,T),t;B,\tau) + (B-K)C_d(F(t,T),t;B,\tau)$$
$$+ \frac{F(t,T)}{B}\left\{C_{bs}\left(\frac{B^2}{F(t,T)},t;K,\tau\right)\right.$$
$$- \left[C_{bs}\left(\frac{B^2}{F(t,T)},t;B,\tau\right)\right.$$
$$\left.\left. + (B-K)C_d\left(\frac{B^2}{F(t,T)},t;B,\tau\right)\right]\right\}$$

$$
C_{d/o}\left(F(t,T),t;K,\tau\right) =
\begin{cases}
\begin{aligned}
& C_{bs}\left(F(t,T),t;K,\tau\right) \\
& -\frac{F(t,T)}{B}C_{bs}\left(\frac{B^2}{F(t,T)},t;K,\tau\right) & \text{if } B \le K
\end{aligned} \\[2ex]
\begin{aligned}
& C_{bs}\left(F(t,T),t;\tau,B\right) \\
& +(B-K)C_d\left(F(t,T),t;B,\tau\right) \\
& -\frac{F(t,T)}{B}\left[C_{bs}\left(\frac{B^2}{F(t,T)},t;B,\tau\right)\right. & \text{if } B > K \\
& \left. +(B-K)C_d\left(\frac{B^2}{F(t,T)},t;B,\tau\right)\right]
\end{aligned}
\end{cases}
$$

$$
C_{d/i}\left(F(t,T),t;K,\tau\right) =
\begin{cases}
\begin{aligned}
& \frac{F(t,T)}{B}C_{bs}\left(\frac{B^2}{F(t,T)},t;K,\tau\right) & \text{if } B \le K
\end{aligned} \\[2ex]
\begin{aligned}
& C_{bs}\left(F(t,T),t;K,\tau\right) \\
& -C_{bs}\left(F(t,T),t;B,\tau\right) \\
& -(B-K)C_d\left(F(t,T),t;B,\tau\right) \\
& +\frac{F(t,T)}{B}\left[C_{bs}\left(\frac{B^2}{F(t,T)},t;B,\tau\right)\right. & \text{if } B > K \\
& \left. +(B-K)C_d\left(\frac{B^2}{F(t,T)},t;B,\tau\right)\right]
\end{aligned}
\end{cases}
$$

$$
P_{u/o}\left(F(t,T),t;K,\tau\right) =
\begin{cases}
\begin{aligned}
& P_{bs}\left(F(t,T),t;K,\tau\right) \\
& -\frac{F(t,T)}{B}P_{bs}\left(\frac{B^2}{F(t,T)},t;K,\tau\right) & \text{if } B \ge K
\end{aligned} \\[2ex]
\begin{aligned}
& P_{bs}\left(F(t,T),t;B,\tau\right) \\
& +(K-B)P_d\left(F(t,T),t;B,\tau\right) \\
& -\frac{F(t,T)}{B}\left[P_{bs}\left(\frac{B^2}{F(t,T)},t;B,\tau\right)\right. & \text{if } B < K \\
& \left. +(K-B)P_d\left(\frac{B^2}{F(t,T)},t;B,\tau\right)\right]
\end{aligned}
\end{cases}
$$

$$
P_{u/i}\left(F(t,T),t;K,\tau\right) =
\begin{cases}
\begin{aligned}
& \frac{F(t,T)}{B}P_{bs}\left(\frac{B^2}{F(t,T)},t;K,\tau\right) & \text{if } B \ge K
\end{aligned} \\[2ex]
\begin{aligned}
& \frac{F(t,T)}{B}\left[P_{bs}\left(\frac{B^2}{F(t,T)},t;B,\tau\right)\right. \\
& \left. +(K-B)P_d\left(\frac{B^2}{F(t,T)},t;B,\tau\right)\right] & \text{if } B < K \\
& -(K-B)P_d\left(F(t,T),t;B,\tau\right)
\end{aligned}
\end{cases}
$$

$$P_{d/o}(F(t,T),t;K,\tau) = P_{bs}(F(t,T),t;K,\tau)$$
$$- \left[P_{bs}(F(t,T),t;B,\tau) + (K-B)P_d(F(t,T),t;B,\tau) \right]$$
$$- \frac{F(t,T)}{B} \left\{ P_{bs}\left(\frac{B^2}{F(t,T)},t;K,\tau\right) \right.$$
$$- \left[P_{bs}\left(\frac{B^2}{F(t,T)},t;B,\tau\right) \right.$$
$$\left. \left. + (K-B)P_d\left(\frac{B^2}{F(t,T)},t;B,\tau\right) \right] \right\}$$

$$P_{d/i}(F(t,T),t;K,\tau) = P_{bs}(F(t,T),t;B,\tau) + (K-B)P_d(F(t,T),t;B,\tau)$$
$$+ \frac{F(t,T)}{B} \left\{ P_{bs}\left(\frac{B^2}{F(t,T)},t;K,\tau\right) \right.$$
$$- \left[P_{bs}\left(\frac{B^2}{F(t,T)},t;B,\tau\right) \right.$$
$$\left. \left. + (K-B)C_d\left(\frac{B^2}{F(t,T)},t;B,\tau\right) \right] \right\}$$

where $C_{bs}(X,t;Y,\tau)$ and $C_d(X,t;Y,\tau)$ are the vanilla and digital call options on futures defined as

$$C_{bs}(X,t;Y,\tau) = e^{-r(T-t)} \left[X\Phi\left(\frac{\log(X/Y) + \frac{1}{2}\sigma^2(\tau-t)}{\sigma(\tau-t)}\right) \right.$$
$$\left. -Y\Phi\left(\frac{\log(X/Y) - \frac{1}{2}\sigma^2(\tau-t)}{\sigma(\tau-t)}\right) \right]$$

and

$$C_d(X,t;Y,\tau) = e^{-r(T-t)}\Phi\left(\frac{\log(X/Y) - \frac{1}{2}\sigma^2(\tau-t)}{\sigma(\tau-t)}\right)$$

and $P_{bs}(X,t;Y,\tau)$ and $P_d(X,t;Y,\tau)$ are the vanilla and digital put options on futures defined as

$$P_{bs}(X,t;Y,\tau) = e^{-r(T-t)} \left[Y\Phi\left(\frac{-\log(X/Y) + \frac{1}{2}\sigma^2(\tau-t)}{\sigma(\tau-t)}\right) \right.$$
$$\left. -X\Phi\left(\frac{-\log(X/Y) - \frac{1}{2}\sigma^2(\tau-t)}{\sigma(\tau-t)}\right) \right]$$

and

$$P_d(X,t;Y,\tau) = e^{-r(T-t)}\Phi\left(\frac{-\log(X/Y) + \frac{1}{2}\sigma^2(\tau-t)}{\sigma(\tau-t)}\right)$$

respectively. Note that $\Phi(x) = \int_{-\infty}^{x} \frac{1}{\sqrt{2\pi}}e^{-\frac{1}{2}u^2}\,du$ is the cdf of a standard normal.

□

9. *Knock-Out Equity Accumulator.* Assume we are in the Black–Scholes world where at time t, the asset price S_t follows the SDE

$$dS_t = (\mu - D)S_t dt + \sigma S_t dW_t$$

where μ, D and $\sigma > 0$ are the drift, dividend yield and volatility, respectively, W_t is the $\mathbb{P}$-standard Wiener process on the probability space $(\Omega, \mathcal{F}, \mathbb{P})$ and there is a risk-free asset which earns interest at a constant rate r.

An accumulator is a product that accumulates a specific asset at a fixed strike price K every day until the contract expires at time T or the asset price rises above a preset barrier level B. Here, K is set below the asset price S_t at initial time $t < T$ and $K < S_t < B$. By denoting N as the number of days between t and T, show that under the risk-neutral measure $\mathbb{Q}$ the present value of this product at time t is

$$V(S_t,t;K,B,T) = \sum_{i=1}^{N}\left[C_{u/o}(S_t,t;K,B,t_i) - P_{u/o}(S_t,t;K,B,t_i)\right]$$

where $t_i = t + \left(\frac{i-1}{N-1}\right)(T-t)$, $i = 1, 2, \ldots, N$, $C_{u/o}(S_t,t;K,B,t_i)$ and $P_{u/o}(S_t,t;K,B,t_i)$ are the up-and-out European call and put options evaluated at time t with common strike K, barrier B and expiry time t_i, respectively.

Solution: From the definition of the equity accumulator, the payoff on date t_i is a futures contract with a knock-out barrier B where it can be decomposed into a long up-and-out European call option and a short up-and-out European put option (see Figure 4.9) for the construction of the accumulator payoff.

By denoting $\Psi(S_{t_i})$ as the payoff on date t_i, $i = 1, 2, \ldots, N$ we can write

$$\Psi(S_{t_i}) = \max\left\{S_{t_i} - K, 0\right\}\mathbb{1}_{\{\max_{t \le u \le t_i} S_u < B\}}$$
$$- \max\left\{K - S_{t_i}, 0\right\}\mathbb{1}_{\{\max_{t \le u \le t_i} S_u < B\}}$$

and the total accumulated payoff is therefore

$$\Psi(S_{t_1}, S_{t_2}, \ldots, S_{t_n}) = \sum_{i=1}^{N}\Psi(S_{t_i}).$$

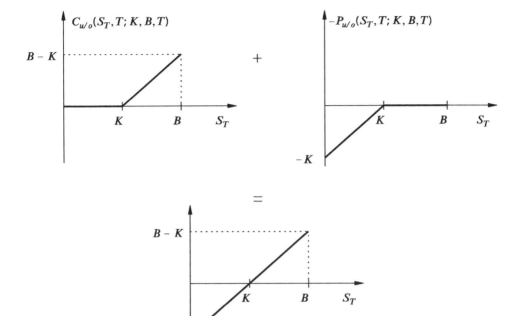

Figure 4.9   Accumulator payoff diagram.

From the risk-neutral measure $\mathbb{Q}$, the value of the accumulator contract at time t is

$$V(S_t, t; K, B, T) = \sum_{i=1}^{N} e^{-r(t_i - t)} \mathbb{E}^{\mathbb{Q}} \left[\Psi(S_{t_i}) \middle| \mathscr{F}_t \right]$$

$$= \sum_{i=1}^{N} e^{-r(t_i - t)} \mathbb{E}^{\mathbb{Q}} \left[\max\left\{ S_{t_i} - K, 0 \right\} \mathbb{1}_{\{ \max_{t \leq u \leq t_i} S_u < B \}} \middle| \mathscr{F}_t \right]$$

$$- \sum_{i=1}^{N} e^{-r(t_i - t)} \mathbb{E}^{\mathbb{Q}} \left[\max\left\{ K - S_{t_i}, 0 \right\} \mathbb{1}_{\{ \max_{t \leq u \leq t_i} S_u < B \}} \middle| \mathscr{F}_t \right]$$

$$= \sum_{i=1}^{N} \left[C_{u/o}(S_t, t; K, B, t_i) - P_{u/o}(S_t, t; K, B, t_i) \right].$$

□

10. *Merton Model for Default of a Company II.* At time t, we assume that the asset A_t of a company satisfies the SDE

$$\frac{dA_t}{A_t} = \mu dt + \sigma dW_t$$

where μ is the drift parameter, $\sigma > 0$ is the volatility and $\{W_t : t \geq 0\}$ is a standard Wiener process on the probability space $(\Omega, \mathcal{F}, \mathbb{P})$. The risk-free interest rate is denoted by r. In financial accounting, the asset A_t is a combination of equity E_t and debt D_t so that

$$A_t = E_t + D_t$$

where, if at any time $t \leq T$, the company will be in default if $A_t < F$ where $F > 0$ is the face value and the debt holders will receive A_t whilst the equity holders will receive nothing. In contrast, if the company is not in default by time $t \leq T$, the debt holders will receive F and the equity holders will receive the rest of the value of the company.

By constructing the payoff diagrams for E_T and D_T, and using the reflection principle, find the values of E_t and D_t for all $t \leq T$ under the Black–Scholes framework.

Solution: Following Problem 2.2.2.30 (page 158) at terminal time T, the payoff diagram for equity shareholders is given in Figure 4.10.

Because the company can default at any time $t \leq T$, we can write E_T as

$$E_T = \max\{A_T - F, 0\} \, \mathbb{1}_{\{\min_{t \leq u \leq T} A_u > F\}}$$

which is a down-and-out European call option on the assets with strike and barrier equal to the face value.

By discounting the entire payoff under the risk-neutral measure $\mathbb{Q}$ and using the reflection principle, we can write E_t as

$$E_t = C(A_t, t; F, T) - \left(\frac{A_t}{F}\right)^{2\alpha} C\left(\frac{F^2}{A_t}, t; F, T\right)$$

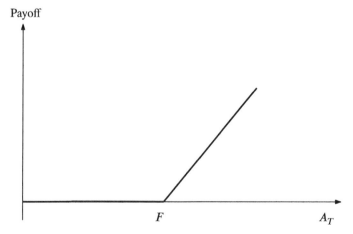

Figure 4.10   Payment to equity holders at time T.

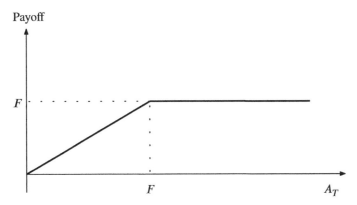

Figure 4.11   Payment to debt holders at time T.

where $\alpha = \dfrac{1}{2}\left(1 - \dfrac{r}{\frac{1}{2}\sigma^2}\right)$, r is the risk-free interest rate,

$$C(X,t;Y,T) = X\Phi\left(\frac{\log(X/Y) + (r + \frac{1}{2}\sigma^2)(T-t)}{\sigma\sqrt{T-t}}\right)$$
$$-Ye^{-r(T-t)}\Phi\left(\frac{\log(X/Y) + (r - \frac{1}{2}\sigma^2)(T-t)}{\sigma\sqrt{T-t}}\right)$$

and $\Phi(x) = \displaystyle\int_{-\infty}^{x} \frac{1}{\sqrt{2\pi}}e^{-\frac{1}{2}u^2}\,du$ is the cdf of a standard normal.

As for payment to the debt holders, the payoff diagram at time T is given in Figure 4.11. Given that the debt at terminal time T is

$$D_T = A_T - E_T$$

by discounting the payoff under the risk-neutral measure $\mathbb{Q}$ and from the results of the equity holders at time t

$$D_t = A_t - E_t$$
$$= A_t - C(A_t,t;F,T) + \left(\frac{A_t}{F}\right)^{2\alpha} C\left(\frac{F^2}{A_t},t;F,T\right).$$

$\square$

11. Consider a binomial tree model for an underlying asset process $\{S_n : 0 \leq n \leq 3\}$ following the Cox–Ross–Rubinstein model. With the initial asset price $S_0 = 100$, let

$$S_{n+1} = \begin{cases} uS_n & \text{with probability } \pi \\ \\ dS_n & \text{with probability } 1 - \pi \end{cases}$$

where $u = e^{\sigma\sqrt{\Delta t}}$ and $d = 1/u$, with σ the volatility and Δt the binomial time step. Assuming the risk-free interest rate $r = 3\%$, continuous dividend yield $D = 1\%$ and volatility $\sigma = 4\%$, find the price of a European-style up-and-out barrier call option at time $t = 0$ with strike $K = 95$, barrier $B = 102$ with expiry time $T = 1$ year in a 3-period binomial tree model.

Solution: Given $S_0 = 100$, $K = 95$, $r = 0.03$, $D = 0.01$, $\sigma = 0.04$ and time step $\Delta t = \frac{1}{3}$, we have

$$u = e^{\sigma\sqrt{\Delta t}} = e^{\frac{0.04}{\sqrt{3}}} = 1.0233$$

and

$$d = e^{-\sigma\sqrt{\Delta t}} = \frac{1}{u} = \frac{1}{1.0233} = 0.9772.$$

Therefore, the risk-neutral probabilities are

$$\pi = \frac{e^{(r-D)\Delta t} - d}{u - d} = 0.6390$$

and

$$1 - \pi = 1 - 0.6390 = 0.3610.$$

The binomial tree in Figure 4.12 shows the price movement of S_0 in a 3-period binomial model.

By setting

$$S_i^{(j)} = u^j d^{i-j} S_0, \quad i = 0, 1, \ldots, n, \quad j = 0, 1, \ldots, i$$

the up-and-out call option price at each of the lattice points is

$$V_i^{(j)} = \begin{cases} e^{-r\Delta t} \left[\pi V_{i+1}^{(j+1)} + (1 - \pi)V_{i+1}^{(j)} \right] & \text{if } S_i^{(j)} < B \\ \\ 0 & \text{if } S_i^{(j)} \geq B \end{cases}$$

where $i = 0, 1, \ldots, n$ and $j = 0, 1, \ldots, i$.

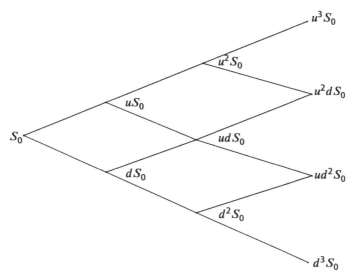

Figure 4.12   A 3-period binomial tree model.

At terminal node $i = n$

$$V_n^{(j)} = \Psi(S_n^{(j)}) = \begin{cases} \max\left\{ S_n^{(j)} - K, 0 \right\} & \text{if } S_n^{(j)} < B \\ \\ 0 & \text{if } S_n^{(j)} \geq B. \end{cases}$$

At time period $n = 3$ (i.e., option expiry time $T = 1$ year)

$$V_3^{(0)} = \Psi(S_3^{(0)})$$

$$= \begin{cases} \max\left\{ d^3 S_0 - K, 0 \right\} & \text{if } d^3 S_0 < B \\ \\ 0 & \text{if } d^3 S_0 \geq B \end{cases}$$

$$= \max\{0.9772^3 \times 100 - 95, 0\}$$

$$= 0$$

$$V_3^{(1)} = \Psi(S_3^{(1)})$$

$$= \begin{cases} \max\left\{ ud^2 S_0 - K, 0 \right\} & \text{if } ud^2 S_0 < B \\ \\ 0 & \text{if } ud^2 S_0 \geq B \end{cases}$$

$$= \max\{1.0233 \times 0.9772^2 \times 100 - 95, 0\}$$

$$= 0.27169$$

$$V_3^{(2)} = \Psi(S_3^{(2)})$$

$$= \begin{cases} \max\left\{u^2 d\, S_0 - K, 0\right\} & \text{if } u^2 d\, S_0 < B \\ 0 & \text{if } u^2 d\, S_0 \geq B \end{cases}$$

$$= 0$$

$$V_3^{(3)} = \Psi(S_3^{(3)})$$

$$= \begin{cases} \max\left\{u^3 S_0 - K, 0\right\} & \text{if } u^3 S_0 < B \\ 0 & \text{if } u^3 S_0 \geq B \end{cases}$$

$$= 0.$$

At time period $n = 2$

$$V_2^{(0)} = \begin{cases} e^{-r\Delta t}\left[\pi V_3^{(1)} + (1-\pi)V_3^{(0)}\right] & \text{if } d^2 S_0 < B \\ 0 & \text{if } d^2 S_0 \geq B \end{cases}$$

$$= e^{-\frac{0.03}{3}}[0.6390 \times 2.7169 + 0.3610 \times 0]$$

$$= 1.7188$$

$$V_2^{(1)} = \begin{cases} e^{-r\Delta t}\left[\pi V_3^{(2)} + (1-\pi)V_3^{(1)}\right] & \text{if } ud\, S_0 < B \\ 0 & \text{if } ud\, S_0 \geq B \end{cases}$$

$$= e^{-\frac{0.03}{3}}[0.6390 \times 0 + 0.3610 \times 2.7169]$$

$$= 0.9710$$

$$V_2^{(2)} = \begin{cases} e^{-r\Delta t}\left[\pi V_3^{(1)} + (1-\pi)V_3^{(0)}\right] & \text{if } u^2 S_0 < B \\ 0 & \text{if } u^2 S_0 \geq B \end{cases}$$

$$= 0.$$

At time period $n = 1$

$$V_1^{(0)} = \begin{cases} e^{-r\Delta t}\left[\pi V_2^{(1)} + (1-\pi)V_2^{(0)}\right] & \text{if } d\, S_0 < B \\ 0 & \text{if } d\, S_0 \geq B \end{cases}$$

$$= e^{-\frac{0.03}{3}}[0.6390 \times 0.9710 + 0.3610 \times 1.7188]$$

$$= 1.2286$$

$$V_1^{(1)} = \begin{cases} e^{-r\Delta t} \left[\pi V_2^{(2)} + (1-\pi)V_2^{(1)} \right] & \text{if } uS_0 < B \\ 0 & \text{if } uS_0 \geq B \end{cases}$$

$$= 0.$$

Finally, at time period $n = 0$

$$V_0^{(0)} = \begin{cases} e^{-r\Delta t} \left[\pi V_1^{(1)} + (1-\pi)V_1^{(0)} \right] & \text{if } S_0 < B \\ 0 & \text{if } S_0 \geq B \end{cases}$$

$$= e^{-\frac{0.03}{3}} [0.6390 \times 0 + 0.3610 \times 1.2286]$$

$$= 0.4391.$$

Therefore, the price of the up-and-out call option based on a 3-period binomial model is $V_0^{(0)} = 0.4391$.

□

12. Table 4.1 shows the up-and-in call option $C_{u/i}(S_t, t; K, B, T)$ prices on an asset $S_t = \$30$, strike $K = \$35$, time to expiry $T - t = 9$ months for various barrier values B.

Table 4.1 European call up-and-in prices for different barriers.

B	$C_{u/i}(S_t, t; K, B, T)$
0	1.76119
10	1.76100
20	1.76076
30	1.76061
40	1.66433
50	0.75711
60	0.19322

By considering the following payoff

$$\Psi(S_T) = \begin{cases} 3\max\{S_T - K, 0\} & \text{if } 0 \leq S_T < 40 \\ 2\max\{S_T - K, 0\} & \text{if } 40 \leq S_T < 60 \\ 0 & \text{if } S_T \geq 60 \end{cases}$$

calculate the price of this 9-month 35-strike European "partial barrier" option.

Solution: By setting $B_1 = 40$ and $B_2 = 60$, the payoff $\Psi(S_T)$ can be constructed by adding two payoffs $\Psi_1(S_T) = 3\max\{S_T - K, 0\} \, \mathbb{1}_{0 \leq S_T < B_1}$ and $\Psi_2(S_T) = 2\max\{S_T - K, 0\} \, \mathbb{1}_{B_1 \leq S_T < B_2}$ (see Figure 4.13).

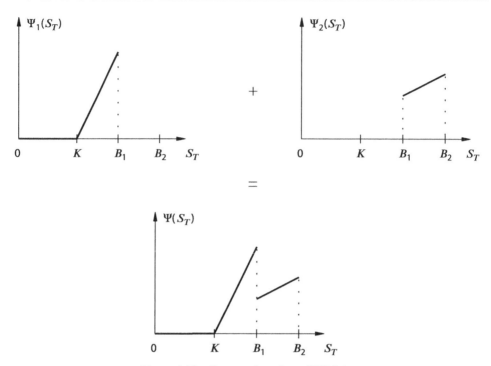

Figure 4.13 Construction of payoff $\Psi(S_T)$.

For payoff $\Psi_1(S_T)$ it is essentially a multiple of an up-and-out call option $C_{u/o}(S_T, T; K, B_1, T)$ such that

$$\Psi_1(S_T) = 3C_{u/o}(S_T, T; K, B_1, T)$$
$$= 3\left[C(S_T, T; K, T) - C_{u/i}(S_T, T; K, B_1, T)\right]$$

where $C(S_T, T; K, T)$ is the European call option payoff with strike K.

In contrast, for payoff $\Psi_2(S_T)$ it can be constructed as in Figure 4.14.

This is a difference between two multiples of up-and-in call options

$$\Psi_2(S_T) = 2\left[C_{u/i}(S_T, T; K, B_1, T) - C_{u/i}(S_T, T; K, B_2, T)\right].$$

Collectively we can express $\Psi(S_T)$ as

$$\Psi(S_T) = \Psi_1(S_T) + \Psi_2(S_T)$$
$$= 3\left[C(S_T, T; K, T) - C_{u/i}(S_T, T; K, B_1, T)\right]$$
$$+ 2\left[C_{u/i}(S_T, T; K, B_1, T) - C_{u/i}(S_T, T; K, B_2, T)\right]$$
$$= 3C(S_T, T; K, T) - C_{u/i}(S_T, T; K, B_1, T) - 2C_{u/i}(S_T, T; K, B_2, T)$$

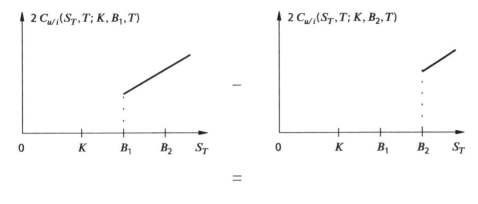

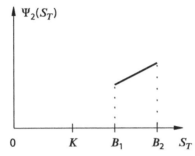

Figure 4.14 Construction of payoff $\Psi_2(S_T)$.

and by discounting the payoff back to time t, the option price is

$$V(S_t, t; K, B_1, B_2, T) = 3C(S_t, t; K, T) - C_{u/i}(S_t, t; K, B_1, T)$$
$$-2C_{u/i}(S_t, t; K, B_2, T)$$
$$= 3 \times 1.76110 - 1.66433 - 2 \times 0.19322$$
$$= \$3.23253$$

since $C(S_t, t; K, T) = C_{u/i}(S_t, t; K, 0, T)$ for barrier $B = 0$.

□

5

Asian Options

In this chapter we look at the pricing of Asian options or average options, which are another popular variant of exotic options. However, unlike barrier options which are weakly path-dependent, Asian options are truly path-dependent options as their payoffs depend on the history of the underlying asset price during its contract period. In the simplest terms, Asian options have payoffs that depend on the average price of the underlying asset over a predetermined period of time as opposed to the options' expiry time. Given that the average of an underlying asset price is less volatile than the asset path, Asian options can be cheaper than their equivalent European or American options.

5.1 INTRODUCTION

In general, an Asian option is an option whose payoff depends on the average of the asset price over some prespecified period of time and observation frequency during the option contract time. For an investor, buying Asian options provides a cost-efficient way of hedging cash or asset flows over extended periods of time as the averaging features make the payoff less susceptible to large asset price movements, including attempts to manipulate the price just before expiry.

There are two kinds of averaging techniques used in Asian options

- arithmetic
- geometric

where the average can be measured discretely or continuously, weighted or unweighted. The majority of Asian options trading in the OTC exchange are mainly arithmetic average prices with European-style payoffs. However, no closed-form solution exists for these options due to the fact that the arithmetic average is not lognormally distributed even when all the individual asset prices follow a lognormal process. As such, the option prices often rely on numerical techniques or approximation methods. In contrast, although being less common in practice, geometric averaging with a European-style payoff has a closed-form solution since geometric averages are also lognormally distributed when all the individual prices follow a lognormal process.

In the discretely sampled arithmetic average case, it is defined as

$$A_n(\tau, T) = \frac{1}{n} \sum_{i=1}^{n} S_{t_i}$$

whilst the discretely sampled geometric average is defined as

$$G_n(\tau, T) = \prod_{i=1}^{n} \left(S_{t_i} \right)^{\frac{1}{n}}$$

where $\tau \le t_1 < t_2 < \cdots < t_{n-1} < t_n \le T$ are the sampling dates over the time period $[\tau, T]$ and S_{t_i}, $i = 1, 2, \ldots, n$ is the asset price at time t_i.

For the continuously sampled arithmetic average, it is defined as

$$A(\tau, T) = \frac{1}{T - \tau} \int_\tau^T S_u \, du$$

and the corresponding continuous geometric average is defined as

$$G(\tau, T) = e^{\frac{1}{T-\tau} \int_\tau^T S_u \, du}$$

where the asset price S_u, $u \in [\tau, T]$ is continuously monitored over the time period $[\tau, T]$.

Within the family of Asian option payoffs, we can group them into average rate (fixed strike) and average strike (floating strike) options payoffs.

Average Rate (Fixed Strike) Option Payoff

For a fixed strike or exercise price K, the average rate (fixed strike) Asian payoff can be subdivided into the following:

- For discretely sampled arithmetic average

$$\Psi(S_T, A_n(\tau, T)) = \begin{cases} \max\left\{ \dfrac{1}{n} \displaystyle\sum_{i=1}^n S_{t_i} - K, 0 \right\} & \text{for call option} \\[4mm] \max\left\{ K - \dfrac{1}{n} \displaystyle\sum_{i=1}^n S_{t_i}, 0 \right\} & \text{for put option.} \end{cases}$$

- For discretely sampled geometric average

$$\Psi(S_T, G_n(\tau, T)) = \begin{cases} \max\left\{ \displaystyle\prod_{i=1}^n \left(S_{t_i} \right)^{\frac{1}{n}} - K, 0 \right\} & \text{for call option} \\[4mm] \max\left\{ K - \displaystyle\prod_{i=1}^n \left(S_{t_i} \right)^{\frac{1}{n}}, 0 \right\} & \text{for put option.} \end{cases}$$

- For continuously sampled arithmetic average

$$\Psi(S_T, A(\tau, T)) = \begin{cases} \max\left\{ \dfrac{1}{T - \tau} \displaystyle\int_\tau^T S_u \, du - K, 0 \right\} & \text{for call option} \\[4mm] \max\left\{ K - \dfrac{1}{T - \tau} \displaystyle\int_\tau^T S_u \, du, 0 \right\} & \text{for put option.} \end{cases}$$

- For continuously sampled geometric average

$$\Psi(S_T, G(\tau, T)) = \begin{cases} \max\left\{ e^{\frac{1}{T-\tau} \int_\tau^T S_u\, du} - K, 0 \right\} & \text{for call option} \\[2mm] \max\left\{ K - e^{\frac{1}{T-\tau} \int_\tau^T S_u\, du}, 0 \right\} & \text{for put option.} \end{cases}$$

Average Strike (Floating Strike) Option Payoff

With S_T being the asset price at the option expiry time T, the average strike (floating strike) Asian payoff can be subdivided into the following:

- For discretely sampled arithmetic average

$$\Psi(S_T, A_n(\tau, T)) = \begin{cases} \max\left\{ S_T - \frac{1}{n}\sum_{i=1}^n S_{t_i}, 0 \right\} & \text{for call option} \\[3mm] \max\left\{ \frac{1}{n}\sum_{i=1}^n S_{t_i} - S_T, 0 \right\} & \text{for put option.} \end{cases}$$

- For discretely sampled geometric average

$$\Psi(S_T, G_n(\tau, T)) = \begin{cases} \max\left\{ S_T - \prod_{i=1}^n \left(S_{t_i} \right)^{\frac{1}{n}}, 0 \right\} & \text{for call option} \\[3mm] \max\left\{ \prod_{i=1}^n \left(S_{t_i} \right)^{\frac{1}{n}} - S_T, 0 \right\} & \text{for put option.} \end{cases}$$

- For continuously sampled arithmetic average

$$\Psi(S_T, A(\tau, T)) = \begin{cases} \max\left\{ S_T - \frac{1}{T-\tau} \int_\tau^T S_u\, du, 0 \right\} & \text{for call option} \\[3mm] \max\left\{ \frac{1}{T-\tau} \int_\tau^T S_u\, du - S_T, 0 \right\} & \text{for put option.} \end{cases}$$

- For continuously sampled geometric average

$$\Psi(S_T, G(\tau, T)) = \begin{cases} \max\left\{ S_T - e^{\frac{1}{T-\tau} \int_\tau^T S_u\, du}, 0 \right\} & \text{for call option} \\[2mm] \max\left\{ e^{\frac{1}{T-\tau} \int_\tau^T S_u\, du} - S_T, 0 \right\} & \text{for put option.} \end{cases}$$

Put–Call Parity

Like its counterparts in European options, there are also put–call parity relationships for European-style Asian options with continuous sampling under the Black–Scholes framework. At time t we assume that the asset price S_t has the following SDE under the risk-neutral measure $\mathbb{Q}$

$$\frac{dS_t}{S_t} = (r - D)dt + \sigma\,dW_t$$

where r is the risk-free interest rate, D is the continuous dividend yield, σ is the volatility and W_t is the $\mathbb{Q}$-standard Wiener process. In addition, let

$$I_t = \int_\tau^t S_u\,du$$

and

$$\overline{D} = \frac{r}{2}\left(\frac{T+t-2\tau}{T-\tau}\right) + \frac{D}{2}\left(\frac{T-t}{T-\tau}\right) + \frac{\sigma^2}{12}\left(\frac{T-t}{T-\tau}\right)\left(\frac{T+2t-3\tau}{T-\tau}\right).$$

By defining $C_{ar}^{(a)}(S_t, I_t, t; K, T)$ $(P_{ar}^{(a)}(S_t, I_t, t; K, T))$ to be the arithmetic average rate call (put) option price written on S_t with strike price K and expiry T, we have the *arithmetic average rate (fixed strike) put–call* relation as

$$C_{ar}^{(a)}(S_t, I_t, t; K, T) - P_{ar}^{(a)}(S_t, I_t, t; K, T) = \frac{e^{-D(T-\tau)} - e^{-r(T-\tau)}}{(r-D)(T-\tau)}S_t + \left(\frac{I_t}{T-\tau} - K\right)e^{-r(T-\tau)}.$$

Similarly, by defining $C_{as}^{(a)}(S_t, I_t, t; T)$ $(P_{as}^{(a)}(S_t, I_t, t; T))$ to be the arithmetic average strike call (put) option price written on S_t with floating strike price $\dfrac{I_T}{T-\tau}$ and expiry T, we have the *arithmetic average strike (floating strike) put–call* relation as

$$C_{as}^{(a)}(S_t, I_t, t; T) - P_{as}^{(a)}(S_t, I_t, t; T)$$

$$= \frac{e^{-D(T-\tau)} - e^{-r(T-\tau)}}{(r-D)(T-\tau)}((r-D)(T-\tau) - 1)\,S_t + \left(S_t - \frac{I_t}{T-\tau}\right)e^{-r(T-\tau)}.$$

In contrast, by defining $C_{ar}^{(g)}(S_t, I_t, t; K, T)$ $(P_{ar}^{(g)}(S_t, I_t, t; K, T))$ to be the geometric average rate call (put) option price written on S_t with strike price K and expiry T, we have the *geometric average rate (fixed strike) put–call* relation as

$$C_{ar}^{(g)}(S_t, I_t, t; K, T) - P_{ar}^{(g)}(S_t, I_t, t; K, T) = e^{\frac{I_t}{T-\tau}}S_t^{\frac{T-t}{T-\tau}}e^{-\overline{D}(T-t)} - Ke^{-r(T-t)}.$$

Finally, by defining $C_{as}^{(g)}(S_t, I_t, t; T)$ $(P_{as}^{(g)}(S_t, I_t, t; T))$ to be the geometric average strike call (put) option price written on S_t with floating strike price $\dfrac{I_T}{T-\tau}$ and expiry T, we have the *geometric average strike (floating strike) put–call relation* as

$$C_{ar}^{(g)}(S_t, I_t, t; T) - P_{ar}^{(g)}(S_t, I_t, t; T) = S_t e^{-D(T-t)} - e^{\frac{I_t}{T-\tau}} S_t^{\frac{T-t}{T-\tau}} e^{-\overline{D}(T-t)}.$$

5.2 PROBLEMS AND SOLUTIONS

5.2.1 Discrete Sampling

1. *Limit of Discrete Arithmetic Average.* Let the time interval $[\tau, T]$ be partitioned into n equal subintervals each of length $\Delta t = \dfrac{T-\tau}{n}$ and let S_{t_i}, $t_i = \tau + i\Delta t$ be the stock price at the end of the ith interval, $i = 1, 2, \dots, n$. By denoting the discretely measured arithmetic average of the stock price as

$$A_n(\tau, T) = \frac{1}{n} \sum_{i=1}^{n} S_{t_i}$$

show that in the limit $n \to \infty$,

$$\lim_{n \to \infty} A_n(\tau, T) = \frac{1}{T-\tau} \int_{\tau}^{T} S_u \, du.$$

Solution: By definition

$$\int_{\tau}^{T} S_u \, du = \lim_{n \to \infty} \sum_{i=1}^{n} S_{t_i}(t_{i+1} - t_i) = \lim_{n \to \infty} \sum_{i=1}^{n} S_{t_i} \Delta t = \lim_{n \to \infty} \frac{T-\tau}{n} \sum_{i=1}^{n} S_{t_i}$$

and hence

$$\lim_{n \to \infty} \frac{1}{n} \sum_{i=1}^{n} S_{t_i} = \frac{1}{T-\tau} \int_{\tau}^{T} S_u \, du.$$

□

2. *Limit of Discrete Geometric Average.* Let the time interval $[\tau, T]$ be partitioned into n equal subintervals each of length $\Delta t = (T-\tau)/n$ and let S_{t_i}, $t_i = \tau + i\Delta t$ be the stock price at the end of the ith interval, $i = 1, 2, \dots, n$. By denoting the discretely measured geometric average of the stock price as

$$G_n(\tau, T) = \left(\prod_{i=1}^{n} S_{t_i} \right)^{\frac{1}{n}}$$

show that in the limit $n \to \infty$,

$$\lim_{n \to \infty} G_n(\tau, T) = e^{\frac{1}{T-\tau} \int_\tau^T \log S_u \, du}.$$

Solution: Given $G_n(\tau, T) = \left(\prod_{i=1}^n S_{t_i} \right)^{\frac{1}{n}}$ we can write

$$\log G_n(\tau, T) = \frac{1}{n} \log \left(\prod_{i=1}^n S_{t_i} \right) = \frac{1}{n} \sum_{i=1}^n \log S_{t_i}$$

or

$$G_n(\tau, T) = e^{\frac{1}{n} \sum_{i=1}^n \log S_{t_i}}.$$

From Problem 5.2.1.1 (page 443) we can deduce that

$$\lim_{n \to \infty} \frac{1}{n} \sum_{i=1}^n \log S_{t_i} = \frac{1}{T-\tau} \int_\tau^T \log S_u \, du$$

and hence

$$\lim_{n \to \infty} \left(\prod_{i=1}^n S_{t_i} \right)^{\frac{1}{n}} = e^{\frac{1}{T-\tau} \int_\tau^T \log S_u \, du}.$$

$\square$

3. Let the time interval $[\tau, T]$ be partitioned into n equal subintervals each of length $\Delta t = (T - \tau)/n$ and let S_{t_i}, $t_i = \tau + i \Delta t$ be the stock price at the end of the ith interval, $i = 1, 2, \ldots, n$. By defining the discretely measured arithmetic average as

$$A_n(\tau, T) = \frac{1}{n} \sum_{i=1}^n S_{t_i}$$

and the discretely measured geometric average as

$$G_n(\tau, T) = \left(\prod_{i=1}^n S_{t_i} \right)^{\frac{1}{n}}$$

show that

$$G_n(\tau, T) \leq A_n(\tau, T).$$

Solution: From the MacLaurin series expansion of e^x, $x \in \mathbb{R}$

$$e^x = 1 + x + \frac{x^2}{2!} + \frac{x^3}{3!} + \dots$$

and because $e^x > 0$ we can therefore deduce that

$$e^x \geq 1 + x, \qquad x \in \mathbb{R}.$$

Let

$$x_i = \frac{S_{t_i}}{A(\tau,T)} - 1, \qquad i = 1, 2, \dots, n$$

so that

$$e^{\frac{S_{t_i}}{A_n(\tau,T)} - 1} \geq 1 + \frac{S_{t_i}}{A_n(\tau,T)} - 1 = \frac{S_{t_i}}{A_n(\tau,T)}.$$

Since

$$\frac{S_{t_i}}{A_n(\tau,T)} \leq e^{\frac{S_{t_i}}{A_n(\tau,T)} - 1}$$

multiplying by the inequality for $i = 1, 2, \dots, n$ yields

$$\frac{S_{t_1}}{A_n(\tau,T)} \cdot \frac{S_{t_2}}{A_n(\tau,T)} \cdots \frac{S_{t_n}}{A_n(\tau,T)} \leq \left(e^{\frac{S_{t_1}}{A_n(\tau,T)} - 1} \right) \left(e^{\frac{S_{t_2}}{A_n(\tau,T)} - 1} \right) \cdots \left(e^{\frac{S_{t_n}}{A_n(\tau,T)} - 1} \right)$$

and hence

$$\frac{\prod_{i=1}^{n} S_{t_i}}{A_n(\tau,T)^n} \leq e^{\frac{\sum_{i=1}^{n} S_{t_i}}{A_n(\tau,T)} - n} = e^{\frac{n A_n(\tau,T)}{A_n(\tau,T)} - n} = 1$$

or

$$\left(\prod_{i=1}^{n} S_{t_i} \right)^{\frac{1}{n}} \leq A_n(\tau,T).$$

Since $G_n(\tau,T) = \left(\prod_{i=1}^{n} S_{t_i} \right)^{\frac{1}{n}}$, then $G_n(\tau,T) \leq A_n(\tau,T)$.

$\square$

4. *Arithmetic–Geometric Average Rate (Fixed Strike) Identity.* Let the asset price S_t follow the GBM

$$\frac{dS_t}{S_t} = (\mu - D) + \sigma \, dW_t$$

where W_t is the $\mathbb{P}$-standard Wiener process on the probability space $(\Omega, \mathcal{F}, \mathbb{P})$, μ, D and σ are the drift parameter, continuous dividend yield and volatility, respectively. In addition, let r be the risk-free interest rate.

Let the time interval $[\tau, T]$ be partitioned into n equal subintervals each of length $\Delta t = (T - \tau)/n$ and let S_{t_i}, $t_i = \tau + i\Delta t$ be the stock price at the end of the ith interval, $i = 1, 2, \ldots, n$. Define the discretely measured arithmetic average as

$$A_n(\tau, T) = \frac{1}{n} \sum_{i=1}^{n} S_{t_i}$$

and the discretely measured geometric average as

$$G_n(\tau, T) = \left(\prod_{i=1}^{n} S_{t_i} \right)^{\frac{1}{n}}.$$

At time t, for a common strike value K and expiry time $T > t$, let the arithmetic average rate (fixed strike) Asian call and put options be

$$C_{ar}^{(a)}(S_t, A_n(\tau, T), t; K, T) = e^{-r(T-t)} \mathbb{E}^{\mathbb{Q}} \left[\max\{A_n(\tau, T) - K, 0\} \big| \mathcal{F}_t \right]$$
$$P_{ar}^{(a)}(S_t, A_n(\tau, T), t; K, T) = e^{-r(T-t)} \mathbb{E}^{\mathbb{Q}} \left[\max\{K - A_n(\tau, T), 0\} \big| \mathcal{F}_t \right]$$

where the expectation is defined under the risk-neutral measure $\mathbb{Q}$.

In contrast, let the corresponding geometric average rate (fixed strike) Asian call and put options be

$$C_{ar}^{(g)}(S_t, G_n(\tau, T), t; K, T) = e^{-r(T-t)} \mathbb{E}^{\mathbb{Q}} \left[\max\{G_n(\tau, T) - K, 0\} \big| \mathcal{F}_t \right]$$
$$P_{ar}^{(g)}(S_t, G_n(\tau, T), t; K, T) = e^{-r(T-t)} \mathbb{E}^{\mathbb{Q}} \left[\max\{K - G_n(\tau, T), 0\} \big| \mathcal{F}_t \right].$$

Show that

$$C_{ar}^{(g)}(S_t, G_n(\tau, T), t; K, T) \leq C_{ar}^{(a)}(S_t, A_n(\tau, T), t; K, T)$$

$$\leq C_{ar}^{(g)}(S_t, G_n(\tau, T), t; K, T) + e^{-r(T-t)} \left\{ \mathbb{E}^{\mathbb{Q}} \left[A_n(\tau, T) \big| \mathcal{F}_t \right] - \mathbb{E}^{\mathbb{Q}} \left[G_n(\tau, T) \big| \mathcal{F}_t \right] \right\}$$

and

$$P_{ar}^{(g)}(S_t, G_n(\tau, T), t; K, T) - e^{-r(T-t)} \left\{ \mathbb{E}^{\mathbb{Q}} \left[A_n(\tau, T) \big| \mathcal{F}_t \right] - \mathbb{E}^{\mathbb{Q}} \left[G_n(\tau, T) \big| \mathcal{F}_t \right] \right\}$$

$$\leq P_{ar}^{(a)}(S_t, A_n(\tau, T), t; K, T) \leq P_{ar}^{(g)}(S_t, G_n(\tau, T), t; K, T).$$

Solution: From Problem 5.2.1.3 (see page 444) we have $G_n(\tau, T) \leq A_n(\tau, T)$, therefore

$$e^{-r(T-t)} \mathbb{E}^{\mathbb{Q}} \left[\max\{G_n(\tau, T) - K, 0\} \big| \mathcal{F}_t \right] \leq e^{-r(T-t)} \mathbb{E}^{\mathbb{Q}} \left[\max\{A_n(\tau, T) - K, 0\} \big| \mathcal{F}_t \right]$$

or

$$C_{ar}^{(g)}(S_t, G_n(\tau, T), t; K, T) \leq C_{ar}^{(a)}(S_t, A_n(\tau, T), t; K, T).$$

In addition, we note that

$$
\begin{aligned}
\max\{A_n(\tau, T) - K, 0\} &= \max\{A_n(\tau, T) - G_n(\tau, T) + G_n(\tau, T) - K, 0\} \\
&\leq A_n(\tau, T) - G_n(\tau, T) + \max\{G_n(\tau, T) - K, 0\}.
\end{aligned}
$$

Thus,

$$
\begin{aligned}
C_{ar}^{(a)}(S_t, A_n(\tau, T), t; K, T) &= e^{-r(T-t)} \mathbb{E}^{\mathbb{Q}} \left[\max\{A_n(\tau, T) - K, 0\} \big| \mathcal{F}_t \right] \\
&\leq e^{-r(T-T)} \mathbb{E}^{\mathbb{Q}} \left[A_n(\tau, T) - G_n(\tau, T) \big| \mathcal{F}_t \right] \\
&\quad + e^{-r(T-T)} \mathbb{E}^{\mathbb{Q}} \left[\max\{G_n(\tau, T) - K, 0\} \big| \mathcal{F}_t \right] \\
&= e^{-r(T-T)} \left\{ \mathbb{E}^{\mathbb{Q}} \left[A_n(\tau, T) \big| \mathcal{F}_t \right] - \mathbb{E}^{\mathbb{Q}} \left[G_n(\tau, T) \big| \mathcal{F}_t \right] \right\} \\
&\quad + C_{ar}^{(g)}(S_t, G_n(\tau, T), t; K, T).
\end{aligned}
$$

In contrast, for the average rate put options

$$e^{-r(T-t)} \mathbb{E}^{\mathbb{Q}} \left[\max\{K - A_n(\tau, T), 0\} \big| \mathcal{F}_t \right] \leq e^{-r(T-t)} \mathbb{E}^{\mathbb{Q}} \left[\max\{K - G_n(\tau, T), 0\} \big| \mathcal{F}_t \right]$$

or

$$P_{ar}^{(a)}(S_t, A_n(\tau, T), t; K, T) \leq P_{ar}^{(g)}(S_t, G_n(\tau, T), t; K, T).$$

Further, we note that

$$
\begin{aligned}
\max\{K - A_n(\tau, T), 0\} &= \max\{K - G_n(\tau, T) + G_n(\tau, T) - A_n(\tau, T), 0\} \\
&= \max\{K - G_n(\tau, T) - (A_n(\tau, T) - G_n(\tau, T)), 0\} \\
&\geq \max\{K - G_n(\tau, T), 0\} - (A_n(\tau, T) - G_n(\tau, T)).
\end{aligned}
$$

Therefore,

$$
\begin{aligned}
P_{ar}^{(a)}(S_t, A_n(\tau, T), t; K, T) &= e^{-r(T-t)} \mathbb{E}^{\mathbb{Q}} \left[\max\{K - A_n(\tau, T), 0\} \big| \mathcal{F}_t \right] \\
&\geq e^{-r(T-t)} \mathbb{E}^{\mathbb{Q}} \left[\max\{K - G_n(\tau, T), 0\} \big| \mathcal{F}_t \right] \\
&\quad - e^{-r(T-t)} \mathbb{E}^{\mathbb{Q}} \left[A_n(\tau, T) - G_n(\tau, T) \big| \mathcal{F}_t \right] \\
&= P_{ar}^{(g)}(S_t, G_n(\tau, T), t; K, T) \\
&\quad - e^{-r(T-t)} \left\{ \mathbb{E}^{\mathbb{Q}} \left[A_n(\tau, T) \big| \mathcal{F}_t \right] - \mathbb{E}^{\mathbb{Q}} \left[G_n(\tau, T) \big| \mathcal{F}_t \right] \right\}.
\end{aligned}
$$

$\square$

5. *Arithmetic–Geometric Average Strike (Floating Strike) Identity.* Let the asset price S_t follow the GBM

$$\frac{dS_t}{S_t} = (\mu - D) + \sigma \, dW_t$$

where W_t is the $\mathbb{P}$-standard Wiener process on the probability space $(\Omega, \mathcal{F}, \mathbb{P})$, μ, D and σ are the drift parameter, continuous dividend yield and volatility, respectively. In addition, let r be the risk-free interest rate.

Let the time interval $[\tau, T]$ be partitioned into n equal subintervals each of length $\Delta t = (T - \tau)/n$ and let S_{t_i}, $t_i = \tau + i\Delta t$ be the stock price at the end of the ith interval, $i = 1, 2, \dots, n$. Define the discretely measured arithmetic average as

$$A_n(\tau, T) = \frac{1}{n} \sum_{i=1}^{n} S_{t_i}$$

and the discretely measured geometric average as

$$G_n(\tau, T) = \left(\prod_{i=1}^{n} S_{t_i} \right)^{\frac{1}{n}}.$$

At time t, for a common strike value K and expiry time $T > t$, let the arithmetic average strike (floating strike) Asian call and put options be

$$C_{as}^{(a)}(S_t, A_n(\tau, T), t; T) = e^{-r(T-t)} \mathbb{E}^{\mathbb{Q}} \left[\max\{S_T - A_n(\tau, T), 0\} \middle| \mathcal{F}_t \right]$$

$$P_{as}^{(a)}(S_t, A_n(\tau, T), t; T) = e^{-r(T-t)} \mathbb{E}^{\mathbb{Q}} \left[\max\{A_n(\tau, T) - S_T, 0\} \middle| \mathcal{F}_t \right]$$

where the expectation is under the risk-neutral measure $\mathbb{Q}$.

In contrast, let the corresponding geometric average strike (floating strike) Asian call and put options be

$$C_{as}^{(g)}(S_t, G_n(\tau, T), t; T) = e^{-r(T-t)} \mathbb{E}^{\mathbb{Q}} \left[\max\{S_T - G_n(\tau, T), 0\} \middle| \mathcal{F}_t \right]$$

$$P_{as}^{(g)}(S_t, G_n(\tau, T), t; T) = e^{-r(T-t)} \mathbb{E}^{\mathbb{Q}} \left[\max\{G_n(\tau, T) - S_T, 0\} \middle| \mathcal{F}_t \right].$$

Show that

$$C_{as}^{(a)}(S_t, A_n(\tau, T), t; T) \leq C_{as}^{(g)}(S_t, G_n(\tau, T), t; T)$$

$$\leq C_{as}^{(a)}(S_t, A_n(\tau, T), t; T) + e^{-r(T-t)} \left\{ \mathbb{E}^{\mathbb{Q}} \left[A_n(\tau, T) \middle| \mathcal{F}_t \right] - \mathbb{E}^{\mathbb{Q}} \left[G_n(\tau, T) \middle| \mathcal{F}_t \right] \right\}$$

and

$$P_{as}^{(a)}(S_t, A_n(\tau, T), t; T) - e^{-r(T-t)} \left\{ \mathbb{E}^{\mathbb{Q}} \left[A_n(\tau, T) \middle| \mathcal{F}_t \right] - \mathbb{E}^{\mathbb{Q}} \left[G_n(\tau, T) \middle| \mathcal{F}_t \right] \right\}$$

$$\leq P_{as}^{(g)}(S_t, G_n(\tau, T), t; T) \leq P_{as}^{(a)}(S_t, A_n(\tau, T), t; T).$$

Solution: Following Problem 5.2.1.3 (see page 444) we have $G_n(\tau, T) \le A_n(\tau, T)$, therefore

$$e^{-r(T-t)}\mathbb{E}^{\mathbb{Q}}\left[\max\{S_T - A_n(\tau, T), 0\}\big|\,\mathcal{F}_t\right] \le e^{-r(T-t)}\mathbb{E}^{\mathbb{Q}}\left[\max\{S_T - G_n(\tau, T), 0\}\big|\,\mathcal{F}_t\right]$$

or

$$C_{as}^{(a)}(S_t, A_n(\tau, T), t; T) \le C_{as}^{(g)}(S_t, G_n(\tau, T), t; T).$$

In addition, we note that

$$\begin{aligned}
\max\{S_T - G_n(\tau, T), 0\} &= \max\{S_T - A_n(\tau, T) + A_n(\tau, T) - G_n(\tau, T), 0\} \\
&\le \max\{S_T - A_n(\tau, T), 0\} + A_n(\tau, T) - G_n(\tau, T).
\end{aligned}$$

Thus,

$$\begin{aligned}
C_{as}^{(g)}(S_t, G_n(\tau, T), t; T) &= e^{-r(T-t)}\mathbb{E}^{\mathbb{Q}}\left[\max\{S_T - G_n(\tau, T), 0\}\big|\,\mathcal{F}_t\right] \\
&\le e^{-r(T-T)}\mathbb{E}^{\mathbb{Q}}\left[\max\{S_T - A_n(\tau, T), 0\}\big|\,\mathcal{F}_t\right] \\
&\quad + e^{-r(T-T)}\mathbb{E}^{\mathbb{Q}}\left[A_n(\tau, T) - G_n(\tau, T)\big|\,\mathcal{F}_t\right] \\
&= C_{as}^{(a)}(S_t, A_n(\tau, T), t; T) \\
&\quad + e^{-r(T-T)}\left\{\mathbb{E}^{\mathbb{Q}}\left[A_n(\tau, T)\big|\,\mathcal{F}_t\right] - \mathbb{E}^{\mathbb{Q}}\left[G_n(\tau, T)\big|\,\mathcal{F}_t\right]\right\}.
\end{aligned}$$

In contrast, for the average strike put options

$$e^{-r(T-t)}\mathbb{E}^{\mathbb{Q}}\left[\max\{G_n(\tau, T) - S_T, 0\}\big|\,\mathcal{F}_t\right] \le e^{-r(T-t)}\mathbb{E}^{\mathbb{Q}}\left[\max\{A_n(\tau, T) - S_T, 0\}\big|\,\mathcal{F}_t\right]$$

or

$$P_{as}^{(g)}(S_t, G_n(\tau, T), t; T) \le P_{as}^{(a)}(S_t, A_n(\tau, T), t; T).$$

In addition, we note that

$$\begin{aligned}
\max\{G_n(\tau, T) - S_T, 0\} &= \max\{G_n(\tau, T) - A_n(\tau, T) + A_n(\tau, T) - S_T, 0\} \\
&= \max\{A_n(\tau, T) - S_T - (A_n(\tau, T) - G_n(\tau, T)), 0\} \\
&\ge \max\{A_n(\tau, T) - S_T, 0\} - (A_n(\tau, T) - G_n(\tau, T)).
\end{aligned}$$

Therefore,

$$\begin{aligned}
P_{as}^{(g)}(S_t, G_n(\tau, T), t; T) &= e^{-r(T-t)}\mathbb{E}^{\mathbb{Q}}\left[\max\{G_n(\tau, T) - S_T, 0\}\big|\,\mathcal{F}_t\right] \\
&\ge e^{-r(T-t)}\mathbb{E}^{\mathbb{Q}}\left[\max\{A_n(\tau, T) - S_T, 0\}\big|\,\mathcal{F}_t\right] \\
&\quad - e^{-r(T-t)}\mathbb{E}^{\mathbb{Q}}\left[A_n(\tau, T) - G_n(\tau, T)\big|\,\mathcal{F}_t\right] \\
&= P_{as}^{(a)}(S_t, A_n(\tau, T), t; T) \\
&\quad - e^{-r(T-t)}\left\{\mathbb{E}^{\mathbb{Q}}\left[A_n(\tau, T)\big|\,\mathcal{F}_t\right] - \mathbb{E}^{\mathbb{Q}}\left[G_n(\tau, T)\big|\,\mathcal{F}_t\right]\right\}.
\end{aligned}$$

$\square$

6. *Discrete Geometric Average Rate (Fixed Strike) Asian Option*. Let the asset price S_t follow the GBM

$$\frac{dS_t}{S_t} = (\mu - D) + \sigma\,dW_t$$

where W_t is the $\mathbb{P}$-standard Wiener process on the probability space $(\Omega, \mathscr{F}, \mathbb{P})$, μ, D and σ are the drift parameter, continuous dividend yield and volatility, respectively. In addition, let r be the risk-free interest rate.

Let the time interval $[\tau, T]$ be partitioned into n equal subintervals each of length $\Delta t = (T - \tau)/n$ and let S_{t_i}, $t_i = \tau + i\Delta t$ be the asset price at the end of the ith interval, $i = 1, 2, \ldots, n$. We define the discretely measured geometric average of asset prices as

$$G_n(\tau, T) = \left(\prod_{i=1}^{n} S_{t_i}\right)^{\frac{1}{n}}$$

and we consider a fixed strike geometric Asian call option at expiry $T > t > \tau$ with payoff

$$\Psi(S_T, G_n(\tau, T)) = \max\{G_n(\tau, T) - K, 0\}$$

where $K > 0$ is the strike price.

Show that if $X \sim \mathcal{N}(\mu_x, \sigma_x^2)$ then for a constant $K > 0$

$$\mathbb{E}\left[\max\{\delta(e^X - K), 0\}\right] = \delta e^{\mu_x + \frac{1}{2}\sigma_x^2} \Phi\left(\frac{\delta(\mu_x + \sigma_x^2 - \log K)}{\sigma_x}\right) - \delta K \Phi\left(\frac{\delta(\mu_x - \log K)}{\sigma_x}\right)$$

where $\delta \in \{-1, 1\}$ and $\Phi(\cdot)$ denotes the cdf of a standard normal.

Suppose $S_{t_1}, S_{t_2}, \ldots, S_{t_k}, 1 \le k \le n - 1$ have been observed and let $t_k \le t < t_{k+1}$ where $t = t_k + \epsilon\Delta t$, $\epsilon \in [0, 1)$. Show that under the risk-neutral measure $\mathbb{Q}$

$$G_n(\tau, T) = \left(\prod_{i=1}^{k} S_{t_i}\right)^{\frac{1}{n}} S_t^{\frac{n-k}{n}} \left[\left(\frac{S_{t_n}}{S_{t_{n-1}}}\right)\left(\frac{S_{t_{n-1}}}{S_{t_{n-2}}}\right)^2 \left(\frac{S_{t_{n-2}}}{S_{t_{n-3}}}\right)^3 \cdots \left(\frac{S_{t_{k+1}}}{S_t}\right)^{n-k}\right]^{\frac{1}{n}}$$

and deduce that

$$\log G_n(\tau, T) \sim \mathcal{N}(m, s^2)$$

where

$$
m = \log\left[\left(\prod_{i=1}^{k} S_{t_i}\right)^{\frac{1}{n}} S_t^{\frac{n-k}{n}}\right]
$$

$$
+ \left(r - D - \frac{1}{2}\sigma^2\right)\left[\frac{(n-k-1)(n-k)}{2n} + \frac{(n-k)(1-\epsilon)}{n}\right]\Delta t
$$

and

$$
s^2 = \sigma^2\left[\frac{(n-k-1)(n-k)(2n-2k-1)}{6n^2} + \frac{(n-k)^2(1-\epsilon)}{n^2}\right]\Delta t.
$$

Using the above information show that under the risk-neutral measure $\mathbb{Q}$, the discrete geo-metric average rate Asian call option price at time t, $\tau < t < T$ is

$$
C_{ar}^{(g)}(S_t, G_n(\tau, T), t; K, T) = \left(\prod_{i=1}^{k} S_{t_i}\right)^{\frac{1}{n}} S_t^{\frac{n-k}{n}} e^{-\overline{D}_n(T-t)}\Phi(\overline{d}_+^{(n)}) - Ke^{-r(T-t)}\Phi(\overline{d}_-^{(n)})
$$

where

$$
\overline{d}_{\pm}^{(n)} = \frac{\log\left[\left(\prod_{i=1}^{k} S_{t_i}\right)^{\frac{1}{n}} S_t^{\frac{n-k}{n}}\right] - \log K + \left(r - D_n \pm \frac{1}{2}\sigma_n^2\right)(T-t)}{\sigma_n\sqrt{T-t}}
$$

$$
\overline{D}_n = r\left[\frac{n(T-t)}{T-\tau} - \frac{(n-k-1)(n-k)}{2n} - \frac{(n-k)(1-\epsilon)}{n}\right]\frac{\Delta t}{T-t}
$$

$$
+ D\left[\frac{(n-k-1)(n-k)}{2n} + \frac{(n-k)(1-\epsilon)}{n}\right]\frac{\Delta t}{T-t}
$$

$$
+ \frac{\sigma^2}{2}\left[\frac{(n-k-1)(n-k)}{2n} - \frac{(n-k-1)(n-k)(2n-2k-1)}{6n^2}\right.
$$

$$
\left. + \frac{(n-k)(1-\epsilon)}{n} - \frac{(n-k)^2(1-\epsilon)}{n}\right]\frac{\Delta t}{T-t}
$$

and

$$
\overline{\sigma}_n^2 = \sigma^2\left[\frac{(n-k-1)(n-k)(2n-2k-1)}{6n^2} + \frac{(n-k)^2(1-\epsilon)}{n^2}\right]\frac{\Delta t}{T-t}.
$$

Finally, show that in the limit $n \to \infty$,

$$
\lim_{n\to\infty} C_{ar}^{(g)}(S_t, G_n(\tau, T), t; K, T) = e^{\frac{I_t}{t}} S_t^{\frac{T-t}{T}} e^{-\overline{D}(T-t)}\Phi(\overline{d}_+) - Ke^{-r(T-t)}\Phi(\overline{d}_-)
$$

where

$$I_t = \int_\tau^t \log S_u \, du$$

$$\overline{d}_\pm = \frac{\dfrac{I_t}{T-\tau} + \left(\dfrac{T-t}{T-\tau}\right)\log S_t - \log K + \left(r - \overline{D} \pm \dfrac{1}{2}\overline{\sigma}^2\right)(T-t)}{\overline{\sigma}\sqrt{T-t}}$$

$$\overline{D} = \frac{r}{2}\left(\frac{T+t-2\tau}{T-\tau}\right) + \frac{D}{2}\left(\frac{T-t}{T-\tau}\right) + \frac{\sigma^2}{12}\left(\frac{T-t}{T-\tau}\right)\left(\frac{T+2t-3\tau}{T-\tau}\right)$$

$$\overline{\sigma}^2 = \frac{\sigma^2}{3}\left(\frac{T-t}{T-\tau}\right)^2.$$

Solution: For the first part of the results refer to Problem 1.2.2.7 of *Problems and Solutions in Mathematical Finance, Volume 1: Stochastic Calculus*.

From Girsanov's theorem, under the risk-neutral measure $\mathbb{Q}$, the asset price S_t follows

$$\frac{dS_t}{S_t} = (r - D)dt + \sigma \, dW_t^{\mathbb{Q}}$$

where $W_t^{\mathbb{Q}}$ is a $\mathbb{Q}$-standard Wiener process.

Let the time interval $[\tau, T]$ be partitioned into n equal subintervals each of length $\Delta t = (T - \tau)/n$ and let S_{t_i}, $t_i = \tau + i\Delta t$ be the asset price at the end of the ith interval. Suppose $S_{t_1}, S_{t_2}, \ldots, S_{t_k}$, $1 \le k \le n - 1$ have been observed and let $t_k \le t < t_{k+1}$ where $t = t_k + \epsilon\Delta t$, $\epsilon \in [0, 1)$. By definition

$$G_n(\tau, T) = \left(\prod_{i=1}^n S_{t_i}\right)^{\frac{1}{n}}$$

$$= \left(\prod_{i=1}^k S_{t_i}\right)^{\frac{1}{n}}\left(\prod_{i=k+1}^n S_{t_i}\right)^{\frac{1}{n}}$$

$$= \left(\prod_{i=1}^k S_{t_i}\right)^{\frac{1}{n}}\left(S_{t_n} S_{t_{n-1}} S_{t_{n-3}} \cdots S_{t_{k+2}} S_{t_{k+1}}\right)^{\frac{1}{n}}$$

$$= \left(\prod_{i=1}^k S_{t_i}\right)^{\frac{1}{n}} S_t^{\frac{n-k}{n}}\left[\left(\frac{S_{t_n}}{S_{t_{n-1}}}\right)\left(\frac{S_{t_{n-1}}}{S_{t_{n-2}}}\right)^2\left(\frac{S_{t_{n-2}}}{S_{t_{n-3}}}\right)^3 \cdots \left(\frac{S_{t_{k+1}}}{S_t}\right)^{n-k}\right]^{\frac{1}{n}}.$$

From Itō's lemma we can easily show for $i = k + 2, k + 3, \ldots, n - 1, n$

$$\log\left(\frac{S_{t_i}}{S_{t_{i-1}}}\right) = \left(r - D - \frac{1}{2}\sigma^2\right)(t_i - t_{i-1}) + \sigma W_{t_i - t_{i-1}}^{\mathbb{Q}}$$

$$= \left(r - D - \frac{1}{2}\sigma^2\right)\Delta t + \sigma W_{t_i - t_{i-1}}^{\mathbb{Q}}$$

and

$$\log\left(\frac{S_{t_{k+1}}}{S_t}\right) = \left(r - D - \frac{1}{2}\sigma^2\right)(t_{k+1} - t) + \sigma W^Q_{t_{k+1}-t}$$

$$= \left(r - D - \frac{1}{2}\sigma^2\right)(1 - \epsilon)\Delta t + \sigma W^Q_{t_{k+1}-t}.$$

From the independent increment property of the standard Wiener process we can deduce that

$$\log\left(\frac{S_{t_n}}{S_{t_{n-1}}}\right), \quad \log\left(\frac{S_{t_{n-1}}}{S_{t_{n-2}}}\right), \quad \log\left(\frac{S_{t_{n-2}}}{S_{t_{n-3}}}\right), \quad \ldots, \quad \log\left(\frac{S_{t_{k+2}}}{S_{t_{k+1}}}\right), \quad \log\left(\frac{S_{t_{k+1}}}{S_t}\right)$$

are mutually independent. Thus,

$$\log G_n(\tau, T) = \log\left[\left(\prod_{i=1}^{k} S_{t_i}\right)^{\frac{1}{n}} S_t^{\frac{n-k}{n}}\right]$$

$$+ \frac{1}{n}\left[\log\left(\frac{S_{t_n}}{S_{t_{n-1}}}\right) + 2\log\left(\frac{S_{t_{n-1}}}{S_{t_{n-2}}}\right)\right.$$

$$\left. + 3\log\left(\frac{S_{t_{n-2}}}{S_{t_{n-3}}}\right) + \ldots + (n - k)\log\left(\frac{S_{t_{k+1}}}{S_t}\right)\right]$$

and because

$$\log S_{t_i} \sim \mathcal{N}\left[\log S_{t_{i-1}} + \left(r - D - \frac{1}{2}\sigma^2\right)\Delta t, \sigma^2 \Delta t\right], \quad i = k + 2, k + 3, \ldots, n$$

$$\log S_{t_{k+1}} \sim \mathcal{N}\left[\log S_t + \left(r - D - \frac{1}{2}\sigma^2\right)(1 - \epsilon)\Delta t, \sigma^2(1 - \epsilon)\Delta t\right]$$

we have

$$\mathbb{E}^Q\left[\log G_n(\tau, T)\right] = \log\left[\left(\prod_{i=1}^{k} S_{t_i}\right)^{\frac{1}{n}} S_t^{\frac{n-k}{n}}\right]$$

$$+ \frac{1}{n}\left(r - D - \frac{1}{2}\sigma^2\right)$$

$$\times (1 + 2 + 3 + \ldots + (n - k - 1) + (n - k)(1 - \epsilon))\Delta t$$

$$= \log\left[\left(\prod_{i=1}^{k} S_{t_i}\right)^{\frac{1}{n}} S_t^{\frac{n-k}{n}}\right]$$

$$+ \left(r - D - \frac{1}{2}\sigma^2\right)\left[\frac{(n - k - 1)(n - k)}{2n} + \frac{(n - k)(1 - \epsilon)}{n}\right]\Delta t$$

and

$$\mathrm{Var}^{\mathbb{Q}}\left[\log G_n(\tau, T)\right] = \frac{\sigma^2}{n^2} \left(1^2 + 2^2 + 3^2 + \ldots + (n-k-1)^2 + (n-k)^2(1-\epsilon)\right) \Delta t$$

$$= \sigma^2 \left[\frac{(n-k-1)(n-k)(2n-2k-1)}{6n^2} + \frac{(n-k)^2(1-\epsilon)}{n^2}\right] \Delta t.$$

Thus, using the above information we can deduce that the discrete geometric average rate Asian call option price at time $\tau < t < T$ is

$$C_{ar}^{(g)}(S_t, G_n(\tau, T), t; K, T) = e^{-r(T-t)}\mathbb{E}^{\mathbb{Q}}\left[\max\{G_n(\tau, T) - K, 0\} \mid \mathcal{F}_t\right]$$

$$= e^{m + \frac{1}{2}s^2 - r(T-t)}\Phi(\overline{d}_+^{(n)}) - Ke^{-r(T-t)}\Phi(\overline{d}_-^{(n)})$$

where

$$m = \log\left[\left(\prod_{i=1}^{k} S_{t_i}\right)^{\frac{1}{n}} S_t^{\frac{n-k}{n}}\right]$$

$$+ \left(r - D - \frac{1}{2}\sigma^2\right)\left[\frac{(n-k-1)(n-k)}{2n} + \frac{(n-k)(1-\epsilon)}{n}\right]\Delta t,$$

$$s^2 = \sigma^2 \left[\frac{(n-k-1)(n-k)(2n-2k-1)}{6n^2} + \frac{(n-k)^2(1-\epsilon)}{n^2}\right]\Delta t,$$

$$\overline{d}_+^{(n)} = \frac{m + s^2 - \log K}{s}$$

and

$$\overline{d}_-^{(n)} = d_+^{(n)} - s.$$

Therefore,

$$e^{m + \frac{1}{2}s^2 - r(T-t)} = \left(\prod_{i=1}^{k} S_{t_i}\right)^{\frac{1}{n}} S_t^{\frac{n-k}{n}} e^{-\overline{D}_n(T-t)}$$

$$\overline{d}_\pm^{(n)} = \frac{\log\left[\left(\prod_{i=1}^{k} S_{t_i}\right)^{\frac{1}{n}} S_t^{\frac{n-k}{n}}\right] - \log K + \left(r - \overline{D}_n \pm \frac{1}{2}\overline{\sigma}_n^2\right)(T-t)}{\overline{\sigma}_n \sqrt{T-t}}$$

where

$$\overline{D}_n = r - \left(r - D - \frac{1}{2}\sigma^2\right)\left[\frac{(n-k-1)(n-k)}{2n} + \frac{(n-k)(1-\epsilon)}{n}\right]\frac{\Delta t}{T-t}$$

$$-\frac{\sigma^2}{2}\left[\frac{(n-k-1)(n-k)(2n-2k-1)}{6n^2} + \frac{(n-k)^2(1-\epsilon)}{n^2}\right]\frac{\Delta t}{T-t}$$

$$= r\left[\frac{n(T-t)}{T-\tau} - \frac{(n-k-1)(n-k)}{2n} - \frac{(n-k)(1-\epsilon)}{n}\right]\frac{\Delta t}{T-t}$$

$$+D\left[\frac{(n-k-1)(n-k)}{2n} + \frac{(n-k)(1-\epsilon)}{n}\right]\frac{\Delta t}{T-t}$$

$$+\frac{\sigma^2}{2}\left[\frac{(n-k-1)(n-k)}{2n} - \frac{(n-k-1)(n-k)(2n-2k-1)}{6n^2}\right.$$

$$\left.+\frac{(n-k)(1-\epsilon)}{n} - \frac{(n-k)^2(1-\epsilon)}{n}\right]\frac{\Delta t}{T-t}$$

and

$$\overline{\sigma}_n^2 = \sigma^2\left[\frac{(n-k-1)(n-k)(2n-2k-1)}{6n^2} + \frac{(n-k)^2(1-\epsilon)}{n^2}\right]\frac{\Delta t}{T-t}.$$

Thus, we can write the discrete geometric average rate Asian call option price at time t, $\tau < t < T$ as

$$C_{ar}^{(g)}(S_t, G_n(\tau, T), t; K, T) = \left(\prod_{i=1}^{k} S_{t_i}\right)^{\frac{1}{n}} S_t^{\frac{n-k}{n}} e^{-\overline{D}_n(T-t)}\Phi(\overline{d}_+^{(n)}) - Ke^{-r(T-t)}\Phi(\overline{d}_-^{(n)}).$$

For the limiting case, we note that since $T = \tau + n\Delta t$ and $t = t_k + \epsilon\Delta t = \tau + (k + \epsilon)\Delta t$, $\epsilon \in [0, 1)$ therefore

$$\lim_{n\to\infty}(n-k)\Delta t = \lim_{n\to\infty}(T - t + \epsilon\Delta t) = T - t$$

$$\lim_{n\to\infty}(n-k-1)\Delta t = \lim_{n\to\infty}(T - t + (\epsilon - 1)\Delta t) = T - t$$

and

$$\lim_{n\to\infty}(2n - 2k - 1)\Delta t = \lim_{n\to\infty}(2(T - t + \epsilon\Delta t) + \Delta t) = 2(T - t).$$

By setting $I_t = \int_\tau^t \log S_u\, d u,$

$$\lim_{n\to\infty} \left(\prod_{i=1}^n S_{t_i}\right)^{\frac{1}{n}} S_t^{\frac{n-k}{n}} = \lim_{n\to\infty} \left(\prod_{i=1}^n S_{t_i}\right)^{\frac{1}{n}} \lim_{n\to\infty} S_t^{\frac{n-k}{n}}$$

$$= \lim_{n\to\infty} e^{\frac{1}{T-\tau}\sum_{i=1}^k \log S_{t_i}\Delta t} \cdot \lim_{n\to\infty} S_t^{\frac{(n-k)\Delta t}{n\Delta t}}$$

$$= e^{\frac{1}{T-\tau}\int_\tau^t \log S_u\, du} S_t^{\frac{T-t}{T-\tau}}$$

$$= e^{\frac{I_t}{T}} S_t^{\frac{T-t}{T-\tau}}$$

$$\lim_{n\to\infty} \overline{D}_n = \lim_{n\to\infty} r\left[\frac{n(T-t)}{T-\tau} - \frac{(n-k-1)(n-k)}{2n} - \frac{(n-k)(1-\epsilon)}{n}\right]\frac{\Delta t}{T-t}$$

$$+ \lim_{n\to\infty} D\left[\frac{(n-k-1)(n-k)}{2n} + \frac{(n-k)(1-\epsilon)}{n}\right]\frac{\Delta t}{T-t}$$

$$+ \lim_{n\to\infty} \frac{\sigma^2}{2}\left[\frac{(n-k-1)(n-k)}{2n} - \frac{(n-k-1)(n-k)(2n-2k-1)}{6n^2}\right.$$

$$+ \left.\frac{(n-k)(1-\epsilon)}{n} - \frac{(n-k)^2(1-\epsilon)}{n}\right]\frac{\Delta t}{T-t}$$

$$= \lim_{n\to\infty} r\left[1 - \frac{(n-k-1)(n-k)\Delta t^2}{2n\Delta t(T-t)} - \frac{(n-k)(1-\epsilon)\Delta t^2}{n\Delta t(T-t)}\right]$$

$$+ \lim_{n\to\infty} D\left[\frac{(n-k-1)(n-k)\Delta t^2}{2n\Delta t(T-t)} + \frac{(n-k)(1-\epsilon)\Delta t^2}{n\Delta t(T-t)}\right]$$

$$+ \lim_{n\to\infty} \frac{\sigma^2}{2}\left[\frac{(n-k-1)(n-k)\Delta t^2}{2n\Delta t(T-t)} - \frac{(n-k-1)(n-k)(2n-2k-1)\Delta t^3}{6n^2\Delta t^2(T-t)}\right.$$

$$+ \left.\frac{(n-k)(1-\epsilon)\Delta t^2}{n\Delta t(T-t)} - \frac{(n-k)^2(1-\epsilon)\Delta t^2}{n\Delta t(T-t)}\right]$$

$$= r\left(1 - \frac{T-t}{2(T-\tau)}\right) + D\left(\frac{T-t}{2(T-\tau)}\right) + \frac{\sigma^2}{2}\left[\frac{T-t}{2(T-\tau)} + \frac{(T-t)^2}{3(T-\tau)^2}\right]$$

$$= \frac{r}{2}\left(\frac{T+t-2\tau}{T-\tau}\right) + \frac{D}{2}\left(\frac{T-t}{T-\tau}\right) + \frac{\sigma^2}{12}\left(\frac{T-t}{T-\tau}\right)\left(\frac{T+2t-3\tau}{T-\tau}\right)$$

and

$$\lim_{n\to\infty} \overline{\sigma}_n^2 = \lim_{n\to\infty} \sigma^2\left[\frac{(n-k-1)(n-k)(2n-2k-1)}{6n^2} + \frac{(n-k)^2(1-\epsilon)}{n^2}\right]\frac{\Delta t}{T-t}$$

$$= \lim_{n\to\infty} \sigma^2\left[\frac{(n-k-1)(n-k)(2n-2k-1)\Delta t^3}{6n^2\Delta t^2(T-t)} + \frac{(n-k)^2(1-\epsilon)\Delta t^3}{n^2\Delta t^2(T-t)}\right]$$

$$= \frac{\sigma^2}{3}\left(\frac{T-t}{T-\tau}\right)^2.$$

Thus, in the limit $n \to \infty$,

$$\lim_{n \to \infty} C_{ar}^{(g)}(S_t, G_n(\tau, T), t; K, T) = e^{\frac{I_t}{T-\tau}} S_t^{\frac{T-t}{T-\tau}} e^{-\overline{D}(T-t)} \Phi(\overline{d}_+) - K e^{-r(T-t)} \Phi(\overline{d}_-)$$

where

$$\overline{d}_\pm = \frac{\dfrac{I_t}{T-\tau} + \left(\dfrac{T-t}{T-\tau}\right) \log S_t - \log K + \left(r - \overline{D} \pm \dfrac{1}{2} \overline{\sigma}^2\right)(T-t)}{\overline{\sigma}\sqrt{T-t}}$$

$$\overline{D} = \frac{r}{2}\left(\frac{T+t-2\tau}{T-\tau}\right) + \frac{D}{2}\left(\frac{T-t}{T-\tau}\right) + \frac{\sigma^2}{12}\left(\frac{T-t}{T-\tau}\right)\left(\frac{T+2t-3\tau}{T-\tau}\right)$$

and

$$\overline{\sigma}^2 = \frac{\sigma^2}{3}\left(\frac{T-t}{T-\tau}\right)^2.$$

$\square$

7. *Levy Approximation – Discrete Arithmetic Average Rate (Fixed Strike) Asian Option.* Let the asset price S_t follow the GBM

$$\frac{dS_t}{S_t} = (\mu - D)dt + \sigma\, dW_t$$

where W_t is the $\mathbb{P}$-standard Wiener process on the probability space $(\Omega, \mathcal{F}, \mathbb{P})$, μ, D and σ are the drift parameter, continuous dividend yield and volatility, respectively. In addition, let r be the risk-free interest rate.

Let the time interval $[\tau, T]$ be partitioned into n equal subintervals each of length $\Delta t = (T - \tau)/n$ and let S_{t_i}, $t_i = \tau + i\Delta t$ be the asset price at the end of the ith interval, $i = 1, 2, \ldots, n$. We define the discretely measured arithmetic average of asset prices as

$$A_n(\tau, T) = \frac{1}{n} \sum_{i=1}^{n} S_{t_i}$$

and we consider an arithmetic average rate Asian put option with expiry $T > t > \tau$ and payoff

$$\Psi(S_T, A_n(\tau, T)) = \max\{K - A_n(\tau, T), 0\}$$

where $K > 0$ is the strike price.

Show that if $X \sim \mathcal{N}(\mu_x, \sigma_x^2)$ then for a constant $K > 0$ and $\alpha \in \mathbb{N}$,

$$\mathbb{E}(X^\alpha) = e^{\alpha\mu_x + \frac{1}{2}\alpha^2\sigma_x^2}$$

and

$$\mathbb{E}\left[\max\{\delta(e^X - K), 0\}\right] = \delta e^{\mu_x + \frac{1}{2}\sigma_x^2} \Phi\left(\frac{\delta(\mu_x + \sigma_x^2 - \log K)}{\sigma_x}\right) - \delta K \Phi\left(\frac{\delta(\mu_x - \log K)}{\sigma_x}\right)$$

where $\delta \in \{-1, 1\}$ and $\Phi(\cdot)$ denotes the cdf of a standard normal.

Suppose $S_{t_1}, S_{t_2}, \ldots, S_{t_k}, 1 \leq k \leq n - 1$ have been observed and let $t_k \leq t < t_{k+1}$ where $t = t_k + \epsilon \Delta t, \epsilon \in [0, 1)$ and

$$A_n(\tau, T) = A_n(t_1, t_k) + A_n(t_{k+1}, t_n)$$

where $A_n(t_1, t_k) = \dfrac{1}{n} \displaystyle\sum_{i=1}^{k} S_{t_i}$ and $A_n(t_{k+1}, t_n) = \dfrac{1}{n} \displaystyle\sum_{i=k+1}^{n} S_{t_i}$. Show that under the risk-neutral measure $\mathbb{Q}$

$$\mathbb{E}^{\mathbb{Q}}\left[S_{t_i} \,\middle|\, S_t\right] = S_t e^{(r-D)(i-k-\epsilon)\Delta t}$$

$$\mathbb{E}^{\mathbb{Q}}\left[S_{t_i} S_{t_j} \,\middle|\, \mathscr{F}_t\right] = S_t^2 e^{(r-D)(i+j-2k-2\epsilon)\Delta t + \sigma^2(\min\{i,j\}-k-\epsilon)\Delta t}$$

where $t_i, t_j > t_k$.

By assuming

$$A_n(t_{k+1}, t_n) \doteq \log\text{-}\mathcal{N}(m, s^2)$$

and using the moment-matching technique up to second order show that

$$m \approx 2 \log \mathbb{E}^{\mathbb{Q}}\left[A_n(t_{k+1}, t_n) \,\middle|\, S_t\right] - \frac{1}{2} \log \mathbb{E}^{\mathbb{Q}}\left[A_n(t_{k+1}, t_n)^2 \,\middle|\, S_t\right]$$

and

$$s^2 \approx \log \mathbb{E}^{\mathbb{Q}}\left[A_n(t_{k+1}, t_n)^2 \,\middle|\, S_t\right] - 2 \log \mathbb{E}^{\mathbb{Q}}\left[A_n(t_{k+1}, t_n) \,\middle|\, S_t\right].$$

Find $\mathbb{E}^{\mathbb{Q}}\left[A_n(t_{k+1}, t_n) \,\middle|\, S_t\right]$ and $\mathbb{E}^{\mathbb{Q}}\left[A_n(t_{k+1}, t_n)^2 \,\middle|\, S_t\right]$, and hence show that the discrete arithmetic average rate Asian put option at time $\tau < t < T$ can be approximated by

$$P_{ar}^{(a)}(S_t, A_n(t_{k+1}, t_n), t; K, T) \approx \overline{K} e^{-r(T-t)} \Phi(-\overline{d}_-^{(n)}) - e^{m + \frac{1}{2}s^2 - r(T-t)} \Phi(-\overline{d}_+^{(n)})$$

where $\overline{K} = K - A_n(t_1, t_k)$, $\overline{d}_+^{(n)} = \dfrac{m + s^2 - \log \overline{K}}{s}$ and $\overline{d}_-^{(n)} = d_+ - s$.

Finally, show that in the limit $n \to \infty$,

$$\lim_{n \to \infty} \mathbb{E}^{\mathbb{Q}}\left[A_n(t_{k+1}, t_n) \,\middle|\, S_t\right] = \frac{S_t(e^{(r-D)(T-t)} - 1)}{(r - D)(T - \tau)}$$

and

$$\lim_{n \to \infty} \mathbb{E}^{\mathbb{Q}} \left[A_n(t_{k+1}, t_n)^2 \,\middle|\, S_t \right] = \frac{S_t^2}{(r - D)(T - \tau)^2} \left[\frac{2 \left(e^{(r-D+\sigma^2)(T-t)} - 1 \right) e^{(r-D)(T-t)}}{r - D + \sigma^2} \right.$$

$$\left. - \frac{\left(e^{2(r-D+\frac{1}{2}\sigma^2)(T-t)} - 1 \right)}{r - D + \frac{1}{2}\sigma^2} \right].$$

Solution: For the first two parts of the results see Problems 1.2.2.7 and 1.2.2.10 of *Problems and Solutions in Mathematical Finance, Volume 1: Stochastic Calculus*.

Under the risk-neutral measure $\mathbb{Q}$, S_t follows

$$\frac{dS_t}{S_t} = (r - D)dt + \sigma \, dW_t^{\mathbb{Q}}$$

where $W_t^{\mathbb{Q}} = \left(\dfrac{\mu - r}{\sigma} \right) t + W_t$ is a $\mathbb{Q}$-standard Wiener process. Thus, conditional on S_t for $t_i \neq t_j, t_i, t_j > t$

$$S_{t_i} = S_t e^{(r-D-\frac{1}{2}\sigma^2)(t_i - t) + \sigma W_{t_i - t}}$$

$$S_{t_i} S_{t_j} = S_t^2 e^{(r-D-\frac{1}{2}\sigma^2)(t_i - t + t_j - t) + \sigma(W_{t_i - t} + W_{t_j - t})}.$$

Since $t = t_k + \epsilon \Delta t$ and $t_j = \tau + j \Delta t$, $j = i, k$ we have

$$\mathbb{E}^{\mathbb{Q}} \left[S_{t_i} \,\middle|\, S_t \right] = S_t e^{(r-D)(t_i - t)} = S_t e^{(r-D)(t_i - t_k - \epsilon \Delta t)} = S_t e^{(r-D)(i-k-\epsilon)\Delta t}.$$

From Problem 2.2.1.4 of *Problems and Solutions in Mathematical Finance, Volume 1: Stochastic Calculus* we can deduce

$$\text{Cov}(W_{t_i - t}, W_{t_j - t}) = \min\{t_i - t, t_j - t\} = \min\{t_i, t_j\} - t$$

and hence

$$W_{t_i - t} + W_{t_j - t} \sim \mathcal{N}(0, t_i + t_j + 2\min\{t_i, t_j\} - 4t).$$

Therefore, conditional on S_t

$$
\begin{aligned}
\mathbb{E}^{\mathbb{Q}}\left[S_{t_i}S_{t_j}\middle|S_t\right] &= S_t^2 e^{(r-D-\frac{1}{2}\sigma^2)(t_i+t_j-2t)+\frac{1}{2}\sigma^2(t_i+t_j+2\min\{t_i,t_j\}-4t)} \\
&= S_t^2 e^{(r-D)(t_i+t_j-2t)+\sigma^2(\min\{t_i,t_j\}-t)} \\
&= S_t^2 e^{(r-D)(t_i+t_j-2t_k-2\epsilon\Delta t)+\sigma^2(\min\{t_i,t_j\}-t_k-\epsilon\Delta)} \\
&= S_t^2 e^{(r-D)(i+j-2k-2\epsilon)\Delta t+\sigma^2(\min\{i,j\}-k-\epsilon)\Delta t}.
\end{aligned}
$$

Let $A_n(t_{k+1},t_k) = \dfrac{1}{n}\displaystyle\sum_{i=k+1}^{n} S_{t_i} \approx \log\text{-}\mathcal{N}(m,s^2)$ and by matching the moments up to second order we have

$$
\mathbb{E}^{\mathbb{Q}}\left[A_n(t_{k+1},t_k)\middle|S_t\right] \approx e^{m+\frac{1}{2}s^2} \quad\text{and}\quad \mathbb{E}^{\mathbb{Q}}\left[A_n(t_{k+1},t_n)^2\middle|S_t\right] \approx e^{2m+2s^2}
$$

or

$$
m+\frac{1}{2}s^2 \approx \log\mathbb{E}^{\mathbb{Q}}\left[A_n(t_{k+1},t_n)\middle|S_t\right] \quad\text{and}\quad m+s^2 \approx \frac{1}{2}\log\mathbb{E}^{\mathbb{Q}}\left[A_n(t_{k+1},t_n)^2\middle|S_t\right].
$$

Solving the approximate equations simultaneously we have

$$
m \approx 2\log\mathbb{E}^{\mathbb{Q}}\left[A_n(t_{k+1},t_n)\middle|S_t\right] - \frac{1}{2}\log\mathbb{E}^{\mathbb{Q}}\left[A_n(t_{k+1},t_n)^2\middle|S_t\right]
$$

and

$$
s^2 \approx \log\mathbb{E}^{\mathbb{Q}}\left[A_n(t_{k+1},t_n)^2\middle|S_t\right] - 2\log\mathbb{E}^{\mathbb{Q}}\left[A_n(t_{k+1},t_n)\middle|S_t\right].
$$

By definition

$$
\begin{aligned}
\mathbb{E}^{\mathbb{Q}}\left[A_n(t_{k+1},t_n)\middle|S_t\right] &= \frac{1}{n}\sum_{i=k+1}^{n}\mathbb{E}^{\mathbb{Q}}\left[S_{t_i}\middle|S_t\right] \\
&= \frac{1}{n}\sum_{i=k+1}^{n}S_t e^{(r-D)(i-k-\epsilon)\Delta t} \\
&= \frac{S_t e^{-(r-D)(k+\epsilon)\Delta t}}{n}\sum_{i=k+1}^{n}e^{(r-D)i\Delta t} \\
&= \frac{S_t e^{-(r-D)(k+\epsilon)\Delta t}}{n}\left[\frac{e^{(r-D)(k+1)\Delta t}\left(1-e^{(r-D)(n-k)\Delta t}\right)}{1-e^{(r-D)\Delta t}}\right] \\
&= \frac{S_t e^{(r-D)(1-\epsilon)\Delta t}}{n}\left[\frac{1-e^{(r-D)(n-k)\Delta t}}{1-e^{(r-D)\Delta t}}\right]
\end{aligned}
$$

whilst for

$$\mathbb{E}^{Q}\left[A_n(t_{k+1},t_n)^2\middle| S_t\right] = \frac{1}{n^2}\sum_{i=k+1}^{n}\sum_{j=k+1}^{n}\mathbb{E}^{Q}\left[S_{t_i}S_{t_j}\middle| S_t\right]$$

$$= \frac{S_t^2 e^{-2(r-D+\frac{1}{2}\sigma^2)\epsilon\Delta t}}{n^2}$$

$$\times \sum_{i=k+1}^{n}\sum_{j=k+1}^{n} e^{(r-D)(i+j-2k)\Delta t + \sigma^2(\min\{i,j\}-k)\Delta t}$$

$$= \frac{S_t^2 e^{-2(r-D+\frac{1}{2}\sigma^2)\epsilon\Delta t}}{n^2}(B_1 + B_2 + B_3)$$

where

$$B_1 = \sum_{\substack{i=k+1\\i=j}}^{n}\sum_{j=k+1}^{n} e^{(r-D)(i+j-2k)\Delta t + \sigma^2(\min\{i,j\}-k)\Delta t}$$

$$B_2 = \sum_{\substack{i=k+1\\i<j}}^{n}\sum_{j=k+1}^{n} e^{(r-D)(i+j-2k)\Delta t + \sigma^2(\min\{i,j\}-k)\Delta t}$$

and

$$B_3 = \sum_{\substack{i=k+1\\i>j}}^{n}\sum_{j=k+1}^{n} e^{(r-D)(i+j-2k)\Delta t + \sigma^2(\min\{i,j\}-k)\Delta t}.$$

For the case

$$B_1 = \sum_{\substack{i=k+1\\i=j}}^{n}\sum_{j=k+1}^{n} e^{(r-D)(i+j-2k)\Delta t + \sigma^2(\min\{i,j\}-k)\Delta t}$$

$$= \sum_{i=k+1}^{n} e^{2(r-D)(i-k)\Delta t + \sigma^2(i-k)\Delta t}$$

$$= e^{-2(r-D+\frac{1}{2}\sigma^2)k\Delta t}\left[\frac{e^{2(r-D+\frac{1}{2}\sigma^2)(k+1)\Delta t}\left(1 - e^{2(r-D+\frac{1}{2}\sigma^2)(n-k)\Delta t}\right)}{1 - e^{2(r-D+\frac{1}{2}\sigma^2)\Delta t}}\right]$$

$$= \frac{e^{2(r-D+\frac{1}{2}\sigma^2)\Delta t}\left(1 - e^{2(r-D+\frac{1}{2}\sigma^2)(n-k)\Delta t}\right)}{1 - e^{2(r-D+\frac{1}{2}\sigma^2)\Delta t}}$$

whilst for

$$B_2 = \sum_{\substack{i=k+1 \\ i<j}}^{n} \sum_{j=k+1}^{n} e^{(r-D)(i+j-2k)\Delta t + \sigma^2(\min\{i,j\}-k)\Delta t}$$

$$= \sum_{i=k+1}^{n} \sum_{j=i+1}^{n} e^{(r-D)(i+j-2k)\Delta t + \sigma^2(i-k)\Delta t}$$

$$= e^{\sigma^2 \Delta t} \sum_{j=k+2}^{n} e^{(r-D)(j-k+1)\Delta t} + e^{2\sigma^2 \Delta t} \sum_{j=k+3}^{n} e^{(r-D)(j-k+2)\Delta t}$$

$$+ e^{3\sigma^2 \Delta t} \sum_{j=k+4}^{n} e^{(r-D)(j-k+3)\Delta t} + \ldots + e^{(n-k-1)\sigma^2 \Delta t} e^{(r-D)(2n-2k-1)\Delta t}$$

and given each term is a geometric series

$$B_2 = e^{\sigma^2 \Delta t} \left[\frac{e^{3(r-D)\Delta t} \left(1 - e^{(r-D)(n-k-1)\Delta t}\right)}{1 - e^{(r-D)\Delta t}} \right]$$

$$+ e^{2\sigma^2 \Delta t} \left[\frac{e^{5(r-D)\Delta t} \left(1 - e^{(r-D)(n-k-2)\Delta t}\right)}{1 - e^{(r-D)\Delta t}} \right]$$

$$+ e^{3\sigma^2 \Delta t} \left[\frac{e^{7(r-D)\Delta t} \left(1 - e^{(r-D)(n-k-3)\Delta t}\right)}{1 - e^{(r-D)\Delta t}} \right]$$

$$+ \ldots + e^{(n-k-1)\sigma^2 \Delta t} \left[\frac{e^{(r-D)(2n-2k-1)\Delta t} \left(1 - e^{(r-D)\Delta t}\right)}{1 - e^{(r-D)\Delta t}} \right]$$

$$= \frac{e^{(3(r-D)+\sigma^2)\Delta t} + e^{(5(r-D)+2\sigma^2)\Delta t} + \ldots + e^{(2n-2k-1)(r-D)+(n-k-1)\sigma^2}}{1 - e^{(r-D)\Delta t}}$$

$$- \frac{e^{((n-k+2)(r-D)+\sigma^2)\Delta t} + e^{((n-k+3)(r-D)+2\sigma^2)\Delta t} + \ldots + e^{((2n-2k-1)(r-D)+(n-k-1)\sigma^2)\Delta t}}{1 - e^{(r-D)\Delta t}}$$

$$= \frac{e^{(3(r-D)+\sigma^2)\Delta t} \left(1 - e^{2(r-D+\frac{1}{2}\sigma^2)(n-k-1)\Delta t}\right)}{\left(1 - e^{(r-D)\Delta t}\right) \left(1 - e^{2(r-D+\frac{1}{2}\sigma^2)\Delta t}\right)}$$

$$- \frac{e^{((n-k+2)(r-D)+\sigma^2)\Delta t} \left(1 - e^{(r-D+\sigma^2)(n-k-1)\Delta t}\right)}{\left(1 - e^{(r-D)\Delta t}\right) \left(1 - e^{(r-D+\sigma^2)\Delta t}\right)}.$$

Using similar steps we would eventually have

$$B_3 = \sum_{\substack{i=k+1 \\ i>j}}^{n} \sum_{j=k+1}^{n} e^{(r-D)(i+j-2k)\Delta t + \sigma^2(\min\{i,j\}-k)\Delta t}$$

$$= \sum_{i=k+1}^{n} \sum_{j=k+1}^{i-1} e^{(r-D)(i+j-2k)\Delta t + \sigma^2(j-k)\Delta t}$$

$$= \frac{e^{(3(r-D)+\sigma^2)\Delta t}\left(1 - e^{2(r-D+\frac{1}{2}\sigma^2)(n-k-1)\Delta t}\right)}{\left(1 - e^{(r-D)\Delta t}\right)\left(1 - e^{2(r-D+\frac{1}{2}\sigma^2)\Delta t}\right)}$$

$$- \frac{e^{((n-k+2)(r-D)+\sigma^2)\Delta t}\left(1 - e^{(r-D+\sigma^2)(n-k-1)\Delta t}\right)}{\left(1 - e^{(r-D)\Delta t}\right)\left(1 - e^{(r-D+\sigma^2)\Delta t}\right)}.$$

Therefore

$$\mathbb{E}^Q\left[A_n(t_{k+1},t_n)^2 \Big| S_t\right] = \frac{S_t^2 e^{-2(r-D+\frac{1}{2}\sigma^2)\epsilon\Delta t}}{n^2}\left[\frac{e^{2(r-D+\frac{1}{2}\sigma^2)\Delta t}\left(1 - e^{2(r-D+\frac{1}{2}\sigma^2)(n-k)\Delta t}\right)}{1 - e^{2(r-D+\frac{1}{2}\sigma^2)\Delta t}}\right.$$

$$+ \frac{2e^{(3(r-D)+\sigma^2)\Delta t}\left(1 - e^{2(r-D+\frac{1}{2}\sigma^2)(n-k-1)\Delta t}\right)}{\left(1 - e^{(r-D)\Delta t}\right)\left(1 - e^{2(r-D+\frac{1}{2}\sigma^2)\Delta t}\right)}$$

$$\left. - \frac{2e^{((n-k+2)(r-D)+\sigma^2)\Delta t}\left(1 - e^{(r-D+\sigma^2)(n-k-1)\Delta t}\right)}{\left(1 - e^{(r-D)\Delta t}\right)\left(1 - e^{(r-D+\sigma^2)\Delta t}\right)}\right].$$

Thus, using the above information we can deduce that the discrete arithmetic average rate Asian put option price at time $t < T$ can be approximated by

$$P_{ar}^{(a)}(S_t, A_n, t; K, T) = e^{-r(T-t)}\mathbb{E}^Q\left[\max\left\{K - \frac{1}{n}\sum_{i=1}^{n}S_{t_i}, 0\right\}\Big|\mathscr{F}_t\right]$$

$$\approx \overline{K}e^{-r(T-t)}\Phi(-\overline{d}_{-}^{(n)}) - e^{m+\frac{1}{2}s^2 - r(T-t)}\Phi(-\overline{d}_{+}^{(n)})$$

where

$$\overline{K} = K - A_n(t_1, t_k)$$

$$\overline{d}_+^{(n)} = \frac{m + s^2 - \log \overline{K}}{s}$$

$$\overline{d}_-^{(n)} = \overline{d}_+^{(n)} - s$$

$$m \approx 2 \log \mathbb{E}^{\mathbb{Q}} \left[A_n(t_{k+1}, t_n) \middle| S_t \right] - \frac{1}{2} \log \mathbb{E}^{\mathbb{Q}} \left[A_n(t_{k+1}, t_n)^2 \middle| S_t \right]$$

$$s^2 \approx \log \mathbb{E}^{\mathbb{Q}} \left[A_n(t_{k+1}, t_n)^2 \middle| S_t \right] - 2 \log \mathbb{E}^{\mathbb{Q}} \left[A_n(t_{k+1}, t_n) \middle| S_t \right].$$

Since $T = \tau + n\Delta t$ and $t = t_k + \epsilon\Delta t = \tau + (k + \epsilon)\Delta t$, $\epsilon \in [0, 1)$ therefore

$$\lim_{n \to \infty} (n - k)\Delta t = \lim_{n \to \infty} (T - t + \epsilon\Delta t) = T - t$$

and

$$\lim_{n \to \infty} (n - k - 1)\Delta t = \lim_{n \to \infty} (T - t + (\epsilon - 1)\Delta t) = T - t.$$

Taking limits $n \to \infty$,

$$\begin{aligned}
\lim_{n \to \infty} \mathbb{E}^{\mathbb{Q}} \left[A_n(t_{k+1}, t_n) \middle| S_t \right] &= \lim_{n \to \infty} \frac{S_t e^{(r-D)(1-\epsilon)\Delta t}}{n} \left[\frac{1 - e^{(r-D)(n-k)\Delta t}}{1 - e^{(r-D)\Delta t}} \right] \\
&= \lim_{n \to \infty} \frac{S_t e^{(r-D)(1-\epsilon)\Delta t}(1 - e^{(r-D)(n-k)\Delta t})}{n\Delta t} \\
&\quad \times \lim_{\Delta t \to 0} \frac{\Delta t}{1 - e^{(r-D)\Delta t}} \\
&= \frac{S_t(1 - e^{(r-D)(T-t)})}{T - \tau} \lim_{\Delta t \to 0} \frac{\Delta t}{1 - e^{(r-D)\Delta t}}.
\end{aligned}$$

From L'Hôpital's rule

$$\lim_{\Delta t \to 0} \frac{\Delta t}{1 - e^{(r-D)\Delta t}} = \lim_{\Delta t \to 0} \frac{1}{-(r-D)e^{(r-D)\Delta t}} = -\frac{1}{r - D}$$

and hence

$$\lim_{n \to \infty} \mathbb{E}^{\mathbb{Q}} \left[A_n(t_{k+1}, t_n) \middle| S_t \right] = \frac{S_t(e^{(r-D)(T-t)} - 1)}{(r - D)(T - \tau)}.$$

In contrast,

$$
\lim_{n\to\infty} \mathbb{E}^{\mathbb{Q}}\left[A_n(t_{k+1}, t_n)^2 \,\middle|\, S_t \right] = \lim_{n\to\infty} \frac{S_t^2 e^{-2(r-D+\frac{1}{2}\sigma^2)\epsilon\Delta t}}{n^2}
$$

$$
\times \left[\frac{e^{2(r-D+\frac{1}{2}\sigma^2)\Delta t}\left(1 - e^{2(r-D+\frac{1}{2}\sigma^2)(n-k)\Delta t}\right)}{1 - e^{2(r-D+\frac{1}{2}\sigma^2)\Delta t}} \right.
$$

$$
+ \frac{2e^{(3(r-D)+\sigma^2)\Delta t}\left(1 - e^{2(r-D+\frac{1}{2}\sigma^2)(n-k-1)\Delta t}\right)}{\left(1 - e^{(r-D)\Delta t}\right)\left(1 - e^{2(r-D+\frac{1}{2}\sigma^2)\Delta t}\right)}
$$

$$
\left. - \frac{2e^{((n-k+2)(r-D)+\sigma^2)\Delta t}\left(1 - e^{(r-D+\sigma^2)(n-k-1)\Delta t}\right)}{\left(1 - e^{(r-D)\Delta t}\right)\left(1 - e^{(r-D+\sigma^2)\Delta t}\right)} \right]
$$

$$
= \lim_{n\to\infty} \frac{S_t^2 e^{-2(r-D+\frac{1}{2}\sigma^2)\epsilon\Delta t}}{n^2 \Delta t^2}
$$

$$
\times \left[\frac{e^{2(r-D+\frac{1}{2}\sigma^2)\Delta t}\left(1 - e^{2(r-D+\frac{1}{2}\sigma^2)(n-k)\Delta t}\right)\Delta t^2}{1 - e^{2(r-D+\frac{1}{2}\sigma^2)\Delta t}} \right.
$$

$$
+ \frac{2e^{(3(r-D)+\sigma^2)\Delta t}\left(1 - e^{2(r-D+\frac{1}{2}\sigma^2)(n-k-1)\Delta t}\right)\Delta t^2}{\left(1 - e^{(r-D)\Delta t}\right)\left(1 - e^{2(r-D+\frac{1}{2}\sigma^2)\Delta t}\right)}
$$

$$
\left. - \frac{2e^{((n-k+2)(r-D)+\sigma^2)\Delta t}\left(1 - e^{(r-D+\sigma^2)(n-k-1)\Delta t}\right)\Delta t^2}{\left(1 - e^{(r-D)\Delta t}\right)\left(1 - e^{(r-D+\sigma^2)\Delta t}\right)} \right]
$$

$$
= C_1 + C_2 - C_3
$$

where

$$
C_1 = \lim_{n\to\infty} \frac{S_t^2 e^{2(r-D+\frac{1}{2}\sigma^2)(1-\epsilon)\Delta t}\left(1 - e^{2(r-D+\frac{1}{2}\sigma^2)(n-k)\Delta t}\right)}{n^2 \Delta t^2}
$$

$$
\times \lim_{\Delta t\to 0} \frac{\Delta t^2}{1 - e^{2(r-D+\frac{1}{2}\sigma^2)\Delta t}}
$$

$$C_2 = \lim_{n \to \infty} \frac{2S_t^2 e^{2(r-D+\frac{1}{2}\sigma^2)(1-\epsilon)\Delta t} \left(1 - e^{2(r-D+\frac{1}{2}\sigma^2)(n-k-1)\Delta t}\right) e^{(r-D)\Delta t}}{n^2 \Delta t^2}$$

$$\times \lim_{\Delta t \to 0} \frac{\Delta t^2}{\left(1 - e^{(r-D)\Delta t}\right)\left(1 - e^{2(r-D+\frac{1}{2}\sigma^2)\Delta t}\right)}$$

and

$$C_3 = \lim_{n \to \infty} \frac{2S_t^2 e^{2(r-D+\frac{1}{2}\sigma^2)(1-\epsilon)\Delta t} \left(1 - e^{(r-D+\sigma^2)(n-k-1)\Delta t}\right) e^{(r-D)(n-k)\Delta t}}{n^2 \Delta t^2}$$

$$\times \lim_{\Delta t \to 0} \frac{\Delta t^2}{\left(1 - e^{(r-D)\Delta t}\right)\left(1 - e^{(r-D+\sigma^2)\Delta t}\right)}.$$

By taking limits $n \to \infty$ and by applying L'Hôpital's rule

$$C_1 = \frac{S_t^2 \left(1 - e^{2(r-D+\frac{1}{2}\sigma^2)(T-t)}\right)}{(T-\tau)^2} \lim_{\Delta t \to 0} \frac{2\Delta t}{-2\left(r - D + \frac{1}{2}\sigma^2\right) e^{2(r-D+\frac{1}{2}\sigma^2)\Delta t}} = 0$$

$$C_2 = \frac{2S_t^2 \left(1 - e^{2(r-D+\frac{1}{2}\sigma^2)(T-t)}\right)}{(T-\tau)^2}$$

$$\times \lim_{\Delta t \to 0} \frac{2\Delta t}{\left[\begin{array}{l} -(r - D)e^{(r-D)\Delta t}\left(1 - e^{2(r-D+\frac{1}{2}\sigma^2)\Delta t}\right) \\[2mm] -2\left(r - D + \frac{1}{2}\sigma^2\right) e^{2(r-D+\frac{1}{2}\sigma^2)\Delta t}\left(1 - e^{(r-D)\Delta t}\right) \end{array} \right]}$$

$$= \frac{2S_t^2 \left(1 - e^{2(r-D+\frac{1}{2}\sigma^2)(T-t)}\right)}{(T-\tau)^2}$$

$$\times \lim_{\Delta t \to 0} \frac{2}{\left[\begin{array}{l} -(r - D)^2 e^{(r-D)\Delta t}\left(1 - e^{2(r-D+\frac{1}{2}\sigma^2)\Delta t}\right) \\[2mm] +4(r - D)\left(r - D + \frac{1}{2}\sigma^2\right) e^{(3(r-D)+\sigma^2)\Delta t} \\[2mm] -4\left(r - D + \frac{1}{2}\sigma^2\right)^2 e^{2(r-D+\frac{1}{2}\sigma^2)\Delta t}\left(1 - e^{(r-D)\Delta t}\right) \end{array} \right]}$$

$$= \frac{S_t^2 \left(1 - e^{2(r-D+\frac{1}{2}\sigma^2)(T-t)}\right)}{(r - D)\left(r - D + \frac{1}{2}\sigma^2\right)(T-\tau)^2}$$

and

$$C_3 = \frac{2S_t^2 \left(1 - e^{(r-D+\sigma^2)(T-t)}\right) e^{(r-D)(T-t)}}{(T-\tau)^2}$$

$$\times \lim_{\Delta t \to 0} \frac{2\Delta t}{\begin{bmatrix} -(r-D)e^{(r-D)\Delta t}\left(1 - e^{(r-D+\sigma^2)\Delta t}\right) \\ \\ -(r-D+\sigma^2)e^{(r-D+\sigma^2)(1-e^{(r-D)\Delta t})} \end{bmatrix}}$$

$$= \frac{2S_t^2 \left(1 - e^{(r-D+\sigma^2)(T-t)}\right) e^{(r-D)(T-t)}}{(T-\tau)^2}$$

$$\times \lim_{\Delta t \to 0} \frac{2}{\begin{bmatrix} -(r-D)^2 e^{(r-D)\Delta t}\left(1 - e^{(r-D+\sigma^2)\Delta t}\right) \\ \\ +2(r-D)(r-D+\sigma^2)e^{2(r-D+\frac{1}{2}\sigma^2)\Delta t} \\ \\ -(r-D+\sigma^2)e^{(r-D+\sigma^2)\Delta t}\left(1 - e^{(r-D)\Delta t}\right) \end{bmatrix}}$$

$$= \frac{2S_t^2 \left(1 - e^{(r-D+\sigma^2)(T-t)}\right) e^{(r-D)(T-t)}}{(r-D)(r-D+\sigma^2)(T-\tau)^2}.$$

Thus,

$$\lim_{n \to \infty} \mathbb{E}^Q \left[A_n(t_{k+1}, t_n)^2 \big| S_t \right] = \frac{S_t^2}{(r-D)(T-\tau)^2} \left[\frac{2\left(e^{(r-D+\sigma^2)(T-t)} - 1\right) e^{(r-D)(T-t)}}{r-D+\sigma^2} \right.$$

$$\left. - \frac{\left(e^{2(r-D+\frac{1}{2}\sigma^2)(T-t)} - 1\right)}{r-D+\frac{1}{2}\sigma^2} \right].$$

□

8. *Curran Approximation – Discrete Arithmetic Average Rate (Fixed Strike) Asian Option.*
   Let the asset price S_t follow the GBM

$$\frac{dS_t}{S_t} = (\mu - D)dt + \sigma \, dW_t$$

where W_t is the $\mathbb{P}$-standard Wiener process on the probability space $(\Omega, \mathscr{F}, \mathbb{P})$, μ, D and σ are the drift parameter, continuous dividend yield and volatility, respectively. In addition, let r be the risk-free interest rate.

Let the time interval $[\tau, T]$ be partitioned into n equal subintervals each of length $\Delta t = (T - \tau)/n$ and let S_{t_i}, $t_i = \tau + i\Delta t$ be the asset price at the end of the ith interval, $i = 1, 2, \dots, n$. We define the discretely measured arithmetic average of asset prices as

$$A_n(\tau, T) = \frac{1}{n} \sum_{i=1}^{n} S_{t_i}$$

and the discretely measured geometric average of asset prices as

$$G_n(\tau, T) = \left(\prod_{i=1}^{n} S_{t_i} \right)^{\frac{1}{n}}.$$

We consider an arithmetic average rate Asian call option with expiry $T > t > \tau$ and payoff

$$\Psi(S_T, A_n(\tau, T)) = \max\{A_n(\tau, T) - K, 0\}$$

where $K > 0$ is the strike price.

Show that if the random variables X and Y follow a joint normal distribution

$$(X, Y) \sim \mathcal{N}_2(\boldsymbol{\mu}, \boldsymbol{\Sigma})$$

where $\boldsymbol{\mu} = \begin{bmatrix} \mu_x \\ \mu_y \end{bmatrix}$ and $\boldsymbol{\Sigma} = \begin{bmatrix} \text{Var}(X) & \text{Cov}(X, Y) \\ \text{Cov}(X, Y) & \text{Var}(Y) \end{bmatrix} = \begin{bmatrix} \sigma_x^2 & \rho_{xy}\sigma_x\sigma_y \\ \rho_{xy}\sigma_x\sigma_y & \sigma_y^2 \end{bmatrix}$ where μ_x, μ_y are the means, σ_x^2, σ_y^2 are the variances and $\rho_{xy} \in (-1, 1)$ is the correlation coefficient, then the conditional distribution

$$X \mid Y = y \sim \mathcal{N}\left(\mu_x + \rho_{xy}\frac{\sigma_x}{\sigma_y}(y - \mu_y), (1 - \rho_{xy}^2)\sigma_x^2 \right).$$

Suppose $S_{t_1}, S_{t_2}, \dots, S_{t_k}$, $1 \leq k \leq n - 1$ have been observed and let $t_k \leq t < t_{k+1}$ where $t = t_k + \epsilon\Delta t$, $\epsilon \in [0, 1)$. Show that under the risk-neutral measure $\mathbb{Q}$, for $t_i > t_k$

$$\log S_{t_i} \sim \mathcal{N}(\mu_i, \sigma_i^2)$$
$$\log G_n(\tau, T) \sim \mathcal{N}(\mu_G, \sigma_G^2)$$

where

$$\mu_i = \log S_t + \left(r - D - \frac{1}{2}\sigma^2 \right)(i - k - \epsilon)\Delta t$$
$$\sigma_i^2 = \sigma^2(i - k - \epsilon)\Delta t$$

and

$$\mu_G = \log\left[\left(\prod_{j=1}^{k} S_{t_j}\right)^{\frac{1}{n}} S_t^{\frac{n-k}{n}}\right]$$

$$+ \left(r - D - \frac{1}{2}\sigma^2\right)\left[\frac{(n-k-1)(n-k)}{2n} + \frac{(1-\epsilon)(n-k)}{n}\right]\Delta t$$

$$\sigma_G^2 = \sigma^2\left[\frac{(n-k)(2(n-k)-1)(n-k-1)}{6n^2} + \frac{(1-\epsilon)(n-k)^2}{n^2}\right]\Delta t.$$

Given the pair of random variables $\left(\log S_{t_i}, \log G_n(\tau, T)\right)$, $t_i > t_k$ show that it has the covariance matrix

$$\Sigma = \begin{bmatrix} \sigma_i^2 & \sigma_{iG} \\ \sigma_{iG} & \sigma_G^2 \end{bmatrix}$$

where

$$\sigma_{iG} = \frac{\sigma^2}{2n}\left[(i-k-\epsilon)(2n-i-k) + (1-\epsilon)(i-k)\right]\Delta t$$

and $\left(\log S_{t_i}, \log G_n(\tau, T)\right)$ follows a bivariate normal distribution.

Hence, deduce that the conditional distribution of $\log S_{t_i}$, $t_i > t_k$ given $\log G_n(\tau, T)$ is

$$\log S_{t_i} | \log G_n(\tau, T) = y \sim \mathcal{N}\left(\mu_i + (y - \mu_G)\frac{\sigma_{iG}}{\sigma_G^2}, \sigma_i^2 - \frac{\sigma_{iG}^2}{\sigma_G^2}\right).$$

Show that for any random variable Z under the filtration $\mathcal{G}$,

$$0 \leq \mathbb{E}\left(\max\{Z, 0\} | \mathcal{G}\right) - \max\left\{\mathbb{E}(Z | \mathcal{G}), 0\right\} \leq \frac{1}{2}\sqrt{\text{Var}(Z | \mathcal{G})}.$$

By defining the arithmetic average rate (fixed strike) call option price at time t, $\tau < t_k < t < T$ as

$$C_{ar}^{(a)}(S_t, A_n(\tau, T), t; K, T) = e^{-r(T-t)}\mathbb{E}^{\mathbb{Q}}\left[\max\{A_n(\tau, T) - K, 0\} | \mathcal{F}_t\right]$$

and by setting $A_n(t_1, t_k) = \frac{1}{n}\sum_{j=1}^{k} S_{t_j}$ and using the following tower property

$$\mathbb{E}^{\mathbb{Q}}\left[\max\{A_n(\tau, T) - K, 0\} | \mathcal{F}_t\right] = \mathbb{E}^{\mathbb{Q}}\left[\mathbb{E}^{\mathbb{Q}}\left[\max\{A_n(\tau, T) - K, 0\} | G_n(\tau, T)\right] \middle| \mathcal{F}_t\right]$$

show that

$$C_{lower} \leq C_{ar}^{(a)}(S_t, A_n(\tau, T), t; K, T) \leq C_{upper}$$

where

$$C_{lower} = e^{-r(T-t)} \left[\frac{1}{n} \sum_{i=k+1}^{n} e^{\mu_i + \frac{1}{2}\sigma_i^2} \Phi\left(\frac{\mu_G - \log \widetilde{K} + \sigma_{iG}}{\sigma_G} \right) \right.$$

$$\left. + \left(A_n(t_1, t_k) - K \right) \Phi\left(\frac{\mu_G - \log \widetilde{K}}{\sigma_G} \right) \right]$$

$$C_{upper} = C_{lower} + \frac{1}{2} e^{-r(T-t)} \mathbb{E}^Q \left[\sqrt{Var\left[\frac{1}{n} \sum_{i=k+1}^{n} S_{t_i} \middle| G_n(\tau, T) \right]} \middle| \mathcal{F}_t \right]$$

$$\widetilde{K} = \left\{ z \middle| A_n(\tau, t_k) + \frac{1}{n} \sum_{i=k+1}^{n} e^{\mu_i + (\log z - \mu_G)\sigma_{iG}/\sigma_G^2 + \frac{1}{2}(\sigma_i^2 - \sigma_{iG}^2/\sigma_G^2)} = K \right\}$$

and $\Phi(x) = \int_{-\infty}^{x} \frac{1}{\sqrt{2\pi}} e^{-\frac{1}{2}u^2} du$ is the cdf of a standard normal.

Solution: If (X, Y) follows a bivariate normal distribution then the joint pdf is given as

$$f_{XY}(x, y) = \frac{1}{2\pi\sigma_x\sigma_y\sqrt{1-\rho_{xy}^2}} e^{-\frac{1}{2(1-\rho_{xy}^2)}\left[\left(\frac{x-\mu_x}{\sigma_x}\right)^2 - 2\rho_{xy}\left(\frac{x-\mu_x}{\sigma_x}\right)\left(\frac{y-\mu_y}{\sigma_y}\right) + \left(\frac{y-\mu_y}{\sigma_y}\right)^2 \right]}.$$

The pdf of the conditional distribution

$$f_{X|Y}(x|y) = \frac{f_{XY}(x, y)}{f_Y(y)}$$

$$= \frac{\frac{1}{2\pi\sigma_x\sigma_y\sqrt{1-\rho_{xy}^2}} e^{-\frac{1}{2(1-\rho_{xy}^2)}\left[\left(\frac{x-\mu_x}{\sigma_x}\right)^2 - 2\rho_{xy}\left(\frac{x-\mu_x}{\sigma_x}\right)\left(\frac{y-\mu_y}{\sigma_y}\right) + \left(\frac{y-\mu_y}{\sigma_y}\right)^2 \right]}}{\frac{1}{\sigma_y\sqrt{2\pi}} e^{-\frac{1}{2}\left(\frac{y-\mu_y}{\sigma_y}\right)^2}}$$

$$= \frac{1}{\sqrt{2\pi}\sigma_x\sqrt{1-\rho_{xy}^2}} e^{-\frac{1}{2(1-\rho_{xy}^2)}\left[\left(\frac{x-\mu_x}{\sigma_x}\right)^2 - 2\rho_{xy}\left(\frac{x-\mu_x}{\sigma_x}\right)\left(\frac{y-\mu_y}{\sigma_y}\right) + \rho_{xy}^2\left(\frac{y-\mu_y}{\sigma_y}\right)^2 \right]}$$

$$= \frac{1}{\sqrt{2\pi}\sigma_x\sqrt{1-\rho_{xy}^2}} e^{-\frac{1}{2}\left[\frac{x - \left(\mu_x + \rho_{xy}\frac{\sigma_x}{\sigma_y}(y-\mu_y)\right)}{\sigma_x\sqrt{1-\rho_{xy}^2}} \right]^2}.$$

Hence, $X\,|\,Y = y \sim \mathcal{N}\left(\mu_x + \rho_{xy}\dfrac{\sigma_x}{\sigma_y}(y - \mu_y), (1 - \rho_{xy}^2)\sigma_x^2\right)$.

Under the risk-neutral measure $\mathbb{Q}$, S_t follows

$$\frac{dS_t}{S_t} = (r - D)dt + \sigma\, dW_t^{\mathbb{Q}}$$

where $W_t^{\mathbb{Q}} = \left(\dfrac{\mu - r}{\sigma}\right)t + W_t$ is a $\mathbb{Q}$-standard Wiener process.

Thus, conditional on S_t for $t_i > t_k$

$$S_{t_i} = S_t e^{(r - D - \frac{1}{2}\sigma^2)(t_i - t) + \sigma W_{t_i - t}}$$

or

$$\log S_{t_i} = \log S_t + \left(r - D - \frac{1}{2}\sigma^2\right)(t_i - t) + \sigma W_{t_i - t}$$

where $W_{t_i - t} \sim \mathcal{N}(0, t_i - t)$. Hence, we can easily deduce that

$$\log S_{t_i} \sim \mathcal{N}(\mu_i, \sigma_i^2)$$

where $\mu_i = \mathbb{E}^{\mathbb{Q}}\left[\log S_{t_i} \,\middle|\, S_t\right]$ and $\sigma_i^2 = \text{Var}^{\mathbb{Q}}\left[\log S_{t_i} \,\middle|\, S_t\right]$.

Since $t = t_k + \epsilon\Delta t$, $t_i = \tau + i\Delta t$ and $t_k = \tau + k\Delta t$,

$$\begin{aligned}
\mu_i &= \mathbb{E}^{\mathbb{Q}}\left[\log S_{t_i} \,\middle|\, S_t\right] \\
&= \log S_t + \left(r - D - \frac{1}{2}\sigma^2\right)(t_i - t) \\
&= \log S_t + \left(r - D - \frac{1}{2}\sigma^2\right)(i - k - \epsilon)\Delta t
\end{aligned}$$

and

$$\begin{aligned}
\sigma_i^2 &= \text{Var}^{\mathbb{Q}}\left[\log S_{t_i} \,\middle|\, S_t\right] \\
&= \sigma^2(t_i - t) \\
&= \sigma^2(i - k - \epsilon)\Delta t.
\end{aligned}$$

For the geometric average, since $S_{t_1}, S_{t_2}, \ldots, S_{t_k}$, $1 \le k \le n - 1$ have been observed, by taking logarithms

$$\begin{aligned}
\log G_n(\tau, T) &= \frac{1}{n}\log\left(\prod_{j=1}^{n} S_{t_j}\right) \\
&= \frac{1}{n}\sum_{j=1}^{n} \log S_{t_j} \\
&= \frac{1}{n}\sum_{j=1}^{k} \log S_{t_j} + \frac{1}{n}\sum_{j=k+1}^{n} \log S_{t_j}
\end{aligned}$$

$$= \frac{1}{n} \sum_{j=1}^{k} \log S_{t_j} + \frac{1}{n} \sum_{j=k+1}^{n} \left[\log S_t + \left(r - D - \frac{1}{2}\sigma^2 \right)(t_j - t) + \sigma W_{t_j - t} \right]$$

$$= \log \left[\left(\prod_{j=1}^{k} S_{t_j} \right)^{\frac{1}{n}} S_t^{\frac{n-k}{n}} \right] + \frac{1}{n} \left(r - D - \frac{1}{2}\sigma^2 \right) \sum_{j=k+1}^{n} (t_j - t)$$

$$+ \frac{\sigma}{n} \sum_{j=k+1}^{n} W_{t_j - t}.$$

Since $W_{t_j - t} \sim \mathcal{N}(0, t_j - t)$ and because the sum of normal variates is also normal, we can therefore deduce

$$\log G_n(\tau, T) \sim \mathcal{N}(\mu_G, \sigma_G^2)$$

with $\mu_G = \mathbb{E}^{\mathbb{Q}}\left[\log G_n(\tau, T) \middle| S_t \right]$ and $\sigma_G^2 = \text{Var}^{\mathbb{Q}}\left[\log G_n(\tau, T) \middle| S_t \right]$.

Since $t = t_k + \epsilon \Delta t$, $t_j = \tau + j\Delta t$ and $t_k = \tau + k\Delta t$,

$$\mu_G = \mathbb{E}^{\mathbb{Q}}\left[\log G_n(\tau, T) \middle| S_t \right]$$

$$= \log \left[\left(\prod_{j=1}^{k} S_{t_j} \right)^{\frac{1}{n}} S_t^{\frac{n-k}{n}} \right] + \frac{1}{n} \left(r - D - \frac{1}{2}\sigma^2 \right) \sum_{j=k+1}^{n} (t_i - t)$$

$$= \log \left[\left(\prod_{j=1}^{k} S_{t_j} \right)^{\frac{1}{n}} S_t^{\frac{n-k}{n}} \right] + \frac{1}{n} \left(r - D - \frac{1}{2}\sigma^2 \right) \sum_{j=k+1}^{n} (i - k - \epsilon)\Delta t$$

$$= \log \left[\left(\prod_{j=1}^{k} S_{t_j} \right)^{\frac{1}{n}} S_t^{\frac{n-k}{n}} \right]$$

$$+ \left(r - D - \frac{1}{2}\sigma^2 \right) \left(\frac{n-k}{n} \right) (n - k + 1 - 2\epsilon) \Delta t$$

$$= \log \left[\left(\prod_{j=1}^{k} S_{t_j} \right)^{\frac{1}{n}} S_t^{\frac{n-k}{n}} \right]$$

$$+ \left(r - D - \frac{1}{2}\sigma^2 \right) \left[\frac{(n-k-1)(n-k)}{2n} + \frac{(1-\epsilon)(n-k)}{n} \right] \Delta t$$

and because

$$\sum_{k=1}^{n} k^2 = \frac{1}{6}n(n+1)(2n+1)$$

the variance is

$$\sigma_G^2 = \text{Var}^Q \left[\log G_n(\tau, T) \,\middle|\, S_t \right]$$

$$= \text{Cov}^Q \left(\frac{\sigma}{n} \sum_{p=k+1}^{n} W_{t_p-t}, \frac{\sigma}{n} \sum_{q=k+1}^{n} W_{t_q-t} \right)$$

$$= \frac{\sigma^2}{n^2} \sum_{p=k+1}^{n} \sum_{q=k+1}^{n} \text{Cov}^Q \left(W_{t_p-t}, W_{t_q-t} \right)$$

$$= \frac{\sigma^2}{n^2} \sum_{p=k+1}^{n} \sum_{q=k+1}^{n} \min\{t_p - t, t_q - t\}$$

$$= \frac{\sigma^2}{n^2} \sum_{p=k+1}^{n} \left[\sum_{q=k+1}^{p} \min\{t_p - t, t_q - t\} \right.$$

$$\left. + \sum_{q=p+1}^{n} \min\{t_p - t, t_q - t\} \right]$$

$$= \frac{\sigma^2}{n^2} \left[\sum_{p=k+1}^{n} \sum_{q=k+1}^{p} (t_q - t) + \sum_{p=k+1}^{n} \sum_{q=p+1}^{n} (t_p - t) \right]$$

$$= \frac{\sigma^2}{n^2} \left[\sum_{p=k+1}^{n} \sum_{q=k+1}^{p} (q - k - \epsilon)\Delta t + \sum_{p=k+1}^{n} \sum_{q=p+1}^{n} (p - k - \epsilon)\Delta t \right]$$

$$= \frac{\sigma^2}{n^2} \left[\sum_{p=k+1}^{n} \left(\frac{p-k}{2} \right) (p - k + 1 - 2\epsilon)\Delta t \right.$$

$$\left. + \sum_{p=k+1}^{n} (n - p)(p - k - \epsilon)\Delta t \right]$$

$$= \frac{\sigma^2}{2n^2} \left[\sum_{p=k+1}^{n} (2(n-k)+1)(p-k) - \sum_{p=k+1}^{n} (p-k)^2 \right.$$

$$\left. - \sum_{p=k+1}^{n} 2(n-k)\epsilon \right] \Delta t$$

$$= \frac{\sigma^2}{2n^2} \left[\frac{(2(n-k)+1)(n-k)(n-k+1)}{2} \right.$$

$$\left. - \frac{(2(n-k)+1)(n-k+1)(n-k)}{6} - 2(n-k)^2\epsilon \right] \Delta t$$

$$= \sigma^2 \left[\frac{(2(n-k)+1)(n-k)(n-k+1)}{6n^2} - \frac{(n-k)^2\epsilon}{n^2} \right] \Delta t$$

$$= \sigma^2 \left[\frac{(n-k)(2(n-k)-1)(n-k-1)}{6n^2} + \frac{(1-\epsilon)(n-k)^2}{n^2} \right] \Delta t.$$

To find the covariance of the random variables $(\log S_{t_i}, \log G_n(\tau, T))$, by definition

$$\text{Cov}\left(\log S_{t_i}, \log G_n(\tau, T)\right) = \text{Cov}\left(\log S_{t_i}, \frac{1}{n}\sum_{j=1}^{n}\log S_{t_j}\right)$$

$$= \text{Cov}\left(\log S_{t_i}, \frac{1}{n}\sum_{j=k+1}^{n}\log S_{t_j}\right)$$

$$= \frac{1}{n}\sum_{j=k+1}^{n}\text{Cov}\left(\log S_{t_i}, \log S_{t_j}\right)$$

$$= \frac{1}{n}\left[\sum_{j=k+1}^{i}\text{Cov}\left(\log S_{t_i}, \log S_{t_j}\right)\right.$$

$$\left. + \sum_{j=i+1}^{n}\text{Cov}\left(\log S_{t_i}, \log S_{t_j}\right)\right]$$

$$= \frac{1}{n}\left[\sum_{j=k+1}^{i}\sigma^2\min\{t_i - t, t_j - t\}\right.$$

$$\left. + \sum_{j=i+1}^{n}\sigma^2\min\{t_i - t, t_j - t\}\right]$$

$$= \frac{1}{n}\left[\sigma^2\sum_{j=k+1}^{i}(t_j - t) + \sigma^2(n - i)(t_i - t)\right]$$

$$= \frac{\sigma^2}{n}\left[\left(\frac{i-k}{2}\right)(t_{k+1} + t_i - 2t) + (n - i)(t_i - t)\right]$$

$$= \frac{\sigma^2}{n}\left[\left(\frac{i-k}{2}\right)(t_{k+1} + t_i - 2(t_k + \epsilon\Delta t))\right.$$

$$\left. + (n - i)(t_i - t_k - \epsilon\Delta t)\right]$$

$$= \frac{\sigma^2}{n}\left[\left(\frac{i-k}{2}\right)(i - k + 1 - 2\epsilon) + (n - i)(i - k - \epsilon)\right]\Delta t$$

$$= \frac{\sigma^2}{2n}\left[(i - k - \epsilon)(2n - i - k) + (1 - \epsilon)(i - k)\right]\Delta t.$$

To show that the pair $(\log S_{t_i}, \log G_n(\tau, T))$ follows a bivariate normal distribution, let

$$\log S_{t_i} = \mu_i + \sigma_i Z_1$$

$$\log G_n(\tau, T) = \mu_G + \sigma_G\left(\rho Z_1 + \sqrt{1 - \rho^2}Z_2\right)$$

where $Z_1, Z_2 \sim \mathcal{N}(0, 1)$, $Z_1 \perp\!\!\!\perp Z_2$ and $\rho = \dfrac{\sigma_{iG}}{\sigma_i \sigma_G}$.

From the definition of the moment-generating function, for $\theta_1, \theta_2 \in \mathbb{R}$

$$\mathbb{E}^{\mathbb{Q}}\left[e^{\theta_1 \log S_{t_i} + \theta_2 \log G_n(\tau,T)}\right] = \mathbb{E}^{\mathbb{Q}}\left[e^{\theta_1(\mu_i + \sigma_i Z_1) + \theta_2(\mu_G + \sigma_G(\rho Z_1 + \sqrt{1-\rho^2} Z_2))}\right]$$

$$= e^{\theta_1 \mu_i + \theta_2 \mu_G}\mathbb{E}^{\mathbb{Q}}\left[e^{(\theta_1 \sigma_i + \theta_2 \rho \sigma_{iG})Z_1 + (\theta_2 \sigma_{iG}\sqrt{1-\rho^2})Z_2}\right]$$

$$= e^{\theta_1 \mu_i + \theta_2 \mu_G}\mathbb{E}^{\mathbb{Q}}\left[e^{(\theta_1 \sigma_i + \theta_2 \rho \sigma_{iG})Z_1}\right]\mathbb{E}^{\mathbb{Q}}\left[e^{(\theta_2 \sigma_{iG}\sqrt{1-\rho^2})Z_2}\right]$$

$$= e^{\theta_1 \mu_i + \theta_2 \mu_G}e^{\frac{1}{2}(\theta_1 \sigma_i + \theta_2 \rho \sigma_{iG})^2}e^{\frac{1}{2}\theta_2^2 \sigma_{iG}^2(1-\rho^2)}$$

$$= e^{\theta_1 \mu_i + \theta_2 \mu_G + \frac{1}{2}(\theta_1^2 \sigma_i^2 + 2\rho\theta_1\theta_2 \sigma_i \sigma_G + \theta_2^2 \sigma_G^2)}$$

which is the moment-generating function of a bivariate normal distribution. Hence $(\log S_{t_i}, \log G_n(\tau, T)) \sim \mathcal{N}_2(\boldsymbol{\mu}, \boldsymbol{\Sigma})$ where $\boldsymbol{\mu} = \begin{bmatrix} \mu_i \\ \mu_G \end{bmatrix}$ and $\boldsymbol{\Sigma} = \begin{bmatrix} \sigma_i^2 & \sigma_{iG} \\ \sigma_{iG} & \sigma_G^2 \end{bmatrix}$.

By setting $\rho = \dfrac{\sigma_{iG}}{\sigma_i \sigma_G}$ and following the result of the conditional distribution of normal distribution, we have

$$\log S_{t_i} \mid \log G_n(\tau,T) = y \sim \mathcal{N}\left(\mu_i + (y - \mu_G)\frac{\sigma_{iG}}{\sigma_G^2}, \sigma_i^2 - \frac{\sigma_{iG}^2}{\sigma_G^2}\right).$$

To show that for any random variable Z under the filtration $\mathscr{G}$

$$0 \le \mathbb{E}\left(\max\{Z,0\} \mid \mathscr{G}\right) - \max\left\{\mathbb{E}(Z \mid \mathscr{G}), 0\right\} \le \frac{1}{2}\sqrt{\text{Var}(Z \mid \mathscr{G})}$$

we note that since $\max\{x,0\}$ is a non-negative convex function, from the conditional Jensen's inequality (see Problem 1.2.3.14 of *Problems and Solutions in Mathematical Finance, Volume 1: Stochastic Calculus*)

$$\mathbb{E}\left(\max\{Z,0\} \mid \mathscr{G}\right) \ge \max\left\{\mathbb{E}(Z \mid \mathscr{G}), 0\right\}.$$

For a random variable U we can set

$$|U| = \max\{U,0\} - \min\{U,0\}$$
$$U = \max\{U,0\} + \min\{U,0\}.$$

Thus, we can write

$$\mathbb{E}(|Z| \mid \mathscr{G}) = \mathbb{E}\left(\max\{Z,0\} \mid \mathscr{G}\right) - \mathbb{E}\left(\min\{Z,0\} \mid \mathscr{G}\right)$$
$$= \mathbb{E}\left(\max\{Z,0\} \mid \mathscr{G}\right) - [\mathbb{E}(Z \mid \mathscr{G}) - \mathbb{E}\left(\max\{Z,0\} \mid \mathscr{G}\right)]$$
$$= 2\mathbb{E}\left(\max\{Z,0\} \mid \mathscr{G}\right) - \mathbb{E}(Z \mid \mathscr{G})$$

or

$$\mathbb{E}\left(\max\{Z,0\}|\,\mathcal{G}\right) = \frac{1}{2}\left\{\mathbb{E}\left(|Z||\,\mathcal{G}\right) + \mathbb{E}\left(Z|\,\mathcal{G}\right)\right\}.$$

Further, we can write

$$|\mathbb{E}\left(Z|\,\mathcal{G}\right)| = \max\left\{\mathbb{E}\left(Z|\,\mathcal{G}\right),0\right\} - \min\left\{\mathbb{E}\left(Z|\,\mathcal{G}\right),0\right\}$$
$$\mathbb{E}\left(Z|\,\mathcal{G}\right) = \max\left\{\mathbb{E}\left(Z|\,\mathcal{G}\right),0\right\} + \min\left\{\mathbb{E}\left(Z|\,\mathcal{G}\right),0\right\}$$

and by adding the two equations,

$$\max\left\{\mathbb{E}\left(Z|\,\mathcal{G}\right),0\right\} = \frac{1}{2}\left\{|\mathbb{E}\left(Z|\,\mathcal{G}\right)| + \mathbb{E}\left(Z|\,\mathcal{G}\right)\right\}.$$

Thus,

$$\mathbb{E}\left(\max\{Z,0\}|\,\mathcal{G}\right) - \max\left\{\mathbb{E}\left(Z|\,\mathcal{G}\right),0\right\} = \frac{1}{2}\left\{\mathbb{E}\left(|Z||\,\mathcal{G}\right) - \mathbb{E}\left(Z|\,\mathcal{G}\right)\right\}$$
$$\leq \frac{1}{2}\mathbb{E}\left(|Z - \mathbb{E}\left(Z|\,\mathcal{G}\right)||\,\mathcal{G}\right)$$
$$\leq \frac{1}{2}\sqrt{\text{Var}\left(Z|\,\mathcal{G}\right)}.$$

From the definition of the average rate call option price at time t, $\tau < t_k < t < T$

$$C(S_t, A_n(\tau,T), t; K, T) = e^{-r(T-t)}\mathbb{E}^{\mathbb{Q}}\left[\max\{A_n(\tau,T) - K, 0\}|\,\mathcal{F}_t\right]$$
$$= e^{-r(T-t)}\mathbb{E}^{\mathbb{Q}}\left[\mathbb{E}^{\mathbb{Q}}\left[\max\{A_n(\tau,T) - K, 0\}|\,G_n(\tau,T)\right]\bigg|\,\mathcal{F}_t\right].$$

Using the inequality

$$\max\left\{\mathbb{E}\left(Z|\,\mathcal{G}\right),0\right\} \leq \mathbb{E}\left(\max\{Z,0\}|\,\mathcal{G}\right) \leq \max\left\{\mathbb{E}\left(Z|\,\mathcal{G}\right),0\right\} + \frac{1}{2}\sqrt{\text{Var}\left(Z|\,\mathcal{G}\right)}$$

for a random variable Z, C_{lower} and C_{upper} are

$$C_{lower} = e^{-r(T-t)}\mathbb{E}^{\mathbb{Q}}\left[\max\left\{\mathbb{E}^{\mathbb{Q}}\left[A_n(\tau,T) - K|\,G_n(\tau,T)\right],0\right\}\bigg|\,\mathcal{F}_t\right]$$

and

$$C_{upper} = C_{lower} + \frac{1}{2}e^{-r(T-t)}\mathbb{E}^{\mathbb{Q}}\left[\sqrt{\text{Var}\left[A_n(\tau,T) - K|\,G_n(\tau,T)\right]}\,\bigg|\,\mathcal{F}_t\right]$$
$$= C_{lower}$$
$$\quad + \frac{1}{2}e^{-r(T-t)}\mathbb{E}^{\mathbb{Q}}\left[\sqrt{\text{Var}\left[A_n(\tau,t_k) + \frac{1}{n}\sum_{i=k+1}^{n}S_{t_i} - K\,\bigg|\,G_n(\tau,T)\right]}\,\bigg|\,\mathcal{F}_t\right]$$
$$= C_{lower} + \frac{1}{2}e^{-r(T-t)}\mathbb{E}^{\mathbb{Q}}\left[\sqrt{\text{Var}\left[\frac{1}{n}\sum_{i=k+1}^{n}S_{t_i}\,\bigg|\,G_n(\tau,T)\right]}\,\bigg|\,\mathcal{F}_t\right].$$

By setting $g(z)$ as the pdf of $G_n(\tau, T)$ and because $A_n(\tau, T) \geq G_n(\tau, T)$

$$
\begin{aligned}
C_{lower} &= e^{-r(T-t)} \mathbb{E}^Q \left[\max \left\{ \mathbb{E}^Q \left[A_n(\tau, T) - K | G_n(\tau, T) \right], 0 \right\} \Big| \mathcal{F}_t \right] \\
&= e^{-r(T-t)} \int_0^\infty \max \left\{ \mathbb{E}^Q \left[A_n(\tau, T) - K | G_n(\tau, T) = z \right], 0 \right\} g(z) \, dz \\
&= e^{-r(T-t)} \int_0^K \max \left\{ \mathbb{E}^Q \left[A_n(\tau, T) - K | G_n(\tau, T) = z \right], 0 \right\} g(z) \, dz \\
&\quad + e^{-r(T-t)} \int_K^\infty \max \left\{ \mathbb{E}^Q \left[A_n(\tau, T) - K | G_n(\tau, T) = z \right], 0 \right\} g(z) \, dz \\
&= e^{-r(T-t)} \int_0^K \max \left\{ \mathbb{E}^Q \left[A_n(\tau, T) - K | G_n(\tau, T) = z \right], 0 \right\} g(z) \, dz \\
&\quad + e^{-r(T-t)} \int_K^\infty \mathbb{E}^Q \left[A_n(\tau, T) - K | G_n(\tau, T) = z \right] g(z) \, dz \\
&= e^{-r(T-t)} \int_{\widetilde{K}}^K \mathbb{E}^Q \left[A_n(\tau, T) - K | G_n(\tau, T) = z \right] g(z) \, dz \\
&\quad + e^{-r(T-t)} \int_K^\infty \mathbb{E}^Q \left[A_n(\tau, T) - K | G_n(\tau, T) = z \right] g(z) \, dz \\
&= e^{-r(T-t)} \int_{\widetilde{K}}^\infty \mathbb{E}^Q \left[A_n(\tau, T) - K | G_n(\tau, T) = z \right] g(z) \, dz
\end{aligned}
$$

where

$$
\widetilde{K} = \left\{ z | \mathbb{E}^Q \left[A_n(\tau, T) | G_n(\tau, T) = z \right] = K \right\}.
$$

To find $\widetilde{K}$, we note that

$$
\begin{aligned}
\mathbb{E}^Q \left[A_n(\tau, T) | G_n(\tau, T) = z \right] &= A_n(\tau, t_k) + \mathbb{E}^Q \left[\frac{1}{n} \sum_{i=k+1}^n S_{t_i} \Big| G_n(\tau, T) = z \right] \\
&= A_n(\tau, t_k) + \mathbb{E}^Q \left[\frac{1}{n} \sum_{i=k+1}^n S_{t_i} \Big| \log G_n(\tau, T) = \log z \right].
\end{aligned}
$$

Since

$$
\log S_{t_i} | \log G_n(\tau, T) = y \sim \mathcal{N} \left(\mu_i + (y - \mu_G) \frac{\sigma_{iG}}{\sigma_G^2}, \sigma_i^2 - \frac{\sigma_{iG}^2}{\sigma_G^2} \right)
$$

then

$$
S_{t_i} | \log G_n(\tau, T) = y \sim \log{-\mathcal{N}} \left(\mu_i + (y - \mu_G) \frac{\sigma_{iG}}{\sigma_G^2}, \sigma_i^2 - \frac{\sigma_{iG}^2}{\sigma_G^2} \right).
$$

Hence,

$$\mathbb{E}^Q \left[\frac{1}{n} \sum_{i=k+1}^{n} S_{t_i} \middle| \log G_n(\tau, T) = \log z \right] = \frac{1}{n} \sum_{i=k+1}^{n} e^{\mu_i + (\log z - \mu_G)\sigma_{iG}/\sigma_G^2 + \frac{1}{2}(\sigma_i^2 - \sigma_{iG}^2/\sigma_G^2)}$$

and by finding the root of the equation

$$A_n(\tau, t_k) + \frac{1}{n} \sum_{i=k+1}^{n} e^{\mu_i + (\log z - \mu_G)\sigma_{iG}/\sigma_G^2 + \frac{1}{2}(\sigma_i^2 - \sigma_{iG}^2/\sigma_G^2)} = K$$

we can obtain a value for $\widetilde{K}$.

Therefore,

$$\begin{aligned}
C_{lower} &= e^{-r(T-t)} \int_{\widetilde{K}}^{\infty} \mathbb{E}^Q \left[A_n(\tau, T) - K \middle| G_n(\tau, T) = z \right] g(z)\, dz \\
&= e^{-r(T-t)} \int_{\widetilde{K}}^{\infty} \mathbb{E}^Q \left[A_n(\tau, T) \middle| G_n(\tau, T) = z \right] g(z)\, dz \\
&\quad - K e^{-r(T-t)} \int_{\widetilde{K}}^{\infty} g(z)\, dz \\
&= e^{-r(T-t)} \int_{\widetilde{K}}^{\infty} \left\{ A_n(\tau, t_k) + \mathbb{E}^Q \left[\frac{1}{n} \sum_{i=k+1}^{n} S_{t_i} \middle| G_n(\tau, T) = z \right] \right\} g(z)\, dz \\
&\quad - K e^{-r(T-t)} \int_{\widetilde{K}}^{\infty} g(z)\, dz \\
&= e^{-r(T-t)} \int_{\widetilde{K}}^{\infty} \mathbb{E}^Q \left[\frac{1}{n} \sum_{i=k+1}^{n} S_{t_i} \middle| G_n(\tau, T) = z \right] g(z)\, dz \\
&\quad + e^{-r(T-t)} \left(A_n(\tau, t_k) - K \right) \int_{\widetilde{K}}^{\infty} g(z)\, dz.
\end{aligned}$$

Since

$$g(z) = \frac{1}{\sqrt{2\pi}\sigma_G z} e^{-\frac{1}{2}\left(\frac{\log z - \mu_G}{\sigma_G}\right)^2}$$

therefore

$$\int_{\widetilde{K}}^{\infty} g(z)\, dz = \Phi \left(\frac{\mu_G - \log \widetilde{K}}{\sigma_G} \right)$$

and

$$\int_{\widetilde{K}}^{\infty} \mathbb{E}^{Q}\left[S_{t_i} \middle| G_n(\tau, T) = z\right] g(z)\, dz$$

$$= \int_{\widetilde{K}}^{\infty} \mathbb{E}^{Q}\left[S_{t_i} \middle| \log G_n(\tau, T) = \log z\right] g(z)\, dz$$

$$= \int_{\widetilde{K}}^{\infty} e^{\mu_i + (\log z - \mu_G)\sigma_{iG}/\sigma_G^2 + \frac{1}{2}(\sigma_i^2 - \sigma_{iG}^2/\sigma_G^2)} g(z)\, dz$$

$$= \int_{\widetilde{K}}^{\infty} e^{\mu_i + (\log z - \mu_G)\sigma_{iG}/\sigma_G^2 + \frac{1}{2}(\sigma_i^2 - \sigma_{iG}^2/\sigma_G^2)} \times \frac{1}{\sqrt{2\pi}\sigma_G z} e^{-\frac{1}{2}\left(\frac{\log z - \mu_G}{\sigma_G}\right)^2}\, dz$$

$$= e^{\mu_i + \frac{1}{2}\sigma_i^2} \int_{\widetilde{K}}^{\infty} \frac{1}{\sqrt{2\pi}\sigma_G z} e^{(\log z - \mu_G)\sigma_{iG}/\sigma_G^2 - \frac{1}{2}\left(\frac{(\log z - \mu_G)^2 + \sigma_{iG}^2}{\sigma_G^2}\right)}\, dz.$$

By setting

$$v = \frac{\log z - \mu_G - \sigma_{iG}}{\sigma_G} \Rightarrow \frac{dv}{dz} = \frac{1}{\sigma_G z}$$

therefore

$$e^{\mu_i + \frac{1}{2}\sigma_i^2} \int_{\widetilde{K}}^{\infty} \frac{1}{\sqrt{2\pi}\sigma_G z} e^{(\log z - \mu_G)\sigma_{iG}/\sigma_G^2 - \frac{1}{2}\left(\frac{(\log z - \mu_G)^2 + \sigma_{iG}^2}{\sigma_G^2}\right)}\, dz$$

$$= e^{\mu_i + \frac{1}{2}\sigma_i^2} \int_{\frac{\log \widetilde{K} - \mu_G - \sigma_{iG}}{\sigma_G}}^{\infty} \frac{1}{\sqrt{2\pi}} e^{-\frac{1}{2}v^2}\, dv$$

$$= e^{\mu_i + \frac{1}{2}\sigma_i^2} \Phi\left(\frac{\mu_G - \log \widetilde{K} + \sigma_{iG}}{\sigma_G}\right).$$

Thus, the lower bound of the arithmetic average rate call option is

$$C_{lower} = e^{-r(T-t)} \left\{ \frac{1}{n} \sum_{i=k+1}^{n} e^{\mu_i + \frac{1}{2}\sigma_i^2} \Phi\left(\frac{\mu_G - \log \widetilde{K} + \sigma_{iG}}{\sigma_G}\right) \right.$$

$$\left. + \left(A_n(\tau, t_k) - K\right) \Phi\left(\frac{\mu_G - \log \widetilde{K}}{\sigma_G}\right) \right\}.$$

$\square$

5.2.2   Continuous Sampling

1. *Black–Scholes Equation for Asian Option.* Let $\{W_t : t \geq 0\}$ be a $\mathbb{P}$-standard Wiener process on the probability space $(\Omega, \mathcal{F}, \mathbb{P})$ and let the asset price S_t follow a GBM with the following SDE

$$\frac{dS_t}{S_t} = (\mu - D)dt + \sigma\, dW_t$$

where μ is the drift parameter, D is the continuous dividend yield, σ is the volatility parameter and r denotes the risk-free interest rate.

Let $V(S_t, I_t, t)$ be the exotic path-dependent Asian option price at time t which depends on

$$S_t \text{ and } I_t = \int_\tau^t f(S_u, u)\, d u$$

where the function f is a function of S_t and t, so that I_t is the integral of the asset price function from initial time τ up to time t. By considering a hedging portfolio involving both an option $V(S_t, I_t, t)$ which cannot be exercised before its expiry time T, $\tau < t < T$ and an asset price S_t, show that $V(S_t, I_t, t)$ satisfies the PDE

$$\frac{\partial V}{\partial t} + \frac{1}{2}\sigma^2 S_t^2 \frac{\partial^2 V}{\partial S_t^2} + (r - D)S_t \frac{\partial V}{\partial S_t} + f(S_t, t)\frac{\partial V}{\partial I_t} - rV(S_t, I_t, t) = 0.$$

Solution: At time t we let the value of a portfolio Π_t be

$$\Pi_t = V(S_t, I_t, t) - \Delta S_t$$

where it involves buying one unit of option $V(S_t, I_t, t)$ and selling Δ units of S_t. Since we receive $DS_t dt$ for every asset held, the change in portfolio Π_t is therefore

$$d\Pi_t = dV - \Delta(dS_t + DS_t dt) = dV - \Delta dS_t - \Delta DS_t dt.$$

Expanding $V(S_t, I_t, t)$ using Taylor's series

$$dV = \frac{\partial V}{\partial t}dt + \frac{\partial V}{\partial S_t}dS_t + \frac{\partial V}{\partial I_t}dI_t + \frac{1}{2}\frac{\partial^2 V}{\partial S_t^2}(dS_t)^2 + \frac{1}{2}\frac{\partial^2 V}{\partial I_t^2}(dI_t)^2$$
$$+ \frac{\partial^2 V}{\partial S_t \partial I_t}(dS_t dI_t) + \dots$$

and by substituting $dS_t = (\mu - D)S_t dt + \sigma S_t dW_t$, $dI_t = f(S_t, t)dt$ and applying Itō's lemma we have

$$dV = \left(\frac{\partial V}{\partial t} + \frac{1}{2}\sigma^2 S_t^2 \frac{\partial^2 V}{\partial S_t^2} + (\mu - D)S_t \frac{\partial V}{\partial S_t} + f(S_t, t)\frac{\partial V}{\partial I_t}\right)dt + \sigma S_t \frac{\partial V}{\partial S_t}\, dW_t.$$

Substituting the above expression into $d\Pi_t$ and rearranging terms, we have

$$d\Pi_t = \left(\frac{\partial V}{\partial t} + \frac{1}{2}\sigma^2 S_t^2 \frac{\partial^2 V}{\partial S_t^2} + (\mu - D)S_t \frac{\partial V}{\partial S_t} + f(S_t, t)\frac{\partial V}{\partial I_t} \right) dt$$
$$+ \sigma S_t \frac{\partial V}{\partial S_t} dW_t - \Delta \left[(\mu - D)S_t dt + \sigma S_t dW_t + DS_t dt \right]$$
$$= \left(\frac{\partial V}{\partial t} + \frac{1}{2}\sigma^2 S_t^2 \frac{\partial^2 V}{\partial S_t^2} + (\mu - D)S_t \frac{\partial V}{\partial S_t} + f(S_t, t)\frac{\partial V}{\partial I_t} - \mu \Delta S_t \right) dt$$
$$+ \sigma S_t \left(\frac{\partial V}{\partial S_t} - \Delta \right) dW_t.$$

To eliminate the random component we choose

$$\Delta = \frac{\partial V}{\partial S_t}$$

which leads to

$$d\Pi_t = \left(\frac{\partial V}{\partial t} + \frac{1}{2}\sigma^2 S_t^2 \frac{\partial^2 V}{\partial S_t^2} - DS_t \frac{\partial V}{\partial S_t} + f(S_t, t)\frac{\partial V}{\partial I_t} \right) dt.$$

Under the no-arbitrage condition the return on the amount I_t invested in a risk-free interest rate would see a growth of

$$d\Pi_t = r\Pi_t dt$$

and hence we can set

$$r\Pi_t dt = \left(\frac{\partial V}{\partial t} + \frac{1}{2}\sigma^2 S_t^2 \frac{\partial^2 V}{\partial S_t^2} - DS_t \frac{\partial V}{\partial S_t} + f(S_t, t)\frac{\partial V}{\partial I_t} \right) dt$$
$$r\left(V(S_t, I_t, t) - \Delta S_t \right) = \frac{\partial V}{\partial t} + \frac{1}{2}\sigma^2 S_t^2 \frac{\partial^2 V}{\partial S_t^2} - DS_t \frac{\partial V}{\partial S_t} + f(S_t, t)\frac{\partial V}{\partial I_t}$$
$$r\left(V(S_t, I_t, t) - S_t \frac{\partial V}{\partial S_t} \right) = \frac{\partial V}{\partial t} + \frac{1}{2}\sigma^2 S_t^2 \frac{\partial^2 V}{\partial S_t^2} - DS_t \frac{\partial V}{\partial S_t} + f(S_t, t)\frac{\partial V}{\partial I_t}.$$

Rearranging terms, we finally have the Black–Scholes equation for Asian options given by

$$\frac{\partial V}{\partial t} + \frac{1}{2}\sigma^2 S_t^2 \frac{\partial^2 V}{\partial S_t^2} + (r - D)S_t \frac{\partial V}{\partial S_t} + f(S_t, t)\frac{\partial V}{\partial I_t} - rV(S_t, I_t, t) = 0.$$

$\square$

2. *Similarity Reduction I.* Let $\{W_t : t \geq 0\}$ be the $\mathbb{P}$-standard Wiener process on the proba-bility space $(\Omega, \mathcal{F}, \mathbb{P})$ and let the asset price S_t follow the SDE

$$\frac{dS_t}{S_t} = (\mu - D)dt + \sigma\, dW_t$$

where μ is the drift parameter, D is the continuous dividend yield, σ is the volatility param-eter and let r be the risk-free interest rate from the money-market account.

Let $V(S_t, I_t, t)$ be a path-dependent Asian option price at time t, $\tau < t < T$ which depends on

$$S_t \text{ and } I_t = \int_\tau^t S_u\, du$$

where τ is the initial time and the option can only be exercised at expiry time T. Assume that $V(S_t, I_t, t)$ satisfies the following PDE

$$\frac{\partial V}{\partial t} + \frac{1}{2}\sigma^2 S_t^2 \frac{\partial^2 V}{\partial S_t^2} + (r - D)S_t \frac{\partial V}{\partial S_t} + S_t \frac{\partial V}{\partial I_t} - rV(S_t, I_t, t) = 0$$

with payoff

$$\Psi(S_T, I_T) = S_T^\alpha F\left(I_T/S_T\right)$$

for some constant α and function F. By considering the change of variables

$$V(S_t, I_t, t) = S_t^\alpha H(x, t), \quad x = I_t/S_t$$

show that $H(x, t)$ satisfies

$$\frac{\partial H}{\partial t} + \frac{1}{2}\sigma^2 x^2 \frac{\partial^2 H}{\partial x^2} + \left[1 + \left\{(1 - \alpha)\sigma^2 - (r - D)\right\} x\right]\frac{\partial H}{\partial x}$$
$$- \left[(1 - \alpha)\left(\frac{1}{2}\alpha\sigma^2 + r\right) + \alpha D\right] H(x, t) = 0$$

with payoff

$$H(x, T) = F(x).$$

Solution: Based on the change of variables

$$V(S_t, I_t, t) = S_t^\alpha H(x, t), \quad x = I_t/S_t$$

we have

$$\frac{\partial V}{\partial t} = S_t^\alpha \frac{\partial H}{\partial t}; \quad \frac{\partial V}{\partial I_t} = S_t^\alpha \frac{\partial H}{\partial x}\frac{\partial x}{\partial I_t} = S_t^{\alpha-1}\frac{\partial H}{\partial x}$$

$$
\frac{\partial V}{\partial S_t} = \alpha S_t^{\alpha-1} H(x,t) + S_t^{\alpha} \frac{\partial H}{\partial x} \frac{\partial x}{\partial S_t} = S_t^{\alpha-1}\left(\alpha H(x,t) - x \frac{\partial H}{\partial x}\right)
$$

$$
\frac{\partial^2 V}{\partial S_t^2} = \frac{\partial}{\partial S_t}\left[S_t^{\alpha-1}\left(\alpha H(x,t) - x \frac{\partial H}{\partial x}\right)\right]
$$

$$
= (\alpha - 1)S_t^{\alpha-2}\left(\alpha H(x,t) - x \frac{\partial H}{\partial x}\right)
$$

$$
+ S_t^{\alpha-1}\left(\alpha \frac{\partial H}{\partial x}\frac{\partial x}{\partial S_t} - \frac{\partial x}{\partial S_t}\frac{\partial H}{\partial x} - x \frac{\partial^2 H}{\partial x^2}\frac{\partial x}{\partial S_t}\right)
$$

$$
= (\alpha - 1)S_t^{\alpha-2}\left(\alpha H(x,t) - x \frac{\partial H}{\partial x}\right)
$$

$$
+ S_t^{\alpha-2}\left(x^2 \frac{\partial^2 H}{\partial x^2} - (\alpha - 1)x \frac{\partial H}{\partial x}\right)
$$

$$
= S_t^{\alpha-2}\left(x^2 \frac{\partial^2 H}{\partial x^2} - 2(\alpha - 1)x \frac{\partial H}{\partial x} + \alpha(\alpha - 1)H(x,t)\right).
$$

By substituting the above expressions into the PDE, we have

$$
S_t^{\alpha}\frac{\partial H}{\partial t} + \frac{1}{2}\sigma^2 S_t^{\alpha}\left(x^2 \frac{\partial^2 H}{\partial x^2} - 2(\alpha - 1)x \frac{\partial H}{\partial x} + \alpha(\alpha - 1)H(x,t)\right)
$$

$$
+ (r - D)S_t^{\alpha}\left(\alpha H(x,t) - x \frac{\partial H}{\partial x}\right) + S_t^{\alpha}\frac{\partial H}{\partial x} - rS_t^{\alpha} H(x,t) = 0
$$

and taking out S_t^{α} and rearranging terms we eventually have

$$
\frac{\partial H}{\partial t} + \frac{1}{2}\sigma^2 x^2 \frac{\partial^2 H}{\partial x^2} + \left[1 + \left\{(1-\alpha)\sigma^2 - (r - D)\right\}x\right]\frac{\partial H}{\partial x}
$$

$$
- \left[(1-\alpha)\left(\frac{1}{2}\alpha\sigma^2 + r\right) + \alpha D\right]H(x,t) = 0
$$

with payoff

$$
H(x,T) = F(x)
$$

since $V(S_T, I_T, T) = S_T^{\alpha} F(I_T/S_T) = S_T^{\alpha} H(I_T/S_T, T)$ and $x = I_T/S_T$.   □

3. *Similarity Reduction II.* Let $\{W_t : t \geq 0\}$ be the $\mathbb{P}$-standard Wiener process on the probability space $(\Omega, \mathcal{F}, \mathbb{P})$ and let the asset price S_t follow the SDE

$$
\frac{dS_t}{S_t} = (\mu - D)dt + \sigma\, dW_t
$$

where μ is the drift parameter, D is the continuous dividend yield, σ is the volatility parameter and let r be the risk-free interest rate from the money-market account.

Let $V(S_t, I_t, t)$ be a path-dependent Asian option price at time t, $\tau < t < T$ which depends on

$$S_t \text{ and } I_t = \int_\tau^t \log S_u \, du$$

where τ is the initial time and the option can only be exercised at expiry time T. Assume that $V(S_t, I_t, t)$ satisfies the following PDE

$$\frac{\partial V}{\partial t} + \frac{1}{2}\sigma^2 S_t^2 \frac{\partial^2 V}{\partial S_t^2} + (r - D)S_t \frac{\partial V}{\partial S_t} + \log S_t \frac{\partial V}{\partial I_t} - rV(S_t, I_t, t) = 0$$

with payoff

$$\Psi(S_T, I_T) = F(I_T)$$

where F is only a function of I_T. By considering the change of variables

$$V(S_t, I_t, t) = H(x, t), \quad x = \frac{I_t + (T - t)\log S_t}{T - \tau}$$

show that $H(x, t)$ satisfies

$$\frac{\partial H}{\partial t} + \frac{1}{2}\left(\frac{\sigma(T - t)}{T - \tau}\right)^2 \frac{\partial^2 H}{\partial x^2} + \left(r - D - \frac{1}{2}\sigma^2\right)\left(\frac{T - t}{T - \tau}\right)\frac{\partial H}{\partial x} - rH(x, t) = 0$$

with payoff

$$H(x, T) = F(x(T - \tau)).$$

Solution: Using the technique of changing variables

$$V(S_t, I_t, t) = H(x, t), \quad x = \frac{I_t + (T - t)\log S_t}{T - \tau}$$

we have

$$\frac{\partial V}{\partial t} = \frac{\partial H}{\partial x}\frac{\partial x}{\partial t} + \frac{\partial H}{\partial t} = \frac{\partial H}{\partial t} - \frac{\log S_t}{T - \tau}\frac{\partial H}{\partial x}$$

$$\frac{\partial V}{\partial I_t} = \frac{\partial H}{\partial x}\frac{\partial x}{\partial I_t} = \frac{1}{T - \tau}\frac{\partial H}{\partial x}$$

$$\frac{\partial V}{\partial S_t} = \frac{\partial H}{\partial x}\frac{\partial x}{\partial S_t} = \frac{1}{S_t}\left(\frac{T-t}{T-\tau}\right)\frac{\partial H}{\partial x}$$

$$\frac{\partial^2 V}{\partial S_t^2} = \frac{\partial}{\partial S_t}\left[\frac{1}{S_t}\left(\frac{T-t}{T-\tau}\right)\frac{\partial H}{\partial x}\right]$$

$$= \left(\frac{T-t}{T-\tau}\right)\left(-\frac{1}{S_t^2}\frac{\partial H}{\partial x} + \frac{1}{S_t}\frac{\partial^2 H}{\partial x^2}\frac{\partial x}{\partial S_t}\right)$$

$$= \left(\frac{T-t}{T-\tau}\right)\left[\frac{1}{S_t^2}\left(\frac{T-t}{T-\tau}\right)\frac{\partial^2 H}{\partial x^2} - \frac{1}{S_t^2}\frac{\partial H}{\partial x}\right]$$

$$= \frac{1}{S_t^2}\left(\frac{T-t}{T-\tau}\right)\left[\left(\frac{T-t}{T-\tau}\right)\frac{\partial^2 H}{\partial x^2} - \frac{\partial H}{\partial x}\right].$$

By substituting the above expressions into the PDE, we have

$$\frac{\partial H}{\partial t} - \frac{\log S_t}{T-\tau}\frac{\partial H}{\partial x} + \frac{1}{2}\sigma^2\left(\frac{T-t}{T-\tau}\right)\left[\left(\frac{T-t}{T-\tau}\right)\frac{\partial^2 H}{\partial x^2} - \frac{\partial H}{\partial x}\right]$$

$$+(r-D)\left(\frac{T-t}{T-\tau}\right)\frac{\partial H}{\partial x} + \frac{\log S_t}{T-\tau}\frac{\partial H}{\partial x} - rH(x,t) = 0$$

or

$$\frac{\partial H}{\partial t} + \frac{1}{2}\left(\frac{\sigma(T-t)}{T-\tau}\right)^2\frac{\partial^2 H}{\partial x^2} + \left(r-D-\frac{1}{2}\sigma^2\right)\left(\frac{T-t}{T-\tau}\right)\frac{\partial H}{\partial x} - rH(x,t) = 0$$

with payoff

$$H(x,T) = F(x(T-\tau))$$

since $V(S_T, I_T, T) = F(I_T) = H(x,T)$ and $x = I_T/(T-\tau)$.

$\square$

4. *Similarity Reduction III.* Let $\{W_t : t \geq 0\}$ be the $\mathbb{P}$-standard Wiener process on the probability space $(\Omega, \mathcal{F}, \mathbb{P})$ and let the asset price S_t follow the SDE

$$\frac{dS_t}{S_t} = (\mu - D)dt + \sigma\, dW_t$$

where μ is the drift parameter, D is the continuous dividend yield, σ is the volatility parameter and let r be the risk-free interest rate from the money-market account.

Let $V(S_t, I_t, t)$ be a path-dependent Asian option price at time t, $\tau < t < T$ which depends on

$$S_t \quad \text{and} \quad I_t = \int_\tau^t \log S_u\, du$$

where $\tau \geq 0$ is the initial time and the option can only be exercised at expiry time T. Assume that $V(S_t, I_t, t)$ satisfies the following PDE

$$\frac{\partial V}{\partial t} + \frac{1}{2}\sigma^2 S_t^2 \frac{\partial^2 V}{\partial S_t^2} + (r - D)S_t \frac{\partial V}{\partial S_t} + \log S_t \frac{\partial V}{\partial I_t} - rV(S_t, I_t, t) = 0$$

with payoff

$$\Psi(S_T, I_T) = S_T^\alpha F\left(\frac{e^{I_T/(T-\tau)}}{S_T}\right)$$

for some constant α and function F. By considering the change of variables

$$V(S_t, I_t, t) = S_t^\alpha H(x, t), \quad x = \frac{I_t - (t - \tau)\log S_t}{T - \tau}$$

show that $H(x, t)$ satisfies

$$\frac{\partial H}{\partial t} + \frac{1}{2}\sigma^2 \left(\frac{t - \tau}{T - \tau}\right)^2 \frac{\partial^2 H}{\partial x^2} - \left[r - D + \frac{1}{2}(2\alpha - 1)\sigma^2 \left(\frac{t - \tau}{T - \tau}\right)\right] \frac{\partial H}{\partial x}$$

$$+ \left[\frac{1}{2}\alpha(\alpha - 1)\sigma^2 + \alpha(r - D) - r\right] H(x, t) = 0$$

with payoff

$$H(x, T) = F(e^x).$$

Solution: Using the change of variables

$$V(S_t, I_t, t) = S_t^\alpha H(x, t), \quad x = \frac{I_t - (t - \tau)\log S_t}{T - \tau}$$

we have

$$\frac{\partial V}{\partial t} = S_t^\alpha \left(\frac{\partial H}{\partial x}\frac{\partial x}{\partial t} + \frac{\partial H}{\partial t}\right) = S_t^\alpha \left(\frac{\partial H}{\partial t} - \frac{\log S_t}{T - \tau}\frac{\partial H}{\partial x}\right)$$

$$\frac{\partial V}{\partial I_t} = S_t^\alpha \frac{\partial H}{\partial x}\frac{\partial x}{\partial I_t} = \frac{S_t^\alpha}{T - \tau}\frac{\partial H}{\partial x}$$

$$\frac{\partial V}{\partial S_t} = \alpha S_t^{\alpha-1} H(x, t) + S_t^\alpha \frac{\partial H}{\partial x}\frac{\partial x}{\partial S_t} = \alpha S_t^{\alpha-1} H(x, t) - S_t^{\alpha-1}\left(\frac{t - \tau}{T - \tau}\right)\frac{\partial H}{\partial x}$$

and

$$\frac{\partial^2 V}{\partial S_t^2} = \alpha(\alpha-1)S_t^{\alpha-2}H(x,t) + \alpha S_t^{\alpha-1}\frac{\partial H}{\partial x}\frac{\partial x}{\partial S_t}$$

$$-(\alpha-1)S_t^{\alpha-2}\left(\frac{t-\tau}{T-\tau}\right)\frac{\partial H}{\partial x} - S_t^{\alpha-1}\left(\frac{t-\tau}{T-\tau}\right)\frac{\partial^2 H}{\partial x^2}\frac{\partial x}{\partial S_t}$$

$$= S_t^{\alpha-2}\left[\alpha(\alpha-1)H(x,t) - \alpha\left(\frac{t-\tau}{T-\tau}\right)\frac{\partial H}{\partial x}\right.$$

$$\left. -(\alpha-1)\left(\frac{t-\tau}{T-\tau}\right)\frac{\partial H}{\partial x} + \left(\frac{t-\tau}{T-\tau}\right)^2\frac{\partial^2 H}{\partial x^2}\right]$$

$$= S_t^{\alpha-2}\left[\left(\frac{t-\tau}{T-\tau}\right)^2\frac{\partial^2 H}{\partial x^2} - (2\alpha-1)\left(\frac{t-\tau}{T-\tau}\right)\frac{\partial H}{\partial x} + \alpha(\alpha-1)H(x,t)\right].$$

By substituting the above expressions into the PDE, we have

$$S_t^\alpha\left(\frac{\partial H}{\partial t} - \frac{\log S_t}{T}\frac{\partial H}{\partial x}\right) + \frac{1}{2}\sigma^2 S_t^\alpha\left[\left(\frac{t-\tau}{T-\tau}\right)^2\frac{\partial^2 H}{\partial x^2}\right.$$

$$\left. -(2\alpha-1)\left(\frac{t-\tau}{T-\tau}\right)\frac{\partial H}{\partial x} + \alpha(\alpha-1)H(x,t)\right] + \alpha(r-D)S_t^\alpha H(x,t)$$

$$-(r-D)S_t^\alpha\left(\frac{t-\tau}{T-\tau}\right)\frac{\partial H}{\partial x} + S_t^\alpha\frac{\log S_t}{T-\tau}\frac{\partial H}{\partial x} - rS_t^\alpha H(x,t) = 0.$$

By removing S_t^α and rearranging terms, we have

$$\frac{\partial H}{\partial t} + \frac{1}{2}\sigma^2\left(\frac{t-\tau}{T-\tau}\right)^2\frac{\partial^2 H}{\partial x^2} - \left[r - D + \frac{1}{2}(2\alpha-1)\sigma^2\left(\frac{t-\tau}{T-\tau}\right)\right]\frac{\partial H}{\partial x}$$

$$+ \left[\frac{1}{2}\alpha(\alpha-1)\sigma^2 + \alpha(r-D) - r\right]H(x,t) = 0$$

with payoff

$$H(x,T) = F(e^x)$$

since $V(S_T, I_T, T) = S_T^\alpha F\left(\dfrac{e^{I_T/(T-\tau)}}{S_T}\right) = S_T^\alpha H(x,T)$ and $x = \dfrac{I_T}{T-\tau} - \log S_T$.

$\square$

5. *Arithmetic Average Rate (Fixed Strike) Asian Option (PDE Approach).* Let $\{W_t : t \geq 0\}$ be the $\mathbb{P}$-standard Wiener process on the probability space $(\Omega, \mathcal{F}, \mathbb{P})$ and let the asset price S_t follow the SDE

$$\frac{dS_t}{S_t} = (\mu - D)dt + \sigma\, dW_t$$

where μ is the drift parameter, D is the continuous dividend yield, σ is the volatility parameter and let r be the risk-free interest rate from the money-market account.

We define

$$I_t = \int_\tau^t S_u \, du$$

to be the asset running sum from initial time $\tau \geq 0$ until time t and consider the arithmetic average rate call option with payoff

$$\Psi(S_T, I_T) = \max\left\{\frac{I_T}{T - \tau} - K, 0\right\}$$

where $K > 0$ is the strike price and T is the option expiry time. Assume that the arithmetic average rate call option price at time $t < T$, $C_{ar}^{(a)}(S_t, I_t, t; K, T)$ satisfies the PDE

$$\frac{\partial C_{ar}^{(a)}}{\partial t} + \frac{1}{2}\sigma^2 S_t^2 \frac{\partial^2 C_{ar}^{(a)}}{\partial S_t^2} + (r - D)S_t \frac{\partial C_{ar}^{(a)}}{\partial S_t} + S_t \frac{\partial C_{ar}^{(a)}}{\partial I_t} - r C_{ar}^{(a)}(S_t, t; K, T) = 0$$

with boundary condition

$$C_{ar}^{(a)}(S_T, I_T, T; K, T) = \max\left\{\frac{I_T}{T - \tau} - K, 0\right\}.$$

By considering the change of variables

$$C_{ar}^{(a)}(S_t, I_t, t; K, T) = S_t u(x, t), \quad x = \frac{I_t - K(T - \tau)}{S_t(T - \tau)}$$

show that $u(x, t)$ satisfies

$$\frac{\partial u}{\partial t} + \frac{1}{2}\sigma^2 x^2 \frac{\partial^2 u}{\partial x^2} + \left[\frac{1}{T - \tau} - (r - D)x\right]\frac{\partial u}{\partial x} - Du(x, t) = 0$$

with boundary condition

$$u(x, T) = \max\{x, 0\}.$$

By setting

$$u(x, t) = a(t)x + b(t)$$

show that $a(t)$ and $b(t)$ satisfy the ODEs

$$\frac{da}{dt} - r\,a(t) = 0 \quad \text{and} \quad \frac{db}{dt} - Db(t) = -\frac{a(t)}{T - \tau}.$$

Hence, show that for $x \geq 0$ and $r \neq D$ the arithmetic average rate call option price at time $t, \tau < t < T$ is

$$C_{ar}^{(a)}(S_t, I_t, t; K, T) = \left(\frac{1}{T - \tau} \int_{\tau}^{t} S_u \, du - K\right) e^{-r(T-t)} + \left(\frac{e^{-D(T-t)} - e^{-r(T-t)}}{(r - D)(T - \tau)}\right) S_t.$$

What is the solution if $r \to D$?

Solution: From the change of variables

$$C_{ar}^{(a)}(S_t, I_t, t; K, T) = S_t u(x, t), \quad x = \frac{I_t - K(T - \tau)}{S_t(T - \tau)}$$

we have

$$\frac{\partial C_{ar}^{(a)}}{\partial t} = S_t \frac{\partial u}{\partial t}$$

$$\frac{\partial C_{ar}^{(a)}}{\partial I_t} = S_t \frac{\partial u}{\partial x} \frac{\partial x}{\partial I_t} = S_t \frac{\partial u}{\partial x} \frac{1}{S_t(T - \tau)} = \frac{1}{T - \tau} \frac{\partial u}{\partial x}$$

$$\frac{\partial C_{ar}^{(a)}}{\partial S_t} = u(x, t) + S_t \frac{\partial u}{\partial x} \frac{\partial x}{\partial S_t} = u(x, t) - x \frac{\partial u}{\partial x}$$

$$\frac{\partial^2 C_{ar}^{(a)}}{\partial S_t^2} = \frac{\partial u}{\partial x} \frac{\partial x}{\partial S_t} - x \frac{\partial^2 u}{\partial x^2} \frac{\partial x}{\partial S_t} - \frac{\partial u}{\partial x} \frac{\partial x}{\partial S_t} = x \frac{\partial^2 u}{\partial x^2} \left(\frac{I_t - K(T - \tau)}{S_t^2(T - \tau)}\right) = \frac{x^2}{S_t} \frac{\partial^2 u}{\partial x^2}.$$

By substituting the above results into the PDE, we have

$$S_t \frac{\partial u}{\partial t} + \frac{1}{2} \sigma^2 S_t^2 \left(\frac{x^2}{S_t}\right) \frac{\partial^2 u}{\partial x^2} + (r - D)S_t \left(u(x, t) - x \frac{\partial u}{\partial x}\right) + \frac{S_t}{T - \tau} \frac{\partial u}{\partial x} - rS_t u(x, t) = 0$$

or

$$\frac{\partial u}{\partial t} + \frac{1}{2} \sigma^2 x^2 \frac{\partial^2 u}{\partial x^2} + \left[\frac{1}{T - \tau} - (r - D)x\right] \frac{\partial u}{\partial x} - Du(x, t) = 0$$

with boundary condition

$$u(x, T) = \max\{x, 0\}$$

since

$$C_{ar}^{(a)}(S_T, I_T, T; K, T) = \max\left\{\frac{I_T}{T - \tau} - K, 0\right\}$$

$$= S_T \max\left\{\frac{I_T - K(T - \tau)}{S_T(T - \tau)}, 0\right\}$$

$$= S_T \max\{x, 0\}.$$

Let $u(x, t) = a(t)x + b(t)$ so that

$$\frac{\partial u}{\partial t} = x\frac{da}{dt} + \frac{db}{dt}; \quad \frac{\partial u}{\partial x} = a(t); \quad \frac{\partial^2 u}{\partial x^2} = 0$$

and by substituting the results into the PDE satisfied by $u(x, t)$

$$x\frac{da}{dt} + \frac{db}{dt} + \left(\frac{1}{T-\tau} - (r-D)x\right)a(t) - Da(t)x - Db(t) = 0$$

or

$$x\left(\frac{da}{dt} - r\,a(t)\right) + \frac{db}{dt} - Db(t) + \frac{a(t)}{T-\tau} = 0.$$

Hence, we can set

$$\frac{da}{dt} - r\,a(t) = 0 \quad \text{and} \quad \frac{db}{dt} - Db(t) = -\frac{a(t)}{T-\tau}.$$

To solve $\dfrac{da}{dt} - ra(t) = 0$ we let the integrating factor $I_a = e^{-\int r\,dt} = e^{-rt}$ and therefore

$$\frac{d}{dt}\left(a(t)e^{-rt}\right) = 0 \text{ or } a(t)e^{-rt} = C_1$$

where C_1 is a constant. Hence, $a(t) = C_1 e^{rt}$.

In contrast, for $\dfrac{db}{dt} - Db(t) = -\dfrac{a(t)}{T-\tau}$ we let the integrating factor $I_b = e^{-\int D\,dt} = e^{-Dt}$. Therefore,

$$\frac{d}{dt}\left(b(t)e^{-Dt}\right) = -\frac{a(t)}{T-\tau}e^{-Dt}$$

$$b(t)e^{-Dt} = -\frac{1}{T-\tau}\int a(t)e^{-Dt}\,dt.$$

Substituting $a(t) = C_1 e^{rt}$ we have

$$b(t)e^{-Dt} = -\frac{C_1}{T-\tau}\int e^{(r-D)t}\,dt$$

$$= -\frac{C_1 e^{(r-D)t}}{(r-D)(T-\tau)} + C_2$$

where C_2 is a constant. Thus,

$$u(x, t) = C_1 e^{rt}x - \frac{C_1 e^{rt}}{(r-D)(T-\tau)} + C_2 e^{Dt}.$$

At the boundary condition for $x \geq 0$, $u(x, T) = x$ we therefore have

$$C_1 e^{rT} x - \frac{C_1 e^{rT}}{(r - D)(T - \tau)} + C_2 e^{DT} = x$$

and by equating coefficients

$$C_1 = e^{-rT} \quad \text{and} \quad C_2 = \frac{e^{-DT}}{(r - D)(T - \tau)}$$

which leads to

$$u(x, t) = x e^{-r(T-t)} + \frac{e^{-D(T-t)} - e^{-r(T-t)}}{(r - D)(T - \tau)}.$$

Thus, for $x \geq 0$ or $\dfrac{1}{T - \tau} \displaystyle\int_\tau^t S_u \, du \geq K$

$$C_{ar}^{(a)}(S_t, I_t, t; K, T) = S_t u(x, t)$$

$$= S_t \left(\frac{I_t - K(T - \tau)}{S_t(T - \tau)} \right) e^{-r(T-t)} + \left(\frac{e^{-D(T-t)} - e^{-r(T-t)}}{(r - D)(T - \tau)} \right) S_t$$

$$= \left(\frac{1}{T - \tau} \int_\tau^t S_u \, du - K \right) e^{-r(T-t)} + \left(\frac{e^{-D(T-t)} - e^{-r(T-t)}}{(r - D)(T - \tau)} \right) S_t.$$

Finally, for the case $r \to D$ and from the application of L'Hôpital's rule

$$\lim_{r \to D} C_{ar}^{(a)}(S_t, I_t, t; K, T) = \lim_{r \to D} \left(\frac{1}{T - \tau} \int_0^t S_u \, du - K \right) e^{-r(T-t)}$$

$$+ \lim_{r \to D} \left(\frac{e^{-D(T-t)} - e^{-r(T-t)}}{(r - D)(T - \tau)} \right) S_t$$

$$= \left(\frac{1}{T - \tau} \int_\tau^t S_u \, du - K \right) e^{-D(T-t)} + \lim_{r \to D} \frac{-r e^{-r(T-t)}}{T - \tau} S_t$$

$$= \left(\frac{1}{T - \tau} \int_\tau^t S_u \, du - K \right) e^{-D(T-t)} - \frac{DS_t}{T - \tau} e^{-D(T-t)}$$

$$= \left[\frac{1}{T - \tau} \left(\int_\tau^t S_u \, du - DS_t \right) - K \right] e^{-D(T-t)}.$$

$\square$

6. *Arithmetic Average Strike (Floating Strike) Asian Option (PDE Approach).* Let $\{W_t : t \geq 0\}$ be the $\mathbb{P}$-standard Wiener process on the probability space $(\Omega, \mathcal{F}, \mathbb{P})$ and let the asset price S_t follow the SDE

$$\frac{dS_t}{S_t} = (\mu - D)dt + \sigma \, dW_t$$

where μ is the drift parameter, D is the continuous dividend yield, σ is the volatility parameter and let r be the risk-free interest rate from the money-market account.

We define

$$I_t = \int_\tau^t S_u \, du$$

to be the asset running sum from initial time $\tau \geq 0$ until time t and consider the arithmetic average strike put option with payoff

$$\Psi(S_T, I_T) = \max\left\{\frac{I_T}{T - \tau} - S_T, 0\right\}$$

where $T > t$ is the option expiry time. Assume that the arithmetic average strike put option price at time t, $\tau < t < T$, $P_{as}^{(a)}(S_t, I_t, t; T)$ satisfies the PDE

$$\frac{\partial P_{as}^{(a)}}{\partial t} + \frac{1}{2}\sigma^2 S_t^2 \frac{\partial^2 P_{as}^{(a)}}{\partial S_t^2} + (r - D)S_t \frac{\partial P_{as}^{(a)}}{\partial S_t} + S_t \frac{\partial P_{as}^{(a)}}{\partial I_t} - r P_{as}^{(a)}(S_t, I_t, t; T) = 0$$

with boundary condition

$$P_{as}^{(a)}(S_T, I_T, T; T) = \max\left\{\frac{I_T}{T - \tau} - S_T, 0\right\}.$$

By considering the change of variables

$$P_{as}^{(a)}(S_t, I_t, t; T) = S_t u(x, t), \quad x = \frac{I_t - S_t(T - \tau)}{S_t(T - \tau)}$$

show that $u(x, t)$ satisfies

$$\frac{\partial u}{\partial t} + \frac{1}{2}\sigma^2(x + 1)^2 \frac{\partial^2 u}{\partial x^2} + \left[\frac{1}{T - \tau} - (r - D)(x + 1)\right]\frac{\partial u}{\partial x} - Du(x, t) = 0$$

with boundary condition

$$u(x, T) = \max\{x, 0\}.$$

By setting

$$u(x, t) = a(t)x + b(t)$$

show that $a(t)$ and $b(t)$ satisfy the ODEs

$$\frac{da}{dt} - r a(t) = 0 \quad \text{and} \quad \frac{db}{dt} - Db(t) = -\left[\frac{1}{T - \tau} - (r - D)\right]a(t).$$

Hence, show that for $x \geq 0$ and $r \neq D$ the arithmetic average strike put option price at time t, $\tau < t < T$ is

$$P_{as}^{(a)}(S_t, I_t, t; T) = \left(\frac{1}{T - \tau} \int_{\tau}^{t} S_u \, du - S_t \right) e^{-r(T-t)}$$

$$+ \left(\frac{1 - (r - D)(T - \tau)}{(r - D)(T - \tau)} \right) \left(e^{-D(T-t)} - e^{-r(T-t)} \right) S_t.$$

What is the solution if $r \to D$?

Solution: From the change of variables

$$P_{as}^{(a)}(S_t, I_t, t; T) = S_t u(x, t), \quad x = \frac{I_t - S_t(T - \tau)}{S_t(T - \tau)}$$

we have

$$\frac{\partial P_{as}^{(a)}}{\partial t} = S_t \frac{\partial u}{\partial t}$$

$$\frac{\partial P_{as}^{(a)}}{\partial I_t} = S_t \frac{\partial u}{\partial x} \frac{\partial x}{\partial I_t} = S_t \frac{\partial u}{\partial x} \frac{1}{S_t(T - \tau)} = \frac{1}{T - \tau} \frac{\partial u}{\partial x}$$

$$\frac{\partial P_{as}^{(a)}}{\partial S_t} = u(x, t) + S_t \frac{\partial u}{\partial x} \frac{\partial x}{\partial S_t}$$

$$= u(x, t) - S_t \frac{\partial u}{\partial x} \left(\frac{I_t}{S_t^2(T - \tau)} \right)$$

$$= u(x, t) - (x + 1) \frac{\partial u}{\partial x}$$

and

$$\frac{\partial^2 P_{as}^{(a)}}{\partial S_t^2} = \frac{\partial u}{\partial x} \frac{\partial x}{\partial S_t} - (x + 1) \frac{\partial^2 u}{\partial x^2} \frac{\partial x}{\partial S_t} - \frac{\partial u}{\partial x} \frac{\partial x}{\partial S_t}$$

$$= (x + 1) \frac{\partial^2 u}{\partial x^2} \left(\frac{I_t}{S_t^2(T - \tau)} \right)$$

$$= \frac{(x + 1)^2}{S_t} \frac{\partial^2 u}{\partial x^2}.$$

By substituting the above results into the PDE, we have

$$S_t \frac{\partial u}{\partial t} + \frac{1}{2}\sigma^2 S_t^2 \left(\frac{(x+1)^2}{S_t}\right)\frac{\partial^2 u}{\partial x^2} + (r-D)S_t \left(u(x,t) - (x+1)\frac{\partial u}{\partial x}\right)$$
$$+ \frac{S_t}{T-\tau}\frac{\partial u}{\partial x} - rS_t u(x,t) = 0$$

or

$$\frac{\partial u}{\partial t} + \frac{1}{2}\sigma^2(x+1)^2\frac{\partial^2 u}{\partial x^2} + \left[\frac{1}{T} - (r-D)(x+1)\right]\frac{\partial u}{\partial x} - Du(x,t) = 0$$

with boundary condition

$$u(x,T) = \max\{x,0\}$$

since

$$P_{as}^{(a)}(S_T, I_T, T; T) = \max\left\{\frac{I_T}{T-\tau} - S_T, 0\right\}$$
$$= S_T \max\left\{\frac{I_T - S_T(T-\tau)}{S_T(T-\tau)}, 0\right\}$$
$$= S_T \max\{x,0\}.$$

Let $u(x,t) = a(t)x + b(t)$ so that

$$\frac{\partial u}{\partial t} = x\frac{da}{dt} + \frac{db}{dt}; \quad \frac{\partial u}{\partial x} = a(t); \quad \frac{\partial^2 u}{\partial x^2} = 0$$

and by substituting the results into the PDE satisfied by $u(x,t)$ we have

$$x\frac{da}{dt} + \frac{db}{dt} + \left(\frac{1}{T-\tau} - (r-D)(x+1)\right)a(t) - Da(t)x - Db(t) = 0$$

or

$$x\left(\frac{da}{dt} - ra(t)\right) + \frac{db}{dt} - Db(t) + \left(\frac{1}{T-\tau} - (r-D)\right)a(t) = 0.$$

Hence, we can set

$$\frac{da}{dt} - ra(t) = 0 \quad \text{and} \quad \frac{db}{dt} - Db(t) = -\left(\frac{1}{T-\tau} - (r-D)\right)a(t).$$

To solve $\frac{da}{dt} - ra(t) = 0$ we let the integrating factor $I_a = e^{-\int r dt} = e^{-rt}$ and therefore

$$\frac{d}{dt}\left(a(t)e^{-rt}\right) = 0 \text{ or } a(t)e^{-rt} = C_1$$

where C_1 is a constant. Hence, $a(t) = C_1 e^{rt}$.

In contrast, for $\dfrac{db}{dt} - Db(t) = -\left(\dfrac{1}{T-\tau} - (r-D)\right) a(t)$ we let the integrating factor $I_b = e^{-\int Ddt} = e^{-Dt}$. Therefore,

$$\frac{d}{dt}\left(b(t)e^{-Dt}\right) = -\left(\frac{1}{T-\tau} - (r-D)\right) a(t)e^{-Dt}$$

$$b(t)e^{-Dt} = -\left(\frac{1}{T-\tau} - (r-D)\right) \int a(t)e^{-Dt}dt.$$

Substituting $a(t) = C_1 e^{rt}$ we have

$$b(t)e^{-Dt} = -C_1\left(\frac{1}{T-\tau} - (r-D)\right) \int e^{(r-D)t}dt$$

$$= -C_1\left(\frac{1-(r-D)(T-\tau)}{(r-D)(T-\tau)}\right) e^{(r-D)t} + C_2$$

$$= -C_1\left(\frac{1-(r-D)(T-\tau)}{(r-D)(T-\tau)}\right) e^{rt} + C_2 e^{Dt}$$

where C_2 is a constant. Thus,

$$u(x,t) = C_1 e^{rt}x - C_1\left(\frac{1-(r-D)(T-\tau)}{(r-D)(T-\tau)}\right) e^{rt} + C_2 e^{Dt}.$$

At the boundary condition for $x \geq 0$, $u(x,T) = x$ we therefore have

$$C_1 e^{rT}x - C_1\left(\frac{1-(r-D)(T-\tau)}{(r-D)(T-\tau)}\right) e^{rT} + C_2 e^{DT} = x$$

and by equating coefficients

$$C_1 = e^{-rT} \quad \text{and} \quad C_2 = \left(\frac{1-(r-D)(T-\tau)}{(r-D)(T-\tau)}\right) e^{-DT}$$

which leads to

$$u(x,t) = xe^{-r(T-t)} + \left(\frac{1-(r-D)(T-\tau)}{(r-D)(T-\tau)}\right)\left(e^{-D(T-t)} - e^{-r(T-t)}\right)$$

and hence

$$P_{as}^{(a)}(S_t, I_t, t; T) = S_t u(x,t)$$

$$= \left(\frac{1}{T-\tau}\int_\tau^t S_u\,du - S_t\right) e^{-r(T-t)}$$

$$+ \left(\frac{1-(r-D)(T-\tau)}{(r-D)(T-\tau)}\right)\left(e^{-D(T-t)} - e^{-r(T-t)}\right) S_t.$$

Finally, for the case $r \to D$ and using L'Hôpital's rule

$$
\lim_{r \to D} P_{as}^{(a)}(S_t, I_t, t; T) = \lim_{r \to D} \left(\frac{1}{T - \tau} \int_0^t S_u \, du - S_t \right) e^{-r(T-t)}
$$

$$
+ \lim_{r \to D} \left(\frac{e^{-D(T-t)} - e^{-r(T-t)}}{(r - D)(T - \tau)} \right) S_t
$$

$$
- \lim_{r \to D} \left(e^{-D(T-t)} - e^{-r(T-t)} \right) S_t
$$

$$
= \left(\frac{1}{T - \tau} \int_0^t S_u \, du - S_t \right) e^{-D(T-t)} - \lim_{r \to D} \frac{re^{-r(T-t)}}{T - \tau} S_t
$$

$$
= \left(\frac{1}{T - \tau} \int_\tau^t S_u \, du - S_t \right) e^{-D(T-t)} - \frac{DS_t}{T - \tau} e^{-D(T-t)}
$$

$$
= \left[\frac{1}{T - \tau} \left(\int_\tau^t S_u \, du - DS_t \right) - S_t \right] e^{-D(T-t)}.
$$

$\square$

7. *Put–Call Parity for Arithmetic Average Options (Probabilistic Approach).* Let $\{W_t : t \geq 0\}$ be the $\mathbb{P}$-standard Wiener process on the probability space $(\Omega, \mathcal{F}, \mathbb{P})$ and let the asset price S_t follow the SDE

$$
\frac{dS_t}{S_t} = (\mu - D)dt + \sigma \, dW_t
$$

where μ is the drift parameter, D is the continuous dividend yield, σ is the volatility parameter and let r be the risk-free interest rate from the money-market account.

We define

$$
I_t = \int_\tau^t S_u \, du
$$

to be the asset running sum within the time period $[\tau, t]$, $0 \leq \tau < t$ and consider the arithmetic average option with zero-strike call payoff

$$
\Psi(S_T, I_T) = \frac{I_T}{T - \tau}
$$

where T is the option expiry time. Using the risk-neutral valuation method find the arbitrage-free arithmetic average option price at time t, $\tau < t < T$.

Consider the payoffs of arithmetic average rate options

$$
C_{ar}^{(a)}(S_T, I_T, T; K, T) = \max \left\{ \frac{I_T}{T - \tau} - K, 0 \right\}
$$

$$
P_{ar}^{(a)}(S_T, I_T, T; K, T) = \max \left\{ K - \frac{I_T}{T - \tau}, 0 \right\}
$$

and arithmetic average strike options

$$C_{as}^{(a)}(S_T, I_T, T; T) = \max\left\{ S_T - \frac{I_T}{T - \tau}, 0 \right\}$$

$$P_{as}^{(a)}(S_T, I_T, T; T) = \max\left\{ \frac{I_T}{T - \tau} - S_T, 0 \right\}.$$

Show that the put–call relation for the arithmetic average rate and arithmetic average strike options are

$$C_{ar}^{(a)}(S_t, I_t, t; K, T) - P_{ar}^{(a)}(S_t, I_t, t; K, T)$$

$$= \left(\frac{1}{T - \tau} \int_\tau^t S_u du - K \right) e^{-r(T-t)} + \left(\frac{e^{-D(T-t)} - e^{-r(T-t)}}{(r - D)(T - \tau)} \right) S_t$$

and

$$C_{as}^{(a)}(S_t, I_t, t; T) - P_{as}^{(a)}(S_t, I_t, t; T)$$

$$= \left(S_t - \frac{1}{T - \tau} \int_\tau^t S_u du \right) e^{-r(T-t)} + \left(\frac{(r - D)(T - \tau) - 1}{(r - D)(T - \tau)} \right) \left(e^{-D(T-t)} - e^{-r(T-t)} \right) S_t$$

respectively.

Solution: From Girsanov's theorem, under the risk-neutral measure $\mathbb{Q}$, S_t follows

$$\frac{dS_t}{S_t} = (r - D)dt + \sigma \, dW_t^{\mathbb{Q}}$$

where $W_t^{\mathbb{Q}} = W_t + \left(\frac{\mu - r}{\sigma} \right)t$ is a $\mathbb{Q}$-standard Wiener process.

Hence, using the risk-neutral valuation method, the price of the option at time $t < T$ with payoff

$$\Psi(S_T, I_T) = \frac{1}{T - \tau} \int_\tau^T S_u \, du$$

is

$$V(S_t, I_t, t; T) = e^{-r(T-t)} \mathbb{E}^{\mathbb{Q}} \left[\Psi(S_T, I_T) \middle| \mathscr{F}_t \right]$$

$$= e^{-r(T-t)} \mathbb{E}^{\mathbb{Q}} \left[\frac{1}{T-\tau} \int_\tau^T S_u \, du \middle| \mathscr{F}_t \right]$$

$$= \frac{1}{T-\tau} e^{-r(T-t)} \mathbb{E}^{\mathbb{Q}} \left[\int_\tau^t S_u \, du + \int_t^T S_u \, du \middle| \mathscr{F}_t \right]$$

$$= \left(\frac{1}{T-\tau} \int_\tau^t S_u \, du \right) e^{-r(T-t)} + \frac{1}{T-\tau} e^{-r(T-t)} \mathbb{E}^{\mathbb{Q}} \left[\int_t^T S_u \, du \middle| \mathscr{F}_t \right]$$

$$= \left(\frac{1}{T-\tau} \int_\tau^t S_u \, du \right) e^{-r(T-t)} + \frac{1}{T-\tau} e^{-r(T-t)} \int_t^T \mathbb{E}^{\mathbb{Q}} \left[S_u \middle| \mathscr{F}_t \right] du.$$

Using Itō's lemma we can easily show that for $u > t$

$$S_u = S_t e^{(r-D-\frac{1}{2}\sigma^2)(u-t) + \sigma W_{u-t}^{\mathbb{Q}}}, \quad W_{u-t}^{\mathbb{Q}} \sim \mathcal{N}(0, u-t).$$

Hence, $\mathbb{E}^{\mathbb{Q}} \left[S_u \middle| \mathscr{F}_t \right] = S_t e^{(r-D)(u-t)}$ and the option price becomes

$$V(S_t, I_t, t; T) = \left(\frac{1}{T-\tau} \int_\tau^t S_u \, du \right) e^{-r(T-t)} + \frac{1}{T-\tau} e^{-r(T-t)} \int_t^T S_t e^{(r-D)(u-t)} \, du$$

$$= \left(\frac{1}{T-\tau} \int_\tau^t S_u \, du \right) e^{-r(T-t)} + \frac{1}{T-\tau} S_t e^{-r(T-t)-(r-D)t} \left[\frac{e^{(r-D)u}}{r-D} \right]_t^T$$

$$= \left(\frac{1}{T-\tau} \int_\tau^t S_u \, du \right) e^{-r(T-t)} + \left(\frac{e^{-D(T-t)} - e^{-r(T-t)}}{(r-D)(T-\tau)} \right) S_t.$$

At expiry time T, the put–call parity for arithmetic average rate options is

$$C_{ar}^{(a)}(S_T, I_T, T; K, T) - P_{ar}^{(a)}(S_T, I_T, T; K, T)$$

$$= \begin{cases} \dfrac{1}{T-\tau} \displaystyle\int_\tau^T S_u \, du - K & \text{if } \dfrac{1}{T-\tau} \displaystyle\int_\tau^T S_u \, du > K \\[4mm] \dfrac{1}{T-\tau} \displaystyle\int_\tau^T S_u \, du - K & \text{if } \dfrac{1}{T-\tau} \displaystyle\int_\tau^T S_u \, du \leq K. \end{cases}$$

By discounting the payoffs back to time t under the risk-neutral measure $\mathbb{Q}$, we have

$$
\begin{aligned}
C_{ar}^{(a)}(S_t, I_t, t; K, T) - P_{ar}^{(a)}(S_t, I_t, t; K, T) &= e^{-r(T-t)} \mathbb{E}^{\mathbb{Q}} \left[\frac{1}{T-\tau} \int_\tau^T S_u \, du - K \, \middle| \, \mathscr{F}_t \right] \\
&= e^{-r(T-t)} \mathbb{E}^{\mathbb{Q}} \left[\frac{1}{T-\tau} \int_\tau^T S_u \, du \, \middle| \, \mathscr{F}_t \right] \\
&\quad - K e^{-r(T-t)} \\
&= \left(\frac{1}{T-\tau} \int_\tau^t S_u \, du \right) e^{-r(T-t)} \\
&\quad + \left(\frac{e^{-D(T-t)} - e^{-r(T-t)}}{(r-D)(T-\tau)} \right) S_t - K e^{-r(T-t)} \\
&= \left(\frac{1}{T-\tau} \int_\tau^t S_u \, du - K \right) e^{-r(T-t)} \\
&\quad + \left(\frac{e^{-D(T-t)} - e^{-r(T-t)}}{(r-D)(T-\tau)} \right) S_t.
\end{aligned}
$$

In contrast, at expiry time T the put–call parity for arithmetic average strike options is

$$
\begin{aligned}
&C_{as}^{(a)}(S_T, I_T, T; T) - P_{as}^{(a)}(S_T, I_T, T; T) \\
&= \begin{cases} S_T - \dfrac{1}{T-\tau} \displaystyle\int_\tau^T S_u \, du & \text{if } S_T > \dfrac{1}{T-\tau} \displaystyle\int_\tau^T S_u \, du \\[4mm] S_T - \dfrac{1}{T-\tau} \displaystyle\int_\tau^T S_u \, du & \text{if } S_T \le \dfrac{1}{T-\tau} \displaystyle\int_\tau^T S_u \, du. \end{cases}
\end{aligned}
$$

By discounting the payoffs back to time t under the risk-neutral measure $\mathbb{Q}$, we have

$$
\begin{aligned}
C_{as}^{(a)}(S_t, I_t, t; T) - P_{as}^{(a)}(S_t, I_t, t; T) &= e^{-r(T-t)} \mathbb{E}^{\mathbb{Q}} \left[S_T - \frac{1}{T-\tau} \int_\tau^T S_u \, du \, \middle| \, \mathscr{F}_t \right] \\
&= e^{-r(T-t)} \mathbb{E}^{\mathbb{Q}} \left[S_T \, \middle| \, \mathscr{F}_t \right] \\
&\quad - e^{-r(T-t)} \mathbb{E}^{\mathbb{Q}} \left[\frac{1}{T-\tau} \int_\tau^T S_u \, du \, \middle| \, \mathscr{F}_t \right] \\
&= S_t e^{-D(T-t)} - \left(\frac{1}{T-\tau} \int_\tau^t S_u \, du \right) e^{-r(T-t)} \\
&\quad - \left(\frac{e^{-D(T-t)} - e^{-r(T-t)}}{(r-D)(T-\tau)} \right) S_t
\end{aligned}
$$

$$= \left(S_t - \frac{1}{T-\tau} \int_\tau^t S_u \, du \right) e^{-r(T-t)}$$
$$+ \left(\frac{(r-D)(T-\tau)-1}{(r-D)(T-\tau)} \right)$$
$$\times \left(e^{-D(T-t)} - e^{-r(T-t)} \right) S_t.$$

□

8. *Geometric Average Rate (Fixed Strike) Asian Option (PDE Approach).* Let $\{W_t : t \geq 0\}$ be the $\mathbb{P}$-standard Wiener process on the probability space $(\Omega, \mathcal{F}, \mathbb{P})$ and let the asset price S_t follow the SDE

$$\frac{dS_t}{S_t} = (\mu - D)dt + \sigma \, dW_t$$

where μ is the drift parameter, D is the continuous dividend yield, σ is the volatility parameter and let r be the risk-free interest rate from the money-market account.

We define

$$I_t = \int_\tau^t \log S_u \, du$$

to be the geometric sum of an asset from initial time $\tau \geq 0$ until time t and consider the geometric average rate call option with payoff

$$\Psi(S_T, I_T) = \max \left\{ e^{\frac{I_T}{T-\tau}} - K, 0 \right\}$$

where $K > 0$ is the strike price and T is the option expiry time. Assume that the geometric average rate call option price at time t, $\tau < t < T$, $C_{ar}^{(g)}(S_t, I_t, t; K, T)$ satisfies the PDE

$$\frac{\partial C_{ar}^{(g)}}{\partial t} + \frac{1}{2}\sigma^2 S_t^2 \frac{\partial^2 C_{ar}^{(g)}}{\partial S_t^2} + (r-D)S_t \frac{\partial C_{ar}^{(g)}}{\partial S_t} + \log S_t \frac{\partial C_{ar}^{(g)}}{\partial I_t} - rC_{ar}^{(g)}(S_t, I_t, t; K, T) = 0$$

with boundary condition

$$C_{ar}^{(g)}(S_T, I_T, T; K, T) = \max \left\{ e^{\frac{I_T}{T-\tau}} - K, 0 \right\}.$$

By considering the change of variables

$$C_{ar}^{(g)}(S_t, I_t, t; K, T) = H(x, t), \quad x = \frac{I_t + (T-t)\log S_t}{T-\tau}$$

show that $H(x,t)$ satisfies

$$\frac{\partial H}{\partial t} + \frac{1}{2}\sigma^2 \left(\frac{T-t}{T-\tau}\right)^2 \frac{\partial^2 H}{\partial x^2} + \left(r - D - \frac{1}{2}\sigma^2\right)\left(\frac{T-t}{T-\tau}\right)\frac{\partial H}{\partial x} - rH(x,t) = 0$$

with boundary condition

$$H(x,T) = \max\{e^x - K, 0\}.$$

By setting

$$\widehat{S}_t = e^x$$

show that the PDE can be transformed into

$$\frac{\partial H}{\partial t} + \frac{1}{2}\sigma^2 \left(\frac{T-t}{T-\tau}\right)^2 \widehat{S}_t^2 \frac{\partial^2 H}{\partial \widehat{S}_t^2} + \left[r - D - \frac{1}{2}\sigma^2 \left(\frac{t-\tau}{T-\tau}\right)\right]\left(\frac{T-t}{T-\tau}\right)\widehat{S}_t \frac{\partial H}{\partial \widehat{S}_t}$$
$$-rH(\widehat{S}_t, t) = 0$$

with terminal payoff

$$H(\widehat{S}_T, T) = \max\{\widehat{S}_T - K, 0\}.$$

Hence, deduce from the European option price formula that the geometric average rate call option price at time t, $\tau < t < T$ is

$$C_{ar}^{(g)}(S_t, I_t, t; K, T) = e^{\frac{I_t}{T-\tau}} S_t^{\frac{T-t}{T-\tau}} e^{-\overline{D}(T-t)}\Phi(\overline{d}_+) - Ke^{-r(T-t)}\Phi(\overline{d}_-)$$

where

$$\overline{d}_\pm = \frac{\dfrac{I_t}{T-\tau} + \left(\dfrac{T-t}{T-\tau}\right)\log S_t - \log K + \left(r - \overline{D} \pm \frac{1}{2}\overline{\sigma}^2\right)(T-t)}{\overline{\sigma}\sqrt{T-t}}$$

$$\overline{D} = \frac{r}{2}\left(\frac{T+t-2\tau}{T-\tau}\right) + \frac{\sigma^2}{12}\left(\frac{T-t}{T-\tau}\right)\left(\frac{T+2t-3\tau}{T-\tau}\right) + \frac{D}{2}\left(\frac{T-t}{T-\tau}\right)$$

$$\overline{\sigma}^2 = \frac{\sigma^2}{3}\left(\frac{T-t}{T-\tau}\right)^2$$

and $\Phi(\cdot)$ is the cdf of a standard normal.

Solution: To obtain the PDEs satisfied by $C_{ar}^{(g)}(S_t, I_t, t; K, T)$ and $H(x,t)$, see Problem 5.2.2.3 (page 483).

By setting $\widehat{S}_t = e^x$ we can express

$$\frac{\partial H}{\partial x} = \frac{\partial H}{\partial \widehat{S}_t}\frac{\partial \widehat{S}_t}{\partial x} = e^x \frac{\partial H}{\partial \widehat{S}_t} = \widehat{S}_t \frac{\partial H}{\partial \widehat{S}_t}$$

$$\frac{\partial^2 H}{\partial x^2} = \frac{\partial \widehat{S}_t}{\partial x}\frac{\partial H}{\partial \widehat{S}_t} + \widehat{S}_t \frac{\partial^2 H}{\partial \widehat{S}_t^2}\frac{\partial \widehat{S}_t}{\partial x} = e^x \frac{\partial H}{\partial \widehat{S}_t} + e^x \widehat{S}_t \frac{\partial^2 H}{\partial \widehat{S}_t^2} = \widehat{S}_t \frac{\partial H}{\partial \widehat{S}_t} + \widehat{S}_t^2 \frac{\partial^2 H}{\partial \widehat{S}_t^2}.$$

By substituting the above results into the PDE satisfied by $H(x,t)$ we have

$$\frac{\partial H}{\partial t} + \frac{1}{2}\sigma^2 \left(\frac{T-t}{T-\tau}\right)^2 \left(\widehat{S}_t \frac{\partial H}{\partial \widehat{S}_t} + \widehat{S}_t^2 \frac{\partial^2 H}{\partial \widehat{S}_t^2}\right) + \left(r - D - \frac{1}{2}\sigma^2\right)\left(\frac{T-t}{T-\tau}\right)\widehat{S}_t \frac{\partial H}{\partial \widehat{S}_t}$$
$$-rH(\widehat{S}_t, t) = 0$$

or

$$\frac{\partial H}{\partial t} + \frac{1}{2}\sigma^2 \left(\frac{T-t}{T-\tau}\right)^2 \widehat{S}_t^2 \frac{\partial^2 H}{\partial \widehat{S}_t^2} + \left[r - D - \frac{1}{2}\sigma^2\left(\frac{t-\tau}{T-\tau}\right)\right]\left(\frac{T-t}{T-\tau}\right)\widehat{S}_t \frac{\partial H}{\partial \widehat{S}_t}$$
$$-rH(\widehat{S}_t, t) = 0$$

with payoff

$$H(\widehat{S}_T, T) = \max\{\widehat{S}_T - K, 0\}$$

which is a Black–Scholes equation with time-dependent dividend yield

$$\widehat{D}(t) = \left[r + \frac{1}{2}\sigma^2 \left(\frac{T-t}{T-\tau}\right)\right]\left(\frac{t-\tau}{T-\tau}\right) + D\left(\frac{T-t}{T-\tau}\right)$$

and volatility

$$\widehat{\sigma}(t) = \sigma\left(\frac{T-t}{T-\tau}\right).$$

Hence, we can deduce that

$$H(\widehat{S}_t, t) = \widehat{S}_t e^{-\int_t^T \widehat{D}(u)\,du}\Phi(\widehat{d}_+) - Ke^{-r(T-t)}\Phi(\widehat{d}_-)$$

where

$$\widehat{d}_\pm = \frac{\log(\widehat{S}_t/K) + \int_t^T (r - \widehat{D}(u) \pm \frac{1}{2}\widehat{\sigma}(u)^2)\,du}{\sqrt{\int_t^T \widehat{\sigma}(u)^2\,du}}$$

with

$$\int_t^T \hat{D}(u)\,du = \int_t^T \left\{ \left[r + \frac{1}{2}\sigma^2 \left(\frac{T-u}{T-\tau} \right) \right] \left(\frac{u-\tau}{T-\tau} \right) + D \left(\frac{T-u}{T-\tau} \right) \right\} du$$

$$= \int_t^T \left\{ \frac{r(u-\tau)}{T-\tau} + \frac{1}{2}\sigma^2 \left(\frac{T-u}{T-\tau} \right) \left(\frac{u-\tau}{T-\tau} \right) + D \left(\frac{T-u}{T-\tau} \right) \right\} du$$

$$= \frac{r(u-\tau)^2}{2(T-\tau)} + \frac{\sigma^2}{2} \left(\frac{(T-u)(u-\tau)^2}{2} + \frac{(u-\tau)^3}{6} \right) - D\frac{(T-u)^2}{2(T-\tau)} \Bigg|_t^T$$

$$= \frac{r(T+t-2\tau)(T-t)}{2(T-\tau)}$$

$$+ \frac{\sigma^2}{12} \left[\frac{(T-t)((T-\tau)^2 + (t-\tau)(T-\tau) + (t-\tau)^2)}{(T-\tau)^2} \right.$$

$$\left. - \frac{2(T-t)(t-\tau)^2}{(T-\tau)^2} \right] + \frac{D(T-t)^2}{2(T-\tau)}$$

$$= \left[\frac{r}{2} \left(\frac{T+t-2\tau}{T-\tau} \right) + \frac{\sigma^2}{12} \left(\frac{T-t}{T-\tau} \right) \left(\frac{T+2t-3\tau}{T-\tau} \right) \right.$$

$$\left. + \frac{D}{2} \left(\frac{T-t}{T-\tau} \right) \right] (T-t)$$

and

$$\int_t^T \hat{\sigma}(u)^2\,du = \int_t^T \sigma^2 \left(\frac{T-u}{T-\tau} \right)^2 du$$

$$= - \frac{\sigma^2(T-u)^3}{3(T-\tau)^2} \Bigg|_t^T$$

$$= \frac{\sigma^2}{3} \left(\frac{T-t}{T-\tau} \right)^2 (T-t).$$

Thus, we can rewrite $H(\hat{S}_t, t)$ as

$$H(\hat{S}_t, t) = \hat{S}_t e^{-\overline{D}(T-t)} \Phi(\overline{d}_+) - K e^{-r(T-t)} \Phi(\overline{d}_-)$$

where

$$\overline{d}_\pm = \frac{\log(\hat{S}_t / K) + (r - \overline{D} \pm \frac{1}{2}\overline{\sigma}^2)(T-t)}{\overline{\sigma}\sqrt{T-t}}$$

$$\overline{D} = \frac{1}{T-t} \int_t^T \hat{D}(u)\,du$$

and

$$\overline{\sigma}^2 = \frac{1}{T-t} \int_t^T \widehat{\sigma}(u)^2 \, du.$$

By substituting $\widehat{S}_t = e^x = e^{\frac{I_t + (T-t)\log S_t}{T-\tau}} = e^{\frac{I_t}{T-\tau}} S_t^{\frac{T-t}{T-\tau}}$, the geometric average rate call option price is

$$C_{ar}^{(g)}(S_t, I_t, t; K, T) = e^{\frac{I_t}{T-\tau}} S_t^{\frac{T-t}{T-\tau}} e^{-\overline{D}(T-t)} \Phi(\overline{d}_+) - K e^{-r(T-t)} \Phi(\overline{d}_-)$$

where

$$\overline{d}_\pm = \frac{\frac{I_t}{T-\tau} + \left(\frac{T-t}{T-\tau}\right)\log S_t - \log K + \left(r - \overline{D} \pm \frac{1}{2}\overline{\sigma}^2\right)(T-t)}{\overline{\sigma}\sqrt{T-t}}.$$

$\square$

9. *Geometric Average Strike (Floating Strike) Asian Option (PDE Approach).* Let $\{W_t : t \geq 0\}$ be the $\mathbb{P}$-standard Wiener process on the probability space $(\Omega, \mathcal{F}, \mathbb{P})$ and let the asset price S_t follow the SDE

$$\frac{dS_t}{S_t} = (\mu - D)dt + \sigma \, dW_t$$

where μ is the drift parameter, D is the continuous dividend yield, σ is the volatility parameter and let r be the risk-free interest rate from the money-market account.

We define

$$I_t = \int_\tau^t \log S_u \, du$$

to be the geometric sum of an asset in the time period $[\tau, t]$, $\tau \geq 0$ and consider the geometric average strike put option with payoff

$$\Psi(S_T, I_T) = \max\left\{ e^{\frac{I_T}{T-\tau}} - S_T, 0 \right\}$$

where T is the option expiry time. Assume that the geometric average strike put option price at time t, $\tau < t < T$, $P_{as}^{(g)}(S_t, I_t, t; T)$ satisfies the PDE

$$\frac{\partial P_{as}^{(g)}}{\partial t} + \frac{1}{2}\sigma^2 S_t^2 \frac{\partial^2 P_{as}^{(g)}}{\partial S_t^2} + (r-D)S_t \frac{\partial P_{as}^{(g)}}{\partial S_t} + \log S_t \frac{\partial P_{as}^{(g)}}{\partial I_t} - r P_{as}^{(g)}(S_t, I_t, t; T) = 0$$

with boundary condition

$$P_{as}^{(g)}(S_T, I_T, T; T) = \max\left\{ e^{\frac{I_T}{T-\tau}} - S_T, 0 \right\}.$$

By considering the change of variables

$$P_{as}^{(g)}(S_t, I_t, t; T) = S_t H(x, t), \quad x = \frac{I_t - (t - \tau)\log S_t}{T - \tau}$$

show that $H(x, t)$ satisfies

$$\frac{\partial H}{\partial t} + \frac{1}{2}\sigma^2 \left(\frac{t-\tau}{T-\tau}\right)^2 \frac{\partial^2 H}{\partial x^2} - \left(r - D + \frac{1}{2}\sigma^2\right)\left(\frac{t-\tau}{T-\tau}\right)\frac{\partial H}{\partial x} - DH(x, t) = 0$$

with boundary condition

$$H(x, T) = \max\{e^x - 1, 0\}.$$

By setting

$$\widehat{S}_t = e^x$$

show that the PDE can be transformed into

$$\frac{\partial H}{\partial t} + \frac{1}{2}\sigma^2 \left(\frac{t-\tau}{T-\tau}\right)^2 \widehat{S}_t^2 \frac{\partial^2 H}{\partial \widehat{S}_t^2} - \left[r - D + \frac{1}{2}\sigma^2 \left(\frac{T-t}{T-\tau}\right)\right]\left(\frac{t-\tau}{T-\tau}\right)\widehat{S}_t \frac{\partial H}{\partial \widehat{S}_t}$$
$$- DH(\widehat{S}_t, t) = 0$$

with terminal payoff

$$H(\widehat{S}_T, T) = \max\{\widehat{S}_T - 1, 0\}.$$

Hence, deduce from the European option price formula that the geometric average strike put option price at time t, $\tau < t < T$ is

$$P_{as}^{(g)}(S_t, I_t, t; T) = e^{\frac{I_t}{T-\tau}} S_t^{\frac{T-t}{T-\tau}} e^{-\overline{D}(T-t)}\Phi(\overline{d}_+) - S_t e^{-D(T-t)}\Phi(\overline{d}_-)$$

where

$$
\overline{d}_\pm = \frac{\dfrac{I_t}{T-\tau} - \dfrac{t-\tau}{T-\tau}\log S_t + \left(r - \overline{D} \pm \frac{1}{2}\overline{\sigma}^2\right)(T-t)}{\overline{\sigma}\sqrt{T-t}}
$$

$$
\overline{D} = \frac{r}{2}\left(\frac{T+t-2\tau}{T-\tau}\right) + \frac{D}{2}\left(\frac{T-t}{T-\tau}\right) + \frac{\sigma^2}{12}\left(\frac{T-t}{T-\tau}\right)\left(\frac{T+2t-3\tau}{T-\tau}\right)
$$

$$
\overline{\sigma}^2 = \frac{\sigma^2}{3}\left(\frac{(T-\tau)^2 + (t-\tau)(T-\tau) + (t-\tau)^2}{(T-\tau)^2}\right)
$$

and $\Phi(\cdot)$ is the cdf of a standard normal.

Solution: To obtain the PDEs satisfied by $P_{as}^{(g)}(S_t, I_t, t; T)$ and $H(x,t)$, see Problem 5.2.2.4 (page 485).

By setting $\widehat{S}_t = e^x$ we can express

$$
\frac{\partial H}{\partial x} = \frac{\partial H}{\partial S_t}\frac{\partial \widehat{S}_t}{\partial x} = e^x\frac{\partial H}{\partial \widehat{S}_t} = \widehat{S}_t\frac{\partial H}{\partial \widehat{S}_t}
$$

$$
\frac{\partial^2 H}{\partial x^2} = \frac{\partial \widehat{S}_t}{\partial x}\frac{\partial H}{\partial \widehat{S}_t} + \widehat{S}_t\frac{\partial^2 H}{\partial \widehat{S}_t^2}\frac{\partial \widehat{S}_t}{\partial x} = e^x\frac{\partial H}{\partial \widehat{S}_t} + e^x\widehat{S}_t\frac{\partial^2 H}{\partial \widehat{S}_t^2} = \widehat{S}_t\frac{\partial H}{\partial \widehat{S}_t} + \widehat{S}_t^2\frac{\partial^2 H}{\partial \widehat{S}_t^2}.
$$

By substituting the above results into the PDE satisfied by $H(x,t)$ we can write

$$
\frac{\partial H}{\partial t} + \frac{1}{2}\sigma^2\left(\frac{t-\tau}{T-\tau}\right)^2\left(\widehat{S}_t\frac{\partial H}{\partial \widehat{S}_t} + \widehat{S}_t^2\frac{\partial^2 H}{\partial \widehat{S}_t^2}\right) - \left(r - D + \frac{1}{2}\sigma^2\right)\left(\frac{t-\tau}{T-\tau}\right)\widehat{S}_t\frac{\partial H}{\partial \widehat{S}_t}
$$

$$
-DH(\widehat{S}_t,t) = 0
$$

or

$$
\frac{\partial H}{\partial t} + \frac{1}{2}\sigma^2\left(\frac{t-\tau}{T-\tau}\right)^2\widehat{S}_t^2\frac{\partial^2 H}{\partial \widehat{S}_t^2} - \left[r - D + \frac{1}{2}\sigma^2\left(\frac{T-t}{T-\tau}\right)\right]\left(\frac{t-\tau}{T-\tau}\right)\widehat{S}_t\frac{\partial H}{\partial \widehat{S}_t}
$$

$$
-DH(\widehat{S}_t,t) = 0
$$

with payoff

$$
H(\widehat{S}_T, T) = \max\{\widehat{S}_T - 1, 0\}
$$

which is a Black–Scholes equation with interest rate D, time-dependent dividend yield

$$
\widehat{D}(t) = r\left(\frac{t-\tau}{T-\tau}\right) + D\left(\frac{T-t}{T-\tau}\right) + \frac{1}{2}\sigma^2\left(\frac{T-t}{T-\tau}\right)\left(\frac{t-\tau}{T-\tau}\right)
$$

and volatility

$$\widehat{\sigma}(t) = \frac{\sigma(t - \tau)}{T - \tau}.$$

Hence, we can deduce that

$$H(\widehat{S}_t, t) = \widehat{S}_t e^{-\int_t^T \widehat{D}(u) du} \Phi(\widehat{d}_+) - e^{-D(T-t)} \Phi(\widehat{d}_-)$$

with

$$\widehat{d}_{\pm} = \frac{\log \widehat{S}_t + \int_t^T (D - \widehat{D}(u) \pm \frac{1}{2} \widehat{\sigma}(u)^2) \, du}{\sqrt{\int_t^T \widehat{\sigma}(u)^2 \, du}}$$

where

$$\int_t^T \widehat{D}(u) \, du = \int_t^T r \left(\frac{u - \tau}{T - \tau} \right) + D \left(\frac{T - u}{T - \tau} \right) + \frac{1}{2} \sigma^2 \left(\frac{T - u}{T - \tau} \right) \left(\frac{u - \tau}{T - \tau} \right) du$$

$$= \frac{r(u - \tau)^2}{2(T - \tau)} - D \frac{(T - u)^2}{2(T - \tau)} + \frac{\sigma^2}{2} \left(\frac{(T - u)(u - \tau)^2}{2} + \frac{(u - \tau)^3}{6} \right) \Bigg|_t^T$$

$$= \frac{r(T + t - 2\tau)(T - t)}{2(T - \tau)} + \frac{D(T - t)^2}{2(T - \tau)}$$

$$+ \frac{\sigma^2}{12} \left[\frac{(T - t)((T - \tau)^2 + (t - \tau)(T - \tau) + (t - \tau)^2)}{(T - \tau)^2} \right.$$

$$\left. - \frac{2(T - t)(t - \tau)^2}{(T - \tau)^2} \right]$$

$$= \left[\frac{r}{2} \left(\frac{T + t - 2\tau}{T - \tau} \right) + \frac{D}{2} \left(\frac{T - t}{T - \tau} \right) \right.$$

$$\left. + \frac{\sigma^2}{12} \left(\frac{T - t}{T - \tau} \right) \left(\frac{T + 2t - 3\tau}{T - \tau} \right) \right] (T - t)$$

and

$$\int_t^T \widehat{\sigma}(u)^2 \, du = \int_t^T \frac{\sigma^2 (u - \tau)^2}{(T - \tau)^2} \, du$$

$$= \frac{\sigma^2}{3} \frac{(u - \tau)^3}{(T - \tau)^2} \Bigg|_t^T$$

$$= \frac{\sigma^2}{3} \left(\frac{(T - \tau)^3 - (t - \tau)^3}{(T - \tau)^2} \right)$$

$$= \frac{\sigma^2}{3} \frac{\left((T - \tau)^2 + (t - \tau)(T - \tau) + (t - \tau)^2 \right) (T - t)}{(T - \tau)^2}.$$

Hence, we can rewrite $H(\widehat{S}_t, t)$ as

$$H(\widehat{S}_t, t) = \widehat{S}_t e^{-\overline{D}(T-t)} \Phi(\overline{d}_+) - e^{-D(T-t)} \Phi(\overline{d}_-)$$

where

$$\overline{d}_\pm = \frac{\log(\widehat{S}_t/K) + \left(D - \overline{D} \pm \frac{1}{2}\overline{\sigma}^2\right)(T-t)}{\overline{\sigma}\sqrt{T-t}}$$

$$\overline{D} = \frac{1}{T-t} \int_t^T \widehat{D}(u)\,du$$

and

$$\overline{\sigma}^2 = \frac{1}{T-t} \int_t^T \widehat{\sigma}(u)^2\,du.$$

By substituting $\widehat{S}_t = e^x = e^{\frac{I_t - t\log S_t}{T}} = e^{\frac{I_t}{T}} S_t^{-\frac{t}{T}}$, the geometric average strike put option at time $t < T$ is

$$P_{as}^{(g)}(S_t, I_t, t; T) = S_t H(x, t)$$

$$= e^{\frac{I_t}{T}} S_t^{\frac{T-t}{T}} e^{-\overline{D}(T-t)} \Phi(\overline{d}_+) - S_t e^{-D(T-t)} \Phi(\overline{d}_-)$$

where

$$\overline{d}_\pm = \frac{\dfrac{I_t}{T-\tau} - \dfrac{t-\tau}{T-\tau}\log S_t + \left(r - \overline{D} \pm \dfrac{1}{2}\overline{\sigma}^2\right)(T-t)}{\overline{\sigma}\sqrt{T-t}}$$

$$\overline{D} = \frac{r}{2}\left(\frac{T+t-2\tau}{T-\tau}\right) + \frac{D}{2}\left(\frac{T-t}{T-\tau}\right) + \frac{\sigma^2}{12}\left(\frac{T-t}{T-\tau}\right)\left(\frac{T+2t-3\tau}{T-\tau}\right)$$

$$\overline{\sigma}^2 = \frac{\sigma^2}{3}\left(\frac{(T-\tau)^2 + (t-\tau)(T-\tau) + (t-\tau)^2}{(T-\tau)^2}\right).$$

□

10. *Geometric Average Rate (Fixed Strike) Asian Option (Probabilistic Approach).* Let $\{W_t : t \geq 0\}$ be the $\mathbb{P}$-standard Wiener process on the probability space $(\Omega, \mathcal{F}, \mathbb{P})$ and let the asset price S_t follow the SDE

$$\frac{dS_t}{S_t} = (\mu - D)dt + \sigma\,dW_t$$

where μ is the drift parameter, D is the continuous dividend yield, σ is the volatility parameter and let r be the risk-free interest rate from the money-market account.

We define

$$I_t = \int_\tau^t \log S_u \, du$$

to be the geometric sum of the asset in the time period $[\tau, t]$, where $\tau \geq 0$ and consider the geometric average rate put option with payoff

$$\Psi(S_T, I_T) = \max\left\{ K - e^{\frac{I_T}{T-\tau}}, 0 \right\}$$

where $K > 0$ is the strike price and T is the option expiry time.

Show that if $X \sim \mathcal{N}(\mu_x, \sigma_x^2)$ then for a constant $K > 0$

$$\mathbb{E}\left[\max\{\delta(e^X - K, 0)\}\right] = \delta e^{\mu_x + \frac{1}{2}\sigma_x^2}\Phi\left(\frac{\delta(\mu_x + \sigma_x^2 - \log K)}{\sigma_x}\right) - \delta K \Phi\left(\frac{\delta(\mu_x - \log K)}{\sigma_x}\right)$$

where $\delta \in \{-1, 1\}$ and $\Phi(\cdot)$ denotes the cdf of a standard normal.

Given that $W_{u-t} \sim N(0, u - t)$, $u > t$ show, using integration by parts, that

$$\int_t^T W_{u-t} \, du = \int_t^T (T - u) \, dW_u$$

and deduce that

$$\int_t^T W_{u-t} \, du \sim \mathcal{N}\left[0, \frac{(T-t)^3}{3}\right].$$

By considering $e^{\frac{I_T}{T-\tau}}$ and $e^{\frac{I_t}{t-\tau}}$ show under the risk-neutral measure $\mathbb{Q}$ that $\dfrac{I_T}{T-\tau}$ follows a normal distribution with mean

$$\mathbb{E}^{\mathbb{Q}}\left(\frac{I_T}{T}\bigg| \mathcal{F}_t\right) = \frac{1}{T-\tau}\left\{\int_\tau^t \log S_u \, du + (T-t)\log S_t + \frac{1}{2}\left(r - D - \frac{1}{2}\sigma^2\right)(T-t)^2\right\}$$

and variance

$$\text{Var}^{\mathbb{Q}}\left(\frac{I_T}{T-\tau}\bigg| \mathcal{F}_t\right) = \frac{\sigma^2}{3}\frac{(T-t)^3}{(T-\tau)^2}.$$

Hence, deduce that under the risk-neutral measure $\mathbb{Q}$ the geometric average rate put option at time $t < T$ is

$$P_{ar}^{(g)}(S_t, I_t, t; K, T) = Ke^{-r(T-t)}\Phi(-\bar{d}_-) - e^{\frac{I_t}{T}}S_t^{\frac{T-t}{T}}e^{-\bar{D}(T-t)}\Phi(-\bar{d}_+)$$

where

$$
\overline{d}_\pm = \frac{\frac{I_t}{T-\tau} + \left(\frac{T-t}{T-\tau}\right)\log S_t - \log K + \left(r - \overline{D} \pm \frac{1}{2}\overline{\sigma}^2\right)(T-t)}{\overline{\sigma}\sqrt{T-t}}
$$

$$
\overline{D} = \frac{r}{2}\left(\frac{T+t-2\tau}{T-\tau}\right) + \frac{D}{2}\left(\frac{T-t}{T-\tau}\right) + \frac{\sigma^2}{12}\left(\frac{T-t}{T-\tau}\right)\left(\frac{T+2t-3\tau}{T-\tau}\right)
$$

$$
\overline{\sigma}^2 = \frac{\sigma^2}{3}\left(\frac{T-t}{T-\tau}\right)^2 .
$$

Solution: For the first part of the results refer to Problem 1.2.2.7 of *Problems and Solutions in Mathematical Finance, Volume 1: Stochastic Calculus.*

From the stationary increment property of a standard Wiener process

$$
\int_t^T W_{u-t}\,du = \int_t^T (W_u - W_t)\,du
$$
$$
= \int_t^T W_u\,du - W_t\int_t^T du
$$
$$
= \int_t^T W_u\,du - W_t(T-t).
$$

Using integration by parts

$$
\int_t^T W_u\,du = uW_u\big|_t^T - \int_t^T u\,dW_u
$$
$$
= TW_T - tW_t - \int_t^T u\,dW_u
$$

and therefore

$$
\int_t^T W_{u-t}\,du = TW_T - tW_t - \int_t^T u\,dW_u - W_t(T-t)
$$
$$
= TW_{T-t} - \int_t^T u\,dW_u
$$
$$
= \int_t^T (T-u)\,dW_u.
$$

Using the properties of the standard Wiener process we have

$$
\mathbb{E}\left[\int_t^T W_{u-t}\,du\right] = \mathbb{E}\left[\int_t^T (T-u)\,dW_u\right] = 0
$$

and

$$\mathbb{E}\left[\left(\int_t^T W_{u-t}\,du\right)^2\right] = \mathbb{E}\left[\int_t^T (T-u)^2\,du\right] = -\left.\frac{(T-u)^3}{3}\right|_t^T = \frac{(T-t)^3}{3}.$$

Since we can write

$$\int_t^T W_{u-t}\,du = \int_t^T (T-u)\,dW_u = \lim_{n\to\infty}\sum_{i=0}^{n-1}(T-t_i)(W_{t_{i+1}} - W_{t_i})$$

where $t_i = t + i(T-t)/n$, we can see that each term of $W_{t_{i+1}} - W_{t_i}$ is multiplied by a deterministic term. Thus, the product is normal and given that the sum of normal variables is also normal, we can deduce that $\int_t^T W_{u-t}\,du \sim \mathcal{N}\left[0, \frac{(T-t)^3}{3}\right]$.

Under the risk-neutral measure $\mathbb{Q}$, S_t follows

$$\frac{dS_t}{S_t} = (r-D)dt + \sigma\,dW_t^{\mathbb{Q}}$$

where $W_t^{\mathbb{Q}} = W_t + \left(\frac{\mu-r}{\sigma}\right)t$ is a $\mathbb{Q}$-standard Wiener process. Using Itô's lemma

$$d\log S_t = \frac{dS_t}{S_t} - \frac{1}{2}\left(\frac{dS_t}{S_t}\right)^2 + \dots$$

$$= (r-D)dt + \sigma\,dW_t^{\mathbb{Q}} - \frac{1}{2}\sigma^2 dt$$

$$= \left(r - D - \frac{1}{2}\sigma^2\right)dt + \sigma\,dW_t^{\mathbb{Q}}$$

and taking integrals for $t < u < T$ we have

$$\int_t^u d\log S_t = \int_t^u \left(r - D - \frac{1}{2}\sigma^2\right)dt + \sigma\int_t^u dW_t^{\mathbb{Q}}$$

or

$$\log S_u = \log S_t + \left(r - D - \frac{1}{2}\sigma^2\right)(u-t) + \sigma W_{u-t}^{\mathbb{Q}}.$$

For $t < T$, let $G_t = e^{\frac{1}{t-\tau}\int_\tau^t \log S_u\,du} = e^{\frac{I_t}{t-\tau}}$ and $G_T = e^{\frac{1}{T-\tau}\int_\tau^T \log S_u\,du} = e^{\frac{I_T}{T-\tau}}$ so that

$$(t-\tau)\log G_t = \int_\tau^t \log S_u\,du$$

and

$$(T - \tau)\log G_T = \int_\tau^T \log S_u \, du.$$

By subtraction

$$(T - \tau)\log G_T - (t - \tau)\log G_t = \int_\tau^T \log S_u \, du - \int_\tau^t \log S_u \, du$$

$$= \int_t^T \log S_u \, du$$

and substituting $\log S_u = \log S_t + (r - D - \frac{1}{2}\sigma^2)(u - t) + \sigma W^Q_{u-t}$ we have

$$(T - \tau)\log G_T - (t - \tau)\log G_t = \int_t^T \left[\log S_t + \left(r - D - \frac{1}{2}\sigma^2\right)(u - t) + \sigma W^Q_{u-t}\right] du$$

$$= (T - t)\log S_t + \int_t^T (r - D - \frac{1}{2}\sigma^2)(u - t)\, du$$

$$+ \sigma \int_t^T W^Q_{u-t} \, du$$

$$= (T - t)\log S_t + \frac{1}{2}\left(r - D - \frac{1}{2}\sigma^2\right)(T - t)^2$$

$$+ \sigma \int_t^T (T - u)\, dW^Q_{u-t}.$$

Since $\log G_T = \dfrac{I_T}{T - \tau}$ and $\log G_t = \dfrac{I_t}{t - \tau}$, therefore

$$I_T = I_t + (T - t)\log S_t + \frac{1}{2}\left(r - D - \frac{1}{2}\sigma^2\right)(T - t)^2 + \sigma \int_t^T (T - u)\, dW^Q_{u-t}$$

or

$$\frac{I_T}{T - \tau} = \frac{1}{T - \tau}\left\{I_t + (T - t)\log S_t + \frac{1}{2}\left(r - D - \frac{1}{2}\sigma^2\right)(T - t)^2 \right.$$

$$\left. + \sigma \int_t^T (T - u)\, dW^Q_{u-t}\right\}.$$

Since $\int_t^T (T-u)\,dW_{u-t}^{\mathbb{Q}}$ is normally distributed, then conditional on the filtration $\mathscr{F}_t$

$$\frac{I_T}{T-\tau}\bigg|\mathscr{F}_t \sim \mathcal{N}\left[\frac{1}{T-\tau}\left\{I_t+(T-t)\log S_t+\frac{1}{2}\left(r-D-\frac{1}{2}\sigma^2\right)(T-t)^2\right\},\right.$$
$$\left.\frac{\sigma^2}{3}\frac{(T-t)^3}{(T-\tau)^2}\right].$$

Using the identity

$$\mathbb{E}\left[\max\{K-e^X,0\}\right] = K\Phi\left(-\frac{(\mu_x-\log K)}{\sigma_x}\right) - e^{\mu_x+\frac{1}{2}\sigma_x^2}\Phi\left(-\frac{(\mu_x+\sigma_x^2-\log K)}{\sigma_x}\right)$$

for $X \sim \mathcal{N}(\mu_x,\sigma_x^2)$ and $\delta = -1$, under the risk-neutral measure $\mathbb{Q}$ the geometric average rate put option price at time t is

$$P_{ar}^{(g)}(S_t,I_t,t;K,T) = e^{-r(T-t)}\mathbb{E}^{\mathbb{Q}}\left[\max\left\{K-e^{\frac{I_T}{T-\tau}},0\right\}\bigg|\mathscr{F}_t\right]$$
$$= Ke^{-r(T-t)}\Phi(-\overline{d}_-) - e^{\overline{m}+\frac{1}{2}\overline{s}^2-r(T-t)}\Phi(-\overline{d}_+)$$

where

$$\overline{m} = \frac{1}{T-\tau}\left\{I_t+(T-t)\log S_t+\frac{1}{2}\left(r-D-\frac{1}{2}\sigma^2\right)(T-t)^2\right\}$$
$$\overline{s}^2 = \frac{\sigma^2}{3}\frac{(T-t)^3}{(T-\tau)^2}$$
$$\overline{d}_+ = \frac{\overline{m}+\overline{s}^2-\log K}{\overline{s}}$$
$$\overline{d}_- = \overline{d}_+ - s.$$

Hence,

$$e^{\overline{m}+\frac{1}{2}\overline{s}^2-r(T-t)} = e^{\frac{1}{T-\tau}\left\{I_t+(T-t)\log S_t+\frac{1}{2}(r-D-\frac{1}{2}\sigma^2)(T-t)^2\right\}+\frac{\sigma^2}{6}\frac{(T-t)^3}{(T-\tau)^2}-r(T-t)}$$
$$= e^{\frac{I_t}{T-\tau}}S_t^{\frac{T-t}{T-\tau}}e^{-\overline{D}(T-t)}$$

where $\overline{D} = \frac{r}{2}\left(\frac{T+t-2\tau}{T-\tau}\right) + \frac{D}{2}\left(\frac{T-t}{T-\tau}\right) + \frac{\sigma^2}{12}\left(\frac{T-t}{T-\tau}\right)\left(\frac{T+2t-3\tau}{T-\tau}\right).$

In contrast,

$$
\begin{aligned}
\bar{d}_+ &= \frac{\bar{m} + \bar{s}^2 - \log K}{\bar{s}} \\[2mm]
&= \frac{\left[\dfrac{1}{T-\tau}\left\{I_t + (T-t)\log S_t + \dfrac{1}{2}\left(r - D - \dfrac{1}{2}\sigma^2\right)(T-t)^2\right\} \atop{+\dfrac{\sigma^2}{3}\dfrac{(T-t)^3}{(T-\tau)^2} - \log K}\right]}{\sqrt{\dfrac{\sigma^2}{3}\dfrac{(T-t)^3}{(T-\tau)^2}}} \\[2mm]
&= \frac{\dfrac{I_t}{T-\tau} + \left(\dfrac{T-t}{T-\tau}\right)\log S_t - \log K + \left(r - \overline{D} + \dfrac{1}{2}\overline{\sigma}^2\right)(T-t)}{\overline{\sigma}\sqrt{T-t}}
\end{aligned}
$$

and

$$
\begin{aligned}
\bar{d}_- &= \bar{d}_+ - \bar{s} \\
&= \bar{d}_+ - \overline{\sigma}\sqrt{T-t} \\
&= \frac{\dfrac{I_t}{T-\tau} + \left(\dfrac{T-t}{T-\tau}\right)\log S_t - \log K + \left(r - \overline{D} - \dfrac{1}{2}\overline{\sigma}^2\right)(T-t)}{\overline{\sigma}\sqrt{T-t}}
\end{aligned}
$$

where $\overline{\sigma}^2 = \dfrac{\sigma^2}{3}\left(\dfrac{T-t}{T-\tau}\right)^2$.

Hence,

$$
P_{ar}^{(g)}(S_t, I_t, t; K, T) = Ke^{-r(T-t)}\Phi(-\bar{d}_-) - e^{\frac{I_t}{T}}S_t^{\frac{T-t}{T}}e^{-\overline{D}(T-t)}\Phi(-\bar{d}_+)
$$

where $\bar{d}_{\pm} = \dfrac{\dfrac{I_t}{T-\tau} + \left(\dfrac{T-t}{T-\tau}\right)\log S_t - \log K + \left(r - \overline{D} \pm \dfrac{1}{2}\overline{\sigma}^2\right)(T-t)}{\overline{\sigma}\sqrt{T-t}}.$

$\square$

11. *Geometric Average Strike (Floating Strike) Asian Option (Probabilistic Approach).* Let $\{W_t : t \geq 0\}$ be the $\mathbb{P}$-standard Wiener process on the probability space $(\Omega, \mathcal{F}, \mathbb{P})$ and let the asset price S_t follow the SDE

$$
\frac{dS_t}{S_t} = (\mu - D)dt + \sigma\,dW_t
$$

where μ is the drift parameter, D is the continuous dividend yield, σ is the volatility parameter and let r be the risk-free interest rate from the money-market account.

We define

$$I_t = \int_\tau^t \log S_u \, du$$

to be the geometric sum of the asset in the time period $[\tau, t]$, where $\tau \geq 0$ and consider the geometric average strike call option with payoff

$$\Psi(S_T, I_T) = \max \left\{ S_T - e^{\frac{I_T}{T-\tau}}, 0 \right\}$$

where T is the option expiry time.

Show that if $X \sim \mathcal{N}(\mu_x, \sigma_x^2)$ and $Y \sim \mathcal{N}(\mu_y, \sigma_y^2)$ have a joint bivariate normal distribution with correlation coefficient $\rho_{xy} \in (-1, 1)$, then

$$\mathbb{E}\left[\max\{e^X - e^Y, 0\} \right]$$

$$= e^{\mu_x + \frac{1}{2}\sigma_x^2} \Phi\left(\frac{\mu_x - \mu_y + \sigma_x(\sigma_x - \rho_{xy}\sigma_y)}{\sqrt{\sigma_x^2 - 2\rho_{xy}\sigma_x\sigma_y + \sigma_y^2}} \right) - e^{\mu_y + \frac{1}{2}\sigma_y^2} \Phi\left(\frac{\mu_x - \mu_y - \sigma_y(\sigma_y - \rho_{xy}\sigma_x)}{\sqrt{\sigma_x^2 - 2\rho_{xy}\sigma_x\sigma_y + \sigma_y^2}} \right)$$

where $\Phi(\cdot)$ is the cdf of a standard normal.

Show that the pair of random variables $\left(W_{T-t}, \int_t^T W_{u-t} \, du \right)$ has the covariance matrix

$$\Sigma = \begin{bmatrix} T-t & \frac{1}{2}(T-t)^2 \\ \frac{1}{2}(T-t)^2 & \frac{1}{3}(T-t)^3 \end{bmatrix}$$

with correlation coefficient $\dfrac{\sqrt{3}}{2}$ and $\left(W_{T-t}, \int_t^T W_{u-t} \, du \right)$ follows a bivariate normal distribution.

Using Itô's formula show that under the risk-neutral measure, for $t < T$

$$\log S_T = \log S_t + \left(r - D - \frac{1}{2}\sigma^2 \right)(T-t) + \sigma W_{T-t}^{\mathbb{Q}}$$

$$\log \left(\frac{I_T}{T-\tau} \right) = \frac{1}{T-\tau} \left\{ I_t + (T-t)\log S_t + \frac{1}{2}\left(r - D - \frac{1}{2}\sigma^2 \right)(T-t)^2 \right.$$

$$\left. + \sigma \int_t^T W_{u-t}^{\mathbb{Q}} \, du \right\}$$

where $W_t^{\mathbb{Q}}$ is a $\mathbb{Q}$-standard Wiener process.

Finally, deduce that under the risk-neutral measure $\mathbb{Q}$ the geometric average strike call option at time $t, \tau < t < T$ is

$$C_{as}^{(g)}(S_t, I_t, t; T) = S_t e^{-D(T-t)} \Phi(-\overline{d}_-) - e^{\frac{I_t}{T-\tau}} S_t^{\frac{T-t}{T-\tau}} e^{-\overline{D}(T-t)} \Phi(-\overline{d}_+)$$

where

$$\overline{d}_\pm = \frac{\dfrac{I_t}{T-\tau} - \dfrac{t}{T-\tau} \log S_t + \left(D - \overline{D} \pm \dfrac{1}{2}\overline{\sigma}^2 \right)(T-t)}{\overline{\sigma}\sqrt{T-t}}$$

$$\overline{D} = \frac{r}{2}\left(\frac{T+t-2\tau}{T}\right) + \frac{D}{2}\left(\frac{T-t}{T-\tau}\right) + \frac{\sigma^2}{12}\left(\frac{T-t}{T-\tau}\right)\left(\frac{T+2t-3\tau}{T-\tau}\right)$$

$$\overline{\sigma}^2 = \frac{\sigma^2}{3}\left(\frac{(T-\tau)^2 + (t-\tau)(T-\tau) + (t-\tau)^2}{(T-\tau)^2}\right).$$

Solution: For the first part of the results see Problem 1.2.2.17 in *Problems and Solutions in Mathematical Finance, Volume 1: Stochastic Calculus*.

By definition, the covariance matrix for the pair of random variables $(W_{T-t}, \int_t^T W_{u-t}\,du)$ is

$$\Sigma = \begin{bmatrix} \mathrm{Var}(W_{T-t}) & \mathrm{Cov}\left(W_{T-t}, \int_t^T W_{u-t}\,du\right) \\ \mathrm{Cov}\left(W_{T-t}, \int_t^T W_{u-t}\,du\right) & \mathrm{Var}\left(\int_t^T W_{u-t}\,du\right) \end{bmatrix}.$$

Given that $W_{T-t} \sim \mathcal{N}(0, T-t)$ and from Problem 5.2.2.10 (page 508), we have

$$\mathrm{Var}(W_{T-t}) = T - t$$

and

$$\mathrm{Var}\left(\int_t^T W_{u-t}\,du\right) = \mathrm{Var}\left(\int_t^T (T-u)\,dW_u\right)$$

$$= \mathbb{E}\left(\int_t^T (T-u)^2\,du\right) - \mathbb{E}\left(\int_t^T (T-u)\,du\right)^2$$

$$= \frac{1}{3}(T-t)^3.$$

For the case $\mathrm{Cov}\left(W_{T-t}, \int_t^T W_{u-t}\, du\right)$ we can write

$$\mathrm{Cov}\left(W_{T-t}, \int_t^T W_{u-t}\, du\right) = \mathbb{E}\left(W_{T-t} \int_t^T W_{u-t}\, du\right)$$

$$-\mathbb{E}(W_{T-t})\mathbb{E}\left(\int_t^T W_{u-t}\, du\right)$$

$$= \mathbb{E}\left(W_{T-t} \int_t^T W_{u-t}\, du\right)$$

$$= \mathbb{E}\left(\int_t^T W_{T-t}W_{u-t}\, du\right)$$

$$= \int_t^T \mathbb{E}\left(W_{T-t}W_{u-t}\right)\, du$$

$$= \int_t^T \mathbb{E}\left[W_{u-t}(W_{T-t} - W_{u-t}) + W_{u-t}^2\right]\, du.$$

From the independent increment property of a standard Wiener process we have

$$\mathrm{Cov}\left(W_{T-t}, \int_t^T W_{u-t}\, du\right) = \int_t^T \mathbb{E}(W_{u-t})\mathbb{E}(W_{T-t} - W_{u-t})\, du$$

$$+ \int_t^T \mathbb{E}(W_{u-t}^2)\, ds$$

$$= \int_t^T \mathbb{E}(W_{u-t}^2)\, ds$$

$$= \int_t^T (u - t)\, du$$

$$= \frac{1}{2}(T - t)^2.$$

Therefore, the covariance matrix is

$$\Sigma = \begin{bmatrix} T - t & \frac{1}{2}(T - t)^2 \\ \frac{1}{2}(T - t)^2 & \frac{1}{3}(T - t)^3 \end{bmatrix}$$

with correlation coefficient

$$\rho = \frac{\mathrm{Cov}\left(W_{T-t}, \int_t^T W_{u-t}\, du\right)}{\sqrt{\mathrm{Var}(W_{T-t})\mathrm{Var}\left(\int_t^T W_{u-t}\, du\right)}} = \frac{\frac{1}{2}(T - t)^2}{\sqrt{\frac{1}{3}(T - t)^4}} = \frac{\sqrt{3}}{2}.$$

By expressing

$$W_{T-t} = \sqrt{T-t}Z_1$$

$$\int_t^T W_{u-t}\,du = \sqrt{\frac{(T-t)^3}{3}}\left(\rho Z_1 + \sqrt{1-\rho^2}Z_2\right)$$

where $Z_1, Z_2 \sim \mathcal{N}(0,1)$ and $Z_1 \perp\!\!\!\perp Z_2$, for constants θ_1 and θ_2

$$\mathbb{E}\left(e^{\theta W_{T-t}+\theta_2 \int_t^T W_{u-t}\,du}\right) = \mathbb{E}\left[e^{\theta_1 \sqrt{T-t}Z_1+\theta_2\sqrt{(T-t)^3/3}(\rho Z_1+\sqrt{1-\rho^2}Z_2)}\right]$$

$$= \mathbb{E}\left[e^{(\theta_1\sqrt{T-t}+\rho\theta_2\sqrt{(T-t)^3/3})Z_1+\theta_2\sqrt{(T-t)^3(1-\rho^2)/3}Z_2}\right]$$

$$= \mathbb{E}\left[e^{(\theta_1\sqrt{T-t}+\rho\theta_2\sqrt{(T-t)^3/3})Z_1}\right]\cdot\mathbb{E}\left[e^{\theta_2\sqrt{(T-t)^3(1-\rho^2)/3}Z_2}\right]$$

$$= e^{\frac{1}{2}(\theta_1\sqrt{T-t}+\rho\theta_2\sqrt{(T-t)^3/3})^2}\cdot e^{\frac{1}{2}\theta_2^2(T-t)^3(1-\rho^2)/3}.$$

By substituting $\rho = \dfrac{\sqrt{3}}{2}$ and setting $\boldsymbol{\theta} = (\theta_1,\theta_2)^T$ we therefore have

$$\mathbb{E}\left(e^{\theta W_{T-t}+\theta_2 \int_t^T W_{u-t}\,du}\right) = e^{\frac{1}{2}\theta_1^2(T-t)+\frac{1}{2}\theta_1\theta_2(T-t)^2+\frac{1}{2}\theta_2^2\frac{(T-t)^3}{3}}$$

$$= e^{\frac{1}{2}\boldsymbol{\theta}^T\boldsymbol{\Sigma}\boldsymbol{\theta}}$$

which is the moment-generating function of a bivariate normal distribution. Hence, $\left(W_{T-t}, \int_t^T W_{u-t}\,du\right)$ follows a bivariate normal distribution.

From Girsanov's theorem, under the risk-neutral measure

$$\frac{dS_t}{S_t} = (r-D)dt + \sigma\,dW_t^{\mathbb{Q}}$$

where $W_t^{\mathbb{Q}} = W_t + \left(\dfrac{\mu-r}{\sigma}\right)t$ is a $\mathbb{Q}$-standard Wiener process. From Itō's formula

$$d\log S_t = \frac{dS_t}{S_t} - \frac{1}{2}\left(\frac{dS_t}{S_t}\right)^2 + \cdots$$

$$= (r-D)dt + \sigma\,dW_t^{\mathbb{Q}} - \frac{1}{2}\sigma^2 dt$$

$$= \left(r - D - \frac{1}{2}\sigma^2\right)dt + \sigma\,dW_t^{\mathbb{Q}}$$

and taking integrals for $t < u < T$ we have

$$\int_t^u d\log S_t = \int_t^u \left(r - D - \frac{1}{2}\sigma^2\right)dt + \sigma\int_t^u dW_t^{\mathbb{Q}}$$

or

$$\log S_u = \log S_t + \left(r - D - \frac{1}{2}\sigma^2\right)(u - t) + \sigma W_{u-t}^Q.$$

For $t < T$, let $G_t = e^{\frac{1}{t-\tau}\int_\tau^t \log S_u\, du} = e^{\frac{I_t}{t-\tau}}$ and $G_T = e^{\frac{1}{T-\tau}\int_\tau^T \log S_u\, du} = e^{\frac{I_T}{T-\tau}}$ so that

$$(t - \tau)\log G_t = \int_\tau^t \log S_u\, du$$

and

$$(T - \tau)\log G_T = \int_\tau^T \log S_u\, du.$$

By subtraction

$$(T - \tau)\log G_T - (t - \tau)\log G_t = \int_\tau^T \log S_u\, du - \int_\tau^t \log S_u\, du = \int_t^T \log S_u\, du$$

and substituting $\log S_u = \log S_t + (r - D - \frac{1}{2}\sigma^2)(u - t) + \sigma W_{u-t}^Q$ we have

$$(T - \tau)\log G_T - (t - \tau)\log G_t = \int_t^T \left[\log S_t + \left(r - D - \frac{1}{2}\sigma^2\right)(u - t) + \sigma W_{u-t}^Q\right] du$$

$$= (T - t)\log S_t + \int_t^T (r - D - \frac{1}{2}\sigma^2)(u - t)\, du$$

$$+ \sigma \int_t^T W_{u-t}^Q\, du$$

$$= (T - t)\log S_t + \frac{1}{2}\left(r - D - \frac{1}{2}\sigma^2\right)(T - t)^2$$

$$+ \sigma \int_t^T W_{u-t}^Q\, du.$$

Since $\log G_T = \dfrac{I_T}{T - \tau}$ and $\log G_t = \dfrac{I_t}{t - \tau}$, therefore

$$I_T = I_t + (T - t)\log S_t + \frac{1}{2}\left(r - D - \frac{1}{2}\sigma^2\right)(T - t)^2 + \sigma \int_t^T W_{u-t}^Q\, du$$

or

$$\frac{I_T}{T - \tau} = \frac{1}{T - \tau}\left\{I_t + (T - t)\log S_t + \frac{1}{2}\left(r - D - \frac{1}{2}\sigma^2\right)(T - t)^2 \right.$$

$$\left. + \sigma \int_t^T W_{u-t}^Q\, du\right\}.$$

Since $W_{T-t}^Q \sim \mathcal{N}(0, T-t)$ and $\int_t^T W_{u-t}^Q \, du \sim \mathcal{N}\left[0, \frac{1}{3}(T-t)^3\right]$, conditional on the filtration $\mathcal{F}_t$

$$\log S_T \mid \mathcal{F}_t \sim \mathcal{N}\left[\log S_t + \left(r - D - \frac{1}{2}\sigma^2\right)(T-t), \sigma^2(T-t)\right]$$

and

$$\frac{I_T}{T-\tau}\bigg| \mathcal{F}_t \sim \mathcal{N}\left[\frac{1}{T-\tau}\left\{I_t + (T-t)\log S_t + \frac{1}{2}\left(r - D - \frac{1}{2}\sigma^2\right)(T-t)^2\right\},\right.$$
$$\left. \frac{\sigma^2}{3}\frac{(T-t)^3}{(T-\tau)^2}\right].$$

In addition, since $\left(W_{T-t}, \int_t^T W_{u-t} \, du\right)$ follows a bivariate normal we can also deduce that $\left(\log S_T, \frac{I_T}{T-\tau}\right)$ also follows a bivariate normal distribution.

From the identity we have

$$\mathbb{E}\left[\max\{e^X - e^Y, 0\}\right]$$

$$= e^{\mu_x + \frac{1}{2}\sigma_x^2}\Phi\left(\frac{\mu_x - \mu_y + \sigma_x(\sigma_x - \rho_{xy}\sigma_y)}{\sqrt{\sigma_x^2 - 2\rho_{xy}\sigma_x\sigma_y + \sigma_y^2}}\right) - e^{\mu_y + \frac{1}{2}\sigma_y^2}\Phi\left(\frac{\mu_x - \mu_y - \sigma_y(\sigma_y - \rho_{xy}\sigma_x)}{\sqrt{\sigma_x^2 - 2\rho_{xy}\sigma_x\sigma_y + \sigma_y^2}}\right)$$

for a bivariate normal distribution such that $X \sim \mathcal{N}(\mu_x, \sigma_x^2)$ and $Y \sim \mathcal{N}(\mu_y, \sigma_y^2)$ with correlation coefficient $\rho_{xy} \in (-1, 1)$. By setting

$$X = \log S_T, \quad \mu_x = \log S_t + \left(r - D - \frac{1}{2}\sigma^2\right)(T-t), \quad \sigma_x^2 = \sigma^2(T-t)$$

$$Y = \frac{I_T}{T-\tau}, \quad \mu_y = \frac{1}{T-\tau}\left[I_t + (T-t)\log S_t + \frac{1}{2}\left(r - D - \frac{1}{2}\sigma^2\right)(T-t)^2\right]$$

$$\sigma_y^2 = \frac{\sigma^2}{3}\frac{(T-t)^3}{(T-\tau)^2} \quad \text{and} \quad \rho_{xy} = \frac{\sqrt{3}}{2}$$

we have

$$e^{\mu_x + \frac{1}{2}\sigma_x^2} = e^{(r - D - \frac{1}{2}\sigma^2)(T-t) + \frac{1}{2}\sigma^2(T-t)}$$

$$= e^{(r-D)(T-t)}$$

$$e^{\mu_y + \frac{1}{2}\sigma_y^2} = e^{\frac{1}{T-\tau}[I_t + (T-t)\log S_t + \frac{1}{2}(r - D - \frac{1}{2}\sigma^2)(T-t)^2] + \frac{\sigma^2}{6}\frac{(T-t)^3}{(T-\tau)^2}}$$

$$= e^{\frac{I_t}{T-\tau}} S_t^{\frac{T-t}{T-\tau}} e^{\frac{r-D}{2}\frac{(T-t)^2}{T-\tau} - \frac{\sigma^2}{12}\left(\frac{T+2t-3\tau}{T-\tau}\right)\frac{(T-t)^2}{T-\tau}}$$

$$= e^{\frac{I_t}{T-\tau}} S_t^{\frac{T-t}{T-\tau}} e^{(r - \overline{D})(T-t)}$$

$$\sigma_x^2 - 2\rho_{xy}\sigma_x\sigma_y + \sigma_y^2 = \sigma^2(T-t) - \frac{\sigma^2(T-t)^2}{T-\tau} + \frac{\sigma^2}{3}\frac{(T-t)^3}{(T-\tau)^2}$$

$$= \frac{\sigma^2}{3}\left[3 - 3\frac{(T-t)}{T-\tau} + \frac{(T-t)^2}{(T-\tau)^2}\right](T-t)$$

$$= \frac{\sigma^2}{3}\left(\frac{(T-\tau)^2 + (t-\tau)(T-\tau) + (t-\tau)^2}{(T-\tau)^2}\right)(T-t)$$

$$= \overline{\sigma}^2(T-t)$$

where

$$\overline{D} = \frac{r}{2}\left(\frac{T+t-2\tau}{T-\tau}\right) + \frac{D}{2}\left(\frac{T-t}{T-\tau}\right) + \frac{\sigma^2}{12}\left(\frac{T-t}{T-\tau}\right)\left(\frac{T+2t-3\tau}{T-\tau}\right)$$

$$\overline{\sigma}^2 = \frac{\sigma^2}{3}\left(\frac{(T-\tau)^2 + (t-\tau)(T-\tau) + (t-\tau)^2}{(T-\tau)^2}\right).$$

In addition,

$$\mu_x - \mu_y + \sigma_x(\sigma_x - \rho_{xy}\sigma_y) = \mu_x - \mu_y + \frac{1}{2}(\sigma_x^2 - 2\rho_{xy}\sigma_x\sigma_y + \sigma_y^2) + \frac{1}{2}\sigma_x^2 - \frac{1}{2}\sigma_y^2$$

$$= \log S_t + \left(r - D - \frac{1}{2}\sigma^2\right)(T-t)$$

$$- \frac{1}{T-\tau}\left[I_t + (T-t)\log S_t + \frac{1}{2}\left(r - D - \frac{1}{2}\sigma^2\right)(T-t)^2\right]$$

$$+ \frac{1}{2}\overline{\sigma}^2(T-t) + \frac{1}{2}\sigma^2(T-t) - \frac{\sigma^2}{6}\frac{(T-t)^2}{(T-\tau)^2}$$

$$= -\frac{I_t}{T-\tau} + \frac{t-\tau}{T-\tau}\log S_t$$

$$+ \left[\frac{r-D}{2}\left(\frac{T+t-2\tau}{T-\tau}\right) + \frac{\sigma^2}{12}\left(\frac{T-t}{T-\tau}\right)\left(\frac{T+2t-3\tau}{T-\tau}\right)\right.$$

$$\left. + \frac{1}{2}\overline{\sigma}^2\right](T-t)$$

$$= -\frac{I_t}{T-\tau} + \frac{t-\tau}{T-\tau}\log S_t - \left(D - \overline{D} - \frac{1}{2}\overline{\sigma}^2\right)(T-t)$$

and

$$\mu_x - \mu_y - \sigma_y(\sigma_y - \rho_{xy}\sigma_x) = \mu_x - \mu_y - \frac{1}{2}(\sigma_x^2 - 2\rho_{xy}\sigma_x\sigma_y + \sigma_y^2) + \frac{1}{2}\sigma_x^2 - \frac{1}{2}\sigma_y^2$$

$$= \log S_t + \left(r - D - \frac{1}{2}\sigma^2\right)(T - t)$$

$$- \frac{1}{T-\tau}\left[I_t + (T-t)\log S_t + \frac{1}{2}\left(r - D - \frac{1}{2}\sigma^2\right)(T-t)^2\right]$$

$$- \frac{1}{2}\overline{\sigma}^2(T-t) + \frac{1}{2}\sigma^2(T-t) - \frac{\sigma^2}{6}\frac{(T-t)^2}{(T-\tau)^2}$$

$$= -\frac{I_t}{T-\tau} + \frac{t-\tau}{T-\tau}\log S_t$$

$$+ \left[\frac{r-D}{2}\left(\frac{T+t-2\tau}{T-\tau}\right) + \frac{\sigma^2}{12}\left(\frac{T-t}{T-\tau}\right)\left(\frac{T+2t-3\tau}{T-\tau}\right)\right.$$

$$\left. - \frac{1}{2}\overline{\sigma}^2\right](T-t)$$

$$= -\frac{I_t}{T-\tau} + \frac{t-\tau}{T-\tau}\log S_t - \left(D - \overline{D} + \frac{1}{2}\overline{\sigma}^2\right)(T-t).$$

Hence, under the risk-neutral measure $\mathbb{Q}$, the geometric average strike call option price at time t is

$$C_{as}^{(g)}(S_t, I_t, t; T) = e^{-r(T-t)}\mathbb{E}^{\mathbb{Q}}\left[\max\left\{S_T - e^{\frac{I_T}{T-\tau}}, 0\right\}\bigg|\mathscr{F}_t\right]$$

$$= S_t e^{-D(T-t)}\Phi(-\overline{d}_-) - e^{\frac{I_t}{T-\tau}}S_t^{\frac{T-t}{T-\tau}}e^{-\overline{D}(T-t)}\Phi(-\overline{d}_+)$$

where $\overline{d}_\pm = \dfrac{\dfrac{I_t}{T-\tau} - \left(\dfrac{t-\tau}{T-\tau}\right)\log S_t + \left(D - \overline{D} \pm \frac{1}{2}\overline{\sigma}^2\right)(T-t)}{\overline{\sigma}\sqrt{T-t}}.$

N.B. The same result can also be obtained if we use the exchange option formula (see Problem 6.2.1.6, page 543).

$\square$

12. *Put–Call Parity for Geometric Average Options (Probabilistic Approach).* Let $\{W_t : t \geq 0\}$ be the $\mathbb{P}$-standard Wiener process on the probability space $(\Omega, \mathscr{F}, \mathbb{P})$ and let the asset price S_t follow the SDE

$$\frac{dS_t}{S_t} = (\mu - D)dt + \sigma\, dW_t$$

where μ is the drift parameter, D is the continuous dividend yield, σ is the volatility parameter and let r be the risk-free interest rate from the money-market account.

We define

$$I_t = \int_\tau^t S_u\, du$$

to be the asset running sum within the time period $[\tau, t]$, $\tau \geq 0$ and consider the geometric average rate option with zero-strike call payoff

$$\Psi(S_T, I_T) = e^{\frac{I_T}{T-\tau}}$$

where T is the option expiry time. Using the risk-neutral valuation method find the arbitrage-free geometric average option price at time t, $\tau < t < T$.

Consider the payoffs of geometric average rate options

$$C_{ar}^{(g)}(S_T, I_T, T; K, T) = \max\left\{ e^{\frac{I_T}{T-\tau}} - K, 0 \right\}$$

$$P_{ar}^{(g)}(S_T, I_T, T; K, T) = \max\left\{ K - e^{\frac{I_T}{T-\tau}}, 0 \right\}$$

and geometric average strike options

$$C_{as}^{(g)}(S_T, I_T, T; T) = \max\left\{ S_T - e^{\frac{I_T}{T-\tau}}, 0 \right\}$$

$$P_{as}^{(g)}(S_T, I_T, T; T) = \max\left\{ e^{\frac{I_T}{T-\tau}} - S_T, 0 \right\}.$$

Show that the put–call relation for the geometric average rate and geometric average strike options are

$$C_{ar}^{(g)}(S_t, I_t, t; K, T) - P_{ar}^{(g)}(S_t, I_t, t; K, T) = e^{\frac{I_t}{T-\tau}} S_t^{\frac{T-t}{T-\tau}} e^{-\overline{D}(T-t)} - Ke^{-r(T-t)}$$

and

$$C_{as}^{(g)}(S_t, I_t, t; T) - P_{as}^{(g)}(S_t, I_t, t; T) = S_t e^{-D(T-t)} - e^{\frac{I_t}{T-\tau}} S_t^{\frac{T-t}{T-\tau}} e^{-\overline{D}(T-t)}$$

respectively where

$$\overline{D} = \frac{r}{2}\left(\frac{T+t-2\tau}{T-\tau}\right) + \frac{D}{2}\left(\frac{T-t}{T-\tau}\right) + \frac{\sigma^2}{12}\left(\frac{T-t}{T-\tau}\right)\left(\frac{T+2t-3\tau}{T-\tau}\right).$$

Solution: From Girsanov's theorem, under the risk-neutral measure $\mathbb{Q}$, S_t follows

$$\frac{dS_t}{S_t} = (r - D)dt + \sigma \, dW_t^{\mathbb{Q}}$$

where $W_t^{\mathbb{Q}} = W_t + \left(\dfrac{\mu - r}{\sigma}\right)t$ is a $\mathbb{Q}$-standard Wiener process.

From Problem 5.2.2.11 (page 514), under the $\mathbb{Q}$ measure

$$\frac{I_T}{T-\tau}\bigg|\,\mathcal{F}_t \sim \mathcal{N}\left[\frac{1}{T-\tau}\left\{I_t + (T-t)\log S_t + \frac{1}{2}\left(r - D - \frac{1}{2}\sigma^2\right)(T-t)^2\right\},\right.$$
$$\left.\frac{\sigma^2}{3}\frac{(T-t)^3}{(T-\tau)^2}\right].$$

Hence, the price of the option at time t, $\tau < t < T$ with payoff $\Psi(S_T, I_T) = e^{\frac{I_T}{T-\tau}}$ is

$$V(S_t, I_t, t; T) = e^{-r(T-t)}\mathbb{E}^{\mathbb{Q}}\left[\Psi(S_T, I_T)\big|\,\mathcal{F}_t\right]$$
$$= e^{-r(T-t)}\mathbb{E}^{\mathbb{Q}}\left[e^{\frac{I_T}{T-\tau}}\big|\,\mathcal{F}_t\right]$$
$$= e^{\frac{1}{T-\tau}\left\{I_t + (T-t)\log S_t + \frac{1}{2}(r-D-\frac{1}{2}\sigma^2)(T-t)^2\right\} + \frac{\sigma^2}{6}\frac{(T-t)^3}{(T-\tau)^2} - r(T-t)}$$
$$= e^{\frac{I_t}{T-\tau}} S_t^{\frac{T-t}{T-\tau}} e^{-\overline{D}(T-t)}$$

where

$$\overline{D} = \frac{r}{2}\left(\frac{T+t-2\tau}{T-\tau}\right) + \frac{D}{2}\left(\frac{T-t}{T-\tau}\right) + \frac{\sigma^2}{12}\left(\frac{T-t}{T-\tau}\right)\left(\frac{T+2t-3\tau}{T-\tau}\right).$$

At option expiry time T, the put–call parity for the geometric average rate option is

$$C_{ar}^{(g)}(S_T, I_T, T; K, T) - P_{ar}^{(g)}(S_T, I_T, T; K, T) = \begin{cases} e^{\frac{I_T}{T-\tau}} - K & \text{if } e^{\frac{I_T}{K}} > K \\[2mm] e^{\frac{I_T}{T-\tau}} - K & \text{if } e^{\frac{I_T}{K}} \leq K \end{cases}$$
$$= e^{\frac{I_T}{T-\tau}} - K.$$

By discounting the payoff back to time t, under the risk-neutral measure $\mathbb{Q}$ we have

$$C_{ar}^{(g)}(S_t, I_t, t; K, T) - P_{ar}^{(g)}(S_t, I_t, t; K, T) = e^{-r(T-t)}\mathbb{E}^{\mathbb{Q}}\left[e^{\frac{I_T}{T-\tau}} - K\big|\,\mathcal{F}_t\right]$$
$$= e^{-r(T-t)}\mathbb{E}^{\mathbb{Q}}\left[e^{\frac{I_T}{T-\tau}}\big|\,\mathcal{F}_t\right] - Ke^{-r(T-t)}$$
$$= e^{\frac{I_t}{T-\tau}} S_t^{\frac{T-t}{T-\tau}} e^{-\overline{D}(T-t)} - Ke^{-r(T-t)}.$$

In contrast, at expiry time T the put–call parity for geometric average strike options is

$$C_{as}^{(g)}(S_T, I_T, T; T) - P_{as}^{(g)}(S_T, I_T, T; T) = \begin{cases} S_T - e^{\frac{I_T}{T-\tau}} & \text{if } S_T > e^{\frac{I_T}{T-\tau}} \\[2mm] S_T - e^{\frac{I_T}{T-\tau}} & \text{if } S_T \le e^{\frac{I_T}{T-\tau}} \end{cases}$$

$$= S_T - e^{\frac{I_T}{T-\tau}}.$$

By discounting the payoffs back to time $t < T$ under the risk-neutral measure $\mathbb{Q}$, and taking note that $\log S_T | \mathcal{F}_t \sim \mathcal{N}\left[\log S_t + \left(r - D - \tfrac{1}{2}\sigma^2\right)(T - t), \sigma^2(T - t)\right]$, we have

$$C_{as}^{(g)}(S_t, I_t, t; T) - P_{as}^{(g)}(S_t, I_t, t; T) = e^{-r(T-t)}\mathbb{E}^{\mathbb{Q}}\left[S_T - e^{\frac{I_T}{T-\tau}}\middle| \mathcal{F}_t\right]$$

$$= e^{-r(T-t)}\mathbb{E}^{\mathbb{Q}}\left[S_T | \mathcal{F}_t\right] - e^{-r(T-t)}\mathbb{E}^{\mathbb{Q}}\left[e^{\frac{I_T}{T-\tau}}\middle| \mathcal{F}_t\right]$$

$$= S_t e^{-D(T-t)} - e^{\frac{I_t}{T-\tau}} S_t^{\frac{T-t}{T-\tau}} e^{-\overline{D}(T-t)}.$$

$\square$

13. *Symmetry of Average Strike (Floating) and Average Rate (Fixed) Strike in Arithmetic Average Options.* Let $\{W_t : t \ge 0\}$ be the $\mathbb{P}$-standard Wiener process on the probability space $(\Omega, \mathcal{F}, \mathbb{P})$ and let the asset price S_t follow the SDE

$$\frac{dS_t}{S_t} = (\mu - D)dt + \sigma \, dW_t$$

where μ is the drift parameter, D is the continuous dividend yield, σ is the volatility parameter and let r be the risk-free interest rate from the money-market account.

Under the risk-neutral measure $\mathbb{Q}$, we consider the arithmetic average option prices at time $t < T$

$$C_{ar}^{(a)}(S_t, t; r, K, T) = e^{-r(T-t)}\mathbb{E}^{\mathbb{Q}}\left[\max\{A(t,T) - K, 0\} | \mathcal{F}_t\right]$$

$$P_{ar}^{(a)}(S_t, t; r, K, T) = e^{-r(T-t)}\mathbb{E}^{\mathbb{Q}}\left[\max\{K - A(t,T), 0\} | \mathcal{F}_t\right]$$

$$C_{as}^{(a)}(S_t, t; r, \lambda, T) = e^{-r(T-t)}\mathbb{E}^{\mathbb{Q}}\left[\max\{\lambda S_T - A(t,T), 0\} | \mathcal{F}_t\right]$$

$$P_{as}^{(a)}(S_t, t; r, \lambda, T) = e^{-r(T-t)}\mathbb{E}^{\mathbb{Q}}\left[\max\{A(t,T) - \lambda S_T, 0\} | \mathcal{F}_t\right]$$

where $\lambda > 0$ is a scaling factor, T is the option expiry and arithmetic average $A(t,T)$ is defined as

$$A(t,T) = \frac{1}{T-t}\int_t^T S_u \, du.$$

Show that the following symmetry results

$$C_{as}^{(a)}(S_t, t; r, \lambda, T) = P_{ar}^{(a)}(S_t, t; D, \lambda S_t, T)$$
$$C_{ar}^{(a)}(S_t, t; r, K, T) = P_{as}^{(a)}(S_t, t; D, K/S_t, T)$$

hold.

Do the above results hold if the arithmetic average takes the form

$$A(\tau, T) = \frac{1}{T - \tau} \int_\tau^T S_u \, du$$

where $\tau < t < T$?

Solution: From Girsanov's theorem, under the risk-neutral measure $\mathbb{Q}$, S_t takes the form

$$\frac{dS_t}{S_t} = (r - D)dt + \sigma \, dW_t^{\mathbb{Q}}$$

where $W_t^{\mathbb{Q}} = W_t + \dfrac{\mu - r}{\sigma} t$ is a $\mathbb{Q}$-standard Wiener process.

For a payoff $\Psi(S_T)$, under the change of numéraire

$$N_t^{(1)} \mathbb{E}^{\mathbb{Q}^{(1)}} \left[\left. \frac{\Psi(S_T)}{N_T^{(1)}} \right| \mathscr{F}_t \right] = N_t^{(2)} \mathbb{E}^{\mathbb{Q}^{(2)}} \left[\left. \frac{\Psi(S_T)}{N_T^{(2)}} \right| \mathscr{F}_t \right]$$

where $N^{(1)}$ and $N^{(2)}$ are numéraires (positive non-dividend-paying assets) and $\mathbb{Q}^{(1)}$ and $\mathbb{Q}^{(2)}$ are the measures under which the asset prices discounted by $N^{(1)}$ and $N^{(2)}$ are $\mathbb{Q}^{(1)}$ and $\mathbb{Q}^{(2)}$-martingales, respectively.

For the first result we have

$$C_{as}^{(a)}(S_t, t; r, \lambda, T) = e^{-r(T-t)} \mathbb{E}^{\mathbb{Q}} \left[\max\{\lambda S_T - A(t, T), 0\} \big| \mathscr{F}_t \right].$$

Under the risk-neutral measure $\mathbb{Q}$, we set

$$N_t^{(1)} = e^{rt} \quad \text{and} \quad N_T^{(1)} = e^{rT}$$

and under the $\mathbb{Q}_S$ measure where $S_t e^{Dt}$ is a non-dividend-paying asset we have

$$N_t^{(2)} = S_t e^{Dt} \quad \text{and} \quad N_T^{(2)} = S_T e^{DT}.$$

Hence, using a change of numéraire

$$C_{as}^{(a)}(S_t, t; r, \lambda, T) = e^{-r(T-t)} \mathbb{E}^{\mathbb{Q}} \left[\max\{\lambda S_T - A(t,T), 0\} \big| \mathcal{F}_t \right]$$

$$= e^{rt} \mathbb{E}^{\mathbb{Q}} \left[\frac{\max\{\lambda S_T - A(t,T), 0\}}{e^{rT}} \bigg| \mathcal{F}_t \right]$$

$$= S_t e^{Dt} \mathbb{E}^{\mathbb{Q}_S} \left[\frac{\max\{\lambda S_T - A(t,T), 0\}}{S_T e^{DT}} \bigg| \mathcal{F}_t \right]$$

$$= e^{-D(T-t)} \mathbb{E}^{\mathbb{Q}_S} \left[\max\left\{ \lambda S_t - \frac{S_t A(t,T)}{S_T}, 0 \right\} \bigg| \mathcal{F}_t \right]$$

$$= e^{-D(T-t)} \mathbb{E}^{\mathbb{Q}_S} \left[\max\left\{ \lambda S_t - A^*(t,T), 0 \right\} \big| \mathcal{F}_t \right]$$

where $A^*(t,T) = \dfrac{S_t A(t,T)}{S_T}$.

Under the $\mathbb{Q}_S$ measure, the discounted money-market account

$$X_t = \left(S_t e^{Dt} \right)^{-1} e^{rt}$$

$$= S_t^{-1} e^{(r-D)t}$$

is a $\mathbb{Q}_S$-martingale.

From Itō's lemma,

$$dX_t = d \left(S_t^{-1} e^{(r-D)t} \right)$$

$$= (r - D)e^{(r-D)t} S_t^{-1} dt + S_t^{-1} e^{(r-D)t} d(S_t^{-1})$$

$$= (r - D)X_t dt + X_t \left(-\frac{dS_t}{S_t} + \left(\frac{dS_t}{S_t} \right)^2 + \ldots \right)$$

$$= (r - D)X_t dt + X_t \left(-(r-D)dt - \sigma \, dW_t^{\mathbb{Q}} + \sigma^2 dt \right)$$

$$= \sigma^2 X_t dt - \sigma X_t \, dW_t^{\mathbb{Q}}$$

$$= -\sigma X_t \, dW_t^S$$

where $W_t^S = W_t^{\mathbb{Q}} - \sigma t$ is a $\mathbb{Q}_S$-standard Wiener process.

Thus, under $\mathbb{Q}_S$

$$\frac{dS_t}{S_t} = (r - D)dt + \sigma \left(dW_t^S + \sigma dt \right)$$

$$= (r - D + \sigma^2)dt + \sigma \, dW_t^S.$$

To find the solution of the SDE, we first expand $d \log S_t$ using Taylor's theorem and by applying Itō's lemma

$$d \log S_t = \frac{d S_t}{S_t} - \frac{1}{2} \left(\frac{d S_t}{S_t} \right)^2 + \dots$$

$$= (r - D + \sigma^2) dt + \sigma \, d W_t^S - \frac{1}{2} \sigma^2 dt$$

$$= \left(r - D + \frac{1}{2} \sigma^2 \right) dt + \sigma \, d W_t^S.$$

Taking integrals,

$$\int_u^T d \log S_t = \int_u^T \left(r - D + \frac{1}{2} \sigma^2 \right) dt + \int_u^T \sigma \, d W_t^S$$

$$\log \left(\frac{S_T}{S_u} \right) = \left(r - D + \frac{1}{2} \sigma^2 \right) (T - u) + \sigma W_{T-u}^S$$

or

$$S_T = S_u e^{(r - D + \frac{1}{2} \sigma^2)(T - u) + \sigma W_{T-u}^S}.$$

By substituting S_T into $A^*(t, T)$,

$$A^*(t, T) = \frac{S_t}{T - t} \int_t^T \frac{S_u}{S_T} \, du$$

$$= \frac{S_t}{T - t} \int_t^T e^{-(r - D + \frac{1}{2} \sigma^2)(T - u) - \sigma W_{T-u}^S} \, du$$

$$= \frac{1}{T - t} \int_t^T S_t e^{(D - r - \frac{1}{2} \sigma^2)(T - u) - \sigma W_{T-u}^S} \, du$$

$$= \frac{1}{T - t} \int_t^T S_t e^{(D - r - \frac{1}{2} \sigma^2)(T - u) + \sigma \widetilde{W}_{T-u}^S} \, du$$

since the reflected standard Wiener process $\widetilde{W}_t^S = -W_t^S$ is also a $\mathbb{Q}_S$-standard Wiener process.

Given that $A^*(t, T)$ is an arithmetic average of the price process of lognormal variates with drift $D - r$, therefore

$$C_{as}^{(a)}(S_t, t; r, \lambda, T) = e^{-D(T-t)} \mathbb{E}^{\mathbb{Q}_S} \left[\max\{ \lambda S_t - A^*(t, T), 0 \} \big| \mathcal{F}_t \right]$$

$$= P_{ar}^{(a)}(S_t, t; D, \lambda S_t, T).$$

For the second result, we note that using the same steps we can also show

$$P_{as}^{(a)}(S_t, t; r, \lambda, T) = C_{ar}^{(a)}(S_t, t; D, \lambda S_t, T).$$

By substituting D with r and λS_t with K so that $\lambda = K/S_t$, we can deduce

$$C_{ar}^{(a)}(S_t, t; r, K, T) = P_{as}^{(a)}(S_t, t; D, K/S_t, T).$$

Note that the symmetry results do not hold if the arithmetic average takes the form

$$A(\tau, T) = \frac{1}{T - \tau} \int_\tau^T S_u \, du$$

where $\tau < t < T$. For example, for an average strike (floating strike) call option payoff

$$\max\{\lambda S_T - A(\tau, T), 0\} = \max\left\{\lambda S_T - \frac{1}{T - \tau} \int_\tau^t S_u \, du - \frac{1}{T - \tau} \int_t^T S_u \, du, 0\right\}$$

and when we divide it by S_T, the known term $\dfrac{1}{T - \tau} \int_\tau^t \dfrac{S_u}{S_T} \, du$ will no longer be a constant value.

$\square$

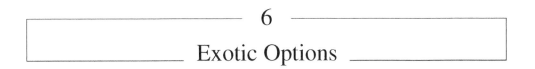

6

Exotic Options

In the last two chapters we came across barrier and Asian options, which are the most popular exotic options traded in the OTC market. In this chapter we continue to discuss other types of exotic options, which are highly customised options that can be used for hedging or speculative purposes. Although these options are less traded and some might just be a two-party transaction, their payoffs have unique features which make them a very interesting subject in their own right. There are many reasons why exotic options are developed in the first place. Most notably, exotic options enable investors or speculators to focus their view on future market behaviour (such as the exchange rate risk or corporate/sovereign credit risk rating).

In this chapter, different types of exotic options are presented and their valuations are discussed in detail. Throughout this chapter, unless otherwise stated, we assume a continuous dividend yield and the volatility of the asset price and the risk-free interest rate are assumed to be constants within the life of the option contract. As the majority of the payoffs discussed in this chapter are based on European-style payoffs, the formulas of many exotic options are analytical.

6.1 INTRODUCTION

Within the family of exotic options, the options can be either path-independent or path-dependent-type options.

Path-Independent Options

For exotic options which are path-independent, their payoffs only depend on the terminal value of the underlying asset price, irrespective of the route taken. Examples of these are the simple digital and asset-or-nothing options, as the payoffs depend exclusively on the asset price at option expiry time. More complicated path-independent options may involve two or more assets, such as exchange options (exchange one asset for another), spread options (difference between asset prices) and rainbow options (best or worst of asset prices).

Path-Dependent Options

For exotic options which are path-dependent, their payoffs may depend on the whole path of the underlying asset price rather than just the terminal value. A great majority of exotic options are path-dependent, such as forward start options (where the option starts at a specified future date), compound options (where the underlying is another option), chooser options (which allow the holder of the option to choose at a specified time whether the contract becomes a European call or a European put) and lookback options (where the maximum or minimum of the underlying asset is attained over a certain period of time).

6.2 PROBLEMS AND SOLUTIONS

6.2.1 Path-Independent Options

1. *Capped Option.* Let $\{W_t : t \geq 0\}$ be a $\mathbb{P}$-standard Wiener process on the probability space $(\Omega, \mathcal{F}, \mathbb{P})$ and let the asset price S_t follow a GBM with the following SDE

$$\frac{dS_t}{S_t} = (\mu - D)\, dt + \sigma dW_t$$

where μ is the drift parameter, D is the continuous dividend yield, σ is the volatility parameter and let r be the risk-free interest-rate parameter from the money-market account.

We consider a capped call option with terminal payoff

$$\Psi(S_T) = \min\{\max\{S_T - K, 0\}, M\}$$

at time $T \geq t$ with strike price $K > 0$ and M the cap value. Show that the capped call option price at time t is

$$C_{cap}(S_t, t; K, M, T) = C_{bs}(S_t, t; K, T) - C_{bs}(S_t, t; K + M, T)$$

where $C_{bs}(X, t; Y, T)$ is the vanilla (or European) call option price defined as

$$C_{bs}(X, t; Y, T) = Xe^{-D(T-t)}\Phi(d_+) - Ye^{-r(T-t)}\Phi(d_-)$$

such that $d_\pm = \dfrac{\log(X/Y) + (r - D \pm \frac{1}{2}\sigma^2)(T - t)}{\sigma\sqrt{T-t}}$ and $\Phi(x) = \displaystyle\int_{-\infty}^{x} \frac{1}{\sqrt{2\pi}} e^{-\frac{1}{2}u^2}\, du$ is the cdf of a standard normal.

Solution: From the definition of a capped call option payoff we can write

$$\Psi(S_T) = \begin{cases} 0 & S_T < K \\ S_T - K & K \leq S_T < K + M \\ M & S_T \geq K + M \end{cases}$$

so that the payoff diagram for the capped call option $C_{cap}(S_T, T; K, M, T)$ can be constructed with the portfolios in Figure 6.1.

Thus, at expiry time T we can write the capped call option price as

$$C_{cap}(S_T, T; K, M, T) = C_{bs}(S_T, T; K, T) - C_{bs}(S_T, T; K + M, T)$$

and by discounting the entire payoff under the risk-neutral measure $\mathbb{Q}$, we can write the solution for the capped call option at time t as

$$C_{cap}(S_t, t; K, M, T) = C_{bs}(S_t, t; K, T) - C_{bs}(S_t, t; K + M, T).$$

$\square$

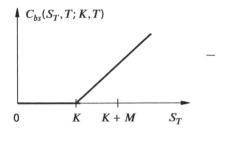

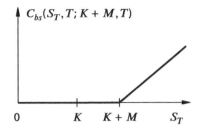

$=$

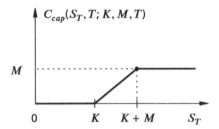

Figure 6.1 Capped call payoff diagram.

2. *Corridor Option.* Let $\{W_t : t \geq 0\}$ be a $\mathbb{P}$-standard Wiener process on the probability space $(\Omega, \mathcal{F}, \mathbb{P})$ and let the asset price S_t follow a GBM with the following SDE

$$\frac{dS_t}{S_t} = (\mu - D)\,dt + \sigma dW_t$$

where μ is the drift parameter, D is the continuous dividend yield, σ is the volatility parameter and let r be the risk-free interest-rate parameter from the money-market account.

We consider a corridor call option with terminal payoff

$$\Psi(S_T) = \begin{cases} 1 & \text{if } K_1 < S_T < K_2 \\ 0 & \text{otherwise} \end{cases}$$

which pays \$1 at expiry time $T \geq t$ if $K_1 < S_T < K_2$ and nothing if $S_T \geq K_2$ or $S_T \leq K_1$, $K_1 < K_2$. Show that the corridor call option price at time t is

$$C_{cor}(S_t, t; K_1, K_2, T) = C_d(S_t, t; K_1, T) - C_d(S_t, t; K_2, T)$$

where $C_d(X, t; Y, T)$ is the European digital call option price defined as

$$C_d(X, t; Y, T) = e^{-r(T-t)}\Phi(d_-)$$

such that $d_- = \dfrac{\log(X/Y) + (r - D - \frac{1}{2}\sigma^2)(T - t)}{\sigma\sqrt{T - t}}$ and $\Phi(x) = \displaystyle\int_{-\infty}^{x} \frac{1}{\sqrt{2\pi}} e^{-\frac{1}{2}u^2}\,du$ is the cdf of a standard normal.

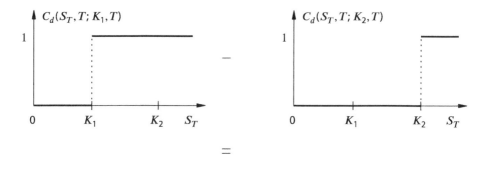

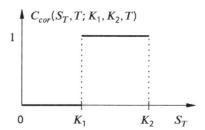

Figure 6.2   Corridor payoff diagram.

Solution: From the corridor option payoff

$$\Psi(S_T) = \begin{cases} 1 & \text{if } K_1 < S_T < K_2 \\ 0 & \text{otherwise} \end{cases}$$

the payoff diagram for $C_{cor}(S_T, T; K_1, K_2, T)$ can be constructed with the portfolios in Figure 6.2.

Thus, at expiry time T we can write the corridor option price as

$$C_{cor}\left(S_T, T; K_1, K_2, T\right) = C_d\left(S_T, T; K_1, T\right) - C_d(S_T, T; K_2, T)$$

and by discounting the entire payoff under the risk-neutral measure $\mathbb{Q}$, we can write the solution for the corridor option at time t as

$$C_{cor}\left(S_t, t; K_1, K_2, T\right) = C_d\left(S_t, t; K_1, T\right) - C_d(S_t, t; K_2, T).$$

$\square$

3. *Power Option.* Let $\{W_t : t \geq 0\}$ be a $\mathbb{P}$-standard Wiener process on the probability space $(\Omega, \mathscr{F}, \mathbb{P})$ and let the stock price S_t follow a GBM with the following SDE

$$\frac{dS_t}{S_t} = (\mu - D) dt + \sigma dW_t$$

where μ is the drift parameter, D is the continuous dividend yield, σ is the volatility parameter and let r be the risk-free interest rate from a money-market account.

We define $Y_t = S_t^n$ for $n \geq 1$. Using Itō's lemma, find the SDE satisfied by Y_t and show that under the risk-neutral measure $\mathbb{Q}$

$$\log\left(\frac{Y_T}{Y_t}\right) \sim \mathcal{N}\left[n\left(r - D - \frac{1}{2}\sigma^2\right)(T-t), n^2\sigma^2(T-t)\right]$$

for $t \leq T$.

By using the European call price formula, deduce that the call option of a power option payoff

$$\Psi(S_T^n) = \max\{S_T^n - K, 0\}$$

for strike price $K > 0$ is

$$C(S_t^n, t; K, T) = S_t^n e^{-nD(T-t)}\Phi(d_+^*) - Ke^{-n(r+\frac{1}{2}(n-1)\sigma^2)(T-t)}\Phi(d_-^*)$$

where $d_+^* = \dfrac{\log(S_t/K^{\frac{1}{n}}) + (r - D + (n - \frac{1}{2})\sigma^2)(T-t)}{\sigma\sqrt{T-t}}$ and $d_-^* = d_+^* - n\sigma\sqrt{T-t}$.

Solution: From Girsanov's theorem, under the risk-neutral measure $\mathbb{Q}$ we can write

$$\frac{dS_t}{S_t} = (r - D)\,dt + \sigma\,dW_t^{\mathbb{Q}}$$

such that $W_t^{\mathbb{Q}} = W_t + \left(\dfrac{\mu - r}{\sigma}\right)t$ is a $\mathbb{Q}$-standard Wiener process. By expanding $d(S_t^n)$ using Taylor's theorem and subsequently with the application of Itō's lemma, we can write

$$d\left(S_t^n\right) = nS_t^{n-1}dS_t + \frac{1}{2}n(n-1)S_t^{n-2}\left(dS_t\right)^2 + \ldots$$

$$= nS_t^n\left(\frac{dS_t}{S_t}\right) + \frac{1}{2}n(n-1)S_t^n\left(\frac{dS_t}{S_t}\right)^2$$

$$= nS_t^n\left[(r - D)dt + \sigma dW_t^{\mathbb{Q}}\right] + \frac{1}{2}n(n-1)S_t^n\sigma^2 dt$$

$$= nS_t^n\left[\left(r - D + \frac{1}{2}(n-1)\sigma^2\right)dt + \sigma dW_t^{\mathbb{Q}}\right]$$

or

$$\frac{dY_t}{Y_t} = n\left(r - D + \frac{1}{2}(n-1)\sigma^2\right)dt + n\sigma dW_t^{\mathbb{Q}}.$$

Using Itō's lemma on $d\left(\log Y_t\right)$ we can write

$$
\begin{aligned}
d\left(\log Y_t\right) &= \frac{dY_t}{Y_t} - \frac{1}{2}\left(\frac{dY_t}{Y_t}\right)^2 + \dots \\
&= n\left(r - D + \frac{1}{2}(n-1)\sigma^2\right)dt + n\sigma dW_t^{\mathbb{Q}} - \frac{1}{2}n^2\sigma^2 dt \\
&= \left(n(r-D) + \frac{1}{2}n(n-1)\sigma^2 - \frac{1}{2}n^2\sigma^2\right)dt + n\sigma dW_t^{\mathbb{Q}} \\
&= \left(n(r-D) - \frac{1}{2}n\sigma^2\right)dt + n\sigma dW_t^{\mathbb{Q}} \\
&= n\left(r - D - \frac{1}{2}\sigma^2\right)dt + n\sigma dW_t^{\mathbb{Q}}.
\end{aligned}
$$

Integrating over time we can write

$$
\int_t^T d\left(\log Y_u\right)du = \int_t^T n\left(r - D - \frac{1}{2}\sigma^2\right)du + n\sigma \int_t^T dW_u^{\mathbb{Q}}
$$

$$
\log\left(\frac{Y_T}{Y_t}\right) = n\left(r - D - \frac{1}{2}\sigma^2\right)(T-t) + n\sigma\left(W_T^{\mathbb{Q}} - W_t^{\mathbb{Q}}\right)
$$

where $W_T^{\mathbb{Q}} - W_t^{\mathbb{Q}} = W_{T-t}^{\mathbb{Q}} \sim \mathcal{N}(0, T-t)$. The expectation and variance are given as

$$
\mathbb{E}^{\mathbb{Q}}\left[\log\left(\frac{Y_T}{Y_t}\right)\right] = n\left(r - D - \frac{1}{2}\sigma^2\right)(T-t) \quad \text{and} \quad \mathrm{Var}^{\mathbb{Q}}\left[\log\left(\frac{Y_T}{Y_t}\right)\right] = n^2\sigma^2(T-t)
$$

or

$$
\log\left(\frac{Y_T}{Y_t}\right) \sim \mathcal{N}\left[n\left(r - D - \frac{1}{2}\sigma^2\right)(T-t), n^2\sigma^2(T-t)\right].
$$

To find the European call price for a power option with payoff $\Psi(S_T^n) = \max\{S_T^n - K, 0\}$ by comparing the SDEs of

$$
dS_t = (r-D)S_t dt + \sigma S_t dW_t^{\mathbb{Q}}
$$

and

$$
dY_t = n\left(r - D + \frac{1}{2}(n-1)\sigma^2\right)Y_t dt + n\sigma Y_t dW_t^{\mathbb{Q}}
$$

we can set

$$
\frac{dY_t}{Y_t} = \left(r^* - D^*\right)dt + \sigma^* dW_t^{\mathbb{Q}}
$$

where $r^* = n\left(r + \frac{1}{2}(n-1)\sigma^2\right)$, $D^* = nD$ and $\sigma^* = n\sigma$. Hence, we can deduce that the call option price at time $t \leq T$ is

$$
C(Y_t, t; K, T) = Y_t e^{-D^*(T-t)}\Phi\left(d_+^*\right) - Ke^{-r^*(T-t)}\Phi\left(d_-^*\right)
$$

where $d_{\pm}^* = \dfrac{\log(Y_t/K) + (r^* - D^* \pm \frac{1}{2}(\sigma^*)^2)(T-t)}{\sigma^*\sqrt{T-t}}.$

By substituting back $Y_t = S_t^n$ we have

$$C(S_t^n, t; K, T) = S_t^n e^{-nD(T-t)}\Phi\left(d_+^*\right) - K e^{-n\left(r + \frac{1}{2}(n-1)\sigma^2\right)(T-t)}\Phi\left(d_-^*\right)$$

where

$$d_+^* = \frac{\log(S_t^n/K) + n(r - D + \frac{1}{2}(n-1)\sigma^2 + \frac{1}{2}n\sigma^2)(T-t)}{n\sigma\sqrt{T-t}}$$

$$= \frac{\log(S_t/K^{\frac{1}{n}}) + (r - D + \frac{1}{2}n\sigma^2 - \frac{1}{2}\sigma^2 + \frac{1}{2}n\sigma^2)(T-t)}{\sigma\sqrt{T-t}}$$

$$= \frac{\log(S_t/K^{\frac{1}{n}}) + (r - D + (n - \frac{1}{2})\sigma^2)(T-t)}{\sigma\sqrt{T-t}}$$

and

$$d_-^* = d_+^* - n\sigma\sqrt{T-t}.$$

$\square$

4. Let $\{W_t^x : t \geq 0\}$ and $\{W_t^y : t \geq 0\}$ be $\mathbb{P}$-standard Wiener processes on the probability space $(\Omega, \mathcal{F}, \mathbb{P})$ and let the asset prices X_t and Y_t satisfy the following diffusion processes

$$dX_t = (\mu_x - D_x)X_t dt + \sigma_x X_t dW_t^x$$
$$dY_t = (\mu_y - D_y)Y_t dt + \sigma_y Y_t dW_t^y$$
$$dW_t^x \cdot dW_t^y = \rho_{xy} dt$$

where μ_x and μ_y are the drifts, D_x and D_y are the continuous dividend yields, σ_x and σ_y are the volatilities, ρ_{xy} is the correlation coefficient such that $\rho_{xy} \in (-1, 1)$ and let r be the risk-free interest rate from a money-market account.

Using a hedging portfolio, show that a European-style option price $V(X_t, Y_t, t)$ which depends on both X_t and Y_t satisfies the following two-dimensional Black–Scholes equation

$$\frac{\partial V}{\partial t} + \frac{1}{2}\sigma_x^2 X_t^2 \frac{\partial^2 V}{\partial X_t^2} + \frac{1}{2}\sigma_y^2 Y_t^2 \frac{\partial^2 V}{\partial Y_t^2} + \rho_{xy}\sigma_x\sigma_y\frac{\partial^2 V}{\partial X_t \partial Y_t} + (r - D_x)X_t\frac{\partial V}{\partial X_t}$$

$$+(r - D_y)Y_t\frac{\partial V}{\partial Y_t} - rV(X_t, Y_t, t) = 0.$$

Solution: At time t we let the portfolio Π_t be

$$\Pi_t = V(X_t, Y_t, t) - \Delta_x X_t - \Delta_y Y_t$$

where the investor is long one unit of option $V(X_t, Y_t, t)$ and short Δ_x and Δ_y units of X_t and Y_t, respectively. Let the change of portfolio be

$$d\Pi_t = dV - \Delta_x(dX_t + D_x X_t dt) - \Delta_y(dY_t + D_y Y_t dt)$$

where the investor receives $D_x X_t dt$ and $D_y Y_t dt$ for holding assets X_t and Y_t, respectively. From Taylor's theorem

$$dV = \frac{\partial V}{\partial t} dt + \frac{\partial V}{\partial X_t} dX_t + \frac{\partial V}{\partial Y_t} dY_t + \frac{1}{2} \frac{\partial^2 V}{\partial X_t^2} (X_t)^2 + \frac{1}{2} \frac{\partial^2 V}{\partial Y_t^2} (Y_t)^2$$
$$+ \frac{\partial^2 V}{\partial X_t \partial Y_t} (dX_t dY_t) + \dots$$

and by substituting $dX_t = (\mu_x - D_x) X_t dt + \sigma_x X_t dW_t^x$, $dY_t = (\mu_y - D_y) Y_t dt + \sigma_y Y_t dW_t^y$, $dW_t^x \cdot dW_t^y = \rho_{xy} dt$ and applying Itō's lemma

$$dV = \left(\frac{\partial V}{\partial t} + \frac{1}{2} \sigma_x^2 X_t^2 \frac{\partial^2 V}{\partial X_t^2} + \frac{1}{2} \sigma_y^2 Y_t^2 \frac{\partial^2 V}{\partial Y_t^2} + \rho_{xy} \sigma_x \sigma_y \frac{\partial^2 V}{\partial X_t \partial Y_t} + (\mu_x - D_x) X_t \frac{\partial V}{\partial X_t} \right.$$
$$\left. + (\mu_y - D_y) Y_t \frac{\partial V}{\partial Y_t} \right) dt + \sigma_x X_t \frac{\partial V}{\partial X_t} dW_t^x + \sigma_y Y_t \frac{\partial V}{\partial Y_t} dW_t^y.$$

Substituting dV back into $d\Pi_t$ we eventually have

$$d\Pi_t = \left(\frac{\partial V}{\partial t} + \frac{1}{2} \sigma_x^2 X_t^2 \frac{\partial^2 V}{\partial X_t^2} + \frac{1}{2} \sigma_y^2 Y_t^2 \frac{\partial^2 V}{\partial Y_t^2} + \rho_{xy} \sigma_x \sigma_y \frac{\partial^2 V}{\partial X_t \partial Y_t} \right.$$
$$\left. + (\mu_x - D_x) X_t \frac{\partial V}{\partial X_t} - \mu_x \Delta_x X_t + (\mu_y - D_y) Y_t \frac{\partial V}{\partial Y_t} - \mu_y \Delta_y Y_t \right) dt$$
$$+ \sigma_x X_t \left(\frac{\partial V}{\partial X_t} - \Delta_x \right) dW_t^x + \sigma_y Y_t \left(\frac{\partial V}{\partial Y_t} - \Delta_y \right) dW_t^y.$$

To eliminate the random components we set

$$\Delta_x = \frac{\partial V}{\partial X_t} \quad \text{and} \quad \Delta_y = \frac{\partial V}{\partial Y_t}$$

which leads to

$$
d\Pi_t = \left(\frac{\partial V}{\partial t} + \frac{1}{2}\sigma_x^2 X_t^2 \frac{\partial^2 V}{\partial X_t^2} + \frac{1}{2}\sigma_y^2 Y_t^2 \frac{\partial^2 V}{\partial Y_t^2} + \rho_{xy}\sigma_x\sigma_y \frac{\partial^2 V}{\partial X_t \partial Y_t} - D_x X_t \frac{\partial V}{\partial X_t} \right.
$$
$$
\left. - D_y Y_t \frac{\partial V}{\partial Y_t} \right) dt.
$$

Under the no-arbitrage condition the return on the amount Π_t invested in a risk-free interest rate r would see a growth of

$$
d\Pi_t = r\Pi_t dt
$$

and therefore we have

$$
r\Pi_t dt = \left(\frac{\partial V}{\partial t} + \frac{1}{2}\sigma_x^2 X_t^2 \frac{\partial^2 V}{\partial X_t^2} + \frac{1}{2}\sigma_y^2 Y_t^2 \frac{\partial^2 V}{\partial Y_t^2} + \rho_{xy}\sigma_x\sigma_y \frac{\partial^2 V}{\partial X_t \partial Y_t} - D_x X_t \frac{\partial V}{\partial X_t} \right.
$$
$$
\left. - D_y Y_t \frac{\partial V}{\partial Y_t} \right) dt
$$

or

$$
r\left(V(X_t, Y_t, t) - \Delta_x X_t - \Delta_y Y_t \right) dt = \left(\frac{\partial V}{\partial t} + \frac{1}{2}\sigma_x^2 X_t^2 \frac{\partial^2 V}{\partial X_t^2} + \frac{1}{2}\sigma_y^2 Y_t^2 \frac{\partial^2 V}{\partial Y_t^2} \right.
$$
$$
+ \rho_{xy}\sigma_x\sigma_y \frac{\partial^2 V}{\partial X_t \partial Y_t} - D_x X_t \frac{\partial V}{\partial X_t}
$$
$$
\left. - D_y Y_t \frac{\partial V}{\partial Y_t} \right) dt
$$

$$
r\left(V(X_t, Y_t, t) - X_t \frac{\partial V}{\partial X_t} - Y_t \frac{\partial V}{\partial Y_t} \right) dt = \left(\frac{\partial V}{\partial t} + \frac{1}{2}\sigma_x^2 X_t^2 \frac{\partial^2 V}{\partial X_t^2} + \frac{1}{2}\sigma_y^2 Y_t^2 \frac{\partial^2 V}{\partial Y_t^2} \right.
$$
$$
+ \rho_{xy}\sigma_x\sigma_y \frac{\partial^2 V}{\partial X_t \partial Y_t} - D_x X_t \frac{\partial V}{\partial X_t}
$$
$$
\left. - D_y Y_t \frac{\partial V}{\partial Y_t} \right) dt.
$$

Finally, by removing dt and rearranging terms we eventually have

$$
\frac{\partial V}{\partial t} + \frac{1}{2}\sigma_x^2 X_t^2 \frac{\partial^2 V}{\partial X_t^2} + \frac{1}{2}\sigma_y^2 Y_t^2 \frac{\partial^2 V}{\partial Y_t^2} + \rho_{xy}\sigma_x\sigma_y \frac{\partial^2 V}{\partial X_t \partial Y_t} + (r - D_x)X_t \frac{\partial V}{\partial X_t}
$$
$$
+ (r - D_y)Y_t \frac{\partial V}{\partial Y_t} - rV(X_t, Y_t, t) = 0.
$$

$\square$

5. *Exchange Option (PDE Approach).* Let $\{W_t^x : t \geq 0\}$ and $\{W_t^y : t \geq 0\}$ be $\mathbb{P}$-standard Wiener processes on the probability space $(\Omega, \mathscr{F}, \mathbb{P})$ and let the asset prices X_t and Y_t satisfy the following diffusion processes

$$dX_t = (\mu_x - D_x)X_t dt + \sigma_x X_t dW_t^x$$
$$dY_t = (\mu_y - D_y)Y_t dt + \sigma_y Y_t dW_t^y$$
$$dW_t^x \cdot dW_t^y = \rho_{xy} dt$$

where μ_x and μ_y are the drifts, D_x and D_y are the continuous dividend yields, σ_x and σ_y are the volatilities, ρ_{xy} is the correlation coefficient such that $\rho_{xy} \in (-1, 1)$ and let r be the risk-free interest rate from a money-market account.

We consider the exchange option with payoff

$$\Psi(X_T, Y_T) = \max\{X_T - Y_T, 0\}$$

at expiry time $T \geq t$ where it gives the option holder the right but not the obligation to exchange asset Y_T for another asset X_T.

Show that if $V(X_t, Y_t, t; T)$ is the price of the exchange option at time t, then it satisfies the two-dimensional Black–Scholes equation

$$\frac{\partial V}{\partial t} + \frac{1}{2}\sigma_x^2 X_t^2 \frac{\partial^2 V}{\partial X_t^2} + \frac{1}{2}\sigma_y^2 Y_t^2 \frac{\partial^2 V}{\partial Y_t^2} + \rho_{xy}\sigma_x\sigma_y \frac{\partial^2 V}{\partial X_t \partial Y_t} + (r - D_x)X_t \frac{\partial V}{\partial X_t}$$
$$+ (r - D_y)Y_t \frac{\partial V}{\partial Y_t} - rV(X_t, Y_t, t; T) = 0$$

with boundary condition

$$V(X_T, Y_T, T; T) = \max\{X_T - Y_T, 0\}.$$

By setting

$$Z_t = \frac{X_t}{Y_t} \quad \text{and} \quad U(Z_t, t; T) = \frac{V(X_t, Y_t, t; T)}{Y_t}$$

show that $U(Z_t, t)$ satisfies

$$\frac{\partial U}{\partial t} + \frac{1}{2}\sigma^2 Z_t^2 \frac{\partial^2 U}{\partial Z_t^2} + (D_y - D_x)Z_t \frac{\partial U}{\partial Z_t} - D_y U(Z_t, t; T) = 0$$

with boundary condition

$$U(Z_T, T; T) = \max\{Z_T - 1, 0\}$$

where $\sigma = \sqrt{\sigma_x^2 - 2\rho_{xy}\sigma_x\sigma_y + \sigma_y^2}$.

Hence, deduce that the exchange option price $V(X_t, Y_t, t; T)$ is

$$V(X_t, Y_t, t; T) = X_t e^{-D_x(T-t)}\Phi(d_+) - Y_t e^{-D_y(T-t)}\Phi(d_-)$$

where $d_\pm = \dfrac{\log(X_t/Y_t) + (D_y - D_x \pm \frac{1}{2}\sigma^2)(T-t)}{\sigma\sqrt{T-t}}$ and $\Phi(x) = \displaystyle\int_{-\infty}^x \dfrac{1}{\sqrt{2\pi}} e^{-\frac{1}{2}u^2}\, du.$

Solution: The first part of the solution can easily be derived following Problem 6.2.1.4 (page 537). As for the second part, we let

$$Z_t = X_t Y_t^{-1} \quad \text{and} \quad V(X_t, Y_t, t; T) = U(Z_t, t; T)Y_t$$

so that

$$\frac{\partial V}{\partial t} = Y_t \frac{\partial U}{\partial t}$$

$$\frac{\partial V}{\partial X_t} = Y_t \frac{\partial U}{\partial Z_t}\frac{\partial Z_t}{\partial X_t} = Y_t \frac{\partial U}{\partial Z_t}Y_t^{-1} = \frac{\partial U}{\partial Z_t}$$

$$\frac{\partial V}{\partial Y_t} = U(Z_t, t) + Y_t \frac{\partial U}{\partial Z_t}\frac{\partial Z_t}{\partial Y_t} = U(Z_t, t) - X_t Y_t^{-1}\frac{\partial U}{\partial Z_t}$$

$$\frac{\partial^2 V}{\partial X_t^2} = \frac{\partial}{\partial X_t}\left(\frac{\partial U}{\partial Z_t}\right) = \frac{\partial^2 U}{\partial Z_t^2}\frac{\partial Z_t}{\partial X_t} = Y_t^{-1}\frac{\partial^2 U}{\partial Z_t^2}$$

$$\frac{\partial^2 V}{\partial Y_t^2} = \frac{\partial U}{\partial Z_t}\frac{\partial Z_t}{\partial Y_t} + X_t Y_t^{-2}\frac{\partial U}{\partial Z_t} - X_t Y_t^{-1}\frac{\partial^2 U}{\partial Z_t^2}\frac{\partial Z_t}{\partial Y_t} = X_t^2 Y_t^{-3}$$

$$\frac{\partial^2 U}{\partial X_t \partial Y_t} = \frac{\partial}{\partial Y_t}\left(\frac{\partial U}{\partial Z_t}\right) = \frac{\partial^2 U}{\partial Z_t^2}\frac{\partial Z_t}{\partial Y_t} = -X_t Y_t^{-2}\frac{\partial^2 U}{\partial Z_t^2}.$$

Hence, by substituting $\dfrac{\partial V}{\partial t}, \dfrac{\partial V}{\partial X_t}, \dfrac{\partial V}{\partial Y_t}, \dfrac{\partial^2 V}{\partial X_t^2}, \dfrac{\partial^2 V}{\partial Y_t^2}$ and $\dfrac{\partial^2 U}{\partial X_t \partial Y_t}$ into

$$\frac{\partial V}{\partial t} + \frac{1}{2}\sigma_x^2 X_t^2 \frac{\partial^2 V}{\partial X_t^2} + \frac{1}{2}\sigma_y^2 Y_t^2 \frac{\partial^2 V}{\partial Y_t^2} + \rho_{xy}\sigma_x\sigma_y \frac{\partial^2 V}{\partial X_t \partial Y_t}$$

$$+ (r - D_x)X_t \frac{\partial V}{\partial X_t} + (r - D_y)Y_t \frac{\partial V}{\partial Y_t} - rV(X_t, Y_t, t; T) = 0$$

in terms of $U(Z_t, t; T)$ and Z_t we eventually have

$$Y_t \left[\frac{\partial U}{\partial t} + \frac{1}{2}(\sigma_x^2 - 2\rho_{xy}\sigma_x\sigma_y + \sigma_y^2)X_t^2 Y_t^{-2}\frac{\partial^2 U}{\partial Z_t^2} \right.$$

$$\left. + (D_y - D_x)X_t Y_t^{-1}\frac{\partial U}{\partial Z_t} - D_y U(Z_t, t; T) \right] = 0$$

or

$$\frac{\partial U}{\partial t} + \frac{1}{2}\sigma^2 Z_t^2 \frac{\partial^2 U}{\partial Z_t^2} + (D_y - D_x)Z_t\frac{\partial U}{\partial Z_t} - D_y U(Z_t, t; T) = 0$$

where $\sigma = \sqrt{\sigma_x^2 - 2\rho_{xy}\sigma_x\sigma_y + \sigma_y^2}$, which is equivalent to a Black–Scholes equation with

$$\text{volatility} = \sigma$$
$$\text{continuous dividend yield} = D_x$$
$$\text{risk-free interest rate} = D_y$$

and boundary condition

$$U(Z_T, T; T) = \max\{X_T - Y_T, 0\}Y_T^{-1}$$
$$= \max\{X_T/Y_T - 1, 0\}$$
$$= \max\{Z_T - 1, 0\}$$

which is the payoff of a European call option with strike price $K = 1$. Hence, following Problem 2.2.2.4 (page 95) we can deduce that

$$U(Z_t, t; T) = Z_t e^{-D_x(T-t)}\Phi(d_+) - e^{-D_y(T-t)}\Phi(d_-)$$

where

$$d_\pm = \frac{\log Z_t + (D_y - D_x \pm \frac{1}{2}\sigma^2)(T - t)}{\sigma\sqrt{T - t}}$$

and substituting

$$U(Z_t, t; T) = V(X_t, Y_t, t)Y_t^{-1} \quad \text{and} \quad Z_t = X_t Y_t^{-1}$$

we have

$$\frac{V(X_t, Y_t, t; T)}{Y_t} = \left(\frac{X_t}{Y_t}\right)e^{-D_x(T-t)}\Phi(d_+) - e^{-D_y(T-t)}\Phi(d_-)$$

or

$$V(X_t, Y_t, t; T) = X_t e^{-D_x(T-t)}\Phi(d_+) - Y_t e^{-D_y(T-t)}\Phi(d_-)$$

where $d_\pm = \dfrac{\log(X_t/Y_t) + (D_y - D_x \pm \frac{1}{2}\sigma^2)(T - t)}{\sigma\sqrt{T - t}}$.

$\square$

6. *Exchange Option (Probabilistic Approach).* Let $\{W_t^x : t \geq 0\}$ and $\{W_t^y : t \geq 0\}$ be $\mathbb{P}$-standard Wiener processes on the probability space $(\Omega, \mathscr{F}, \mathbb{P})$ and let the asset prices X_t and Y_t have the following diffusion processes

$$dX_t = (\mu_x - D_x)X_t dt + \sigma_x X_t dW_t^x$$
$$dY_t = (\mu_y - D_y)Y_t dt + \sigma_y Y_t dW_t^y$$
$$dW_t^x \cdot dW_t^y = \rho_{xy} dt$$

where μ_x and μ_y are the drifts, D_x and D_y are the continuous dividend yields, σ_x and σ_y are the volatilities, ρ_{xy} is the correlation coefficient such that $\rho_{xy} \in (-1, 1)$ and let r be the risk-free interest rate from a money-market account.

By defining two new independent standard Wiener processes $\widehat{W}_t^y$ and $\widehat{W}_t^{y^\perp}$ such that

$$d\widetilde{W}_t^x = \rho_{xy} d\widehat{W}_t^y + \sqrt{1 - \rho_{xy}^2} d\widehat{W}_t^{y^\perp}$$
$$d\widetilde{W}_t^y = d\widehat{W}_t^y$$
$$d\widehat{W}_t^y \cdot d\widehat{W}_t^{y^\perp} = 0$$

where, under the risk-neutral measure $\mathbb{Q}$, $\widetilde{W}_t^x = W_t^x + \left(\dfrac{\mu_x - r}{\sigma_x}\right) t$ and $\widetilde{W}_t^y = W_t^y + \left(\dfrac{\mu_y - r}{\sigma_y}\right) t$ are $\mathbb{Q}$-standard Wiener processes, we define the price of an exchange option at time t with payoff

$$\Psi(X_T, Y_T) = \max\{X_T - Y_T, 0\}$$

at expiry time $T \geq t$ as

$$V(X_t, Y_t, t; T) = e^{-r(T-t)} \mathbb{E}^{\mathbb{Q}}\left[\max\{X_T - Y_T, 0\} \middle| \mathscr{F}_t\right].$$

By denoting $\mathbb{Q}_Y$ as the new measure where $Y_t e^{D_y t}$ is the numéraire and taking note that the discounted money-market account

$$\left(Y_t e^{D_y t}\right)^{-1} e^{rt}$$

is a $\mathbb{Q}_Y$-martingale, show that under $\mathbb{Q}_Y$, X_t and Y_t have the following diffusion processes

$$\frac{dX_t}{X_t} = (r - D_x + \rho_{xy}\sigma_x\sigma_y)dt + \rho_{xy}\sigma_x d\overline{W}_t^y + \sigma_x\sqrt{1 - \rho_{xy}^2} d\widehat{W}_t^{y^\perp}$$
$$\frac{dY_t}{Y_t} = (r - D_y + \sigma_y^2)dt + \sigma_y d\overline{W}_t^y$$

where $\overline{W}_t^y = \widehat{W}_t^y - \sigma_y t$. Hence, by finding the diffusion process for X_t/Y_t under $\mathbb{Q}_Y$ show that

$$\log\left(\frac{X_T}{Y_T}\right) \sim \mathcal{N}\left[\log\left(\frac{X_t}{Y_t}\right) + \left(D_y - D_x - \frac{1}{2}\sigma^2\right)(T-t), \sigma^2(T-t)\right]$$

where $\sigma = \sqrt{\sigma_x^2 - 2\rho_{xy}\sigma_x\sigma_y + \sigma_y^2}$ and finally deduce Margrabe's formula

$$V(X_t, Y_t, t; T) = X_t e^{-D_x(T-t)}\Phi(d_+) - Y_t e^{-D_y(T-t)}\Phi(d_-)$$

where $d_{\pm} = \dfrac{\log(X_t/Y_t) + (D_y - D_x \pm \frac{1}{2}\sigma^2)(T-t)}{\sigma\sqrt{T-t}}$ and $\Phi(x) = \displaystyle\int_{-\infty}^{x} \frac{1}{\sqrt{2\pi}}e^{-\frac{1}{2}u^2}du$.

Solution: From Girsanov's theorem, under the risk-neutral measure $\mathbb{Q}$

$$\frac{dX_t}{X_t} = (r - D_x)dt + \sigma_x d\widetilde{W}_t^x$$

$$\frac{dY_t}{Y_t} = (r - D_y)dt + \sigma_y d\widetilde{W}_t^y$$

$$d\widetilde{W}_t^x \cdot d\widetilde{W}_t^y = \rho_{xy}dt$$

where $\widetilde{W}_t^x = W_t^x + \left(\dfrac{\mu_x - r}{\sigma_x}\right)t$ and $\widetilde{W}_t^y = W_t^y + \left(\dfrac{\mu_y - r}{\sigma_y}\right)t$ are $\mathbb{Q}$-standard Wiener processes. By defining

$$d\widetilde{W}_t^x = \rho_{xy}d\widehat{W}_t^y + \sqrt{1 - \rho_{xy}^2}\,d\widehat{W}_t^{y\perp}$$

$$d\widetilde{W}_t^y = d\widehat{W}_t^y$$

$$d\widehat{W}_t^y \cdot d\widehat{W}_t^{y\perp} = 0$$

we have

$$\frac{dX_t}{X_t} = (r - D_x)dt + \sigma_x\left(\rho_{xy}d\widehat{W}_t^y + \sqrt{1 - \rho_{xy}^2}\,d\widehat{W}_t^{y\perp}\right)$$

$$\frac{dY_t}{Y_t} = (r - D_y)dt + \sigma_y d\widehat{W}_t^y$$

such that

$$\left(\rho_{xy}d\widehat{W}_t^y + \sqrt{1 - \rho_{xy}^2}\,d\widehat{W}_t^{y\perp}\right) \cdot d\widehat{W}_t^y = \rho_{xy}dt.$$

For a payoff $\Psi(X_T, Y_T)$ under the change of numéraire,

$$N_t \mathbb{E}^{\mathbb{Q}} \left[\frac{\Psi(X_T, Y_T)}{N_T} \middle| \mathscr{F}_t \right] = M_t \mathbb{E}^{\mathbb{Q}_Y} \left[\frac{\Psi(X_T, Y_T)}{M_T} \middle| \mathscr{F}_t \right]$$

where N and M are numéraires (positive non-dividend-paying assets) and $\mathbb{Q}$ and $\mathbb{Q}_Y$ are the measures under which the asset prices discounted by N and M are $\mathbb{Q}$ and $\mathbb{Q}_Y$-martingales, respectively.

Under the risk-neutral measure $\mathbb{Q}$ we have

$$N_t = e^{rt} \text{ and } N_T = e^{rT}$$

and under the $\mathbb{Q}_Y$ measure, where $Y_t e^{D_y t}$ is a non-dividend-paying asset we have

$$M_t = Y_t e^{D_y t} \text{ and } M_T = Y_T e^{D_y T}.$$

Using a change of numéraire, the exchange option at time t is

$$
\begin{aligned}
V(X_t, Y_t, t; T) &= e^{-r(T-t)} \mathbb{E}^{\mathbb{Q}} \left[\max\{X_T - Y_T, 0\} \middle| \mathscr{F}_t \right] \\
&= e^{rt} \mathbb{E}^{\mathbb{Q}} \left[\frac{\max\{X_T/Y_T - 1, 0\} Y_T}{e^{rT}} \middle| \mathscr{F}_t \right] \\
&= Y_t e^{D_y t} \mathbb{E}^{\mathbb{Q}_Y} \left[\frac{\max\{X_T/Y_T - 1, 0\} Y_T}{Y_T e^{D_y T}} \middle| \mathscr{F}_t \right] \\
&= Y_t e^{-D_y(T-t)} \mathbb{E}^{\mathbb{Q}_Y} \left[\max\{X_T/Y_T - 1, 0\} \middle| \mathscr{F}_t \right].
\end{aligned}
$$

Under $\mathbb{Q}_Y$ the discounted money-market account

$$
\begin{aligned}
Z_t &= \left(Y_t e^{D_y t} \right)^{-1} e^{rt} \\
&= Y_t^{-1} e^{(r - D_y)t}
\end{aligned}
$$

is a $\mathbb{Q}_Y$-martingale and from Itō's lemma

$$
\begin{aligned}
dZ_t &= (r - D_y) e^{(r-D_y)t} Y_t^{-1} dt + Y_t^{-1} e^{(r-D_y)t} \left(-\frac{dY_t}{Y_t} + \left(\frac{dY_t}{Y_t} \right)^2 + \dots \right) \\
&= (r - D_y) Z_t dt + Z_t \left(-(r - D_y) dt - \sigma_y d\widehat{W}_t^y + \sigma_y^2 dt \right) \\
&= \sigma_y^2 Z_t dt - \sigma_y Z_t d\widehat{W}_t^y \\
&= -\sigma_y Z_t (d\widehat{W}_t^y - \sigma_y dt) \\
&= -\sigma_y Z_t d\overline{W}_t^y
\end{aligned}
$$

where $\overline{W}_t^y = \widehat{W}_t^y - \sigma_y t$ is a $\mathbb{Q}_Y$-standard Wiener process. Because $\widehat{W}_t^{y\perp} \perp \widehat{W}_t^y$, then $\widehat{W}_t^{y\perp}$ is also a $\mathbb{Q}_Y$-standard Wiener process.

Thus, under $\mathbb{Q}_Y$

$$\frac{dX_t}{X_t} = (r - D_x)dt + \sigma_x \left(\rho_{xy} d\widehat{W}_t^y + \sqrt{1 - \rho_{xy}^2} d\widehat{W}_t^{y\perp} \right)$$

$$= (r - D_x)dt + \sigma_x \left(\rho_{xy} d\overline{W}_t^y + \rho_{xy}\sigma_y dt + \sqrt{1 - \rho_{xy}^2} d\widehat{W}_t^{y\perp} \right)$$

$$= (r - D_x + \rho_{xy}\sigma_x\sigma_y)dt + \rho_{xy}\sigma_x d\overline{W}_t^y + \sigma_x\sqrt{1 - \rho_{xy}^2} d\widehat{W}_t^{y\perp}$$

and

$$\frac{dY_t}{Y_t} = (r - D_y)dt + \sigma_y d\widehat{W}_t^y$$

$$= (r - D_y)dt + \sigma_y \left(d\overline{W}_t^y + \sigma_y dt \right)$$

$$= (r - D_y + \sigma_y^2)dt + \sigma_y d\overline{W}_t^y.$$

From Taylor's theorem

$$\frac{d\left(\dfrac{X_t}{Y_t}\right)}{\left(\dfrac{X_t}{Y_t}\right)} = \frac{Y_t}{X_t} \left[\frac{dX_t}{Y_t} - \frac{X_t}{Y_t^2}dY_t + \frac{1}{2!}\left(\frac{2X_t}{Y_t^3}\right)(dY_t)^2 - \frac{dX_t dY_t}{Y_t^2} + \cdots \right]$$

$$= \frac{dX_t}{X_t} - \frac{dY_t}{Y_t} + \left(\frac{dY_t}{Y_t}\right)^2 - \left(\frac{dX_t}{X_t}\right)\left(\frac{dY_t}{Y_t}\right) + \cdots$$

and by substituting dX_t/X_t, dY_t/Y_t and using Itô's lemma

$$\frac{d\left(\dfrac{X_t}{Y_t}\right)}{\left(\dfrac{X_t}{Y_t}\right)} = (r - D_x + \rho_{xy}\sigma_x\sigma_y)dt + \rho_{xy}\sigma_x d\overline{W}_t^y + \sigma_x\sqrt{1 - \rho_{xy}^2} d\widehat{W}_t^{y\perp}$$

$$-(r - D_y + \sigma_y^2)dt - \sigma_y d\overline{W}_t^y + \sigma_y^2 dt - \rho_{xy}\sigma_x\sigma_y dt$$

$$= (D_y - D_x)dt + (\rho_{xy}\sigma_x - \sigma_y)d\overline{W}_t^y + \sigma_x\sqrt{1 - \rho_{xy}^2} d\widehat{W}_t^{y\perp}.$$

To find the distribution of X_t/Y_t we note that

$$d\left(\log\left(\frac{X_t}{Y_t}\right)\right) = \frac{d\left(\dfrac{X_t}{Y_t}\right)}{\left(\dfrac{X_t}{Y_t}\right)} - \frac{1}{2!}\left[\frac{d\left(\dfrac{X_t}{Y_t}\right)}{\left(\dfrac{X_t}{Y_t}\right)}\right]^2 + \cdots$$

$$= \left(D_y - D_x - \frac{1}{2}\sigma^2\right)dt + (\rho_{xy}\sigma_x - \sigma_y)d\overline{W}_t^y + \sigma_x\sqrt{1 - \rho_{xy}^2} d\widehat{W}_t^{y\perp}$$

where $\sigma = \sqrt{\sigma_x^2 - 2\rho_{xy}\sigma_x\sigma_y + \sigma_y^2}$.

Taking integrals

$$\int_t^T d\left(\log\left(\frac{X_u}{Y_u}\right)\right) = \int_t^T \left(D_y - D_x - \frac{1}{2}\sigma^2\right)du + \int_t^T (\rho_{xy}\sigma_x - \sigma_y)d\overline{W}_u^y$$

$$+ \int_t^T \sigma_x\sqrt{1 - \rho_{xy}^2}d\widehat{W}_u^{y\perp}$$

or

$$\log\left(\frac{X_T}{Y_T}\right) = \log\left(\frac{X_t}{Y_t}\right) + \left(D_y - D_x - \frac{1}{2}\sigma^2\right)(T-t) + (\rho_{xy}\sigma_x - \sigma_y)\overline{W}_{T-t}^y$$

$$+ \sigma_x\sqrt{1 - \rho_{xy}^2}\widehat{W}_{T-t}^{y\perp}.$$

Because $\overline{W}_{T-t}^y, \widehat{W}_{T-t}^{y\perp} \sim \mathcal{N}(0, T-t)$ and $\overline{W}_{T-t}^y \perp\!\!\!\perp \widehat{W}_{T-t}^{y\perp}$, hence

$$\log\left(\frac{X_T}{Y_T}\right) \sim \mathcal{N}\left[\log\left(\frac{X_t}{Y_t}\right) + \left(D_y - D_x - \frac{1}{2}\sigma^2\right)(T-t), \sigma^2(T-t)\right].$$

Finally, by analogy with a European call price formula, we can deduce

$$V(X_t, Y_t, t; T) = Y_t e^{-D_y(T-t)}\mathbb{E}^{\mathbb{Q}}\left[\max\left\{\frac{X_T}{Y_T} - 1, 0\right\}\bigg|\mathcal{F}_t\right]$$

$$= Y_t e^{-D_y(T-t)}\left[\frac{X_t}{Y_t}e^{-(D_x-D_y)(T-t)}\Phi(d_+) - \Phi(d_-)\right]$$

$$= X_t e^{-D_x(T-t)}\Phi(d_+) - Y_t e^{-D_y(T-t)}\Phi(d_-)$$

where $d_\pm = \dfrac{\log(X_t/Y_t) + (D_y - D_x \pm \frac{1}{2}\sigma^2)(T-t)}{\sigma\sqrt{T-t}}.$

$\square$

7. *Spread Option I.* Let $\{W_t^x : t \geq 0\}$ and $\{W_t^y : t \geq 0\}$ be $\mathbb{P}$-standard Wiener processes on the probability space $(\Omega, \mathcal{F}, \mathbb{P})$ and let the asset prices X_t and Y_t have the following diffusion processes

$$dX_t = (\mu_x - D_x)X_t dt + \sigma_x X_t dW_t^x$$
$$dY_t = (\mu_y - D_y)Y_t dt + \sigma_y Y_t dW_t^y$$
$$dW_t^x \cdot dW_t^y = \rho_{xy}dt$$

where μ_x and μ_y are the drifts, D_x and D_y are the continuous dividend yields, σ_x and σ_y are the volatilities, ρ_{xy} is the correlation coefficient such that $\rho_{xy} \in (-1, 1)$ and let r be the risk-free interest rate from a money-market account.

By setting two new independent standard Wiener processes $\widehat{W}_t^y$ and $\widehat{W}_t^{y^\perp}$ such that

$$d\widetilde{W}_t^x = \rho_{xy}d\widehat{W}_t^y + \sqrt{1 - \rho_{xy}^2}\,d\widehat{W}_t^{y^\perp}$$
$$d\widetilde{W}_t^y = d\widehat{W}_t^y$$
$$d\widehat{W}_t^y \cdot d\widehat{W}_t^{y^\perp} = 0$$

where, under the risk-neutral measure $\mathbb{Q}$, $\widetilde{W}_t^x = W_t^x + \left(\dfrac{\mu_x - r}{\sigma_x}\right)t$ and $\widetilde{W}_t^y = W_t^y + \left(\dfrac{\mu_y - r}{\sigma_y}\right)t$ are $\mathbb{Q}$-standard Wiener processes, for a strike price $K > 0$ we define the price of a call spread option at time t with payoff

$$\Psi(X_T, Y_T) = \max\{X_T - Y_T - K, 0\}$$

at expiry time $T \geq t$ as

$$C_{sp}(X_t, Y_t, t; K, T) = e^{-r(T-t)}\mathbb{E}^{\mathbb{Q}}\left[\max\{X_T - Y_T - K, 0\}\,\big|\,\mathcal{F}_t\right].$$

For a small strike $K \ll Y_t$, show that under the $\mathbb{Q}$ measure, the process $Z_t = Y_t + Ke^{-r(T-t)}$ is approximately log normal with the following diffusion

$$\frac{dZ_t}{Z_t} = (r - D_z)dt + \sigma_z d\widehat{W}_t^y$$

where $D_z = \dfrac{D_y Y_t}{Y_t + Ke^{-r(T-t)}}$ and $\sigma_z = \dfrac{\sigma_y Y_t}{Y_t + Ke^{-r(T-t)}}$ are assumed to be constants.

By denoting $\mathbb{Q}_Z$ as the new measure where $Z_t e^{D_z t}$ is the numéraire and taking note that the discounted money-market account

$$\left(Z_t e^{D_z t}\right)^{-1}e^{rt}$$

is a $\mathbb{Q}_Z$-martingale, show that under $\mathbb{Q}_Z$, X_t and Z_t have the following diffusion processes

$$\frac{dX_t}{X_t} = (r - D_x + \rho_{xy}\sigma_x\sigma_z)dt + \rho_{xy}\sigma_x d\overline{W}_t^y + \sigma_x\sqrt{1 - \rho_{xy}^2}\,d\widehat{W}_t^{y^\perp}$$
$$\frac{dZ_t}{Z_t} = (r - D_z + \sigma_z^2)dt + \sigma_z d\overline{W}_t^y$$

where $\overline{W}_t^y = \widehat{W}_t^y - \sigma_z t$. Therefore, by finding the diffusion process for X_t/Z_t under $\mathbb{Q}_Z$ show that

$$
\log\left(\frac{X_T}{Y_T}\right) \approx \mathcal{N}\left[\log\left(\frac{X_t}{Y_t + Ke^{-r(T-t)}}\right) + \left(\frac{D_y Y_t}{Y_t + Ke^{-r(T-t)}} - D_x - \frac{1}{2}\sigma^2\right)(T-t),\right.
$$
$$
\left.\sigma^2(T-t)\right]
$$

where $\sigma = \sqrt{\sigma_x^2 - 2\rho_{xy}\sigma_x\sigma_y\left(\dfrac{Y_t}{Y_t + Ke^{-r(T-t)}}\right) + \left(\dfrac{\sigma_y Y_t}{Y_t + Ke^{-r(T-t)}}\right)^2}$ and finally deduce Kirk's approximation formula

$$
C_{sp}(X_t, Y_t, t; K) \approx X_t e^{-D_x(T-t)}\Phi(d_+) - \left(Y_t + Ke^{-r(T-t)}\right)e^{-\left(\frac{D_y Y_t}{Y_t + Ke^{-r(T-t)}}\right)(T-t)}\Phi(d_-)
$$

where

$$
d_\pm = \frac{\log\left(\dfrac{X_t}{Y_t + Ke^{-r(T-t)}}\right) + \left(\dfrac{D_y Y_t}{Y_t + Ke^{-r(T-t)}} - D_x \pm \dfrac{1}{2}\sigma^2\right)(T-t)}{\sigma\sqrt{T-t}}
$$

and

$$
\Phi(x) = \int_{-\infty}^{x} \frac{1}{\sqrt{2\pi}} e^{-\frac{1}{2}u^2} d u.
$$

Solution: From Girsanov's theorem, under the risk-neutral measure $\mathbb{Q}$ we can write

$$
\frac{dX_t}{X_t} = (r - D_x)dt + \sigma_x d\widetilde{W}_t^x
$$
$$
\frac{dY_t}{Y_t} = (r - D_y)dt + \sigma_y d\widetilde{W}_t^y
$$
$$
d\widetilde{W}_t^x \cdot d\widetilde{W}_t^y = \rho_{xy}dt
$$

where $\widetilde{W}_t^x = W_t^x + \left(\dfrac{\mu_x - r}{\sigma_x}\right)t$ and $\widetilde{W}_t^y = W_t^y + \left(\dfrac{\mu_y - r}{\sigma_y}\right)t$ are $\mathbb{Q}$-standard Wiener processes. By defining

$$
d\widetilde{W}_t^x = \rho_{xy}d\widehat{W}_t^y + \sqrt{1 - \rho_{xy}^2}\,d\widehat{W}_t^{y\perp}
$$
$$
d\widetilde{W}_t^y = d\widehat{W}_t^y
$$
$$
d\widehat{W}_t^y \cdot d\widehat{W}_t^{y\perp} = 0
$$

we have

$$\frac{dX_t}{X_t} = (r - D_x)dt + \sigma_x \left(\rho_{xy} d\widehat{W}_t^y + \sqrt{1 - \rho_{xy}^2} d\widehat{W}_t^{y\perp} \right)$$

$$\frac{dY_t}{Y_t} = (r - D_y)dt + \sigma_y d\widehat{W}_t^y$$

such that

$$\left(\rho_{xy} d\widehat{W}_t^y + \sqrt{1 - \rho_{xy}^2} d\widehat{W}_t^{y\perp} \right) \cdot d\widehat{W}_t^y = \rho_{xy} dt.$$

For a small strike $K \ll Y_t$, the diffusion process for $Z_t = Y_t + Ke^{-r(T-t)}$ is

$$\begin{aligned}
dZ_t &= dY_t + rKe^{-r(T-t)}dt \\
&= (r - D_y)Y_t dt + \sigma_y Y_t d\widehat{W}_t^y + rKe^{-r(T-t)}dt \\
&= r\left(Y_t + Ke^{-r(T-t)} \right) dt - D_y Y_t dt + \sigma_y Y_t d\widehat{W}_t^y \\
&= rZ_t dt - D_y Y_t dt + \sigma_y Y_t d\widehat{W}_t^y
\end{aligned}$$

or

$$\frac{dZ_t}{Z_t} = (r - D_z)dt + \sigma_z d\widehat{W}_t^y$$

where $D_z = \dfrac{D_y Y_t}{Y_t + Ke^{-r(T-t)}}$ and $\sigma_z = \dfrac{\sigma_y Y_t}{Y_t + Ke^{-r(T-t)}}$. By expanding $d(\log Z_t)$ using Itō's lemma we have

$$\begin{aligned}
d(\log Z_t) &= \frac{dZ_t}{Z_t} - \frac{1}{2!} \left(\frac{dZ_t}{Z_t} \right)^2 + \cdots \\
&= \left(r - D_z - \frac{1}{2}\sigma_z^2 \right) dt + \sigma_z d\widehat{W}_t^y.
\end{aligned}$$

By assuming both D_z and σ_z to be constants and taking integrals

$$\int_t^T d(\log Z_u) = \int_t^T \left(r - D_z - \frac{1}{2}\sigma_z^2 \right) du + \int_t^T \sigma_z d\widehat{W}_u^y$$

$$\log\left(\frac{Z_T}{Z_t} \right) = \left(r - D_z - \frac{1}{2}\sigma_z^2 \right)(T-t) + \int_t^T \sigma_z d\widehat{W}_u^y$$

we can therefore deduce that

$$\log\left(\frac{Y_T + K}{Y_t + Ke^{-r(T-t)}}\right) \doteq \mathcal{N}\left[\left(r - D_z - \frac{1}{2}\sigma_y^2\right)(T-t), \sigma_z^2(T-t)\right].$$

For a payoff $\Psi(X_T, Y_T)$ under the change of numéraire

$$N_t \mathbb{E}^{\mathbb{Q}}\left[\frac{\Psi(X_T, Y_T)}{N_T}\middle|\mathcal{F}_t\right] = M_t \mathbb{E}^{\mathbb{Q}_Z}\left[\frac{\Psi(X_T, Y_T)}{M_T}\middle|\mathcal{F}_t\right]$$

where N and M are numéraires (positive non-dividend-paying assets) and $\mathbb{Q}$ and $\mathbb{Q}_Z$ are the measures under which the asset prices discounted by N and M are $\mathbb{Q}$ and $\mathbb{Q}_Z$-martingales, respectively.

Under the risk-neutral, measure $\mathbb{Q}$ we have

$$N_t = e^{rt} \text{ and } N_T = e^{rT}$$

and under the $\mathbb{Q}_Z$ measure, where $Z_t e^{D_z t}$ is a non-dividend-paying asset, we have

$$M_t = Z_t e^{D_z t} \text{ and } M_T = Z_T e^{D_z T}.$$

Using a change of numéraire, the call spread option at time t is

$$C_{sp}(X_t, Y_t, t; K, T) = e^{-r(T-t)}\mathbb{E}^{\mathbb{Q}}\left[\max\{X_T - Y_T - K, 0\}\middle|\mathcal{F}_t\right]$$

$$= e^{rt}\mathbb{E}^{\mathbb{Q}}\left[\frac{\max\left\{\dfrac{X_T}{Y_T + K} - 1, 0\right\}(Y_T + K)}{e^{rT}}\middle|\mathcal{F}_t\right]$$

$$= (Y_t + Ke^{-r(T-t)})e^{D_z t}$$

$$\times \mathbb{E}^{\mathbb{Q}_Z}\left[\frac{\max\left\{\dfrac{X_T}{Y_T + K} - 1, 0\right\}(Y_T + K)}{(Y_T + K)e^{D_z T}}\middle|\mathcal{F}_t\right]$$

$$= (Y_t + Ke^{-r(T-t)})e^{-D_z(T-t)}$$

$$\times \mathbb{E}^{\mathbb{Q}_Z}\left[\max\left\{\frac{X_T}{Y_T + K} - 1, 0\right\}\middle|\mathcal{F}_t\right]$$

$$= Z_t e^{-D_z(T-t)}\mathbb{E}^{\mathbb{Q}_Z}\left[\max\left\{\frac{X_T}{Z_T} - 1, 0\right\}\middle|\mathcal{F}_t\right].$$

Under $\mathbb{Q}_Z$, the discounted money-market account

$$\overline{Z}_t = \left(Z_t e^{D_z t}\right)^{-1} e^{rt}$$
$$= Z_t^{-1} e^{(r - D_z)t}$$

is a $\mathbb{Q}_Z$-martingale and from Itō's lemma

$$d\overline{Z}_t = (r - D_z)e^{(r-D_z)t} Z_t^{-1} dt + Z_t^{-1} e^{(r-D_z)t}\left(-\frac{dZ_t}{Z_t} + \left(\frac{dZ_t}{Z_t}\right)^2 + \dots\right)$$

$$= (r - D_z)\overline{Z}_t dt + \overline{Z}_t\left(-(r - D_z)dt - \sigma_z d\widehat{W}_t^y + \sigma_z^2 dt\right)$$

$$= \sigma_z^2 \overline{Z}_t dt - \sigma_z \overline{Z}_t d\widehat{W}_t^y$$

$$= -\sigma_z \overline{Z}_t (d\widehat{W}_t^y - \sigma_z dt)$$

$$= -\sigma_z \overline{Z}_t d\overline{W}_t^y$$

where $\overline{W}_t^y = \widehat{W}_t^y - \sigma_z t$ is a $\mathbb{Q}_Z$-standard Wiener process. Because $\widehat{W}_t^{y\perp} \perp \widehat{W}_t^y$, then therefore $\widehat{W}_t^{y\perp}$ is also a $\mathbb{Q}_Z$-standard Wiener process.

Thus, under $\mathbb{Q}_Z$

$$\frac{dX_t}{X_t} = (r - D_x)dt + \sigma_x\left(\rho_{xy} d\widehat{W}_t^y + \sqrt{1 - \rho_{xy}^2}\, d\widehat{W}_t^{y\perp}\right)$$

$$= (r - D_x)dt + \sigma_x\left(\rho_{xy} d\overline{W}_t^y + \rho_{xy}\sigma_z dt + \sqrt{1 - \rho_{xy}^2}\, d\widehat{W}_t^{y\perp}\right)$$

$$= (r - D_x + \rho_{xy}\sigma_x\sigma_z)dt + \rho_{xy}\sigma_x d\overline{W}_t^y + \sigma_x\sqrt{1 - \rho_{xy}^2}\, d\widehat{W}_t^{y\perp}$$

and

$$\frac{dZ_t}{Z_t} = (r - D_z)dt + \sigma_z d\widehat{W}_t^y$$

$$= (r - D_z)dt + \sigma_z\left(d\overline{W}_t^y + \sigma_z dt\right)$$

$$= (r - D_z + \sigma_z^2)dt + \sigma_z d\overline{W}_t^y.$$

From Taylor's theorem

$$\frac{d\left(\dfrac{X_t}{Z_t}\right)}{\left(\dfrac{X_t}{Z_t}\right)} = \frac{Z_t}{X_t}\left[\frac{dX_t}{Z_t} - \frac{X_t}{Z_t^2} dZ_t + \frac{1}{2!}\left(\frac{2X_t}{Z_t^3}\right)(dZ_t)^2 - \frac{dX_t dZ_t}{Z_t^2} + \dots\right]$$

$$= \frac{dX_t}{X_t} - \frac{dZ_t}{Z_t} + \left(\frac{dZ_t}{Z_t}\right)^2 - \left(\frac{dX_t}{X_t}\right)\left(\frac{dZ_t}{Z_t}\right) + \dots$$

and by substituting dX_t/X_t, dZ_t/Z_t and using Itō's lemma

$$
\frac{d\left(\dfrac{X_t}{Z_t}\right)}{\left(\dfrac{X_t}{Z_t}\right)} = (r - D_x + \rho_{xy}\sigma_x\sigma_z)dt + \rho_{xy}\sigma_x d\overline{W}_t^y + \sigma_x\sqrt{1 - \rho_{xy}^2}\,d\widehat{W}_t^{y\perp}
$$

$$
-(r - D_y + \sigma_z^2)dt - \sigma_z d\overline{W}_t^y + \sigma_z^2 dt - \rho_{xy}\sigma_x\sigma_z dt
$$

$$
= (D_z - D_x)dt + (\rho_{xy}\sigma_x - \sigma_z)d\overline{W}_t^y + \sigma_x\sqrt{1 - \rho_{xy}^2}\,d\widehat{W}_t^{y\perp}.
$$

To find the distribution of X_t/Z_t we note that

$$
d\left(\log\left(\frac{X_t}{Z_t}\right)\right) = \frac{d\left(\dfrac{X_t}{Z_t}\right)}{\left(\dfrac{X_t}{Z_t}\right)} - \frac{1}{2!}\left[\frac{d\left(\dfrac{X_t}{Z_t}\right)}{\left(\dfrac{X_t}{Z_t}\right)}\right]^2 + \ldots
$$

$$
= \left(D_z - D_x - \frac{1}{2}\sigma^2\right)dt + (\rho_{xy}\sigma_x - \sigma_z)d\overline{W}_t^y
$$

$$
+ \sigma_x\sqrt{1 - \rho_{xy}^2}\,d\widehat{W}_t^{y\perp}
$$

where $\sigma = \sqrt{\sigma_x^2 - 2\rho_{xy}\sigma_x\sigma_z + \sigma_z^2}$.

Since we are assuming D_z and σ_z to be constants and taking integrals

$$
\int_t^T d\left(\log\left(\frac{X_u}{Z_u}\right)\right) = \int_t^T \left(D_z - D_x - \frac{1}{2}\sigma^2\right)du + \int_t^T (\rho_{xy}\sigma_x - \sigma_z)d\overline{W}_u^y
$$

$$
+ \int_t^T \sigma_x\sqrt{1 - \rho_{xy}^2}\,d\widehat{W}_u^{y\perp}
$$

or

$$
\log\left(\frac{X_T}{Z_T}\right) = \log\left(\frac{X_t}{Z_t}\right) + \left(D_z - D_x - \frac{1}{2}\sigma^2\right)(T - t) + (\rho_{xy}\sigma_x - \sigma_z)\overline{W}_{T-t}^y
$$

$$
+ \sigma_x\sqrt{1 - \rho_{xy}^2}\,\widehat{W}_{T-t}^{y\perp}.
$$

Because $\overline{W}_{T-t}^y$, $\widehat{W}_{T-t}^{y\perp} \sim \mathcal{N}(0, T - t)$ and $\overline{W}_{T-t}^y \perp\!\!\!\perp \widehat{W}_{T-t}^{y\perp}$, hence

$$
\log\left(\frac{X_T}{Z_T}\right) \approx \mathcal{N}\left[\log\left(\frac{X_t}{Z_t}\right) + \left(D_z - D_x - \frac{1}{2}\sigma^2\right)(T - t), \sigma^2(T - t)\right].
$$

Finally, by analogy with a European call price formula we can deduce Kirk's approximation formula

$$
\begin{aligned}
C_{sp}(X_t, Y_t, t; K, T) &= Z_t e^{-D_z(T-t)} \mathbb{E}^{\mathbb{Q}_Z}\left[\max\left\{ \frac{X_T}{Z_T} - 1, 0 \right\} \middle| \mathscr{F}_t \right] \\
&\approx Z_t e^{-D_z(T-t)} \left[\frac{X_t}{Z_t} e^{-(D_x - D_z)(T-t)} \Phi(d_+) - \Phi(d_-) \right] \\
&= X_t e^{-D_x(T-t)} \Phi(d_+) \\
&\quad - \left(Y_t + K e^{-r(T-t)} \right) e^{-\left(\frac{D_y Y_t}{Y_t + K e^{-r(T-t)}} \right)(T-t)} \Phi(d_-)
\end{aligned}
$$

where $d_{\pm} = \dfrac{\log\left(\dfrac{X_t}{Y_t + K e^{-r(T-t)}} \right) + \left(\dfrac{D_y Y_t}{Y_t + K e^{-r(T-t)}} - D_x \pm \dfrac{1}{2}\sigma^2 \right)(T-t)}{\sigma\sqrt{T-t}}$.

□

8. *Spread Option II.* Let $\{W_t^{(1)} : t \geq 0\}$ and $\{W_t^{(2)} : t \geq 0\}$ be $\mathbb{P}$-standard Wiener processes on the probability space $(\Omega, \mathscr{F}, \mathbb{P})$ and let the asset prices $S_t^{(1)}$ and $S_t^{(2)}$ follow ABMs of the form

$$
\begin{aligned}
dS_t^{(1)} &= (\mu_1 - D_1)dt + \sigma_1 dW_t^{(1)} \\
dS_t^{(2)} &= (\mu_2 - D_2)dt + \sigma_2 dW_t^{(2)} \\
dW_t^{(1)} \cdot dW_t^{(2)} &= \rho dt
\end{aligned}
$$

where μ_1 and μ_2 are the drifts, D_1 and D_2 are the continuous dividend yields, σ_1 and σ_2 are the volatilities, $\rho \in (-1, 1)$ is the correlation coefficient and let r be the risk-free interest rate from a money-market account.

Using Itô's lemma show that under the risk-neutral measure $\mathbb{Q}$ for $T > t$, the conditional distribution of $S_T^{(2)} - S_T^{(1)}$ given $S_t^{(1)}$ and $S_t^{(2)}$ is

$$
S_T^{(2)} - S_T^{(1)} \middle| S_t^{(1)}, S_t^{(2)} \sim \mathcal{N}\left(m, s^2 \right)
$$

where

$$
m = S_t^{(2)} e^{-D_2(T-t)} - S_t^{(1)} e^{-D_1(T-t)}
$$

and

$$
\begin{aligned}
s^2 &= \frac{\sigma_1^2}{2(r - D_1)}\left[e^{2(r-D_1)(T-t)} - 1 \right] + \frac{\sigma_2^2}{2(r - D_2)}\left[e^{2(r-D_2)(T-t)} - 1 \right] \\
&\quad - \frac{2\rho\sigma_1\sigma_2}{2r - D_1 - D_2}\left[e^{(2r-D_1-D_2)(T-t)} - 1 \right].
\end{aligned}
$$

Using the risk-neutral valuation approach show that for a strike price $K > 0$, the price of a call spread option at time $t < T$ with payoff

$$\Psi(S_T^{(1)}, S_T^{(2)}) = \max\{S_T^{(2)} - S_T^{(1)} - K, 0\}$$

is

$$C_{sp}(S_t^{(1)}, S_t^{(2)}, t; K, T) = \left(S_t^{(2)}e^{-D_2(T-t)} - S_t^{(1)}e^{-D_1(T-t)} - Ke^{-r(T-t)}\right)\Phi(d) + \sigma\Phi'(d)$$

where

$$d = \frac{S_t^{(2)}e^{-D_2(T-t)} - S_t^{(1)}e^{-D_1(T-t)} - Ke^{-r(T-t)}}{\sigma}$$

$$\sigma^2 = \frac{\sigma_1^2}{2(r - D_1)}\left[e^{-2D_1(T-t)} - e^{-2r(T-t)}\right] + \frac{\sigma_2^2}{2(r - D_2)}\left[e^{-2D_2(T-t)} - e^{-2r(T-t)}\right]$$

$$- \frac{2\rho\sigma_1\sigma_2}{2r - D_1 - D_2}\left[e^{-(D_1+D_2)(T-t)} - e^{-2r(T-t)}\right]$$

and $\Phi(x) = \int_{-\infty}^{x} \frac{1}{\sqrt{2\pi}}e^{-\frac{1}{2}u^2}\,du$ is the standard normal cdf.

Solution: Under the risk-neutral measure $\mathbb{Q}$,

$$dS_t^{(1)} = (r - D_1)S_t^{(1)}dt + \sigma_1 d\widetilde{W}_t^{(1)}$$
$$dS_t^{(2)} = (r - D_2)S_t^{(2)}dt + \sigma_2 d\widetilde{W}_t^{(2)}$$

where $\widetilde{W}_t^{(1)} = W_t^{(1)} + \left(\dfrac{\mu_1 - rS_t^{(1)}}{\sigma_1}\right)t$ and $\widetilde{W}_t^{(2)} = W_t^{(2)} + \left(\dfrac{\mu_2 - rS_t^{(2)}}{\sigma_2}\right)t$ are $\mathbb{Q}$-standard Wiener processes (see Problem 4.2.3.7, *Problems and Solutions in Mathematical Finance, Volume 1: Stochastic Calculus*).

From Problem 2.2.2.8 (page 109) we can easily show that for $t < T$,

$$S_T^{(1)} = S_t^{(1)}e^{(r-D_1)(T-t)} + \sigma_1 \int_t^T e^{(r-D_1)(T-u)}d\widetilde{W}_u^{(1)}$$

and

$$S_T^{(2)} = S_t^{(2)}e^{(r-D_2)(T-t)} + \sigma_2 \int_t^T e^{(r-D_2)(T-u)}d\widetilde{W}_u^{(2)}.$$

Thus,

$$\mathbb{E}^{\mathbb{Q}}\left(S_T^{(2)} - S_T^{(1)}\middle|\mathcal{F}_t\right) = S_t^{(2)}e^{(r-D_2)(T-t)} - S_t^{(1)}e^{(r-D_1)(T-t)}$$

and

$$\text{Var}^{\mathbb{Q}}\left(S_T^{(2)} - S_T^{(1)}\middle|\mathcal{F}_t\right)$$

$$= \text{Var}^{\mathbb{Q}}\left(S_T^{(1)}\middle|\mathcal{F}_t\right) + \text{Var}^{\mathbb{Q}}\left(S_T^{(2)}\middle|\mathcal{F}_t\right) - 2\text{Cov}^{\mathbb{Q}}\left(S_T^{(1)}, S_T^{(2)}\middle|\mathcal{F}_t\right)$$

$$= \sigma_1^2\mathbb{E}^{\mathbb{Q}}\left[\left(\int_t^T e^{(r-D_1)(T-u)}d\widetilde{W}_u^{(1)}\right)^2\middle|\mathcal{F}_t\right]$$

$$+\sigma_2^2\mathbb{E}^{\mathbb{Q}}\left[\left(\int_t^T e^{(r-D_2)(T-u)}d\widetilde{W}_u^{(2)}\right)^2\middle|\mathcal{F}_t\right]$$

$$-2\sigma_1\sigma_2\text{Cov}^{\mathbb{Q}}\left[\int_t^T e^{(r-D_1)(T-u)}d\widetilde{W}_u^{(1)}, \int_t^T e^{(r-D_2)(T-u)}d\widetilde{W}_u^{(2)}\middle|\mathcal{F}_t\right]$$

$$= \sigma_1^2\mathbb{E}^{\mathbb{Q}}\left[\int_t^T e^{2(r-D_1)(T-u)}du\middle|\mathcal{F}_t\right] + \sigma_2^2\mathbb{E}^{\mathbb{Q}}\left[\int_t^T e^{2(r-D_2)(T-u)}du\middle|\mathcal{F}_t\right]$$

$$-2\sigma_1\sigma_2\text{Cov}^{\mathbb{Q}}\left[\int_t^T e^{(r-D_1)(T-u)}d\widetilde{W}_u^{(1)}, \int_t^T e^{(r-D_2)(T-u)}d\widetilde{W}_u^{(2)}\middle|\mathcal{F}_t\right].$$

By setting

$$d\widetilde{W}_t^{(2)} = \rho d\widetilde{W}_t^{(1)} + \sqrt{1-\rho^2}d\widehat{W}_t^{(1)}$$

so that $d\widehat{W}_t^{(1)} \cdot d\widetilde{W}_t^{(1)} = 0$, then

$$\text{Var}^{\mathbb{Q}}\left(S_T^{(2)} - S_T^{(1)}\middle|\mathcal{F}_t\right)$$

$$= \sigma_1^2\mathbb{E}^{\mathbb{Q}}\left[\int_t^T e^{2(r-D_1)(T-u)}du\middle|\mathcal{F}_t\right] + \sigma_2^2\mathbb{E}^{\mathbb{Q}}\left[\int_t^T e^{2(r-D_2)(T-u)}du\middle|\mathcal{F}_t\right]$$

$$-2\sigma_1\sigma_2\text{Cov}^{\mathbb{Q}}\left[\int_t^T e^{(r-D_1)(T-u)}d\widetilde{W}_u^{(1)},\right.$$

$$\rho \int_t^T e^{(r-D_2)(T-u)} d\widetilde{W}_u^{(1)} + \sqrt{1-\rho^2} \int_t^T e^{(r-D_2)(T-u)} d\widehat{W}_u^{(1)} \Bigg| \mathcal{F}_t \Bigg]$$

$$= \sigma_1^2 \int_t^T e^{2(r-D_1)(T-u)} du + \sigma_2^2 \int_t^T e^{2(r-D_2)(T-u)} du$$

$$-2\rho\sigma_1\sigma_2 \mathbb{E}^{\mathbb{Q}} \left[\int_t^T e^{(r-D_1)(T-u)} d\widetilde{W}_u^{(1)} \cdot \int_t^T e^{(r-D_2)(T-u)} d\widetilde{W}_u^{(1)} \Bigg| \mathcal{F}_t \right]$$

$$= \sigma_1^2 \int_t^T e^{2(r-D_1)(T-u)} du + \sigma_2^2 \int_t^T e^{2(r-D_2)(T-u)} du$$

$$-2\rho\sigma_1\sigma_2 \mathbb{E}^{\mathbb{Q}} \left[\int_t^T e^{(2r-D_1-D_2)(T-u)} du \right]$$

$$= \sigma_1^2 \int_t^T e^{2(r-D_1)(T-u)} du + \sigma_2^2 \int_t^T e^{2(r-D_2)(T-u)} du$$

$$-2\rho\sigma_1\sigma_2 \int_t^T e^{(2r-D_1-D_2)(T-u)} du.$$

Solving the integrals, we have

$$\text{Var}^{\mathbb{Q}} \left(S_T^{(2)} - S_T^{(1)} \Big| \mathcal{F}_t \right) = \frac{\sigma_1^2}{2(r-D_1)} \left[e^{2(r-D_1)(T-t)} - 1 \right]$$

$$+ \frac{\sigma_2^2}{2(r-D_2)} \left[e^{2(r-D_2)(T-t)} - 1 \right]$$

$$- \frac{2\rho\sigma_1\sigma_2}{2r-D_1-D_2} \left[e^{(2r-D_1-D_2)(T-t)} - 1 \right].$$

Since

$$S_T^{(1)} \Big| S_t^{(1)} \sim \mathcal{N} \left(S_t^{(1)} e^{(r-D_1)(T-t)}, \frac{\sigma_1^2}{2(r-D_1)} \left[e^{2(r-D_1)(T-t)} - 1 \right] \right)$$

and

$$S_T^{(2)} \Big| S_t^{(2)} \sim \mathcal{N} \left(S_t^{(2)} e^{(r-D_2)(T-t)}, \frac{\sigma_2^2}{2(r-D_2)} \left[e^{2(r-D_2)(T-t)} - 1 \right] \right)$$

therefore

$$S_T^{(2)} - S_T^{(1)} \Big| S_t^{(1)}, S_t^{(2)} \sim \mathcal{N}(m, s^2)$$

where

$$m = S_t^{(2)} e^{(r-D_2)(T-t)} - S_t^{(1)} e^{(r-D_1)(T-t)}$$

and

$$s^2 = \frac{\sigma_1^2}{2(r - D_1)} \left[e^{2(r-D_1)(T-t)} - 1 \right] + \frac{\sigma_2^2}{2(r - D_2)} \left[e^{2(r-D_2)(T-t)} - 1 \right]$$
$$- \frac{2\rho\sigma_1\sigma_2}{2r - D_1 - D_2} \left[e^{(2r-D_1-D_2)(T-t)} - 1 \right].$$

Using the same steps as described in Problem 2.2.2.8 (page 109), we can easily show that the call spread option price at time $t < T$ is

$$C_{sp}(S_t^{(1)}, S_t^{(2)}, t; K, T) = e^{-r(T-t)} \mathbb{E}^{\mathbb{Q}} \left[\max\{S_T^{(2)} - S_T^{(1)} - K, 0\} \middle| \mathcal{F}_t \right]$$
$$= e^{-r(T-t)} \left[(m - K)\Phi\left(\frac{m - K}{s} \right) + s\Phi'\left(\frac{m - K}{s} \right) \right]$$
$$= \left(S_t^{(2)} e^{-D_2(T-t)} - S_t^{(1)} e^{-D_1(T-t)} - Ke^{-r(T-t)} \right) \Phi(d)$$
$$+ \sigma\Phi'(d)$$

where

$$d = \frac{S_t^{(2)} e^{-D_2(T-t)} - S_t^{(1)} e^{-D_1(T-t)} - Ke^{-r(T-t)}}{\sigma}$$

and

$$\sigma^2 = \frac{\sigma_1^2}{2(r - D_1)} \left[e^{-2D_1(T-t)} - e^{-2r(T-t)} \right] + \frac{\sigma_2^2}{2(r - D_2)} \left[e^{-2D_2(T-t)} - e^{-2r(T-t)} \right]$$
$$- \frac{2\rho\sigma_1\sigma_2}{2r - D_1 - D_2} \left[e^{-(D_1+D_2)(T-t)} - e^{-2r(T-t)} \right].$$

$\square$

9. *Rainbow Option I.* Let $X \sim \mathcal{N}(\mu_x, \sigma_x^2)$ and $Y \sim \mathcal{N}(\mu_y, \sigma_y^2)$ be jointly normally distributed with correlation coefficient $\rho_{xy} \in (-1, 1)$. If $Z = \min\{X, Y\}$ show that the probability density function (pdf) of Z is

$$f_Z(z) = \Phi\left(\frac{-z + \mu_y + \dfrac{\rho_{xy}\sigma_y}{\sigma_x}(z - \mu_x)}{\sigma_y\sqrt{1 - \rho_{xy}^2}} \right) f_X(z) + \Phi\left(\frac{-z + \mu_x + \dfrac{\rho_{xy}\sigma_x}{\sigma_y}(z - \mu_y)}{\sigma_x\sqrt{1 - \rho_{xy}^2}} \right) f_Y(z)$$

where $f_X(z) = \dfrac{1}{\sigma_x\sqrt{2\pi}} e^{-\frac{1}{2}\left(\frac{z-\mu_x}{\sigma_x}\right)^2}$, $f_Y(z) = \dfrac{1}{\sigma_y\sqrt{2\pi}} e^{-\frac{1}{2}\left(\frac{z-\mu_y}{\sigma_y}\right)^2}$ and Φ denotes the cumulative distribution function of a standard normal.

Hence, show that

$$\mathbb{E}\left[\max\left\{e^Z - K, 0\right\}\right]$$

$$= e^{\mu_x + \frac{1}{2}\sigma_x^2}\Phi\left(\frac{\mu_x + \sigma_x^2 - \log K}{\sigma_x}, \frac{\mu_y - \mu_x - \sigma_x(\sigma_x - \rho_{xy}\sigma_y)}{\sqrt{\sigma_x^2 - 2\rho_{xy}\sigma_x\sigma_y + \sigma_y^2}}, \frac{\sigma_x - \rho_{xy}\sigma_y}{\sqrt{\sigma_x^2 - 2\rho_{xy}\sigma_x\sigma_y + \sigma_y^2}}\right)$$

$$+ e^{\mu_y + \frac{1}{2}\sigma_y^2}\Phi\left(\frac{\mu_y + \sigma_y^2 - \log K}{\sigma_y}, \frac{\mu_x - \mu_y - \sigma_y(\sigma_y - \rho_{xy}\sigma_x)}{\sqrt{\sigma_x^2 - 2\rho_{xy}\sigma_x\sigma_y + \sigma_y^2}}, \frac{\sigma_y - \rho_{xy}\sigma_x}{\sqrt{\sigma_x^2 - 2\rho_{xy}\sigma_x\sigma_y + \sigma_y^2}}\right)$$

$$- K\left[\Phi\left(\frac{\mu_x - \log K}{\sigma_x}, \frac{\mu_y - \mu_x}{\sqrt{\sigma_x^2 - 2\rho_{xy}\sigma_x\sigma_y + \sigma_y^2}}, \frac{\sigma_x - \rho_{xy}\sigma_y}{\sqrt{\sigma_x^2 - 2\rho_{xy}\sigma_x\sigma_y + \sigma_y^2}}\right)\right.$$

$$\left.+ \Phi\left(\frac{\mu_y - \log K}{\sigma_y}, \frac{\mu_x - \mu_y}{\sqrt{\sigma_x^2 - 2\rho_{xy}\sigma_x\sigma_y + \sigma_y^2}}, \frac{\sigma_y - \rho_{xy}\sigma_x}{\sqrt{\sigma_x^2 - 2\rho_{xy}\sigma_x\sigma_y + \sigma_y^2}}\right)\right]$$

where $K > 0$, $\mathbb{E}$ denotes the expectation with respect to e^Z distribution and Φ denotes the cumulative distribution function of a standard bivariate normal distribution given as

$$\Phi(u, v, \rho_{uv}) = \int_{-\infty}^{u}\int_{-\infty}^{v}\frac{1}{2\pi\sqrt{1 - \rho_{uv}^2}}e^{-\frac{1}{2(1-\rho_{uv}^2)}(x^2 - 2\rho_{uv}xy + y^2)}\,dy\,dx$$

where $\rho_{uv} \in (-1, 1)$.

Let the asset prices $S_t^{(1)}$ and $S_t^{(2)}$ have the following diffusion processes

$$dS_t^{(1)} = (\mu_1 - D_1)S_t^{(1)}dt + \sigma_1 S_t^{(1)}dW_t^{(1)}$$
$$dS_t^{(2)} = (\mu_2 - D_2)S_t^{(2)}dt + \sigma_2 S_t^{(2)}dW_t^{(2)}$$
$$dW_t^{(1)} \cdot dW_t^{(2)} = \rho dt$$

where $\{W_t^{(1)} : t \geq 0\}$ and $\{W_t^{(2)} : t \geq 0\}$ are $\mathbb{P}$-standard Wiener processes on the probability space $(\Omega, \mathscr{F}, \mathbb{P})$, μ_1 and μ_2 are the drift parameters, D_1 and D_2 are the continuous dividend yields, σ_1 and σ_2 are the volatilities, $\rho \in (-1, 1)$ is the correlation coefficient and let r be the risk-free interest rate from a money market account.

Show that $(W_t^{(1)}, W_t^{(2)})$ follows a bivariate normal distribution.

Given the payoff of a rainbow call on the minimum option is defined as

$$\Psi(S_T^{(1)}, S_T^{(2)}) = \max\left\{\min\{S_T^{(1)}, S_T^{(2)}\} - K, 0\right\}$$

where $K > 0$ is the strike price, $T \geq t$ is the option expiry time, using the above results find the rainbow call on the minimum option price at time t under the risk-neutral measure $\mathbb{Q}$.

Solution: The first part of the results follows from Problem 1.2.2.15 of *Problems and Solutions in Mathematical Finance, Volume 1: Stochastic Calculus.*

To calculate the closed-form solution of

$$\mathbb{E}\left[\max\left\{e^Z - K, 0\right\}\right]$$

where $Z = \min\{X, Y\}$, $X \sim \mathcal{N}(\mu_x, \sigma_x^2)$, $Y \sim \mathcal{N}(\mu_y, \sigma_y^2)$, $Cov(X, Y) = \rho_{xy}\sigma_x\sigma_y$, $\rho_{xy} \in (-1, 1)$ and $K > 0$, the expectation can be written as

$$\mathbb{E}\left[\max\left\{e^Z - K, 0\right\}\right] = \int_{-\infty}^{+\infty} \max\left\{e^z - K, 0\right\} f_Z(z) dz$$

where $f_Z(z)$ is the pdf of Z.

By substituting the pdf of Z we have

$$\mathbb{E}\left[\max\left\{e^Z - K, 0\right\}\right] = \int_{\log K}^{+\infty} \left(e^z - K\right) f_Z(z)\, dz$$

$$= \int_{\log K}^{+\infty} \left(e^z - K\right) \Phi\left(\frac{-z + \mu_y + \dfrac{\rho_{xy}\sigma_y}{\sigma_x}(z - \mu_x)}{\sigma_y\sqrt{1 - \rho_{xy}^2}}\right) f_X(z)\, dz$$

$$+ \int_{\log K}^{+\infty} \left(e^z - K\right) \Phi\left(\frac{-z + \mu_x + \dfrac{\rho_{xy}\sigma_x}{\sigma_y}(z - \mu_y)}{\sigma_x\sqrt{1 - \rho_{xy}^2}}\right) f_Y(z)\, dz$$

$$= A_1 + A_2 - B_1 - B_2$$

where

$$A_1 = \int_{\log K}^{+\infty} e^z \Phi\left(\frac{-z + \mu_y + \dfrac{\rho_{xy}\sigma_y}{\sigma_x}(z - \mu_x)}{\sigma_y\sqrt{1 - \rho_{xy}^2}}\right) f_X(z)\, dz$$

$$A_2 = \int_{\log K}^{+\infty} e^z \Phi\left(\frac{-z + \mu_x + \dfrac{\rho_{xy}\sigma_x}{\sigma_y}(z - \mu_y)}{\sigma_x\sqrt{1 - \rho_{xy}^2}}\right) f_Y(z)\, dz$$

$$B_1 = K \int_{\log K}^{+\infty} \Phi\left(\frac{-z + \mu_y + \dfrac{\rho_{xy}\sigma_y}{\sigma_x}(z - \mu_x)}{\sigma_y\sqrt{1 - \rho_{xy}^2}}\right) f_X(z)\, dz$$

$$B_2 = K \int_{\log K}^{+\infty} \Phi\left(\frac{-z + \mu_x + \dfrac{\rho_{xy}\sigma_x}{\sigma_y}(z - \mu_y)}{\sigma_x\sqrt{1 - \rho_{xy}^2}}\right) f_Y(z)\, dz.$$

For the case

$$A_1 = \int_{\log K}^{+\infty} e^z \Phi \left(\frac{-z + \mu_y + \dfrac{\rho_{xy}\sigma_y}{\sigma_x}(z - \mu_x)}{\sigma_y\sqrt{1 - \rho_{xy}^2}} \right) f_X(z)\,dz$$

we let $w = \dfrac{z - \mu_x}{\sigma_x}$ and therefore

$$A_1 = \int_{w=\frac{\log K - \mu_x}{\sigma_x}}^{+\infty} e^{\mu_x + w\sigma_x} \Phi \left(\frac{\mu_y - \mu_x - w(\sigma_x - \rho_{xy}\sigma_y)}{\sigma_y\sqrt{1 - \rho_{xy}^2}} \right) \frac{1}{\sqrt{2\pi}} e^{-\frac{1}{2}w^2}\,dw$$

$$= \int_{w=\frac{\log K - \mu_x}{\sigma_x}}^{+\infty} e^{\mu_x + \frac{1}{2}\sigma_x^2} \left(\int_{-\infty}^{y=\frac{\mu_y - \mu_x - w(\sigma_x - \rho_{xy}\sigma_y)}{\sigma_y\sqrt{1 - \rho_{xy}^2}}} \frac{1}{\sqrt{2\pi}} e^{-\frac{1}{2}y^2}\,dy \right) \frac{1}{\sqrt{2\pi}} e^{-\frac{1}{2}(w-\sigma_x)^2}\,dw.$$

Let $v = w - \sigma_x$ and we then have

$$A_1 = \int_{v=\frac{\log K - \mu_x - \sigma_x^2}{\sigma_x}}^{+\infty} e^{\mu_x + \frac{1}{2}\sigma_x^2} \left(\int_{-\infty}^{y=\frac{\mu_y - \mu_x - (v+\sigma_x)(\sigma_x - \rho_{xy}\sigma_y)}{\sigma_y\sqrt{1 - \rho_{xy}^2}}} \frac{1}{\sqrt{2\pi}} e^{-\frac{1}{2}y^2}\,dy \right) \frac{1}{\sqrt{2\pi}} e^{-\frac{1}{2}v^2}\,dv$$

$$= e^{\mu_x + \frac{1}{2}\sigma_x^2} \int_{-\infty}^{v=\frac{\mu_x + \sigma_x^2 - \log K}{\sigma_x}} \int_{-\infty}^{y=\frac{\mu_y - \mu_x - \sigma_x(\sigma_x - \rho_{xy}\sigma_y)}{\sigma_y\sqrt{1 - \rho_{xy}^2}} - \frac{v(\sigma_x - \rho_{xy}\sigma_y)}{\sigma_y\sqrt{1 - \rho_{xy}^2}}} \frac{1}{2\pi} e^{-\frac{1}{2}(y^2 + v^2)}\,dy\,dv.$$

Let $u = y + \dfrac{v(\sigma_x - \rho_{xy}\sigma_y)}{\sigma_y\sqrt{1 - \rho_{xy}^2}}$ and by setting $\sigma^2 = \sigma_x^2 - 2\rho_{xy}\sigma_x\sigma_y + \sigma_y^2$ we will have

$$A_1 = e^{\mu_x + \frac{1}{2}\sigma_x^2} \int_{-\infty}^{v=\frac{\mu_x + \sigma_x^2 - \log K}{\sigma_x}} \int_{-\infty}^{u=\frac{\mu_y - \mu_x - \sigma_x(\sigma_x - \rho_{xy}\sigma_y)}{\sigma_y\sqrt{1 - \rho_{xy}^2}}} f(u, v)\,du\,dv$$

such that

$$f(u, v) = \frac{1}{2\pi} e^{-\frac{1}{2}\left[u^2 - \frac{2(\sigma_x - \rho_{xy}\sigma_y)}{\sigma_y\sqrt{1 - \rho_{xy}^2}}uv + \left(1 + \frac{(\sigma_x - \rho_{xy}\sigma_y)^2}{\sigma_y^2(1 - \rho_{xy}^2)}\right)v^2 \right]}$$

$$= \frac{1}{2\pi} e^{-\frac{1}{2}\left(\frac{\sigma^2}{\sigma_y^2(1 - \rho_{xy}^2)} \right) \left[\frac{u^2}{\left(\frac{\sigma^2}{\sigma_y^2(1 - \rho_{xy}^2)} \right)} - \frac{2(\sigma_x - \rho_{xy}\sigma_y)\sigma_y\sqrt{1 - \rho_{xy}^2}}{\sigma^2}uv + v^2 \right]}.$$

By setting $\bar{u} = \dfrac{u}{\left(\dfrac{\sigma}{\sigma_y \sqrt{1 - \rho_{xy}^2}} \right)}$ and $\bar{\rho}_{xy} = \dfrac{\sigma_x - \rho_{xy}\sigma_y}{\sigma}$ we have

$$A_1 = e^{\mu_x + \frac{1}{2}\sigma_x^2} \int_{-\infty}^{v = \frac{\mu_x + \sigma_x^2 - \log K}{\sigma_x}} \int_{-\infty}^{\bar{u} = \frac{\mu_y - \mu_x - \sigma_x(\sigma_x - \rho_{xy}\sigma_y)}{\sigma}} f(\bar{u}, v) \, d\bar{u} \, dv$$

where

$$f(\bar{u}, v) = \frac{1}{2\pi} \left(\frac{\sigma}{\sigma_y \sqrt{1 - \rho_{xy}^2}} \right) e^{-\frac{1}{2}\left(\frac{\sigma}{\sigma_y \sqrt{1 - \rho_{xy}^2}} \right)^2 \left(\bar{u}^2 - \frac{2(\sigma_x - \rho_{xy}\sigma_y)}{\sigma}\bar{u}v + v^2 \right)}$$

$$= \frac{1}{2\pi \sqrt{1 - \bar{\rho}_{xy}^2}} e^{-\frac{1}{2(1 - \bar{\rho}_{xy}^2)}(\bar{u}^2 - 2\bar{\rho}_{xy}\bar{u}v + v^2)}.$$

Hence,

$$A_1 = e^{\mu_x + \frac{1}{2}\sigma_x^2} \Phi \left(\frac{\mu_x + \sigma_x^2 - \log K}{\sigma_x}, \frac{\mu_y - \mu_x - \sigma_x(\sigma_x - \rho_{xy}\sigma_y)}{\sqrt{\sigma_x^2 + \sigma_y^2 - 2\rho_{xy}\sigma_x\sigma_y}}, \frac{\sigma_x - \rho_{xy}\sigma_y}{\sqrt{\sigma_x^2 - 2\rho_{xy}\sigma_x\sigma_y + \sigma_y^2}} \right).$$

Using the same techniques as discussed above we have

$$A_2 = e^{\mu_y + \frac{1}{2}\sigma_y^2} \Phi \left(\frac{\mu_y + \sigma_y^2 - \log K}{\sigma_y}, \frac{\mu_x - \mu_y - \sigma_y(\sigma_y - \rho_{xy}\sigma_x)}{\sqrt{\sigma_x^2 - 2\rho_{xy}\sigma_x\sigma_y + \sigma_y^2}}, \frac{\sigma_y - \rho_{xy}\sigma_x}{\sqrt{\sigma_x^2 - 2\rho_{xy}\sigma_x\sigma_y + \sigma_y^2}} \right).$$

For the case

$$B_1 = K \int_{\log K}^{+\infty} \Phi \left(\frac{-z + \mu_y + \frac{\rho_{xy}\sigma_y}{\sigma_x}(z - \mu_x)}{\sigma_y \sqrt{1 - \rho_{xy}^2}} \right) f_X(z) \, dz$$

we let $w = \dfrac{z - \mu_x}{\sigma_x}$ and therefore

$$B_1 = K \int_{w=\frac{\log K - \mu_x}{\sigma_x}}^{+\infty} \Phi\left(\frac{\mu_y - \mu_x - w(\sigma_x - \rho_{xy}\sigma_y)}{\sigma_y\sqrt{1-\rho_{xy}^2}}\right) \frac{1}{\sqrt{2\pi}} e^{-\frac{1}{2}w^2} dw$$

$$= K \int_{w=\frac{\log K - \mu_x}{\sigma_x}}^{+\infty} \left(\int_{-\infty}^{y=\frac{\mu_y - \mu_x - w(\sigma_x - \rho_{xy}\sigma_y)}{\sigma_y\sqrt{1-\rho_{xy}^2}}} \frac{1}{\sqrt{2\pi}} e^{-\frac{1}{2}y^2} dy\right) \frac{1}{\sqrt{2\pi}} e^{-\frac{1}{2}w^2} dw$$

$$= K \int_{-\infty}^{w=\frac{\mu_x - \log K}{\sigma_x}} \int_{-\infty}^{y=\frac{\mu_y - \mu_x}{\sigma_y\sqrt{1-\rho_{xy}^2}} - \frac{w(\sigma_x - \rho_{xy}\sigma_y)}{\sigma_y\sqrt{1-\rho_{xy}^2}}} \frac{1}{2\pi} e^{-\frac{1}{2}\left(y^2 + w^2\right)} dy\, dw.$$

Let $u = y + \dfrac{w(\sigma_x - \rho_{xy}\sigma_y)}{\sigma_y\sqrt{1-\rho_{xy}^2}}$ and by setting $\sigma^2 = \sigma_x^2 + \sigma_y^2 - 2\rho_{xy}\sigma_x\sigma_y$ we will have

$$B_1 = K \int_{-\infty}^{w=\frac{\mu_x - \log K}{\sigma_x}} \int_{-\infty}^{u=\frac{\mu_y - \mu_x}{\sigma_y\sqrt{1-\rho_{xy}^2}}} g(u, w)\, du\, dw$$

such that

$$g(u, w) = \frac{1}{2\pi} e^{-\frac{1}{2}\left(u^2 - \frac{2(\sigma_x - \rho_{xy}\sigma_y)}{\sigma_y\sqrt{1-\rho_{xy}^2}} uw + \left(1 + \frac{(\sigma_x - \rho_{xy}\sigma_y)^2}{\sigma_y^2(1-\rho_{xy}^2)}\right)w^2\right)}$$

$$= \frac{1}{2\pi} e^{-\frac{1}{2}\left(\frac{\sigma^2}{\sigma_y^2(1-\rho_{xy}^2)}\right)\left(\frac{u^2}{\left(\frac{\sigma^2}{\sigma_y^2(1-\rho_{xy}^2)}\right)} - \frac{2(\sigma_x - \rho_{xy}\sigma_y)\sigma_y\sqrt{1-\rho_{xy}^2}}{\sigma^2} uw + w^2\right)}.$$

By setting $\bar{u} = \dfrac{u}{\left(\dfrac{\sigma}{\sigma_y\sqrt{1-\rho_{xy}^2}}\right)}$ and $\bar{\rho}_{xy} = \dfrac{\sigma_x - \rho_{xy}\sigma_y}{\sigma}$ we have

$$B_1 = K \int_{-\infty}^{w=\frac{\mu_x - \log K}{\sigma_x}} \int_{-\infty}^{\bar{u}=\frac{\mu_y - \mu_x}{\sigma}} g(\bar{u}, w)\, d\bar{u}\, dw$$

where

$$g(\bar{u}, w) = \frac{1}{2\pi} \left(\frac{\sigma}{\sigma_y \sqrt{1 - \rho_{xy}^2}} \right) e^{-\frac{1}{2} \left(\frac{\sigma}{\sigma_y \sqrt{1-\rho_{xy}^2}} \right)^2 \left(\bar{u}^2 - \frac{2(\sigma_x - \rho_{xy}\sigma_y)}{\sigma} \bar{u}w + w^2 \right)}$$

$$= \frac{1}{2\pi \sqrt{1 - \bar{\rho}_{xy}^2}} e^{-\frac{1}{2(1-\bar{\rho}_{xy}^2)}(\bar{u}^2 - 2\bar{\rho}_{xy}\bar{u}w + w^2)}.$$

Hence,

$$B_1 = K\Phi\left(\frac{\mu_x - \log K}{\sigma_x}, \frac{\mu_y - \mu_x}{\sqrt{\sigma_x^2 - 2\rho_{xy}\sigma_x\sigma_y + \sigma_y^2}}, \frac{\sigma_x - \rho_{xy}\sigma_y}{\sqrt{\sigma_x^2 - 2\rho_{xy}\sigma_x\sigma_y + \sigma_y^2}} \right).$$

In the same vein, we can also show

$$B_2 = K\Phi\left(\frac{\mu_y - \log K}{\sigma_y}, \frac{\mu_x - \mu_y}{\sqrt{\sigma_x^2 - 2\rho_{xy}\sigma_x\sigma_y + \sigma_y^2}}, \frac{\sigma_y - \rho_{xy}\sigma_x}{\sqrt{\sigma_x^2 - 2\rho_{xy}\sigma_x\sigma_y + \sigma_y^2}} \right).$$

Hence, by substituting A_1, A_2, B_1 and B_2 back to $\mathbb{E}\left[\max\left\{e^Z - K, 0\right\}\right]$ we have

$$\mathbb{E}\left[\max\left\{e^Z - K, 0\right\}\right]$$

$$= e^{\mu_x + \frac{1}{2}\sigma_x^2} \Phi\left(\frac{\mu_x + \sigma_x^2 - \log K}{\sigma_x}, \frac{\mu_y - \mu_x - \sigma_x(\sigma_x - \rho_{xy}\sigma_y)}{\sqrt{\sigma_x^2 - 2\rho_{xy}\sigma_x\sigma_y + \sigma_y^2}}, \frac{\sigma_x - \rho_{xy}\sigma_y}{\sqrt{\sigma_x^2 - 2\rho_{xy}\sigma_x\sigma_y + \sigma_y^2}} \right)$$

$$+ e^{\mu_y + \frac{1}{2}\sigma_y^2} \Phi\left(\frac{\mu_y + \sigma_y^2 - \log K}{\sigma_y}, \frac{\mu_x - \mu_y - \sigma_y(\sigma_y - \rho_{xy}\sigma_x)}{\sqrt{\sigma_x^2 - 2\rho_{xy}\sigma_x\sigma_y + \sigma_y^2}}, \frac{\sigma_y - \rho_{xy}\sigma_x}{\sqrt{\sigma_x^2 - 2\rho_{xy}\sigma_x\sigma_y + \sigma_y^2}} \right)$$

$$- K\left[\Phi\left(\frac{\mu_x - \log K}{\sigma_x}, \frac{\mu_y - \mu_x}{\sqrt{\sigma_x^2 - 2\rho_{xy}\sigma_x\sigma_y + \sigma_y^2}}, \frac{\sigma_x - \rho_{xy}\sigma_y}{\sqrt{\sigma_x^2 - 2\rho_{xy}\sigma_x\sigma_y + \sigma_y^2}} \right) \right.$$

$$\left. + \Phi\left(\frac{\mu_y - \log K}{\sigma_y}, \frac{\mu_x - \mu_y}{\sqrt{\sigma_x^2 - 2\rho_{xy}\sigma_x\sigma_y + \sigma_y^2}}, \frac{\sigma_y - \rho_{xy}\sigma_x}{\sqrt{\sigma_x^2 - 2\rho_{xy}\sigma_x\sigma_y + \sigma_y^2}} \right) \right].$$

Since $W_t^{(1)}, W_t^{(2)} \sim \mathcal{N}(0, t)$ with $\text{Cov}(W_t^{(1)}, W_t^{(2)}) = \rho t$ then by expressing

$$W_t^{(1)} = \sqrt{t} Z_1$$
$$W_t^{(2)} = \sqrt{t} \left(\rho Z_1 + \sqrt{1 - \rho^2} Z_2 \right)$$

where $Z_1, Z_2 \sim \mathcal{N}(0, 1)$ and $Z_1 \perp Z_2$, therefore for constants θ_1 and θ_2,

$$
\begin{aligned}
\mathbb{E}\left(e^{\theta W_t^{(1)} + \theta_2 W_t^{(2)}} \right) &= \mathbb{E}\left[e^{\theta_1 \sqrt{t} Z_1 + \theta_2 \sqrt{t}(\rho Z_1 + \sqrt{1 - \rho^2} Z_2)} \right] \\
&= \mathbb{E}\left[e^{(\theta_1 \sqrt{t} + \rho \theta_2 \sqrt{t})Z_1 + \theta_2 \sqrt{t(1 - \rho^2)} Z_2} \right] \\
&= \mathbb{E}\left[e^{(\theta_1 \sqrt{t} + \rho \theta_2 \sqrt{t})Z_1} \right] \cdot \mathbb{E}\left[e^{\theta_2 \sqrt{t(1 - \rho^2)} Z_2} \right] \\
&= e^{\frac{1}{2}(\theta_1 \sqrt{t} + \rho \theta_2 \sqrt{t})^2} \cdot e^{\frac{1}{2} \theta_2^2 t(1 - \rho^2)}.
\end{aligned}
$$

By setting $\theta = (\theta_1, \theta_2)^T$ and $\Sigma = \begin{bmatrix} t & \frac{1}{2}\rho t \\ \frac{1}{2}\rho t & t \end{bmatrix}$ we therefore have

$$
\begin{aligned}
\mathbb{E}\left(e^{\theta W_t^{(1)} + \theta_2 W_t^{(2)}} \right) &= e^{\frac{1}{2}\theta_1^2 t + \rho \theta_1 \theta_2 t + \frac{1}{2}\theta_2^2 t} \\
&= e^{\frac{1}{2}\theta^T \Sigma \theta}
\end{aligned}
$$

which is the moment generating function of a bivariate normal distribution. Hence, $(W_t^{(1)}, W_t^{(2)})$ follows a bivariate normal distribution.

From the definition of a rainbow call on the minimum option at time t under risk-neutral measure $\mathbb{Q}$, we have

$$C_{\min}(S_t^{(1)}, S_t^{(2)}, t; T, K) = e^{-r(T-t)} \mathbb{E}^{\mathbb{Q}}\left[\max\left\{ \min\{S_T^{(1)}, S_T^{(2)}\} - K, 0 \right\} \middle| \mathcal{F}_t \right]$$

where

$$
\begin{aligned}
dS_t^{(1)} &= (r - D_1)S_t^{(1)} dt + \sigma_1 S_t^{(1)} d\widetilde{W}_t^{(1)} \\
dS_t^{(2)} &= (r - D_2)S_t^{(2)} dt + \sigma_2 S_t^{(2)} d\widetilde{W}_t^{(2)} \\
d\widetilde{W}_t^{(1)} \cdot d\widetilde{W}_t^{(2)} &= \rho dt
\end{aligned}
$$

such that $\widetilde{W}_t^{(1)} = W_t^{(1)} + \left(\dfrac{\mu_1 - r}{\sigma_1} \right) t$ and $\widetilde{W}_t^{(2)} = W_t^{(2)} + \left(\dfrac{\mu_2 - r}{\sigma_2} \right) t$ are $\mathbb{Q}$-standard Wiener processes.

By setting $S_T^{(1)} = e^{\log S_T^{(1)}}$ and $S_T^{(2)} = e^{\log S_T^{(2)}}$ we can write

$$C_{\min}(S_t^{(1)}, S_t^{(2)}, t; K, T) = e^{-r(T-t)}\mathbb{E}^{\mathbb{Q}}\left[\max\left\{\min\left\{e^{\log S_T^{(1)}}, e^{\log S_T^{(2)}}\right\} - K, 0\right\}\bigg|\mathscr{F}_t\right]$$

$$= e^{-r(T-t)}\mathbb{E}^{\mathbb{Q}}\left[\max\left\{e^{\min\left\{\log S_T^{(1)}, \log S_T^{(2)}\right\}} - K, 0\right\}\bigg|\mathscr{F}_t\right]$$

$$= e^{-r(T-t)}\mathbb{E}^{\mathbb{Q}}\left[\max\left\{e^Z - K, 0\right\}\bigg|\mathscr{F}_t\right]$$

where $Z = \min\{X, Y\}$, $X = e^{\log S_T^{(1)}}$ and $Y = e^{\log S_T^{(2)}}$ such that $(\log S_T^{(1)}, \log S_T^{(2)})$ follows a bivariate normal distribution.

From Itō's formula we can show that

$$\log S_T^{(1)} \sim \mathcal{N}\left[\log S_t^{(1)} + \left(r - D_1 - \frac{1}{2}\sigma_1^2\right)(T-t), \sigma_1^2(T-t)\right]$$

$$\log S_T^{(2)} \sim \mathcal{N}\left[\log S_t^{(2)} + \left(r - D_2 - \frac{1}{2}\sigma_2^2\right)(T-t), \sigma_2^2(T-t)\right].$$

By setting

$$\mu_x = \log S_t^{(1)} + \left(r - D_1 - \frac{1}{2}\sigma_1^2\right)(T-t)$$

$$\sigma_x^2 = \sigma_1^2(T-t)$$

$$\mu_y = \log S_t^{(2)} + \left(r - D_2 - \frac{1}{2}\sigma_2^2\right)(T-t)$$

$$\sigma_y^2 = \sigma_2^2(T-t)$$

and after some algebraic manipulations we will have

$$e^{\mu_x + \frac{1}{2}\sigma_x^2} = S_t^{(1)}e^{(r-D_1)(T-t)}$$

$$e^{\mu_y + \frac{1}{2}\sigma_y^2} = S_t^{(2)}e^{(r-D_2)(T-t)}$$

$$\frac{\mu_x + \sigma_x^2 - \log K}{\sigma_x} = \frac{\log(S_t^{(1)}/K) + (r - D_1 + \frac{1}{2}\sigma_1^2)(T-t)}{\sigma_1\sqrt{T-t}}$$

$$\frac{\mu_y + \sigma_y^2 - \log K}{\sigma_y} = \frac{\log(S_t^{(2)}/K) + (r - D_2 + \frac{1}{2}\sigma_2^2)(T-t)}{\sigma_2\sqrt{T-t}}$$

$$\frac{\mu_y - \mu_x - \sigma_x(\sigma_x - \rho_{xy}\sigma_y)}{\sqrt{\sigma_x^2 - 2\rho_{xy}\sigma_x\sigma_y + \sigma_y^2}} = \frac{\log(S_t^{(2)}/S_t^{(1)}) + \left(D_1 - D_2 - \frac{1}{2}(\sigma_1^2 - 2\rho\sigma_1\sigma_2 + \sigma_2^2)\right)(T-t)}{\sqrt{(\sigma_1^2 - 2\rho\sigma_1\sigma_2 + \sigma_2^2)(T-t)}}$$

$$\frac{\mu_x - \mu_y - \sigma_y(\sigma_y - \rho_{xy}\sigma_x)}{\sqrt{\sigma_x^2 - 2\rho_{xy}\sigma_x\sigma_y + \sigma_y^2}} = \frac{\log(S_t^{(1)}/S_t^{(2)}) + \left(D_2 - D_1 - \frac{1}{2}(\sigma_1^2 - 2\rho\sigma_1\sigma_2 + \sigma_2^2)\right)(T-t)}{\sqrt{(\sigma_1^2 - 2\rho\sigma_1\sigma_2 + \sigma_2^2)(T-t)}}$$

$$\frac{\sigma_x - \rho_{xy}\sigma_y}{\sqrt{\sigma_x^2 - 2\rho_{xy}\sigma_x\sigma_y + \sigma_y^2}} = \frac{\sigma_1 - \rho\sigma_2}{\sqrt{(\sigma_1^2 - 2\rho\sigma_1\sigma_2 + \sigma_2^2)(T - t)}}$$

$$\frac{\sigma_y - \rho_{xy}\sigma_x}{\sqrt{\sigma_x^2 - 2\rho_{xy}\sigma_x\sigma_y + \sigma_y^2}} = \frac{\sigma_2 - \rho\sigma_1}{\sqrt{(\sigma_1^2 - 2\rho\sigma_1\sigma_2 + \sigma_2^2)(T - t)}}$$

$$\frac{\mu_x - \log K}{\sigma_x} = \frac{\log(S_t^{(1)}/K) + (r - D_1 - \frac{1}{2}\sigma_1^2)(T - t)}{\sigma_1(T - t)}$$

$$\frac{\mu_y - \log K}{\sigma_y} = \frac{\log(S_t^{(2)}/K) + (r - D_2 - \frac{1}{2}\sigma_2^2)(T - t)}{\sigma_2(T - t)}$$

$$\frac{\mu_y - \mu_x}{\sqrt{\sigma_x^2 - 2\rho_{xy}\sigma_x\sigma_y + \sigma_y^2}} = \frac{\log(S_t^{(2)}/S_t^{(1)}) + \left(D_1 - D_2 + \frac{1}{2}(\sigma_1^2 - \sigma_2^2)\right)(T - t)}{\sqrt{(\sigma_1^2 - 2\rho\sigma_1\sigma_2 + \sigma_2^2)(T - t)}}$$

$$\frac{\mu_x - \mu_y}{\sqrt{\sigma_x^2 - 2\rho_{xy}\sigma_x\sigma_y + \sigma_y^2}} = \frac{\log(S_t^{(1)}/S_t^{(2)}) + \left(D_2 - D_1 + \frac{1}{2}(\sigma_2^2 - \sigma_1^2)\right)(T - t)}{\sqrt{(\sigma_1^2 - 2\rho\sigma_1\sigma_2 + \sigma_2^2)(T - t)}}$$

By setting $\sigma = \sqrt{\sigma_1^2 - 2\rho\sigma_1\sigma_2 + \sigma_2^2}$ and substituting the above expressions into $C_{\min}(S_t^{(1)}, S_t^{(2)}, t; K, T)$, the rainbow call on the minimum option at time t, $t < T$ is therefore

$$C_{\min}(S_t^{(1)}, S_t^{(2)}, t; K, T) = S_t^{(1)}e^{-D_1(T-t)}\Phi(\alpha_+^{(1)}, \beta_+, \rho^{(1)}) + S_t^{(2)}e^{-D_2(T-t)}\Phi(\alpha_+^{(2)}, \beta_-, \rho^{(2)})$$
$$- Ke^{-r(T-t)}\Phi(\alpha_-^{(1)}, \gamma_+, \rho^{(1)}) - Ke^{-r(T-t)}\Phi(\alpha_-^{(2)}, \gamma_-, \rho^{(2)})$$

where

$$\alpha_\pm^{(1)} = \frac{\log(S_t^{(1)}/K) + (r - D_1 \pm \frac{1}{2}\sigma_1^2)(T - t)}{\sigma_1\sqrt{T - t}},$$

$$\beta_\pm = \frac{\pm\log(S_t^{(2)}/S_t^{(1)}) \pm (D_1 - D_2 \mp \frac{1}{2}\sigma^2)(T - t)}{\sigma\sqrt{T - t}},$$

$$\alpha_\pm^{(2)} = \frac{\log(S_t^{(2)}/K) + (r - D_2 \pm \frac{1}{2}\sigma_2^2)(T - t)}{\sigma_2\sqrt{T - t}},$$

$$\gamma_\pm = \frac{\pm\log(S_t^{(2)}/S_t^{(1)}) \pm (D_1 - D_2 \pm \frac{1}{2}(\sigma_1^2 - \sigma_2^2))(T - t)}{\sigma\sqrt{T - t}},$$

$$\rho^{(1)} = \frac{\sigma_1 - \rho\sigma_2}{\sigma\sqrt{T - t}},$$

$$\rho^{(2)} = \frac{\sigma_2 - \rho\sigma_1}{\sigma\sqrt{T - t}}.$$

$\square$

10. *Rainbow Option II*. Let $X \sim \mathcal{N}(\mu_x, \sigma_x^2)$ and $Y \sim \mathcal{N}(\mu_y, \sigma_y^2)$ be jointly normally distributed with correlation coefficient $\rho_{xy} \in (-1, 1)$. If $Z = \max\{X, Y\}$ show that the pdf of Z is

$$f_Z(z) = \Phi\left(\frac{z - \mu_y - \dfrac{\rho_{xy}\sigma_y}{\sigma_x}(z - \mu_x)}{\sigma_y\sqrt{1 - \rho_{xy}^2}}\right) f_X(z) + \Phi\left(\frac{z - \mu_x - \dfrac{\rho_{xy}\sigma_x}{\sigma_y}(z - \mu_y)}{\sigma_x\sqrt{1 - \rho_{xy}^2}}\right) f_Y(z)$$

where $f_X(z) = \dfrac{1}{\sigma_x\sqrt{2\pi}} e^{-\frac{1}{2}\left(\frac{z - \mu_x}{\sigma_x}\right)^2}$, $f_Y(z) = \dfrac{1}{\sigma_y\sqrt{2\pi}} e^{-\frac{1}{2}\left(\frac{z - \mu_y}{\sigma_y}\right)^2}$ and $\Phi(\cdot)$ denotes the cdf of a standard normal.

Hence, show that

$$\mathbb{E}\left[\max\left\{e^Z - K, 0\right\}\right]$$

$$= e^{\mu_x + \frac{1}{2}\sigma_x^2} \Phi\left(\frac{\mu_x + \sigma_x^2 - \log K}{\sigma_x}, \frac{-\mu_y + \mu_x + \sigma_x(\sigma_x - \rho_{xy}\sigma_y)}{\sqrt{\sigma_x^2 - 2\rho_{xy}\sigma_x\sigma_y + \sigma_y^2}}, \frac{-\sigma_x + \rho_{xy}\sigma_y}{\sqrt{\sigma_x^2 - 2\rho_{xy}\sigma_x\sigma_y + \sigma_y^2}}\right)$$

$$+ e^{\mu_y + \frac{1}{2}\sigma_y^2} \Phi\left(\frac{\mu_y + \sigma_y^2 - \log K}{\sigma_y}, \frac{-\mu_x + \mu_y + \sigma_y(\sigma_y - \rho_{xy}\sigma_x)}{\sqrt{\sigma_x^2 - 2\rho_{xy}\sigma_x\sigma_y + \sigma_y^2}}, \frac{-\sigma_y + \rho_{xy}\sigma_x}{\sqrt{\sigma_x^2 - 2\rho_{xy}\sigma_x\sigma_y + \sigma_y^2}}\right)$$

$$- K\left[\Phi\left(\frac{\mu_x - \log K}{\sigma_x}, \frac{-\mu_y + \mu_x}{\sqrt{\sigma_x^2 - 2\rho_{xy}\sigma_x\sigma_y + \sigma_y^2}}, \frac{-\sigma_x + \rho_{xy}\sigma_y}{\sqrt{\sigma_x^2 - 2\rho_{xy}\sigma_x\sigma_y + \sigma_y^2}}\right)\right.$$

$$\left. + \Phi\left(\frac{\mu_y - \log K}{\sigma_y}, \frac{-\mu_x + \mu_y}{\sqrt{\sigma_x^2 - 2\rho_{xy}\sigma_x\sigma_y + \sigma_y^2}}, \frac{-\sigma_y + \rho_{xy}\sigma_x}{\sqrt{\sigma_x^2 - 2\rho_{xy}\sigma_x\sigma_y + \sigma_y^2}}\right)\right]$$

where $K > 0$, $\mathbb{E}$ denotes the expectation with respect to the e^Z distribution and Φ denotes the cumulative standard bivariate normal distribution function given as

$$\Phi(u, v, \rho_{uv}) = \int_{-\infty}^{u} \int_{-\infty}^{v} \frac{1}{2\pi\sqrt{1 - \rho_{uv}^2}} e^{-\frac{1}{2(1 - \rho_{uv}^2)}(x^2 - 2\rho_{uv}xy + y^2)}\, dy\, dx$$

where $\rho_{uv} \in (-1, 1)$.

Let the asset prices $S_t^{(1)}$ and $S_t^{(2)}$ have the following diffusion processes

$$dS_t^{(1)} = (\mu_1 - D_1)S_t^{(1)}dt + \sigma_1 S_t^{(1)}dW_t^{(1)}$$
$$dS_t^{(2)} = (\mu_2 - D_2)S_t^{(2)}dt + \sigma_2 S_t^{(2)}dW_t^{(2)}$$
$$dW_t^{(1)} \cdot dW_t^{(2)} = \rho dt$$

where $\{W_t^{(1)} : t \geq 0\}$ and $\{W_t^{(2)} : t \geq 0\}$ are $\mathbb{P}$-standard Wiener processes on the probability space $(\Omega, \mathcal{F}, \mathbb{P})$, μ_1 and μ_2 are the drift parameters, D_1 and D_2 are the continuous dividend yields, σ_1 and σ_2 are the volatilities, $\rho \in (-1, 1)$ is the correlation coefficient and let r be the risk-free interest rate from a money-market account.

Show that $(W_t^{(1)}, W_t^{(2)})$ follows a bivariate normal distribution.

Given the payoff of a rainbow call on the maximum option is defined as

$$\Psi(S_T^{(1)}, S_T^{(2)}) = \max \left\{ \max\{S_T^{(1)}, S_T^{(2)}\} - K, 0 \right\}$$

where $K > 0$ is the strike price, $T \geq t$ is the option expiry time, using the above results find the rainbow call on the maximum option price at time t under the risk-neutral measure $\mathbb{Q}$.

Solution: The first part of the results follows from Problem 1.2.2.15 of *Problems and Solutions in Mathematical Finance, Volume 1: Stochastic Calculus.*

Following Problem 6.2.1.9 (page 558), it can easily be shown that for $K > 0$

$$\mathbb{E}\left[\max\left\{e^Z - K, 0\right\}\right]$$

$$= e^{\mu_x + \frac{1}{2}\sigma_x^2}\Phi\left(\frac{\mu_x + \sigma_x^2 - \log K}{\sigma_x}, \frac{-\mu_y + \mu_x + \sigma_x(\sigma_x - \rho_{xy}\sigma_y)}{\sqrt{\sigma_x^2 - 2\rho_{xy}\sigma_x\sigma_y + \sigma_y^2}}, \frac{-\sigma_x + \rho_{xy}\sigma_y}{\sqrt{\sigma_x^2 - 2\rho_{xy}\sigma_x\sigma_y + \sigma_y^2}}\right)$$

$$+ e^{\mu_y + \frac{1}{2}\sigma_y^2}\Phi\left(\frac{\mu_y + \sigma_y^2 - \log K}{\sigma_y}, \frac{-\mu_x + \mu_y + \sigma_y(\sigma_y - \rho_{xy}\sigma_x)}{\sqrt{\sigma_x^2 - 2\rho_{xy}\sigma_x\sigma_y + \sigma_y^2}}, \frac{-\sigma_y + \rho_{xy}\sigma_x}{\sqrt{\sigma_x^2 - 2\rho_{xy}\sigma_x\sigma_y + \sigma_y^2}}\right)$$

$$- K\left[\Phi\left(\frac{\mu_x - \log K}{\sigma_x}, \frac{-\mu_y + \mu_x}{\sqrt{\sigma_x^2 - 2\rho_{xy}\sigma_x\sigma_y + \sigma_y^2}}, \frac{-\sigma_x + \rho_{xy}\sigma_y}{\sqrt{\sigma_x^2 - 2\rho_{xy}\sigma_x\sigma_y + \sigma_y^2}}\right)\right.$$

$$\left. + \Phi\left(\frac{\mu_y - \log K}{\sigma_y}, \frac{-\mu_x + \mu_y}{\sqrt{\sigma_x^2 - 2\rho_{xy}\sigma_x\sigma_y + \sigma_y^2}}, \frac{-\sigma_y + \rho_{xy}\sigma_x}{\sqrt{\sigma_x^2 - 2\rho_{xy}\sigma_x\sigma_y + \sigma_y^2}}\right)\right].$$

To show that $(W_t^{(1)}, W_t^{(2)})$ follows a bivariate normal distribution, see Problem 6.2.1.9 (page 558).

The rainbow call on the maximum option at time t under the risk-neutral measure $\mathbb{Q}$ is defined as

$$C_{\max}(S_t^{(1)}, S_t^{(2)}, t; K, T) = e^{-r(T-t)}\mathbb{E}^{\mathbb{Q}}\left[\max\left\{\max\{S_T^{(1)}, S_T^{(2)}\} - K, 0\right\}\Big|\mathcal{F}_t\right]$$

where

$$dS_t^{(1)} = (r - D_1)S_t^{(1)}dt + \sigma_1 S_t^{(1)} d\widetilde{W}_t^{(1)}$$
$$dS_t^{(2)} = (r - D_2)S_t^{(2)}dt + \sigma_2 S_t^{(2)} d\widetilde{W}_t^{(2)}$$
$$d\widetilde{W}_t^{(1)} \cdot d\widetilde{W}_t^{(2)} = \rho dt$$

such that $\widetilde{W}_t^{(1)} = W_t^{(1)} + \left(\dfrac{\mu_1 - r}{\sigma_1}\right)t$ and $\widetilde{W}_t^{(2)} = W_t^{(2)} + \left(\dfrac{\mu_2 - r}{\sigma_2}\right)t$ are $\mathbb{Q}$-standard Wiener processes.

By setting $S_T^{(1)} = e^{\log S_T^{(1)}}$ and $S_T^{(2)} = e^{\log S_T^{(2)}}$ we can write

$$C_{\max}(S_t^{(1)}, S_t^{(2)}, t; K, T) = e^{-r(T-t)}\mathbb{E}^{\mathbb{Q}}\left[\max\left\{\max\left\{e^{\log S_T^{(1)}}, e^{\log S_T^{(2)}}\right\} - K, 0\right\}\Big|\mathcal{F}_t\right]$$

$$= e^{-r(T-t)}\mathbb{E}^{\mathbb{Q}}\left[\max\left\{e^{\max\left\{\log S_T^{(1)}, \log S_T^{(2)}\right\}} - K, 0\right\}\Big|\mathcal{F}_t\right]$$

$$= e^{-r(T-t)}\mathbb{E}^{\mathbb{Q}}\left[\max\left\{e^Z - K, 0\right\}\Big|\mathcal{F}_t\right]$$

where $Z = \max\{X, Y\}$, $X = e^{\log S_T^{(1)}}$ and $Y = e^{\log S_T^{(2)}}$ such that $(\log S_T^{(1)}, \log S_T^{(2)})$ follows a bivariate normal distribution.

From Itō's formula we can easily show that

$$\log S_T^{(1)} \sim \mathcal{N}\left[\log S_t^{(1)} + \left(r - D_1 - \frac{1}{2}\sigma_1^2\right)(T - t), \sigma_1^2(T - t)\right]$$
$$\log S_T^{(2)} \sim \mathcal{N}\left[\log S_t^{(2)} + \left(r - D_2 - \frac{1}{2}\sigma_2^2\right)(T - t), \sigma_2^2(T - t)\right].$$

By setting

$$\mu_x = \log S_t^{(1)} + \left(r - D_1 - \frac{1}{2}\sigma_1^2\right)(T - t)$$
$$\sigma_x^2 = \sigma_1^2(T - t)$$
$$\mu_y = \log S_t^{(2)} + \left(r - D_2 - \frac{1}{2}\sigma_2^2\right)(T - t)$$
$$\sigma_y^2 = \sigma_2^2(T - t)$$

and after some algebraic manipulations we have

$$e^{\mu_x + \frac{1}{2}\sigma_x^2} = S_t^{(1)} e^{(r-D_1)(T-t)}$$

$$e^{\mu_y + \frac{1}{2}\sigma_y^2} = S_t^{(2)} e^{(r-D_2)(T-t)}$$

$$\frac{\mu_x + \sigma_x^2 - \log K}{\sigma_x} = \frac{\log(S_t^{(1)}/K) + (r - D_1 + \frac{1}{2}\sigma_1^2)(T-t)}{\sigma_1\sqrt{T-t}}$$

$$\frac{\mu_y + \sigma_y^2 - \log K}{\sigma_y} = \frac{\log(S_t^{(2)}/K) + (r - D_2 + \frac{1}{2}\sigma_2^2)(T-t)}{\sigma_2\sqrt{T-t}}$$

$$\frac{-\mu_y + \mu_x + \sigma_x(\sigma_x - \rho_{xy}\sigma_y)}{\sqrt{\sigma_x^2 - 2\rho_{xy}\sigma_x\sigma_y + \sigma_y^2}} = \frac{\log(S_t^{(1)}/S_t^{(2)}) - \left(D_1 - D_2 - \frac{1}{2}(\sigma_1^2 - 2\rho\sigma_1\sigma_2 + \sigma_2^2)\right)(T-t)}{\sqrt{(\sigma_1^2 - 2\rho\sigma_1\sigma_2 + \sigma_2^2)(T-t)}}$$

$$\frac{-\mu_x + \mu_y + \sigma_y(\sigma_y - \rho_{xy}\sigma_x)}{\sqrt{\sigma_x^2 - 2\rho_{xy}\sigma_x\sigma_y + \sigma_y^2}} = \frac{\log(S_t^{(2)}/S_t^{(1)}) - \left(D_2 - D_1 - \frac{1}{2}(\sigma_1^2 - 2\rho\sigma_1\sigma_2 + \sigma_2^2)\right)(T-t)}{\sqrt{(\sigma_1^2 - 2\rho\sigma_1\sigma_2 + \sigma_2^2)(T-t)}}$$

$$\frac{-\sigma_x + \rho_{xy}\sigma_y}{\sqrt{\sigma_x^2 - 2\rho_{xy}\sigma_x\sigma_y + \sigma_y^2}} = \frac{-\sigma_1 + \rho\sigma_2}{\sqrt{(\sigma_1^2 - 2\rho\sigma_1\sigma_2 + \sigma_2^2)(T-t)}}$$

$$\frac{-\sigma_y + \rho_{xy}\sigma_x}{\sqrt{\sigma_x^2 - 2\rho_{xy}\sigma_x\sigma_y + \sigma_y^2}} = \frac{-\sigma_2 + \rho\sigma_1}{\sqrt{(\sigma_1^2 - 2\rho\sigma_1\sigma_2 + \sigma_2^2)(T-t)}}$$

$$\frac{\mu_x - \log K}{\sigma_x} = \frac{\log(S_t^{(1)}/K) + (r - D_1 - \frac{1}{2}\sigma_1^2)(T-t)}{\sigma_1(T-t)}$$

$$\frac{\mu_y - \log K}{\sigma_y} = \frac{\log(S_t^{(2)}/K) + (r - D_2 - \frac{1}{2}\sigma_2^2)(T-t)}{\sigma_2(T-t)}$$

$$\frac{-\mu_y + \mu_x}{\sqrt{\sigma_x^2 - 2\rho_{xy}\sigma_x\sigma_y + \sigma_y^2}} = \frac{\log(S_t^{(1)}/S_t^{(2)}) - \left(D_1 - D_2 + \frac{1}{2}(\sigma_1^2 - \sigma_2^2)\right)(T-t)}{\sqrt{(\sigma_1^2 - 2\rho\sigma_1\sigma_2 + \sigma_2^2)(T-t)}}$$

$$\frac{-\mu_x + \mu_y}{\sqrt{\sigma_x^2 - 2\rho_{xy}\sigma_x\sigma_y + \sigma_y^2}} = \frac{\log(S_t^{(2)}/S_t^{(1)}) - \left(D_2 - D_1 + \frac{1}{2}(\sigma_2^2 - \sigma_1^2)\right)(T-t)}{\sqrt{(\sigma_1^2 - 2\rho\sigma_1\sigma_2 + \sigma_2^2)(T-t)}}.$$

By setting $\sigma = \sqrt{\sigma_1^2 - 2\rho\sigma_1\sigma_2 + \sigma_2^2}$ and substituting the above expressions into the option price $C_{\max}(S_t^{(1)}, S_t^{(2)}, t; K, T)$, the rainbow call on the maximum option at time t is therefore

$$
\begin{aligned}
C_{\max}(S_t^{(1)}, S_t^{(2)}, t; K, T) = {} & S_t^{(1)} e^{-D_1(T-t)} \Phi(\alpha_+^{(1)}, -\beta_+, -\rho^{(1)}) \\
& + S_t^{(2)} e^{-D_2(T-t)} \Phi(\alpha_+^{(2)}, -\beta_-, -\rho^{(2)}) \\
& - K e^{-r(T-t)} \Phi(\alpha_-^{(1)}, -\gamma_+, -\rho^{(1)}) \\
& - K e^{-r(T-t)} \Phi(\alpha_-^{(2)}, -\gamma_-, -\rho^{(2)})
\end{aligned}
$$

where

$$
\alpha_\pm^{(1)} = \frac{\log(S_t^{(1)}/K) + (r - D_1 \pm \frac{1}{2}\sigma_1^2)(T-t)}{\sigma_1\sqrt{T-t}}
$$

$$
\beta_\pm = \frac{\pm\log(S_t^{(2)}/S_t^{(1)}) \pm (D_1 - D_2 \mp \frac{1}{2}\sigma^2)(T-t)}{\sigma\sqrt{T-t}}
$$

$$
\alpha_\pm^{(2)} = \frac{\log(S_t^{(2)}/K) + (r - D_2 \pm \frac{1}{2}\sigma_2^2)(T-t)}{\sigma_2\sqrt{T-t}}
$$

$$
\gamma_\pm = \frac{\pm\log(S_t^{(2)}/S_t^{(1)}) \pm (D_1 - D_2 \pm \frac{1}{2}(\sigma_1^2 - \sigma_2^2))(T-t)}{\sigma\sqrt{T-t}}
$$

$$
\rho^{(1)} = \frac{\sigma_1 - \rho\sigma_2}{\sigma\sqrt{T-t}}
$$

$$
\rho^{(2)} = \frac{\sigma_2 - \rho\sigma_1}{\sigma\sqrt{T-t}}.
$$

$\square$

11. *Black–Scholes Equation for Cross-Currency Option.* Let $(\Omega, \mathcal{F}, \mathbb{P})$ be a probability space and let $\{W_t^s : t \geq 0\}$ and $\{W_t^x : t \geq 0\}$ be $\mathbb{P}$-standard Wiener processes such that $dW_t^s \cdot dW_t^x = \rho dt$, $\rho \in (-1, 1)$. Suppose that S_t denotes the asset price quoted in foreign currency having the following SDE

$$
\frac{dS_t}{S_t} = (\mu_s - D_s)\,dt + \sigma_s dW_t^s
$$

where μ_s is the drift parameter, D_s is the continuous dividend yield, σ_s is the volatility parameter and let r_f denote the foreign risk-free interest rate. Let X_t be the foreign-to-domestic exchange rate having the SDE

$$
\frac{dX_t}{X_t} = \mu_x dt + \sigma_x dW_t^x
$$

where μ_x is the exchange rate drift, σ_x is the exchange rate volatility parameter and let r_d be the domestic risk-free interest rate. Here, $X_t S_t$ is the foreign asset price quoted in domestic currency.

By considering a hedging portfolio involving a cross-currency option $V(S_t, X_t, t)$ denoted in domestic currency that can only be exercised at expiry time T, $t \leq T$, with asset price $X_t S_t$ and exchange rate X_t, show that $V(S_t, X_t, t)$ satisfies the two-dimensional PDE

$$\frac{\partial V}{\partial t} + \frac{1}{2}\sigma_s^2 S_t^2 \frac{\partial^2 V}{\partial S_t^2} + \frac{1}{2}\sigma_x^2 X_t^2 \frac{\partial^2 V}{\partial X_t^2} + \rho\sigma_x\sigma_s X_t S_t \frac{\partial^2 V}{\partial X_t \partial S_t}$$

$$+ (r_f - D_s - \rho\sigma_x\sigma_s)S_t \frac{\partial V}{\partial S_t} + (r_d - r_f)X_t \frac{\partial V}{\partial X_t} - r_d V(S_t, X_t, t) = 0.$$

Solution: To eliminate both asset risk and exchange rate risk, at time t we let the value of a portfolio Π_t be

$$\Pi_t = V(S_t, X_t, t) - \Delta_1(X_t S_t) - \Delta_2 X_t$$

where it involves buying one unit of cross-currency option $V(S_t, X_t, t)$, selling Δ_1 units of foreign assets $X_t S_t$ converted into domestic currency and selling Δ_2 units of X_t. Since we receive $D_s S_t dt$ for every asset held, and because we hold $-\Delta_1 X_t S_t$, our portfolio changes by an amount $-\Delta D_s X_t S_t dt$. In addition, given that X_t will also grow at the foreign risk-free rate r_f, the change in portfolio Π_t is

$$d\Pi_t = dV - \Delta_1(d(X_t S_t) + D_s X_t S_t dt) - \Delta_2(dX_t + r_f X_t dt)$$
$$= dV - \Delta_1(S_t dX_t + X_t dS_t + \rho\sigma_x\sigma_s X_t S_t dt + D_s X_t S_t dt)$$
$$- \Delta_2(dX_t + r_f X_t dt)$$

where $d(X_t S_t) = S_t dX_t + X_t dS_t + dX_t dS_t$ and from Itō's lemma we can write $dX_t dS_t = \rho\sigma_x\sigma_s X_t S_t dt$.

Expanding $V(S_t, X_t, t)$ using Taylor's theorem

$$dV = \frac{\partial V}{\partial t}dt + \frac{\partial V}{\partial S_t}dS_t + \frac{\partial V}{\partial X_t}dX_t$$

$$+ \frac{1}{2}\left[\frac{\partial^2 V}{\partial S_t^2}(dS_t)^2 + \frac{\partial^2 V}{\partial X_t^2}(dX_t)^2 + 2\frac{\partial^2 V}{\partial X_t \partial S_t}(dX_t dS_t)\right] + \ldots$$

and by substituting $dS_t = (\mu_s - D_s)S_t dt + \sigma_s S_t dW_t^s$, $dX_t = \mu_x X_t dt + \sigma_x X_t dW_t^x$ and subsequently applying Itō's lemma we have

$$dV = \left[\frac{\partial V}{\partial t} + \frac{1}{2}\sigma_s^2 S_t^2 \frac{\partial^2 V}{\partial S_t^2} + \frac{1}{2}\sigma_x^2 X_t^2 \frac{\partial^2 V}{\partial X_t^2} + \rho\sigma_x\sigma_s X_t S_t \frac{\partial^2 V}{\partial X_t \partial S_t}\right.$$

$$\left. + (\mu_s - D_s)S_t \frac{\partial V}{\partial S_t} + \mu_x X_t \frac{\partial V}{\partial X_t}\right]dt + \sigma_s S_t \frac{\partial V}{\partial S_t}dW_t^s + \sigma_x X_t \frac{\partial V}{\partial X_t}dW_t^x.$$

Substituting back into $d\Pi_t$ and rearranging terms, we have

$$d\Pi_t = \left[\frac{\partial V}{\partial t} + \frac{1}{2}\sigma_s^2 S_t^2 \frac{\partial^2 V}{\partial S_t^2} + +\frac{1}{2}\sigma_x^2 X_t^2 \frac{\partial^2 V}{\partial X_t^2} + \rho\sigma_x\sigma_s X_t S_t \frac{\partial^2 V}{\partial X_t \partial S_t}\right.$$
$$+(\mu_s - D_s)S_t\frac{\partial V}{\partial S_t} + \mu_x X_t \frac{\partial V}{\partial X_t} - \Delta_1(\mu_x + \mu_s + \rho\sigma_x\sigma_s)X_t S_t$$
$$\left. -\Delta_2(\mu_x + r_f)X_t\right]dt + \sigma_s\left(\frac{\partial V}{\partial S_t} - \Delta_1 X_t\right)S_t dW_t^s$$
$$+\sigma_x\left(\frac{\partial V}{\partial X_t} - \Delta_1 S_t - \Delta_2\right)X_t dW_t^x.$$

To eliminate the dW_t^s and dW_t^x terms we have

$$\Delta_1 = \frac{1}{X_t}\frac{\partial V}{\partial S_t} \text{ and } \Delta_2 = \frac{1}{X_t}\left(X_t\frac{\partial V}{\partial X_t} - S_t\frac{\partial V}{\partial S_t}\right)$$

which leads to

$$d\Pi_t = \left[\frac{\partial V}{\partial t} + \frac{1}{2}\sigma_s^2 S_t^2 \frac{\partial^2 V}{\partial S_t^2} + \frac{1}{2}\sigma_x^2 X_t^2 \frac{\partial^2 V}{\partial X_t^2} + \rho\sigma_x\sigma_s X_t S_t \frac{\partial^2 V}{\partial X_t \partial S_t}\right.$$
$$\left. +(r_f - D_s - \rho\sigma_x\sigma_s)S_t\frac{\partial V}{\partial S_t} - r_f X_t \frac{\partial V}{\partial X_t}\right]dt.$$

Under the no-arbitrage condition the return on the amount Π_t invested in a risk-free interest rate in domestic currency would see a growth of

$$d\Pi_t = r_d\Pi_t dt$$
$$= r_d[V(S_t, X_t, t) - \Delta_1(X_t S_t) - \Delta_2 X_t]dt$$
$$= r_d\left[V(S_t, X_t, t) - X_t\frac{\partial V}{\partial X_t}\right]dt$$

and hence we have

$$r_d\Pi_t dt = \left[\frac{\partial V}{\partial t} + \frac{1}{2}\sigma_s^2 S_t^2 \frac{\partial^2 V}{\partial S_t^2} + \frac{1}{2}\sigma_x^2 X_t^2 \frac{\partial^2 V}{\partial X_t^2}\right.$$
$$+\rho\sigma_x\sigma_s X_t S_t \frac{\partial^2 V}{\partial X_t \partial S_t} + (r_f - D_s - \rho\sigma_x\sigma_s)S_t\frac{\partial V}{\partial S_t}$$
$$\left. -r_f X_t\frac{\partial V}{\partial X_t}\right]dt$$

$$r_d\left[V(S_t, X_t, t) - X_t\frac{\partial V}{\partial X_t}\right]dt = \left[\frac{\partial V}{\partial t} + \frac{1}{2}\sigma_s^2 S_t^2 \frac{\partial^2 V}{\partial S_t^2} + \frac{1}{2}\sigma_x^2 X_t^2 \frac{\partial^2 V}{\partial X_t^2}\right.$$
$$+\rho\sigma_x\sigma_s X_t S_t \frac{\partial^2 V}{\partial X_t \partial S_t} + (r_f - D_s - \rho\sigma_x\sigma_s)S_t\frac{\partial V}{\partial S_t}$$
$$\left. -r_f X_t\frac{\partial V}{\partial X_t}\right]dt$$

and finally

$$\frac{\partial V}{\partial t} + \frac{1}{2}\sigma_s^2 S_t^2 \frac{\partial^2 V}{\partial S_t^2} + \frac{1}{2}\sigma_x^2 X_t^2 \frac{\partial^2 V}{\partial X_t^2} + \rho\sigma_x\sigma_s X_t S_t \frac{\partial^2 V}{\partial X_t \partial S_t}$$

$$+(r_f - D_s - \rho\sigma_x\sigma_s)S_t \frac{\partial V}{\partial S_t} + (r_d - r_f)X_t \frac{\partial V}{\partial X_t} - r_d V(S_t, X_t, t) = 0$$

which is a two-dimensional PDE.

$\square$

12. *Cross-Currency Option (PDE Approach).* Let $(\Omega, \mathcal{F}, \mathbb{P})$ be a probability space and let $\{W_t^s : t \geq 0\}$ and $\{W_t^x : t \geq 0\}$ be $\mathbb{P}$-standard Wiener processes. Let S_t and X_t denote the asset price quoted in foreign currency and the foreign-to-domestic exchange rate respectively each having the following SDEs

$$\frac{dS_t}{S_t} = (\mu_s - D_s)dt + \sigma_s dW_t^s$$

$$\frac{dX_t}{X_t} = \mu_x dt + \sigma_x dW_t^x$$

$$dW_t^s \cdot dW_t^x = \rho dt, \quad \rho \in (-1, 1)$$

where μ_s is the asset drift parameter, D_s is the asset continuous dividend yield, σ_s is the asset volatility parameter, μ_x is exchange rate drift, σ_x is the exchange rate volatility parameter and let r_f be the foreign risk-free interest rate and r_d be the domestic risk-free interest rate.

For a strike price $K > 0$ and expiry time T, let $C(S_t, X_t, t; K, T)$ be the European-style call option price at time $t \leq T$ denoted in domestic currency satisfying the two-dimensional partial differential equation

$$\frac{\partial C}{\partial t} + \frac{1}{2}\sigma_s^2 S_t^2 \frac{\partial^2 C}{\partial S_t^2} + \frac{1}{2}\sigma_x^2 X_t^2 \frac{\partial^2 C}{\partial X_t^2} + \rho\sigma_x\sigma_s X_t S_t \frac{\partial^2 C}{\partial X_t \partial S_t}$$

$$+(r_f - D_s - \rho\sigma_x\sigma_s)S_t \frac{\partial C}{\partial S_t} + (r_d - r_f)X_t \frac{\partial C}{\partial X_t} - r_d C(S_t, X_t, t; K, T) = 0.$$

Using the above partial differentiation equation find the call option price at time $t \leq T$ for each of the payoffs at expiry time T:

(a) A Foreign Equity Option Converted to Domestic Currency

$$\Psi(S_T, X_T) = X_T \max\{S_T - K_s, 0\}$$

(b) A Foreign Equity Option Struck in Domestic Currency (or Compo Option)

$$\Psi(S_T, X_T) = \max\{X_T S_T - \hat{K}, 0\}$$

(c) A Foreign Equity Option Struck in Pre-Determined Domestic Currency (or Quanto Option)

$$\Psi(S_T, X_T) = \overline{X} \max\{S_T - K_s, 0\}$$

(d) An FX Option Denoted in Domestic Currency

$$\Psi(S_T, X_T) = S_T \max\{X_T - K_x, 0\}$$

where at expiry time T, S_T is the asset price in foreign currency, X_T is the foreign-to-domestic exchange rate, K_s is the strike price in foreign currency, $\hat{K}$ is the strike price in domestic currency, K_x is the strike price on the exchange rate and $\overline{X}$ is some pre-determined fixed exchange rate.

Solution:
(a) For the payoff $\Psi(S_T, X_T) = X_T \max\{S_T - K_s, 0\}$ we can set

$$C(S_t, X_t, t; K_s, T) = X_t f(S_t, t)$$

where $f(S_T, T) = \max\{S_T - K_s, 0\}$. With a change of variables we have

$$\frac{\partial C}{\partial t} = X_t \frac{\partial f}{\partial t}; \quad \frac{\partial C}{\partial S_t} = X_t \frac{\partial f}{\partial S_t}; \quad \frac{\partial C}{\partial X_t} = f(S_t, t)$$

$$\frac{\partial^2 C}{\partial S_t^2} = X_t \frac{\partial^2 f}{\partial S_t^2}; \quad \frac{\partial^2 C}{\partial X_t^2} = 0; \quad \frac{\partial^2 C}{\partial X_t \partial S_t} = \frac{\partial f}{\partial S_t}$$

and by substituting the above results into the two-dimensional partial differential equation we have

$$X_t \frac{\partial f}{\partial t} + \frac{1}{2}\sigma_s^2 S_t^2 X_t \frac{\partial^2 f}{\partial S_t^2} + \rho \sigma_x \sigma_s X_t S_t \frac{\partial f}{\partial S_t} + (r_f - D_s - \rho \sigma_x \sigma_s) X_t S_t \frac{\partial f}{\partial S_t}$$
$$+ (r_d - r_f) X_t f(S_t, t) - r_d X_t f(S_t, t) = 0$$

or

$$\frac{\partial f}{\partial t} + \frac{1}{2}\sigma_s^2 S_t^2 \frac{\partial^2 f}{\partial S_t^2} + (r_f - D_s) S_t \frac{\partial f}{\partial S_t} - r_f f(S_t, t) = 0$$

which is a Black–Scholes equation with volatility σ_s, foreign risk-free interest rate r_f and continuous dividend yield D_s. Given that $f(S_T, T) = \max\{S_T - K_s, 0\}$ is a European call option payoff therefore we can deduce that

$$f(S_t, t) = S_t e^{-D_s(T-t)} \Phi(d_+) - K_s e^{-r_f(T-t)} \Phi(d_-)$$

where $d_\pm = \dfrac{\log(S_t/K_s) + (r_f - D_s \pm \frac{1}{2}\sigma_s^2)(T-t)}{\sigma_s \sqrt{T-t}}$ and $\Phi(\cdot)$ is the cumulative distribution function of a standard normal. Hence, the call option price at time t is

$$C(S_t, X_t, t; K_s, T) = X_t \left[S_t e^{-D_s(T-t)} \Phi(d_+) - K_s e^{-r_f(T-t)} \Phi(d_-) \right].$$

(b) For payoff $\Psi(S_T, X_T) = \max\{X_T S_T - \hat{K}, 0\}$ we define $\hat{S}_t = X_t S_t$ and we consider the option price at time t as

$$C(S_t, X_t, t; \hat{K}, T) = g(\hat{S}_t, t)$$

where $g(\hat{S}_T, T) = \max\{X_T S_T - \hat{K}, 0\}$. From the change of variables we can write

$$\frac{\partial C}{\partial t} = \frac{\partial g}{\partial t}; \quad \frac{\partial C}{\partial S_t} = \frac{\partial g}{\partial \hat{S}_t}\frac{\partial \hat{S}_t}{\partial S_t} = X_t\frac{\partial g}{\partial \hat{S}_t}; \quad \frac{\partial C}{\partial X_t} = \frac{\partial g}{\partial \hat{S}_t}\frac{\partial \hat{S}_t}{\partial X_t} = S_t\frac{\partial g}{\partial \hat{S}_t}$$

$$\frac{\partial^2 C}{\partial S_t^2} = \frac{\partial}{\partial S_t}\left(X_t\frac{\partial g}{\partial \hat{S}_t}\right) = X_t\frac{\partial^2 g}{\partial \hat{S}_t^2}\frac{\partial \hat{S}_t}{\partial S_t} = X_t^2\frac{\partial^2 g}{\partial \hat{S}_t^2};$$

$$\frac{\partial^2 C}{\partial X_t^2} = \frac{\partial}{\partial X_t}\left(S_t\frac{\partial g}{\partial \hat{S}_t}\right) = S_t\frac{\partial^2 g}{\partial \hat{S}_t^2}\frac{\partial \hat{S}}{\partial X_t} = S_t^2\frac{\partial^2 g}{\partial \hat{S}_t^2}$$

$$\frac{\partial^2 C}{\partial X_t \partial S_t} = \frac{\partial}{\partial X_t}\left(X_t\frac{\partial g}{\partial \hat{S}_t}\right) = \frac{\partial g}{\partial \hat{S}_t} + X_t\frac{\partial^2 g}{\partial \hat{S}_t^2}\frac{\partial \hat{S}_t}{\partial X_t} = \frac{\partial g}{\partial \hat{S}_t} + X_t S_t\frac{\partial^2 g}{\partial \hat{S}_t^2}.$$

By substituting the above results into the two-dimensional partial differentiation equation we have

$$\frac{\partial g}{\partial t} + \frac{1}{2}\sigma_s^2(X_t S_t)^2\frac{\partial^2 g}{\partial \hat{S}_t^2} + \frac{1}{2}\sigma_x^2(X_t S_t)^2\frac{\partial^2 g}{\partial \hat{S}_t^2} + \rho\sigma_x\sigma_s(X_t S_t)^2\frac{\partial^2 g}{\partial \hat{S}_t^2}$$

$$+ (r_f - D_s - \rho\sigma_x\sigma_s)X_t S_t\frac{\partial g}{\partial \hat{S}_t} + \rho\sigma_x\sigma_s X_t S_t\frac{\partial g}{\partial \hat{S}_t} + (r_d - r_f)X_t S_t\frac{\partial g}{\partial \hat{S}_t}$$

$$- r_d g(\hat{S}_t, t) = 0$$

or

$$\frac{\partial g}{\partial t} + \frac{1}{2}(\sigma_x^2 + 2\rho\sigma_x\sigma_s + \sigma_s^2)\hat{S}_t^2\frac{\partial^2 g}{\partial \hat{S}_t^2} + (r_d - D_s)\hat{S}_t\frac{\partial g}{\partial \hat{S}_t} - r_d g(\hat{S}_t, t) = 0$$

which is a Black–Scholes equation with volatility $\sigma_g = \sqrt{\sigma_x^2 + 2\rho\sigma_x\sigma_s + \sigma_s^2}$, domestic risk-free interest rate r_d and continuous dividend yield D_s. Since

$$C(S_T, X_T, T; K_x, T) = g(\hat{S}_T, T) = \max\{\hat{S}_T - \hat{K}, 0\}$$

is the payoff of a European call option therefore the call option at time t is

$$C(S_t, X_t, t; \hat{K}, T) = \hat{S}_t e^{-D_s(T-t)} \Phi(d_+) - \hat{K} e^{-r_d(T-t)} \Phi(d_-)$$
$$= X_t S_t e^{-D_s(T-t)} \Phi(d_+) - \hat{K} e^{-r_d(T-t)} \Phi(d_-)$$

where $d_\pm = \dfrac{\log((X_t S_t)/\hat{K}) + (r_d - D_s \pm \frac{1}{2}\sigma_g^2)(T-t)}{\sigma_g \sqrt{T-t}}$ and $\Phi(\cdot)$ is the cumulative distribution function of a standard normal.

(c) For the payoff $\Psi(S_T, X_T) = \overline{X} \max\{S_T - K_s, 0\}$ we can write

$$C(S_t, X_t, t; K_s, T) = \overline{X} h(S_t, t)$$

such that $h(S_T, T) = \max\{S_T - K_s, 0\}$. Hence, we can express

$$\frac{\partial C}{\partial t} = \overline{X}\frac{\partial h}{\partial t}; \quad \frac{\partial C}{\partial S_t} = \overline{X}\frac{\partial h}{\partial S_t}; \quad \frac{\partial C}{\partial X_t} = 0$$
$$\frac{\partial^2 C}{\partial S_t^2} = \overline{X}\frac{\partial^2 C}{\partial S_t^2}; \quad \frac{\partial^2 C}{\partial X_t^2} = 0; \quad \frac{\partial^2 C}{\partial X_t \partial S_t} = 0.$$

By substituting the above expressions into the two-dimensional partial differentiation equation we have

$$\overline{X}\frac{\partial h}{\partial t} + \frac{1}{2}\sigma_s^2 S_t^2 \overline{X}\frac{\partial^2 h}{\partial S_t^2} + (r_f - D_s - \rho\sigma_x\sigma_s)S_t\overline{X}\frac{\partial h}{\partial S_t} - r_d\overline{X}h(S_t, t) = 0$$

or

$$\frac{\partial h}{\partial t} + \frac{1}{2}\sigma_s^2 S_t^2 \frac{\partial^2 h}{\partial S_t^2} + (r_f - D_s - \rho\sigma_x\sigma_s)S_t\frac{\partial h}{\partial S_t} - r_d h(S_t, t) = 0$$

which is a Black–Scholes equation with volatility σ_s, domestic risk-free interest rate r_d and continuous dividend yield $D_h = r_d - r_f + D_s + \rho\sigma_x\sigma_s$. Given that

$$h(S_T, T) = \max\{S_T - K_s, 0\}$$

is a European call option payoff therefore we can deduce that

$$h(S_t, t) = S_t e^{-D_h(T-t)} \Phi(d_+) - K_s e^{-r_d(T-t)} \Phi(d_-)$$

where $d_\pm = \dfrac{\log(S_t/K_s) + (r_d - D_h \pm \frac{1}{2}\sigma_s^2)(T-t)}{\sigma_s \sqrt{T-t}}$ and $\Phi(\cdot)$ is the cumulative distribution function of a standard normal. Hence, the call option price at time t is

$$C(S_t, X_t, t; K_s, T) = \overline{X}\left[S_t e^{-D_h(T-t)} \Phi(d_+) - K_s e^{-r_d(T-t)} \Phi(d_-) \right].$$

(d) For payoff $\Psi(S_T, X_T) = S_T \max\{X_T - K_x, 0\}$ we can define

$$C(S_t, X_t, t; K_x, T) = S_t u(X_t, t)$$

where $u(X_T, T) = \max\{X_T - K_x, 0\}$. From the change of variables we can set

$$\frac{\partial C}{\partial t} = S_t \frac{\partial u}{\partial t}; \quad \frac{\partial C}{\partial S_t} = u(X_t, t), \quad \frac{\partial C}{\partial X_t} = S_t \frac{\partial u}{\partial X_t}$$

$$\frac{\partial^2 C}{\partial S_t^2} = 0; \quad \frac{\partial^2 C}{\partial X_t^2} = S_t \frac{\partial^2 u}{\partial X_t^2}, \quad \frac{\partial^2 u}{\partial X_t \partial S_t} = \frac{\partial u}{\partial X_t}.$$

By substituting the above results into the two-dimensional partial differentiation equation we have

$$S_t \frac{\partial u}{\partial t} + \frac{1}{2} \sigma_x^2 X_t^2 S_t \frac{\partial^2 u}{\partial X_t^2} + \rho \sigma_x \sigma_s X_t S_t \frac{\partial u}{\partial X_t} + (r_f - D_s - \rho \sigma_x \sigma_s) S_t u(X_t, t)$$

$$+ (r_d - r_f) X_t S_t \frac{\partial u}{\partial X_t} - r_d S_t u(X_t, t) = 0$$

or

$$\frac{\partial u}{\partial t} + \frac{1}{2} \sigma_x^2 X_t^2 \frac{\partial^2 u}{\partial X_t^2} + (r_d - r_f + \rho \sigma_x \sigma_s) \frac{\partial u}{\partial X_t} - (r_d - r_f + D_s + \rho \sigma_x \sigma_s) u(X_t, t) = 0$$

which is a Black–Scholes equation with volatility σ_x, risk-free interest rate $r_u = r_d - r_f + D_s + \rho \sigma_x \sigma_s$ and continuous dividend yield D_s. Since

$$u(X_T, T) = \max\{X_T - K_x, 0\}$$

is the payoff of a European call option therefore

$$u(X_t, t) = X_t e^{-D_s(T-t)} \Phi(d_+) - K_x e^{-r_u(T-t)} \Phi(d_-)$$

where $d_\pm = \dfrac{\log(X_t/K_x) + (r_u - D_s \pm \frac{1}{2}\sigma_x^2)(T-t)}{\sigma_x \sqrt{T-t}}$ and $\Phi(\cdot)$ is the cumulative distribution function of a standard normal. Hence, the call option price at time t is

$$C(S_t, X_t, t; K_x, T) = S_t \left[X_t e^{-D_s(T-t)} \Phi(d_+) - K_x e^{-r_u(T-t)} \Phi(d_-) \right].$$

□

13. *Cross-Currency Option (Probabilistic Approach).* Let $(\Omega, \mathcal{F}, \mathbb{P})$ be a probability space and let $\{W_t^s : t \geq 0\}$ and $\{W_t^x : t \geq 0\}$ be $\mathbb{P}$-standard Wiener processes. Let S_t and X_t

denote the asset price quoted in foreign currency and the foreign-to-domestic exchange rate respectively each having the following SDEs

$$\frac{dS_t}{S_t} = (\mu_s - D_s)dt + \sigma_s dW_t^s$$

$$\frac{dX_t}{X_t} = \mu_x dt + \sigma_x dW_t^x$$

$$dW_t^s \cdot dW_t^x = \rho dt, \quad \rho \in (-1, 1)$$

where μ_s is the asset drift parameter, D_s is the asset continuous dividend yield, σ_s is the asset volatility parameter, μ_x is exchange rate drift, σ_x is the exchange rate volatility parameter and let r_f be the foreign risk-free interest rate and r_d be the domestic risk-free interest rate.

Show that under the domestic risk-neutral measure $\mathbb{Q}_d$, the diffusion processes for the exchange rate X_t, asset price denominated in foreign currency S_t, asset price denominated in domestic currency $X_t S_t$ are

$$\frac{dX_t}{X_t} = (r_d - r_f)dt + \sigma_x dW_t^{x_d}$$

$$\frac{dS_t}{S_t} = (r_f - \rho\sigma_x\sigma_s - D_s)dt + \sigma_s dW_t^{s_d}$$

$$\frac{d(X_t S_t)}{X_t S_t} = (r_d - D_s)dt + \sqrt{\sigma_x^2 + 2\rho\sigma_x\sigma_s + \sigma_s^2}\,dW_t^{x s_d}$$

where $W_t^{x_d}$, $W_t^{s_d}$ and $W_t^{x s_d}$ are $\mathbb{Q}_d$-standard Wiener processes.

Find the call option price at time $t \leq T$ for each of the payoffs (denominated in domestic currency) at expiry time T:

(a) A Foreign Equity Option Converted to Domestic Currency

$$\Psi(S_T, X_T) = X_T \max\{S_T - K_s, 0\}$$

(b) A Foreign Equity Option Struck in Domestic Currency (or Compo Option)

$$\Psi(S_T, X_T) = \max\{X_T S_T - \hat{K}, 0\}$$

(c) A Foreign Equity Option Struck in Pre-Determined Domestic Currency (or Quanto Option)

$$\Psi(S_T, X_T) = \overline{X} \max\{S_T - K_s, 0\}$$

(d) An FX Option Denoted in Domestic Currency

$$\Psi(S_T, X_T) = S_T \max\{X_T - K_x, 0\}$$

where S_T is the asset price in foreign currency, X_T is the foreign-to-domestic exchange rate, K_s is the strike price in foreign currency, $\hat{K}$ is the strike price in domestic currency, K_x is the strike price on the exchange rate and $\overline{X}$ is some pre-determined fixed exchange rate.

Solution: To show the diffusion processes of X_t and $X_t S_t$ under the domestic risk-neutral measure $\mathbb{Q}_d$ see Problems 4.2.3.15 and 4.2.3.17 of *Problems and Solutions of Mathematical Finance, Volume 1: Stochastic Calculus.*

For the case of asset price, let the diffusion process of S_t under $\mathbb{Q}_d$-measure be

$$\frac{dS_t}{S_t} = \mu_s^d dt + \sigma_s dW_t^{Sd}$$

where μ_s^d is the drift and W_t^{Sd} is the $\mathbb{Q}_d$-standard Wiener process.

Since under the $\mathbb{Q}_d$ measure

$$\frac{dX_t}{X_t} = (r_d - r_f)dt + \sigma_x dW_t^{Xd}$$

$$\frac{d(X_t S_t)}{X_t S_t} = (r_d - D_s)dt + \sqrt{\sigma_x^2 + 2\rho\sigma_x\sigma_s + \sigma_s^2}\, dW_t^{XSd}$$

where W_t^{Xd} and W_t^{XSd} are $\mathbb{Q}_d$-standard Wiener processes, then from Itō's lemma,

$$
\begin{aligned}
d(X_t S_t) &= X_t dS_t + S_t dX_t + (dX_t)(dS_t) \\
&= \mu_s^d X_t S_t dt + \sigma_s X_t S_t dW_t^{Sd} \\
&\quad + (r_d - r_f)X_t S_t dt + \sigma_x X_t S_t dW_t^{Xd} + \rho\sigma_x\sigma_s dt \\
&= (\mu_s^d + r_d - r_f + \rho\sigma_x\sigma_s)X_t S_t dt + \sqrt{\sigma_x^2 + 2\rho\sigma_x\sigma_s + \sigma_s^2}\, X_t S_t dW_t^{XSd}
\end{aligned}
$$

where $W_t^{XSd} = \dfrac{\sigma_x W_t^{Xd} + \sigma_s W_t^{Sd}}{\sqrt{\sigma_x^2 + 2\rho\sigma_x\sigma_s + \sigma_s^2}}$ is a $\mathbb{Q}_d$-standard Wiener process.

Hence, by comparing with

$$\frac{d(X_t S_t)}{X_t S_t} = (r_d - D_s)dt + \sqrt{\sigma_x^2 + 2\rho\sigma_x\sigma_s + \sigma_s^2}\, dW_t^{XSd}$$

we can deduce

$$\mu_s^d = r_f - \rho\sigma_x\sigma_s - D_s.$$

Thus, under the domestic risk-neutral measure $\mathbb{Q}_d$

$$\frac{dS_t}{S_t} = (r_f - \rho\sigma_x\sigma_s - D_s)dt + \sigma_s dW_t^{Sd}.$$

Denoting $\Phi(\cdot)$ as the cumulative distribution function of a standard normal we note:
(a) For the payoff $\Psi(S_T, X_T) = X_T \max\{S_T - K_s, 0\}$, and since we can write

$$X_T = X_t e^{(r_d - r_f - \frac{1}{2}\sigma_x^2)(T-t) + \sigma_x W_{T-t}^{Xd}}$$

the call option price at time t is

$$
\begin{aligned}
&C(S_t, X_t, t; K_s, T) \\
&= e^{-r_d(T-t)} \mathbb{E}^{\mathbb{Q}_d} \left[X_T \max\{ S_T - K_s, 0 \} \middle| \mathscr{F}_t \right] \\
&= e^{-r_d(T-t)} \mathbb{E}^{\mathbb{Q}_d} \left[X_t e^{(r_d - r_f - \frac{1}{2}\sigma_x^2)(T-t) + \sigma_x W_{T-t}^{x_d}} \max\{ S_T - K_s, 0 \} \middle| \mathscr{F}_t \right] \\
&= X_t e^{-r_f(T-t)} \mathbb{E}^{\mathbb{Q}_d} \left[e^{-\frac{1}{2}\sigma_x^2(T-t) + \sigma_x W_{T-t}^{x_d}} \max\{ S_T - K_s, 0 \} \middle| \mathscr{F}_t \right].
\end{aligned}
$$

We define a new probability measure $\widetilde{\mathbb{Q}}$ on the filtration $\mathscr{F}_s$, $0 \le s \le t$ where we set the Radon–Nikodým derivative as

$$
\left. \frac{d\widetilde{\mathbb{Q}}}{d\mathbb{Q}_d} \right|_{\mathscr{F}_t} = e^{-\int_0^t (-\sigma_x) dW_u^{x_d} - \frac{1}{2}\int_0^t (-\sigma_x)^2 du}
$$

where the process $\widetilde{W}_t^x = W_t^{x_d} - \sigma_x t$ follows a $\widetilde{\mathbb{Q}}$-standard Wiener process.
    Since we can also write

$$
W_t^{x_d} = \rho W_t^{s_d} + \sqrt{1 - \rho^2} Y_t^d
$$

where $W_t^{s_d}$ and Y_t^d are $\mathbb{Q}_d$-standard Wiener processes and $W_t^{s_d} \perp\!\!\!\perp Y_t^d$, the Radon–Nikodým derivative can be expressed as

$$
\begin{aligned}
\left. \frac{d\widetilde{\mathbb{Q}}}{d\mathbb{Q}_d} \right|_{\mathscr{F}_t} &= e^{-\int_0^t (-\sigma_x) dW_u^{x_d} - \frac{1}{2}\int_0^t (-\sigma_x)^2 du} \\
&= e^{-\int_0^t (-\sigma_x)(\rho dW_t^{s_d} + \sqrt{1-\rho^2} dY_t^d) - \frac{1}{2}\int_0^t (-\sigma_x)^2 du} \\
&= e^{-\int_0^t (-\rho\sigma_x) dW_u^{s_d} - \frac{1}{2}\int_0^t (-\rho\sigma_x)^2 du} \cdot e^{-\int_0^t (-\sqrt{1-\rho^2}\sigma_x) dY_u^d - \frac{1}{2}\int_0^t (-\sqrt{1-\rho^2}\sigma_x)^2 du}
\end{aligned}
$$

such that from the two-dimension Girsanov's theorem

$$
\widetilde{W}_t^s = W_t^{s_d} - \rho\sigma_x t
$$

and

$$
\widetilde{Y}_t = Y_t^d - \sqrt{1 - \rho^2}\,\sigma_x t
$$

are $\widetilde{\mathbb{Q}}$-standard Wiener process and $\widetilde{W}_t^s \perp\!\!\!\perp \widetilde{Y}_t$.
    Thus, under the $\widetilde{\mathbb{Q}}$-measure, the call option price is

$$
V(S_t, X_t, t; K_s, T) = X_t e^{-r_f(T-t)} \mathbb{E}^{\widetilde{\mathbb{Q}}} \left[\max\{ S_T - K_s, 0 \} \middle| \mathscr{F}_t \right]
$$

with the dynamics of S_t under the $\widetilde{\mathbb{Q}}$-measure being

$$\frac{dS_t}{S_t} = (r_f - \rho\sigma_x\sigma_s - D_s)dt + \sigma_s dW_t^{S_d}$$

$$= (r_f - \rho\sigma_x\sigma_s - D_s)dt + \sigma_s \left(d\widetilde{W}_t^s + \rho\sigma_x dt\right)$$

$$= (r_f - D_s)dt + \sigma_s d\widetilde{W}_t^s.$$

Hence, the call option price at time $t \leq T$ is

$$C(S_t, X_t, t; K_s, T) = X_t e^{-r_f(T-t)} \mathbb{E}^{\widetilde{\mathbb{Q}}} \left[\max\{S_T - K_s, 0\}\big| \mathcal{F}_t\right]$$

$$= X_t \left[S_t e^{-D_s(T-t)}\Phi(d_+) - K_s e^{-r_f(T-t)}\Phi(d_-)\right]$$

where

$$d_{\pm} = \frac{\log(S_t/K_s) + (r_f - D_s \pm \frac{1}{2}\sigma_s^2)(T-t)}{\sigma_s\sqrt{T-t}}.$$

(b) For the payoff $\Psi(S_T, X_T) = \max\{X_T S_T - \hat{K}, 0\}$ which is denominated in domestic currency, we note that the diffusion process $X_t S_t$ under the $\mathbb{Q}_d$ measure is

$$\frac{d(X_t S_t)}{X_t S_t} = (r_d - D_s)dt + \sqrt{\sigma_x^2 + 2\rho\sigma_x\sigma_s + \sigma_s^2}dW_t^{XS_d}$$

where $W_t^{XS_d}$ is a $\mathbb{Q}_d$-standard Wiener process.

Thus, the call option price of the foreign equity option struck in domestic currency can be easily deduced as

$$C(S_t, X_t, t; \hat{K}, T) = e^{-r_d(T-t)} \mathbb{E}^{\mathbb{Q}_d} \left[\max\left\{X_T S_T - \hat{K}, 0\right\}\Big| \mathcal{F}_t\right]$$

$$= X_t S_t e^{-D_s(T-t)}\Phi(d_+) - \hat{K}e^{-r_d(T-t)}\Phi(d_-)$$

where

$$d_{\pm} = \frac{\log((X_t S_t)/\hat{K}) + (r_d - D_s \pm \frac{1}{2}(\sigma_x^2 + 2\rho\sigma_x\sigma_s + \sigma_s^2))(T-t)}{\sqrt{(\sigma_x^2 + 2\rho\sigma_x\sigma_s + \sigma_s^2)(T-t)}}.$$

(c) For the quanto option payoff $\Psi(S_T, X_T) = \overline{X}\max\{S_T - K_s, 0\}$, under the domestic risk-neutral measure $\mathbb{Q}_d$, S_t follows

$$\frac{dS_t}{S_t} = (r_f - \rho\sigma_x\sigma_s - D_s)dt + \sigma_s dW_t^{S_d}$$

or

$$\frac{dS_t}{S_t} = (r_d - (r_d - r_f + \rho\sigma_x\sigma_s + D_s))dt + \sigma_s dW_t^{Sd}$$

$$= (r_d - \overline{D}_s)dt + \sigma_s dW_t^{Sd}$$

where $\overline{D}_s = r_d - r_f + \rho\sigma_x\sigma_s + D_s$ and W_t^{Sd} is a $\mathbb{Q}_d$-standard Wiener process.

Because $\overline{X}$ is a fixed exchange rate, the call option price at time t can be deduced as

$$C(S_t, X_t, t; K_s, T) = \overline{X}e^{-r_d(T-t)}\mathbb{E}^{\mathbb{Q}_d}\left[\max\{S_T - K_s, 0\}\big|\,\mathscr{F}_t\right]$$

$$= \overline{X}\left[S_t e^{-\overline{D}_s(T-t)}\Phi(d_+) - K_s e^{-r_d(T-t)}\Phi(d_-)\right]$$

where

$$d_\pm = \frac{\log(S_t/K_s) + (r_d - \overline{D}_s \pm \frac{1}{2}\sigma_s^2)(T-t)}{\sigma_s\sqrt{T-t}}.$$

(d) For the terminal payoff $\Psi(S_T, X_T) = S_T \max\{X_T - K_x, 0\}$ which is denominated in the domestic currency, under the domestic risk-neutral measure $\mathbb{Q}_d$, S_t follows

$$\frac{dS_t}{S_t} = (r_f - \rho\sigma_x\sigma_s - D_s)dt + \sigma_s dW_t^{Sd}$$

where W_t^{Sd} is the $\mathbb{Q}_d$-standard Wiener process.

Thus, by solving the SDE for S_t we can write

$$S_T = S_t e^{(r_f - \rho\sigma_x\sigma_s - D_s - \frac{1}{2}\sigma_x^2)(T-t) + \sigma_s W_{T-t}^{Sd}}$$

and the call option price at time t is

$$C(S_t, X_t, t; K_x, T)$$

$$= e^{-r_d(T-t)}\mathbb{E}^{\mathbb{Q}_d}\left[S_T \max\{X_T - K_x, 0\}\big|\,\mathscr{F}_t\right]$$

$$= e^{-r_d(T-t)}\mathbb{E}^{\mathbb{Q}_d}\left[S_t e^{(r_f - \rho\sigma_x\sigma_s - D_s - \frac{1}{2}\sigma_x^2)(T-t) + \sigma_s W_{T-t}^{Sd}}\max\{X_T - K_x, 0\}\big|\,\mathscr{F}_t\right]$$

$$= S_t e^{-\overline{r}(T-t)}\mathbb{E}^{\mathbb{Q}_d}\left[e^{-\frac{1}{2}\sigma_s^2(T-t) + \sigma_s W_{T-t}^{Sd}}\max\{X_T - K_x, 0\}\big|\,\mathscr{F}_t\right].$$

where $\overline{r} = r_d - r_f + \rho\sigma_x\sigma_s + D_s$.

We define a new probability measure $\overline{\mathbb{Q}}$ on the filtration $\mathscr{F}_s, 0 \leq s \leq t$ where we set the Radon–Nikodým derivative as

$$\left.\frac{d\overline{\mathbb{Q}}}{d\mathbb{Q}_d}\right|_{\mathscr{F}_t} = e^{-\int_0^t (-\sigma_s)dW_u^{Sd} - \frac{1}{2}\int_0^t (-\sigma_s)^2 du}$$

where the process $\overline{W}_t^s = W_t^{Sd} - \sigma_s t$ follows a $\overline{\mathbb{Q}}$-standard Wiener process.

Since we can also write

$$W_t^{Sd} = \rho W_t^{Xd} + \sqrt{1-\rho^2} Z_t^d$$

where W_t^{Xd} and Z_t^d are $\mathbb{Q}_d$-standard Wiener processes and $W_t^{Xd} \perp Z_t^d$, the Radon–Nikodým derivative can be expressed as

$$\left.\frac{d\overline{\mathbb{Q}}}{d\mathbb{Q}_d}\right|_{\mathscr{F}_t} = e^{-\int_0^t (-\sigma_s)dW_u^{Sd} - \frac{1}{2}\int_0^t (-\sigma_s)^2 du}$$

$$= e^{-\int_0^t (-\sigma_s)(\rho dW_t^{Xd} + \sqrt{1-\rho^2}dZ_t^d) - \frac{1}{2}\int_0^t (-\sigma_s)^2 du}$$

$$= e^{-\int_0^t (-\rho\sigma_s)dW_u^{Xd} - \frac{1}{2}\int_0^t (-\rho\sigma_s)^2 du} \cdot e^{-\int_0^t (-\sqrt{1-\rho^2}\sigma_s)dZ_u^d - \frac{1}{2}\int_0^t (-\sqrt{1-\rho^2}\sigma_s)^2 du}$$

such that from the two-dimension Girsanov's theorem

$$\overline{W}_t^x = W_t^{Xd} - \rho\sigma_s t$$

and

$$\overline{Z}_t = Z_t^d - \sqrt{1-\rho^2}\sigma_s t$$

are $\overline{\mathbb{Q}}$-standard Wiener process and $\overline{W}_t^x \perp \overline{Z}_t$.

Thus, under the $\overline{\mathbb{Q}}$-measure, the call option price is

$$V(S_t, X_t, t; K_x, T) = S_t e^{-\bar{r}(T-t)} \mathbb{E}^{\overline{\mathbb{Q}}}\left[\max\{X_T - K_x, 0\} \mid \mathscr{F}_t\right]$$

with the dynamics of X_t under the $\overline{\mathbb{Q}}$-measure being

$$\frac{dX_t}{X_t} = (r_d - r_f)dt + \sigma_x dW_t^{Xd}$$

$$= (r_d - r_f)dt + \sigma_x \left(d\overline{W}_t^x + \rho\sigma_s dt\right)$$

$$= (r_d - r_f + \rho\sigma_x\sigma_s)dt + \sigma_x d\overline{W}_t^x$$

$$= (\bar{r} - D_s)dt + \sigma_x d\overline{W}_t^x.$$

Hence, the call option price at time $t \leq T$ is

$$C(S_t, X_t, t; K_x, T) = S_t e^{-\bar{r}(T-t)} \mathbb{E}^{\overline{\mathbb{Q}}} \left[\max\{X_T - K_x, 0\} \,\middle|\, \mathscr{F}_t \right]$$

$$= S_t \left[X_t e^{-D_s(T-t)} \Phi(d_+) - K_x e^{-\bar{r}(T-t)} \Phi(d_-) \right]$$

where

$$d_\pm = \frac{\log(X_t/K_x) + (\bar{r} - D_s \pm \frac{1}{2}\sigma_x^2)(T-t)}{\sigma_x \sqrt{T-t}}$$

N.B. For terminal payoffs in (a) and (d), we can also express them as exchange option payoffs and the solutions follow from applying the formula given in Problem 6.2.1.6 (page 543).

$\square$

6.2.2 Path-Dependent Options

1. *Forward Start Option.* Let $\{W_t : t \geq 0\}$ be a $\mathbb{P}$-standard Wiener process on the probability space $(\Omega, \mathscr{F}, \mathbb{P})$ and let the asset price S_t follow a GBM with the following SDE

$$\frac{dS_t}{S_t} = (\mu - D)dt + \sigma dW_t$$

where μ is the drift parameter, D is the continuous dividend yield and σ is the volatility parameter. In addition, we let r be the risk-free interest rate.

A forward start call option gives the holder the right to buy at time T_1 an at-the-money European call option with an expiry date of $T_2 > T_1$, where the strike price K is set as $K = S_{T_1}$. Hence, the payoff of this option at T_2 is

$$\Psi(S_{T_1}, S_{T_2}) = \max\{S_{T_2} - S_{T_1}, 0\}.$$

By considering $T_1 < t \leq T_2, t = T_1$ and $t < T_1$, show that the forward call option price is

$$C_{fs}(S_t, t; T_1, T_2) = \begin{cases} S_t e^{-D(T-t)} \left[e^{-D(T_2-T_1)} \Phi(\bar{d}_+) - e^{-r(T_2-T_1)} \Phi(\bar{d}_-) \right] & t \leq T_1 \\[2mm] S_t e^{-D(T_2-t)} \Phi(d_+) - S_{T_1} e^{-r(T_2-t)} \Phi(d_-) & T_1 < t \leq T_2 \end{cases}$$

where $\displaystyle \bar{d}_\pm = \frac{(r - D \pm \frac{1}{2}\sigma^2)(T_2 - T_1)}{\sigma\sqrt{T_2 - T_1}}$, $\displaystyle d_\pm = \frac{\log(S_t/S_{T_1}) + (r - D \pm \frac{1}{2}\sigma^2)(T_2 - t)}{\sigma\sqrt{T_2 - t}}$ and $\Phi(\cdot)$ is the cdf of a standard normal.

Solution: From Girsanov's theorem, under the risk-neutral measure $\mathbb{Q}$

$$\frac{dS_t}{S_t} = (r - D)dt + \sigma dW_t^{\mathbb{Q}}$$

where $W_t^{\mathbb{Q}} = W_t + \left(\dfrac{\mu - r}{\sigma}\right)t$ is a $\mathbb{Q}$-standard Wiener process.

For $T_1 < t \leq T_2$, as S_{T_1} is known then

$$C_{fs}\left(S_t, t; T_1, T_2\right) = e^{-r(T_2-t)}\mathbb{E}^{\mathbb{Q}}\left[\max\{S_{T_2} - S_{T_1}, 0\}\middle|\mathscr{F}_t\right]$$
$$= C_{bs}(S_t, t; S_{T_1}, T_2)$$
$$= S_t e^{-D(T_2-t)}\Phi(d_+) - S_{T_1}e^{-r(T_2-t)}\Phi(d_-)$$

which is a regular European call option price $C_{bs}(S_t, t; K, T_2)$ with strike price $K = S_{T_1}$
at expiry time T_2 such that $d_\pm = \dfrac{\log(S_t/S_{T_1}) + (r - D \pm \frac{1}{2}\sigma^2)(T_2 - t)}{\sigma\sqrt{T_2 - t}}$.

At $t = T_1$, $S_t = S_{T_1}$ and therefore

$$C_{fs}(S_t, t; T_1, T_2) = C_{bs}(S_{T_1}, T_1; S_{T_1}, T_2)$$
$$= S_{T_1}e^{-D(T_2-T_1)}\Phi(\bar{d}_+) - S_{T_1}e^{-r(T_2-T_1)}\Phi(\bar{d}_-)$$
$$= S_{T_1}\left[e^{-D(T_2-T_1)}\Phi(\bar{d}_+) - e^{-r(T_2-T_1)}\Phi(\bar{d}_-)\right]$$

where

$$\bar{d}_\pm = \frac{\log(S_{T_1}/S_{T_1}) + (r - D \pm \frac{1}{2}\sigma^2)(T_2 - T_1)}{\sigma\sqrt{T_2 - T_1}} = \frac{(r - D \pm \frac{1}{2}\sigma^2)(T_2 - T_1)}{\sigma\sqrt{T_2 - T_1}}.$$

Finally, for $t < T_1$

$$C_{fs}(S_t, t; T_1, T_2) = e^{-r(T_1-t)}\mathbb{E}^{\mathbb{Q}}\left[C_{fs}(S_{T_1}, T_1; T_1, T_2)\middle|\mathscr{F}_t\right]$$
$$= e^{-r(T_1-t)}\mathbb{E}^{\mathbb{Q}}\left[S_{T_1}\left[e^{-D(T_2-T_1)}\Phi(\bar{d}_+) - e^{-r(T_2-T_1)}\Phi(\bar{d}_-)\right]\middle|\mathscr{F}_t\right]$$
$$= e^{-r(T_1-t)}\left[e^{-D(T_2-T_1)}\Phi(\bar{d}_+) - e^{-r(T_2-T_1)}\Phi(\bar{d}_-)\right]\mathbb{E}^{\mathbb{Q}}\left[S_{T_1}\middle|\mathscr{F}_t\right]$$

since $\bar{d}_+$ and $\bar{d}_-$ do not depend on S_{T_1}. From Itō's lemma

$$S_{T_1} = S_t e^{(r-D-\frac{1}{2}\sigma^2)(T_1-t)+\sigma W^{\mathbb{Q}}_{T_1-t}}$$

therefore

$$\mathbb{E}^{\mathbb{Q}}[S_{T_1}|\mathscr{F}_t] = S_t e^{(r-D)(T_1-t)}$$

and hence

$$C_{fs}(S_t, t; T_1, T_2) = S_t e^{-D(T_1-t)}\left[e^{-D(T_2-T_1)}\Phi(\bar{d}_+) - e^{-r(T_2-T_1)}\Phi(\bar{d}_-)\right].$$

Collectively, we therefore have

$$C_{fs}(S_t, t; T_1, T_2)$$
$$= \begin{cases} S_t e^{-D(T-t)} \left[e^{-D(T_2-T_1)} \Phi(\bar{d}_+) - e^{-r(T_2-T_1)} \Phi(\bar{d}_-) \right] & t \leq T_1 \\ S_t e^{-D(T_2-t)} \Phi(d_+) - S_{T_1} e^{-r(T_2-t)} \Phi(d_-) & T_1 < t \leq T_2. \end{cases}$$

N.B. Using similar arguments we can also show the forward start put option as

$$P_{fs}(S_t, t; T_1, T_2)$$
$$= \begin{cases} S_t e^{-D(T-t)} \left[e^{-r(T_2-T_1)} \Phi(-\bar{d}_-) - e^{-D(T_2-T_1)} \Phi(-\bar{d}_+) \right] & t \leq T_1 \\ S_{T_1} e^{-r(T_2-t)} \Phi(-d_-) - S_t e^{-D(T_2-t)} \Phi(-d_+) & T_1 < t \leq T_2. \end{cases}$$

$\square$

2. *Rachet/Cliquet Option.* Let $\{W_t : t \geq 0\}$ be a $\mathbb{P}$-standard Wiener process on the probability space $(\Omega, \mathscr{F}, \mathbb{P})$ and let the asset price S_t follow the following SDE

$$\frac{dS_t}{S_t} = (\mu - D)dt + \sigma dW_t$$

where μ is the drift parameter, D is the continuous dividend yield and σ is the volatility parameter. In addition, let r be the risk-free interest rate from a money-market account.

A rachet or cliquet option is a series of forward start options where at the end of a typical leg, from T_{i-1} to T_i the option allows the holder to "lock in" intermediate profits

$$\max\{S_{T_i} - K_{i-1}, 0\} = \max\{S_{T_i} - S_{T_{i-1}}, 0\}$$

which will be paid out at expiry time T where the strike K_{i-1} is reset to the asset price $S_{T_{i-1}}$ at time $T_{i-1}, T_{i-1} < T_i$.

We consider a 3-leg rachet call option with initial strike K_0 at time T_0. At time $T_1 > T_0$ the strike is reset to $K_1 = S_{T_1}$, which is the asset price at time T_1. At time $T_2 > T_1$ the strike is reset again to $K_2 = S_{T_2}$, which is the asset price at time T_2. Finally, at the option expiry time $T > T_2$ the holder of the call rachet will receive the call payoff with strike $K_2 = S_{T_2}$ and "locked-in" amounts of $\max\{S_{T_1} - K_0, 0\}$ and $\{S_{T_2} - K_1, 0\}$.

From the above information
(a) Write down the overall payoff $\Psi(S_T)$ noting that the strike is being reset to the spot price at each reset date.
(b) By working back from the expiry, determine the option price $C_{ra}(S_t, t; K_0, T_1, T_2, T)$ under the risk-neutral measure $\mathbb{Q}$, for $T_0 < t \leq T_1, T_1 < t \leq T_2$ and $T_2 < t \leq T$.

Solution:
(a) The overall payoff at expiry time T is given as

$$\Psi(S_T) = \max\{S_T - K_2, 0\} + \max\{K_2 - K_1, 0\} + \max\{K_1 - K_0, 0\}$$
$$= \max\{S_T - S_{T_2}, 0\} + \max\{S_{T_2} - S_{T_1}, 0\} + \max\{S_{T_1} - K_0, 0\}.$$

(b) Under the risk-neutral measure $\mathbb{Q}$, the asset price S_t follows

$$\frac{dS_t}{S_t} = (r - D)dt + \sigma dW_t^{\mathbb{Q}}$$

where r is the risk-free interest rate and $W_t^{\mathbb{Q}} = W_t + \left(\frac{\mu - r}{\sigma}\right)t$ is the $\mathbb{Q}$-standard Wiener process.

For $T_2 < t \leq T$, under the filtration $\mathcal{F}_t$ the information at T_1 and T_2 is known, therefore we can write the option price as

$$
\begin{aligned}
C_{ra}\left(S_t, t; K_0, T_1, T_2, T\right) &= e^{-r(T-t)}\mathbb{E}^{\mathbb{Q}}\left[\Psi(S_T)\middle|\mathcal{F}_t\right] \\
&= e^{-r(T-t)}\mathbb{E}^{\mathbb{Q}}\left[\max\{S_T - S_{T_2}, 0\}\middle|\mathcal{F}_t\right] \\
&\quad + e^{-r(T-t)}\mathbb{E}^{\mathbb{Q}}\left[\max\{S_{T_2} - S_{T_1}, 0\}\middle|\mathcal{F}_t\right] \\
&\quad + e^{-r(T-t)}\mathbb{E}^{\mathbb{Q}}\left[\max\{S_{T_1} - K_0, 0\}\middle|\mathcal{F}_t\right] \\
&= C_{bs}(S_t, t; S_{T_2}, T) + e^{-r(T-t)}\max\{S_{T_2} - S_{T_1}, 0\} \\
&\quad + e^{-r(T-t)}\max\{S_{T_1} - K_0, 0\}
\end{aligned}
$$

where $C_{bs}(S_t, t; S_{T_2}, T)$ is the European call option price with strike S_{T_2} and expiry time T.

For $T_1 < t \leq T_2$, under the filtration $\mathcal{F}_t$ the information up to T_1 is known, therefore we can write the payoff as

$$
\begin{aligned}
\Psi(S_{T_2}) &= C_{ra}(S_{T_2}, T_2; K_0, T_1, T_2, T) \\
&= C_{bs}(S_{T_2}, T_2; S_{T_2}, T) + e^{-r(T-T_2)}\max\{S_{T_2} - S_{T_1}, 0\} \\
&\quad + e^{-r(T-T_2)}\max\{S_{T_1} - K_0, 0\}
\end{aligned}
$$

and the option price at time $T_1 < t \leq T_2$ is

$$
\begin{aligned}
C_{ra}&\left(S_t, t; K_0, T_1, T_2, T\right) \\
&= e^{-r(T_2-t)}\mathbb{E}^{\mathbb{Q}}\left[\Psi(S_{T_2})\middle|\mathcal{F}_t\right] \\
&= e^{-r(T_2-t)}\mathbb{E}^{\mathbb{Q}}\left[C_{bs}(S_{T_2}, T_2; S_{T_2}, T)\middle|\mathcal{F}_t\right] \\
&\quad + e^{-r(T_2-t)}\mathbb{E}^{\mathbb{Q}}\left[e^{-r(T-T_2)}\max\{S_{T_2} - S_{T_1}, 0\}\middle|\mathcal{F}_t\right] \\
&\quad + e^{-r(T_2-t)}\mathbb{E}^{\mathbb{Q}}\left[e^{-r(T-T_2)}\max\{S_{T_1} - K_0, 0\}\middle|\mathcal{F}_t\right] \\
&= e^{-r(T_2-t)}\mathbb{E}^{\mathbb{Q}}\left[S_{T_2}\left(e^{-D(T-T_2)}\Phi(d_+) - e^{-r(T-T_2)}\Phi(d_-)\right)\middle|\mathcal{F}_t\right] \\
&\quad + e^{-r(T-T_2)}\mathbb{E}^{\mathbb{Q}}\left[e^{-r(T_2-t)}\max\{S_{T_2} - S_{T_1}, 0\}\middle|\mathcal{F}_t\right] \\
&\quad + e^{-r(T_2-t)}e^{-r(T-T_2)}\max\{S_{T_1} - K_0, 0\}
\end{aligned}
$$

where

$$d_{\pm} = \frac{\log(S_{T_2}/S_{T_2}) + (r \pm \frac{1}{2}\sigma^2)(T - T_2)}{\sigma\sqrt{T - T_2}} = \frac{(r \pm \frac{1}{2}\sigma^2)(T - T_2)}{\sigma\sqrt{T - T_2}}.$$

Since $\mathbb{E}^{\mathbb{Q}}\left[S_{T_2}\middle|\mathcal{F}_t\right] = S_t e^{r(T_2-t)}$ and $d_{\pm}$ is independent of the filtration $\mathcal{F}_t$, we therefore have

$$C_{ra}(S_t, t; K_0, T_1, T_2, T) = S_t \left(e^{-D(T-T_2)}\Phi(d_+) - e^{-r(T-T_2)}\Phi(d_-)\right)$$

$$+ e^{-r(T-T_2)}C_{bs}(S_t, t; S_{T_1}, T_2)$$

$$+ e^{-r(T-t)}\max\{S_{T_1} - K_0, 0\}$$

where $C_{bs}(S_t, t; S_{T_1}, T_2)$ is a European call option price with strike price S_{T_1} and expiry time T_2.

Finally, for $T_0 < t \leq T_1$ the payoff is

$$\Psi(S_{T_1}) = C_{ra}(S_{T_1}, T_1; K_0, T_1, T_2, T)$$

$$= S_{T_1}\left(e^{-D(T-T_2)}\Phi(d_+) - e^{-r(T-T_2)}\Phi(d_-)\right)$$

$$+ e^{-r(T-T_2)}C_{bs}(S_{T_1}, T_1; S_{T_1}, T_2) + e^{-r(T-T_1)}\max\{S_{T_1} - K_0, 0\}$$

and the option price at time $T_0 < t \leq T_1$ is

$$C_{ra}\left(S_t, t; K_0, T_1, T_2, T\right)$$

$$= e^{-r(T_1-t)}\mathbb{E}^{\mathbb{Q}}\left[\Psi(S_{T_1})|\mathcal{F}_t\right]$$

$$= e^{-r(T_1-t)}\mathbb{E}^{\mathbb{Q}}\left[S_{T_1}\left(e^{-D(T-T_2)}\Phi(d_+) - e^{-r(T-T_2)}\Phi(d_-)\right)\middle|\mathcal{F}_t\right]$$

$$+ e^{-r(T_1-t)}\mathbb{E}^{\mathbb{Q}}\left[S_{T_1}\left(e^{-D(T_2-T_1)}\Phi(\hat{d}_+) - e^{-r(T_2-T_1)}\Phi(\hat{d}_-)\right)\middle|\mathcal{F}_t\right]$$

$$+ e^{-r(T_1-t)}\mathbb{E}^{\mathbb{Q}}\left[e^{-r(T-T_1)}\max\{S_{T_1} - K_0, 0\}|\mathcal{F}_t\right]$$

where

$$\hat{d}_{\pm} = \frac{\log(S_{T_1}/S_{T_1}) + (r \pm \frac{1}{2}\sigma^2)(T_2 - T_1)}{\sigma\sqrt{T_2 - T_1}} = \frac{(r \pm \frac{1}{2}\sigma^2)\left(T_2 - T_1\right)}{\sigma\sqrt{T_2 - T_1}}.$$

Since both $d_{\pm}$ and $\hat{d}_{\pm}$ are independent of the filtration $\mathscr{F}_t$, and because $\mathbb{E}^Q\left[S_{T_1}\middle|\mathscr{F}_t\right] = S_t e^{r(T_1-t)}$, therefore

$$
\begin{aligned}
C_{ra}(S_t,t;K_0,T_1,T_2,T) &= S_t\left(e^{-D(T-T_2)}\Phi(d_+) - e^{-r(T-T_2)}\Phi(d_-)\right)\\
&+S_t\left(e^{-D(T_2-T_1)}\Phi(\hat{d}_+) - e^{-r(T_2-T_1)}\Phi(\hat{d}_-)\right)\\
&+e^{-r(T-T_1)}\mathbb{E}^Q\left[e^{-r(T_1-t)}\max\{S_{T_1}-K_0,0\}\middle|\mathscr{F}_t\right]\\
&= S_t\left(e^{-D(T-T_2)}\Phi(d_+) - e^{-r(T-T_2)}\Phi(d_-)\right)\\
&+S_t\left(e^{-D(T_2-T_1)}\Phi(\hat{d}_+) - e^{-r(T_2-T_1)}\Phi(\hat{d}_-)\right)\\
&+e^{-r(T-T_1)}C_{bs}(S_t,t;K_0,T_1)
\end{aligned}
$$

where $C_{bs}(S_t,t;K_0,T_1)$ is a European call option at time t with strike price K_0 and expiry time T_1.

$\square$

3. *Compound Option I.* Let $\{W_t : t \geq 0\}$ be a $\mathbb{P}$-standard Wiener process on the probability space $(\Omega,\mathscr{F},\mathbb{P})$ and let the asset price S_t follow

$$
\frac{dS_t}{S_t} = (\mu - D)dt + \sigma dW_t
$$

where μ is the drift parameter, D is the continuous dividend yield and σ is the volatility parameter. In addition, we let r be the risk-free interest rate.

Consider a European call-on-a-call option price with payoff

$$
\Psi(S_{T_1}) = \max\{C_{bs}(S_{T_1},T_1;K_2,T_2) - K_1,0\}
$$

where on the first expiry date T_1, the option holder has the right to buy the underlying European call option worth

$$
\begin{aligned}
C_{bs}(S_{T_1},T_1;K_2,T_2) &= S_{T_1}e^{-D(T_2-T_1)}\Phi(d_+) - K_2 e^{-r(T_2-T_1)}\Phi(d_-)\\
d_{\pm} &= \frac{\log(S_{T_1}/K_2) + (r - D \pm \frac{1}{2}\sigma^2)(T_2 - T_1)}{\sigma\sqrt{T_2 - T_1}}
\end{aligned}
$$

by paying the first strike price K_1. Here the underlying European call option gives the holder the right but not the obligation to buy the underlying asset by paying the second strike price K_2 at expiry date $T_2 \geq T_1$.

Using the risk-neutral measure valuation, show that the European call-on-a-call option price at time $t \leq T_1 \leq T_2$ is

$$
\begin{aligned}
C_c(S_t,t;K_1,T_1,K_2,T_2) &= S_t e^{-D(T_2-t)}\Phi(\alpha_+,\beta_+,\rho) - K_2 e^{-r(T_2-t)}\Phi(\alpha_-,\beta_-,\rho)\\
&-K_1 e^{-r(T_1-t)}\Phi(\alpha_-)
\end{aligned}
$$

where

$$\alpha_\pm = \frac{\log(S_t/\widetilde{S}_{T_1}) + (r - D \pm \frac{1}{2}\sigma^2)(T_1 - t)}{\sigma\sqrt{T_1 - t}}, \beta_\pm = \frac{\log(S_t/K_2) + (r - D \pm \frac{1}{2}\sigma^2)(T_2 - t)}{\sigma\sqrt{T_2 - t}},$$

$\rho = \sqrt{\dfrac{T_1 - t}{T_2 - t}}$ and $\widetilde{S}_{T_1}$ satisfies $C_{bs}(\widetilde{S}_{T_1}, T_1; K_2, T_2) = K_1$, $\Phi(x, y, \rho_{xy})$ is the cdf of a standard bivariate normal with correlation coefficient $\rho_{xy} \in (-1, 1)$ and $\Phi(x)$ is the cdf of a standard normal.

Finally, deduce the put-on-a-call option price at time $t \leq T_1 \leq T_2$ with payoff

$$\Psi(S_{T_1}) = \max\{K_1 - C_{bs}(S_{T_1}, T_1; K_2, T_2), 0\}.$$

Solution: Under the risk-neutral measure $\mathbb{Q}$, S_t follows

$$\frac{dS_t}{S_t} = (r - D)dt + \sigma dW_t^{\mathbb{Q}}$$

where $W_t^{\mathbb{Q}} = W_t + \left(\dfrac{\mu - r}{\sigma}\right)t$ is a $\mathbb{Q}$-standard Wiener process. From Itō's lemma we can easily show for $T > t$

$$\log\left(\frac{S_T}{S_t}\right) \sim \mathcal{N}\left[\left(r - D - \frac{1}{2}\sigma^2\right)(T - t), \sigma^2(T - t)\right]$$

with density function

$$f(S_T|S_t) = \frac{1}{S_T\sigma\sqrt{2\pi(T - t)}}e^{-\frac{1}{2}\left(\frac{\log(S_T/S_t) - (r - D - \frac{1}{2}\sigma^2)(T - t)}{\sigma\sqrt{T - t}}\right)^2}.$$

By definition, the call-on-a-call option at time $t \leq T_1 \leq T_2$ is

$$\begin{aligned}
C_c&(S_t, t; K_1, T_1, K_2, T_2)\\
&= e^{-r(T_1 - t)}\mathbb{E}^{\mathbb{Q}}\left[\max\left\{C_{bs}(S_{T_1}, T_1; K_2, T_2) - K_1, 0\right\}\Big|\mathcal{F}_t\right]\\
&= e^{-r(T_1 - t)}\int_0^\infty \max\left\{C_{bs}(S_{T_1}, T_1; K_2, T_2) - K_1, 0\right\}f(S_{T_1}|S_t)\,dS_{T_1}\\
&= e^{-r(T_1 - t)}\int_{\widetilde{S}_{T_1}}^\infty \left[C_{bs}(S_{T_1}, T_1; K_2, T_2) - K_1\right]f(S_{T_1}|S_t)\,dS_{T_1}\\
&= A_1 - A_2 - A_3
\end{aligned}$$

where $\widetilde{S}_{T_1}$ satisfies the equation $C_{bs}(S_{T_1}, T_1; K_2, T_2) = K_1$ and

$$A_1 = e^{-r(T_1-t)} \int_{\widetilde{S}_{T_1}}^{\infty} S_{T_1} e^{-D(T_2-T_1)} \Phi(d_+) f(S_{T_1}|S_t) \, dS_{T_1}$$

$$A_2 = e^{-r(T_1-t)} \int_{\widetilde{S}_{T_1}}^{\infty} K_2 e^{-r(T_2-T_1)} \Phi(d_-) f(S_{T_1}|S_t) \, dS_{T_1}$$

$$A_3 = K_1 e^{-r(T_1-t)} \int_{\widetilde{S}_{T_1}}^{\infty} f(S_{T_1}|S_t) \, dS_{T_1}.$$

For the case

$$A_1 = e^{-r(T_1-t)-D(T_2-T_1)}$$

$$\times \int_{\widetilde{S}_{T_1}}^{\infty} S_{T_1} \Phi\left(\frac{\log(S_{T_1}/K_2) + (r - D + \frac{1}{2}\sigma^2)(T_2 - T_1)}{\sigma\sqrt{T_2 - T_1}}\right) f(S_{T_1}|S_t) \, dS_{T_1}$$

and by setting $x = \dfrac{\log(S_{T_1}/S_t) - (r - D - \frac{1}{2}\sigma^2)(T_1 - t)}{\sigma\sqrt{T_1 - t}}$ we have

$$A_1 = S_t e^{-r(T_1-t)-D(T_2-T_1)+(r-D-\frac{1}{2}\sigma^2)(T_1-t)}$$

$$\times \int_{\alpha}^{\infty} \Phi\left(\frac{m + x\sigma\sqrt{T_1 - t}}{\sigma\sqrt{T_2 - T_1}}\right) \frac{1}{\sqrt{2\pi}} e^{-\frac{1}{2}(x^2 - 2x\sigma\sqrt{T_2-t})} \, dx$$

or

$$A_1 = S_t e^{-D(T_2-t)} \int_{\alpha}^{\infty} \Phi\left(\frac{m + x\sigma\sqrt{T_1 - t}}{\sigma\sqrt{T_2 - T_1}}\right) \frac{1}{\sqrt{2\pi}} e^{-\frac{1}{2}(x-\sigma\sqrt{T_1-t})^2} \, dx$$

where

$$\alpha = \frac{\log(\widetilde{S}_{T_1}/S_t) - (r - D - \frac{1}{2}\sigma^2)(T_1 - t)}{\sigma\sqrt{T_1 - t}}$$

and

$$m = \log(S_t/K_2) + (r - D + \frac{1}{2}\sigma^2)(T_2 - T_1) + (r - D - \frac{1}{2}\sigma^2)(T_1 - t).$$

By setting $y = -(x - \sigma\sqrt{T_1 - t})$ and from Problem 1.2.2.16 of *Problems and Solutions in Mathematical Finance, Volume 1: Stochastic Calculus* we have

$$A_1 = -S_t e^{-D(T_2-t)} \int_{\alpha_+}^{-\infty} \Phi\left(\frac{m + \sigma^2(T_1 - t) - y\sigma\sqrt{T_1 - t}}{\sigma\sqrt{T_2 - T_1}}\right) \frac{1}{\sqrt{2\pi}} e^{-\frac{1}{2}y^2} dy$$

$$= S_t e^{-D(T_2-t)} \int_{-\infty}^{\alpha_+} \Phi\left(\frac{m + \sigma^2(T_1 - t) - y\sigma\sqrt{T_1 - t}}{\sigma\sqrt{T_2 - T_1}}\right) \frac{1}{\sqrt{2\pi}} e^{-\frac{1}{2}y^2} dy$$

$$= S_t e^{-D(T_2-t)} \int_{-\infty}^{\alpha_+} \Phi\left(\frac{\beta_+ - \rho y}{\sqrt{1 - \rho^2}}\right) \frac{1}{\sqrt{2\pi}} e^{-\frac{1}{2}y^2} dy$$

$$= S_t e^{-D(T_2-t)} \Phi(\alpha_+, \beta_+, \rho)$$

where

$$\alpha_+ = \frac{\log(S_t/\widetilde{S}_{T_1}) + (r - D + \frac{1}{2}\sigma^2)(T_1 - t)}{\sigma\sqrt{T_1 - t}}, \quad \beta_+ = \frac{\log(S_t/K_2) + (r - D + \frac{1}{2}\sigma^2)(T_2 - t)}{\sigma\sqrt{T_2 - t}}$$

and $\rho = \sqrt{\dfrac{T_1 - t}{T_2 - t}}$.

In contrast, for

$$A_2 = K_2 e^{-r(T_2-t)}$$

$$\times \int_{\widetilde{S}_{T_1}}^{\infty} \Phi\left(\frac{\log(S_{T_1}/K_2) + (r - D - \frac{1}{2}\sigma^2)(T_2 - T_1)}{\sigma\sqrt{T_2 - T_1}}\right) f(S_{T_1}|S_t) \, dS_{T_1}$$

and by setting $x = \dfrac{\log(S_{T_1}/S_t) - (r - D - \frac{1}{2}\sigma^2)(T_1 - t)}{\sigma\sqrt{T_1 - t}}$ we have

$$A_2 = K_2 e^{-r(T_2-t)}$$

$$\times \int_{-\alpha_-}^{\infty} \Phi\left(\frac{\log(S_t/K_2) + (r - D - \frac{1}{2}\sigma^2)(T_2 - t) + x\sigma\sqrt{T_1 - t}}{\sigma\sqrt{T_2 - T_1}}\right) \frac{1}{\sqrt{2\pi}} e^{-\frac{1}{2}x^2} dx$$

where $\alpha_- = \dfrac{\log(S_t/\widetilde{S}_{T_1}) + (r - D - \frac{1}{2}\sigma^2)(T_1 - t)}{\sigma\sqrt{T_1 - t}}$.

Setting $y = -x$

$$A_2 = -K_2 e^{-r(T_2-t)} \int_{\alpha_-}^{-\infty} \Phi\left(\frac{\beta_- - \rho y}{\sqrt{1 - \rho^2}}\right) \frac{1}{\sqrt{2\pi}} e^{-\frac{1}{2}y^2} dy$$

$$= K_2 e^{-r(T_2-t)} \int_{-\infty}^{\alpha_-} \Phi\left(\frac{\beta_- - \rho y}{\sqrt{1 - \rho^2}}\right) \frac{1}{\sqrt{2\pi}} e^{-\frac{1}{2}y^2} dy$$

$$= K_2 e^{-r(T_2-t)} \Phi(\alpha_-, \beta_-, \rho)$$

where $\beta_- = \dfrac{\log(S_t/K_2) + (r - D - \frac{1}{2}\sigma^2)(T_2 - t)}{\sigma\sqrt{T_2 - t}}$.

Finally, because $W^{\mathbb{Q}}_{T_1-t} \sim \mathcal{N}(0, T_1 - t)$ we have

$$A_3 = K_1 e^{-r(T_1-t)} \int_{\widetilde{S}_{T_1}}^{\infty} f(S_{T_1}|S_t)\, dS_{T_1}$$

$$= K_1 e^{-r(T_1-t)} \mathbb{Q}\left(S_{T_1} > \widetilde{S}_{T_1} \,\middle|\, S_t \right)$$

$$= K_1 e^{-r(T_1-t)} \mathbb{Q}\left(S_t e^{(r-D-\frac{1}{2}\sigma^2)(T_1-t)+\sigma W^{\mathbb{Q}}_{T_1-t}} > \widetilde{S}_{T_1} \,\middle|\, S_t \right)$$

$$= K_1 e^{-r(T_1-t)} \mathbb{Q}\left(W^{\mathbb{Q}}_{T_1-t} > \frac{\log(\widetilde{S}_{T_1}/S_t) - (r - D - \frac{1}{2}\sigma^2)(T_1 - t)}{\sigma} \,\middle|\, S_t \right)$$

$$= K_1 e^{-r(T_1-t)} \Phi(\alpha_-).$$

Thus, the call-on-a-call option price at time $t \le T_1 \le T_2$ is

$$C_c(S_t, t; K_1, T_1, K_2, T_2) = S_t e^{-D(T_2-t)} \Phi(\alpha_+, \beta_+, \rho) - K_2 e^{-r(T_2-t)} \Phi(\alpha_-, \beta_-, \rho)$$
$$- K_1 e^{-r(T_1-t)} \Phi(\alpha_-).$$

For the case of a put-on-a-call option, the payoff at time T_1 is

$$P_c(S_{T_1}, T_1; K_1, T_1) = \max\{K_1 - C_{bs}(S_{T_1}, T_1; K_2, T_2), 0\}$$

whilst the payoff at time T_1 for a call-on-a-call option is

$$C_c(S_{T_1}, T_1; K_1, T_1) = \max\{C_{bs}(S_{T_1}, T_1; K_2, T_2) - K_1, 0\}.$$

Hence,

$$C_c(S_{T_1}, T_1; K_1, T_1, K_2, T_2) - P_c(S_{T_1}, T_1; K_1, T_1, K_2, T_2)$$

$$= \begin{cases} C_{bs}(S_{T_1}, T_1; K_2, T_2) - K_1 & \text{if } C_{bs}(S_{T_1}, T_1; K_2, T_2) > K_1 \\ C_{bs}(S_{T_1}, T_1; K_2, T_2) - K_1 & \text{if } C_{bs}(S_{T_1}, T_1; K_2, T_2) \le K_1 \end{cases}$$

$$= C_{bs}(S_{T_1}, T_1; K_2, T_2) - K_1.$$

By discounting the payoff back to time t under the risk-neutral measure $\mathbb{Q}$, we have

$$C_c(S_t, t; K_1, T_1, K_2, T_2) - P_c(S_t, t; K_1, T_1, K_2, T_2) = C_{bs}(S_t, t; K_2, T_2) - K_1 e^{-r(T_1-t)}$$

or

$$P_c(S_t, t; K_1, T_1, K_2, T_2) = C_c(S_t, t; K_1, T_1, K_2, T_2) - C_{bs}(S_t, t; K_2, T_2) + K_1 e^{-r(T_1-t)}.$$

$\square$

4. *Compound Option II.* Let $\{W_t : t \geq 0\}$ be a $\mathbb{P}$-standard Wiener process on the probability space $(\Omega, \mathcal{F}, \mathbb{P})$ and let the asset price S_t follow

$$\frac{dS_t}{S_t} = (\mu - D)dt + \sigma dW_t$$

where μ is the drift parameter, D is the continuous dividend yield and σ is the volatility parameter. In addition, we let r be the risk-free interest rate.

Consider a European put-on-a-put option price with payoff

$$\Psi(S_{T_1}) = \max\{K_1 - P_{bs}(S_{T_1}, T_1; K_2, T_2), 0\}$$

where on the first expiry date T_1, the option holder has the right to sell the underlying European put option

$$P_{bs}(S_{T_1}, T_1; K_2, T_2) = K_2 e^{-r(T_2 - T_1)}\Phi(-d_-) - S_{T_1} e^{-D(T_2 - T_1)}\Phi(-d_+)$$

$$d_{\pm} = \frac{\log(S_{T_1}/K_2) + (r - D \pm \frac{1}{2}\sigma^2)(T_2 - T_1)}{\sigma\sqrt{T_2 - T_1}}$$

at the first strike price K_1. Here the underlying European put option gives the holder the right but not the obligation to sell the underlying asset by receiving the second strike price K_2 at expiry date $T_2 \geq T_1$.

Using the risk-neutral measure valuation, show that the European put-on-a-put option price at time $t \leq T_1 \leq T_2$ is

$$P_p(S_t, t; K_1, T_1, K_2, T_2) = K_1 e^{-r(T_1 - t)}\Phi(-\alpha_-) - K_2 e^{-r(T_2 - t)}\Phi(-\alpha_-, -\beta_-, \rho)$$

$$+ S_t e^{-D(T_2 - t)}\Phi(-\alpha_+, -\beta_+, \rho)$$

where

$$\alpha_{\pm} = \frac{\log(S_t/\widehat{S}_{T_1}) + (r - D \pm \frac{1}{2}\sigma^2)(T_1 - t)}{\sigma\sqrt{T_1 - t}}, \quad \beta_{\pm} = \frac{\log(S_t/K_2) + (r - D \pm \frac{1}{2}\sigma^2)(T_2 - t)}{\sigma\sqrt{T_2 - t}},$$

$\rho = \sqrt{\dfrac{T_1 - t}{T_2 - t}}$ and $\widehat{S}_{T_1}$ satisfies $P_{bs}(\widehat{S}_{T_1}, T_1; K_2, T_2) = K_1$, $\Phi(x, y, \rho_{xy})$ is the cdf of a standard bivariate normal with correlation coefficient $\rho_{xy} \in (-1, 1)$ and $\Phi(x)$ is the cdf of a standard normal.

Finally, deduce the call-on-a-put option price at time $t \leq T_1 \leq T_2$ with option payoff

$$\Psi(S_{T_1}) = \max\{P_{bs}(S_{T_1}, T_1; K_2, T_2) - K_1, 0\}.$$

Solution: From Girsanov's theorem, under the risk-neutral measure $\mathbb{Q}$, S_t follows

$$\frac{dS_t}{S_t} = (r - D)dt + \sigma dW_t^{\mathbb{Q}}$$

where $W_t^{\mathbb{Q}} = W_t + \left(\dfrac{\mu - r}{\sigma}\right)t$ is a $\mathbb{Q}$-standard Wiener process. Using Itō's lemma we can easily show for $T > t$

$$\log\left(\frac{S_T}{S_t}\right) \sim \mathcal{N}\left[\left(r - D - \frac{1}{2}\sigma^2\right)(T - t), \sigma^2(T - t)\right]$$

with density function

$$f(S_T|S_t) = \frac{1}{S_T\sigma\sqrt{2\pi(T-t)}}e^{-\frac{1}{2}\left(\frac{\log(S_T/S_t)-(r-D-\frac{1}{2}\sigma^2)(T-t)}{\sigma\sqrt{T-t}}\right)^2}.$$

By definition the put-on-a-put option at time $t \le T_1 \le T_2$ is

$$
\begin{aligned}
&P_p(S_t, t; K_1, T_1, K_2, T_2) \\
&= e^{-r(T_1-t)}\mathbb{E}^{\mathbb{Q}}\left[\max\left\{K_1 - P_{bs}(S_{T_1}, T_1; K_2, T_2), 0\right\}\middle|\mathcal{F}_t\right] \\
&= e^{-r(T_1-t)}\int_0^\infty \max\left\{K_1 - P_{bs}(S_{T_1}, T_1; K_2, T_2), 0\right\} f(S_{T_1}|S_t)\, dS_{T_1} \\
&= e^{-r(T_1-t)}\int_0^{\hat{S}_{T_1}}\left[K_1 - P_{bs}(S_{T_1}, T_1; K_2, T_2)\right] f(S_{T_1}|S_t)\, dS_{T_1} \\
&= B_1 - B_2 + B_3
\end{aligned}
$$

where $\hat{S}_{T_1}$ satisfies the equation $P_{bs}(S_{T_1}, T_1; K_2, T_2) = K_1$ and

$$B_1 = K_1 e^{-r(T_1-t)}\int_0^{\hat{S}_{T_1}} f(S_{T_1}|S_t)\, dS_{T_1}$$

$$B_2 = e^{-r(T_1-t)}\int_0^{\hat{S}_{T_1}} K_2 e^{-r(T_2-T_1)}\Phi(-d_-)f(S_{T_1}|S_t)\, dS_{T_1}$$

$$B_3 = e^{-r(T_1-t)}\int_0^{\hat{S}_{T_1}} S_{T_1} e^{-D(T_2-T_1)}\Phi(-d_+)f(S_{T_1}|S_t)\, dS_{T_1}.$$

Given $W^{\mathbb{Q}}_{T_1-t} \sim \mathcal{N}(0, T_1-t)$ we have

$$
\begin{aligned}
B_1 &= K_1 e^{-r(T_1-t)}\int_0^{\hat{S}_{T_1}} f(S_{T_1}|S_t)\, dS_{T_1} \\
&= K_1 e^{-r(T_1-t)}\mathbb{Q}\left(S_{T_1} < \hat{S}_{T_1}\middle|S_t\right) \\
&= K_1 e^{-r(T_1-t)}\mathbb{Q}\left(S_t e^{(r-D-\frac{1}{2}\sigma^2)(T_1-t)+\sigma W^{\mathbb{Q}}_{T_1-t}} < \hat{S}_{T_1}\middle|S_t\right) \\
&= K_1 e^{-r(T_1-t)}\mathbb{Q}\left(W^{\mathbb{Q}}_{T_1-t} < \frac{\log(\hat{S}_{T_1}/S_t)-(r-D-\frac{1}{2}\sigma^2)(T_1-t)}{\sigma}\middle|S_t\right) \\
&= K_1 e^{-r(T_1-t)}\Phi(-\alpha_-)
\end{aligned}
$$

where $\alpha_- = \dfrac{\log(S_t/\hat{S}_{T_1}) + (r - D - \frac{1}{2}\sigma^2)(T_1 - t)}{\sigma\sqrt{T_1 - t}}.$

As for the case

$$B_2 = K_2 e^{-r(T_2-t)}$$

$$\times \int_0^{\hat{S}_{T_1}} \Phi\left(\frac{-\log(S_{T_1}/K_2) - (r - D - \frac{1}{2}\sigma^2)(T_2 - T_1)}{\sigma\sqrt{T_2 - T_1}} \right) f(S_{T_1}|S_t)\, dS_{T_1}$$

and by setting $x = \dfrac{\log(S_{T_1}/S_t) - (r - D - \frac{1}{2}\sigma^2)(T_1 - t)}{\sigma\sqrt{T_1 - t}}$ we have

$$B_2 = K_2 e^{-r(T_2-t)}$$

$$\times \int_{-\infty}^{-\alpha_-} \Phi\left(\frac{\log(K_2/S_t) - (r - D - \frac{1}{2}\sigma^2)(T_2 - t) - x\sigma\sqrt{T_1 - t}}{\sigma\sqrt{T_2 - T_1}} \right) \frac{1}{\sqrt{2\pi}} e^{-\frac{1}{2}x^2}\, dx.$$

By simplifying the integrands and from Problem 1.2.2.16 of *Problems and Solutions in Mathematical Finance, Volume 1: Stochastic Calculus* we can write

$$B_2 = K_2 e^{-r(T_2-t)} \int_{-\infty}^{-\alpha_-} \Phi\left(\frac{-\beta_- - \rho x}{\sqrt{1 - \rho^2}} \right) \frac{1}{\sqrt{2\pi}} e^{-\frac{1}{2}x^2}\, dx$$

$$= K_2 e^{-r(T_2-t)} \Phi(-\alpha_-, -\beta_-, \rho)$$

where $\beta_- = \dfrac{\log(S_t/K_2) + (r - D - \frac{1}{2}\sigma^2)(T_2 - t)}{\sigma\sqrt{T_2 - t}}$ and $\rho = \sqrt{\dfrac{T_1 - t}{T_2 - t}}$.

Finally, for the case

$$B_3 = e^{-r(T_1-t)-D(T_2-T_1)}$$

$$\times \int_0^{\hat{S}_{T_1}} S_{T_1} \Phi\left(\frac{\log(K_2/S_{T_1}) - (r - D + \frac{1}{2}\sigma^2)(T_2 - T_1)}{\sigma\sqrt{T_2 - T_1}} \right) f(S_{T_1}|S_t)\, dS_{T_1}$$

and by setting $x = \dfrac{\log(S_{T_1}/S_t) - (r - D - \frac{1}{2}\sigma^2)(T_1 - t)}{\sigma\sqrt{T_1 - t}}$ we have

$$B_3 = S_t e^{-r(T_1-t)-D(T_2-T_1)+(r-D-\frac{1}{2}\sigma^2)(T_1-t)}$$

$$\times \int_{-\infty}^{\alpha} \Phi\left(\frac{m + x\sigma\sqrt{T_1 - t}}{\sigma\sqrt{T_2 - T_1}} \right) \frac{1}{\sqrt{2\pi}} e^{-\frac{1}{2}(x^2 - 2x\sigma\sqrt{T_2-t})}\, dx$$

or

$$B_3 = S_t e^{-D(T_2-t)} \int_{-\infty}^{\alpha} \Phi\left(\frac{m - x\sigma\sqrt{T_1 - t}}{\sigma\sqrt{T_2 - T_1}} \right) \frac{1}{\sqrt{2\pi}} e^{-\frac{1}{2}(x - \sigma\sqrt{T_1-t})^2}\, dx$$

where

$$\alpha = \frac{\log(\widetilde{S}_{T_1}/S_t) - (r - D - \frac{1}{2}\sigma^2)(T_1 - t)}{\sigma\sqrt{T_1 - t}}$$

$$m = \log(K_2/S_t) - (r - D + \frac{1}{2}\sigma^2)(T_2 - T_1) - (r - D - \frac{1}{2}\sigma^2)(T_1 - t).$$

By setting $y = x - \sigma\sqrt{T_1 - t}$ we have

$$B_3 = S_t e^{-D(T_2-t)} \int_{-\infty}^{-\alpha_+} \Phi\left(\frac{m - \sigma^2(T_1 - t) - y\sigma\sqrt{T_1 - t}}{\sigma\sqrt{T_2 - T_1}}\right) \frac{1}{\sqrt{2\pi}} e^{-\frac{1}{2}y^2} dy$$

$$= S_t e^{-D(T_2-t)} \int_{-\infty}^{-\alpha_+} \Phi\left(\frac{-\beta_+ - \rho y}{\sqrt{1-\rho^2}}\right) \frac{1}{\sqrt{2\pi}} e^{-\frac{1}{2}y^2} dy$$

$$= S_t e^{-D(T_2-t)} \Phi(-\alpha_+, -\beta_+, \rho).$$

Thus, the put-on-a-put option price at time $t \leq T_1 \leq T_2$ is

$$P_p(S_t, t; K_1, T_1, K_2, T_2) = K_1 e^{-r(T_1-t)} \Phi(-\alpha_-) - K_2 e^{-r(T_2-t)} \Phi(-\alpha_-, -\beta_-, \rho)$$
$$+ S_t e^{-D(T_2-t)} \Phi(-\alpha_+, -\beta_+, \rho).$$

For the case of a call-on-a-put option, the payoff at time T_1 is

$$C_p(S_{T_1}, T_1; K_1, T_1, K_2, T_2) = \max\{P_{bs}(S_{T_1}, T_1; K_2, T_2) - K_1, 0\}$$

whilst the payoff at time T_1 for a put-on-a-put option is

$$P_p(S_{T_1}, T_1; K_1, T_1, K_2, T_2) = \max\{K_1 - P_{bs}(S_{T_1}, T_1; K_2, T_2), 0\}.$$

Hence,

$$C_p(S_{T_1}, T_1; K_1, T_1, K_2, T_2) - P_p(S_{T_1}, T_1; K_1, T_1, K_2, T_2)$$

$$= \begin{cases} P_{bs}(S_{T_1}, T_1; K_2, T_2) - K_1 & \text{if } P_{bs}(S_{T_1}, T_1; K_2, T_2) > K_1 \\ P_{bs}(S_{T_1}, T_1; K_2, T_2) - K_1 & \text{if } P_{bs}(S_{T_1}, T_1; K_2, T_2) \leq K_1 \end{cases}$$

$$= P_{bs}(S_{T_1}, T_1; K_2, T_2) - K_1.$$

By discounting the payoff back to time t under the risk-neutral measure $\mathbb{Q}$, we have

$$C_p(S_t, t; K_1, T_1, K_2, T_2) - P_p(S_t, t; K_1, T_1, K_2, T_2) = P_{bs}(S_t, t; K_2, T_2) - K_1 e^{-r(T_1-t)}$$

or

$$C_p(S_t, t; K_1, T_1, K_2, T_2) = P_p(S_t, t; K_1, T_1, K_2, T_2) + P_{bs}(S_t, t; K_2, T_2) - K_1 e^{-r(T_1-t)}.$$

$\square$

5. *Simple Chooser Option.* Let $\{W_t : t \geq 0\}$ be a $\mathbb{P}$-standard Wiener process on the probability space $(\Omega, \mathcal{F}, \mathbb{P})$ and let the asset price S_t follow a GBM with the following SDE

$$\frac{dS_t}{S_t} = (\mu - D)dt + \sigma dW_t$$

where μ is the drift parameter, D is the continuous dividend yield and σ is the volatility
parameter. In addition, we let r be the risk-free interest rate.

A simple chooser option is an option contract whereby it gives the holder of the option
at a fixed time τ, $t \leq \tau \leq T$ the right but not the obligation to decide whether the contract
is a European call or put option with the following payoff

$$\Psi\left(S_\tau\right) = \max\{C_{bs}(S_\tau, \tau; K, T), P_{bs}(S_\tau, \tau; K, T)\}$$

where S_τ is the stock price at time τ, T is the chooser option expiry time, K is the strike
price,

$$C_{bs}(S_\tau, \tau; K, T) = S_\tau e^{-D(T-\tau)}\Phi(d_+) - Ke^{-r(T-\tau)}\Phi(d_-)$$

and

$$P_{bs}(S_\tau, \tau; K, T) = Ke^{-r(T-\tau)}\Phi(-d_-) - S_\tau e^{-D(T-\tau)}\Phi(-d_+)$$

are the European call and put options at time τ, respectively with

$$d_\pm = \frac{\log(S_\tau/K) + (r - D \pm \frac{1}{2}\sigma^2)(T - \tau)}{\sigma\sqrt{T - \tau}}$$

and $\Phi(\cdot)$ is the cdf of a standard normal.

Show that $e^{-rt}V_{bs}(S_t, t; K, T)$ is a martingale under the risk-neutral measure $\mathbb{Q}$, where
$V_{bs}(S_t, t; K, T)$ is the price of a European option at time t given as

$$V_{bs}(S_t, t; K, T) = \begin{cases} C_{bs}(S_t, t; K, T) & \text{if payoff } \Psi(S_T) = \max\{S_T - K, 0\} \\ \\ P_{bs}(S_t, t; K, T) & \text{if payoff } \Psi(S_T) = \max\{K - S_T, 0\}. \end{cases}$$

Given the simple chooser option is valued at time t, $t \leq \tau$ show using the put–call parity
that the payoff at intermediate time τ can be expressed as

$$\Psi(S_\tau) = C_{bs}(S_\tau, \tau; K, T) + e^{-D(T-\tau)}\max\{\widetilde{K} - S_\tau, 0\}$$

where $\widetilde{K} = Ke^{-(r-D)(T-\tau)}$.

Hence, show that the simple chooser option price at time $t \leq \tau \leq T$ is

$$V_{sc}(S_t, t; \widetilde{K}, \tau, K, T) = C_{bs}(S_t, t; K, T) + e^{-D(T-\tau)}P_{bs}(S_t, t; \widetilde{K}, \tau).$$

Solution: Under the risk-neutral measure $\mathbb{Q}$, S_t follows

$$\frac{dS_t}{S_t} = (r - D)dt + \sigma dW_t^{\mathbb{Q}}$$

where $W_t^{\mathbb{Q}} = W_t + \left(\dfrac{\mu - r}{\sigma}\right) t$ is a $\mathbb{Q}$-standard Wiener process. To show that $e^{-rt}V_{bs}(S_t, t; K, T)$ is a $\mathbb{Q}$-martingale, see Problem 2.2.2.8 (page 109).

From the simple chooser payoff at time $\tau \le T$

$$\Psi(S_\tau) = \max\{C_{bs}(S_\tau, \tau; K, T), P_{bs}(S_\tau, \tau; K, T)\}$$

and knowing the put–call parity at time τ is

$$P_{bs}(S_\tau, \tau; K, T) = C_{bs}(S_\tau, \tau; K, T) + Ke^{-r(T-\tau)} - S_\tau e^{-D(T-\tau)}$$

we can rewrite the payoff as

$$
\begin{aligned}
\Psi(S_\tau) &= \max\{C_{bs}(S_\tau, \tau; K, T), C_{bs}(S_\tau, \tau; K, T) + Ke^{-r(T-\tau)} - S_\tau e^{-D(T-\tau)}\} \\
&= C_{bs}(S_\tau, \tau; K, T) + \max\{0, Ke^{-r(T-\tau)} - S_\tau e^{-D(T-\tau)}\} \\
&= C_{bs}(S_\tau, \tau; K, T) + e^{-D(T-\tau)} \max\{Ke^{-(r-D)(T-\tau)} - S_\tau, 0\} \\
&= C_{bs}(S_\tau, \tau; K, T) + e^{-D(T-\tau)} \max\{\widetilde{K} - S_\tau, 0\}
\end{aligned}
$$

where $\widetilde{K} = Ke^{-(r-D)(T-\tau)}$.

Therefore, the price of a simple chooser option at time $t \le \tau \le T$ is

$$
\begin{aligned}
V_{sc}(S_t, t; \widetilde{K}, \tau, K, T) &= e^{-r(\tau-t)}\mathbb{E}^{\mathbb{Q}}\left[\Psi(S_\tau)|\mathcal{F}_t\right] \\
&= e^{-r(\tau-t)} \\
&\quad \times \mathbb{E}^{\mathbb{Q}}\left[C_{bs}(S_\tau, \tau; K, T) + e^{-D(T-\tau)}\max\{\widetilde{K} - S_\tau, 0\}\Big|\mathcal{F}_t\right] \\
&= e^{-r(\tau-t)} \cdot e^{r(\tau-t)}C_{bs}(S_t, t; K, T) \\
&\quad + e^{-D(T-\tau)} \cdot e^{-r(\tau-t)}\mathbb{E}^{\mathbb{Q}}\left[\max\{\widetilde{K} - S_\tau, 0\}\Big|\mathcal{F}_t\right] \\
&= C_{bs}(S_t, t; K, T) + e^{-D(T-\tau)}P_{bs}(S_t, t; \widetilde{K}, \tau)
\end{aligned}
$$

since $\mathbb{E}^{\mathbb{Q}}\left[e^{-r\tau}C_{bs}(S_\tau, \tau; K, T)\big|\mathcal{F}_t\right] = e^{-rt}C_{bs}(S_t, t; K, T)$ is a $\mathbb{Q}$-martingale.

$\square$

6. *Complex Chooser Option.* Let $\{W_t : t \ge 0\}$ be a $\mathbb{P}$-standard Wiener process on the probability space $(\Omega, \mathcal{F}, \mathbb{P})$ and let the asset price S_t follow a GBM with the following SDE

$$\frac{dS_t}{S_t} = (\mu - D)dt + \sigma dW_t$$

where μ is the drift parameter, D is the continuous dividend yield and σ is the volatility parameter. In addition, we let r be the risk-free interest rate.

A complex chooser option is an option contract whereby it gives the holder of the option at a fixed time τ, $t \leq \tau \leq \min\{T_c, T_p\}$ the right to decide whether the contract is a European call or put option of different time to expiry and strike prices with the following payoff

$$\Psi\left(S_\tau\right) = \max\{C_{bs}(S_\tau, \tau; K_c, T_c), P_{bs}(S_\tau, \tau; K_p, T_p)\}$$

where S_τ is the stock price at time τ, T_c is the call option expiry time, T_p is the put option expiry time, K_c is the call option strike, K_p is the put option strike so that

$$C_{bs}(S_\tau, \tau; K_c, T_c) = S_\tau e^{-D(T_c - \tau)}\Phi(d_+^c) - K_c e^{-r(T_c - \tau)}\Phi(d_-^c)$$

and

$$P_{bs}(S_\tau, \tau; K, T_p) = K_p e^{-r(T_p - \tau)}\Phi(-d_-^p) - S_\tau e^{-D(T_p - \tau)}\Phi(-d_+^p)$$

are the European call and put options at time τ, respectively with
$$d_\pm^c = \frac{\log(S_\tau/K_c) + (r - D \pm \frac{1}{2}\sigma^2)(T_c - \tau)}{\sigma\sqrt{T_c - \tau}}, \quad d_\pm^p = \frac{\log(S_\tau/K_p) + (r - D \pm \frac{1}{2}\sigma^2)(T_p - \tau)}{\sigma\sqrt{T_p - \tau}}$$
and $\Phi(\cdot)$ is the cdf of a standard normal.

Show that under the risk-neutral measure $\mathbb{Q}$, the complex chooser option price at time $t \leq \tau$ is

$$\begin{aligned}
V_{cc}(S_t, t; \tau, K_c, T_c, K_p, T_p) &= S_t e^{-D(T_c - t)}\Phi(\alpha_+, \beta_+, \rho_c) \\
&\quad - K_c e^{-r(T_c - t)}\Phi(\alpha_-, \beta_-, \rho_c) \\
&\quad + K_p e^{-r(T_p - t)}\Phi(-\alpha_-, -\gamma_-, \rho_p) \\
&\quad - S_t e^{-D(T_p - t)}\Phi(-\alpha_+, -\gamma_+, \rho_p)
\end{aligned}$$

where

$$\alpha_\pm = \frac{\log(S_t/X) + (r - D \pm \frac{1}{2}\sigma^2)(\tau - t)}{\sigma\sqrt{\tau - t}}, \quad \beta_\pm = \frac{\log(S_t/K_c) + (r - D \pm \frac{1}{2}\sigma^2)(T_c - t)}{\sigma\sqrt{T_c - t}},$$

$$\gamma_\pm = \frac{\log(S_t/K_p) + (r - D \pm \frac{1}{2}\sigma^2)(T_p - t)}{\sigma\sqrt{T_p - t}}, \quad \rho_c = \sqrt{\frac{\tau - t}{T_c - t}}, \quad \rho_p = \sqrt{\frac{\tau - t}{T_p - t}}, \quad X \text{ solves the}$$

equation $C_{bs}(X, \tau; K_c, T_c) = P_{bs}(X, \tau; K_p, T_p)$ and $\Phi(u, v, \rho_{uv})$ is the cdf of a standard bivariate normal with correlation coefficient $\rho_{uv} \in (-1, 1)$.

Solution: Under the risk-neutral measure $\mathbb{Q}$, the asset price S_t follows

$$\frac{dS_t}{S_t} = (r - D)dt + \sigma dW_t^{\mathbb{Q}}$$

where $W_t^{\mathbb{Q}} = W_t + \left(\dfrac{\mu - r}{\sigma}\right) t$ is a $\mathbb{Q}$-standard Wiener process. From Itō's lemma we can easily show for $T > t$

$$\log\left(\frac{S_T}{S_t}\right) \sim \mathcal{N}\left[\left(r - D - \frac{1}{2}\sigma^2\right)(T - t), \sigma^2(T - t)\right]$$

with density function

$$f(S_T|S_t) = \frac{1}{S_T\sigma\sqrt{2\pi(T - t)}} e^{-\frac{1}{2}\left(\frac{\log(S_T/S_t)-(r-D-\frac{1}{2}\sigma^2)(T-t)}{\sigma\sqrt{T-t}}\right)^2}.$$

By definition, the complex chooser option price at time t, $t \leq \tau \leq \min\{T_c, T_p\}$ is

$$V_{cc}(S_t, t; \tau, K_c, T_c, K_p, T_p)$$
$$= e^{-r(\tau-t)}\mathbb{E}^{\mathbb{Q}}\left[\max\{C_{bs}(S_\tau, \tau; K_c, T_c), P_{bs}(S_\tau, \tau; K_p, T_p)\}\,\Big|\,\mathscr{F}_t\right]$$
$$= e^{-r(\tau-t)}\int_0^\infty \max\{C_{bs}(S_\tau, \tau; K_c, T_c), P_{bs}(S_\tau, \tau; K_p, T_p)\}f(S_\tau|S_t)\,dS_\tau.$$

Let X solve the nonlinear equation $C_{bs}(X, \tau; K_c, T_c) = P_{bs}(X, \tau; K_p, T_p)$, then we can rewrite

$$V_{cc}(S_t, t; \tau, K_c, T_c, K_p, T_p) = e^{-r(\tau-t)}\int_0^X P_{bs}(S_\tau, \tau; K_p, T_p)f(S_\tau|S_t)\,dS_\tau$$
$$+ e^{-r(\tau-t)}\int_X^\infty C_{bs}(S_\tau, \tau; K_c, T_c)f(S_\tau|S_t)\,dS_\tau.$$

From Problem 6.2.2.3 (page 591) we can deduce that

$$e^{-r(\tau-t)}\int_X^\infty C_{bs}(S_\tau, \tau; K_c, T_c)f(S_\tau|S_t)\,dS_\tau$$
$$= e^{-r(\tau-t)}\int_X^\infty S_\tau e^{-D(T_c-\tau)}\Phi\left(d_+^c\right)f(S_\tau|S_t)\,dS_\tau$$
$$- e^{-r(\tau-t)}\int_X^\infty K_c e^{-r(T_c-\tau)}\Phi\left(d_-^c\right)f(S_\tau|S_t)\,dS_\tau$$
$$= S_t e^{-D(T_c-t)}\Phi(\alpha_+, \beta_+, \rho_c) - K_c e^{-r(T_c-t)}\Phi(\alpha_-, \beta_-, \rho_c)$$

where $\alpha_\pm = \dfrac{\log(S_t/X) + (r - D \pm \frac{1}{2}\sigma^2)(\tau - t)}{\sigma\sqrt{\tau - t}}$, $\beta_\pm = \dfrac{\log(S_t/K_c) + (r - D \pm \frac{1}{2}\sigma^2)(T_c - t)}{\sigma\sqrt{T_c - t}}$

and $\rho_c = \sqrt{\dfrac{\tau - t}{T_c - t}}$.

Furthermore, from Problem 6.2.2.4 (page 596) we can also deduce that

$$
e^{-r(\tau-t)} \int_0^X P_{bs}(S_\tau, \tau; K_p, T_p) f(S_\tau | S_t) \, dS_\tau
$$

$$
= e^{-r(\tau-t)} \int_0^X K_p e^{-r(T_p-\tau)} \Phi\left(-d_-^p\right) f(S_\tau | S_t) \, dS_\tau
$$

$$
- e^{-r(\tau-t)} \int_0^X S_\tau e^{-D(T_p-\tau)} \Phi\left(-d_+^p\right) f(S_\tau | S_t) \, dS_\tau
$$

$$
= K_p e^{-r(T_p-t)} \Phi(-\alpha_-, -\gamma_-, \rho_p) - S_t e^{-D(T_p-t)} \Phi(-\alpha_+, -\gamma_+, \rho_p)
$$

where $\gamma_\pm = \dfrac{\log(S_t/K_p) + (r - D \pm \frac{1}{2}\sigma^2)(T_p - t)}{\sigma\sqrt{T_p - t}}$ and $\rho_p = \sqrt{\dfrac{\tau - t}{T_p - t}}$.

Hence, the price of a complex chooser option at time $t \le \tau$ is

$$
V_{cc}(S_t, t; \tau, K_c, T_c, K_p, T_p) = S_t e^{-D(T_c-t)} \Phi(\alpha_+, \beta_+, \rho_c)
$$

$$
- K_c e^{-r(T_c-t)} \Phi(\alpha_-, \beta_-, \rho_c)
$$

$$
+ K_p e^{-r(T_p-t)} \Phi(-\alpha_-, -\gamma_-, \rho_p)
$$

$$
- S_t e^{-D(T_p-t)} \Phi(-\alpha_+, -\gamma_+, \rho_p).
$$

$\square$

7. *Black–Scholes Equation for Lookback Option I.* Let $\{W_t : t \ge 0\}$ be a $\mathbb{P}$-standard Wiener process on the probability space $(\Omega, \mathcal{F}, \mathbb{P})$ and let the stock price S_t follow a GBM

$$
\frac{dS_t}{S_t} = (\mu - D)dt + \sigma dW_t
$$

where μ is the drift parameter, D is the continuous dividend yield and σ is the volatility parameter. In addition, we let r be the risk-free interest rate.

Consider a European-style lookback option with terminal payoff

$$
V(S_T, M_T, T) = \Psi(S_T, M_T)
$$

which depends on the maximum of the stock price M_T reached within the lookback time period $[t_0, T]$, $t_0 \ge 0$ where T, $T > t$ is the option expiry time.

By defining

$$
M_t^{(n)} = \left[\int_{t_0}^t S_u^n \, du \right]^{\frac{1}{n}} \quad \text{and} \quad M_t = \max_{t_0 \le u \le t} S_u
$$

for $n \in \mathbb{N}$, show that

$$
\lim_{n \to \infty} M_t^{(n)} = M_t.
$$

Explain why, when the current stock price equals its current maximum, we would have the following result

$$\left.\frac{\partial V}{\partial M_t}\right|_{S_t=M_t} = 0.$$

By considering a hedging portfolio involving both lookback option $V(S_t, M_t^{(n)}, t)$ and stock price S_t, show that for $0 < S_t < M_t^{(n)}$, $V(S_t, M_t^{(n)}, t)$ satisfies the following PDE

$$\frac{\partial V}{\partial t} + \frac{1}{n} \frac{S_t^n}{\left[M_t^{(n)}\right]^{n-1}} \frac{\partial V}{\partial M_t^{(n)}} + \frac{1}{2}\sigma^2 S_t^2 \frac{\partial^2 V}{\partial S_t^2} + (r - D)S_t \frac{\partial V}{\partial S_t} - rV(S_t, M_t^{(n)}, t) = 0.$$

Finally, by taking $n \to \infty$, show that for $0 < S_t < M_t$, $V(S_t, M_t, t)$ satisfies

$$\frac{\partial V}{\partial t} + \frac{1}{2}\sigma^2 S_t^2 \frac{\partial^2 V}{\partial S_t^2} + (r - D)S_t \frac{\partial V}{\partial S_t} - rV(S_t, M_t, t) = 0$$

subject to the boundary conditions

$$V(S_T, M_T, T) = \Psi(S_T, M_T) \quad \text{and} \quad \left.\frac{\partial V}{\partial M_t}\right|_{S_t=M_t} = 0.$$

Solution: By definition, for $n \in \mathbb{N}$

$$M_t^{(n)} = \left[\int_{t_0}^t S_u^n \, du\right]^{\frac{1}{n}} \quad \text{and} \quad M_t = \max_{t_0 \le u \le t} S_u$$

and because S_t is continuous within the interval $[t_0, t]$, therefore the integral $\int_{t_0}^t S_u^n \, du$ exists as well as the maximum $M_t^{(n)}$ and M_t.

Since $S_u \le M_t$, $t_0 \le u \le t$, therefore for any $n \in \mathbb{N}$

$$0 < \int_{t_0}^t S_u^n \, du \le \int_{t_0}^t M_t^n \, du = M_t^n(t - t_0)$$

and hence

$$\left[\int_{t_0}^t S_u^n \, du\right]^{\frac{1}{n}} \le (t - t_0)^{\frac{1}{n}} M_t.$$

Taking limits $n \to \infty$

$$\lim_{n \to \infty} \left[\int_{t_0}^t S_u^n \, du\right]^{\frac{1}{n}} \le \lim_{n \to \infty} (t - t_0)^{\frac{1}{n}} M_t$$

we therefore have

$$\lim_{n \to \infty} M_t^{(n)} \le M_t.$$

We next choose a small $\epsilon > 0$ and define $\mathcal{A}_\epsilon(t)$ to be the set of $u \in [t_0, t]$ for which

$$S_u \ge M_t - \epsilon, \quad u \in [t_0, t]$$

and let

$$\lambda_\epsilon(t) = \int_{\mathcal{A}_\epsilon(t)} du$$

be the total length of the interval in which $S_u \ge M_t - \epsilon$.

Since S_u is continuous for $u \in [t_0, t]$, $\lambda_\epsilon(t) > 0$ and $\lambda_\epsilon(t) \le t - t_0$ therefore

$$\int_{t_0}^{t} S_u^n \, du \ge \int_{\mathcal{A}_\epsilon(t)} S_u^n \, du \ge \int_{\mathcal{A}_\epsilon(t)} (M_t - \epsilon)^n \, du = (M_t - \epsilon)^n \lambda_\epsilon(t)$$

and hence

$$\left[\int_{t_0}^{t} S_u^n \, du \right]^{\frac{1}{n}} \ge \lambda_\epsilon(t)^{\frac{1}{n}} (M_t - \epsilon).$$

Taking limits $n \to \infty$

$$\lim_{n \to \infty} M_t^{(n)} \ge M_t - \epsilon$$

and thus we have

$$M_t - \epsilon \le \lim_{n \to \infty} M_t^{(n)} \le M_t$$

and because $\epsilon > 0$ is a small number we can deduce that

$$\lim_{n \to \infty} M_t^{(n)} = M_t.$$

To show that $\dfrac{\partial V}{\partial M_t} = 0$ on $S_t = M_t$, we note that if $S_t = M_t$ then

$$M_T = \max_{t_0 \le u \le T} S_u = \max \left\{ \max_{t_0 \le u \le t} S_u, \max_{t \le u \le T} S_u \right\} \ge \max_{t_0 \le u \le t} S_u = M_t$$

and hence $\mathbb{P}(M_T = M_t) = 0$, which shows that M_t cannot be the final maximum at option expiry time T.

Since $M_T \neq M_t$, this implies that the lookback option $V(S_t, M_t, t)$ at time t is insensitive to small changes in M_t. Therefore,

$$\left. \frac{\partial V}{\partial M_t} \right|_{S_t=M_t} = 0.$$

To find the PDE satisfied by $V(S_t, M_t^{(n)}, t)$ we first construct a Δ-hedged portfolio having one option $V(S_t, M_t^{(n)}, t)$ and $-\Delta$ number of shares S_t. Thus, the hedged portfolio Π_t at time t is

$$\Pi_t = V(S_t, M_t^{(n)}, t) - \Delta S_t.$$

From t to $t + dt$, and because the holder receives $DS_t dt$ for every asset held, the portfolio value changes by an amount

$$d\Pi_t = dV - \Delta(dS_t + DS_t dt)$$

where

$$dV = \frac{\partial V}{\partial t}dt + \frac{\partial V}{\partial S_t}dS_t + \frac{\partial V}{\partial M_t^{(n)}}dM_t^{(n)} + \frac{1}{2}\frac{\partial^2 V}{\partial S_t^2}(dS_t)^2 + \frac{1}{2}\frac{\partial^2 V}{\partial (M_t^{(n)})^2}(dM_t^{(n)})^2 + \dots$$

and

$$dS_t = (\mu - D)S_t dt + \sigma S_t dW_t.$$

Since $M_t^{(n)} = \left[\int_{t_0}^t S_u^n du \right]^{\frac{1}{n}}$ we have

$$dM_t^{(n)} = \frac{1}{n}\left[\int_{t_0}^t S_u^n du \right]^{\frac{1}{n}-1} S_t^n dt = \frac{1}{n}\frac{S_t^n}{(M_t^{(n)})^{n-1}}dt.$$

From Itô's lemma

$$dV = \frac{\partial V}{\partial t}dt + \frac{\partial V}{\partial S_t}\left[(\mu - D)S_t dt + \sigma S_t dW_t\right] + \frac{1}{n}\frac{S_t^n}{(M_t^{(n)})^{n-1}}\frac{\partial V}{\partial M_t^{(n)}}dt$$

$$+ \frac{1}{2}\sigma^2 S_t^2 \frac{\partial^2 V}{\partial S_t^2}dt$$

$$= \left[\frac{\partial V}{\partial t} + \frac{1}{n}\frac{S_t^n}{(M_t^{(n)})^{n-1}}\frac{\partial V}{\partial M_t^{(n)}} + \frac{1}{2}\sigma^2 S_t^2 \frac{\partial^2 V}{\partial S_t^2} + (\mu - D)S_t\frac{\partial V}{\partial S_t} \right]dt$$

$$+ \sigma S_t \frac{\partial V}{\partial S_t}dW_t$$

and by substituting the above equation back into $d\Pi_t$ and rearranging terms, we have

$$d\Pi_t = \left[\frac{\partial V}{\partial t} + \frac{1}{n}\frac{S_t^n}{(M_t^{(n)})^{n-1}}\frac{\partial V}{\partial M_t^{(n)}} + \frac{1}{2}\sigma^2 S_t^2 \frac{\partial^2 V}{\partial S_t^2} + (\mu - D)S_t\frac{\partial V}{\partial S_t} - \mu\Delta S_t\right]dt$$
$$+ \sigma S_t\left(\frac{\partial V}{\partial S_t} - \Delta\right)dW_t.$$

To eliminate the random term we set

$$\Delta = \frac{\partial V}{\partial S_t}$$

and hence

$$d\Pi_t = \left[\frac{\partial V}{\partial t} + \frac{1}{n}\frac{S_t^n}{(M_t^{(n)})^{n-1}}\frac{\partial V}{\partial M_t^{(n)}} + \frac{1}{2}\sigma^2 S_t^2 \frac{\partial^2 V}{\partial S_t^2} - DS_t\frac{\partial V}{\partial S_t}\right]dt.$$

Under the no-arbitrage condition, the return on the amount Π_t invested in a risk-free interest rate would see a growth of

$$d\Pi_t = r\Pi_t dt$$

and therefore

$$r\Pi_t dt = \left[\frac{\partial V}{\partial t} + \frac{1}{n}\frac{S_t^n}{(M_t^{(n)})^{n-1}}\frac{\partial V}{\partial M_t^{(n)}} + \frac{1}{2}\sigma^2 S_t^2 \frac{\partial^2 V}{\partial S_t^2}\right.$$
$$\left. - DS_t\frac{\partial V}{\partial S_t}\right]dt$$

$$r\left(V(S_t, M_t^{(n)}, t) - \Delta S_t\right)dt = \left[\frac{\partial V}{\partial t} + \frac{1}{n}\frac{S_t^n}{(M_t^{(n)})^{n-1}}\frac{\partial V}{\partial M_t^{(n)}} + \frac{1}{2}\sigma^2 S_t^2 \frac{\partial^2 V}{\partial S_t^2}\right.$$
$$\left. - DS_t\frac{\partial V}{\partial S_t}\right]dt$$

$$r\left(V(S_t, M_t^{(n)}, t) - S_t\frac{\partial V}{\partial S_t}\right)dt = \left[\frac{\partial V}{\partial t} + \frac{1}{n}\frac{S_t^n}{(M_t^{(n)})^{n-1}}\frac{\partial V}{\partial M_t^{(n)}} + \frac{1}{2}\sigma^2 S_t^2 \frac{\partial^2 V}{\partial S_t^2}\right.$$
$$\left. - DS_t\frac{\partial V}{\partial S_t}\right]dt.$$

By removing dt and rearranging terms, we finally have

$$\frac{\partial V}{\partial t} + \frac{1}{n}\frac{S_t^n}{(M_t^{(n)})^{n-1}}\frac{\partial V}{\partial M_t^{(n)}} + \frac{1}{2}\sigma^2 S_t^2 \frac{\partial^2 V}{\partial S_t^2} + (r - D)S_t\frac{\partial V}{\partial S_t} - rV(S_t, M_t^{(n)}, t) = 0.$$

If we take the limit $n \to \infty$ then $\lim_{n\to\infty} M_t^{(n)} = M_t$ and since $S_t \leq \max_{t_0 \leq u \leq t} S_u = M_t$ we have

$$\lim_{n\to\infty} \frac{1}{n} \frac{S_t^n}{(M_t^{(n)})^{n-1}} = 0.$$

Thus, in the limit $V(S_t, M_t, t)$ satisfies

$$\frac{\partial V}{\partial t} + \frac{1}{2}\sigma^2 S_t^2 \frac{\partial^2 V}{\partial S_t^2} + (r - D)S_t \frac{\partial V}{\partial S_t} - rV(S_t, M_t, t) = 0$$

with boundary conditions

$$V(S_T, M_T, T) = \Psi(S_T, M_T) \quad \text{and} \quad \left. \frac{\partial V}{\partial M_t} \right|_{S_t=M_t} = 0.$$

$\square$

8. *Stop-Loss Option.* At time t, let the asset price S_t follow a GBM

$$\frac{dS_t}{S_t} = (\mu - D)dt + \sigma dW_t$$

where W_t is a standard Wiener process on the probability space $(\Omega, \mathscr{F}, \mathbb{P})$, μ is the drift parameter, D is the continuous dividend yield and σ is the volatility parameter. In addition, let r be the risk-free interest rate.

Consider a stop-loss option $V(S_t, M_t)$, which is a perpetual barrier lookback option with a rebate λM_t where $\lambda \in (0, 1)$ is a fixed proportion of the maximum realised asset price at time t, $M_t = \max_{t_0 \leq u \leq t} S_u$ where $t_0 \geq 0$. By setting a time-dependent barrier $B_t = \lambda M_t$ such that if $S_t \leq B_t$ then the option pays the holder B_t, and because the option is time independent, the option is not triggered until the barrier is hit.

From the above information show that for $B_t < S_t < M_t$, the stop-loss option price $V(S_t, M_t)$ satisfies

$$\frac{1}{2}\sigma^2 S_t^2 \frac{\partial^2 V}{\partial S_t^2} + (r - D)S_t \frac{\partial V}{\partial S_t} - rV(S_t, M_t) = 0$$

with boundary conditions

$$V(B_t, M_t) = B_t \quad \text{and} \quad \left. \frac{\partial V}{\partial M_t} \right|_{S_t=M_t} = 0.$$

By considering the change of variables

$$V(S_t, M_t) = M_t \phi(\xi), \quad \xi = S_t / M_t$$

show that for $\lambda < \xi < 1$, $\phi(\xi)$ satisfies

$$\frac{1}{2}\sigma^2\xi^2\frac{d^2\phi}{d\xi^2} + (r - D)\xi\frac{d\phi}{d\xi} - r\phi(\xi) = 0$$

with boundary conditions

$$\phi(\lambda) = \lambda \quad \text{and} \quad \phi(1) = \frac{d\phi}{d\xi}\bigg|_{\xi=1}.$$

By setting $\phi(\xi) = C\xi^m$ where C and m are constants, show that the stop-loss option price is

$$V(S_t, M_t) = \lambda M_t \left[\frac{(1-\beta)\left(S_t/M_t\right)^\alpha - (1-\alpha)\left(S_t/M_t\right)^\beta}{(1-\beta)\lambda^\alpha - (1-\alpha)\lambda^\beta}\right]$$

where

$$\alpha = \frac{-(r - D - \frac{1}{2}\sigma^2) + \sqrt{(r - D - \frac{1}{2}\sigma^2)^2 + 2\sigma^2 r}}{\sigma^2}$$

and

$$\beta = \frac{-(r - D - \frac{1}{2}\sigma^2) - \sqrt{(r - D - \frac{1}{2}\sigma^2)^2 + 2\sigma^2 r}}{\sigma^2}.$$

What is the option price if $D = 0$?

Solution: Following the steps given in Problem 6.2.1.7 (page 547), we first define

$$M_t^{(n)} = \left[\int_{t_0}^t S_u^n \, du\right]^{\frac{1}{n}}.$$

To find the PDE satisfied by $V(S_t, M_t^{(n)})$ we construct a Δ-hedged portfolio

$$\Pi_t = V(S_t, M_t^{(n)}) - \Delta S_t$$

having one option $V(S_t, M_t^{(n)})$ and short Δ number of shares S_t. Using similar steps as described in Problem 6.2.1.7 (page 547), we can easily show that

$$\frac{1}{n}\frac{S_t^n}{(M_t^{(n)})^{n-1}}\frac{\partial V}{\partial M_t^{(n)}} + \frac{1}{2}\sigma^2 S_t^2\frac{\partial^2 V}{\partial S_t^2} + (r - D)S_t\frac{\partial V}{\partial S_t} - rV(S_t, M_t^{(n)}) = 0.$$

By taking $\lim_{n \to \infty} M_t^{(n)} = M_t$ then $V(S_t, M_t)$ will satisfy

$$\frac{1}{2}\sigma^2 S_t^2 \frac{\partial^2 V}{\partial S_t^2} + (r - D)S_t \frac{\partial V}{\partial S_t} - rV(S_t, M_t, t) = 0$$

for $\lambda M_t < S_t < M_t$ with boundary conditions

$$V(\lambda M_t, M_t) = \lambda M_t \quad \text{and} \quad \left. \frac{\partial V}{\partial M_t} \right|_{S_t = M_t} = 0.$$

Setting $V(S_t, M_t) = M_t \phi(\xi)$ with $\xi = S_t / M_t$ we have

$$\frac{\partial V}{\partial S_t} = M_t \frac{d\phi}{d\xi} \frac{d\xi}{dS_t} = \frac{d\phi}{d\xi}, \quad \frac{\partial^2 V}{\partial S_t^2} = \frac{d^2\phi}{d\xi^2} \frac{d\xi}{dS_t} = \frac{1}{M_t} \frac{d^2\phi}{d\xi^2}$$

$$\frac{\partial V}{\partial M_t} = \phi(\xi) + M_t \frac{d\phi}{d\xi} \frac{d\xi}{dM_t} = \phi(\xi) + M_t \frac{d\phi}{d\xi} \left(-\frac{S_t}{M_t^2} \right) = \phi(\xi) - \xi \frac{d\phi}{d\xi}$$

$$V(\lambda M_t, M_t) = \lambda M_t \implies M_t \phi \left(\frac{\lambda M_t}{M_t} \right) = \lambda M_t \quad \text{or} \quad \phi(\lambda) = \lambda$$

and

$$\left. \frac{\partial V}{\partial M_t} \right|_{S_t = M_t} = \phi(1) - \left. \frac{d\phi}{d\xi} \right|_{\xi=1} = 0.$$

Substituting the above results into the PDE and boundary conditions, and because $\xi = S_t / M_t$, we will eventually arrive at a second-order ODE

$$\frac{1}{2}\sigma^2 \xi^2 \frac{d^2\phi}{d\xi^2} + (r - D)\xi \frac{d\phi}{d\xi} - r\phi(\xi) = 0$$

for $\lambda < \xi < 1$ with boundary conditions

$$\phi(\lambda) = \lambda \quad \text{and} \quad \phi(1) = \left. \frac{d\phi}{d\xi} \right|_{\xi=1}.$$

To solve the ODE we let

$$\phi(\xi) = C\xi^m$$

where C and m are constants. Substituting

$$\phi(\xi) = C\xi^m, \quad \frac{d\phi}{d\xi} = mC\xi^{m-1}, \quad \frac{d^2\phi}{d\xi^2} = m(m-1)C\xi^{m-2}$$

into the ODE we have

$$\frac{1}{2}\sigma^2 m(m-1) + (r-D)m - r = 0$$

or

$$\frac{1}{2}\sigma^2 m^2 + \left(r - D - \frac{1}{2}\sigma^2\right)m - r = 0.$$

Therefore,

$$m = \frac{-(r - D - \frac{1}{2}\sigma^2) \pm \sqrt{(r - D - \frac{1}{2}\sigma^2)^2 + 2\sigma^2 r}}{\sigma^2}.$$

Since

$$\sqrt{(r - D - \frac{1}{2}\sigma^2)^2 + 2\sigma^2 r} > (r - D - \frac{1}{2}\sigma^2)$$

the solution of the ODE must be of the form

$$\phi(\xi) = A\xi^\alpha + B\xi^\beta$$

where A and B are unknown constants,

$$\alpha = \frac{-(r - D - \frac{1}{2}\sigma^2) + \sqrt{(r - D - \frac{1}{2}\sigma^2)^2 + 2\sigma^2 r}}{\sigma^2} > 0$$

and

$$\beta = \frac{-(r - D - \frac{1}{2}\sigma^2) - \sqrt{(r - D - \frac{1}{2}\sigma^2)^2 + 2\sigma^2 r}}{\sigma^2} < 0.$$

Substituting $\phi(\xi) = A\xi^\alpha + B\xi^\beta$ into the boundary conditions

$$\phi(\lambda) = \lambda \quad \text{and} \quad \phi(1) = \phi'(1)$$

we have

$$A\lambda^\alpha + B\lambda^\beta = \lambda \quad \text{and} \quad A(\alpha - 1) + B(\alpha - 1) = 0.$$

Solving the two equations simultaneously, we have

$$A = \frac{(1-\beta)\lambda}{(1-\beta)\lambda^\alpha + (\alpha-1)\lambda^\beta} \quad \text{and} \quad B = \frac{-(1-\alpha)\lambda}{(1-\beta)\lambda^\alpha + (\alpha-1)\lambda^\beta}$$

and hence

$$\phi(\xi) = A\xi^\alpha + B\xi^\beta = \frac{(1-\beta)\lambda\xi^\alpha - (1-\alpha)\lambda\xi^\beta}{(1-\beta)\lambda^\alpha + (\alpha-1)\lambda^\beta}.$$

Because $V(S_t, M_t) = M_t\phi(\xi)$ and $\xi = S_t/M_t$, the stop-loss option price at time t is

$$V(S_t, M_t) = \lambda M_t \left[\frac{(1-\beta)\left(S_t/M_t\right)^\alpha - (1-\alpha)\left(S_t/M_t\right)^\beta}{(1-\beta)\lambda^\alpha - (1-\alpha)\lambda^\beta} \right].$$

Finally, if $D = 0$ then $\alpha = 1$ and $\beta = 0$, and therefore $A = 1$ and $B = 0$. Thus, $\phi(\xi) = \xi$ is independent of λ and hence the stop-loss option price is

$$V(S_t, M_t) = M_t\phi(\xi) = M_t\xi = S_t$$

which is equivalent to the underlying stock price S_t.

$\square$

9. *Perpetual American Fixed Strike Lookback Option.* At time t let the asset price S_t follow a GBM

$$\frac{dS_t}{S_t} = (\mu - D)dt + \sigma dW_t$$

where W_t is a standard Wiener process on the probability space $(\Omega, \mathcal{F}, \mathbb{P})$, μ is the drift parameter, D is the continuous dividend yield and σ is the volatility parameter. In addition, let r be the risk-free interest rate.

Consider a perpetual American fixed strike lookback option $V(S_t, M_t; K)$ which gives the holder the right to buy at the specified fixed strike $K > 0$ with the intrinsic payoff $\max\{M_t - K, 0\}$, $M_t = \max_{t_0 \leq u \leq t} S_u$, $t_0 \geq 0$ up to the date chosen by the option holder. Let $S^\infty < M_t$ where $S^\infty > K$ is the unknown optimal exercise boundary such that for $S_t \geq S^\infty$ the option should be exercised whilst for $S_t < S^\infty$ the option should be held. Show that for $0 < S_t < S^\infty < M_t$, the option price $V(S_t, M_t; K)$ satisfies

$$\frac{1}{2}\sigma^2 S_t^2 \frac{\partial^2 V}{\partial S_t^2} + (r-D)S_t\frac{\partial V}{\partial S_t} - rV(S_t, M_t; K) = 0$$

with boundary conditions

$$V(S^\infty, M_t; K) = M_t - K \quad \text{and} \quad \left.\frac{\partial V}{\partial M_t}\right|_{S_t = M_t} = 0.$$

By considering the change of variables

$$V(S_t, M_t; K) = M_t \phi(\xi), \quad \xi = S_t/M_t$$

show that for $0 < \xi < \xi^\infty < 1$ where $\xi^\infty = S^\infty/M_t$, then $\phi(\xi)$ satisfies

$$\frac{1}{2}\sigma^2\xi^2\frac{d^2\phi}{d\xi^2} + (r-D)\xi\frac{d\phi}{d\xi} - r\phi(\xi) = 0$$

with boundary conditions

$$\phi(\xi^\infty) = \frac{M_t - K}{M_t}, \quad \frac{d\phi}{d\xi}\Big|_{\xi=\xi^\infty} = -\frac{K}{S^\infty} \quad \text{and} \quad \phi(1) = \frac{d\phi}{d\xi}\Big|_{\xi=1}.$$

By setting $\phi(\xi) = C\xi^m$ where C and m are constants, show that the option price is

$$V(S_t, M_t; K)$$

$$= \begin{cases} \dfrac{1}{\alpha-\beta}\left\{\left[\dfrac{(M_t-K)\alpha+K}{M_t}\right]\left(\dfrac{\xi}{\xi^\infty}\right)^\beta \right. \\ \qquad\qquad \left. -\left[\dfrac{(M_t-K)\beta+K}{M_t}\right]\left(\dfrac{\xi}{\xi^\infty}\right)^\alpha\right\} & \text{if } S_t < S^\infty \\[4mm] M_t - K & \text{if } S_t \geq S^\infty \end{cases}$$

where

$$\alpha = \frac{-(r-D-\frac{1}{2}\sigma^2) + \sqrt{(r-D-\frac{1}{2}\sigma^2)^2 + 2\sigma^2 r}}{\sigma^2}$$

$$\beta = \frac{-(r-D-\frac{1}{2}\sigma^2) - \sqrt{(r-D-\frac{1}{2}\sigma^2)^2 + 2\sigma^2 r}}{\sigma^2}$$

and

$$\xi^\infty = \left\{\frac{(\beta-1)\left[(M_t-K)\alpha+K\right]}{(\alpha-1)\left[(M_t-K)\beta+K\right]}\right\}^{\frac{1}{\beta-\alpha}}.$$

What is the option price if $D = 0$?

Solution: To show that $V(S_t, M_t; K)$ satisfies

$$\frac{1}{2}\sigma^2 S_t^2\frac{\partial^2 V}{\partial S_t^2} + (r-D)S_t\frac{\partial V}{\partial S_t} - rV(S_t, M_t; K) = 0$$

with boundary condition $\dfrac{\partial V}{\partial M_t}\Big|_{S_t=M_t} = 0$, see Problem 6.2.2.8 (page 609).

Let $K < S^\infty < M_t$ be the optimal exercise boundary such that $S_t \geq S^\infty$, then the perpetual American fixed strike lookback option price is equal to its intrinsic value $V(S^\infty, M_t; K) = M_t - K$. In contrast, for $S_t < S^\infty$ the option should be held. Thus, for $0 < S_t < S^\infty < M_t$ the option problem can be expressed as

$$\frac{1}{2}\sigma^2 S_t^2 \frac{\partial^2 V}{\partial S_t^2} + (r - D)S_t \frac{\partial^2 V}{\partial S_t} - rV(S_t, M_t; K) = 0$$

with boundary conditions

$$V(S^\infty, M_t; K) = M_t - K \quad \text{and} \quad \left.\frac{\partial V}{\partial M_t}\right|_{S_t=M_t} = 0.$$

Using the change of variables

$$V(S_t, M_t; K) = M_t\phi(\xi), \quad \xi = S_t/M_t \quad \text{and} \quad \xi^\infty = S^\infty/M_t$$

and following the steps given in Problem 6.2.2.8 (page 609), we can easily show that $\phi(\xi)$ satisfies

$$\frac{1}{2}\sigma^2 \xi^2 \frac{d^2\phi}{d\xi^2} + (r - D)\xi \frac{d\phi}{d\xi} - r\phi(\xi) = 0$$

for $0 < \xi < \xi^\infty < 1$.

As for the boundary conditions, we note that for $V(S^\infty, M_t; K) = M_t - K$

$$M_t\phi(\xi^\infty) = M_t - K \quad \text{or} \quad \phi(\xi^\infty) = \frac{M_t - K}{M_t}.$$

In addition, because

$$\frac{\partial V}{\partial M_t} = \phi(\xi) + M_t \frac{d\phi}{d\xi} \frac{d\xi}{dM_t} = \phi(\xi) - \xi \frac{d\phi}{d\xi}$$

therefore $\left.\dfrac{\partial V}{\partial M_t}\right|_{S_t=S^\infty} = 1$ becomes

$$\phi(\xi^\infty) - \xi^\infty \left.\frac{d\phi}{d\xi}\right|_{\xi=\xi^\infty} = 1 \quad \text{or} \quad \left.\frac{d\phi}{d\xi}\right|_{\xi=\xi^\infty} = -\frac{K}{S^\infty}$$

since $\phi(\xi^\infty) = \dfrac{M_t - K}{M_t}$.

Finally, $\left.\dfrac{\partial V}{\partial M_t}\right|_{S_t=M_t} = 0$ becomes

$$\phi(1) - \left.\frac{d\phi}{d\xi}\right|_{\xi=1} = 0.$$

Therefore, for $0 < \xi < \xi^\infty < 1$, $\phi(\xi)$ satisfies

$$\frac{1}{2}\sigma^2\xi^2\frac{d^2\phi}{d\xi^2} + (r - D)\xi\frac{d\phi}{d\xi} - r\phi(\xi) = 0$$

with boundary conditions

$$\phi(\xi^\infty) = \frac{M_t - K}{M_t}, \quad \frac{d\phi}{d\xi}\bigg|_{\xi=\xi^\infty} = -\frac{K}{S^\infty} \quad \text{and} \quad \phi(1) = \frac{d\phi}{d\xi}\bigg|_{\xi=1}.$$

By setting $\phi(\xi) = C\xi^m$ where C and m are constants, then following Problem 6.2.2.8 (page 609) the solution of the Cauchy–Euler equation is

$$\phi(\xi) = A\xi^\alpha + B\xi^\beta$$

where A and B are constants to be determined with

$$\alpha = \frac{-(r - D - \frac{1}{2}\sigma^2) + \sqrt{(r - D - \frac{1}{2}\sigma^2)^2 + 2\sigma^2 r}}{\sigma^2}$$

and

$$\beta = \frac{-(r - D - \frac{1}{2}\sigma^2) - \sqrt{(r - D - \frac{1}{2}\sigma^2)^2 + 2\sigma^2 r}}{\sigma^2}.$$

Substituting $\phi(\xi) = A\xi^\alpha + B\xi^\beta$ and $\phi'(\xi) = \alpha A\xi^{\alpha-1} + \beta B\xi^{\beta-1}$ into the boundary conditions, we have

$$A(\xi^\infty)^\alpha + B(\xi^\infty)^\beta = \frac{M_t - K}{M_t}$$

$$\alpha A(\xi^\infty)^{\alpha-1} + \beta B(\xi^\infty)^{\beta-1} = -\frac{K}{S^\infty}$$

$$(\alpha - 1)A + (\beta - 1)B = 0.$$

By solving

$$A(\xi^\infty)^\alpha + B(\xi^\infty)^\beta = \frac{M_t - K}{M_t} \quad \text{and} \quad \alpha A(\xi^\infty)^{\alpha-1} + \beta B(\xi^\infty)^{\beta-1} = -\frac{K}{S^\infty}$$

simultaneously we have

$$A = \frac{(M_t - K)\beta + K}{M_t(\beta - \alpha)(\xi^\infty)^\alpha} \quad \text{and} \quad B = \frac{(M_t - K)\alpha + K}{M_t(\alpha - \beta)(\xi^\infty)^\beta}.$$

By substituting the expressions for A and B into $\alpha A(\xi^\infty)^{\alpha-1} + \beta B(\xi^\infty)^{\beta-1} = 0$ we have the identity

$$(\alpha - 1)\left[(M_t - K)\beta + K\right](\xi^\infty)^\beta = (\beta - 1)\left[(M_t - K)\alpha + K\right](\xi^\infty)^\alpha$$

and hence

$$\xi^\infty = \left\{ \frac{(\beta - 1)\left[(M_t - K)\alpha + K\right]}{(\alpha - 1)\left[(M_t - K)\beta + K\right]} \right\}^{\frac{1}{\beta - \alpha}}.$$

Therefore,

$$
\begin{aligned}
\phi(\xi) &= A\xi^\alpha + B\xi^\beta \\
&= \frac{1}{M_t(\alpha - \beta)} \left\{ \left[\frac{(M_t - K)\alpha + K}{M_t}\right]\left(\frac{\xi}{\xi^\infty}\right)^\beta - \left[\frac{(M_t - K)\beta + K}{M_t}\right]\left(\frac{\xi}{\xi^\infty}\right)^\alpha \right\}
\end{aligned}
$$

and hence the option price for $0 < S_t < S^\infty < M_t$ is

$$
\begin{aligned}
&V(S_t, M_t; K) \\
&= \frac{1}{\alpha - \beta} \left\{ \left[\frac{(M_t - K)\alpha + K}{M_t}\right]\left(\frac{\xi}{\xi^\infty}\right)^\beta - \left[\frac{(M_t - K)\beta + K}{M_t}\right]\left(\frac{\xi}{\xi^\infty}\right)^\alpha \right\}.
\end{aligned}
$$

Collectively, we can therefore write

$$
V(S_t, M_t; K)
= \begin{cases}
\dfrac{1}{\alpha - \beta} \left\{ \left[\dfrac{(M_t - K)\alpha + K}{M_t}\right]\left(\dfrac{\xi}{\xi^\infty}\right)^\beta \right. & \\
\qquad \left. - \left[\dfrac{(M_t - K)\beta + K}{M_t}\right]\left(\dfrac{\xi}{\xi^\infty}\right)^\alpha \right\} & \text{if } S_t < S^\infty \\[2ex]
M_t - K & \text{if } S_t \geq S^\infty.
\end{cases}
$$

When the continuous dividend yield $D = 0$ then $\alpha = 1$ and $\beta = -\dfrac{2r}{\sigma^2}$. Thus, ξ^∞ is undefined, which implies that the option price problem does not have a solution. This shows that it is never optimal to hold such an option unless S_t pays a continuous stream of dividends.

N.B. For the case when $K = 0$, the option is known as a Russian option, which pays out the maximum realised asset price M_t up to the date chosen by the holder.

□

10. *Black–Scholes Equation for Lookback Option II.* Let $\{W_t : t \geq 0\}$ be a $\mathbb{P}$-standard Wiener process on the probability space $(\Omega, \mathscr{F}, \mathbb{P})$ and let the stock price S_t follow a GBM

$$\frac{dS_t}{S_t} = (\mu - D)dt + \sigma dW_t$$

where μ is the drift parameter, D is the continuous dividend yield and σ is the volatility parameter.

Consider a European-style lookback option with terminal payoff

$$V(S_T, m_T, T) = \Psi(S_T, m_T)$$

which depends on the minimum of the stock price m_T reached within the lookback time period $[t_0, T]$, $t_0 \geq 0$ where $T > t$ is the option expiry time. By defining

$$m_t^{(n)} = \left[\int_{t_0}^{t} S_u^{-n} du \right]^{-\frac{1}{n}} \quad \text{and} \quad m_t = \min_{t_0 \leq u \leq t} S_u$$

for $n \in \mathbb{N}$, show that

$$\lim_{n \to \infty} m_t^{(n)} = m_t.$$

Explain why, when the current stock price equals its current minimum, we would have the following result

$$\left. \frac{\partial V}{\partial m_t} \right|_{S_t = m_t} = 0.$$

By considering a hedging portfolio involving both lookback option $V(S_t, m_t^{(n)}, t)$ and stock S_t, show that for $S_t > m_t^{(n)} > 0$, $V(S_t, m_t^{(n)}, t)$ satisfies the following PDE

$$\frac{\partial V}{\partial t} - \frac{1}{n} \frac{\left[m_t^{(n)} \right]^{n+1}}{S_t^n} \frac{\partial V}{\partial m_t^{(n)}} + \frac{1}{2} \sigma^2 S_t^2 \frac{\partial^2 V}{\partial S_t^2} + (r - D)S_t \frac{\partial V}{\partial S_t} - rV(S_t, M_t^{(n)}, t) = 0.$$

Finally, by taking $n \to \infty$, show that for $S_t > m_t > 0$, $V(S_t, m_t, t)$ satisfies

$$\frac{\partial V}{\partial t} + \frac{1}{2} \sigma^2 S_t^2 \frac{\partial^2 V}{\partial S_t^2} + (r - D)S_t \frac{\partial V}{\partial S_t} - rV(S_t, m_t, t) = 0$$

subject to the boundary conditions

$$V(S_T, m_T, T) = \Psi(S_T, m_T) \quad \text{and} \quad \left. \frac{\partial V}{\partial m_t} \right|_{S_t = m_t} = 0.$$

Solution: By definition, for $n \in \mathbb{N}$

$$m_t^{(n)} = \left[\int_{t_0}^{t} S_u^n \, du \right]^{\frac{1}{n}} \quad \text{and} \quad m_t = \min_{t_0 \leq u \leq t} S_u$$

and because S_t is continuous within the interval $[t_0, t]$, therefore the integral $\int_{t_0}^{t} S_u^{-n} \, du$ exists as well as the minimum $m_t^{(n)}$ and m_t.

Since we can write

$$m_t = \left[\max_{t_0 \leq u \leq t} S_u^{-1} \right]^{-1}$$

therefore

$$m_t^{-1} = \max_{t_0 \leq u \leq t} S_u^{-1}$$

and for any $n \in \mathbb{N}$

$$\int_{t_0}^{t} m_t^{-n} du \geq \int_{t_0}^{t} S_u^{-n} \, du$$

or

$$m_t^{-n}(t - t_0) \geq \int_{0}^{t} S_u^{-n} \, du$$

and hence

$$m_t (t - t_0)^{-\frac{1}{n}} \leq \left[\int_{0}^{t} S_u^{-n} \, du \right]^{-\frac{1}{n}}.$$

Taking limits $n \to \infty$

$$\lim_{n \to \infty} m_t (t - t_0)^{-\frac{1}{n}} \leq \lim_{n \to \infty} \left[\int_{0}^{t} S_u^{-n} \, du \right]^{-\frac{1}{n}}$$

we therefore have

$$m_t \leq \lim_{n \to \infty} m_t^{(n)}.$$

We next choose a small $\epsilon > 0$ and define $\mathcal{A}_\epsilon(t)$ to be the set of $u \in [t_0, t]$ for which

$$S_u \leq m_t + \epsilon, \quad u \in [t_0, t]$$

and let

$$\lambda_\epsilon(t) = \int_{A_\epsilon(t)} du$$

be the total length of the interval in which $S_u \leq m_t + \epsilon$ (or $S_u^{-1} \geq (m_t + \epsilon)^{-1}$).
Since S_u is continuous for $u \in [t_0, t]$, $\lambda_\epsilon(t) > 0$ and $\lambda_\epsilon(t) \leq t - t_0$ therefore

$$\int_{t_0}^{t} S_u^{-n}\, du \geq \int_{A_\epsilon(t)} S_u^{-n}\, du \geq \int_{A_\epsilon(t)} (m_t + \epsilon)^{-n}\, du = (m_t + \epsilon)^{-n} \lambda_\epsilon(t)$$

and hence

$$\left[\int_{t_0}^{t} S_u^{-n}\, du \right]^{-\frac{1}{n}} \leq \lambda_\epsilon(t)^{-\frac{1}{n}} (m_t + \epsilon).$$

Taking limits $n \to \infty$

$$\lim_{n \to \infty} m_t^{(n)} \leq m_t + \epsilon$$

and thus we have

$$m_t \leq \lim_{n \to \infty} M_t^{(n)} \leq m_t + \epsilon$$

and because $\epsilon > 0$ is a small number we can deduce that

$$\lim_{n \to \infty} m_t^{(n)} = m_t.$$

To show that $\dfrac{\partial V}{\partial m_t} = 0$ on $S_t = m_t$ we note that if $S_t = m_t$ then

$$m_T = \min_{t_0 \leq u \leq T} S_u = \min \left\{ \min_{t_0 \leq u \leq t} S_u, \min_{t \leq u \leq T} S_u \right\} \leq \min_{0 \leq u \leq t} S_u = m_t$$

and hence $\mathbb{P}(m_T = m_t) = 0$, which shows that m_t cannot be the final maximum at option expiry time T.

Since $m_T \neq m_t$, this implies that the lookback option $V(S_t, m_t, t)$ at time t is insensitive to small changes in m_t. Therefore,

$$\left. \frac{\partial V}{\partial m_t} \right|_{S_t = m_t} = 0.$$

To find the PDE satisfied by $V(S_t, m_t^{(n)}, t)$ we first construct a Δ-hedged portfolio having one option $V(S_t, m_t^{(n)}, t)$ and shorting Δ number of shares S_t. Thus, the hedged portfolio Π_t at time t is

$$\Pi_t = V(S_t, m_t^{(n)}, t) - \Delta S_t.$$

From t to $t + dt$, and because the holder receives $DS_t dt$ for every asset held, the portfolio value changes by an amount

$$d\Pi_t = dV - \Delta(dS_t + DS_t dt)$$

where

$$dV = \frac{\partial V}{\partial t} dt + \frac{\partial V}{\partial S_t} dS_t + \frac{\partial V}{\partial m_t^{(n)}} dm_t^{(n)} + \frac{1}{2}\frac{\partial^2 V}{\partial S_t^2}(dS_t)^2 + \frac{1}{2}\frac{\partial^2 V}{\partial (m_t^{(n)})^2}(dm_t^{(n)})^2 + \dots$$

and

$$dS_t = (\mu - D)S_t dt + \sigma S_t dW_t.$$

Since $m_t^{(n)} = \left[\int_{t_0}^{t} S_u^{-n} du \right]^{-\frac{1}{n}}$ we have

$$dm_t^{(n)} = -\frac{1}{n}\left[\int_0^t S_u^{-n} du \right]^{-\frac{1}{n}-1} S_t^{-n} dt = -\frac{1}{n}\frac{(m_t^{(n)})^{n+1}}{S_t^n} dt.$$

From Itō's lemma

$$dV = \frac{\partial V}{\partial t} dt + \frac{\partial V}{\partial S_t}\left[(\mu - D)S_t dt + \sigma S_t dW_t \right] - \frac{1}{n}\frac{(m_t^{(n)})^{n+1}}{S_t^n}\frac{\partial V}{\partial m_t^{(n)}} dt$$

$$+ \frac{1}{2}\sigma^2 S_t^2 \frac{\partial^2 V}{\partial S_t^2} dt$$

$$= \left[\frac{\partial V}{\partial t} - \frac{1}{n}\frac{(m_t^{(n)})^{n+1}}{S_t^n}\frac{\partial V}{\partial m_t^{(n)}} + \frac{1}{2}\sigma^2 S_t^2 \frac{\partial^2 V}{\partial S_t^2} + (\mu - D)S_t\frac{\partial V}{\partial S_t} \right] dt$$

$$+ \sigma S_t \frac{\partial V}{\partial S_t} dW_t$$

and by substituting dV into $d\Pi_t$ and rearranging terms, we have

$$d\Pi_t = \left[\frac{\partial V}{\partial t} - \frac{1}{n}\frac{(m_t^{(n)})^{n+1}}{S_t^n}\frac{\partial V}{\partial m_t^{(n)}} + \frac{1}{2}\sigma^2 S_t^2 \frac{\partial^2 V}{\partial S_t^2} + (\mu - D)S_t\frac{\partial V}{\partial S_t} - \mu\Delta S_t \right] dt$$

$$+ \sigma S_t \left(\frac{\partial V}{\partial S_t} - \Delta \right) dW_t.$$

To eliminate the random term we set

$$\Delta = \frac{\partial V}{\partial S_t}$$

and hence

$$d\Pi_t = \left[\frac{\partial V}{\partial t} - \frac{1}{n}\frac{(m_t^{(n)})^{n+1}}{S_t^n}\frac{\partial V}{\partial m_t^{(n)}} + \frac{1}{2}\sigma^2 S_t^2 \frac{\partial^2 V}{\partial S_t^2} - DS_t\frac{\partial V}{\partial S_t} \right] dt.$$

Under the no-arbitrage condition, the return on the amount Π_t invested in a risk-free interest rate would see a growth of

$$d\Pi_t = r\Pi_t dt$$

and therefore

$$r\Pi_t dt = \left[\frac{\partial V}{\partial t} - \frac{1}{n} \frac{(m_t^{(n)})^{n+1}}{S_t^n} \frac{\partial V}{\partial m_t^{(n)}} + \frac{1}{2}\sigma^2 S_t^2 \frac{\partial^2 V}{\partial S_t^2} \right.$$
$$\left. -DS_t \frac{\partial V}{\partial S_t} \right] dt$$

$$r\left(V(S_t, m_t^{(n)}, t) - \Delta S_t \right) dt = \left[\frac{\partial V}{\partial t} - \frac{1}{n} \frac{(m_t^{(n)})^{n+1}}{S_t^n} \frac{\partial V}{\partial M_t^{(n)}} + \frac{1}{2}\sigma^2 S_t^2 \frac{\partial^2 V}{\partial S_t^2} \right.$$
$$\left. -DS_t \frac{\partial V}{\partial S_t} \right] dt$$

$$r\left(V(S_t, m_t^{(n)}, t) - S_t \frac{\partial V}{\partial S_t} \right) dt = \left[\frac{\partial V}{\partial t} - \frac{1}{n} \frac{(m_t^{(n)})^{n+1}}{S_t^n} \frac{\partial V}{\partial m_t^{(n)}} + \frac{1}{2}\sigma^2 S_t^2 \frac{\partial^2 V}{\partial S_t^2} \right.$$
$$\left. -DS_t \frac{\partial V}{\partial S_t} \right] dt.$$

By removing dt and rearranging terms, we finally have

$$\frac{\partial V}{\partial t} - \frac{1}{n} \frac{(m_t^{(n)})^{n+1}}{S_t^n} \frac{\partial V}{\partial m_t^{(n)}} + \frac{1}{2}\sigma^2 S_t^2 \frac{\partial^2 V}{\partial S_t^2} + (r-D)S_t \frac{\partial V}{\partial S_t} - rV(S_t, m_t^{(n)}, t) = 0.$$

If we take the limit $n \to \infty$ then $\lim_{n\to\infty} m_t^{(n)} = m_t$, and since $m_t = \min_{t_0 \leq u \leq t} S_u \leq S_t$, we have

$$\lim_{n\to\infty} \frac{1}{n} \frac{(m_t^{(n)})^{n+1}}{S_t^n} = \lim_{n\to\infty} \frac{1}{n} \left(\frac{m_t^{(n)}}{S_t} \right)^n m_t^{(n)} = 0.$$

Thus, in the limit, $V(S_t, m_t, t)$ satisfies

$$\frac{\partial V}{\partial t} + \frac{1}{2}\sigma^2 S_t^2 \frac{\partial^2 V}{\partial S_t^2} + (r-D)S_t \frac{\partial V}{\partial S_t} - rV(S_t, m_t, t) = 0$$

with boundary conditions

$$V(S_T, m_T, T) = \Psi(S_T, m_T) \quad \text{and} \quad \left. \frac{\partial V}{\partial m_t} \right|_{S_t = m_t} = 0.$$

$\square$

11. *Perpetual American Floating Strike Lookback Option.* At time t let the asset price S_t follow a GBM

$$\frac{dS_t}{S_t} = (\mu - D)dt + \sigma dW_t$$

where W_t is a standard Wiener process on the probability space $(\Omega, \mathcal{F}, \mathbb{P})$, μ is the drift parameter, D is the continuous dividend yield and σ is the volatility parameter. In addition, we let r be the risk-free interest rate.

Consider a perpetual American floating strike lookback option $V(S_t, m_t)$ which gives the holder the right but not the obligation to buy at the lowest realised asset price with the intrinsic payoff $\max\{S_t - m_t, 0\}$, $m_t = \min_{t_0 \leq u \leq t} S_u$, $t_0 \geq 0$ up to the date chosen by the option holder.

Let $S^* > m_t$ be the unknown optimal exercise boundary such that for $S_t \geq S^*$ the option should be exercised whilst for $S_t < S^*$ the option should be held.

Show that for $m_t < S_t < S^*$, the option price $V(S_t, m_t)$ satisfies

$$\frac{1}{2}\sigma^2 S_t^2 \frac{\partial^2 V}{\partial S_t^2} + (r - D)S_t \frac{\partial V}{\partial S_t} - rV(S_t, m_t) = 0$$

with boundary conditions

$$V(S^*, m_t) = S^* - m_t \quad \text{and} \quad \left.\frac{\partial V}{\partial m_t}\right|_{S_t = m_t} = 0.$$

By considering the change of variables

$$V(S_t, m_t) = S_t \varphi(\zeta), \zeta = m_t/S_t$$

show that for $0 < \zeta^* < \zeta < 1$, where $\zeta^* = m_t/S^*$, then $\varphi(\zeta)$ satisfies

$$\frac{1}{2}\sigma^2 \zeta^2 \frac{d^2\varphi}{d\zeta^2} + (D - r)\zeta \frac{d\varphi}{d\zeta} - D\varphi(\zeta) = 0$$

with boundary conditions

$$\varphi(\zeta^*) = 1 - \zeta^*, \quad \left.\frac{d\varphi}{d\zeta}\right|_{\zeta=\zeta^*} = -1 \quad \text{and} \quad \varphi(1) = \left.\frac{d\varphi}{d\zeta}\right|_{\zeta=1}.$$

By setting $\varphi(\zeta) = C\zeta^m$ where C and m are constants, show that the option price $V(S_t, m_t)$ is

$$V(S_t, m_t)$$
$$= \begin{cases} \dfrac{1}{\alpha - \beta}\left\{\left[(1 - \alpha)\zeta^* + \alpha\right]\left(\dfrac{\zeta}{\zeta^*}\right)^\beta - \left[(1 - \beta)\zeta^* + \beta\right]\left(\dfrac{\zeta}{\zeta^*}\right)^\alpha\right\} & \text{if } S_t < S^* \\[3mm] S^* - m_t & \text{if } S_t \geq S^* \end{cases}$$

where

$$\alpha = \frac{-(D - r - \frac{1}{2}\sigma^2) + \sqrt{(D - r - \frac{1}{2}\sigma^2)^2 + 2\sigma^2 D}}{\sigma^2}$$

$$\beta = \frac{-(D - r - \frac{1}{2}\sigma^2) - \sqrt{(D - r - \frac{1}{2}\sigma^2)^2 + 2\sigma^2 D}}{\sigma^2}$$

and $0 < \zeta^* < 1$ satisfies $f(\zeta^*) = 0$ where

$$f(\zeta) = \beta(1 - \alpha)\zeta^{\alpha-\beta+1} + \alpha\beta\zeta^{\alpha-\beta} - \alpha(1 - \beta)\zeta - \alpha\beta.$$

Show that if $D > 0$ then $f(\zeta) = 0$ has a unique solution in $\zeta \in (0, 1)$.
What is the option price when $D = 0$?

Solution: To show that $V(S_t, m_t)$ satisfies

$$\frac{1}{2}\sigma^2 S_t^2 \frac{\partial^2 V}{\partial S_t^2} + (r - D)S_t \frac{\partial V}{\partial S_t} - rV(S_t, m_t) = 0$$

with boundary condition $\left. \dfrac{\partial V}{\partial m_t} \right|_{S_t=m_t} = 0$, see Problem 6.2.2.10 (page 618) and Problem
6.2.2.8 (page 609).

Given that S^* is the optimal exercise boundary then for $S_t \geq S^*$, the option price is
equal to its intrinsic value $V(S^*, m_t) = S^* - m_t$. Therefore, for $m_t < S_t < S^*$, $V(S_t, m_t)$
satisfies

$$\frac{1}{2}\sigma^2 S_t^2 \frac{\partial^2 V}{\partial S_t^2} + (r - D)S_t \frac{\partial V}{\partial S_t} - rV(S_t, m_t) = 0$$

with boundary conditions

$$V(S^*, m_t) = S^* - m_t \quad \text{and} \quad \left. \frac{\partial V}{\partial m_t} \right|_{S_t=m_t} = 0.$$

By the change of variables

$$V(S_t, m_t) = S_t \varphi(\zeta), \quad \zeta = m_t/S_t \quad \text{and} \quad \zeta^* = m_t/S^*$$

we have

$$\frac{\partial V}{\partial S_t} = \varphi(\zeta) + S_t \frac{d\varphi}{d\zeta} \frac{d\zeta}{dS_t} = \varphi(\zeta) - \zeta \frac{d\varphi}{d\zeta}$$

$$\frac{\partial^2 V}{\partial S_t^2} = \frac{d\varphi}{d\zeta} \frac{d\zeta}{dS_t} - \frac{d\zeta}{dS_t} \frac{d\varphi}{d\zeta} - \zeta \frac{d^2\varphi}{d\zeta^2} \frac{d\zeta}{dS_t} = \frac{\zeta^2}{S_t} \frac{d^2\varphi}{d\zeta^2}$$

$$\frac{\partial V}{\partial m_t} = S_t \frac{d\varphi}{d\zeta} \frac{d\zeta}{dm_t} = \frac{d\varphi}{d\zeta}$$

$$\left. \frac{\partial V}{\partial m_t} \right|_{S_t=m_t} = \left. \frac{d\varphi}{d\zeta} \right|_{\zeta=1} \quad \text{and} \quad \left. \frac{\partial V}{\partial m_t} \right|_{S_t=S^*} = \left. \frac{d\varphi}{d\zeta} \right|_{\zeta=\zeta^*}.$$

Substituting the above results into the PDE and because $\zeta = m_t/S_t$, we eventually arrive at a second-order ODE of the form

$$\frac{1}{2}\sigma^2\xi^2\frac{d^2\varphi}{d\zeta^2} + (D-r)\zeta\frac{d\varphi}{d\zeta} - D\varphi(\zeta) = 0$$

for $0 < \zeta^* < \zeta < 1$. As for the boundary conditions, we note that for $V(S^*, m_t) = S^* - m_t$

$$S^*\varphi(\zeta^*) = S^* - m_t \quad \text{or} \quad \varphi(\zeta^*) = 1 - \zeta^*.$$

In addition, because $\left.\dfrac{\partial V}{\partial m_t}\right|_{S_t=S^*} = -1$ we have $\left.\dfrac{d\varphi}{d\zeta}\right|_{\zeta=\zeta^*} = -1$ and $\left.\dfrac{\partial V}{\partial m_t}\right|_{S_t=m_t} = 0$

becomes $\left.\dfrac{d\varphi}{d\zeta}\right|_{\zeta=1} = 0.$

Therefore, for $0 < \zeta^* < \zeta < 1$, $\varphi(\zeta)$ satisfies

$$\frac{1}{2}\sigma^2\xi^2\frac{d^2\varphi}{d\zeta^2} + (D-r)\zeta\frac{d\varphi}{d\zeta} - D\varphi(\zeta) = 0$$

with boundary conditions

$$\varphi(\zeta^*) = 1 - \zeta^*, \quad \left.\frac{d\varphi}{d\zeta}\right|_{\zeta=\zeta^*} = -1 \quad \text{and} \quad \left.\frac{d\varphi}{d\zeta}\right|_{\zeta=1} = 0.$$

By setting $\varphi(\zeta) = C\zeta^n$ where C and n are constants, then following Problem 6.2.2.8 (page 609) the solution of the ODE is

$$\varphi(\zeta) = A\zeta^\alpha + B\zeta^\beta$$

where A and B are constants to be determined with

$$\alpha = \frac{-(D-r-\frac{1}{2}\sigma^2) + \sqrt{(D-r-\frac{1}{2}\sigma^2)^2 + 2\sigma^2 D}}{\sigma^2}$$

and

$$\beta = \frac{-(D-r-\frac{1}{2}\sigma^2) - \sqrt{(D-r-\frac{1}{2}\sigma^2)^2 + 2\sigma^2 D}}{\sigma^2}.$$

Substituting $\varphi(\zeta) = A\zeta^\alpha + B\zeta^\beta$ and $\varphi'(\xi) = \alpha A\zeta^{\alpha-1} + \beta B\zeta^{\beta-1}$ into the boundary conditions we have

$$A(\zeta^*)^\alpha + B(\zeta^*)^\beta = 1 - \zeta^*$$
$$\alpha A(\zeta^*)^{\alpha-1} + \beta B(\zeta^*)^{\beta-1} = -1$$
$$\alpha A + \beta B = 0.$$

By solving

$$A(\zeta^*)^\alpha + B(\zeta^*)^\beta = 1 - \zeta^* \quad \text{and} \quad \alpha A(\zeta^*)^{\alpha-1} + \beta B(\zeta^*)^{\beta-1} = -1$$

simultaneously we have

$$A = \frac{(1-\beta)\zeta^* + \beta}{(\beta-\alpha)(\zeta^*)^\alpha} \quad \text{and} \quad B = \frac{(1-\alpha)\zeta^* + \alpha}{(\alpha-\beta)(\zeta^*)^\beta}.$$

By substituting the expressions for A and B into $\alpha A + \beta B = 0$ we have

$$\frac{\beta(1-\alpha)\zeta^* + \alpha\beta}{(\alpha-\beta)(\zeta^*)^\beta} = \frac{\alpha(1-\beta)\zeta^* + \alpha\beta}{(\alpha-\beta)(\zeta^*)^\alpha}$$

or

$$\beta(1-\alpha)(\zeta^*)^{\alpha-\beta+1} + \alpha\beta(\zeta^*)^{\alpha-\beta} - \alpha(1-\beta)\zeta^* - \alpha\beta = 0.$$

Thus, $0 < \zeta^* < 1$ satisfies $f(\zeta) = 0$ where

$$f(\zeta) = \beta(1-\alpha)\zeta^{\alpha-\beta+1} + \alpha\beta\zeta^{\alpha-\beta} - \alpha(1-\beta)\zeta - \alpha\beta.$$

To show that $\zeta^* \in (0,1)$ is unique for $D > 0$, we note that

$$\sqrt{(D-r-\tfrac{1}{2}\sigma^2)^2 + 2\sigma^2 D} = \sqrt{(D-r)^2 - (D-r)\sigma^2 + \tfrac{1}{4}\sigma^4 + 2\sigma^2 D}$$

$$= \sqrt{(D-r)^2 + (D+r)\sigma^2 + \tfrac{1}{4}\sigma^4}$$

$$> \sqrt{(D-r)^2 + (D-r)\sigma^2 + \tfrac{1}{4}\sigma^4}$$

$$= D - r + \tfrac{1}{2}\sigma^2$$

and hence

$$\alpha = \frac{-(D-r-\tfrac{1}{2}\sigma^2) + \sqrt{(D-r+\tfrac{1}{2}\sigma^2)^2 + 2\sigma^2 D}}{\sigma^2} > 1$$

and

$$\beta = \frac{-(D-r-\tfrac{1}{2}\sigma^2) - \sqrt{(D-r+\tfrac{1}{2}\sigma^2)^2 + 2\sigma^2 D}}{\sigma^2} < 0.$$

Since

$$f(0) = -\alpha\beta > 0 \quad \text{and} \quad f(1) = \beta - \alpha < 0$$

then from the intermediate value theorem, f must have at least one root in the interval $(0,1)$.

For $\zeta \in (0, 1)$ and because

$$\beta(1 - \alpha)(\alpha - \beta + 1) > 0, \quad \alpha\beta(\alpha - \beta) > 0 \quad \text{and} \quad \alpha - \beta > 1$$

therefore

$$
\begin{aligned}
f'(\zeta) &= \beta(1 - \alpha)(\alpha - \beta + 1)\zeta^{\alpha-\beta} + \alpha\beta(\alpha - \beta)\zeta^{\alpha-\beta-1} - \alpha(1 - \beta) \\
&< \beta(1 - \alpha)(\alpha - \beta + 1) + \alpha\beta(\alpha - \beta) - \alpha(1 - \beta) \\
&= (\alpha - \beta)(\beta - 1) \\
&< 0.
\end{aligned}
$$

Thus, f is a monotonically decreasing function in $\zeta \in (0, 1)$ which implies that $f(\zeta) = 0$ has a unique solution in $(0, 1)$.

Finally, when $D = 0$ then

$$\alpha = \frac{2r}{\sigma^2} + 1 \quad \text{and} \quad \beta = 0$$

and hence $\zeta^* = 0$ since $f(\zeta) = -\left(\dfrac{2r}{\sigma^2} + 1\right)\zeta$, which implies that the option problem does not have a solution. This shows that it is never optimal to hold such an option in the absence of an asset paying continuous dividend yields.

$\qquad\qquad\qquad\qquad\qquad\qquad\qquad\qquad\qquad\qquad\qquad\qquad\qquad\qquad\qquad\quad\Box$

12. *European Fixed Strike Lookback Option I.* Let $\{W_t : t \geq 0\}$ be a $\mathbb{P}$-standard Wiener process on the probability space $(\Omega, \mathcal{F}, \mathbb{P})$ and let the asset price S_t follow a GBM with the following SDE

$$\frac{dS_t}{S_t} = (\mu - D)\, dt + \sigma dW_t$$

where μ is the drift parameter, D is the continuous dividend yield and σ is the volatility parameter.

Consider a European-style fixed strike lookback call option with terminal payoff

$$\Psi(S_T) = \max\left\{\max_{t_0 \leq u \leq T} S_u - K, 0\right\}$$

which depends on the maximum of the asset price reached within the lookback period $[t_0, T]$, $t_0 \geq 0$ where T is the expiry time and $K > 0$ is the strike price.

By definition, under the risk-neutral measure $\mathbb{Q}$, the value of a fixed strike lookback call option at time t, $t_0 \leq t \leq T$ is

$$C_F(S_t, t; K, T) = e^{-r(T-t)}\mathbb{E}^{\mathbb{Q}}\left[\max\left\{\max\left\{\max_{t_0 \leq u \leq t} S_u, \max_{t \leq u \leq T} S_u\right\} - K, 0\right\}\bigg| \mathcal{F}_t\right]$$

where r is the risk-free interest rate.

By considering two cases $\max_{t_0 \leq u \leq t} S_u \leq K$ and $\max_{t_0 \leq u \leq t} S_u > K$, show that $C_F(S_t, t; K, T)$ can be written as

$$C_F(S_t, t; K, T) = e^{-r(T-t)} \max \left\{ \max_{t_0 \leq u \leq t} S_u - K, 0 \right\} + \hat{C}_F(S_t, t; \hat{K}, T)$$

where $\hat{C}_F(S_t, t; \hat{K}, T) = e^{-r(T-t)} \mathbb{E}^{\mathbb{Q}} \left[\max \left\{ \max_{t \leq u \leq T} S_u - \hat{K}, 0 \right\} \middle| \mathcal{F}_t \right]$ such that

$\hat{K} = \max \left\{ \max_{t_0 \leq u \leq t} S_u, K \right\}$.

Using the identity

$$\frac{1}{\sqrt{2\pi\tau}} \int_L^U e^{aw - \frac{1}{2}\left(\frac{w}{\sqrt{\tau}}\right)^2} \, dw = e^{\frac{1}{2}a^2\tau} \left[\Phi\left(\frac{U - a\tau}{\sqrt{\tau}}\right) - \Phi\left(\frac{L - a\tau}{\sqrt{\tau}}\right) \right]$$

show that

$$\hat{C}_F(S_t, t; \hat{K}, T) = C_{bs}(S_t, t; \hat{K}, T)$$
$$+ \left(\frac{S_t}{\alpha}\right) \left[e^{-D(T-t)} \Phi(\hat{d}_+) - \left(\frac{S_t}{\hat{K}}\right)^{-\alpha} e^{-r(T-t)} \Phi(\hat{d}_-) \right]$$

where $C_{bs}(S_t, t; \hat{K}, T)$ is the vanilla (or European) call option price defined as

$$C_{bs}(S_t, t; \hat{K}, T) = S_t e^{-D(T-t)} \Phi(d_+) - \hat{K} e^{-r(T-t)} \Phi(d_-)$$

with

$$d_\pm = \frac{\log(S_t/\hat{K}) + (r - D \pm \frac{1}{2}\sigma^2)(T - t)}{\sigma\sqrt{T - t}}$$

$$\hat{d}_\pm = \frac{\log(S_t/\hat{K}) \pm (r - D \pm \frac{1}{2}\sigma^2)(T - t)}{\sigma\sqrt{T - t}}$$

$\alpha = \dfrac{r - D}{\frac{1}{2}\sigma^2}$ and $\Phi(x) = \displaystyle\int_{-\infty}^x \frac{1}{\sqrt{2\pi}} e^{-\frac{1}{2}u^2} \, du$ is the cdf of a standard normal.

Solution: Under the risk-neutral measure $\mathbb{Q}$, S_t follows

$$\frac{dS_t}{S_t} = (r - D)dt + \sigma dW_t^{\mathbb{Q}}$$

where $W_t^{\mathbb{Q}} = W_t + \left(\dfrac{\mu - r}{\sigma}\right) t$ is a $\mathbb{Q}$-standard Wiener process.

By writing

$$\max_{t_0 \leq u \leq t} S_u = S_{t-t_0}^{\max}, \qquad \max_{t \leq u \leq T} S_u = S_{T-t}^{\max}$$

hence

$$C_F(S_t, t; K, T) = e^{-r(T-t)}\mathbb{E}^{\mathbb{Q}}\left[\max\left\{\max\left\{\max_{t_0\leq u\leq t} S_u, \max_{t\leq u\leq T} S_u\right\} - K, 0\right\}\bigg|\mathscr{F}_t\right]$$

$$= e^{-r(T-t)}\mathbb{E}^{\mathbb{Q}}\left[\max\left\{\max\left\{S_{t-t_0}^{\max}, S_{T-t}^{\max}\right\} - K, 0\right\}\bigg|\mathscr{F}_t\right].$$

If $S_{t-t_0}^{\max} \leq K$ then

$$\max\left\{\max\left\{S_{t-t_0}^{\max}, S_{T-t}^{\max}\right\} - K, 0\right\} = \max\left\{S_{T-t}^{\max} - K, 0\right\}$$

and if $S_{t-t_0}^{\max} > K$ then

$$\max\left\{\max\left\{S_{t-t_0}^{\max}, S_{T-t}^{\max}\right\} - K, 0\right\} = S_{t-t_0}^{\max} - K + \max\left\{S_{T-t}^{\max} - S_{t-t_0}^{\max}, 0\right\}.$$

Thus, we can write

$$\max\left\{\max\left\{S_{t-t_0}^{\max}, S_{T-t}^{\max}\right\} - K, 0\right\} = \max\left\{S_{t-t_0}^{\max} - K, 0\right\}$$
$$+ \max\left\{S_{T-t}^{\max} - \max\{S_{t-t_0}^{\max}, K\}, 0\right\}.$$

By substituting this back into the fixed strike lookback option price, we have

$$C_F(S_t, t; K, T)$$
$$= e^{-r(T-t)}\mathbb{E}^{\mathbb{Q}}\left[\max\left\{S_{t-t_0}^{\max} - K, 0\right\} + \max\left\{S_{T-t}^{\max} - \max\{S_{t-t_0}^{\max}, K\}, 0\right\}\bigg|\mathscr{F}_t\right]$$
$$= e^{-r(T-t)}\max\left\{S_{t-t_0}^{\max} - K, 0\right\}$$
$$+ e^{-r(T-t)}\mathbb{E}^{\mathbb{Q}}\left[\max\left\{S_{T-t}^{\max} - \max\{S_{t-t_0}^{\max}, K\}, 0\right\}\bigg|\mathscr{F}_t\right]$$
$$= e^{-r(T-t)}\max\left\{S_{t-t_0}^{\max} - K, 0\right\} + \widehat{C}_F(S_t, t; \widehat{K}, T)$$

where $\widehat{C}_F(S_t, t; \widehat{K}, T) = e^{-r(T-t)}\mathbb{E}^{\mathbb{Q}}\left[\max\left\{S_{T-t}^{\max} - \widehat{K}, 0\right\}\bigg|\mathscr{F}_t\right]$, $\widehat{K} = \max\left\{S_{t-t_0}^{\max}, K\right\}$.

From Itô's lemma we can write

$$S_{T-t}^{\max} = \max_{t\leq u\leq T} S_u$$
$$= \max_{t\leq u\leq T} S_t e^{(r-D-\frac{1}{2}\sigma^2)(u-t)+\sigma W_{u-t}^{\mathbb{Q}}}$$
$$= S_t e^{M_{T-t}}$$

where $M_{T-t} = \max_{t \le u \le T} v(u - t) + \sigma W^{\mathbb{Q}}_{u-t}$ such that $v = r - D - \frac{1}{2}\sigma^2$. From Problem 4.2.2.15 of *Problems and Solutions in Mathematical Finance, Volume 1: Stochastic Calculus*,

$$\mathbb{Q}\left(M_{T-t} \le x\right) = \Phi\left(\frac{x - v(T - t)}{\sigma\sqrt{T - t}}\right) - e^{\frac{2vx}{\sigma^2}} \Phi\left(\frac{-x - v(T - t)}{\sigma\sqrt{T - t}}\right), \quad x \ge 0$$

and hence

$$\hat{C}_F(S_t, t; \hat{K}, T) = e^{-r(T-t)}\mathbb{E}^{\mathbb{Q}}\left[\max\left\{S_t e^{M_{T-t}} - \hat{K}, 0\right\} \Big| \mathscr{F}_t\right]$$

$$= e^{-r(T-t)} \int_{\hat{K}}^{\infty} \mathbb{Q}\left(S_t e^{M_{T-t}} \ge x\right) dx$$

$$= e^{-r(T-t)} \int_{\hat{K}}^{\infty} \mathbb{Q}\left(e^{M_{T-t}} \ge \frac{x}{S_t}\right) dx$$

$$= e^{-r(T-t)} \int_{\hat{K}}^{\infty} \mathbb{Q}\left(M_{T-t} \ge \log\left(\frac{x}{S_t}\right)\right) dx.$$

By substituting $y = \log\left(x/S_t\right)$ we have

$$\hat{C}_F(S_t, t; \hat{K}, T)$$

$$= e^{-r(T-t)} \int_{\log(\hat{K}/S_t)}^{\infty} S_t e^y \mathbb{Q}\left(M_{T-t} \ge y\right) dy$$

$$= S_t e^{-r(T-t)} \int_{\log(\hat{K}/S_t)}^{\infty} e^y \left[\Phi\left(\frac{-y + v(T - t)}{\sigma\sqrt{T - t}}\right) + e^{\frac{2vy}{\sigma^2}} \Phi\left(\frac{-y - v(T - t)}{\sigma\sqrt{T - t}}\right)\right] dy$$

$$= A_1 + A_2$$

where

$$A_1 = S_t e^{-r(T-t)} \int_{\log(\hat{K}/S_t)}^{\infty} e^y \Phi\left(\frac{-y + v(T - t)}{\sigma\sqrt{T - t}}\right) dy$$

and

$$A_2 = S_t e^{-r(T-t)} \int_{\log(\hat{K}/S_t)}^{\infty} e^{\left(1+\frac{2v}{\sigma^2}\right)y} \Phi\left(\frac{-y - v(T - t)}{\sigma\sqrt{T - t}}\right) dy.$$

For the case $A_1 = S_t e^{-r(T-t)} \int_{\log(\hat{K}/S_t)}^{\infty} e^y \Phi\left(\dfrac{-y + v(T-t)}{\sigma\sqrt{T-t}}\right) dy$ and using integration by parts with

$$\frac{dU}{dy} = e^y \Rightarrow U = e^y$$

$$V = \Phi\left(\frac{-y + v(T-t)}{\sigma\sqrt{T-t}}\right) \Rightarrow \frac{dV}{dy} = -\frac{1}{\sigma\sqrt{2\pi(T-t)}} e^{-\frac{1}{2}\left(\frac{-y+v(T-t)}{\sigma\sqrt{T-t}}\right)^2}$$

we can write

$$A_1 = S_t e^{-r(T-t)} \left\{ \left[e^y \Phi\left(\frac{-y + v(T-t)}{\sigma\sqrt{T-t}}\right) \right]_{\log(\hat{K}/S_t)}^{\infty} \right.$$

$$\left. + \int_{\log(\hat{K}/S_t)}^{\infty} \frac{1}{\sigma\sqrt{2\pi(T-t)}} e^{y - \frac{1}{2}\left(\frac{-y+v(T-t)}{\sigma\sqrt{T-t}}\right)^2} dy \right\}$$

$$= -Ke^{-r(T-t)} \Phi\left(\frac{\log(S_t/\hat{K}) + v(T-t)}{\sigma\sqrt{T-t}}\right)$$

$$+ S_t e^{-\left(r + \frac{v^2}{2\sigma^2}\right)(T-t)} \int_{\log(\hat{K}/S_t)}^{\infty} \frac{1}{\sigma\sqrt{2\pi(T-t)}} e^{\left(1 + \frac{v}{\sigma^2}\right)y - \frac{1}{2}\left(\frac{y}{\sigma\sqrt{T-t}}\right)^2} dy.$$

From the identity

$$\frac{1}{\sqrt{2\pi\tau}} \int_L^U e^{aw - \frac{1}{2}\left(\frac{w}{\sqrt{\tau}}\right)^2} dw = e^{\frac{1}{2}a^2\tau} \left[\Phi\left(\frac{U - a\tau}{\sqrt{\tau}}\right) - \Phi\left(\frac{L - a\tau}{\sqrt{\tau}}\right) \right]$$

we have

$$A_1 = -Ke^{-r(T-t)} \Phi\left(\frac{\log(S_t/\hat{K}) + v(T-t)}{\sigma\sqrt{T-t}}\right)$$

$$+ S_t e^{-\left(r + \frac{v^2}{2\sigma^2}\right)(T-t) + \frac{1}{2}\left(1 + \frac{v}{\sigma^2}\right)^2 \sigma^2(T-t)} \left[1 - \Phi\left(\frac{\log(\hat{K}/S_t) - \left(1 + \frac{v}{\sigma^2}\right)\sigma^2(T-t)}{\sigma\sqrt{T-t}}\right) \right]$$

$$= -\hat{K}e^{-r(T-t)} \Phi\left(\frac{\log(S_t/\hat{K}) + v(T-t)}{\sigma\sqrt{T-t}}\right)$$

$$+ S_t e^{\left(v + \frac{1}{2}\sigma^2 - r\right)(T-t)} \Phi\left(\frac{\log(S_t/\hat{K}) + \left(1 + \frac{v}{\sigma^2}\right)\sigma^2(T-t)}{\sigma\sqrt{T-t}}\right).$$

By substituting $v = r - D - \frac{1}{2}\sigma^2$ we obtain

$$A_1 = S_t e^{-D(T-t)}\Phi(d_+) - \widehat{K}e^{-r(T-t)}\Phi(d_-)$$

such that $d_\pm = \dfrac{\log(S_t/\widehat{K}) + (r - D \pm \frac{1}{2}\sigma^2)(T-t)}{\sigma\sqrt{T-t}}.$

Finally, for the case $A_2 = S_t e^{-r(T-t)} \displaystyle\int_{\log(\widehat{K}/S_t)}^{\infty} e^{\left(1+\frac{2v}{\sigma^2}\right)y} \Phi\left(\dfrac{-y + v(T-t)}{\sigma\sqrt{T-t}}\right) dy$ and

using integration by parts with

$$\frac{dU}{dy} = e^{\left(1+\frac{2v}{\sigma^2}\right)y} \Rightarrow U = \left(1 + \frac{2v}{\sigma^2}\right)^{-1} e^{\left(1+\frac{2v}{\sigma^2}\right)y}$$

$$V = \Phi\left(\frac{-y - v(T-t)}{\sigma\sqrt{T-t}}\right) \Rightarrow \frac{dV}{dy} = -\frac{1}{\sigma\sqrt{2\pi(T-t)}} e^{-\frac{1}{2}\left(\frac{-y-v(T-t)}{\sigma\sqrt{T-t}}\right)^2}$$

we can write

$$A_2 = \frac{S_t e^{-r(T-t)}}{\left(1 + \frac{2v}{\sigma^2}\right)} \left\{ \left[e^{\left(1+\frac{2v}{\sigma^2}\right)y} \Phi\left(\frac{-y - v(T-t)}{\sigma\sqrt{T-t}}\right) \right]_{\log(\widehat{K}/S_t)}^{\infty} \right.$$

$$\left. + \int_{\log(\widehat{K}/S_t)}^{\infty} \frac{1}{\sigma\sqrt{2\pi(T-t)}} e^{\left(1+\frac{2v}{\sigma^2}\right)y - \frac{1}{2}\left(\frac{-y-v(T-t)}{\sigma\sqrt{T-t}}\right)^2} dy \right\}$$

$$= -\frac{S_t e^{-r(T-t)}}{\left(1 + \frac{2v}{\sigma^2}\right)} \left(\frac{S_t}{\widehat{K}}\right)^{-\left(1+\frac{2v}{\sigma^2}\right)} \Phi\left(\frac{\log(S_t/\widehat{K}) - v(T-t)}{\sigma\sqrt{T-t}}\right)$$

$$+ \frac{S_t e^{-\left(r+\frac{v^2}{2\sigma^2}\right)(T-t)}}{\left(1 + \frac{2v}{\sigma^2}\right)} \int_{\log(\widehat{K}/S_t)}^{\infty} \frac{1}{\sigma\sqrt{2\pi(T-t)}} e^{\left(1+\frac{v}{\sigma^2}\right)y - \frac{1}{2}\left(\frac{y}{\sigma\sqrt{T-t}}\right)^2} dy.$$

Using the identity

$$\frac{1}{\sqrt{2\pi\tau}} \int_L^U e^{aw - \frac{1}{2}\left(\frac{w}{\sqrt{\tau}}\right)^2} dw = e^{\frac{1}{2}a^2\tau} \left[\Phi\left(\frac{U - a\tau}{\sqrt{\tau}}\right) - \Phi\left(\frac{L - a\tau}{\sqrt{\tau}}\right) \right]$$

again we have

$$
A_2 = -\frac{S_t e^{-r(T-t)}}{\left(1 + \frac{2v}{\sigma^2}\right)} \left(\frac{S_t}{\widehat{K}}\right)^{-\left(1 + \frac{2v}{\sigma^2}\right)} \Phi\left(\frac{\log(S_t/\widehat{K}) - v(T-t)}{\sigma\sqrt{T-t}}\right)
$$

$$
+ \frac{S_t e^{-\left(r + \frac{v^2}{2\sigma^2}\right)(T-t) + \frac{1}{2}\left(1 + \frac{v}{\sigma^2}\right)^2 \sigma^2(T-t)}}{\left(1 + \frac{2v}{\sigma^2}\right)} \left[1 - \Phi\left(\frac{\log(\widehat{K}/S_t) - \left(1 + \frac{v}{\sigma^2}\right)\sigma^2(T-t)}{\sigma\sqrt{T-t}}\right)\right]
$$

$$
= -\frac{S_t e^{-r(T-t)}}{\left(1 + \frac{2v}{\sigma^2}\right)} \left(\frac{S_t}{\widehat{K}}\right)^{-\left(1 + \frac{2v}{\sigma^2}\right)} \Phi\left(\frac{\log(S_t/\widehat{K}) - v(T-t)}{\sigma\sqrt{T-t}}\right)
$$

$$
+ \frac{(v + \frac{1}{2}\sigma^2 - r)(T-t)}{\left(1 + \frac{2v}{\sigma^2}\right)} \Phi\left(\frac{\log(S_t/\widehat{K}) + \left(1 + \frac{v}{\sigma^2}\right)\sigma^2(T-t)}{\sigma\sqrt{T-t}}\right).
$$

By substituting $v = r - D - \frac{1}{2}\sigma^2$ and setting $\alpha = \dfrac{r - D}{\frac{1}{2}\sigma^2}$ we obtain

$$
A_2 = \frac{S_t e^{-D(T-t)}}{\alpha} \Phi(\widehat{d}_+) - \frac{S_t e^{-r(T-t)}}{\alpha} \left(\frac{S_t}{\widehat{K}}\right)^{-\alpha} \Phi(\widehat{d}_-)
$$

where $\widehat{d}_\pm = \dfrac{\log(S_t/\widehat{K}) \pm (r - D \pm \frac{1}{2}\sigma^2)(T-t)}{\sigma\sqrt{T-t}}.$

Hence,

$$
\widehat{C}_F(S_t, t; \widehat{K}, T) = C_{bs}(S_t, t; \widehat{K}, T)
$$

$$
+ \left(\frac{S_t}{\alpha}\right) \left[e^{-D(T-t)}\Phi(\widehat{d}_+) - \left(\frac{S_t}{\widehat{K}}\right)^{-\alpha} e^{-r(T-t)}\Phi(\widehat{d}_-)\right].
$$

By gathering all the results, we finally have

$$
C_F(S_t, t; K, T) = e^{-r(T-t)} \max\left\{S_{t-t_0}^{\max} - K, 0\right\} + C_{bs}(S_t, t; \widehat{K}, T)
$$

$$
+ \left(\frac{S_t}{\alpha}\right) \left[e^{-D(T-t)}\Phi(\widehat{d}_+) - \left(\frac{S_t}{\widehat{K}}\right)^{-\alpha} e^{-r(T-t)}\Phi(\widehat{d}_-)\right]
$$

where $\widehat{K} = \max\left\{S_{t-t_0}^{\max}, K\right\}.$

$\square$

13. *European Fixed Strike Lookback Option II.* Let $\{W_t : t \geq 0\}$ be a $\mathbb{P}$-standard Wiener process on the probability space $(\Omega, \mathcal{F}, \mathbb{P})$ and let the asset price S_t follow a GBM with the following SDE

$$\frac{dS_t}{S_t} = (\mu - D)\,dt + \sigma\,dW_t$$

where μ is the drift parameter, D is the continuous dividend yield and σ is the volatility parameter.

We consider a European-style fixed strike lookback put option with terminal payoff

$$\Psi(S_T) = \max\left\{K - \min_{t_0 \leq u \leq T} S_u, 0\right\}$$

which depends on the minimum of the asset price reached within the lookback period $[t_0, T]$, $t_0 \geq 0$ where T is the expiry time and $K > 0$ is the strike price.

By definition, under the risk-neutral measure $\mathbb{Q}$ the value of a fixed strike lookback put option at time t, $t_0 \leq t \leq T$ is

$$P_F(S_t, t; K, T) = e^{-r(T-t)}\mathbb{E}^{\mathbb{Q}}\left[\max\left\{K - \min\left\{\min_{t_0 \leq u \leq t} S_u, \min_{t \leq u \leq T} S_u\right\}, 0\right\}\middle| \mathcal{F}_t\right]$$

where r is the risk-free interest rate.

By considering two cases $\min_{t_0 \leq u \leq t} S_u \leq K$ and $\min_{t_0 \leq u \leq t} S_u > K$, show that $P_F(S_t, t; K, T)$ can be written as

$$P_F(S_t, t; K, T) = e^{-r(T-t)}\max\left\{K - \min_{t_0 \leq u \leq t} S_u, 0\right\} + \hat{P}_F(S_t, t; \hat{K}, T)$$

where $\hat{P}_F(S_t, t; \hat{K}, T) = e^{-r(T-t)}\mathbb{E}^{\mathbb{Q}}\left[\max\left\{\hat{K} - \min_{t \leq u \leq T} S_u, 0\right\}\middle| \mathcal{F}_t\right]$ such that $\hat{K} = \min\left\{\min_{t_0 \leq u \leq t} S_u, K\right\}$.

Using the identity

$$\frac{1}{\sqrt{2\pi\tau}}\int_L^U e^{aw - \frac{1}{2}\left(\frac{w}{\sqrt{\tau}}\right)^2}\,dw = e^{\frac{1}{2}a^2\tau}\left[\Phi\left(\frac{U - a\tau}{\sqrt{\tau}}\right) - \Phi\left(\frac{L - a\tau}{\sqrt{\tau}}\right)\right]$$

show that

$$\hat{P}_F(S_t, t; \hat{K}, T) = P_{bs}(S_t, t; \hat{K}, T)$$
$$+ \left(\frac{S_t}{\alpha}\right)\left[\left(\frac{S_t}{\hat{K}}\right)^{-\alpha}e^{-r(T-t)}\Phi(-\hat{d}_-) - e^{-D(T-t)}\Phi(-\hat{d}_+)\right]$$

where $P_{bs}(S_t, t; \widehat{K}, T)$ is the vanilla (or European) put option price defined as

$$P_{bs}(S_t, t; \widehat{K}, T) = \widehat{K} e^{-r(T-t)} \Phi(-d_-) - S_t e^{-D(T-t)} \Phi(-d_+)$$

with

$$d_\pm = \frac{\log(S_t/\widehat{K}) + (r - D \pm \frac{1}{2}\sigma^2)(T-t)}{\sigma\sqrt{T-t}}$$

$$\widehat{d}_\pm = \frac{\log(S_t/\widehat{K}) \pm (r - D \pm \frac{1}{2}\sigma^2)(T-t)}{\sigma\sqrt{T-t}}$$

$\alpha = \dfrac{r-D}{\frac{1}{2}\sigma^2}$ and $\Phi(x) = \displaystyle\int_{-\infty}^{x} \frac{1}{\sqrt{2\pi}} e^{-\frac{1}{2}u^2}\, du$ is the cdf of a standard normal.

Solution: From Girsanov's theorem, under the risk-neutral measure $\mathbb{Q}$, S_t follows

$$\frac{dS_t}{S_t} = (r - D)dt + \sigma dW_t^{\mathbb{Q}}$$

where $W_t^{\mathbb{Q}} = W_t + \left(\dfrac{\mu - r}{\sigma}\right) t$ is a $\mathbb{Q}$-standard Wiener process.

By writing

$$\min_{t_0 \le u \le t} S_u = S_{t-t_0}^{\min}, \qquad \min_{t \le u \le T} S_u = S_{T-t}^{\min}$$

hence

$$P_F(S_t, t; K, T) = e^{-r(T-t)} \mathbb{E}^{\mathbb{Q}}\left[\max\left\{ K - \min\left\{ \min_{t_0 \le u \le t} S_u, \min_{t \le u \le T} S_u \right\}, 0 \right\} \middle| \mathscr{F}_t \right]$$

$$= e^{-r(T-t)} \mathbb{E}^{\mathbb{Q}}\left[\max\left\{ K - \min\left\{ S_{t-t_0}^{\min}, S_{T-t}^{\min} \right\}, 0 \right\} \middle| \mathscr{F}_t \right].$$

If $S_{t-t_0}^{\min} \le K$ then

$$\max\left\{ K - \min\left\{ S_{t-t_0}^{\min}, S_{T-t}^{\min} \right\}, 0 \right\} = K - S_{t-t_0}^{\min} + \max\left\{ S_{t-t_0}^{\min} - S_{T-t}^{\min}, 0 \right\}$$

and if $S_{t-t_0}^{\min} > K$ then

$$\max\left\{ K - \min\left\{ S_{t-t_0}^{\min}, S_{T-t}^{\min} \right\}, 0 \right\} = \max\left\{ K - S_{T-t}^{\min}, 0 \right\}.$$

Thus, we can write

$$\max\left\{K - \min\left\{S_{t-t_0}^{\min}, S_{T-t}^{\min}\right\}, 0\right\} = \max\left\{K - S_{t-t_0}^{\min}, 0\right\}$$
$$+ \max\left\{\min\{S_{t-t_0}^{\min}, K\} - S_{T-t}^{\min}, 0\right\}.$$

By substituting this back into the fixed strike lookback option price, we have

$$P_F(S_t, t; K, T)$$
$$= e^{-r(T-t)}\mathbb{E}^{\mathbb{Q}}\left[\max\left\{K - S_{t-t_0}^{\min}, 0\right\} + \max\left\{\min\{S_{t-t_0}^{\min}, K\} - S_{T-t}^{\min}, 0\right\}\bigg| \mathscr{F}_t\right]$$
$$= e^{-r(T-t)}\max\left\{K - S_{t-t_0}^{\min}, 0\right\}$$
$$+ e^{-r(T-t)}\mathbb{E}^{\mathbb{Q}}\left[\max\left\{\min\{S_{t-t_0}^{\min}, K\} - S_{T-t}^{\min}, 0\right\}\bigg| \mathscr{F}_t\right]$$
$$= e^{-r(T-t)}\max\left\{K - S_{t-t_0}^{\min}, 0\right\} + \hat{P}_F(S_t, t; \hat{K}, T)$$

where $\hat{P}_F(S_t, t; \hat{K}, T) = e^{-r(T-t)}\mathbb{E}^{\mathbb{Q}}\left[\max\left\{\hat{K} - S_{T-t}^{\min}, 0\right\}\bigg| \mathscr{F}_t\right]$, $\hat{K} = \min\left\{S_{t-t_0}^{\min}, K\right\}$.

From Itō's lemma we can write

$$S_{T-t}^{\max} = \min_{t \leq u \leq T} S_u$$
$$= \min_{t \leq u \leq T} S_t e^{(r-D-\frac{1}{2}\sigma^2)(u-t)+\sigma W_{u-t}^{\mathbb{Q}}}$$
$$= S_t e^{m_{T-t}}$$

where $m_{T-t} = \min_{t \leq u \leq T} v(u - t) + \sigma W_{u-t}^{\mathbb{Q}}$ such that $v = r - D - \frac{1}{2}\sigma^2$. From Problem 4.2.2.15 of *Problems and Solutions in Mathematical Finance, Volume 1: Stochastic Calculus*

$$\mathbb{Q}\left(m_{T-t} \leq x\right) = \Phi\left(\frac{x - v(T-t)}{\sigma\sqrt{T-t}}\right) + e^{\frac{2vx}{\sigma^2}}\Phi\left(\frac{x + v(T-t)}{\sigma\sqrt{T-t}}\right), \quad x \leq 0.$$

Hence,

$$\hat{P}_F(S_t, t; \hat{K}, T) = e^{-r(T-t)}\mathbb{E}^{\mathbb{Q}}\left[\max\left\{\hat{K} - S_t e^{m_{T-t}}, 0\right\}\bigg| \mathscr{F}_t\right]$$
$$= e^{-r(T-t)}\int_{-\infty}^{\hat{K}}\mathbb{Q}\left(S_t e^{m_{T-t}} \leq x\right) dx$$
$$= e^{-r(T-t)}\int_{-\infty}^{\hat{K}}\mathbb{Q}\left(e^{m_{T-t}} \leq \frac{x}{S_t}\right) dx$$
$$= e^{-r(T-t)}\int_{-\infty}^{\hat{K}}\mathbb{Q}\left(m_{T-t} \leq \log\left(\frac{x}{S_t}\right)\right) dx.$$

By substituting $y = \log\left(x/S_t\right)$ we have

$$\widehat{P}_F(S_t, t; \widehat{K}, T) = e^{-r(T-t)} \int_{-\infty}^{\log(\widehat{K}/S_t)} S_t e^y \mathbb{Q}\left(m_{T-t} \leq y\right) dy$$

$$= S_t e^{-r(T-t)}$$

$$\times \int_{-\infty}^{\log(\widehat{K}/S_t)} e^y \left[\Phi\left(\frac{y - v(T-t)}{\sigma\sqrt{T-t}}\right) + e^{\frac{2vy}{\sigma^2}}\Phi\left(\frac{y + v(T-t)}{\sigma\sqrt{T-t}}\right)\right] dy$$

$$= B_1 + B_2$$

where

$$B_1 = S_t e^{-r(T-t)} \int_{-\infty}^{\log(\widehat{K}/S_t)} e^y \Phi\left(\frac{y - v(T-t)}{\sigma\sqrt{T-t}}\right) dy$$

and

$$B_2 = S_t e^{-r(T-t)} \int_{-\infty}^{\log(\widehat{K}/S_t)} e^{\left(1+\frac{2v}{\sigma^2}\right)y}\Phi\left(\frac{y + v(T-t)}{\sigma\sqrt{T-t}}\right) dy.$$

For the case $B_1 = S_t e^{-r(T-t)} \int_{-\infty}^{\log(\widehat{K}/S_t)} e^y \Phi\left(\frac{y - v(T-t)}{\sigma\sqrt{T-t}}\right) dy$ and using integration by

parts with

$$\frac{dU}{dy} = e^y \Rightarrow U = e^y$$

$$V = \Phi\left(\frac{y - v(T-t)}{\sigma\sqrt{T-t}}\right) \Rightarrow \frac{dV}{dy} = \frac{1}{\sigma\sqrt{2\pi(T-t)}} e^{-\frac{1}{2}\left(\frac{y-v(T-t)}{\sigma\sqrt{T-t}}\right)^2}$$

we can write

$$B_1 = S_t e^{-r(T-t)} \left\{ \left[e^y \Phi\left(\frac{y - v(T-t)}{\sigma\sqrt{T-t}}\right)\right]_{-\infty}^{\log(\widehat{K}/S_t)} \right.$$

$$\left. - \int_{-\infty}^{\log(\widehat{K}/S_t)} \frac{1}{\sigma\sqrt{2\pi(T-t)}} e^{y-\frac{1}{2}\left(\frac{y-v(T-t)}{\sigma\sqrt{T-t}}\right)^2} dy \right\}$$

$$= Ke^{-r(T-t)}\Phi\left(\frac{\log(\widehat{K}/S_t) - v(T-t)}{\sigma\sqrt{T-t}}\right)$$

$$- S_t e^{-\left(r+\frac{v^2}{2\sigma^2}\right)(T-t)} \int_{-\infty}^{\log(\widehat{K}/S_t)} \frac{1}{\sigma\sqrt{2\pi(T-t)}} e^{\left(1+\frac{v}{\sigma^2}\right)y-\frac{1}{2}\left(\frac{y}{\sigma\sqrt{T-t}}\right)^2} dy.$$

From the identity

$$\frac{1}{\sqrt{2\pi\tau}} \int_L^U e^{aw - \frac{1}{2}\left(\frac{w}{\sqrt{\tau}}\right)^2} dw = e^{\frac{1}{2}a^2\tau} \left[\Phi\left(\frac{U - a\tau}{\sqrt{\tau}}\right) - \Phi\left(\frac{L - a\tau}{\sqrt{\tau}}\right) \right]$$

we have

$$B_1 = Ke^{-r(T-t)}\Phi\left(\frac{\log(\widehat{K}/S_t) - v(T-t)}{\sigma\sqrt{T-t}}\right)$$

$$- S_t e^{-\left(r + \frac{v^2}{2\sigma^2}\right)(T-t) + \frac{1}{2}\left(1 + \frac{v}{\sigma^2}\right)^2\sigma^2(T-t)} \Phi\left(\frac{\log(\widehat{K}/S_t) - \left(1 + \frac{v}{\sigma^2}\right)\sigma^2(T-t)}{\sigma\sqrt{T-t}}\right)$$

$$= \widehat{K}e^{-r(T-t)}\Phi\left(\frac{\log(\widehat{K}/S_t) - v(T-t)}{\sigma\sqrt{T-t}}\right)$$

$$- S_t e^{\left(v + \frac{1}{2}\sigma^2 - r\right)(T-t)} \Phi\left(\frac{\log(\widehat{K}/S_t) - \left(1 + \frac{v}{\sigma^2}\right)\sigma^2(T-t)}{\sigma\sqrt{T-t}}\right).$$

By substituting $v = r - D - \frac{1}{2}\sigma^2$ we have

$$B_1 = \widehat{K}e^{-r(T-t)}\Phi\left(-d_-\right) - S_t e^{-D(T-t)}\Phi\left(-d_+\right)$$

such that $d_\pm = \dfrac{\log(S_t/\widehat{K}) + (r - D \pm \frac{1}{2}\sigma^2)(T-t)}{\sigma\sqrt{T-t}}$.

Finally, for the case $B_2 = S_t e^{-r(T-t)} \displaystyle\int_{-\infty}^{\log(\widehat{K}/S_t)} e^{\left(1 + \frac{2v}{\sigma^2}\right)y} \Phi\left(\frac{y + v(T-t)}{\sigma\sqrt{T-t}}\right) dy$ and using integration by parts with

$$\frac{dU}{dy} = e^{\left(1 + \frac{2v}{\sigma^2}\right)y} \Rightarrow U = \left(1 + \frac{2v}{\sigma^2}\right)^{-1} e^{\left(1 + \frac{2v}{\sigma^2}\right)y}$$

$$V = \Phi\left(\frac{y + v(T-t)}{\sigma\sqrt{T-t}}\right) \Rightarrow \frac{dV}{dy} = \frac{1}{\sigma\sqrt{2\pi(T-t)}} e^{-\frac{1}{2}\left(\frac{y + v(T-t)}{\sigma\sqrt{T-t}}\right)^2}$$

we can write

$$
B_2 = \frac{S_t e^{-r(T-t)}}{\left(1 + \frac{2v}{\sigma^2}\right)} \left\{ \left[e^{\left(1 + \frac{2v}{\sigma^2}\right)y} \Phi\left(\frac{y + v(T-t)}{\sigma\sqrt{T-t}}\right) \right]_{-\infty}^{\log(\widehat{K}/S_t)} \right.
$$

$$
\left. - \int_{-\infty}^{\log(\widehat{K}/S_t)} \frac{1}{\sigma\sqrt{2\pi(T-t)}} e^{\left(1 + \frac{2v}{\sigma^2}\right)y - \frac{1}{2}\left(\frac{y + v(T-t)}{\sigma\sqrt{T-t}}\right)^2} dy \right\}
$$

$$
= \frac{S_t e^{-r(T-t)}}{\left(1 + \frac{2v}{\sigma^2}\right)} \left(\frac{S_t}{\widehat{K}}\right)^{-\left(1 + \frac{2v}{\sigma^2}\right)} \Phi\left(\frac{\log(\widehat{K}/S_t) + v(T-t)}{\sigma\sqrt{T-t}}\right)
$$

$$
- \frac{S_t e^{-\left(r + \frac{v^2}{2\sigma^2}\right)(T-t)}}{\left(1 + \frac{2v}{\sigma^2}\right)} \int_{-\infty}^{\log(\widehat{K}/S_t)} \frac{1}{\sigma\sqrt{2\pi(T-t)}} e^{\left(1 + \frac{v}{\sigma^2}\right)y - \frac{1}{2}\left(\frac{y}{\sigma\sqrt{T-t}}\right)^2} dy.
$$

Using the identity

$$
\frac{1}{\sqrt{2\pi\tau}} \int_L^U e^{aw - \frac{1}{2}\left(\frac{w}{\sqrt{\tau}}\right)^2} dw = e^{\frac{1}{2}a^2\tau} \left[\Phi\left(\frac{U - a\tau}{\sqrt{\tau}}\right) - \Phi\left(\frac{L - a\tau}{\sqrt{\tau}}\right) \right]
$$

once again we have

$$
B_2 = \frac{S_t e^{-r(T-t)}}{\left(1 + \frac{2v}{\sigma^2}\right)} \left(\frac{S_t}{\widehat{K}}\right)^{-\left(1 + \frac{2v}{\sigma^2}\right)} \Phi\left(\frac{\log(\widehat{K}/S_t) + v(T-t)}{\sigma\sqrt{T-t}}\right)
$$

$$
- \frac{S_t e^{-\left(r + \frac{v^2}{2\sigma^2}\right)(T-t) + \frac{1}{2}\left(1 + \frac{v}{\sigma^2}\right)^2 \sigma^2(T-t)}}{\left(1 + \frac{2v}{\sigma^2}\right)} \Phi\left(\frac{\log(\widehat{K}/S_t) - \left(1 + \frac{v}{\sigma^2}\right)\sigma^2(T-t)}{\sigma\sqrt{T-t}}\right)
$$

$$
= \frac{S_t e^{-r(T-t)}}{\left(1 + \frac{2v}{\sigma^2}\right)} \left(\frac{S_t}{\widehat{K}}\right)^{-\left(1 + \frac{2v}{\sigma^2}\right)} \Phi\left(\frac{\log(\widehat{K}/S_t) + v(T-t)}{\sigma\sqrt{T-t}}\right)
$$

$$
- \frac{(v + \frac{1}{2}\sigma^2 - r)(T-t)}{\left(1 + \frac{2v}{\sigma^2}\right)} \Phi\left(\frac{\log(\widehat{K}/S_t) - \left(1 + \frac{v}{\sigma^2}\right)\sigma^2(T-t)}{\sigma\sqrt{T-t}}\right).
$$

By substituting $v = r - D - \frac{1}{2}\sigma^2$ and setting $\alpha = \dfrac{r - D}{\frac{1}{2}\sigma^2}$ we obtain

$$B_2 = \frac{S_t e^{-r(T-t)}}{\alpha} \left(\frac{S_t}{\widehat{K}}\right)^{-\alpha} \Phi(-\widehat{d}_-) - \frac{S_t e^{-D(T-t)}}{\alpha} \Phi(-\widehat{d}_+)$$

where $\widehat{d}_\pm = \dfrac{\log(S_t/\widehat{K}) \pm (r - D \pm \frac{1}{2}\sigma^2)(T - t)}{\sigma\sqrt{T - t}}$.

Hence,

$$\widehat{P}_F(S_t, t; \widehat{K}, T) = P_{bs}(S_t, t; \widehat{K}, T)$$
$$+ \left(\frac{S_t}{\alpha}\right)\left[\left(\frac{S_t}{\widehat{K}}\right)^{-\alpha} e^{-r(T-t)}\Phi(-\widehat{d}_-) - e^{-D(T-t)}\Phi(-\widehat{d}_+)\right].$$

By gathering all the results, we finally have

$$P_F(S_t, t; K, T) = e^{-r(T-t)} \max\left\{K - S_{t-t_0}^{\min}, 0\right\} + P_{bs}(S_t, t; \widehat{K}, T)$$
$$+ \left(\frac{S_t}{\alpha}\right)\left[\left(\frac{S_t}{\widehat{K}}\right)^{-\alpha} e^{-r(T-t)}\Phi(-\widehat{d}_-) - e^{-D(T-t)}\Phi(-\widehat{d}_+)\right]$$

where $\widehat{K} = \min\left\{S_{t-t_0}^{\min}, K\right\}$.

$\square$

14. *European Floating Strike Lookback Option I.* Let $\{W_t : t \geq 0\}$ be a $\mathbb{P}$-standard Wiener process on the probability space $(\Omega, \mathscr{F}, \mathbb{P})$ and let the asset price S_t follow a GBM with the following SDE

$$\frac{dS_t}{S_t} = (\mu - D)dt + \sigma dW_t$$

where μ is the drift parameter, D is the continuous dividend yield and σ is the volatility parameter.

We consider a European-style floating strike lookback call option with terminal payoff

$$\Psi(S_T) = \max\{S_T - K_{\min}, 0\}$$

where the floating strike price $K_{\min}$ is defined as $K_{\min} = \min\left\{\min_{t_0 \leq u \leq t} S_u, \min_{t \leq u \leq T} S_u\right\}$, which depends on the minimum of the asset price reached within the lookback period $[t_0, T]$, $t_0 \geq 0$ where T is the option expiry time.

By definition, under the risk-neutral measure $\mathbb{Q}$ the value of a floating strike lookback call option at time t, $t_0 \leq t \leq T$ is

$$C_f(S_t, t; K_{\min}, T) = e^{-r(T-t)}\mathbb{E}^{\mathbb{Q}}\left[\max\{S_T - K_{\min}, 0\}\big| \mathscr{F}_t\right]$$

where r is the risk-free interest rate. By setting $S_{t-t_0}^{\min} = \min_{t_0 \le u \le t} S_u$, show that

$$C_f(S_t, t; K_{\min}, T) = S_t - e^{-r(T-t)} S_{t-t_0}^{\min} + \hat{P}_F(S_t, t; S_{t-t_0}^{\min}, T)$$

where

$$\hat{P}_F(S_t, t; S_{t-t_0}^{\min}, T) = P_{bs}(S_t, t; S_{t-t_0}^{\min}, T)$$
$$+ \left(\frac{S_t}{\alpha}\right) \left[\left(\frac{S_t}{S_{t-t_0}^{\min}}\right)^{-\alpha} e^{-r(T-t)} \Phi(-\hat{d}_-) - e^{-D(T-t)} \Phi(-\hat{d}_+)\right]$$

such that $P_{bs}(S_t, t; S_{t-t_0}^{\min}, T)$ is the European put option price defined as

$$P_{bs}(S_t, t; S_{t-t_0}^{\min}, T) = S_{t-t_0}^{\min} e^{-r(T-t)} \Phi(-d_-) - S_t e^{-D(T-t)} \Phi(-d_+)$$

with

$$d_\pm = \frac{\log(S_t / S_{t-t_0}^{\min}) + (r - D \pm \frac{1}{2}\sigma^2)(T - t)}{\sigma\sqrt{T - t}}$$

$$\hat{d}_\pm = \frac{\log(S_t / S_{t-t_0}^{\min}) \pm (r - D \pm \frac{1}{2}\sigma^2)(T - t)}{\sigma\sqrt{T - t}}$$

$\alpha = \dfrac{r - D}{\frac{1}{2}\sigma^2}$ and $\Phi(x) = \displaystyle\int_{-\infty}^{x} \frac{1}{\sqrt{2\pi}} e^{-\frac{1}{2}u^2} du$ is the cdf of a standard normal.

Solution: By setting $S_{t-t_0}^{\min} = \min_{t_0 \le u \le t} S_u$ and $S_{T-t}^{\min} = \min_{t \le u \le T} S_u$, we can write the payoff as

$$\Psi(S_T) = \max\left\{S_T - K_{\min}, 0\right\}$$
$$= \max\left\{S_T - \min\left\{S_{t-t_0}^{\min}, S_{T-t}^{\min}\right\}, 0\right\}$$
$$= \begin{cases} \max\left\{S_T - S_{t-t_0}^{\min}, 0\right\} & \text{if } S_{t-t_0}^{\min} \le S_{T-t}^{\min} \\[2mm] \max\left\{S_T - S_{T-t}^{\min}, 0\right\} & \text{if } S_{t-t_0}^{\min} > S_{T-t}^{\min} \end{cases}$$
$$= \begin{cases} S_T - S_{t-t_0}^{\min} & \text{if } S_{t-t_0}^{\min} \le S_{T-t}^{\min} \\[2mm] S_T - S_{T-t}^{\min} & \text{if } S_{t-t_0}^{\min} > S_{T-t}^{\min} \end{cases}$$
$$= S_T - \min\left\{S_{t-t_0}^{\min}, S_{T-t}^{\min}\right\}$$
$$= S_T - S_{t-t_0}^{\min} + \max\left\{S_{t-t_0}^{\min} - S_{T-t}^{\min}, 0\right\}.$$

Under the risk-neutral measure $\mathbb{Q}$, S_t follows

$$\frac{dS_t}{S_t} = (r - D)dt + \sigma dW_t^{\mathbb{Q}}$$

where $W_t^{\mathbb{Q}} = W_t + \left(\dfrac{\mu - r}{\sigma}\right) t$ is a $\mathbb{Q}$-standard Wiener process. Thus, the option price at time t, $t_0 \leq t \leq T$ is

$$C_f(S_t, t; K_{\min}, T)$$

$$= e^{-r(T-t)} \mathbb{E}^{\mathbb{Q}}\left[S_T - S_{t-t_0}^{\min} + \max\left\{ S_{t-t_0}^{\min} - S_{T-t}^{\min}, 0 \right\} \middle| \mathscr{F}_t \right]$$

$$= e^{-r(T-t)} \mathbb{E}^{\mathbb{Q}}\left[S_T - S_{t-t_0}^{\min} \middle| \mathscr{F}_t \right] + e^{-r(T-t)} \mathbb{E}^{\mathbb{Q}}\left[\max\left\{ S_{t-t_0}^{\min} - S_{T-t}^{\min}, 0 \right\} \middle| \mathscr{F}_t \right]$$

$$= e^{-r(T-t)} \left(S_t e^{r(T-t)} - S_{t-t_0}^{\min} \right) + e^{-r(T-t)} \mathbb{E}^{\mathbb{Q}}\left[\max\left\{ S_{t-t_0}^{\min} - S_{T-t}^{\min}, 0 \right\} \middle| \mathscr{F}_t \right]$$

$$= S_t - e^{-r(T-t)} S_{t-t_0}^{\min} + e^{-r(T-t)} \mathbb{E}^{\mathbb{Q}}\left[\max\left\{ S_{t-t_0}^{\min} - S_{T-t}^{\min}, 0 \right\} \middle| \mathscr{F}_t \right].$$

From Problem 6.2.2.13 (page 634) we can write

$$\widehat{P}_F(S_t, t; S_{t-t_0}^{\min}, T) = e^{-r(T-t)} \mathbb{E}^{\mathbb{Q}}\left[\max\left\{ S_{t-t_0}^{\min} - S_{T-t}^{\min}, 0 \right\} \middle| \mathscr{F}_t \right]$$

where

$$\widehat{P}_F(S_t, t; S_{t-t_0}^{\min}, T) = P_{bs}(S_t, t; S_{t-t_0}^{\min}, T)$$

$$+ \left(\frac{S_t}{\alpha}\right) \left[\left(\frac{S_t}{S_{t-t_0}^{\min}}\right)^{-\alpha} e^{-r(T-t)} \Phi(-\widehat{d}_-) - e^{-D(T-t)} \Phi(-\widehat{d}_+) \right]$$

such that $P_{bs}(S_t, t; S_{t-t_0}^{\min}, T)$ is the European put option price defined as

$$P_{bs}(S_t, t; S_{t-t_0}^{\min}, T) = S_{t-t_0}^{\min} e^{-r(T-t)} \Phi(-d_-) - S_t e^{-D(T-t)} \Phi(-d_+)$$

with

$$d_\pm = \frac{\log(S_t / S_{t-t_0}^{\min}) + (r - D \pm \frac{1}{2}\sigma^2)(T - t)}{\sigma\sqrt{T - t}}$$

$$\widehat{d}_\pm = \frac{\log(S_t / S_{t-t_0}^{\min}) \pm (r - D \pm \frac{1}{2}\sigma^2)(T - t)}{\sigma\sqrt{T - t}}$$

and $\alpha = \dfrac{r - D}{\frac{1}{2}\sigma^2}$.

Hence,

$$C_f(S_t, t; K_{\min}, T) = S_t - e^{-r(T-t)} S_{t-t_0}^{\min} + \hat{P}_F(S_t, t; S_{t-t_0}^{\min}, T).$$

$\square$

15. *European Floating Strike Lookback Option II.* Let $\{W_t : t \geq 0\}$ be a $\mathbb{P}$-standard Wiener process on the probability space $(\Omega, \mathcal{F}, \mathbb{P})$ and let the asset price S_t follow a GBM with the following SDE

$$\frac{dS_t}{S_t} = (\mu - D)dt + \sigma dW_t$$

where μ is the drift parameter, D is the continuous dividend yield and σ is the volatility parameter.

We consider a European-style floating strike lookback put option with terminal payoff

$$\Psi(S_T) = \max\{K_{\max} - S_T, 0\}$$

where the floating strike price $K_{\max}$ is defined as $K_{\max} = \max \left\{ \max_{t_0 \leq u \leq t} S_u, \max_{t \leq u \leq T} S_u \right\}$ which depends on the maximum of the asset price reached within the lookback period $[t_0, T]$, $t_0 \geq 0$ where T is the option expiry time.

By definition, under the risk-neutral measure $\mathbb{Q}$ the value of a floating strike lookback put option at time t, $t_0 \leq t \leq T$ is

$$P_f(S_t, t; K_{\max}, T) = e^{-r(T-t)} \mathbb{E}^{\mathbb{Q}} \left[\max\{K_{\max} - S_T, 0\} \mid \mathcal{F}_t \right]$$

where r is the risk-free interest rate. By setting $S_{t-t_0}^{\max} = \max_{t_0 \leq u \leq t} S_u$, show that

$$P_f(S_t, t; K_{\max}, T) = \hat{C}_F(S_t, t; S_{t-t_0}^{\max}, T) + e^{-r(T-t)} S_{t-t_0}^{\max} - S_t$$

where

$$\hat{C}_F(S_t, t; S_{t-t_0}^{\max}, T) = C_{bs}(S_t, t; S_{t-t_0}^{\max}, T)$$
$$+ \left(\frac{S_t}{\alpha} \right) \left[e^{-D(T-t)} \Phi(\hat{d}_+) - \left(\frac{S_t}{S_{t-t_0}^{\max}} \right)^{-\alpha} e^{-r(T-t)} \Phi(\hat{d}_-) \right]$$

such that $C_{bs}(S_t, t; S_{t-t_0}^{\max}, T)$ is the European call option price defined as

$$C_{bs}(S_t, t; S_{t-t_0}^{\max}, T) = S_t e^{-D(T-t)} \Phi\left(d_+\right) - S_{t-t_0}^{\max} e^{-r(T-t)} \Phi\left(d_-\right)$$

with

$$d_\pm = \frac{\log(S_t / S_{t-t_0}^{\max}) + (r - D \pm \frac{1}{2}\sigma^2)(T - t)}{\sigma\sqrt{T - t}}$$

$$\hat{d}_{\pm} = \frac{\log(S_t/S_{t-t_0}^{\max}) \pm (r - D \pm \frac{1}{2}\sigma^2)(T - t)}{\sigma\sqrt{T - t}}$$

$\alpha = \dfrac{r - D}{\frac{1}{2}\sigma^2}$ and $\Phi(x) = \displaystyle\int_{-\infty}^{x} \frac{1}{\sqrt{2\pi}} e^{-\frac{1}{2}u^2}\, du$ is the cdf of a standard normal.

Solution: By setting $S_{t-t_0}^{\max} = \displaystyle\max_{t_0 \leq u \leq t} S_u$ and $S_{T-t}^{\max} = \displaystyle\max_{t \leq u \leq T} S_u$, we can write the payoff as

$$
\begin{aligned}
\Psi(S_T) &= \max\left\{K_{\max} - S_T, 0\right\} \\
&= \max\left\{\max\left\{S_{t-t_0}^{\max}, S_{T-t}^{\max}\right\} - S_T, 0\right\} \\
&= \begin{cases} \max\left\{S_{t-t_0}^{\max} - S_T, 0\right\} & \text{if } S_{T-t}^{\max} \leq S_{t-t_0}^{\max} \\[2mm] \max\left\{S_{T-t}^{\max} - S_T, 0\right\} & \text{if } S_{T-t}^{\max} > S_{t-t_0}^{\max} \end{cases} \\
&= \begin{cases} S_{t-t_0}^{\max} - S_T & \text{if } S_{T-t}^{\max} \leq S_{t-t_0}^{\max} \\[2mm] S_{T-t}^{\max} - S_T & \text{if } S_{T-t}^{\max} > S_{t-t_0}^{\max} \end{cases} \\
&= \max\left\{S_{t-t_0}^{\max}, S_{T-t}^{\max}\right\} - S_T \\
&= \max\left\{S_{T-t}^{\max} - S_{t-t_0}^{\max}, 0\right\} + S_{t-t_0}^{\max} - S_T.
\end{aligned}
$$

Under the risk-neutral measure $\mathbb{Q}$, S_t follows

$$\frac{dS_t}{S_t} = (r - D)dt + \sigma dW_t^{\mathbb{Q}}$$

where $W_t^{\mathbb{Q}} = W_t + \left(\dfrac{\mu - r}{\sigma}\right) t$ is a $\mathbb{Q}$-standard Wiener process. Hence, the option price at time t, $t_0 \leq t \leq T$ is

$$
\begin{aligned}
&P_f(S_t, t; K_{\max}, T) \\
&= e^{-r(T-t)}\mathbb{E}^{\mathbb{Q}}\left[\max\left\{S_{T-t}^{\max} - S_{t-t_0}^{\max}, 0\right\} + S_{t-t_0}^{\max} - S_T \,\middle|\, \mathcal{F}_t\right] \\
&= e^{-r(T-t)}\mathbb{E}^{\mathbb{Q}}\left[\max\left\{S_{T-t}^{\max} - S_{t-t_0}^{\max}, 0\right\}\,\middle|\, \mathcal{F}_t\right] + e^{-r(T-t)}\mathbb{E}^{\mathbb{Q}}\left[S_{t-t_0}^{\max} - S_T\,\middle|\, \mathcal{F}_t\right] \\
&= e^{-r(T-t)}\mathbb{E}^{\mathbb{Q}}\left[\max\left\{S_{T-t}^{\max} - S_{t-t_0}^{\max}, 0\right\}\,\middle|\, \mathcal{F}_t\right] + e^{-r(T-t)}\left(S_{t-t_0}^{\max} - S_t e^{r(T-t)}\right) \\
&= e^{-r(T-t)}\mathbb{E}^{\mathbb{Q}}\left[\max\left\{S_{T-t}^{\max} - S_{t-t_0}^{\max}, 0\right\}\,\middle|\, \mathcal{F}_t\right] + e^{-r(T-t)}S_{t-t_0}^{\max} - S_t.
\end{aligned}
$$

From Problem 6.2.2.12 (page 627) we can write

$$\hat{C}_F(S_t, t; S^{\max}_{t-t_0}, T) = e^{-r(T-t)}\mathbb{E}^Q\left[\max\left\{S^{\max}_{T-t} - S^{\max}_{t-t_0}, 0\right\}\bigg| \mathscr{F}_t\right]$$

where

$$\hat{C}_F(S_t, t; S^{\max}_{t-t_0}, T) = C_{bs}(S_t, t; S^{\max}_{t-t_0}, T)$$

$$+ \left(\frac{S_t}{\alpha}\right)\left[e^{-D(T-t)}\Phi(\hat{d}_+) - \left(\frac{S_t}{S^{\max}_{t-t_0}}\right)^{-\alpha} e^{-r(T-t)}\Phi(\hat{d}_-)\right]$$

such that $C_{bs}(S_t, t; S^{\max}_{t-t_0}, T)$ is the European call option price defined as

$$C_{bs}(S_t, t; S^{\max}_{t-t_0}, T) = S_t e^{-D(T-t)}\Phi\left(d_+\right) - S^{\max}_{t-t_0} e^{-r(T-t)}\Phi\left(d_-\right)$$

with

$$d_\pm = \frac{\log(S_t/S^{\max}_{t-t_0}) + (r - D \pm \frac{1}{2}\sigma^2)(T - t)}{\sigma\sqrt{T - t}}$$

$$\hat{d}_\pm = \frac{\log(S_t/S^{\max}_{t-t_0}) \pm (r - D \pm \frac{1}{2}\sigma^2)(T - t)}{\sigma\sqrt{T - t}}$$

and $\alpha = \dfrac{r - D}{\frac{1}{2}\sigma^2}$.

Thus,

$$P_f(S_t, t; K_{\max}, T) = \hat{C}_F(S_t, t; S^{\max}_{t-t_0}, T) + e^{-r(T-t)}S^{\max}_{t-t_0} - S_t.$$

$\square$

Volatility Models

Within the framework of the Black–Scholes model, one of the incorrect assumptions of the model is that the volatility of the underlying asset or stock price is constant. Empirical studies have found that by equating the theoretical Black–Scholes formula with market-quoted European option prices, different volatility values are obtained for different strikes and option expiries. However, this is due to the inherent property of the geometric Brownian motion model, which tries to fit the log returns of asset prices that do not conform to the normality assumption as observed in the market. In this chapter we will discuss further developments beyond the Black–Scholes framework where the volatility takes centre stage.

7.1 INTRODUCTION

In this section we consider different types of volatility which are used by practitioners as a form of risk measurement.

Historical Volatility

Historical volatility reflects the past price movements of the underlying asset observed in the market and is also referred to as the asset's actual, realised or statistical volatility. In general, historical volatility can also be considered as a standard deviation, which is a measure of the amount of variation or dispersion for a specified period of asset prices. Thus, a higher dispersion value implies a higher risk that future asset prices will be further away from the current price. To estimate the volatility parameter of a diffusion model, the most systematic way is to use the maximum-likelihood method.

Suppose we have a sequence of random variables $X_1, X_2, \ldots, X_n$ having a joint density $f_{X_1, X_2, \ldots, X_n}(x_1, x_2, \ldots, x_n | \theta)$ which depends on an unknown parameter θ. Here, θ may be a vector. Given the observed values $X_i = x_i$ where $i = 1, 2, \ldots, n$, the likelihood of θ as a function of $x_1, x_2, \ldots, x_n$ is defined as

$$\ell(\theta) = f_{X_1, X_2, \ldots, X_n}(x_1, x_2, \ldots, x_n | \theta).$$

The maximum-likelihood estimate (mle) of θ is that the value of θ is chosen via optimisation to maximise the joint density $f_{X_1, X_2, \ldots, X_n}(x_1, x_2, \ldots, x_n | \theta)$.

If the random variables $X_1, X_2, \ldots, X_n$ are assumed to be independent and identically distributed, their joint density is the product of the marginal densities, and the likelihood becomes

$$\ell(\theta) = f_{X_1}(x_1 | \theta) f_{X_2}(x_2 | \theta) \ldots f_{X_n}(x_n | \theta).$$

In contrast, if $X_1, X_2, \ldots, X_n$ are assumed to follow a Markov process, the joint density can be represented as a product of conditional densities

$$\ell(\theta) = f_{X_1}(x_1 | \theta) f_{X_2 | X_1}(x_2 | x_1, \theta) \ldots f_{X_n | X_{n-1}}(x_n | x_{n-1}, \theta).$$

For certain probability density functions, rather than maximising the likelihood function, it is more efficient to maximise the natural logarithm (since the logarithm is a monotone function). Hence, for an independent and identically distributed sample, the log-likelihood in terms of marginal densities is

$$\log \ell(\theta) = \log f_{X_1}(x_1 | \theta) + \log f_{X_2}(x_2 | \theta) + \ldots + \log f_{X_n}(x_n | \theta)$$

whilst for the conditional densities

$$\log \ell(\theta) = \log f_{X_1}(x_1 | \theta) + \log f_{X_2 | X_1}(x_2 | x_1, \theta) + \ldots + \log f_{X_n | X_{n-1}}(x_n | x_{n-1}, \theta).$$

In statistics, the maximum-likelihood estimate for a parameter θ is denoted by $\hat{\theta}$, and is obtained by solving the first-order necessary condition of a local maximiser

$$\left. \frac{\partial \ell(\theta)}{\partial \theta} \right|_{\theta = \hat{\theta}} = 0 \text{ or } \left. \frac{\partial \log \ell(\theta)}{\partial \theta} \right|_{\theta = \hat{\theta}} = 0.$$

Implied Volatility

Recall that the Black–Scholes formula for a European option price $V_{bs}(S_t, t; K, T)$ at time t, written on asset price S_t with strike price K and expiry $T > t$, is

$$V_{bs}(S_t, t; K, T) = \begin{cases} S_t e^{-D(T-t)} \Phi(d_+) - K e^{-r(T-t)} \Phi(d_-) & \text{for call option} \\ K e^{-r(T-t)} \Phi(-d_-) - S_t e^{-D(T-t)} \Phi(-d_+) & \text{for put option} \end{cases}$$

with

$$d_\pm = \frac{\log(S_t / K) + (r + D \pm \frac{1}{2} \sigma^2 (T - t))}{\sigma \sqrt{T - t}}, \Phi(x) = \int_{-\infty}^{x} \frac{1}{\sqrt{2\pi}} e^{-\frac{1}{2} u^2} du$$

where r is the risk-free interest rate, D is the continuous dividend yield on the underlying asset and σ is the asset price volatility which is the only parameter that is not directly observed. In the simplest terms, the volatility parameter can be estimated from historical price data on the asset price S_t, and with the calibrated value it can then be used in the Black–Scholes formula to value any contingent claim written on S_t. In addition, all other options can also be priced with the same estimated volatility irrespective of the strike price K and expiry time T. Although this approach is feasible and easy to implement, there is no single calculation for historical volatility. For example, the choice of the number of historical days for the volatility estimation will have a direct impact on the calculation and hence, the estimated volatility might be unreliable.

Instead of relying on historical price movements of the asset price, an alternate volatility estimation can be calculated involving the Black–Scholes theoretical formula. As the volatility σ is the only unobservable parameter, and given that the vega of the Black–Scholes formula of either a call or put option is positive,

$$\frac{\partial V_{bs}}{\partial \sigma} > 0$$

for all σ, therefore if we know the market price of the European option V_{mkt} written on asset price S_t and traded at time t with strike K and expiry T, then there exists a unique $\sigma = \sigma_{imp}$ known as the *implied volatility* such that

$$V_{bs}(S_t, t; K, T, \sigma_{imp}) = V_{mkt}$$

provided V_{mkt} lies between

$$V_{mkt} \leq \begin{cases} S_t & \text{for call option} \\ \\ K & \text{for put option} \end{cases}$$

and

$$V_{mkt} \geq \begin{cases} \max\left\{S_t e^{-D(T-t)} - K e^{-r(T-t)}, 0\right\} & \text{for call option} \\ \\ \max\left\{K e^{-r(T-t)} - S_t e^{-D(T-t)}, 0\right\} & \text{for put option.} \end{cases}$$

According to the Black–Scholes assumptions, the implied volatility calculated at time t should be a constant value or time dependent across all strike prices K and option expiries T. However, in reality, it shows variations with both strike (known as *volatility smile* or *volatility skew*) and expiry T (known as *term structure of volatility*). Given that the implied volatility $\sigma_{imp}(K,T)$ for a certain strike K and expiry T has a fixed value, the relation $\sigma_{imp}(K,T)$ is called an *implied volatility surface*.

Local Volatility

As the calculated implied volatility is not a constant value by varying the strike and option expiry, the most straightforward strategy is to modify the Black–Scholes model by assuming the asset price volatility $\sigma(S_t, t)$ is a function of both the underlying asset price and time. By doing so, not only will it be able to accommodate the implied volatility for discrete strike prices and expiry times, but it will also allow us to price options consistently at any moment in time. In a local volatility model, the underlying asset price S_t follows a modified SDE of the form

$$\frac{dS_t}{S_t} = (\mu - D)dt + \sigma(S_t, t)dW_t$$

where W_t is the standard Wiener process, μ is the drift, D is the continuous dividend yield and $\sigma(S_t, t)$ is the local volatility function depending on the asset price S_t and time t.

By substituting the constant or time-dependent volatility with $\sigma(S_t, t)$, the Black–Scholes PDE satisfied by a European-style option $V(S_t, t; K, T)$ with strike K, expiry $T > t$ and having a payoff $\Psi(S_T)$,

$$\frac{\partial V}{\partial t} + \frac{1}{2}\sigma(S_t, t)^2 S_t^2 \frac{\partial^2 V}{\partial S_t^2} + (r - D)S_t \frac{\partial V}{\partial S_t} - rV(S_t, t; K, T) = 0$$

$$V(S_T, T; K, T) = \Psi(S_T)$$

still remains valid and the option price at time t,

$$V(S_t, t; K, T) = e^{-r(T-t)} \mathbb{E}^{\mathbb{Q}}\left[\Psi(S_T) \big| \mathscr{F}_t\right]$$

as the present value of the expected payoff under the risk-neutral measure $\mathbb{Q}$ remains the same. However, given that the volatility is now a function of the underlying asset price and time, the Black–Scholes analytical solution is not extended for this model.

Given the current asset price S_t, the local volatility function $\sigma(S_t, t)$ can be obtained uniquely from market quotes of European call option prices $C(S_t, t; K, T)$ (or put option prices $P(S_t, t; K, T)$) across all strikes K and expiry times T through the *Dupire formula*

$$\sigma(K, T) = \begin{cases} \sqrt{\dfrac{\left(\dfrac{\partial C}{\partial T} + (r - D)K\dfrac{\partial C}{\partial K} + DC(S_t, t; K, T)\right)}{K^2 \dfrac{\partial^2 C}{\partial K^2}}} & \text{for European call option} \\[3em] \sqrt{\dfrac{\left(\dfrac{\partial P}{\partial T} + (r - D)K\dfrac{\partial P}{\partial K} + DP(S_t, t; K, T)\right)}{K^2 \dfrac{\partial^2 P}{\partial K^2}}} & \text{for European put option.} \end{cases}$$

If we have a sequence of market-quoted European call (or put) option prices $C_{\text{mkt}}(S_t, t; K_i, T_j)$ (or $P_{\text{mkt}}(S_t, t; K_i, T_j)$) of different strikes K_i, $i = 1, 2, \ldots, N$ and expiries T_j, $j = 1, 2, \ldots, M$, we can first interpolate and extrapolate these prices to produce a smooth surface. Assuming that the surface is twice continuously differentiable in K and T, we can then subsequently utilise the Dupire formula to determine the local volatility for any arbitrary strikes and expiries.

In addition, the local volatility function can also be expressed in terms of the implied volatility σ_{imp}, given as

$$\sigma(K, T) = \sqrt{\dfrac{2\left(\dfrac{\partial \sigma_{\text{imp}}}{\partial T} + (r - D)K\dfrac{\partial \sigma_{\text{imp}}}{\partial K} + \dfrac{1}{2}\dfrac{\sigma_{\text{imp}}}{T - t}\right)}{K^2 \dfrac{\partial^2 \sigma_{\text{imp}}}{\partial K^2} + \dfrac{2Kd_+^{\text{imp}}}{\sigma_{\text{imp}}\sqrt{T-t}}\dfrac{\partial \sigma_{\text{imp}}}{\partial K} + \dfrac{K^2 d_+^{\text{imp}} d_-^{\text{imp}}}{\sigma_{\text{imp}}}\left(\dfrac{\partial \sigma_{\text{imp}}}{\partial K}\right)^2 + \dfrac{1}{\sigma_{\text{imp}}\sqrt{T-t}}}}$$

such that

$$
d_{\pm}^{\text{imp}} = \frac{\log(S_t/K) + (r - D \pm \frac{1}{2}\sigma_{\text{imp}}^2)(T - t)}{\sigma_{\text{imp}}\sqrt{T - t}}
$$

where, analogous to the Dupire formula, an implied volatility surface is first produced using the market-quoted European call (or put) option prices for a range of strikes and expiries before utilising the above formula to calculate the local volatility function for any arbitrary strikes and expiries.

Stochastic Volatility

As observed in the market, the distribution of the returns of the asset prices shows that it is highly peaked and fat-tailed, which deviates from the assumption of normality. To resolve this shortcoming of the Black–Scholes model, we can either choose a jump-diffusion model or we can assume that the volatility of the underlying asset price is a stochastic process (i.e., a stochastic volatility model). When modelling the asset price as a jump-diffusion model, we assume that the prices do not move continuously in time and we can then let the model make discrete jumps based on a Poisson process. In contrast, when modelling the asset price volatility as a stochastic process we assume that the volatility is a continuous random variable in order to describe the fat-tailed distribution of the asset price returns.

In a general stochastic volatility model, the underlying asset price return and its instantaneous volatility have the following diffusion processes

$$
\frac{dS_t}{S_t} = \mu(S_t, Y_t, t)dt + \sigma(Y_t, t)dW_t^S
$$
$$
dY_t = \alpha(S_t, Y_t, t)dt + \beta(S_t, Y_t, t)dW_t^Y
$$
$$
dW_t^S \cdot dW_t^Y = \rho dt
$$

where $\{W_t^S : t \geq 0\}$ and $\{W_t^Y : t \geq 0\}$ are two correlated standard Wiener processes under the physical measure $\mathbb{P}$ with correlation value $\rho \in (-1, 1)$, S_t is the underlying asset price, $\mu(S_t, Y_t, t)$ is the asset price drift and $\sigma(Y_t, t)$ is the asset instantaneous volatility, which is assumed to be a stochastic process having drift $\alpha(S_t, Y_t, t)$ and volatility (known as vol-of-vol) $\beta(S_t, Y_t, t)$.

Like the jump-diffusion model, the market we have described above is incomplete since there is only one traded asset and two sources of uncertainty (Wiener processes W_t^S and W_t^Y). In addition, the modelling of the volatility as a stochastic process is more challenging, since it is a hidden process and is not directly observable. Thus, the calibration of the model parameters against existing market data is harder as it contains more parameters to estimate than a simple Black–Scholes model.

7.2 PROBLEMS AND SOLUTIONS

7.2.1 Historical and Implied Volatility

1. *Estimation of Geometric Brownian Motion Parameters.* Let $S_t, S_{t+\Delta t}, S_{t+2\Delta t}, \ldots, S_{t+N\Delta t}$ with $\Delta t = (T - t)/N$ be a sequence of discrete values observed at regular time intervals $\Delta t > 0$ which are assumed to follow a GBM process

$$dS_t = \mu S_t dt + \sigma S_t dW_t$$

where the drift μ and volatility σ are constant parameters and W_t is a standard Wiener process on the probability space $(\Omega, \mathcal{F}, \mathbb{P})$.

Using maximum-likelihood estimation or otherwise, calculate the historical estimates of μ and σ.

Solution: From Itō's formula

$$d \log S_t = \frac{dS_t}{S_t} - \frac{1}{2}\left(\frac{dS_t}{S_t}\right)^2 + \ldots$$

$$= \left(\mu - \frac{1}{2}\sigma^2\right) dt + \sigma dW_t$$

and taking integrals

$$\int_t^{t+\Delta t} d \log S_u = \int_t^{t+\Delta t} \left(\mu - \frac{1}{2}\sigma^2\right) du + \int_t^{t+\Delta t} \sigma dW_u$$

$$\log\left(\frac{S_{t+\Delta t}}{S_t}\right) = \left(\mu - \frac{1}{2}\sigma^2\right) \Delta t + \sigma W_{\Delta t}$$

where $W_{\Delta t} \sim \mathcal{N}(0, \Delta t)$.

Therefore,

$$\log\left(\frac{S_{t+\Delta t}}{S_t}\right) \sim \mathcal{N}\left[\left(\mu - \frac{1}{2}\sigma^2\right)\Delta t, \sigma^2 \Delta t\right].$$

Maximum-Likelihood Estimation Method

Using the maximum-likelihood method, the likelihood function is the joint density of $\log\left(\frac{S_{t+\Delta t}}{S_t}\right), \log\left(\frac{S_{t+2\Delta t}}{S_{t+\Delta t}}\right), \ldots, \log\left(\frac{S_{t+N\Delta t}}{S_{t+(N-1)\Delta t}}\right)$ which is a product of their marginal densities

$$\ell(\mu, \sigma) = \prod_{i=1}^{N} \frac{1}{\sigma\sqrt{2\pi\Delta t}} \exp\left[-\frac{1}{2}\left(\frac{\log\left(\frac{S_{t+i\Delta t}}{S_{t+(i-1)\Delta t}}\right) - \left(\mu - \frac{1}{2}\sigma^2\right)\Delta t}{\sigma\sqrt{\Delta t}}\right)^2\right]$$

$$= \prod_{i=1}^{N} \frac{1}{\sigma\sqrt{2\pi\Delta t}} \exp\left[-\frac{1}{2}\left(\frac{R_i - \left(\mu - \frac{1}{2}\sigma^2\right)\Delta t}{\sigma\sqrt{\Delta t}}\right)^2\right]$$

where $R_i = \log \left(\dfrac{S_{t+i\Delta t}}{S_{t+(i-1)\Delta t}} \right)$, $i = 1, 2, \ldots, N$.

Taking the log-likelihood

$$\log \ell(\mu, \sigma) = -N \log \sigma - \frac{N}{2} \log(2\pi \Delta t) - \frac{1}{2\sigma^2 \Delta t} \sum_{i=1}^{N} \left(R_i - \left(\mu - \frac{1}{2}\sigma^2 \right) \Delta t \right)^2$$

and partial differentials with respect to μ and σ,

$$\frac{\partial \log \ell}{\partial \mu} = \frac{1}{\sigma^2} \sum_{i=1}^{N} \left(R_i - \left(\mu - \frac{1}{2}\sigma^2 \right) \Delta t \right)$$

$$\frac{\partial \log \ell}{\partial \sigma} = -\frac{N}{\sigma} + \frac{1}{\sigma^3 \Delta t} \sum_{i=1}^{N} \left(R_i - \left(\mu - \frac{1}{2}\sigma^2 \right) \Delta t \right)^2 - \frac{1}{\sigma} \sum_{i=1}^{N} \left(R_i - \left(\mu - \frac{1}{2}\sigma^2 \right) \Delta t \right).$$

By setting $\dfrac{\partial \log \ell}{\partial \mu} = 0$ and $\dfrac{\partial \log \ell}{\partial \sigma} = 0$, the maximum-likelihood estimates $\hat{\mu}$ and $\hat{\sigma}$ satisfy

$$\left(\hat{\mu} - \frac{1}{2}\hat{\sigma}^2 \right) \Delta t = \bar{R}$$

and

$$-\frac{N}{\hat{\sigma}} + \frac{1}{\hat{\sigma}^3 \Delta t} \sum_{i=1}^{N} (R_i - \bar{R})^2 - \frac{1}{\hat{\sigma}} \sum_{i=1}^{N} (R_i - \bar{R}) = 0$$

where $\bar{R} = \dfrac{1}{N} \sum_{i=1}^{N} R_i$.

Thus, we have

$$\hat{\mu} = \frac{1}{\Delta t} \left(\bar{R} + \frac{1}{2N} \sum_{i=1}^{N} (R_i - \bar{R})^2 \right) \quad \text{and} \quad \hat{\sigma} = \sqrt{\frac{1}{N\Delta t} \sum_{i=1}^{N} (R_i - \bar{R})^2}.$$

Moment-Matching Estimation Method

Since

$$\mathbb{E}^Q \left[\log \left(\frac{S_{t+\Delta t}}{S_t} \right) \Big| \mathscr{F}_t \right] = \left(\mu - \frac{1}{2}\sigma^2 \right) \Delta t$$

$$\text{Var}^Q \left[\log \left(\frac{S_{t+\Delta t}}{S_t} \right) \Big| \mathscr{F}_t \right] = \sigma^2 \Delta t$$

and by setting the logarithm return

$$R_i = \log\left(\frac{S_{t+i\Delta t}}{S_{t+(i-1)\Delta t}}\right)$$

where $R_i = 1, 2, \ldots, N$ are independent and identically distributed, the estimates of $\hat{\mu}$ and $\hat{\sigma}$ are given by

$$\left(\hat{\mu} - \frac{1}{2}\hat{\sigma}^2\right)\Delta t = \bar{R}$$

and

$$\hat{\sigma}^2 \Delta t = \frac{1}{(N-1)\Delta t}\sum_{i=1}^{N}\left(R_i - \bar{R}\right)^2$$

where $\bar{R} = \dfrac{1}{N}\sum_{i=1}^{N} R_i$. Thus, we have

$$\hat{\mu} = \frac{1}{\Delta t}\left(\bar{R} + \frac{1}{2(N-1)}\sum_{i=1}^{N}(R_i - \bar{R})^2\right) \quad\text{and}\quad \hat{\sigma} = \sqrt{\frac{1}{(N-1)\Delta t}\sum_{i=1}^{N}(R_i - \bar{R})^2}.$$

$\square$

2. *Estimation of Ornstein–Uhlenbeck Process Parameters.* Let S_t, $S_{t+\Delta t}$, $S_{t+2\Delta t}$, ..., $S_{t+N\Delta t}$ with $\Delta t = (T - t)/N$ be a sequence of discrete values observed at regular time intervals $\Delta t > 0$ which are assumed to follow an Ornstein–Uhlenbeck process

$$dS_t = \kappa(\theta - S_t)dt + \sigma dW_t$$

where the mean-reversion rate κ, long-term mean θ and volatility σ are constant parameters and W_t is a standard Wiener process on the probability space $(\Omega, \mathcal{F}, \mathbb{P})$.

Using maximum-likelihood estimation or otherwise, calculate the historical estimates of κ, θ and σ.

Solution: From the Ornstein–Uhlenbeck process

$$dS_t = \kappa(\theta - S_t)dt + \sigma dW_t$$

and by applying Itō's formula on $e^{\kappa t}S_t$ we have

$$\begin{aligned}
d(e^{\kappa t}S_t) &= \kappa e^{\kappa t}S_t dt + e^{\kappa t}dS_t + \frac{1}{2}\kappa^2 e^{\kappa t}S_t(dt)^2 + \ldots\\
&= \kappa e^{\kappa t}S_t dt + e^{\kappa t}\left(\kappa(\theta - S_t)dt + \sigma dW_t\right)\\
&= \kappa\theta e^{\kappa t}dt + \sigma e^{\kappa t}dW_t.
\end{aligned}$$

Integrating the above expression,

$$\int_t^{t+\Delta t} d(e^{\kappa u}S_u) = \int_t^{t+\Delta t} \kappa\theta e^{\kappa u}du + \int_t^{t+\Delta t} \sigma e^{\kappa u}dW_u$$

$$S_{t+\Delta t} = S_t e^{-\kappa\Delta t} + \theta\left(1 - e^{-\kappa\Delta t}\right) + \int_t^{t+\Delta t}\sigma e^{-\kappa(t+\Delta t-u)}dW_u.$$

Given that both $\{W_t : t \geq 0\}$ and $\{W_t^2 - t : t \geq 0\}$ are $\mathbb{P}$-martingales, we have

$$\mathbb{E}\left[\int_t^{t+\Delta t}\sigma e^{-\kappa(t+\Delta t-u)}dW_u \,\middle|\, \mathcal{F}_t\right] = 0$$

and

$$\mathbb{E}\left[\left(\int_t^{t+\Delta t}\sigma e^{-\kappa(t+\Delta t-u)}dW_u\right)^2 \,\middle|\, \mathcal{F}_t\right] = \mathbb{E}\left[\int_t^{t+\Delta t}\sigma^2 e^{-2\kappa(t+\Delta t-u)}du \,\middle|\, \mathcal{F}_t\right]$$

$$= \frac{\sigma^2}{2\kappa}\left(1 - e^{-2\kappa\Delta t}\right)$$

and following the arguments given in Problem 2.2.2.31 (page 161) we can deduce

$$S_{t+\Delta t}\,|\,S_t \sim \mathcal{N}\left(S_t e^{-\kappa\Delta t} + \theta\left(1 - e^{-\kappa\Delta t}\right), \frac{\sigma^2}{2\kappa}\left(1 - e^{-2\kappa\Delta t}\right)\right).$$

To calculate the estimates of κ, θ and σ, we consider two approaches.

Maximum-Likelihood Estimation Method
By setting $s^2 = \dfrac{\sigma^2}{2\kappa}\left(1 - e^{-2\kappa\Delta t}\right)$, the likelihood function is the joint density of S_t, $S_{t+\Delta t}$, ..., $S_{t+N\Delta t}$ such that

$$\ell(\kappa,\theta,s) = \prod_{i=1}^N \frac{1}{s\sqrt{2\pi}}\exp\left[-\frac{1}{2}\left(\frac{S_{t+i\Delta t} - S_{t+(i-1)\Delta t}e^{-\kappa\Delta t} - \theta(1 - e^{-\kappa\Delta t})}{s}\right)^2\right]$$

and taking the log-likelihood

$$\log\ell(\kappa,\theta,s) = -N\log s - \frac{N}{2}\log(2\pi)$$

$$-\frac{1}{2s^2}\sum_{i=1}^N\left[S_{t+i\Delta t} - S_{t+(i-1)\Delta t}e^{-\kappa\Delta t} - \theta\left(1 - e^{-\kappa\Delta t}\right)\right]^2.$$

Taking partial differentials with respect to κ, θ and s,

$$\frac{\partial \log \ell}{\partial \kappa} = -\frac{1}{s^2} \sum_{i=1}^{N} \left[S_{t+i\Delta t} - S_{t+(i-1)\Delta t} e^{-\kappa \Delta t} - \theta \left(1 - e^{-\kappa \Delta t}\right) \right] \left[S_{t+(i-1)\Delta t} - \theta \right] \Delta t e^{-\kappa \Delta t}$$

$$= -\frac{\Delta t e^{-\kappa \Delta t}}{s^2} \sum_{i=1}^{N} \left[\left(S_{t+i\Delta t} - \theta \right) \left(S_{t+(i-1)\Delta t} - \theta \right) - \left(S_{t+(i-1)\Delta t} - \theta \right)^2 e^{-\kappa \Delta t} \right]$$

$$\frac{\partial \log \ell}{\partial \theta} = \frac{1 - e^{-\kappa \Delta t}}{s^2} \sum_{i=1}^{N} \left[S_{t+i\Delta t} - S_{t+(i-1)\Delta t} e^{-\kappa \Delta t} - \theta \left(1 - e^{-\kappa \Delta t}\right) \right]$$

$$\frac{\partial \log \ell}{\partial s} = -\frac{N}{s} + \frac{1}{s^3} \sum_{i=1}^{N} \left[S_{t+i\Delta t} - S_{t+(i-1)\Delta t} e^{-\kappa \Delta t} - \theta \left(1 - e^{-\kappa \Delta t}\right) \right]^2 .$$

By setting $\frac{\partial \log \ell}{\partial \kappa} = 0$, $\frac{\partial \log \ell}{\partial \theta} = 0$ and $\frac{\partial \log \ell}{\partial s} = 0$, the maximum-likelihood estimates $\hat{\kappa}$, $\hat{\theta}$ and $\hat{s}$ are

$$\hat{\kappa} = -\frac{1}{\Delta t} \log \left[\frac{\sum_{i=1}^{N} (S_{t+i\Delta t} - \hat{\theta})(S_{t+(i-1)\Delta t} - \hat{\theta})}{\sum_{i=1}^{N} (S_{t+(i-1)\Delta t} - \hat{\theta})^2} \right]$$

$$\hat{\theta} = \frac{\sum_{i=1}^{N} (S_{t+i\Delta t} - S_{t+(i-1)\Delta t} e^{-\hat{\kappa} \Delta t})}{N(1 - e^{-\hat{\kappa} \Delta t})}$$

$$\hat{s}^2 = \frac{1}{N} \sum_{i=1}^{N} \left[S_{t+i\Delta t} - \hat{\theta} - (S_{t+(i-1)\Delta t} - \hat{\theta}) e^{-\hat{\kappa} \Delta t} \right]^2 .$$

Letting

$$S_x = \sum_{i=1}^{N} S_{t+(i-1)\Delta t}, \quad S_y = \sum_{i=1}^{N} S_{t+i\Delta t}$$

$$S_{xx} = \sum_{i=1}^{N} S_{t+(i-1)\Delta t}^2, \quad S_{yy} = \sum_{i=1}^{N} S_{t+i\Delta t}^2, \quad S_{xy} = \sum_{i=1}^{N} S_{t+(i-1)\Delta t} S_{t+i\Delta t}$$

we have

$$\hat{\kappa} = -\frac{1}{\Delta t} \log \left[\frac{S_{xy} - \hat{\theta}(S_x + S_y) + N\hat{\theta}^2}{S_{xx} - 2\hat{\theta}S_x + N\hat{\theta}^2} \right]$$

$$\hat{\theta} = \frac{S_y - S_x e^{-\hat{\kappa} \Delta t}}{N(1 - e^{-\hat{\kappa} \Delta t})}$$

$$\hat{s}^2 = \frac{1}{N} \left[S_{yy} - 2S_{xy} e^{-\hat{\kappa} \Delta t} + S_{xx} e^{-2\hat{\kappa} \Delta t} - 2\hat{\theta}(S_y - S_x e^{-\hat{\kappa} \Delta t})(1 - e^{-\hat{\kappa} \Delta t}) \right.$$
$$\left. + N\hat{\theta}^2 (1 - e^{-\hat{\kappa} \Delta t})^2 \right] .$$

Substituting $\hat{\kappa}$ into $\hat{\theta}$,

$$N\hat{\theta} = \frac{S_y(S_{xx} - 2\hat{\theta} + N\hat{\theta}^2) - S_x(S_{xy} - \hat{\theta}S_x - \hat{\theta}S_y + N\hat{\theta}^2)}{S_{xx} - S_{xy} + \hat{\theta}(S_y - S_x)}$$

$$= \frac{S_yS_{xx} - S_xS_{xy} + \hat{\theta}(S_x^2 - S_xS_y) + N\hat{\theta}^2(S_y - S_x)}{S_{xx} - S_{xy} + \hat{\theta}(S_y - S_x)}$$

or

$$N\hat{\theta}(S_{xx} - S_{xy}) + N\hat{\theta}^2(S_y - S_x) = S_yS_{xx} - S_xS_{xy} + \hat{\theta}(S_x^2 - S_xS_y) + N\hat{\theta}^2(S_y - S_x)$$

and hence

$$\hat{\theta} = \frac{S_yS_{xx} - S_xS_{xy}}{N(S_{xx} - S_{xy}) - S_x^2 + S_xS_y}$$

with the maximum-likelihood estimates of mean-reversion rate $\hat{\kappa}$ and volatility $\hat{\sigma}$ being

$$\hat{\kappa} = -\frac{1}{\Delta t}\log\left[\frac{S_{xy} - \hat{\theta}(S_x + S_y) + N\hat{\theta}^2}{S_{xx} - 2\hat{\theta}S_x + N\hat{\theta}^2}\right] \quad \text{and} \quad \hat{\sigma} = \sqrt{\frac{2\hat{\kappa}\hat{s}}{1 - e^{-2\hat{\kappa}\Delta t}}}$$

respectively.

Ordinary Least-Squares Method
We let the relationship between consecutive $S_t, S_{t+\Delta t}, \ldots, S_{t+N\Delta t}$ be

$$S_{t+\Delta t} = mS_t + c + \epsilon_t, \epsilon_t \sim \mathcal{N}(0, \sigma_\epsilon^2)$$

where m and c are the regression parameters, ϵ_t is normally distributed and is independent and identically distributed.

By comparing the relationship between the linear fit and the solution of the Ornstein–Uhlenbeck process model

$$S_{t+\Delta t} = S_t e^{-\kappa\Delta t} + \theta\left(1 - e^{-\kappa\Delta t}\right) + \int_t^{t+\Delta t} \sigma e^{-\kappa(t+\Delta t-u)}dW_u$$

where $\int_t^{t+\Delta t} \sigma e^{-\kappa(t+\Delta t-u)}dW_u \sim \mathcal{N}\left(0, \frac{\sigma^2}{2\kappa}\left(1 - e^{-2\kappa\Delta t}\right)\right)$, the Ornstein–Uhlenbeck parameters can be equated as

$$\kappa = -\frac{\log m}{\Delta t}, \quad \theta = \frac{c}{1 - m} \quad \text{and} \quad \sigma = \sigma_\epsilon\sqrt{\frac{2\kappa}{1 - e^{-2\kappa\Delta t}}}.$$

As for estimating the pair (m, c), we can compute it by solving the following ordinary least-squares problem

$$OLS \left\{ \begin{array}{c} \text{minimise} \\ m,c \in \mathbb{R} \end{array} \sum_{i=1}^{N} \left(S_{t+i\Delta t} - m S_{t+(i-1)\Delta t} - c \right)^2 \right. .$$

By setting $f(m, c) = \sum_{i=1}^{N} \left(S_{t+i\Delta t} - m S_{t+(i-1)\Delta t} - c \right)^2$ and taking partial derivatives with respect to m and c,

$$\frac{\partial f}{\partial m} = -2 \sum_{i=1}^{N} \left(S_{t+i\Delta t} - m S_{t+(i-1)\Delta t} - c \right) S_{t+(i-1)\Delta t} = -2(S_{xy} - m S_{xx} - c S_x)$$

$$\frac{\partial f}{\partial c} = -2 \sum_{i=1}^{N} \left(S_{t+i\Delta t} - m S_{t+(i-1)\Delta t} - c \right) = -2(S_y - m S_x - cN)$$

where

$$S_x = \sum_{i=1}^{N} S_{t+(i-1)\Delta t}, \quad S_y = \sum_{i=1}^{N} S_{t+i\Delta t}$$

$$S_{xx} = \sum_{i=1}^{N} S_{t+(i-1)\Delta t}^2, \quad S_{yy} = \sum_{i=1}^{N} S_{t+i\Delta t}^2, \quad S_{xy} = \sum_{i=1}^{N} S_{t+(i-1)\Delta t} S_{t+i\Delta t}.$$

By setting the partial derivatives to zero and solving the linear equations simultaneously, the estimates $\hat{m}$ and $\hat{c}$ that minimise OLS are given as

$$\hat{m} = \frac{N S_{xy} - S_x S_y}{N S_{xx} - S_x^2}, \quad \hat{c} = \frac{S_y - \hat{m} S_x}{N}$$

with the unbiased estimated standard error $\hat{\sigma}_\epsilon$ given as

$$\hat{\sigma}_\epsilon = \sqrt{\frac{\sum_{i=1}^{N} \left(S_{t+i\Delta t} - \hat{m} S_{t+(i-1)\Delta t} - \hat{c} \right)^2}{N - 2}}.$$

Take note that the divisor $N - 2$ is used instead of N because two parameters m and c have been estimated, thus giving $N - 2$ degrees of freedom.

□

3. *Estimation of Geometric Mean-Reverting Process Parameters.* Let S_t, $S_{t+\Delta t}$, $S_{t+2\Delta t}$, ..., $S_{t+N\Delta t}$ with $\Delta t = (T - t)/N$ be a sequence of discrete values observed at regular time intervals $\Delta t > 0$ which are assumed to follow a geometric mean-reverting process with

the following SDE

$$dS_t = \kappa(\theta - \log S_t)S_t dt + \sigma S_t dW_t, \quad S_0 > 0$$

where the mean-reversion rate κ, long-term mean θ and volatility σ are constant parameters and W_t is a standard Wiener process on the probability space $(\Omega, \mathcal{F}, \mathbb{P})$.

Using maximum-likelihood estimation or otherwise, calculate the historical estimates of κ, θ and σ.

Solution: By expanding $\log S_t$ using Taylor's formula and subsequently applying Itô's formula we have

$$d(\log S_t) = \frac{1}{S_t}dS_t - \frac{1}{2S_t^2}\left(dS_t\right)^2 + \dots$$

$$= \kappa\left(\theta - \log S_t\right)dt + \sigma dW_t - \frac{1}{2}\sigma^2 dt$$

$$= \left(\kappa\left(\theta - \log S_t\right) - \frac{1}{2}\sigma^2\right)dt + \sigma dW_t$$

and setting $X_t = \log S_t$ we can rewrite the SDE as

$$dX_t = \left(\kappa(\theta - X_t) - \frac{1}{2}\sigma^2\right)dt + \sigma dW_t$$

$$= \kappa(\vartheta - X_t)dt + \sigma dW_t$$

where $\vartheta = \theta - \dfrac{\sigma^2}{2\kappa}$.

By letting

$$S_x = \sum_{i=1}^{N} \log S_{t+(i-1)\Delta t}, \quad S_y = \sum_{i=1}^{N} \log S_{t+i\Delta t} \quad S_{xx} = \sum_{i=1}^{N} \left(\log S_{t+(i-1)\Delta t}\right)^2,$$

$$S_{yy} = \sum_{i=1}^{N} \left(\log S_{t+i\Delta t}\right)^2 \quad S_{xy} = \sum_{i=1}^{N} \left(\log S_{t+(i-1)\Delta t}\right)\left(\log S_{t+i\Delta t}\right)$$

then from analogy with the Ornstein–Uhlenbeck process estimation of parameters (see Problem 7.2.1.2, page 654), the maximum-likelihood estimates of ϑ, κ and σ are

$$\hat{\vartheta} = \frac{S_y S_{xx} - S_x S_{xy}}{N(S_{xx} - S_{xy}) - S_x^2 + S_x S_y}$$

$$\hat{\kappa} = -\frac{1}{\Delta t}\log\left[\frac{S_{xy} - \hat{\vartheta}(S_x + S_y) + N\hat{\vartheta}^2}{S_{xx} - 2\hat{\vartheta}S_x + N\hat{\vartheta}^2}\right]$$

$$\hat{\sigma} = \sqrt{\frac{2\hat{\kappa}\hat{s}}{1 - e^{-2\hat{\kappa}\Delta t}}}$$

where

$$\hat{s}^2 = \frac{1}{N} \left[S_{yy} - 2S_{xy}e^{-\hat{\kappa}\Delta t} + S_{xx}e^{-2\hat{\kappa}\Delta t} - 2\hat{\vartheta}(S_y - S_x e^{-\hat{\kappa}\Delta t})(1 - e^{-\hat{\kappa}\Delta t}) \right.$$
$$\left. + N\hat{\vartheta}^2(1 - e^{-\hat{\kappa}\Delta t})^2 \right].$$

Alternatively, using ordinary least squares, the estimates of ϑ, κ and σ are

$$\hat{\vartheta} = \frac{\hat{c}}{1 - \hat{m}}, \quad \hat{\kappa} = -\frac{\log \hat{m}}{\Delta t} \quad \text{and} \quad \hat{\sigma} = \hat{\sigma}_\epsilon \sqrt{\frac{2\hat{\kappa}}{1 - e^{-2\hat{\kappa}\Delta t}}}$$

where

$$\hat{m} = \frac{N S_{xy} - S_x S_y}{N S_{xx} - S_x^2}$$

$$\hat{c} = \frac{S_y - \hat{m} S_x}{N}$$

$$\hat{\sigma}_\epsilon = \sqrt{\frac{\sum_{i=1}^{N} \left(\log S_{t+i\Delta t} - \hat{m} \log S_{t+(i-1)\Delta t} - \hat{c} \right)^2}{N - 2}}.$$

From the relationship $\vartheta = \theta - \frac{\sigma^2}{2\kappa}$, the estimate $\hat{\theta}$ is recovered from

$$\hat{\theta} = \hat{\vartheta} + \frac{\hat{\sigma}^2}{2\hat{\kappa}}.$$

$\square$

4. *Generalised Historical Volatility.* Let $S_t, S_{t+\Delta t}, S_{t+2\Delta t}, \ldots, S_{t+N\Delta t}$ with $\Delta t = (T - t)/N$ be a sequence of discrete asset prices observed at regular time intervals $\Delta t > 0$. Assume that the asset prices follow a lognormal model with daily closing prices (i.e., $\Delta t = 1$ trading day) and let σ_{sd} be the standard deviation of logarithm returns of asset prices.

Assuming 252 trading days per year, find the estimated annualised, monthly and weekly volatilities.

Solution: Following Problem 7.2.1.1 (page 651) using the maximum-likelihood method, the biased standard deviation σ_{sd} of the logarithm returns of asset prices can be estimated as

$$\sigma_{sd} = \sqrt{\frac{1}{N} \sum_{i=1}^{N} \left(R_i - \bar{R} \right)^2}$$

where $R_i = \log \left(\frac{S_{t+i\Delta t}}{S_{t+(i-1)\Delta t}} \right)$, $i = 1, 2, \ldots, N$ and $\bar{R} = \frac{1}{N} \sum_{i=1}^{N} R_i$.

For the case of annualised volatility, we set $\Delta t = \frac{1}{252}$ and have

$$\sigma_{\text{annualised}} = \frac{\sigma_{\text{sd}}}{\sqrt{\Delta t}} = \frac{\sigma_{\text{sd}}}{\sqrt{\frac{1}{252}}} = \sigma_{\text{sd}} \sqrt{252}.$$

For the case of monthly volatility, we set $\Delta t = \frac{12}{252}$ and therefore

$$\sigma_{\text{monthly}} = \frac{\sigma_{\text{sd}}}{\sqrt{\Delta t}} = \frac{\sigma_{\text{sd}}}{\sqrt{\frac{12}{252}}} = \sigma_{\text{sd}} \sqrt{\frac{252}{12}}.$$

Finally, for the case of weekly volatility, we set $\Delta t = \frac{52}{252}$ and hence

$$\sigma_{\text{weekly}} = \frac{\sigma_{\text{sd}}}{\sqrt{\Delta t}} = \frac{\sigma_{\text{sd}}}{\sqrt{\frac{52}{252}}} = \sigma_{\text{sd}} \sqrt{\frac{252}{52}}.$$

$\square$

5. *Brenner–Subrahmanyam Approximation.* Show that the cdf of a standard normal

$$\Phi(x) = \frac{1}{\sqrt{2\pi}} \int_{-\infty}^{x} e^{-\frac{1}{2}u^2} du$$

can be expressed as

$$\Phi(x) = \frac{1}{2} + \frac{1}{\sqrt{2\pi}} \left(x - \frac{1}{2^1 \cdot 1! \cdot 3} x^3 + \frac{1}{2^2 \cdot 2! \cdot 5} x^5 - \frac{1}{2^3 \cdot 3! \cdot 7} x^7 + \ldots \right).$$

Let the Black–Scholes formula for the value of a European option $V(S_t, t; K, T)$ be

$$V(S_t, t; K, T) = \begin{cases} S_t e^{-D(T-t)} \Phi(d_+) - K e^{-r(T-t)} \Phi(d_-) & \text{for call option} \\ K e^{-r(T-t)} \Phi(-d_-) - S_t e^{-D(T-t)} \Phi(-d_+) & \text{for put option} \end{cases}$$

where

$$d_\pm = \frac{\log(S_t/K) + (r - D \pm \frac{1}{2}\sigma^2)(T - t)}{\sigma \sqrt{T - t}}$$

such that $\Phi(\cdot)$ is the cumulative distribution of a standard normal, S_t is the spot price at time $t < T$, T is the option expiry time, K is the strike price, r is the risk-free interest rate, D is the continuous dividend yield and σ is the volatility.

By defining ATM as $S_t e^{-D(T-t)} = K e^{-r(T-t)}$ (i.e., continuously paid dividend stock price equal to discounted strike price) and taking a linear approximation of the cumulative distribution of a standard normal, show that the implied volatility $\sigma_{\text{imp}}^{\text{atm}}$ of an ATM option in a forward sense ($F(t,T) = S_t e^{(r-D)(T-t)} = K$) satisfying

$$V(S_t, t; K, T, \sigma_{\text{imp}}^{\text{atm}}) = V_{\text{mkt}}$$

where V_{mkt} is the market-observed ATM European option price can be approximated as

$$\sigma_{\text{imp}}^{\text{atm}} \approx \frac{V_{\text{mkt}}}{S_t e^{-D(T-t)}} \sqrt{\frac{2\pi}{T-t}}.$$

Solution: Given that $e^{-\frac{1}{2}x^2}$ is an even function

$$\Phi(x) = \frac{1}{\sqrt{2\pi}} \int_{-\infty}^{x} e^{-\frac{1}{2}u^2} du$$

$$= \frac{1}{2} + \frac{1}{\sqrt{2\pi}} \int_{0}^{x} e^{-\frac{1}{2}u^2} du$$

and using Taylor's expansion of $f(u) = e^{-\frac{1}{2}u^2}$ about $u = 0$ so that

$$f(u) = f(0) + f'(0)u + \frac{1}{2!}f''(0)u^2 + \frac{1}{3!}f'''(0)u^3 + \dots$$

we have

$$f'(u) = -uf(u), \quad f''(u) = (u^2 - 1)f(u), \quad f'''(u) = (-u^3 + 3u)f(u)$$

$$f^{(4)}(u) = (u^4 - 6u^2 + 3)f(u), \quad f^{(5)}(u) = (-u^5 + 10u^3 - 15u)f(u)$$

$$f^{(6)}(u) = (u^6 - 15u^4 + 45u^2 + 15)f(u), \quad f^{(7)}(u) = (-u^7 + 21u^5 - 105u^3 + 75u)f(u)$$

$$\vdots$$

Hence,

$$\int_0^x e^{-\frac{1}{2}u^2} du = \int_0^x \left(1 - \frac{1}{2!}u^2 + \frac{3}{4!}u^4 - \frac{15}{6!}u^6 + \dots\right) du$$

$$= \int_0^x \left(1 - \frac{1}{2!}u^2 + \frac{1}{2^2 \cdot 2!}u^4 - \frac{1}{2^3 \cdot 3!}u^6 + \dots\right) du$$

$$= x - \frac{1}{2! \cdot 3}x^3 + \frac{1}{2^2 \cdot 2! \cdot 5}x^5 - \frac{1}{2^3 \cdot 3! \cdot 7}x^7 + \dots$$

and therefore

$$\Phi(x) = \frac{1}{2} + \frac{1}{\sqrt{2\pi}}\left(x - \frac{1}{2^1 \cdot 1! \cdot 3}x^3 + \frac{1}{2^2 \cdot 2! \cdot 5}x^5 - \frac{1}{2^3 \cdot 3! \cdot 7}x^7 + \ldots\right).$$

Setting $S_t e^{-D(T-t)} = K e^{-r(T-t)}$ so that

$$d_{\pm} = \pm\frac{1}{2}\sigma\sqrt{T-t}$$

and taking a linear approximation of $\Phi(d_{\pm})$,

$$\Phi(d_{\pm}) \approx \frac{1}{2} \pm \frac{1}{2}\sigma\sqrt{\frac{T-t}{2\pi}}.$$

By equating the Black–Scholes theoretical price with the European option market price

$$V_{\mathrm{mkt}} = \delta S_t e^{-D(T-t)}\Phi(\delta d_+) - \delta K e^{-r(T-t)}\Phi(\delta d_-)$$

where $\delta \in \{-1, 1\}$ and substituting $\Phi(d_{\pm}) \approx \frac{1}{2} \pm \frac{1}{2}\sigma_{\mathrm{imp}}^{\mathrm{atm}}\sqrt{\frac{T-t}{2\pi}}$, we have

$$V_{\mathrm{mkt}} \approx \delta S_t e^{-D(T-t)}\left(\frac{\delta}{2} + \frac{\delta\sigma_{\mathrm{imp}}^{\mathrm{atm}}}{2}\sqrt{\frac{T-t}{2\pi}}\right) - \delta S_t e^{-D(T-t)}\left(\frac{\delta}{2} - \frac{\delta\sigma_{\mathrm{imp}}^{\mathrm{atm}}}{2}\sqrt{\frac{T-t}{2\pi}}\right)$$

$$= \sigma_{\mathrm{imp}}^{\mathrm{atm}} S_t e^{-D(T-t)}\sqrt{\frac{T-t}{2\pi}}$$

since $\delta^2 = 1$.

Therefore, the implied volatility can approximated by

$$\sigma_{\mathrm{imp}}^{\mathrm{atm}} \approx \frac{V_{\mathrm{mkt}}}{S_t e^{-D(T-t)}}\sqrt{\frac{2\pi}{T-t}}.$$

$\square$

6. *Li ATM Volatility Approximation.* Prove the following trigonometry identity

$$\cos 3\theta = 4\cos^3\theta - 3\cos\theta.$$

Consider the depressed cubic equation

$$x^3 + px + q = 0$$

where $p, q \in \mathbb{R}$. By setting $x = 2y\sqrt{\dfrac{|p|}{3}}$, show that the cubic equation can be expressed as

$$4y^3 + 3\operatorname{sgn}(p)y = C$$

where $C = -\dfrac{3q}{2|p|}\sqrt{\dfrac{3}{|p|}}$. Hence, if $p < 0$ and $|C| < 1$ then show that the roots of the depressed cubic equation are

$$x = 2\sqrt{\frac{|p|}{3}}\cos\left(\frac{1}{3}\cos^{-1}C\right), 2\sqrt{\frac{|p|}{3}}\cos\left(\frac{2\pi}{3} \pm \frac{1}{3}\cos^{-1}C\right).$$

Let the Black–Scholes theoretical price for the value of a European option $V(S_t, t; K, T)$ be

$$V(S_t, t; K, T) = \begin{cases} S_t e^{-D(T-t)}\Phi(d_+) - Ke^{-r(T-t)}\Phi(d_-) & \text{for call option} \\[2mm] Ke^{-r(T-t)}\Phi(-d_-) - S_t e^{-D(T-t)}\Phi(-d_+) & \text{for put option} \end{cases}$$

where

$$d_\pm = \frac{\log(S_t/K) + (r - D \pm \frac{1}{2}\sigma^2)(T - t)}{\sigma\sqrt{T - t}}$$

such that $\Phi(\cdot)$ is the cdf of a standard normal, S_t is the spot price at time $t < T$, T is the option expiry time, K is the strike price, r is the risk-free interest rate, D is the continuous dividend yield and σ is the volatility.

By taking the third-order approximation of

$$\Phi(x) = \frac{1}{2} + \frac{1}{\sqrt{2\pi}}\left(x - \frac{1}{2^1 \cdot 1! \cdot 3}x^3 + \frac{1}{2^2 \cdot 2! \cdot 5}x^5 - \frac{1}{2^3 \cdot 3! \cdot 7}x^7 + \dots\right)$$

and by considering an ATM option in a forward sense such that $S_t e^{-D(T-t)} = Ke^{-r(T-t)}$, show that by equating

$$V(S_t, t; K, T, \sigma_{\text{imp}}^{\text{atm}}) = V_{\text{mkt}}$$

where V_{mkt} is the market-observed ATM European option price, the corresponding ATM implied volatility $\sigma_{\text{imp}}^{\text{atm}}$ can be approximated as

$$\sigma_{\text{imp}}^{\text{atm}} \approx 4\sqrt{\frac{2}{T - t}}\cos\left(\frac{2\pi}{3} - \frac{1}{3}\cos^{-1}C\right)$$

where $C = -\dfrac{3\sqrt{\pi}V_{mkt}}{4S_t e^{-D(T-t)}}$.

Solution: For $i = \sqrt{-1}$, from De Moivre's formula

$$(\cos\theta + i\sin\theta)^3 = \cos 3\theta + i\sin 3\theta$$
$$\cos^3\theta + 3i\cos^2\theta\sin\theta - 3\cos\theta\sin^2\theta - i\sin^3\theta = \cos 3\theta + i\sin 3\theta$$
$$(\cos^3\theta - 3\cos\theta\sin^2\theta) + i(3\cos^2\theta\sin\theta - \sin^3\theta) = \cos 3\theta + i\sin 3\theta.$$

By equating the real terms and because $\cos^2\theta + \sin^2\theta = 1$, we have

$$\cos 3\theta = \cos^3\theta - 3\cos\theta\sin^2\theta$$
$$= \cos^3\theta - 3\cos\theta(1 - \cos^2\theta)$$

or

$$\cos 3\theta = 4\cos^3\theta - 3\cos\theta.$$

By substituting $x = 2\sqrt{\dfrac{|p|}{3}}y$ into the depressed cubic equation

$$\frac{8|p|}{3}\sqrt{\frac{|p|}{3}}y^3 + 2p\sqrt{\frac{|p|}{3}}y + q = 0$$
$$4y^3 + 3\frac{p}{|p|}y = -\frac{3q}{2|p|}\sqrt{\frac{3}{|p|}}$$
$$4y^3 + 3\,\mathrm{sgn}(p)y = -\frac{3q}{2|p|}\sqrt{\frac{3}{|p|}}$$

or

$$4y^3 + 3\,\mathrm{sgn}(p)y = C$$

where $C = -\dfrac{3q}{2|p|}\sqrt{\dfrac{3}{|p|}}$.

For $p < 0$ and $|C| \le 1$ we let $y = \cos\theta$ so that the domain of $y \in [-1, 1]$. Therefore,

$$4\cos^3\theta - 3\cos\theta = C$$

or

$$\cos 3\theta = C.$$

Hence,

$$3\theta = \cos^{-1}C, 2\pi + \cos^{-1}C, 2\pi - \cos^{-1}C$$

or

$$\theta = \frac{1}{3}\cos^{-1}C, \frac{2\pi}{3} + \frac{1}{3}\cos^{-1}C, \frac{2\pi}{3} - \frac{1}{3}\cos^{-1}C.$$

Thus, the roots of the depressed cubic equation are

$$x = 2\sqrt{-\frac{p}{3}}\cos\left(\frac{1}{3}\cos^{-1}C\right), 2\sqrt{-\frac{p}{3}}\cos\left(\frac{2\pi}{3} \pm \frac{1}{3}\cos^{-1}C\right).$$

By setting $S_t e^{-D(T-t)} = K e^{-r(T-t)}$ so that

$$d_{\pm} = \pm\frac{1}{2}\sigma\sqrt{T-t}$$

and taking the cubic approximation of $\Phi(d_{\pm})$ we have

$$\Phi(d_{\pm}) \approx \frac{1}{2} \pm \frac{1}{\sqrt{2\pi}}\xi \mp \frac{1}{6\sqrt{2\pi}}\xi^3$$

where $\zeta = \frac{1}{2}\sigma\sqrt{T-t}$.

Equating the Black–Scholes theoretical price with the European ATM option market price

$$V_{\text{mkt}} = \delta S_t e^{-D(T-t)}\Phi(\delta d_+) - \delta K e^{-r(T-t)}\Phi(\delta d_-)$$

where $\delta \in \{-1,1\}$ and substituting $S_t e^{-D(T-t)} = K e^{-r(T-t)}$, $\Phi(d_{\pm}) \approx \frac{1}{2} \pm \frac{1}{\sqrt{2\pi}}\xi \mp$

$\frac{1}{6\sqrt{2\pi}}\xi^3$, $\xi = \frac{1}{2}\sigma_{\text{imp}}^{\text{atm}}\sqrt{T-t}$ and because $\delta^2 = 1$ we have

$$V_{\text{mkt}} \approx \delta^2 S_t e^{-D(T-t)}\left(\frac{1}{2} + \frac{1}{\sqrt{2\pi}}\xi - \frac{1}{6\sqrt{2\pi}}\xi^3\right)$$

$$-\delta^2 S_t e^{-D(T-t)}\left(\frac{1}{2} - \frac{1}{\sqrt{2\pi}}\xi + \frac{1}{6\sqrt{2\pi}}\xi^3\right)$$

$$= \frac{S_t e^{-D(T-t)}}{\sqrt{2\pi}}\left(2\xi - \frac{1}{3}\xi^3\right)$$

or

$$\xi^3 - 6\xi + \frac{3\sqrt{2\pi}V_{\text{mkt}}}{S_t e^{-D(T-t)}} \approx 0.$$

By setting $p = -6$ and $q = \dfrac{3\sqrt{2\pi}V_{\text{mkt}}}{S_t e^{-D(T-t)}}$ in the depressed cubic equation we have

$$C = -\frac{3\sqrt{\pi}V_{\text{mkt}}}{4S_t e^{-D(T-t)}}$$

and hence the roots of the cubic equation are

$$\xi \approx 2\sqrt{2}\cos\left(\frac{1}{3}\cos^{-1}C\right), 2\sqrt{2}\cos\left(\frac{2\pi}{3}\pm\frac{1}{3}\cos^{-1}C\right).$$

Since $\sigma_{\text{imp}}^{\text{atm}} \in (0,1)$, $V_{\text{mkt}} > 0$ and $S_t e^{-D(T-t)} > 0$ we only consider the case when $-1 < C < 0$, which implies

$$-1 < -\frac{3\sqrt{\pi}V_{\text{mkt}}}{4S_t e^{-D(T-t)}} < 0$$

or

$$\frac{V_{\text{mkt}}}{S_t e^{-D(T-t)}} < \frac{4}{3\sqrt{\pi}} < 1$$

and thus

$$V_{\text{mkt}} < S_t e^{-D(T-t)}(= Ke^{-r(T-t)})$$

which is valid for all ATM European call or put options.

As $C \in (-1,0)$ then, because $\dfrac{\pi}{2} < \cos^{-1}C < \pi$, we have

$$\frac{1}{2} < \cos\left(\frac{1}{3}\cos^{-1}C\right) < \frac{\sqrt{3}}{2}$$

$$-\frac{\sqrt{3}}{2} < \cos\left(\frac{2\pi}{3}+\frac{1}{3}\cos^{-1}C\right) < -1$$

and

$$0 < \cos\left(\frac{2\pi}{3}-\frac{1}{3}\cos^{-1}C\right) < \frac{1}{2}.$$

Since $\sigma_{\text{imp}}^{\text{atm}} \in (0,1)$, the first two inequalities are inappropriate and we only consider the root

$$\xi \approx 2\sqrt{2}\cos\left(\frac{2\pi}{3}-\frac{1}{3}\cos^{-1}C\right).$$

By equating

$$\frac{1}{2}\sigma_{\text{imp}}^{\text{atm}}\sqrt{T-t} \approx 2\sqrt{2}\cos\left(\frac{2\pi}{3} - \frac{1}{3}\cos^{-1}C\right)$$

the implied ATM volatility can be estimated as

$$\sigma_{\text{imp}}^{\text{atm}} \approx 4\sqrt{\frac{2}{T-t}}\cos\left(\frac{2\pi}{3} - \frac{1}{3}\cos^{-1}C\right)$$

where $C = -\dfrac{3\sqrt{\pi}V_{\text{mkt}}}{4S_t e^{-D(T-t)}}$.

□

7. *Li Non-ATM Volatility Approximation.* Let the Black–Scholes price for the value of a European option $V(S_t, t; K, T, \sigma)$ be

$$V(S_t, t; K, T, \sigma) = \delta S_t e^{-D(T-t)}\Phi(\delta d_+) - \delta K e^{-r(T-t)}\Phi(\delta d_-)$$

$$\delta = \begin{cases} +1 & \text{for call option} \\ -1 & \text{for put option} \end{cases}$$

where

$$d_\pm = \frac{\log(S_t/K) + (r - D \pm \frac{1}{2}\sigma^2)(T-t)}{\sigma\sqrt{T-t}}$$

such that $\Phi(\cdot)$ is the cdf of a standard normal, S_t is the spot price at time $t < T$, T is the option expiry time, K is the strike price, r is the risk-free interest rate, D is the continuous dividend yield and σ is the volatility.

By defining

$$m = \frac{S_t e^{-D(T-t)}}{K e^{-r(T-t)}}$$

as the measure of moneyness of an option, show that the Black–Scholes formula can be expressed as

$$f(m) = \delta m\Phi(\delta d_+) - \delta\Phi(\delta d_-)$$

where $f(m) = \dfrac{V(S_t, t; K, T, \sigma)}{K e^{-r(T-t)}}$, $d_\pm = \dfrac{\log m}{2\xi} \pm \xi$ and $\xi = \frac{1}{2}\sigma\sqrt{T-t}$.

From the expansion of the normal distribution function

$$\Phi(x) = \frac{1}{2} + \frac{1}{\sqrt{2\pi}}\left(x - \frac{1}{2^1 \cdot 1! \cdot 3}x^3 + \frac{1}{2^2 \cdot 2! \cdot 5}x^5 - \frac{1}{2^3 \cdot 3! \cdot 7}x^7 + \dots\right)$$

and taking a quadratic approximation of $f(m)$ centred at $m = 1$, show that

$$f(m) = \frac{\delta(m-1)}{2} + \frac{m+1}{\sqrt{2\pi}}\xi + \frac{(m-1)^2}{4\sqrt{2\pi}\xi} + O(\xi(m-1)^2).$$

Equating

$$V(S_t, t; K, T, \sigma_{imp}) = V_{mkt}$$

where V_{mkt} is the market-observed European price, show that by ignoring higher terms of $\xi(m-1)^2$ the implied volatility σ_{imp} can be approximated as

$$\sigma_{imp} \approx \sqrt{\frac{2\pi}{T-t}} \frac{1}{\bar{S}_t + \bar{K}} \left\{ \left(V_{mkt} - \delta\left(\frac{\bar{S}_t - \bar{K}}{2}\right)\right) \right.$$

$$\left. + \sqrt{\left(V_{mkt} - \delta\left(\frac{\bar{S}_t - \bar{K}}{2}\right)\right)^2 - \frac{(\bar{S}_t - \bar{K})^2}{\pi} \frac{(1+\bar{S}_t/\bar{K})}{2}} \right\}$$

where $\bar{S}_t = S_t e^{-D(T-t)}$ and $\bar{K} = Ke^{-r(T-t)}$ are the dividend paid stock price and discounted strike price, respectively.

Discuss the limitations of this approximation.

Under what conditions for V_{mkt} is this approximation valid?

Finally, what is the value of σ_{imp} when $m = 1$?

Solution: From the Black–Scholes theoretical price formula, we can rewrite

$$\frac{V(S_t, t; K, T, \sigma)}{Ke^{-r(T-t)}} = \delta \frac{S_t e^{-D(T-t)}}{Ke^{-r(T-t)}} \Phi(\delta d_+) - \delta \Phi(\delta d_-)$$

where

$$d_\pm = \frac{\log\left(\dfrac{S_t e^{-D(T-t)}}{Ke^{-r(T-t)}}\right) \pm \frac{1}{2}\sigma^2(T-t)}{\sigma\sqrt{T-t}}.$$

By writing $m = \dfrac{S_t e^{-D(T-t)}}{Ke^{-r(T-t)}}$, $\xi = \dfrac{1}{2}\sigma\sqrt{T-t}$ and $f(m) = \dfrac{V(S_t, t; K, T, \sigma)}{Ke^{-r(T-t)}}$, the Black–Scholes formula becomes

$$f(m) = \delta m\Phi(\delta d_+) - \delta\Phi(\delta d_-)$$

such that $d_\pm = \dfrac{\log m}{2\xi} \pm \xi.$

From Taylor's theorem,

$$f(m) = f(1) + f'(1)(m-1) + \frac{1}{2}f''(1)(m-1)^2 + O((m-1)^3)$$

where

$$f(m) = \delta m \Phi(\delta d_+) - \delta \Phi(\delta d_-)$$

$$f'(m) = \delta \Phi(\delta d_+) + \frac{\delta}{2\xi}\left(\frac{\partial \Phi(\delta d_+)}{\partial d_+} - \frac{1}{m}\frac{\partial \Phi(\delta d_-)}{\partial d_-}\right)$$

and

$$f''(m) = \frac{\delta}{2m\xi}\left(\frac{\partial \Phi(\delta d_+)}{\partial d_+} + \frac{1}{m}\frac{\partial \Phi(\delta d_-)}{\partial d_-}\right) + \frac{\delta}{4m\xi^2}\left(\frac{\partial^2 \Phi(\delta d_+)}{\partial d_+^2} - \frac{1}{m}\frac{\partial^2 \Phi(\delta d_-)}{\partial d_-^2}\right).$$

Since

$$\Phi(\delta d_\pm) = \frac{1}{2} + \frac{\delta}{\sqrt{2\pi}}\left(d_\pm - \frac{1}{6}d_\pm^3 + \frac{1}{40}d_\pm^5 - \frac{1}{336}d_\pm^7 + \dots\right)$$

$$\frac{\partial \Phi(\delta d_\pm)}{\partial d_\pm} = \frac{\delta}{\sqrt{2\pi}}\left(1 - \frac{1}{2}d_\pm^2 + \frac{1}{8}d_\pm^4 - \frac{1}{48}d_\pm^6 + \dots\right)$$

$$\frac{\partial^2 \Phi(\delta d_\pm)}{\partial d_\pm^2} = \frac{\delta}{\sqrt{2\pi}}\left(-d_\pm + \frac{1}{2}d_\pm^3 - \frac{1}{8}d_\pm^5 + \dots\right)$$

therefore

$$\Phi(\delta d_\pm)\big|_{m=1} = \frac{1}{2} \pm \frac{\delta}{\sqrt{2\pi}}\left(\xi - \frac{1}{6}\xi^3 + \frac{1}{40}\xi^5 - \frac{1}{336}\xi^6 + \dots\right)$$

$$\frac{\partial \Phi(\delta d_\pm)}{\partial d_\pm}\bigg|_{m=1} = \frac{\delta}{\sqrt{2\pi}}\left(1 - \frac{1}{2}\xi^2 + \frac{1}{8}\xi^4 - \frac{1}{48}\xi^6 + \dots\right)$$

$$\frac{\partial^2 \Phi(\delta d_\pm)}{\partial d_\pm^2}\bigg|_{m=1} = \pm\frac{\delta}{\sqrt{2\pi}}\left(-\xi + \frac{1}{2}\xi^3 - \frac{1}{8}\xi^5 + \dots\right).$$

Given $\Phi'(x) - \Phi'(-x) = 0$, thus

$$f(1) = \delta\left(\Phi(\delta\xi) - \Phi(-\delta\xi)\right)$$
$$f'(1) = \delta\Phi(\delta\xi)$$
$$f''(1) = \frac{\delta}{2\xi}\left(\frac{\partial \Phi(\delta d_+)}{\partial d_+}\bigg|_{m=1} + \frac{\partial \Phi(\delta d_-)}{\partial d_-}\bigg|_{m=1}\right)$$
$$+ \frac{\delta}{4\xi^2}\left(\frac{\partial^2 \Phi(\delta d_+)}{\partial d_+^2}\bigg|_{m=1} - \frac{\partial^2 \Phi(\delta d_-)}{\partial d_-^2}\bigg|_{m=1}\right)$$

and hence

$$
\begin{aligned}
f(m) &= \delta \left(m\Phi(\delta\xi) - \Phi(-\delta\xi) \right) + \frac{\delta}{4\xi} \left(\left. \frac{\partial \Phi(\delta d_+)}{\partial d_+} \right|_{m=1} + \left. \frac{\partial \Phi(\delta d_-)}{\partial d_-} \right|_{m=1} \right) (m-1)^2 \\
&+ \frac{\delta}{8\xi^2} \left(\left. \frac{\partial^2 \Phi(\delta d_+)}{\partial d_+^2} \right|_{m=1} - \left. \frac{\partial^2 \Phi(\delta d_-)}{\partial d_-^2} \right|_{m=1} \right) (m-1)^2 + O((m-1)^3).
\end{aligned}
$$

Since $\delta^2 = 1$, we have

$$
\delta \left(m\Phi(\delta\xi) - \Phi(-\delta\xi) \right) = \frac{\delta(m-1)}{2} + \frac{\xi}{\sqrt{2\pi}}(m+1) + O(\xi^3)
$$

$$
\frac{\delta}{2\xi} \left(\left. \frac{\partial \Phi(\delta d_+)}{\partial d_+} \right|_{m=1} + \left. \frac{\partial \Phi(\delta d_-)}{\partial d_-} \right|_{m=1} \right) (m-1)^2 = \frac{(m-1)^2}{2\xi\sqrt{2\pi}} - \frac{\xi(m-1)^2}{4\sqrt{2\pi}} \\
+ O(\xi^3(m-1)^2)
$$

$$
\frac{\delta}{8\xi^2} \left(\left. \frac{\partial^2 \Phi(\delta d_+)}{\partial d_+^2} \right|_{m=1} - \left. \frac{\partial^2 \Phi(\delta d_-)}{\partial d_-^2} \right|_{m=1} \right) (m-1)^2 = -\frac{(m-1)^2}{4\xi\sqrt{2\pi}} + \frac{\xi(m-1)^2}{8\sqrt{2\pi}} \\
+ O(\xi^3(m-1)^2)
$$

and hence

$$
f(m) = \frac{\delta(m-1)}{2} + \frac{m+1}{\sqrt{2\pi}}\xi + \frac{(m-1)^2}{4\sqrt{2\pi}\xi} + O(\xi(m-1)^2).
$$

By equating

$$
V(S_t, t; K, T, \sigma_{\text{imp}}) = V_{\text{mkt}}
$$

and setting $\bar{S}_t = S_t e^{-D(T-t)}$, $\bar{K} = Ke^{-r(T-t)}$ and ignoring higher orders of $\xi(m-1)^2$, we can write

$$
\frac{V_{\text{mkt}}}{\bar{K}} \approx \frac{\delta(m-1)}{2} + \frac{m+1}{\sqrt{2\pi}}\xi + \frac{(m-1)^2}{4\sqrt{2\pi}\xi}
$$

or

$$
2\xi^2 - \alpha\xi + \beta \approx 0
$$

where $\alpha = \dfrac{\sqrt{2\pi}}{m+1} \left(\dfrac{2V_{\text{mkt}}}{\bar{K}} - \delta(m-1) \right)$ and $\beta = \dfrac{1}{2} \dfrac{(m-1)^2}{m+1}$.

Since $\xi = \frac{1}{2}\sigma_{\text{imp}}\sqrt{T-t}$ and because $0 < \sigma_{\text{imp}} < 1$, we choose

$$\xi \approx \frac{\alpha + \sqrt{\alpha^2 - 8\beta}}{2}$$

or

$$\sigma_{\text{imp}} \approx \frac{\alpha + \sqrt{\alpha^2 - 8\beta}}{\sqrt{T-t}}.$$

By substituting $m = \bar{S}_t/\bar{K}$, we have

$$\alpha = \frac{2\sqrt{2\pi}}{\bar{S}_t + \bar{K}}\left(V_{\text{mkt}} - \delta\left(\frac{\bar{S}_t - \bar{K}}{2}\right)\right) \quad \text{and} \quad \beta = \frac{1}{2\bar{K}}\frac{(\bar{S}_t - \bar{K})^2}{\bar{S}_t + \bar{K}}$$

and thus

$$\sigma_{\text{imp}} \approx \sqrt{\frac{2\pi}{T-t}}\frac{1}{\bar{S}_t + \bar{K}}\left\{\left(V_{\text{mkt}} - \delta\left(\frac{\bar{S}_t - \bar{K}}{2}\right)\right)\right.$$
$$\left. + \sqrt{\left(V_{\text{mkt}} - \delta\left(\frac{\bar{S}_t - \bar{K}}{2}\right)\right)^2 - \frac{(\bar{S}_t - \bar{K})^2}{\pi}\frac{(1 + \bar{S}_t/\bar{K})}{2}}\right\}.$$

On the issue of the limitations of this approximation, one can see that in some cases the square-root term might not have a real solution.

In order for the approximation to have a real solution, we require

$$\left(V_{\text{mkt}} - \delta\left(\frac{\bar{S}_t - \bar{K}}{2}\right)\right)^2 - \frac{(\bar{S}_t - \bar{K})^2}{\pi}\frac{(1 + \bar{S}_t/\bar{K})}{2} \geq 0$$

or

$$\left[V_{\text{mkt}} - (\bar{S}_t - \bar{K})\left(\frac{1}{2}\delta - \sqrt{\frac{1 + \bar{S}_t/\bar{K}}{2\pi}}\right)\right]\left[V_{\text{mkt}} - (\bar{S}_t - \bar{K})\left(\frac{1}{2}\delta + \sqrt{\frac{1 + \bar{S}_t/\bar{K}}{2\pi}}\right)\right] \geq 0.$$

Therefore,

$$V_{\text{mkt}} \geq \max\left\{(\bar{S}_t - \bar{K})\left(\frac{1}{2}\delta - \sqrt{\frac{1 + \bar{S}_t/\bar{K}}{2\pi}}\right), (\bar{S}_t - \bar{K})\left(\frac{1}{2}\delta + \sqrt{\frac{1 + \bar{S}_t/\bar{K}}{2\pi}}\right)\right\}$$

or

$$
V_{\text{mkt}} \leq \min\left\{ (\bar{S}_t - \bar{K})\left(\frac{1}{2}\delta - \sqrt{\frac{1 + \bar{S}_t/\bar{K}}{2\pi}}\right), (\bar{S}_t - \bar{K})\left(\frac{1}{2}\delta + \sqrt{\frac{1 + \bar{S}_t/\bar{K}}{2\pi}}\right) \right\}.
$$

Finally, for the case when $m = 1$ or $\bar{S}_t = \bar{K}$, the implied volatility formula will be reduced to the Brenner–Subrahmanyam approximation, i.e.

$$
\sigma_{\text{imp}} \approx \frac{V_{\text{mkt}}}{\bar{S}_t}\sqrt{\frac{2\pi}{T-t}}.
$$

$\square$

8. *Corrado–Miller–Hallerbach Approximation.* Let the Black–Scholes price for the value of a European option $V(S_t, t; K, T, \sigma)$ be

$$
V(S_t, t; K, T, \sigma) = \delta S_t e^{-D(T-t)}\Phi(\delta d_+) - \delta K e^{-r(T-t)}\Phi(\delta d_-)
$$

$$
\delta = \begin{cases} +1 & \text{for call option} \\ -1 & \text{for put option} \end{cases}
$$

where

$$
d_\pm = \frac{\log(S_t/K) + (r - D \pm \frac{1}{2}\sigma^2)(T - t)}{\sigma\sqrt{T - t}}
$$

such that $\Phi(\cdot)$ is the cdf of a standard normal, S_t is the spot price at time $t < T$, T is the option expiry time, K is the strike price, r is the risk-free interest rate, D is the continuous dividend yield and σ is the volatility.

From the definition

$$
\tanh^{-1} x = \frac{1}{2}\log\left(\frac{1 + x}{1 - x}\right), \quad |x| < 1
$$

show that

$$
\log z = 2\sum_{n=0}^{\infty} \frac{1}{2n + 1}\left(\frac{z - 1}{z + 1}\right)^{2n+1}
$$

for any real number $z > 0$.

By setting

$$
\bar{S}_t = S_t e^{-D(T-t)} \quad \text{and} \quad \bar{K} = K e^{-r(T-t)}
$$

and equating

$$V(S_t, t; K, T, \sigma_{\text{imp}}) = V_{\text{mkt}}$$

where V_{mkt} is the market-observed European price, and by ignoring the third-order and higher terms of the normal distribution function

$$\Phi(x) = \frac{1}{2} + \frac{1}{\sqrt{2\pi}} \left(x - \frac{1}{2^1 \cdot 1! \cdot 3} x^3 + \frac{1}{2^2 \cdot 2! \cdot 5} x^5 - \frac{1}{2^3 \cdot 3! \cdot 7} x^7 + \ldots \right)$$

and taking a linear approximation of $\log(\bar{S}_t / \bar{K})$, show that the implied volatility σ_{imp} is approximated by

$$\sigma_{\text{imp}} \approx \sqrt{\frac{2\pi}{T-t}} \left(\frac{V_{\text{mkt}} - \delta \left(\dfrac{\bar{S}_t - \bar{K}}{2} \right)}{\bar{S}_t + \bar{K}} \right)$$

$$+ \sqrt{\frac{2\pi}{T-t} \left(\frac{V_{\text{mkt}} - \delta \left(\dfrac{\bar{S}_t - \bar{K}}{2} \right)}{\bar{S}_t + \bar{K}} \right)^2 - \frac{4}{T-t} \left(\frac{\bar{S}_t - \bar{K}}{\bar{S}_t + \bar{K}} \right)^2}.$$

Solution: Since

$$\tanh^{-1} x = \frac{1}{2} \log \left(\frac{1+x}{1-x} \right)$$

$$= \frac{1}{2} (\log(1+x) - \log(1-x))$$

and from the MacLaurin series

$$\log(1+x) = x - \frac{1}{2}x^2 + \frac{1}{3}x^3 - \frac{1}{4}x^4 + \ldots, x \in (-1, 1]$$

$$\log(1-x) = -x - \frac{1}{2}x^2 - \frac{1}{3}x^3 - \frac{1}{4}x^4 + \ldots, |x| < 1$$

we have

$$\tanh^{-1} x = x + \frac{1}{3}x^3 + \frac{1}{5}x^5 + \frac{1}{7}x^7 + \ldots, |x| < 1.$$

By setting

$$z = \frac{1+x}{1-x}$$

and expressing x in terms of z,

$$x = \frac{z-1}{z+1}.$$

By substituting the above information into $\tanh^{-1} x$,

$$\begin{aligned}
\log z &= 2\tanh^{-1}\left(\frac{z-1}{z+1}\right) \\
&= 2\left(\frac{z-1}{z+1} + \frac{1}{3}\left(\frac{z-1}{z+1}\right)^3 + \frac{1}{5}\left(\frac{z-1}{z+1}\right)^5 + \frac{1}{7}\left(\frac{z-1}{z+1}\right)^7 + \dots\right) \\
&= 2\sum_{n=0}^{\infty} \frac{1}{2n+1}\left(\frac{z-1}{z+1}\right)^{2n+1}
\end{aligned}$$

for $z > 0$.

By equating $V_{\text{mkt}} = V(S_t, t; K, T, \sigma_{\text{imp}})$ and taking a linear approximation of $\Phi(\delta d_{\pm})$ such that

$$d_{\pm} = \frac{\log(\bar{S}_t/\bar{K})}{\sigma_{\text{imp}}\sqrt{T-t}} \pm \frac{1}{2}\sigma\sqrt{T-t}$$

we have

$$\begin{aligned}
V_{\text{mkt}} &= \delta\bar{S}_t\Phi(\delta d_+) - \delta\bar{K}\Phi(\delta d_-) \\
&\approx \delta\bar{S}_t\left(\frac{1}{2} + \frac{\delta}{\sqrt{2\pi}d_+}\right) - \delta\bar{K}\left(\frac{1}{2} + \frac{\delta}{\sqrt{2\pi}d_-}\right) \\
&= \delta\left(\frac{\bar{S}_t - \bar{K}}{2}\right) + \frac{(\bar{S}_t - \bar{K})\log(\bar{S}_t/\bar{K})}{\sigma_{\text{imp}}\sqrt{2\pi(T-t)}} + \frac{1}{2}\sqrt{\frac{T-t}{2\pi}}(\bar{S}_t + \bar{K})
\end{aligned}$$

since $\delta^2 = 1$.

Thus,

$$(\bar{S}_t + \bar{K})(T-t)\sigma_{\text{imp}}^2 - 2\sqrt{2\pi(T-t)}\left(V_{\text{mkt}} - \delta\left(\frac{\bar{S}_t - \bar{K}}{2}\right)\right)\sigma_{\text{imp}}$$

$$+ 2(\bar{S}_t - \bar{K})\log(\bar{S}_t/\bar{K}) \approx 0$$

and taking the largest root,

$$
\sigma_{\text{imp}} \approx \sqrt{\frac{2\pi}{T-t}} \left| \frac{V_{\text{mkt}} - \delta\left(\dfrac{\bar{S}_t - \bar{K}}{2}\right)}{\bar{S}_t + \bar{K}} \right|
$$

$$
+ \sqrt{\frac{2\pi}{T-t}\left(\frac{V_{\text{mkt}} - \delta\left(\dfrac{\bar{S}_t - \bar{K}}{2}\right)}{\bar{S}_t + \bar{K}}\right)^2 - \frac{2}{T-t}\left(\frac{\bar{S}_t - \bar{K}}{\bar{S}_t + \bar{K}}\right)\log(\bar{S}_t/\bar{K})}.
$$

Taking a linear approximation of $\log(\bar{S}_t/\bar{K}) \approx 2(\bar{S}_t - \bar{K})/(\bar{S}_t + \bar{K})$,

$$
\sigma_{\text{imp}} \approx \sqrt{\frac{2\pi}{T-t}} \left| \frac{V_{\text{mkt}} - \delta\left(\dfrac{\bar{S}_t - \bar{K}}{2}\right)}{\bar{S}_t + \bar{K}} \right|
$$

$$
+ \sqrt{\frac{2\pi}{T-t}\left(\frac{V_{\text{mkt}} - \delta\left(\dfrac{\bar{S}_t - \bar{K}}{2}\right)}{\bar{S}_t + \bar{K}}\right)^2 - \frac{4}{T-t}\left(\frac{\bar{S}_t - \bar{K}}{\bar{S}_t + \bar{K}}\right)^2}.
$$

$\square$

9. We consider the Black–Scholes formula for the value of a European option $V(S_t, t; K, T, \sigma)$ such that

$$
V(S_t, t; K, T, \sigma) = \begin{cases} S_t e^{-D(T-t)}\Phi(d_+) - Ke^{-r(T-t)}\Phi(d_-) & \text{for call option} \\[2ex] Ke^{-r(T-t)}\Phi(-d_-) - S_t e^{-D(T-t)}\Phi(-d_+) & \text{for put option} \end{cases}
$$

with

$$
d_{\pm} = \frac{\log(S_t/K) + (r - D \pm \frac{1}{2}\sigma^2)(T-t)}{\sigma\sqrt{T-t}}
$$

such that $\Phi(\cdot)$ is the cdf of a standard normal, S_t is the spot price at time $t < T$, T is the option expiry time, K is the strike price, r is the risk-free interest rate, D is the continuous dividend yield and σ is the spot volatility.

Show that $V(S_t, t; K, T, \sigma)$ is a monotonically increasing function in σ over $(0, \infty)$.

We define σ_{imp}^{∞} as the implied volatility such that

$$V(S_t, t; K, T, \sigma_{imp}^{\infty}) = V_{mkt}$$

that is we equate the Black–Scholes theoretical price with the observed European option price obtained in the market, V_{mkt}.

Under what conditions does there exist a unique solution σ_{imp}^{∞}?

Solution: From Problem 2.2.4.6 (page 224), the vega of a European option is

$$\frac{\partial V}{\partial \sigma} = \sqrt{\frac{T-t}{2\pi}} S_t e^{-D(T-t)} e^{-\frac{1}{2}d_+^2}.$$

Since $S_t > 0$, therefore $\dfrac{\partial V}{\partial \sigma} > 0$ for all $\sigma \in (0, \infty)$. Thus, $V(S_t, t; K, T)$ is a monotonically increasing function in $\sigma \in (0, \infty)$.

From Problems 2.2.1.3 (page 74), 2.2.1.4 (page 75), 2.2.1.5 (page 75) and 2.2.1.6 (page 76), $V(S_t, t; K, T)$ satisfies

$$V(S_t, t; K, T, \sigma) \geq \begin{cases} \max\{S_t e^{-D(T-t)} - Ke^{-r(T-t)}, 0\} & \text{for call option} \\ \max\{Ke^{-r(T-t)} - S_t e^{-D(T-t)}, 0\} & \text{for put option} \end{cases}$$

and

$$V(S_t, t; K, T, \sigma) \leq \begin{cases} S_t & \text{for call option} \\ K & \text{for put option.} \end{cases}$$

If the market price V_{mkt} lies between the bounded region as described above for either a call or put option, and from the monotonicity and continuity of $V(S_t, t; K, T, \sigma)$ in $\sigma \in (0, \infty)$, then σ_{imp}^{∞} exists and is a unique solution of $V(S_t, t; K, T, \sigma_{imp}^{\infty}) = V_{mkt}$. □

10. *Manaster–Koehler Method.* Consider the Black–Scholes formula for the value of a European option $V(S_t, t; K, T, \sigma)$ such that

$$V(S_t, t; K, T, \sigma) = \begin{cases} S_t e^{-D(T-t)}\Phi(d_+) - Ke^{-r(T-t)}\Phi(d_-) & \text{for call option} \\ Ke^{-r(T-t)}\Phi(-d_-) - S_t e^{-D(T-t)}\Phi(-d_+) & \text{for put option} \end{cases}$$

with

$$d_\pm = \frac{\log(S_t/K) + (r - D \pm \frac{1}{2}\sigma^2)(T-t)}{\sigma\sqrt{T-t}}$$

such that $\Phi(\cdot)$ is the cdf of a standard normal, S_t is the spot price at time $t < T$, T is the
option expiry time, K is the strike price, r is the risk-free interest rate, D is the continuous
dividend yield and σ is the spot volatility.

Show that $\dfrac{\partial V}{\partial \sigma}$ is maximised at

$$\sigma_{\max} = \sqrt{\left| \frac{2}{T-t} \left(\log(S_t/K) + (r-D)(T-t) \right) \right|}$$

and prove that

$$\frac{\partial^2 V}{\partial \sigma^2} = \frac{\partial V}{\partial \sigma} \left(\frac{T-t}{4\sigma^3} \right) \left(\sigma_{\max}^4 - \sigma^4 \right)$$

for all $\alpha \in (0, \infty)$.

We define $\sigma_{\text{imp}}^\infty$ as the implied volatility such that

$$V(S_t, t; K, T, \sigma_{\text{imp}}^\infty) = V_{\text{mkt}}$$

where V_{mkt} is the option price obtained in the market. Deduce that $V(S_t, t; K, T, \sigma)$ is
strictly convex if $\sigma_{\text{imp}}^\infty < \sigma_{\max}$ and $V(S_t, t; K, T, \sigma)$ is strictly concave if $\alpha^\infty > \sigma_{\max}$.

Finally, if the sequence $\{\sigma_n\}$ is generated by the Newton–Raphson method

$$\sigma_{n+1} = \sigma_n - \left\{ \frac{V(S_t, t; K, T, \sigma_n) - V_{\text{mkt}}}{\left. \dfrac{\partial V}{\partial \sigma} \right|_{\sigma=\sigma_n}} \right\}, n \geq 0$$

with initial iterate $\sigma_0 = \sigma_{\max}$ and if $V(S_t, t; K, T, \sigma_{\text{imp}}^\infty) = V_{\text{mkt}}$ has a solution, show that
$\{\sigma_n\}$ converges monotonically to the unique solution $\sigma_{\text{imp}}^\infty$ with a quadratic rate of convergence, i.e.

$$|\sigma_{n+1} - \sigma_{\text{imp}}^\infty| = O(|\sigma_n - \sigma_{\text{imp}}^\infty|^2).$$

Solution: From Problem 2.2.4.6 (page 224), the vega of a European option is

$$\frac{\partial V}{\partial \sigma} = \sqrt{\frac{T-t}{2\pi}} S_t e^{-D(T-t)} e^{-\frac{1}{2} d_+^2}.$$

To find the local extrema of $\dfrac{\partial V}{\partial \sigma}$, we first differentiate $\dfrac{\partial V}{\partial \sigma}$ with respect to σ

$$\frac{\partial^2 V}{\partial \sigma^2} = -\sqrt{\frac{T-t}{2\pi}} S_t e^{-D(T-t)} d_+ \frac{\partial d_+}{\partial \sigma} e^{-\frac{1}{2} d_+^2}$$

and since

$$\frac{\partial d_+}{\partial \sigma} = \frac{\sigma^2 (T-t)^{3/2} - \left(\log(S_t/K) + (r - D + \frac{1}{2}\sigma^2)\right)\sqrt{T-t}}{\sigma^2 (T-t)}$$

$$= -d_-$$

therefore

$$\frac{\partial^2 V}{\partial \sigma^2} = d_+ d_- \sqrt{\frac{T-t}{2\pi}} S_t e^{-D(T-t)} e^{-\frac{1}{2}d_+^2}$$

$$= \left(\frac{d_+ d_-}{\sigma}\right)\frac{\partial V}{\partial \sigma}.$$

By setting $\dfrac{\partial^2 V}{\partial \sigma^2} = 0$, we have either $d_+ = 0$ or $d_- = 0$, which implies

$$\sigma^2 = -\frac{2}{T-t}\left(\log(S_t/K) + r - D\right)$$

or

$$\sigma^2 = \frac{2}{T-t}\left(\log(S_t/K) + r - D\right).$$

Taking second derivatives of $\dfrac{\partial V}{\partial \sigma}$

$$\frac{\partial^3 V}{\partial \sigma^3} = -\left(\frac{d_+ d_-}{\sigma}\right)\frac{\partial V}{\partial \sigma} + \frac{\partial d_+}{\partial \sigma}\left(\frac{d_-}{\sigma}\right)\frac{\partial V}{\partial \sigma} + \frac{\partial d_-}{\partial \sigma}\left(\frac{d_+}{\sigma}\right)\frac{\partial V}{\partial \sigma} + \left(\frac{d_+ d_-}{\sigma}\right)\frac{\partial^2 V}{\partial \sigma^2}$$

$$= -\left(\frac{d_+ d_-}{\sigma}\right)\frac{\partial V}{\partial \sigma} - \frac{d_-^2}{\sigma}\frac{\partial V}{\partial \sigma} - \frac{d_+^2}{\sigma}\frac{\partial V}{\partial \sigma} + \left(\frac{d_+ d_-}{\sigma}\right)\frac{\partial^2 V}{\partial \sigma^2}$$

and substituting $\sigma^2 = -\dfrac{2}{T-t}\left(\log(S_t/K) + r - D\right)$ or $\sigma^2 = \dfrac{2}{T-t}\left(\log(S_t/K) + r - D\right)$ gives

$$\frac{\partial^3 V}{\partial \sigma^3} < 0.$$

Hence,

$$\sigma_{\max} = \sqrt{\left|\frac{2}{T-t}\left(\log(S_t/K) + (r - D)(T-t)\right)\right|}$$

is the maximum point of $\dfrac{\partial V}{\partial \sigma}$ (since $\sigma_{\max}$ is the only extremum point).

From

$$\sigma_{\max} = \sqrt{\left| \frac{2}{T-t} \left(\log(S_t/K) + (r-D)(T-t) \right) \right|}$$

we can write

$$\sigma_{\max}^4 = \frac{4}{(T-t)^2} \left(\log(S_t/K) + (r-D)(T-t) \right)^2$$

or

$$\left(\log(S_t/K) + (r-D)(T-t) \right)^2 = \frac{\sigma_{\max}^4 (T-t)^2}{4}.$$

Expanding $d_+ d_-$,

$$d_+ d_- = \frac{\left(\log(S_t/K) + (r-D+\frac{1}{2}\sigma^2)(T-t) \right) \left(\log(S_t/K) + (r-D-\frac{1}{2}\sigma^2)(T-t) \right)}{\sigma^2(T-t)}$$

$$= \frac{\left(\log(S_t/K) + (r-D)(T-t) \right)^2 - \frac{1}{4}\sigma^4(T-t)^2}{\sigma^2(T-t)}$$

$$= \frac{T-t}{4\sigma^2} \left(\sigma_{\max}^4 - \sigma^4 \right).$$

Therefore,

$$\frac{\partial^2 V}{\partial \sigma^2} = \frac{\partial V}{\partial \sigma} \left(\frac{T-t}{4\sigma^3} \right) \left(\sigma_{\max}^4 - \sigma^4 \right)$$

for all $\sigma \in (0, \infty)$.

If the implied volatility $\sigma^\infty < \sigma_{\max}$ we have $\frac{\partial^2 V}{\partial \sigma^2} > 0$, which implies $\frac{\partial V}{\partial \sigma}$ is a monotonically increasing function in $\sigma \in [\sigma_{\text{imp}}^\infty, \sigma_{\max}]$, and hence $V(S_t, t; K, T, \sigma)$ is strictly convex in $\sigma \in [\sigma_{\text{imp}}^\infty, \sigma_{\max}]$.

In contrast, if $\sigma^\infty > \sigma_{\max}$ we have $\frac{\partial^2 V}{\partial \sigma^2} < 0$, which implies $\frac{\partial V}{\partial \sigma}$ is a monotonically decreasing function in $\sigma \in [\sigma_{\text{imp}}^\infty, \sigma_{\max}]$, and hence $V(S_t, t; K, T, \sigma)$ is strictly concave in $\sigma \in [\sigma_{\text{imp}}^\infty, \sigma_{\max}]$.

To show that the sequence $\{\sigma_n\}$ is monotonic and bounded, we note that from the Newton–Raphson formula

$$\sigma_{n+1} = \sigma_n - \left\{ \frac{V(S_t, t; K, T, \sigma_n) - V_{\text{mkt}}}{\left. \frac{\partial V}{\partial \sigma} \right|_{\sigma=\sigma_n}} \right\}, \quad n \geq 0$$

and by expanding $V(S_t, t; K, T, \sigma_n)$ at σ_{imp}^{∞} up to the first order

$$\left| \frac{\sigma_{n+1} - \sigma_{imp}^{\infty}}{\sigma_n - \sigma_{imp}^{\infty}} \right| = \left| 1 - \left(\frac{V(S_t, t; K, T, \sigma_n) - V(S_t, t; K, T, \sigma_{imp}^{\infty})}{\sigma_n - \sigma_{imp}^{\infty}} \right) \frac{1}{\left. \frac{\partial V}{\partial \sigma} \right|_{\sigma=\sigma_n}} \right|$$

$$= \left| 1 - \left(\left. \frac{\partial V}{\partial \sigma} \right|_{\sigma=\sigma_n^*} \right) \Big/ \left(\left. \frac{\partial V}{\partial \sigma} \right|_{\sigma=\sigma_n} \right) \right|$$

where σ_n^* lies between σ_n and σ_{imp}^{∞}.

For $n = 0$

$$\left| \frac{\sigma_1 - \sigma_{imp}^{\infty}}{\sigma_0 - \sigma_{imp}^{\infty}} \right| = \left| 1 - \left(\left. \frac{\partial V}{\partial \sigma} \right|_{\sigma=\sigma_0^*} \right) \Big/ \left(\left. \frac{\partial V}{\partial \sigma} \right|_{\sigma=\sigma_0} \right) \right|$$

and because $\sigma_0 = \sigma_{max}$ maximises $\dfrac{\partial V}{\partial \sigma}$ and $\dfrac{\partial V}{\partial \sigma} > 0$ for all $\sigma \in (0, \infty)$, thus

$$0 < \left. \frac{\partial V}{\partial \sigma} \right|_{\sigma=\sigma_0^*} < \left. \frac{\partial V}{\partial \sigma} \right|_{\sigma=\sigma_0}$$

and we obtain

$$\left| \frac{\sigma_1 - \sigma_{imp}^{\infty}}{\sigma_0 - \sigma_{imp}^{\infty}} \right| < 1.$$

Assume the result

$$\left| \frac{\sigma_{k+1} - \sigma_{imp}^{\infty}}{\sigma_k - \sigma_{imp}^{\infty}} \right| < 1$$

is true for $n = k$ such that

$$0 < \left. \frac{\partial V}{\partial \sigma} \right|_{\sigma=\sigma_k^*} < \left. \frac{\partial V}{\partial \sigma} \right|_{\sigma=\sigma_k}$$

where σ_k^* is between σ_k and σ_{imp}^{∞}.

For $n = k + 1$

$$\left| \frac{\sigma_{k+2} - \sigma_{imp}^{\infty}}{\sigma_{k+1} - \sigma_{imp}^{\infty}} \right| = \left| 1 - \left(\left. \frac{\partial V}{\partial \sigma} \right|_{\sigma=\sigma_{k+1}^*} \right) \Big/ \left(\left. \frac{\partial V}{\partial \sigma} \right|_{\sigma=\sigma_{k+1}} \right) \right|$$

where σ_{k+1}^* is between σ_{k+1} and σ_{imp}^∞. Because $\sigma_0 = \sigma_{max}$ is a maximum point of $\dfrac{\partial V}{\partial \sigma}$ and $\dfrac{\partial V}{\partial \sigma} > 0$ for all $\sigma \in (0, \infty)$, thus

$$0 < \frac{\partial V}{\partial \sigma}\bigg|_{\sigma=\sigma_{k+1}^*} < \frac{\partial V}{\partial \sigma}\bigg|_{\sigma=\sigma_0}$$

and

$$0 < \frac{\partial V}{\partial \sigma}\bigg|_{\sigma=\sigma_{k+1}} < \frac{\partial V}{\partial \sigma}\bigg|_{\sigma=\sigma_0}$$

and hence

$$\left| \frac{\sigma_{k+2} - \sigma_{imp}^\infty}{\sigma_{k+1} - \sigma_{imp}^\infty} \right| = \left| 1 - \left(\frac{\partial V}{\partial \sigma}\bigg|_{\sigma=\sigma_{k+1}^*} \right) \bigg/ \left(\frac{\partial V}{\partial \sigma}\bigg|_{\sigma=\sigma_{k+1}} \right) \right|$$

$$< \left| 1 - \left(\frac{\partial V}{\partial \sigma}\bigg|_{\sigma=\sigma_{k+1}^*} \right) \bigg/ \left(\frac{\partial V}{\partial \sigma}\bigg|_{\sigma=\sigma_0} \right) \right|$$

$$< 1.$$

Thus, the result is also true for $n = k + 1$. Using mathematical induction, we have proved that

$$\left| \frac{\sigma_{n+1} - \sigma_{imp}^\infty}{\sigma_n - \sigma_{imp}^\infty} \right| < 1$$

for all $n \geq 0$, which shows that the sequence $\{\sigma_n\}$ is monotone and bounded, and therefore converges to a limit σ_{imp}^∞.

By expanding $V(S_t, t; K, T, \sigma_{imp}^\infty)$ about σ_n using Taylor's theorem

$$V(S_t, t; K, T, \sigma_{imp}^\infty) = V(S_t, t; K, T, \sigma_n) + (\sigma_{imp}^\infty - \sigma_n) \frac{\partial V}{\partial \sigma}\bigg|_{\sigma=\sigma_n}$$

$$+ \frac{1}{2}(\sigma_{imp}^\infty - \sigma_n)^2 \frac{\partial^2 V}{\partial \sigma^2}\bigg|_{\sigma=\sigma_n^*}$$

where σ_n^* is between σ_n and σ_{imp}^∞ and substituting it into the Newton–Raphson formula, and since

$$V(S_t, t; K, T, \sigma_{imp}^\infty) = V_{mkt}$$

we have

$$\sigma_{n+1} - \sigma_{\text{imp}}^{\infty} = \frac{1}{2} \left\{ \left(\frac{\partial^2 V}{\partial \sigma^2} \bigg|_{\sigma=\sigma_n^*} \right) \bigg/ \left(\frac{\partial V}{\partial \sigma} \bigg|_{\sigma=\sigma_n} \right) \right\} (\sigma_n - \sigma_{\text{imp}}^{\infty})^2.$$

Taking absolute values on both sides gives

$$\left| \sigma_{n+1} - \sigma_{\text{imp}}^{\infty} \right| = \left| \frac{1}{2} \left\{ \left(\frac{\partial^2 V}{\partial \sigma^2} \bigg|_{\sigma=\sigma_n^*} \right) \bigg/ \left(\frac{\partial V}{\partial \sigma} \bigg|_{\sigma=\sigma_n} \right) \right\} \right| (\sigma_n - \sigma_{\text{imp}}^{\infty})^2.$$

Since $\frac{\partial V}{\partial \sigma} > 0$, $\frac{\partial^2 V}{\partial \sigma^2} = \frac{\partial V}{\partial \sigma} \left(\frac{T-t}{4\sigma^3} \right) \left(\sigma_{\text{max}}^4 - \sigma^4 \right)$ is finite and if $V(S_t, t; K, T, \sigma_{\text{imp}}^{\infty}) = V_{\text{mkt}}$ has a solution (see Problem 7.2.1.9, page 676 for the existence and uniqueness conditions of a solution $\sigma_{\text{imp}}^{\infty}$) then, with a starting point $\sigma_0 = \sigma_{\text{max}}$, the sequence $\{\sigma_n\}$ converges monotonically to a unique solution $\sigma_{\text{imp}}^{\infty}$ with the rate of convergence of the iterates being quadratic, i.e.

$$|\sigma_{n+1} - \sigma_{\text{imp}}^{\infty}| = O(|\sigma_n - \sigma_{\text{imp}}^{\infty}|^2).$$

$\square$

11. *Chambers–Nawalkha Approximation.* Let the Black–Scholes formula for the value of a European option $V(S_t, t; K, T, \sigma)$ be

$$V(S_t, t; K, T, \sigma) = \begin{cases} S_t e^{-D(T-t)} \Phi(d_+) - K e^{-r(T-t)} \Phi(d_-) & \text{for call option} \\[2mm] K e^{-r(T-t)} \Phi(-d_-) - S_t e^{-D(T-t)} \Phi(-d_+) & \text{for put option} \end{cases}$$

where

$$d_{\pm} = \frac{\log(S_t/K) + (r - D \pm \frac{1}{2}\sigma^2)(T - t)}{\sigma\sqrt{T - t}}$$

such that $\Phi(\cdot)$ is the cdf of a standard normal, S_t is the spot price at time $t < T$, T is the option expiry time, K is the strike price, r is the risk-free interest rate, D is the continuous dividend yield and σ is the spot volatility.

By defining the ATM option as $S_t e^{-D(T-t)} = K e^{-r(T-t)}$ with the corresponding implied volatility $\sigma_{\text{imp}}^{\text{atm}}$, show that by expanding $V(S_t, t; K, T, \sigma)$ up to second order about $\sigma = \sigma_{\text{imp}}^{\text{atm}}$, the non-ATM volatility σ can be approximated as

$$\sigma \approx \sigma_{\text{imp}}^{\text{atm}} + \frac{\beta - \frac{\partial V}{\partial \sigma} \bigg|_{\sigma=\sigma_{\text{imp}}^{\text{atm}}}}{\frac{\partial^2 V}{\partial \sigma^2} \bigg|_{\sigma=\sigma_{\text{imp}}^{\text{atm}}}}$$

where

$$
\beta = \sqrt{\left(\frac{\partial V}{\partial \sigma}\bigg|_{\sigma=\sigma_{\text{imp}}^{\text{atm}}}\right)^2 - 2\left(\frac{\partial^2 V}{\partial \sigma^2}\bigg|_{\sigma=\sigma_{\text{imp}}^{\text{atm}}}\right)\left(V(S_t,t;K,T,\sigma_{\text{imp}}^{\text{atm}}) - V(S_t,t;K,T,\sigma)\right)}.
$$

Solution: Expanding $V(S_t,t;K,T,\sigma)$ using Taylor's theorem about $\sigma = \sigma_{\text{imp}}^{\text{atm}}$ up to second order

$$
V(S_t,t;K,T,\sigma) \approx V(S_t,t;K,T,\sigma_{\text{imp}}^{\text{atm}}) + \frac{\partial V}{\partial \sigma}\bigg|_{\sigma=\sigma_{\text{imp}}^{\text{atm}}}(\sigma - \sigma_{\text{imp}}^{\text{atm}})
$$

$$
+\frac{1}{2}\frac{\partial^2 V}{\partial \sigma^2}\bigg|_{\sigma=\sigma_{\text{imp}}^{\text{atm}}}(\sigma - \sigma_{\text{imp}}^{\text{atm}})^2.
$$

Rearranging the terms,

$$
\frac{1}{2}\frac{\partial^2 V}{\partial \sigma^2}\bigg|_{\sigma=\sigma_{\text{imp}}^{\text{atm}}}(\sigma - \sigma_{\text{imp}}^{\text{atm}})^2 + \frac{\partial V}{\partial \sigma}\bigg|_{\sigma=\sigma_{\text{imp}}^{\text{atm}}}(\sigma - \sigma_{\text{imp}}^{\text{atm}}) + V(S_t,t;K,T,\sigma_{\text{imp}}^{\text{atm}})
$$

$$
-V(S_t,t;K,T,\sigma) \approx 0
$$

and solving the quadratic equation,

$$
\sigma - \sigma_{\text{imp}}^{\text{atm}} \approx \frac{-\dfrac{\partial V}{\partial \sigma}\bigg|_{\sigma=\sigma_{\text{imp}}^{\text{atm}}} \pm \beta}{\dfrac{\partial^2 V}{\partial \sigma^2}\bigg|_{\sigma=\sigma_{\text{imp}}^{\text{atm}}}}
$$

where

$$
\beta = \sqrt{\left(\frac{\partial V}{\partial \sigma}\bigg|_{\sigma=\sigma_{\text{imp}}^{\text{atm}}}\right)^2 - 2\left(\frac{\partial^2 V}{\partial \sigma^2}\bigg|_{\sigma=\sigma_{\text{imp}}^{\text{atm}}}\right)\left(V(S_t,t;K,T,\sigma_{\text{imp}}^{\text{atm}}) - V(S_t,t;K,T,\sigma)\right)}.
$$

Since $\sigma > 0$, we choose

$$
\sigma \approx \sigma_{\text{imp}}^{\text{atm}} + \frac{\beta - \dfrac{\partial V}{\partial \sigma}\bigg|_{\sigma=\sigma_{\text{imp}}^{\text{atm}}}}{\dfrac{\partial^2 V}{\partial \sigma^2}\bigg|_{\sigma=\sigma_{\text{imp}}^{\text{atm}}}}.
$$

$\square$

7.2.2 Local Volatility

1. Let $\{W_t : t \geq 0\}$ be a standard Wiener process on the probability space $(\Omega, \mathcal{F}, \mathbb{P})$. Suppose the asset price S_t has the following dynamics

$$\frac{dS_t}{S_t} = (\mu - D)dt + \sigma_t dW_t$$

where μ, D are constants and the volatility σ_t is a continuous process. In addition, let r be the risk-free interest rate from a money-market account.

By considering a European call option $C(S_t, t; K, T)$ written at time t on S_t with strike price K and expiry time T $(T > t)$, show the following identities

$$C(S_t, t; K, T) = K C(S_t/K, t; 1; T)$$
$$C(S_t, t; K, T) = S_t \frac{\partial C}{\partial S_t} + K \frac{\partial C}{\partial K}$$
$$S_t^2 \frac{\partial^2 C}{\partial S_t^2} = K^2 \frac{\partial^2 C}{\partial K^2}.$$

By substituting the above identities into the Black–Scholes equation, find the Dupire equation and payoff satisfied by $C(S_t, t; K, T)$ as a function of strike K and time t.

Solution: From the Black–Scholes formula

$$C(S_t, t; K, T) = S_t e^{-D(T-t)} \Phi(d_+) - K e^{-r(T-t)} \Phi(d_-)$$

where

$$d_\pm = \frac{\log(S_t/K) + (r - D \pm \frac{1}{2}\bar{\alpha}^2)(T - t)}{\bar{\alpha}\sqrt{T - t}}$$

$$\bar{\alpha}^2 = \frac{1}{T - t} \int_t^T \sigma_u^2 \, du$$

and $\Phi(\cdot)$ is the cdf of a standard normal.
Thus,

$$C(S_t, t; K, T) = K \left(S_t/K e^{-D(T-t)} \Phi(d_+) - e^{-r(T-t)} \Phi(d_-) \right)$$
$$= K C(S_t/K, t; 1, T).$$

To show $C(S_t, t; K, T) = S_t \dfrac{\partial C}{\partial S_t} + K \dfrac{\partial C}{\partial K}$ we note that

$$\frac{\partial C}{\partial S_t} = e^{-D(T-t)} \Phi(d_+) + S_t e^{-D(T-t)} \frac{\partial \Phi(d_+)}{\partial S_t} - K e^{-r(T-t)} \frac{\partial \Phi(d_-)}{\partial S_t}$$

$$\frac{\partial C}{\partial K} = S_t e^{-D(T-t)} \frac{\partial \Phi(d_+)}{\partial K} - e^{-r(T-t)} \Phi(d_-) - K e^{-r(T-t)} \frac{\partial \Phi(d_-)}{\partial K}$$

so that

$$S_t \frac{\partial C}{\partial S_t} + K \frac{\partial C}{\partial K} = C(S_t.t; K, T)$$

$$+ S_t \left(S_t e^{-D(T-t)} \frac{\partial \Phi(d_+)}{\partial S_t} - K e^{-r(T-t)} \frac{\partial \Phi(d_-)}{\partial S_t} \right)$$

$$+ K \left(S_t e^{-D(T-t)} \frac{\partial \Phi(d_+)}{\partial K} - K e^{-r(T-t)} \frac{\partial \Phi(d_-)}{\partial K} \right).$$

From Problem 2.2.4.1 (page 218),

$$S_t e^{-D(T-t)} \frac{\partial \Phi(d_+)}{\partial S_t} = K e^{-r(T-t)} \frac{\partial \Phi(d_-)}{\partial S_t}$$

$$S_t e^{-D(T-t)} \frac{\partial \Phi(d_+)}{\partial K} = K e^{-r(T-t)} \frac{\partial \Phi(d_-)}{\partial K}.$$

Hence,

$$C(S_t.t; K, T) = S_t \frac{\partial C}{\partial S_t} + K \frac{\partial C}{\partial K}.$$

To show $S_t^2 \frac{\partial^2 C}{\partial S_t^2} = K^2 \frac{\partial^2 C}{\partial K^2}$, we first differentiate $C(S_t, t; K, T) = S_t \frac{\partial C}{\partial S_t} + K \frac{\partial C}{\partial K}$ with respect to S_t so that

$$\frac{\partial C}{\partial S_t} = \frac{\partial C}{\partial S_t} + S_t \frac{\partial^2 C}{\partial S_t^2} + K \frac{\partial^2 C}{\partial S_t \partial K}$$

or

$$S_t \frac{\partial^2 C}{\partial S_t^2} = -K \frac{\partial^2 C}{\partial S_t \partial K}.$$

Multiplying the above expression with S_t and using the identity

$$C(S_t, t; K, T) = S_t \frac{\partial C}{\partial S_t} + K \frac{\partial C}{\partial K}$$

we have

$$S_t^2 \frac{\partial^2 C}{\partial S_t^2} = -S_t K \frac{\partial^2 C}{\partial S_t \partial K}$$

$$= -K \frac{\partial}{\partial K} \left(S_t \frac{\partial C}{\partial S_t} \right)$$

$$= -K \frac{\partial}{\partial K} \left(C(S_t, t; K, T) - K \frac{\partial C}{\partial K} \right)$$

$$= -K \frac{\partial C}{\partial K} + K \left(\frac{\partial C}{\partial K} + K \frac{\partial^2 C}{\partial K^2} \right)$$

$$= K^2 \frac{\partial^2 C}{\partial K^2}.$$

By substituting the identities into the Black–Scholes equation,

$$\frac{\partial C}{\partial t} + \frac{1}{2} \sigma_t^2 S_t^2 \frac{\partial^2 C}{\partial S_t^2} + (r - D) S_t \frac{\partial C}{\partial S_t} - rC(S_t, t; K, T) = 0$$

we have

$$\frac{\partial C}{\partial t} + \frac{1}{2} \sigma_t^2 K^2 \frac{\partial^2 C}{\partial K^2} + (r - D) S_t \left(C(S_t, t; K, T) - K \frac{\partial C}{\partial K} \right) - rC(S_t, t; K, T) = 0$$

or

$$\frac{\partial C}{\partial t} + \frac{1}{2} \sigma_t^2 K^2 \frac{\partial^2 C}{\partial K^2} + (D - r) K \frac{\partial C}{\partial K} - DC(S_t, t; K, T) = 0$$

with payoff

$$C(S_T, T; K, T) = \max\{S_T - K, 0\}.$$

□

2. *Backward Kolmogorov Equation – Local Volatility Model.* Let $\{W_t : t \geq 0\}$ be a $\mathbb{P}$-standard Wiener process on the probability space $(\Omega, \mathcal{F}, \mathbb{P})$ and let the asset price S_t follow a local volatility model with the following SDE

$$\frac{dS_t}{S_t} = (\mu - D) \, dt + \sigma(S_t, t) dW_t$$

where μ is the drift parameter, D is the continuous dividend yield, $\sigma(S_t, t)$ is the local volatility function and let r be the risk-free interest-rate parameter from the money-market account.

Using Taylor's series, show for a definite integral of a smooth function $f(x)$ that

$$\int_a^b f(u)\, du = f\left(\frac{a+b}{2}\right)(b-a) + O\left((b-a)^3\right)$$

and hence show, under the risk-neutral measure $\mathbb{Q}$, that

$$\mathbb{E}^{\mathbb{Q}}\left[S_{t+\Delta t} - S_t\,\middle|\, \mathcal{F}_t\right] = (r - D)S_{t+\frac{1}{2}\Delta t}\Delta t + O\left((\Delta t)^3\right)$$

$$\mathbb{E}^{\mathbb{Q}}\left[\left(S_{t+\Delta t} - S_t\right)^2\,\middle|\, \mathcal{F}_t\right] = \sigma\left(S_{t+\frac{1}{2}\Delta t}, t + \frac{1}{2}\Delta t\right)^2 S^2_{t+\frac{1}{2}\Delta t}\Delta t + O\left((\Delta t)^2\right)$$

$$\mathbb{E}^{\mathbb{Q}}\left[\left(S_{t+\Delta t} - S_t\right)^3\,\middle|\, \mathcal{F}_t\right] = O\left((\Delta t)^2\right)$$

for $\Delta t > 0$.

Let $p(S_t, t; S_T, T)$ be the transition pdf for the asset price where the asset price is S_t at time t given that the asset price is S_T at time $T > t$. From the Chapman–Kolmogorov equation for $\Delta t > 0$,

$$p(S_t, t - \Delta t; S_T, T) = \int_0^\infty p(S_t, t - \Delta t; z, t)p(z, t; S_T, T)\, dz$$

show that by expanding $p(z, t; S_T, T)$ using Taylor series centred on S_t up to second order and taking limits $\Delta t \to 0$, $p(S_t, t; S_T, T)$ satisfies the backward Kolmogorov equation

$$\frac{\partial}{\partial t}p(S_t, t; S_T, T) + \frac{1}{2}\sigma(S_t, t)^2 S_t^2 \frac{\partial^2}{\partial S_t^2}p(S_t, t; S_T, T) + (r - D)S_t\frac{\partial}{\partial S_t}p(S_t, t; S_T, T) = 0$$

with boundary condition

$$p(S_t, t; S_T, t) = \delta(S_t - S_T), \quad \forall t.$$

Solution: From Taylor's theorem

$$f(x) = f\left(\frac{a+b}{2}\right) + f'\left(\frac{a+b}{2}\right)\left(x - \frac{1}{2}(a+b)\right)$$
$$+ \frac{1}{2}f''\left(\frac{a+b}{2}\right)\left(x - \frac{1}{2}(a+b)\right)^2 + O\left(\left(x - \frac{1}{2}(a+b)\right)^3\right)$$

and taking integrals

$$
\int_a^b f(u)\,du = \int_a^b f\left(\frac{a+b}{2}\right) du + \int_a^b f'\left(\frac{a+b}{2}\right)\left(u - \frac{1}{2}(a+b)\right) du
$$

$$
+ \int_a^b \frac{1}{2} f''\left(\frac{a+b}{2}\right)\left(u - \frac{1}{2}(a+b)\right)^2 du
$$

$$
+ \int_a^b O\left(\left(u - \frac{1}{2}(a+b)\right)^3\right) du
$$

$$
= f\left(\frac{a+b}{2}\right)(b-a) + \frac{1}{2} f'\left(\frac{a+b}{2}\right)\left(u - \frac{1}{2}(a+b)\right)^2 \Bigg|_a^b
$$

$$
+ \frac{1}{3!} f'\left(\frac{a+b}{2}\right)\left(u - \frac{1}{2}(a+b)\right)^3 \Bigg|_a^b + O\left(\left(u - \frac{1}{2}(a+b)\right)^4\right) \Bigg|_a^b
$$

$$
= f\left(\frac{a+b}{2}\right)(b-a) + O\left((b-a)^3\right).
$$

From Girsanov's theorem, under the risk-neutral measure $\mathbb{Q}$, S_t follows

$$
\frac{dS_t}{S_t} = (r - D)dt + \sigma(S_t, t)dW_t^{\mathbb{Q}}
$$

where $W_t^{\mathbb{Q}} = W_t + \int_0^t \frac{\mu - r}{\sigma(S_u, u)} du$ is a $\mathbb{Q}$-standard Wiener process.

By using the risk-neutral dynamics

$$
dS_t = (r - D)S_t + \sigma(S_t, t)S_t dW_t^{\mathbb{Q}}
$$

and taking integrals we have

$$
\int_t^{t+\Delta t} dS_u = \int_t^{t+\Delta t} (r - D)S_u\,du + \int_t^{t+\Delta t} \sigma(S_u, u)S_u dW_u^{\mathbb{Q}}
$$

or

$$
S_{t+\Delta t} - S_t = \int_t^{t+\Delta t} (r - D)S_u\,du + \int_t^{t+\Delta t} \sigma(S_u, u)S_u\,dW_u^{\mathbb{Q}}.
$$

Thus, by taking expectations and using the approximation integration formula as well as the Itō calculus property,

$$
\mathbb{E}^{\mathbb{Q}}\left[S_{t+\Delta t} - S_t \big| \mathscr{F}_t\right] = \int_t^{t+\Delta t} (r - D)S_u\,du + \mathbb{E}^{\mathbb{Q}}\left[\int_t^{t+\Delta t} \sigma(S_u, u)S_u\,dW_u^{\mathbb{Q}} \bigg| \mathscr{F}_t\right]
$$

$$
= \int_t^{t+\Delta t} (r - D)S_u\,du
$$

$$
= (r - D)S_{t+\frac{1}{2}\Delta t}\Delta t + O\left((\Delta t)^3\right)
$$

$$\mathbb{E}^{\mathbb{Q}}\left[\left(S_{t+\Delta t} - S_t\right)^2 \Big| \mathscr{F}_t\right]$$

$$= (r-D)^2 \left(\int_t^{t+\Delta t} S_u\, du\right)^2$$

$$+ 2(r-D)\left(\int_t^{t+\Delta t} S_u\, du\right) \mathbb{E}^{\mathbb{Q}}\left[\left(\int_t^{t+\Delta t} \sigma(S_u,u)S_u\, dW_u^{\mathbb{Q}}\right)\Big| \mathscr{F}_t\right]$$

$$+ \mathbb{E}^{\mathbb{Q}}\left[\left(\int_t^{t+\Delta t} \sigma(S_u,u)S_u\, dW_u^{\mathbb{Q}}\right)^2 \Big| \mathscr{F}_t\right]$$

$$= (r-D)^2 \left(\int_t^{t+\Delta t} S_u\, du\right)^2$$

$$+ 2(r-D)\left(\int_t^{t+\Delta t} S_u\, du\right) \mathbb{E}^{\mathbb{Q}}\left[\left(\int_t^{t+\Delta t} \sigma(S_u,u)S_u\, dW_u^{\mathbb{Q}}\right)\Big| \mathscr{F}_t\right]$$

$$+ \int_t^{t+\Delta t} \sigma(S_u,u)^2 S_u^2\, du$$

$$= \sigma\left(S_{t+\frac{1}{2}\Delta t}, t+\frac{1}{2}\Delta t\right)^2 S_{t+\frac{1}{2}\Delta t}^2 \Delta t + O\left((\Delta t)^2\right)$$

and

$$\mathbb{E}^{\mathbb{Q}}\left[\left(S_{t+\Delta t} - S_t\right)^3 \Big| \mathscr{F}_t\right]$$

$$= (r-D)^3 \left(\int_t^{t+\Delta t} S_u\, du\right)^3$$

$$+ 2(r-D)^2 \left(\int_t^{t+\Delta t} S_u\, du\right)^2 \mathbb{E}^{\mathbb{Q}}\left[\left(\int_t^{t+\Delta t} \sigma(S_u,u)S_u\, dW_u^{\mathbb{Q}}\right)\Big| \mathscr{F}_t\right]$$

$$+ (r-D)\left(\int_t^{t+\Delta t} S_u\, du\right)\left(\int_t^{t+\Delta t} \sigma(S_u,u)^2 S_u^2\, du\right)$$

$$+ (r-D)^2 \left(\int_t^{t+\Delta t} S_u\, du\right)^2 \mathbb{E}^{\mathbb{Q}}\left[\left(\int_t^{t+\Delta t} \sigma(S_u,u)S_u\, dW_u^{\mathbb{Q}}\right)\Big| \mathscr{F}_t\right]$$

$$+ 2(r-D)\left(\int_t^{t+\Delta t} S_u\, du\right)\left(\int_t^{t+\Delta t} \sigma(S_u,u)^2 S_u^2\, du\right)$$

$$+ \left(\int_t^{t+\Delta t} \sigma(S_u,u)^2 S_u^2\, du\right) \mathbb{E}^{\mathbb{Q}}\left[\left(\int_t^{t+\Delta t} \sigma(S_u,u)S_u\, dW_u^{\mathbb{Q}}\right)\Big| \mathscr{F}_t\right]$$

$$= O\left((\Delta t)^2\right).$$

From the Chapman–Kolmogorov equation we have

$$p(S_t, t - \Delta t; S_T, T) = \int_0^\infty p(S_t, t - \Delta t; z, t) p(z, t; S_T, T) \, dz$$

and expanding $p(z, t; S_T, T)$ using Taylor series centred on S_t up to second order yields

$$p(z, t; S_T, T) = p(S_t, t; S_T, T) + (z - S_t) \frac{\partial}{\partial S_t} p(S_t, t; S_T, T)$$

$$+ \frac{1}{2}(z - S_t)^2 \frac{\partial^2}{\partial S_t^2} p(S_t, t; S_T, T) + O((z - S_t)^3).$$

By substituting the Taylor series into the Chapman–Kolmogorov equation we have

$$p(S_t, t - \Delta t; S_T, T) = p(S_t, t; S_T, T) \int_0^\infty p(S_t, t - \Delta t; z, t) \, dz$$

$$+ \frac{\partial}{\partial S_t} p(S_t, t; S_T, T) \int_0^\infty (z - S_t) p(S_t, t - \Delta t; z, t) \, dz$$

$$+ \frac{1}{2} \frac{\partial^2}{\partial S_t^2} p(S_t, t; S_T, T) \int_0^\infty (z - S_t)^2 p(S_t, t - \Delta t; z, t) \, dz$$

$$+ O\left(\int_0^\infty (z - S_t)^3 p(S_t, t - \Delta t; z, t) \, dz \right).$$

Since

$$\int_0^\infty p(S_t, t - \Delta t; z, t) \, dz = 1$$

$$\int_0^\infty (z - S_t) p(S_t, t - \Delta t; z, t) \, dz = (r - D) S_{t + \frac{1}{2}\Delta t} \Delta t + O((\Delta t)^2)$$

$$\int_0^\infty (z - S_t)^2 p(S_t, t - \Delta t; z, t) \, dz = \sigma \left(S_{t + \frac{1}{2}\Delta t}, t + \frac{1}{2}\Delta t \right)^2 S_{t + \frac{1}{2}\Delta t}^2 \Delta t + O((\Delta t)^2)$$

$$\int_0^\infty (z - S_t)^3 p(S_t, t - \Delta t; z, t) \, dz = O((\Delta t)^2)$$

then by taking limits $\Delta t \to 0$,

$$\lim_{\Delta t \to 0} \frac{p(S_t, t - \Delta t; S_T, T) - p(S_t, t; S_T, T)}{\Delta t}$$

$$= (r - D) S_t \frac{\partial}{\partial S_t} p(S_t, t; S_T, T)$$

$$+ \frac{1}{2} \lim_{\Delta t \to 0} \sigma \left(S_{t + \frac{1}{2}\Delta t}, t + \frac{1}{2}\Delta t \right)^2 S_t^2 \frac{\partial^2}{\partial S_t^2} p(S_t, t; S_T, T) + \lim_{\Delta t \to 0} O((\Delta t)^2)$$

we have

$$-\frac{\partial}{\partial t}p(S_t,t;S_T,T) = (r-D)S_t\frac{\partial}{\partial S_t}p(S_t,t;S_T,T) + \frac{1}{2}\sigma(S_t,t)^2 S_t^2\frac{\partial^2}{\partial S_t^2}p(S_t,t;S_T,T)$$

or

$$\frac{\partial}{\partial t}p(S_t,t;S_T,T) + \frac{1}{2}\sigma(S_t,t)^2 S_t^2\frac{\partial^2}{\partial S_t^2}p(S_t,t;S_T,T) + (r-D)S_t\frac{\partial}{\partial S_t}p(S_t,t;S_T,T) = 0$$

with boundary condition

$$p(S_t,t;S_T,t) = \delta(S_t - S_T)$$

for all t.

$\square$

3. *Black–Scholes Equation – Local Volatility Model.* Under the risk-neutral measure $\mathbb{Q}$, let $\{\widetilde{W}_t : t \geq 0\}$ be a $\mathbb{Q}$-standard Wiener process on the probability space $(\Omega, \mathcal{F}, \mathbb{Q})$ and let the asset price S_t follow a local volatility model with the following SDE

$$\frac{dS_t}{S_t} = (r-D)\,dt + \sigma(S_t,t)d\widetilde{W}_t$$

where r is the risk-free interest-rate parameter from the money-market account, D is the continuous dividend yield and $\sigma(S_t,t)$ is the local volatility function.

Let $p(S_t,t;S_T,T)$ be the transition pdf of the asset price where the asset price is S_t at time t given that the asset price is S_T at time $T > t$. We consider a European option written on S_t with strike price $K > 0$ expiring at time $T > t$ with payoff $\Psi(S_T)$, where the option price at time t under the risk-neutral measure $\mathbb{Q}$ is

$$V(S_t,t;K,T) = e^{-r(T-t)}\mathbb{E}^{\mathbb{Q}}\left[\Psi(S_T)\middle|\,\mathcal{F}_t\right]$$
$$= e^{-r(T-t)}\int_0^\infty \Psi(z)p(S_t,t;z,T)\,dz.$$

By using the backward Kolmogorov equation, show that $V(S_t,t;K,T)$ satisfies the Black–Scholes equation

$$\frac{\partial V}{\partial t} + \frac{1}{2}\sigma(S_t,t)^2 S_t^2\frac{\partial^2 V}{\partial S_t^2} + (r-D)S_t\frac{\partial V}{\partial S_t} - rV(S_t,t;K,T) = 0$$

with boundary condition

$$V(S_T,T;K,T) = \Psi(S_T).$$

From the above PDE and boundary condition, can we price a European option analytically?

Solution: Given

$$V(S_t, t; K, T) = e^{-r(T-t)} \int_0^\infty \Psi(z) p(S_t, t; z, T) \, dz$$

by taking first and second-order differentials we have

$$\frac{\partial V}{\partial t} = re^{-r(T-t)} \int_0^\infty \Psi(z) p(S_t, t; z, T) \, dz + e^{-r(T-t)} \int_0^\infty \Psi(z) \frac{\partial}{\partial t} p(S_t, t; z, T) \, dz$$

$$= rV(S_t, t; K, T) + e^{-r(T-t)} \int_0^\infty \Psi(z) \frac{\partial}{\partial t} p(S_t, t; z, T) \, dz$$

$$\frac{\partial V}{\partial S_t} = e^{-r(T-t)} \int_0^\infty \Psi(z) \frac{\partial}{\partial S_t} p(S_t, t; z, T) \, dz$$

$$\frac{\partial^2 V}{\partial S_t^2} = e^{-r(T-t)} \int_0^\infty \Psi(z) \frac{\partial^2}{\partial S_t^2} p(S_t, t; z, T) \, dz$$

and from Problem 7.2.2.2 (page 687), the backward Kolmogorov equation satisfied by $p(S_t, t; S_T, T)$ is

$$\frac{\partial}{\partial t} p(S_t, t; S_T, T) + \frac{1}{2}\sigma(S_t, t)^2 S_t^2 \frac{\partial^2}{\partial S_t^2} p(S_t, t; S_T, T) + (r - D)S_t \frac{\partial}{\partial S_t} p(S_t, t; S_T, T) = 0$$

with boundary condition

$$p(S_t, T; S_T, T) = \delta(S_t - S_T)$$

for all t.

By multiplying the backward Kolmogorov equation with $\Psi(S_T)$ and taking integrals we have

$$\int_0^\infty \Psi(z) \frac{\partial}{\partial t} p(S_t, t; z, T) \, dz + \frac{1}{2}\sigma(S_t, t)^2 S_t^2 \int_0^\infty \Psi(z) \frac{\partial^2}{\partial S_t^2} p(S_t, t; z, T) \, dz$$

$$+ (r - D)S_t \int_0^\infty \Psi(z) \frac{\partial}{\partial S_t} p(S_t, t; z, T) \, dz = 0.$$

Writing the above equation in terms of $\dfrac{\partial V}{\partial t}, \dfrac{\partial V}{\partial S_t}$ and $\dfrac{\partial^2 V}{\partial S_t^2}$,

$$e^{-r(T-t)} \left[\frac{\partial V}{\partial t} - rV(S_t, t; K, T) + \frac{1}{2}\sigma(S_t, t)^2 S_t^2 \frac{\partial^2 V}{\partial S_t^2} + (r - D)S_t \frac{\partial V}{\partial S_t} \right] = 0$$

or

$$\frac{\partial V}{\partial t} + \frac{1}{2}\sigma(S_t, t)^2 S_t^2 \frac{\partial^2 V}{\partial S_t^2} + (r - D)S_t \frac{\partial V}{\partial S_t} - rV(S_t, t; K, T) = 0.$$

Finally, for the boundary condition we note that

$$V(S_T, T; K, T) = \int_0^\infty \Psi(z) p(S_T, T; z, T) \, dz$$

and from the definition of the Dirac delta function

$$
\begin{aligned}
V(S_T, T; K, T) &= \int_0^\infty \Psi(z) p(S_T, T; z, T) \, dz \\
&= \int_0^\infty \Psi(z) \delta(S_T - z) \, dz \\
&= \Psi(S_T).
\end{aligned}
$$

Given that the solution of $V(S_t, t; K, T)$ depends on the unknown local volatility function, we cannot rely on the analytical Black–Scholes formula to price a European option. In general, this PDE has to be solved numerically.

$\square$

4. *Forward Kolmogorov Equation – Local Volatility Model.* Let $\{W_t : t \geq 0\}$ be a $\mathbb{P}$-standard Wiener process on the probability space $(\Omega, \mathcal{F}, \mathbb{P})$. We consider an asset price S_t following a local volatility model SDE

$$\frac{dS_t}{S_t} = (\mu - D) \, dt + \sigma(S_t, t) dW_t$$

where μ is the drift parameter, D is the continuous dividend yield, $\sigma(S_t, t)$ is the local volatility function and let r be the risk-free interest-rate parameter.

Using Girsanov's theorem, show that under the risk-neutral measure $\mathbb{Q}$, the above SDE is

$$\frac{dS_t}{S_t} = (r - D) \, dt + \sigma(S_t, t) d\widetilde{W}_t$$

where $\widetilde{W}_t$ is a $\mathbb{Q}$-standard Wiener process.

Let $p(S_t, t; S_T, T)$ be the transition pdf of the asset price where the asset price is S_t at time t given that the asset price is S_T at time $T > t$. From the Chapman–Kolmogorov equation for $\Delta T > 0$,

$$p(S_t, t; S_T, T + \Delta T) = \int_0^\infty p(S_t, t; z, T) p(z, T; S_T, T + \Delta T) \, dz$$

show that in the limit $\Delta T \to 0$,

$$\frac{\partial}{\partial T} p(S_t, t; S_T, T) = -\int_0^\infty p(S_t, t; z, T) \frac{\partial}{\partial T} p(z, T; S_T, T) \, dz.$$

Finally, using the backward Kolmogorov equation, show that $p(S_t, t; S_T, T)$ satisfies the forward Kolmogorov equation

$$\frac{\partial}{\partial T} p(S_t, t; S_T, T) - \frac{1}{2} \frac{\partial^2}{\partial S_T^2} \left[\sigma(S_T, T)^2 S_T^2 p(S_t, t; S_T, T) \right]$$

$$+ (r - D) \frac{\partial}{\partial S_T} \left[S_T p(S_t, t; S_T, T) \right] = 0$$

with boundary condition

$$p(S_t, t; S_T, t) = \delta(S_t - S_T), \quad \forall t.$$

Solution: At time t, the portfolio Π_t is valued as

$$\Pi_t = \phi_t S_t + \psi_t B_t$$

where B_t is the risk-free asset having the following diffusion $d B_t = r B_t dt$. Since the holder of the portfolio will receive $DS_t dt$ for every stock held, then in differential form

$$\begin{aligned}
d\Pi_t &= \phi_t \left(dS_t + DS_t dt \right) + \psi_t d B_t \\
&= \phi_t \left(\mu S_t dt + \sigma(S_t, t) S_t dW_t \right) + \psi_t r B_t dt \\
&= r\Pi_t dt + \phi_t(\mu - r) S_t dt + \phi_t \sigma(S_t, t) S_t dW_t \\
&= r\Pi_t dt + \phi_t \sigma(S_t, t) S_t \left(\lambda_t dt + dW_t \right)
\end{aligned}$$

where $\lambda_t = \dfrac{\mu - r}{\sigma(S_t, t)}$.

From the discounted portfolio,

$$\begin{aligned}
d(e^{-rt} \Pi_t) &= -re^{-rt} \Pi_t dt + e^{-rt} d\Pi_t \\
&= e^{-rt} \phi_t \sigma(S_t, t) S_t \left(\lambda_t dt + dW_t \right) \\
&= \phi_t \sigma(S_t, t) e^{-rt} d\widetilde{W}_t
\end{aligned}$$

where

$$\widetilde{W}_t = W_t + \int_0^t \frac{\mu - r}{\sigma(S_u, u)} du.$$

From Girsanov's theorem, there exists an equivalent martingale measure or risk-neutral measure $\mathbb{Q}$ on the filtration $\mathcal{F}_s$, $0 \le s \le t$ defined by the Radon–Nikodým derivative

$$Z_s = e^{-\int_0^t \lambda_u^2 du - \frac{1}{2} \int_0^t \lambda_u dW_u}$$

so that $\widetilde{W}_t$ is a $\mathbb{Q}$-standard Wiener process. Given that under the risk-neutral measure $\mathbb{Q}$, the discounted portfolio has no dt term, therefore $e^{-rt} \Pi_t$ is a $\mathbb{Q}$-martingale.

By substituting

$$dW_t = d\widetilde{W}_t - \frac{\mu - r}{\sigma(S_t, t)} dt$$

into

$$\frac{dS_t}{S_t} = (\mu - D) \, dt + \sigma(S_t, t) dW_t$$

the asset price diffusion process under $\mathbb{Q}$ becomes

$$\frac{dS_t}{S_t} = (r - D) \, dt + \sigma(S_t, t) d\widetilde{W}_t.$$

From the Chapman–Kolmogorov equation for $\Delta T > 0$,

$$p(S_t, t; S_T, T + \Delta T) = \int_0^\infty p(S_t, t; z, T) p(z, T; S_T, T + \Delta T) \, dz$$

we can write

$$
\begin{aligned}
&p(S_t, t; S_T, T + \Delta T) - p(S_t, t; S_T, T) \\
&= \int_0^\infty p(S_t, t; z, T) p(z, T; S_T, T + \Delta T) \, dz - p(S_t, t; S_T, T) \\
&= \int_0^\infty p(S_t, t; z, T) p(z, T; S_T, T + \Delta T) \, dz \\
&\quad - \int_0^\infty p(S_t, t; z, T) p(z, T; S_T, T) \, dz \\
&= \int_0^\infty p(S_t, t; z, T) p(z, T; S_T, T + \Delta T) \, dz \\
&\quad - \int_0^\infty p(S_t, t; z, T) \delta(z - S_T) \, dz.
\end{aligned}
$$

By dividing the expression with ΔT and taking limits $\Delta T \to 0$,

$$
\begin{aligned}
&\lim_{\Delta T \to 0} \frac{p(S_t, t; S_T, T + \Delta T) - p(S_t, t; S_T, T)}{\Delta T} \\
&= \lim_{\Delta t \to 0} \int_0^\infty \frac{p(S_t, t; z, T) p(z, T; S_T, T + \Delta T)}{\Delta T} \, dz \\
&\quad - \lim_{\Delta T \to 0} \int_0^\infty \frac{p(S_t, t; z, T) \delta(z - S_T)}{\Delta T} \, dz \\
&= \lim_{\Delta T \to 0} \int_0^\infty p(S_t, t; z, T) \left[\frac{p(z, T; S_T, T + \Delta T) - \delta(z - S_T)}{\Delta T} \right] dz \\
&= \lim_{\Delta T \to 0} \int_0^\infty p(S_t, t; z, T) \left[\frac{p(z, T; S_T, T + \Delta T) - p(z, T + \Delta T; S_T, T + \Delta T)}{\Delta T} \right] dz.
\end{aligned}
$$

Since

$$\lim_{\Delta T \to 0} \frac{p(S_t, t; S_T, T + \Delta T) - p(S_t, t; S_T, T)}{\Delta T} = \frac{\partial}{\partial T} p(S_t, t; S_T, T)$$

and

$$\lim_{\Delta T \to 0} \frac{p(z, T; S_T, T + \Delta T) - p(z, T + \Delta T; S_T, T + \Delta T)}{\Delta T} = -\frac{\partial}{\partial T} p(z, T; S_T, T)$$

thus

$$\frac{\partial}{\partial T} p(S_t, t; S_T, T) = -\int_0^\infty p(S_t, t; z, T) \frac{\partial}{\partial T} p(z, T; S_T, T) \, dz.$$

From the backward Kolmogorov equation on $p(z, t; S_T, T)$ for the local volatility model

$$\frac{\partial}{\partial t} p(z, t; S_T, T) + \frac{1}{2}\sigma(z, t)^2 z^2 \frac{\partial^2}{\partial z^2} p(z, t; S_T, T) + (r - D)z \frac{\partial}{\partial z} p(z, t; S_T, T) = 0$$

we have

$$\frac{\partial}{\partial T} p(S_t, t; S_T, T)$$
$$= \int_0^\infty p(S_t, t; z, T) \left[(r - D)z \frac{\partial}{\partial} z \, p(z, T; S_T, T) + \frac{1}{2}\sigma(z, T)^2 z^2 \frac{\partial^2}{\partial z^2} p(z, T; S_T, T) \right] dz$$
$$= \int_0^\infty (r - D)z \, p(S_t, t; z, T) \frac{\partial}{\partial z} p(z, T; S_T, T) \, dz$$
$$+ \int_0^\infty \frac{1}{2}\sigma(z, T)^2 z^2 p(S_t, t; z, T) \frac{\partial^2}{\partial z^2} p(z, T; S_T, T) \, dz.$$

Integrating by parts for $\int_0^\infty (r - D)z \, p(S_t, t; z, T) \frac{\partial}{\partial z} p(z, T; S_T, T) \, dz$, we let

$$u = (r - D)z \, p(S_t, t; z, T) \quad \text{and} \quad \frac{dv}{dz} = \frac{\partial}{\partial z} p(z, T; S_T, T)$$

so that

$$\frac{du}{dz} = \frac{\partial}{\partial z} \left[(r - D)z \, p(S_t, t; z, T) \right] \quad \text{and} \quad v = p(z, T; S_T, T).$$

We then have

$$
\int_0^\infty (r-D)z\, p(S_t,t;z,T)\frac{\partial}{\partial z} p(z,T;S_T,T)dz
$$

$$
= (r-D)z\, p(S_t,t;z,T)p(z,T;S_T,T)\Big|_0^\infty
$$

$$
- \int_0^\infty p(z,T;S_T,T)\frac{\partial}{\partial z}\left[(r-D)z\, p(S_t,t;z,T)\right]dz
$$

$$
= - \int_0^\infty p(z,T;S_T,T)\frac{\partial}{\partial z}\left[(r-D)z\, p(S_t,t;z,T)\right]dz.
$$

Taking integration by parts for $\displaystyle\int_0^\infty \frac{1}{2}\sigma(z,T)^2 z^2 p(S_t,t;z,T)\frac{\partial^2}{\partial z^2}p(z,T;S_T,T)\,dz$, we let

$$
u = \frac{1}{2}\sigma(z,T)^2 z^2 p(S_t,t;z,T) \quad\text{and}\quad \frac{dv}{dz} = \frac{\partial^2}{\partial z^2}p(z,T;S_T,T)
$$

so that

$$
\frac{du}{dz} = \frac{\partial}{\partial z}\left[\frac{1}{2}\sigma(z,T)^2 z^2 p(S_t,t;z,T)\right] \quad\text{and}\quad v = \frac{\partial}{\partial z}p(z,T;S_T,T)
$$

and hence

$$
\int_0^\infty \frac{1}{2}\sigma(z,T)^2 z^2 p(S_t,t;z,T)\frac{\partial^2}{\partial z^2}p(z,T;S_T,T)\,dz
$$

$$
= \frac{1}{2}\sigma(z,T)^2 z^2 p(S_t,t;z,T)\frac{\partial}{\partial z}p(z,T;S_T,T)\Big|_0^\infty
$$

$$
- \int_0^\infty \frac{\partial}{\partial z}p(z,T;S_T,T)\frac{\partial}{\partial z}\left[\frac{1}{2}\sigma(z,T)^2 z^2 p(S_t,t;z,T)\right]dz
$$

$$
= - \int_0^\infty \frac{\partial}{\partial z}p(z,T;S_T,T)\frac{\partial}{\partial z}\left[\frac{1}{2}\sigma(z,T)^2 z^2 p(S_t,t;z,T)\right]dz.
$$

Using integration by parts again, we let

$$
u = \frac{\partial}{\partial z}\left[\frac{1}{2}\sigma(z,T)^2 z^2 p(S_t,t;z,T)\right] \quad\text{and}\quad \frac{dv}{dz} = \frac{\partial}{\partial z}p(z,T;S_T,T)
$$

so that

$$
\frac{du}{dz} = \frac{\partial^2}{\partial z^2}\left[\frac{1}{2}\sigma(z,T)^2 z^2 p(S_t,t;z,T)\right] \quad\text{and}\quad v = p(z,T;S_T,T)
$$

and therefore

$$\int_0^\infty \frac{1}{2}\sigma(z,T)^2 z^2 p(S_t,t;z,T)\frac{\partial^2}{\partial z^2}p(z,T;S_T,T)\,dz$$

$$= -\frac{\partial}{\partial z}\left[\frac{1}{2}\sigma(z,T)^2 z^2 p(S_t,t;z,T)\right]p(z,T;S_T,T)\Big|_0^\infty$$

$$+\int_0^\infty p(z,T;S_T,T)\frac{\partial^2}{\partial z^2}\left[\frac{1}{2}\sigma(z,T)^2 z^2 p(S_t,t;z,T)\right]dz$$

$$= \int_0^\infty p(z,T;S_T,T)\frac{\partial^2}{\partial z^2}\left[\frac{1}{2}\sigma(z,T)^2 z^2 p(S_t,t;z,T)\right]dz.$$

Thus,

$$\frac{\partial}{\partial T}p(S_t,t;S_T,T)$$

$$= -\int_0^\infty p(z,T;S_T,T)\frac{\partial}{\partial z}\left[(r-D)z\,p(S_t,t;z,T)\right]dz$$

$$+\int_0^\infty p(z,T;S_T,T)\frac{\partial^2}{\partial z^2}\left[\frac{1}{2}\sigma(z,T)^2 z^2 p(S_t,t;z,T)\right]dz$$

$$= \int_0^\infty\left\{\frac{\partial^2}{\partial z^2}\left[\frac{1}{2}\sigma(z,T)^2 z^2 p(S_t,t;z,T)\right]-\frac{\partial}{\partial z}\left[(r-D)z\,p(S_t,t;z,T)\right]\right\}\delta(z-S_T)\,dz$$

$$= \frac{\partial^2}{\partial S_T^2}\left[\frac{1}{2}\sigma(S_T,T)^2 S_T^2 p(S_t,t;S_T,T)\right]-\frac{\partial}{\partial S_T}\left[(r-D)S_T p(S_t,t;S_T,T)\right]$$

and rearranging terms we have the forward Kolmogorov equation

$$\frac{\partial}{\partial T}p(S_t,t;S_T,T)-\frac{1}{2}\frac{\partial^2}{\partial S_T^2}\left[\sigma(S_T,T)^2 S_T^2 p(S_t,t;S_T,T)\right]$$

$$+(r-D)\frac{\partial}{\partial S_T}\left[S_T p(S_t,t;S_T,T)\right]=0$$

with boundary condition

$$p(S_t,t;S_T,t)=\delta(S_t-S_T),\forall t.$$

$\square$

5. *Dupire Equation.* Let $\{W_t:t\geq 0\}$ be a $\mathbb{P}$-standard Wiener process on the probability space $(\Omega,\mathscr{F},\mathbb{P})$ and let the stock price S_t follow a local volatility model with the following SDE

$$\frac{dS_t}{S_t}=(\mu-D)\,dt+\sigma(S_t,t)dW_t$$

where μ is the drift parameter, D is the continuous dividend yield, $\sigma(S_t,t)$ is the local volatility function and let r be the risk-free interest rate.

Let $p(S_t, t; S_T, T)$ be the transition pdf of the stock price where the stock is worth S_t at time t given that the stock price is S_T at time $T > t$. We consider a European call option written on S_t with strike price $K > 0$ expiring at time $T > t$ with payoff $\Psi(S_T) = \max\{S_T - K, 0\}$ where, under the risk-neutral measure $\mathbb{Q}$, the option price at time t is

$$C(S_t, t; K, T) = e^{-r(T-t)}\mathbb{E}^{\mathbb{Q}}\left[\max\{S_T - K, 0\}\,|\,\mathcal{F}_t\right]$$

$$= e^{-r(T-t)}\int_0^\infty \max\{z - K, 0\}p(S_t, t; z, T)\,dz.$$

Show that the following identities are true

$$z\frac{\partial}{\partial K}(z - K) = K\frac{\partial}{\partial K}(z - K) - (z - K)$$

$$\frac{\partial}{\partial z}(z - K) = -\frac{\partial}{\partial K}(z - K)$$

$$\frac{\partial^2}{\partial z^2}(z - K) = \frac{\partial^2}{\partial K^2}(z - K).$$

By using the forward Kolmogorov equation and the above identities or otherwise, show that $C(S_t, t; K, T)$ satisfies the Dupire equation

$$\frac{\partial C}{\partial T} - \frac{1}{2}\sigma(K, T)^2 K^2\frac{\partial^2 C}{\partial K^2} + (r - D)K\frac{\partial C}{\partial K} + DC(S_t, t; K, T) = 0$$

with boundary condition

$$C(S_T, T; K, T) = \max\{S_T - K, 0\}.$$

Explain the significance of this equation.

Finally, deduce that a European put option price $P(S_t, t; K, T)$ written on S_t at time t, with payoff $\Psi(S_T) = \max\{K - S_T, 0\}$ expiring at time $T > t$, satisfies

$$\frac{\partial P}{\partial T} - \frac{1}{2}\sigma(K, T)^2 K^2\frac{\partial^2 P}{\partial K^2} + (r - D)K\frac{\partial P}{\partial K} + DP(S_t, t; K, T) = 0$$

with boundary condition

$$P(S_T, T; K, T) = \max\{K - S_T, 0\}.$$

Solution: To show the first identity, we can write

$$z\frac{\partial}{\partial K}(z - K) = (z - K + K)\frac{\partial}{\partial K}(z - K)$$

$$= (z - K)\frac{\partial}{\partial K}(z - K) + K\frac{\partial}{\partial K}(z - K)$$

$$= -(z - K) + K\frac{\partial}{\partial K}(z - K)$$

$$= K\frac{\partial}{\partial K}(z - K) - (z - K).$$

As for the second identity, we note that

$$\frac{\partial}{\partial z}(z - K) = 1 = -\frac{\partial}{\partial K}(z - K).$$

Finally,

$$\frac{\partial^2}{\partial z^2}(z - K) = \frac{\partial}{\partial z}\left[\frac{\partial}{\partial z}(z - K)\right]$$

$$= -\frac{\partial}{\partial z}\left[\frac{\partial}{\partial K}(z - K)\right]$$

$$= -\frac{\partial}{\partial K}\left[\frac{\partial}{\partial z}(z - K)\right]$$

$$= \frac{\partial^2}{\partial K^2}(z - K).$$

By definition

$$C(S_t, t; K, T) = e^{-r(T-t)}\mathbb{E}^{\mathbb{Q}}\left[\max\{S_T - K, 0\} \mid \mathscr{F}_t\right]$$

$$= e^{-r(T-t)}\int_0^\infty \max\{z - K, 0\}p(S_t, t; z, T)\,dz$$

$$= e^{-r(T-t)}\int_K^\infty (z - K)p(S_t, t; z, T)\,dz.$$

Differentiating $C(S_t, t; K, T)$ with respect to T and from the forward Kolmogorov equation

$$\frac{\partial}{\partial T}p(S_t, t; S_T, T) - \frac{1}{2}\frac{\partial^2}{\partial S_T^2}\left[\sigma(S_T, T)^2 S_T^2 p(S_t, t; S_T, T)\right]$$

$$+(r - D)\frac{\partial}{\partial S_T}\left[S_T p(S_t, t; S_T, T)\right] = 0$$

we have

$$\frac{\partial C}{\partial T} = -re^{-r(T-t)} \int_K^\infty (z-K)p(S_t,t;z,T)\,dz$$

$$+ e^{-r(T-t)} \int_K^\infty (z-K)\frac{\partial}{\partial T}p(S_t,t;z,T)\,dz$$

$$= -rC(S_t,t;K,T) + \frac{1}{2}e^{-r(T-t)} \int_K^\infty (z-K)\frac{\partial^2}{\partial z^2}\left[\sigma(z,T)^2 z^2 p(S_t,t;z,T)\right]dz$$

$$-(r-D)e^{-r(T-t)} \int_K^\infty (z-K)\frac{\partial}{\partial z}\left[z\,p(S_t,t;z,T)\right]dz.$$

Integrate by parts for $\int_K^\infty (z-K)\frac{\partial}{\partial z}\left[z\,p(S_t,t;z,T)\right]dz$ and let

$$u = (z-K), \quad \frac{dv}{dz} = \frac{\partial}{\partial z}\left[z\,p(S_t,t;z,T)\right]$$

so that

$$\frac{du}{dz} = \frac{\partial}{\partial z}(z-K) = -\frac{\partial}{\partial K}(z-K) \quad \text{and} \quad v = z\,p(S_t,t;z,T).$$

Therefore,

$$\int_K^\infty (z-K)\frac{\partial}{\partial z}\left[z\,p(S_t,t;z,T)\right]dz$$

$$= (z-K)z\,p(S_t,t;z,T)\Big|_K^\infty + \int_K^\infty z\,p(S_t,t;z,T)\frac{\partial}{\partial K}(z-K)\,dz$$

$$= \int_K^\infty p(S_t,t;z,T)z\frac{\partial}{\partial K}(z-K)\,dz$$

$$= \int_K^\infty \left[K\frac{\partial}{\partial K}(z-K) - (z-K)\right]p(S_t,t;z,T)\,dz$$

$$= K\int_K^\infty \frac{\partial}{\partial K}\left[(z-K)p(S_t,t;z,T)\right]dz - \int_K^\infty (z-K)p(S_t,t;z,T)\,dz$$

and hence

$$e^{-r(T-t)} \int_K^\infty (z-K)\frac{\partial}{\partial z}\left[z\,p(S_t,t;z,T)\right]dz$$

$$= Ke^{-r(T-t)} \int_K^\infty \frac{\partial}{\partial K}\left[(z-K)p(S_t,t;z,T)\right]dz$$

$$- e^{-r(T-t)} \int_K^\infty (z-K)p(S_t,t;z,T)\,dz$$

$$= K\frac{\partial C}{\partial K} - C(S_t,t;K,T).$$

For $\displaystyle\int_K^\infty (z-K)\frac{\partial^2}{\partial z^2}\left[\sigma(z,T)^2 z^2 p(S_t,t;z,T)\right]dz$ we let

$$u=(z-K) \quad\text{and}\quad \frac{dv}{dz}=\frac{\partial^2}{\partial z^2}\left[\sigma(z,T)^2 z^2 p(S_t,t;z,T)\right]$$

so that

$$\frac{du}{dz}=\frac{\partial}{\partial z}(z-K)\quad\text{and}\quad v=\frac{\partial}{\partial z}\left[\sigma(z,T)^2 z^2 p(S_t,t;z,T)\right]$$

and therefore

$$\int_K^\infty (z-K)\frac{\partial^2}{\partial z^2}\left[\sigma(z,T)^2 z^2 p(S_t,t;z,T)\right]dz$$

$$=(z-K)\frac{\partial}{\partial z}\left[\sigma(z,T)^2 z^2 p(S_t,t;z,T)\right]\Big|_K^\infty$$

$$-\int_K^\infty \frac{\partial}{\partial z}(z-K)\frac{\partial}{\partial z}\left[\sigma(z,T)^2 z^2 p(S_t,t;z,T)\right]dz$$

$$=-\int_K^\infty \frac{\partial}{\partial z}(z-K)\frac{\partial}{\partial z}\left[\sigma(z,T)^2 z^2 p(S_t,t;z,T)\right]dz.$$

To integrate $\displaystyle-\int_K^\infty \frac{\partial}{\partial z}(z-K)\frac{\partial}{\partial z}\left[\sigma(z,T)^2 z^2 p(S_t,t;z,T)\right]dz$ we set

$$u=\frac{\partial}{\partial z}(z-K)\quad\text{and}\quad \frac{dv}{dz}=\frac{\partial}{\partial z}\left[\sigma(z,T)^2 z^2 p(S_t,t;z,T)\right]$$

so that

$$\frac{du}{dz}=\frac{\partial^2}{\partial z^2}(z-K)\quad\text{and}\quad v=\sigma(z,T)^2 z^2 p(S_t,t;z,T)$$

and hence

$$-\int_K^\infty (z-K)\frac{\partial^2}{\partial z^2}\left[\sigma(z,T)^2 z^2 p(S_t,t;z,T)\right]dz$$

$$=-\sigma(z,T)^2 z^2 p(S_t,t;z,T)\frac{\partial}{\partial z}(z-K)\Big|_K^\infty$$

$$+\int_K^\infty \sigma(z,T)^2 z^2 p(S_t,t;z,T)\frac{\partial^2}{\partial z^2}(z-K)\,dz$$

$$=\sigma(K,T)^2 K^2 p(S_t,t;K,T)+\int_K^\infty \sigma(z,T)^2 z^2 p(S_t,t;z,T)\frac{\partial^2}{\partial K^2}(z-K)\,dz$$

$$=\sigma(K,T)^2 K^2 p(S_t,t;K,T)$$

since $\displaystyle\frac{\partial}{\partial z}(z-K)=1$ and $\displaystyle\frac{\partial^2}{\partial z^2}(z-K)=\frac{\partial^2}{\partial K^2}(z-K)=0.$

Given that

$$
\begin{aligned}
\frac{\partial^2 C}{\partial K^2} &= \frac{\partial}{\partial K}\left(\frac{\partial C}{\partial K}\right) \\
&= \frac{\partial}{\partial K}\left[e^{-r(T-t)}\int_K^\infty \frac{\partial}{\partial K}\left[(z-K)p(S_t,t;z,T)\right]dz\right] \\
&= e^{-r(T-t)}\left[-p(S_t,t;K,T)\frac{\partial}{\partial K}(z-K)+\int_K^\infty \frac{\partial^2}{\partial K^2}(z-K)p(S_t,t;z,T)\,dz\right] \\
&= e^{-r(T-t)}p(S_t,t;K,T)
\end{aligned}
$$

therefore

$$
\frac{1}{2}e^{-r(T-t)}\int_K^\infty (z-K)\frac{\partial^2}{\partial z^2}\left[\sigma(z,T)^2 z^2 p(S_t,t;z,T)\right]dz = \frac{1}{2}\sigma(K,T)^2 K^2 \frac{\partial^2 C}{\partial K^2}.
$$

Thus,

$$
\frac{\partial C}{\partial T} = -rC(S_t,t;K,T)+\frac{1}{2}\sigma(K,T)^2 K^2\frac{\partial^2 C}{\partial K^2}-(r-D)\left[K\frac{\partial C}{\partial K}-C(S_t,t;K,T)\right]
$$

or

$$
\frac{\partial C}{\partial T}-\frac{1}{2}\sigma(K,T)^2 K^2\frac{\partial^2 C}{\partial K^2}+(r-D)K\frac{\partial C}{\partial K}+DC(S_t,t;K,T)=0
$$

with boundary condition

$$
C(S_T,T;K,T)=\max\{S_T-K,0\}.
$$

From the equation, we can write

$$
\sigma(K,T)^2 = \frac{2\left(\dfrac{\partial C}{\partial T}+(r-D)K\dfrac{\partial C}{\partial K}+DC(S_t,t;K,T)\right)}{K^2\dfrac{\partial^2 C}{\partial K^2}}
$$

such that given the current spot price S_t, the local volatility function $\sigma(S_t,t)$ can be obtained from market quotes of call options of arbitrary strikes K and expiry times T.

From the put–call parity

$$
C(S_t,t;K,T)=P(S_t,t;K,T)+S_t e^{-D(T-t)}-Ke^{-r(T-t)}
$$

we have

$$\frac{\partial C}{\partial T} = \frac{\partial P}{\partial T} - DS_t e^{-D(T-t)} + rKe^{-r(T-t)}$$

$$\frac{\partial C}{\partial K} = \frac{\partial P}{\partial K} - e^{-r(T-t)}$$

$$\frac{\partial^2 C}{\partial K^2} = \frac{\partial^2 P}{\partial K^2}.$$

Substituting the above information into the Dupire equation for $C(S_t, t; K, T)$, we have

$$\frac{\partial P}{\partial T} - DS_t e^{-D(T-t)} + rKe^{-r(T-t)} - \frac{1}{2}\sigma(K,T)^2 \frac{\partial^2 P}{\partial K^2} + (r-D)K \left[\frac{\partial P}{\partial K} - e^{-r(T-t)} \right]$$

$$+ D \left[P(S_t, t; K, T) + S_t e^{-D(T-t)} - Ke^{-r(T-t)} \right] = 0$$

or

$$\frac{\partial P}{\partial T} - \frac{1}{2}\sigma(K,T)^2 K^2 \frac{\partial^2 P}{\partial K^2} + (r-D)K \frac{\partial P}{\partial K} + DP(S_t, t; K, T) = 0$$

with boundary condition

$$P(S_T, T; K, T) = \max\{K - S_T, 0\}.$$

$\square$

6. *Time-Dependent Volatility.* Consider a time-dependent (or term-structure) volatility function $\sigma(t)$ and the implied volatility function $\sigma_{\text{imp}}(t, T)$, which is a function of t and T, $T > t$ and assume their relationship is defined by

$$\sigma_{\text{imp}}^2(t, T) = \frac{1}{T-t} \int_t^T \sigma^2(u)\, du.$$

For two given expiry times $T_1 < T_2$, show that

$$\int_{T_1}^{T_2} \sigma^2(u)\, du = (T_2 - t)\sigma_{\text{imp}}^2(t, T_2) - (T_1 - t)\sigma_{\text{imp}}^2(t, T_1).$$

If the volatility is a piecewise constant over the time interval $[T_1, T_2]$, find $\sigma(u)$, $T_1 < u < T_2$.

Solution: By definition

$$\int_{T_1}^{T_2} \sigma^2(u)\, du = \int_t^{T_2} \sigma^2(u)\, du - \int_t^{T_1} \sigma^2(u)\, du$$

$$= (T_2 - t)\sigma_{\text{imp}}^2(t, T_2) - (T_1 - t)\sigma_{\text{imp}}^2(t, T_1).$$

Assuming

$$\int_{T_1}^{T_2} \sigma^2(u)\, du = \sigma^2(u)(T_2 - T_1), T_1 < u < T_2$$

and using the above result, we have

$$\sigma^2(u)(T_2 - T_1) = (T_2 - t)\sigma_{\mathrm{imp}}^2(t, T_2) - (T_1 - t)\sigma_{\mathrm{imp}}^2(t, T_1)$$

or

$$\sigma(u) = \sqrt{\frac{(T_2 - t)\sigma_{\mathrm{imp}}^2(t, T_2) - (T_1 - t)\sigma_{\mathrm{imp}}^2(t, T_1)}{T_2 - T_1}}, T_1 < u < T_2.$$

$\square$

7. *Relationship Between Local Volatility and Implied Volatility.* Let the relationship between the market-quoted call prices $C(S_t, t; K, T)$ and their corresponding implied volatilities $\sigma_{\mathrm{imp}}(S_t, t; K, T)$ be given by the Black–Scholes formula

$$C(S_t, t; K, T) = S_t e^{-D(T-t)}\Phi(d_+^{\mathrm{imp}}) - K e^{-r(T-t)}\Phi(d_-^{\mathrm{imp}})$$

$$d_\pm = \frac{\log(S_t/K) + (r - D \pm \frac{1}{2}\sigma_{\mathrm{imp}}^2)(T - t)}{\sigma_{\mathrm{imp}}\sqrt{T - t}}$$

where $\Phi(x) = \dfrac{1}{\sqrt{2\pi}}\displaystyle\int_{-\infty}^{x} e^{-\frac{1}{2}x^2}\, dx$ is the cdf of a standard normal and $\sigma_{\mathrm{imp}} \equiv \sigma_{\mathrm{imp}}(S_t, t; K, T)$.

From the Dupire equation, the local volatility $\sigma(K, T)$ is extracted from

$$\sigma(K, T)^2 = \frac{2\left(\dfrac{\partial C}{\partial T} + (r - D)K\dfrac{\partial C}{\partial K} + DC(S_t, t; K, T)\right)}{K^2 \dfrac{\partial^2 C}{\partial K^2}}.$$

By writing the Black–Scholes formula in the form

$$C(S_t, t; K, T) = S_t N_1 - K N_2$$

where $N_1 = e^{-D(T-t)}\Phi(d_+^{\mathrm{imp}})$, $N_2 = e^{-r(T-t)}\Phi(d_-^{\mathrm{imp}})$ and using the property

$$d_+^{\mathrm{imp}} = d_-^{\mathrm{imp}} + \sigma_{\mathrm{imp}}(S_t, t; K, T)\sqrt{T - t}$$

show that

(a) $S_t \dfrac{\partial N_1}{\partial d_+^{\mathrm{imp}}} - K \dfrac{\partial N_2}{\partial d_-^{\mathrm{imp}}} = 0$

(b) $\dfrac{\partial d_+^{\mathrm{imp}}}{\partial T} - \dfrac{\partial d_-^{\mathrm{imp}}}{\partial T} = \dfrac{\sigma_{\mathrm{imp}}}{2\sqrt{T-t}} + \sqrt{T-t}\dfrac{\partial \sigma_{\mathrm{imp}}}{\partial T}$

(c) $\dfrac{\partial d_+^{\mathrm{imp}}}{\partial K} - \dfrac{\partial d_-^{\mathrm{imp}}}{\partial K} = \sqrt{T-t}\dfrac{\partial \sigma_{\mathrm{imp}}}{\partial K}$

(d) $\dfrac{\partial d_-^{\mathrm{imp}}}{\partial K} = -\dfrac{1}{K\sigma_{\mathrm{imp}}\sqrt{T-t}} - \left(\dfrac{d_-^{\mathrm{imp}}}{\sigma_{\mathrm{imp}}} + \sqrt{T-t}\right)\dfrac{\partial \sigma_{\mathrm{imp}}}{\partial K}.$

Hence, using the above properties or otherwise, show that the local volatility function in terms of implied volatility is

$$\sigma(K,T)^2 = \frac{2\left(\dfrac{\partial \sigma_{\mathrm{imp}}}{\partial T} + (r-D)K\dfrac{\partial \sigma_{\mathrm{imp}}}{\partial K} + \dfrac{1}{2}\dfrac{\sigma_{\mathrm{imp}}}{T-t}\right)}{K^2\dfrac{\partial^2 \sigma_{\mathrm{imp}}}{\partial K^2} + \dfrac{2Kd_+^{\mathrm{imp}}}{\sigma_{\mathrm{imp}}\sqrt{T-t}}\dfrac{\partial \sigma_{\mathrm{imp}}}{\partial K} + \dfrac{K^2 d_+^{\mathrm{imp}} d_-^{\mathrm{imp}}}{\sigma_{\mathrm{imp}}}\left(\dfrac{\partial \sigma_{\mathrm{imp}}}{\partial K}\right)^2 + \dfrac{1}{\sigma_{\mathrm{imp}}\sqrt{T-t}}}.$$

Solution:

(a) Using the identity $d_+^{\mathrm{imp}} = d_-^{\mathrm{imp}} - \sigma_{\mathrm{imp}}\sqrt{T-t}$, from Problem 2.2.4.1 (page 218), we can easily show that

$$S_t e^{-D(T-t)} e^{-\frac{1}{2}(d_+^{\mathrm{imp}})^2} = K e^{-r(T-t)} e^{-\frac{1}{2}(d_-^{\mathrm{imp}})^2}$$

or

$$S_t e^{-D(T-t)} \frac{1}{\sqrt{2\pi}} e^{-\frac{1}{2}(d_+^{\mathrm{imp}})^2} = K e^{-r(T-t)} \frac{1}{\sqrt{2\pi}} e^{-\frac{1}{2}(d_-^{\mathrm{imp}})^2}$$

which implies

$$S_t \frac{\partial N_1}{\partial d_+^{\mathrm{imp}}} = K \frac{\partial N_2}{\partial d_-^{\mathrm{imp}}}$$

and hence

$$S_t \frac{\partial N_1}{\partial d_+^{\mathrm{imp}}} - K \frac{\partial N_2}{\partial d_-^{\mathrm{imp}}} = 0.$$

(b) From $d_+^{\mathrm{imp}} - d_-^{\mathrm{imp}} = \sigma_{\mathrm{imp}}\sqrt{T-t}$ and taking partial derivatives with respect to T, we have

$$\frac{\partial d_+^{\mathrm{imp}}}{\partial T} - \frac{\partial d_-^{\mathrm{imp}}}{\partial T} = \frac{\sigma_{\mathrm{imp}}}{2\sqrt{T-t}} + \sqrt{T-t}\frac{\partial \sigma_{\mathrm{imp}}}{\partial T}.$$

(c) From $d_+^{\text{imp}} - d_-^{\text{imp}} = \sigma_{\text{imp}} \sqrt{T - t}$ and taking partial derivatives with respect to K, we have

$$\frac{\partial d_+^{\text{imp}}}{\partial K} - \frac{\partial d_-^{\text{imp}}}{\partial K} = \sqrt{T - t} \frac{\partial \sigma_{\text{imp}}}{\partial K}.$$

(d) From $d_-^{\text{imp}} = \dfrac{\log(S_t/K) + (r - D - \frac{1}{2}\sigma_{\text{imp}}^2)(T - t)}{\sigma_{\text{imp}} \sqrt{T - t}}$ and taking partial derivatives with respect to K, we have

$$\frac{\partial d_-^{\text{imp}}}{\partial K} = \frac{-\sigma_{\text{imp}} \sqrt{T - t} \left(\dfrac{1}{K} + \sigma_{\text{imp}} \dfrac{\partial \sigma_{\text{imp}}}{\partial K}(T - t) \right)}{\sigma_{\text{imp}}^2 (T - t)}$$

$$- \frac{\sqrt{T - t} \dfrac{\partial \sigma_{\text{imp}}}{\partial K} \left(\log(S_t/K) + \left(r - D - \dfrac{1}{2}\sigma_{\text{imp}}^2 \right)(T - t) \right)}{\sigma_{\text{imp}}^2 (T - t)}$$

$$= -\frac{1}{K \sigma_{\text{imp}} \sqrt{T - t}} - \sqrt{T - t} \frac{\partial \sigma_{\text{imp}}}{\partial K} - \frac{d_-^{\text{imp}}}{\sigma_{\text{imp}}} \frac{\partial \sigma_{\text{imp}}}{\partial K}$$

$$= -\frac{1}{K \sigma_{\text{imp}} \sqrt{T - t}} - \left(\frac{d_-^{\text{imp}}}{\sigma_{\text{imp}}} + \sqrt{T - t} \right) \frac{\partial \sigma_{\text{imp}}}{\partial K}.$$

Using the above information,

$$\frac{\partial C}{\partial T} = -DS_t e^{-D(T-t)} \Phi(d_+^{\text{imp}}) + S_t e^{-D(T-t)} \Phi'(d_+^{\text{imp}}) \frac{\partial d_+^{\text{imp}}}{\partial T}$$

$$+ rKe^{-r(T-t)} \Phi(d_-^{\text{imp}}) - Ke^{-r(T-t)} \Phi'(d_-^{\text{imp}}) \frac{\partial d_-^{\text{imp}}}{\partial T}$$

$$= -DS_t N_1 + rK N_2 + S_t \frac{\partial N_1}{\partial d_+^{\text{imp}}} \frac{\partial d_+^{\text{imp}}}{\partial T} - K \frac{\partial N_2}{\partial d_-^{\text{imp}}} \frac{\partial d_-^{\text{imp}}}{\partial T}$$

$$= -DS_t N_1 + rK N_2 + K \frac{\partial N_2}{\partial d_-^{\text{imp}}} \left(\frac{\partial d_+^{\text{imp}}}{\partial T} - \frac{\partial d_-^{\text{imp}}}{\partial T} \right)$$

$$= -DS_t N_1 + rK N_2 + K \frac{\partial N_2}{\partial d_-^{\text{imp}}} \left(\frac{\sigma_{\text{imp}}}{2\sqrt{T - t}} + \sqrt{T - t} \frac{\partial \sigma_{\text{imp}}}{\partial T} \right)$$

$$(r-D)K\frac{\partial C}{\partial K} = (r-D)K\left[S_t e^{-D(T-t)}\Phi'(d_+^{\text{imp}})\frac{\partial d_+^{\text{imp}}}{\partial K} - e^{-r(T-t)}\Phi(d_-^{\text{imp}})\right.$$

$$\left. -Ke^{-r(T-t)}\Phi'(d_-^{\text{imp}})\frac{\partial d_-^{\text{imp}}}{\partial K}\right]$$

$$= (r-D)K\left[Ke^{-r(T-t)}\Phi'(d_-^{\text{imp}})\left(\frac{\partial d_+^{\text{imp}}}{\partial K} - \frac{\partial d_-^{\text{imp}}}{\partial K}\right)\right.$$

$$\left. -e^{-r(T-t)}\Phi(d_-^{\text{imp}})\right]$$

$$= (r-D)K^2\frac{\partial N_2}{\partial d_-^{\text{imp}}}\sqrt{T-t}\frac{\partial \sigma_{\text{imp}}}{\partial K} - (r-D)KN_2$$

$$DC(S_t,t;K,T) = DS_t N_1 - DKN_2$$

and

$$K^2\frac{\partial^2 C}{\partial K^2} = K^2\left[\frac{\partial}{\partial K}\left(K\frac{\partial N_2}{\partial d_-^{\text{imp}}}\sqrt{T-t}\frac{\partial \sigma_{\text{imp}}}{\partial K} - N_2\right)\right]$$

$$= K^2\left[\frac{\partial N_2}{\partial d_-}\sqrt{T-t}\frac{\partial \sigma_{\text{imp}}}{\partial K} - Kd_-^{\text{imp}}\frac{\partial N_2}{\partial d_-^{\text{imp}}}\frac{\partial d_-^{\text{imp}}}{\partial K}\sqrt{T-t}\frac{\partial \sigma_{\text{imp}}}{\partial K}\right.$$

$$\left. +K\frac{\partial N_2}{\partial d_-^{\text{imp}}}\sqrt{T-t}\frac{\partial^2 \sigma_{\text{imp}}}{\partial K^2} - \frac{\partial N_2}{\partial d_-^{\text{imp}}}\frac{\partial d_-^{\text{imp}}}{\partial K}\right]$$

$$= K^2\frac{\partial N_2}{\partial d_-^{\text{imp}}}\left[\sqrt{T-t}\frac{\partial \sigma_{\text{imp}}}{\partial K} - K\sqrt{T-t}d_-^{\text{imp}}\frac{\partial d_-^{\text{imp}}}{\partial K}\frac{\partial \sigma_{\text{imp}}}{\partial K}\right.$$

$$\left. +K\sqrt{T-t}\frac{\partial^2 \sigma_{\text{imp}}}{\partial K^2} - \frac{\partial d_-^{\text{imp}}}{\partial K}\right]$$

$$= K^2\frac{\partial N_2}{\partial d_-^{\text{imp}}}\left[\sqrt{T-t}\frac{\partial \sigma_{\text{imp}}}{\partial K} + K\sqrt{T-t}\frac{\partial^2 \sigma_{\text{imp}}}{\partial K^2}\right.$$

$$\left. +\left(Kd_-^{\text{imp}}\sqrt{T-t}\frac{\partial \sigma_{\text{imp}}}{\partial K} + 1\right)\left(\frac{1}{K\sigma_{\text{imp}}\sqrt{T-t}} + \left(\frac{d_-^{\text{imp}}}{\sigma_{\text{imp}}} + \sqrt{T-t}\right)\frac{\partial \sigma_{\text{imp}}}{\partial K}\right)\right]$$

$$= K^2\frac{\partial N_2}{\partial d_-^{\text{imp}}}\left[2\left(\frac{d_-^{\text{imp}}}{\sigma_{\text{imp}}} + \sqrt{T-t}\right)\frac{\partial \sigma_{\text{imp}}}{\partial K} + K\sqrt{T-t}\frac{\partial^2 \sigma_{\text{imp}}}{\partial K^2}\right.$$

$$\left. +Kd_-^{\text{imp}}\sqrt{T-t}\left(\frac{d_-^{\text{imp}}}{\sigma_{\text{imp}}} + \sqrt{T-t}\right)\left(\frac{\partial \sigma_{\text{imp}}}{\partial K}\right)^2 + \frac{1}{K\sigma_{\text{imp}}\sqrt{T-t}}\right]$$

$$
= K^2 \frac{\partial N_2}{\partial d_-^{\text{imp}}} \left[\frac{2d_+^{\text{imp}}}{\sigma_{\text{imp}}} \frac{\partial \sigma_{\text{imp}}}{\partial K} + K\sqrt{T-t} \frac{\partial^2 \sigma_{\text{imp}}}{\partial K^2} \right.
$$

$$
\left. + K \left(\frac{d_+^{\text{imp}} d_-^{\text{imp}}}{\sigma_{\text{imp}}} \right) \sqrt{T-t} \left(\frac{\partial \sigma_{\text{imp}}}{\partial K} \right)^2 + \frac{1}{K \sigma_{\text{imp}} \sqrt{T-t}} \right]
$$

$$
= K \frac{\partial N_2}{\partial d_-} \sqrt{T-t} \left[K^2 \frac{\partial^2 \sigma_{\text{imp}}}{\partial K^2} + \frac{2K d_+^{\text{imp}}}{\sigma_{\text{imp}} \sqrt{T-t}} \frac{\partial \sigma_{\text{imp}}}{\partial K} \right.
$$

$$
\left. + \frac{K^2 d_+^{\text{imp}} d_-^{\text{imp}}}{\sigma_{\text{imp}}} \left(\frac{\partial \sigma_{\text{imp}}}{\partial K} \right)^2 + \frac{1}{\sigma_{\text{imp}} \sqrt{T-t}} \right].
$$

Gathering all this information, we have

$$
\sigma(K,T)^2 = \frac{2 \left(\dfrac{\partial \sigma_{\text{imp}}}{\partial T} + (r-D)K \dfrac{\partial \sigma_{\text{imp}}}{\partial K} + \dfrac{1}{2} \dfrac{\sigma_{\text{imp}}}{T-t} \right)}{K^2 \dfrac{\partial^2 \sigma_{\text{imp}}}{\partial K^2} + \dfrac{2K d_+^{\text{imp}}}{\sigma_{\text{imp}} \sqrt{T-t}} \dfrac{\partial \sigma_{\text{imp}}}{\partial K} + \dfrac{K^2 d_+^{\text{imp}} d_-^{\text{imp}}}{\sigma_{\text{imp}}} \left(\dfrac{\partial \sigma_{\text{imp}}}{\partial K} \right)^2 + \dfrac{1}{\sigma_{\text{imp}} \sqrt{T-t}}}.
$$

$\square$

7.2.3 Stochastic Volatility

1. *Generalised Stochastic Volatility Model.* Let $\{W_t^S : t \geq 0\}$ and $\{W_t^Y : t \geq 0\}$ be two correlated $\mathbb{P}$-standard Wiener processes on the probability space $(\Omega, \mathcal{F}, \mathbb{P})$. Suppose we have a stochastic volatility model having the following diffusion processes

$$
dS_t = \mu(S_t, Y_t, t)S_t dt + \sigma(Y_t, t)S_t dW_t^S
$$
$$
dY_t = \alpha(S_t, Y_t, t)dt + \beta(S_t, Y_t, t)dW_t^Y
$$
$$
dW_t^S \cdot dW_t^Y = \rho dt
$$

where S_t is the asset price which pays no dividends, $\sigma(Y_t, t)$ is the volatility process, $\mu(S_t, Y_t, t)$, $\alpha(S_t, Y_t, t)$ and $\beta(S_t, Y_t, t)$ are continuous functions and $\rho \in (-1, 1)$ is the correlation. In addition, let B_t be a risk-free asset having the following differential equation

$$
dB_t = r B_t dt
$$

where r is a constant risk-free interest rate.

By defining $\{W_t : t \geq 0\}$ as a standard Wiener process where $W_t \perp\!\!\!\perp W_t^Y$, show that we can write

$$
W_t^S = \rho W_t^Y + \sqrt{1-\rho^2} W_t.
$$

Using the two-dimensional Girsanov's theorem, show that under the risk-neutral measure $\mathbb{Q}$,

$$dS_t = rS_t dt + \sigma(Y_t,t)S_t \left(\rho d\widetilde{W}_t^Y + \sqrt{1-\rho^2} d\widetilde{W}_t \right)$$
$$dY_t = \left[\alpha(S_t,Y_t,t) - \gamma_t \beta(S_t,Y_t,t) \right] dt + \beta(S_t,Y_t,t) d\widetilde{W}_t^Y$$

where $\widetilde{W}_t$ and $\widetilde{W}_t^Y$ are $\mathbb{Q}$-standard Wiener processes and γ_t is the market price of volatility risk.

Solution: For the first part of the solution, from $W_t^S = \rho W_t^Y + \sqrt{1-\rho^2} W_t$ we have

$$\mathbb{E}(W_t^S) = \mathbb{E}(\rho W_t^Y + \sqrt{1-\rho^2} W_t) = \rho \mathbb{E}(W_t^Y) + \sqrt{1-\rho^2} \mathbb{E}(W_t) = 0$$

and

$$\text{Var}(W_t^S) = \text{Var}(\rho W_t^Y + \sqrt{1-\rho^2} W_t) = \rho^2 \text{Var}(W_t^Y) + (1-\rho^2)\text{Var}(W_t) = t.$$

Given both $W_t^Y \sim \mathcal{N}(0,t)$, $W_t \sim \mathcal{N}(0,t)$ and $W_t^Y \perp\!\!\!\perp W_t$ therefore

$$\rho W_t^Y + \sqrt{1-\rho^2} W_t \sim \mathcal{N}(0,t).$$

In addition, using Itō's formula and taking note that $W_t^Y \perp\!\!\!\perp W_t$,

$$\begin{aligned}
dW_t^S \cdot dW_t^Y &= d(\rho W_t^Y + \sqrt{1-\rho^2} W_t) \cdot dW_t^Y \\
&= (\rho dW_t^Y + \sqrt{1-\rho^2} dW_t) \cdot dW_t^Y \\
&= \rho (dW_t^Y)^2 + \sqrt{1-\rho^2} dW_t \cdot dW_t^Y \\
&= \rho dt.
\end{aligned}$$

Thus, we can write $W_t^S = \rho W_t^Y + \sqrt{1-\rho^2} W_t$.

Under the $\mathbb{P}$-measure we have

$$dS_t = \mu(S_t,Y_t,t)S_t dt + \sigma(Y_t,t)S_t \left(\sqrt{1-\rho^2} dW_t + \rho dW_t^Y \right)$$
$$dY_t = \alpha(S_t,Y_t,t)dt + \beta(S_t,Y_t,t)dW_t^Y$$

and by defining

$$\widetilde{W}_t^Y = W_t^Y + \int_0^t \gamma_u \, du$$

$$\widetilde{W}_t = W_t + \int_0^t \lambda_u \, du$$

where γ_t is the market price of volatility risk and λ_t is the market price of asset price risk, and since $W_t \perp\!\!\!\perp W_t^Y$, therefore $\widetilde{W}_t \perp\!\!\!\perp \widetilde{W}_t^Y$.

From the two-dimensional Girsanov's theorem, there exists a risk-neutral measure $\mathbb{Q}$ on the filtration $\mathcal{F}_s$, $0 \leq s \leq t$ defined by the Radon–Nikodým process

$$\frac{d\mathbb{Q}}{d\mathbb{P}} = Z_t = e^{-\frac{1}{2}\int_0^t \lambda_u^2 du - \int_0^t \lambda_u dW_u} \cdot e^{-\frac{1}{2}\int_0^t \gamma_u^2 du - \int_0^t \gamma_u dW_u^Y}$$

so that $\widetilde{W}_t$ and $\widetilde{W}_t^Y$ are $\mathbb{Q}$-standard Wiener processes and $\widetilde{W}_t \perp\!\!\!\perp \widetilde{W}_t^Y$.

Let $X_t = e^{-rt} S_t$ be the discounted asset price, and from the application of Itō's formula

$$dX_t = \frac{\partial X_t}{\partial t} dt + \frac{\partial X_t}{\partial S_t} dS_t + \frac{1}{2}\frac{\partial^2 X_t}{\partial t^2}(dt)^2 + \frac{1}{2}\frac{\partial^2 X_t}{\partial S_t^2}(dS_t)^2 + \dots$$

$$= -re^{-rt} S_t dt + e^{-rt}\left(\mu(S_t, Y_t, t) S_t dt + \sqrt{1-\rho^2}\sigma(Y_t, t) S_t dW_t \right.$$

$$\left. + \rho\sigma(Y_t, t) S_t dW_t^Y \right)$$

$$= -rX_t dt + \mu(S_t, Y_t, t) X_t dt + \sqrt{1-\rho^2}\sigma(Y_t, t) X_t dW_t + \rho\sigma(Y_t, t) X_t dW_t^Y$$

$$= \sigma(Y_t, t) X_t \left[\left(\frac{\mu(S_t, Y_t, t) - r}{\sigma(Y_t, t)} \right) dt + \sqrt{1-\rho^2} dW_t + \rho dW_t^Y \right]$$

$$= \sigma(Y_t, t) X_t \left[\left(\frac{\mu(S_t, Y_t, t) - r}{\sigma(Y_t, t)} \right) dt + \sqrt{1-\rho^2}\left(d\widetilde{W}_t - \lambda_t dt \right) \right.$$

$$\left. + \rho\left(d\widetilde{W}_t^Y - \gamma_t dt \right) \right]$$

$$= \sigma(Y_t, t) X_t \left[\left\{ \left(\frac{\mu(S_t, Y_t, t) - r}{\sigma(Y_t, t)} \right) - \sqrt{1-\rho^2}\lambda_t - \rho\gamma_t \right\} dt \right.$$

$$\left. + \sqrt{1-\rho^2} d\widetilde{W}_t + \rho d\widetilde{W}_t^Y \right].$$

To ensure that $e^{-rt} S_t$ is a $\mathbb{Q}$-martingale, we therefore set

$$\sqrt{1-\rho^2}\lambda_t + \rho\gamma_t = \frac{\mu(S_t, Y_t, t) - r}{\sigma(Y_t, t)}.$$

Using the above relationship and substituting

$$dW_t = d\widetilde{W}_t - \lambda_t dt$$
$$dW_t^Y = d\widetilde{W}_t^Y - \gamma_t dt$$

into

$$dS_t = \mu(S_t, Y_t, t) S_t dt + \sigma(Y_t, t) S_t \left(\sqrt{1-\rho^2} dW_t + \rho dW_t^Y \right)$$
$$dY_t = \alpha(S_t, Y_t, t) dt + \beta(S_t, Y_t, t) dW_t^Y$$

the asset price under the risk-neutral measure $\mathbb{Q}$ becomes

$$dS_t = \mu(S_t, Y_t, t)S_t dt + \sqrt{1 - \rho^2}\sigma(Y_t, t)S_t \left(d\widetilde{W}_t - \lambda_t dt\right)$$

$$+ \rho\sigma(Y_t, t)S_t \left(d\widetilde{W}_t^Y - \gamma_t dt\right)$$

$$= rS_t dt + \sqrt{1 - \rho^2}\sigma(Y_t, t)S_t d\widetilde{W}_t + \rho\sigma(Y_t, t)S_t d\widetilde{W}_t^Y$$

and the stochastic volatility under the risk-neutral measure $\mathbb{Q}$ is

$$dY_t = \left[\alpha(S_t, Y_t, t) - \gamma_t \beta(S_t, Y_t, t)\right] dt + \beta(S_t, Y_t, t)d\widetilde{W}_t^Y.$$

$\square$

2. *Backward Kolmogorov Equation – Stochastic Volatility Model.* Let $\{W_t^S : t \geq 0\}$ and $\{W_t^\sigma : t \geq 0\}$ be two correlated $\mathbb{P}$-standard Wiener processes on the probability space $(\Omega, \mathcal{F}, \mathbb{P})$ and let the asset price S_t follow a stochastic volatility model with the following SDEs

$$\frac{dS_t}{S_t} = (\mu - D) dt + \sigma_t dW_t^S$$

$$d\sigma_t = \alpha(\sigma_t, t)dt + \beta(\sigma_t, t)dW_t^\sigma$$

$$dW_t^S \cdot dW_t^\sigma = \rho dt$$

where μ is the drift parameter, D is the continuous dividend yield, σ_t is the volatility process, $\alpha(\sigma_t, t)$ and $\beta(\sigma_t, t)$ are continuous functions, $\rho \in (-1, 1)$ is the correlation parameter, and let r be the risk-free interest-rate parameter from the money-market account.

By introducing $\{Z_t : t \geq 0\}$ as a standard Wiener process, independent of W_t^σ, show that we can write

$$W_t^S = \rho W_t^\sigma + \sqrt{1 - \rho^2}Z_t.$$

Using the two-dimensional Girsanov's theorem, show that under the risk-neutral measure $\mathbb{Q}$,

$$dS_t = (r - D)S_t dt + \sigma_t S_t d\widetilde{W}_t^S$$

$$d\sigma_t = \widetilde{\alpha}(\sigma_t, t)dt + \beta(\sigma_t, t)d\widetilde{W}_t^\sigma$$

where $\widetilde{W}_t^S = \rho\widetilde{W}_t^\sigma + \sqrt{1 - \rho^2}\widetilde{Z}_t$, $\widetilde{W}_t^\sigma$ and $\widetilde{Z}_t$ are $\mathbb{Q}$-standard Wiener processes, $\widetilde{W}_t^\sigma \perp\!\!\!\perp \widetilde{Z}_t$ and $\widetilde{\alpha}(\sigma_t, t) = \alpha(\sigma_t, t) - \gamma_t \beta(\sigma_t, t)$ such that γ_t is the market price of volatility risk.

Using Taylor's series, show that for a definite integral of a smooth function $f(x)$,

$$\int_a^b f(u) \, du = f\left(\frac{a+b}{2}\right)(b - a) + O\left((b - a)^3\right)$$

and hence show that under the risk-neutral measure $\mathbb{Q}$,

$$\mathbb{E}^{\mathbb{Q}}\left[S_{t+\Delta t} - S_t \middle| \mathcal{F}_t\right] = (r - D)S_{t+\frac{1}{2}\Delta t}\Delta t + O\left((\Delta t)^3\right)$$

$$\mathbb{E}^{\mathbb{Q}}\left[\sigma_{t+\Delta t} - \sigma_t \middle| \mathcal{F}_t\right] = \tilde{\alpha}\left(\sigma_{t+\frac{1}{2}\Delta t}, t + \frac{1}{2}\Delta t\right)\Delta t + O\left((\Delta t)^2\right)$$

$$\mathbb{E}^{\mathbb{Q}}\left[(S_{t+\Delta t} - S_t)^2 \middle| \mathcal{F}_t\right] = \sigma^2_{t+\frac{1}{2}\Delta t}S^2_{t+\frac{1}{2}\Delta t}\Delta t + O\left((\Delta t)^2\right)$$

$$\mathbb{E}^{\mathbb{Q}}\left[(\sigma_{t+\Delta t} - \sigma_t)^2 \middle| \mathcal{F}_t\right] = \beta\left(\sigma_{t+\frac{1}{2}\Delta t}, t + \frac{1}{2}\Delta t\right)^2\Delta t + O\left((\Delta t)^2\right)$$

$$\mathbb{E}^{\mathbb{Q}}\left[(S_{t+\Delta t} - S_t)(\sigma_{t+\Delta t} - \sigma_t) \middle| \mathcal{F}_t\right] = \rho\beta\left(\sigma_{t+\frac{1}{2}\Delta t}, t + \frac{1}{2}\Delta t\right)\sigma_{t+\frac{1}{2}\Delta t}S_{t+\frac{1}{2}\Delta t}\Delta t$$
$$+ O\left((\Delta t)^2\right)$$

$$\mathbb{E}^{\mathbb{Q}}\left[(S_{t+\Delta t} - S_t)^3 \middle| \mathcal{F}_t\right] = O\left((\Delta t)^2\right)$$

$$\mathbb{E}^{\mathbb{Q}}\left[(S_{t+\Delta t} - S_t)^2(\sigma_{t+\Delta t} - \sigma_t) \middle| \mathcal{F}_t\right] = O\left((\Delta t)^2\right)$$

$$\mathbb{E}^{\mathbb{Q}}\left[(S_{t+\Delta t} - S_t)(\sigma_{t+\Delta t} - \sigma_t)^2 \middle| \mathcal{F}_t\right] = O\left((\Delta t)^2\right)$$

$$\mathbb{E}^{\mathbb{Q}}\left[(\sigma_{t+\Delta t} - \sigma_t)^3 \middle| \mathcal{F}_t\right] = O\left((\Delta t)^2\right)$$

for $\Delta t > 0$.

Let $p(S_t, \sigma_t, t; S_T, \sigma_T, T)$ be the transition pdf of the asset price, where the asset price and volatility are S_t and σ_t at time t, respectively given that the asset price and volatility are S_T and σ_T at time $T > t$, respectively. From the Chapman–Kolmogorov equation for $\Delta t > 0$,

$$p(S_t, \sigma_t, t - \Delta t; S_T, \sigma_T, T) = \int_0^\infty \int_0^\infty p(S_t, \sigma_t, t - \Delta t; x, y, t)p(x, y, t; S_T, \sigma_T, T)\, dx\, dy$$

show that by expanding $p(x, y, t; S_T, \sigma_T, T)$ using Taylor series centred on S_t and σ_t up to second order and taking limits $\Delta t \to 0$, $p(S_t, \sigma_t, t; S_T, \sigma_T, T)$ satisfies the backward Kolmogorov equation

$$\frac{\partial}{\partial t}p(S_t, \sigma_t, t; S_T, \sigma_T, T) + \frac{1}{2}\sigma_t^2 S_t^2 \frac{\partial^2}{\partial S_t^2}p(S_t, \sigma_t, t; S_T, \sigma_T, T)$$

$$+ \frac{1}{2}\beta(\sigma_t, t)^2 \frac{\partial^2}{\partial \sigma_t^2}p(S_t, \sigma_t, t; S_T, \sigma_T, T) + \rho\beta(\sigma_t, t)\sigma_t S_t \frac{\partial^2}{\partial \sigma_t \partial S_t}p(S_t, \sigma_t, t; S_T, \sigma_T, T)$$

$$+ (r - D)S_t \frac{\partial}{\partial S_t}p(S_t, \sigma_t, t; S_T, \sigma_T, T) + \tilde{\alpha}(\sigma_t, t)\frac{\partial}{\partial \sigma_t}p(S_t, \sigma_t, t; S_T, \sigma_T, T) = 0$$

with boundary condition

$$p(S_t, \sigma_t, t; S_T, \sigma_T, t) = \delta(S_t - S_T)\delta(\sigma_t - \sigma_T), \quad \forall t.$$

Note that if $\{W_t : t \geq 0\}$ *and* $\{B_t : t \geq 0\}$ *are two correlated standard Wiener processes on the probability space* $(\Omega, \mathcal{F}, \mathbb{P})$ *with correlation* $\rho \in (-1, 1)$, *and if* f *and* g *are simple processes, then the covariance between the Itō integrals*

$$I_t = \int_0^t f(W_s, s) \, dW_s \text{ and } J_t = \int_0^t g(B_s, s) \, dB_s$$

is

$$\mathbb{E}\left[\left(\int_0^t f(W_s, s) \, dW_s\right)\left(\int_0^t g(B_s, s) \, dB_s\right)\right]$$

$$= \mathbb{E}\left(\int_0^t f(W_s, s) g(B_s, s) \, d\langle W, B\rangle_s\right)$$

$$= \rho \mathbb{E}\left(\int_0^t f(W_s, s) g(B_s, s) \, ds\right)$$

where

$$\langle W, B\rangle_t = \lim_{n\to\infty} \sum_{i=0}^{n-1}(W_{t_{i+1}} - W_{t_i})(B_{t_{i+1}} - B_{t_i})$$

such that $t_i = it/n$, $0 = t_0 < t_1 < t_2 < \cdots < t_{n-1} < t_n = t$, $n \in \mathbb{N}$.

Solution: To show that we can set $W_t^S = \rho W_t^\sigma + \sqrt{1 - \rho^2} Z_t$, $Z_t \perp\!\!\!\perp W_t^\sigma$, see Problem 7.2.2.1 (page 685).

We define

$$\widetilde{Z}_t = Z_t + \int_0^t \lambda_u \, du$$

$$\widetilde{W}_t^\sigma = W_t^\sigma + \int_0^t \gamma_u \, du$$

where λ_t is the market price of asset risk and γ_t is the market price of volatility risk. Since $Z_t \perp\!\!\!\perp W_t^\sigma$, we can easily deduce that $\widetilde{Z}_t \perp\!\!\!\perp \widetilde{W}_t^\sigma$.

Let the portfolio Π_t be defined as

$$\Pi_t = \phi_t S_t + \psi_t B_t$$

where ϕ_t units are invested in risky asset S_t and ψ_t units are invested in risk-free asset B_t. Given that the holder of the portfolio will receive $DS_t dt$ for every risky asset held, thus

$$d\Pi_t = \phi_t\left(dS_t + DS_t dt\right) + \psi_t d B_t$$

$$= \phi_t\left(\mu S_t dt + \sigma_t S_t dW_t^S\right) + \psi_t\left(r B_t dt\right)$$

$$= r\Pi_t dt + \phi_t S_t\left[(\mu - r)dt + \sigma_t\left(\rho dW_t^\sigma + \sqrt{1 - \rho^2} dZ_t\right)\right].$$

By substituting

$$dW_t^\sigma = d\widetilde{W}_t^\sigma - \gamma_t dt$$
$$dZ_t = d\widetilde{Z}_t - \lambda_t dt$$

into $d\Pi_t$ we have

$$d\Pi_t = r\Pi_t dt$$
$$+ \phi_t S_t \left[(\mu - r)dt + \sigma_t \left(\rho d\widetilde{W}_t^\sigma - \rho\gamma_t dt + \sqrt{1 - \rho^2} d\widetilde{Z}_t - \sqrt{1 - \rho^2}\lambda_t dt \right) \right]$$
$$= r\Pi_t dt$$
$$+ \phi_t S_t \left[\left(\mu - r - \left(\rho\gamma_t + \sqrt{1 - \rho^2}\lambda_t \right) \sigma_t \right) dt + \sigma_t \left(\rho d\widetilde{W}_t^\sigma + \sqrt{1 - \rho^2} d\widetilde{Z}_t \right) \right].$$

Since $\widetilde{W}_t^\sigma$ and $\widetilde{Z}_t$ are $\mathbb{Q}$-martingales, and in order for the discounted portfolio $e^{-rt}\Pi_t$ to be a $\mathbb{Q}$-martingale,

$$d(e^{-rt}\Pi_t) = -r e^{-rt}\Pi_t dt + e^{-rt} d\Pi_t$$
$$= e^{-rt}\phi_t S_t \left[\left(\mu - r - \left(\rho\gamma_t + \sqrt{1 - \rho^2}\lambda_t \right) \sigma_t \right) dt \right.$$
$$\left. + \sigma_t \left(\rho d\widetilde{W}_t^\sigma + \sqrt{1 - \rho^2} d\widetilde{Z}_t \right) \right]$$

we set

$$\rho\gamma_t + \sqrt{1 - \rho^2}\lambda_t = \frac{\mu - r}{\sigma_t}.$$

Hence, by substituting

$$dW_t^\sigma = d\widetilde{W}_t^\sigma - \gamma_t dt$$
$$dZ_t = d\widetilde{Z}_t - \lambda_t dt$$
$$\rho\gamma_t + \sqrt{1 - \rho^2}\lambda_t = \frac{\mu - r}{\sigma_t}$$

into $dS_t = (\mu - D)S_t dt + \sigma_t S_t \left(\rho dW_t^\sigma + \sqrt{1 - \rho^2} dZ_t \right)$, we have

$$dS_t = (\mu - D)S_t dt + \sigma_t S_t \left(\rho d\widetilde{W}_t^\sigma - \rho\gamma_t dt + \sqrt{1 - \rho^2} d\widetilde{Z}_t - \sqrt{1 - \rho^2}\lambda_t dt \right)$$
$$= (\mu - D)S_t dt + \sigma_t S_t \left(\rho d\widetilde{W}_t^\sigma + \sqrt{1 - \rho^2} d\widetilde{Z}_t \right) - \sigma_t S_t \left(\rho\gamma_t + \sqrt{1 - \rho^2}\lambda_t \right) dt$$
$$= (\mu - D)S_t dt + \sigma_t S_t \left(\rho d\widetilde{W}_t^\sigma + \sqrt{1 - \rho^2} d\widetilde{Z}_t \right) - \sigma_t S_t \left(\frac{\mu - r}{\sigma_t} \right) dt$$
$$= (r - D)S_t dt + \sigma_t S_t \left(\rho d\widetilde{W}_t^\sigma + \sqrt{1 - \rho^2} d\widetilde{Z}_t \right)$$
$$= (r - D)S_t dt + \sigma_t S_t d\widetilde{W}_t^S.$$

In contrast, by substituting

$$dW_t^\sigma = d\widetilde{W}_t^\sigma - \gamma_t dt$$

into $d\sigma_t = \alpha(\sigma_t, t)dt + \beta(\sigma_t, t)dW_t^\sigma$, the instantaneous volatility under the $\mathbb{Q}$ measure becomes

$$
\begin{aligned}
d\sigma_t &= \alpha(\sigma_t, t)dt + \beta(\sigma_t, t)\left(d\widetilde{W}_t^\sigma - \gamma_t dt\right) \\
&= \left(\alpha(\sigma_t, t) - \gamma_t \beta(\sigma_t, t)\right)dt + \beta(\sigma_t, t)d\widetilde{W}_t^\sigma \\
&= \widetilde{\alpha}(\sigma_t, t)dt + \beta(\sigma_t, t)d\widetilde{W}_t^\sigma
\end{aligned}
$$

where $\widetilde{\alpha}(\sigma_t, t) = \alpha(\sigma_t, t) - \gamma_t \beta(\sigma_t, t)$.

To show that

$$\int_a^b f(u)\, du = f\left(\frac{a+b}{2}\right)(b-a) + O\left((b-a)^3\right)$$

for a smooth function f, see Problem 7.2.2.2 (see page 687).

From

$$
\begin{aligned}
dS_t &= (r - D)S_t dt + \sigma_t S_t d\widetilde{W}_t^S \\
d\sigma_t &= \widetilde{\alpha}(\sigma_t, t)dt + \beta(\sigma_t, t)d\widetilde{W}_t^\sigma \\
d\widetilde{W}_t^S \cdot d\widetilde{W}_t^\sigma &= \rho dt
\end{aligned}
$$

and taking integrals

$$
\begin{aligned}
\int_t^{t+\Delta t} dS_u &= \int_t^{t+\Delta t} (r-D)S_u\, du + \int_t^{t+\Delta t} \sigma_u S_u\, d\widetilde{W}_u^S \\
\int_t^{t+\Delta t} d\sigma_u &= \int_t^{t+\Delta t} \widetilde{\alpha}(\sigma_u, u)\, du + \int_t^{t+\Delta t} \beta(\sigma_u, u)\, d\widetilde{W}_u^\sigma
\end{aligned}
$$

we have

$$
\begin{aligned}
S_{t+\Delta t} - S_t &= \int_t^{t+\Delta t} (r-D)S_u\, du + \int_t^{t+\Delta t} \sigma_u S_u\, d\widetilde{W}_u^S \\
\sigma_{t+\Delta t} - \sigma_t &= \int_t^{t+\Delta t} \widetilde{\alpha}(\sigma_u, u)\, du + \int_t^{t+\Delta t} \beta(\sigma_u, u)\, d\widetilde{W}_u^\sigma.
\end{aligned}
$$

Taking expectations, using the approximate integral formula and Itō calculus,

$$
\begin{aligned}
\mathbb{E}^{\mathbb{Q}}\left[S_{t+\Delta t} - S_t \,|\, \mathcal{F}_t\right] &= (r-D)\int_t^{t+\Delta t} S_u\, du + \mathbb{E}^{\mathbb{Q}}\left[\int_t^{t+\Delta t} \sigma_u S_u\, d\widetilde{W}_u^S \,\Big|\, \mathcal{F}_t\right] \\
&= (r-D)S_{t+\frac{1}{2}\Delta t}\Delta t + O((\Delta t)^3)
\end{aligned}
$$

$$\mathbb{E}^{Q}\left[\sigma_{t+\Delta t} - \sigma_{t}\middle|\mathcal{F}_{t}\right] = \int_{t}^{t+\Delta t}\widetilde{\alpha}(\sigma_{u}, u)\,du + \mathbb{E}^{Q}\left[\int_{t}^{t+\Delta t}\beta(\sigma_{u}, u)d\widetilde{W}_{u}^{\sigma}\middle|\mathcal{F}_{t}\right]$$

$$= \widetilde{\alpha}\left(\sigma_{t+\frac{1}{2}\Delta t}, t + \frac{1}{2}\Delta t\right)\Delta t + O((\Delta t)^{3})$$

$$\mathbb{E}^{Q}\left[(S_{t+\Delta t} - S_{t})^{2}\middle|\mathcal{F}_{t}\right] = (r - D)^{2}\left(\int_{t}^{t+\Delta t}S_{u}\,du\right)^{2}$$

$$+ 2(r - D)\left(\int_{t}^{t+\Delta t}S_{u}\,du\right)\mathbb{E}^{Q}\left[\int_{t}^{t+\Delta t}\sigma_{u}S_{u}\,d\widetilde{W}_{u}^{S}\middle|\mathcal{F}_{t}\right]$$

$$+ \mathbb{E}^{Q}\left[\left(\int_{t}^{t+\Delta t}\sigma_{u}S_{u}\,d\widetilde{W}_{u}^{S}\right)^{2}\middle|\mathcal{F}_{t}\right]$$

$$= (r - D)^{2}\left(\int_{t}^{t+\Delta t}S_{u}\,du\right)^{2} + \int_{t}^{t+\Delta t}\sigma_{u}^{2}S_{u}^{2}\,du$$

$$= \sigma_{t+\frac{1}{2}\Delta t}^{2}S_{t+\frac{1}{2}\Delta t}^{2}\Delta t + O((\Delta t)^{2})$$

$$\mathbb{E}^{Q}\left[(\sigma_{t+\Delta t} - \sigma_{t})^{2}\middle|\mathcal{F}_{t}\right] = \left(\int_{t}^{t+\Delta t}\widetilde{\alpha}(\sigma_{u}, u)\,du\right)^{2}$$

$$+ 2\left(\int_{t}^{t+\Delta t}\widetilde{\alpha}(\sigma_{u}, u)\,du\right)\mathbb{E}^{Q}\left[\int_{t}^{t+\Delta t}\beta(\sigma_{u}, u)\,d\widetilde{W}_{u}^{\sigma}\middle|\mathcal{F}_{t}\right]$$

$$+ \mathbb{E}^{Q}\left[\left(\int_{t}^{t+\Delta t}\beta(\sigma_{u}, u)\,d\widetilde{W}_{u}^{\sigma}\right)^{2}\middle|\mathcal{F}_{t}\right]$$

$$= \left(\int_{t}^{t+\Delta t}\widetilde{\alpha}(\sigma_{u}, u)\,du\right)^{2} + \int_{t}^{t+\Delta t}\beta(\sigma_{u}, u)^{2}\,du$$

$$= \beta\left(\sigma_{t+\frac{1}{2}\Delta t}, t + \frac{1}{2}\Delta t\right)^{2}\Delta t + O((\Delta t)^{2})$$

$$\mathbb{E}^{Q}\left[(S_{t+\Delta t} - S_{t})(\sigma_{t+\Delta t} - \sigma_{t})\middle|\mathcal{F}_{t}\right]$$

$$= (r - D)\left(\int_{t}^{t+\Delta t}S_{u}\,du\right)\left(\int_{t}^{t+\Delta t}\widetilde{\alpha}(\sigma_{u}, u)\,du\right)$$

$$+ (r - D)\left(\int_{t}^{t+\Delta t}S_{u}\,du\right)\mathbb{E}^{Q}\left[\int_{t}^{t+\Delta t}\beta(\sigma_{u}, u)\,d\widetilde{W}_{u}^{\sigma}\middle|\mathcal{F}_{t}\right]$$

$$+ \left(\int_{t}^{t+\Delta t}\widetilde{\alpha}(\sigma_{u}, u)\,du\right)\mathbb{E}^{Q}\left[\int_{t}^{t+\Delta t}\sigma_{u}S_{u}\,d\widetilde{W}_{u}^{S}\middle|\mathcal{F}_{t}\right]$$

$$+ \mathbb{E}^{Q}\left[\left(\int_{t}^{t+\Delta t}\sigma_{u}S_{u}\,d\widetilde{W}_{u}^{S}\right)\left(\int_{t}^{t+\Delta t}\beta(\sigma_{u}, u)\,d\widetilde{W}_{u}^{\sigma}\right)\middle|\mathcal{F}_{t}\right]$$

$$= (r - D)\left(\int_{t}^{t+\Delta t}S_{u}\,du\right)\left(\int_{t}^{t+\Delta t}\widetilde{\alpha}(\sigma_{u}, u)\,du\right)$$

$$+\mathbb{E}^{\mathbb{Q}}\left[\left(\int_t^{t+\Delta t}\sigma_u\beta(\sigma_u,u)S_u\,d\langle\widetilde{W}^S,\widetilde{W}^\sigma\rangle_u\right)\middle|\mathcal{F}_t\right]$$

$$=(r-D)\left(\int_t^{t+\Delta t}S_u\,du\right)\left(\int_t^{t+\Delta t}\widetilde{\alpha}(\sigma_u,u)\,du\right)+\rho\int_t^{t+\Delta t}\sigma_u\beta(\sigma_u,u)S_u\,du$$

$$=\rho\beta\left(\sigma_{t+\frac{1}{2}\Delta t},t+\frac{1}{2}\Delta t\right)\sigma_{t+\frac{1}{2}\Delta t}S_{t+\frac{1}{2}\Delta t}\Delta t+O((\Delta t)^2)$$

$$\mathbb{E}^{\mathbb{Q}}\left[(S_{t+\Delta t}-S_t)^3\middle|\mathcal{F}_t\right]$$

$$=(r-D)^3\left(\int_t^{t+\Delta t}S_u\,du\right)^3$$

$$+3(r-D)^2\left(\int_t^{t+\Delta t}S_u\,du\right)^2\mathbb{E}^{\mathbb{Q}}\left[\int_t^{t+\Delta t}\sigma_uS_u\,dW_u^S\middle|\mathcal{F}_t\right]$$

$$+3(r-D)\left(\int_t^{t+\Delta t}S_u\,du\right)\left(\int_t^{t+\Delta t}\sigma_u^2S_u^2\,du\right)$$

$$+\left(\int_t^{t+\Delta t}\sigma_u^2S_u^2\,du\right)\mathbb{E}^{\mathbb{Q}}\left[\int_t^{t+\Delta t}\sigma_uS_u\,dW_u^S\middle|\mathcal{F}_t\right]$$

$$=O((\Delta t)^2)$$

$$\mathbb{E}^{\mathbb{Q}}\left[(S_{t+\Delta t}-S_t)^2\left(\sigma_{t+\Delta t}-\sigma_t\right)\middle|\mathcal{F}_t\right]$$

$$=(r-D)^2\left(\int_t^{t+\Delta t}S_u\,du\right)^2\left(\int_t^{t+\Delta t}\widetilde{\alpha}(\sigma_u,u)\,du\right)$$

$$+2(r-D)\left(\int_t^{t+\Delta t}S_u\,du\right)\left(\int_t^{t+\Delta t}\widetilde{\alpha}(\sigma_u,u)\,du\right)$$

$$\times\mathbb{E}^{\mathbb{Q}}\left[\int_t^{t+\Delta t}\sigma_uS_u\,dW_u^S\middle|\mathcal{F}_t\right]$$

$$+\left(\int_t^{t+\Delta t}\widetilde{\alpha}(\sigma_u,u)\,du\right)\left(\int_t^{t+\Delta t}\sigma_u^2S_u^2\,du\right)$$

$$+(r-D)^2\left(\int_t^{t+\Delta t}S_u\,du\right)^2\mathbb{E}^{\mathbb{Q}}\left[\left(\int_t^{t+\Delta t}\beta(\sigma_u,u)\,dW_u^\sigma\right)\middle|\mathcal{F}_t\right]$$

$$+2(r-D)\left(\int_t^{t+\Delta t}S_u\,du\right)$$

$$\times\mathbb{E}^{\mathbb{Q}}\left[\left(\int_t^{t+\Delta t}\sigma_uS_u\,dW_u^S\right)\left(\int_t^{t+\Delta t}\beta(\sigma_u,u)\,dW_u^\sigma\right)\middle|\mathcal{F}_t\right]$$

$$+\left(\int_t^{t+\Delta t}\sigma_u^2S_u^2\,du\right)\mathbb{E}^{\mathbb{Q}}\left[\left(\int_t^{t+\Delta t}\beta(\sigma_u,u)\,dW_u^\sigma\right)\middle|\mathcal{F}_t\right]$$

$$=O((\Delta t)^2)$$

$$\mathbb{E}^{\mathbb{Q}}\left[\left(S_{t+\Delta t}-S_t\right)\left(\sigma_{t+\Delta t}-\sigma_t\right)^2\middle|\mathcal{F}_t\right]$$

$$= (r-D)\left(\int_t^{t+\Delta t} S_u\,du\right)\left(\int_t^{t+\Delta t}\widetilde{\alpha}(\sigma_u,u)\,du\right)^2$$

$$+2(r-D)\left(\int_t^{t+\Delta t} S_u\,du\right)\left(\int_t^{t+\Delta t}\widetilde{\alpha}(\sigma_u,u)\,du\right)$$

$$\times\mathbb{E}^{\mathbb{Q}}\left[\int_t^{t+\Delta t}\beta(\sigma_u,u)\,dW_u^\sigma\middle|\mathcal{F}_t\right]$$

$$+(r-D)\left(\int_t^{t+\Delta t} S_u\,du\right)\left(\int_t^{t+\Delta t}\beta(\sigma_u,u)^2\,du\right)$$

$$+\left(\int_t^{t+\Delta t}\widetilde{\alpha}(\sigma_u,u)\,du\right)^2\mathbb{E}^{\mathbb{Q}}\left[\int_t^{t+\Delta t}\sigma_u S_u\,dW_u^S\middle|\mathcal{F}_t\right]$$

$$+2\left(\int_t^{t+\Delta t}\widetilde{\alpha}(\sigma_u,u)\,du\right)$$

$$\times\mathbb{E}^{\mathbb{Q}}\left[\left(\int_t^{t+\Delta t}\sigma_u S_u\,dW_u^S\right)\left(\int_t^{t+\Delta t}\beta(\sigma_u,u)\,dW_u^\sigma\right)\middle|\mathcal{F}_t\right]$$

$$+\left(\int_t^{t+\Delta t}\beta(\sigma_u,u)^2\,du\right)\mathbb{E}^{\mathbb{Q}}\left[\int_t^{t+\Delta t}\sigma_u S_u\,dW_u^S\middle|\mathcal{F}_t\right]$$

$$= O((\Delta t)^2)$$

and

$$\mathbb{E}^{\mathbb{Q}}\left[\left(\sigma_{t+\Delta t}-\sigma_t\right)^3\middle|\mathcal{F}_t\right]$$

$$= \left(\int_t^{t+\Delta t}\widetilde{\alpha}(\sigma_u,u)\,du\right)^3$$

$$+3\left(\int_t^{t+\Delta t}\widetilde{\alpha}(\sigma_u,u)\,du\right)^2\mathbb{E}^{\mathbb{Q}}\left[\int_t^{t+\Delta t}\beta(\sigma_u,u)\,dW_u^\sigma\middle|\mathcal{F}_t\right]$$

$$+3\left(\int_t^{t+\Delta t}\widetilde{\alpha}(\sigma_u,u)\,du\right)\left(\int_t^{t+\Delta t}\beta(\sigma_u,u)^2\,du\right)$$

$$+\left(\int_t^{t+\Delta t}\beta(\sigma_u,u)^2\,du\right)\mathbb{E}^{\mathbb{Q}}\left[\int_t^{t+\Delta t}\beta(\sigma_u,u)\,dW_u^\sigma\middle|\mathcal{F}_t\right]$$

$$= O((\Delta t)^2).$$

From the Chapman–Kolmogorov equation we have

$$p(S_t,\sigma_t,t-\Delta t;S_T,T)=\int_0^\infty\int_0^\infty p(S_t,\sigma_t,t-\Delta t;x,y,t)p(x,y,t;S_T,\sigma_T,T)\,dy\,dx$$

and expanding $p(x, y, t; S_T, \sigma_T, T)$ using Taylor series centred on S_t and σ_t,

$$
\begin{aligned}
p(x, y, t; S_T, \sigma_T, T) &= p(S_t, \sigma_t, t; S_T, \sigma_T, T) \\
&+ (x - S_t) \frac{\partial}{\partial S_t} p(S_t, \sigma_t, t; S_T, \sigma_T, T) \\
&+ (y - \sigma_t) \frac{\partial}{\partial \sigma_t} p(S_t, \sigma_t, t; S_T, \sigma_T, T) \\
&+ \frac{1}{2}(x - S_t)^2 \frac{\partial^2}{\partial S_t^2} p(S_t, \sigma_t, t; S_T, \sigma_T, T) \\
&+ \frac{1}{2}(y - \sigma_t)^2 \frac{\partial^2}{\partial \sigma_t^2} p(S_t, \sigma_t, t; S_T, \sigma_T, T) \\
&+ (x - S_t)(y - \sigma_t) \frac{\partial^2}{\partial \sigma_t \partial S_t} p(S_t, \sigma_t, t; S_T, \sigma_T, T) \\
&+ O((x - S_t)^3) + O((x - S_t)^2(y - \sigma_t)) \\
&+ O((x - S_t)(y - \sigma_t)^2) + O((y - \sigma_t)^3).
\end{aligned}
$$

Substituting Taylor's expansion into the Chapman–Kolmogorov equation yields

$$
\begin{aligned}
&p(S_t, \sigma_t, t - \Delta t; S_T, T) \\
&= p(S_t, \sigma_t, t; S_T, \sigma_T, T) \int_0^\infty \int_0^\infty p(S_t, \sigma_t, t - \Delta t; x, y, t) \, dy dx \\
&+ \frac{\partial}{\partial S_t} p(S_t, \sigma_t, t; S_T, \sigma_T, T) \int_0^\infty \int_0^\infty (x - S_t) p(S_t, \sigma_t, t - \Delta t; x, y, t) \, dy dx \\
&+ \frac{\partial}{\partial \sigma_t} p(S_t, \sigma_t, t; S_T, \sigma_T, T) \int_0^\infty \int_0^\infty (y - \sigma_t) p(S_t, \sigma_t, t - \Delta t; x, y, t) \, dy dx \\
&+ \frac{1}{2} \frac{\partial^2}{\partial S_t^2} p(S_t, \sigma_t, t; S_T, \sigma_T, T) \int_0^\infty \int_0^\infty (x - S_t)^2 p(S_t, \sigma_t, t - \Delta t; x, y, t) \, dy dx \\
&+ \frac{1}{2} \frac{\partial^2}{\partial \sigma_t^2} p(S_t, \sigma_t, t; S_T, \sigma_T, T) \int_0^\infty \int_0^\infty (y - \sigma_t)^2 p(S_t, \sigma_t, t - \Delta t; x, y, t) \, dy dx \\
&+ \frac{\partial^2}{\partial \sigma_t \partial S_t} p(S_t, \sigma_t, t; S_T, \sigma_T, T) \\
&\times \int_0^\infty \int_0^\infty (x - S_t)(y - \sigma_t) p(S_t, \sigma_t, t - \Delta t; x, y, t) \, dy dx \\
&+ O\left(\int_0^\infty \int_0^\infty (x - S_t)^3 p(S_t, \sigma_t, t - \Delta t; x, y, t) \, dy dx \right) \\
&+ O\left(\int_0^\infty \int_0^\infty (x - S_t)^2(y - \sigma_t) p(S_t, \sigma_t, t - \Delta t; x, y, t) \, dy dx \right) \\
&+ O\left(\int_0^\infty \int_0^\infty (x - S_t)(y - \sigma_t)^2 p(S_t, \sigma_t, t - \Delta t; x, y, t) \, dy dx \right) \\
&+ O\left(\int_0^\infty \int_0^\infty (y - \sigma_t)^3 p(S_t, \sigma_t, t - \Delta t; x, y, t) \, dy dx \right).
\end{aligned}
$$

Since

$$\int_0^\infty \int_0^\infty p(S_t, \sigma_t, t - \Delta t; x, y, t) \, dy \, dx = 1$$

$$\int_0^\infty \int_0^\infty (x - S_t) p(S_t, \sigma_t, t - \Delta t; x, y, t) \, dy \, dx = (r - D) S_{t+\frac{1}{2}\Delta t} \Delta t$$
$$+ O\left((\Delta t)^3\right)$$

$$\int_0^\infty \int_0^\infty (y - \sigma_t) p(S_t, \sigma_t, t - \Delta t; x, y, t) \, dy \, dx = \tilde{\alpha}\left(\sigma_{t+\frac{1}{2}\Delta t}, t + \frac{1}{2}\Delta t\right) \Delta t$$
$$+ O\left((\Delta t)^2\right)$$

$$\int_0^\infty \int_0^\infty (x - S_t)^2 p(S_t, \sigma_t, t - \Delta t; x, y, t) \, dy \, dx = \sigma_{t+\frac{1}{2}\Delta t}^2 S_{t+\frac{1}{2}\Delta t}^2 \Delta t$$
$$+ O\left((\Delta t)^2\right)$$

$$\int_0^\infty \int_0^\infty (y - \sigma_t)^2 p(S_t, \sigma_t, t - \Delta t; x, y, t) \, dy \, dx = \beta\left(\sigma_{t+\frac{1}{2}\Delta t}, t + \frac{1}{2}\Delta t\right)^2 \Delta t$$
$$+ O\left((\Delta t)^2\right)$$

$$\int_0^\infty \int_0^\infty (x - S_t)(y - \sigma_t) p(S_t, \sigma_t, t - \Delta t; x, y, t) \, dy \, dx = \rho\beta\left(\sigma_{t+\frac{1}{2}\Delta t}, t + \frac{1}{2}\Delta t\right)$$
$$\times \sigma_{t+\frac{1}{2}\Delta t} S_{t+\frac{1}{2}\Delta t} \Delta t$$
$$+ O\left((\Delta t)^2\right)$$

$$\int_0^\infty \int_0^\infty (x - S_t)^3 p(S_t, \sigma_t, t - \Delta t; x, y, t) \, dy \, dx = O\left((\Delta t)^2\right)$$

$$\int_0^\infty \int_0^\infty (x - S_t)^2 (y - \sigma_t) p(S_t, \sigma_t, t - \Delta t; x, y, t) \, dy \, dx = O\left((\Delta t)^2\right)$$

$$\int_0^\infty \int_0^\infty (x - S_t)(y - \sigma_t)^2 p(S_t, \sigma_t, t - \Delta t; x, y, t) \, dy \, dx = O\left((\Delta t)^2\right)$$

$$\int_0^\infty \int_0^\infty (y - \sigma_t)^3 p(S_t, \sigma_t, t - \Delta t; x, y, t) \, dy \, dx = O\left((\Delta t)^2\right)$$

then by taking limits $\Delta t \to 0$,

$$\lim_{\Delta t \to 0} \frac{p(S_t, \sigma_t, t - \Delta t; S_T, T) - p(S_t, \sigma_t, t; S_T, \sigma_T, T)}{\Delta t}$$

$$= (r - D) \lim_{\Delta t \to 0} S_{t+\frac{1}{2}\Delta t} \frac{\partial}{\partial S_t} p(S_t, \sigma_t, t; S_T, \sigma_T, T)$$

$$+ \lim_{\Delta t \to 0} \tilde{\alpha}\left(\sigma_{t+\frac{1}{2}\Delta t}, t + \frac{1}{2}\Delta t\right) \frac{\partial}{\partial \sigma_t} p(S_t, \sigma_t, t; S_T, \sigma_T, T)$$

$$+ \frac{1}{2} \lim_{\Delta t \to 0} \sigma_{t+\frac{1}{2}\Delta t}^2 S_{t+\frac{1}{2}\Delta t}^2 \frac{\partial^2}{\partial S_t^2} p(S_t, \sigma_t, t; S_T, \sigma_T, T)$$

$$+ \frac{1}{2} \lim_{\Delta t \to 0} \beta\left(\sigma_{t+\frac{1}{2}\Delta t}, t + \frac{1}{2}\Delta t\right)^2 \frac{\partial^2}{\partial \sigma_t^2} p(S_t, \sigma_t, t; S_T, \sigma_T, T)$$

$$+\rho \lim_{\Delta t \to 0} \beta \left(\sigma_{t+\frac{1}{2}\Delta t}, t + \frac{1}{2}\Delta t \right) \sigma_{t+\frac{1}{2}\Delta t} S_{t+\frac{1}{2}\Delta t} \frac{\partial^2}{\partial S_t \partial \sigma_t} p(S_t, \sigma_t, t; S_T, \sigma_T, T)$$

$$+ \lim_{\Delta t \to 0} O(\Delta t)$$

and hence

$$-\frac{\partial}{\partial t} p(S_t, \sigma_t, t; S_T, \sigma_T, T) = \frac{1}{2} \sigma_t^2 S_t^2 \frac{\partial^2}{\partial S_t^2} p(S_t, \sigma_t, t; S_T, \sigma_T, T)$$

$$+ \frac{1}{2} \beta(\sigma_t, t)^2 \frac{\partial^2}{\partial \sigma_t^2} p(S_t, \sigma_t, t; S_T, \sigma_T, T) + \rho \beta(\sigma_t, t) \sigma_t S_t \frac{\partial^2}{\partial \sigma_t \partial S_t} p(S_t, \sigma_t, t; S_T, \sigma_T, T)$$

$$+ (r - D) S_t \frac{\partial}{\partial S_t} p(S_t, \sigma_t, t; S_T, \sigma_T, T) + \tilde{\alpha}(\sigma_t, t) \frac{\partial}{\partial \sigma_t} p(S_t, \sigma_t, t; S_T, \sigma_T, T)$$

or

$$\frac{\partial}{\partial t} p(S_t, \sigma_t, t; S_T, \sigma_T, T) + \frac{1}{2} \sigma_t^2 S_t^2 \frac{\partial^2}{\partial S_t^2} p(S_t, \sigma_t, t; S_T, \sigma_T, T)$$

$$+ \frac{1}{2} \beta(\sigma_t, t)^2 \frac{\partial^2}{\partial \sigma_t^2} p(S_t, \sigma_t, t; S_T, \sigma_T, T) + \rho \beta(\sigma_t, t) \sigma_t S_t \frac{\partial^2}{\partial \sigma_t \partial S_t} p(S_t, \sigma_t, t; S_T, \sigma_T, T)$$

$$+ (r - D) S_t \frac{\partial}{\partial S_t} p(S_t, \sigma_t, t; S_T, \sigma_T, T) + \tilde{\alpha}(\sigma_t, t) \frac{\partial}{\partial \sigma_t} p(S_t, \sigma_t, t; S_T, \sigma_T, T) = 0$$

with boundary condition

$$p(S_t, \sigma_t, t; S_T, \sigma_T, t) = \delta(S_t - S_T)\delta(\sigma_t - \sigma_T), \forall t.$$

□

3. *Black–Scholes Equation – Stochastic Volatility Model.* Under the risk-neutral measure $\mathbb{Q}$, let $\{\widetilde{W}_t^S : t \geq 0\}$ and $\{\widetilde{W}_t^\sigma : t \geq 0\}$ be two correlated $\mathbb{Q}$-standard Wiener processes on the probability space $(\Omega, \mathcal{F}, \mathbb{Q})$ with correlation $\rho \in (-1, 1)$. Let the asset price S_t under the $\mathbb{Q}$ measure follow a stochastic volatility model with the following dynamics

$$dS_t = (r - D)S_t dt + \sigma_t S_t d\widetilde{W}_t^S$$
$$d\sigma_t = \tilde{\alpha}(\sigma_t, t)dt + \beta(\sigma_t, t)d\widetilde{W}_t^\sigma$$
$$d\widetilde{W}_t^S \cdot d\widetilde{W}_t^\sigma = \rho dt$$

where r is the risk-free interest-rate parameter from the money-market account, D is the continuous dividend yield, σ_t is the volatility process, $\tilde{\alpha}(\sigma_t, t)$ and $\beta(\sigma_t, t)$ are continuous functions.

Let $p(S_t, \sigma_t, t; S_T, \sigma_T, T)$ be the transition pdf of the asset price, where the asset price and volatility are S_t and σ_t at time t, respectively, given that the asset price and volatility are S_T and σ_T at time $T > t$, respectively. We consider a European option written on S_t

with strike price $K > 0$ expiring at time $T > t$ with payoff $\Psi(S_T)$, where the option price at time t under the risk-neutral measure $\mathbb{Q}$ is

$$V(S_t, \sigma_t, t; K, T) = e^{-r(T-t)} \mathbb{E}^{\mathbb{Q}} \left[\Psi(S_T) \mid \mathscr{F}_t \right]$$

$$= e^{-r(T-t)} \int_0^\infty \int_0^\infty \Psi(x) p(S_t, \sigma_t, t; x, y, T) \, dy \, dx.$$

By using the backward Kolmogorov equation, show that $V(S_t, \sigma_t, t; K, T)$ satisfies the two-dimensional Black–Scholes equation

$$\frac{\partial V}{\partial t} + \frac{1}{2} \sigma_t^2 S_t^2 \frac{\partial^2 V}{\partial S_t^2} + \frac{1}{2} \beta(\sigma_t, t)^2 \frac{\partial^2 V}{\partial \sigma_t^2} + \rho \beta(\sigma_t, t) \sigma_t S_t \frac{\partial^2 V}{\partial \sigma_t \partial S_t}$$

$$+ (r - D) S_t \frac{\partial V}{\partial S_t} + \widetilde{\alpha}(\sigma_t, t) \frac{\partial V}{\partial \sigma_t} - rV(S_t, \sigma_t, t; K, T) = 0$$

with boundary condition

$$V(S_T, \sigma_T, T; K, T) = \Psi(S_T).$$

Solution: Given

$$V(S_t, \sigma_t, t; K, T) = e^{-r(T-t)} \int_0^\infty \int_0^\infty \Psi(x) p(S_t, \sigma_t, t; x, y, T) \, dy \, dx$$

by taking first and second-order differentials, we have

$$\frac{\partial V}{\partial t} = re^{-r(T-t)} \int_0^\infty \int_0^\infty \Psi(x) p(S_t, \sigma_t, t; x, y, T) \, dy \, dx$$

$$+ e^{-r(T-t)} \int_0^\infty \int_0^\infty \Psi(x) \frac{\partial}{\partial t} p(S_t, \sigma_t, t; x, y, T) \, dy \, dx$$

$$= re^{-r(T-t)} V(S_t, \sigma_t, t; K, T)$$

$$+ e^{-r(T-t)} \int_0^\infty \int_0^\infty \Psi(x) \frac{\partial}{\partial t} p(S_t, \sigma_t, t; x, y, T) \, dy \, dx$$

$$\frac{\partial V}{\partial S_t} = e^{-r(T-t)} \int_0^\infty \int_0^\infty \Psi(x) \frac{\partial}{\partial S_t} p(S_t, \sigma_t, t; x, y, T) \, dy \, dx$$

$$\frac{\partial V}{\partial \sigma_t} = e^{-r(T-t)} \int_0^\infty \int_0^\infty \Psi(x) \frac{\partial}{\partial \sigma_t} p(S_t, \sigma_t, t; x, y, T) \, dy \, dx$$

$$\frac{\partial^2 V}{\partial S_t^2} = e^{-r(T-t)} \int_0^\infty \int_0^\infty \Psi(x) \frac{\partial^2}{\partial S_t^2} p(S_t, \sigma_t, t; x, y, T) \, dy \, dx$$

$$\frac{\partial^2 V}{\partial \sigma_t^2} = e^{-r(T-t)} \int_0^\infty \int_0^\infty \Psi(x) \frac{\partial^2}{\partial \sigma_t^2} p(S_t, \sigma_t, t; x, y, T) \, dy \, dx$$

$$\frac{\partial^2 V}{\partial \sigma_t \partial S_t} = e^{-r(T-t)} \int_0^\infty \int_0^\infty \Psi(x) \frac{\partial^2}{\partial \sigma_t \partial S_t} p(S_t, \sigma_t, t; x, y, T) \, dy \, dx.$$

From Problem 7.2.3.2 (page 713), the backward Kolmogorov equation satisfied by the transition probability $p(S_t, \sigma_t, t; S_T, \sigma_T, T)$ is

$$\frac{\partial}{\partial t} p(S_t, \sigma_t, t; S_T, \sigma_T, T) + \frac{1}{2} \sigma_t^2 S_t^2 \frac{\partial^2}{\partial S_t^2} p(S_t, \sigma_t, t; S_T, \sigma_T, T)$$

$$+ \frac{1}{2} \beta(\sigma_t, t)^2 \frac{\partial^2}{\partial \sigma_t^2} p(S_t, \sigma_t, t; S_T, \sigma_T, T) + \rho \beta(\sigma_t, t) \sigma_t S_t \frac{\partial^2}{\partial \sigma_t \partial S_t} p(S_t, \sigma_t, t; S_T, \sigma_T, T)$$

$$+ (r - D) S_t \frac{\partial}{\partial S_t} p(S_t, \sigma_t, t; S_T, \sigma_T, T) + \tilde{\alpha}(\sigma_t, t) \frac{\partial}{\partial \sigma_t} p(S_t, \sigma_t, t; S_T, \sigma_T, T) = 0$$

with boundary condition

$$p(S_t, \sigma_t, t; S_T, \sigma_T, T) = \delta(S_t - S_T)\delta(\sigma_t - \sigma_T)$$

for all t.

By multiplying the backward Kolmogorov equation with $\Psi(S_T)$ and taking double integrals we have

$$\int_0^\infty \int_0^\infty \Psi(x) \frac{\partial}{\partial t} p(S_t, \sigma_t, t; x, y, T) \, dy \, dx$$

$$+ \frac{1}{2} \sigma_t^2 S_t^2 \int_0^\infty \int_0^\infty \Psi(x) \frac{\partial^2}{\partial S_t^2} p(S_t, \sigma_t, t; x, y, T) \, dy \, dx$$

$$+ \frac{1}{2} \beta(\sigma_t, t)^2 \int_0^\infty \int_0^\infty \Psi(x) \frac{\partial^2}{\partial \sigma_t^2} p(S_t, \sigma_t, t; x, y, T) \, dy \, dx$$

$$+ \rho \beta(\sigma_t, t) \sigma_t S_t \int_0^\infty \int_0^\infty \Psi(x) \frac{\partial^2}{\partial \sigma_t \partial S_t} p(S_t, \sigma_t, t; x, y, T) \, dy \, dx$$

$$+ (r - D) S_t \int_0^\infty \int_0^\infty \Psi(x) \frac{\partial}{\partial S_t} p(S_t, \sigma_t, t; x, y, T) \, dy \, dx$$

$$+ \tilde{\alpha}(\sigma_t, t) \int_0^\infty \int_0^\infty \Psi(x) \frac{\partial}{\partial \sigma_t} p(S_t, \sigma_t, t; x, y, T) \, dy \, dx = 0.$$

By writing the above equation in terms of $\dfrac{\partial V}{\partial t}, \dfrac{\partial V}{\partial S_t}, \dfrac{\partial V}{\partial \sigma_t}, \dfrac{\partial^2 V}{\partial S_t^2}, \dfrac{\partial^2 V}{\partial \sigma_t^2}$ and $\dfrac{\partial^2 V}{\partial \sigma_t \partial S_t}$ we have

$$e^{-r(T-t)} \left[\frac{\partial V}{\partial t} - rV(S_t, \sigma_t, t; K, T) + \frac{1}{2} \sigma_t^2 S_t^2 \frac{\partial^2 V}{\partial S_t^2} + \frac{1}{2} \beta(\sigma_t, t)^2 \frac{\partial^2 V}{\partial \sigma_t^2} \right.$$

$$\left. + \rho \beta(\sigma_t, t) \sigma_t S_t \frac{\partial^2 V}{\partial \sigma_t \partial S_t} + (r - D) S_t \frac{\partial V}{\partial S_t} + \tilde{\alpha}(\sigma_t, t) \frac{\partial V}{\partial \sigma_t} \right] = 0$$

or

$$\frac{\partial V}{\partial t} + \frac{1}{2}\sigma_t^2 S_t^2 \frac{\partial^2 V}{\partial S_t^2} + \frac{1}{2}\beta(\sigma_t,t)^2 \frac{\partial^2 V}{\partial \sigma_t^2} + \rho\beta(\sigma_t,t)\sigma_t S_t \frac{\partial^2 V}{\partial \sigma_t \partial S_t}$$

$$+(r-D)S_t\frac{\partial V}{\partial S_t} + \widetilde{\alpha}(\sigma_t,t)\frac{\partial V}{\partial \sigma_t} - rV(S_t,\sigma_t,t;K,T) = 0.$$

Finally, for the boundary condition we note that

$$V(S_T,\sigma_T,T;K,T) = \int_0^\infty \int_0^\infty \Psi(x)p(S_T,\sigma_T,T;x,y,T)\,dy\,dx$$

and from the definition of the Dirac delta function,

$$V(S_T,\sigma_T,T;K,T) = \int_0^\infty \int_0^\infty \Psi(x)p(S_T,\sigma_T,T;x,y,T)\,dy\,dx$$

$$= \int_0^\infty \int_0^\infty \Psi(x)\delta(S_T - x)\delta(\sigma_T - y)\,dy\,dx$$

$$= \Psi(S_T).$$

$\square$

4. *Forward Kolmogorov Equation – Stochastic Volatility Model.* Let $\{W_t^S : t \geq 0\}$ and $\{W_t^\sigma : t \geq 0\}$ be two correlated $\mathbb{P}$-standard Wiener processes on the probability space $(\Omega, \mathcal{F}, \mathbb{P})$ and let the asset price S_t follow a stochastic volatility model with the following SDEs

$$\frac{dS_t}{S_t} = (\mu - D)\,dt + \sigma_t dW_t^S$$

$$d\sigma_t = \alpha(\sigma_t,t)dt + \beta(\sigma_t,t)dW_t^\sigma$$

$$dW_t^S \cdot dW_t^\sigma = \rho dt$$

where μ is the drift parameter, D is the continuous dividend yield, σ_t is the volatility process, $\alpha(\sigma_t,t)$ and $\beta(\sigma_t,t)$ are continuous functions, $\rho \in (-1,1)$ is the correlation parameter, and let r be the risk-free interest-rate parameter from the money-market account.

By introducing $\{Z_t : t \geq 0\}$ as a standard Wiener process, independent of W_t^σ, show that we can write

$$W_t^S = \rho W_t^\sigma + \sqrt{1-\rho^2}Z_t.$$

Using the two-dimensional Girsanov's theorem, show that under the risk-neutral measure $\mathbb{Q}$,

$$dS_t = (r-D)S_t dt + \sigma_t S_t d\widetilde{W}_t^S$$

$$d\sigma_t = \widetilde{\alpha}(\sigma_t,t)dt + \beta(\sigma_t,t)d\widetilde{W}_t^\sigma$$

where $\widetilde{W}_t^S = \rho\widetilde{W}_t^\sigma + \sqrt{1-\rho^2}\widetilde{Z}_t$, $\widetilde{W}_t^\sigma$ and $\widetilde{Z}_t$ are $\mathbb{Q}$-standard Wiener processes, $\widetilde{W}_t^\sigma \perp\!\!\!\perp \widetilde{Z}_t$ and $\widetilde{\alpha}(\sigma_t,t) = \alpha(\sigma_t,t) - \gamma_t\beta(\sigma_t,t)$ such that γ_t is the market price of volatility risk.

Let $p(S_t, \sigma_t, t; S_T, \sigma_T, T)$ be the transition pdf of the asset price, where the asset price and volatility are S_t and σ_t at time t, respectively, given that the asset price and volatility are S_T and σ_T at time $T > t$, respectively. From the Chapman–Kolmogorov equation for $\Delta T > 0$,

$$p(S_t, \sigma_t, t; S_T, \sigma_T, T + \Delta T)$$
$$= \int_0^\infty \int_0^\infty p(S_t, \sigma_t, t; x, y, T) p(x, y, T; S_T, \sigma_T, T + \Delta T) \, dy dx$$

show that in the limit $\Delta T \to 0$,

$$\frac{\partial}{\partial T} p(S_t, t; S_T, T) = -\int_0^T \int_0^\infty p(S_t, \sigma_t, t; x, y, T) \frac{\partial}{\partial T} p(x, y, T; S_T, \sigma_T, T) \, dy dx.$$

Finally, using the backward Kolmogorov equation, show that $p(S_t, \sigma_t, t; S_T, \sigma_T, T)$ satisfies the forward Kolmogorov equation

$$\frac{\partial}{\partial T} p(S_t, \sigma_t, t; S_T, \sigma_T, T) - \frac{1}{2} \frac{\partial^2}{\partial S_T^2} \left[\sigma_T^2 S_T^2 p(S_t, \sigma_t, t; S_T, \sigma_T, T) \right]$$

$$- \frac{1}{2} \frac{\partial^2}{\partial \sigma_T^2} \left[\beta(\sigma_T, T)^2 p(S_t, \sigma_t, t; S_T, \sigma_T, T) \right]$$

$$- \rho \frac{\partial^2}{\partial \sigma_T \partial S_T} \left[\beta(\sigma_T, T) \sigma_T S_T p(S_t, \sigma_t, t; S_T, \sigma_T, T) \right]$$

$$+ (r - D) \frac{\partial}{\partial S_T} \left[S_T p(S_t, \sigma_t, t; S_T, \sigma_T, T) \right] + \frac{\partial}{\partial \sigma_T} \left[\tilde{\alpha}(\sigma_T, T) p(S_t, \sigma_t, t; S_T, \sigma_T, T) \right] = 0$$

with boundary condition

$$p(S_t, \sigma_t, t; S_T, \sigma_T, T) = \delta(S_t - S_T) \delta(\sigma_t - \sigma_T), \quad \forall t.$$

Solution: To show that under the risk-neutral measure $\mathbb{Q}$, the asset price and the volatility follow the dynamics

$$dS_t = (r - D)S_t dt + \sigma_t S_t d\widetilde{W}_t^S$$
$$d\sigma_t = \tilde{\alpha}(\sigma_t, t) dt + \beta(\sigma_t, t) d\widetilde{W}_t^\sigma$$

see Problem 7.2.3.2 (page 713).

From the Chapman–Kolmogorov equation for $\Delta T > 0$,

$$p(S_t, \sigma_t, t; S_T, \sigma_T, T + \Delta T)$$
$$= \int_0^\infty \int_0^\infty p(S_t, \sigma_t, t; x, y, T) p(x, y, T; S_T, \sigma_T, T + \Delta T) \, dy dx$$

we can write

$$p(S_t, \sigma_t, t; S_T, \sigma_T, T + \Delta T) - p(S_t, \sigma_t, t; S_T, \sigma_T, T)$$

$$= \int_0^\infty \int_0^\infty p(S_t, \sigma_t, t; x, y, T) p(x, y, T; S_T, \sigma_T, T + \Delta T) \, dy \, dx$$

$$- p(S_t, \sigma_t, t; S_T, \sigma_T, T)$$

$$= \int_0^\infty \int_0^\infty p(S_t, \sigma_t, t; x, y, T) p(x, y, T; S_T, \sigma_T, T + \Delta T) \, dy \, dx$$

$$- \int_0^\infty \int_0^\infty p(S_t, \sigma_t, t; x, y, T) p(x, y, T; S_T, \sigma_T, T) \, dy \, dx$$

$$= \int_0^\infty \int_0^\infty p(S_t, \sigma_t, t; x, y, T) p(x, y, T; S_T, \sigma_T, T + \Delta T) \, dy \, dx$$

$$- \int_0^\infty \int_0^\infty p(S_t, \sigma_t, t; x, y, T) \delta(x - S_T) \delta(y - \sigma_T) \, dy \, dx.$$

By dividing the expression with ΔT and taking limits $\Delta T \to 0$,

$$\lim_{\Delta T \to 0} \frac{p(S_t, \sigma_t, t; S_T, \sigma_T, T + \Delta T) - p(S_t, \sigma_t, t; S_T, \sigma_T, T)}{\Delta T}$$

$$= \lim_{\Delta t \to 0} \int_0^\infty \int_0^\infty \frac{p(S_t, \sigma_t, t; x, y, T) p(x, y, T; S_T, \sigma_T, T + \Delta T)}{\Delta T} \, dy \, dx$$

$$- \lim_{\Delta T \to 0} \int_0^\infty \int_0^\infty \frac{p(S_t, \sigma_t, t; x, y, T) \delta(x - S_T) \delta(y - \sigma_T)}{\Delta T} \, dy \, dx$$

$$= \lim_{\Delta T \to 0} \int_0^\infty \int_0^\infty \left\{ p(S_t, \sigma_t, t; x, y, T) \right.$$

$$\times \left. \left[\frac{p(x, y, T; S_T, \sigma_T, T + \Delta T) - \delta(x - S_T) \delta(y - \sigma_T)}{\Delta T} \right] \right\} dy \, dx$$

$$= \lim_{\Delta T \to 0} \int_0^\infty \int_0^\infty \left\{ p(S_t, \sigma_t, t; x, y, T) \right.$$

$$\times \left. \left[\frac{p(x, y, T; S_T, \sigma_T, T + \Delta T) - p(x, y, T + \Delta T; S_T, \sigma_T, T + \Delta T)}{\Delta T} \right] \right\} dy \, dx.$$

Since

$$\lim_{\Delta T \to 0} \frac{p(S_t,\sigma_t,t; S_T,\sigma_T,T+\Delta T) - p(S_t,\sigma_t,t; S_T,\sigma_T,T)}{\Delta T}$$

$$= \frac{\partial}{\partial T} p(S_t,\sigma_t,t; S_T,\sigma_T,T)$$

and

$$\lim_{\Delta T \to 0} \frac{p(x,y,T; S_T,\sigma_T,T+\Delta T) - p(x,y,T+\Delta T; S_T,\sigma_T,T+\Delta T)}{\Delta T}$$

$$= -\frac{\partial}{\partial T} p(x,y,T; S_T,\sigma_T,T)$$

thus

$$\frac{\partial}{\partial T} p(S_t,\sigma_t,t; S_T,\sigma_T,T)$$

$$= -\int_0^\infty \int_0^\infty p(S_t,\sigma_t,t; x,y,T) \frac{\partial}{\partial T} p(x,y,T; S_T,\sigma_T,T)\,dy dx.$$

From the backward Kolmogorov equation on $p(x,y,t; S_T,\sigma_T,T)$ for the stochastic volatility model

$$\frac{\partial}{\partial t} p(x,y,t; S_T,\sigma_T,T) + \frac{1}{2} y^2 x^2 \frac{\partial^2}{\partial x^2} p(x,y,t; S_T,\sigma_T,T)$$

$$+ \frac{1}{2} \beta(y,t)^2 \frac{\partial^2}{\partial y^2} p(x,y,t; S_T,\sigma_T,T) + \rho\beta(y,t)yx \frac{\partial^2}{\partial y\partial x} p(x,y,t; S_T,\sigma_T,T)$$

$$+ (r-D)x \frac{\partial}{\partial x} p(x,y,t; S_T,\sigma_T,T) + \tilde{\alpha}(y,t) \frac{\partial}{\partial y} p(x,y,t; S_T,\sigma_T,T) = 0$$

we have

$$\frac{\partial}{\partial T} p(S_t,\sigma_t,t; S_T,\sigma_T,T)$$

$$= \int_0^\infty \int_0^\infty p(S_t,\sigma_t,t; x,y,T) \left[(r-D)x \frac{\partial}{\partial x} p(x,y,T; S_T,\sigma_T,T) \right.$$

$$+ \tilde{\alpha}(y,T) \frac{\partial}{\partial y} p(x,y,T; S_T,\sigma_T,T) + \frac{1}{2} y^2 x^2 \frac{\partial^2}{\partial x^2} p(x,y,T; S_T,\sigma_T,T)$$

$$+ \frac{1}{2} \beta(y,T)^2 \frac{\partial^2}{\partial y^2} p(x,y,T; S_T,\sigma_T,T)$$

$$\left. + \rho\beta(y,T)yx \frac{\partial^2}{\partial y\partial x} p(x,y,T; S_T,\sigma_T,T) \right] dy dx$$

$$= \int_0^\infty \int_0^\infty (r - D)xp(S_t, \sigma_t, t; x, y, T)\frac{\partial}{\partial x}p(x, y, T; S_T, \sigma_T, T)\, dy\, dx$$

$$+ \int_0^\infty \int_0^\infty \tilde{\alpha}(y, T)p(S_t, \sigma_t, t; x, y, T)\frac{\partial}{\partial y}p(x, y, T; S_T, \sigma_T, T)\, dy\, dx$$

$$+ \int_0^\infty \int_0^\infty \frac{1}{2}y^2x^2 p(S_t, \sigma_t, t; x, y, T)\frac{\partial^2}{\partial x^2}p(x, y, T; S_T, \sigma_T, T)\, dy\, dx$$

$$+ \int_0^\infty \int_0^\infty \frac{1}{2}\beta(y, T)^2 p(S_t, \sigma_t, t; x, y, T)\frac{\partial^2}{\partial y^2}p(x, y, T; S_T, \sigma_T, T)\, dy\, dx$$

$$+ \int_0^\infty \int_0^\infty \rho\beta(y, T)yxp(S_t, \sigma_t, t; x, y, T)\frac{\partial^2}{\partial y\partial x}p(x, y, T; S_T, \sigma_T, T)\, dy\, dx.$$

Integrating by parts for

$$\int_0^\infty \int_0^\infty (r - D)x\, p(S_t, \sigma_t, t; x, y, T)\frac{\partial}{\partial x}p(x, y, T; S_T, \sigma_T, T)\, dy\, dx$$

we let

$$u = (r - D)xp(S_t, \sigma_t, t; x, y, T) \quad \text{and} \quad \frac{dv}{dx} = \frac{\partial}{\partial x}p(x, y, T; S_T, \sigma_T, T)$$

so that

$$\frac{du}{dx} = \frac{\partial}{\partial x}\left[(r - D)x\, p(S_t, \sigma_t, t; x, y, T)\right] \quad \text{and} \quad v = p(x, y, T; S_T, \sigma_T, T).$$

Thus, we have

$$\int_0^\infty \int_0^\infty (r - D)x\, p(S_t, \sigma_t, t; x, y, T)\frac{\partial}{\partial x}p(x, y, T; S_T, \sigma_T, T)\, dy\, dx$$

$$= \int_0^\infty (r - D)x\, p(S_t, \sigma_t, t; x, y, T)p(x, y, T; S_T, \sigma_T, T)\Big|_0^\infty\, dy$$

$$- \int_0^\infty \int_0^\infty p(x, y, T; S_T, \sigma_T, T)\frac{\partial}{\partial x}\left[(r - D)x\, p(S_t, \sigma_t, t; x, y, T)\right]\, dy\, dx$$

$$= -\int_0^\infty \int_0^\infty p(x, y, T; S_T, \sigma_T, T)\frac{\partial}{\partial x}\left[(r - D)xp(S_t, \sigma_t, t; x, y, T)\right]\, dy\, dx.$$

For the case of integration by parts for

$$\int_0^\infty \int_0^\infty \tilde{\alpha}(y,T)p(S_t,\sigma_t,t;x,y,T)\frac{\partial}{\partial y}p(x,y,T;S_T,\sigma_T,T)\,dy\,dx$$

we let

$$u = \tilde{\alpha}(y,T)p(S_t,\sigma_t,t;x,y,T) \quad \text{and} \quad \frac{dv}{dy} = \frac{\partial}{\partial y}p(x,y,T;S_T,\sigma_T,T)$$

so that

$$\frac{du}{dy} = \frac{\partial}{\partial y}\left[\tilde{\alpha}(y,T)p(S_t,\sigma_t,t;x,y,T)\right] \quad \text{and} \quad v = p(x,y,T;S_T,\sigma_T,T).$$

Hence,

$$\int_0^\infty \int_0^\infty \tilde{\alpha}(y,T)p(S_t,\sigma_t,t;x,y,T)\frac{\partial}{\partial y}p(x,y,T;S_T,\sigma_T,T)\,dy\,dx$$

$$= \int_0^\infty \tilde{\alpha}(y,T)p(S_t,\sigma_t,t;x,y,T)p(x,y,T;S_T,\sigma_T,T)\Big|_0^\infty\,dx$$

$$- \int_0^\infty \int_0^\infty \frac{\partial}{\partial y}\left[\tilde{\alpha}(y,T)p(S_t,\sigma_t,t;x,y,T)\right]p(x,y,T;S_T,\sigma_T,T)\,dy\,dx$$

$$= -\int_0^\infty \int_0^\infty \frac{\partial}{\partial y}\left[\tilde{\alpha}(y,T)p(S_t,\sigma_t,t;x,y,T)\right]p(x,y,T;S_T,\sigma_T,T)\,dy\,dx.$$

For the case of

$$\int_0^\infty \int_0^\infty \frac{1}{2}y^2x^2p(S_t,\sigma_t,t;x,y,T)\frac{\partial^2}{\partial x^2}p(x,y,T;S_T,\sigma_T,T)\,dy\,dx$$

and solving the integral by parts, we let

$$u = \frac{1}{2}y^2x^2p(S_t,\sigma_t,t;x,y,T) \quad \text{and} \quad \frac{dv}{dx} = \frac{\partial^2}{\partial x^2}p(x,y,T;S_T,\sigma_T,T)$$

so that

$$\frac{du}{dx} = \frac{\partial}{\partial x}\left[\frac{1}{2}y^2x^2p(S_t,\sigma_t,t;x,y,T)\right] \quad \text{and} \quad v = \frac{\partial}{\partial x}p(x,y,T;S_T,\sigma_T,T).$$

Hence,

$$\int_0^\infty \int_0^\infty \frac{1}{2} y^2 x^2 p(S_t, \sigma_t, t; x, y, T) \frac{\partial^2}{\partial x^2} p(x, y, T; S_T, \sigma_T, T) \, dy \, dx$$

$$= \int_0^\infty \frac{1}{2} y^2 x^2 p(S_t, \sigma_t, t; x, y, T) \frac{\partial}{\partial x} p(x, y, T; S_T, \sigma_T, T) \Big|_0^\infty \, dx$$

$$- \int_0^\infty \int_0^\infty \frac{\partial}{\partial x} p(x, y, T; S_T, \sigma_T, T) \frac{\partial}{\partial x} \left[\frac{1}{2} y^2 x^2 p(S_t, \sigma_t, t; x, y, T) \right] dy \, dx$$

$$= - \int_0^\infty \int_0^\infty \frac{\partial}{\partial x} p(x, y, T; S_T, \sigma_T, T) \frac{\partial}{\partial x} \left[\frac{1}{2} y^2 x^2 p(S_t, \sigma_t, t; x, y, T) \right] dy \, dx.$$

Integrating by parts again, we let

$$u = \frac{\partial}{\partial x} \left[\frac{1}{2} y^2 x^2 p(S_t, \sigma_t, t; x, y, T) \right] \quad \text{and} \quad \frac{dv}{dx} = \frac{\partial}{\partial x} p(x, y, T; S_T, \sigma_T, T)$$

so that

$$\frac{du}{dx} = \frac{\partial^2}{\partial x^2} \left[\frac{1}{2} y^2 x^2 p(S_t, \sigma_t, t; x, y, T) \right] \quad \text{and} \quad v = p(x, y, T; S_T, \sigma_T, T).$$

Thus, we have

$$\int_0^\infty \int_0^\infty \frac{1}{2} y^2 x^2 p(S_t, \sigma_t, t; x, y, T) \frac{\partial^2}{\partial x^2} p(x, y, T; S_T, \sigma_T, T) \, dy \, dx$$

$$= - \int_0^\infty \frac{\partial}{\partial x} \left[\frac{1}{2} y^2 x^2 p(S_t, \sigma_t, t; x, y, T) \right] p(x, y, T; S_T, \sigma_T, T) \Big|_0^\infty \, dy$$

$$+ \int_0^\infty \int_0^\infty \frac{\partial^2}{\partial x^2} \left[\frac{1}{2} y^2 x^2 p(S_t, \sigma_t, t; x, y, T) \right] p(x, y, T; S_T, \sigma_T, T) \, dy \, dx$$

$$= \int_0^\infty \int_0^\infty \frac{\partial^2}{\partial x^2} \left[\frac{1}{2} y^2 x^2 p(S_t, \sigma_t, t; x, y, T) \right] p(x, y, T; S_T, \sigma_T, T) \, dy \, dx.$$

Taking integration by parts of

$$\int_0^\infty \int_0^\infty \frac{1}{2} \beta(y, T)^2 p(S_t, \sigma_t, t; x, y, T) \frac{\partial^2}{\partial y^2} p(x, y, T; S_T, \sigma_T, T) dy \, dx$$

we let

$$u = \frac{1}{2} \beta(y, T)^2 p(S_t, \sigma_t, t; x, y, T) \quad \text{and} \quad \frac{dv}{dy} = \frac{\partial^2}{\partial y^2} p(x, y, T; S_T, \sigma_T, T)$$

so that

$$\frac{du}{dy} = \frac{\partial}{\partial y}\left[\frac{1}{2}\beta(y,T)^2 p(S_t,\sigma_t,t;x,y,T)\right] \quad \text{and} \quad v = \frac{\partial}{\partial y}p(x,y,T;S_T,\sigma_T,T).$$

Therefore,

$$\int_0^\infty \int_0^\infty \frac{1}{2}\beta(y,T)^2 p(S_t,\sigma_t,t;x,y,T)\frac{\partial^2}{\partial y^2}p(x,y,T;S_T,\sigma_T,T)\,dy\,dx$$

$$= \int_0^\infty \frac{1}{2}\beta(y,T)^2 p(S_t,\sigma_t,t;x,y,T)\frac{\partial}{\partial y}p(x,y,T;S_T,\sigma_T,T)\Big|_0^\infty \,dx$$

$$- \int_0^\infty \int_0^\infty \frac{\partial}{\partial y}\left[\frac{1}{2}\beta(y,T)^2 p(S_t,\sigma_t,t;x,y,T)\right]\frac{\partial}{\partial y}p(x,y,T;S_T,\sigma_T,T)\,dy\,dx$$

$$= -\int_0^\infty \int_0^\infty \frac{\partial}{\partial y}\left[\frac{1}{2}\beta(y,T)^2 p(S_t,\sigma_t,t;x,y,T)\right]\frac{\partial}{\partial y}p(x,y,T;S_T,\sigma_T,T)\,dy\,dx.$$

Integrating by parts again, we let

$$u = \frac{\partial}{\partial y}\left[\frac{1}{2}\beta(y,T)^2 p(S_t,\sigma_t,t;x,y,T)\right] \quad \text{and} \quad \frac{dv}{dy} = \frac{\partial}{\partial y}p(x,y,T;S_T,\sigma_T,T)$$

so that

$$\frac{du}{dy} = \frac{\partial^2}{\partial y^2}\left[\frac{1}{2}\beta(y,T)^2 p(S_t,\sigma_t,t;x,y,T)\right] \quad \text{and} \quad v = p(x,y,T;S_T,\sigma_T,T)$$

and hence

$$\int_0^\infty \int_0^\infty \frac{1}{2}\beta(y,T)^2 p(S_t,\sigma_t,t;x,y,T)\frac{\partial^2}{\partial y^2}p(x,y,T;S_T,\sigma_T,T)\,dy\,dx$$

$$= -\int_0^\infty \frac{\partial}{\partial y}\left[\frac{1}{2}\beta(y,T)^2 p(S_t,\sigma_t,t;x,y,T)\right]p(x,y,T;S_T,\sigma_T,T)\Big|_0^\infty \,dx$$

$$+ \int_0^\infty \int_0^\infty \frac{\partial^2}{\partial y^2}\left[\frac{1}{2}\beta(y,T)^2 p(S_t,\sigma_t,t;x,y,T)\right]p(x,y,T;S_T,\sigma_T,T)\,dy\,dx$$

$$= \int_0^\infty \int_0^\infty \frac{\partial^2}{\partial y^2}\left[\frac{1}{2}\beta(y,T)^2 p(S_t,\sigma_t,t;x,y,T)\right]p(x,y,T;S_T,\sigma_T,T)\,dy\,dx.$$

Finally, for

$$\int_0^\infty \int_0^\infty \rho\beta(y,T)yx p(S_t,\sigma_t,t;x,y,T)\frac{\partial^2}{\partial y\partial x}p(x,y,T;S_T,\sigma_T,T)\,dy\,dx$$

we let

$$u = \rho\beta(y,T)yxp(S_t,\sigma_t,t;x,y,T) \quad \text{and} \quad \frac{dv}{dy} = \frac{\partial^2}{\partial y \partial x}p(x,y,T;S_T,\sigma_T,T)$$

so that

$$\frac{du}{dy} = \frac{\partial}{\partial y}\left[\rho\beta(y,T)yxp(S_t,\sigma_t,t;x,y,T)\right] \quad \text{and} \quad v = \frac{\partial}{\partial x}p(x,y,T;S_T,\sigma_T,T).$$

Therefore,

$$\int_0^\infty \int_0^\infty \rho\beta(y,T)yxp(S_t,\sigma_t,t;x,y,T)\frac{\partial^2}{\partial y \partial x}p(x,y,T;S_T,\sigma_T,T)\,dy\,dx$$

$$= \int_0^\infty \rho\beta(y,T)yxp(S_t,\sigma_t,t;x,y,T)\frac{\partial}{\partial x}p(x,y,T;S_T,\sigma_T,T)\Big|_0^\infty dx$$

$$- \int_0^\infty \int_0^\infty \frac{\partial}{\partial y}\left[\rho\beta(y,T)yxp(S_t,\sigma_t,t;x,y,T)\right]\frac{\partial}{\partial x}p(x,y,T;S_T,\sigma_T,T)\,dy\,dx$$

$$= - \int_0^\infty \int_0^\infty \frac{\partial}{\partial y}\left[\rho\beta(y,T)yxp(S_t,\sigma_t,t;x,y,T)\right]\frac{\partial}{\partial x}p(x,y,T;S_T,\sigma_T,T)\,dy\,dx.$$

Using integration by parts again, we let

$$u = \frac{\partial}{\partial y}\left[\rho\beta(y,T)yxp(S_t,\sigma_t,t;x,y,T)\right] \quad \text{and} \quad \frac{dv}{dx} = \frac{\partial}{\partial x}p(x,y,T;S_T,\sigma_T,T)$$

so that

$$\frac{du}{dx} = \frac{\partial^2}{\partial y \partial x}\left[\rho\beta(y,T)yxp(S_t,\sigma_t,t;x,y,T)\right] \quad \text{and} \quad v = p(x,y,T;S_T,\sigma_T,T)$$

and therefore,

$$\int_0^\infty \int_0^\infty \rho\beta(y,T)yxp(S_t,\sigma_t,t;x,y,T)\frac{\partial^2}{\partial y \partial x}p(x,y,T;S_T,\sigma_T,T)\,dy\,dx$$

$$= - \int_0^\infty \frac{\partial}{\partial y}\left[\rho\beta(y,T)yxp(S_t,\sigma_t,t;x,y,T)\right]p(x,y,T;S_T,\sigma_T,T)\Big|_0^\infty dy$$

$$+ \int_0^\infty \int_0^\infty \frac{\partial^2}{\partial y \partial x}\left[\rho\beta(y,T)yxp(S_t,\sigma_t,t;x,y,T)\right]p(x,y,T;S_T,\sigma_T,T)\,dy\,dx$$

$$= \int_0^\infty \int_0^\infty \frac{\partial^2}{\partial y \partial x}\left[\rho\beta(y,T)yxp(S_t,\sigma_t,t;x,y,T)\right]p(x,y,T;S_T,\sigma_T,T)\,dy\,dx.$$

Thus

$$
\frac{\partial}{\partial T} p(S_t, \sigma_t, t; S_T, \sigma_T, T)
$$

$$
= -\int_0^\infty \int_0^\infty \frac{\partial}{\partial x} \left[(r - D) x p(S_t, \sigma_t, t; x, y, T) \right] p(x, y, T; S_T, \sigma_T, T) \, dy \, dx
$$

$$
- \int_0^\infty \int_0^\infty \frac{\partial}{\partial y} \left[\widetilde{\alpha}(y, T) p(S_t, \sigma_t, t; x, y, T) \right] p(x, y, T; S_T, \sigma_T, T) \, dy \, dx
$$

$$
+ \int_0^\infty \int_0^\infty \frac{\partial^2}{\partial x^2} \left[\frac{1}{2} y^2 x^2 p(S_t, \sigma_t, t; x, y, T) \right] p(x, y, T; S_T, \sigma_T, T) \, dy \, dx
$$

$$
+ \int_0^\infty \int_0^\infty \frac{\partial^2}{\partial y^2} \left[\frac{1}{2} \beta(y, T)^2 p(S_t, \sigma_t, t; x, y, T) \right] p(x, y, T; S_T, \sigma_T, T) \, dy \, dx
$$

$$
+ \int_0^\infty \int_0^\infty \frac{\partial^2}{\partial y \partial x} \left[\rho \beta(y, T) y x p(S_t, \sigma_t, t; x, y, T) \right] p(x, y, T; S_T, \sigma_T, T) \, dy \, dx
$$

or

$$
\frac{\partial}{\partial T} p(S_t, \sigma_t, t; S_T, \sigma_T, T)
$$

$$
= -\int_0^\infty \int_0^\infty \frac{\partial}{\partial x} \left[(r - D) x p(S_t, \sigma_t, t; x, y, T) \right] \delta(x - S_T) \delta(y - \sigma_T) \, dy \, dx
$$

$$
- \int_0^\infty \int_0^\infty \frac{\partial}{\partial y} \left[\widetilde{\alpha}(y, T) p(S_t, \sigma_t, t; x, y, T) \right] \delta(x - S_T) \delta(y - \sigma_T) \, dy \, dx
$$

$$
+ \int_0^\infty \int_0^\infty \frac{\partial^2}{\partial x^2} \left[\frac{1}{2} y^2 x^2 p(S_t, \sigma_t, t; x, y, T) \right] \delta(x - S_T) \delta(y - \sigma_T) \, dy \, dx
$$

$$
+ \int_0^\infty \int_0^\infty \frac{\partial^2}{\partial y^2} \left[\frac{1}{2} \beta(y, T)^2 p(S_t, \sigma_t, t; x, y, T) \right] \delta(x - S_T) \delta(y - \sigma_T) \, dy \, dx
$$

$$
+ \int_0^\infty \int_0^\infty \frac{\partial^2}{\partial y \partial x} \left[\rho \beta(y, T) y x p(S_t, \sigma_t, t; x, y, T) \right] \delta(x - S_T) \delta(y - \sigma_T) \, dy \, dx.
$$

Hence,

$$
\frac{\partial}{\partial T} p(S_t, \sigma_t, t; S_T, \sigma_T, T) = -\frac{\partial}{\partial S_T} \left[(r - D) S_T p(S_t, \sigma_t, t; S_T, \sigma_T, T) \right]
$$

$$
- \frac{\partial}{\partial \sigma_T} \left[\widetilde{\alpha}(\sigma_T, T) p(S_t, \sigma_t, t; S_T, \sigma_T, T) \right]
$$

$$
+ \frac{\partial^2}{\partial S_T^2} \left[\frac{1}{2} \sigma_T^2 S_T^2 p(S_t, \sigma_t, t; S_T, \sigma_T, T) \right]
$$

$$
+ \frac{\partial^2}{\partial \sigma_T^2} \left[\frac{1}{2} \beta(\sigma_T, T)^2 p(S_t, \sigma_t, t; S_T, \sigma_T, T) \right]
$$

$$
+ \frac{\partial^2}{\partial \sigma_T \partial S_T} \left[\rho \beta(\sigma_T, T) \sigma_T S_T p(S_t, \sigma_t, t; S_T, \sigma_T, T) \right]
$$

and rearranging terms we have the forward Kolmogorov equation for the stochastic volatility model

$$\frac{\partial}{\partial T} p(S_t,\sigma_t,t; S_T,\sigma_T,T) - \frac{1}{2}\frac{\partial^2}{\partial S_T^2}\left[\sigma_T^2 S_T^2 p(S_t,\sigma_t,t; S_T,\sigma_T,T)\right]$$

$$-\frac{1}{2}\frac{\partial^2}{\partial \sigma_T^2}\left[\beta(\sigma_T,T)^2 p(S_t,\sigma_t,t; S_T,\sigma_T,T)\right]$$

$$-\rho\frac{\partial^2}{\partial \sigma_T \partial S_T}\left[\beta(\sigma_T,T)\sigma_T S_T p(S_t,\sigma_t,t; S_T,\sigma_T,T)\right]$$

$$+(r-D)\frac{\partial}{\partial S_T}\left[S_T p(S_t,\sigma_t,t; S_T,\sigma_T,T)\right] + \frac{\partial}{\partial \sigma_T}\left[\widetilde{\alpha}(\sigma_T,T)p(S_t,\sigma_t,t; S_T,\sigma_T,T)\right] = 0$$

with boundary condition

$$p(S_t,\sigma_t,t; S_T,\sigma_T,t) = \delta(S_t - S_T)\delta(\sigma_t - \sigma_T)$$

for all t.

$\square$

5. Under the risk-neutral measure $\mathbb{Q}$, let $\{\widetilde{W}_t^S : t \geq 0\}$ and $\{\widetilde{W}_t^\sigma : t \geq 0\}$ be two correlated $\mathbb{Q}$-standard Wiener processes on the probability space $(\Omega,\mathcal{F},\mathbb{Q})$ with correlation $\rho \in (-1,1)$. Let the asset price S_t under the $\mathbb{Q}$ measure follow a stochastic volatility model with the following dynamics

$$dS_t = (r-D)S_t dt + \sigma_t S_t d\widetilde{W}_t^S$$
$$d\sigma_t = \widetilde{\alpha}(\sigma_t,t)dt + \beta(\sigma_t,t)d\widetilde{W}_t^\sigma$$
$$d\widetilde{W}_t^S \cdot d\widetilde{W}_t^\sigma = \rho dt$$

where r is the risk-free interest-rate parameter from the money-market account, D is the continuous dividend yield, σ_t is the volatility process, $\widetilde{\alpha}(\sigma_t,t)$ and $\beta(\sigma_t,t)$ are continuous functions.

Let $p(S_t,\sigma_t,t; S_T,\sigma_T,T)$ be the transition pdf of the asset price, where the asset price and volatility are S_t and σ_t at time t, respectively, given that the asset price and volatility are S_T and σ_T at time $T > t$, respectively. We consider a European call option written on S_t with strike price $K > 0$ expiring at time $T > t$ with payoff $\Psi(S_T) = \max\{S_T - K, 0\}$ where, under the risk-neutral measure $\mathbb{Q}$, the option price at time t is

$$C(S_t,\sigma_t,t; K,T) = e^{-r(T-t)}\mathbb{E}^{\mathbb{Q}}\left[\max\{S_T - K, 0\}|\mathcal{F}_t\right]$$

$$= e^{-r(T-t)}\int_0^\infty \int_0^\infty \max\{x - K, 0\}p(S_t,\sigma_t,t; x,y,T)\,dy\,dx.$$

Show that the following identities are true

$$x\frac{\partial}{\partial K}(x-K) = K\frac{\partial}{\partial K}(x-K) - (x-K)$$

$$\frac{\partial}{\partial x}(x-K) = -\frac{\partial}{\partial K}(x-K)$$

$$\frac{\partial^2}{\partial z^2}(z-K) = \frac{\partial^2}{\partial K^2}(z-K).$$

By using the forward Kolmogorov equation and the above identities or otherwise, show that $C(S_t, \sigma_t, t; K, T)$ satisfies

$$\frac{\partial C}{\partial T} - \frac{1}{2}\mathbb{E}^{\mathbb{Q}}\left[\sigma_T^2\bigg| S_T = K, S_t, \sigma_t\right]K^2\frac{\partial^2 C}{\partial K^2} + (r-D)K\frac{\partial C}{\partial K} + DC(S_t, t; K, T) = 0$$

with boundary condition

$$C(S_T, \sigma_T, T; K, T) = \max\{S_T - K, 0\}.$$

Explain the significance of this equation.

Deduce that for a European put option price $P(S_t, \sigma_t, t; K, T)$ written on S_t at time t with payoff $\Psi(S_T) = \max\{K - S_T, 0\}$ expiring at time $T > t$, $P(S_t, t; K, T)$ satisfies

$$\frac{\partial P}{\partial T} - \frac{1}{2}\mathbb{E}^{\mathbb{Q}}\left[\sigma_T^2\bigg| S_T = K, S_t, \sigma_t\right]K^2\frac{\partial^2 P}{\partial K^2} + (r-D)K\frac{\partial P}{\partial K} + DP(S_t, t; K, T) = 0$$

with boundary condition

$$P(S_T, \sigma_T, T; K, T) = \max\{K - S_T, 0\}.$$

Under what condition do both the stochastic volatility and local volatility models price European options equally?

Solution: For the proof of the three identities, see Problem 7.2.2.5 (page 699).

By definition,

$$C(S_t, \sigma_t, t; K, T) = e^{-r(T-t)}\mathbb{E}^{\mathbb{Q}}\left[\max\{S_T - K, 0\}\big| \mathcal{F}_t\right]$$

$$= e^{-r(T-t)}\int_0^\infty \int_0^\infty \max\{x - K, 0\}p(S_t, \sigma_t, t; x, y, T)\,dy\,dx$$

$$= e^{-r(T-t)}\int_K^\infty \int_0^\infty (x - K)p(S_t, \sigma_t, t; x, y, T)\,dy\,dx.$$

Differentiating $C(S_t, \sigma_t, t; K, T)$ with respect to T and from the forward Kolmogorov equation for the stochastic volatility model

$$\frac{\partial}{\partial T} p(S_t, \sigma_t, t; S_T, \sigma_T, T) - \frac{1}{2} \frac{\partial^2}{\partial S_T^2} \left[\sigma_T^2 S_T^2 p(S_t, \sigma_t, t; S_T, \sigma_T, T) \right]$$

$$- \frac{1}{2} \frac{\partial^2}{\partial \sigma_T^2} \left[\beta(\sigma_T, T)^2 p(S_t, \sigma_t, t; S_T, \sigma_T, T) \right]$$

$$- \rho \frac{\partial^2}{\partial \sigma_T \partial S_T} \left[\beta(\sigma_T, T) \sigma_T S_T p(S_t, \sigma_t, t; S_T, \sigma_T, T) \right]$$

$$+ (r - D) \frac{\partial}{\partial S_T} \left[S_T p(S_t, \sigma_t, t; S_T, \sigma_T, T) \right] + \frac{\partial}{\partial \sigma_T} \left[\tilde{\alpha}(\sigma_T, T) p(S_t, \sigma_t, t; S_T, \sigma_T, T) \right] = 0$$

we have

$$\frac{\partial C}{\partial T} = -r e^{-r(T-t)} \int_K^\infty \int_0^\infty (x - K) p(S_t, \sigma_t, t; x, y, T) \, dy \, dx$$

$$+ e^{-r(T-t)} \int_K^\infty \int_0^\infty (x - K) \frac{\partial}{\partial T} p(S_t, \sigma_t, t; x, y, T) \, dy \, dx$$

$$= -r C(S_t, \sigma_t, t; K, T)$$

$$+ \frac{1}{2} e^{-r(T-t)} \int_K^\infty \int_0^\infty (x - K) \frac{\partial^2}{\partial x^2} \left[y^2 x^2 p(S_t, \sigma_t, t; x, y, T) \right] dy \, dx$$

$$+ \frac{1}{2} e^{-r(T-t)} \int_K^\infty \int_0^\infty (x - K) \frac{\partial^2}{\partial y^2} \left[\beta(y, T)^2 p(S_t, \sigma_t, t; x, y, T) \right] dy \, dx$$

$$+ \rho e^{-r(T-t)} \int_K^\infty \int_0^\infty (x - K) \frac{\partial^2}{\partial y \partial x} \left[\beta(y, T) y x p(S_t, \sigma_t, t; x, y, T) \right] dy \, dx$$

$$- (r - D) e^{-r(T-t)} \int_K^\infty \int_0^\infty (x - K) \frac{\partial}{\partial x} \left[x p(S_t, \sigma_t, t; x, y, T) \right] dy \, dx$$

$$- e^{-r(T-t)} \int_K^\infty \int_0^\infty (x - K) \frac{\partial}{\partial y} \left[\tilde{\alpha}(y, T) p(S_t, \sigma_t, t; x, y, T) \right] dy \, dx.$$

Given that the payoff does not depend on σ_T, using integration by parts, all partial derivatives with respect to σ_T will vanish. Hence,

$$\int_K^\infty \int_0^\infty (x - K) \frac{\partial^2}{\partial y^2} \left[\beta(y, T)^2 p(S_t, \sigma_t, t; x, y, T) \right] dy \, dx = 0$$

$$\int_K^\infty \int_0^\infty (x - K) \frac{\partial^2}{\partial y \partial x} \left[\beta(y, T) y x p(S_t, \sigma_t, t; x, y, T) \right] dy \, dx = 0$$

$$\int_K^\infty \int_0^\infty (x - K) \frac{\partial}{\partial y} \left[\tilde{\alpha}(y, T) p(S_t, \sigma_t, t; x, y, T) \right] dy \, dx = 0$$

and we can rewrite the equation as

$$\frac{\partial C}{\partial T} = -rC(S_t, \sigma_t, t; K, T)$$

$$+ \frac{1}{2}e^{-r(T-t)} \int_0^\infty \int_K^\infty (x - K)\frac{\partial^2}{\partial x^2} \left[y^2 x^2 p(S_t, \sigma_t, t; x, y, T)\right] dx dy$$

$$- (r - D)e^{-r(T-t)} \int_0^\infty \int_K^\infty (x - K)\frac{\partial}{\partial x} \left[x p(S_t, \sigma_t, t; x, y, T)\right] dx dy.$$

Integrating by parts for the inner integral

$$\int_K^\infty (x - K)\frac{\partial}{\partial x} \left[x p(S_t, \sigma_t, t; x, y, T)\right] dx$$

we let

$$u = (x - K) \quad \text{and} \quad \frac{dv}{dx} = \frac{\partial}{\partial x} \left[x \, p(S_t, \sigma_t, t; x, y, T)\right]$$

so that

$$\frac{du}{dx} = \frac{\partial}{\partial x}(x - K) = -\frac{\partial}{\partial K}(x - K) \quad \text{and} \quad v = x \, p(S_t, \sigma_t, t; x, y, T).$$

Therefore,

$$\int_K^\infty (x - K)\frac{\partial}{\partial x} \left[x p(S_t, \sigma_t, t; x, y, T)\right] dx$$

$$= (x - K)x \, p(S_t, \sigma_t, t; x, y, T)\big|_K^\infty + \int_K^\infty x p(S_t, \sigma_t, t; x, y, T)\frac{\partial}{\partial K}(x - K) dx$$

$$= \int_K^\infty p(S_t, \sigma_t, t; x, y, T)z\frac{\partial}{\partial K}(x - K) dx$$

$$= \int_K^\infty \left[K\frac{\partial}{\partial K}(x - K) - (x - K)\right] p(S_t, \sigma_t, t; x, y, T) dx$$

$$= K \int_K^\infty \frac{\partial}{\partial K} \left[(x - K)p(S_t, \sigma_t, t; x, y, T)\right] dx$$

$$- \int_K^\infty (x - K)p(S_t, \sigma_t, t; x, y, T) dx$$

and hence,

$$e^{-r(T-t)} \int_0^\infty \int_K^\infty (x - K)\frac{\partial}{\partial x}\left[x\, p(S_t, \sigma_t, t; x, y, T)\right] dx\, dy$$

$$= K\, e^{-r(T-t)} \int_0^\infty \int_K^\infty \frac{\partial}{\partial K}\left[(x - K)p(S_t, \sigma_t, t; x, y, T)\right] dx\, dy$$

$$- e^{-r(T-t)} \int_0^\infty \int_K^\infty (x - K)p(S_t, \sigma_t, t; x, y, T)\, dx\, dy$$

$$= K\frac{\partial C}{\partial K} - C(S_t, \sigma_t, t; K, T).$$

For the case of the inner integral

$$\int_K^\infty (x - K)\frac{\partial^2}{\partial z^2}\left[y^2 x^2 p(S_t, \sigma_t, t; x, y, T)\right] dx$$

we let

$$u = (x - K) \quad \text{and} \quad \frac{dv}{dx} = \frac{\partial^2}{\partial x^2}\left[y^2 x^2 p(S_t, \sigma_t, t; x, y, T)\right]$$

so that

$$\frac{du}{dx} = \frac{\partial}{\partial x}(x - K) \quad \text{and} \quad v = \frac{\partial}{\partial x}\left[y^2 x^2 p(S_t, \sigma_t, t; x, y, T)\right]$$

and therefore

$$\int_K^\infty (x - K)\frac{\partial^2}{\partial x^2}\left[y^2 x^2 p(S_t, \sigma_t, t; x, y, T)\right] dx$$

$$= (x - K)\frac{\partial}{\partial x}\left[y^2 x^2 p(S_t, \sigma_t, t; x, y, T)\right]\bigg|_K^\infty$$

$$- \int_K^\infty \frac{\partial}{\partial x}(x - K)\frac{\partial}{\partial x}\left[y^2 x^2 p(S_t, \sigma_t, t; x, y, T)\right] dx$$

$$= - \int_K^\infty \frac{\partial}{\partial x}(x - K)\frac{\partial}{\partial x}\left[y^2 x^2 p(S_t, \sigma_t, t; x, y, T)\right] dx.$$

To integrate

$$- \int_K^\infty \frac{\partial}{\partial x}(x - K)\frac{\partial}{\partial x}\left[y^2 x^2 p(S_t, \sigma_t, t; x, y, T)\right] dx$$

we set

$$u = \frac{\partial}{\partial x}(x - K) \quad \text{and} \quad \frac{dv}{dx} = \frac{\partial}{\partial x}\left[y^2 x^2 p(S_t, \sigma_t, t; x, y, T)\right]$$

so that

$$\frac{du}{dx} = \frac{\partial^2}{\partial x^2}(x - K) \quad \text{and} \quad v = y^2 x^2 p(S_t, \sigma_t, t; x, y, T)$$

and hence

$$-\int_K^\infty (x - K)\frac{\partial^2}{\partial x^2}\left[y^2 x^2 p(S_t, \sigma_t, t; x, y, T)\right] dx$$

$$= -y^2 x^2 p(S_t, \sigma_t, t; x, y, T)\frac{\partial}{\partial x}(x - K)\Big|_K^\infty + \int_K^\infty y^2 x^2 p(S_t, \sigma_t, t; x, y, T)\frac{\partial^2}{\partial x^2}(x - K)\,dx$$

$$= y^2 K^2 p(S_t, \sigma_t, t; K, y, T) + \int_K^\infty y^2 x^2 p(S_t, \sigma_t, t; x, y, T)\frac{\partial^2}{\partial K^2}(x - K)\,dx$$

$$= y^2 K^2 p(S_t, \sigma_t, t; K, y, T)$$

since $\frac{\partial}{\partial x}(x - K) = 1$ and $\frac{\partial^2}{\partial x^2}(x - K) = \frac{\partial^2}{\partial K^2}(x - K) = 0$.

Therefore,

$$\frac{1}{2}e^{-r(T-t)}\int_0^\infty \int_K^\infty (x - K)\frac{\partial^2}{\partial x^2}\left[y^2 x^2 p(S_t, \sigma_t, t; x, y, T)\right] dxdy$$

$$= \frac{1}{2}e^{-r(T-t)}\int_0^\infty y^2 K^2 p(S_t, \sigma_t, t; K, y, T)\,dy$$

$$= \frac{1}{2}K^2\left[e^{-r(T-t)}\int_0^\infty y^2 p(S_t, \sigma_t, t; K, y, T)\,dy\right].$$

Given that

$$\frac{\partial^2 C}{\partial K^2} = \frac{\partial}{\partial K}\left(\frac{\partial C}{\partial K}\right)$$

$$= \frac{\partial}{\partial K}\left[e^{-r(T-t)}\int_0^\infty \int_K^\infty \frac{\partial}{\partial K}\left[(x - K)p(S_t, \sigma_t, t; x, y, T)\right] dxdy\right]$$

$$= e^{-r(T-t)}\int_0^\infty \left[-p(S_t, t; K, T)\frac{\partial}{\partial K}(x - K)\right.$$

$$\left. + \int_K^\infty \frac{\partial^2}{\partial K^2}(x - K)p(S_t, \sigma_t, t; x, y, T)\,dx\right] dy$$

$$= e^{-r(T-t)}\int_0^\infty p(S_t, \sigma_t, t; K, y, T)\,dy$$

$$= e^{-r(T-t)}p(S_t, \sigma_t, t; S_T = K, T)$$

and from the identity

$$p(S_t, \sigma_t, t; K, y, T) = p(S_t, \sigma_t, t; S_T = K, T)p(S_T = K, S_t, \sigma_t, t; y)$$

we have

$$\frac{1}{2}e^{-r(T-t)} \int_0^\infty \int_K^\infty (x-K)\frac{\partial^2}{\partial x^2}\left[y^2 x^2 p(S_t, \sigma_t, t; x, y, T)\right] dx dy$$

$$= \frac{1}{2}e^{-r(T-t)} \int_0^\infty y^2 K^2 p(S_t, \sigma_t, t; K, y, T)\, dy$$

$$= \frac{1}{2}K^2 \left[e^{-r(T-t)}\int_0^\infty y^2 p(S_t, \sigma_t, t; K, y, T)\, dy\right]$$

$$= \frac{1}{2}K^2 \left[e^{-r(T-t)}p(S_t, \sigma_t, t; S_T = K, T)\int_0^\infty y^2 p(S_T = K, S_t, \sigma_t, t; y)\, dy\right]$$

$$= \frac{1}{2}K^2 \frac{\partial^2 C}{\partial K^2}\int_0^\infty y^2 p(S_T = K, S_t, \sigma_t, t; y)\, dy$$

$$= \frac{1}{2}\mathbb{E}^Q\left[\sigma_T^2 \Big| S_T = K, S_t, \sigma_t, t\right] K^2 \frac{\partial^2 C}{\partial K^2}.$$

Thus,

$$\frac{\partial C}{\partial T} = -rC(S_t, \sigma_t, t; K, T) + \frac{1}{2}\mathbb{E}^Q\left[\sigma_T^2 \Big| S_T = K, S_t, \sigma_t, t\right] K^2 \frac{\partial^2 C}{\partial K^2}$$
$$-(r-D)\left[K\frac{\partial C}{\partial K} - C(S_t, \sigma_t, t; K, T)\right]$$

or

$$\frac{\partial C}{\partial T} - \frac{1}{2}\mathbb{E}^Q\left[\sigma_T^2 \Big| S_T = K, S_t, \sigma_t, t\right] K^2 \frac{\partial^2 C}{\partial K^2} + (r-D)K\frac{\partial C}{\partial K} + DC(S_t, \sigma_t, t; K, T) = 0$$

with boundary condition

$$C(S_T, \sigma_T, T; K, T) = \max\{S_T - K, 0\}.$$

From the PDE expression, we can write

$$\mathbb{E}^Q\left[\sigma_T^2 \Big| S_T = K, S_t, \sigma_t, t\right] = \frac{2\left(\frac{\partial C}{\partial T} + (r-D)K\frac{\partial C}{\partial K} + DC(S_t, \sigma_t, t; K, T)\right)}{K^2 \frac{\partial^2 C}{\partial K^2}}$$

such that given the market prices of call options written on S_t with arbitrary strikes K and expiries T, the expected volatility at time T can be extracted given that the asset price is $S_T = K$ at time T.

From the put–call parity

$$C(S_t, \sigma_t, t; K, T) = P(S_t, \sigma_t, t; K, T) + S_t e^{-D(T-t)} - K e^{-r(T-t)}$$

we have

$$\frac{\partial C}{\partial T} = \frac{\partial P}{\partial T} - DS_t e^{-D(T-t)} + rK e^{-r(T-t)}$$

$$\frac{\partial C}{\partial K} = \frac{\partial P}{\partial K} - e^{-r(T-t)}$$

$$\frac{\partial^2 C}{\partial K^2} = \frac{\partial^2 P}{\partial K^2}.$$

Substituting the above information into the PDE for $C(S_t, \sigma_t, t; K, T)$,

$$\frac{\partial P}{\partial T} - DS_t e^{-D(T-t)} + rK e^{-r(T-t)} - \frac{1}{2}\mathbb{E}^{\mathbb{Q}}\left[\sigma_T^2 \Big| S_T = K, S_t, \sigma_t, t\right]\frac{\partial^2 P}{\partial K^2}$$

$$+(r - D)K\left[\frac{\partial P}{\partial K} - e^{-r(T-t)}\right] + D\left[P(S_t, \sigma_t, t; K, T) + S_t e^{-D(T-t)} - K e^{-r(T-t)}\right] = 0$$

or

$$\frac{\partial P}{\partial T} - \frac{1}{2}\mathbb{E}^{\mathbb{Q}}\left[\sigma_T^2 \Big| S_T = K, S_t, \sigma_t, t\right]K^2\frac{\partial^2 P}{\partial K^2} + (r - D)K\frac{\partial P}{\partial K} + DP(S_t, \sigma_t, t; K, T) = 0$$

with boundary condition

$$P(S_T, \sigma_T, T; K, T) = \max\{K - S_T, 0\}.$$

Take note that if the volatility is a function of asset price and time, then

$$\mathbb{E}^{\mathbb{Q}}\left[\sigma_T^2 \Big| S_T = K, S_t, \sigma_t, t\right] = \mathbb{E}^{\mathbb{Q}}\left[\sigma(S_T, T)^2 \Big| S_T = K, S_t, \sigma_t, t\right] = \sigma(K, T)^2$$

and the PDE becomes the Dupire equation. Thus, a local volatility model and stochastic volatility model will price a European option equally provided the above relationship is satisfied.

$\square$

6. *Hull–White Model.* Let $\{W_t^S : t \geq 0\}$ and $\{W_t^\sigma : t \geq 0\}$ be two independent standard Wiener processes on the probability space $(\Omega, \mathscr{F}, \mathbb{P})$. Suppose the asset price S_t and its

instantaneous variance σ_t^2 have the following diffusion processes

$$dS_t = (\mu - D)S_t dt + \sigma_t S_t dW_t^S$$
$$d\sigma_t^2 = \alpha\sigma_t^2 dt + \xi\sigma_t^2 dW_t^\sigma$$
$$dW_t^S \cdot dW_t^\sigma = \rho dt$$

where μ, D, α and ξ are constants. In addition, let B_t be the risk-free asset with the differential equation

$$dB_t = r B_t dt$$

where r is the risk-free interest rate.

By using the two-dimensional Girsanov's theorem, show that under the risk-neutral measure $\mathbb{Q}$,

$$dS_t = (r - D)S_t dt + \sigma_t S_t d\widetilde{W}_t^S$$
$$d\sigma_t^2 = (\alpha - \xi\gamma)\sigma_t^2 dt + \xi\sigma_t^2 d\widetilde{W}_t^\sigma$$

where $\widetilde{W}_t^S$ and $\widetilde{W}_t^\sigma$ are $\mathbb{Q}$-standard Wiener processes, $\widetilde{W}_t^S \perp \widetilde{W}_t^\sigma$ and γ is the market price of volatility risk.

Is the market arbitrage free and complete under the $\mathbb{Q}$ measure?

By letting $\tilde{\alpha} = \alpha - \xi\gamma$, and conditional on $\mathscr{F}_t$ and $\{\sigma_u : t \le u \le T\}$, show that under the risk-neutral measure $\mathbb{Q}$

$$\log\left(\frac{S_T}{S_t}\right) \bigg| \mathscr{F}_t, \{\sigma_u : t \le u \le T\}$$

$$\sim \mathcal{N}\left[\left(r - D - \frac{1}{2}\sigma_{\text{RMS}}^2(t,T)\right)(T-t), \sigma_{\text{RMS}}^2(t,T)(T-t)\right]$$

and conditional on $\mathscr{F}_t$ show that under the risk-neutral measure $\mathbb{Q}$

$$\log\left(\frac{\sigma_T^2}{\sigma_t^2}\right) \bigg| \mathscr{F}_t \sim \mathcal{N}\left[\left(\tilde{\alpha} - \frac{1}{2}\xi^2\right)(T-t), \xi^2(T-t)\right]$$

where

$$\sigma_{\text{RMS}}^2(t,T) = \frac{1}{T-t}\int_t^T \sigma_u^2 du$$

is known as the mean variance over the time interval $[t,T]$.

Show that

$$\mathbb{E}^{\mathbb{Q}}\left[\sigma_{\text{RMS}}^2(t,T) \big| \mathscr{F}_t\right] = \frac{\sigma_t^2}{\tilde{\alpha}(T-t)}\left(e^{\tilde{\alpha}(T-t)} - 1\right)$$

and

$$
\mathrm{Var}^{\mathbb{Q}}\left[\sigma_{\mathrm{RMS}}^2(t,T)\Big|\mathcal{F}_t\right] = \frac{\sigma_t^2}{(T-t)^2}\left[\frac{2e^{(2\tilde{\alpha}+\xi^2)(T-t)}}{(\tilde{\alpha}+\xi^2)(2\tilde{\alpha}+\xi^2)}\right.
$$

$$
\left. +\frac{2}{\tilde{\alpha}}\left(\frac{1}{2\tilde{\alpha}+\xi^2} - \frac{e^{\tilde{\alpha}(T-t)}}{\tilde{\alpha}+\xi^2}\right) - \frac{\left(e^{\tilde{\alpha}(T-t)}-1\right)^2}{\tilde{\alpha}^2}\right].
$$

We consider a European option price $V(S_t,\sigma_t^2,t;K,T)$ at time t written on S_t with expiry time $T > t$, strike price K, continuous dividend yield D and instantaneous variance σ_t^2,

$$
V(S_t,\sigma_t^2,t;K,T) = e^{-r(T-t)}\mathbb{E}^{\mathbb{Q}}\left[\Psi(S_T)\big|\mathcal{F}_t\right]
$$

where the payoff

$$
\Psi(S_T) = \begin{cases} \max\{S_T - K, 0\} & \text{for call option} \\[2mm] \max\{K - S_T, 0\} & \text{for put option.} \end{cases}
$$

Using the tower property, show that the price of a European option at time t is

$$
V(S_t,\sigma_t^2,t;K,T) = \mathbb{E}^{\mathbb{Q}}\left[V_{bs}\left(S_t,\sigma_{\mathrm{RMS}}^2(t,T),t;K,T\right)\Big|\mathcal{F}_t\right]
$$

where $V_{bs}(S_t,\sigma_{\mathrm{RMS}}^2(t,T),t;K,T)$ denotes the Black–Scholes formula for a European option at time t with spot price S_t, strike price K, time-dependent (or term-structure) variance $\sigma_{\mathrm{RMS}}^2(t,T)$ and option expiry time $T > t$.

By expanding $V_{bs}(S_t,\sigma_{\mathrm{RMS}}^2(t,T),t;K,T)$ about its expected value

$$
\overline{\sigma}_{\mathrm{RMS}}^2(t,T) = \mathbb{E}^{\mathbb{Q}}\left[\sigma_{\mathrm{RMS}}^2(t,T)\big|\mathcal{F}_t\right]
$$

up to second order, show that the option price can be approximated by

$$
V(S_t,\sigma_t^2,t;K,T) \approx V_{bs}(S_t,\overline{\sigma}_{\mathrm{RMS}}^2(t,T),t;K,T)
$$

$$
+\frac{1}{4\overline{\sigma}_{\mathrm{RMS}}^2(t,T)}\sqrt{\frac{T-t}{2\pi}}S_t e^{-D(T-t)}e^{-\frac{1}{2}(d_+^{\mathrm{RMS}})^2}
$$

$$
\times\left(d_+^{\mathrm{RMS}}d_-^{\mathrm{RMS}} - 1\right)\mathrm{Var}^{\mathbb{Q}}\left[\sigma_{\mathrm{RMS}}^2(t,T)\big|\mathcal{F}_t\right]
$$

where

$$
d_{\pm}^{\mathrm{RMS}} = \frac{\log(S_t/K) + (r - D \pm \frac{1}{2}\overline{\sigma}_{\mathrm{RMS}}^2(t,T))(T-t)}{\overline{\sigma}_{\mathrm{RMS}}(t,T)\sqrt{T-t}}.
$$

Solution: We first define

$$\widetilde{W}_t^S = W_t^S + \int_0^t \lambda_u \, du$$

$$\widetilde{W}_t^\sigma = W_t^\sigma + \int_0^t \gamma_u \, du$$

where λ_t is the market price of asset risk and γ_t is the market price of volatility risk. Since $W_t^S \perp\!\!\!\perp W_t^\sigma$, we can deduce $\widetilde{W}_t^S \perp\!\!\!\perp \widetilde{W}_t^\sigma$.

Let the portfolio Π_t be defined as

$$\Pi_t = \phi_t S_t + \psi_t B_t$$

where ϕ_t units are invested in risky asset S_t and ψ_t units are invested in risk-free asset B_t. Given that the holder of the portfolio will receive $DS_t dt$ for every risky asset held,

$$\begin{aligned}
d\Pi_t &= \phi_t \left(dS_t + DS_t dt \right) + \psi_t d B_t \\
&= \phi_t \left(\mu S_t dt + \sigma_t S_t dW_t^S \right) + \psi_t \left(r B_t dt \right) \\
&= r\Pi_t dt + \psi_t S_t \left[(\mu - r)dt + \sigma_t dW_t^S \right].
\end{aligned}$$

Substituting

$$dW_t^S = d\widetilde{W}_t^S - \lambda_t dt$$

$$dW_t^\sigma = d\widetilde{W}_t^\sigma - \gamma_t dt$$

into $d\Pi_t$ we have

$$\begin{aligned}
d\Pi_t &= r\Pi_t dt + \psi_t S_t \left[(\mu - r)dt + \sigma_t \left(d\widetilde{W}_t^S - \lambda_t dt \right) \right] \\
&= r\Pi_t dt + \psi_t S_t \left[\left(\mu - r - \lambda_t \sigma_t \right) dt + \sigma_t d\widetilde{W}_t^S \right].
\end{aligned}$$

Since $\widetilde{W}_t^S$ is a $\mathbb{Q}$-martingale, and in order for the discounted portfolio $e^{-rt}\Pi_t$ to be a $\mathbb{Q}$-martingale,

$$\begin{aligned}
d(e^{-rt}\Pi_t) &= -r e^{-rt}\Pi_t dt + e^{-rt} d\Pi_t \\
&= e^{-rt}\psi_t S_t \left[\left(\mu - r - \lambda_t \sigma_t \right) dt + \sigma_t d\widetilde{W}_t^S \right]
\end{aligned}$$

we set

$$\lambda_t = \frac{\mu - r}{\sigma_t}.$$

Hence, by substituting

$$dW_t^S = d\widetilde{W}_t^S - \lambda_t dt$$

into $dS_t = (\mu - D)S_t dt + \sigma_t S_t dW_t^S$, the asset price dynamics under the $\mathbb{Q}$ measure becomes

$$dS_t = (\mu - D)S_t dt + \sigma_t S_t \left(d\widetilde{W}_t^S - \lambda_t dt \right)$$

$$= (\mu - D)S_t dt + \sigma_t S_t \left(d\widetilde{W}_t^S - \left(\frac{\mu - r}{\sigma_t} \right) dt \right)$$

or

$$dS_t = (r - D)S_t dt + \sigma_t S_t d\widetilde{W}_t^S.$$

As for the case of the instantaneous variance, given that σ_t^2 is not a traded security, we can set

$$\gamma_t = \gamma$$

where γ is a constant. By substituting

$$dW_t^\sigma = d\widetilde{W}_t^\sigma - \gamma dt$$

into $d\sigma_t^2 = \alpha \sigma_t^2 dt + \xi \sigma_t^2 dW_t^\sigma$, the instantaneous variance under the $\mathbb{Q}$ measure is

$$d\sigma_t^2 = \alpha \sigma_t^2 dt + \xi \sigma_t^2 \left(d\widetilde{W}_t^\sigma - \gamma dt \right)$$

or

$$d\sigma_t^2 = (\alpha - \xi\gamma) \sigma_t^2 dt + \xi \sigma_t^2 d\widetilde{W}_t^\sigma.$$

The market is arbitrage free since we can construct a risk-neutral measure $\mathbb{Q}$ on the filtration $\mathcal{F}_s, 0 \le s \le t$. However, the market is not complete as $\mathbb{Q}$ is not unique, since σ_t^2 is not a traded security.

Expanding $d \log S_t$ and applying Itō's lemma,

$$d \log S_t = \frac{dS_t}{S_t} - \frac{1}{2} \left(\frac{dS_t}{S_t} \right)^2 + \dots$$

$$= (r - D)dt + \sigma_t d\widetilde{W}_t^S - \frac{1}{2}\sigma_t^2 dt$$

$$= \left(r - D - \frac{1}{2}\sigma_t^2 \right) dt + \sigma_t d\widetilde{W}_t^S.$$

Taking integrals,

$$\int_t^T d\log S_u = \int_t^T \left(r - D - \frac{1}{2}\sigma_u^2\right) du + \int_t^T \sigma_u \, d\widetilde{W}_u^S$$

$$\log\left(\frac{S_T}{S_t}\right) = \left(r - D - \frac{1}{2}\sigma_{\text{RMS}}^2(t,T)\right)(T-t) + \int_t^T \sigma_u \, d\widetilde{W}_u^S$$

where

$$\sigma_{\text{RMS}}^2(t,T) = \frac{1}{T-t}\int_t^T \sigma_u^2 \, du.$$

From the properties of the Itō integral,

$$\mathbb{E}^{\mathbb{Q}}\left[\log\left(\frac{S_T}{S_t}\right)\bigg|\mathscr{F}_t, \{\sigma_u : t \leq u \leq T\}\right] = \left(r - D - \frac{1}{2}\sigma_{\text{RMS}}^2(t,T)\right)(T-t)$$

and

$$\text{Var}^{\mathbb{Q}}\left[\log\left(\frac{S_T}{S_t}\right)\bigg|\mathscr{F}_t, \{\sigma_u : t \leq u \leq T\}\right]$$

$$= \text{Var}^{\mathbb{Q}}\left[\int_t^T \sigma_u d\widetilde{W}_u^S\bigg|\mathscr{F}_t, \{\sigma_u : t \leq u \leq T\}\right]$$

$$= \mathbb{E}^{\mathbb{Q}}\left[\left(\int_t^T \sigma_u d\widetilde{W}_u^S\right)^2\bigg|\mathscr{F}_t, \{\sigma_u : t \leq u \leq T\}\right]$$

$$- \left\{\mathbb{E}^{\mathbb{Q}}\left[\int_t^T \sigma_u d\widetilde{W}_u^S\bigg|\mathscr{F}_t, \{\sigma_u : t \leq u \leq T\}\right]\right\}^2$$

$$= \mathbb{E}^{\mathbb{Q}}\left[\int_t^T \sigma_u^2 du\bigg|\mathscr{F}_t, \{\sigma_u : t \leq u \leq T\}\right]$$

$$= \sigma_{\text{RMS}}^2(t,T)(T-t).$$

Thus, conditional on $\mathscr{F}_t$ and $\{\sigma_u : t \leq u \leq T\}$, we can easily deduce that

$$\log\left(\frac{S_T}{S_t}\right)\bigg|\mathscr{F}_t, \{\sigma_u : t \leq u \leq T\}$$

$$\sim \mathcal{N}\left[\left(r - D - \frac{1}{2}\sigma_{RMS}^2\right)(T-t), \sigma_{RMS}^2(T-t)\right].$$

In contrast, by expanding $d \log \sigma_t^2$ and applying Itō's lemma,

$$d \log \sigma_t^2 = \frac{d\sigma_t^2}{\sigma_t^2} - \frac{1}{2} \left(\frac{d\sigma_t^2}{\sigma_t^2} \right)^2 + \dots$$

$$= \widetilde{\alpha} dt + \xi d\widetilde{W}_t^\sigma - \frac{1}{2} \xi^2 dt$$

$$= \left(\widetilde{\alpha} - \frac{1}{2} \xi^2 \right) dt + \xi d\widetilde{W}_t^\sigma$$

and taking integrals,

$$\int_t^T d \log \sigma_u^2 = \int_t^T \left(\widetilde{\alpha} - \frac{1}{2} \xi^2 \right) du + \int_t^T \xi d\widetilde{W}_u^\sigma$$

$$\log \left(\frac{\sigma_T^2}{\sigma_t^2} \right) = \left(\widetilde{\alpha} - \frac{1}{2} \xi^2 \right) (T - t) + \xi \widetilde{W}_{T-t}^\sigma.$$

Thus, using Itō integral properties,

$$\log \left(\frac{\sigma_T^2}{\sigma_t^2} \right) \bigg| \mathscr{F}_t \sim \mathcal{N} \left[\left(\widetilde{\alpha} - \frac{1}{2} \xi^2 \right) (T - t), \xi^2 (T - t) \right].$$

To find $\mathbb{E}^Q \left[\sigma_{\mathrm{RMS}}^2 (t, T) \big| \mathscr{F}_t \right]$ we note that

$$\mathbb{E}^Q \left[\sigma_{\mathrm{RMS}}^2 (t, T) \big| \mathscr{F}_t \right] = \mathbb{E}^Q \left[\frac{1}{T-t} \int_t^T \sigma_u^2 du \bigg| \mathscr{F}_t \right]$$

$$= \frac{1}{T-t} \int_t^T \mathbb{E}^Q \left[\sigma_u^2 \big| \mathscr{F}_t \right] du$$

$$= \frac{1}{T-t} \int_t^T \sigma_t^2 e^{\widetilde{\alpha}(u-t)} du$$

$$= \frac{\sigma_t^2}{\widetilde{\alpha}(T-t)} \left(e^{\widetilde{\alpha}(T-t)} - 1 \right).$$

For the case of $\mathrm{Var}^Q \left[\sigma_{\mathrm{RMS}}^2 (t, T) \big| \mathscr{F}_t \right]$, we first note

$$\mathbb{E}^Q \left[\sigma_{\mathrm{RMS}}^4 (t, T) \big| \mathscr{F}_t \right] = \mathbb{E}^Q \left[\frac{1}{(T-t)^2} \left(\int_t^T \sigma_u^2 du \right) \left(\int_t^T \sigma_v^2 dv \right) \bigg| \mathscr{F}_t \right]$$

$$= \frac{1}{(T-t)^2} \int_{u=t}^{u=T} \int_{v=t}^{v=T} \mathbb{E}^Q \left[\sigma_u^2 \sigma_v^2 \big| \mathscr{F}_t \right] dv du.$$

Since

$$\sigma_u^2 = \sigma_t^2 e^{(\tilde{\alpha} - \frac{1}{2}\xi^2)(u-t) + \xi \widetilde{W}_{u-t}^\sigma} \quad \text{and} \quad \sigma_v^2 = \sigma_t^2 e^{(\tilde{\alpha} - \frac{1}{2}\xi^2)(v-t) + \xi \widetilde{W}_{v-t}^\sigma}$$

we have

$$\sigma_u^2 \sigma_v^2 = \sigma_t^4 e^{(\tilde{\alpha} - \frac{1}{2}\xi^2)(u+v-2t) + \xi(\widetilde{W}_{u-t}^\sigma + \widetilde{W}_{v-t}^\sigma)}$$

where

$$\widetilde{W}_{u-t}^\sigma + \widetilde{W}_{v-t}^\sigma \sim \mathcal{N}\left(0, u + v - 2t + 2\min\{u - t, v - t\}\right)$$

since

$$\text{Cov}\left(\widetilde{W}_{u-t}^\sigma, \widetilde{W}_{v-t}^\sigma\right) = \min\{u - t, v - t\}.$$

Thus,

$$
\begin{aligned}
\mathbb{E}^{\mathbb{Q}}\left[\sigma_{\text{RMS}}^4(t,T)\,\middle|\,\mathscr{F}_t\right] &= \frac{\sigma_t^2 e^{-2\tilde{\alpha}t}}{(T-t)^2} \int_{u=t}^{u=T} \int_{v=t}^{v=T} e^{\tilde{\alpha}(u+v) + \xi^2 \min\{u-t, v-t\}}\, dv\, du \\[4pt]
&= \frac{\sigma_t^2 e^{-2\tilde{\alpha}t}}{(T-t)^2} \int_{u=t}^{u=T} \int_{v=t}^{v=u} e^{\tilde{\alpha}(u+v) + \xi^2 (v-t)}\, dv\, du \\[4pt]
&\quad + \frac{\sigma_t^2 e^{-2\tilde{\alpha}t}}{(T-t)^2} \int_{u=t}^{u=T} \int_{v=u}^{v=T} e^{\tilde{\alpha}(u+v) + \xi^2 (u-t)}\, dv\, du \\[4pt]
&= \frac{\sigma_t^2 e^{-(2\tilde{\alpha}+\xi^2)t}}{(T-t)^2} \int_{u=t}^{u=T} \int_{v=t}^{v=u} e^{(\tilde{\alpha}+\xi^2)v + \tilde{\alpha}u}\, dv\, du \\[4pt]
&\quad + \frac{\sigma_t^2 e^{-(2\tilde{\alpha}+\xi^2)t}}{(T-t)^2} \int_{u=t}^{u=T} \int_{v=u}^{v=T} e^{(\tilde{\alpha}+\xi^2)u + \tilde{\alpha}v}\, dv\, du.
\end{aligned}
$$

Since

$$\int_{u=t}^{u=T} \int_{v=t}^{v=u} e^{(\tilde{\alpha}+\xi^2)v + \tilde{\alpha}u}\, dv\, du = \frac{e^{(2\tilde{\alpha}+\xi^2)T}}{(\tilde{\alpha}+\xi^2)(2\tilde{\alpha}+\xi^2)} - \frac{e^{\tilde{\alpha}T} e^{(\tilde{\alpha}+\xi^2)t}}{\tilde{\alpha}(\tilde{\alpha}+\xi^2)}$$

$$\qquad\qquad\qquad\qquad\qquad - \frac{e^{(2\tilde{\alpha}+\xi^2)t}}{(\tilde{\alpha}+\xi^2)(2\tilde{\alpha}+\xi^2)} + \frac{e^{(2\tilde{\alpha}+\xi^2)t}}{\tilde{\alpha}(\tilde{\alpha}+\xi^2)}$$

$$\int_{u=t}^{u=T} \int_{v=u}^{v=T} e^{(\tilde{\alpha}+\xi^2)u + \tilde{\alpha}v}\, dv\, du = \frac{e^{(2\tilde{\alpha}+\xi^2)T}}{\tilde{\alpha}(\tilde{\alpha}+\xi^2)} - \frac{e^{(2\tilde{\alpha}+\xi^2)T}}{\tilde{\alpha}(2\tilde{\alpha}+\xi^2)} - \frac{e^{\tilde{\alpha}T} e^{(\tilde{\alpha}+\xi^2)t}}{\tilde{\alpha}(\tilde{\alpha}+\xi^2)}$$

$$\qquad\qquad\qquad\qquad\qquad + \frac{e^{(2\tilde{\alpha}+\xi^2)t}}{\tilde{\alpha}(2\tilde{\alpha}+\xi^2)}$$

and after some algebraic manipulations, we eventually arrive at

$$\mathbb{E}^{\mathbb{Q}}\left[\sigma_{\text{RMS}}^4(t,T)\,\middle|\,\mathscr{F}_t\right] = \frac{\sigma_t^2}{(T-t)^2}\left[\frac{2e^{(2\widetilde{\alpha}+\xi^2)(T-t)}}{(\widetilde{\alpha}+\xi^2)(2\widetilde{\alpha}+\xi^2)}\right.$$
$$\left.+\frac{2}{\widetilde{\alpha}}\left(\frac{1}{2\widetilde{\alpha}+\xi^2}-\frac{e^{\widetilde{\alpha}(T-t)}}{\widetilde{\alpha}+\xi^2}\right)\right].$$

Thus,

$$\text{Var}^{\mathbb{Q}}\left[\sigma_{\text{RMS}}^2(t,T)\,\middle|\,\mathscr{F}_t\right] = \mathbb{E}^{\mathbb{Q}}\left[\sigma_{\text{RMS}}^4(t,T)\,\middle|\,\mathscr{F}_t\right]-\left\{\mathbb{E}^{\mathbb{Q}}\left[\sigma_{\text{RMS}}^2(t,T)\,\middle|\,\mathscr{F}_t\right]\right\}^2$$
$$=\frac{\sigma_t^2}{(T-t)^2}\left[\frac{2e^{(2\widetilde{\alpha}+\xi^2)(T-t)}}{(\widetilde{\alpha}+\xi^2)(2\widetilde{\alpha}+\xi^2)}\right.$$
$$\left.+\frac{2}{\widetilde{\alpha}}\left(\frac{1}{2\widetilde{\alpha}+\xi^2}-\frac{e^{\widetilde{\alpha}(T-t)}}{\widetilde{\alpha}+\xi^2}\right)-\frac{\left(e^{\widetilde{\alpha}(T-t)}-1\right)^2}{\widetilde{\alpha}^2}\right].$$

Conditional on $\mathscr{F}_t$ and $\{\sigma_u : t\le u\le T\}$, S_T is log normal with initial value S_t and from the tower property,

$$V(S_t,\sigma_t^2,t;K,T) = e^{-r(T-t)}\mathbb{E}^{\mathbb{Q}}\left[\Psi(S_T)\,\middle|\,\mathscr{F}_t\right]$$
$$= \mathbb{E}^{\mathbb{Q}}\left[e^{-r(T-t)}\mathbb{E}^{\mathbb{Q}}\left[\Psi(S_T)\,\middle|\,\mathscr{F}_t,\{\sigma_u:t\le u\le T\}\right]\,\middle|\,\mathscr{F}_t\right]$$
$$= \mathbb{E}^{\mathbb{Q}}\left[V_{bs}(S_t,\sigma_{\text{RMS}}^2(t,T),t;K,T)\,\middle|\,\mathscr{F}_t\right]$$

where the inner expectation is the Black–Scholes formula with initial value S_t and time-dependent (or term-structure) variance $\sigma_{\text{RMS}}^2(t,T) = \frac{1}{T-t}\int_t^T \sigma_u^2\,du$. Thus, the option price under stochastic volatility is the average value over all possible volatility paths.

By expanding $V_{bs}(S_t,\sigma_{\text{RMS}}^2(t,T),t;K,T)$ about its expected value

$$\overline{\sigma}_{\text{RMS}}^2(t,T) = \mathbb{E}^{\mathbb{Q}}\left[\sigma_{\text{RMS}}^2(t,T)\,\middle|\,\mathscr{F}_t\right]$$

up to second order,

$$V_{bs}(S_t,\sigma_{\text{RMS}}^2(t,T),t;K,T)$$

$$\approx V_{bs}(S_t,\overline{\sigma}_{\text{RMS}}^2(t,T),t;K,T)$$

$$+\left.\frac{\partial V_{bs}}{\partial(\sigma_{\text{RMS}}^2(t,T))}\right|_{\sigma_{\text{RMS}}^2(t,T)=\overline{\sigma}_{\text{RMS}}^2(t,T)}\left(\sigma_{\text{RMS}}^2(t,T)-\overline{\sigma}_{\text{RMS}}^2(t,T)\right)$$

$$+\left.\frac{\partial^2 V_{bs}}{\partial(\sigma_{\text{RMS}}^2(t,T))^2}\right|_{\sigma_{\text{RMS}}^2(t,T)=\overline{\sigma}_{\text{RMS}}^2(t,T)}\left(\sigma_{\text{RMS}}^2(t,T)-\overline{\sigma}_{\text{RMS}}^2(t,T)\right)^2.$$

From Problems 2.2.2.6 (page 105) and 2.2.4.7 (page 226), we have

$$\frac{\partial V}{\partial \sigma} = \sqrt{\frac{T-t}{2\pi}} S_t e^{-D(T-t)} e^{-\frac{1}{2}d_+^2}$$

$$\frac{\partial^2 V}{\partial \sigma^2} = \sqrt{\frac{T-t}{2\pi}} S_t e^{-D(T-t)} e^{-\frac{1}{2}d_+^2} \frac{d_+ d_-}{\sigma}$$

where

$$d_\pm = \frac{\log(S_t/K) + (r - D \pm \frac{1}{2}\sigma^2)(T-t)}{\sigma\sqrt{T-t}}.$$

By setting $v = \sigma^2$,

$$\frac{\partial V}{\partial \sigma^2} = \frac{\partial V}{\partial \sigma} \frac{\partial \sigma}{\partial v}$$

$$= \frac{1}{2\sigma} \sqrt{\frac{T-t}{2\pi}} S_t e^{-D(T-t)} e^{-\frac{1}{2}d_+^2}$$

$$\frac{\partial^2 V}{\partial (\sigma^2)^2} = \frac{\partial}{\partial \sigma}\left(\frac{\partial V}{\partial \sigma}\frac{\partial \sigma}{\partial v}\right)$$

$$= \frac{\partial^2 V}{\partial \sigma^2}\frac{\partial \sigma}{\partial v} + \frac{\partial V}{\partial \sigma}\frac{\partial^2 \sigma}{\partial \sigma \partial v}$$

$$= \frac{1}{2\sigma^2} \sqrt{\frac{T-t}{2\pi}} S_t e^{-D(T-t)} e^{-\frac{1}{2}d_+^2} d_+ d_-$$

$$\quad - \frac{1}{2\sigma^2} \sqrt{\frac{T-t}{2\pi}} S_t e^{-D(T-t)} e^{-\frac{1}{2}d_+^2}$$

$$= \frac{1}{2\sigma^2} \sqrt{\frac{T-t}{2\pi}} S_t e^{-D(T-t)} e^{-\frac{1}{2}d_+^2} \left(d_+ d_- - 1\right).$$

Thus,

$$\left.\frac{\partial V_{bs}}{\partial(\sigma_{\mathrm{RMS}}^2(t,T))}\right|_{\sigma_{\mathrm{RMS}}^2(t,T)=\bar{\sigma}_{\mathrm{RMS}}^2(t,T)} = \frac{1}{2\bar{\sigma}_{\mathrm{RMS}}^2(t,T)} \sqrt{\frac{T-t}{2\pi}} S_t e^{-D(T-t)} e^{-\frac{1}{2}(d_+^{\mathrm{RMS}})^2}$$

$$\left.\frac{\partial^2 V_{bs}}{\partial(\sigma_{\mathrm{RMS}}^2(t,T))^2}\right|_{\sigma_{\mathrm{RMS}}^2(t,T)=\bar{\sigma}_{\mathrm{RMS}}^2(t,T)} = \frac{1}{2\bar{\sigma}_{\mathrm{RMS}}^2(t,T)} \sqrt{\frac{T-t}{2\pi}} S_t e^{-D(T-t)} e^{-\frac{1}{2}(d_+^{\mathrm{RMS}})^2}$$

$$\times \left(d_+^{\mathrm{RMS}} d_-^{\mathrm{RMS}} - 1\right).$$

Therefore,

$$
V(S_t, \sigma_t^2, t; K, T)
$$

$$
\approx V_{bs}(S_t, \overline{\sigma}_{\text{RMS}}^2(t, T), t; K, T)
$$

$$
+ \frac{1}{2\overline{\sigma}_{\text{RMS}}^2(t, T)} \sqrt{\frac{T-t}{2\pi}} S_t e^{-D(T-t)} e^{-\frac{1}{2}(d_+^{\text{RMS}})^2} \mathbb{E}^{\mathbb{Q}} \left[\sigma_{\text{RMS}}^2(t, T) - \overline{\sigma}_{\text{RMS}}^2(t, T) \Big| \mathcal{F}_t \right]
$$

$$
+ \frac{1}{4\overline{\sigma}_{\text{RMS}}^2(t, T)} \sqrt{\frac{T-t}{2\pi}} S_t e^{-D(T-t)} e^{-\frac{1}{2}(d_+^{\text{RMS}})^2} \left(d_+^{\text{RMS}} d_-^{\text{RMS}} - 1 \right)
$$

$$
\times \mathbb{E}^{\mathbb{Q}} \left[\left(\sigma_{\text{RMS}}^2(t, T) - \overline{\sigma}_{\text{RMS}}^2(t, T) \right)^2 \Big| \mathcal{F}_t \right]
$$

$$
= V_{bs}(S_t, \overline{\sigma}_{\text{RMS}}^2(t, T), t; K, T)
$$

$$
+ \frac{1}{4\overline{\sigma}_{\text{RMS}}^2(t, T)} \sqrt{\frac{T-t}{2\pi}} S_t e^{-D(T-t)} e^{-\frac{1}{2}(d_+^{\text{RMS}})^2} \left(d_+^{\text{RMS}} d_-^{\text{RMS}} - 1 \right)
$$

$$
\times \text{Var}^{\mathbb{Q}} \left[\sigma_{\text{RMS}}^2(t, T) \Big| \mathcal{F}_t \right].
$$

$\square$

7. *Heston Model.* Let $\{W_t^S : t \geq 0\}$ and $\{W_t^\sigma : t \geq 0\}$ be two standard Wiener processes on the probability space $(\Omega, \mathcal{F}, \mathbb{P})$ with correlation $\rho \in (-1, 1)$. Suppose that the asset price S_t and its instantaneous variance σ_t^2 have the following dynamics

$$
dS_t = (\mu - D)S_t dt + \sigma_t S_t dW_t^S
$$

$$
d\sigma_t^2 = \kappa(\theta - \sigma_t^2)dt + \alpha\sigma_t dW_t^\sigma
$$

$$
dW_t^S \cdot dW_t^\sigma = \rho dt
$$

where μ, D, κ, θ and α are constants. In addition, let B_t be the risk-free asset with differential equation

$$
dB_t = r B_t dt
$$

where r is the risk-free interest rate.

By introducing $\{Z_t : t \geq 0\}$ as a standard Wiener process, independent of W_t^σ, show that we can write

$$
W_t^S = \rho W_t^\sigma + \sqrt{1 - \rho^2} Z_t.
$$

Using the two-dimensional Girsanov's theorem, show that under the risk-neutral measure $\mathbb{Q}$,

$$
dS_t = (r - D)S_t dt + \sigma_t S_t \left(\rho d\widetilde{W}_t^\sigma + \sqrt{1 - \rho^2} d\widetilde{Z}_t \right)
$$

$$
d\sigma_t^2 = \left(\kappa(\theta - \sigma_t^2) - \alpha\gamma_t\sigma_t \right) dt + \alpha\sigma_t d\widetilde{W}_t^\sigma
$$

where $\widetilde{W}_t^\sigma$ and $\widetilde{Z}_t$ are Q-standard Wiener processes, $\widetilde{W}_t^\sigma \perp\!\!\!\perp \widetilde{Z}_t$ and γ_t is the market price of volatility risk.

Is the market arbitrage free and complete under the Q measure?

By assuming the market price of volatility risk is proportional to the instantaneous volatility σ_t,

$$\gamma_t = c\sigma_t$$

where c is a positive constant, show that the dynamics of the model can be described by

$$dS_t = (r - D)S_t dt + \sigma_t S_t \left(\rho d\widetilde{W}_t^\sigma + \sqrt{1 - \rho^2} d\widetilde{Z}_t \right)$$
$$d\sigma_t^2 = \tilde{\kappa}(\tilde{\theta} - \sigma_t^2)dt + \alpha\sigma_t d\widetilde{W}_t^\sigma$$

such that $\tilde{\kappa} = \kappa + \alpha c$ and $\tilde{\theta} = \kappa\theta(\kappa + \alpha c)^{-1}$.

Hence, conditional on $\mathcal{F}_t$ and $\{\sigma_u : t \le u \le T\}$ show that

$$\log\left(\frac{S_T/\xi_T}{S_t/\xi_t} \right)\Bigg| \mathcal{F}_t, \{\sigma_u : t \le u \le T\}$$

$$\sim \mathcal{N}\left[\left(r - D - \frac{1}{2}\sigma_{RMS}^2(t,T)\right)(T-t), \sigma_{RMS}^2(t,T)(T-t) \right]$$

where

$$\xi_s = e^{\rho \int_0^s \sigma_u d\widetilde{W}_u^\sigma - \frac{1}{2}\rho^2 \int_0^s \sigma_u^2 du} \quad \text{and} \quad \sigma_{RMS}^2(t,T) = \frac{1 - \rho^2}{T - t} \int_t^T \sigma_u^2 du.$$

We consider a European option price $V(S_t, \sigma_t^2, t; K, T)$ at time t written on S_t with expiry time $T > t$, strike price K, continuous dividend yield D and instantaneous variance σ_t,

$$V(S_t, \sigma_t^2, t; K, T) = e^{-r(T-t)}\mathbb{E}^Q\left[\Psi(S_T) \big| \mathcal{F}_t \right]$$

where the payoff is

$$\Psi(S_T) = \begin{cases} \max\{S_T - K, 0\} & \text{for call option} \\ \max\{K - S_T, 0\} & \text{for put option.} \end{cases}$$

Using the tower property, show that the price of a European option at time t can be expressed by

$$V(S_t, \sigma_t^2, t; K, T) = \mathbb{E}^Q\left[\frac{\xi_T}{\xi_t} V_{bs}\left(S_t, \sigma_{RMS}^2(t,T), t; K/(\xi_T/\xi_t), T\right) \Bigg| \mathcal{F}_t \right]$$

where $V_{bs}(S_t, \sigma^2_{\text{RMS}}(t,T), t; K, T)$ denotes the Black–Scholes formula for a European option at time t with spot price S_t, strike price K, variance $\sigma^2_{\text{RMS}}(t,T)$ and option expiry time $T > t$.

Finally, by denoting $\mathbb{Q}^\xi$ as a new measure where ξ_t is used as numéraire, show that

$$V(S_t, \sigma^2_t, t; K, T) = \mathbb{E}^{\mathbb{Q}^\xi}\left[V_{bs}\left(S_t, \sigma^2_{\text{RMS}}(t,T), t; K/(\xi_T/\xi_t), T\right)\Big|\mathscr{F}_t\right].$$

Solution: For the first two results, see Problem 7.2.2.2 (page 687).

The market is arbitrage free since we can construct a risk-neutral measure $\mathbb{Q}$ on the filtration $\mathscr{F}_s$, $0 \le s \le t$. However, the market is not complete since σ^2_t is not a traded asset and therefore $\mathbb{Q}$ is not unique. Thus, the risk-neutral measure $\mathbb{Q}$ is an equivalent market measure.

By setting $\gamma = c\sigma_t$,

$$\begin{aligned}
d\sigma^2_t &= \left(\kappa(\theta - \sigma^2_t) - \alpha c\sigma^2_t\right)dt + \alpha\sigma_t d\widetilde{W}^\sigma_t \\
&= \left(\kappa\theta - (\kappa + \alpha c)\sigma^2_t\right)dt + \alpha\sigma_t d\widetilde{W}^\sigma_t \\
&= \tilde{\kappa}(\tilde{\theta} - \sigma^2_t)dt + \alpha\sigma_t d\widetilde{W}^\sigma_t
\end{aligned}$$

such that $\tilde{\kappa} = \kappa + \alpha c$ and $\tilde{\theta} = \kappa\theta(\kappa + \alpha c)^{-1}$.

To show that

$$\log\left(\frac{S_T/\xi_T}{S_t/\xi_t}\right)\Bigg|\mathscr{F}_t, \{\sigma_u : t \le u \le T\}$$

$$\sim \mathcal{N}\left[\left(r - D - \frac{1}{2}\sigma^2_{\text{RMS}}(t,T)\right)(T-t), \sigma^2_{\text{RMS}}(t,T)(T-t)\right]$$

where

$$\xi_s = e^{\rho\int_0^s \sigma_u d\widetilde{W}^\sigma_u - \frac{1}{2}\rho^2\int_0^s \sigma^2_u du} \quad \text{and} \quad \sigma^2_{\text{RMS}}(t,T) = \frac{1-\rho^2}{T-t}\int_t^T \sigma^2_u du$$

see Problem 3.2.3.10 of *Problems and Solutions in Mathematical Finance, Volume 1: Stochastic Calculus.*

Conditional on $\mathscr{F}_t$ and $\{\sigma_u : t \le u \le T\}$, S_T is log normal with initial value $S_t\xi_T/\xi_t$ and using the tower property,

$$\begin{aligned}
V(S_t, \sigma^2_t, t; K, T) &= e^{-r(T-t)}\mathbb{E}^{\mathbb{Q}}\left[\Psi(S_T)\big|\mathscr{F}_t\right] \\
&= \mathbb{E}^{\mathbb{Q}}\left[e^{-r(T-t)}\mathbb{E}^{\mathbb{Q}}\left[\Psi(S_T)\big|\mathscr{F}_t, \{\sigma_u : t \le u \le T\}\right]\Big|\mathscr{F}_t\right]
\end{aligned}$$

such that the inner expectation is the Black–Scholes formula with initial value $S_t\xi_T/\xi_t$ and term-structure variance $\sigma^2_{\text{RMS}}(t,T) = \dfrac{1-\rho^2}{T-t}\displaystyle\int_t^T \sigma^2_u du$.

Thus,

$$V(S_t, \sigma_t^2, t; K, T) = \mathbb{E}^{\mathbb{Q}} \left[V_{bs} \left(\frac{S_t \xi_T}{\xi_t}, \sigma_{\mathrm{RMS}}^2(t, T), t; K, T \right) \middle| \mathscr{F}_t \right].$$

For a constant value $\pi > 0$, the Black–Scholes formula with a constant or time-dependent volatility σ has the following identity (see Problem 2.2.2.8, page 109)

$$V_{bs} \left(\pi S_t, \sigma^2, t; K, T \right) = \pi V_{bs}(S_t, \sigma^2, t; K/\pi, T)$$

and therefore

$$V(S_t, \sigma_t^2, t; K, T) = \mathbb{E}^{\mathbb{Q}} \left[\frac{\xi_T}{\xi_t} V_{bs} \left(S_t, \sigma_{\mathrm{RMS}}^2(t, T), t; K/(\xi_T/\xi_t), T \right) \middle| \mathscr{F}_t \right].$$

Under the change of numéraire for a payoff X_T

$$N_t^{(1)} \mathbb{E}^{\mathbb{Q}^{(1)}} \left[\frac{X_T}{N_T^{(1)}} \middle| \mathscr{F}_t \right] = N_t^{(2)} \mathbb{E}^{\mathbb{Q}^{(2)}} \left[\frac{X_T}{N_T^{(2)}} \middle| \mathscr{F}_t \right]$$

where for $i = 1, 2$, $N^{(i)}$ is a numéraire and $\mathbb{Q}^{(i)}$ is the measure under which the asset prices discounted by $N^{(i)}$ are $\mathbb{Q}^{(i)}$-martingales.

Under the risk-neutral measure $\mathbb{Q}$ we have

$$N_t^{(1)} = 1 \quad \text{and} \quad N_T^{(1)} = 1$$

and under the measure $\mathbb{Q}^\xi$

$$N_t^{(2)} = \xi_t \quad \text{and} \quad N_T^{(2)} = \xi_T.$$

By setting $X_T = \frac{\xi_T}{\xi_t} V_{bs} \left(S_t, \sigma_{\mathrm{RMS}}^2(t, T), t; K, T \right)$, the option price under the measure $\mathbb{Q}^\xi$ is

$$V(S_t, \sigma_t^2, t; K, T) = \xi_t \mathbb{E}^{\mathbb{Q}^\xi} \left[\frac{\xi_T}{\xi_t} \frac{V_{bs} \left(S_t, \sigma_{\mathrm{RMS}}^2(t, T), t; K/(\xi_T/\xi_t), T \right)}{\xi_T} \middle| \mathscr{F}_t \right]$$

$$= \mathbb{E}^{\mathbb{Q}^\xi} \left[V_{bs} \left(S_t, \sigma_{\mathrm{RMS}}^2(t, T), t; K/(\xi_T/\xi_t), T \right) \middle| \mathscr{F}_t \right].$$

$\square$

8. *Heston Model – Black–Scholes Equation.* Let $(\Omega, \mathscr{F}, \mathbb{P})$ be a probability space and let $\{W_t^S : t \geq 0\}$ and $\{W_t^v : t \geq 0\}$ be two correlated Wiener processes. Suppose that the

asset price S_t and the instantaneous variance v_t follow the diffusion processes

$$dS_t = (\mu - D)S_t dt + \sqrt{v_t} S_t dW_t^S$$
$$dv_t = \kappa(\theta - v_t)dt + \xi\sqrt{v_t} dW_t^v$$
$$dW_t^S \cdot dW_t^v = \rho dt$$

where μ is the drift, D is the continuous dividend yield, $\kappa, \theta, \xi > 0$ are constant parameters, ρ is the correlation coefficient such that $\rho \in (-1, 1)$ and let r be the risk-free interest rate from a money-market account.

By considering a hedging portfolio consisting of two European-style options $V(S_t, v_t, t; T_1)$ and $V(S_t, v_t, t; T_2)$ of different expiry dates T_1 and T_2 and the underlying asset S_t, show that

$$\frac{\partial V}{\partial t} + \frac{1}{2}v_t S_t^2 \frac{\partial^2 V}{\partial S_t^2} + \frac{1}{2}\xi^2 v_t \frac{\partial^2 V}{\partial v_t^2} + \rho\xi v_t S_t \frac{\partial^2 V}{\partial S_t \partial v_t}$$

$$+(r - D)S_t\frac{\partial V}{\partial S_t} + \left(\kappa(\theta - v_t) - \lambda(S_t, v_t)\right)\frac{\partial V}{\partial v_t} - rV(S_t, v_t, t; T) = 0$$

where $\lambda(S_t, v_t)$ is the market price of volatility risk independent of the expiry time T.

Solution: Let $V(S_t, v_t, t; T)$ denote the price of an option at time $t < T$ with expiry time T. By applying Itō's lemma, dV is given by

$$dV = \frac{\partial V}{\partial t}dt + \frac{\partial V}{\partial S_t}dS_t + \frac{\partial V}{\partial v_t}dv_t + \frac{1}{2}\frac{\partial^2 V}{\partial S_t^2}(dS_t)^2 + \frac{1}{2}\frac{\partial^2 V}{\partial v_t^2}(dv_t)^2$$

$$+\frac{\partial^2 V}{\partial S_t \partial v_t}(dS_t)(dv_t) + \dots$$

$$= \frac{\partial V}{\partial t}dt + \frac{\partial V}{\partial S_t}\left((\mu - D)S_t dt + \sqrt{v_t} S_t dW_t^S\right)$$

$$+\frac{\partial V}{\partial v_t}\left(\kappa(\theta - v_t)dt + \xi\sqrt{v_t} dW_t^v\right)$$

$$+\frac{1}{2}\frac{\partial^2 V}{\partial S_t^2}\left(v_t S_t^2 dt\right) + \frac{1}{2}\frac{\partial^2 V}{\partial v_t^2}(\xi^2 v_t dt) + \frac{\partial^2 V}{\partial S_t \partial v_t}(\rho\xi v_t S_t dt)$$

$$= \left(\frac{\partial V}{\partial t} + \frac{1}{2}v_t S_t^2 \frac{\partial^2 V}{\partial S_t^2} + \frac{1}{2}\xi^2 v_t \frac{\partial^2 V}{\partial v_t^2} + \rho\xi v_t S_t \frac{\partial^2 V}{\partial S_t \partial v_t} + (\mu - D)S_t\frac{\partial V}{\partial S_t}\right.$$

$$\left.+ \kappa(\theta - v_t)\frac{\partial V}{\partial v_t}\right)dt + \sqrt{v_t}S_t\frac{\partial V}{\partial S_t}dW_t^S + \xi\sqrt{v_t}\frac{\partial V}{\partial v_t}dW_t^v.$$

Let the portfolio Π_t consist of buying one option with expiry date T_1, $V(S_t, v_t, t; T_1)$, selling Δ_1 units of asset S_t and selling Δ_2 units of the option with expiry date T_2, $V(S_t, v_t, t; T_2)$, where $T_1 \neq T_2$. By setting

$$V_1(S_t, v_t, t; T_1) = V(S_t, v_t, t; T_1)$$
$$V_2(S_t, v_t, t; T_2) = V(S_t, v_t, t; T_2)$$

at time t, the value of the portfolio is

$$\Pi_t = V_1(S_t, v_t, t; T_1) - \Delta_1 S_t - \Delta_2 V_2(S_t, v_t, t; T_2).$$

Since we receive $DS_t dt$ for every asset held, the change in portfolio Π_t is

$d\Pi_t$

$$= dV_1 - \Delta_1 \left(dS_t + DS_t dt\right) - \Delta_2 dV_2$$

$$= \left(\frac{\partial V_1}{\partial t} + \frac{1}{2} v_t S_t^2 \frac{\partial^2 V_1}{\partial S_t^2} + \frac{1}{2} \xi^2 v_t \frac{\partial^2 V_1}{\partial v_t^2} + \rho \xi v_t S_t \frac{\partial^2 V_1}{\partial S_t \partial v_t} + (\mu - D) S_t \frac{\partial V_1}{\partial S_t} \right.$$

$$\left. + \kappa(\theta - v_t) \frac{\partial V_1}{\partial v_t} \right) dt - \Delta_2 \left(\frac{\partial V_2}{\partial t} + \frac{1}{2} v_t S_t^2 \frac{\partial^2 V_2}{\partial S_t^2} + \frac{1}{2} \xi^2 v_t \frac{\partial^2 V_2}{\partial v_t^2} + \rho \xi v_t S_t \frac{\partial^2 V_2}{\partial S_t \partial v_t} \right.$$

$$\left. + (\mu - D) S_t \frac{\partial V_2}{\partial S_t} + \kappa(\theta - v_t) \frac{\partial V_2}{\partial v_t} \right) dt - \Delta_1 \mu S_t dt$$

$$+ \left(\frac{\partial V_1}{\partial S_t} - \Delta_1 - \Delta_2 \frac{\partial V_2}{\partial S_t} \right) \sqrt{v_t} S_t dW_t^S + \left(\frac{\partial V_1}{\partial S_t} - \Delta_2 \frac{\partial V_2}{\partial v_t} \right) \xi \sqrt{v_t} dW_t^v.$$

To eliminate both the asset and volatility risk, we have

$$\frac{\partial V_1}{\partial S_t} = \Delta_1 + \Delta_2 \frac{\partial V_2}{\partial S_t} \quad \text{and} \quad \frac{\partial V_1}{\partial S_t} = \Delta_2 \frac{\partial V_2}{\partial v_t}$$

or

$$\Delta_1 = \frac{\partial V_1}{\partial S_t} - \left(\frac{\partial V_1}{\partial S_t} \frac{\partial V_2}{\partial S_t} \right) \bigg/ \frac{\partial V_2}{\partial v_t} \quad \text{and} \quad \Delta_2 = \frac{\partial V_1}{\partial S_t} \bigg/ \frac{\partial V_2}{\partial v_t}.$$

Under the no-arbitrage condition, the return on the portfolio Π_t invested in a risk-free interest rate would see a growth of

$$d\Pi_t = r\Pi_t dt$$

and therefore we have

$$\frac{\partial V_1}{\partial t} + \frac{1}{2}v_t S_t^2 \frac{\partial^2 V_1}{\partial S_t^2} + \frac{1}{2}\xi^2 v_t \frac{\partial^2 V_1}{\partial v_t^2} + \rho\xi v_t S_t \frac{\partial^2 V_1}{\partial S_t \partial v_t} + (\mu - D)S_t \frac{\partial V_1}{\partial S_t} + \kappa(\theta - v_t)\frac{\partial V_1}{\partial v_t}$$

$$- \left(\frac{\partial V_1}{\partial S_t} \middle/ \frac{\partial V_2}{\partial v_t}\right)\left(\frac{\partial V_2}{\partial t} + \frac{1}{2}v_t S_t^2 \frac{\partial^2 V_2}{\partial S_t^2} + \frac{1}{2}\xi^2 v_t \frac{\partial^2 V_2}{\partial v_t^2} + \rho\xi v_t S_t \frac{\partial^2 V_2}{\partial S_t \partial v_t}\right.$$

$$+ (\mu - D)S_t \frac{\partial V_2}{\partial S_t} + \kappa(\theta - v_t)\frac{\partial V_2}{\partial v_t}\right) - \left(\frac{\partial V_1}{\partial S_t} - \left(\frac{\partial V_1}{\partial S_t}\frac{\partial V_2}{\partial S_t}\right) \middle/ \frac{\partial V_2}{\partial v_t}\right)\mu S_t$$

$$= r\left[V_1(S_t, v_t, t; T_1) - \left(\frac{\partial V_1}{\partial S_t} - \left(\frac{\partial V_1}{\partial S_t}\frac{\partial V_2}{\partial S_t}\right) \middle/ \frac{\partial V_2}{\partial v_t}\right)S_t\right.$$

$$- \left(\frac{\partial V_1}{\partial S_t} \middle/ \frac{\partial V_2}{\partial v_t}\right)V_2(S_t, v_t, t; T_2)\right].$$

By gathering together all V_1 terms on the left-hand side and all V_2 terms on the right-hand side

$$\frac{\left[\begin{array}{c} \dfrac{\partial V_1}{\partial t} + \dfrac{1}{2}v_t S_t^2 \dfrac{\partial^2 V_1}{\partial S_t^2} + \dfrac{1}{2}\xi^2 v_t \dfrac{\partial^2 V_1}{\partial v_t^2} + \rho\xi v_t S_t \dfrac{\partial^2 V_1}{\partial S_t \partial v_t} \\[3mm] + (r - D)S_t \dfrac{\partial V_1}{\partial S_t} + \kappa(\theta - v_t)\dfrac{\partial V_1}{\partial v_t} - rV_1(S_t, v_t, t; T_1) \end{array}\right]}{\dfrac{\partial V_1}{\partial v_t}}$$

$$= \frac{\left[\begin{array}{c} \dfrac{\partial V_2}{\partial t} + \dfrac{1}{2}v_t S_t^2 \dfrac{\partial^2 V_2}{\partial S_t^2} + \dfrac{1}{2}\xi^2 v_t \dfrac{\partial^2 V_2}{\partial v_t^2} + \rho\xi v_t S_t \dfrac{\partial^2 V_2}{\partial S_t \partial v_t} \\[3mm] + (r - D)S_t \dfrac{\partial V_2}{\partial S_t} + \kappa(\theta - v_t)\dfrac{\partial V_2}{\partial v_t} - rV_2(S_t, v_t, t; T_2) \end{array}\right]}{\dfrac{\partial V_2}{\partial v_t}}.$$

Since the left-hand side is a function of T_1 and the right-hand side is a function of T_2, the only way for the equality to hold is for both sides to be equal to a common function $\lambda(S_t, v_t)$ independent of the expiry time T. By dropping the subscripts we have

$$\frac{\left[\begin{array}{c} \dfrac{\partial V}{\partial t} + \dfrac{1}{2}v_t S_t^2 \dfrac{\partial^2 V}{\partial S_t^2} + \dfrac{1}{2}\xi^2 v_t \dfrac{\partial^2 V}{\partial v_t^2} + \rho\xi v_t S_t \dfrac{\partial^2 V}{\partial S_t \partial v_t} \\[3mm] + (r - D)S_t \dfrac{\partial V}{\partial S_t} + \kappa(\theta - v_t)\dfrac{\partial V}{\partial v_t} - rV(S_t, v_t, t; T_1) \end{array}\right]}{\dfrac{\partial V}{\partial v_t}} = \lambda(S_t, v_t).$$

Thus,

$$\frac{\partial V}{\partial t} + \frac{1}{2}v_t S_t^2 \frac{\partial^2 V}{\partial S_t^2} + \frac{1}{2}\xi^2 v_t \frac{\partial^2 V}{\partial v_t^2} + \rho \xi v_t S_t \frac{\partial^2 V}{\partial S_t \partial v_t}$$

$$+(r-D)S_t \frac{\partial V}{\partial S_t} + \left(\kappa(\theta - v_t) - \lambda(S_t, v_t)\right)\frac{\partial V}{\partial v_t} - rV(S_t, v_t, t; T) = 0.$$

$\square$

9. *Heston Model – European Option Price.* Let $\{W_t^S : t \geq 0\}$ and $\{W_t^v : t \geq 0\}$ be two standard Wiener processes on the probability space $(\Omega, \mathcal{F}, \mathbb{P})$ with correlation $\rho \in (-1, 1)$. Suppose that the asset price S_t and its instantaneous variance v_t follow

$$dS_t = (\mu - D)S_t dt + \sqrt{v_t} S_t dW_t^S$$
$$dv_t = \kappa(\theta - v_t)dt + \xi\sqrt{v_t}dW_t^v$$
$$dW_t^S \cdot dW_t^v = \rho dt$$

where μ is the asset drift, D is the continuous dividend yield, κ is the variance mean-reversion rate, θ is the variance long-term mean, ξ is the vol-of-vol and $\rho \in (-1, 1)$ is the correlation coefficient. In addition, we let r be the risk-free interest rate from a money-market account.

Let $C(S_t, v_t, t; K, T)$ denote the price of a European call option at time t with strike price K and expiry time $T > t$, satisfying the Black–Scholes equation

$$\frac{\partial C}{\partial t} + \frac{1}{2}v_t S_t^2 \frac{\partial^2 C}{\partial S_t^2} + \frac{1}{2}\xi^2 v_t \frac{\partial^2 C}{\partial v_t^2} + \rho \xi v_t S_t \frac{\partial^2 C}{\partial S_t \partial v_t}$$

$$+(r-D)S_t \frac{\partial C}{\partial S_t} + \left(\kappa(\theta - v_t) - \lambda(S_t, v_t)\right)\frac{\partial C}{\partial v_t} - rC(S_t, v_t, t; K, T) = 0$$

such that $\lambda(S_t, v_t)$ is the market price of volatility risk, with boundary condition

$$C(S_T, v_T, T; K, T) = \max\{S_T - K, 0\}.$$

By introducing x_t as the logarithm of the spot price

$$x_t = \log S_t$$

and assuming $\lambda(S_t, v_t) = \lambda v_t$ where λ is a constant value, show that $C(x_t, v_t, t; K, T)$ satisfies the following PDE

$$\frac{\partial C}{\partial t} + \frac{1}{2}v_t \frac{\partial^2 C}{\partial x_t^2} + \frac{1}{2}\xi^2 v_t \frac{\partial^2 C}{\partial v_t^2} + \rho \xi v_t \frac{\partial^2 C}{\partial x_t \partial v_t}$$

$$+\left(r - D - \frac{1}{2}v_t\right)\frac{\partial C}{\partial x_t} + \left(\kappa(\theta - v_t) - \lambda v_t\right)\frac{\partial C}{\partial v_t} - rC(x_t, v_t, t; K, T) = 0$$

with boundary condition

$$C(x_T, v_T, T; K, T) = \max\left\{e^{x_T} - K, 0\right\}.$$

By analogy with the Black–Scholes formula, let the solution of the call price take the form

$$C(x_t, v_t, t; K, T) = e^{x_t} e^{-D(T-t)} P_1(x_t, v_t, t; K, T) - K e^{-r(T-t)} P_2(x_t, v_t, t; K, T)$$

where $P_1(x_t, v_t, t; K, T)$ and $P_2(x_t, v_t, t; K, T)$ are the risk-neutral probabilities that the call option is ITM at expiry time T. By substituting the proposed solution into the PDE, show that $P_1(x_t, v_t, t; K, T)$ and $P_2(x_t, v_t, t; K, T)$ satisfy the PDEs

$$\frac{\partial P_j}{\partial t} + \frac{1}{2} v_t \frac{\partial^2 P_j}{\partial x_t^2} + \frac{1}{2} \xi^2 v_t \frac{\partial^2 P_j}{\partial v_t^2} + \rho \xi v_t \frac{\partial^2 P_j}{\partial x_t \partial v_t} + \left(r - D + u_j v_t\right) \frac{\partial P_j}{\partial x_t}$$

$$+ \left(a - b_j v_t\right) \frac{\partial P_j}{\partial v_t} = 0$$

for $j = 1, 2$ where

$$u_1 = \frac{1}{2}, \quad u_2 = -\frac{1}{2}, \quad a = \kappa\theta, \quad b_1 = \kappa + \lambda - \rho\xi, \quad b_2 = \kappa + \lambda$$

subject to the boundary condition

$$P_j(x_T, v_T, T; K, T) = \mathbb{1}_{x_T \geq \log K}.$$

Let $\hat{P}_j(m, v_t, t; K, T)$ be the Fourier transform of $P_j(x_t, v_t, t; K, T)$, where

$$\hat{P}_j(m, v_t, t; K, T) = \int_{-\infty}^{\infty} e^{-imx_t} P_j(x_t, v_t, t; K, T) \, dx_t, \quad j = 1, 2$$

and show that $\hat{P}_j(m, v_t, t; K, T)$ satisfies

$$\frac{\partial \hat{P}_j}{\partial t} + \frac{1}{2} \xi^2 v_t \frac{\partial^2 \hat{P}_j}{\partial v_t^2} + \left(a - b_j v_t + im\rho\xi v_t\right) \frac{\partial \hat{P}_j}{\partial v_t}$$

$$+ \left((r - D + u_j v_t)im - \frac{1}{2} m^2 v_t\right) \hat{P}_j(m, v_t, t; K, T) \quad = \quad 0$$

with boundary condition

$$\hat{P}_j(m, v_T, T; K, T) = \frac{e^{-im \log K}}{im}.$$

By seeking an exponential affine solution of the form

$$\hat{P}_j(m, \upsilon_t, t; K, T) = e^{A(t,T)+B(t,T)\upsilon_t} \hat{P}_j(m, \upsilon_T, T; K, T)$$

with $A(T, T) = 0$ and $B(T, T) = 0$, show that

$$\frac{\partial B}{\partial t} = \gamma \left(B(t, T) - \pi_+ \right) \left(B(t, T) - \pi_- \right)$$

$$\frac{\partial A}{\partial t} = \delta B(t, T) + \varepsilon$$

where

$$\alpha = \frac{1}{2}m^2 - imu_j, \quad \beta = b_j - im\rho\xi, \quad \gamma = -\frac{1}{2}\xi^2$$

$$\delta = -1, \quad \varepsilon = -(r - D)im, \quad \pi_\pm = \frac{-\beta \pm \sqrt{\beta^2 - 4\alpha\gamma}}{2\gamma}.$$

Solving the two differential equations, show that

$$A(t, T) = \frac{\delta\pi_-}{\eta} \left[\left(\frac{\tilde{\pi} - 1}{\tilde{\pi}} \right) \log \left(\frac{1 - \tilde{\pi}e^{\eta(T-t)}}{1 - \tilde{\pi}} \right) - \eta(T - t) \right] - \varepsilon(T - t)$$

$$B(t, T) = \frac{\pi_- \left(1 - e^{\eta(T-t)} \right)}{1 - \tilde{\pi}e^{\eta(T-t)}}$$

where

$$\tilde{\pi} = \pi_-/\pi_+ \quad \text{and} \quad \eta = \sqrt{\beta^2 - 4\alpha\gamma}.$$

Finally, by taking the Fourier inversion of $\hat{P}_j(m, \upsilon_t, t; K, T)$,

$$P_j(x_t, \upsilon_t, t; K, T) = \frac{1}{2\pi} \int_{-\infty}^{\infty} e^{imx_t} \hat{P}_j(m, \upsilon_t, t; K, T) \, dm$$

show that the European call option at time t is

$$C(x_t, \upsilon_t, t; K, T) = e^{x_t}e^{-D(T-t)}P_1(x_t, \upsilon_t, t; K, T) - Ke^{-r(T-t)}P_2(x_t, \upsilon_t, t; K, T)$$

where

$$P_j(x_t, \upsilon_t, t; K, T) = \frac{1}{2\pi} \int_{-\infty}^{\infty} \frac{e^{im(x_t - \log K) + A(t,T) + B(t,T)\upsilon_t}}{im} \, dm, \quad j = 1, 2.$$

Solution: From the PDE satisfied by $C(S_t, v_t, t; K, T)$,

$$\frac{\partial C}{\partial t} + \frac{1}{2} v_t S_t^2 \frac{\partial^2 C}{\partial S_t^2} + \frac{1}{2} \xi^2 v_t \frac{\partial^2 C}{\partial v_t^2} + \rho \xi v_t S_t \frac{\partial^2 C}{\partial S_t \partial v_t}$$

$$+ (r - D) S_t \frac{\partial C}{\partial S_t} + \left(\kappa(\theta - v_t) - \lambda(S_t, v_t) \right) \frac{\partial C}{\partial v_t} - r C(S_t, v_t, t; K, T) = 0$$

such that $\lambda(S_t, v_t)$ is the market price of volatility risk, with boundary condition

$$C(S_T, v_T, T; K, T) = \max\{S_T - K, 0\}$$

and by substituting $\lambda(S_t, v_t) = \lambda v_t$ and $x_t = \log S_t$, we have

$$\frac{\partial C}{\partial S_t} = \frac{\partial C}{\partial x_t} \frac{\partial x_t}{\partial S_t} = \frac{1}{S_t} \frac{\partial C}{\partial x_t}$$

$$\frac{\partial^2 C}{\partial S_t^2} = \frac{\partial}{\partial S_t} \left(\frac{1}{S_t} \frac{\partial C}{\partial x_t} \right) = -\frac{1}{S_t^2} \frac{\partial C}{\partial x_t} + \frac{1}{S_t} \frac{\partial}{\partial S_t} \left(\frac{\partial C}{\partial x_t} \right) = \frac{1}{S_t^2} \left(\frac{\partial^2 C}{\partial x_t^2} - \frac{\partial C}{\partial x_t} \right)$$

and

$$\frac{\partial^2 C}{\partial S_t \partial v_t} = \frac{1}{S_t} \frac{\partial}{\partial v_t} \left(\frac{\partial C}{\partial x_t} \right) = \frac{1}{S_t} \frac{\partial^2 C}{\partial x_t \partial v_t}.$$

Hence, by substituting the above equations into the Black–Scholes PDE we have

$$\frac{\partial C}{\partial t} + \frac{1}{2} v_t \frac{\partial^2 C}{\partial x_t^2} + \frac{1}{2} \xi^2 v_t \frac{\partial^2 C}{\partial v_t^2} + \rho \xi v_t \frac{\partial^2 C}{\partial x_t \partial v_t}$$

$$+ \left(r - D - \frac{1}{2} v_t \right) \frac{\partial C}{\partial x_t} + \left(\kappa(\theta - v_t) - \lambda v_t \right) \frac{\partial C}{\partial v_t} - r C(x_t, v_t, t; K, T) = 0$$

with boundary condition

$$C(x_T, v_T, T; K, T) = \max\left\{ e^{x_T} - K, 0 \right\} = \left(e^{x_T} - K \right) \mathbb{1}_{x_T \geq \log K}.$$

Setting the solution of the call price in the form

$$C(x_t, v_t, t; K, T) = e^{x_t} e^{-D(T-t)} P_1(x_t, v_t, t; K, T) - K e^{-r(T-t)} P_2(x_t, v_t, t; K, T)$$

we have

$$\frac{\partial C}{\partial t} = De^{x_t}e^{-D(T-t)}P_1(x_t, v_t, t; K, T) + e^{x_t}e^{-D(T-t)}\frac{\partial P_1}{\partial t}$$

$$-rKe^{-r(T-t)}P_2(x_t, v_t, t; K, T) - Ke^{-r(T-t)}\frac{\partial P_2}{\partial t}$$

$$\frac{\partial C}{\partial x_t} = e^{x_t}e^{-D(T-t)}P_1(x_t, v_t, t; K, T) + e^{x_t}e^{-D(T-t)}\frac{\partial P_1}{\partial x_t} - Ke^{-r(T-t)}\frac{\partial P_2}{\partial x_t}$$

$$\frac{\partial^2 C}{\partial x_t^2} = e^{x_t}e^{-D(T-t)}P_1(x_t, v_t, t; K, T) + 2e^{x_t}e^{-D(T-t)}\frac{\partial P_1}{\partial x_t} + e^{x_t}e^{-D(T-t)}\frac{\partial^2 P_1}{\partial x_t^2}$$

$$-Ke^{-r(T-t)}\frac{\partial^2 P_2}{\partial x_t^2}$$

$$\frac{\partial^2 C}{\partial v_t \partial x_t} = e^{x_t}e^{-D(T-t)}\frac{\partial P_1}{\partial v_t} + e^{x_t}e^{-D(T-t)}\frac{\partial^2 P_1}{\partial v_t \partial x_t} - Ke^{-r(T-t)}\frac{\partial^2 P_2}{\partial v_t \partial x_t}$$

$$\frac{\partial C}{\partial v_t} = e^{x_t}e^{-D(T-t)}\frac{\partial P_1}{\partial v_t} - Ke^{-r(T-t)}\frac{\partial P_2}{\partial v_t}$$

$$\frac{\partial^2 C}{\partial v_t^2} = e^{x_t}e^{-D(T-t)}\frac{\partial^2 P_1}{\partial v_t^2} - Ke^{-r(T-t)}\frac{\partial^2 P_2}{\partial v_t^2}.$$

At expiry time T,

$$C(S_T, v_T, T; K, T) = \max\{e^{x_T} - K, 0\} = \left(e^{x_T} - K\right)\mathbb{1}_{x_T \geq \log K}$$

which is equivalent to

$$e^{x_T}P_1(x_T, v_T, T; K, T) - KP_2(x_T, v_T, T; k, T) = e^{x_T}\mathbb{1}_{x_T \geq \log K} - K\mathbb{1}_{x_T \geq \log K}.$$

Hence, the boundary condition becomes

$$P_1(x_T, v_T, T; K, T) = \mathbb{1}_{x_T \geq \log K} \quad \text{and} \quad P_2(x_T, v_T, T; K, T) = \mathbb{1}_{x_T \geq \log K}.$$

Substituting the above equations into the PDE satisfied by $C(x_t, v_t, t; K, T)$, $P_1(x_t, v_t, t; K, T)$ will satisfy

$$\frac{\partial P_1}{\partial t} + \frac{1}{2}v_t\frac{\partial^2 P_1}{\partial x_t^2} + \frac{1}{2}\xi^2 v_t\frac{\partial^2 P_1}{\partial v_t^2} + \rho\xi v_t\frac{\partial^2 P_1}{\partial x_t \partial v_t} + \left(r - D + \frac{1}{2}v_t\right)\frac{\partial P_1}{\partial x_t}$$

$$+ \left(\kappa\theta - (\kappa + \lambda - \rho\xi)v_t\right)\frac{\partial P_1}{\partial v_t} = 0$$

with boundary condition

$$P_1(x_T, v_T, T; K, T) = \mathbb{1}_{x_T \geq \log K}.$$

In contrast, $P_2(x_t, v_t, t; K, T)$ will satisfy

$$\frac{\partial P_2}{\partial t} + \frac{1}{2} v_t \frac{\partial^2 P_2}{\partial x_t^2} + \frac{1}{2} \xi^2 v_t \frac{\partial^2 P_2}{\partial v_t^2} + \rho \xi v_t \frac{\partial^2 P_2}{\partial x_t \partial v_t} + \left(r - D - \frac{1}{2} v_t \right) \frac{\partial P_2}{\partial x_t}$$
$$+ \left(\kappa \theta - (\kappa + \lambda) v_t \right) \frac{\partial P_2}{\partial v_t} = 0$$

with boundary condition

$$P_2(x_T, v_T, T; K, T) = \mathbb{1}_{x_T \geq \log K}.$$

From the definition of the Fourier transform,

$$\widehat{P}_j(m, v_t, t; K, T) = \int_{-\infty}^{\infty} e^{-imx_t} P_j(x_t, v_t, t; K, T) \, dx_t, \quad j = 1, 2$$

and taking Fourier transforms of the PDE satisfied by $P_j(x_t, v_t, t; K, T), j = 1, 2$ we have

$$\int_{-\infty}^{\infty} e^{-imx_t} \frac{\partial P_j}{\partial t} \, dx_t + \frac{1}{2} v_t \int_{-\infty}^{\infty} e^{-imx_t} \frac{\partial^2 P_j}{\partial x_t^2} \, dx_t + \frac{1}{2} \xi^2 v_t \int_{-\infty}^{\infty} e^{-imx_t} \frac{\partial^2 P_j}{\partial v_t^2} \, dx_t$$
$$+ \rho \xi v_t \int_{-\infty}^{\infty} e^{-imx_t} \frac{\partial^2 P_j}{\partial x_t \partial v_t} \, dx_t + \left(r - D + u_j v_t \right) \int_{-\infty}^{\infty} e^{-imx_t} \frac{\partial P_j}{\partial x_t} \, dx_t$$
$$+ \left(a - b_j v_t \right) \int_{-\infty}^{\infty} e^{-imx_t} \frac{\partial P_j}{\partial v_t} \, dx_t = 0.$$

Using integration by parts for partial derivatives with respect to x_t,

$$\int_{-\infty}^{\infty} e^{-imx_t} \frac{\partial P_j}{\partial x_t} \, dx_t = im \int_{-\infty}^{\infty} e^{-imx_t} P_j(x_t, v_t, t; K, T) \, dx_t = im \widehat{P}_j(m, v_t, t; K, T)$$

$$\int_{-\infty}^{\infty} e^{-imx_t} \frac{\partial^2 P_j}{\partial x_t^2} \, dx_t = im \int_{-\infty}^{\infty} e^{-imx_t} \frac{\partial P_j}{\partial x_t} \, dx_t = -m^2 \widehat{P}_j(m, v_t, t; K, T)$$

$$\int_{-\infty}^{\infty} e^{-imx_t} \frac{\partial^2 P_j}{\partial x_t \partial v_t} \, dx_t = im \int_{-\infty}^{\infty} e^{-imx_t} \frac{\partial P_j}{\partial v_t} \, dx_t = im \frac{\partial \widehat{P}_j}{\partial v_t}$$

and since

$$\int_{-\infty}^{\infty} e^{-imx_t} \frac{\partial P_j}{\partial t} \, dx_t = \frac{\partial \widehat{P}_j}{\partial t}, \quad \int_{-\infty}^{\infty} e^{-imx_t} \frac{\partial P_j}{\partial v_t} \, dx_t = \frac{\partial \widehat{P}_j}{\partial v_t}$$

and

$$\int_{-\infty}^{\infty} e^{-imx_t} \frac{\partial^2 P_j}{\partial v_t^2} \, dx_t = \frac{\partial^2 \widehat{P}_j}{\partial v_t^2}$$

by substituting them into the Fourier-transformed PDE, we eventually have

$$\frac{\partial \widehat{P}_j}{\partial t} + \frac{1}{2} \xi^2 v_t \frac{\partial^2 \widehat{P}_j}{\partial v_t^2} + \left(a - b_j v_t + im\rho\xi v_t \right) \frac{\partial \widehat{P}_j}{\partial v_t}$$

$$+ \left((r - D + u_j v_t)im - \frac{1}{2} m^2 v_t \right) \widehat{P}_j(m, v_t, t; K, T) = 0$$

with boundary condition

$$\widehat{P}_j(m, v_T, T; K, T) = \int_{-\infty}^{\infty} e^{-imx_T} \, \mathbb{1}_{\{x_T \geq \log K\}} \, dx_T$$

$$= \int_{\log K}^{\infty} e^{-imx_T} \, dx_T$$

$$= -\frac{e^{-imx_T}}{im} \Big|_{\log K}^{\infty}$$

$$= \frac{e^{-im \log K}}{im}$$

for $j = 1, 2$.

Setting the solution of the Fourier-transformed PDE as

$$\widehat{P}_j(m, v_t, t; K, T) = e^{A(t,T)+B(t,T)v_t} \widehat{P}_j(m, v_T, T; K, T)$$

and in order to satisfy the boundary condition, we therefore have

$$A(T, T) = 0 \quad \text{and} \quad B(T, T) = 0.$$

Substituting

$$\frac{\partial \widehat{P}_j}{\partial t} = \left(\frac{\partial A}{\partial t} + \frac{\partial B}{\partial t} v_t \right) \widehat{P}_j(m, v_T, T; K, T), \quad \frac{\partial \widehat{P}_j}{\partial v_t} = B(t, T)\widehat{P}_j(m, v_t, t; K, T)$$

and

$$\frac{\partial^2 \widehat{P}_j}{\partial v_t^2} = B(t, T)^2 \widehat{P}_j(m, v_t, t; K, T)$$

into the Fourier-transformed PDE and removing the common factor $\widehat{P}_j(m, v_t, t; K, T)$,

$$\frac{\partial A}{\partial t} + \frac{\partial B}{\partial t} v_t + \frac{1}{2}\xi^2 v_t B(t, T)^2 + \left(a - b_j v_t + im\rho\xi v_t\right) B(t, T)$$

$$+(r - D + u_j v_t)im - \frac{1}{2}m^2 v_t = 0.$$

Thus, by equating coefficients we have

$$\frac{\partial B}{\partial t} + i\,mu_j - \frac{1}{2}m^2 + (i\,m\rho\xi - b_j)B(t, T) + \frac{1}{2}\xi^2 B(t, T)^2 = 0$$

$$\frac{\partial A}{\partial t} + aB(t, T) + (r - D)i\,m = 0$$

with boundary conditions

$$A(T, T) = 0 \quad \text{and} \quad B(T, T) = 0.$$

By setting

$$\alpha = \frac{1}{2}m^2 - i\,mu_j, \quad \beta = b_j - i\,m\rho\xi, \quad \gamma = -\frac{1}{2}\xi^2$$

$$\delta = -1, \quad \varepsilon = -(r - D)i\,m, \quad \pi_\pm = \frac{-\beta \pm \sqrt{\beta^2 - 4\alpha\gamma}}{2\gamma}$$

the above differential equations can be written as

$$\frac{\partial B}{\partial t} = \alpha + \beta B(t, T) + \gamma B(t, T)^2 = \gamma(B(t, T) - \pi_+)(B(t, T) - \pi_-)$$

$$\frac{\partial A}{\partial t} = \delta B(t, T) + \varepsilon$$

with boundary conditions

$$A(T, T) = 0 \quad \text{and} \quad B(T, T) = 0.$$

Solving the differential equation for $B(t, T)$,

$$\int \frac{dB}{(B(t, T) - \pi_+)(B(t, T) - \pi_-)} = \int \gamma\, dt$$

$$\frac{1}{\pi_- - \pi_+}\left[\int \frac{dB}{B - \pi_-} - \int \frac{dB}{B - \pi_+}\right] = \int \gamma\, dt$$

$$\frac{1}{\pi_- - \pi_+} \log\left(\frac{B - \pi_-}{B - \pi_+}\right) = \gamma t + C$$

where C is a constant.

At $t = T$, $B(T,T) = 0$ and so

$$C = \frac{1}{\pi_- - \pi_+} \log\left(\frac{\pi_-}{\pi_+}\right) - \gamma T.$$

Thus,

$$B(t,T) = \frac{\pi_-\left(1 - e^{(\pi_+ - \pi_-)\gamma(T-t)}\right)}{1 - \widetilde{\pi} e^{(\pi_+ - \pi_-)\gamma(T-t)}} = \frac{\pi_-\left(1 - e^{\eta(T-t)}\right)}{1 - \widetilde{\pi} e^{\eta(T-t)}}$$

where

$$\widetilde{\pi} = \pi_-/\pi_+ \quad \text{and} \quad \eta = (\pi_+ - \pi_-)\gamma = \sqrt{\beta^2 - 4\alpha\gamma}.$$

Finally, for the case of $A(t,T)$ we can rewrite $B(t,T)$ as

$$B(t,T) = \frac{\pi_-\left(1 - e^{\eta(T-t)}\right)}{1 - \widetilde{\pi} e^{\eta(T-t)}} = \pi_- \left[\frac{e^{-\eta(T-t)}}{e^{-\eta(T-t)} - \widetilde{\pi}} - \frac{e^{\eta(T-t)}}{1 - \widetilde{\pi} e^{\eta(T-t)}} \right]$$

and solving for $A(t,T)$,

$$\int dA = \int B(t,T)\, dt + \int \varepsilon\, dt$$

$$= \delta\pi_- \left[\int \frac{e^{-\eta(T-t)}}{e^{-\eta(T-t)} - \widetilde{\pi}}\, dt - \int \frac{e^{\eta(T-t)}}{1 - \widetilde{\pi} e^{\eta(T-t)}}\, dt \right] + \int \varepsilon\, dt$$

$$A(t,T) = \frac{\delta\pi_-}{\eta} \left[\log\left(e^{-\eta(T-t)} - \widetilde{\pi}\right) - \frac{1}{\widetilde{\pi}} \log\left(1 - \widetilde{\pi} e^{\eta(T-t)}\right) \right] + \varepsilon t + C$$

where C is a constant.

From the boundary condition $A(T,T) = 0$, we have

$$C = -\left\{ \frac{\delta\pi_-}{\eta} \left[\left(\frac{\widetilde{\pi} - 1}{\widetilde{\pi}}\right) \log(1 - \widetilde{\pi}) \right] + \varepsilon T \right\}$$

and therefore

$$A(t,T) = \frac{\delta\pi_-}{\eta} \left[\left(\frac{\widetilde{\pi} - 1}{\widetilde{\pi}}\right) \log\left(\frac{1 - \widetilde{\pi} e^{\eta(T-t)}}{1 - \widetilde{\pi}}\right) - \eta(T - t) \right] - \varepsilon(T - t).$$

Hence, for $j = 1, 2$,

$$\widetilde{P}_j(m, v_t.t; K, T) = \frac{e^{A(t,T) + B(t,T)v_t - i\,m \log K}}{i\,m}$$

and from the Fourier inversion theorem

$$P_j(x_t, v_t, t; K, T) = \frac{1}{2\pi} \int_{-\infty}^{\infty} e^{imx_t} \widetilde{P}_j(m, v_t.t; K, T) \, dm$$

$$= \frac{1}{2\pi} \int_{-\infty}^{\infty} \frac{e^{im(x_t - \log K) + A(t,T) + B(t,T)v_t}}{i\,m} \, dm, j = 1, 2$$

such that the European call option price at time t is

$$C(x_t, v_t, t; K, T) = e^{x_t} e^{-D(T-t)} P_1(x_t, v_t, t; K, T) - K e^{-r(T-t)} P_2(x_t, v_t, t; K, T).$$

$\square$

7.2.4   Volatility Derivatives

1. *Variance Swap.* Let $\{W_t : t \geq 0\}$ be a standard Wiener process on the probability space $(\Omega, \mathscr{F}, \mathbb{P})$. Suppose that the asset price S_t has the following dynamics

$$\frac{dS_t}{S_t} = (\mu - D)dt + \sigma_t dW_t$$

where μ, D are constants and the volatility σ_t is a continuous (possibly stochastic) process. In addition, let r be the risk-free interest rate from a money-market account.

By considering a European call option $C(S_t, t; K, T)$ written at time t on S_t with strike price K and expiry time T $(T > t)$, state the Dupire equation and payoff satisfied by $C(S_t, t; K, T)$ as a function of strike K and time t.

Sketch the call option payoff as a function of strike K.

Assume that for European call options, all strikes are available and we wish to replicate a payoff $\Psi(S_T)$ by synthesising from the following

$$\Psi(S_T) = \int_0^{\infty} \phi(K) \max\{S_T - K, 0\} \, dK$$

where $\phi(K)$ is a density function of European call option payoffs with strike K.

Show that

$$\phi(K) = \Psi''(K).$$

Under what conditions can the payoff $\Psi(S_T)$ be synthesised using the above expression?

Hence, deduce that the payoff $\Psi(S_T)$ can be constructed using a combination of European put, call, asset and cash of the form

$$\Psi(S_T) = \int_0^{K_0} \phi_P(K) \max\{K - S_T, 0\} dK + \int_{K_0}^{\infty} \phi_C(K) \max\{S_T - K, 0\} \, dK$$
$$+ \alpha S_T + \beta$$

where α, β and K_0 are constants, $\phi_P(K)$ and $\phi_C(K)$ are density functions of European put and call option payoffs with strike K, respectively.

Find the replicating portfolio for the payoff $\Psi(S_T) = \log S_T$ in terms of K_0.

A variance swap is a contract with payoff

$$\Psi(\sigma_T) = \int_t^T \sigma_u^2 \, du - K_{var}$$

in which the constant K_{var} is chosen so that there is no upfront fee to be paid when the contract is initiated at time t.

Show that

$$\int_t^T \sigma_u^2 \, du = 2 \left[\int_t^T \frac{dS_u}{S_u} - \log\left(\frac{S_T}{S_t}\right) \right]$$

and using the replicating portfolio for $\log S_T$ or otherwise, deduce that this contract can be replicated with a combination of European call, put, cash and asset.

Solution: The Dupire equation is

$$\frac{\partial C}{\partial T} + \frac{1}{2}\sigma_t^2 K^2 \frac{\partial^2 C}{\partial K^2} + (D - r)K \frac{\partial C}{\partial K} - DC(S_t, t; K, T) = 0$$

with payoff

$$C(S_T, T; K, T) = \max\{S_T - K, 0\}.$$

The call option payoff as a function of strike K is illustrated in Figure 7.1.

Given that

$$\Psi(S_T) = \int_0^\infty \phi(K) \max\{S_T - K, 0\} \, dK$$

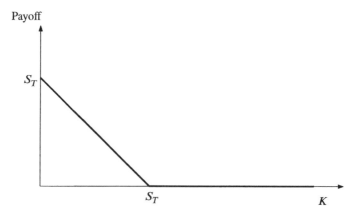

Figure 7.1 Call option payoff as a function of strike K.

by differentiating the expression with respect to S_T,

$$\Psi'(S_T) = \frac{\partial}{\partial S_T} \int_0^\infty \phi(K) \max\{S_T - K, 0\} \, dK$$

$$= \frac{\partial}{\partial S_T} \left[\int_0^{S_T} \phi(K) \max\{S_T - K, 0\} \, dK \right.$$

$$\left. + \int_{S_T}^\infty \phi(K) \max\{S_T - K, 0\} \, dK \right]$$

$$= \frac{\partial}{\partial S_T} \int_0^{S_T} \phi(K)(S_T - K) \, dK$$

$$= \int_0^{S_T} \phi(K) \, dK.$$

Differentiating it again

$$\Psi''(S_T) = \frac{\partial}{\partial S_T} \int_0^{S_T} \phi(K) \, dK$$

$$= \phi(S_T).$$

Therefore,

$$\Psi''(K) = \phi(K).$$

From the above information, the conditions under which the payoff $\Psi(S_T)$ can be synthesised are
- $\Psi(S_T)$ has gradient continuity
- $\Psi''(S_T)$ is bounded for small or large S_T values.
  If $\Psi(S_T)$ has a gradient discontinuity say at $S_T = K_0$, then

$$\lim_{S_T \to K_0^-} \Psi'(S_T) \neq \lim_{S_T \to K_0^+} \Psi'(S_T)$$

and hence $\Psi'(S_T)$ and subsequently $\Psi''(S_T)$ is not continuous at $S_T = K_0$. Thus, $\phi(S_T)$ is also not defined at $S_T = K_0$.

In contrast, if $\Psi''(S_T)$ is not bounded for small or large S_T, the integral will not converge (i.e., trading options with unbounded strikes).

Since $\phi(S_T) = \Psi''(S_T)$ there is a unique $\phi(S_T)$ corresponding to each $\Psi(S_T)$. Therefore, depending on the position of the arbitrary constant K_0 with respect to S_T, the synthesising portfolio can also accommodate a put option and also a linear function of S_T as well. To show how this portfolio is synthesised, for a constant K_0 we can set

$$\Psi''(S_T) = \phi(S_T)$$

$$= \begin{cases} \phi_C(S_T) & \text{for } 0 < K_0 < S_T < \infty \\[2mm] \phi_P(S_T) & \text{for } 0 < S_T < K_0 < \infty \end{cases}$$

where $\phi_C(S_T)$ and $\phi_P(S_T)$ are density functions of European call and put option payoffs with strike $K = S_T$, respectively.

Taking integrals, we can write it as

$$\Psi'(S_T) = \begin{cases} \displaystyle\int_{K_0}^{S_T} \phi_C(K)\,dK + \alpha & \text{for } 0 < K_0 < S_T < \infty \\[4mm] -\displaystyle\int_{S_T}^{K_0} \phi_P(K)\,dK + \alpha & \text{for } 0 < S_T < K_0 < \infty \end{cases}$$

where α is a constant.

Integrating again, we can write it as

$$\Psi(S_T) = \begin{cases} \displaystyle\int_{K_0}^{S_T} \phi_C(K)(S_T - K)\,dK + \alpha S_T + \beta & \text{for } 0 < K_0 < S_T < \infty \\[4mm] \displaystyle\int_{S_T}^{K_0} \phi_P(K)(K - S_T)\,dK + \alpha S_T + \beta & \text{for } 0 < S_T < K_0 < \infty \end{cases}$$

where β is a constant.

Hence,

$$\Psi(S_T) = \begin{cases} \displaystyle\int_{K_0}^{\infty} \phi_C(K)\max\{S_T - K, 0\}\,dK + \alpha S_T + \beta & \text{for } 0 < K_0 < S_T < \infty \\[4mm] \displaystyle\int_{0}^{K_0} \phi_P(K)\max\{K - S_T, 0\}\,dK + \alpha S_T + \beta & \text{for } 0 < S_T < K_0 < \infty \end{cases}$$

or in general,

$$\Psi(S_T) = \int_{0}^{K_0} \phi_P(K)\max\{K - S_T, 0\}\,dK + \int_{K_0}^{\infty} \phi_C(K)\max\{S_T - K, 0\}\,dK$$
$$+ \alpha S_T + \beta.$$

To find the replicating strategy for $\Psi(S_T) = \log S_T$, we consider two cases.

Case 1: $0 < K_0 < S_T < \infty$.

$$\Psi(S_T) = \int_0^{K_0} \phi_P(K) \max\{K - S_T, 0\} \, dK + \int_{K_0}^{\infty} \phi_C(K) \max\{S_T - K, 0\} \, dK$$
$$+ \alpha S_T + \beta$$

$$= \int_{K_0}^{\infty} \phi_C(K) \max\{S_T - K, 0\} \, dK + \alpha S_T + \beta$$

$$= \int_{K_0}^{S_T} \phi_C(K) \max\{S_T - K, 0\} \, dK + \int_{S_T}^{\infty} \phi_C(K) \max\{S_T - K, 0\} \, dK$$
$$+ \alpha S_T + \beta$$

$$= \int_{K_0}^{S_T} \phi_C(K)(S_T - K) \, dK + \alpha S_T + \beta.$$

By setting $\Psi(S_T) = \log S_T$ and differentiating with respect to S_T up to second order,

$$\Psi(S_T) = \log S_T = \int_{K_0}^{S_T} \phi_C(K)(S_T - K) \, dK + \alpha S_T + \beta$$

$$\Psi'(S_T) = \frac{1}{S_T} = \int_{K_0}^{S_T} \phi_C(K) \, dK + \alpha$$

$$\Psi''(S_T) = -\frac{1}{S_T^2} = \phi_C(S_T).$$

At $S_T = K_0$

$$\log K_0 = \alpha K_0 + \beta$$
$$\frac{1}{K_0} = \alpha.$$

Thus,

$$\alpha = \frac{1}{K_0}, \quad \beta = \log K_0 - 1 \quad \text{and} \quad \phi_C(K) = -\frac{1}{K^2}.$$

Case 2: $0 < S_T < K_0 < \infty$.

$$\Psi(S_T) = \int_0^{K_0} \phi_P(K) \max\{K - S_T, 0\} \, dK + \int_{K_0}^{\infty} \phi_C(K) \max\{S_T - K, 0\} \, dK$$
$$+ \alpha S_T + \beta$$

$$= \int_0^{K_0} \phi_P(K) \max\{K - S_T, 0\} \, dK + \alpha S_T + \beta$$

$$= \int_0^{S_T} \phi_P(K) \max\{K - S_T, 0\} \, dK + \int_{S_T}^{K_0} \phi_P(K) \max\{K - S_T, 0\} \, dK$$

$$+ \alpha S_T + \beta$$

$$= \int_{S_T}^{K_0} \phi_P(K)(K - S_T) \, dK + \alpha S_T + \beta.$$

By setting $\Psi(S_T) = \log S_T$ and differentiating with respect to S_T up to second order,

$$\Psi(S_T) = \log S_T = \int_{S_T}^{K_0} \phi_P(K)(K - S_T) \, dK + \alpha S_T + \beta$$

$$\Psi'(S_T) = \frac{1}{S_T} = - \int_{S_T}^{K_0} \phi_P(K) \, dK + \alpha$$

$$\Psi''(S_T) = -\frac{1}{S_T^2} = \phi_P(S_T).$$

At $S_T = K_0$

$$\log K_0 = \alpha K_0 + \beta$$

$$\frac{1}{K_0} = \alpha.$$

Thus,

$$\alpha = \frac{1}{K_0}, \quad \beta = \log K_0 - 1 \quad \text{and} \quad \phi_P(K) = -\frac{1}{K^2}.$$

Combining case 1 and case 2 results we finally have the replicating formula for $\log S_T$ in terms of K_0

$$\log S_T = - \int_0^{K_0} \frac{1}{K^2} \max\{K - S_T, 0\} \, dK - \int_{K_0}^{\infty} \frac{1}{K^2} \max\{S_T - K, 0\} \, dK$$

$$+ \frac{S_T}{K_0} + \log K_0 - 1.$$

Under the risk-neutral measure $\mathbb{Q}$,

$$\frac{dS_t}{S_t} = (r - D)dt + \sigma_t d\widetilde{W}_t$$

where $\widetilde{W}_t = W_t + \int_0^t \frac{\mu - r}{\sigma_u} \, du$ is a $\mathbb{Q}$-standard Wiener process.

From Taylor's expansion and subsequently applying Itō's lemma,

$$d \log S_t = \frac{dS_t}{S_t} - \frac{1}{2}\left(\frac{dS_t}{S_t}\right)^2 + \ldots$$

$$= (r - D)dt + \sigma_t d\widetilde{W}_t - \frac{1}{2}\sigma_t^2 dt$$

$$= \frac{dS_t}{S_t} - \frac{1}{2}\sigma_t^2 dt.$$

Taking integrals,

$$\int_t^T d \log S_u = \int_t^T \frac{dS_u}{S_u} - \frac{1}{2}\int_t^T \sigma_u^2 \, du$$

$$\log\left(\frac{S_T}{S_t}\right) = \int_t^T \frac{dS_u}{S_u} - \frac{1}{2}\int_t^T \sigma_u^2 \, du$$

or

$$\int_t^T \sigma_u^2 \, du = 2\left[\int_t^T \frac{dS_u}{S_u} - \log\left(\frac{S_T}{S_t}\right)\right].$$

For the case of a variance swap payoff

$$\Psi(\sigma_T) = \int_t^T \sigma_u^2 \, du - K_{var}$$

let the value of the swap contract at time t be

$$V(\sigma_t, t; K_{var}, T) = e^{-r(T-t)}\mathbb{E}^{\mathbb{Q}}\left[\left.\int_t^T \sigma_u^2 \, du - K_{var}\right| \mathscr{F}_t\right].$$

Since there is no cash flow at initiation of the contract at time t,

$$V(\sigma_t, t; K_{var}, T) = 0$$

we can then express

$$K_{var} = \mathbb{E}^{\mathbb{Q}}\left[\left.\int_t^T \sigma_u^2 du\right| \mathscr{F}_t\right]$$

$$= 2\left\{\mathbb{E}^{\mathbb{Q}}\left[\left.\int_t^T \frac{dS_u}{S_u} - \log\left(\frac{S_T}{S_t}\right)\right| \mathscr{F}_t\right]\right\}$$

$$= 2\left\{\mathbb{E}^{\mathbb{Q}}\left[\left.\int_t^T \frac{dS_u}{S_u}\right| \mathscr{F}_t\right] - \mathbb{E}^{\mathbb{Q}}\left[\left.\log\left(\frac{S_T}{S_t}\right)\right| \mathscr{F}_t\right]\right\}.$$

From the dynamics

$$\frac{dS_t}{S_t} = (r - D)dt + \sigma_t d\widetilde{W}_t$$

then

$$\mathbb{E}^Q\left[\int_t^T \frac{dS_u}{S_u}\bigg|\mathcal{F}_t\right] = \mathbb{E}^Q\left[\int_t^T (r - D)\,du + \int_t^T \sigma_u\,d\widetilde{W}_u\bigg|\mathcal{F}_t\right]$$

$$= (r - D)(T - t)$$

since

$$\mathbb{E}^Q\left[\int_t^T \sigma_u\,d\widetilde{W}_u\bigg|\mathcal{F}_t\right] = 0.$$

As for $\log(S_T/S_t)$, for an arbitrary constant K_0 we can write

$$\log\left(\frac{S_T}{S_t}\right) = \log\left(\frac{S_T}{K_0}\right) + \log\left(\frac{K_0}{S_t}\right)$$

and from the results of $\log S_T$,

$$\log\left(\frac{S_T}{S_t}\right) = -\int_0^{K_0} \frac{1}{K^2}\max\{K - S_T, 0\}\,dK - \int_{K_0}^{\infty} \frac{1}{K^2}\max\{S_T - K, 0\}\,dK$$

$$+ \frac{S_T}{K_0} - 1 + \log\left(\frac{K_0}{S_t}\right).$$

Since

$$\mathbb{E}^Q\left[\max\{S_T - K, 0\}\big|\mathcal{F}_t\right] = e^{r(T-t)}C(S_t, t; K, T)$$

$$\mathbb{E}^Q\left[\max\{K - S_T, 0\}\big|\mathcal{F}_t\right] = e^{r(T-t)}P(S_t, t; K, T)$$

$$\mathbb{E}^Q\left[S_T\big|\mathcal{F}_t\right] = S_t e^{r(T-t)}$$

the parameter K_{var} becomes

$$K_{var} = 2\left\{\mathbb{E}^Q\left[\int_t^T \frac{dS_u}{S_u}\bigg|\mathcal{F}_t\right] - \mathbb{E}^Q\left[\log\left(\frac{S_T}{S_t}\right)\bigg|\mathcal{F}_t\right]\right\}$$

$$= 2\left\{(r - D)(T - t) + \mathbb{E}^Q\left[\int_0^{K_0} \frac{1}{K^2}\max\{K - S_T, 0\}\,dK\bigg|\mathcal{F}_t\right]\right.$$

$$+ \mathbb{E}^Q\left[\int_0^{K_0} \frac{1}{K^2}\max\{S_T - K, 0\}\,dK\bigg|\mathcal{F}_t\right] - \frac{1}{K_0}\mathbb{E}^Q\left[S_T\big|\mathcal{F}_t\right]$$

$$\left. - \left[\log\left(\frac{K_0}{S_t} - 1\right)\right]\right\}$$

$$= 2 \left\{ (r - D)(T - t) + e^{(r-D)(T-t)} \int_0^{K_0} \frac{1}{K^2} P(S_t, t; K, T) \, dK \right.$$

$$+ e^{(r-D)(T-t)} \int_{K_0}^{\infty} \frac{1}{K^2} C(S_t, t; K, T) \, dK - \frac{S_t e^{(r-D)(T-t)}}{K_0}$$

$$\left. - \left[\log \left(\frac{K_0}{S_t} - 1 \right) \right] \right\}.$$

$\square$

2. Let the asset price S_t and its instantaneous variance σ_t^2 have the following dynamics

$$dS_t = (\mu - D)S_t dt + \sigma_t S_t dW_t^S$$

$$d\sigma_t^2 = \kappa(\theta - \sigma_t^2) dt + \alpha \sigma_t dW_t^\sigma$$

$$dW_t^S \cdot dW_t^\sigma = \rho dt$$

where μ, D, κ, θ and α are constants, $\{W_t^S : t \geq 0\}$ and $\{W_t^\sigma : t \geq 0\}$ are two standard Wiener processes on the probability space $(\Omega, \mathcal{F}, \mathbb{P})$ with correlation $\rho \in (-1, 1)$. In addition, we let B_t be a risk-free asset with the differential equation

$$dB_t = r B_t dt$$

where r is the risk-free interest rate.

We consider a variance swap with payoff

$$\Psi(\sigma_T) = \int_t^T \sigma_u^2 \, du - K_{var}$$

where K_{var} is chosen so that no cash flows are exchanged when the contract is initiated at time t.

Assuming that the market price of volatility risk is zero, calculate the fair value of K_{var}.

Solution: Following Problem 7.2.3.7 (page 753), it can be shown that under the risk-neutral measure $\mathbb{Q}$,

$$dS_t = (r - D)S_t dt + \sigma_t S_t d\widetilde{W}_t^S$$

$$d\sigma_t^2 = \left(\kappa(\theta - \sigma_t^2) - \alpha \gamma_t \sigma_t \right) dt + \alpha \sigma_t d\widetilde{W}_t^\sigma$$

where $\widetilde{W}_t^S = \rho \widetilde{W}_t^\sigma + \sqrt{1 - \rho^2} \widetilde{Z}_t$, $\widetilde{W}_t^\sigma$ and $\widetilde{Z}_t$ are $\mathbb{Q}$-standard Wiener processes, $\widetilde{W}_t^\sigma \perp \widetilde{Z}_t$ and γ_t is the market price of volatility risk.

By assuming that the market price of volatility risk is zero,

$$dS_t = (r - D)S_t dt + \sigma_t S_t d\widetilde{W}_t^S$$

$$d\sigma_t^2 = \kappa(\theta - \sigma_t^2) dt + \alpha \sigma_t d\widetilde{W}_t^\sigma.$$

Let the variance swap payoff at expiry time T be

$$\Psi(\sigma_T) = \int_t^T \sigma_u^2 \, du - K_{var}$$

then under the risk-neutral measure $\mathbb{Q}$, the value of the contract at time t is

$$V(\sigma_t, t; K_{var}, T) = e^{-r(T-t)} \mathbb{E}^{\mathbb{Q}} \left[\Psi(\sigma_T) \middle| \mathscr{F}_t \right]$$

$$= e^{-r(T-t)} \mathbb{E}^{\mathbb{Q}} \left[\int_t^T \sigma_u^2 \, du - K_{var} \middle| \mathscr{F}_t \right].$$

Since there is no cash flow when the contract is initiated, we can set

$$V(\sigma_t, t; K_{var}, T) = 0$$

and the fair value of K_{var} is defined as

$$K_{var} = \mathbb{E}^{\mathbb{Q}} \left[\int_t^T \sigma_u^2 \, du \middle| \mathscr{F}_t \right].$$

From the stochastic volatility model under the risk-neutral measure $\mathbb{Q}$,

$$d\sigma_t^2 = \kappa(\theta - \sigma_t^2) dt + \alpha \sigma_t d\widetilde{W}_t^\sigma$$

and taking integrals on both sides we have

$$\int_t^T d\sigma_u^2 = \int_t^T \kappa(\theta - \sigma_u^2) \, du + \int_t^T \alpha \sigma_u \, d\widetilde{W}_u^\sigma$$

Taking expectations under the filtration $\mathscr{F}_t$,

$$\mathbb{E}^{\mathbb{Q}} \left[\int_t^T d\sigma_u^2 \middle| \mathscr{F}_t \right] = \mathbb{E}^{\mathbb{Q}} \left[\int_t^T \kappa(\theta - \sigma_u^2) \, du \middle| \mathscr{F}_t \right] + \mathbb{E}^{\mathbb{Q}} \left[\int_t^T \alpha \sigma_u \, d\widetilde{W}_u^\sigma \middle| \mathscr{F}_t \right]$$

$$\int_t^T \mathbb{E}^{\mathbb{Q}} \left[d\sigma_u^2 \middle| \mathscr{F}_t \right] = \int_t^T \mathbb{E}^{\mathbb{Q}} \left[\kappa(\theta - \sigma_u^2) \, du \middle| \mathscr{F}_t \right]$$

since $\mathbb{E}^{\mathbb{Q}} \left[\int_t^T \alpha \sigma_u \, d\widetilde{W}_u^\sigma \middle| \mathscr{F}_t \right] = 0$.

Simplifying further,

$$\int_t^T d\mathbb{E}^{\mathbb{Q}} \left[\sigma_u^2 \middle| \mathscr{F}_t \right] = \int_t^T \left[\kappa\theta - \kappa\mathbb{E}^{\mathbb{Q}} \left[\sigma_u^2 \middle| \mathscr{F}_t \right] \right] du.$$

By differentiating with respect to T,

$$\frac{d}{dT}\mathbb{E}^Q\left[\sigma_T^2\,\middle|\,\mathscr{F}_t\right] = \kappa\theta - \kappa\mathbb{E}^Q\left[\sigma_T^2\,\middle|\,\mathscr{F}_t\right]$$

or

$$\frac{d}{dT}\mathbb{E}^Q\left[\sigma_T^2\,\middle|\,\mathscr{F}_t\right] + \kappa\mathbb{E}^Q\left[\sigma_T^2\,\middle|\,\mathscr{F}_t\right] = \kappa\theta.$$

To solve the first-order differential equation, we set the particular integral

$$I = e^{\int \kappa dT} = e^{\kappa T}$$

and multiplying I with the differential equation

$$\frac{d}{dT}\left[e^{\kappa T}\mathbb{E}^Q\left[\sigma_T^2\,\middle|\,\mathscr{F}_t\right]\right] = \kappa\theta e^{\kappa T}$$

and then taking integrals,

$$e^{\kappa T}\mathbb{E}^Q\left[\sigma_T^2\,\middle|\,\mathscr{F}_t\right] = \theta e^{\kappa T} + C$$

where C is a constant.

When the contract is initialised at time t,

$$\mathbb{E}^Q\left[\sigma_t^2\,\middle|\,\mathscr{F}_t\right] = \sigma_t^2$$

so that

$$C = e^{\kappa t}(\sigma_t^2 - \theta).$$

Therefore,

$$\mathbb{E}^Q\left[\sigma_T^2\,\middle|\,\mathscr{F}_t\right] = \theta + e^{-\kappa(T-t)}(\sigma_t^2 - \theta)$$

and finally the fair value K_{var} takes the form

$$
\begin{aligned}
K_{var} &= \int_t^T \mathbb{E}^Q\left[\sigma_u^2\,\middle|\,\mathscr{F}_t\right]du \\
&= \int_t^T \left[\theta + e^{-\kappa(u-t)}(\sigma_t^2 - \theta)\right]du \\
&= \theta(T-t) + \left(\frac{\sigma_t^2 - \theta}{\kappa}\right)\left(1 - e^{-\kappa(T-t)}\right).
\end{aligned}
$$

$\square$

3. Let $\{W_t : t \geq 0\}$ be a standard Wiener process on the probability space $(\Omega, \mathcal{F}, \mathbb{P})$. Suppose that the asset price S_t has the following dynamics

$$\frac{dS_t}{S_t} = (\mu - D)dt + \sigma_t dW_t$$

where μ, D are constants and the volatility σ_t is a continuous (possibly stochastic) process. In addition, let r be the risk-free interest rate from a money-market account.

By dividing the time interval $[t, T]$ into n equal intervals with corresponding asset price values S_{t_0}, S_{t_1}, ..., S_{t_n}, $t_i = t + i\Delta t$, $\Delta t = (T - t)/n$, $t = t_0 < t_1 < \cdots < t_{n-1} < t_n = T$, show that the realised integrated variance $\int_t^T \sigma_u^2 \, du$ and volatility $\int_t^T \sigma_u \, du$ can be approximated by

$$\int_t^T \sigma_u^2 \, du = \lim_{n \to \infty} \sum_{i=0}^{n-1} \left(\frac{S_{t_{i+1}} - S_{t_i}}{S_{t_i}} \right)^2$$

and

$$\int_t^T \sigma_u \, du = \lim_{n \to \infty} \sqrt{\frac{\pi}{2} \left(\frac{T - t}{n} \right)} \sum_{i=0}^{n-1} \left| \frac{S_{t_{i+1}} - S_{t_i}}{S_{t_i}} \right|$$

respectively.

We consider a call option on the realised integrated variance having payoff

$$\Psi(\sigma_T) = \max \left\{ \int_t^T \sigma_u^2 \, du - K, 0 \right\}.$$

Explain how to value the call option at time t as a discretely sampled Asian option.

Solution: From the diffusion process

$$\frac{dS_t}{S_t} = (\mu - D) \, dt + \sigma_t dW_t$$

and using Itō's lemma

$$
\begin{aligned}
\left(\frac{dS_t}{S_t} \right)^2 &= \left[(\mu - D)dt + \sigma_t dW_t \right]^2 \\
&= (\mu - D)^2 (dt)^2 + 2(\mu - D)\sigma_t dW_t t + \sigma_t^2 (dW_t)^2 \\
&= \sigma_t^2 dt.
\end{aligned}
$$

Thus, for a small time interval Δt,

$$\sigma_t^2 \Delta t = \left(\frac{S_{t_{i+1}} - S_{t_i}}{S_{t_i}} \right)^2$$

and the realised integrated variance is

$$\int_t^T \sigma_u^2 \, du \approx \sum_{i=0}^{n-1} \left(\frac{S_{t_{i+1}} - S_{t_i}}{S_{t_i}} \right)^2.$$

Therefore, as $n \to \infty$,

$$\int_t^T \sigma_u^2 \, du = \lim_{n \to \infty} \sum_{i=0}^{n-1} \left(\frac{S_{t_{i+1}} - S_{t_i}}{S_{t_i}} \right)^2.$$

From Itō's lemma

$$\sigma_t^2 (dW_t)^2 = \left(\frac{dS_t}{S_t} \right)^2$$

we can set

$$\sigma_t |dW_t| = \left| \frac{dS_t}{S_t} \right|.$$

Since $|dW_t|$ follows a folded normal distribution $|dW_t| \sim \mathcal{N}_f(0, dt)$ with mean

$$\mathbb{E}(|dW_t|) = \sqrt{\frac{2dt}{\pi}}$$

informally we can write

$$|dW_t| = \sqrt{\frac{2dt}{\pi}}.$$

For small Δt,

$$\sigma_t \sqrt{\frac{2\Delta t}{\pi}} = \left| \frac{S_{t_{i+1}} - S_{t_i}}{S_{t_i}} \right|$$

or

$$\sigma_t \Delta t = \sqrt{\frac{\pi \Delta t}{2}} \left| \frac{S_{t_{i+1}} - S_{t_i}}{S_{t_i}} \right|.$$

Hence, the realised integrated volatility can be approximated by

$$\int_t^T \sigma_u \, du \approx \sqrt{\frac{\pi}{2} \left(\frac{T-t}{n} \right)} \sum_{i=0}^{n-1} \left| \frac{S_{t_{i+1}} - S_{t_i}}{S_{t_i}} \right|$$

and in the limit $n \to \infty$,

$$\int_t^T \sigma_u \, du = \lim_{n \to \infty} \sqrt{\frac{\pi}{2} \left(\frac{T-t}{n} \right)} \sum_{i=0}^{n-1} \left| \frac{S_{t_{i+1}} - S_{t_i}}{S_{t_i}} \right|.$$

By definition, the call option price at time t under the risk-neutral measure $\mathbb{Q}$ is

$$C_{var}(\sigma_t, t; K, T) = e^{-r(T-t)} \mathbb{E}^{\mathbb{Q}} \left[\max \left\{ \int_t^T \sigma_u^2 \, du - K, 0 \right\} \middle| \mathcal{F}_t \right]$$

and since we can approximate

$$\int_t^T \sigma_u^2 \, du \approx \sum_{i=0}^{n-1} \left(\frac{S_{t_{i+1}} - S_{t_i}}{S_{t_i}} \right)^2$$

the payoff can be written as

$$\Psi(\sigma_T) \approx \max \left\{ \sum_{i=0}^{n-1} \left(\frac{S_{t_{i+1}} - S_{t_i}}{S_{t_i}} \right)^2 - K, 0 \right\}.$$

To value the option as a discretely sampled Asian option, we let

$$\Psi(\sigma_T^{(j)}) \approx \max \left\{ \sum_{i=0}^{n-1} \left(\frac{S_{t_{i+1}}^{(j)} - S_{t_i}^{(j)}}{S_{t_i}^{(j)}} \right)^2 - K, 0 \right\}, \quad j = 1, 2, \ldots, m$$

where $\Psi(\sigma_T^{(j)})$ is the jth realisation of the payoff.

Thus, the call option price at time t, which is the discounted expected payoff, is approximated by

$$C_{var}(\sigma_t, t; K, T) \approx e^{-r(T-t)} \left[\frac{1}{m} \sum_{j=1}^{m} \max \left\{ \sum_{i=0}^{n-1} \left(\frac{S_{t_{i+1}}^{(j)} - S_{t_i}^{(j)}}{S_{t_i}^{(j)}} \right)^2 - K, 0 \right\} \right]$$

$$= e^{-r(T-t)} \max \left\{ \frac{1}{m} \sum_{j=1}^{m} \sum_{i=0}^{n-1} \left(\frac{S_{t_{i+1}}^{(j)} - S_{t_i}^{(j)}}{S_{t_i}^{(j)}} \right)^2 - K, 0 \right\}.$$

$\square$

4. *Timer Option.* Under the risk-neutral measure $\mathbb{Q}$, let $\{\widetilde{W}_t^S : t \geq 0\}$ and $\{\widetilde{W}_t^V : t \geq 0\}$ be two correlated $\mathbb{Q}$-standard Wiener processes on the probability space $(\Omega, \mathcal{F}, \mathbb{Q})$ with correlation $\rho \in (-1, 1)$. Let the asset price S_t under the $\mathbb{Q}$ measure follow a stochastic volatility model with the following dynamics

$$\frac{dS_t}{S_t} = (r - D)dt + \sqrt{V_t}d\widetilde{W}_t^S$$

$$dV_t = \alpha(V_t, t)dt + \beta(V_t, t)d\widetilde{W}_t^V$$

$$d\widetilde{W}_t^S \cdot d\widetilde{W}_t^V = \rho dt$$

where r is the risk-free interest-rate parameter from the money-market account, D is the continuous dividend yield, $\sqrt{V_t}$ is the volatility process, $\alpha(V_t, t)$ and $\beta(V_t, t)$ are continuous functions.

We denote τ as the random expiry time of a call option written on S_t at time t with strike price $K > 0$,

$$\tau = \inf \left\{ u > t : \int_t^u V_s\, ds = \widetilde{V} \right\}$$

where it is the first hitting time of the realised integrated variance to the variance budget $\widetilde{V}$.

Show that the timer call option price at time t is equal to

$$C_{timer}(S_t, V_t, t; K, \tau) = \mathbb{E}^{\mathbb{Q}} \left[\max \left\{ S_t e^{-D(\tau-t) - \frac{1}{2}\widetilde{V} + B_{\widetilde{V}}} - Ke^{-r(\tau-t)}, 0 \right\} \Big| \mathcal{F}_t \right]$$

where

$$B_{\widetilde{V}} = \int_t^\tau \sqrt{V_u} \left(\rho d\widetilde{W}_u^V + \sqrt{1 - \rho^2} d\widetilde{Z}_u \right)$$

such that $\widetilde{Z}_t$ is a $\mathbb{Q}$-standard Wiener process and $\widetilde{Z}_t \perp \widetilde{W}_t^V$.
Is there an explicit solution for the above timer call option?

Discuss under what conditions we can expect the timer call option to have closed-form solutions.

Finally, show that the put–call parity of timer options is

$$C_{timer}(S_t, V_t, t; K, \tau) - P_{timer}(S_t, V_t, t; K, \tau)$$
$$= \mathbb{E}^Q\left[\left.S_\tau e^{-r(\tau-t)}\right| \mathcal{F}_t\right] - K\mathbb{E}^Q\left[\left.e^{-r(\tau-t)}\right| \mathcal{F}_t\right]$$

where $P_{timer}(S_t, V_t, t; K, \tau)$ is the timer put option written on S_t at time t with strike price K and random expiry time τ.

Solution: By expanding $d\log S_t$ using Taylor's series and subsequently applying Itō's lemma,

$$d\log S_t = \frac{dS_t}{S_t} - \frac{1}{2}\left(\frac{dS_t}{S_t}\right)^2 + \dots$$
$$= (r-D)dt + \sqrt{V_t}\,dW_t^S - \frac{1}{2}V_t\,dt$$
$$= \left(r - D - \frac{1}{2}V_t\right)dt + \sqrt{V_t}\,dW_t^S.$$

Since we can set

$$dW_t^S = \rho\,d\widetilde{W}_t^V + \sqrt{1-\rho^2}\,d\widetilde{Z}_t$$

where $\widetilde{W}_t^V \perp \widetilde{Z}_t$, we can set

$$d\log S_t = \left(r - D - \frac{1}{2}V_t\right)dt + \sqrt{V_t}\left(\rho\,d\widetilde{W}_t^V + \sqrt{1-\rho^2}\,d\widetilde{Z}_t\right).$$

Taking integrals,

$$\int_t^\tau d\log S_u = \int_t^\tau (r-D)\,du - \frac{1}{2}\int_t^\tau V_u\,du$$
$$+ \int_t^\tau \sqrt{V_u}\left(\rho\,d\widetilde{W}_u^V + \sqrt{1-\rho^2}\,d\widetilde{Z}_u\right)$$
$$\log\left(\frac{S_\tau}{S_t}\right) = (r-D)(\tau-t) - \frac{1}{2}\widetilde{V} + B_{\widetilde{V}}$$

or

$$S_\tau = S_t e^{(r-D)(\tau-t) - \frac{1}{2}\widetilde{V} + B_{\widetilde{V}}}.$$

Given that the payoff of a timer call option is paid at random time τ, the price of a timer call option at time t is

$$C_{timer}(S_t, V_t, t; K, \tau) = \mathbb{E}^Q\left[e^{-r(\tau - t)} \max\left\{S_\tau - K, 0\right\} \middle| \mathcal{F}_t\right]$$

$$= \mathbb{E}^Q\left[e^{-r(\tau - t)} \max\left\{S_t e^{(r-D)(\tau - t) + B_{\widetilde{V}} - \frac{1}{2}\widetilde{V}} - K, 0\right\} \middle| \mathcal{F}_t\right]$$

$$= \mathbb{E}^Q\left[\max\left\{S_t e^{-D(\tau - t) - \frac{1}{2}\widetilde{V} + B_{\widetilde{V}}} - Ke^{-r(\tau - t)}, 0\right\} \middle| \mathcal{F}_t\right].$$

From the timer call option price expression, there is no explicit solution since $B_{\widetilde{V}}$ and the random expiry time τ can be correlated and the conditional distribution of $B_{\widetilde{V}}\middle| \tau$ is not a normal distribution.

Conditions where we expect the timer call option to have closed-form solutions are as follows.

(a) $K = 0$ and $D = 0$

By setting $K = 0$ and $D = 0$, the timer call option is reduced to a timer share contract with random expiry time τ.

Hence, we can set

$$C_{timer}(S_t, V_t, t; K, \tau) = \mathbb{E}^Q\left[e^{-r(\tau - t)} S_\tau \middle| \mathcal{F}_t\right]$$

$$= S_t$$

by assuming, under the general stochastic volatility model, that $e^{rt} S_t$ is a martingale (i.e., putting restrictions on $\alpha(V_t, t)$ and $\beta(V_t, t)$).

(b) $r = 0$ and $D = 0$

By setting $r = 0$ and $D = 0$, we have

$$C_{timer}(S_t, V_t, t; K, \tau) = \mathbb{E}^Q\left[\max\left\{S_t e^{-\frac{1}{2}\widetilde{V} + B_{\widetilde{V}}} - K, 0\right\} \middle| \mathcal{F}_t\right].$$

Note that the difference between the timer option and a European option is only the expiry time τ, which is random when $r = D = 0$, then the exact date when the cash flow occurs is no longer applicable. Thus, the timer option is not dependent on τ and following the Black–Scholes formula we have

$$C_{timer}(S_t, V_t, t; K) = S_t \Phi(d_+) - K\Phi(d_-)$$

where

$$d_\pm = \frac{\log(S_t/K) \pm \frac{1}{2}\widetilde{V}}{\sqrt{\widetilde{V}}}$$

and $\Phi(\cdot)$ is the cdf of a standard normal.

(c) $\beta(V_t, t) = 0$

When $\beta(V_t, t) = 0$, the instantaneous variance process is deterministic and hence we know exactly when to exercise the timer call option. By solving the first-order PDE

$$\frac{dV_t}{dt} = \alpha(V_t, t)$$

to find the solution V_t, let $T_{\widetilde{V}}$ be the time for the realised integrated variance to reach the variance budget $\widetilde{V}$, i.e.

$$\int_t^{T_{\widetilde{V}}} V_u\, du = \widetilde{V}.$$

Thus, the solution of the timer call option reduces to the Black–Scholes formula

$$C_{timer}(S_t, V_t, t; K) = S_t e^{-D(T_{\widetilde{V}} - t)} \Phi(d_+) - K e^{-r(T_{\widetilde{V}} - t)} \Phi(d_-)$$

where

$$d_\pm = \frac{\log(S_t/K) + (r - D)(T_{\widetilde{V}} - t) \pm \frac{1}{2}\widetilde{V}}{\sqrt{\widetilde{V}}}$$

and $\Phi(\cdot)$ is the cdf of a standard normal.

For the put–call parity relationship, from the identity

$$\max\{S_\tau - K, 0\} - \max\{K - S_\tau, 0\} = S_\tau - K.$$

Taking expectations under the risk-neutral measure $\mathbb{Q}$,

$$\mathbb{E}^{\mathbb{Q}}\left[e^{-r(\tau - t)} \max\{S_\tau - K, 0\}\,\middle|\,\mathcal{F}_t\right] - \mathbb{E}^{\mathbb{Q}}\left[e^{-r(\tau - t)} \max\{S_\tau - K, 0\}\,\middle|\,\mathcal{F}_t\right]$$
$$= \mathbb{E}^{\mathbb{Q}}\left[e^{-r(\tau - t)}(S_\tau - K)\,\middle|\,\mathcal{F}_t\right]$$

or

$$C_{timer}(S_t, V_t, t; K, \tau) - P_{timer}(S_t, V_t, t; K, \tau)$$
$$= \mathbb{E}^{\mathbb{Q}}\left[e^{-r(\tau - t)} S_\tau\,\middle|\,\mathcal{F}_t\right] - K\mathbb{E}^{\mathbb{Q}}\left[e^{-r(\tau - t)}\,\middle|\,\mathcal{F}_t\right].$$

From the put–call parity, we can see that the first term on the right-hand side is the price of a timer share contract at time t, whilst the second term is the price of a timer cash contract at time t.

$\square$

Appendix A
Mathematics Formulae

Indices

$$x^a x^b = x^{a+b}, \quad \frac{x^a}{x^b} = x^{a-b}, \quad (x^a)^b = (x^b)^a = x^{ab}$$

$$x^{-a} = \frac{1}{x^a}, \quad \left(\frac{x}{y}\right)^a = \frac{x^a}{y^a}, \quad x^0 = 1.$$

Surds

$$x^{\frac{1}{a}} = \sqrt[a]{x}, \quad \sqrt[a]{xy} = \sqrt[a]{x}\sqrt[a]{y}, \quad \sqrt[a]{x/y} = \frac{\sqrt[a]{x}}{\sqrt[a]{y}}$$

$$\left(\sqrt[a]{x}\right)^a = x, \quad \sqrt[a]{\sqrt[b]{x}} = \sqrt[ab]{x}, \quad \left(\sqrt[a]{x}\right)^b = \sqrt[a]{x^b} = x^{\frac{b}{a}}.$$

Exponential and Natural Logarithm

$$e^x e^y = e^{x+y}, \quad (e^x)^y = (e^y)^x = e^{xy}, \quad e^0 = 1$$

$$\log(xy) = \log x + \log y, \quad \log\left(\frac{x}{y}\right) = \log x - \log y, \quad \log x^y = y \log x$$

$$\log e^x = x, \quad e^{\log x} = x, \quad e^{a \log x} = x^a.$$

Quadratic Equation

For constants a, b and c, the roots of a quadratic equation $ax^2 + bx + c = 0$ are

$$x = \frac{-b \pm \sqrt{b^2 - 4ac}}{2a}.$$

Binomial Formula

$$\binom{n}{k} = \frac{n!}{k!(n-k)!}, \quad \binom{n}{k} + \binom{n}{k+1} = \binom{n+1}{k+1}$$

$$(x+y)^n = \sum_{k=0}^{n} \binom{n}{k} x^{n-k} y^k = \sum_{k=0}^{n} \frac{n!}{k!(n-k)!} x^{n-k} y^k.$$

Series

Arithmetic: For initial term a and common difference d, the nth term is

$$T_n = a + (n-1)d$$

and the sum of n terms is

$$S_n = \frac{1}{2}n\,[2a + (n-1)d]\,.$$

Geometric: For initial term a and common ratio r, the nth term is

$$T_n = ar^{n-1}$$

the sum of n terms is

$$S_n = \frac{a(1-r^n)}{1-r}$$

and the sum of infinite terms is

$$\lim_{n\to\infty} S_n = \frac{a}{1-r}, \quad |r| < 1.$$

Summation

For $n \in \mathbb{Z}^+$,

$$\sum_{k=1}^{n} k = \frac{1}{2}n(n+1), \quad \sum_{k=1}^{n} k^2 = \frac{1}{6}n(n+1)(2n+1), \quad \sum_{k=1}^{n} k^3 = \left[\frac{1}{2}n(n+1)\right]^2.$$

Let $a_1, a_2, \ldots$ be a sequence of numbers.

- If $\sum a_n < \infty \Longrightarrow \lim_{n\to\infty} a_n = 0$.
- If $\lim_{n\to\infty} a_n \neq 0 \Longrightarrow \sum a_n = \infty$.

Trigonometric Functions

$$\sin(-x) = -\sin x, \quad \cos(-x) = \cos x, \quad \tan x = \frac{\sin x}{\cos x}$$

$$\csc x = \frac{1}{\sin x}, \quad \sec x = \frac{1}{\cos x}, \quad \cot x = \frac{1}{\tan x}$$

$$\cos^2 x + \sin^2 x = 1, \quad \tan^2 x + 1 = \sec^2 x, \quad \cot^2 x + 1 = \csc^2 x$$

$$\sin(x \pm y) = \sin x \cos y \pm \cos x \sin y$$

$$\cos(x \pm y) = \cos x \cos y \mp \sin x \sin y$$

$$\tan(x \pm y) = \frac{\tan x \pm \tan y}{1 \mp \tan x \tan y}$$

$$\sin(0) = 0, \quad \sin\left(\frac{\pi}{6}\right) = \frac{1}{2}, \quad \sin\left(\frac{\pi}{4}\right) = \frac{1}{\sqrt{2}}, \quad \sin\left(\frac{\pi}{3}\right) = \frac{\sqrt{3}}{2}, \quad \sin\left(\frac{\pi}{2}\right) = 1$$

$$\cos(0) = 1, \quad \cos\left(\frac{\pi}{6}\right) = \frac{\sqrt{3}}{2}, \quad \cos\left(\frac{\pi}{4}\right) = \frac{1}{\sqrt{2}}, \quad \cos\left(\frac{\pi}{3}\right) = \frac{1}{2}, \quad \cos\left(\frac{\pi}{2}\right) = 0$$

$$\tan(0) = 0, \quad \tan\left(\frac{\pi}{6}\right) = \frac{1}{\sqrt{3}}, \quad \tan\left(\frac{\pi}{4}\right) = 1, \quad \tan\left(\frac{\pi}{3}\right) = \sqrt{3}, \quad \tan\left(\frac{\pi}{2}\right) = \infty.$$

Hyperbolic Functions

$$\sinh x = \frac{e^x - e^{-x}}{2}, \quad \cosh x = \frac{e^x + e^{-x}}{2}, \quad \tanh x = \frac{\sinh x}{\cosh x} = \frac{e^x - e^{-x}}{e^x + e^{-x}}$$

$$\text{csch} x = \frac{1}{\sinh x}, \quad \text{sech} x = \frac{1}{\cosh x}, \quad \coth x = \frac{1}{\tanh x}$$

$$\sinh(-x) = -\sinh x, \quad \cosh(-x) = \cosh x, \quad \tanh(-x) = -\tanh x$$

$$\cosh^2 x - \sinh^2 x = 1, \quad \coth^2 x - 1 = \text{csch}^2 x, \quad 1 - \tanh^2 x = \text{sech}^2 x$$

$$\sinh(x \pm y) = \sinh x \cosh y \pm \cosh x \sinh y$$

$$\cosh(x \pm y) = \cosh x \cosh y \pm \sinh x \sinh y$$

$$\tanh(x \pm y) = \frac{\tanh x \pm \tanh y}{1 \pm \tanh x \tanh y}.$$

Complex Numbers

Let $w = u + iv$ and $z = x + iy$ where $u, v, x, y \in \mathbb{R}$, $i = \sqrt{-1}$ and $i^2 = -1$, then

$$w \pm z = (u \pm x) + (v \pm y)i, \quad wz = (ux - vy) + (vx + uy)i$$

$$\frac{w}{z} = \left(\frac{ux + vy}{x^2 + y^2}\right) + \left(\frac{vx - uy}{x^2 + y^2}\right)i$$

$$\bar{z} = x - iy, \quad \bar{\bar{z}} = z, \quad \overline{w + z} = \bar{w} + \bar{z}, \quad \overline{wz} = \bar{w}\bar{z}, \quad \overline{\left(\frac{w}{z}\right)} = \frac{\bar{w}}{\bar{z}}.$$

De Moivre's Formula: Let $z = x + iy$ where $x, y \in \mathbb{R}$ and we can write

$$z = r(\cos\theta + i\sin\theta), \quad r = \sqrt{x^2 + y^2}, \quad \theta = \tan^{-1}\left(\frac{y}{x}\right).$$

For $n \in \mathbb{Z}$

$$[r(\cos\theta + i\sin\theta)]^n = r^n\left[\cos(n\theta) + i\sin(n\theta)\right].$$

Euler's Formula: For $\theta \in \mathbb{R}$

$$e^{i\theta} = \cos\theta + i\sin\theta.$$

Derivatives

If $f(x)$ and $g(x)$ are differentiable functions of x and a and b are constants

Sum Rule:

$$\frac{d}{dx}(af(x) + bg(x)) = af'(x) + bg'(x)$$

Product/Chain Rule:

$$\frac{d}{dx}(f(x)g(x)) = f(x)g'(x) + f'(x)g(x)$$

Quotient Rule:

$$\frac{d}{dx}\left(\frac{f(x)}{g(x)}\right) = \frac{f'(x)g(x) - f(x)g'(x)}{g(x)^2}, \quad g(x) \neq 0$$

where $\dfrac{d}{dx}f(x) = f'(x)$ and $\dfrac{d}{dx}g(x) = g'(x)$.

If $f(z)$ is a differentiable function of z and $z = z(x)$ is a differentiable function of x, then

$$\frac{d}{dx}f(z(x)) = f'(z(x))z'(x).$$

If $x = x(s)$, $y = y(s)$ and $F(s) = f(x(s), y(s))$, then

$$\frac{d}{ds}F(s) = \frac{\partial f}{\partial x} \cdot \frac{\partial x}{\partial s} + \frac{\partial f}{\partial y} \cdot \frac{\partial y}{\partial s}.$$

If $x = x(u, v)$, $y = y(u, v)$ and $F(u, v) = f(x(u, v), y(u, v))$, then

$$\frac{\partial F}{\partial u} = \frac{\partial f}{\partial x} \cdot \frac{\partial x}{\partial u} + \frac{\partial f}{\partial y} \cdot \frac{\partial y}{\partial u}, \frac{\partial F}{\partial v} = \frac{\partial f}{\partial x} \cdot \frac{\partial x}{\partial v} + \frac{\partial f}{\partial y} \cdot \frac{\partial y}{\partial v}.$$

Standard Differentiations

If $f(x)$ and $g(x)$ are differentiable functions of x and a and b are constants

$$\frac{d}{dx}a = 0, \quad \frac{d}{dx}[f(x)]^n = n[f(x)]^{n-1}f'(x)$$

$$\frac{d}{dx}e^{f(x)} = f'(x)e^{f(x)}, \quad \frac{d}{dx}\log f(x) = \frac{f'(x)}{f(x)}, \quad \frac{d}{dx}a^{f(x)} = f'(x)a^{f(x)}\log a$$

$$\frac{d}{dx}\sin(ax) = a\cos x, \quad \frac{d}{dx}\cos(ax) = -a\sin(ax), \quad \frac{d}{dx}\tan(ax) = a\sec^2 x$$

$$\frac{d}{dx}\sinh(ax) = a\cosh(ax), \quad \frac{d}{dx}\cosh(ax) = a\sinh(ax), \quad \frac{d}{dx}\tanh(ax) = a\operatorname{sech}^2(ax)$$

where $f'(x) = \frac{d}{dx}f(x)$.

Taylor Series

If $f(x)$ is an analytic function of x, then for small h

$$f(x_0 + h) = f(x_0) + f'(x_0)h + \frac{1}{2!}f''(x_0)h^2 + \frac{1}{3!}f'''(x_0)h^3 + \dots$$

If $f(x, y)$ is an analytic function of x and y, then for small $\Delta x, \Delta y$

$$f(x_0 + \Delta x, y_0 + \Delta y) = f(x_0, y_0) + \frac{\partial f(x_0, y_0)}{\partial x}\Delta x + \frac{\partial f(x_0, y_0)}{\partial y}\Delta y$$

$$+ \frac{1}{2!}\left[\frac{\partial^2 f(x_0, y_0)}{\partial x^2}(\Delta x)^2 + 2\frac{\partial^2 f(x_0, y_0)}{\partial x \partial y}\Delta x \Delta y + \frac{\partial^2 f(x_0, y_0)}{\partial y^2}(\Delta y)^2\right]$$

$$+ \frac{1}{3!}\left[\frac{\partial^3 f(x_0, y_0)}{\partial x^3}(\Delta x)^3 + 3\frac{\partial^3 f(x_0, y_0)}{\partial x^2 \partial y}(\Delta x)^2 \Delta y\right.$$

$$\left. + 3\frac{\partial^3 f(x_0, y_0)}{\partial x \partial y^2}\Delta x(\Delta y)^2 + \frac{\partial^3 f(x_0, y_0)}{\partial y^3}(\Delta y)^3\right] + \dots$$

Maclaurin Series

Taylor series expansion of a function about $x_0 = 0$:

$$\frac{1}{1+x} = 1 - x + x^2 - x^3 + \dots, \quad |x| < 1$$

$$\frac{1}{1-x} = 1 + x + x^2 + x^3 + \dots, \quad |x| < 1$$

$$e^x = 1 + x + \frac{1}{2!}x^2 + \frac{1}{3!}x^3 + \dots, \quad \text{for all } x$$

$$e^{-x} = 1 - x + \frac{1}{2!}x^2 - \frac{1}{3!}x^3 + \ldots, \quad \text{for all } x$$

$$\log(1 + x) = x - \frac{1}{2}x^2 + \frac{1}{3}x^3 - \frac{1}{4}x^4 + \ldots, \quad x \in (-1, 1]$$

$$\log(1 - x) = -x - \frac{1}{2}x^2 - \frac{1}{3}x^3 - \frac{1}{4}x^4 + \ldots, \quad |x| < 1$$

$$\sin x = x - \frac{1}{3!}x^3 + \frac{1}{5!}x^5 - \frac{1}{7!}x^7 + \ldots, \quad \text{for all } x$$

$$\cos x = 1 - \frac{1}{2!}x^2 + \frac{1}{4!}x^4 - \frac{1}{6!}x^6 + \ldots, \quad \text{for all } x$$

$$\tan x = x + \frac{1}{3}x^3 + \frac{2x^5}{15} + \frac{17}{315}x^7 + \ldots, \quad |x| < \frac{\pi}{2}$$

$$\sinh x = x + \frac{1}{3!}x^3 + \frac{1}{5!}x^5 + \frac{1}{7!}x^7 + \ldots, \quad \text{for all } x$$

$$\cosh x = 1 + \frac{1}{2!}x^2 + \frac{1}{4!}x^4 + \frac{1}{6!}x^6 + \ldots, \quad \text{for all } x$$

$$\tanh x = x - \frac{1}{3}x^3 + \frac{2x^5}{15} - \frac{17}{315}x^7 + \ldots, \quad |x| < \frac{\pi}{2}.$$

Landau Symbols and Asymptotics

Let $f(x)$ and $g(x)$ be two functions defined on some subsets of real numbers, then as $x \to x_0$

- $f(x) = O(g(x))$ if there exists a constant $K > 0$ and $\delta > 0$ such that $|f(x)| \leq K|g(x)|$ for $|x - x_0| < \delta$
- $f(x) = o(g(x))$ if $\lim\limits_{x \to x_0} \frac{f(x)}{g(x)} = 0$
- $f(x) \sim g(x)$ if $\lim\limits_{x \to x_0} \frac{f(x)}{g(x)} = 1$.

L'Hôpital's Rule

Let f and g be differentiable on $a \in \mathbb{R}$ such that $g'(x) \neq 0$ in an interval around a, except possibly at a itself. Suppose that

$$\lim_{x \to a} f(x) = \lim_{x \to a} g(x) = 0$$

or

$$\lim_{x \to a} f(x) = \lim_{x \to a} g(x) = \pm\infty$$

then

$$\lim_{x \to a} \frac{f(x)}{g(x)} = \lim_{x \to a} \frac{f'(x)}{g'(x)}.$$

Indefinite Integrals

If $F(x)$ is a differentiable function and $f(x)$ is its derivative, then

$$\int f(x)\,dx = F(x) + c$$

where $F'(x) = \dfrac{d}{dx}F(x) = f(x)$ and c is an arbitrary constant.
If $f(x)$ is a continuous function then

$$\frac{d}{dx}\int f(x)\,dx = f(x).$$

Standard Indefinite Integrals

If $f(x)$ is a differentiable function of x and a and b are constants

$$\int a\,dx = ax + c, \qquad \int (ax+b)^n\,dx = \frac{(ax+b)^{n+1}}{a(n+1)} + c, \quad n \neq -1$$

$$\int \frac{f'(x)}{f(x)}\,dx = \log|f(x)| + c, \qquad \int e^{f(x)}\,dx = \frac{1}{f'(x)}e^{f(x)} + c$$

$$\int \log(ax)\,dx = x\log(ax) - ax + c, \qquad \int a^x\,dx = \frac{a^x}{\log a} + c$$

$$\int \sin(ax)\,dx = -\frac{1}{a}\cos(ax) + c, \qquad \int \cos(ax)\,dx = \frac{1}{a}\sin(ax) + c$$

$$\int \sinh(ax)\,dx = \frac{1}{a}\cosh(ax) + c, \qquad \int \cosh(ax)\,dx = \frac{1}{a}\sinh(ax) + c$$

where c is an arbitrary constant.

Definite Integrals

If $F(x)$ is a differentiable function and $f(x)$ is its derivative and is continuous on a closed interval $[a, b]$, then

$$\int_a^b f(x)\,dx = F(b) - F(a)$$

where $F'(x) = \dfrac{d}{dx}F(x) = f(x)$.

If $f(x)$ and $g(x)$ are integrable functions then

$$\int_a^a f(x)\,dx = 0, \quad \int_a^b f(x)\,dx = -\int_b^a f(x)\,dx$$

$$\int_a^b [\alpha f(x) + \beta g(x)]\,dx = \alpha \int_a^b f(x)\,dx + \beta \int_a^b g(x)\,dx, \quad \alpha, \beta \text{ are constants}$$

$$\int_a^b f(x)\,dx = \int_a^c f(x)\,dx + \int_c^b f(x)\,dx, \quad c \in [a,b].$$

Derivatives of Definite Integrals

If $f(t)$ is a continuous function of t and $a(x)$ and $b(x)$ are continuous functions of x

$$\frac{d}{dx}\int_{a(x)}^{b(x)} f(t)\,dt = f(b(x))\frac{d}{dx}b(x) - f(a(x))\frac{d}{dx}a(x)$$

$$\frac{d}{dx}\int_{a(x)}^{b(x)} dt = \frac{d}{dx}b(x) - \frac{d}{dx}a(x).$$

If $g(x,t)$ is a differentiable function of two variables then

$$\frac{d}{dx}\int_{a(x)}^{b(x)} g(x,t)\,dt = g(x,b(x))\frac{d}{dx}b(x) - g(x,a(x))\frac{d}{dx}a(x) + \int_{a(x)}^{b(x)} \frac{\partial g(x,t)}{\partial x}\,dt.$$

Integration by Parts

For definite integrals

$$\int_a^b u(x)v'(x)\,dx = u(x)v(x)\Big|_a^b - \int_a^b v(x)u'(x)\,dx$$

where $u'(x) = \dfrac{d}{dx}u(x)$ and $v'(x) = \dfrac{d}{dx}v(x)$.

Integration by Substitution

If $f(x)$ is a continuous function of x and g' is continuous on the closed interval $[a,b]$, then

$$\int_{g(b)}^{g(a)} f(x)\,dx = \int_a^b f(g(u))g'(u)\,du.$$

Gamma Function

The gamma function is defined as

$$\Gamma(z) = \int_0^\infty t^{z-1} e^{-t}\, dt$$

such that

$$\Gamma(z+1) = z\Gamma(z), \quad \Gamma\left(\frac{1}{2}\right) = \sqrt{\pi}, \quad \Gamma(n) = (n-1)! \text{ for } n \in \mathbb{N}.$$

Beta Function

The beta function is defined as

$$B(x, y) = \int_0^1 t^{x-1}(1-t)^{y-1}\, dt \text{ for } x > 0, y > 0$$

such that

$$B(x, y) = B(y, x), \quad B(x, y) = \frac{\Gamma(x)\Gamma(y)}{\Gamma(x+y)}.$$

In addition

$$\int_0^u t^{x-1}(u-t)^{y-1}\, dt = u^{x+y-1} B(x, y).$$

Convex Function

A set Ω in a vector space over $\mathbb{R}$ is called a convex set if for $x, y \in \Omega$, $x \neq y$ and for any $\lambda \in (0, 1)$,

$$\lambda x + (1 - \lambda)y \in \Omega.$$

Let Ω be a convex set in a vector space over $\mathbb{R}$. A function $f : \Omega \longmapsto \mathbb{R}$ is called a convex function if for $x, y \in \Omega$, $x \neq y$ and for any $\lambda \in (0, 1)$,

$$f(\lambda x + (1 - \lambda)y) \leq \lambda f(x) + (1 - \lambda) f(y).$$

- If the inequality is strict then f is strictly convex.
- If f is convex and differentiable on $\mathbb{R}$ then $f(x) \geq f(y) + f'(y)(x - y)$.
- If f is a twice continuously differentiable function on $\mathbb{R}$ then f is convex if and only if $f'' \geq 0$. If $f'' > 0$ then f is strictly convex.
- f is a (strictly) concave function if $-f$ is a (strictly) convex function.

Dirac Delta Function

The Dirac delta function is defined as

$$\delta(x) = \begin{cases} 0 & x \neq 0 \\ \infty & x = 0 \end{cases}$$

and for a continuous function $f(x)$ and a constant a we have

$$\int_{-\infty}^{\infty} \delta(x)\, dx = 1, \quad \int_{-\infty}^{\infty} f(x)\delta(x)\, dx = f(0), \quad \int_{-\infty}^{\infty} f(x)\delta(x-a)\, dx = f(a).$$

Heaviside Step Function

The Heaviside step function $H(x)$ is defined as the integral of the Dirac delta function given as

$$H(x) = \int_{-\infty}^{x} \delta(s)\, ds = \begin{cases} 0 & x < 0 \\ 1 & x > 0. \end{cases}$$

Fubini's Theorem

Suppose that $f(x, y)$ is $A \times B$ measurable and if $\displaystyle\int_{A \times B} |f(x, y)|\, d(x, y) < \infty$, then

$$\int_{A \times B} f(x, y)\, d(x, y) = \int_A \left(\int_B f(x, y)\, dy \right) dx = \int_B \left(\int_A f(x, y)\, dx \right) dy.$$

Appendix B
Probability Theory Formulae

Probability Concepts

Let A and B be events of the sample space Ω with probabilities $\mathbb{P}(A) \in [0, 1]$ and $\mathbb{P}(B) \in [0, 1]$, then

Complement:

$$\mathbb{P}(A^c) = 1 - \mathbb{P}(A).$$

Conditional:

$$\mathbb{P}(A|B) = \frac{\mathbb{P}(A \cap B)}{\mathbb{P}(B)}.$$

Independence: The events A and B are independent if and only if

$$\mathbb{P}(A \cap B) = \mathbb{P}(A) \cdot \mathbb{P}(B).$$

Mutually Exclusive: The events A and B are mutually exclusive if and only if

$$\mathbb{P}(A \cap B) = 0.$$

Addition:

$$\mathbb{P}(A \cup B) = \mathbb{P}(A) + \mathbb{P}(B) - \mathbb{P}(A \cap B).$$

Multiplication:

$$\mathbb{P}(A \cap B) = \mathbb{P}(A|B)\mathbb{P}(B) = \mathbb{P}(B|A)\mathbb{P}(A).$$

Partition:

$$\mathbb{P}(A) = \mathbb{P}(A \cap B) + \mathbb{P}(A \cap B^c) = \mathbb{P}(A|B)\mathbb{P}(B) + \mathbb{P}(A|B^c)\mathbb{P}(B^c).$$

Bayes' Rule

Let A and B be events of the sample space Ω with probabilities $\mathbb{P}(A) \in [0, 1]$ and $\mathbb{P}(B) \in [0, 1]$, then

$$\mathbb{P}(A|B) = \frac{\mathbb{P}(B|A)\mathbb{P}(A)}{\mathbb{P}(B)}.$$

Indicator Function

The indicator function $\mathbb{I}_A$ of an event A of a sample space Ω is a function $\mathbb{I}_A : \Omega \longmapsto \mathbb{R}$ defined as

$$\mathbb{I}_A(\omega) = \begin{cases} 1 & \text{if } \omega \in A \\ 0 & \text{if } \omega \in A^c. \end{cases}$$

Properties: For events A and B of the sample space Ω

$$\mathbb{I}_{A^c} = 1 - \mathbb{I}_A, \quad \mathbb{I}_{A \cap B} = \mathbb{I}_A \mathbb{I}_B, \quad \mathbb{I}_{A \cup B} = \mathbb{I}_A + \mathbb{I}_B - \mathbb{I}_A \mathbb{I}_B$$

$$\mathbb{E}(\mathbb{I}_A) = \mathbb{P}(A), \quad \text{Var}(\mathbb{I}_A) = \mathbb{P}(A)\mathbb{P}(A^c), \quad \text{Cov}(\mathbb{I}_A, \mathbb{I}_B) = \mathbb{P}(A \cap B) - \mathbb{P}(A)\mathbb{P}(B).$$

Discrete Random Variables

Univariate Case

Let X be a discrete random variable whose possible values are $x = x_1, x_2, \ldots$ and let $P(X = x)$ be the probability mass function.

Total Probability of All Possible Values:

$$\sum_{k=1}^{\infty} \mathbb{P}(X = x_k) = 1.$$

Cumulative Distribution Function:

$$\mathbb{P}(X \leq x_n) = \sum_{k=1}^{n} \mathbb{P}(X = x_k).$$

Expectation:

$$\mathbb{E}(X) = \mu = \sum_{k=1}^{\infty} x_k \mathbb{P}(X = x_k).$$

Variance:

$$\begin{aligned}
\text{Var}(X) &= \sigma^2 \\
&= \mathbb{E}\left[(X - \mu)^2\right] \\
&= \sum_{k=1}^{\infty} (x_k - \mu)^2 \mathbb{P}(X = x_k) \\
&= \sum_{k=1}^{\infty} x_k^2 \mathbb{P}(X = x_k) - \mu^2 \\
&= \mathbb{E}(X^2) - [\mathbb{E}(X)]^2.
\end{aligned}$$

Moment-Generating Function:

$$M_X(t) = \mathbb{E}\left(e^{tX}\right) = \sum_{k=1}^{\infty} e^{tx_k} \mathbb{P}(X = x_k), \quad t \in \mathbb{R}.$$

Characteristic Function:

$$\varphi_X(t) = \mathbb{E}\left(e^{itX}\right) = \sum_{k=1}^{\infty} e^{itx_k} \mathbb{P}(X = x_k), \quad i = \sqrt{-1} \text{ and } t \in \mathbb{R}.$$

Bivariate Case

Let X and Y be discrete random variables whose possible values are $x = x_1, x_2, \ldots$ and $y = y_1, y_2, \ldots$, respectively, and let $P(X = x, Y = y)$ be the joint probability mass function.

Total Probability of All Possible Values:

$$\sum_{j=1}^{\infty} \sum_{k=1}^{\infty} \mathbb{P}(X = x_j, Y = y_k) = 1.$$

Joint Cumulative Distribution Function:

$$\mathbb{P}(X \leq x_n, Y \leq y_m) = \sum_{j=1}^{n} \sum_{k=1}^{m} \mathbb{P}(X = x_j, Y = y_k).$$

Marginal Probability Mass Function:

$$\mathbb{P}(X = x) = \sum_{k=1}^{\infty} \mathbb{P}(X = x, Y = y_k), \quad \mathbb{P}(Y = y) = \sum_{j=1}^{\infty} \mathbb{P}(X = x_j, Y = y).$$

Conditional Probability Mass Function:

$$\mathbb{P}(X = x | Y = y) = \frac{\mathbb{P}(X = x, Y = y)}{\mathbb{P}(Y = y)}, \quad \mathbb{P}(Y = y | X = x) = \frac{\mathbb{P}(X = x, Y = y)}{\mathbb{P}(X = x)}.$$

Conditional Expectation:

$$\mathbb{E}(X | Y) = \mu_{x|y} = \sum_{j=1}^{n} x_j \mathbb{P}(X = x_j | Y = y), \quad \mathbb{E}(Y | X) = \mu_{y|x} = \sum_{k=1}^{n} y_k \mathbb{P}(Y = y_k | X = x).$$

Conditional Variance:

$$\text{Var}(X|Y) = \sigma_{x|y}^2$$

$$= \mathbb{E}\left[(X - \mu_{x|y})^2 \,\middle|\, Y\right]$$

$$= \sum_{j=1}^{\infty}(x_j - \mu_{x|y})^2 \mathbb{P}(X = x_j | Y = y)$$

$$= \sum_{j=1}^{\infty} x_j^2 \mathbb{P}(X = x_j | Y = y) - \mu_{x|y}^2$$

$$\text{Var}(Y|X) = \sigma_{y|x}^2$$

$$= \mathbb{E}\left[(Y - \mu_{y|x})^2 \,\middle|\, X\right]$$

$$= \sum_{k=1}^{\infty}(y_k - \mu_{y|x})^2 \mathbb{P}(Y = y_k | X = x)$$

$$= \sum_{k=1}^{\infty} y_k^2 \mathbb{P}(Y = y_k | X = x) - \mu_{y|x}^2.$$

Covariance:
For $\mathbb{E}(X) = \mu_x$ and $\mathbb{E}(Y) = \mu_y$

$$\text{Cov}(X, Y) = \mathbb{E}\left[(X - \mu_x)(Y - \mu_y)\right]$$

$$= \sum_{j=1}^{\infty}\sum_{k=1}^{\infty}(x_j - \mu_x)(y_k - \mu_y)\mathbb{P}(X = x_j, Y = y_k)$$

$$= \sum_{j=1}^{\infty}\sum_{k=1}^{\infty} x_j y_k \mathbb{P}(X = x_j, Y = y_k) - \mu_x \mu_y$$

$$= \mathbb{E}(XY) - \mathbb{E}(X)\mathbb{E}(Y).$$

Joint Moment-Generating Function:
For $s, t \in \mathbb{R}$

$$M_{XY}(s, t) = \mathbb{E}\left(e^{sX + tY}\right) = \sum_{j=1}^{\infty}\sum_{k=1}^{\infty} e^{sx_j + ty_k}\mathbb{P}(X = x_j, Y = y_k).$$

Joint Characteristic Function:
For $i = \sqrt{-1}$ and $s, t \in \mathbb{R}$

$$\varphi_{XY}(s, t) = \mathbb{E}\left(e^{isX + itY}\right) = \sum_{j=1}^{\infty}\sum_{k=1}^{\infty} e^{isx_j + ity_k}\mathbb{P}(X = x_j, Y = y_k).$$

Independence:
X and Y are independent if and only if

- $\mathbb{P}(X = x, Y = y) = \mathbb{P}(X = x)\mathbb{P}(Y = y).$
- $M_{XY}(s, t) = \mathbb{E}\left(e^{sX+tY}\right) = \mathbb{E}\left(e^{sX}\right)\mathbb{E}\left(e^{tY}\right) = M_X(s)M_Y(t).$
- $\varphi_{XY}(s, t) = \mathbb{E}\left(e^{isX+itY}\right) = \mathbb{E}\left(e^{isX}\right)\mathbb{E}\left(e^{itY}\right) = \varphi_X(s)\varphi_Y(t).$

Continuous Random Variables

Univariate Case

Let X be a continuous random variable whose values $x \in \mathbb{R}$ and let $f_X(x)$ be the probability density function.

Total Probability of All Possible Values:

$$\int_{-\infty}^{\infty} f_X(x)\,dx = 1.$$

Evaluating Probability:

$$\mathbb{P}(a \le X \le b) = \int_a^b f_X(x)\,dx.$$

Cumulative Distribution Function:

$$F_X(x) = \mathbb{P}(X \le x) = \int_{-\infty}^x f_X(x)\,dx.$$

Probability Density Function:

$$f_X(x) = \frac{d}{dx}F_X(x).$$

Expectation:

$$\mathbb{E}(X) = \mu = \int_{-\infty}^{\infty} x f_X(x)\,dx.$$

Variance:

$$\text{Var}(X) = \sigma^2 = \int_{-\infty}^{\infty} (x - \mu)^2 f_X(x)\,dx = \int_{-\infty}^{\infty} x^2 f_X(x)\,dx - \mu^2 = \mathbb{E}(X^2) - [\mathbb{E}(X)]^2.$$

Moment-Generating Function:

$$M_X(t) = \mathbb{E}\left(e^{tX}\right) = \int_{-\infty}^{\infty} e^{tx} f_X(x)\,dx, t \in \mathbb{R}.$$

Characteristic Function:

$$\varphi_X(t) = \mathbb{E}\left(e^{itX}\right) = \int_{-\infty}^{\infty} e^{itx} f_X(x)\, dx, \quad i = \sqrt{-1} \text{ and } t \in \mathbb{R}.$$

Probability Density Function of a Dependent Variable:
Let the random variable $Y = g(X)$. If g is monotonic then the probability density function of Y is

$$f_Y(y) = f_X\left(g^{-1}(y)\right) \left| \frac{d}{dy} g^{-1}(y) \right|^{-1}$$

where g^{-1} denotes the inverse function.

Bivariate Case

Let X and Y be two continuous random variables whose values $x \in \mathbb{R}$ and $y \in \mathbb{R}$, and let $f_{XY}(x, y)$ be the joint probability density function.

Total Probability of All Possible Values:

$$\int_{-\infty}^{\infty} \int_{-\infty}^{\infty} f_{XY}(x, y)\, dx\, dy = \int_{-\infty}^{\infty} \int_{-\infty}^{\infty} f_{XY}(x, y)\, dy\, dx = 1.$$

Joint Cumulative Distribution Function:

$$F_{XY}(x, y) = \mathbb{P}(X \le x, Y \le y) = \int_{-\infty}^{x} \int_{-\infty}^{y} f_{XY}(x, y)\, dy\, dx = \int_{-\infty}^{y} \int_{-\infty}^{x} f_{XY}(x, y)\, dx\, dy.$$

Evaluating Joint Probability:

$$\mathbb{P}(x_a \le X \le x_b, y_a \le Y \le y_b) = \int_{x_a}^{x_b} \int_{y_a}^{y_b} f_{XY}(x, y)\, dy\, dx$$

$$= \int_{y_a}^{y_b} \int_{x_a}^{x_b} f_{XY}(x, y)\, dx\, dy$$

$$= F_{XY}(x_b, y_b) - F_{XY}(x_b, y_a) - F_{XY}(x_a, y_b) + F_{XY}(x_a, y_a).$$

Joint Probability Density Function:

$$f_{XY}(x, y) = \frac{\partial^2}{\partial x \partial y} F_{XY}(x, y) = \frac{\partial^2}{\partial y \partial x} F_{XY}(x, y).$$

Marginal Probability Density Function:

$$f_X(x) = \int_{-\infty}^{\infty} f_{XY}(x, y)\, dy, \quad f_Y(y) = \int_{-\infty}^{\infty} f_{XY}(x, y)\, dx.$$

Conditional Probability Density Function:

$$f_{X|Y}(x|y) = \frac{f_{XY}(x, y)}{f_Y(y)}, \quad f_{Y|X}(y|x) = \frac{f_{XY}(x, y)}{f_X(x)}.$$

Conditional Expectation:

$$\mathbb{E}(X|Y) = \mu_{x|y} = \int_{-\infty}^{\infty} x f_{X|Y}(x|y)\, dx, \quad \mathbb{E}(Y|X) = \mu_{y|x} = \int_{-\infty}^{\infty} y f_{Y|X}(y|x)\, dy.$$

Conditional Variance:

$$\text{Var}(X|Y) = \sigma_{x|y}^2$$
$$= \mathbb{E}\left[(X - \mu_{x|y})^2 \,\middle|\, Y\right]$$
$$= \int_{-\infty}^{\infty} (x - \mu_{x|y})^2 f_{X|Y}(x|y)\, dx$$
$$= \int_{-\infty}^{\infty} x^2 f_{X|Y}(x|y)\, dx - \mu_{x|y}^2$$

$$\text{Var}(Y|X) = \sigma_{y|x}^2$$
$$= \mathbb{E}\left[(Y - \mu_{y|x})^2 \,\middle|\, X\right]$$
$$= \int_{-\infty}^{\infty} (y - \mu_{y|x})^2 f_{Y|X}(y|x)\, dy$$
$$= \int_{-\infty}^{\infty} y^2 f_{Y|X}(y|x)\, dy - \mu_{y|x}^2.$$

Covariance:
For $\mathbb{E}(X) = \mu_x$ and $\mathbb{E}(Y) = \mu_y$

$$\text{Cov}(X, Y) = \mathbb{E}\left[(X - \mu_x)(Y - \mu_y)\right]$$
$$= \int_{-\infty}^{\infty} \int_{-\infty}^{\infty} (x - \mu_x)(y - \mu_y) f_{XY}(x, y)\, dy\, dx$$
$$= \int_{-\infty}^{\infty} \int_{-\infty}^{\infty} xy f_{XY}(x, y)\, dy\, dx - \mu_x \mu_y$$
$$= \mathbb{E}(XY) - \mathbb{E}(X)\mathbb{E}(Y).$$

Joint Moment-Generating Function:
For $t, s \in \mathbb{R}$

$$M_{XY}(s, t) = \mathbb{E}\left(e^{sX + tY}\right) = \int_{-\infty}^{\infty} \int_{-\infty}^{\infty} e^{sx + ty} f_{XY}(x, y)\, dy\, dx.$$

Joint Characteristic Function:
For $i = \sqrt{-1}$ and $t, s \in \mathbb{R}$

$$\varphi_{XY}(s,t) = \mathbb{E}\left(e^{isX+itY}\right) = \int_{-\infty}^{\infty} \int_{-\infty}^{\infty} e^{isx+ity} f_{XY}(x,y) \, dy \, dx.$$

Independence:
X and Y are independent if and only if

- $f_{XY}(x,y) = f_X(x)f_Y(y)$.
- $M_{XY}(s,t) = \mathbb{E}\left(e^{sX+tY}\right) = \mathbb{E}\left(e^{sX}\right)\mathbb{E}\left(e^{tY}\right) = M_X(s)M_Y(t)$.
- $\varphi_{XY}(s,t) = \mathbb{E}\left(e^{isX+itY}\right) = \mathbb{E}\left(e^{isX}\right)\mathbb{E}\left(e^{itY}\right) = \varphi_X(s)\varphi_Y(t)$.

Joint Probability Density Function of Dependent Variables:

Let the random variables $U = g(X,Y)$, $V = h(X,Y)$. If $u = g(x,y)$ and $v = h(x,y)$ can be uniquely solved for x and y in terms of u and v with solutions given by, say, $x = p(u,v)$ and $y = q(u,v)$ and the functions g and h have continuous partial derivatives at all points (x,y) such that the determinant

$$J(x,y) = \begin{vmatrix} \dfrac{\partial g}{\partial x} & \dfrac{\partial g}{\partial y} \\[2mm] \dfrac{\partial h}{\partial x} & \dfrac{\partial h}{\partial y} \end{vmatrix} = \frac{\partial g}{\partial x}\frac{\partial h}{\partial y} - \frac{\partial g}{\partial y}\frac{\partial h}{\partial x} \neq 0$$

then the joint probability density function of U and V is

$$f_{UV}(u,v) = f_{XY}(x,y)\,|J(x,y)|^{-1}$$

where $x = p(u,v)$ and $y = q(u,v)$.

Properties of Expectation and Variance

Let X and Y be two random variables and for constants a and b

$$\mathbb{E}(aX + b) = a\mathbb{E}(X) + b, \ \mathrm{Var}(aX + b) = a^2\mathrm{Var}(X)$$

$$\mathbb{E}(aX + bY) = a\mathbb{E}(X) + b\mathbb{E}(Y), \quad \mathrm{Var}(aX + bY) = a^2\mathrm{Var}(X) + b^2\mathrm{Var}(Y) + 2ab\mathrm{Cov}(X,Y).$$

Properties of Moment-Generating and Characteristic Functions

If a random variable X has moments up to kth order where k is a non-negative integer, then

$$\mathbb{E}(X^k) = \frac{d^k}{dt^k}M_X(t)\bigg|_{t=0} = i^{-k}\frac{d^k}{dt^k}\varphi_X(t)\bigg|_{t=0}$$

where $i = \sqrt{-1}$.

If the bivariate random variables X and Y have moments up to $m + n = k$ where m, n and k are non-negative integers, then

$$\mathbb{E}(X^m Y^n) = \frac{d^k}{d s^m d t^n} M_{XY}(s,t)\bigg|_{s=0,t=0} = i^{-k} \frac{d^k}{d s^m d t^n} \varphi_{XY}(s,t)\bigg|_{s=0,t=0}$$

where $i = \sqrt{-1}$.

Correlation Coefficient

Let X and Y be two random variables with means μ_x and μ_y and variances σ_x^2 and σ_y^2. The correlation coefficient ρ_{xy} between X and Y is defined as

$$\rho_{xy} = \frac{\mathrm{Cov}(X,Y)}{\sqrt{\mathrm{Var}(X)\mathrm{Var}(Y)}} = \frac{\mathbb{E}\left[(X - \mu_x)(Y - \mu_y)\right]}{\sigma_x \sigma_y}.$$

Important information:

- ρ_{xy} measures only the linear dependency between X and Y.
- $-1 \le \rho_{xy} \le 1$.
- If $\rho_{xy} = 0$ then X and Y are uncorrelated.
- If X and Y are independent then $\rho_{xy} = 0$. However the converse is not true.
- If X and Y are jointly normally distributed then X and Y are independent if and only if $\rho_{XY} = 0$.

Convolution

If X and Y are independent discrete random variables with probability mass functions $\mathbb{P}(X = x)$ and $\mathbb{P}(Y = y)$, respectively, then the probability mass function for $Z = X + Y$ is

$$\mathbb{P}(Z = z) = \sum_x \mathbb{P}(X = x)\mathbb{P}(Y = z - x) = \sum_y \mathbb{P}(X = z - y)\mathbb{P}(Y = y).$$

If X and Y are independent continuous random variables with probability density functions $f_X(x)$ and $f_Y(y)$, respectively, then the probability density function for $Z = X + Y$ is

$$f_Z(z) = \int_{-\infty}^{\infty} f_X(x)f_Y(z - x)\,dx = \int_{-\infty}^{\infty} f_X(z - y)f_Y(y)\,dy.$$

Discrete Distributions

Bernoulli: A random variable X is said to follow a Bernoulli distribution, $X \sim \text{Bernoulli}(p)$ where $p \in [0, 1]$ is the probability of success and the probability mass function is given as

$$P(X = x) = p^x(1 - p)^{1-x}, \quad x = 0, 1$$

where $\mathbb{E}(X) = p$ and $\text{Var}(X) = p - p^2$. The moment-generating function is

$$M_X(t) = 1 - p + pe^t, \quad t \in \mathbb{R}$$

and the corresponding characteristic function is

$$\varphi_X(t) = 1 - p + pe^{it}, \quad i = \sqrt{-1} \text{ and } t \in \mathbb{R}.$$

Geometric: A random variable X is said to follow a geometric distribution, $X \sim \text{Geometric}(p)$ where $p \in [0, 1]$ is the probability of success and the probability mass function is given as

$$\mathbb{P}(X = x) = p(1 - p)^{x-1}, \quad x = 1, 2, \ldots$$

where $\mathbb{E}(X) = \dfrac{1}{p}$ and $\text{Var}(X) = \dfrac{1 - p}{p^2}$. The moment-generating function is

$$M_X(t) = \frac{p}{1 - (1 - p)e^t}, \quad t \in \mathbb{R}$$

and the corresponding characteristic function is

$$\varphi_X(t) = \frac{p}{1 - (1 - p)e^{it}}, \quad i = \sqrt{-1} \text{ and } t \in \mathbb{R}.$$

Binomial: A random variable X is said to follow a binomial distribution, $X \sim \text{Binomial}(n, p)$, $p \in [0, 1]$ where $p \in [0, 1]$ is the probability of success and $n \in \mathbb{N}_0$ is the number of trials and the probability mass function is given as

$$\mathbb{P}(X = x) = \binom{n}{x} p^x (1 - p)^{n-x}, \quad x = 0, 1, 2, \ldots, n$$

where $\mathbb{E}(X) = np$ and $\text{Var}(X) = np(1 - p)$. The moment-generating function is

$$M_X(t) = (1 - p + pe^t)^n, \quad t \in \mathbb{R}$$

and the corresponding characteristic function is

$$\varphi_X(t) = (1 - p + pe^{it})^n, \quad i = \sqrt{-1} \text{ and } t \in \mathbb{R}.$$

Negative Binomial: A random variable X is said to follow a negative binomial distribution, $X \sim \text{NB}(r, p)$ where $p \in [0, 1]$ is the probability of success and r is the number of successes accumulated and the probability mass function is given as

$$\mathbb{P}(X = x) = \binom{x - 1}{r - 1} p^r (1 - p)^{n-r}, \quad x = r, r + 1, r + 2, \ldots$$

where $\mathbb{E}(X) = \dfrac{r}{p}$ and $\mathrm{Var}(X) = \dfrac{r(1-p)}{p^2}$. The moment-generating function is

$$M_X(t) = \left(\frac{1-p}{1-pe^t}\right)^r, \quad t < -\log p$$

and the corresponding characteristic function is

$$M_X(t) = \left(\frac{1-p}{1-pe^{it}}\right)^r, \quad i = \sqrt{-1} \text{ and } t \in \mathbb{R}.$$

Poisson: A random variable X is said to follow a Poisson distribution, $X \sim \mathrm{Poisson}(\lambda)$, $\lambda > 0$ with probability mass function given as

$$\mathbb{P}(X = x) = \frac{e^{-\lambda}\lambda^x}{x!}, \quad x = 0,1,2,\dots$$

where $\mathbb{E}(X) = \lambda$ and $\mathrm{Var}(X) = \lambda$. The moment-generating function is

$$M_X(t) = e^{\lambda(e^t-1)}, \quad t \in \mathbb{R}$$

and the corresponding characteristic function is

$$\varphi_X(t) = e^{\lambda(e^{it}-1)}, \quad i = \sqrt{-1} \text{ and } t \in \mathbb{R}.$$

Continuous Distributions

Uniform: A random variable X is said to follow a uniform distribution, $X \sim \mathcal{U}(a,b)$, $a < b$ with probability density function given as

$$f_X(x) = \frac{1}{b-a}, \quad a < x < b$$

where $\mathbb{E}(X) = \dfrac{a+b}{2}$ and $\mathrm{Var}(X) = \dfrac{(b-a)^2}{12}$. The moment-generating function is

$$M_X(t) = \frac{e^{tb} - e^{ta}}{t(b-a)}, \quad t \in \mathbb{R}$$

and the corresponding characteristic function is

$$\varphi_X(t) = \frac{e^{tb} - e^{ita}}{it(b-a)}, \quad i = \sqrt{-1} \text{ and } t \in \mathbb{R}.$$

Normal: A random variable X is said to follow a normal distribution, $X \sim \mathcal{N}(\mu, \sigma)$, $\mu \in \mathbb{R}$, $\sigma^2 > 0$ with probability density function given as

$$f_X(x) = \frac{1}{\sigma\sqrt{2\pi}} e^{-\frac{1}{2}\left(\frac{x-\mu}{\sigma}\right)^2}, \quad x \in \mathbb{R}$$

where $\mathbb{E}(X) = \mu$ and $\mathrm{Var}(X) = \sigma^2$. The moment-generating function is

$$M_X(t) = e^{\mu t + \frac{1}{2}\sigma^2 t^2}, \quad t \in \mathbb{R}$$

and the corresponding characteristic function is

$$\varphi_X(t) = e^{i\mu t - \frac{1}{2}\sigma^2 t^2}, \quad i = \sqrt{-1} \text{ and } t \in \mathbb{R}.$$

Lognormal: A random variable X is said to follow a lognormal distribution, $X \sim \log\text{-}\mathcal{N}(\mu, \sigma)$, $\mu \in \mathbb{R}$, $\sigma^2 > 0$ with probability density function given as

$$f_X(x) = \frac{1}{x\sigma\sqrt{2\pi}} e^{-\frac{1}{2}\left(\frac{\log(x)-\mu}{\sigma}\right)^2}, \quad x > 0$$

where $\mathbb{E}(X) = e^{\mu + \frac{1}{2}\sigma^2}$ and $\mathrm{Var}(X) = (e^{\sigma^2} - 1)e^{2\mu + \sigma^2}$. The moment-generating function is

$$M_X(t) = \sum_{n=0}^{\infty} \frac{t^n}{n!} e^{n\mu + \frac{1}{2}n^2\sigma^2}, \quad t \leq 0$$

and the corresponding characteristic function is

$$\varphi_X(t) = \sum_{n=0}^{\infty} \frac{(it)^n}{n!} e^{n\mu + \frac{1}{2}n^2\sigma^2}, \quad i = \sqrt{-1} \text{ and } t \in \mathbb{R}.$$

Exponential: A random variable X is said to follow an exponential distribution, $X \sim \mathrm{Exp}(\lambda)$, $\lambda > 0$ with probability density function

$$f_X(x) = \lambda e^{-\lambda x}, \quad x \geq 0$$

where $\mathbb{E}(X) = \frac{1}{\lambda}$ and $\mathrm{Var}(X) = \frac{1}{\lambda^2}$. The moment-generating function is

$$M_X(t) = \frac{\lambda}{\lambda - t}, \quad t < \lambda$$

and the corresponding characteristic function is

$$\varphi_X(t) = \frac{\lambda}{\lambda - it}, \quad i = \sqrt{-1} \text{ and } t \in \mathbb{R}.$$

Gamma: A random variable X is said to follow a gamma distribution, $X \sim \text{Gamma}(\alpha, \lambda)$, $\alpha, \lambda > 0$ with probability density function given as

$$f_X(x) = \frac{\lambda e^{-\lambda x}(\lambda x)^{\alpha-1}}{\Gamma(\alpha)}, \quad x \geq 0$$

such that

$$\Gamma(\alpha) = \int_0^\infty e^{-x} x^{\alpha-1} dx$$

where $\mathbb{E}(X) = \frac{\alpha}{\lambda}$ and $\text{Var}(X) = \frac{\alpha}{\lambda^2}$. The moment-generating function is

$$M_X(t) = \left(\frac{\lambda}{\lambda - t}\right)^\alpha, \quad t < \lambda$$

and the corresponding characteristic function is

$$\varphi_X(t) = \left(\frac{\lambda}{\lambda - it}\right)^\alpha, \quad i = \sqrt{-1} \text{ and } t \in \mathbb{R}.$$

Chi-Square: A random variable X is said to follow a chi-square distribution, $X \sim \chi^2(v), v \in \mathbb{N}$ with probability density function given as

$$f_X(x) = \frac{1}{2^{\frac{v}{2}}\Gamma\left(\frac{v}{2}\right)} x^{\frac{v}{2}-1} e^{-\frac{x}{2}}, \quad x \geq 0$$

such that

$$\Gamma\left(\frac{v}{2}\right) = \int_0^\infty e^{-x} x^{\frac{v}{2}-1} dx$$

where $\mathbb{E}(X) = v$ and $\text{Var}(X) = 2v$. The moment-generating function is

$$M_X(t) = (1 - 2t)^{-\frac{v}{2}}, \quad -\frac{1}{2} < t < \frac{1}{2}$$

and the corresponding characteristic function is

$$M_X(t) = (1 - 2it)^{-\frac{v}{2}}, \quad i = \sqrt{-1} \text{ and } t \in \mathbb{R}.$$

Bivariate Normal: The random variables X and Y with means μ_x, μ_y, variances σ_x^2, σ_y^2 and correlation coefficient $\rho_{xy} \in (-1, 1)$ is said to follow a joint normal distribution, $(X, Y) \sim$

$\mathcal{N}_2\left(\boldsymbol{\mu}, \boldsymbol{\Sigma}\right)$ where $\boldsymbol{\mu} = \begin{bmatrix} \mu_x \\ \mu_y \end{bmatrix}$ and $\boldsymbol{\Sigma} = \begin{bmatrix} \text{Var}(X) & \text{Cov}(X,Y) \\ \text{Cov}(X,Y) & \text{Var}(Y) \end{bmatrix} = \begin{bmatrix} \sigma_x^2 & \rho_{xy}\sigma_x\sigma_y \\ \rho_{xy}\sigma_x\sigma_y & \sigma_y^2 \end{bmatrix}$ with

joint probability density function given as

$$f_{XY}(x,y) = \frac{1}{2\pi\sigma_x\sigma_y\sqrt{1-\rho_{xy}^2}} e^{-\frac{1}{2(1-\rho_{xy}^2)}\left[\left(\frac{x-\mu_x}{\sigma_x}\right)^2 - 2\rho\left(\frac{x-\mu_x}{\sigma_x}\right)\left(\frac{y-\mu_y}{\sigma_y}\right) + \left(\frac{y-\mu_y}{\sigma_y}\right)^2\right]}, x,y \in \mathbb{R}.$$

The moment-generating function is

$$M_{XY}(s,t) = e^{\mu_x s + \mu_y t + \frac{1}{2}(\sigma_x^2 s^2 + 2\rho_{xy}\sigma_x\sigma_y st + \sigma_y^2 t^2)}, \quad s,t \in \mathbb{R}$$

and the corresponding characteristic function is

$$\varphi_{XY}(s,t) = e^{i\mu_x s + i\mu_y t - \frac{1}{2}(\sigma_x^2 s^2 + 2\rho_{xy}\sigma_x\sigma_y st + \sigma_y^2 t^2)}, \quad i = \sqrt{-1} \text{ and } s,t \in \mathbb{R}.$$

Multivariate Normal: The random vector $\mathbf{X} = (X_1, X_2, \ldots, X_n)$ is said to follow a multivariate normal distribution, $\mathbf{X} \sim \mathcal{N}_n\left(\boldsymbol{\mu}, \boldsymbol{\Sigma}\right)$ where

$$\boldsymbol{\mu} = \begin{bmatrix} \mathbb{E}(X_1) \\ \mathbb{E}(X_2) \\ \vdots \\ \mathbb{E}(X_n) \end{bmatrix} \text{ and } \boldsymbol{\Sigma} = \begin{bmatrix} \text{Var}(X_1) & \text{Cov}(X_1, X_2) & \ldots & \text{Cov}(X_1, X_n) \\ \text{Cov}(X_1, X_2) & \text{Var}(X_2) & \ldots & \text{Cov}(X_2, X_n) \\ \vdots & \vdots & \ddots & \vdots \\ \text{Cov}(X_1, X_n) & \text{Cov}(X_2, X_n) & \ldots & \text{Var}(X_n) \end{bmatrix}$$

with probability density function given as

$$f_{\mathbf{X}}(x_1, x_2, \ldots, x_n) = \frac{1}{(2\pi)^{\frac{n}{2}} |\boldsymbol{\Sigma}|^{\frac{1}{2}}} e^{-\frac{1}{2}\mathbf{X}^T \boldsymbol{\Sigma}^{-1} \mathbf{X}}.$$

The moment-generating function is

$$M_{\mathbf{X}}(t_1, t_2, \ldots, t_n) = e^{\boldsymbol{\mu}^T \mathbf{t} + \frac{1}{2}\mathbf{t}^T \boldsymbol{\Sigma} \mathbf{t}}, \quad \mathbf{t} = (t_1, t_2, \ldots, t_n)^T$$

and the corresponding characteristic function is

$$\varphi_{\mathbf{X}}(t_1, t_2, \ldots, t_n) = e^{i\boldsymbol{\mu}^T \mathbf{t} - \frac{1}{2}\mathbf{t}^T \boldsymbol{\Sigma} \mathbf{t}}, \quad \mathbf{t} = (t_1, t_2, \ldots, t_n)^T.$$

Integrable and Square-Integrable Random Variables

Let X be a real-valued random variable.

- If $\mathbb{E}(|X|) < \infty$ then X is an integrable random variable.
- If $\mathbb{E}(X^2) < \infty$ then X is a square-integrable random variable.

Convergence of Random Variables

Let $X_1, X_2, \ldots, X_n$ be a sequence of random variables. Then

(a) $X_n \xrightarrow{a.s} X$ converges almost surely if

$$\mathbb{P}\left(\lim_{n\to\infty} X_n = X\right) = 1.$$

(b) $X_n \xrightarrow{r} X$ converges in the rth mean, $r \geq 1$, if $\mathbb{E}(|X_n^r|) < \infty$ and

$$\lim_{n\to\infty} \mathbb{E}\left(|X_n - X|^r\right) = 0.$$

(c) $X_n \xrightarrow{P} X$ converges in probability, if for all $\varepsilon > 0$,

$$\lim_{n\to\infty} \mathbb{P}\left(|X_n - X| \geq \varepsilon\right) = 0.$$

(d) $X_n \xrightarrow{D} X$ converges in distribution, if for all $x \in \mathbb{R}$,

$$\lim_{n\to\infty} \mathbb{P}(X_n \leq x) = \mathbb{P}(X \leq x).$$

Relationship Between Modes of Convergence

For any $r \geq 1$

$$\left\{\begin{array}{c} X_n \xrightarrow{a.s} X \\ X_n \xrightarrow{r} X \end{array}\right\} \Longrightarrow \left\{X_n \xrightarrow{P} X\right\} \Longrightarrow \left\{X_n \xrightarrow{D} X\right\}.$$

If $r > s \geq 1$ then

$$\left\{X_n \xrightarrow{r} X\right\} \Longrightarrow \left\{X_n \xrightarrow{s} X\right\}.$$

Dominated Convergence Theorem

If $X_n \xrightarrow{a.s} X$ and for any $n \in \mathbb{N}$ we have $|X_n| < Y$ for some Y such that $\mathbb{E}(|Y|) < \infty$, then $\mathbb{E}(|X_n|) < \infty$ and

$$\lim_{n\to\infty} \mathbb{E}(X_n) = \mathbb{E}(X).$$

Monotone Convergence Theorem

If $0 \leq X_n \leq X_{n+1}$ and $X_n \xrightarrow{a.s} X$ for any $n \in \mathbb{N}$ then

$$\lim_{n\to\infty} \mathbb{E}(X_n) = \mathbb{E}(X).$$

The Weak Law of Large Numbers

Let $X_1, X_2, \ldots, X_n$ be a sequence of independent and identically distributed random variables with common mean $\mu \in \mathbb{R}$. Then for any $\varepsilon > 0$,

$$\mathbb{P}\left(\lim_{n \to \infty} \left| \frac{X_1 + X_2 + \ldots + X_n}{n} - \mu \right| \geq \varepsilon \right) = 0.$$

The Strong Law of Large Numbers

Let $X_1, X_2, \ldots, X_n$ be a sequence of independent and identically distributed random variables with common mean $\mu \in \mathbb{R}$. Then

$$\mathbb{P}\left(\lim_{n \to \infty} \frac{X_1 + X_2 + \ldots + X_n}{n} = \mu \right) = 1.$$

The Central Limit Theorem

Let $X_1, X_2, \ldots, X_n$ be a sequence of independent and identically distributed random variables with common mean $\mu \in \mathbb{R}$ and variance $\sigma^2 > 0$ and we denote the sample mean as

$$\overline{X} = \frac{X_1 + X_2 + \ldots + X_n}{n}$$

where $\mathbb{E}(\overline{X}) = \mu$ and $\mathrm{Var}(\overline{X}) = \dfrac{\sigma^2}{n}$. By defining

$$Z_n = \frac{\overline{X} - \mathbb{E}(\overline{X})}{\sqrt{\mathrm{Var}(\overline{X})}} = \frac{\overline{X} - \mu}{\sigma/\sqrt{n}}$$

then for $n \to \infty$,

$$\lim_{n \to \infty} Z_n = \lim_{n \to \infty} \frac{\overline{X} - \mu}{\sigma/\sqrt{n}} \xrightarrow{D} \mathcal{N}(0, 1)$$

that is Z_n follows a standard normal distribution asymptotically.

Appendix C
Differential Equations Formulae

Separable Equations

The form

$$\frac{dy}{dx} = f(x)g(y)$$

has a solution

$$\int \frac{1}{g(y)}\, dy = \int f(x)\, dx.$$

If $g(y)$ is a linear equation and if y_1 and y_2 are two solutions, then $y_3 = ay_1 + by_2$ is also a solution for constant a and b.

First-Order Ordinary Differential Equations

General Linear Equation: The general form of a first-order ordinary differential equation

$$\frac{dy}{dx} + f(x)y = g(x)$$

has a solution

$$y = I(x)^{-1} \int I(u)g(u)\, du + C$$

where $I(x) = e^{\int f(x)dx}$ is the integrating factor and C is a constant.

Bernoulli Differential Equation: For $n \neq 1$, the Bernoulli differential equation has the form

$$\frac{dy}{dx} + P(x)y = Q(x)y^n$$

which, by setting $w = \dfrac{1}{y^{n-1}}$, can be transformed to a general linear ordinary differential equation of the form

$$\frac{dw}{dx} + (1-n)P(x)w = (1-n)Q(x)$$

with a particular solution

$$w = (1 - n)I(x)^{-1} \int I(u)Q(u) \, du$$

where $I(x) = e^{(1-n) \int P(x)dx}$ is the integrating factor. The solution to the Bernoulli differential equation becomes

$$y = \left\{ (1 - n)I(x)^{-1} \int I(u)Q(u) \, du \right\}^{-\frac{1}{n-1}} + C$$

where C is a constant value.

Second-Order Ordinary Differential Equations

General Linear Equation: For a homogeneous equation

$$a\frac{d^2y}{dx^2} + b\frac{dy}{dx} + cy = 0$$

by setting $y = e^{ux}$ the differential equation has a general solution based on the characteristic equation

$$au^2 + bu + c = 0$$

such that m_1 and m_2 are the roots of the quadratic equation, and if

- $m_1, m_2 \in \mathbb{R}, m_1 \neq m_2$ then $y = Ae^{m_1 x} + Be^{m_2 x}$
- $m_1, m_2 \in \mathbb{R}, m_1 = m_2 = m$ then $y = e^{mx}(A + Bx)$
- $m_1, m_2 \in \mathbb{C}, m_1 = \alpha + i\beta, m_2 = \alpha - i\beta$ then $y = e^{\alpha x}[A\cos(\beta x) + B\sin(\beta x)]$

where A, B are constants.

Cauchy–Euler Equation: For a homogeneous equation

$$ax^2\frac{d^2y}{dx^2} + bx\frac{dy}{dx} + cy = 0$$

by setting $y = x^u$ the Cauchy–Euler equation has a general solution based on the characteristic equation

$$au^2 + (b - a)u + c = 0$$

such that m_1 and m_2 are the roots of the quadratic equation, and if

- $m_1, m_2 \in \mathbb{R}, m_1 \neq m_2$ then $y = Ax^{m_1} + Bx^{m_2}$
- $m_1, m_2 \in \mathbb{R}, m_1 = m_2 = m$ then $y = x^m(A + B\log x)$
- $m_1, m_2 \in \mathbb{C}, m_1 = \alpha + i\beta, m_2 = \alpha - i\beta$ then $y = x^\alpha[A\cos(\beta \log x) + B\sin(\beta \log x)]$

where A, B are constants.

Variation of Parameters: For a general non-homogeneous second-order differential equation

$$a(x)\frac{d^2y}{dx^2} + b(x)\frac{dy}{dx} + c(x) = f(x)$$

has the solution

$$y = y_c + y_p$$

where y_c, the complementary function, satisfies the homogeneous equation

$$a(x)\frac{d^2y_c}{dx^2} + b(x)\frac{dy_c}{dx} + c(x) = 0$$

and y_p, the particular integral, satisfies

$$a(x)\frac{d^2y_p}{dx^2} + b(x)\frac{dy_p}{dx} + c(x) = f(x).$$

Let $y_c = C_1 y_c^{(1)}(x) + C_2 y_c^{(2)}(x)$ where C_1 and C_2 are constants, then the particular solution to the non-homogeneous second-order differential equation is

$$y_p = -y_c^{(1)}(x) \int \frac{y_c^{(2)}(x)f(x)}{a(x)W(y_c^{(1)}(x), y_c^{(2)}(x))}\, dx + y_c^{(2)}(x) \int \frac{y_c^{(1)}(x)f(x)}{a(x)W(y_c^{(1)}(x), y_c^{(2)}(x))}\, dx$$

where $W(y_c^{(1)}(x), y_c^{(2)}(x))$ is the Wronskian defined as

$$W(y_c^{(1)}(x), y_c^{(2)}(x)) = \begin{vmatrix} y_c^{(1)}(x) & y_c^{(2)}(x) \\ \dfrac{d}{dx}y_c^{(1)}(x) & \dfrac{d}{dx}y_c^{(2)}(x) \end{vmatrix} = y_c^{(1)}(x)\frac{d}{dx}y_c^{(2)}(x) - y_c^{(2)}(x)\frac{d}{dx}y_c^{(1)}(x) \neq 0.$$

Homogeneous Heat Equations

Initial Value Problem on an Infinite Interval: The diffusion equation of the form

$$\frac{\partial u}{\partial t} = \alpha\frac{\partial^2 u}{\partial x^2}, \quad \alpha > 0, \quad -\infty < x < \infty, \quad t > 0$$

with initial condition $u(x, 0) = f(x)$ has a solution

$$u(x, t) = \frac{1}{2\sqrt{\pi\alpha t}} \int_{-\infty}^{\infty} f(z)e^{-\frac{(x-z)^2}{4\alpha t}}\, dz.$$

Initial Value Problem on a Semi-Infinite Interval: The diffusion equation of the form

$$\frac{\partial u}{\partial t} = \alpha \frac{\partial^2 u}{\partial x^2}, \quad \alpha > 0, \quad 0 \leq x < \infty, \quad t > 0$$

with

- initial condition $u(x,0) = f(x)$ and boundary condition $u(0,t) = 0$ has a solution

$$u(x,t) = \frac{1}{2\sqrt{\pi \alpha t}} \int_0^\infty f(z) \left[e^{-\frac{(x-z)^2}{4\alpha t}} - e^{-\frac{(x+z)^2}{4\alpha t}} \right] dz$$

- initial condition $u(x,0) = f(x)$ and boundary condition $u_x(0,t) = 0$ has a solution

$$u(x,t) = \frac{1}{2\sqrt{\pi \alpha t}} \int_0^\infty f(z) \left[e^{-\frac{(x-z)^2}{4\alpha t}} + e^{-\frac{(x+z)^2}{4\alpha t}} \right] dz$$

- initial condition $u(x,0) = 0$ and boundary condition $u(0,t) = g(t)$ has a solution

$$u(x,t) = \frac{x}{2\sqrt{\pi \alpha}} \int_0^t \frac{1}{\sqrt{t-w}} g(w) e^{-\frac{x^2}{4\alpha(t-w)}} \, dw.$$

Stochastic Differential Equations

Suppose that X_t, Y_t and Z_t are Itō processes satisfying the following stochastic differential equations:

$$dX_t = \mu(X_t,t)dt + \sigma(X_t,t)dW_t^x$$
$$dY_t = \mu(Y_t,t)dt + \sigma(Y_t,t))dW_t^y$$
$$dZ_t = \mu(Z_t,t)dt + \sigma(Z_t,t)dW_t^z$$

where W_t^x, W_t^y and W_t^z are standard Wiener processes.

Reciprocal:

$$\frac{d\left(\frac{1}{X_t}\right)}{\left(\frac{1}{X_t}\right)} = -\frac{dX_t}{X_t} + \left(\frac{dX_t}{X_t}\right)^2.$$

Product:

$$\frac{d(X_t Y_t)}{X_t Y_t} = \frac{dX_t}{X_t} + \frac{dY_t}{Y_t} + \frac{dX_t}{X_t}\frac{dY_t}{Y_t}.$$

Quotient:

$$\frac{d\left(\dfrac{X_t}{Y_t}\right)}{\left(\dfrac{X_t}{Y_t}\right)} = \frac{dX_t}{X_t} - \frac{dY_t}{Y_t} - \frac{dX_t}{X_t}\frac{dY_t}{Y_t} + \left(\frac{dY_t}{Y_t}\right)^2.$$

Product and Quotient I:

$$\frac{d\left(\dfrac{X_tY_t}{Z_t}\right)}{\left(\dfrac{X_tY_t}{Z_t}\right)} = \frac{dX_t}{X_t} + \frac{dY_t}{Y_t} - \frac{dZ_t}{Z_t} + \frac{dX_t}{X_t}\frac{dY_t}{Y_t} - \frac{dX_t}{X_t}\frac{dZ_t}{Z_t} - \frac{dY_t}{Y_t}\frac{dZ_t}{Z_t} + \left(\frac{dZ_t}{Z_t}\right)^2.$$

Product and Quotient II:

$$\frac{d\left(\dfrac{X_t}{Y_tZ_t}\right)}{\left(\dfrac{X_t}{Y_tZ_t}\right)} = \frac{dX_t}{X_t} - \frac{dY_t}{Y_t} - \frac{dZ_t}{Z_t} - \frac{dX_t}{X_t}\frac{dY_t}{Y_t} - \frac{dX_t}{X_t}\frac{dZ_t}{Z_t} + \frac{dY_t}{Y_t}\frac{dZ_t}{Z_t}.$$

Black–Scholes Model

Black–Scholes Equation (Continuous Dividend Yield): At time t, let the asset price S_t follow a geometric Brownian motion

$$\frac{dS_t}{S_t} = (\mu - D)dt + \sigma dW_t$$

where μ is the drift parameter, D is the continuous dividend yield, σ is the volatility parameter and W_t is a standard Wiener process. For a European-style derivative $V(S_t, t)$ written on the asset S_t, it satisfies the Black–Scholes equation with continuous dividend yield

$$\frac{\partial V}{\partial t} + \frac{1}{2}\sigma^2 S_t^2 \frac{\partial^2 V}{\partial S_t^2} + (r - D)S_t\frac{\partial V}{\partial S_t} - rV(S_t, t) = 0$$

where r is the risk-free interest rate. The parameters μ, r, D and σ can be either constants, deterministic functions or stochastic processes.

European Options: For a European option having the payoff

$$\Psi(S_T) = \max\{\delta(S_T - K), 0\}$$

where $\delta \in \{-1, 1\}$, K is the strike price and T is the option expiry time, and if r, D and σ are constants the European option price at time $t < T$ is

$$V(S_t, t; K, T) = \delta S_t e^{-D(T-t)}\Phi(\delta d_+) - \delta K e^{-r(T-t)}\Phi(\delta d_-)$$

where $d_{\pm} = \dfrac{\log(S_t/K) + (r - D \pm \frac{1}{2}\sigma^2)(T - t)}{\sigma\sqrt{T - t}}$ and $\Phi(\cdot)$ is the cumulative distribution function of a standard normal.

Reflection Principle: If $V(S_t, t)$ is a solution of the Black–Scholes equation then for a constant $B > 0$, the function

$$U(S_t, t) = \left(\frac{S_t}{B}\right)^{2\alpha} V\left(\frac{B^2}{S_t}, t\right), \quad \alpha = \frac{1}{2}\left(1 - \frac{r - D}{\frac{1}{2}\sigma^2}\right)$$

also satisfies the Black–Scholes equation.

Black Model

Black Equation: At time t, let the asset price S_t follow a geometric Brownian motion

$$\frac{dS_t}{S_t} = (\mu - D)dt + \sigma dW_t$$

where μ is the drift parameter, D is the continuous dividend yield, σ is the volatility parameter and W_t is a standard Wiener process. Consider the price of a futures contract maturing at time $T > t$ on the asset S_t as

$$F(t, T) = S_t e^{(r-D)(T-t)}$$

where r is the risk-free interest rate. For a European option on futures $V(F(t, T), t)$ written on a futures contract $F(t, T)$, it satisfies the Black equation

$$\frac{\partial V}{\partial t} + \frac{1}{2}\sigma^2 F(t, T)^2 \frac{\partial^2 V}{\partial F^2} - rV(F(t, T), t) = 0.$$

The parameters μ, r, D and σ can be either constants, deterministic functions or stochastic processes.

European Options on Futures: For a European option on futures having the payoff

$$\Psi(F(T, T)) = \max\{\delta(F(T, T) - K), 0\}$$

where $\delta \in \{-1, 1\}$, K is the strike price and T is the option expiry time, and if r and σ are constants then the price of a European option on futures at time $t < T$ is

$$V(F(t, T), t; K, T) = \delta e^{-r(T-t)} \left[F(t, T)\Phi(\delta d_+) - K\Phi(\delta d_-)\right]$$

where $d_{\pm} = \dfrac{\log(F(t, T)/K) \pm \frac{1}{2}\sigma^2(T - t)}{\sigma\sqrt{T - t}}$ and $\Phi(\cdot)$ is the cumulative distribution function of a standard normal.

Reflection Principle: If $V(F(t,T),t)$ is a solution of the Black equation then for a constant $B > 0$ the function

$$U(F(t,T),t) = \frac{F(t,T)}{B} V\left(\frac{B^2}{F(t,T)}, t\right)$$

also satisfies the Black equation.

Garman–Kohlhagen Model

Garman–Kohlhagen Equation: At time t, let the foreign-to-domestic exchange rate X_t follow a geometric Brownian motion

$$\frac{dX_t}{X_t} = \mu dt + \sigma dW_t$$

where μ is the drift parameter, σ is the volatility parameter and W_t is a standard Wiener process. For a European-style derivative $V(X_t,t)$ which depends on X_t, it satisfies the Garman–Kohlhagen equation

$$\frac{\partial V}{\partial t} + \frac{1}{2}\sigma^2 X_t^2 \frac{\partial^2 V}{\partial X_t^2} + (r_d - r_f)X_t\frac{\partial V}{\partial X_t} - r_d V(X_t,t) = 0$$

where r_d and r_f are the domestic and foreign currencies' risk-free interest rates. The parameters μ, r_d, r_f and σ can be either constants, deterministic functions or stochastic processes.

European Options: For a European option having the payoff

$$\Psi(X_T) = \max\{\delta(X_T - K), 0\}$$

where $\delta \in \{-1, 1\}$, K is the strike price and T is the option expiry time, and if r_d, r_f and σ are constants then the European option price (domestic currency in one unit of foreign currency) at time $t < T$ is

$$V(X_t, t; K, T) = \delta X_t e^{-r_f(T-t)}\Phi(\delta d_+) - \delta K\, e^{-r_d(T-t)}\Phi(\delta d_-)$$

where $d_\pm = \dfrac{\log(X_t/K) + (r_d - r_f \pm \frac{1}{2}\sigma^2)(T - t)}{\sigma\sqrt{T - t}}$ and $\Phi(\cdot)$ is the cumulative distribution function of a standard normal.

Reflection Principle: If $V(X_t,t)$ is a solution of the Garman–Kohlhagen equation then for a constant $B > 0$, the function

$$U(X_t,t) = \left(\frac{X_t}{B}\right)^{2\alpha} V\left(\frac{B^2}{X_t}, t\right), \quad \alpha = \frac{1}{2}\left(1 - \frac{r_d - r_f}{\frac{1}{2}\sigma^2}\right)$$

also satisfies the Garman–Kohlhagen equation.

Bibliography

Abramovitz, M. and Stegun, I.A. (1970). *Handbook of Mathematical Functions: with Formulas, Graphs and Mathematical Tables*. Dover Publications, New York.

Barlow, M.T. (2002). A diffusion model for electricity prices. *Mathematical Finance*, 12(4), pp. 287–298.

Baz, J. and Chacko, G. (2004). *Financial Derivatives: Pricing, Applications and Mathematics*. Cambridge University Press, Cambridge.

Bernard, C. and Cui, Z. (2011). Pricing of timer options. *Journal of Computational Finance*, 15(1), pp. 69–104.

Black, F. (1975). Fact and fantasy in the use of options. *Financial Analysts Journal*, Jul/Aug, pp. 36–72.

Black, F. and Scholes, M. (1973). The pricing of options and corporate liabilities. *Journal of Political Economy*, 81, pp. 637–654.

Bos, M. and Vandermark, S. (2002). Finessing fixed dividends. *Risk Magazine*, 15(9).

Bossu, S. (2014). *Advanced Equity Derivatives, Volatility and Correlation*. John Wiley and Sons, Hoboken, NJ.

Bossu, S. and Henrotte, P. (2012). *An Introduction to Equity Derivatives: Theory and Practice*, 2nd edn. John Wiley and Sons, Chichester, UK.

Boyle, P.P. (1988). A lattice framework for option pricing with two state variables. *Journal of Financial and Quantitative Analysis*, 23(1), pp. 1–12.

Brenner, M. and Subrahmanyam, M.G. (1988). A simple formula to compute the implied standard deviation. *Financial Analyst Journal*, 5, pp. 80–83.

Brezeźniak, Z. and Zastawniak, T. (1999). *Basic Stochastic Processes*. Springer-Verlag, Berlin.

Capiński, M., Kopp, E. and Traple, J. (2012). *Stochastic Calculus for Finance*. Cambridge University Press, Cambridge.

Carr, P. and Lee, R. (2010). Volatility derivatives. *Annual Review of Financial Economics*, 1, pp. 319–339.

Carr, P. and Sun, J. (2007). A new approach for option pricing under stochastic volatility. *Review of Derivatives Research*, 10, pp. 87–150.

Chambers, D.R. and Nawalkha, S.J. (2001). An improved approach to computing implied volatility. *The Financial Review*, 38, pp. 89–100.

Chance, D.M. (1996). Leap into the unknown. *Risk*, 6, pp. 60–66.

Chance, D.M. (1996). A generalized simple formula to compute the implied volatility. *The Financial Review*, 4, pp. 859–867.

Chin, E., Nel, D. and Ólafsson, S. (2014). *Problems and Solutions in Mathematical Finance, Volume 1: Stochastic Calculus*. John Wiley and Sons, Chichester, UK.

Clewlow, S. and Strickland, C. (1999). Valuing energy options in a one factor model fitted to forward prices. Working Paper, School of Finance and Economics, University of Technology, Sydney, Australia.

Cont, R. and Tankov, P. (2003). *Financial Modelling with Jump Processes*. Chapman and Hall/CRC, London.

Conze, A. and Viswanathan (1991). Path dependent options: The case of lookback options. *The Journal of Finance*, XLVI(5), pp. 1893–1907.

Corrado, C.J. and Miller, T.W. Jr. (1994). A note on a simple, accurate formula to compute implied standard deviations. *Journal of Banking & Finance*, 20, pp. 595–603.

Cox, J.C. (1996). The constant elasticity of variance option pricing model. *The Journal of Portfolio Management, Special Issue*, pp. 15–17.

Cox, J.C., Ingersoll, J.E. and Ross, S.A. (1985). A theory of the term structure of interest rates. *Econometrica*, 53, pp. 385–407.

Curran, M. (1994). Valuing Asian and portfolio options by conditioning on the geometric mean price. *Management Science*, 40(12), pp. 1705–1711.

Dai, M. (2000). A closed-form solution for perpetual American floating strike lookback options. *Journal of Computational Finance*, 4(2), pp. 63–68.

Demeterfi, K., Derman, E., Kamal, M. and Zou, J. (1999). More than you ever wanted to know about volatility swaps. *Quantitative Strategies Research Notes*, Goldman Sachs.

Dupire, B. (2004). Pricing with a smile. *Risk*, pp. 1–10.

Fouque, J., Papanicolaou, G., Sircar, R. and Sølna, K. (2011). *Multiscale Stochastic Volatility for Equity, Interest Rate, and Credit Derivatives*. Cambridge University Press, Cambridge.

Girsanov, I. (1960). On transforming a certain class of stochastic processes by absolutely continuous substitution of measures. *SIAM Theory of Probability and Applications*, 5(3), pp. 285–301.

Gradshteyn, I.S. and Ryzhik, I.M. (1980). *Table of Integrals, Series and Products*, A. Jeffrey (ed.). Academic Press, New York.

Grimmett, G. and Strizaker, D. (2001). *Probability and Random Processes*, 3rd edn. Oxford University Press, Oxford.

Hallerbach, W.G. (2004). An improved estimator for Black–Scholes–Merton implied volatility. ERIM Report Series Research in Management, ERS-2004-054-F&A, Erasmus Universiteit Rotterdam.

Haug, E.G. (2007). *The Complete Guide to Option Pricing Formulas*, 2nd edn. McGraw-Hill Professional, New York.

Henderson, V. and Wojakowski, R. (2002). On the equivalence of floating- and fixed-strike Asian options. *Journal of Applied Probability*, 39(2), pp. 391–394.

Heston, S.L. (1993). A closed-form solution for options with stochastic volatility with applications to bond and currency options. *The Review of Financial Studies*, 6(2), pp. 327–343.

Howison, S., Rafailidis, A. and Rasmussen, H. (2004). On the pricing and hedging of volatility derivatives. *Applied Mathematical Finance*, 11, pp. 317–348.

Hsu, Y.L., Lin, T.I. and Lee, C.F. (2008). Constant elasticity of variance (CEV) option pricing model: Integration and detailed derivation. *Mathematics and Computers in Simulation*, 79(1), pp. 60–71.

Hull, J. (2014). *Options, Futures, and Other Derivatives*, 9th edn. Prentice Hall, Englewood Cliffs, NJ.

Hull, J. and White, A. (2003). The pricing of options on assets with stochastic volatilities. *The Journal of Finance*, 42(2), pp. 281–300.

Itō, K. (1951). On stochastic differential equations: Memoirs. *American Mathematical Society*, 4, pp. 1–51.

Joshi, M. (2008). *The Concepts and Practice of Mathematical Finance*, 2nd edn. Cambridge University Press, Cambridge.

Joshi, M. (2011). *More Mathematical Finance*. Pilot Whale Press, Melbourne.

Kamrad, B. and Ritchken, P. (1991). Multinomial approximating models for options with k state variables. *Management Science*, 37(12), pp. 1640–1652.

Karatzas, I. and Shreve, S.E. (2004). *Brownian Motion and Stochastic Calculus*, 2nd edn. Springer-Verlag, Berlin.

Knoblock, J. (1988). *Xunzi, A Translation and Study of the Complete Works, Volume I, Books 1–6*, Stanford University Press, Stanford, CA.

Kou, S.G. (2002). A jump-diffusion model for option pricing. *Management Science*, 48, pp. 1086–1101.

Kwok, Y.K. (2008). *Mathematical Models of Financial Derivatives*, 2nd edn. Springer-Verlag, Berlin.

Leland, H.E. (1985). Option pricing and replication with transactions costs. *The Journal of Finance*, 40(5), pp. 1283–1301.

Levy, E. (1992). Pricing European average rate currency options. *Journal of International Money and Finance*, 11, pp. 474–491.

Li, S. (2003). The estimation of implied volatility from the Black–Scholes model: Some new formulas and their applications. Discussion Papers in Economics, Finance and International Competitiveness, No. 14, Queensland University of Technology, Australia.

Li, S. (2005). A new formula for computing implied volatility. *Applied Mathematics and Computation*, 170(1), pp. 611–625.

Li, M. and Mercurio, F. (2013). Closed-form approximation of timer option prices under general stochastic volatility models. MPRA Paper, No. 47465.

Maller, R.A., Müller, G. and Szimayer, A. (2009). Ornstein–Uhlenbeck processes and extensions. *Handbook of Financial Time Series*. Springer-Verlag, Berlin, pp. 421–437.

Manaster, S. and Koehler, G. (1982). The calculation of implied volatility from the Black–Scholes model: A note. *The Journal of Finance*, 38(1), pp. 227–230.

Marsaglia, G. (2004). Evaluating the normal distribution. *Journal of Statistical Software*, 11(4), pp. 1–11.

Merton, R. (1973). The theory of rational option pricing. *Bell Journal of Economics and Management Science*, 4, pp. 141–183.

Merton, R. (1976). Option pricing when underlying stock returns are discontinuous. *Journal of Financial Economics*, 3, pp. 125–144.

Musiela, M. and Rutkowski, M. (2007). *Martingale Methods in Financial Modelling*, 2nd edn. Springer-Verlag, Berlin.

Nielsen, J.A. and Sandmann, K. (2003). Pricing bounds on Asian options. *The Journal of Financial Quantitative Analysis*, 38(2), pp. 449–473.

Øksendal, B. (2003). *Stochastic Differential Equations: An Introduction with Applications*, 6th edn. Springer-Verlag, Berlin.

Rabinovitch, R. (1989). Pricing stock and bond options when the default-free rate is stochastic. *Journal of Financial and Quantitative Analysis*, 24(4), pp. 447–457.

Rebonato, R. (2004). *Volatility and Correlation*. John Wiley and Sons, Chichester, UK.

Renault, E. and Touzi, N. (1996). Option hedging and implied volatilities in a stochastic volatility model. *Mathematical Finance*, 6(4), pp. 279–302.

Rice, J.A. (2007). *Mathematical Statistics and Data Analysis*, 3rd edn. Duxbury Advanced Series. Brooks/Cole.

Rogers, L.C.G. and Shi, Z. (1995). The value of an Asian option. *Journal of Applied Probability*, 32, pp. 1077–1088.

Romano, M. and Touzi, N. (1997). Contingent claims and market completeness in a stochastic volatility model. *Mathematical Finance*, 7(4), pp. 399–410.

Ross, S. (2002). *A First Course in Probability*, 6th edn. Prentice Hall, Englewood Cliffs, NJ.

Shreve, S.E. (2005). *Stochastic Calculus for Finance, Volume I: The Binomial Asset Pricing Models*. Springer-Verlag, New York.

Shreve, S.E. (2008). *Stochastic Calculus for Finance, Volume II: Continuous-Time Models*. Springer-Verlag, New York.

Stulz, R.M. (1982). Options on the minimum or the maximum of two risky assets: Analysis and applications. *Journal of Financial Economics*, 10, pp. 161–185.

Turnbull, S.M. and Wakeman L.M. (1991). A quick algorithm for pricing European average options. *Journal of Financial and Quantitative Methods*, 26(3), pp. 377–389.

Whalley, A.E. and Wilmott, P. (1997). An asymptotic analysis of an optimal hedging model for option pricing with transaction costs. *Mathematical Finance*, 7(3), pp. 307–324.

Wilmott, P. (1994). Discrete charms. *Risk Magazine*, 7(3), pp. 48–51.

Wilmott, P. (2006). *Paul Wilmott on Quantitative Finance*, 2nd edn. John Wiley and Sons, Chichester, UK.

Wilmott, P., Dewynne, J. and Howison, S. (1993). *Option Pricing: Mathematical Models and Computation*. Oxford Financial Press, Oxford.

Notation

SET NOTATION

$\in$	is an element of
$\notin$	is not an element of
Ω	sample space
$\mathscr{E}$	universal set
$\varnothing$	empty set
A	subset of Ω
A^c	complement of set A
$|A|$	cardinality of A
$\mathbb{N}$	set of natural numbers, $\{1, 2, 3, \ldots\}$
$\mathbb{N}_0$	set of natural numbers including zero, $\{0, 1, 2, \ldots\}$
$\mathbb{Z}$	set of integers, $\{0, \pm 1, \pm 2, \pm 3, \ldots\}$
$\mathbb{Z}^+$	set of positive integers, $\{1, 2, 3, \ldots\}$
$\mathbb{R}$	set of real numbers
$\mathbb{R}^+$	set of positive real numbers, $\{x \in \mathbb{R} : x > 0\}$
$\mathbb{C}$	set of complex numbers
$A \times B$	cartesian product of sets A and B, $A \times B = \{(a, b) : a \in A, b \in B\}$
$a \sim b$	a is equivalent to b
$\subseteq$	subset
$\subset$	proper subset
$\cap$	intersection
$\cup$	union
$\backslash$	difference
$\triangle$	symmetric difference
sup	supremum or least upper bound
inf	infimum or greatest lower bound
$[a, b]$	the closed interval $\{x \in \mathbb{R} : a \le x \le b\}$
$[a, b)$	the interval $\{x \in \mathbb{R} : a \le x < b\}$
$(a, b]$	the interval $\{x \in \mathbb{R} : a < x \le b\}$
(a, b)	the open interval $\{x \in \mathbb{R} : a < x < b\}$
$\mathscr{F}, \mathscr{G}, \mathscr{H}$	σ-algebra (or σ-fields)

MATHEMATICAL NOTATION

x^+	$\max\{x, 0\}$
x^-	$\min\{x, 0\}$
$\lfloor x \rfloor$	largest integer not greater than or equal to x, $\max\{m \in \mathbb{Z} \mid m \leq x\}$
$\lceil x \rceil$	smallest integer greater than or equal to x, $\min\{n \in \mathbb{Z} \mid n \geq x\}$
$x \vee y$	$\max\{x, y\}$
$x \wedge y$	$\min\{x, y\}$
i	$\sqrt{-1}$
∞	infinity
$\exists$	there exists
$\exists!$	there exists a unique
$\forall$	for all
$\approx$	approximately equal to
$p \Longrightarrow q$	p implies q
$p \Longleftarrow q$	p is implied by q
$p \Longleftrightarrow q$	p implies and is implied by q
$f : X \mapsto Y$	f is a function where every element of X has an image in Y
$f(x)$	the value of the function f at x
$\lim_{x \to a} f(x)$	limit of $f(x)$ as x tends to a
$\delta x, \Delta x$	increment of x
$f^{-1}(x)$	the inverse function of the function $f(x)$
$f'(x), f''(x)$	first and second-order derivative of the function $f(x)$
$\dfrac{dy}{dx}, \dfrac{d^2y}{dx^2}$	first and second-order derivative of y with respect to x
$\displaystyle\int y\,dx, \int_a^b y\,dx$	the indefinite and definite integral of y with respect to x
$\dfrac{\partial f}{\partial x_i}, \dfrac{\partial^2 f}{\partial x_i^2}$	first and second-order partial derivative of f with respect to x_i
	where f is a function on $(x_1, x_2, \ldots, x_n)$
$\dfrac{\partial^2 f}{\partial x_i \partial x_j}$	second-order partial derivative of f with respect to x_i and x_j
	where f is a function on $(x_1, x_2, \ldots, x_n)$
$\log_a x$	logarithm of x to the base of a
$\log x$	natural logarithm of x
$\displaystyle\sum_{i=1}^{n} a_i$	$a_1 + a_2 + \ldots + a_n$
$\displaystyle\prod_{i=1}^{n} a_i$	$a_1 \times a_2 \times \ldots \times a_n$
$|a|$	modulus of a
$\left(\sqrt[n]{a}\right)^m$	$a^{\frac{m}{n}}$
$n!$	n factorial
$\dbinom{n}{k}$	$\dfrac{n!}{k!(n-k)!}$ for $n, k \in \mathbb{Z}^+$

$\delta(x)$	Dirac delta function
$H(x)$	Heaviside step function
$\Gamma(t)$	gamma function
$B(x, y)$	beta function
$\mathbf{a}$	a vector $\mathbf{a}$
$|\mathbf{a}|$	magnitude of a vector $\mathbf{a}$
$\mathbf{a} \cdot \mathbf{b}$	scalar or dot product of vectors $\mathbf{a}$ and $\mathbf{b}$
$\mathbf{a} \times \mathbf{b}$	vector or cross product of vectors $\mathbf{a}$ and $\mathbf{b}$
$\mathbf{M}$	a matrix $\mathbf{M}$
$\mathbf{M}^T$	transpose of a matrix $\mathbf{M}$
$\mathbf{M}^{-1}$	inverse of a square matrix $\mathbf{M}$
$|\mathbf{M}|$	determinant of a square matrix $\mathbf{M}$

PROBABILITY NOTATION

A, B, C	events
$\mathbb{I}_A$	indicator of the event A
$\mathbb{P}, \mathbb{Q}$	probability measures
$\mathbb{P}(A)$	probability of event A
$\mathbb{P}(A|B)$	probability of event A conditional on event B
X, Y, Z	random variables
$\mathbf{X}, \mathbf{Y}, \mathbf{Z}$	random vectors
$P(X = x)$	probability mass function of a discrete random variable X
$f_X(x)$	probability density function of a continuous random variable X
$F_X(x), \mathbb{P}(X \leq x)$	cumulative distribution function of random variable X
$M_X(t)$	moment-generating function of a random variable X
$\varphi_X(t)$	characteristic function of a random variable X
$P(X = x, Y = y)$	joint probability mass function of discrete variables X and Y
$f_{XY}(x, y)$	joint probability density function of continuous random variables X and Y
$F_{XY}(x, y), \mathbb{P}(X \leq x, Y \leq y)$	joint cumulative distribution function of random variables X and Y
$M_{XY}(s, t)$	joint moment generating function of random variables X and Y
$\varphi_{XY}(s, t)$	joint characteristic function of random variables X and Y
$p(x, t; y, T)$	transition probability density of y at time T starting at time t at point x
$\sim$	is distributed as
$\nsim$	is not distributed as
$\dot{\sim}$	is approximately distributed as
$\xrightarrow{a.s}$	converges almost surely
$\xrightarrow{r}$	converges in the r-th mean

$\xrightarrow{P}$	converges in probability
$\xrightarrow{D}$	converges in distribution
$X \overset{d}{=} Y$	X and Y are identically distributed random variables
$X \perp\!\!\!\perp Y$	X and Y are independent random variables
$X \not\!\perp\!\!\!\perp Y$	X and Y are not independent random variables
$\mathbb{E}(X)$	expectation of random variable X
$\mathbb{E}^{\mathbb{Q}}(X)$	expectation of random variable X under the probability measure $\mathbb{Q}$
$\mathbb{E}[g(X)]$	expectation of $g(X)$
$\mathbb{E}(X \mid \mathscr{F})$	conditional expectation of X
$\text{Var}(X)$	variance of random variable X
$\text{Var}(X \mid \mathscr{F})$	conditional variance of X
$\text{Cov}(X, Y)$	covariance of random variables X and Y
ρ_{xy}	correlation between random variables X and Y
Bernoulli(p)	Bernoulli distribution with mean p and variance $p(1 - p)$
Geometric(p)	geometric distribution with mean p^{-1} and variance $(1 - p)p^{-2}$
Binomial(n, p)	binomial distribution with mean np and variance $np(1 - p)$
BN(n, r)	negative binomial distribution with mean rp^{-1} and variance $r(1 - p)p^{-2}$
Poisson(λ)	Poisson distribution with mean λ and variance λ
Exp(λ)	exponential distribution with mean λ^{-1} and variance λ^{-2}
Gamma(α, λ)	gamma distribution with mean $\alpha\lambda^{-1}$ and variance $\alpha\lambda^{-2}$
$\mathcal{U}(a, b)$	uniform distribution with mean $\frac{1}{2}(a + b)$ and variance $\frac{1}{12}(b - a)^2$
$\mathcal{N}(\mu, \sigma^2)$	normal distribution with mean μ and variance σ^2
log-$\mathcal{N}(\mu, \sigma^2)$	lognormal distribution with mean $e^{\mu + \frac{1}{2}\sigma^2}$ and variance $(e^{\sigma^2} - 1)e^{2\mu + \sigma^2}$
$\chi^2(k)$	chi-square distribution with mean k and variance $2k$
$\mathcal{N}_n(\mu, \Sigma)$	multivariate normal distribution with n-dimensional mean vector μ and $n \times n$ covariance matrix Σ
$\Phi(\cdot), \Phi(x)$	cumulative distribution function of a standard normal
$\Phi(x, y, \rho_{xy})$	cumulative distribution function of a standard bivariate normal with correlation coefficient ρ_{xy}
W_t	standard Wiener process, $W_t \sim \mathcal{N}(0, t)$
N_t	Poisson process, $N_t \sim$ Poisson(λt)

Index

Printed and bound by CPI Group (UK) Ltd, Croydon, CR0 4YY

23/04/2025

14660949-0005